Contents/Índice

Proprietary terms

This dictionary includes some words which are, or are asserted to be, proprietary names or trade marks. Their inclusion does not imply that they have acquired for legal purposes a non-proprietary or general significance, nor is any other judgement implied concerning their legal status. In cases where the editor has some evidence that a word is used as a proprietary name or trade mark this is indicated by the symbol ®, but no judgement concerning the legal status of such words is made or implied thereby.

Nomes comerciais

Este dicionário inclui algumas palavras que são, ou acredita-se ser, nomes comerciais ou marcas registadas. A sua inclusão no dicionário não implica que elas tenham adquirido para fins legais um significado geral ou não-comercial, assim como não afeta em nenhum dos conceitos implícitos o seu status legal. Nos casos em que o editor tenha prova suficiente de que uma palavra seja usada como um nome comercial ou marca registada, este emprego é indicado pelo símbolo ®, mas nenhuma apreciação relativa ao status legal de tais palavras é feita ou sugerida por esta indicação.

OXFORD
UNIVERSITY PRESS

Great Clarendon Street, Oxford, OX2 6DP,
United Kingdom

Oxford University Press is a department of the University of Oxford.
It furthers the University's objective of excellence in research, scholarship,
and education by publishing worldwide. Oxford is a registered trade mark of
Oxford University Press in the UK and in certain other countries

First published as the Oxford Portuguese Mini Dictionary in 2006
First Edition published in 2009
Second Edition published in 2012

Impression: 2

British Library Cataloguing in Publication Data
Data available

Library of Congress Cataloguing in Publication Data
Data available

ISBN 978-0-19-964097-3

Printed in Great Britain by Clays Ltd, St Ives plc

Contributors/Colaboradores

Portuguese–English *compiled by John Whitlam*
English–Portuguese *compiled by Lia Correia Raitt*
Revisions for the second edition: *Vanda Meneses Santos, Teresa Barbosa, Daniel Grassi, Helen Newstead, Catarina Fouto, Alison Aiken, Mike Harland, Sarah Bailey, Mariana Cunha, Susana Valdez*

Thanks are due to/Agradecimentos a: Dr John Sykes, Prof. A. W. Raitt, Comandante Virgílio Correia, Marcelo Affonso, Eng. Pedro Carvalho, Eng. Vasco Carvalho, Dr Iva Correia, Dr Ida Reis de Carvalho, Eng. J. Reis de Carvalho, Prof. A. Falcão, Bispo Manuel Falcão, Dr M. Luísa Falcão, Prof. J. Ferraz, Prof. M. de Lourdes Ferraz, Drs Ana e Jorge Fonseca, Mr Robert Howes, Eng. Hugo Pires, Prof. M. Laura Pires, Dr M. Alexandre Pires, Embaixador L. Pazos Alonso, Dr Teresa Pinto Pereira, Dr Isabel Tully, Carlos Wallenstein, e Dr H. Martins e os membros de sua Mesa Lusófona do St Anthony's College, em Oxford.

Introduction

This new edition of the *Oxford Essential Portuguese Dictionary* is designed as a practical reference tool for tourists, students and business people alike, and it includes a host of new features to help the user get the most out of the dictionary.

The wordlist has been updated to include the latest words and meanings in both languages (e.g. *blogger*, *carbon footprint*, *social networking*; *avatar*, *ciberespeculador*, *mídia social*), and all the Portuguese text has been revised in line with the latest spelling reform (see also page xiv). This new edition also includes notes on life and culture in the United Kingdom and the United States (e.g. *Congress*, *Edinburgh Festival*, *gap year*), as well as special treatment of complex grammatical words in both languages, such as *do*, *have*; *de*, *estar*. These expanded entries are presented in boxes to help the user find them more easily, and contain language notes to warn of possible pitfalls.

The dictionary has an easy-to-use, streamlined layout. Bullets separate parts of speech within an entry, and different meanings are signposted using indicators or typical collocates with which the headword frequently occurs. The swung dash (~) is used to replace a headword, or that part of a headword preceding the vertical bar (|).

In both English and Portuguese, only irregular plural forms are given. Plural forms of Portuguese nouns and adjectives ending in a single vowel are formed by adding an s (e.g. *livro*, *livros*). Those ending in *n*, *r*, *s* where the stress falls on the final syllable, and *z*, add *es* (e.g. *mulher*, *mulheres*, *falaz*, *falazes*). Nouns and adjectives ending in *m* change the final *m* to *ns* (e.g. *homem*, *homens*, *bom*, *bons*); those ending in *ol* change their ending to *óis* (e.g. *lençol*, *lençois*); and nouns ending in *al* change their ending to *ais* (e.g. *casal*, *casais*). Most of those ending in *ão* change their ending to *ões* (e.g. *estação*, *estações*).

Portuguese nouns and adjectives ending in an unstressed *o* form the feminine by changing the *o* to *a* (e.g. *belo*, *bela*). Those ending in *or* become *ora* (e.g. *trabalhador*, *trabalhadora*). All other masculine–feminine changes are shown at the main headword.

English and Portuguese pronunciation is given by means of the International Phonetic Alphabet. It is shown for all headwords, and for those derived words whose pronunciation is not easily deduced from that of a headword.

Portuguese verb tables will be found in the appendix.

Introdução

Esta nova edição do *Oxford Essential Portuguese Dictionary* foi concebida como uma ferramenta de referência prática para turistas, estudantes e profissionais, e inclui uma série de novos recursos para ajudar o utilizador a tirar o máximo proveito do dicionário.

A lista de vocábulos foi atualizada de modo a incluir palavras e significados mais recentes em ambas as línguas (ex. *blogger*, *carbon footprint*, *social networking*; *avatar*, *ciberespeculador*, *mídia social*) e todo o português foi revisto à luz do Acordo Ortográfico. Esta nova edição também inclui notas culturais sobre o Reino Unido e os Estados Unidos (ex. *Congress*, *Edinburgh Festival*, *gap year*), bem como um tratamento especial a palavras gramaticais complexas em português e inglês, tais como *do*, *have*; *de*, *estar*. Estes verbetes mais detalhados encontram-se destacados dentro de caixas, de modo a facilitar a sua identificação, e contêm anotações linguísticas alertando o utilizador para possíveis armadilhas.

O dicionário possui uma apresentação visual simplificada e fácil de usar. Em cada verbete, as categorias gramaticais estão separadas por itens e os significados distintos encontram-se sinalizados através de indicadores ou colocações típicas utilizadas no contexto em que a palavra frequentemente ocorre. O sinal (~) é usado para substituir o verbete, ou parte deste precedendo a barra vertical (|).

Tanto em inglês como em português, somente as formas irregulares do plural são dadas. As formas regulares do plural dos substantivos ingleses recebem um *s* (ex. *teacher*, *teachers*), ou *es* quando terminarem em *ch*, *sh*, *s*, *ss*, *us*, *x* ou *z* (ex. *sash*, *sashes*). Os substantivos terminados em *y* e precedidos por uma consoante, mudam no plural para *ies* (ex. *baby*, *babies*).

O passado e o particípio passado dos verbos regulares ingleses são formados pelo acréscimo de *ed* à forma infinitiva (ex. *last*, *lasted*). Os verbos terminados em *e* recebem *d* (ex. *move*, *moved*). Aqueles terminados em *y* têm o *y* substituído por *ied* (*carry*, *carried*). As formas irregulares dos verbos aparecem no dicionário por ordem alfabética, remetidas à forma infinitiva, e também na lista de verbos no apêndice.

As pronúncias inglesa e portuguesa são dadas em acordo com o Alfabeto Fonético Internacional. A pronúncia é dada para todos os verbetes, assim como para aquelas palavras derivadas cuja pronúncia não seja facilmente deduzida a partir do verbete.

Portuguese Pronunciation

The phonetics shown in this dictionary are for Brazilian Portuguese. The main differences in the pronunciation of European Portuguese are shown at the end of this section.

Vowels and Diphthongs

a, à, á, â	/ã/	cham*a*m, *a*mbos, *a*ntes	1) before *m* at the end of a word, or before *m* or *n* and another consonant, is nasalized
	/a /	*aba*, *à*, *acolá*, des*â*nimo	2) in other positions is like *a* in English r*a*ther
ã	/ã/	irm*ã*	is nasalized
e	/ẽ/	sem, venda	1) before *m* at the end of a word, or before *m* or *n* and another consonant, is nasalized
	/i/	art*e*	2) at the end of a word is like *y* in English happy
	/e/	menas	3) in other positions is like *e* in English they
é	/ɛ/	artéria	is like *e* in English get
ê	/e/	fêmur	is like *e* in English they
i	/ĩ/	s*i*m, vindo	1) before *m* at the end of a word, or before *m* or *n* and another consonant, is nasalized
	/i/	f*i*la	2) in other positions is like *ee* in English *see*
o	/õ/	com, sombra, *o*nda	1) before *m* at the end of a word, or before *m* or *n* and another consonant, is nasalized
	/u/	muito	2) at the end of a word, unstressed, is like *u* in English rule
	/o/	comover	3) in other positions, unstressed, is like *o* in English pole
	/o/	bobo	4) stressed, is like *o* in
	/ɔ/	loja	English pole or *o* in shop
ó	/o/	ópera	is like o in English shop
ô	/o/	tônica	is like o in English pole

u, ú		g*u*erra, g*u*isado, q*u*e, q*u*ilo	1) is usually silent in *gue*, *gui*, *que*, and *qui* but is sometimes pronounced /w/, as in tranq*u*ilo, cinq*u*enta, ung*u*ento
	/u/	m*u*la, p*ú*rp*u*ra	2) in other positions is like *u* in English r*u*le
ãe	/ãj/	m*ãe*, p*ãe*s, alem*ãe*s	is like *y* in English b*y*, but nasalized
ai	/aj/	v*ai*, p*ai*, s*ai*, c*ai*xa	is like *y* in English b*y*
ao, au	/aw/	*ao*s, *au*todefesa	is like *ow* in English h*ow*
ão	/ãw/	n*ão*	is like *ow* in English h*ow*, but nasalized
ei	/ej/	l*ei*	is like *ey* in English th*ey*
eu	/ew/	d*eu*s, fl*eu*gma	both vowels pronounced separately
õe	/õj/	eleiç*õe*s	is like *oi* in English c*oi*n, but nasalized
oi	/oj/	n*oi*te	is like *oi* in English c*oi*n
ou	/o/	p*ou*co	is like *o* in English p*o*le

Consonants

b	/b/	*b*anho	is like *b* in English *b*all
c	/s/	*c*inza, *c*em	1) before *e* or *i* is like *s* in English *s*it
	/k/	*c*asa	2) in other positions is like *c* in English *c*at
ç	/s/	esta*ç*ão	is like *s* in English *s*it
ch	/ʃ/	*ch*á	is like *sh* in English *sh*out
d	/dʒ/	*d*izer, don*d*e	1) before *i* or final unstressed *e* is like *j* in English *j*oin
	/d/	*d*ar	2) in other positions is like *d* in English *d*og
f	/f/	*f*alar	is like *f* in English *f*all
g	/g/	a*g*ente, *g*iro	1) before *e* or *i* is like *s* in English vi*s*ion
	/g/	*g*ato	2) in other positions is like *g* in English *g*et
h		haver	is silent in Portuguese, but see *ch*, *lh*, *nh*
j	/ʒ/	*j*unta	is like *s* in English vi*s*ion
k	/k/	*k*it	is like *k* in English *k*ey
l	/w/	fa*l*ta	1) between a vowel and a consonant, or following a vowel at the end of a word, is like *w* in English *w*ater
	/l/	*l*ata	2) in other positions is like *l* in English *l*ike
l	/ʎ/	calhar	is like *lli* in English mi*lli*on
m		a*m*bas/ãbuʃ/ co*m*/kõ/	1) between a vowel and a consonant, or after a vowel at the end of a word, *m* nasalizes the preceding vowel
	/m/	*m*ato, *m*ão	2) in other positions is like *m* in English *m*other

n		ci*n*za/'sĩza/	1) between a vowel and a consonant, *n* nasalizes the preceding vowel
	/n/	be*n*igno	2) in other positions is like *n* in English *n*ear
nh	/ɲ/	ba*nh*o	is like *ni* in English opin*i*on
p	/p/	*p*az	is like *p* in English *p*oor
q	/k/	*q*ue, in*q*uieto	1) *qu* before *e* or *i* is like English *k*
	/kw/	*q*uase, *q*uórum	2) *qu* before *a* or *o*, or *qü* before *e* or *i*, is like *qu* in English *qu*een
r	/ɾ/	apa*r*ato, go*r*do	1) between two vowels, or between a vowel and a consonant, is trilled
	/x/	*r*ato, ga*rr*a, mel*r*o, gen*r*o, Is*r*ael	2) at the beginning of a word, or in *rr*, or after *l*, *n*, or *s*, is like *ch* in Scottish lo*ch*
s	/ʃ/	depoi*s*	1) at the end of a word is like *sh* in English *sh*oot
	/z/	a*s*a, de*s*de, abi*s*mo, I*s*rael	2) between two vowels, or before *b*, *d*, *g*, *l*, *m*, *n*, *r*, *v*, is like *z* in English *z*ebra
	/s/	*s*uave	3) in other positions is like *s* in English *s*it
t	/tʃ/	*t*io, an*t*es	1) before *i* or final unstressed *e* is like *ch* in English *ch*eese
	/tʃi/	ki*t*	2) at the end of a word is like *chy* in English it*chy*
	/t/	a*t*ar	3) in other positions is like *t* in English *t*ap
v	/v/	lu*v*a	is like *v* in English *v*ain
w	/u/	*w*att	is shorter than English *w*
x	/z/	e*x*ato, e*x*emplo	1) in the prefix *ex* before a vowel, is pronounced like *z* in *z*ero
	/ʃ/	*x*ícara, bai*x*o, pei*x*e, frou*x*o	2) at the beginning of a word or after *ai*, *ei* or *ou*, is pronounced like *sh* in *sh*ow
	/s/	e*x*plodir, au*x*iliar	3) is like *s* in English *s*it
	/ks/	a*x*ila, fi*x*o	4) is like *x* in English e*x*it
			5) in the combination *xce*, *xci*, *x* is not pronounced in Portuguese e.g. excelente, excitar
z	/s/	fala*z*	1) at the end of a word, is like *s* in English *s*it
	/z/	di*z*er	2) in other positions, is like English *z*

European Portuguese Pronunciation

The main differences in pronunciation are:

d	/d/	*d*ar, *d*izer, bal*d*e, don*d*e	1) at the beginning of a word, or after *l*, or *n*, is like *d* in English *d*og
	/ð/	ci*d*a*d*e, me*d*roso	2) in other positions is a sound between *d* in English *d*og and *th* in English *th*is
e	/ə/	art*e*	at the end of a word, is like *e* in English quarr*e*l
r	/rr/	*r*ato, ga*rr*a, mel*r*o, gen*r*o, Is*r*ael, guel*r*a, ten*r*o, is*r*aelense	at the beginning of a word, or in *rr*, or after *l*, *n*, or *s*, is strongly trilled
s	/ʃ/	depoi*s*, a*s*co, ra*s*par, co*s*tura	1) at the end of a word, or before *c*, *f*, *p*, *qu*, or *t*, is like English *sh*
	/ʒ/	de*s*de, I*s*lã, abi*s*mo, I*s*rael	2) before *b*, *d*, *g*, *l*, *m*, *n*, *r*, or *u* is like *s* in English vi*s*ion
t	/t/	*t*ar, an*t*es, *t*io	is like *t* in English *t*ap
z	/ʃ/	fala*z*	at the end of a word, is like *sh* in English *sh*ake

Portuguese spelling reform

Brazil and Portugal are in the process of implementing a new spelling reform, which was agreed between all Portuguese-speaking countries in 1990. The aim of the Portuguese spelling reform is to standardize spellings across all Portuguese-speaking countries, and many of the spelling differences that used to exist between Brazilian and European Portuguese have been eliminated. Brazil and Portugal introduced the new spellings in 2009 and 2008 respectively, but there will be a transition period of four years (in Brazil) and six years (in Portugal) in which both spellings will be accepted.

All the spellings in this dictionary have been updated in line with the new reform. Here follows a summary of the main changes:

– Silent consonants -c- and -p- are omitted in words in which the consonants are not pronounced, e.g.

Pre-spelling reform	**Post-spelling reform**
Br ator, *Port* actor	ator
Br correto, *Port* correcto	correto
Br ótimo, *Port* óptimo	ótimo

Note, however, that the consonant remains in cases where the pronunciation differs between the two countries, e.g. *Br* fato, *Port* facto; *Br* súdito, *Port* súbdito.

– Accents are suppressed in the diphthongs -éi- and -ói- in penultimate syllables:

Pre-spelling reform	**Post-spelling reform**
Br/Port bóia	boia
Br idéia, *Port* ideia	ideia

– Words ending in -êem and -ôo lose their accents:

Pre-spelling reform	**Post-spelling reform**
Br/Port vêem	veem
Br vôo, *Port* voo	voo

– Accents used to differentiate homographs, such as *pára* (verb) and *para* (preposition) have been removed. An important exception is *pôr* (verb) and *por* (preposition), which have not been harmonized.

– The diaeresis is no longer present in -güe-, -güi-, and -qüe-, -qüi-:

Pre-spelling reform	**Post-spelling reform**
Br agüentar, *Port* aguentar	aguentar
Br cinqüenta, *Port* cinquenta	cinquenta

– Certain hyphenated compounds lose their hyphens:

Pre-spelling reform	**Post-spelling reform**
Br/Port auto-escola	autoescola
Br/Port mini-saia	minissaia

However, a few differences between European Portuguese and Brazilian spellings still remain, mostly to reflect how the words are pronounced. An important difference to remember is when a written accent is required on *o* or *e* before *m* and *n*, Brazilian Portuguese uses a circumflex, whereas European Portuguese uses an acute accent, e.g. *econômico* (Br), *económico* (Port); *gêmeo* (Br), *gémeo* (Port); *tênis* (Br), *ténis* (Port). Due to the size of the dictionary, it has not been possible to show all European Portuguese spelling variants in the entries. However, the most common European Portuguese lexical variants are included (e.g. *chávena*, *comboio*, *pequeno-almoço*, *telemóvel*).

Pronúncia inglesa

Vogais e Ditongos

/iː/	see, tea	como *i* em giro
/ɪ/	sit, happy	é um som mais breve do que *i* em li
/e/	set	como *e* em tépido
/æ/	hat	é um som mais breve do que *a* em amor
/ɑː/	arm, calm	como *a* em cartaz
/ɒ/	got	como *o* em exótico
/ɔː/	saw, more	como *o* em corte
/ʊ/	put, look	como *u* em murro
/uː/	too, due	como *u* em duro
/ʌ/	cup, some	como *a* em pano
/ɜː/	firm, fur	como *e* em enxerto
/ə/	ago, weather	como *e* no português europeu parte
/eɪ/	page, pain, pay	como *ei* em leite
/əʊ/	home, roam	é um som mais longo do que *o* em coma
/aɪ/	fine, by, guy	como *ai* em sai
/aɪə/	fire, tyre	como *ai* em sai seguido por /ə/
/aʊ/	now, shout	como *au* em aula
/aʊə/	hour, flower	como *au* em aula seguido por /ə/
/ɔɪ/	join, boy	como *oi* em dói
/ɪə/	dear, here, beer	como *ia* em dia
/eə/	hair, care, bear, there	como *e* em etéreo
/ʊə/	poor, during	como *ua* em sua

Consoantes

/p/	snap	como *p* em pato
/b/	bath	como *b* em bala
/t/	tap	como *t* em tela
/d/	dip	como *d* em dar
/k/	cat, kite, stomach, pique	como *c* em casa
/ks/	exercise	como *x* em axila
/g/	got	como *g* em gato
/tʃ/	chin	como *t* em tio
/dʒ/	June, general, judge	como *d* em dizer
/f/	fall	como *f* em faca

/v/	*v*ine, o*f*	como *v* em *v*aca
/θ/	*th*in, mo*th*	não tem equivalente, soa como um *s* entre os dentes
/ð/	*th*is	não tem equivalente, soa com um *z* entre os dentes
/s/	*s*o, voi*c*e	como *s* em *s*uave
/z/	*z*oo, ro*s*e	como *z* em fa*z*er
/ʃ/	*sh*e, lun*ch*	como *ch* em *ch*egar
/ʒ/	mea*s*ure, vi*s*ion	como *j* em *j*amais
/h/	*h*ow	*h* aspirado
/m/	*m*an	como *m* em *m*ala
/n/	*n*o*n*e	como *n* em *n*ada
/ŋ/	si*ng*	como *n* em ci*n*to
/l/	*l*eg	como *l* em *l*uva
/r/	*r*ed, w*r*ite	como *r* em ca*r*a
/j/	*y*es, *y*oke	como *i* em *i*oga
/w/	*w*eather, s*w*itch	como *u* em ág*u*a

ˈ indica a sílaba tônica, e.g. abusar /abuˈzar/

Abbreviations/Abreviaturas

adjective	*a*	adjetivo
abbreviation	*abbr/abr*	abreviatura
adverb	*adv*	advérbio
article	*art*	artigo
American (English)	*Amer*	(inglês) americano
anatomy	*anat*	anatomia
architecture	*arquit*	arquitetura
astrology	*astr/astrol*	astrologia
motoring	*auto*	automobilismo
aviation	*aviat*	aviação
biology	*biol*	biologia
botany	*bot*	botânica
Brazilian Portuguese	*Br*	português do Brasil
cinema	*cine*	cinema
colloquial	*colloq*	coloquial
commerce	*comm/com*	comércio
computing	*comput*	computação
conjunction	*conj*	conjunção
cookery	*culin*	cozinha
electricity	*electr/eletr*	eletricidade
feminine	*f*	feminina
familiar	*fam*	familiar
figurative	*fig*	figurativo
geography	*geog*	geografia
grammar	*gramm/gram*	gramática
infinitive	*inf*	infinitivo
interjection	*int*	interjeição
interrogative	*interr*	interrogativo
invariable	*invar*	invariável
legal, law	*jur/jurid*	jurídico
language	*lang*	linguagem
literal	*lit*	literal
masculine	*m*	masculino
mathematics	*mat*	matemática
mechanics	*mech*	mecânica

medicine	*med*	medicina
military	*mil*	militar
music	*mus*	música
noun	*n*	substantivo
nautical	*naut*	náutico
negative	*neg*	negativo
oneself	*o.s.*	se, si mesmo
European Portuguese	*P*	português de Portugal
pejorative	*pej*	pejorativo
philosophy	*phil*	filosofia
plural	*pl*	plural
politics	*pol*	política
European Portuguese	*Port*	português de Portugal
past participle	*pp*	particípio passado
prefix	*pref*	prefixo
preposition	*prep*	preposição
present	*pres*	presente
present participle	*pres p*	particípio presente
pronoun	*pron*	pronome
psychology	*psych/psic*	psicologia
past tense	*pt*	pretérito
relative	*rel*	relativo
religion	*relig*	religião
somebody	*sb*	alguém
singular	*sing*	singular
slang	*sl*	gíria
something	*sth*	algo
subjunctive	*subj*	subjuntivo
technology	*techn/tecn*	tecnologia
theatre	*theat/teat*	teatro
television	*TV*	televisão
United Kingdom	*UK*	Reino Unido
United States	*US*	Estados Unidos
university	*univ*	universidade
auxiliary verb	*v aux*	verbo auxiliar
intransitive verb	*vi*	verbo intransitivo
pronominal verb	*vpr*	verbo pronominal
transitive verb	*vt*	verbo transitivo
transitive & intransitive verb	*vt/i*	verbo transitivo e intransitivo

Aa

a /a/ ● *artigo*

····➤ the; **~ casa** the house; **~ Maria ainda não chegou** Maria hasn't arrived yet

! O artigo é omitido em inglês com nomes próprios, ou com parentes: **a vovó já chegou** *grandma has arrived*; **onde está a Joana?** *where's Joana?*

····➤ (*com partes do corpo, roupa*) **ela quebrou ~ perna** she broke her leg; **~ sua camisa está do lado contrário** your shirt is back to front

! Em português, utiliza-se em geral o artigo para se referir a partes do corpo, enquanto no inglês usa-se o pronome possessivo.

● *pron*

····➤ (*mulher*) her

····➤ (*coisa*) it

····➤ (*você*) you

● *prep*

····➤ (*direção*) to; **vou ~ São Paulo** I am going to São Paulo

····➤ (*posição*) **à esquerda** on the left; **ao meu lado** by my side

····➤ (*distância*) **~ dez quilômetros daqui** ten kilometres from here

····➤ (*frequência*) **uma vez ao ano** once a year; **tenho aulas de dança às sextas** I have dance classes on Fridays

····➤ (*esporte*) **ganharam de 2 ~ zero** they won 2 nil

····➤ (*modo, meio*) **ir ~ pé** go on foot; **lavar à mão** handwash; **escrever (ao computador)** type

····➤ (*com preço, medida*) **cinco libras ~ hora** five pounds an hour; **às centenas** by the hundreds; **vender às dúzias** sell by the dozen

····➤ (*com tempo, idade, parte do dia*) **às onze** at eleven; **aos cinquenta anos** at (the age of) 50; **à noite** at night

····➤ (*com velocidade*) **estão ~ 100 quilômetros por hora** they're going at 100 kilometres per hour

····➤ (*seguido de infinitivo*) **fomos os primeiros ~ chegar** we were the first to arrive

····➤ (*complemento indireto*) to; **dê isto à sua tia** give this to your aunt

····➤ (*em expressões*) **provar por ~ mais b** prove beyond doubt

à /a/ = **a** *prep*

aba /'aba/ *f* (*de chapéu*) brim; (*de camisa*) tail; (*de mesa*) flap

abacate /aba'katʃi/ *m* avocado (pear)

abacaxi /abaka'ʃi/ *m* pineapple; **!** (*problema*) pain, headache

aba|de /a'badʒi/ *m* abbot. **~dia** *f* abbey

aba|fado /aba'fadu/ *a* (*tempo*) humid, close; (*quarto*) stuffy. **~far** *vt* (*asfixiar*) stifle; muffle ‹*som*›; smother ‹*fogo*›; suppress ‹*informação*›; cover up ‹*escândalo, assunto*›

abagunçar /abagu'sar/ *vt* mess up

abaixar /aba'ʃar/ *vt* lower; turn down ‹*som, rádio*›. **~-se** *vpr* bend down

abaixo /a'baʃu/ *adv* down; **~ de** below; **mais ~** further down. **~-assinado** *m* petition

abajur /aba'ʒur/ *m* (*quebra-luz*) lampshade; (*lâmpada*) (table) lamp

aba|lar /aba'lar/ *vt* shake; *fig* shock. **~lar-se** *vpr* be shocked, be shaken. **~lo** *m* shock

abanar /aba'nar/ *vt* shake, wave; wag ‹*rabo*›; (*com leque*) fan

abando|nar /abãdo'nar/ *vt* abandon; (*deixar*) leave. **~no** /o/ *m* abandonment; (*estado*) neglect

abarcar /abar'kar/ *vt* comprise, cover

abarro|tado /abaxo'tadu/ *a* crammed full; (*lotado*) crowded, packed. **~tar** *vt* cram full, stuff

abastado /abas'tadu/ *a* wealthy

abaste|cer /abaste'ser/ *vt* supply; fuel ‹*motor*›; fill up (with petrol) ‹*carro*›; refuel ‹*avião*›. **~cimento** *m* supply; (*de carro, avião*) refuelling

aba|ter /aba'ter/ *vt* knock down; cut down, fell ‹*árvore*›; shoot down ‹*avião, ave*›; slaughter ‹*gado*›; knock down, cut ‹*preço*›; **~ter alguém** ‹*trabalho*› get sb down, wear sb out; ‹*má notícia*› sadden sb; ‹*doença*› lay sb low, knock the stuffing out of sb. **~tido** *a* dispirited, dejected; ‹*cara*› haggard, worn. **~timento** *m* dejection; (*de preço*) reduction

abaulado /abaw'ladu/ *a* convex; ‹*estrada*› cambered

abcesso /ab'sɛsu/ *m Port* ▶ ABSCESSO

abdi|cação /abidʒika'sãw/ *f* abdication. **~car** *vt/i* abdicate

abdômen /abi'domẽ/ *m* abdomen

abecedário /abese'dariu/ *m* alphabet, ABC

abeirar-se /abe'rarsi/ *vr* draw near

abe|lha /a'beʎa/ *f* bee. **~lhudo** *a* inquisitive, nosy

abençoar /abẽso'ar/ *vt* bless

aber|to /a'bɛrtu/ *pp de* ▶ ABRIR ● *a* open; ‹*céu*› clear; ‹*gás, torneira*› on; ‹*sinal*› green. **~tura** *f* opening; *Foto* aperture; *Pol* liberalization

abeto /a'betu/ *m* fir (tree)

abis|mado /abiz'madu/ *a* astonished. **~mo** *m* abyss

abjeto /abi'ʒɛtu/ *a* abject

abóbada /a'bɔbada/ *f* vault

abobalhado /aboba'ʎadu/ *a* silly

abóbora /a'bɔbora/ *f* pumpkin

abobrinha /abo'briɲa/ *f* courgette, *Amer* zucchini

abo|lição /aboli'sãw/ *f* abolition. **~lir** *vt* abolish

abomi|nação /abomina'sãw/ *f* abomination. **~nável** (*pl* **~náveis**) *a* abominable

abo|nar /abo'nar/ *vt* guarantee ‹*dívida*›; give a bonus to ‹*empregado*›. **~no** /o/ *m* guarantee; (*no salário*) bonus; (*subsídio*) allowance, benefit; (*reforço*) endorsement

abordar /abor'dar/ *vt* approach ‹*pessoa*›; broach, tackle ‹*assunto*›; *Naut* board

aborre|cer /aboxe'ser/ *vt* (*irritar*) annoy; (*entediar*) bore. **~cer-se** *vpr* get annoyed; get bored. **~cido** *a* annoyed; bored. **~cimento** *m* annoyance; boredom

abor|tar /abor'tar/ *vi* miscarry, have a miscarriage ● *vt* abort. **~to** /o/ *m* abortion; (*natural*) miscarriage

aboto|adura /abotoa'dura/ *f* cufflink. **~ar** *vt* button (up) ● *vi* bud

abra|çar /abra'sar/ *vt* hug, embrace; embrace ‹*causa*›. **~ço** *m* hug, embrace

abrandar /abrã'dar/ *vt* ease ‹*dor*›; temper ‹*calor, frio*›; mollify, appease, placate ‹*povo*›; tone down, smooth over ‹*escândalo*› ● *vi* ‹*dor*› ease; ‹*calor, frio*› become less extreme; ‹*tempestade*› die down

abranger /abrã'ʒer/ *vt* cover; (*entender*) take in, grasp; **~ a** extend to

abrasileirar /abrazile'rar/ *vt* Brazilianize

abre-|garrafas /abriga'xafas/ *m invar Port* bottle opener. **~latas** *m invar Port* can opener

abreugrafia /abrewgra'fia/ *f* X-ray

abrevi|ar /abrevi'ar/ *vt* abbreviate ‹*palavra*›; abridge ‹*livro*›. **~atura** *f* abbreviation

abridor /abri'dor/ *m* **~ (de lata)** can opener; **~ de garrafa** bottle opener

abri|gar /abri'gar/ *vt* shelter; house ‹*sem-teto*›. **~gar-se** *vpr* (take) shelter. **~go** *m* shelter

abril /a'briw/ *m* April

abrir /a'brir/ *vt* open; (*a chave*) unlock; turn on ‹*gás, torneira*›; make ‹*buraco, exceção*› ● *vi* open; ‹*céu, tempo*› clear (up); ‹*sinal*› turn green. **~-se** *vpr* open; (*desabafar*) open up

abrupto /a'bruptu/ *a* abrupt

abrutalhado /abruta'ʎadu/ *a* ‹*sapato*› heavy; ‹*pessoa*› coarse

abscesso /abi'sɛsu/ *m* abscess

absolu|tamente /abisoluta'mẽtʃi/ *adv* absolutely; (*não*) not at all. **~to** *a* absolute; **em ~to** not at all, absolutely not

absol|ver /abisow'ver/ *vt* absolve; *Jurid* acquit. **~vição** *f* absolution; *Jurid* acquittal

absor|ção /abisor'sãw/ *f* absorption. **~to** *a* absorbed. **~vente** *a* ‹*tecido*› absorbent; ‹*livro*› absorbing. **~ver** *vt* absorb. **~ver-se** *vpr* get absorbed

abs|têmio /abis'temiu/ *a* abstemious; (*de álcool*) teetotal ● *m* teetotaller. **~tenção** *f* abstention. **~tencionista** *a* abstaining ● *m/f* abstainer. **~ter-se** *vpr* abstain; **~ter-se de** refrain from. **~tinência** *f* abstinence; **síndrome de ~tinência** withdrawal symptoms *pl*

abstra|ção /abistra'sãw/ *f* abstraction; (*mental*) distraction. **~ir** *vt* separate. **~to** *a* abstract

absurdo /abi'surdu/ *a* absurd ● *m* nonsense

abun|dância /abũ'dãsia/ *f* abundance. **~dante** *a* abundant. **~dar** *vi* abound

abu|sar /abu'zar/ *vi* go too far; **~sar de** abuse; (*aproveitar-se*) take advantage of. **~so** *m* abuse

abutre /a'butri/ *m* vulture

aca|bado /aka'badu/ *a* finished; (*exausto*) exhausted; (*velho*) decrepit. **~bamento** *m* finish. **~bar** *vt* finish ● *vi* finish, end; (*esgotar-se*) run out; **~bar com** put an end to, end; (*abolir, matar*) do away with; split up with ‹*namorado*›; wipe out ‹*adversário*›; **~bou de chegar** he has just arrived; **~bar fazendo** ou **por fazer** end up doing. **~bar-se** *vpr* end, be over; (*esgotar-se*) run out

acabrunhado /akabru'ɲadu/ *a* dejected

aca|demia /akade'mia/ *f* academy; (*de ginástica etc*) gym. **~dêmico** *a & m* academic

> **Academia Brasileira de Letras**
> The *Academia Brasileira de Letras* is responsible for promoting Brazilian language and literature, and was founded in Rio de Janeiro in 1897. It was modelled on the French Academy, and comprises 40 life members, known as the *Imortais* (Immortals), including writers, poets, essayists, playwrights and intellectuals.

açafrão /asa'frãw/ *m* saffron

acalentar /akalẽ'tar/ *vt* lull to sleep ‹*bebê*›; cherish ‹*esperanças*›; have in mind ‹*planos*›

acalmar /akaw'mar/ *vt* calm (down) ● *vi* ‹*vento*› drop; ‹*mar*› grow calm. **~-se** *vpr* calm down

acam|pamento /akãpa'mẽtu/ *m* camp; (*ato*) camping. **~par** *vi* camp

aca|nhado /aka'ɲadu/ *a* shy. **~nhamento** *m* shyness. **~nhar-se** *vpr* be shy

ação /a'sãw/ *f* action; *Jurid* lawsuit; *Com* share

acariciar /akarisi'ar/ *vt* (*com a mão*) caress, stroke; (*adular*) make a fuss of; cherish ‹*esperanças*›

acarretar /akaxe'tar/ *vt* bring, cause

acasalar /akaza'lar/ *vt* mate. **~-se** *vpr* mate

acaso /a'kazu/ *m* chance; **ao ~** at random; **por ~** by chance

aca|tamento /akata'mẽtu/ *m* respect, deference. **~tar** *vt* respect, defer to ‹*pessoa, opinião*›; obey, abide by ‹*leis, ordens*›; take in ‹*criança*›

acautelar-se /akawte'larsi/ *vpr* be cautious

acei|tação /asejta'sãw/ *f* acceptance. **~tar** *vt* accept. **~tável** (*pl* **~táveis**) *a* acceptable

acele|ração /aselera'sãw/ *f* acceleration. **~rador** *m* accelerator. **~rar** *vi* accelerate ● *vt* speed up

acenar /ase'nar/ *vi* signal; (*saudando*) wave; **~ com** promise, offer

acender /asẽ'der/ *vt* light ‹*cigarro, fogo, vela*›; switch on ‹*luz*›; heat up ‹*debate*›

aceno /a'senu/ *m* signal; (*de saudação*) wave

acen|to /a'sẽtu/ *m* accent. **~tuar** *vt* accentuate; accent ‹*letra*›

acepção /asep'sãw/ *f* sense

acepipes /ase'pipʃ/ *m pl Port* cocktail snacks

acerca /a'serka/ **~ de** *prep* about, concerning

acercar-se /aser'karsi/ *vpr* **~ de** approach

acertar /aser'tar/ *vt* find ‹(*com o*) *caminho*, (*a*) *casa*›; put right, set ‹*relógio*›; get right ‹*pergunta*›; guess (correctly) ‹*solução*›; hit ‹*alvo*›; make ‹*acordo, negócio*›; fix, arrange ‹*encontro*› ● *vi* (*ter razão*) be right; (*atingir o alvo*) hit the mark; **~ com** find, happen upon; **~ em** hit

acervo /a'servu/ *m* collection; *Jurid* estate

aceso /a'sezu/ *pp de* ▶ ACENDER ● *a* ‹*luz*› on; ‹*fogo*› alight

aces|sar /ase'sar/ *vt* access. **~sível** (*pl* **~síveis**) *a* accessible; affordable ‹*preço*›. **~so** /ɛ/ *m* access; (*de raiva, tosse*) fit; (*de febre*) attack. **~sório** *a & m* accessory

acetona /ase'tona/ *f* (*para unhas*) nail varnish remover

achado /a'ʃadu/ *m* find

achaque /a'ʃaki/ *m* ailment

achar /a'ʃar/ *vt* find; (*pensar*) think. **~-se** *vpr* (*estar*) be; (*considerar-se*) think that one is; **acho que sim/não** I think so/ I don't think so

achatar /aʃa'tar/ *vt* flatten; cut ‹*salário*›

aciden|tado /asidẽ'tadu/ *a* rough ‹*terreno*›; bumpy ‹*estrada*›; eventful ‹*viagem, vida*›; injured ‹*pessoa*›. **~tal** (*pl* **~tais**) *a* accidental. **~te** *m* accident

acidez /asi'des/ *f* acidity

ácido /'asidu/ *a & m* acid

acima /a'sima/ *adv* above; **~ de** above; **mais ~** higher up

acio|nar /asio'nar/ *vt* operate; *Jurid* sue. **~nista** *m/f* shareholder

acirrado /asi'xadu/ *a* stiff, tough

a

acla|mação /aklama'sãw/ *f* acclaim; (*de rei*) acclamation. **~mar** *vt* acclaim

aclarar /akla'rar/ *vt* clarify, clear up ● *vi* clear up. **~-se** *vpr* become clear

aclimatar /aklima'tar/ *vt* acclimatize, *Amer* acclimate. **~-se** *vpr* get acclimatized, *Amer* get acclimated

aço /'asu/ *m* steel; **~ inoxidável** stainless steel

acocorar-se /akoko'rarsi/ *vpr* squat (down)

acolá /ako'la/ *adv* over there

acolcho|ado /akowʃo'adu/ *m* quilt. **~ar** *vt* quilt; upholster ‹*móveis*›

aco|lhedor /akoʎe'dor/ *a* welcoming. **~lher** *vt* welcome ‹*hóspede*›; take in ‹*criança, refugiado*›; accept ‹*decisão, convite*›; respond to ‹*pedido*›. **~lhida** *f*, **~lhimento** *m* welcome; (*abrigo*) refuge

acomodar /akomo'dar/ *vt* accommodate; (*ordenar*) arrange; (*tornar cômodo*) make comfortable. **~-se** *vpr* make o.s. comfortable

acompa|nhamento /akõpaɲa'mẽtu/ *m Mus* accompaniment; (*prato*) side dish; (*comitiva*) escort. **~nhante** *m/f* companion; *Mus* accompanist. **~nhar** *vt* accompany, go with; watch ‹*jogo, progresso*›; keep up with ‹*eventos, caso*›; keep up with, follow ‹*aula, conversa*›; share ‹*política, opinião*›; *Mus* accompany; **a estrada ~nha o rio** the road runs alongside the river

aconche|gante /akõʃe'gãtʃi/ *a* cosy, *Amer* cozy. **~gar** *vt* (*chegar a si*) cuddle; (*agasalhar*) wrap up; (*na cama*) tuck up; (*tornar cômodo*) make comfortable. **~gar-se** *vpr* ensconce o.s.; **~gar-se com** snuggle up to. **~go** /e/ *m* cosiness, *Amer* coziness; (*abraço*) cuddle

acondicionar /akõdʒisio'nar/ *vt* condition; pack, package ‹*mercadoria*›

aconse|lhar /akõse'ʎar/ *vt* advise; **~lhar alguém a** advise sb to; **~lhar algo a alguém** recommend sth to sb. **~lhar-se** *vpr* consult. **~lhável** (*pl* **~lháveis**) *a* advisable

aconte|cer /akõte'ser/ *vi* happen. **~cimento** *m* event

acordar /akor'dar/ *vt/i* wake up

acorde /a'kɔrdʒi/ *m* chord

acordeão /akordʒi'ãw/ *m* accordion

acordo /a'kordu/ *m* agreement; **de ~ com** in agreement with ‹*pessoa*›; in accordance with ‹*lei etc*›; **estar de ~** agree

Açores /a'soris/ *m pl* Azores

açoriano /asori'ano/ *a & m* Azorean

acorrentar /akoxẽ'tar/ *vt* chain (up)

acossar /ako'sar/ *vt* hound, badger

acos|tamento /akosta'mẽtu/ *m* hard shoulder, *Amer* berm. **~tar-se** *vpr* lean back

acostu|mado /akostu'madu/ *a* usual, customary; **estar ~mado a** be used to. **~mar** *vt* accustom; **~mar-se a** get used to

acotovelar /akotove'lar/ *vt* (*empurrar*) jostle; (*para avisar*) nudge

açou|gue /a'sogi/ *m* butcher's (shop). **~gueiro** *m* butcher

acovardar /akovar'dar/ *vt* cow, intimidate

acre /'akri/ *a* ‹*gosto*› bitter; ‹*aroma*› acrid, pungent; ‹*tom*› harsh

acredi|tar /akredʒi'tar/ *vt* believe; accredit ‹*representante*›; **~tar em** believe ‹*pessoa, história*›; believe in ‹*Deus, fantasmas*›; (*ter confiança*) have faith in. **~tável** (*pl* **~táveis**) *a* believable

acre-doce /akri'dosi/ *a* sweet and sour

acrescentar /akresẽ'tar/ *vt* add

acres|cer /akre'ser/ *vt* (*juntar*) add; (*aumentar*) increase ● *vi* increase; **~cido de** with the addition of; **~ce que** add to that the fact that

acréscimo /a'krɛsimu/ *m* addition; (*aumento*) increase

acriançado /akriã'sadu/ *a* childish

acrílico /a'kriliku/ *a* acrylic

acroba|cia /akroba'sia/ *f* acrobatics. **~ta** *m/f* acrobat

acuar /aku'ar/ *vt* corner

açúcar /a'sukar/ *m* sugar

açuca|rar /asuka'rar/ *vt* sweeten; sugar ‹*café, chá*›. **~reiro** *m* sugar bowl

açude /a'sudʒi/ *m* dam

acudir /aku'dʒir/ *vt/i* **~ (a)** come to the rescue (of)

acumular /akumu'lar/ *vt* accumulate; combine ‹*cargos*›

acupuntura /akupũ'tura/ *f* acupuncture

acu|sação /akuza'sãw/ *f* accusation. **~sar** *vt* accuse; *Jurid* charge; (*revelar*) reveal, show up; acknowledge ‹*recebimento*›

acústi|ca /a'kustʃika/ *f* acoustics. **~co** *a* acoustic

adap|tação /adapta'sãw/ *f* adaptation. **~tado** *a* ‹*criança*› well-adjusted. **~tar** *vt* adapt; (*para encaixar*) tailor. **~tar-se** *vpr* adapt. **~tável** (*pl* **~táveis**) *a* adaptable

adega /a'dɛga/ *f* wine cellar

adentro /a'dẽtru/ *adv* inside; **selva ~** into the jungle

adepto /a'dɛptu/ *m* follower; *Port* (*de equipa*) supporter

ade|quado /ade'kwadu/ *a* appropriate, suitable. **~quar** *vt* adapt, tailor

adereços /ade'resus/ *m pl* props

ade|rente /ade'rẽtʃi/ *m/f* follower. **~rir** *vi* (*colar*) stick; join ‹*a partido, causa*›; follow ‹*a moda*›. **~são** *f* adhesion; (*apoio*) support. **~sivo** *a* sticky, adhesive ● *m* sticker

ades|trado /ades'tradu/ *a* skilled. **~trador** *m* trainer. **~trar** *vt* train; break in ‹*cavalo*›

adeus /a'dews/ *int* goodbye ● *m* goodbye, farewell

adian|tado /adʒiã'tadu/ *a* advanced; ‹*relógio*› fast; **chegar ~tado** be early. **~tamento** *m* progress; (*pagamento*) advance. **~tar** *vt* advance ‹*dinheiro*›; put forward ‹*relógio*›; bring forward ‹*data, reunião*›; get ahead with ‹*trabalho*› ● *vi* ‹*relógio*› gain; (*ter efeito*) be of use; **não ~ta (fazer)** it's no use (doing). **~tar-se** *vpr* progress, get ahead. **~te** *adv* ahead

adi|ar /adʒi'ar/ *vt* postpone; adjourn ‹*sessão*›. **~amento** *m* postponement, adjournment

adi|ção /adʒi'sãw/ *f* addition. **~cionar** *vt* add. **~do** *m* attaché

adivi|nhação /adʒiviɲa'sãw/ *f* guesswork; (*por adivinho*) fortune telling. **~nhar** *vt* guess; tell ‹*futuro, sorte*›; read ‹*pensamento*›. **~nho** *m* fortune teller

adjetivo /adʒe'tʃivu/ *m* adjective

adminis|tração /adʒiministra'sãw/ *f* administration; (*de empresas*) management. **~trador** *m* administrator; manager. **~trar** *vt* administer; manage ‹*empresa*›

admi|ração /adʒimira'sãw/ *f* admiration; (*assombro*) wonder(ment). **~rado** *a* admired; (*surpreso*) amazed, surprised. **~rador** *m* admirer ● *a* admiring. **~rar** *vt* admire; (*assombrar*) amaze. **~rar-se** *vpr* be amazed. **~rável** (*pl* **~ráveis**) *a* admirable; (*assombroso*) amazing

admis|são /adʒimi'sãw/ *f* admission; (*de escola*) intake. **~sível** (*pl* **~síveis**) *a* admissible

admitir /adʒimi'tʃir/ *vt* admit; (*permitir*) permit, allow; (*contratar*) take on

adoçante /ado'sãtʃi/ *m* sweetener

adoção /ado'sãw/ *f* adoption

ado|çar /ado'sar/ *vt* sweeten. **~cicado** *a* slightly sweet

adoecer /adoe'ser/ *vi* fall ill ● *vt* make ill

adoles|cência /adole'sẽsia/ *f* adolescence. **~cente** *a & mf* adolescent

adorar /ado'rar/ *vt* (*amar*) adore; worship ‹*deus*›; [!] (*gostar de*) love

adorme|cer /adorme'ser/ *vi* fall asleep; ‹*perna*› go to sleep, go numb. **~cido** *a* sleeping; ‹*perna*› numb

ador|nar /ador'nar/ *vt* adorn. **~no** /o/ *m* adornment

ado|tar /ado'tar/ *vt* adopt. **~tivo** *a* adopted

adquirir /adʒiki'rir/ *vt* acquire

adu|bar /adu'bar/ *vt* fertilize. **~bo** *m* fertilizer

adu|lação /adula'sãw/ *f* flattery; (*do público*) adulation. **~lar** *vt* make a fuss of; (*com palavras*) flatter

adulterar /aduwte'rar/ *vt* adulterate; cook, doctor ‹*contas*› ● *vi* commit adultery

adul|tério /aduw'tɛriu/ *m* adultery. **~to** *a & m* adult

adúltero /a'duwteru/ *m* adulterer (*f* -ess) ● *a* adulterous

advento /adʒi'vẽtu/ *m* advent

advérbio /adʒi'vɛrbiu/ *m* adverb

adver|sário /adʒiver'sariu/ *m* opponent; (*inimigo*) adversary. **~sidade** *f* adversity. **~so** *a* adverse; (*adversário*) opposed

adver|tência /adʒiver'tẽsia/ *f* warning. **~tir** *vt* warn

advo|cacia /adʒivoka'sia/ *f* legal practice. **~gado** *m* lawyer. **~gar** *vt* advocate; *Jurid* plead ● *vi* practise law

aéreo /a'ɛriu/ *a* air

aeróbica /'aɛ'rɔbika/ *f* aerobics

ae|rodinâmica /aerodʒi'namika/ *f* aerodynamics. **~rodinâmico** *a* aerodynamic. **~ródromo** *m* airfield. **~romoça** /o/ *f* air hostess. **~ronauta** *m* airman (*f* -woman). **~ronáutica** *f* (*força*) air force; (*ciência*) aeronautics. **~ronave** *f* aircraft. **~roporto** /o/ *m* airport

aeros|sol /aero'sɔw/ (*pl* **~sóis**) *m* aerosol

afabilidade /afabili'dadʒi/ *f* friendliness, kindness

a

afagar /afa'gar/ *vt* stroke

afamado /afa'madu/ *a* renowned, famed

afas|tado /afas'tadu/ *a* remote; ‹*parente*› distant; **~tado de** (far) away from. **~tamento** *m* removal; (*distância*) distance; (*de candidato*) rejection. **~tar** *vt* move away; (*tirar*) remove; ward off ‹*perigo, ameaça*›; put out of one's mind ‹*ideia*›. **~tar-se** *vpr* move away; (*distanciar-se*) distance o.s.; (*de cargo*) step down

afá|vel /a'favew/ (*pl* **~veis**) *a* friendly, genial

afazeres /afa'zeris/ *m pl* business; **~ domésticos** (household) chores

Afeganistão /afeganis'tãw/ *m* Afghanistan

afe|gão /afe'gãw/ *a* & *m* (*f* **~gã**) Afghan

afeição /afej'sãw/ *f* affection, fondness

afeiçoado /afejsu'adu/ *a* (*devoto*) devoted; (*amoroso*) fond

afeminado /afemi'nadu/ *a* effeminate

aferir /afe'rir/ *vt* check, inspect ‹*pesos, medidas*›; (*avaliar*) assess; (*cotejar*) compare

aferrar /afe'xar/ *vt* grasp; **~se a** cling to

afe|tação /afeta'sãw/ *f* affectation. **~tado** *a* affected. **~tar** *vt* affect. **~tivo** *a* (*carinhoso*) affectionate; (*sentimental*) emotional. **~to** /ɛ/ *m* affection. **~tuoso** /o/ *a* affectionate

afi|ado /afi'adu/ *a* sharp; skilled ‹*pessoa*›. **~ar** *vt* sharpen

aficionado /afisio'nadu/ *m* enthusiast

afilhado /afi'ʎadu/ *m* godson (*f* -daughter)

afili|ação /afilia'sãw/ *f* affiliation. **~ada** *f* affiliate. **~ar** *vt* affiliate

afim /a'fĩ/ *a* related, similar

afinado /afi'nadu/ *a* in tune

afinal /afi'naw/ *adv* **~ (de contas)** (*por fim*) in the end; (*pensando bem*) after all

afinar /afi'nar/ *vt* tune ● *vi* taper

afinco /a'fĩku/ *m* perseverance, determination

afinidade /afini'dadʒi/ *f* affinity

afir|mação /afirma'sãw/ *f* assertion. **~mar** *vt* claim, assert. **~mativo** *a* affirmative

afivelar /afive'lar/ *vt* buckle

afixar /afik'sar/ *vt* stick, post

afli|ção /afli'sãw/ *f* (*física*) affliction; (*cuidado*) anxiety. **~gir** *vt* ‹*doença*› afflict; (*inquietar*) trouble. **~gir-se** *vpr* worry. **~to** *a* troubled, worried

afluente /aflu'ẽtʃi/ *m* tributary

afo|bação /afoba'sãw/ *f* fluster, flap. **~bado** *a* in a flap, flustered. **~bar** *vt* fluster. **~bar-se** *vpr* get flustered, get in a flap

afo|gado /afo'gadu/ *a* drowned; **morrer ~gado** drown. **~gador** *m* choke. **~gar** *vt/i* drown; *Auto* flood. **~gar-se** *vpr* (*matar-se*) drown o.s.

afoito /a'fojtu/ *a* bold, daring

afora /a'fɔra/ *adv* **pelo mundo ~** throughout the world

afortunado /afortu'nadu/ *a* fortunate

afresco /a'fresku/ *m* fresco

África /'afrika/ *f* Africa; **~ do Sul** South Africa

africano /afri'kanu/ *a* & *m* African

afrodisíaco /afrodʒi'ziaku/ *a* & *m* aphrodisiac

afron|ta /a'frõta/ *f* affront, insult. **~tar** *vt* affront, insult

afrouxar /afro'ʃar/ *vt/i* loosen; (*de rapidez*) slow down; (*de disciplina*) relax

afta /'afta/ *f* (mouth) ulcer

afugentar /afuʒẽ'tar/ *vt* drive away; rout ‹*inimigo*›

afundar /afũ'dar/ *vt* sink. **~se** *vpr* sink

agachar /aga'ʃar/ *vi*, **~se** *vpr* bend down

agarrar /aga'xar/ *vt* grab, snatch. **~se** *vpr* **~se a** cling to, hold on to

agasa|lhar /agaza'ʎar/ *vt*, **~lhar-se** *vpr* wrap up (warmly). **~lho** *m* (*casaco*) coat; (*suéter*) sweater

agência /a'ʒẽsia/ *f* agency; **~ de correio** post office; **~ de viagens** travel agency

agenda /a'ʒẽda/ *f* diary

agente /a'ʒẽtʃi/ *m/f* agent

ágil /'aʒiw/ (*pl* **ágeis**) *a* ‹*pessoa*› agile; ‹*serviço*› quick, efficient

agili|dade /aʒili'dadʒi/ *f* agility; (*rapidez*) speed. **~zar** *vt* speed up, streamline

ágio /'aʒiu/ *m* premium

agiota /aʒi'ɔta/ *m/f* loan shark

agir /a'ʒir/ *vi* act

agi|tado /aʒi'tadu/ *a* agitated; ‹*mar*› rough. **~tar** *vt* wave ‹*braços*›; wag ‹*rabo*›; shake ‹*garrafa*›; (*perturbar*) agitate. **~tar-se** *vpr* get agitated; ‹*mar*› get rough

aglome|ração /aglomera'sãw/ *f* collection; (*de pessoas*) crowd; **~rar** *vt* collect. **~rar-se** *vpr* gather

agonia /ago'nia/ *f* anguish; (*da morte*) death throes

agora /a'gɔra/ *adv* now; (*há pouco*) just now; **~ mesmo** right now; **de ~ em diante** from now on; **até ~** so far, up till now

agosto /a'gostu/ *m* August

agouro /a'goru/ *m* omen

agraciar /agrasi'ar/ *vt* decorate

agra|dar /agra'dar/ *vt* please; (*fazer agrados*) be nice to, fuss over ● *vi* be pleasing, please; (*cair no gosto*) go down well. **~dável** (*pl* **~dáveis**) *a* pleasant

agrade|cer /agrade'ser/ *vt* **~cer algo a alguém, ~cer a alguém por algo** thank sb for sth ● *vi* say thank you. **~cido** *a* grateful. **~cimento** *m* gratitude; *pl* thanks

agrado /a'gradu/ *m* **fazer ~s a** be nice to, make a fuss of

agra|far /agra'far/ *vt Port* staple. **~fador** *m* stapler

agrário /a'grariu/ *a* land, agrarian

agra|vante /agra'vãtʃi/ *a* aggravating ● *f* aggravating circumstance. **~var** *vt* aggravate, make worse. **~var-se** *vpr* get worse

agredir /agre'dʒir/ *vt* attack

agregado /agre'gadu/ *m* (*em casa*) lodger

agres|são /agre'sãw/ *f* aggression; (*ataque*) assault. **~sivo** *a* aggressive. **~sor** *m* aggressor

agreste /a'grɛstʃi/ *a* rural

agrião /agri'ãw/ *m* watercress

agrícola /a'grikola/ *a* agricultural

agricul|tor /agrikuw'tor/ *m* farmer. **~tura** *f* agriculture, farming

agridoce /agri'dosi/ *a* bittersweet

agropecuá|ria /agropeku'aria/ *f* farming. **~rio** *a* agricultural

agru|pamento /agrupa'mẽtu/ *m* grouping. **~par** *vt* group. **~par-se** *vpr* group (together)

água /'agwa/ *f* water; **dar ~ na boca** be mouth-watering; **ir por ~ abaixo** go down the drain; **~ benta** holy water; **~ de coco** coconut water; **~ doce** fresh water; **~ mineral** mineral water; **~ salgada** salt water; **~ sanitária** household bleach

aguaceiro /agwa'seru/ *m* downpour

água-colônia *f* eau de cologne

aguado /a'gwadu/ *a* watery

aguardar /agwar'dar/ *vt* wait for, await ● *vi* wait

aguardente /agwar'dẽtʃi/ *f* spirit

aguarrás /agwa'xas/ *m* turpentine

água-viva /agwa'viva/ *f* jellyfish

agu|çado /agu'sadu/ *a* pointed; ‹*sentidos*› acute. **~çar** *vt* sharpen. **~deza** *f* sharpness; (*mental*) perceptiveness. **~do** *a* sharp; ‹*som*› shrill; *fig* acute

aguentar /agwẽ'tar/ *vt* stand, put up with; hold ‹*peso*› ● *vi* ‹*pessoa*› hold out; ‹*suporte*› hold

águia /'agia/ *f* eagle

agulha /a'guʎa/ *f* needle

ai /aj/ *m* sigh; (*de dor*) groan ● *int* ah!; (*de dor*) ouch!

aí /a'i/ *adv* there; (*então*) then

aidético /aj'dɛtʃiku/ *a* suffering from Aids ● *m* Aids sufferer

AIDS /'ajdʒis/ *f* Aids; **vírus da ~** AIDS virus

ainda /a'ĩda/ *adv* still; **melhor ~** even better; **não ... ~** not ... yet; **~ assim** even so; **~ bem** just as well; **~ por cima** moreover, in addition; **~ que** even if

aipim /aj'pĩ/ *m* cassava

aipo /'ajpu/ *m* celery

ajeitar /aʒej'tar/ *vt* (*arrumar*) sort out; (*arranjar*) arrange; (*ajustar*) adjust. **~-se** *vpr* adapt; (*dar certo*) turn out right, sort o.s. out

ajoe|lhado /aʒoe'ʎadu/ *a* kneeling (down). **~lhar** *vi*, **~lhar-se** *vpr* kneel (down)

aju|da /a'ʒuda/ *f* help. **~dante** *m/f* helper. **~dar** *vt* help

ajuizado /aʒui'zadu/ *a* sensible

ajus|tar /aʒus'tar/ *vt* adjust; settle ‹*disputa*›; take in ‹*roupa*›. **~tar-se** *vpr* conform. **~tável** (*pl* **~táveis**) *a* adjustable. **~te** *m* adjustment; (*acordo*) settlement

ala /'ala/ *f* wing

ala|gação /alaga'sãw/ *f* flooding. **~gadiço** *a* marshy ● *m* marsh. **~gar** *vt* flood

alameda /ala'meda/ *f* avenue

álamo /'alamu/ *m* poplar (tree)

alarde /a'lardʒi/ *m* **fazer ~ de** flaunt; make a big thing of ‹*notícia*›. **~ar** *vt/i* flaunt

alargar /alar'gar/ *vt* widen; *fig* broaden; let out ‹*roupa*›

alarido /ala'ridu/ *m* outcry

a

alar|ma /a'larma/ *m* alarm. **~mante** *a* alarming. **~mar** *vt* alarm. **~me** *m* alarm. **~mista** *a & m* alarmist

alastrar /alas'trar/ *vt* scatter; (*disseminar*) spread ● *vi* spread

alavanca /ala'vãka/ *f* lever; **~ de mudanças** gear lever

alba|nês /awba'nes/ *a & m* (*f* **~nesa**) Albanian

Albânia /aw'bania/ *f* Albania

albergue /aw'bɛrgi/ *m* hostel

álbum /'awbũ/ *m* album

alça /'awsa/ *f* handle; (*de roupa*) strap; (*de fusil*) sight

alcachofra /awka'ʃofra/ *f* artichoke

alçada /aw'sada/ *f* competence, power

Alcaida /'aw'kaida/ *f Port* ▶ **AL-QAEDA**

álcali /'awkali/ *m* alkali

alcan|çar /awkã'sar/ *vt* reach; (*conseguir*) attain; (*compreender*) understand ● *vi* reach. **~çável** (*pl* **~çáveis**) *a* reachable; attainable. **~ce** *m* reach; (*de tiro*) range; (*importância*) consequence; (*compreensão*) understanding

alcaparra /awka'paxa/ *f* caper

alcatra /aw'katra/ *f* rump steak

alcatrão /awka'trãw/ *m* tar

álcool /'awkɔw/ *m* alcohol

alcoó|latra /awko'ɔlatra/ *m/f* alcoholic. **~lico** *a & m* alcoholic

alcunha /aw'kuɲa/ *f* nickname

aldeia /aw'deja/ *f* village

aleatório /alia'tɔriu/ *a* random, arbitrary

alecrim /ale'krĩ/ *m* rosemary

ale|gação /alega'sãw/ *f* allegation. **~gar** *vt* allege

ale|goria /alego'ria/ *f* allegory. **~górico** *a* allegorical

ale|grar /ale'grar/ *vt* cheer up; brighten up ‹*casa*›. **~grar-se** *vpr* cheer up. **~gre** /ɛ/ *a* cheerful; ‹*cores*› bright. **~gria** *f* joy

alei|jado /ale'ʒadu/ *a* crippled ● *m* cripple. **~jar** *vt* cripple

alei|tamento /alejta'mẽtu/ *m* breastfeeding. **~tar** *vt* breastfeed

além /a'lẽj/ *adv* beyond; **~ de** (*ao lado de lá de*) beyond; (*mais de*) over; (*ademais de*) apart from

Alemanha /ale'maɲa/ *f* Germany

ale|mão /ale'mãw/ (*pl* **~mães**) *a & m* (*f* **~mã**) German

alen|tador /alẽta'dor/ *a* encouraging. **~tar** *vt* encourage. **~tar-se** *vpr* cheer up. **~to** *m* courage; (*fôlego*) breath

alergia /aler'ʒia/ *f* allergy

alérgico /a'lɛrʒiku/ *a* allergic (**a** to)

aler|ta /a'lɛrta/ *a & m* alert ● *adv* on the alert. **~tar** *vt* alert

alfa|bético /awfa'bɛtʃiku/ *a* alphabetical. **~betização** *f* literacy. **~betizar** *vt* teach to read and write. **~beto** *m* alphabet

alface /aw'fasi/ *f* lettuce

alfaiate /awfaj'atʃi/ *m* tailor

al|fândega /aw'fãdʒiga/ *f* customs. **~fandegário** *a* customs ● *m* customs officer

alfine|tada /awfine'tada/ *f* prick; (*dor*) stabbing pain; *fig* dig. **~te** /e/ *m* pin; **~te de segurança** safety pin

alforreca /alfo'xeka/ *f Port* jellyfish

alga /'awga/ *f* seaweed

algarismo /awga'rizmu/ *m* numeral

algazarra /awga'zaxa/ *f* uproar, racket

alge|mar /awʒe'mar/ *vt* handcuff. **~mas** /e/ *f pl* handcuffs

algibeira /alʒi'bejra/ *f Port* pocket

algo /'awgu/ *pron* something; (*numa pergunta*) anything ● *adv* somewhat

algodão /awgo'dãw/ *m* cotton; **~(-doce)** candy floss, *Amer* cotton candy; **~ (hidrófilo)** cotton wool, *Amer* absorbent cotton

alguém /aw'gẽj/ *pron* somebody, someone; (*numa pergunta*) anybody, anyone

al|gum /aw'gũ/ (*f* **~guma**) *a* some; (*numa pergunta*) any; (*nenhum*) no, not one ● *pron pl* some; **~guma coisa** something

algures /aw'guris/ *adv* somewhere

alheio /a'ʎeju/ *a* (*de outra pessoa*) someone else's; (*de outras pessoas*) other people's; **~ a** foreign to; (*impróprio*) irrelevant to; (*desatento*) unaware of; **~ de** removed from

alho /'aʎu/ *m* garlic. **~-poró** *m* leek

ali /a'li/ *adv* (over) there

ali|ado /ali'adu/ *a* allied ● *m* ally. **~ança** *f* alliance; (*anel*) wedding ring. **~ar** *vt*, **~ar-se** *vpr* ally

aliás /a'ljaʃ/ *adv* (*além disso*) what's more, furthermore; (*no entanto*) however; (*diga-se de passagem*) by the way, incidentally; (*senão*) otherwise

álibi /'alibi/ *m* alibi

alicate /ali'katʃi/ *m* pliers; **~ de unhas** nail clippers

alicerce /ali'sɛrsi/ *m* foundation; *fig* basis

alie|nado /alie'nadu/ *a* alienated; (*demente*) insane. **~nar** *vt* alienate; transfer ‹*bens*›. **~nígena** *a & m/f* alien

alimen|tação /alimẽta'sãw/ *f* (*ato*) feeding; (*comida*) food; *Tecn* supply. **~tar** *a* food; ‹*hábitos*› eating ● *vt* feed; *fig* nurture; **~tar-se de** live on. **~tício** *a* **gêneros ~tícios** foodstuffs. **~to** *m* food

ali|nhado /ali'ɲadu/ *a* aligned; ‹*pessoa*› smart, *Amer* sharp. **~nhar** *vt* align

alíquota /a'likwota/ *f* (*de imposto*) bracket

alisar /ali'zar/ *vt* smooth (out); straighten ‹*cabelo*›

alistar /alis'tar/ *vt* recruit. **~-se** *vpr* enlist

aliviar /alivi'ar/ *vt* relieve

alívio /a'liviu/ *m* relief

alma /'awma/ *f* soul

almanaque /awma'naki/ *m* yearbook

almejar /awme'ʒar/ *vt* long for

almirante /awmi'rãtʃi/ *m* admiral

almo|çar /awmo'sar/ *vi* have lunch ● *vt* have for lunch. **~ço** /o/ *m* lunch

almofada /awmo'fada/ *f* cushion; *Port* (*de cama*) pillow

almôndega /aw'mõdʒiga/ *f* meatball

almoxarifado /awmoʃari'fadu/ *m* storeroom

alô /a'lo/ *int* hallo

alocar /alo'kar/ *vt* allocate

alo|jamento /aloʒa'mẽtu/ *m* accommodation, *Amer* accommodations; (*habitação*) housing. **~jar** *vt* accommodate; house ‹*sem-teto*›. **~jar-se** *vpr* stay

alongar /alõ'gar/ *vt* lengthen; extend, stretch out ‹*braço*›

alpendre /aw'pẽdri/ *m* shed; (*pórtico*) porch

Alpes /'awpis/ *m pl* Alps

alpinis|mo /awpi'nizmu/ *m* mountaineering. **~ta** *m/f* mountaineer

Al-Qaeda /aw'kaida/ *f BR* Al-Qaeda

alqueire /aw'keri/ *m*: = 4.84 hectares; (*in São Paulo*) = 2.42 hectares

alquimi|a /awki'mia/ *f* alchemy. **~sta** *mf* alchemist

alta /'awta/ *f* rise; **dar ~ a** discharge; **ter ~** be discharged

altar /aw'tar/ *m* altar

alterar /awte'rar/ *vt* alter; (*falsificar*) falsify. **~-se** *vpr* change; (*zangar-se*) get angry

alter|nado /awter'nadu/ *a* alternate. **~nar** *vt/i*, **~nar-se** *vpr* alternate. **~nativa** *f* alternative. **~nativo** *a* alternative; ‹*corrente*› alternating

al|teza /aw'teza/ *f* highness. **~titude** *f* altitude

altifalante /awtʃifa'lãtʃi/ *m Port* ▶ **ALTO-FALANTE**

alti|vez /awtʃi'ves/ *f* arrogance. **~vo** *a* arrogant; (*elevado*) majestic

alto /'awtu/ *a* high; ‹*pessoa*› tall; ‹*barulho*› loud ● *adv* high; ‹*falar*› loud(ly); ‹*ler*› aloud ● *m* top; **os ~s e baixos** the ups and downs ● *int* halt!. **~-falante** *m* loudspeaker

altura /aw'tura/ *f* height; (*momento*) moment; **ser à ~ de** be up to

aluci|nação /alusina'sãw/ *f* hallucination. **~nante** *a* mind-boggling, crazy

aludir /alu'dʒir/ *vi* allude (**a** to)

alu|gar /alu'gar/ *vt* rent ‹*casa*›; hire, rent ‹*carro*›; ‹*locador*› let, rent out, hire out. **~guel**, *Port* **~guer** /ɛ/ *m* rent; (*ato*) renting

alumiar /alumi'ar/ *vt* light (up)

alumínio /alu'miniu/ *m* aluminium, *Amer* aluminum

aluno /a'lunu/ *m* pupil

alusão /alu'zãw/ *f* allusion (**a** to)

alvará /awva'ra/ *m* permit, licence

alve|jante /awve'ʒãtʃi/ *m* bleach. **~jar** *vt* bleach; (*visar*) aim at

alvenaria /awvena'ria/ *f* masonry

alvo /'awvu/ *m* target

alvorada /awvo'rada/ *f* dawn

alvoro|çar /awvoro'sar/ *vt* stir up, agitate; (*entusiasmar*) excite. **~ço** /o/ *m* (*tumulto*) uproar; (*entusiasmo*) excitement

amabilidade /amabili'dadʒi/ *f* kindness

amaci|ante /amasi'ãtʃi/ *m* (*de roupa*) (fabric) conditioner. **~ar** *vt* soften; run in ‹*carro*›

amador /ama'dor/ *a & m* amateur. **~ismo** *m* amateurism. **~ístico** *a* amateurish

amadurecer /amadure'ser/ *vt/i* ‹*fruta*› ripen; *fig* mature

âmago /'amagu/ *m* heart, core; (*da questão*) crux

amaldiçoar /amawdʒiso'ar/ *vt* curse

amamentar /amamẽ'tar/ *vt* breastfeed

amanhã /ama'ɲã/ *m & adv* tomorrow; **depois de ~** the day after tomorrow

amanhecer /amaɲe'ser/ *vi & m* dawn

amansar /amã'sar/ *vt* tame; *fig* placate ‹*pessoa*›

a|mante /a'mãtʃi/ *m/f* lover. **~mar** *vt/i* love

amarelo /ama'rɛlu/ *a & m* yellow

amar|go /a'margu/ *a* bitter. **~gura** *f* bitterness. **~gurar** *vt* embitter; (*sofrer*) endure

amarrar /ama'xar/ *vt* tie (up); *Naut* moor; **~ a cara** frown, scowl

amarrotar /amaxo'tar/ *vt* crease

amassar /ama'sar/ *vt* crush, squash; screw up ‹*papel*›; crease ‹*roupa*›; dent ‹*carro*›; knead ‹*pão*›; mash ‹*batatas*›

amá|vel /a'mavew/ (*pl* **~veis**) *a* kind

Ama|zonas /ama'zonas/ *m* Amazon. **~zônia** *f* Amazonia

> **Amazônia** The Amazon region is home to the world's largest rainforest, covering 7 million square kilometres, half of which is in Brazilian territory. It is made up of the Amazon Basin, which has the highest flow of river water in the world, and the Amazon Rainforest, and is home to vast biodiversity, including more than sixty thousand types of trees.

âmbar /'ãbar/ *m* amber

ambi|ção /ãbi'sãw/ *f* ambition. **~cionar** *vt* aspire to. **~cioso** /o/ *a* ambitious

ambien|tal /ãbiẽ'taw/ (*pl* **~tais**) *a* environmental. **~tar** *vt* set ‹*filme, livro*›; set up ‹*casa*›. **~tar-se** *vpr* settle in. **~te** *m* environment; (*atmosfera*) atmosphere

am|biguidade /ãbigwi'dadʒi/ *f* ambiguity. **~bíguo** *a* ambiguous

âmbito /'ãbitu/ *m* scope, range

ambos /'ãbus/ *a & pron* both

ambu|lância /ãbu'lãsia/ *f* ambulance. **~lante** *a* (*que anda*) walking; ‹*músico*› wandering; ‹*venda*› mobile. **~latório** *m* outpatient clinic

amea|ça /ami'asa/ *f* threat. **~çador** *a* threatening. **~çar** *vt* threaten

ameba /a'mɛba/ *f* amoeba

amedrontar /amedrõ'tar/ *vt* scare. **~-se** *vpr* get scared

ameixa /a'meʃa/ *f* plum; (*passa*) prune

amém /a'mẽj/ *int* amen ● *m* agreement; **dizer ~ a** go along with

amêndoa /a'mẽdoa/ *f* almond

amendoim /amẽdo'ĩ/ *m* peanut

ame|nidade /ameni'dadʒi/ *f* pleasantness; pleasantries, small talk. **~nizar** *vt* ease; calm ‹*ânimos*›; settle ‹*disputa*›; tone down ‹*repreensão*›. **~no** /e/ *a* pleasant; mild ‹*clima*›

América /a'mɛrika/ *f* America; **~ do Norte/Sul** North/South America

america|nizar /amerikani'zar/ *vt* Americanize. **~no** *a & m* American

amestrar /ames'trar/ *vt* train

ametista /ame'tʃista/ *f* amethyst

amianto /ami'ãtu/ *m* asbestos

ami|gar-se /ami'garsi/ *vpr* make friends. **~gável** (*pl* **~gáveis**) *a* amicable

amígdala /a'migdala/ *f* tonsil

amigdalite /amigda'litʃi/ *f* tonsillitis

amigo /a'migu/ *a* friendly ● *m* friend; **~ da onça** false friend

amistoso /amis'tozu/ *a & m* friendly

amiúde /ami'udʒi/ *adv* often

amizade /ami'zadʒi/ *f* friendship

amnésia /ami'nɛzia/ *f* amnesia

amnistia /amnis'tia/ *f Port* ▶ **ANISTIA**

amo|lação /amola'sãw/ *f* annoyance. **~lante** *a* annoying. **~lar** *vt* annoy, bother; sharpen ‹*faca*›. **~lar-se** *vpr* get annoyed

amolecer /amole'ser/ *vt/i* soften

amol|gadura /amowga'dura/ *f* dent. **~gar** *vt* dent

amoníaco /amo'niaku/ *m* ammonia

amontoar /amõto'ar/ *vt* pile up; amass ‹*riquezas*›. **~-se** *vpr* pile up

amor /a'mor/ *m* love

amora /a'mɔra/ *f* **~ preta**, *Port* **~ silvestre** blackberry

amordaçar /amorda'sar/ *vt* gag

amoroso /amo'rozu/ *a* loving

amor-perfeito /amorper'fejtu/ *m* pansy

amor-próprio /amor'propriu/ *m* self-esteem

amorte|cedor /amortese'dor/ *m* shock absorber. **~cer** *vt* deaden; absorb ‹*impacto*›; break ‹*queda*› ● *vi* fade

amostra /a'mɔstra/ *f* sample

ampa|rar /ãpa'rar/ *vt* support; *fig* protect. **~rar-se** *vpr* lean. **~ro** *m* (*apoio*) support; (*proteção*) protection; (*ajuda*) aid

ampere /ã'pɛri/ *m* amp(ere)
ampli|ação /ãplia'sãw/ *f* (*de foto*) enlargement; (*de casa*) extension. **~ar** *vt* enlarge ‹*foto*›; extend ‹*casa*›; broaden ‹*conhecimentos*›
amplifi|cador /ãplifika'dor/ *m* amplifier. **~car** *vt* amplify
amplo /'ãplu/ *a* ‹*sala*› spacious; ‹*roupa*› full; ‹*sentido, conhecimento*› broad
ampola /ã'pola/ *f* ampoule
amputar /ãpu'tar/ *vt* amputate
Amsterdã /amister'dã/ *f*, *Port* **Amsterdão** /amiʃter'dãw/ *m* Amsterdam
amu|ado /amu'adu/ *a* in a sulk, sulky. **~ar** *vi* sulk
amuleto /amu'leto/ *m* charm
amuo /a'muu/ *m* sulk
ana|crônico /ana'kroniku/ *a* anachronistic. **~cronismo** *m* anachronism
anais /a'najs/ *m pl* annals
analfabeto /anawfa'bɛtu/ *a & m* illiterate
analgésico /anaw'ʒɛziku/ *m* painkiller
analisar /anali'zar/ *vt* analyse
análise /a'nalizi/ *f* analysis
ana|lista /ana'lista/ *m/f* analyst. **~lítico** *a* analytical
analogia /analo'ʒia/ *f* analogy
análogo /a'nalogu/ *a* analogous
ananás /ana'naʃ/ *m invar Port* pineapple
anão /a'nãw/ *a & m* (*f* **anã**) dwarf
anarquia /anar'kia/ *f* anarchy; *fig* chaos
anárquico /a'narkiku/ *a* anarchic
anarquista /anar'kista/ *m/f* anarchist
ana|tomia /anato'mia/ *f* anatomy. **~tômico** *a* anatomical
anca /'ãka/ *f* (*de pessoa*) hip; (*de animal*) rump
anchova /ã'ʃova/ *f* anchovy
ancinho /ã'siɲu/ *m* rake
âncora /'ãkora/ *f* anchor
anco|radouro /ãkora'doru/ *m* anchorage. **~rar** *vt/i* anchor
andaime /ã'dajmi/ *m* scaffolding
an|damento /ãda'mẽtu/ *m* (*progresso*) progress; (*rumo*) course; **dar ~damento a** set in motion. **~dar** *m* (*jeito de andar*) gait, walk; (*de prédio*) floor; *Port* (*apartamento*) flat, *Amer* apartment ● *vi* (*ir a pé*) walk; (*de trem, ônibus*) travel; (*a cavalo, de bicicleta*) ride; (*funcionar, progredir*) go; **ele ~da deprimido** he's been depressed lately
Andes /'ãdʒis/ *m pl* Andes
andorinha /ãdo'riɲa/ *f* swallow
anedota /ane'dɔta/ *f* anecdote
anel /a'nɛw/ (*pl* **anéis**) *m* ring; (*no cabelo*) curl; **~ viário** ring road
anelado /ane'ladu/ *a* curly
anemia /ane'mia/ *f* anaemia
anêmico /a'nemiku/ *a* anaemic
anes|tesia /aneste'zia/ *f* anaesthesia; (*droga*) anaesthetic. **~tesiar** *vt* anaesthetize. **~tésico** *a & m* anaesthetic. **~tesista** *m/f* anaesthetist
ane|xar /anek'sar/ *vt* annex ‹*terras*›; (*em carta*) enclose; (*juntar*) attach. **~xo** /a'nɛksu/ *a* attached; (*em carta*) enclosed ● *m* annexe; (*em carta*) enclosure; *Comput* attachment
anfetamina /ãfeta'mina/ *f* amphetamine
anfíbio /ã'fibiu/ *a* amphibious ● *m* amphibian
anfiteatro /ãfitʃi'atru/ *m* amphitheatre; (*no teatro*) dress circle
anfi|trião /ãfitri'ãw/ *m* (*f* **~triã**) host (*f* -ess)
angariar /ãgari'ar/ *vt* raise ‹*fundos*›; canvass for ‹*votos*›; win ‹*adeptos, simpatia*›
angli|cano /ãgli'kanu/ *a & m* Anglican. **~cismo** *m* Anglicism
anglo-saxônico /ãglusak'soniku/ *a* Anglo-Saxon
Angola /ã'gɔla/ *f* Angola
angolano /ãgo'lanu/ *a & m* Angolan
angra /'ãgra/ *f* inlet, cove
angular /ãgu'lar/ *a* angular
ângulo /'ãgulu/ *m* angle
angústia /ã'gustʃia/ *f* anguish, anxiety
angustiante /ãgustʃi'ãtʃi/ *a* distressing; ‹*momento*› anxious
ani|mado /ani'madu/ *a* (*vivo*) lively; (*alegre*) cheerful; (*entusiasmado*) enthusiastic. **~mador** *a* encouraging ● *m* presenter. **~mal** (*pl* **~mais**) *a & m* animal. **~mar** *vt* encourage; liven up ‹*festa*›. **~mar-se** *vpr* cheer up; ‹*festa*› liven up
ânimo /'animu/ *m* courage, spirit; tempers
animosidade /animozi'dadʒi/ *f* animosity

aniquilar /aniki'lar/ *vt* destroy; (*prostrar*) shatter

anis /a'nis/ *m* aniseed

anistia /anis'tʃia/ *f* amnesty

aniver|sariante /aniversari'ãtʃi/ *m/f* birthday boy (*f* girl). **~sário** *m* birthday; (*de casamento etc*) anniversary

anjo /'ãʒu/ *m* angel

ano /'anu/ *m* year; **fazer ~s** have a birthday; **~ bissexto** leap year; **~ letivo** academic year. **~-bom** *m* New Year

anoite|cer /anojte'ser/ *m* nightfall ● *vi* **~ceu** night fell

anomalia /anoma'lia/ *f* anomaly

anonimato /anoni'matu/ *m* anonymity

anônimo /a'nonimu/ *a* anonymous

anorexia /anorek'sia/ *f* anorexia

anoréxico /ano'rɛksiku/ *a & m* anorexic

anor|mal /anor'maw/ (*pl* **~mais**) *a* abnormal

ano|tação /anota'sãw/ *f* note. **~tar** *vt* note down, write down

ânsia /'ãsia/ *f* anxiety; (*desejo*) longing; **~s de vômito** nausea

ansi|ar /ãsi'ar/ *vi* **~ por** long for. **~edade** *f* anxiety; (*desejo*) eagerness. **~oso** /o/ *a* anxious

antártico /ã'tartʃiku/ *a & m* Antarctic

antebraço /ãtʃi'brasu/ *m* forearm

antece|dência /ãtese'dẽsia/ *f* **com ~dência** in advance. **~dente** *a* preceding. **~dentes** *m pl* record, past

antecessor /ãtese'sor/ *m* (*f* **~a**) predecessor

anteci|pação /ãtʃisipa'sãw/ *f* anticipation; **com ~pação** in advance. **~padamente** *adv* in advance. **~pado** *a* advance. **~par** *vt* anticipate, forestall; (*adiantar*) bring forward. **~par-se** *vpr* be previous

antena /ã'tena/ *f* aerial, *Amer* antenna; (*de inseto*) feeler

anteontem /ãtʃi'õtẽ/ *adv* the day before yesterday

antepassado /ãtʃipa'sadu/ *m* ancestor

anterior /ãteri'or/ *a* previous; (*dianteiro*) front

antes /'ãtʃis/ *adv* before; (*ao contrário*) rather; **~ de/que** before

antessala /ãtʃi'sala/ *f* anteroom

anti|biótico /ãtʃibi'ɔtʃiku/ *a & m* antibiotic. **~caspa** *a* anti-dandruff. **~concepcional** (*pl* **~concepcionais**) *a & m* contraceptive. **~congelante** *m* antifreeze. **~corpo** *m* antibody

antídoto /ã'tʃidotu/ *m* antidote

antiético /ãtʃi'ɛtʃiku/ *a* unethical

antigamente /ãtʃiga'mẽtʃi/ *adv* formerly

anti|go /ã'tʃigu/ *a* old; (*da antiguidade*) ancient; ‹*móveis etc*› antique; (*anterior*) former. **~guidade** *f* antiquity; (*numa firma*) seniority; (*monumentos*) antiquities; (*móveis etc*) antiques

anti-|higiênico /ãtʃiʒi'eniku/ *a* unhygienic. **~histamínico** *a & m* antihistamine. **~horário** *a* anticlockwise

antilhano /ãtʃi'ʎanu/ *a & m* West Indian

Antilhas /ã'tʃiʎas/ *f pl* West Indies

anti|patia /ãtʃipa'tʃia/ *f* dislike. **~pático** *a* unpleasant, unfriendly

antiquado /ãtʃi'kwadu/ *a* antiquated, outdated

antis|semitismo /ãtʃisemi'tʃizmu/ *m* anti-Semitism. **~séptico** *a & m* antiseptic. **~social** (*pl* **~sociais**) *a* antisocial

antítese /ã'tʃitezi/ *f* antithesis

antologia /ãtolo'ʒia/ *f* anthology

antônimo /ã'tonimu/ *m* antonym

antro /'ãtru/ *m* cavern; (*de animal*) lair; (*de ladrões*) den

antro|pófago /ãtro'pɔfagu/ *a* man-eating. **~pologia** *f* anthropology. **~pólogo** *m* anthropologist

anu|al /anu'aw/ (*pl* **~ais**) *a* annual, yearly

anu|lação /anula'sãw/ *f* cancellation. **~lar** *vt* cancel; annul ‹*casamento*›; (*compensar*) cancel out ● *m* ring finger

anunciar /anũsi'ar/ *vt* announce; advertise ‹*produto*›

anúncio /a'nũsiu/ *m* announcement; (*propaganda, classificado*) advert(isement); (*cartaz*) notice

ânus /'anus/ *m invar* anus

an|zol /ã'zɔw/ (*pl* **~zóis**) *m* fish hook

aonde /a'õdʒi/ *adv* where

apadrinhar /apadri'ɲar/ *vt* be godfather to ‹*afilhado*›; be best man for ‹*noivo*›; (*proteger*) protect; (*patrocinar*) support

apa|gado /apa'gadu/ *a* ‹*fogo*› out; ‹*luz, TV*› off; (*indistinto*) faint; ‹*pessoa*› dull. **~gar** *vt* put out ‹*cigarro, fogo*›; blow out ‹*vela*›; switch off ‹*luz, TV*›; rub out ‹*erro*›; clean ‹*quadro-negro*›.

~gar-se *vpr* ‹*fogo, luz*› go out; ‹*lembrança*› fade; (*desmaiar*) pass out; [!] (*dormir*) nod off

apaixo|nado /apaʃo'nadu/ *a* in love (**por** with). **~nante** *a* captivating. **~nar-se** *vpr* fall in love (**por** with)

apalpar /apaw'par/ *vt* touch, feel; ‹*médico*› examine

apanhar /apa'ɲar/ *vt* catch; (*do chão*) pick up; pick ‹*flores, frutas*›; (*ir buscar*) pick up; (*alcançar*) catch up ● *vi* be beaten

aparafusar /aparafu'zar/ *vt* screw

apa|ra-lápis /apara'lapiʃ/ *m invar Port* pencil sharpener. **~rar** *vt* catch ‹*bola*›; parry ‹*golpe*›; trim ‹*cabelo*›; sharpen ‹*lápis*›

aparato /apa'ratu/ *m* pomp, ceremony

apare|cer /apare'ser/ *vi* appear; **~ça!** do drop in!. **~cimento** *m* appearance

apare|lhagem /apare'ʎaʒẽ/ *f* equipment. **~lhar** *vt* equip. **~lho** /e/ *m* apparatus; (*máquina*) machine; (*de chá*) set, service; (*fone*) phone

aparência /apa'rẽsia/ *f* appearance; **na ~** apparently

aparen|tado /aparẽ'tadu/ *a* related. **~tar** *vt* show; (*fingir*) feign. **~te** *a* apparent

apartado /apar'tadu/ *m Port* PO Box

apar|tamento /aparta'mẽtu/ *m* flat, *Amer* apartment. **~tar** *vt*, **~tar-se** *vpr* separate. **~te** *m* aside

apatia /apa'tʃia/ *f* apathy

apático /a'patʃiku/ *a* apathetic

apavo|rante /apavo'rãtʃi/ *a* terrifying. **~rar** *vt* terrify. **~rar-se** *vpr* be terrified

apaziguar /apazi'gwar/ *vt* appease

apear-se /api'arsi/ *vpr* (*de cavalo*) dismount; (*de ônibus*) alight

ape|gar-se /ape'garsi/ *vpr* become attached (**a** to). **~go** /e/ *m* attachment

ape|lação /apela'sãw/ *f* appeal; *fig* exhibitionism. **~lar** *vi* appeal (**de** against); **~lar para** appeal to; *fig* resort to

apeli|dar /apeli'dar/ *vt* nickname. **~do** *m* nickname

apelo /a'pelu/ *m* appeal

apenas /a'penas/ *adv* only

apêndice /a'pẽdʒisi/ *m* appendix

apendicite /apẽdʒi'sitʃi/ *f* appendicitis

aperceber-se /aperse'bersi/ *vpr* **~ (de)** notice, realize

aperfeiçoar /aperfejso'ar/ *vt* perfect

aperitivo /aperi'tʃivu/ *m* aperitif

aper|tado /aper'tadu/ *a* tight; (*sem dinheiro*) hard-up. **~tar** *vt* (*segurar*) hold tight; tighten ‹*cinto*›; press ‹*botão*›; squeeze ‹*esponja*›; take in ‹*vestido*›; fasten ‹*cinto de segurança*›; step up ‹*vigilância*›; cut down on ‹*despesas*›; break ‹*coração*›; *fig* pressurize ‹*pessoa*›; **~tar a mão de alguém** shake hands with sb ● *vi* ‹*sapato*› pinch; ‹*chuva, frio*› get worse; ‹*estrada*› narrow. **~tar-se** *vpr* (*gastar menos*) tighten one's belt; (*não ter dinheiro*) feel the pinch. **~to** /e/ *m* pressure; (*de botão*) press; (*dificuldade*) tight spot, jam; **~to de mãos** handshake

apesar /ape'zar/ **~ de** *prep* in spite of

apeti|te /ape'tʃitʃi/ *m* appetite. **~toso** /o/ *a* appetizing

apetrechos /ape'treʃus/ *m pl* gear; (*de pesca*) tackle

apimentado /apimẽ'tadu/ *a* spicy, hot

apinhar /api'ɲar/ *vt* crowd, pack. **~-se** *vpr* crowd

api|tar /api'tar/ *vi* whistle ● *vt* referee ‹*jogo*›. **~to** *m* whistle

aplanar /apla'nar/ *vt* level ‹*terreno*›; *fig* smooth ‹*caminho*›; smooth over ‹*problema*›

aplau|dir /aplaw'dʒir/ *vt* applaud. **~so(s)** *m*(*pl*) applause

apli|cação /aplika'sãw/ *f* application; (*de dinheiro*) investment; (*de lei*) enforcement. **~car** *vt* apply; invest ‹*dinheiro*›; enforce ‹*lei*›. **~car-se** *vpr* apply (**a** to); (*ao estudo etc*) apply o.s. (**a** to). **~que** *m* hairpiece

apoderar-se /apode'rarsi/ *vpr* **~ de** take possession of; ‹*raiva*› take hold of

apodrecer /apodre'ser/ *vt/i* rot

apoi|ar /apoj'ar/ *vt* lean; *fig* support; (*basear*) base. **~ar-se** *vpr*, **~ar-se em** lean on; *fig* be based on, rest on. **~o** *m* support

apólice /a'pɔlisi/ *f* policy; (*ação*) bond

apon|tador /apõta'dor/ *m* pencil sharpener. **~tar** *vt* (*com o dedo*) point at, point to; point out ‹*erro, caso interessante*›; aim ‹*arma*›; name ‹*nomes*›; put forward ‹*razão*› ● *vi* ‹*sol, planta*› come up; (*com o dedo*) point (**para** to)

apoquentar /apokẽ'tar/ *vt* annoy

aporrinhar /apoxi'ɲar/ *vt* annoy

após /a'pɔs/ *adv* after; **loção ~-barba** aftershave (lotion)

aposen|tado /apozẽ'tadu/ *a* retired ● *m* pensioner. **~tadoria** *f* retirement; (*pensão*) pension. **~tar** *vt*, **~tar-se** *vpr* retire. **~to** *m* room

após-guerra /apɔz'gɛxa/ *m* post-war period

apos|ta /a'pɔsta/ *f* bet. **~tar** *vt* bet (**em** on); *fig* have faith (**em** in)

apostila /apos'tʃila/ *f* revision aid, book of key facts

apóstolo /a'pɔstolu/ *m* apostle

apóstrofo /a'pɔstrofu/ *m* apostrophe

apre|ciação /apresia'sãw/ *f* appreciation. **~ciar** *vt* appreciate; think highly of ‹*pessoa*›. **~ciativo** *a* appreciative. **~ciável** (*pl* **~ciáveis**) *a* appreciable. **~ço** /e/ *m* regard

apreen|der /apriẽ'der/ *vt* seize ‹*contrabando*›; apprehend ‹*criminoso*›; grasp ‹*sentido*›. **~são** *f* apprehension; (*de contrabando*) seizure. **~sivo** *a* apprehensive

apregoar /aprego'ar/ *vt* proclaim; cry ‹*mercadoria*›

apren|der /aprẽ'der/ *vt/i* learn. **~diz** *m/f* (*de ofício*) apprentice; (*de direção*) learner. **~dizado** *m*, **~dizagem** *f* (*de ofício*) apprenticeship; (*de profissão*) training; (*escolar*) learning

apresen|tação /aprezẽta'sãw/ *f* presentation; (*teatral etc*) performance; (*de pessoas*) introduction. **~tador** *m* presenter. **~tar** *vt* present; introduce ‹*pessoa*›. **~tar-se** *vpr* (*identificar-se*) introduce o.s.; ‹*ocasião, problema*› present o.s., arise; **~tar-se a** report to ‹*polícia etc*›; go in for ‹*exame*›; stand for ‹*eleição*›. **~tável** (*pl* **~táveis**) *a* presentable

apres|sado /apre'sadu/ *a* hurried. **~sar** *vt* hurry. **~sar-se** *vpr* hurry (up)

aprimorar /aprimo'rar/ *vt* perfect, refine

aprofundar /aprofũ'dar/ *vt* deepen; study carefully ‹*questão*›. **~-se** *vpr* get deeper; **~-se em** go deeper into

aprontar /aprõ'tar/ *vt* get ready; pick ‹*briga*› ● *vi* act up. **~-se** *vpr* get ready

apropriado /apropri'adu/ *a* appropriate, suitable

apro|vação /aprova'sãw/ *f* approval; (*num exame*) pass. **~var** *vt* approve of; approve ‹*lei*› ● *vi* make the grade; **ser ~vado** (*num exame*) pass

aprovei|tador /aprovejta'dor/ *m* opportunist. **~tamento** *m* utilization. **~tar** *vt* take advantage of; take ‹*ocasião*›; (*utilizar*) use ● *vi* make the most of it; *Port* (*adiantar*) be of use. **~tar-se** *vpr* take advantage (**de** of); **~te!** (*divirta-se*) have a good time!

aproxi|mação /aprosima'sãw/ *f* (*chegada*) approach; (*estimativa*) approximation. **~mado** *a* ‹*valor*› approximate. **~mar** *vt* move nearer; (*aliar*) bring together. **~mar-se** *vpr* approach, get nearer (**de** to)

ap|tidão /aptʃi'dãw/ *f* aptitude, suitability. **~to** *a* suitable

apunhalar /apuɲa'lar/ *vt* stab

apu|rado /apu'radu/ *a* refined. **~rar** *vt* (*aprimorar*) refine; (*descobrir*) ascertain; investigate ‹*caso*›; collect ‹*dinheiro*›; count ‹*votos*›. **~rar-se** *vpr* (*com a roupa*) dress smartly. **~ro** *m* refinement; (*no vestir*) elegance; (*dificuldade*) difficulty; *pl* trouble

aquarela /akwa'rɛla/ *f* watercolour

aquariano /akwari'anu/ *a & m* Aquarian

aquário /a'kwariu/ *m* aquarium; **Aquário** Aquarius

aquartelar /akwarte'lar/ *vt* billet

aquático /a'kwatʃiku/ *a* aquatic, water

aque|cedor /akese'dor/ *m* heater. **~cer** *vt* heat ● *vi*, **~cer-se** *vpr* heat up. **~cimento** /akesi'mẽtu/ *m* heating; **~cimento global** global warming

aqueduto /ake'dutu/ *m* aqueduct

aquele /a'keli/ *a* that; those ● *pron* that one; those; **~ que** the one that

àquele =A + AQUELE

aqui /a'ki/ *adv* here

aquilo /a'kilu/ *pron* that

àquilo =A + AQUILO

aquisi|ção /akizi'sãw/ *f* acquisition. **~tivo** *a* **poder ~tivo** purchasing power

ar /ar/ *m* air; (*aspecto*) look, air; *Port* (*no carro*) choke; **ao ~ livre** in the open air; **no ~** *fig* up in the air; *TV* on air; **~ condicionado** air conditioning

árabe /'arabi/ *a & m* Arab; *Lang* Arabic

Arábia /a'rabia/ *f* Arabia; **~ Saudita** Saudi Arabia

arado /a'radu/ *m* plough, *Amer* plow

aragem /a'raʒẽ/ *f* breeze

arame /a'rami/ *m* wire; **~ farpado** barbed wire

aranha /a'raɲa/ *f* spider

arar /a'rar/ *vt* plough, *Amer* plow

arara /a'rara/ *f* parrot

arbi|trar /arbi'trar/ *vt/i* referee ‹*jogo*›; arbitrate ‹*disputa*›. **~trário** *a* arbitrary

arbítrio /ar'bitriu/ *m* judgement; **livre ~** free will

árbitro /'arbitru/ *m* arbiter ‹*da moda etc*›; *Jurid* arbitrator; (*de futebol*) referee; (*de tênis*) umpire

arborizado /arbori'zadu/ *a* wooded, green; ‹*rua*› tree-lined

arbusto /ar'bustu/ *m* shrub

ar|ca /'arka/ *f* **~ca de Noé** Noah's Ark. **~cada** *f* (*galeria*) arcade; (*arco*) arch

arcaico /ar'kajku/ *a* archaic

arcar /ar'kar/ *vt* **~ com** deal with

arcebispo /arse'bispu/ *m* archbishop

arco /'arku/ *m Arquit* arch; (*arma, Mus*) bow; *Eletr, Mat* arc. **~-da-velha** *m* **coisa do ~-da-velha** amazing thing; **~-íris** *m invar* rainbow

ar|dente /ar'dẽtʃi/ *a* burning; *fig* ardent. **~der** *vi* burn; ‹*olhos, ferida*› sting

ar|dil /ar'dʒiw/ (*pl* **~dis**) *m* trick, ruse

ardor /ar'dor/ *m* heat; *fig* ardour; **com ~** ardently

árduo /'arduu/ *a* strenuous, arduous

área /'aria/ *f* area; **(grande) ~** penalty area; **~ (de serviço)** yard

arear /ari'ar/ *vt* scour ‹*panela*›

areia /a'reja/ *f* sand

arejar /are'ʒar/ *vt* air ● *vi*, **~-se** *vpr* get some air; (*descansar*) have a breather

are|na /a'rena/ *f* arena. **~noso** /o/ *a* sandy

arenque /a'rẽki/ *m* herring

argamassa /arga'masa/ *f* mortar

Argélia /ar'ʒɛlia/ *f* Algeria

argelino /arʒe'linu/ *a & m* Algerian

Argentina /arʒẽ'tʃina/ *f* Argentina

argentino /arʒẽ'tʃinu/ *a & m* Argentinian

argila /ar'ʒila/ *f* clay

argola /ar'gɔla/ *f* ring

arguido /ar'gwidu/ *m* defendant

argumen|tar /argumẽ'tar/ *vt/i* argue. **~to** *m* argument; (*de filme etc*) subject matter

ariano /ari'anu/ *a & m* (*do signo Aries*) Arian

árido /'aridu/ *a* arid; barren ‹*deserto*›; *fig* dull, dry

Áries /'aris/ *m* Aries

arisco /a'risku/ *a* timid

aristo|cracia /aristokra'sia/ *f* aristocracy. **~crata** *m/f* aristocrat. **~crático** *a* aristocratic

aritmética /aritʃ'mɛtʃika/ *f* arithmetic

arma /'arma/ *f* weapon; arms; **~ de fogo** firearm

ar|mação /arma'sãw/ *f* frame; (*de óculos*) frames; *Naut* rigging. **~madilha** *f* trap. **~madura** *f* suit of armour; (*armação*) framework. **~mar** *vt* (*dar armas a*) arm; (*montar*) put up, assemble; set up ‹*máquina*›; set, lay ‹*armadilha*›; fit out ‹*navio*›; hatch ‹*plano, complô*›; cause ‹*briga*›. **~mar-se** *vpr* arm o.s.

armarinho /arma'riɲu/ *m* haberdashery, *Amer* notions

armário /ar'mariu/ *m* cupboard; (*de roupa*) wardrobe

arma|zém /arma'zẽj/ *m* warehouse; (*loja*) general store; (*depósito*) storeroom. **~zenagem** *f*, **~zenamento** *m* storage. **~zenar** *vt* store

Armênia /ar'menia/ *f* Armenia

armênio /ar'meniu/ *a & m* Armenian

aro /'aru/ *m* (*de roda, óculos*) rim; (*de porta*) frame

aro|ma /a'roma/ *m* aroma; (*perfume*) fragrance. **~mático** *a* aromatic; fragrant

ar|pão /ar'pãw/ *m* harpoon. **~poar** *vt* harpoon

arquear /arki'ar/ *vt* arch. **~-se** *vpr* bend, bow

arque|ologia /arkiolo'ʒia/ *f* archaeology. **~ológico** *a* archaeological. **~ólogo** *m* archaeologist

arquétipo /ar'kɛtʃipu/ *m* archetype

arquibancada /arkibã'kada/ *f* terraces, *Amer* bleachers

arquipélago /arki'pɛlagu/ *m* archipelago

arquite|tar /arkite'tar/ *vt* think up. **~to** /ɛ/ *m* architect. **~tônico** *a* architectural. **~tura** *f* architecture

arqui|var /arki'var/ *vt* file ‹*papéis*›; shelve ‹*plano, processo*›. **~vista** *m/f* archivist. **~vo** *m* file; (*conjunto*) files; (*móvel*) filing cabinet; (*do Estado etc*) archives

arran|cada /axã'kada/ *f* lurch; (*de atleta*) *fig* spurt. **~car** *vt* pull out ‹*cabelo etc*›; pull off ‹*botão etc*›; pull up ‹*erva daninha etc*›; take out ‹*dente*›; (*das mãos de alguém*) wrench, snatch; extract ‹*confissão, dinheiro*› ● *vi* ‹*carro*› roar off; ‹*pessoa*› take off; (*dar solavanco*) lurch forward. **~car-se** *vpr* take off. **~co** *m* pull, tug

arranha-céu /axaɲa'sɛw/ *m* skyscraper

arra|nhadura /axaɲa'dura/ *f* scratch. **~nhão** *m* scratch. **~nhar** *vt* scratch; have a smattering of ‹*língua*›

arran|jar /axã'ʒar/ *vt* arrange; (*achar*) get, find; (*resolver*) settle, sort out. **~jar-se** *vpr* manage. **~jo** *m* arrangement

arrasar /axa'zar/ *vt* devastate; raze, flatten ‹*casa, cidade*›. **~-se** *vpr* be devastated

arrastar /axas'tar/ *vt* drag; ‹*corrente, avalancha*› sweep away; (*atrair*) draw ● *vi* trail. **~-se** *vpr* crawl; ‹*tempo*› drag; ‹*processo*› drag out

arreba|tador /axebata'dor/ *a* entrancing; shocking ‹*notícia*›. **~tar** *vt* (*enlevar*) entrance, send; (*chocar*) shock

arreben|tação /axebẽta'sãw/ *f* surf. **~tar** *vi* ‹*bomba*› explode; ‹*corda*› snap, break; ‹*balão, pessoa*› burst; ‹*onda*› break; ‹*guerra, incêndio*› break out ● *vt* snap, break ‹*corda*›; burst ‹*balão*›; break down ‹*porta*›

arrebitar /axebi'tar/ *vt* turn up ‹*nariz*›; prick up ‹*orelhas*›

arreca|dação /axekada'sãw/ *f* (*dinheiro*) tax revenue. **~dar** *vt* collect

arredar /axe'dar/ *vt* **não ~ pé** stand one's ground

arredio /axe'dʒiu/ *a* withdrawn

arredondar /axedõ'dar/ *vt* round up ‹*quantia*›; round off ‹*ângulo*›

arredores /axe'dɔris/ *m pl* surroundings; (*de cidade*) outskirts

arrefecer /axefe'ser/ *vt/i* cool

arregaçar /axega'sar/ *vt* roll up

arrega|lado /axega'ladu/ *a* ‹*olhos*› wide. **~lar** *vt* **~lar os olhos** be wide-eyed with amazement

arreganhar /axega'ɲar/ *vt* bare ‹*dentes*›. **~-se** *vpr* grin

arrema|tar /axema'tar/ *vt* finish off; (*no tricô*) cast off. **~te** *m* conclusion; (*na costura*) finishing off; (*no futebol*) finishing

arremes|sar /axeme'sar/ *vt* hurl. **~so** /e/ *m* throw

arrendar /axẽ'dar/ *vt* rent

arrepen|der-se /axepẽ'dersi/ *vpr* be sorry; ‹*pecador*› repent; **~der-se de** regret. **~dido** *a* sorry; ‹*pecador*› repentant. **~dimento** *m* regret; (*de pecado, crime*) repentance

arrepi|ado /axepi'adu/ *a* ‹*cabelo*› standing on end; ‹*pele, pessoa*› covered in goose pimples. **~ar** *vt* (*dar calafrios*) make shudder; make stand on end ‹*cabelo*›; **me ~a (a pele)** it gives me goose pimples. **~ar-se** *vpr* (*estremecer*) shudder; ‹*cabelo*› stand on end; (*na pele*) get goose pimples. **~o** *m* shudder; **me dá ~os** it makes me shudder

arris|cado /axis'kadu/ *a* risky. **~car** *vt* risk. **~car-se** *vpr* take a risk, risk it

arroba /a'xoba/ *m Comput* @, at sign

arro|char /axo'ʃar/ *vt* tighten up ● *vi* be tough. **~cho** /o/ *m* squeeze

arro|gância /axo'gãsia/ *f* arrogance. **~gante** *a* arrogant

arro|jado /axo'ʒadu/ *a* bold. **~jar** *vt* throw

arrombar /axõ'bar/ *vt* break down ‹*porta*›; break into ‹*casa*›; crack ‹*cofre*›

arro|tar /axo'tar/ *vi* burp, belch. **~to** /o/ *m* burp

arroz /a'xoz/ *m* rice; **~ doce** rice pudding. **~al** (*pl* **~ais**) *m* rice field

arrua|ça /axu'asa/ *f* riot. **~ceiro** *m* rioter

arruela /axu'ɛla/ *f* washer

arruinar /axui'nar/ *vt* ruin. **~-se** *vpr* be ruined

arru|madeira /axuma'dera/ *f* (*de hotel*) chambermaid. **~mar** *vt* tidy (up) ‹*casa*›; sort out ‹*papéis, vida*›; pack ‹*mala*›; (*achar*) find, get; make up ‹*desculpa*›; (*vestir*) dress up. **~mar-se** *vpr* (*aprontar-se*) get ready; (*na vida*) sort o.s. out

arse|nal /arse'naw/ (*pl* **~nais**) *m* arsenal

arsênio /ar'seniu/ *m* arsenic

arte /'artʃi/ *f* art; **fazer ~** ‹*criança*› get up to mischief. **~fato** *m* product, article

arteiro /ar'teru/ *a* mischievous

artéria /ar'tɛria/ *f* artery

artesa|nal /arteza'naw/ (*pl* **~nais**) *a* craft. **~nato** *m* craftwork

arte|são /arte'zãw/ (*pl* **~s**) *m* (*f* **~sã**) artisan, craftsman (*f* -woman)

ártico /'artʃiku/ *a* & *m* arctic

articu|lação /artʃikula'sãw/ *f* articulation; *Anat, Tecn* joint. **~lar** *vt* articulate

arti|ficial /artʃifisi'aw/ (*pl* **~ficiais**) *a* artificial. **~fício** *m* trick

artigo /ar'tʃigu/ *m* article; *Com* item

arti|lharia /artʃiʎa'ria/ *f* artillery. **~lheiro** *m Mil* gunner; (*no futebol*) striker

artimanha /artʃi'maɲa/ *f* trick; (*método*) clever way

ar|tista /ar'tʃista/ *m/f* artist. **~tístico** *a* artistic

artrite /ar'tritʃi/ *f* arthritis

árvore /'arvori/ *f* tree

arvoredo /arvo'redu/ *m* grove

ás /as/ *m* ace

às ▶ A

asa /'aza/ *f* wing; (*de xícara*) handle. **~-delta** *f* hang-glider

ascen|dência /asẽ'dẽsia/ *f* ancestry; (*superioridade*) ascendancy. **~dente** *a* rising. **~der** *vi* rise; ascend ‹*ao trono*›. **~são** *f* rise; *Relig* Ascension; **em ~são** rising; *fig* up and coming. **~sor** *m* lift, *Amer* elevator. **~sorista** *m/f* lift operator

asco /'asku/ *m* revulsion, disgust; **dar ~** be revolting

asfalto /as'fawtu/ *m* asphalt

asfixiar /asfiksi'ar/ *vt/i* asphyxiate

Ásia /'azia/ *f* Asia

asiático /azi'atʃiku/ *a & m* Asian

asilo /a'zilu/ *m* (*refúgio*) asylum; (*de velhos, crianças*) home

as|ma /'azma/ *f* asthma. **~mático** *a & m* asthmatic

asneira /az'nera/ *f* stupidity; (*uma*) stupid thing

aspargo /as'pargu/ *m* asparagus

aspas /'aspas/ *f pl* inverted commas

aspecto /as'pɛktu/ *m* appearance, look; (*de um problema*) aspect

aspereza /aspe'reza/ *f* roughness; (*do clima, de um som*) harshness; *fig* rudeness

áspero /'asperu/ *a* rough; ‹*clima, som*› harsh; *fig* rude

aspi|ração /aspira'sãw/ *f* aspiration; *Med* inhalation. **~rador** *m* vacuum cleaner. **~rar** *vt* inhale, breathe in ‹*ar, fumaça*›; suck up ‹*líquido*›; **~rar a** aspire to

aspirina /aspi'rina/ *f* aspirin

asqueroso /aske'rozu/ *a* revolting, disgusting

assa|do /a'sadu/ *a & m* roast. **~dura** *f* (*na pele*) sore patch

assalariado /asalari'adu/ *a* salaried ● *m* salaried worker

assal|tante /asaw'tãtʃi/ *m/f* robber; (*na rua*) mugger; (*de casa*) burglar. **~tar** *vt* rob; burgle, *Amer* burglarize ‹*casa*›. **~to** *m* (*roubo*) robbery; (*a uma casa*) burglary; (*ataque*) assault; (*no boxe*) round

assanhado /asa'ɲadu/ *a* worked up; ‹*criança*› excitable; (*erótico*) amorous

assar /a'sar/ *vt* roast

assassi|nar /asasi'nar/ *vt* murder; *Pol* assassinate. **~nato** *m* murder; *Pol* assassination. **~no** *m* murderer; *Pol* assassin

asseado /asi'adu/ *a* well-groomed

as|sediar /asedʒi'ar/ *vt* besiege ‹*cidade*›; *fig* harass. **~sédio** *m* siege; *fig* pestering; **~sédio sexual** sexual harassment

assegurar /asegu'rar/ *vt* (*tornar seguro*) secure; (*afirmar*) guarantee; **~ a alguém algo/que** assure s.o. of sth/that; **~-se de/que** make sure of/that

assembleia /asẽ'blɛja/ *f Pol* assembly; *Com* meeting

> *i* **Assembleia da República** The Portuguese Assembly of the Republic, located in the Palácio de São Bento, Lisbon, is the Portuguese parliament. The Assembly's 230 seats are allocated by proportional representation, and the members collectively represent the country's twenty-two constituencies and the two autonomous regions, Madeira and the Azores.

assemelhar /aseme'ʎar/ *vt* liken. **~-se** *vpr* be alike; **~-se a** resemble, be like

assen|tar /asẽ'tar/ *vt* (*estabelecer*) establish, define; settle ‹*povo*›; lay ‹*tijolo*›; **~tar com** go with; **~tar a** ‹*roupa*› suit ● *vi* ‹*pó*› settle. **~tar-se** *vpr* settle down. **~to** *m* seat; *fig* basis; **tomar ~to** take a seat; ‹*pó*› settle

assen|tir /asẽ'tʃir/ *vi* agree. **~timento** *m* agreement

assertivo /aser'tʃivu/ *a* assertive

assessor /ase'sor/ *m* adviser. **~ar** *vt* advise

assexuado /aseksu'adu/ *a* asexual

assiduidade /asidui'dadʒi/ *f* (*à escola*) regular attendance; (*diligência*) diligence

assíduo /a'siduu/ *a* (*que frequenta*) regular; (*diligente*) assiduous

assim /a'sĩ/ *adv* like this, like that; (*portanto*) therefore; **e ~ por diante** and so on; **~ como** as well as; **~ que** as soon as

assimétrico /asi'mɛtriku/ *a* asymmetrical

a

assimilar /asimi'lar/ *vt* assimilate. **~-se** *vpr* be assimilated

assinalar /asina'lar/ *vt* (*marcar*) mark; (*distinguir*) distinguish; (*apontar*) point out

assi|nante /asi'nãtʃi/ *m/f* subscriber. **~nar** *vt/i* sign. **~natura** *f* (*nome*) signature; (*de revista*) subscription

assis|tência /asis'tẽsia/ *f* assistance; (*presença*) attendance; (*público*) audience. **~tente** *a* assistant ● *m/f* assistant; **~tente social** social worker. **~tir (a)** *vt/i* (*ver*) watch; (*presenciar*) attend; assist ‹*doente*›

assoalho /aso'aʎu/ *m* floor

assoar /aso'ar/ *vt* **~ o nariz**, *Port* **~-se** blow one's nose

assobi|ar /asobi'ar/ *vt/i* whistle. **~o** *m* whistle

associ|ação /asosia'sãw/ *f* association. **~ado** *a & m* associate. **~ar** *vt* associate (**a** with). **~ar-se** *vpr* associate; *Com* go into partnership (**a** with)

assolar /aso'lar/ *vt* devastate

assom|bração /asõbra'sãw/ *f* ghost. **~brar** *vt* astonish, amaze. **~brar-se** *vpr* be amazed. **~bro** *m* amazement, astonishment; (*coisa*) marvel. **~broso** /o/ *a* astonishing, amazing

assoprar /aso'prar/ *vi* blow ● *vt* blow; blow out ‹*vela*›

assoviar *etc* ▶ **ASSOBIAR** *etc*

assu|mido /asu'midu/ *a* (*confesso*) confirmed, self-confessed. **~mir** *vt* assume, take on; accept, admit ‹*defeito*› ● *vi* take office

assunto /a'sũtu/ *m* subject; (*negócio*) matter

assus|tador /asusta'dor/ *a* frightening. **~tar** *vt* frighten, scare. **~tar-se** *vpr* get frightened, get scared

asterisco /aste'risku/ *m* asterisk

as|tral /as'traw/ (*pl* **~trais**) *m* [!] state of mind. **~tro** *m* star. **~trologia** *f* astrology. **~trólogo** *m* astrologer. **~tronauta** *m/f* astronaut. **~tronave** *f* spaceship. **~tronomia** *f* astronomy. **~tronômico** *a* astronomical. **~trônomo** *m* astronomer

as|túcia /as'tusia/ *f* cunning. **~tuto** *a* cunning; ‹*comerciante*› astute

ata /'ata/ *f* minutes

ataca|dista /ataka'dʒista/ *m/f* wholesaler. **~do** *m* **por ~do** wholesale

ata|cante /ata'kãtʃi/ *a* attacking ● *m/f* attacker. **~car** *vt* attack; tackle ‹*problema*›

atadura /ata'dura/ *f* bandage

ata|lhar /ata'ʎar/ *vi* take a shortcut. **~lho** *m* shortcut

ataque /a'taki/ *m* attack; (*de raiva, riso*) fit; **~ aéreo** air strike

atar /a'tar/ *vt* tie

atarantado /atarã'tadu/ *a* flustered, in a flap

atarefado /atare'fadu/ *a* busy

atarracado /ataxa'kadu/ *a* stocky

atarraxar /ataxa'ʃar/ *vt* screw

até /a'tɛ/ *prep* (up) to, as far as; (*tempo*) until ● *adv* even; **~ logo** goodbye; **~ que** until

ateia /a'tɛja/ *a & f* ▶ **ATEU**

ateliê /ateli'e/ *m* studio

atemorizar /atemori'zar/ *vt* frighten

Atenas /a'tenas/ *f* Athens

aten|ção /atẽ'sãw/ *f* attention; *pl* (*bondade*) thoughtfulness; **com ~ção** attentively. **~cioso** *a* thoughtful, considerate

aten|der /atẽ'der/ **~der (a)** *vt/i* answer ‹*telefone, porta*›; answer to ‹*nome*›; serve ‹*freguês*›; see ‹*paciente, visitante*›; grant, meet ‹*pedido*›; heed ‹*conselho*›. **~dimento** *m* service; (*de médico etc*) consultation

aten|tado /atẽ'tadu/ *m* murder attempt; *Pol* assassination attempt; (*ataque*) attack (**contra** on). **~tar** *vi* **~tar contra** make an attempt on

atento /a'tẽtu/ *a* attentive; **~ a** mindful of

aterrador /atexa'dor/ *a* terrifying

ater|ragem /ate'xaʒẽ/ *f Port* landing. **~rar** *vi Port* land

aterris|sagem /atexi'saʒẽ/ *f* landing. **~sar** *vi* land

aterro /a'texu/ *m* **~ (sanitário)** landfill

ater-se /a'tersi/ *vpr* **~ a** keep to, go by

ates|tado /ates'tadu/ *m* certificate. **~tar** *vt* attest (to)

ateu /a'tew/ *a & m* (*f* **ateia**) atheist

atiçar /atʃi'sar/ *vt* poke ‹*fogo*›; stir up ‹*ódio, discórdia*›; arouse ‹*pessoa*›

atinar /atʃi'nar/ *vt* work out, guess; **~ com** find; **~ em** notice

atingir /atʃĩ'ʒir/ *vt* reach; hit ‹*alvo*›; (*conseguir*) attain; (*afetar*) affect

atirar /atʃi'rar/ *vt* throw ● *vi* shoot; **~ em** fire at

atitude /atʃi'tudʒi/ *f* attitude; **tomar uma ~** take action

ati|va /a'tʃiva/ *f* active service. **~var** *vt* activate. **~vidade** *f* activity. **~vo** *a* active ● *m Com* assets

Atlântico /at'lãtʃiku/ *m* Atlantic

atlas /'atlas/ *m* atlas

at|leta /at'lɛta/ *m/f* athlete. **~lético** *a* athletic. **~letismo** *m* athletics

atmosfera /atʃimos'fɛra/ *f* atmosphere

ato /'atu/ *m* act; (*ação*) action; **no ~** on the spot

ato|lar /ato'lar/ *vt* bog down. **~lar-se** *vpr* get bogged down. **~leiro** *m* bog; *fig* fix, spot of trouble

atômico /a'tomiku/ *a* atomic

atomizador /atomiza'dor/ *m* atomizer spray

átomo /'atomu/ *m* atom

atônito /a'tonitu/ *a* astonished, stunned

ator /a'tor/ *m* actor

atordoar /atordo'ar/ *vt* ‹*golpe, notícia*› stun; ‹*som*› deafen; (*alucinar*) bewilder

atormentar /atormẽ'tar/ *vt* plague, torment

atração /atra'sãw/ *f* attraction

atracar /atra'kar/ *vt/i Naut* moor. **~-se** *vpr* grapple; [!] neck

atraente /atra'ẽtʃi/ *a* attractive

atraiçoar /atrajso'ar/ *vt* betray

atrair /atra'ir/ *vt* attract

atrapalhar /atrapa'ʎar/ *vt/i* (*confundir*) confuse; (*estorvar*) hinder; (*perturbar*) disturb. **~-se** *vpr* get mixed up

atrás /a'traʃ/ *adv* behind; (*no fundo*) at the back; **~ de** behind; (*depois de, no encalço de*) after; **um mês ~** a month ago; **ficar ~** be left behind

atra|sado /atra'zadu/ *a* late; ‹*país, criança*› backward; ‹*relógio*› slow; ‹*pagamento*› overdue; ‹*ideias*› old-fashioned. **~sar** *vt* delay; put back ‹*relógio*› ● *vi* be late; ‹*relógio*› lose. **~sar-se** *vpr* be late; (*num trabalho*) get behind; (*no pagar*) get into arrears. **~so** *m* delay; (*de país etc*) backwardness; *pl Com* arrears; **com ~so** late

atrativo /atra'tʃivu/ *m* attraction

através /atra'vɛs/ **~ de** *prep* through; (*de um lado ao outro*) across

atravessado /atrave'sadu/ *a* ‹*espinha*› stuck; **estar com alguém ~ na garganta** be fed up with sb

atravessar /atrave'sar/ *vt* go through; cross ‹*rua, rio*›

atre|ver-se /atre'versi/ *vpr* dare; **~ver-se a** dare to. **~vido** *a* daring; (*insolente*) impudent. **~vimento** *m* daring, boldness; (*insolência*) impudence

atribu|ir /atribu'ir/ *vt* attribute (**a** to); confer ‹*prêmio, poderes*› (**a** on); attach ‹*importância*› (**a** to). **~to** *m* attribute

atrito /a'tritu/ *m* friction; (*desavença*) disagreement

atriz /a'tris/ *f* actress

atrocidade /atrosi'dadʒi/ *f* atrocity

atrope|lar /atrope'lar/ *vt* run over, knock down ‹*pedestre*›; (*empurrar*) jostle; mix up ‹*palavras*›; **~lamento** *m* (*de pedestre*) running over. **~lo** /e/ *m* scramble

atroz /a'tros/ *a* awful, terrible; heinous ‹*crime*›; cruel ‹*pessoa*›

atuação /atua'sãw/ *f* (*ação*) action; (*desempenho*) performance

atu|al /atu'aw/ (*pl* **~ais**) *a* current, present; ‹*assunto, interesse*› topical; ‹*pessoa, carro*› up-to-date. **~alidade** *f* (*presente*) present (time); (*de um livro*) topicality; *pl* current affairs. **~alizado** *a* up-to-date. **~alizar** *vt* update. **~alizar-se** *vpr* bring o.s. up to date. **~almente** *adv* at present, currently

atum /a'tũ/ *m* tuna

aturdir /atur'dʒir/ *vt* ▶ ATORDOAR

audácia /aw'dasia/ *f* boldness; (*insolência*) audacity

audi|ção /awdʒi'sãw/ *f* hearing; (*concerto*) recital. **~ência** *f* audience; *Jurid* hearing

audiovisu|al /awdʒiovizu'aw/ (*pl* **~ais**) *a* audiovisual

auditório /awdʒi'tɔriu/ *m* auditorium; **programa de ~** variety show

auge /'awʒi/ *m* peak, height

aula /'awla/ *f* class, lesson; **dar ~** teach

aumen|tar /awmẽ'tar/ *vt* increase; raise ‹*preço, salário*›; extend ‹*casa*›; (*com lente*) magnify; (*acrescentar*) add ● *vi* increase; ‹*preço, salário*› go up. **~to** *m* increase; (*de salário*) rise, *Amer* raise

au|sência /aw'zẽsia/ *f* absence. **~sente** *a* absent ● *m/f* absentee

aus|pícios /aws'pisius/ *m pl* auspices. **~picioso** /o/ *a* auspicious

auste|ridade /awsteri'dadʒi/ *f* austerity. **~ro** /ɛ/ *a* austere

Austrália /aw'stralia/ *f* Australia

australiano /awstrali'anu/ *a & m* Australian

Áustria /'awstria/ *f* Austria

a

austríaco /aws'triaku/ *a & m* Austrian

autarquia /awtar'kia/ *f* public authority

autêntico /aw'tẽtʃiku/ *a* authentic; genuine ‹*pessoa*›; true ‹*fato*›

autobio|grafia /awtobiogra'fia/ *f* autobiography. **~gráfico** *a* autobiographical

autocarro /awto'kaxu/ *m Port* bus

autocrata /awto'krata/ *a* autocratic

autodefesa /awtode'feza/ *f* self-defence

autodidata /awtodʒi'data/ *a & m/f* self-taught (person)

autódromo /aw'tɔdromu/ *m* race track

autoescola /awtois'kɔla/ *f* driving school

autoestrada /awtois'trada/ *f* motorway, *Amer* expressway

autógrafo /aw'tɔgrafu/ *m* autograph

auto|mação /awtoma'sãw/ *f* automation. **~mático** *a* automatic. **~matizar** *vt* automate

auto|mobilismo /awtomobi-'lizmu/ *m* motoring; (*esporte*) motor racing. **~móvel** (*pl* **~móveis**) *m* motor car, *Amer* automobile

automutilação /awtomutʃila'sãw/ *f* self-harm

au|tonomia /awtono'mia/ *f* autonomy. **~tônomo** *a* autonomous; ‹*trabalhador*› self-employed

autopeça /awto'pɛsa/ *f* car spare

autópsia /aw'tɔpsia/ *f* autopsy

autor /aw'tor/ *m* (*f* **~a**) author; (*de crime*) perpetrator; *Jurid* plaintiff

autoria /awto'ria/ *f* authorship; (*de crime*) responsibility (**de** for)

autori|dade /awtori'dadʒi/ *f* authority. **~zação** *f* authorization. **~zar** *vt* authorize

autorretrato /awtoxe'tratu/ *m* self-portrait

autuar /awtu'ar/ *vt* sue

au|xiliar /awsili'ar/ *a* auxiliary ● *m/f* assistant ● *vt* assist. **~xílio** *m* assistance, aid

aval /a'vaw/ (*pl* **avais**) *m* endorsement; *Com* guarantee

avali|ação /avalia'sãw/ *f* (*de preço*) valuation; *fig* evaluation. **~ar** *vt* value ‹*quadro etc*› (**em** at); assess ‹*danos, riscos*›; *fig* evaluate

avan|çar /avã'sar/ *vt* move forward ● *vi* move forward; *Mil fig* advance; **~çar a** (*montar*) amount to. **~ço** *m* advance

avar|eza /ava'reza/ *f* meanness. **~ento** *a* mean

ava|ria /ava'ria/ *f* damage; (*de máquina*) breakdown. **~riado** *a* damaged; ‹*máquina*› out of order; ‹*carro*› broken down. **~riar** *vt* damage ● *vi* be damaged; ‹*máquina*› break down

avatar /ava'tar/ *m* avatar

ave /'avi/ *f* bird; **~ de rapina** bird of prey

aveia /a'veja/ *f* oats

avelã /ave'lã/ *f* hazelnut

avenida /ave'nida/ *f* avenue

aven|tal /avẽ'taw/ (*pl* **~tais**) *m* apron

aventu|ra /avẽ'tura/ *f* adventure; (*amorosa*) fling. **~rar** *vt* venture. **~rar-se** *vpr* venture (**a** to). **~reiro** *a* adventurous ● *m* adventurer

averiguar /averi'gwar/ *vt* check (out)

avermelhado /averme'ʎadu/ *a* reddish

aver|são /aver'sãw/ *f* aversion. **~so** *a* averse (**a** to)

aves|sas /a'vɛsas/ **às ~sas** the wrong way round; (*de cabeça para baixo*) upside down. **~so** /e/ *m* **ao ~so** inside out

avestruz /aves'trus/ *m* ostrich

avi|ação /avia'sãw/ *f* aviation. **~ão** *m* (aero)plane, *Amer* (air)plane; **~ão a jato** jet

avi|dez /avi'des/ *f* (*cobiça*) greediness

ávido /'avidu/ *a* greedy

avi|sar /avi'zar/ *vt* (*informar*) tell, let know; (*advertir*) warn. **~so** *m* notice; (*advertência*) warning

avistar /avis'tar/ *vt* catch sight of

avo /'avu/ *m* **um doze ~s** one twelfth

avó /a'vɔ/ *f* grandmother. **~s** *m pl* grandparents

avô /a'vo/ *m* grandfather

avoado /avo'adu/ *a* dizzy, scatterbrained

avulso /a'vuwsu/ *a* loose, odd

avultado /avuw'tadu/ *a* bulky

axila /ak'sila/ *f* armpit

azaléia /aza'lɛja/ *f* azalea

azar /a'zar/ *m* bad luck; **ter ~** be unlucky. **~ado, ~ento** *a* unlucky

aze|dar /aze'dar/ *vt* sour ● *vi* go sour. **~do** /e/ *a* sour

azei|te /a'zejtʃi/ *m* oil. **~tona** /o/ *f* olive

azevinho /aze'viɲu/ *m* holly
azia /a'zia/ *f* heartburn
azucrinar /azukri'nar/ *vt* annoy
azul /a'zuw/ (*pl* **azuis**) *a* blue
azulejo /azu'leʒu/ *m* (ceramic) tile
azul-marinho /azuwma'riɲu/ *a invar* navy blue

Bb

babá /ba'ba/ *f* nanny; **~ eletrônica** baby alarm
ba|bado /ba'badu/ *m* frill. **~bador** *m* bib. **~bar** *vt/i*, **~bar-se** *vpr* drool (**por** over); ‹*bebê*› dribble. **~beiro** *Port m* bib
baby-sitter /bejbi'siter/ (*pl* **~s**) *m/f* babysitter
bacalhau /baka'ʎaw/ *m* cod

> **bacalhau** *Bacalhau* is the Portuguese word for 'cod', although it is most commonly used to refer to salt (or dried) cod. Salt cod originated during the time of the Portuguese discoveries, when people needed a way to preserve fish before the advent of refrigeration. It's a hugely popular food, so much so that it's commonly said there are 365 ways to cook *bacalhau*, one for each day of the year, but in reality, there are many more.

bacana /ba'kana/ *a* ! great
bacha|rel /baʃa'rɛw/ (*pl* **~réis**) *m* bachelor. **~relado** *m* bachelor's degree. **~relar-se** *vpr* graduate
bacia /ba'sia/ *f* basin; (*da privada*) bowl; *Anat* pelvis
backup /bɛ'kap/ *m Port Comput* backup
baço /'basu/ *m* spleen
bacon /'bejkõ/ *m* bacon
bactéria /bak'tɛria/ *f* bacterium; *pl* bacteria
bada|lado /bada'ladu/ *a* ! talked about. **~lar** *vt* ring ‹*sino*› ● *vi* ring; ! go out and about. **~lativo** *a* ! fun-loving
badejo /ba'dɛʒu/ *m* sea bass
baderna /ba'dɛrna/ *f* (*tumulto*) commotion; (*desordem*) mess
badulaque /badu'laki/ *m* trinket
bafafá /bafa'fa/ *m* ! to-do, kerfuffle
ba|fo /'bafu/ *m* bad breath. **~fômetro** *m* Breathalyser. **~forada** *f* puff
bagaço /ba'gasu/ *m* pulp; *Port* (*aguardente*) brandy
baga|geiro /baga'ʒeru/ *m* (*de carro*) roof rack; *Port* (*homem*) porter. **~gem** *f* luggage; (*cultural etc*) baggage
bagatela /baga'tɛla/ *f* trifle
Bagdá /bagi'da/ *f* Baghdad
bago /'bagu/ *m* berry; (*de chumbo*) pellet
bagulho /ba'guʎu/ *m* piece of junk; *pl* junk; **ele é um ~** he's as ugly as sin
bagun|ça /ba'gũsa/ *f* mess. **~çar** *vt* mess up. **~ceiro** *a* messy
baía /ba'ia/ *f* bay
baiano /ba'janu/ *a & m* Bahian
baila /'bajla/ *f* **trazer/vir à ~** bring/come up
bai|lar /baj'lar/ *vt/i* dance. **~larino** *m* ballet dancer. **~le** *m* dance; (*de gala*) ball
bainha /ba'iɲa/ *f* (*de vestido*) hem; (*de arma*) sheath
baioneta /bajo'neta/ *f* bayonet
bairro /'bajxu/ *m* neighbourhood, area
baixa /'baʃa/ *f* drop, fall; (*de guerra*) casualty; (*dispensa*) discharge. **~-mar** *f* low tide
baixar /ba'ʃar/ *vt* lower; issue ‹*ordem*›; pass ‹*lei*›; *Comput* download ● *vi* drop, fall; ! (*pintar*) turn up
baixaria /baʃa'ria/ *f* sordidness; (*uma*) sordid thing
baixela /ba'ʃɛla/ *f* set of cutlery
baixeza /ba'ʃeza/ *f* baseness
baixo /'baʃu/ *a* low; ‹*pessoa*› short; ‹*som, voz*› quiet, soft; ‹*cabeça, olhos*› lowered; (*vil*) sordid ● *adv* low; ‹*falar*› softly, quietly ● *m* bass; **em ~** underneath; (*em casa*) downstairs; **em ~ de** under; **para ~** down; (*em casa*) downstairs; **por ~ de** under(neath)
baju|lador /baʒula'dor/ *a* obsequious ● *m* sycophant. **~lar** *vt* fawn on
bala /'bala/ *f* (*de revólver*) bullet; (*doce*) sweet
balada /ba'lada/ *f* ballad
balaio /ba'laju/ *m* linen basket
balan|ça /ba'lãsa/ *f* scales; **Balança** (*signo*) Libra; **~ça de pagamentos** balance of payments. **~çar** *vt/i* (*no ar*) swing; (*numa cadeira etc*) rock; ‹*carro, avião*› shake; ‹*navio*› roll. **~çar-se** *vpr* swing. **~cete** /e/ *m* trial balance. **~ço** *m Com* balance sheet; (*brinquedo*) swing; (*movimento no ar*) swinging; (*de carro,*

avião) shaking; (*de navio*) rolling; (*de cadeira*) rocking; **fazer um ~ço de** *fig* take stock of

b

balangandã /balãgã'dã/ *m* bauble

balão /ba'lãw/ *m* balloon; **soltar um ~ de ensaio** *fig* put out feelers

balar /ba'lar/ *vi* bleat

balbu|ciar /bawbusi'ar/ *vt/i* babble. **~cio** *m* babble, babbling

balbúrdia /baw'burdʒia/ *f* hubbub

bal|cão /baw'kãw/ *m* (*em loja*) counter; (*de informações, bilhetes*) desk; (*de cozinha*) worktop, *Amer* counter; (*no teatro*) circle. **~conista** *m/f* shop assistant

balde /'bawdʒi/ *m* bucket

baldeação /bawdʒia'sãw/ *f* **fazer ~** change (trains)

baldio /baw'dʒiu/ *a* fallow; **terreno ~** (piece of) waste ground

balé /ba'lɛ/ *m* ballet

balear /bali'ar/ *vt* shoot

baleia /ba'leja/ *f* whale

balido /ba'lidu/ *m* bleat, bleating

balísti|ca /ba'listʃika/ *f* ballistics. **~co** *a* ballistic

bali|za /ba'liza/ *f* marker; (*luminosa*) beacon. **~zar** *vt* mark out

balneário /bawni'ariu/ *m* seaside resort

balofo /ba'lofu/ *a* fat, tubby

baloiço, balouço /ba'lojsu, ba'losu/ *Port m* (*de criança*) swing

balsa /'bawsa/ *f* (*de madeira etc*) raft; (*que vai e vem*) ferry

bálsamo /'bawsamu/ *m* balm

báltico /'bawtʃiku/ *a & m* Baltic

baluarte /balu'artʃi/ *m* bulwark

bambo /'bãbu/ *a* loose, slack; ‹*pernas*› limp; ‹*mesa*› wobbly

bambo|lê /bãbo'le/ *m* hula hoop. **~lear** *vi* ‹*pessoa*› sway, totter; ‹*coisa*› wobble

bambu /bã'bu/ *m* bamboo

ba|nal /ba'naw/ (*pl* **~nais**) *a* banal. **~nalidade** *f* banality

bana|na /ba'nana/ *f* banana ● *m/f* 🅸 wimp. **~nada** *f* banana fudge. **~neira** *f* banana tree; **plantar ~neira** do a handstand

banca /'bãka/ *f* (*de trabalho*) bench; (*de jornais*) news stand; **~ examinadora** examining board. **~da** *f Pol* bench

bancar /bã'kar/ *vt* (*custear*) finance; (*fazer papel de*) play; (*fingir*) pretend

bancário /bã'kariu/ *a* bank ● *m* bank employee

bancarrota /bãka'xota/ *f* bankruptcy; **ir à ~** go bankrupt

banco /'bãku/ *m Com* bank; (*no parque*) bench; (*na cozinha, num bar*) stool; (*de bicicleta*) saddle; (*de carro*) seat; **~ de areia** sandbank; **~ de dados** database

banda /'bãda/ *f* band; (*lado*) side; **de ~** sideways on; **nestas ~s** in these parts; **~ desenhada** *Port* cartoon; **~ larga** broadband

bandei|ra /bã'dera/ *f* flag; (*divisa*) banner; **dar ~ra** 🅸 give o.s. away. **~rante** *m/f* pioneer ● *f* girl guide. **~rinha** *m* linesman

bandeja /bã'deʒa/ *f* tray

bandido /bã'dʒidu/ *m* bandit

bando /'bãdu/ *m* (*de pessoas*) band; (*de pássaros*) flock

bandolim /bãdo'lĩ/ *m* mandolin

bangalô /bãga'lo/ *m* bungalow

Bangcoc /bã'koki/ *f* Bangkok

bangue-bangue /bãgi'bãgi/ *m* 🅸 western

banguela /bã'gɛla/ *a* toothless

banha /'baɲa/ *f* lard; *pl* (*no corpo*) flab

banhar /ba'ɲar/ *vt* (*molhar*) bathe; (*lavar*) bath. **~-se** *vpr* bathe

banhei|ra /ba'ɲera/ *f* bath, *Amer* bathtub. **~ro** *m* bathroom; *Port* lifeguard

banhista /ba'ɲista/ *m/f* bather

banho /'baɲu/ *m* bath; (*no mar*) bathe, dip; **tomar ~** have a bath; (*no chuveiro*) have a shower; **tomar um ~ de loja/cultura** go on a shopping/cultural spree; **~ de espuma** bubble bath; **~ de sol** sunbathing. **~-maria** (*pl* **~s-maria**) *m* bain-marie

ba|nimento /bani'mẽtu/ *m* banishment. **~nir** *vt* banish

banjo /'bãʒu/ *m* banjo

banqueiro /bã'keru/ *m* banker

banqueta /bã'keta/ *f* footstool

banque|te /bã'ketʃi/ *m* banquet. **~teiro** *m* caterer

banzé /bã'zɛ/ *m* 🅸 commotion, uproar

baque /'baki/ *m* thud, crash; (*revés*) blow. **~ar** *vi* topple over ● *vt* hit hard, knock for six

bar /bar/ *m* bar

barafunda /bara'fũda/ *f* jumble; (*barulho*) racket

bara|lhada /bara'ʎada/ *f* jumble. **~lho** *m* pack of cards, *Amer* deck of cards

barão /ba'rãw/ *m* baron

barata /ba'rata/ *f* cockroach

bara|tear /baratʃi'ar/ *vt* cheapen. **~teiro** *a* cheap

baratinar /baratʃi'nar/ *vt* fluster; (*transtornar*) rattle, shake up

barato /ba'ratu/ *a* cheap ● *adv* cheaply ● *m* [!] **um ~** great; **que ~!** that's brilliant!

barba /'barba/ *f* beard; *pl* (*de gato etc*) whiskers; **fazer a ~** shave. **~da** *f* walkover; (*cavalo*) favourite. **~do** *a* bearded

barbante /bar'bãtʃi/ *m* string

bar|baridade /barbari'dadʒi/ *f* barbarity; [!] (*muito dinheiro*) fortune. **~bárie** *f*, **~barismo** *m* barbarism

bárbaro /'barbaru/ *m* barbarian ● *a* barbaric; [!] (*forte, bom*) terrific

barbatana /barba'tana/ *f* fin

bar|beador /barbia'dor/ *m* shaver. **~bear** *vt* shave. **~bear-se** *vpr* shave. **~bearia** *f* barber's shop. **~beiragem** *f* [!] bit of bad driving. **~beiro** *m* barber; [!] (*motorista*) bad driver

bar|ca /'barka/ *f* barge; (*balsa*) ferry. **~caça** *f* barge. **~co** *m* boat; **~co a motor** motor boat; **~co a remo/vela** rowing/sailing boat, *Amer* rowboat/sailboat

barga|nha /bar'gaɲa/ *f* bargain. **~nhar** *vt/i* bargain

barítono /ba'ritonu/ *m* baritone

barômetro /ba'rometru/ *m* barometer

baronesa /baro'neza/ *f* baroness

barra /'baxa/ *f* bar; (*sinal gráfico*) slash, stroke; [!] (*situação*) situation; **segurar a ~** hold out; **forçar a ~** force the issue

barra|ca /ba'xaka/ *f* (*de acampar*) tent; (*na feira*) stall; (*casinha*) hut; (*guarda-sol*) sunshade. **~cão** *m* shed. **~co** *m* shack, shanty

barragem /ba'xaʒẽ/ *f* (*represa*) dam

barra-pesada /baxape'zada/ *a invar* [!] ‹*bairro*› rough; ‹*pessoa*› shady; (*difícil*) tough

bar|rar /ba'xar/ *vt* bar. **~reira** *f* barrier; (*em corrida*) hurdle; (*em futebol*) wall

barrento /ba'xẽtu/ *a* muddy

barricada /baxi'kada/ *f* barricade

barri|ga /ba'xiga/ *f* stomach, *Amer* belly; **~ga da perna** calf. **~gudo** *a* pot-bellied

bar|ril /ba'xiw/ (*pl* **~ris**) *m* barrel

barro /'baxu/ *m* (*argila*) clay; (*lama*) mud

barroco /ba'xoku/ *a & m* baroque

barrote /ba'xɔtʃi/ *m* beam, joist

baru|lheira /baru'ʎera/ *f* racket, din. **~lhento** *a* noisy. **~lho** *m* noise

base /'bazi/ *f* base; *fig* (*fundamento*) basis; **com ~ em** on the basis of; **na ~ de** based on. **~ado** *a* based; (*firme*) well-founded ● *m* [!] joint. **~ar** *vt* base; **~ar-se em** be based on

básico /'baziku/ *a* basic

basquete /bas'kɛtʃi/ *m*, **basquetebol** /baskɛtʃi'bɔw/ *m* basketball

bas|ta /'basta/ *m* **dar um ~ta em** call a halt to. **~tante** *a* (*muito*) quite a lot of; (*suficiente*) enough ● *adv* (*com adjetivo, advérbio*) quite; (*com verbo*) quite a lot; (*suficientemente*) enough

bastão /bas'tãw/ *m* stick; (*num revezamento, de comando*) baton

bastar /bas'tar/ *vi* be enough

bastidores /bastʃi'doris/ *m pl* (*no teatro*) wings; **nos ~** *fig* behind the scenes

bata /'bata/ *f* (*de mulher*) smock; (*de médico etc*) overall

bata|lha /ba'taʎa/ *f* battle. **~lhador** *a* plucky, feisty ● *m* fighter. **~lhão** *m* battalion. **~lhar** *vi* battle; (*esforçar-se*) fight hard ● *vt* fight hard to get

batata /ba'tata/ *f* potato; **~ doce** sweet potato; **~ frita** chips, *Amer* French fries; (*salgadinhos*) crisps, *Amer* potato chips

bate-boca /batʃi'boka/ *m* row, argument

bate|deira /bate'dera/ *f* whisk; (*de manteiga*) churn. **~dor** *m* (*policial etc*) outrider; (*no criquete*) batsman; (*no beisebol*) batter; (*de caça*) beater; **~dor de carteiras** pickpocket

batelada /bate'lada/ *f* batch; **~s de** heaps of

batente /ba'tẽtʃi/ *m* (*de porta*) doorway; **para o/no ~** [!] (*ao trabalho*) to/at work

bate-papo /batʃi'papu/ *m* chat

bater /ba'ter/ *vt* beat; stamp ‹*pé*›; slam ‹*porta*›; strike ‹*horas*›; take ‹*foto*›; flap ‹*asas*›; (*datilografar*) type; (*lavar*) wash; (*usar muito*) wear a lot ‹*roupa*›; [!] pinch ‹*carteira*›; **~ à máquina** type; **~ à** ou **na porta** knock at the door; **~ em** hit; harp on ‹*assunto*›; **~ com o carro** crash one's car, have a crash; **~ com a cabeça** bang one's head; **ele batia os dentes de frio** his teeth were chattering with cold; **ele não bate bem** [!] he's not all there ● *vi* ‹*coração*› beat; ‹*porta*› slam; ‹*janela*› bang; ‹*horas*› strike; ‹*sino*› ring; (*à porta*) knock; (*com o carro*) crash; ‹*luz, sol*› shine on. **~-se** *vpr* (*lutar*) fight

bate|ria /bate'ria/ *f Eletr* battery; *Mus* drums; **~ria de cozinha** kitchen utensils. **~rista** *m/f* drummer

bati|da /ba'tʃida/ *f* beat; (*à porta*) knock; (*no carro*) crash; (*policial*) raid; (*bebida*) cocktail of rum, sugar and fruit juice. **~do** *a* beaten; ‹*roupa*› well worn; ‹*assunto*› hackneyed ● *m* **~do de leite** *Port* milkshake

batina /ba'tʃina/ *f* cassock

ba|tismo /ba'tʃizmu/ *m* baptism. **~tizado** *m* christening. **~tizar** *vt* baptize; (*pôr nome*) christen

batom /ba'tõ/ *m* lipstick

batu|cada /batu'kada/ *f* samba percussion group. **~car** *vt/i* drum in a samba rhythm. **~que** *m* samba rhythm

batuta /ba'tuta/ *f* baton; **sob a ~ de** under the direction of

baú /ba'u/ *m* trunk

baunilha /baw'niʎa/ *f* vanilla

bazar /ba'zar/ *m* bazaar; (*loja*) stationery and haberdashery shop

bê-a-bá /bea'ba/ *m* ABC

bea|titude /beatʃi'tudʒi/ *f* (*felicidade*) bliss; (*devoção*) piety, devoutness. **~to** *a* (*devoto*) pious, devout; (*feliz*) blissful

bêbado /'bebadu/ *a & m* drunk

bebê /be'be/ *m* baby; **~ de proveta** test-tube baby

bebe|deira /bebe'dera/ *f* (*estado*) drunkenness; (*ato*) drinking bout. **~dor** *m* drinker. **~douro** *m* drinking fountain

beber /be'ber/ *vt/i* drink

bebericar /beberi'kar/ *vt/i* sip

bebida /be'bida/ *f* drink

beca /'bɛka/ *f* gown

beça /'bɛsa/ *f* **à ~** [!] (*com substantivo*) loads of; (*com adjetivo*) really; (*com verbo*) a lot

becape /bɛ'kap/ *m Comput* backup

beco /'beku/ *m* alley; **~ sem saída** dead end

bedelho /be'deʎu/ *m* **meter o ~ (em)** stick one's oar in(to)

bege /'bɛʒi/ *a invar* beige

bei|cinho /bej'siɲu/ *m* **fazer ~cinho** pout. **~ço** *m* lip. **~çudo** *a* thick-lipped

beija-flor /bejʒa'flor/ *m* hummingbird

bei|jar /be'ʒar/ *vt* kiss. **~jo** *m* kiss. **~joca** /ɔ/ *f* peck

bei|ra /'bera/ *f* edge; *fig* (*do desastre etc*) verge, brink; **à ~ra de** at the edge of; *fig* on the verge of. **~rada** *f* edge. **~ra-mar** *f* seaside. **~rar** *vt* (*ficar*) border (on); (*andar*) skirt; *fig* border on, verge on; **ele está ~rando os 30 anos** he's nearing thirty

beisebol /beijsi'bɔw/ *m* baseball

belas-artes /bɛlaʃ'artʃiʃ/ *f pl* fine arts

beldade /bew'dadʒi/ *f*, **beleza** /be'leza/ *f* beauty

belga /'bɛwga/ *a & m* Belgian

Bélgica /'bɛwʒika/ *f* Belgium

beliche /be'liʃi/ *m* bunk

bélico /'bɛliku/ *a* war

belicoso /beli'kozu/ *a* warlike

belis|cão /belis'kãw/ *m* pinch. **~car** *vt* pinch; nibble ‹*comida*›

Belize /be'lizi/ *m* Belize

belo /'bɛlu/ *a* beautiful

beltrano /bew'tranu/ *m* such-and-such

bem /bẽj/ *adv* well; (*bastante*) quite; (*muito*) very ● *m* (*pl* **bens**) good; *pl* goods, property; **está ~** (it's) fine, OK; **fazer ~ a** be good for; **tudo ~?** [!] how's things?; **se ~ que** even though; **~ feito (por você)** [!] it serves you right; **muito ~!** well done!; **de ~ com alguém** on good terms with sb; **~ como** as well as

bem|-apessoado /bẽjapeso'adu/ *a* nice-looking. **~-comportado** *a* well-behaved; **~-disposto** *a* keen, willing; **~-estar** *m* well-being; **~-humorado** *a* good-humoured; **~-intencionado** *a* well-intentioned; **~-passado** *a* ‹*carne*› well-done; **~-sucedido** *a* successful; **~-vindo** *a* welcome; **~-visto** *a* well thought of

bênção /'bẽsãw/ (*pl* **~s**) *f* blessing

bendito /bẽ'dʒitu/ *a* blessed

benefi|cência /benefi'sẽsia/ *f* (*bondade*) goodness, kindness; (*caridade*) charity. **~cente** *a* ‹*associação*› charitable; ‹*concerto, feira*› charity. **~ciado** *m* beneficiary. **~ciar** *vt* benefit. **~ciar-se** *vpr* benefit (**de** from)

benefício /bene'fisiu/ *m* benefit; **em ~ de** in aid of

benéfico /be'nɛfiku/ *a* beneficial (**a** to)

benevolência /benevo'lẽsia/ *f* benevolence

benévolo /be'nɛvolu/ *a* benevolent

benfeitor /bẽfej'tor/ *m* benefactor

bengala /bẽ'gala/ *f* walking stick; (*pão*) French stick

benigno /be'niginu/ *a* benign

ben|to /'bẽtu/ *a* blessed; ‹*água*› holy. **~zer** *vt* bless. **~zer-se** *vpr* cross o.s.

berço /'bersu/ *m* (*de embalar*) cradle; (*caminha*) cot; *fig* birthplace; **ter ~** be from a good family

berimbau /berĩ'baw/ *m*: Brazilian percussion instrument shaped like a bow

berinjela /berĩ'ʒɛla/ *f* aubergine, *Amer* eggplant

Berlim /ber'lĩ/ *f* Berlin

berma /'bɛrma/ *f Port* hard shoulder, *Amer* berm

bermuda /ber'muda/ *f* Bermuda shorts

Berna /'bɛrna/ *f* Berne

ber|rante /be'xãtʃi/ *a* loud, flashy. **~rar** *vi* ‹*pessoa*› shout; ‹*criança*› bawl; ‹*boi*› bellow. **~reiro** *m* (*gritaria*) yelling, shouting; (*choro*) crying, bawling. **~ro** /ɛ/ *m* yell, shout; (*de boi*) bellow; **aos ~ros** shouting

besouro /be'zoru/ *m* beetle

bes|ta /'besta/ *a* (*idiota*) stupid; (*cheio de si*) full of o.s.; (*pedante*) pretentious ● *f* (*pessoa*) dimwit, numbskull; **ficar ~ta** [!] be taken aback. **~teira** *f* stupidity; (*uma*) stupid thing; **falar ~teira** talk rubbish. **~tial** (*pl* **~tiais**) *a* bestial. **~tificar** *vt* astound, dumbfound

besuntar /bezũ'tar/ *vt* coat; (*sujar*) smear

betão /be'tãw/ *Port m* concrete

beterraba /bete'xaba/ *f* beetroot

betoneira /beto'nera/ *f* cement mixer

bexiga /be'ʃiga/ *f* bladder

bezerro /be'zeru/ *m* calf

bibelô /bibe'lo/ *m* ornament

Bíblia /'biblia/ *f* Bible

bíblico /'bibliku/ *a* biblical

biblio|grafia /bibliogra'fia/ *f* bibliography. **~teca** /ɛ/ *f* library. **~tecário** *m* librarian ● *a* library

bica /'bika/ *f* tap; *Port* (*cafezinho*) espresso; **suar em ~s** drip with sweat

bicama /bi'kama/ *f* truckle bed

bicar /bi'kar/ *vt* peck

bíceps /'bisɛps/ *m invar* biceps

bicha /'biʃa/ *f* [!] queer, fairy; *Port* (*fila*) queue

bicheiro /bi'ʃeru/ *m* organizer of illegal numbers game, racketeer

bicho /'biʃu/ *m* animal; (*inseto*) insect, *Amer* bug; **que ~ te mordeu?** what's got into you?. **~-da-seda** (*pl* **~s-da-seda**) *m* silkworm; **~ de sete cabeças** *m* [!] big deal, big thing; **~ do mato** (*pl* **~s do mato**) *m* very shy person

bicho-papão /'biʃupa'pãw/ *m* (*pl* **bichos-papões**) bogeyman

bicicleta /bisi'klɛta/ *f* bicycle, bike

bico /'biku/ *m* (*de ave*) beak; (*de faca*) point; (*de sapato*) toe; (*de bule*) spout; (*de caneta*) nib; (*do seio*) nipple; (*de gás*) jet; [!] (*emprego*) odd job, sideline; (*boca*) mouth

bidê /bi'de/ *m* bidet

bidimensio|nal /bidʒimẽsio'naw/ (*pl* **~nais**) *a* two-dimensional

biela /bi'ɛla/ *f* connecting rod

Bielo-Rússia /bielo'xusia/ *f* Byelorussia

bielo-russo /bielo'xusu/ *a & m* Byelorussian

bie|nal /bie'naw/ (*pl* **~nais**) *a* biennial ● *f* biennial art exhibition

bife /'bifi/ *m* steak

bifo|cal /bifo'kaw/ (*pl* **~cais**) *a* bifocal

bifur|cação /bifurka'sãw/ *f* fork. **~car-se** *vpr* fork

bigamia /biga'mia/ *f* bigamy

bígamo /'bigamu/ *a* bigamous ● *m* bigamist

bigo|de /bi'gɔdʒi/ *m* moustache. **~dudo** *a* with a big moustache

bigorna /bi'gɔrna/ *f* anvil

bijuteria /biʒute'ria/ *f* costume jewellery

bilate|ral /bilate'raw/ (*pl* **~rais**) *a* bilateral

bilhão /bi'ʎãw/ *m* thousand million, *Amer* billion

bilhar /bi'ʎar/ *m* pool, billiards

bilhe|te /bi'ʎetʃi/ *m* ticket; (*recado*) note; **~te de ida e volta** return ticket, *Amer* round-trip ticket; **~te de identidade** *Port* identity card; **o ~te azul** [!] the sack. **~teria** *f*, *Port* **~teira** *f* (*no cinema, teatro*) box office; (*na estação*) ticket office

bilíngue /bi'lĩgwi/ *a* bilingual

bilionário /bilio'nariu/ *a & m* billionaire

bílis /'bilis/ *f* bile

binário /bi'nariu/ *a* binary

bingo /'bĩgu/ *m* bingo

binóculo /bi'nɔkulu/ *m* binoculars

biocombustível /biokõbus'tʃivew/ *m* biofuel

biodegradá|vel /biodegra'davew/ (*pl* **~veis**) *a* biodegradable

biodiesel /bio'dʒizew/ *m* biodiesel

biodiversidade /biodʒiversi'dadʒi/ *f* biodiversity

bio|grafia /biogra'fia/ *f* biography. **~gráfico** *a* biographical

biógrafo /bi'ɔgrafu/ *m* biographer

bio|logia /biolo'ʒia/ *f* biology. **~lógico** *a* biological

biólogo /bi'ɔlogu/ *m* biologist

biombo /bi'õbu/ *m* screen

biônico /bi'oniku/ *a* bionic; *Pol* unelected

biópsia /bi'ɔpsia/ *f* biopsy

bioquími|ca /bio'kimika/ *f* biochemistry. **~co** *a* biochemical ● *m* biochemist

biquíni /bi'kini/ *m* bikini

birma|nês /birma'nes/ *a & m* (*f* **~nesa**) Burmese

Birmânia /bir'mania/ *f* Burma

birô /bi'ro/ *m* bureau

bir|ra /'bixa/ *f* wilfulness; **fazer ~ra** have a tantrum. **~rento** *a* wilful

biruta /bi'ruta/ [!] *a* crazy ● *f* windsock

bis /bis/ *int* encore!, more! ● *m invar* encore

bisa|vó /biza'vɔ/ *f* great-grandmother. **~vós** *m pl* great-grandparents. **~vô** *m* great-grandfather

bisbilho|tar /bizbiʎo'tar/ *vt* pry into ● *vi* pry. **~teiro** *a* prying ● *m* busybody. **~tice** *f* prying

bisca|te /bis'katʃi/ *m* odd job. **~teiro** *m* odd-job man

biscoito /bis'kojtu/ *m* biscuit, *Amer* cookie

bisnaga /biz'naga/ *f* (*pão*) bridge roll; (*tubo*) tube

bisne|ta /biz'nɛta/ *f* great-granddaughter. **~to** /ɛ/ *m* great-grandson; *pl* great-grandchildren

bis|pado /bis'padu/ *m* bishopric. **~po** *m* bishop

bissexto /bi'sestu/ *a* occasional; **ano ~** leap year

bissexu|al /biseksu'aw/ (*pl* **~ais**) *a & m/f* bisexual

bisturi /bistu'ri/ *m* scalpel

bito|la /bi'tɔla/ *f* gauge. **~lado** *a* narrow-minded

bizarro /bi'zaxu/ *a* bizarre

blablablá /blabla'bla/ *m* [!] chit-chat

black /'blɛki/ *m* black market. **~-tie** *m* evening dress

blas|femar /blasfe'mar/ *vi* blaspheme. **~fêmia** *f* blasphemy. **~femo** /e/ *a* blasphemous ● *m* blasphemer

blecaute /ble'kawtʃi/ *m* power cut

ble|far /ble'far/ *vi* bluff. **~fe** /ɛ/ *m* bluff

blin|dado /blĩ'dadu/ *a* armoured. **~dagem** *f* armour plating

blitz /blits/ *f invar* police spot check (on vehicles)

blo|co /'blɔku/ *m* block; *Pol* bloc; (*de papel*) pad; (*no carnaval*) section.

blogar /blo'gar/ *vi* blog

blogue /'blɔgi/ *m* blog

blogueiro /blo'gejru/ *m*, *Port* **bloguista** /blo'giʃta/ *m/f* blogger

blo|quear /blo'kjar/ *vt* block; *Mil* blockade. **~queio** *m* blockage; *Psic* mental block; *Mil* blockade

blusa /'bluza/ *f* shirt; (*de mulher*) blouse; (*de lã*) sweater

blusão /blu'zãw/ *m* jacket

boa /'boa/ *f de* ▶ **BOM** ● **numa ~** [!] well; (*sem problemas*) easily; **estar numa ~** [!] be doing fine. **~-gente** *a invar* [!] nice; **~-nova** (*pl* **~s-novas**) *f* good news. **~-pinta** (*pl* **~s-pintas**) *a* [!] nice-looking; **~-praça** (*pl* **~s-praças**) *a* [!] friendly, sociable

boate /bo'atʃi/ *f* nightclub

boato /bo'atu/ *m* rumour

boa|-vida /boa'vida/ (*pl* **~s-vidas**) *m/f* good-for-nothing, waster. **~zinha** *a* sweet, kind

bo|bagem /bo'baʒẽ/ *f* silliness; (*uma*) silly thing. **~beada** *f* slip-up. **~bear** *vi* slip up. **~beira** *f* ▶ **BOBAGEM**

bobe /'bɔbi/ *m* curler, roller

bobina /bo'bina/ *f* reel; *Eletr* coil

bobo /'bobu/ *a* silly ● *m* fool; (*da corte*) jester. **~ca** /ɔ/ *a* [!] stupid ● *m/f* [!] twit

bo|ca /'boka/ *f* mouth; (*no fogão*) ring; **~ca da noite** nightfall. **~cado** *m* (*na boca*) mouthful; (*pedaço*) piece, bit. **~cal** (*pl* **~cais**) *m* mouthpiece

boce|jar /bose'ʒar/ *vi* yawn. **~jo** /e/ *m* yawn

boche|cha /bo'ʃeʃa/ *f* cheek. **~char** *vi* rinse one's mouth. **~cho** /e/ *m* mouthwash. **~chudo** *a* with puffy cheeks

bodas /'bodas/ *f pl* wedding anniversary; **~ de prata/ouro** silver/golden wedding

bode /'bɔdʒi/ *m* (billy) goat; **~ expiatório** scapegoat

bodega /bo'dɛga/ *f* (*de bebidas*) off-licence, *Amer* liquor store; (*de secos e molhados*) grocer's shop, corner shop
boêmio /bo'emiu/ *a & m* Bohemian
bofe|tada /bofe'tada/ *f*, **bofetão** /bofe'tãw/ *m* slap. **~tear** *vt* slap
boi /boj/ *m* bullock, *Amer* steer
bói /bɔj/ *m* office boy
boia /'bɔja/ *f* (*de balizamento*) buoy; (*de cortiça, isopor etc*) float; (*câmara de borracha*) rubber ring; (*de braço*) armband, water wing; (*na caixa-d'água*) ballcock; [!] (*comida*) grub; **~ salva-vidas** lifebelt. **~-fria** (*pl* **~s-frias**) *m/f* itinerant farm labourer
boiar /bo'jar/ *vt/i* float; [!] be lost
boico|tar /bojko'tar/ *vt* boycott. **~te** /ɔ/ *m* boycott
boiler /'bojler/ (*pl* **~s**) *m* boiler
boina /'bojna/ *f* beret
bo|jo /'boʒu/ *m* bulge. **~judo** *a* (*cheio*) bulging; (*arredondado*) bulbous
bola /'bɔla/ *f* ball; **dar ~ para** [!] give attention to ‹*pessoa*›; care about ‹*coisa*›; **~ de gude** marble; **~ de neve** snowball
bolacha /bo'laʃa/ *f* (*biscoito*) biscuit, *Amer* cookie; (*descanso*) beer mat; [!] (*tapa*) slap
bo|lada /bo'lada/ *f* large sum of money. **~lar** *vt* think up, devise
boleia /bo'lɛja/ *f* cab; *Port* (*carona*) lift
boletim /bole'tʃĩ/ *m* bulletin; (*escolar*) report
bolha /'boʎa/ *f* bubble; (*na pele*) blister ● *m/f* [!] pain
boliche /bo'liʃi/ *m* skittles
Bolívia /bo'livia/ *f* Bolivia
boliviano /bolivi'anu/ *a & m* Bolivian
bolo /'bolu/ *m* cake
bo|lor /bo'lor/ *m* mould, mildew. **~lorento** *a* mouldy

> **bolo rei** A ring-shaped fruit bread, covered in crystallized fruit and nuts, and eaten at Christmas time. Traditionally, a lucky coin or trinket and a *fava* (bean) would be hidden in the cake. In Portugal, whoever found the *fava* would be entitled to make a wish.

bolota /bo'lɔta/ *f* (*glande*) acorn; (*bolinha*) little ball
bol|sa /'bowsa/ *f* bag; **~sa (de estudo)** scholarship; **~sa (de valores)** stock exchange. **~sista** *m/f*, *Port* **~seiro** *m* scholarship student. **~so** /o/ *m* pocket
bom /bõ/ *a* (*f* **boa**) good; (*de saúde*) well; ‹*comida*› nice; **está ~** that's fine
bomba[1] /'bõba/ *f* (*explosiva*) bomb; (*doce*) eclair; *fig* bombshell; **levar ~** [!] fail
bomba[2] /'bõba/ *f* (*de bombear*) pump; **~ de gasolina** *Port* petrol pump
Bombaim /bõba'ĩ/ *f* Bombay
bombar|dear /bõbardʒi'ar/ *vt* bombard; (*do ar*) bomb. **~deio** *m* bombardment; (*do ar*) bombing
bomba|-relógio /bõbaxe'lɔʒiu/ (*pl* **~s-relógio**) *f* time bomb
bom|bear /bõbi'ar/ *vt* pump. **~beiro** *m* fireman; (*encanador*) plumber
bombom /bõ'bõ/ *m* chocolate
bombordo /bõ'bɔrdu/ *m* port
bondade /bõ'dadʒi/ *f* goodness
bonde /'bõdʒi/ *m* tram; (*teleférico*) cable car
bondoso /bõ'dozu/ *a* good(-hearted)
boné /bo'nɛ/ *m* cap
bone|ca /bo'nɛka/ *f* doll. **~co** /ɛ/ *m* dummy
bonificação /bonifika'sãw/ *f* bonus
bonito /bo'nitu/ *a* ‹*mulher*› pretty; ‹*homem*› handsome; ‹*tempo, casa etc*› lovely
bônus /'bonus/ *m invar* bonus
boqui|aberto /bokia'bɛrtu/ *a* open-mouthed, flabbergasted. **~nha** *f* snack
borboleta /borbo'leta/ *f* butterfly; (*roleta*) turnstile
borbotão /borbo'tãw/ *m* spurt
borbu|lha /bor'buʎa/ *f* bubble. **~lhar** *vi* bubble
borda /'bɔrda/ *f* edge. **~do** *a* edged; (*à linha*) embroidered ● *m* embroidery
bordão /bor'dãw/ *m* (*frase*) catchphrase
bordar /bor'dar/ *vt* (*à linha*) embroider
bor|del /bor'dɛw/ (*pl* **~déis**) *m* brothel
bordo /'bɔrdu/ *m* **a ~** aboard
borra /'boxa/ *f* dregs; (*de café*) grounds
borra|cha /bo'xaʃa/ *f* rubber. **~cheiro** *m* tyre fitter
bor|rão /bo'xãw/ *m* (*de tinta*) blot; (*rascunho*) rough draft. **~rar** *vt* (*sujar*) blot; (*riscar*) cross out; (*pintar*) daub
borrasca /bo'xaska/ *f* squall
borri|far /boxi'far/ *vt* sprinkle. **~fo** *m* sprinkling

b

bosque /'bɔski/ *m* wood

bosta /'bɔsta/ *f* (*de animal*) dung; (*chulo*) crap

bota /'bɔta/ *f* boot

botâni|ca /bo'tanika/ *f* botany. **~co** *a* botanical ● *m* botanist

bo|tão /bo'tãw/ *m* button; (*de flor*) bud; **falar com os seus ~tões** say to o.s.

botar /bo'tar/ *vt* put; put on ‹*roupa*›; set ‹*mesa, despertador*›; lay ‹*ovo*›; find ‹*defeito*›

bote[1] /'bɔtʃi/ *m* (*barco*) dinghy; **~ salva-vidas** lifeboat; (*de borracha*) life raft

bote[2] /'bɔtʃi/ *m* (*de animal etc*) lunge

botequim /butʃi'kĩ/ *m* bar

botoeira /boto'era/ *f* buttonhole

boxe /'bɔksi/ *m* boxing. **~ador** *m* boxer

brabo /'brabu/ *a* ‹*animal*› ferocious; ‹*calor, sol*› fierce; ‹*doença*› bad; ‹*prova, experiência*› tough; (*zangado*) angry

bra|çada /bra'sada/ *f* armful; (*em natação*) stroke. **~çadeira** *f* (*faixa*) armband; (*ferragem*) bracket; (*de atleta*) sweatband. **~çal** (*pl* **~çais**) *a* manual. **~celete** /e/ *m* bracelet. **~ço** *m* arm; **~ço direito** *fig* (*pessoa*) right-hand man

bra|dar /bra'dar/ *vt/i* shout. **~do** *m* shout

braguilha /bra'giʎa/ *f* fly, flies

braile /'brajli/ *m* Braille

bra|mido /bra'midu/ *m* roar. **~mir** *vi* roar

branco /'brãku/ *a* white ● *m* (*homem*) white man; (*espaço*) blank; **em ~** ‹*cheque etc*› blank; **noite em ~** sleepless night

bran|do /'brãdu/ *a* gentle; ‹*doença*› mild; (*indulgente*) lenient, soft. **~dura** *f* gentleness; (*indulgência*) softness, leniency

brasa /'braza/ *f* **em ~** red-hot; **mandar ~** [!] go to town

brasão /bra'zãw/ *m* coat of arms

braseiro /bra'zeru/ *m* brazier

Brasil /bra'ziw/ *m* Brazil

brasi|leiro /brazi'leru/ *a & m* Brazilian. **~liense** *a & m/f* (person) from Brasilia

bra|vata /bra'vata/ *f* bravado. **~vio** *a* wild; ‹*mar*› rough. **~vo** *a* (*corajoso*) brave; (*zangado*) angry; ‹*mar*› rough. **~vura** *f* bravery

breca /'brɛka/ *f* **levado da ~** very naughty

brecar /bre'kar/ *vt* stop ‹*carro*›; *fig* curb ● *vi* brake

brecha /'brɛʃa/ *f* gap; (*na lei*) loophole

bre|ga /'brɛga/ *a* [!] tacky, naff. **~guice** *f* [!] tack, tackiness

brejo /'brɛʒu/ *m* marsh; **ir para o ~** *fig* go down the drain

brenha /'brɛɲa/ *f* thicket

breque /'brɛki/ *m* brake

breu /brew/ *m* tar, pitch

bre|ve /'brɛvi/ *a* short, brief; **em ~ve** soon, shortly. **~vidade** *f* shortness, brevity

briga /'briga/ *f* fight; (*bate-boca*) argument

briga|da /bri'gada/ *f* brigade. **~deiro** *m* brigadier; (*doce*) chocolate truffle

bri|gão /bri'gãw/ *a* (*f* **~gona**) belligerent; (*na fala*) argumentative ● *m* (*f* **~gona**) troublemaker. **~gar** *vi* fight; (*com palavras*) argue; ‹*cores*› clash

bri|lhante /bri'ʎãtʃi/ *a* (*reluzente*) shiny; *fig* brilliant. **~lhar** *vi* shine. **~lho** *m* (*de sapatos etc*) shine; (*dos olhos, de metais*) gleam; (*das estrelas*) brightness; (*de uma cor*) brilliance; *fig* (*esplendor*) splendour

brin|cadeira /brĩka'dera/ *f* (*piada*) joke; (*brinquedo, jogo*) game; **de ~cadeira** for fun. **~calhão** (*f* **~calhona**) *a* playful ● *m* joker. **~car** *vi* (*divertir-se*) play; (*gracejar*) joke

brinco /'brĩku/ *m* earring

brin|dar /brĩ'dar/ *vt* (*saudar*) toast, drink to; (*presentear*) give a gift to; **~dar alguém com algo** afford sb sth; (*de presente*) give sb sth as a gift. **~de** *m* (*saudação*) toast; (*presente*) free gift

brinquedo /brĩ'kedu/ *m* toy

brio /'briu/ *m* self-esteem, character. **~so** /o/ *a* self-confident

brisa /'briza/ *f* breeze

britadeira /brita'dera/ *f* pneumatic drill

britânico /bri'taniku/ *a* British ● *m* Briton; **os ~s** the British

broca /'brɔka/ *f* drill

broche /'brɔʃi/ *m* brooch

brochura /bro'ʃura/ *f* **livro de ~** paperback

brócolis /'brɔkulis/ *m pl*, *Port* **brócolos** /'brɔkuluʃ/ *m pl* broccoli

bron|ca /'brõka/ *f* [!] telling-off; **dar uma ~ca em alguém** tell sb off. **~co** *a* coarse, rough

bronquite /brõ'kitʃi/ *f* bronchitis

bronze /'brõzi/ *m* bronze. **~ado** *a* tanned, brown ● *m* (sun)tan. **~ador** *a* tanning ● *m* suntan lotion. **~amento** *m* tanning. **~ar** *vt* tan. **~ar-se** *vpr* go brown, tan

bro|tar /bro'tar/ *vt* sprout ‹*folhas, flores*›; spout ‹*lágrimas, palavras*› ● *vi* ‹*planta*› sprout; ‹*água*› spout; ‹*ideias*› pop up. **~tinho** *m* [!] youngster. **~to** /o/ *m* shoot; [!] youngster

broxa /'brɔʃa/ *f* (large) paint brush ● *a* [!] impotent

bruços /'brusus/ **de ~** face down

bru|ma /'bruma/ *f* mist. **~moso** /o/ *a* misty

brusco /'brusku/ *a* brusque, abrupt

bru|tal /bru'taw/ (*pl* **~tais**) *a* brutal. **~talidade** *f* brutality. **~to** *a* ‹*feições*› coarse; ‹*homem*› brutish; ‹*tom, comentário*› aggressive; ‹*petróleo*› crude; ‹*peso, lucro, salário*› gross ● *m* brute

bruxa /'bruʃa/ *f* witch; (*feia*) hag. **~ria** *f* witchcraft

Bruxelas /bru'ʃɛlas/ *f* Brussels

bruxo /'bruʃu/ *m* wizard

bruxulear /bruʃuli'ar/ *vi* flicker

bucha /'buʃa/ *f* (*tampão*) bung; (*para paredes*) Rawlplug®; **acertar na ~** [!] hit the nail on the head

bucho /'buʃu/ *m* gut; **~ de boi** tripe

budis|mo /bu'dʒizmu/ *m* Buddhism. **~ta** *a & m/f* Buddhist

bueiro /bu'eru/ *m* storm drain

búfalo /'bufalu/ *m* buffalo

bu|fante /bu'fãtʃi/ *a* full, puffed. **~far** *vi* snort; (*reclamar*) grumble, moan

bufê /bu'fe/ *m* (*refeição*) buffet; (*serviço*) catering service; (*móvel*) sideboard

bugiganga /buʒi'gãga/ *f* knick-knack

bujão /bu'ʒãw/ *m* **~ de gás** gas cylinder

bula /'bula/ *f* (*de remédio*) directions; (*do Papa*) bull

bulbo /'buwbu/ *m* bulb

bule /'buli/ *m* (*de chá*) teapot; (*de café etc*) pot

Bulgária /buw'garia/ *f* Bulgaria

búlgaro /'buwgaru/ *a & m* Bulgarian

bulhufas /bu'ʎufas/ *pron* [!] nothing

bulício /bu'lisiu/ *m* bustle

bulimia /buli'mia/ *f* bulimia

bullying /'bʊliɪŋ/ *m* bullying

bumbum /bũ'bũ/ *m* [!] bottom, bum

bunda /'bũda/ *f* bottom

buquê /bu'ke/ *m* bouquet

buraco /bu'raku/ *m* hole; (*de agulha*) eye; (*jogo de cartas*) rummy; **~ da fechadura** keyhole

burburinho /burbu'riɲu/ *m* (*de vozes*) hubbub

burca /'burka/ *f* burka

bur|guês /bur'ges/ *a & m* (*f* **~guesa**) bourgeois. **~guesia** *f* bourgeoisie

burlar /bur'lar/ *vt* get round ‹*lei*›; get past ‹*defesas, vigilância*›

buro|cracia /burokra'sia/ *f* bureaucracy. **~crata** *m/f* bureaucrat. **~crático** *a* bureaucratic. **~cratizar** *vt* make bureaucratic

bur|rice /bu'xisi/ *f* stupidity; (*uma*) stupid thing. **~ro** *a* stupid; (*ignorante*) dim ● *m* (*animal*) donkey; (*pessoa*) halfwit, dunce; **~ro de carga** *fig* workhorse

bus|ca /'buska/ *f* search; **dar ~ca em** search. **~ca-pé** *m* banger. **~car** *vt* fetch; (*de carro*) pick up; **mandar ~car** send for

bússola /'busola/ *f* compass; *fig* guide

busto /'bustu/ *m* bust

butique /bu'tʃiki/ *f* boutique

buzi|na /bu'zina/ *f* horn. **~nada** *f* toot (of the horn). **~nar** *vi* sound the horn, toot the horn

Cc

cá /ka/ *adv* here; **o lado de ~** this side; **para ~** here; **de ~ para lá** back and forth; **de lá para ~** since then; **~ entre nós** between you and me

ca|bal /ka'baw/ (*pl* **~bais**) *a* complete, full; ‹*prova*› conclusive

cabana /ka'bana/ *f* hut; (*casinha no campo*) cottage

cabeça /ka'besa/ *f* head; (*de lista*) top; (*inteligência*) mind ● *m/f* (*chefe*) ringleader; (*pessoa inteligente*) brains; **de ~** off the top of one's head; **de ~ para baixo** upside down; **deu-lhe na ~ de** he took it into his head to; **esquentar a ~** [!] get worked up; **fazer a ~ de alguém** convince sb; **quebrar a ~** rack one's brains; **subir à ~** go to sb's head; **ter a ~ no lugar** have one's head screwed on. **~da** *f* (*no futebol*) header; (*pancada*) head butt; **dar uma ~da no teto** bang one's head on the ceiling. **~ de porco** *f* tenement; **~ de vento** *m/f* scatterbrain, airhead. **~lho** *m* heading

cabe|cear /kabesi'ar/ *vt* head ‹*bola*›. **~ceira** *f* head. **~çudo** *a* pig-headed

cabe|dal /kabe'daw/ (*pl* **~dais**) *m* wealth

cabelei|ra /kabe'lera/ *f* head of hair; (*peruca*) wig. **~reiro** *m* hairdresser

cabe|lo /ka'belu/ *m* hair; **cortar o ~lo** have one's hair cut. **~ludo** *a* hairy; (*difícil*) complicated; ‹*palavra, piada*› dirty

caber /ka'ber/ *vi* fit; (*ter cabimento*) be fitting; **~ a** ‹*mérito, parte*› be due to; ‹*tarefa*› fall to; **cabe a você ir** it is up to you to go; **~ em alguém** fit sb

cabide /ka'bidʒi/ *m* (*peça de madeira, arame etc*) hanger; (*móvel*) hat stand; (*na parede*) coat rack

cabimento /kabi'mẽtu/ *m* **ter ~** be fitting, be appropriate; **não ter ~** be out of the question

cabine /ka'bini/ *f* cabin; (*de avião*) cockpit; (*de loja*) changing room; **~ telefônica** phone box, *Amer* phone booth

cabisbaixo /kabiz'baʃu/ *a* crestfallen

cabí|vel /ka'bivew/ (*pl* **~veis**) *a* appropriate, fitting

cabo[1] /'kabu/ *m* (*militar*) corporal; **ao ~ de** after; **levar a ~** carry out; **~ eleitoral** campaign worker

cabo[2] /'kabu/ *m* (*fio*) cable; (*de panela etc*) handle; **TV por ~** cable TV; **~ de extensão** extension lead; **~ de força** tug of war

caboclo /ka'boklu/ *a & m* mestizo

ca|bra /'kabra/ *f* goat. **~brito** *m* kid

ca|ça /'kasa/ *f* (*atividade*) hunting; (*caçada*) hunt; (*animais*) game ● *m* (*avião*) fighter; **à ~ça de** in pursuit of; **~ça das bruxas** *fig* witch hunt. **~çador** *m* hunter. **~ça-minas** *m invar* minesweeper; **~ça-níqueis** *m invar* slot machine. **~çar** *vt* hunt ‹*animais, criminoso etc*›; (*procurar*) hunt for ● *vi* hunt

cacareco /kaka'rɛku/ *m* piece of junk; *pl* junk

cacare|jar /kakare'ʒar/ *vi* cluck. **~jo** /e/ *m* clucking

caçarola /kasa'rɔla/ *f* saucepan

cacau /ka'kaw/ *m* cocoa

cace|tada /kase'tada/ *f* blow with a club; *fig* annoyance. **~te** /e/ *m* club ● *int* ! damn

cachaça /ka'ʃasa/ *f* white rum

> **cachaça** Also known as *aguardente de cana* (sugar-cane rum), *cachaça* is Brazil's most popular alcoholic drink. It's made by fermenting sugar-cane juice, and is extremely alcoholic. Brazilians refer to the drink informally as *caninha*, *pinga*, or *canha*, and it is mixed with lemon juice and sugar to make *caipirinha*, Brazil's most famous cocktail.

cachê /ka'ʃe/ *m* fee

cache|col /kaʃe'kɔw/ (*pl* **~cóis**) *m* scarf

cachimbo /ka'ʃĩbu/ *m* pipe

cacho /'kaʃu/ *m* (*de banana, uva*) bunch; (*de cabelo*) lock; ! (*caso*) affair

cachoeira /kaʃo'era/ *f* waterfall

cachor|rinho /kaʃo'xiɲu/ *m* (*nado*) doggy paddle. **~ro** /o/ *m* dog; *Port* puppy; (*pessoa*) scoundrel. **~ro-quente** (*pl* **~ros-quentes**) *m* hot dog

cacife /ka'sifi/ *m fig* pull

caci|que /ka'siki/ *m* (*índio*) chief; (*político*) boss. **~quia** *f* leadership

caco /'kaku/ *m* shard; (*pessoa*) old crock

cacto /'kaktu/ *m* cactus

caçula /ka'sula/ *m/f* youngest child ● *a* youngest

cada /'kada/ *a* each; **~ duas horas** every two hours; **custam £5 ~ (um)** they cost £5 each; **~ vez mais** more and more; **~ vez mais fácil** easier and easier; **ele fala ~ coisa** ! he says the most amazing things

cadafalso /kada'fawsu/ *m* gallows

cadarço /ka'darsu/ *m* shoelace

cadas|trar /kadas'trar/ *vt* register. **~tro** *m* register; (*ato*) registration; (*policial, bancário*) records, files; (*imobiliário*) land register

ca|dáver /ka'daver/ *m* (dead) body, corpse. **~davérico** *a* cadaverous, corpse-like; ‹*exame*› post-mortem

cadê /ka'de/ *adv* ! where is/are...?

cadeado /kadʒi'adu/ *m* padlock

cadeia /ka'deja/ *f* (*de eventos, lojas etc*) chain; (*prisão*) prison; (*rádio, TV*) network

cadeira /ka'dera/ *f* (*móvel*) chair; (*no teatro*) stall; (*de político*) seat; (*função de professor*) chair; (*matéria*) subject; *pl Anat* hips; **~ de balanço** rocking chair; **~ de rodas** wheelchair; **~ elétrica** electric chair

ca|dência /ka'dẽsia/ *f Mus* (*da voz*) cadence; (*compasso*) rhythm.

~denciado *a* rhythmic; ‹*passos*› measured

cader|neta /kader'neta/ *f* notebook; (*de professor*) register; (*de banco*) passbook; **~neta de poupança** savings account. **~no** /ɛ/ *m* exercise book; (*pequeno*) notebook; (*no jornal*) section

cadete /ka'detʃi/ *m* cadet

cadu|car /kadu'kar/ *vi* ‹*pessoa*› become senile; ‹*contrato*› lapse. **~co** *a* ‹*pessoa*› senile; ‹*contrato*› lapsed. **~quice** *f* senility

cafajeste /kafa'ʒɛstʃi/ *m* swine

ca|fé /ka'fɛ/ *m* coffee; (*estabelecimento*) cafe; **~fé da manhã** breakfast; **tomar ~fé** have breakfast. **~fé-com-leite** *a invar* coffee-coloured, light brown ● *m* white coffee. **~feeiro** *a* coffee ● *m* coffee plant. **~feicultura** *f* coffee-growing. **~feína** *f* caffein(e)

cafetã /kafe'tã/ *m* caftan

cafetão /kafe'tãw/ *m* pimp

cafe|teira /kafe'tera/ *f* coffee pot; **~ de pistão** cafetière. **~zal** (*pl* **~zais**) *m* coffee plantation. **~zinho** *m* small black coffee

cafo|na /ka'fɔna/ *a* [!] naff, tacky. **~nice** *f* tackiness; (*coisa*) tacky thing

cágado /'kagadu/ *m* turtle

caiar /kaj'ar/ *vt* whitewash

cãibra /'kãjbra/ *f* cramp

caí|da /ka'ida/ *f* fall; ▶ QUEDA. **~do** *a* ‹*árvore etc*› fallen; ‹*beiços etc*› drooping; (*deprimido*) dejected; (*apaixonado*) smitten

caimento /kaj'mẽtu/ *m* fall

caipi|ra /kaj'pira/ *a* ‹*pessoa*› countrified; ‹*festa, música*› country; ‹*sotaque*› rural ● *m/f* country person; (*depreciativo*) country bumpkin. **~rinha** *f* cachaça with limes, sugar and ice

cair /ka'ir/ *vi* fall; ‹*dente, cabelo*› fall out; ‹*botão etc*› fall off; ‹*comércio, trânsito etc*› fall off; ‹*tecido, cortina*› hang; **~ bem/mal** ‹*roupa*› go well/badly; ‹*ato, dito*› go down well/ badly; **estou caindo de sono** I'm really sleepy

cais /kajs/ *m* quay; *Port* (*na estação*) platform

caixa /'kaʃa/ *f* box; (*de loja etc*) cash desk ● *m/f* cashier; **~ de correio** letter box; **~ de entrada** *Comput* inbox; **~ de mudanças**, *Port* **~ de velocidades** gear box; **~ postal** post office box, PO Box; **~ de saída** *Comput* outbox. **~-d'água** (*pl* **~s-d'água**) *f* water tank; **~-forte** (*pl* **~s-fortes**) *f* vault

cai|xão /ka'ʃãw/ *m* coffin. **~xeiro** *m* (*em loja*) assistant; salesman. **~xilho** *m* frame. **~xote** /ɔ/ *m* crate

caju /ka'ʒu/ *m* cashew fruit. **~eiro** *m* cashew tree

cal /kaw/ *f* lime

calado /ka'ladu/ *a* quiet

calafrio /kala'friu/ *m* shudder, shiver

calami|dade /kalami'dadʒi/ *f* calamity. **~toso** /o/ *a* calamitous

calar /ka'lar/ *vi* be quiet ● *vt* keep quiet about ‹*segredo, sentimento*›; silence ‹*pessoa*›. **~-se** *vpr* go quiet

calça /'kawsa/ *f* trousers, *Amer* pants

calça|da /kaw'sada/ *f* pavement, *Amer* sidewalk; *Port* (*rua*) roadway. **~dão** *m* pedestrian precinct. **~deira** *f* shoehorn. **~do** *a* paved ● *m* shoe; *pl* footwear

calcanhar /kawka'ɲar/ *m* heel

calção /kaw'sãw/ *m* shorts; **~ de banho** swimming trunks

calcar /kaw'kar/ *vt* (*pisar*) trample; (*comprimir*) press; **~ algo em** *fig* base sth on, model sth on

calçar /kaw'sar/ *vt* put on ‹*sapatos, luvas*›; take ‹*número*›; pave ‹*rua*›; (*com calço*) wedge ● *vi* ‹*sapato*› fit. **~-se** *vpr* put one's shoes on

calcário /kaw'kariu/ *m* limestone ● *a* ‹*água*› hard

calças /'kawsas/ *f pl* ▶ CALÇA

calcinha /kaw'siɲa/ *f* knickers, *Amer* panties

cálcio /'kawsiu/ *m* calcium

calço /'kawsu/ *m* wedge

calcu|ladora /kawkula'dora/ *f* calculator. **~lar** *vt/i* calculate. **~lista** *a* calculating ● *m/f* opportunist

cálculo /'kawkulu/ *m* calculation; (*diferencial*) calculus; *Med* stone

cal|da /'kawda/ *f* syrup; *pl* hot springs. **~deira** *f* boiler. **~deirão** *m* cauldron. **~do** *m* (*sopa*) broth; (*suco*) juice; **~do de carne/galinha** beef/chicken stock

calefação /kalefa'sãw/ *f* heating

caleidoscópio /kalejdos'kɔpiu/ *m* kaleidoscope

calejado /kale'ʒadu/ *a* ‹*mãos*› calloused; ‹*pessoa*› experienced

calendário /kalẽ'dariu/ *m* calendar

calha /'kaʎa/ *f* (*no telhado*) gutter; (*sulco*) gulley

calhamaço /kaʎa'masu/ *m* tome

calhambeque /kaʎã'bɛki/ *m* [!] banger

C

calhar /ka'ʎar/ *vi* **calhou que** it so happened that; **calhou pegarem o mesmo trem** they happened to get the same train; **~ de** happen to; **vir a ~** come at the right time

cali|brado /kali'bradu/ *a* (*bêbado*) tipsy. **~brar** *vt* calibrate; check (the pressure of) ‹*pneu*›. **~bre** *m* calibre; **coisas desse ~bre** things of this order

cálice /'kalisi/ *m* (*copo*) liqueur glass; (*na missa*) chalice

caligrafia /kaligra'fia/ *f* (*letra*) handwriting; (*arte*) calligraphy

calista /ka'lista/ *m/f* chiropodist, *Amer* podiatrist

cal|ma /'kawma/ *f* calm. **com ~ma** *int* calm down. **~mante** *m* tranquilizer. **~mo** *a* calm

calo /'kalu/ *m* (*na mão*) callus; (*no pé*) corn

calombo /ka'lõbu/ *m* bump

calor /ka'lor/ *m* heat; (*agradável*) *fig* warmth; **estar com ~** be hot

calo|rento /kalo'rẽtu/ *a* ‹*pessoa*› sensitive to heat; ‹*lugar*› hot. **~ria** *f* calorie. **~roso** /o/ *a* warm; ‹*protesto*› lively

calota /ka'lɔta/ *f* hubcap

calo|te /ka'lɔtʃi/ *m* bad debt. **~teiro** *m* bad risk

calouro /ka'loru/ *m* (*na faculdade*) freshman; (*em outros ramos*) novice

ca|lúnia /ka'lunia/ *f* slander. **~luniar** *vt* slander. **~lunioso** /o/ *a* slanderous

cal|vície /kaw'visi/ *f* baldness. **~vo** *a* bald

cama /'kama/ *f* bed; **~ de casal/solteiro** double/single bed. **~-beliche** (*pl* **~s-beliches**) *f* bunk bed

camada /ka'mada/ *f* layer; (*de tinta*) coat

câmara /'kamara/ *f* chamber; (*fotográfica*) camera; **em ~ lenta** in slow motion; **~ de ar** inner tube; **~ digital** digital camera; **~ municipal** town council; *Port* town hall

camarada /kama'rada/ *a* friendly ● *m/f* comrade. **~gem** *f* comradeship; (*convivência agradável*) camaraderie

camarão /kama'rãw/ *m* shrimp; (*maior*) prawn

cama|reira /kama'rera/ *f* chambermaid. **~rim** *m* dressing room. **~rote** /ɔ/ *m* (*no teatro*) box; (*num navio*) cabin

cambada /kã'bada/ *f* gang, horde

cambalacho /kãba'laʃu/ *m* scam

camba|lear /kãbali'ar/ *vi* stagger. **~lhota** *f* somersault

cambi|al /kãbi'aw/ (*pl* **~ais**) *a* exchange. **~ante** *m* shade. **~ar** *vt* change

câmbio /'kãbiu/ *m* exchange; (*taxa*) rate of exchange; **~ oficial/paralelo** official/black market exchange rate

cambista /kã'bista/ *m/f* (*de entradas*) ticket tout, *Amer* scalper; (*de dinheiro*) money changer

Camboja /kã'bɔʒa/ *m* Cambodia

cambojano /kãbo'ʒanu/ *a & m* Cambodian

camburão /kãbu'rãw/ *m* police van

camelo /ka'melu/ *m* camel

camelô /kame'lo/ *m* street vendor

camião /kami'ãw/ *Port m* ▶ CAMINHÃO

caminhada /kami'ɲada/ *f* walk

caminhão /kami'ɲãw/ *m* lorry, *Amer* truck

cami|nhar /kami'ɲar/ *vi* walk; *fig* advance, progress. **~nho** *m* way; (*estrada*) road; (*trilho*) path; **a ~nho** on the way; **a meio ~nho** halfway; **~nho de ferro** *Port* railway, *Amer* railroad

caminho|neiro /kamiɲo'neru/ *m* lorry driver, *Amer* truck driver. **~nete** /ɛ/ *m* van

camio|neta /kamio'neta/ *f* van. **~nista** *Port m/f* ▶ CAMINHONEIRO

cami|sa /ka'miza/ *f* shirt. **~sa de força** straitjacket; **~sa de vênus** condom. **~seta** /e/ *f* T-shirt; (*de baixo*) vest. **~sinha** *f* [!] condom. **~sola** /ɔ/ *f* nightdress; *Port* sweater

camomila /kamo'mila/ *f* camomile

campainha /kãpa'iɲa/ *f* bell; (*da porta*) doorbell

campanário /kãpa'nariu/ *m* belfry

campanha /kã'paɲa/ *f* campaign

campe|ão /kãpi'ãw/ *m* (*f* **~ã**) champion. **~onato** *m* championship

cam|pestre /kã'pɛstri/ *a* rural. **~pina** *f* grassland

cam|ping /'kãpĩ/ *m* camping; (*lugar*) campsite. **~pismo** *Port m* camping

campo /'kãpu/ *m* field; (*interior*) country; (*de futebol*) pitch; (*de golfe*) course; **~ de concentração** concentration camp. **~nês** *m* (*f* **~nesa**) peasant

camu|flagem /kamu'flaʒẽ/ *f* camouflage. **~flar** *vt* camouflage

camundongo /kamũ'dõgu/ *m* mouse

cana /'kana/ *f* cane; **~ de açúcar** sugar cane

Canadá /kana'da/ *m* Canada

canadense /kana'dẽsi/ *a & m* Canadian

ca|nal /ka'naw/ (*pl* **~nais**) *m* channel; (*hidrovia*) canal; **~ de televisão a cabo** cable channel

canalha /ka'naʎa/ *m/f* scoundrel

canali|zação /kanaliza'sãw/ *f* piping. **~zador** *Port m* plumber. **~zar** *vt* channel ‹*líquido, esforço, recursos*›; canalize ‹*rio*›; pipe for water and drainage ‹*cidade*›

canário /ka'nariu/ *m* canary

canastrão /kanas'trãw/ *m* (*f* **~trona**) ham actor, (*f* actress)

canavi|al /kanavi'aw/ (*pl* **~ais**) *m* cane field. **~eiro** *a* sugar cane

canção /kã'sãw/ *f* song

cance|lamento /kãsela'mẽtu/ *m* cancellation. **~lar** *vt* cancel; (*riscar*) cross out

câncer /'kãser/ *m* cancer; **C~** (*signo*) Cancer

cance|riano /kãseri'anu/ *a & m* Cancerian. **~rígeno** *a* carcinogenic. **~roso** /o/ *a* cancerous ● *m* person with cancer

cancro /'kãkru/ *m Port* (*câncer*) cancer; *fig* canker

candango /kã'dãgu/ *m* person from Brasilia

cande|eiro /kãdʒi'eru/ *m* (oil) lamp. **~labro** *m* candelabra

candida|tar-se /kãdʒida'tarsi/ *vpr* (*a vaga*) apply (**a** for); (*à presidência etc*) stand, *Amer* run (**a** for). **~to** *m* candidate (**a** for); (*a vaga*) applicant (**a** for). **~tura** *f* candidature; (*a vaga*) application (**a** for)

cândido /'kãdʒidu/ *a* innocent

candomblê /kãdõ'blɛ/ *m* Afro-Brazilian cult; (*reunião*) candomble meeting

> *i*
> **candomblé** *Candomblé* is one of the principally Afro-Brazilian religions that worship the gods of Western Africa, known as *orixás*. The ceremonies take place in *terreiros* to the sound of percussion, and can include animal sacrifices and the consumption of alcoholic drinks in a bid to 'raise the spirit'. The main festival is the *Festa de Iemanjá*, the Queen of the Ocean, on the 2nd of February.

candura /kã'dura/ *f* innocence

cane|ca /ka'nɛka/ *f* mug. **~co** /ɛ/ *m* tankard

canela[1] /ka'nɛla/ *f* (*condimento*) cinnamon

canela[2] /ka'nɛla/ *f* (*da perna*) shin. **~da** *f* **dar uma ~da em alguém** kick sb in the shins; **dar uma ~da em algo** hit one's shins on sth

cane|ta /ka'neta/ *f* pen; **~ esferográfica** ballpoint pen. **~ta-tinteiro** (*pl* **~tas-tinteiro**) *f* fountain pen

cangote /kã'gɔtʃi/ *m* nape of the neck

canguru /kãgu'ru/ *m* kangaroo

canhão /ka'ɲãw/ *m* (*arma*) cannon; (*vale*) canyon

canhoto /ka'ɲotu/ *a* left-handed ● *m* (*talão*) stub

cani|bal /kani'baw/ (*pl* **~bais**) *m/f* cannibal. **~balismo** *m* cannibalism

caniço /ka'nisu/ *m* reed; (*pessoa*) skinny person

canícula /ka'nikula/ *f* heat wave

ca|nil /ka'niw/ (*pl* **~nis**) *m* kennel

canivete /kani'vɛtʃi/ *m* penknife

canja /'kãʒa/ *f* chicken soup; [!] piece of cake

canjica /kã'ʒika/ *f* corn porridge

cano /'kanu/ *m* pipe; (*de bota*) top; (*de arma de fogo*) barrel

cano|a /ka'noa/ *f* canoe. **~agem** *f* canoeing. **~ista** *m/f* canoeist

canonizar /kanoni'zar/ *vt* canonize

can|saço /kã'sasu/ *m* tiredness. **~sado** *a* tired. **~sar** *vt* tire; (*aborrecer*) bore ● *vi*, **~sar-se** *vpr* get tired. **~sativo** *a* tiring; (*aborrecido*) boring. **~seira** *f* tiredness; (*lida*) toil

can|tada /kã'tada/ *f* [!] chat-up. **~tar** *vt/i* sing; [!] chat up

cântaro /'kãtaru/ *m* **chover a ~s** pour down, bucket down

cantarolar /kãtaro'lar/ *vt/i* hum

cantei|ra /kã'tera/ *f* quarry. **~ro** *m* (*de flores*) flower bed; (*artífice*) stonemason; **~ro de obras** site office

cantiga /kã'tʃiga/ *f* ballad

can|til /kã'tʃiw/ (*pl* **~tis**) *m* canteen. **~tina** *f* canteen

canto[1] /'kãtu/ *m* (*ângulo*) corner

can|to[2] /'kãtu/ *m* (*cantar*) singing. **~tor** *m* singer. **~toria** *f* singing

canudo /ka'nudu/ *m* (*de beber*) straw; (*tubo*) tube; [!] (*diploma*) diploma

cão /kãw/ (*pl* **cães**) *m* dog

caolho /ka'oʎu/ *a* one-eyed

ca|os /kaws/ *m* chaos. **~ótico** *a* chaotic

capa /'kapa/ *f* (*de livro, revista*) cover; (*roupa sem mangas*) cape; **~ de chuva** raincoat

capacete /kapa'setʃi/ *m* helmet

capacho /ka'paʃu/ *m* doormat

capaci|dade /kapasi'dadʒi/ *f* capacity; (*aptidão*) ability. **~tar** *vt* enable; (*convencer*) convince

capataz /kapa'tas/ *m* foreman

capaz /ka'pas/ *a* capable (**de** of); **ser ~ de** (*poder*) be able to; (*ser provável*) be likely to

cape|la /ka'pɛla/ *f* chapel. **~lão** (*pl* **~lães**) *m* chaplain

capen|ga /ka'pẽga/ *a* doddery. **~gar** *vi* dodder

capeta /ka'peta/ *m* (*diabo*) devil; (*criança*) little devil

capilar /kapi'lar/ *a* hair

ca|pim /ka'pĩ/ *m* grass. **~pinar** *vt/i* weed

capi|tal /kapi'taw/ (*pl* **~tais**) *a & m/f* capital. **~talismo** *m* capitalism. **~talista** *a & m/f* capitalist. **~talizar** *vt Com* capitalize; (*aproveitar*) capitalize on

capi|tanear /kapitani'ar/ *vt* captain ‹*navio*›; *fig* lead. **~tania** *f* captaincy; **~tania do porto** port authority. **~tão** (*pl* **~tães**) *m* captain

capitulação /kapitula'sãw/ *f* capitulation, surrender

capítulo /ka'pitulu/ *m* chapter; (*de telenovela*) episode

capô /ka'po/ *m* bonnet, *Amer* hood

capoeira /kapo'era/ *f* Brazilian kick-boxing

> ***i***
> **capoeira** Capoeira was created as a form of self-defence by the descendants of African slaves during the colonial period. When the practice was banned by the colonizers, it developed into a gentle and graceful art form, in which participants are not allowed to touch each other. Capoeira originated in the state of Bahia, and is 'played' in pairs to the sound of percussion instruments, such as the *berimbau*.

capo|ta /ka'pɔta/ *f* roof. **~tar** *vi* overturn

capote /ka'pɔtʃi/ *m* overcoat

capri|char /kapri'ʃar/ *vi* excel o.s.. **~cho** *m* (*esmero*) care; (*desejo*) whim; (*teimosia*) contrariness. **~choso** /o/ *a* (*cheio de caprichos*) capricious; (*com esmero*) painstaking, meticulous

capricorniano /kaprikorni'anu/ *a & m* Capricorn

Capricórnio /kapri'kɔrniu/ *m* Capricorn

cápsula /'kapsula/ *f* capsule

cap|tar /kap'tar/ *vt* pick up ‹*emissão, sinais*›; tap ‹*água*›; catch, grasp ‹*sentido*›; win ‹*simpatia, admiração*›. **~tura** *f* capture. **~turar** *vt* capture

capuz /ka'pus/ *m* hood

caquético /ka'kɛtʃiku/ *a* broken-down, on one's last legs

caqui /ka'ki/ *m* persimmon

cáqui /'kaki/ *a invar & m* khaki

cara /'kara/ *f* face; (*aparência*) look; (*ousadia*) cheek ● *m* [!] guy; **~ a ~** face to face; **de ~** straightaway; **dar de ~ com** run into; **está na ~** it's obvious; **fechar a ~** frown; **~ de pau** cheek ● *a* cheeky, brazen; **~ de tacho** [!] sheepish look

cara|col /kara'kɔw/ (*pl* **~cóis**) *m* snail

caracte|re /karak'tɛri/ *m* character. **~rística** *f* characteristic, feature. **~rístico** *a* characteristic. **~rizar** *vt* characterize. **~rizar-se** *vpr* be characterized

caramba /ka'rãba/ *int* (*de espanto*) wow; (*de desagrado*) damn

caramelo /kara'mɛlu/ *m* caramel; (*bala*) toffee

caramujo /kara'muʒu/ *m* water snail

caranguejo /karã'geʒu/ *m* crab

caratê /kara'te/ *m* karate

caráter /ka'rater/ *m* character

caravana /kara'vana/ *f* caravan

car|boidrato /karboi'dratu/ *m* carbohydrate. **~bono** /kar'bonu/ *m* carbon; **de ~bono neutro** carbon-neutral ‹*produtos, programa*›

carbu|rador /karbura'dor/ *m* carburettor, *Amer* carburator. **~rante** *m* fuel

carcaça /kar'kasa/ *f* carcass; (*de navio etc*) frame

cárcere /'karseri/ *m* jail

carcereiro /karse'reru/ *m* jailer, warder

carcomido /karko'midu/ *a* worm-eaten; ‹*rosto*› pockmarked

cardápio /kar'dapiu/ *m* menu

carde|al /kardʒi'aw/ (*pl* **~ais**) *a* cardinal

cardíaco /kar'dʒiaku/ *a* cardiac; **ataque ~** heart attack

cardinal /kardʒi'naw/ *a* cardinal; **tecla ~** hash key

cardio|lógico /kardʒio'lɔʒiku/ *a* heart. **~logista** *m/f* heart specialist, cardiologist

cardume /kar'dumi/ *m* shoal

careca /ka'rɛka/ *a* bald ● *f* bald patch

ca|recer /kare'ser/ *vt* **~ de** lack. **~rência** *f* lack; (*social*) deprivation; (*afetiva*) lack of affection. **~rente** *a* lacking; (*socialmente*) deprived; (*afetivamente*) in need of affection

carestia /kares'tʃia/ *f* high cost; (*geral*) high cost of living; (*escassez*) shortage

careta /ka'reta/ *f* grimace ● *a* [!] straight, square

car|ga /'karga/ *f* load; (*mercadorias*) cargo; (*elétrica*) charge; (*de cavalaria*) charge; (*de caneta*) refill; *fig* burden; **~ga horária** workload. **~go** *m* (*função*) post, job; **a ~go de** in the charge of. **~gueiro** *m* (*navio*) cargo ship, freighter

cariar /kari'ar/ *vi* decay

Caribe /ka'ribi/ *m* Caribbean

caricatu|ra /karika'tura/ *f* caricature. **~rar** *vt* caricature. **~rista** *m/f* caricaturist

carícia /ka'risia/ *f* (*com a mão*) stroke, caress; (*carinho*) affection

cari|dade /kari'dadʒi/ *f* charity; **obra de ~dade** charity. **~doso** /o/ *a* charitable

cárie /'kari/ *f* tooth decay

carim|bar /karĩ'bar/ *vt* stamp; postmark ‹*carta*›. **~bo** *m* stamp; (*do correio*) postmark

cari|nho /ka'riɲu/ *m* affection; (*um*) caress. **~nhoso** /o/ *a* affectionate

carioca /kari'ɔka/ *a* from Rio de Janeiro ● *m/f* person from Rio de Janeiro ● *Port m* weak coffee

caris|ma /ka'rizma/ *m* charisma. **~mático** *a* charismatic

carna|val /karna'vaw/ (*pl* **~vais**) *m* carnival. **~valesco** /e/ *a* carnival; ‹*roupa*› over the top, overdone ● *m* carnival organizer

Carnaval Carnival is celebrated in Brazil and Portugal in the period just before Lent. The term *Carnaval* originates from the Italian for "to remove meat"; for Roman Catholics, the festivities traditionally preceded a time of abstinence during Lent. The Brazilian carnival is the most famous carnival in the world, and lavish street parties take part across the country for the best part of a week. Carnival is celebrated in Portugal too, mostly on Shrove Tuesday, with street parties and processions throughout the country.

car|ne /'karni/ *f* (*humana etc*) flesh; (*comida*) meat. **~neiro** *m* sheep; (*macho*) ram; (*como comida*) mutton. **~niça** *f* carrion. **~nificina** *f* slaughter. **~nívoro** *a* carnivorous ● *m* carnivore. **~nudo** *a* fleshy

caro /'karu/ *a* expensive; (*querido*) dear ● *adv* ‹*custar, cobrar*› a lot; ‹*comprar, vender*› at a high price; **pagar ~** pay a high price (for)

caroço /ka'rosu/ *m* (*de pêssego etc*) stone; (*de maçã*) core; (*em sopa, molho etc*) lump

carona /ka'rona/ *f* lift

carpete /kar'pɛtʃi/ *m* fitted carpet

carpin|taria /karpĩta'ria/ *f* carpentry. **~teiro** *m* carpenter

carran|ca /ka'xãka/ *f* scowl. **~cudo** *a* ‹*cara*› scowling; ‹*pessoa*› sullen

carrapato /kaxa'patu/ *m* (*animal*) tick; *fig* hanger-on

carrasco /ka'xasku/ *m* executioner; *fig* butcher

carre|gado /kaxe'gadu/ *a* ‹*céu*› dark, black; ‹*cor*› dark; ‹*ambiente*› tense. **~gador** /kaxega'dor/ *m* (*de celular, computador*) charger; (*profissão*) porter; **~ de pilhas** battery charger. **~gamento** *m* loading; (*carga*) load. **~gar** *vt* load ‹*navio, arma, máquina fotográfica*›; (*levar*) carry; charge ‹*bateria, pilha*›; **~gar em** overdo; pronounce strongly ‹*letra*›; *Port* press

carreira /ka'xera/ *f* career

carre|tel /kaxe'tɛw/ (*pl* **~téis**) *m* reel

car|ril /ka'xiw/ (*pl* **~ris**) *Port m* rail

carrinho /ka'xiɲu/ *m* (*para bagagem, compras*) trolley; (*de criança*) pram; **~ de mão** wheelbarrow

carro /'kaxu/ *m* car; (*de bois*) cart; **~ alegórico** float; **~ esporte** sports car; **~ fúnebre** hearse. **~ça** /ɔ/ *f* cart. **~ceria** *f* bodywork. **~-chefe** (*pl* **~s-chefes**) *m* (*no carnaval*) main float; *fig* centrepiece; **~-forte** (*pl* **~s-fortes**) *m* security van

carros|sel /kaxo'sɛw/ (*pl* **~séis**) *m* merry-go-round

carruagem /kaxu'aʒẽ/ *f* carriage

C

carta /'karta/ *f* letter; (*mapa*) chart; (*do baralho*) card; **~ branca** *fig* carte blanche; **~ de condução** *Port* driving licence, *Amer* driver's license. **~-bomba** (*pl* **~s-bomba**) *f* letter bomb. **~da** *f fig* move

cartão /kar'tãw/ *m* card; *Port* (*papelão*) cardboard; **~ de cidadão** *Port* identity card; **~ de crédito** credit card; **~ de visita** visiting card; **~ magnético** swipe card; **~ pré-pago** top-up card; **~ SIM** SIM (card); **~ telefônico** phonecard. **~-postal** (*pl* **cartões-postais**) *m* postcard

> *i*
> **cartão de cidadão** All Portuguese citizens above the age of ten are required to carry an identity card. It can be used instead of a passport for travel within the European Union. The older *bilhete de identidade* (identity card) is gradually being phased out in favour of an electronic *cartão de cidadão*, which combines the identity card together with various social security and electoral documents.

car|taz /kar'tas/ *m* poster, *Amer* bill; **em ~** showing, *Amer* playing. **~teira** *f* (*para dinheiro*) wallet; (*cartão*) card; (*mesa*) desk; **~teira de identidade** identity card; **~teira de motorista** driving licence, *Amer* driver's license. **~teiro** *m* postman

> *i*
> **carteira de identidade** *Carteira de identidade, cédula de identidade* or *registro geral* (*RG*) are all names for the identity card that is used throughout Brazil. This contains the holder's name, date of birth, parents' names, signature and the issue date, as well as the bearer's right thumb print.

car|tel /kar'tɛw/ (*pl* **~téis**) *m* cartel

cárter /'karter/ *m* sump

carto|la /kar'tɔla/ *f* top hat ● *m* director. **~lina** *f* card. **~mante** *m/f* tarot reader, fortune teller

cartório /kar'tɔriu/ *m* registry office

cartucho /kar'tuʃu/ *m* cartridge; (*de dinamite*) stick; (*de amendoim etc*) bag

car|tum /kar'tũ/ *m* cartoon. **~tunista** *m/f* cartoonist

caruncho /ka'rũʃu/ *m* woodworm

carvalho /kar'vaʎu/ *m* oak

car|vão /kar'vãw/ *m* coal; (*de desenho*) charcoal. **~voeiro** *a* coal

casa /'kaza/ *f* house; (*comercial*) firm; (*de tabuleiro*) square; (*de botão*) hole; **em ~** at home; **para ~** home; **na ~ dos 30 anos** in one's thirties; **~ da moeda** mint; **~ de banho** *Port* bathroom; **~ de campo** country house; **~ de saúde** private hospital; **~ decimal** decimal place; **~ popular** council house

casaco /ka'zaku/ *m* (*sobretudo*) coat; (*paletó*) jacket; (*de lã*) pullover

ca|sal /ka'zaw/ (*pl* **~sais**) *m* couple. **~samento** *m* marriage; (*cerimônia*) wedding. **~sar** *vt* marry; *fig* combine ● *vi* get married; *fig* go together. **~sar-se** *vpr* get married; *fig* combine; **~sar-se com** marry

casarão /kaza'rãw/ *m* mansion

casca /'kaska/ *f* (*de árvore*) bark; (*de laranja, limão*) peel; (*de banana*) skin; (*de noz, ovo*) shell; (*de milho*) husk; (*de pão*) crust; (*de ferida*) scab

cascalho /kas'kaʎu/ *m* gravel

cascata /kas'kata/ *f* waterfall; [!] fib

casca|vel /kaska'vɛw/ (*pl* **~véis**) *f* (*cobra*) rattlesnake; (*mulher*) shrew

casco /'kasku/ *m* (*de cavalo etc*) hoof; (*de navio*) hull; (*garrafa vazia*) empty

ca|sebre /ka'zɛbri/ *m* hovel, shack. **~seiro** *a* ‹*comida*› home-made; ‹*pessoa*› home-loving; ‹*vida*› home ● *m* housekeeper

caserna /ka'zɛrna/ *f* barracks

casmurro /kaz'muxu/ *a* sullen

caso /'kazu/ *m* case; (*amoroso*) affair; (*conto*) story ● *conj* in case; **em todo ou qualquer ~** in any case; **fazer ~ de** take notice of; **vir ao ~** be relevant; **~ contrário** otherwise

casório /ka'zɔriu/ *m* [!] wedding

caspa /'kaspa/ *f* dandruff

casquinha /kas'kiɲa/ *f* (*de sorvete*) cone, cornet

cassar /ka'sar/ *vt* revoke, withdraw ‹*direitos, autorização*›; ban ‹*político*›

cassete /ka'sɛtʃi/ *m* cassette

cassetete /kase'tɛtʃi/ *m* truncheon, *Amer* nightstick

cassino /ka'sinu/ *m* casino; **~ de oficiais** officers' mess

casta|nha /kas'taɲa/ *f* chestnut; **~nha de caju** cashew nut. **~nha-do-pará** (*pl* **~nhas-do-pará**) *f* Brazil nut. **~nheiro** *m* chestnut tree. **~nho** *a* chestnut(-coloured). **~nholas** /ɔ/ *f pl* castanets

castelhano /kaste'ʎanu/ *a & m* Castilian

castelo /kas'tɛlu/ *m* castle

casti|çal /kastʃi'saw/ (*pl* **~çais**) *m* candlestick
cas|tidade /kastʃi'dadʒi/ *f* chastity. **~tigar** *vt* punish. **~tigo** *m* punishment. **~to** *a* chaste
castor /kas'tor/ *m* beaver
castrar /kas'trar/ *vt* castrate
casu|al /kazu'aw/ (*pl* **~ais**) *a* chance; (*fortuito*) fortuitous. **~alidade** *f* chance
casulo /ka'zulu/ *m* (*de larva*) cocoon
cata /'kata/ *f* **à ~ de** in search of
cata|lão /kata'lãw/ (*pl* **~lães**) *a & m* (*f* **~lã**) Catalan
catalisador /kataliza'dor/ *m* catalyst; (*de carro*) catalytic convertor
catalogar /katalo'gar/ *vt* catalogue
catálogo /ka'talogu/ *m* catalogue; (*de telefones*) phone book
Catalunha /kata'luɲa/ *f* Catalonia
catapora /kata'pɔra/ *f* chicken pox
catar /ka'tar/ *vt* (*procurar*) search for; (*recolher*) gather; (*do chão*) pick up; sort ‹*arroz, café*›
catarata /kata'rata/ *f* waterfall; (*no olho*) cataract
catarro /ka'taxu/ *m* catarrh
catástrofe /ka'tastrofi/ *f* catastrophe
catastrófico /katas'trɔfiku/ *a* catastrophic
catecismo /kate'sizmu/ *m* catechism
cátedra /'katedra/ *f* chair
cate|dral /kate'draw/ (*pl* **~drais**) *f* cathedral. **~drático** *m* professor
cate|goria /katego'ria/ *f* category; (*social*) class; (*qualidade*) quality. **~górico** *a* categorical. **~gorizar** *vt* categorize
catinga /ka'tʃĩga/ *f* body odour, stink
cati|vante /katʃi'vãtʃi/ *a* captivating. **~var** *vt* captivate. **~veiro** *m* captivity. **~vo** *a & m* captive
catolicismo /katoli'sizmu/ *m* Catholicism
católico /ka'tɔliku/ *a & m* Catholic
catorze /ka'torzi/ *a & m* fourteen
cau|da /'kawda/ *f* tail. **~dal** (*pl* **~dais**) *m* torrent
caule /'kawli/ *m* stem
cau|sa /'kawza/ *f* cause; *Jurid* case; **por ~sa de** because of; **~sa fraturante** divisive issue. **~sar** *vt* cause
caute|la /kaw'tɛla/ *f* caution; (*documento*) ticket. **~loso** /o/ *a* cautious, careful
cava /'kava/ *f* armhole
cava|do /ka'vadu/ *a* ‹*vestido*› low-cut; ‹*olhos*› deep-set. **~dor** *a* hard-working ● *m* hard worker
cava|laria /kavala'ria/ *f* cavalry. **~lariça** *f* stable. **~leiro** *m* horseman; (*na Idade Média*) knight
cavalete /kava'letʃi/ *m* easel
caval|gadura /kavawga'dura/ *f* mount. **~gar** *vt/i* ride; sit astride ‹*muro, banco*›; (*saltar*) jump
cavalhei|resco /kavaʎe'resku/ *a* gallant, gentlemanly. **~ro** *m* gentleman ● *a* gallant, gentlemanly
cavalo /ka'valu/ *m* horse; **a ~** on horseback; **~-vapor** (*pl* **~s-vapor**) horsepower
cavanhaque /kava'ɲaki/ *m* goatee
cavaquinho /kava'kiɲu/ *m* ukulele
cavar /ka'var/ *vt* dig; *fig* go all out for ● *vi* dig; *fig* go all out; **~ em** (*vasculhar*) delve into; **~ a vida** make a living
caveira /ka'vera/ *f* skull
caverna /ka'vɛrna/ *f* cavern
caviar /kavi'ar/ *m* caviar
cavidade /kavi'dadʒi/ *f* cavity
cavilha /ka'viʎa/ *f* peg
cavo /'kavu/ *a* hollow
cavoucar /kavo'kar/ *vt* excavate
caxemira /kaʃe'mira/ *f* cashmere
caxumba /ka'ʃũba/ *f* mumps
Cc /'sese/ *abr* (= **cópia carbono**) Cc
Cco /'seseo/ *abr* (= **com cópia oculta**) Bcc
cear /si'ar/ *vt* have for supper ● *vi* have supper
cebo|la /se'bola/ *f* onion. **~linha** *f* spring onion
ceder /se'der/ *vt* give up; (*dar*) give; (*emprestar*) lend ● *vi* (*não resistir*) give way; **~ a** yield to
cedilha /se'dʒiʎa/ *f* cedilla
cedo /'sedu/ *adv* early; **mais ~ ou mais tarde** sooner or later
cedro /'sɛdru/ *m* cedar
cédula /'sɛdula/ *f* (*de banco*) note, *Amer* bill; (*eleitoral*) ballot paper
ce|gar /se'gar/ *vt* blind; blunt ‹*faca*›; **às ~gas** blindly. **~go** /ɛ/ *a* blind; ‹*faca*› blunt ● *m* blind man
cegonha /se'goɲa/ *f* stork
cegueira /se'gera/ *f* blindness
ceia /'seja/ *f* supper

C

cei|fa /'sejfa/ *f* harvest; (*massacre*) slaughter. **~far** *vt* reap; claim ‹*vidas*›; (*matar*) mow down

cela /'sɛla/ *f* cell

cele|bração /selebra'sãw/ *f* celebration. **~brar** *vt* celebrate

célebre /'sɛlebri/ *a* celebrated

celebridade /selebri'dadʒi/ *f* celebrity

celeiro /se'leru/ *m* granary

célere /'sɛleri/ *a* swift, fast

celeste /se'lɛstʃi/ *a* celestial

celeuma /se'lewma/ *f* pandemonium

celibato /seli'batu/ *m* celibacy

celofane /selo'fani/ *m* cellophane®

celta /'sɛwta/ *a* Celtic ● *m/f* Celt ● *m* (*língua*) Celtic

célula /'sɛlula/ *f* cell; **~ estaminal** *Port* stem cell

celu|lar /selu'lar/ *a* cellular ● *m* mobile, *Amer* cell phone. **~lite** *f* cellulite. **~lose** /ɔ/ *f* cellulose

célula-tronco /'sɛlula'trõku/ *f* (*pl* **células-tronco**) stem cell

cem /sẽj/ *a & m* hundred

cemitério /semi'tɛriu/ *m* cemetery; *fig* graveyard

cena /'sena/ *f* scene; (*palco*) stage; **em ~** on stage

cenário /se'nariu/ *m* scenery; (*de crime etc*) scene

cênico /'seniku/ *a* stage

cenoura /se'nora/ *f* carrot

cen|so /'sẽsu/ *m* census. **~sor** *m* censor. **~sura** *f* (*de jornais etc*) censorship; (*órgão*) censor(s); (*condenação*) censure. **~surar** *vt* censor ‹*jornal, filme etc*›; (*condenar*) censure

centavo /sẽ'tavu/ *m* cent

centeio /sẽ'teju/ *m* rye

centelha /sẽ'teʎa/ *f* spark; *fig* (*de gênio etc*) flash

cente|na /sẽ'tena/ *f* hundred; **uma ~na de** about a hundred; **às ~nas** in their hundreds. **~nário** *m* centenary

centésimo /sẽ'tɛzimu/ *a* hundredth

cen|tígrado /sẽ'tʃigradu/ *m* centigrade. **~tilitro** *m* centilitre. **~tímetro** *m* centimetre

cento /'sẽtu/ *a & m* hundred; **por ~** per cent

cen|tral /sẽ'traw/ (*pl* **~trais**) *a* central ● *f* switchboard; **~tral eólica** wind farm. **~tralizar** *vt* centralize. **~trar** *vt* centre. **~tro** *m* centre

cera /'sera/ *f* wax; **fazer ~** waste time, faff about

cerâmi|ca /se'ramika/ *f* ceramics, pottery. **~co** *a* ceramic

cer|ca /'serka/ *f* fence; **~ca viva** hedge. **~ca de** *adv* around, about. **~cado** *m* enclosure; (*para criança*) playpen. **~car** *vt* surround; (*com muro, cerca*) enclose; (*assediar*) besiege

cercear /sersi'ar/ *vt fig* curtail, restrict

cerco /'serku/ *m Mil* siege; (*policial*) dragnet

cere|al /seri'aw/ (*pl* **~ais**) *m* cereal

cere|bral /sere'braw/ (*pl* **~brais**) *a* cerebral

cérebro /'sɛrebru/ *m* brain; (*inteligência*) intellect

cere|ja /se'reʒa/ *f* cherry. **~jeira** *f* cherry tree

cerimônia /seri'monia/ *f* ceremony; **sem ~** unceremoniously; **fazer ~** stand on ceremony

cerimoni|al /serimoni'aw/ (*pl* **~ais**) *a & m* ceremonial. **~oso** /o/ *a* ceremonious

cer|rado /se'xadu/ *a* ‹*barba, mata*› thick; ‹*punho, dentes*› clenched ● *m* scrubland. **~rar** *vt* close. **~rar-se** *vpr* close; ‹*noites, trevas*› close in

certeiro /ser'teru/ *a* well-aimed, accurate

certeza /ser'teza/ *f* certainty; **com ~** certainly; **ter ~** be sure (**de** of **de que** that)

certidão /sertʃi'dãw/ *f* certificate; **~ de nascimento** birth certificate

certifi|cado /sertʃifi'kadu/ *m* certificate; **~car-se de** make sure of. **~car** *vt* certify

certo /'sɛrtu/ *a* (*correto*) right; (*seguro*) certain; (*algum*) a certain ● *adv* right; **dar ~** work

cerveja /ser'veʒa/ *f* beer. **~ria** *f* brewery; (*bar*) pub

cervo /'sɛrvu/ *m* deer

cer|zidura /serzi'dura/ *f* darning. **~zir** *vt* darn

cesariana /sezari'ana/ *f* Caesarian

césio /'sɛziu/ *m* caesium

cessar /se'sar/ *vt/i* cease

ces|ta /'sesta/ *f* basket; (*de comida*) hamper; **~to de lixo** waste-paper basket. **~to** /e/ *m* basket

ceticismo /setʃi'sizmu/ *m* scepticism

cético /'sɛtʃiku/ *a* sceptical ● *m* sceptic

cetim /se'tʃĩ/ *m* satin
céu /sɛw/ *m* sky; (*na religião*) heaven; ~ **da boca** roof of the mouth
cevada /se'vada/ *f* barley
chá /ʃa/ *m* tea; ~ **de bar** bachelor party, *Amer* stag night; ~ **de panela** hen night, *Amer* wedding shower
cha|cal /ʃa'kaw/ (*pl* **~cais**) *m* jackal
chácara /'ʃakara/ *f* smallholding; (*casa*) country cottage
chaci|na /ʃa'sina/ *f* slaughter. **~nar** *vt* slaughter
chafariz /ʃafa'ris/ *m* fountain
chaga /'ʃaga/ *f* sore
chaleira /ʃa'lera/ *f* kettle
chama /'ʃama/ *f* flame
cha|mada /ʃa'mada/ *f* call; (*dos presentes*) roll call; (*dos alunos*) register. **~mado** *m* call ● *a* (*depois do substantivo*) called; (*antes do substantivo*) so-called. **~mar** *vt* call; (*para sair etc*) ask, invite; attract ‹*atenção*› ● *vi* call; ‹*telefone*› ring. **~mar-se** *vpr* be called. **~mariz** *m* decoy. **~mativo** *a* showy, flashy
chamejar /ʃame'ʒar/ *vi* flare
chaminé /ʃami'nɛ/ *f* (*de casa, fábrica*) chimney; (*de navio, trem*) funnel
champanhe /ʃã'paɲi/ *m* champagne
champu /ʃã'pu/ *Port m* shampoo
chamuscar /ʃamus'kar/ *vt* singe, scorch
chance /'ʃãsi/ *f* chance
chanceler /ʃãse'ler/ *m* chancellor
chanchada /ʃã'ʃada/ *f* (*peça*) second-rate play; (*filme*) B movie
chanta|gear /ʃãtaʒi'ar/ *vt* blackmail. **~gem** *f* blackmail. **~gista** *m/f* blackmailer
chão /ʃãw/ (*pl* **~s**) *m* ground; (*dentro de casa etc*) floor
chapa /'ʃapa/ *f* sheet; (*foto*) plate; ~ **eleitoral** electoral list; ~ **de matrícula** *Port* number plate, *Amer* license plate ● *m* [!] mate
chapéu /ʃa'pɛw/ *m* hat
charada /ʃa'rada/ *f* riddle
char|ge /'ʃarʒi/ *f* (political) cartoon. **~gista** *m/f* cartoonist
charla|tanismo /ʃarlata'nizmu/ *m* charlatanism. **~tão** (*pl* **~tães**) *m* (*f* **~tona**) charlatan
char|me /'ʃarmi/ *m* charm; **fazer ~me** turn on the charm. **~moso** /o/ *a* charming
charneca /ʃar'nɛka/ *f* moor
charuto /ʃa'rutu/ *m* cigar
chassi /ʃa'si/ *m* chassis
chat /'ʃat/ *m* (*na internet*) chat; **sala de ~** chatroom
chata /'ʃata/ *f* (*barca*) barge
chate|ação /ʃatʃia'sãw/ *f* annoyance. **~ar** *vt* annoy. **~ar-se** *vpr* get annoyed
cha|tice /ʃa'tʃisi/ *f* nuisance. **~to** *a* (*tedioso*) boring; (*irritante*) annoying; (*mal-educado*) rude; (*plano*) flat
chauvinis|mo /ʃovi'nizmu/ *m* chauvinism. **~ta** *m/f* chauvinist ● *a* chauvinistic
chavão /ʃa'vãw/ *m* cliché
cha|ve /ʃa've/ *f* key; (*ferramenta*) spanner. **~ve de fenda** screwdriver; **~ve inglesa** wrench; **~veiro** *m* (*aro*) key ring; (*pessoa*) locksmith
chávena /'ʃavena/ *f* soup bowl; *Port* (*xícara*) cup
checar /ʃe'kar/ *vt* check
check-up /ʃe'kap/ *m Med* check-up; **fazer um ~** to have a checkup
che|fe /'ʃɛfi/ *m/f* (*patrão*) boss; (*gerente*) manager; (*dirigente*) leader. **~fia** *f* leadership; (*de empresa*) management; (*sede*) headquarters. **~fiar** *vt* lead; be in charge of ‹*trabalho*›
che|gada /ʃe'gada/ *f* arrival. **~gado** *a* ‹*amigo, relação*› close. **~gar** *vi* arrive; (*deslocar-se*) move up; (*ser suficiente*) be enough ● *vt* bring up ‹*prato, cadeira*›; **~gar a fazer** go as far as doing; **aonde você quer ~gar?** what are you driving at?; **~gar lá** *fig* make it
cheia /'ʃeja/ *f* flood
cheio /'ʃeju/ *a* full; [!] (*farto*) fed up
chei|rar /ʃe'rar/ *vt/i* smell (**a** of). **~roso** /o/ *a* scented
cheque /'ʃɛki/ *m* cheque, *Amer* check; ~ **de viagem** traveller's cheque; ~ **em branco** blank cheque
chi|ado /ʃi'adu/ *m* (*de pneus, freios*) screech; (*de porta*) squeak; (*de vapor, numa fita*) hiss. **~ar** *vi* ‹*porta*› squeak; ‹*pneus, freios*› screech; ‹*vapor, fita*› hiss; ‹*fritura*› sizzle; [!] (*reclamar*) grumble, moan
chiclete /ʃi'klɛtʃi/ *m* chewing gum; ~ **de bola** bubble gum
chico|tada /ʃiko'tada/ *f* lash. **~te** /ɔ/ *m* whip. **~tear** *vt* whip
chi|frar /ʃi'frar/ *vt* [!]cheat on ‹*marido, esposa*›; two-time ‹*namorado, namorada*›. **~fre** *m* horn. **~frudo** *a* horned; [!] cuckolded ● *m* cuckold

C

Chile /'ʃili/ *m* Chile
chileno /ʃi'lenu/ *a & m* Chilean
chilique /ʃi'liki/ [!] *m* funny turn
chil|rear /ʃiwxi'ar/ *vi* chirp, twitter. **~reio** *m* chirping, twittering
chimarrão /ʃima'xãw/ *m* unsweetened maté tea
chimpanzé /ʃĩpã'zɛ/ *m* chimpanzee
China /'ʃina/ *f* China
chinelo /ʃi'nɛlu/ *m* slipper
chi|nês /ʃi'nes/ *a & m* (*f* **~nesa**) Chinese
chinfrim /ʃĩ'frĩ/ *a* tatty, shoddy
chio /'ʃiu/ *m* squeak; (*de pneus*) screech; (*de vapor*) hiss
chique /'ʃiki/ *a* ‹*pessoa, aparência, roupa*› smart, *Amer* sharp; ‹*hotel, bairro, loja etc*› smart, upmarket, posh
chiqueiro /ʃi'keru/ *m* pigsty
chis|pa /'ʃispa/ *f* flash. **~pada** *f* dash. **~par** *vi* (*soltar chispas*) flash; (*correr*) dash
choca|lhar /ʃoka'ʎar/ *vt/i* rattle. **~lho** *m* rattle
cho|cante /ʃo'kãtʃi/ *a* shocking; [!] incredible. **~car** *vt/i* hatch ‹*ovos*›; (*ultrajar*) shock. **~car-se** *vpr* ‹*carros etc*› crash; ‹*teorias etc*› clash
chocho /'ʃoʃu/ *a* dull, insipid
chocolate /ʃoko'latʃi/ *m* chocolate
chofer /ʃo'fɛr/ *m* chauffeur
chope /'ʃopi/ *m* draught lager
choque /'ʃɔki/ *m* shock; (*colisão*) collision; (*conflito*) clash
cho|radeira /ʃora'dera/ *f* fit of crying. **~ramingar** *vi* whine. **~ramingas** *m/f invar* whiner. **~rão** *m* (*salgueiro*) weeping willow ● *a* (*f* **~rona**) tearful. **~rar** *vi* cry. **~ro** /o/ *m* crying. **~roso** /o/ *a* tearful
chouriço /ʃo'risu/ *m* black pudding; *Port* sausage
chover /ʃo'ver/ *vi* rain
chuchu /ʃu'ʃu/ *m* chayote
chucrute /ʃu'krutʃi/ *m* sauerkraut
chumaço /ʃu'masu/ *m* wad
chum|bado /ʃũ'badu/ *a* [!] knocked out. **~bar** *Port vt* fill ‹*dente*›; fail ‹*aluno*› ● *vi* ‹*aluno*› fail. **~bo** *m* lead; *Port* (*obturação*) filling
chu|par /ʃu'par/ *vt* suck; ‹*esponja*› suck up. **~peta** /e/ *f* dummy, *Amer* pacifier
churras|caria /ʃuxaska'ria/ *f* barbecue restaurant. **~co** *m* barbecue. **~queira** *f* barbecue. **~quinho** *m* kebab
chu|tar /ʃu'tar/ *vt/i* kick; [!] (*adivinhar*) guess. **~te** *m* kick. **~teira** *f* football boot
chu|va /'ʃuva/ *f* rain; **~va de pedra** hail. **~varada** *f* torrential rainstorm. **~veiro** *m* shower. **~viscar** *vi* drizzle. **~visco** *m* drizzle. **~voso** /o/ *a* rainy
ciberespaço /siberis'pasu/ *m* cyberspace
ciberespeculador /siberispekula'dor/ *m* cybersquatter
ciberterrorismo /sibertexo'rizmu/ *m* cyberterrorism
cica|triz /sika'tris/ *f* scar. **~trizar** *vt* scar ● *vi* ‹*ferida*› heal
ci|clismo /si'klizmu/ *m* cycling. **~clista** *m/f* cyclist. **~clo** *m* cycle. **~clone** /o/ *m* cyclone. **~clovia** *f* cycle lane
cida|dania /sidada'nia/ *f* citizenship. **~dão** (*pl* **~dãos**) *m* (*f* **~dã**) citizen. **~de** *f* town; (*grande*) city. **~dela** /ɛ/ *f* citadel
ciência /si'ẽsia/ *f* science
cien|te /si'ẽtʃi/ *a* aware. **~tífico** *a* scientific. **~tista** *m/f* scientist
ci|fra /'sifra/ *f* figure; (*código*) cipher. **~frão** *m* dollar sign. **~frar** *vt* encode
cigano /si'ganu/ *a & m* gypsy
cigarra /si'gaxa/ *f* cicada; (*dispositivo*) buzzer
cigar|reira /siga'xera/ *f* cigarette case. **~ro** *m* cigarette
cilada /si'lada/ *f* trap; (*estratagema*) trick
cilindrada /silĩ'drada/ *f* (engine) capacity
cilíndrico /si'lĩdriku/ *a* cylindrical
cilindro /si'lĩdru/ *m* cylinder; (*rolo*) roller
cílio /'siliu/ *m* eyelash
cima /'sima/ *f* **em ~** on top; (*na casa*) upstairs; **em ~ de** on, on top of; **para ~** up; (*na casa*) upstairs; **por ~** over the top; **por ~ de** over; **de ~** from above; **ainda por ~** moreover
címbalo /'sĩbalu/ *m* cymbal
cimeira /si'mera/ *f* crest; *Port* (*cúpula*) summit
cimen|tar /simẽ'tar/ *vt* cement. **~to** *m* cement
cinco /'sĩku/ *a & m* five
cine|asta /sini'asta/ *m/f* film-maker. **~ma** /e/ *m* cinema
cínico /'siniku/ *a* cynical ● *m* cynic
cinismo /si'nizmu/ *m* cynicism
cinquen|ta /sĩ'kwẽta/ *a & m* fifty. **~tão** *a & m* (*f* **~tona**) fifty-year-old
cinti|lante /sĩtʃi'lãtʃi/ *a* glittering. **~lar** *vi* glitter

cin|to /'sĩtu/ *m* belt; **~to de segurança** seat belt. **~tura** *f* waist. **~turão** *m* belt

cin|za /'sĩza/ *f* ash ● *a invar* grey. **~zeiro** *m* ashtray

cin|zel /sĩ'zɛw/ (*pl* **~zéis**) *m* chisel. **~zelar** *vt* carve

cinzento /sĩ'zẽtu/ *a* grey

ci|pó /si'pɔ/ *m* vine, liana. **~poal** (*pl* **~poais**) *m* jungle

cipreste /si'prɛstʃi/ *m* cypress

cipriota /sipri'ɔta/ *a & m* Cypriot

ciranda /si'rãda/ *f fig* merry-go-round

cir|cense /sir'sẽsi/ *a* circus. **~co** *m* circus

circu|ito /sir'kuitu/ *m* circuit. **~lação** *f* circulation. **~lar** *a & f* circular ● *vt* circulate ● *vi* ‹*dinheiro, sangue*› circulate; ‹*carro*› drive; ‹*ônibus*› run; ‹*trânsito*› move; ‹*pessoa*› go round

círculo /'sirkulu/ *m* circle

circunci|dar /sirkũsi'dar/ *vt* circumcise. **~são** *f* circumcision

circun|dar /sirkũ'dar/ *vt* surround. **~ferência** *f* circumference. **~flexo** /ɛks/ *a & m* circumflex. **~scrição** *f* district; **~scrição eleitoral** constituency. **~specto** /ɛ/ *a* circumspect. **~stância** *f* circumstance. **~stanciado** *a* detailed. **~stancial** (*pl* **~stanciais**) *a* circumstantial. **~stante** *m/f* bystander

cirrose /si'xɔzi/ *f* cirrhosis

cirur|gia /sirur'ʒia/ *f* surgery. **~gião** *m* (*f* **~giã**) surgeon

cirúrgico /si'rurʒiku/ *a* surgical

cisão /si'zãw/ *f* split, division

cisco /'sisku/ *m* speck

cisma[1] /'sizma/ *m* schism

cis|ma[2] /'sizma/ *f* (*mania*) fixation; (*devaneio*) imagining, daydream; (*prevenção*) irrational dislike; (*de criança*) whim. **~mar** *vt/i* be lost in thought; ‹*criança*› be insistent; **~mar em** brood over; **~mar de** ou **em fazer** insist on doing; **~mar que** insist on thinking that; **~mar com alguém** take a dislike to sb

cisne /'sizni/ *m* swan

cistite /sis'tʃitʃi/ *f* cystitis

ci|tação /sita'sãw/ *f* quotation; *Jurid* summons. **~tar** *vt* quote; *Jurid* summon

ciúme /si'umi/ *m* jealousy; **ter ~s de** be jealous of

ciu|meira /siu'mera/ *f* fit of jealousy. **~mento** *a* jealous

cívico /'siviku/ *a* civic

ci|vil /si'viw/ (*pl* **~vis**) *a* civil ● *m* civilian. **~vilidade** *f* civility

civili|zação /siviliza'sãw/ *f* civilization. **~zado** *a* civilized. **~zar** *vt* civilize

civismo /si'vizmu/ *m* public spirit

cla|mar /kla'mar/ *vt/i* cry out, clamour (**por** for). **~mor** *m* outcry. **~moroso** /o/ *a* ‹*protesto*› loud, noisy; ‹*erro, injustiça*› blatant

clandestino /klãdes'tʃinu/ *a* clandestine

cla|ra /'klara/ *f* egg white. **~raboia** *f* skylight. **~rão** *m* flash. **~rear** *vt* brighten; clarify ‹*questão*› ● *vi* brighten up; (*fazer-se dia*) become light. **~reira** *f* clearing. **~reza** /e/ *f* clarity. **~ridade** *f* brightness; (*do dia*) daylight

cla|rim /kla'rĩ/ *m* bugle. **~rinete** /e/ *m* clarinet

clarividente /klarivi'dẽtʃi/ *m/f* clairvoyant

claro /'klaru/ *a* clear; ‹*luz*› bright; ‹*cor*› light ● *adv* clearly ● *int* of course; **~ que sim/não** of course/of course not; **às claras** openly; **noite em ~** sleepless night; **já é dia ~** it's already daylight

classe /'klasi/ *f* class; **~ média** middle class

clássico /'klasiku/ *a* classical; (*famoso, exemplar*) classic ● *m* classic

classifi|cação /klasifika'sãw/ *f* classification; (*numa competição esportiva*) placing, place. **~cado** *a* classified; ‹*candidato*› successful; ‹*esportista, time*› qualified. **~car** *vt* classify; (*considerar*) describe (**de** as). **~car-se** *vpr* ‹*candidato, esportista*› qualify; (*chamar-se*) describe o.s. (**de** as). **~catório** *a* qualifying

classudo /kla'sudu/ *a* [!] classy

claustro|fobia /klawstrofo'bia/ *f* claustrophobia. **~fóbico** *a* claustrophobic

cláusula /'klawzula/ *f* clause

cla|ve /'klavi/ *f* clef. **~vícula** *f* collar bone

cle|mência /kle'mẽsia/ *f* clemency. **~mente** *a* ‹*pessoa*› lenient; ‹*tempo*› clement

cleptomaníaco /kleptoma'niaku/ *m* kleptomaniac

clérigo /'klɛrigu/ *m* cleric, clergyman

clero /'klɛru/ *m* clergy

clicar /kli'kar/ *vi Comput* click

clichê /kli'ʃe/ *m* cliché

C

clien|te /kli'ẽtʃi/ *m/f* (*de loja*) customer; (*de advogado, empresa*) client. **~tela** /ɛ/ *f* (*de loja*) customers; (*de restaurante, empresa*) clientele

cli|ma /'klima/ *m* climate. **~mático** /kli'matʃiku/ *a* climatic; **alterações ~máticas** climate change

clímax /'klimaks/ *m invar* climax

clíni|ca /'klinika/ *f* clinic; **~ca geral** general practice. **~co** *a* clinical ● *m* **~co geral** general practitioner, GP

clipe /'klipi/ *m* clip; (*para papéis*) paper clip

clonar /klo'nar/ *vt* clone

clone /'kloni/ *m* clone

cloro /'klɔru/ *m* chlorine

close /'klozi/ *m* close-up

clube /'klubi/ *m* club

coação /koa'sãw/ *f* coercion

coadjuvante /koadʒu'vãtʃi/ *a* ‹*ator*› supporting ● *m/f* (*em peça, filme*) co-star; (*em crime*) accomplice

coador /koa'dor/ *m* strainer; (*de legumes*) colander; (*de café*) filter bag

coadunar /koadu'nar/ *vt* combine

coagir /koa'ʒir/ *vt* compel

coagular /koagu'lar/ *vt/i* clot. **~-se** *vpr* clot

coágulo /ko'agulu/ *m* clot

coalhar /koa'ʎar/ *vt/i* curdle. **~-se** *vpr* curdle

coalizão /koali'zãw/ *f* coalition

coar /ko'ar/ *vt* strain

coaxar /koa'ʃar/ *vi* croak ● *m* croaking

cobaia /ko'baja/ *f* guinea pig

cober|ta /ko'bɛrta/ *f* (*de cama*) bedcover; (*de navio*) deck. **~to** /ɛ/ *a* covered ● *pp de* ▶ COBRIR. **~tor** *m* blanket. **~tura** *f* (*revestimento*) covering; (*reportagem*) coverage; (*seguro*) cover; (*apartamento*) penthouse

cobi|ça /ko'bisa/ *f* greed, covetousness. **~çar** *vt* covet. **~çoso** /o/ *a* covetous

cobra /'kɔbra/ *f* snake

co|brador /kobra'dor/ *m* (*no ônibus*) conductor. **~brança** *f* (*de dívida*) collection; (*de preço*) charging. **~brança de pênalti/falta** penalty (kick)/free kick. **~brar** *vt* collect ‹*dívida*›; ask for ‹*coisa prometida*›; take ‹*pênalti*›; **~brar algo a alguém** (*em dinheiro*) charge sb for sth; *fig* make sb pay for sth; **~brar uma falta** (*no futebol*) take a free kick

cobre /'kɔbri/ *m* copper

cobrir /ko'brir/ *vt* cover. **~-se** *vpr* ‹*pessoa*› cover o.s. up; ‹*coisa*› be covered

cocaína /koka'ina/ *f* cocaine

coçar /ko'sar/ *vt* scratch ● *vi* (*esfregar-se*) scratch; (*comichar*) itch. **~-se** *vpr* scratch o.s.

cócegas /'kɔsegas/ *f pl* **fazer ~ em** tickle; **sentir ~** be ticklish

coceira /ko'sera/ *f* itch

cochi|char /koʃi'ʃar/ *vt/i* whisper. **~cho** *m* whisper

cochi|lada /koʃi'lada/ *f* doze. **~lar** *vi* doze. **~lo** *m* snooze

coco /'koku/ *m* coconut

cócoras /'kɔkoras/ *f pl* **de ~** squatting; **ficar de ~** squat

côdea /'kodʒia/ *f* crust

codificar /kodʒifi'kar/ *vt* encode ‹*mensagem*›; codify ‹*leis*›

código /'kɔdʒigu/ *m* code; **~ de barras** bar code

codinome /kodʒi'nomi/ *m* code name

coeficiente /koefisi'ẽtʃi/ *m* coefficient; *fig* (*fator*) factor

coelho /ko'eʎu/ *m* rabbit

coentro /ko'ẽtru/ *m* coriander

coerção /koer'sãw/ *f* coercion

coe|rência /koe'rẽsia/ *f* (*lógica*) coherence; (*consequência*) consistency. **~rente** *a* (*lógico*) coherent; (*consequente*) consistent

coexis|tência /koezis'tẽsia/ *f* coexistence. **~tir** *vi* coexist

cofre /'kɔfri/ *m* safe; (*de dinheiro público*) coffer

cogi|tação /koʒita'sãw/ *f* contemplation; **fora de ~tação** out of the question. **~tar** *vt/i* contemplate

cogumelo /kogu'mɛlu/ *m* mushroom

coibir /koi'bir/ *vt* restrict; **~-se de** keep o.s. from

coice /'kojsi/ *m* kick

coinci|dência /koĩsi'dẽsia/ *f* coincidence. **~dir** *vi* coincide

coisa /'kojza/ *f* thing

coitado /koj'tadu/ *m* poor thing; **~ do pai** poor father

cola /'kɔla/ *f* glue; (*cópia*) crib

colabo|ração /kolabora'sãw/ *f* collaboration; (*de escritor etc*) contribution. **~rador** *m* collaborator; (*em jornal, livro*) contributor. **~rar** *vi* collaborate; (*em jornal, livro*) contribute (**em** to)

colagem /ko'laʒẽ/ *f* collage

colágeno /ko'laʒenu/ *m* collagen

colapso /ko'lapsu/ *m* collapse

colar[1] /ko'lar/ *m* necklace

colar[2] /ko'lar/ *vt* (*grudar*) stick; (*copiar*) crib ● *vi* stick; (*copiar*) crib; ‹*desculpa etc*› stand up, stick

colarinho /kola'riɲu/ *m* collar; (*de cerveja*) head

colate|ral /kolate'raw/ (*pl* **~rais**) *a* **efeito ~ral** side effect

col|cha /'kowʃa/ *f* bedspread. **~chão** *m* mattress

colchete /kow'ʃetʃi/ *m* fastener; (*sinal de pontuação*) square bracket; **~ de pressão** press stud, popper

colchonete /kowʃo'nɛtʃi/ *m* (foldaway) mattress

coldre /'kɔwdri/ *m* holster

cole|ção /kole'sãw/ *f* collection. **~cionador** *m* collector. **~cionar** *vt* collect

colega /ko'lɛga/ *m/f* (*amigo*) friend; (*de trabalho*) colleague

colegi|al /koleʒi'aw/ (*pl* **~ais**) *a* school ● *m/f* schoolboy (*f* -girl)

colégio /ko'lɛʒiu/ *m* secondary school, *Amer* high school

coleira /ko'lera/ *f* collar

cólera /'kɔlera/ *f* (*doença*) cholera; (*raiva*) fury

colérico /ko'lɛriku/ *a* (*furioso*) furious ● *m* (*doente*) cholera victim

colesterol /koleste'rɔw/ *m* cholesterol

cole|ta /ko'lɛta/ *f* collection. **~tânea** *f* collection. **~tar** *vt* collect

colete /ko'letʃi/ *m* waistcoat, *Amer* vest; **~ salva-vidas** life jacket, *Amer* life preserver

coletivo /kole'tʃivu/ *a* collective; ‹*transporte*› public ● *m* bus

colheita /ko'ʎejta/ *f* harvest; (*produtos colhidos*) crop

colher[1] /ko'ʎɛr/ *f* spoon

colher[2] /ko'ʎer/ *vt* pick ‹*flores, frutos*›; gather ‹*informações*›

colherada /koʎe'rada/ *f* spoonful

colibri /koli'bri/ *m* hummingbird

cólica /'kɔlika/ *f* colic

colidir /koli'dʒir/ *vi* collide

coli|gação /koliga'sãw/ *f Pol* coalition. **~gado** *m Pol* coalition partner. **~gar** *vt* bring together. **~gar-se** *vpr* join forces; *Pol* form a coalition

colina /ko'lina/ *f* hill

colírio /ko'liriu/ *m* eyewash

colisão /koli'zãw/ *f* collision

collant /ko'lã/ (*pl* **~s**) *m* body; (*de ginástica*) leotard

colmeia /kow'meja/ *f* beehive

colo /'kɔlu/ *f* (*regaço*) lap; (*pescoço*) neck

colo|cação /koloka'sãw/ *f* placing; (*emprego*) position; (*exposição de fatos*) statement; (*de aparelho, pneus, carpete etc*) fitting; **~car** put; fit ‹*aparelho, pneus, carpete etc*›; put forward, state ‹*opinião, ideias*›; (*empregar*) get a job for. **~cado** *a* placed; **o primeiro ~cado** (*em ranking*) person in first place. **~cador** *m* fitter

Colômbia /ko'lõbia/ *f* Colombia

colombiano /kolõbi'anu/ *a & m* Colombian

cólon /'kɔlõ/ *m* colon

colônia[1] /ko'lonia/ *f* (*colonos*) colony

colônia[2] /ko'lonia/ *f* (*perfume*) cologne

coloni|al /koloni'aw/ (*pl* **~ais**) *a* colonial. **~alismo** *m* colonialism. **~alista** *a & m/f* colonialist. **~zar** *vt* colonize

colono /ko'lonu/ *m* settler, colonist; (*lavrador*) tenant farmer

coloqui|al /koloki'aw/ (*pl* **~ais**) *a* colloquial

colóquio /ko'lɔkiu/ *m* (*conversa*) conversation; (*congresso*) conference

colo|rido /kolo'ridu/ *a* colourful ● *m* colouring. **~rir** *vt* colour

colu|na /ko'luna/ *f* column; (*vertebral*) spine. **~nável** (*pl* **~náveis**) *a* famous ● *m/f* celebrity . **~nista** *m/f* columnist

com /kõ/ *prep* with; **o comentário foi comigo** the comment was meant for me; **você está ~ a chave?** have you got the key?; **~ seis anos de idade** at six years of age

coma /'koma/ *f* coma

comadre /ko'madri/ *f* (*madrinha*) godmother of one's child; (*mãe do afilhado*) mother of one's godchild; (*urinol*) bedpan

coman|dante /komã'dãtʃi/ *m* commander. **~dar** *vt* lead; (*ordenar*) command; (*elevar-se acima de*) dominate. **~do** *m* command; (*grupo*) commando group

comba|te /kõ'batʃi/ *m* combat; (*a drogas, doença etc*) fight (**a** against). **~ter** *vt/i* fight. **~ter-se** *vpr* fight

combi|nação /kõbina'sãw/ *f* combination; (*acordo*) arrangement; (*plano*) scheme; (*roupa*) petticoat. **~nar**

vt (*juntar*) combine; (*ajustar*) arrange ● *vi* go together, match. **~nar com** go with, match; **~nar de sair** arrange to go out; **~nar-se** *vpr* (*juntar-se*) combine; (*harmonizar-se*) go together, match

C

comboio /kõ'boju/ *m* convoy; *Port* (*trem*) train

combustí|vel /kõbus'tʃivew/ (*pl* **~veis**) *m* fuel

come|çar /kome'sar/ *vt/i* start, begin. **~ço** /e/ *m* beginning, start

comédia /ko'mɛdʒia/ *f* comedy

comediante /komedʒi'ãtʃi/ *m/f* comedian (*f* comedienne)

comemo|ração /komemora'sãw/ *f* (*celebração*) celebration; (*lembrança*) commemoration. **~rar** *vt* (*festejar*) celebrate; (*lembrar*) commemorate

comen|tar /komẽ'tar/ *vt* comment on; (*falar mal de*) make comments about. **~tário** *m* comment; (*de texto, na TV etc*) commentary; **sem ~tários** no comment. **~tarista** *m/f* commentator

comer /ko'mer/ *vt* eat; ‹*ferrugem etc*› eat away; take ‹*peça de xadrez*›; **dar de ~ a** feed ● *vi* eat. **~-se** *vpr* (*de raiva etc*) be consumed (**de** with)

comerci|al /komersi'aw/ (*pl* **~ais**) *a & m* commercial. **~alizar** *vt* market. **~ante** *m/f* trader. **~ar** *vi* do business, trade. **~ário** *m* shopworker

comércio /ko'mɛrsiu/ *m* (*atividade*) trade; (*loja etc*) business; (*lojas*) shops; **~ eletrônico** e-commerce; **~ justo** fair trade

comes /'komis/ *m pl* **~ e bebes** [!] food and drink. **~tíveis** *m pl* foods, food. **~tível** (*pl* **~tíveis**) *a* edible

cometa /ko'meta/ *m* comet

cometer /kome'ter/ *vt* commit ‹*crime*›; make ‹*erro*›

comichão /komi'ʃãw/ *f* itch

comício /ko'misiu/ *m* rally

cômico /'komiku/ *a* (*de comédia*) comic; (*engraçado*) comical

comida /ko'mida/ *f* food; (*uma*) meal

comigo = **com** + **mim**

comi|lão /komi'lãw/ *a* (*f* **~lona**) greedy ● *m* (*f* **~lona**) glutton

cominho /ko'miɲu/ *m* cummin

comiserar-se /komize'rarsi/ *vpr* commiserate (**de** with)

comis|são /komi'sãw/ *f* commission. **~sário** *m* commissioner; **~sário de bordo** (*aéreo*) steward; (*de navio*) purser. **~sionar** *vt* commission

comi|tê /komi'te/ *m* committee. **~tiva** *f* group; (*de uma pessoa*) retinue

como /'komu/ *adv* (*na condição de*) as; (*da mesma forma que*) like; (*de que maneira*) how ● *conj* as; **~?** (*pedindo repetição*) pardon?; **~ se** as if; **assim ~** as well as

cômoda /'komoda/ *f* chest of drawers, *Amer* bureau

como|didade /komodʒi'dadʒi/ *f* comfort; (*conveniência*) convenience. **~dismo** *m* complacency. **~dista** *a* complacent

cômodo /'komodu/ *a* comfortable; (*conveniente*) convenient ● *m* (*aposento*) room

como|vente /komo'vẽtʃi/ *a* moving. **~ver** *vt* move ● *vi* be moving. **~ver-se** *vpr* be moved

compacto /kõ'paktu/ *a* compact ● *m* single

compadecer-se /kõpade'sersi/ *vpr* feel pity (**de** for)

compadre /kõ'padri/ *m* (*padrinho*) godfather of one's child; (*pai do afilhado*) father of one's godchild

compaixão /kõpa'ʃãw/ *f* compassion

companhei|rismo /kõpaɲe-'rizmu/ *m* companionship. **~ro** *m* (*de viagem etc*) companion; (*amigo*) friend, mate

companhia /kõpa'ɲia/ *f* company; **fazer ~ a alguém** keep sb company

compa|ração /kõpara'sãw/ *f* comparison. **~rar** *vt* compare. **~rativo** *a* comparative. **~rável** (*pl* **~ráveis**) *a* comparable

compare|cer /kõpare'ser/ *vi* appear; **~cer a** attend. **~cimento** *m* attendance

comparsa /kõ'parsa/ *m/f* (*ator*) bit player; (*cúmplice*) sidekick

comparti|lhar /kõpartʃi'ʎar/ *vt/i* share (**de** in). **~mento** *m* compartment

compassado /kõpa'sadu/ *a* (*medido*) measured; (*ritmado*) regular

compassivo /kõpa'sivu/ *a* compassionate

compasso /kõ'pasu/ *m Mus* beat, time; (*instrumento*) compass, pair of compasses

compatí|vel /kõpa'tʃivew/ (*pl* **~veis**) *a* compatible

compatriota /kõpatri'ɔta/ *m/f* compatriot, fellow countryman (*f*-woman)

compelir /kõpe'lir/ *vt* compel

compene|tração /kõpenetra'sãw/ *f* conviction. **~trar** *vt* convince. **~trar-se** *vpr* convince o.s.

compen|sação /kõpẽsa'sãw/ *f* compensation; (*de cheques*) clearing; **~sação de carbono** carbon offsetting. **~sar** *vt* make up for ‹*defeitos, danos*›; offset ‹*peso, gastos*›; clear ‹*cheques*› ● *vi* ‹*crime*› pay

compe|tência /kõpe'tẽsia/ *f* competence. **~tente** *a* competent

compe|tição /kõpetʃi'sãw/ *f* competition. **~tidor** *m* competitor. **~tir** *vi* compete; **~tir a** be up to. **~tividade** *f* competitiveness. **~titivo** *a* competitive

compla|cência /kõpla'sẽsia/ *f* complaisance. **~cente** *a* obliging

complemen|tar /kõplemẽ'tar/ *vt* complement ● *a* complementary. **~to** *m* complement

comple|tar /kõple'tar/ *vt* complete; top up ‹*copo, tanque etc*›; **~tar 20 anos** turn 20. **~to** /ɛ/ *a* complete; (*cheio*) full up; **por ~to** completely; **escrever por ~to** write out in full

comple|xado /kõplek'sadu/ *a* with a complex. **~xidade** *f* complexity. **~xo** /ɛ/ *a & m* complex

compli|cação /kõplika'sãw/ *f* complication. **~cado** *a* complicated. **~car** *vt* complicate. **~car-se** *vpr* get complicated

complô /kõ'plo/ *m* conspiracy, plot

com|ponente /kõpo'nẽtʃi/ *a & m* component. **~por** *vt/i* compose. **~por-se** *vpr* (*controlar-se*) compose o.s.; **~por-se de** be composed of

compor|tamento /kõporta'mẽtu/ *m* behaviour. **~tar** *vt* hold; bear ‹*dor, prejuízo*›. **~tar-se** *vpr* behave

composi|ção /kõpozi'sãw/ *f* composition; (*acordo*) conciliation. **~tor** *m* (*de música*) composer; (*gráfico*) compositor

compos|to /kõ'postu/ *pp de* ▶ COMPOR ● *a* compound; ‹*pessoa*› level-headed ● *m* compound; **~to de** made up of. **~tura** *f* composure

compota /kõ'pɔta/ *f* fruit in syrup

com|pra /'kõpra/ *f* purchase; *pl* shopping; **fazer ~pras** go shopping. **~prador** *m* buyer. **~prar** *vt* buy; bribe ‹*oficial, juiz*›; pick ‹*briga*›

compreen|der /kõpriẽ'der/ *vt* (*conter em si*) contain; (*estender-se a*) cover, take in; (*entender*) understand. **~são** *f* understanding. **~sível** (*pl* **~síveis**) *a* understandable. **~sivo** *a* understanding

compres|sa /kõ'prɛsa/ *f* compress. **~são** *f* compression. **~sor** *m* compressor; **rolo ~sor** steamroller

compri|do /kõ'pridu/ *a* long. **~mento** *m* length

compri|mido /kõpri'midu/ *m* pill, tablet ● *a* ‹*ar*› compressed. **~mir** *vt* (*apertar*) press; (*reduzir o volume de*) compress

comprome|tedor /kõpromete'dor/ *a* compromising. **~ter** *vt* (*envolver*) involve; (*prejudicar*) compromise; **~ter alguém a fazer** commit sb to doing. **~ter-se** *vpr* (*obrigar-se*) commit o.s.; (*prejudicar-se*) compromise o.s.. **~tido** *a* (*ocupado*) busy; (*noivo*) spoken for

compromisso /kõpro'misu/ *m* commitment; (*encontro marcado*) appointment; **sem ~** without obligation

compro|vação /kõprova'sãw/ *f* proof. **~vante** *m* receipt. **~var** *vt* prove

compul|são /kõpuw'sãw/ *f* compulsion. **~sivo** *a* compulsive. **~sório** *a* compulsory

compu|tação /kõputa'sãw/ *f* computation; (*matéria, ramo*) computing; **~ na nuvem** cloud computing. **~tador** *m* computer. **~tadorizar** *vt* computerize. **~tar** *vt* compute

comum /ko'mũ/ *a* common; (*não especial*) ordinary; **fora do ~** out of the ordinary; **em ~** ‹*trabalho*› joint; ‹*atuar*› jointly; **ter muito em ~** have a lot in common

comungar /komũ'gar/ *vi* take communion

comunhão /komu'ɲãw/ *f* communion; *Relig* (Holy) Communion

comuni|cação /komunika'sãw/ *f* communication; **~cação social/visual** media studies/ graphic design. **~cado** *m* notice; *Pol* communiqué. **~car** *vt* communicate; (*unir*) connect ● *vi*, **~car-se** *vpr* communicate. **~cativo** *a* communicative

comu|nidade /komuni'dadʒi/ *f* community. **~nismo** *m* communism. **~nista** *a & m/f* communist. **~nitário** *a* (*da comunidade*) community; (*para todos juntos*) communal

côncavo /'kõkavu/ *a* concave

conce|ber /kõse'ber/ *vt* conceive; (*imaginar*) conceive of ● *vi* conceive. **~bível** (*pl* **~bíveis**) *a* conceivable

C

C

conceder /kõse'der/ *vt* grant; **~ em** accede to

concei|to /kõ'sejtu/ *m* concept; (*opinião*) opinion; (*fama*) reputation. **~tuado** *a* highly thought of. **~tuar** *vt* (*imaginar*) conceptualize; (*avaliar*) assess

concen|tração /kõsẽtra'sãw/ *f* concentration; (*de jogadores*) training camp. **~trar** *vt* concentrate. **~trar-se** *vpr* concentrate

concepção /kõsep'sãw/ *f* conception; (*opinião*) view

concernir /kõser'nir/ *vt* **~ a** concern

concerto /kõ'sertu/ *m* concert

conces|são /kõse'sãw/ *f* concession. **~sionária** *f* dealership. **~sionário** *m* dealer

concha /'kõʃa/ *f* (*de molusco*) shell; (*colher*) ladle

concili|ação /kõsilia'sãw/ *f* conciliation. **~ador** *a* conciliatory. **~ar** *vt* reconcile

concílio /kõ'siliu/ *m* council

conci|são /kõsi'zãw/ *f* conciseness. **~so** *a* concise

conclamar /kõkla'mar/ *vt* call ‹*eleição, greve*›; call upon ‹*pessoa*›

conclu|dente /kõklu'dẽtʃi/ *a* conclusive. **~ir** *vt/i* conclude. **~são** *f* conclusion. **~sivo** *a* concluding

concor|dância /kõkor'dãsia/ *f* agreement. **~dante** *a* consistent. **~dar** *vi* agree (**em** to) ● *vt* bring into line. **~data** *f* **abrir ~data** go into liquidation

concórdia /kõ'kɔrdʒia/ *f* concord

concor|rência /kõko'xẽsia/ *f* competition (**a** for). **~rente** *a* competing. **~rer** *vi* compete (**a** for); **~rer para** contribute to. **~rido** *a* popular

concre|tizar /kõkretʃi'zar/ *vt* realize. **~tizar-se** *vpr* be realized. **~to** /ɛ/ *a & m* concrete

concurso /kõ'kursu/ *m* contest; (*prova*) competition

con|dado /kõ'dadu/ *m* county. **~de** *m* count

condeco|ração /kõdekora'sãw/ *f* decoration. **~rar** *vt* decorate

conde|nação /kõdena'sãw/ *f* condemnation; *Jurid* conviction. **~nar** *vt* condemn; *Jurid* convict

conden|sação /kõdẽsa'sãw/ *f* condensation. **~sar** *vt* condense. **~sar-se** *vpr* condense

condescen|dência /kõdesẽ'dẽsia/ *f* acquiescence. **~dente** *a* acquiescent. **~der** *vi* acquiesce; **~der a** comply with ‹*pedido, desejo*›; **~der a ir** condescend to go

condessa /kõ'desa/ *f* countess

condi|ção /kõdʒi'sãw/ *f* condition; (*qualidade*) capacity; **ter ~ção** ou **~ções para** be able to; **em boas ~ções** in good condition. **~cionado** *a* conditioned. **~cional** (*pl* **~cionais**) *a* conditional. **~cionamento** *m* conditioning

condimen|tar /kõdʒimẽ'tar/ *vt* season. **~to** *m* seasoning

condoer-se /kõdo'ersi/ *vpr* **~ de** feel sorry for

condolência /kõdo'lẽsia/ *f* sympathy; *pl* condolences

condomínio /kõdo'miniu/ *m* (*taxa*) service charge

condu|ção /kõdu'sãw/ *f* (*de carro etc*) driving; (*transporte*) transport. **~cente** *a* conducive (**a** to). **~ta** *f* conduct. **~to** *m* conduit. **~tor** *m* (*de carro*) driver; *Eletr* conductor. **~zir** *vt* lead; drive ‹*carro*›; *Eletr* conduct ● *vi* (*de carro*) drive; (*levar*) lead (**a** to)

cone /'koni/ *m* cone

conec|tar /konek'tar/ *vt* connect. **~tado** *a* connected; *Comput* online

conectividade /konektʃivi'dadʒi/ *f* connectivity

cone|xão /konek'sãw/ *f* connection. **~xo** /ɛ/ *a* connected

confec|ção /kõfek'sãw/ *f* (*roupa*) off-the-peg outfit; (*loja*) clothes shop, boutique; (*fábrica*) clothes manufacturer. **~cionar** *vt* make

confederação /kõfedera'sãw/ *f* confederation

confei|tar /kõfej'tar/ *vt* ice. **~taria** *f* cake shop. **~teiro** *m* confectioner

confe|rência /kõfe'rẽsia/ *f* conference; (*palestra*) lecture. **~rencista** *m/f* speaker

conferir /kõfe'rir/ *vt* check (**com** against); (*conceder*) confer (**a** on) ● *vi* (*controlar*) check; (*estar exato*) tally

confes|sar /kõfe'sar/ *vt/i* confess. **~sar-se** *vpr* confess. **~sionário** *m* confessional. **~sor** *m* confessor

confete /kõ'fɛtʃi/ *m* confetti

confi|ança /kõfi'ãsa/ *f* (*convicção*) confidence; (*fé*) trust. **~ante** *a* confident (**em** of). **~ar** *vt/i* (*dar*) entrust; **~ar em** trust. **~ável** (*pl* **~áveis**) *a* reliable. **~dência** *f* confidence. **~dencial**

(*pl* **~denciais**) *a* confidential. **~denciar** *vt* tell in confidence. **~dente** *m/f* confidant (*f* confidante)
configu|ração /kõfigura'sãw/ *f* configuration. **~rar** *vt* (*representar*) represent; (*formar*) shape; *Comput* configure
con|finar /kõfi'nar/ *vi* **~finar com** border on. **~fins** *m pl* borders
confir|mação /kõfirma'sãw/ *f* confirmation. **~mar** *vt* confirm. **~mar-se** *vpr* be confirmed
confis|car /kõfis'kar/ *vt* confiscate. **~co** *m* confiscation
confissão /kõfi'sãw/ *f* confession
confla|gração /kõflagra'sãw/ *f* conflagration. **~grar** *vt* set alight; *fig* throw into turmoil
confli|tante /kõfli'tãtʃi/ *a* conflicting. **~to** *m* conflict
confor|mação /kõforma'sãw/ *f* resignation. **~mado** *a* resigned (**com** to). **~mar** *vt* adapt (**a** to); **~mar-se com** conform to ‹*regra, política*›; resign o.s. to, come to terms with ‹*destino, evento*›. **~me** /ɔ/ *prep* according to ● *conj* depending on; **~me** it depends. **~midade** *f* conformity. **~mismo** *m* conformism. **~mista** *a & m/f* conformist
confor|tar /kõfor'tar/ *vt* comfort. **~tável** (*pl* **~táveis**) *a* comfortable. **~to** /o/ *m* comfort; **comida de ~to** comfort eating; **zona de ~to** comfort zone
confraternizar /kõfraterni'zar/ *vi* fraternize
confron|tação /kõfrõta'sãw/ *f* confrontation. **~tar** *vt* confront; (*comparar*) compare. **~to** *m* confrontation; (*comparação*) comparison
con|fundir /kõfũ'dʒir/ *vt* confuse. **~fundir-se** *vpr* get confused. **~fusão** *f* confusion; (*desordem*) mess; (*tumulto*) commotion. **~fuso** *a* (*confundido*) confused; (*que confunde*) confusing
conge|lador /kõʒela'dor/ *m* freezer. **~lamento** *m* (*de preços etc*) freeze. **~lar** *vt* freeze. **~lar-se** *vpr* freeze
congênito /kõ'ʒenitu/ *a* congenital
congestão /kõʒes'tãw/ *f* congestion
congestio|nado /kõʒestʃio'nadu/ *a* ‹*rua, cidade*› congested; ‹*pessoa, rosto*› flushed; ‹*olhos*› bloodshot. **~namento** *m* (*de trânsito*) traffic jam. **~nar** *vt* congest. **~nar-se** *vpr* ‹*rua*› get congested; ‹*rosto*› flush
conglomerado /kõglome'radu/ *m* conglomerate
congratular /kõgratu'lar/ *vt* congratulate (**por** on)
congre|gação /kõgrega'sãw/ *f* (*na igreja*) congregation; (*reunião*) gathering. **~gar** *vt* bring together. **~gar-se** *vpr* congregate
congresso /kõ'grɛsu/ *m* congress
conhaque /ko'ɲaki/ *m* brandy
conhe|cedor /koɲese'dor/ *a* knowing ● *m* connoisseur. **~cer** *vt* know; (*ser apresentado a*) get to know; (*visitar*) go to, visit. **~cido** *a* known; (*famoso*) well-known ● *m* acquaintance. **~cimento** *m* knowledge; **tomar ~cimento de** learn of; **travar ~cimento com alguém** make sb's acquaintance, become acquainted with sb
cônico /'koniku/ *a* conical
coni|vência /koni'vẽsia/ *f* connivance. **~vente** *a* conniving (**em** at)
conjetu|ra /kõʒe'tura/ *f* conjecture. **~rar** *vt/i* conjecture
conju|gação /kõʒuga'sãw/ *f Ling* conjugation. **~gar** *vt* conjugate ‹*verbo*›
cônjuge /'kõʒuʒi/ *m/f* spouse
conjun|ção /kõʒũ'sãw/ *f* conjunction. **~tivo** *a & m* subjunctive. **~to** *a* joint ● *m* set; (*roupa*) outfit; (*musical*) group; **o ~to de** the body of; **em ~to** jointly. **~tura** *f* state of affairs; (*econômica*) state of the economy
conosco = **com** + **nós**
cono|tação /konota'sãw/ *f* connotation. **~tar** *vt* connote
conquanto /kõ'kwãtu/ *conj* although, even though
conquis|ta /kõ'kista/ *f* conquest; (*proeza*) achievement. **~tador** *m* conqueror ● *a* conquering. **~tar** *vt* conquer ‹*terra, país*›; win ‹*riqueza, independência*›; win over ‹*pessoa*›
consa|gração /kõsagra'sãw/ *f* (*de uma igreja*) consecration; (*dedicação*) dedication. **~grado** *a* ‹*artista, expressão*› established. **~grar** *vt* consecrate ‹*igreja*›; establish ‹*artista, estilo*›; (*dedicar*) dedicate (**a** to); **~grar-se a** dedicate o.s. to
consci|ência /kõsi'ẽsia/ *f* (*moralidade*) conscience; (*sentidos*) consciousness; (*no trabalho*) conscientiousness; (*de um fato etc*) awareness. **~encioso** /o/ *a* conscientious. **~ente** *a* conscious. **~entizar** *vt* make aware (**de** of). **~entizar-se** *vpr* become aware (**de** of)
consecutivo /kõseku'tʃivu/ *a* consecutive

C

conse|guinte /kõse'gĩtʃi/ *a* **por ~guinte** consequently. **~guir** *vt* get; **~guir fazer** manage to do ● *vi* succeed

conse|lheiro /kõse'ʎeru/ *m* counsellor, adviser. **~lho** /e/ *m* piece of advice ● *pl* advice; (*órgão*) council

consen|so /kõ'sẽsu/ *m* consensus. **~timento** *m* consent. **~tir** *vt* allow ● *vi* consent (**em** to)

conse|quência /kõse'kwẽsia/ *f* consequence; **por ~quência** consequently. **~quente** *a* consequent; (*coerente*) consistent

conser|tar /kõser'tar/ *vt* repair. **~to** /e/ *m* repair

conser|va /kõ'sɛrva/ *f* (*em vidro*) preserve; (*em lata*) tinned food. **~vação** *f* preservation. **~vador** *a & m* conservative. **~vadorismo** *m* conservatism. **~vante** *a & m* preservative. **~var** *vt* preserve; (*manter, guardar*) keep. **~var-se** *vpr* keep. **~vatório** *m* conservatory

conside|ração /kõsidera'sãw/ *f* consideration; (*estima*) esteem; **levar em ~ração** take into consideration. **~rar** *vt* consider; (*estimar*) think highly of ● *vi* consider. **~rar-se** *vpr* consider o.s.. **~rável** (*pl* **~ráveis**) *a* considerable

consig|nação /kõsigna'sãw/ *f* consignment. **~nar** *vt* consign

consigo = **com** + **si**

consis|tência /kõsis'tẽsia/ *f* consistency. **~tente** *a* firm. **~tir** *vi* consist (**em** in)

consoante /kõso'ãtʃi/ *f* consonant

conso|lação /kõsola'sãw/ *f* consolation. **~lador** *a* consoling. **~lar** *vt* console. **~lar-se** *vpr* console o.s.

consolidar /kõsoli'dar/ *vt* consolidate; mend ‹*fratura*›

consolo /kõ'solu/ *m* consolation

consórcio /kõ'sɔrsiu/ *m* consortium

consorte /kõ'sɔrtʃi/ *m/f* consort

conspícuo /kõs'pikuu/ *a* conspicuous

conspi|ração /kõspira'sãw/ *f* conspiracy; **teoria da ~ração** conspiracy theory. **~rador** *m* conspirator. **~rar** *vi* conspire

cons|tância /kõs'tãsia/ *f* constancy. **~tante** *a & f* constant. **~tar** *vi* (*em lista etc*) appear; **não me ~ta** I am not aware; **~ta que** it is said that; **~tar de** consist of

consta|tação /kõstata'sãw/ *f* observation. **~tar** *vt* note, notice; certify ‹*óbito*›

conste|lação /kõstela'sãw/ *f* constellation. **~lado** *a* star-studded

conster|nação /kõsterna'sãw/ *f* consternation. **~nar** *vt* dismay

consti|pação /kõstʃipa'sãw/ *f Port* (*resfriado*) cold. **~pado** *a* (*resfriado*) with a cold; (*no intestino*) constipated. **~par-se** *vpr Port* (*resfriar-se*) get a cold

constitu|cional /kõstʃitusio'naw/ (*pl* **~cionais**) *a* constitutional. **~ição** *f* constitution. **~inte** *a* constituent ● *f* **Constituinte** Constituent Assembly. **~ir** *vt* form ‹*governo, sociedade*›; (*representar*) constitute; (*nomear*) appoint

constran|gedor /kõstrãʒe'dor/ *a* embarrassing. **~ger** *vt* embarrass; (*coagir*) constrain. **~ger-se** *vpr* get embarrassed. **~gimento** *m* (*embaraço*) embarrassment; (*coação*) constraint

constru|ção /kõstru'sãw/ *f* construction; (*terreno*) building site. **~ir** *vt* build ‹*casa, prédio*›; *fig* construct. **~tivo** *a* constructive. **~tor** *m* builder. **~tora** *f* building firm

cônsul /'kõsuw/ (*pl* **~es**) *m* consul

consulado /kõsu'ladu/ *m* consulate

consul|ta /kõ'suwta/ *f* consultation. **~tar** *vt* consult. **~tor** *m* consultant. **~toria** *f* consultancy. **~tório** *m* (*médico*) surgery, *Amer* office

consu|mação /kõsuma'sãw/ *f* (*taxa*) minimum charge. **~mado** *a* **fato ~mado** fait accompli. **~mar** *vt* accomplish ‹*projeto*›; carry out ‹*crime, sacrifício*›; consummate ‹*casamento*›

consu|midor /kõsumi'dor/ *a & m* consumer. **~mir** *vt* consume; take up ‹*tempo*›. **~mismo** *m* consumerism. **~mista** *a & m/f* consumerist. **~mo** *m* consumption

conta /'kõta/ *f* (*a pagar*) bill; (*bancária*) account; (*contagem*) count; (*de vidro etc*) bead; *pl Com* accounts; **em ~** economical; **por ~ de** on account of; **por ~ própria** on one's own account; **ajustar ~s** settle up; **dar ~ de** *fig* be up to; **dar ~ do recado** [!] deliver the goods; **dar-se ~ de** realize; **fazer de ~** pretend; **ficar por ~ de** be left to; **levar** ou **ter em ~** take into account; **prestar ~s de** account for; **tomar ~ de** take care of; **~ bancária** bank account; **~ corrente** current account

contabi|lidade /kõtabili'dadʒi/ *f* accountancy; (*contas*) accounts; (*seção*) accounts department. **~lista** *Port m/f* accountant. **~lizar** *vt* write up ‹*quantia*›;

fig notch up

contact- *Port* ▶ **contat-**

conta|dor /kõta'dor/ *m* (*pessoa*) accountant; (*de luz etc*) meter. **~gem** *f* counting; (*de pontos num jogo*) scoring; **~gem regressiva** countdown

contagi|ante /kõtaʒi'ãtʃi/ *a* infectious. **~ar** *vt* infect. **~ar-se** *vpr* become infected

contágio /kõ'taʒiu/ *m* infection

contagioso /kõtaʒi'ozu/ *a* contagious

contami|nação /kõtamina'sãw/ *f* contamination. **~nar** *vt* contaminate

contanto /kõ'tãtu/ *adv* **~ que** provided that

contar /kõ'tar/ *vt/i* count; (*narrar*) tell; **~ com** count on

conta|tar /kõta'tar/ *vt* contact. **~to** *m* contact; **entrar em ~to com** get in touch with; **tomar ~to com** come into contact with

contem|plação /kõtẽpla'sãw/ *f* contemplation. **~plar** *vt* (*considerar*) contemplate; (*dizer respeito a*) concern; **~plar alguém com** treat sb to ● *vi* ponder. **~plativo** *a* contemplative

contemporâneo /kõtẽpo'raniu/ *a & m* contemporary

contenção /kõtẽ'sãw/ *f* containment

conten|cioso /kõtẽsi'ozu/ *a* contentious. **~da** *f* dispute

conten|tamento /kõtẽta'mẽtu/ *m* contentment. **~tar** *vt* satisfy. **~tar-se** *vpr* be content. **~te** *a* (*feliz*) happy; (*satisfeito*) content. **~to** *m* **a ~to** satisfactorily

conter /kõ'ter/ *vt* contain. **~-se** *vpr* contain o.s.

conterrâneo /kõte'xaniu/ *m* fellow countryman (*f* -woman)

contestar /kõtes'tar/ *vt* question; *Jurid* contest

conteúdo /kõte'udu/ *m* (*de recipiente*) contents; *fig* (*de carta etc*) content

contexto /kõ'testu/ *m* context

contigo = **com** + **ti**

continência /kõtʃi'nẽsia/ *f Mil* salute

continen|tal /kõtʃinẽ'taw/ (*pl* **~tais**) *a* continental. **~te** *m* continent

contin|gência /kõtʃĩ'ʒẽsia/ *f* contingency. **~gente** *a* (*eventual*) possible; (*incerto*) contingent ● *m* contingent

continu|ação /kõtʃinua'sãw/ *f* continuation. **~ar** *vt/i* continue; **eles ~am ricos** they are still rich. **~idade** *f* continuity

contínuo /kõ'tʃinuu/ *a* continuous ● *m* office junior

con|tista /kõ'tʃista/ *m/f* (short) story writer. **~to** *m* (short) story; **~to de fadas** fairy tale; **~to do vigário** confidence trick, swindle

contorcer /kõtor'ser/ *vt* twist. **~-se** *vpr* (*de dor*) writhe

contor|nar /kõtor'nar/ *vt* go round; *fig* get round ‹*obstáculo, problema*›; (*cercar*) surround; (*delinear*) outline. **~no** /o/ *m* outline; (*da paisagem*) contour

contra /'kõtra/ *prep* against

contra|-atacar /kõtrata'kar/ *vt* counter-attack. **~-ataque** *m* counter-attack

contrabaixo /kõtra'baʃu/ *m* double bass

contrabalançar /kõtrabalã'sar/ *vt* counterbalance

contraban|dear /kõtrabãdʒi'ar/ *vt* smuggle. **~dista** *m/f* smuggler. **~do** *m* (*ato*) smuggling; (*artigos*) contraband

contração /kõtra'sãw/ *f* contraction

contracenar /kõtrase'nar/ *vi* **~ com** play up to

contraceptivo /kõtrasep'tʃivu/ *a & m* contraceptive

contracheque /kõtra'ʃɛki/ *m* pay slip

contradi|ção /kõtradʒi'sãw/ *f* contradiction. **~tório** *a* contradictory. **~zer** *vt* contradict. **~zer-se** *vpr* ‹*pessoa*› contradict o.s.; ‹*ideias etc*› be contradictory

contragosto /kõtra'gostu/ *m* **a ~** reluctantly

contrair /kõtra'ir/ *vt* contract; pick up ‹*hábito, vício*›. **~-se** *vpr* contract

contramão /kõtra'mãw/ *f* opposite direction ● *a invar* one way

contramestre /kõtra'mɛstri/ *m* supervisor; (*em navio*) bosun

contraofensiva /kõtraofẽ'siva/ *f* counter-offensive

contrapartida /kõtrapar'tʃida/ *f fig* compensation; **em ~** on the other hand

contraproducente /kõtraprodu'sẽtʃi/ *a* counterproductive

contrari|ar /kõtrari'ar/ *vt* go against, run counter to; (*aborrecer*) annoy. **~edade** *f* adversity; (*aborrecimento*) annoyance

contrário /kõ'trariu/ *a* opposite; (*desfavorável*) adverse; **~ a** contrary to; ‹*pessoa*› opposed to ● *m* opposite;

C

C

pelo ou **ao ~** on the contrary; **ao ~ de** contrary to; **em ~** to the contrary

contras|tante /kõtras'tãtʃi/ *a* contrasting. **~tar** *vt/i* contrast. **~te** *m* contrast

contratação /kõtrata'sãw/ *f* (*de empregado*) recruitment; (*de jogador*) signing

contra|tante /kõtra'tãtʃi/ *m/f* contractor. **~tar** *vt* employ, take on ‹*operários*›

contra|tempo /kõtra'tẽpu/ *m* hitch

contra|to /kõ'tratu/ *m* contract. **~tual** (*pl* **~tuais**) *a* contractual

contraven|ção /kõtravẽ'sãw/ *f* contravention. **~tor** *m* offender

contribu|ição /kõtribui'sãw/ *f* contribution. **~inte** *m/f* contributor; (*pagador de impostos*) taxpayer. **~ir** *vt* contribute ● *vi* contribute; (*pagar impostos*) pay tax

contrição /kõtri'sãw/ *f* contrition

contro|lar /kõtro'lar/ *vt* control; (*fiscalizar*) check. **~le** /o/, *Port* **~lo** /o/ *m* control; (*fiscalização*) check; **~le de qualidade** quality control

contro|vérsia /kõtro'vɛrsia/ *f* controversy. **~verso** /ɛ/ *a* controversial

contudo /kõ'tudu/ *conj* nevertheless

contundir /kõtũ'dʒir/ *vt* (*dar hematoma em*) bruise; injure ‹*jogador*›. **~-se** *vpr* bruise o.s.; ‹*jogador*› get injured

conturbado /kõtur'badu/ *a* troubled

contu|são /kõtu'zãw/ *f* bruise; (*de jogador*) injury. **~so** *a* bruised; ‹*jogador*› injured

convales|cença /kõvale'sẽsa/ *f* convalescence. **~cer** *vi* convalesce

convenção /kõvẽ'sãw/ *f* convention

conven|cer /kõvẽ'ser/ *vt* convince. **~cido** *a* (*convicto*) convinced; (*metido*) conceited. **~cimento** *m* (*convicção*) conviction; (*imodéstia*) conceitedness

convencio|nal /kõvẽsio'naw/ (*pl* **~nais**) *a* conventional

conveni|ência /kõveni'ẽsia/ *f* convenience. **~ente** *a* convenient; (*cabível*) appropriate

convênio /kõ'veniu/ *m* agreement

convento /kõ'vẽtu/ *m* convent

convergir /kõver'ʒir/ *vi* converge

conver|sa /kõ'vɛrsa/ *f* conversation; **a ~sa dele** the things he says; **~sa fiada** idle talk. **~sação** *f* conversation. **~sado** *a* ‹*pessoa*› talkative; ‹*assunto*› talked about. **~sador** *a* talkative

conversão /kõver'sãw/ *f* conversion

conversar /kõver'sar/ *vi* talk

conver|sível /kõver'sivew/ (*pl* **~síveis**) *a & m* convertible. **~ter** *vt* convert. **~ter-se** *vpr* be converted. **~tido** *m* convert

con|vés /kõ'vɛs/ (*pl* **~veses**) *m* deck

convexo /kõ'vɛksu/ *a* convex

convic|ção /kõvik'sãw/ *f* conviction. **~to** *a* convinced; (*ferrenho*) confirmed; ‹*criminoso*› convicted

convi|dado /kõvi'dadu/ *m* guest. **~dar** *vt* invite. **~dativo** *a* inviting

convincente /kõvĩ'sẽtʃi/ *a* convincing

convir /kõ'vir/ *vi* (*ficar bem*) be appropriate; (*concordar*) agree (**em** on); **~ a** suit, be convenient for; **convém notar que** one should note that

convite /kõ'vitʃi/ *m* invitation

convi|vência /kõvi'vẽsia/ *f* coexistence; (*relação*) close contact. **~ver** *vi* coexist; (*ter relações*) associate (**com** with)

convívio /kõ'viviu/ *m* association (**com** with)

convocar /kõvo'kar/ *vt* call ‹*eleições, greve*›; call upon ‹*pessoa*› (**a** to); (*ao serviço militar*) call up

convosco = **com** + **vós**

convul|são /kõvuw'sãw/ *f* (*do corpo*) convulsion; (*da sociedade etc*) upheaval. **~sionar** *vt* convulse ‹*corpo*›; *fig* churn up. **~sivo** *a* convulsive

cooper /'kuper/ *m* jogging; **fazer ~** go jogging

coope|ração /koopera'sãw/ *f* cooperation. **~rar** *vi* cooperate. **~rativa** *f* cooperative. **~rativo** *a* cooperative

coorde|nação /koordena'sãw/ *f* coordination. **~nada** *f* coordinate. **~nar** *vt* coordinate

copa /'kɔpa/ *f* (*de árvore*) top; (*aposento*) breakfast room; (*torneio*) cup; *pl* (*naipe*) hearts; **a C~ (do Mundo)** the World Cup. **~-cozinha** (*pl* **~s-cozinhas**) *f* kitchen-diner

cópia /'kɔpia/ *f* copy

copiar /kopi'ar/ *vt* copy

copiloto /kopi'lotu/ *m* co-pilot

copioso /kopi'ozu/ *a* ample; ‹*refeição*› substantial

copo /'kɔpu/ *m* glass

coque /'kɔki/ *m* (*penteado*) bun

coqueiro /ko'keru/ *m* coconut palm

coqueluche /koke'luʃi/ *f* (*doença*) whooping cough; (*mania*) fad

coque|tel /koke'tɛw/ (*pl* **~téis**) *m* cocktail; (*reunião*) cocktail party

cor[1] /kɔr/ *m* **de ~** by heart

cor[2] /kor/ *f* colour; **TV a ~es** colour TV; **pessoa de ~** coloured person

coração /kora'sãw/ *m* heart

cora|gem /ko'raʒẽ/ *f* courage. **~joso** /o/ *a* courageous

co|ral[1] /ko'raw/ (*pl* **~rais**) *m* (*animal*) coral

co|ral[2] /ko'raw/ (*pl* **~rais**) *m* (*de cantores*) choir ● *a* choral

co|rante /ko'rãtʃi/ *a & m* colouring. **~rar** *vt* colour ● *vi* blush

cor|da /'kɔrda/ *f* rope; *Mus* string; (*para roupa lavada*) clothes line; **dar ~da em** wind ‹*relógio*›; **~da bamba** tightrope; **~das vocais** vocal chords. **~dão** *m* cord; (*de sapatos*) lace; (*policial*) cordon

cordeiro /kor'deru/ *m* lamb

cor|del /kor'dɛw/ (*pl* **~déis**) *Port m* string; **literatura de ~del** trash literature

cor-de-rosa /kordʒi'rɔza/ *a invar* pink

cordi|al /kordʒi'aw/ (*pl* **~ais**) *a & m* cordial. **~alidade** *f* cordiality

cordilheira /kordʒi'ʎera/ *f* chain of mountains

coreano /kori'anu/ *a & m* Korean

Coreia /ko'rɛja/ *f* Korea

core|ografia /koriogra'fia/ *f* choreography. **~ógrafo** *m* choreographer

coreto /ko'retu/ *m* bandstand

coriza /ko'riza/ *f* runny nose

corja /'kɔrʒa/ *f* pack; (*de pessoas*) rabble

córner /'kɔrner/ *m* corner

coro /'koru/ *m* chorus

coro|a /ko'roa/ *f* crown; (*de flores etc*) wreath ● *m/f* [!] old man (*f* woman). **~ação** *f* coronation. **~ar** *vt* crown

coro|nel /koro'nɛw/ (*pl* **~néis**) *m* colonel

coronha /ko'roɲa/ *f* butt

corpete /kor'petʃi/ *m* bodice

corpo /'korpu/ *m* body; (*físico de mulher*) figure; (*físico de homem*) physique; **~ a ~** *m invar* pitched battle. **~ de bombeiros** fire brigade; **~ diplomático** diplomatic corps; **~ docente** teaching staff, *Amer* faculty; **~ral** (*pl* **~rais**) *a* physical; ‹*pena*› corporal

corpu|lência /korpu'lẽsia/ *f* stoutness. **~lento** *a* stout

correção /koxe'sãw/ *f* correction

corre-corre /kɔxi'kɔxi/ *m* (*debandada*) stampede; (*correria*) rush

corre|diço /koxe'dʒisu/ *a* ‹*porta*› sliding. **~dor** *m* (*atleta*) runner; (*passagem*) corridor

correia /ko'xeja/ *f* strap; (*peça de máquina*) belt; (*para cachorro*) lead, *Amer* leash

correio /ko'xeju/ *m* post, mail; (*repartição*) post office; **pôr no ~** post, *Amer* mail; **~ aéreo** air mail; **~ de voz** voicemail; **~ eletrônico** email

correlação /koxela'sãw/ *f* correlation

correligionário /koxeliʒio'nariu/ *m* party colleague

corrente /ko'xẽtʃi/ *a* ‹*água*› running; ‹*mês, conta*› current; ‹*estilo*› fluid; (*usual*) common ● *f* (*de água, eletricidade*) current; (*cadeia*) chain; **~ de ar** draught. **~za** /e/ *f* current; (*de ar*) draught

cor|rer /ko'xer/ *vi* (*à pé*) run; (*de carro*) drive fast, speed; (*fazer rápido*) rush; ‹*água, sangue*› flow; ‹*tempo*› elapse; ‹*boato*› go round ● *vt* draw ‹*cortina*›; run ‹*risco*›. **~reria** *f* rush

correspon|dência /koxespõ'dẽsia/ *f* correspondence. **~dente** *a* corresponding ● *m/f* correspondent; (*equivalente*) equivalent. **~der** *vi* **~der a** correspond to; (*retribuir*) return. **~der-se** *vpr* correspond (**com** with)

corre|tivo /koxe'tʃivu/ *a* corrective ● *m* punishment. **~to** /ɛ/ *a* correct

corretor /koxe'tor/ *m* broker; **~ de imóveis** estate agent, *Amer* realtor

corrida /ko'xida/ *f* (*prova*) race; (*ação de correr*) run; (*de taxi*) ride

corrigir /koxi'ʒir/ *vt* correct

corrimão /koxi'mãw/ (*pl* **~s**) *m* handrail; (*de escada*) banister

corriqueiro /koxi'keru/ *a* ordinary, run-of-the-mill

corroborar /koxobo'rar/ *vt* corroborate

corroer /koxo'er/ *vt* corrode ‹*metal*›; *fig* erode. **~-se** *vpr* corrode; *fig* erode

corromper /koxõ'per/ *vt* corrupt. **~-se** *vpr* be corrupted

corro|são /koxo'zãw/ *f* (*de metal*) corrosion; *fig* erosion. **~sivo** *a* corrosive

corrup|ção /koxup'sãw/ *f* corruption. **~to** *a* corrupt

cor|tada /kor'tada/ *f* (*em tênis*) smash; (*em pessoa*) put-down. **~tante** *a* cutting. **~tar** *vt* cut; cut off ‹*luz, telefone, perna etc*›; cut down ‹*árvore*›; cut out ‹*efeito, vício*›; take away ‹*prazer*›; (*com o carro*) cut up; (*desprezar*) cut dead; **~tar o cabelo** (*no cabeleireiro*) get one's hair cut ● *vi* cut. **~te**[1] /ɔ/ *m* cut; (*gume*) blade; (*desenho*) cross-section; **sem ~te** ‹*faca*› blunt; **~te de cabelo** haircut

cor|te[2] /'kortʃi/ *f* court. **~tejar** *vt* court. **~tejo** /e/ *m* (*séquito*) retinue; (*fúnebre*) cortège. **~tês** *a* (*f* **~tesa**) courteous, polite. **~tesão** (*pl* **~tesãos**) *m* courtier. **~tesia** *f* courtesy

corti|ça /kor'tʃisa/ *f* cork. **~ço** *m* (*casa popular*) slum tenement

cortina /kor'tʃina/ *f* curtain

cortisona /kortʃi'zona/ *f* cortisone

coruja /ko'ruʒa/ *f* owl ● *a* ‹*pai, mãe*› proud, doting

coruscar /korus'kar/ *vi* flash

corvo /'korvu/ *m* crow

cós /kɔs/ *m invar* waistband

coser /ko'zer/ *vt/i* sew

cosmético /koz'mɛtʃiku/ *a & m* cosmetic

cósmico /'kɔzmiku/ *a* cosmic

cosmo /'kɔzmu/ *m* cosmos. **~nauta** *m/f* cosmonaut. **~polita** *a* cosmopolitan ● *m/f* globetrotter

costa /'kɔsta/ *f* coast; *pl* (*dorso*) back; **C~ do Marfim** Ivory Coast; **C~ Rica** Costa Rica

costarriquenho /kostaxi'keɲu/ *a & m* Costa Rican

cos|teiro /kos'teru/ *a* coastal. **~tela** /ɛ/ *f* rib. **~teleta** /e/ *f* chop; *pl* (*suíças*) sideburns. **~telinha** *f* (*de porco*) spare rib

costu|mar /kostu'mar/ *vt* **~ma fazer** he usually does; **~mava fazer** he used to do. **~me** *m* (*uso*) custom; (*traje*) costume; **de ~me** usually; **como de ~me** as usual; **ter o ~me de** have a habit of. **~meiro** *a* customary

costu|ra /kos'tura/ *f* sewing. **~rar** *vt/i* sew. **~reira** *f* (*mulher*) dressmaker; (*caixa*) needlework box

co|ta /'kɔta/ *f* quota. **~tação** *f* (*preço*) rate; (*apreço*) rating. **~tado** *a* ‹*ação*› quoted; (*conceituado*) highly rated. **~tar** *vt* rate; quote ‹*ações*›

cote|jar /kote'ʒar/ *vt* compare. **~jo** /e/ *m* comparison

cotidiano /kotʃidʒi'anu/ *a* everyday ● *m* everyday life

cotonete /koto'nɛtʃi/ *m* cotton bud

cotove|lada /kotove'lada/ *f* (*para abrir caminho*) shove; (*para chamar atenção*) nudge. **~lo** /e/ *m* elbow

coura|ça /ko'rasa/ *f* (*armadura*) breastplate; (*de navio, animal*) armour. **~çado** *Port m* battleship

couro /'koru/ *m* leather; **~ cabeludo** scalp

couve /'kovi/ *f* spring greens. **~-de-bruxelas** (*pl* **~s-de-bruxelas**) *f* Brussels sprout; **~-flor** (*pl* **~s-flores**) *f* cauliflower

couvert /ku'vɛr/ (*pl* **~s**) *m* cover charge

cova /'kɔva/ *f* (*buraco*) pit; (*sepultura*) grave

covar|de /ko'vardʒi/ *m/f* coward ● *a* cowardly. **~dia** *f* cowardice

coveiro /ko'veru/ *m* gravedigger

covil /ko'viw/ (*pl* **~vis**) *m* den, lair

covinha /ko'viɲa/ *f* dimple

co|xa /'koʃa/ *f* thigh. **~xear** *vi* hobble

coxia /ko'ʃia/ *f* aisle

coxo /'koʃu/ *a* hobbling; **ser ~** hobble

co|zer /ko'zer/ *vt/i* cook. **~zido** *m* stew, casserole

cozi|nha /ko'ziɲa/ *f* (*aposento*) kitchen; (*comida, ação*) cooking; (*arte*) cookery. **~nhar** *vt/i* cook. **~nheiro** *m* cook

crachá /kra'ʃa/ *m* badge, *Amer* button

crânio /'kraniu/ *m* skull; (*pessoa*) genius

crápula /'krapula/ *m/f* scoundrel

craque /'kraki/ *m* (*de futebol*) soccer star; [!] expert

crase /'krazi/ *f* contraction; **a com ~** a grave (à)

crasso /'krasu/ *a* crass

cratera /kra'tɛra/ *f* crater

cravar /kra'var/ *vt* drive in ‹*prego*›; dig ‹*unha*›; stick ‹*estaca*›; **~ com os olhos** stare at. **~-se** *vpr* stick

cravejar /krave'ʒar/ *vt* nail; (*com balas*) spray, riddle

cravo[1] /'kravu/ *m* (*flor*) carnation; (*condimento*) clove

cravo[2] /'kravu/ *m* (*na pele*) blackhead; (*prego*) nail

cravo[3] /'kravu/ *m* (*instrumento*) harpsichord

creche /'krɛʃi/ *f* crèche

credenci|ais /kredẽsi'ajs/ *f pl* credentials. **~ar** *vt* qualify

credi|ário /kredʒi'ariu/ *m* hire purchase agreement, credit plan. **~bilidade** *f* credibility. **~tar** *vt* credit

credifone® /kredʒi'foni/ *m Port* phonecard

crédito /'krɛdʒitu/ *m* credit; **a ~** on credit

cre|do /'krɛdu/ *m* creed ● *int* heavens. **~dor** *m* creditor ● *a* ‹*saldo*› credit

crédulo /'krɛdulu/ *a* gullible

cre|mação /krema'sãw/ *f* cremation. **~mar** *vt* cremate. **~matório** *m* crematorium

cre|me /'kremi/ *a invar & m* cream; **~me Chantilly** whipped cream; **~me de leite** (sterilized) cream. **~moso** /o/ *a* creamy

cren|ça /'krẽsa/ *f* belief. **~dice** *f* superstition. **~te** *m* believer; (*protestante*) Protestant ● *a* religious; (*protestante*) Protestant; **estar ~te que** believe that

crepe /'krɛpi/ *m* crepe

crepitar /krepi'tar/ *vi* crackle

crepom /kre'põ/ *m* crepe; **papel ~** tissue paper

crepúsculo /kre'puskulu/ *m* twilight

crer /krer/ *vt/i* believe (**em** in); **creio que** I think (that). **~-se** *vpr* believe o.s. to be

cres|cendo /kre'sẽdu/ *m* crescendo. **~cente** *a* growing ● *m* crescent. **~cer** *vi* grow; ‹*bolo*› rise. **~cido** *a* grown. **~cimento** *m* growth

crespo /'krespu/ *a* ‹*cabelo*› frizzy; ‹*mar*› choppy

cretino /kre'tʃinu/ *m* cretin

cria /'kria/ *f* baby; *pl* young

criação /kria'sãw/ *f* creation; (*educação*) upbringing; (*de animais*) raising; (*gado*) livestock

criado /kri'adu/ *m* servant. **~-mudo** (*pl* **~s-mudos**) *m* bedside table

criador /kria'dor/ *m* creator; (*de animais*) farmer, breeder

crian|ça /kri'ãsa/ *f* child ● *a* childish. **~çada** *f* kids. **~cice** *f* childishness; (*uma*) childish thing

criar /kri'ar/ *vt* (*fazer*) create; bring up ‹*filhos*›; rear ‹*animais*›; grow ‹*planta*›; pluck up ‹*coragem*›. **~-se** *vpr* be brought up, grow up

criati|vidade /kriatʃivi'dadʒi/ *f* creativity. **~vo** *a* creative

criatura /kria'tura/ *f* creature

crime /'krimi/ *m* crime

crimi|nal /krimi'naw/ (*pl* **~nais**) *a* criminal. **~nalidade** *f* crime. **~noso** *m* criminal

crina /'krina/ *f* mane

crioulo /kri'olu/ *a & m* Creole; (*negro*) black

cripta /'kripta/ *f* crypt

crisálida /kri'zalida/ *f* chrysalis

crisântemo /kri'zãtemu/ *m* chrysanthemum

crise /'krizi/ *f* crisis

cris|ma /'krizma/ *f* confirmation. **~mar** *vt* confirm. **~mar-se** *vpr* get confirmed

crista /'krista/ *f* crest

cris|tal /kris'taw/ (*pl* **~tais**) *m* crystal; (*vidro*) glass. **~talino** *a* crystal clear. **~talizar** *vt/i* crystallize

cris|tandade /kristã'dadʒi/ *f* Christendom. **~tão** (*pl* **~tãos**) *a & m* (*f* **~tã**) Christian. **~tianismo** *m* Christianity

Cristo /'kristu/ *m* Christ

> **i**
>
> **Cristo Redentor** *Cristo Redentor* (Christ the Redeemer) is a statue of Jesus Christ at the peak of the Corcovado mountain in Rio de Janeiro. Inaugurated in 1931, the monument is 38 metres high, and is situated 710 metres above sea level. From the statue, you can see the centre of Rio de Janeiro, the *Pão de Açúcar* (Sugarloaf mountain), the Rodrigo de Freitas Lagoon, and other tourist attractions.

cri|tério /kri'tɛriu/ *m* discretion; (*norma*) criterion. **~terioso** *a* perceptive, discerning

crítica /'kritʃika/ *f* criticism; (*análise*) critique; (*de filme, livro*) review; (*críticos*) critics

criticar /kritʃi'kar/ *vt* criticize; review ‹*filme, livro*›

crítico /'kritʃiku/ *a* critical ● *m* critic

crivar /kri'var/ *vt* (*furar*) riddle

crí|vel /'krivew/ (*pl* **~veis**) *a* credible

crivo /'krivu/ *m* sieve; *fig* scrutiny

crocante /kro'kãtʃi/ *a* crunchy

crochê /kro'ʃe/ *m* crochet

crocodilo /kroko'dʒilu/ *m* crocodile

cromo /'kromu/ *m* chrome; [!] (*pessoa*) geek [!]

cromossomo /kromo'somu/ *m* chromosome

crôni|ca /'kronika/ *f* (*histórica*) chronicle; (*no jornal*) feature; (*conto*) short story. **~co** *a* chronic

cronista /kro'nista/ *m/f* (*de jornal*) feature writer; (*contista*) short story writer; (*historiador*) chronicler

crono|grama /krono'grama/ *m* schedule. **~logia** *f* chronology. **~lógico** *a* chronological. **~metrar** *vt* time

cronômetro /kro'nometru/ *m* stopwatch

croquete /kro'kɛtʃi/ *m* savoury meatball in breadcrumbs

croqui /kro'ki/ *m* sketch

crosta /'krosta/ *f* crust; (*em ferida*) scab

cru /kru/ *a* (*f* **~a**) raw; ‹*luz, tom, palavra*› harsh; ‹*linguagem*› crude; ‹*verdade*› unvarnished, plain

cruci|al /krusi'aw/ (*pl* **~ais**) *a* crucial

crucifi|cação /krusifika'sãw/ *f* crucifixion. **~car** *vt* crucify. **~xo** /ks/ *m* crucifix

cru|el /kru'ɛw/ (*pl* **~éis**) *a* cruel. **~eldade** *f* cruelty. **~ento** *a* bloody

crupe /'krupi/ *m* croup

crustáceos /krus'tasius/ *m pl* shellfish

cruz /krus/ *f* cross

cruza|da /kru'zada/ *f* crusade. **~do**[1] *m* (*soldado*) crusader

cru|zado[2] /kru'zadu/ *m* (*moeda*) cruzado. **~zador** *m* cruiser. **~zamento** *m* (*de ruas*) crossroads, junction, *Amer* intersection; (*de raças*) cross. **~zar** *vt* cross ● *vi* ‹*navio*› cruise; **~zar com** pass. **~zar-se** *vpr* cross; ‹*pessoas*› pass each other. **~zeiro** *m* (*moeda*) cruzeiro; (*viagem*) cruise; (*cruz*) cross

cu /ku/ *m* (*chulo*) arse, *Amer* ass; **~ de ferro** [!] swot [!]

Cuba /'kuba/ *f* Cuba

cubano /ku'banu/ *a & m* Cuban

cúbico /'kubiku/ *a* cubic

cubículo /ku'bikulu/ *m* cubicle

cubis|mo /ku'bizmu/ *m* cubism. **~ta** *a & m/f* cubist

cubo /'kubu/ *m* cube; (*de roda*) hub

cuca /'kuka/ *f* [!] head

cuco /'kuku/ *m* cuckoo; (*relógio*) cuckoo clock

cueca /ku'ɛka/ *f* underpants; *pl Port* (*de mulher*) knickers

cueiro /ku'eru/ *m* baby wrap

cuia /'kuia/ *f* gourd

cuidado /kui'dadu/ *m* care; **com ~** carefully; **ter** ou **tomar ~** be careful. **~so** /o/ *a* careful

cuidar /kui'dar/ *vi* **~ de** take care of. **~-se** *vpr* look after o.s.

cujo /'kuʒu/ *pron* whose

culatra /ku'latra/ *f* breech; **sair pela ~** *fig* backfire

culiná|ria /kuli'naria/ *f* cookery. **~rio** *a* culinary

culmi|nância /kuwmi'nãsia/ *f* culmination. **~nante** *a* culminating. **~nar** *vi* culminate (**em** in)

cul|pa /'kuwpa/ *f* guilt; **foi ~pa minha** it was my fault; **ter ~pa de** be to blame for. **~pabilidade** *f* guilt. **~pado** *a* guilty ● *m* culprit. **~par** *vt* blame (**de** for); (*na justiça*) find guilty (**de** of). **~par-se** *vpr* take the blame (**de** for). **~pável** (*pl* **~páveis**) *a* culpable, guilty

culti|var /kuwtʃi'var/ *vt* cultivate; grow ‹*plantas*›. **~vo** *m* cultivation; (*de plantas*) growing

cul|to /'kuwtu/ *a* cultured ● *m* cult. **~tura** *f* culture; (*de terra*) cultivation. **~tural** (*pl* **~turais**) *a* cultural

cumbuca /kũ'buka/ *f* bowl

cume /'kumi/ *m* peak

cúmplice /'kũplisi/ *m/f* accomplice

cumplicidade /kũplisi'dadʒi/ *f* complicity

cumprimen|tar /kũprimẽ'tar/ *vt/i* (*saudar*) greet; (*parabenizar*) compliment. **~to** *m* (*saudação*) greeting; (*elogio*) compliment; (*de lei, ordem*) compliance (**de** with); (*de promessa, palavra*) fulfilment

cumprir /kũ'prir/ *vt* keep ‹*promessa, palavra*›; comply with ‹*lei, ordem*›; do ‹*dever*›; carry out ‹*obrigações*›; serve ‹*pena*›; **~ com** keep to ● *vi* **cumpre-nos ir** we should go. **~-se** *vpr* be fulfilled

cúmulo /'kumulu/ *m* height; **é o ~!** that's the limit!

cunha /'kuɲa/ *f* wedge; *Port* (*pessoa influente*) contact

cunha|da /ku'ɲada/ *f* sister-in-law. **~do** *m* brother-in-law

cunhar /'kuɲar/ *vt* coin ‹*palavra, expressão*›; mint ‹*moedas*›

cunho /'kuɲu/ *m* hallmark

cupim /ku'pĩ/ *m* termite

cupom /ku'põ/ *m* coupon

cúpula /'kupula/ *f* (*abóbada*) dome; (*de abajur*) shade; (*chefia*) leadership; **(reunião de) ~** summit (meeting)

cura /'kura/ *f* cure ● *m* curate, priest

curandeiro /kurã'deru/ *m* (*religioso*) faith healer; (*índio*) medicine man; (*charlatão*) quack

curar /ku'rar/ *vt* cure; dress ‹*ferida*›. **~-se** *vpr* be cured

curativo /kura'tʃivu/ *m* dressing

curá|vel /ku'ravew/ (*pl* **~veis**) *a* curable

curin|ga /ku'rĩga/ *m* wild card. **~gão** *m* joker
curio|sidade /kuriozi'dadʒi/ *f* curiosity. **~so** /o/ *a* curious ● *m* (*espectador*) onlooker
cur|ral /ku'xaw/ (*pl* **~rais**) *m* pen
currículo /ku'xikulu/ *m* curriculum; (*resumo*) curriculum vitae, CV
cur|sar /kur'sar/ *vt* attend ‹*escola, aula*›; study ‹*matéria*›. **~so** *m* course. **~sor** *m* cursor
curta|-metragem /kurtame'traʒẽ/ (*pl* **~s-metragens**) *m* short (film)
cur|tição /kurtʃi'sãw/ *f* [!] enjoyment. **~tir** *vt* [!] enjoy; tan ‹*couro*›
curto /'kurtu/ *a* short; ‹*conhecimento, inteligência*› limited. **~-circuito** (*pl* **~s-circuitos**) *m* short circuit
cur|va /'kurva/ *f* curve; (*de estrada, rio*) bend; **~va fechada** hairpin bend. **~var** *vt* bend. **~var-se** *vpr* bend; *fig* bow (**a** to). **~vo** *a* curved; ‹*estrada*› winding
cus|parada /kuspa'rada/ *f* spit. **~pe** *m* spit, spittle. **~pir** *vt/i* spit
cus|ta /'kusta/ *f* **à ~ta de** at the expense of. **~tar** *vt* cost ● *vi* (*ser difícil*) be hard; **~tar a fazer** (*ter dificuldade*) find it hard to do; (*demorar*) take a long time to do. **~tear** *vt* finance, fund. **~teio** *m* funding; (*relação de despesas*) costing. **~to** *m* cost; **a ~to** with difficulty
custódia /kus'tɔdʒia/ *f* custody
cutelo /ku'tɛlu/ *m* cleaver
cutícula /ku'tʃikula/ *f* cuticle
cútis /'kutʃis/ *f invar* complexion
cutucar /kutu'kar/ *vt* (*com o cotovelo, joelho*) nudge; (*com o dedo*) poke; (*com instrumento*) prod
czar /zar/ *m* tsar

Dd

da = **de** + **a**
dádiva /'dadʒiva/ *f* gift; (*donativo*) donation
dado /'dadu/ *m* (*de jogar*) die, dice; (*informação*) fact, piece of information; *pl* data
dador /da'dor/ *m Port* donor
daí /da'i/ *adv* (*no espaço*) from there; (*no tempo*) then; **~ por diante** from then on; **e ~?** [!] so what?
dali /da'li/ *adv* from over there
dália /'dalia/ *f* dahlia
dal|tônico /daw'toniku/ *a* colour-blind. **~tonismo** *m* colour blindness
dama /'dama/ *f* lady; (*em jogos*) queen; *pl* (*jogo*) draughts, *Amer* checkers; **~ de honra** bridesmaid
da|nado /da'nadu/ *a* damned; (*zangado*) angry; (*travesso*) naughty. **~nar-se** *vpr* get angry; **~ne-se!** [!] who cares?
dan|ça /'dãsa/ *f* dance. **~çar** *vt* dance ● *vi* dance; [!] ‹*pessoa*› miss out; ‹*coisa*› go by the board; ‹*crimonoso*› get caught. **~çarino** *m* dancer. **~ceteria** *f* discotheque
da|nificar /danifi'kar/ *vt* damage. **~ninho** *a* undesirable. **~no** *m* (*pl*) damage. **~noso** /o/ *a* damaging
dantes /'dãtʃiʃ/ *adv* formerly
daquela(s), daquele(s) = **de** + **aquela(s), aquele(s)**
daqui /da'ki/ *adv* from here; **~ a 2 dias** in 2 days(' time); **~ a pouco** in a minute; **~ em diante** from now on
daquilo = **de** + **aquilo**
dar /dar/ *vt* give; have ‹*dormida, lida etc*›; do ‹*pulo, cambalhota etc*›; cause ‹*problemas*›; produce ‹*frutas, leite*›; deal ‹*cartas*›; (*lecionar*) teach ● *vi* (*ser possível*) be possible; (*ser suficiente*) be enough; **~ com** come across; **~ em** lead to; **ele dá para ator** he'd make a good actor; **~ por** (*considerar como*) consider to be; (*reparar em*) notice. **~-se** *vpr* ‹*coisa*› happen; ‹*pessoa*› get on
dardo /'dardu/ *m* dart; (*no atletismo*) javelin
das = **de** + **as**
da|ta /'data/ *f* date; **de longa ~** long since. **~tar** *vt/i* date
dati|lografar /datʃilogra'far/ *vt/i* type. **~lografia** *f* typing. **~lógrafo** *m* typist

de /dʒi/ ● *prep*

····➤ (*matéria, conteúdo, qualidade*) of; **um jarro ~ água** a jug of water; **uma mesa ~ madeira** a wooden table; **um livro ~ grande interesse** a book of great interest

····➤ (*em descrições*) with; **a mulher ~ cabelo castanho** the woman with brown hair; **o rapaz ~ calças azuis** the boy in blue trousers; **uma camiseta ~ manga curta** a short-sleeved shirt

d

····➤ (*meio de transporte*) by; **~ avião/trem** by plane/train

····➤ (*com números e expressões de tempo*) **uma nota ~ 10 reais** a 10-real note; **~ dia** during the day

····➤ (*origem, procedência*) from; **eles são ~ São Paulo** they are from São Paulo

····➤ (*posse*) **o cachorro da Ana** Ana's dog; **a chave do carro** the car key; **as pernas da mesa** the table legs

····➤ (*série*) **~ meia em meia hora** every half hour; **~ de dois em dois metros** every two metres

····➤ (*tema, disciplina*) **um livro ~ inglês** an English book; **não entendo nada ~ motores** I don't know a thing about engines

····➤ (*indica autor*) by; **um livro ~ Machado de Assis** a book by Machado de Assis

····➤ (*causa*) **morrer ~ fome** die of hunger; **chorar ~ alegria** cry for joy

debaixo /dʒi'baʃu/ *adv* below; **~ de** under

debalde /dʒi'bawdʒi/ *adv* in vain

debandada /debã'dada/ *f* stampede

deba|te /de'batʃi/ *m* debate; **~te frente a frente** face-to-face debate. **~ter** *vt* debate. **~ter-se** *vpr* grapple

debelar /debe'lar/ *vt* overcome

dé|bil /'dɛbiw/ (*pl* **~beis**) *a* feeble; **~bil mental** retarded (person)

debili|dade /debili'dadʒi/ *f* debility. **~tar** *vt* debilitate. **~tar-se** *vpr* become debilitated

debitar /debi'tar/ *vt* debit

débito /'dɛbitu/ *m* debit

debo|chado /debo'ʃadu/ *a* sardonic. **~char** *vt* mock. **~che** /ɔ/ *m* jibe

debruar /debru'ar/ *vt/i* edge

debruçar-se /debru'sarsi/ *vpr* bend over; **~ sobre** study

debrum /de'brũ/ *m* edging

debulhar /debu'ʎar/ *vt* thresh

debu|tante /debu'tãtʃi/ *f* debutante. **~tar** *vi* debut, make one's debut

década /'dɛkada/ *f* decade; **a ~ dos 60** the sixties

deca|dência /deka'dẽsia/ *f* decadence. **~dente** *a* decadent

decair /deka'ir/ *vi* decline; (*degringolar*) go downhill; ‹*planta*› wilt

decal|car /dekaw'kar/ *vt* trace. **~que** *m* tracing

decapitar /dekapi'tar/ *vt* decapitate

decatlo /de'katlu/ *m* decathlon

de|cência /de'sẽsia/ *f* decency. **~cente** *a* decent

decepar /dese'par/ *vt* cut off

decep|ção /desep'sãw/ *f* disappointment. **~cionar** *vt* disappoint. **~cionar-se** *vpr* be disappointed

decerto /dʒi'sɛrtu/ *adv* certainly

deci|dido /desi'dʒidu/ *a* ‹*pessoa*› determined. **~dir** *vt/i* decide. **~dir-se** *vpr* make up one's mind; **~dir-se por** decide on

decíduo /de'siduu/ *a* deciduous

decifrar /desi'frar/ *vt* decipher

deci|mal /desi'maw/ (*pl* **~mais**) *a & m* decimal

décimo /'dɛsimu/ *a & m* tenth; **~ primeiro** eleventh; **~ segundo** twelfth; **~ terceiro** thirteenth; **~ quarto** fourteenth; **~ quinto** fifteenth; **~ sexto** sixteenth; **~ sétimo** seventeenth; **~ oitavo** eighteenth; **~ nono** nineteenth

deci|são /desi'zãw/ *f* decision. **~sivo** *a* decisive

decla|ração /deklara'sãw/ *f* declaration. **~rado** *a* ‹*inimigo*› sworn; ‹*crente*› avowed; ‹*ladrão*› self-confessed. **~rar** *vt* declare

decli|nação /deklina'sãw/ *f* declension. **~nar** *vt* **~nar (de)** decline ● *vi* decline; ‹*sol*› go down; ‹*chão*› slope down

declínio /de'kliniu/ *m* decline

declive /de'klivi/ *m* (downward) slope, incline

decodificar /dekodʒifi'kar/ *vt* decode

deco|lagem /deko'laʒẽ/ *f* take-off. **~lar** *vi* take off; *fig* get off the ground

decom|por /dekõ'por/ *vt* break down; contort ‹*feições*›. **~por-se** *vpr* break down; ‹*cadáver*› decompose. **~posição** *f* (*de cadáver*) decomposition

deco|ração /dekora'sãw/ *f* decoration; (*aprendizagem*) learning by heart. **~rar** *vt* (*adornar*) decorate; (*aprender*) learn by heart, memorize. **~rativo** *a* decorative. **~reba** /ɛ/ *f* [!] rote learning. **~ro** /o/ *m* decorum. **~roso** /o/ *a* decorous

decor|rência /deko'xẽsia/ *f* consequence. **~rente** *a* resulting (**de** from). **~rer** *vi* ‹*tempo*› elapse; ‹*acontecimento*› pass off; (*resultar*) result (**de** from) ● *m* **no ~rer de** in the course of; **com o ~rer do tempo** in time, with the passing of time

deco|tado /deko'tadu/ *a* low-cut. **~te** /ɔ/ *m* neckline
decrépito /de'krɛpitu/ *a* decrepit
decres|cente /dekre'sẽtʃi/ *a* decreasing. **~cer** *vi* decrease
decre|tar /dekre'tar/ *vt* decree; declare ‹*estado de sítio*›. **~to** /ɛ/ *m* decree. **~to-lei** *m* act
decurso /de'kursu/ *m* course
de|dal /de'daw/ (*pl* **~dais**) *m* thimble. **~dão** *m* (*da mão*) thumb; (*do pé*) big toe
dedetizar /dedetʃi'zar/ *vt* spray with insecticide
dedi|cação /dedʒika'sãw/ *f* dedication. **~car** *vt* dedicate; devote ‹*tempo*›. **~car-se** *vpr* dedicate o.s. (**a** to). **~catória** *f* dedication
dedilhar /dedʒi'ʎar/ *vt* pluck
dedo /'dedu/ *m* finger; (*do pé*) toe; **cheio de ~s** all fingers and thumbs; (*sem graça*) awkward. **~-duro** (*pl* **~s-duros**) *m* sneak; (*político, criminoso*) informer
dedução /dedu'sãw/ *f* deduction
dedurar /dedu'rar/ *vt* sneak on; (*à polícia*) inform on
dedu|tivo /dedu'tʃivu/ *a* deductive. **~zir** *vt* (*descontar*) deduct; (*concluir*) deduce
defa|sado /defa'zadu/ *a* out of step. **~sagem** *f* gap, lag
defecar /defe'kar/ *vi* defecate
defei|to /de'fejtu/ *m* defect; **botar ~to em** find fault with. **~tuoso** /o/ *a* defective
defen|der /defẽ'der/ *vt* defend. **~der-se** *vpr* (*virar-se*) fend for o.s.; (*contra-atacar*) defend o.s. (**de** against). **~siva** *f* **na ~siva** on the defensive. **~sor** *m* defender; (*advogado*) defence counsel
defe|rência /defe'rẽsia/ *f* deference. **~rente** *a* deferential
defesa /de'feza/ *f* defence ● *m* defender
defici|ência /defisi'ẽsia/ *f* deficiency. **~ente** *a* deficient; (*física ou mentalmente*) handicapped ● *m/f* handicapped person
déficit /'dɛfisitʃi/ (*pl* **~s**) *m* deficit
deficitário /defisitʃi'ariu/ *a* in deficit; ‹*empresa*› loss-making
definhar /defi'ɲar/ *vi* waste away; ‹*planta*› wither
defi|nição /defini'sãw/ *f* definition. **~nir** *vt* define. **~nir-se** *vpr* (*descrever-se*) define o.s.; (*decidir-se*) come to a decision; (*explicar-se*) make one's position clear. **~nitivo** *a* definitive. **~nível** (*pl* **~níveis**) *a* definable
defla|ção /defla'sãw/ *f* deflation. **~cionário** *a* deflationary
deflagrar /defla'grar/ *vt* set off ● *vi* break out
defor|mar /defor'mar/ *vt* misshape; deform ‹*corpo*›; distort ‹*imagem*›. **~midade** *f* deformity
defraudar /defraw'dar/ *vt* defraud (**de** of)
defron|tar /defrõ'tar/ *vt* **~tar com** face. **~te** *adv* opposite; **~te de** opposite
defumar /defu'mar/ *vt* smoke
defunto /de'fũtu/ *a & m* deceased
dege|lar /deʒe'lar/ *vt/i* thaw. **~lo** /e/ *m* thaw
degeneração /deʒenera'sãw/ *f* degeneration
degenerar /deʒene'rar/ *vi* degenerate (**em** into)
degolar /dego'lar/ *vt* cut the throat of
degra|dação /degrada'sãw/ *f* degradation. **~dante** *a* degrading. **~dar** *vt* degrade
degrau /de'graw/ *m* step
degringolar /degrĩgo'lar/ *vi* deteriorate, go downhill
degustar /degus'tar/ *vt* taste
dei|tada /dej'tada/ *f* lie-down. **~tado** *a* lying down; (*dormindo*) in bed; [!] (*preguiçoso*) idle. **~tar** *vt* lay down; (*na cama*) put to bed; (*pôr*) put; *Port* (*jogar*) throw ● *vi*, **~tar-se** *vpr* lie down; (*ir para cama*) go to bed
dei|xa /'deʃa/ *f* cue. **~xar** *vt* leave; (*permitir*) let; **~xar de** (*parar*) stop; (*omitir*) fail; **não pôde ~xar de rir** he couldn't help laughing; **~xar alguém nervoso** make sb annoyed; **~xar cair** drop; **~xar a desejar** leave a lot to be desired; **~xa (para lá)** [!] never mind, forget it
dela(s) = **de** + **ela(s)**
delatar /dela'tar/ *vt* report
délavé /dela've/ *a invar* faded
dele(s) = **de** + **ele(s)**
dele|gação /delega'sãw/ *f* delegation; **~gação de autoridade** *Com* empowerment. **~gacia** *f* police station. **~gado** *m* delegate; **~gado de polícia** police chief. **~gar** *vt* delegate
delei|tar /delej'tar/ *vt* delight. **~tar-se** *vpr* delight (**com** in). **~te** *m* delight. **~toso** /o/ *a* delightful
delgado /dew'gadu/ *a* slender

d

delibe|ração /delibera'sãw/ *f* deliberation. **~rar** *vt/i* deliberate
delica|deza /delika'deza/ *f* delicacy; (*cortesia*) politeness. **~do** *a* delicate; (*cortês*) polite
delícia /de'lisia/ *f* delight; **ser uma ~** ‹*comida*› be delicious; ‹*sol etc*› be lovely
d **delici|ar** /delisi'ar/ *vt* delight; **~ar-se** delight (**com** in). **~oso** /o/ *a* delightful, lovely; ‹*comida*› delicious
deline|ador /delinia'dor/ *m* eyeliner. **~ar** *vt* outline
delin|quência /delĩ'kwẽsia/ *f* delinquency. **~quente** *a & m* delinquent
deli|rante /deli'rãtʃi/ *a* rapturous; *Med* delirious. **~rar** *vi* go into raptures; ‹*doente*› be delirious
delírio /de'liriu/ *m* (*febre*) delirium; (*excitação*) raptures
delito /de'litu/ *m* crime
delonga /de'lõga/ *f* delay
delta /'dɛwta/ *m* delta
dema|gogia /demago'ʒia/ *f* demagogy. **~gógico** *a* demagogic. **~gogo** /o/ *m* demagogue
demais /dʒi'majs/ *a & adv* (*muito*) very much; (*em demasia*) too much; **os ~** the rest, the others; **é ~!** [!] it's great!
deman|da /de'mãda/ *f* demand; *Jurid* action. **~dar** *vt* sue
demão /de'mãw/ *f* coat
demar|car /demar'kar/ *vt* demarcate. **~catório** *a* demarcation
demasia /dema'zia/ *f* excess; **em ~** too (much, many)
de|mência /de'mẽsia/ *f* insanity; *Med* dementia. **~mente** *a* insane; *Med* demented
demissão /demi'sãw/ *f* sacking, dismissal; **pedir ~** resign
demitir /demi'tʃir/ *vt* sack, dismiss. **~-se** *vpr* resign
demo|cracia /demokra'sia/ *f* democracy. **~crata** *m/f* democrat. **~crático** *a* democratic. **~cratizar** *vt* democratize. **~grafia** *f* demography. **~gráfico** *a* demographic
demo|lição /demoli'sãw/ *f* demolition. **~lir** *vt* demolish
demônio /de'moniu/ *m* demon
demons|tração /demõstra'sãw/ *f* demonstration. **~trar** *vt* demonstrate. **~trativo** *a* demonstrative
demo|ra /de'mɔra/ *f* delay. **~rado** *a* lengthy. **~rar** *vi* (*levar*) take; (*tardar a voltar, terminar etc*) be long; (*levar muito tempo*) take a long time ● *vt* delay
dendê /dẽ'de/ *m* (*óleo*) palm oil
denegrir /dene'grir/ *vt* denigrate
dengoso /dẽ'gozu/ *a* coy
dengue /'dẽgi/ *m* dengue
denomi|nação /denomina'sãw/ *f* denomination. **~nar** *vt* name
denotar /deno'tar/ *vt* denote
den|sidade /dẽsi'dadʒi/ *f* density. **~so** *a* dense
den|tado /dẽ'tadu/ *a* serrated. **~tadura** *f* (set of) teeth; (*postiça*) dentures, false teeth. **~tal** (*pl* **~tais**) *a* dental. **~tário** *a* dental. **~te** *m* tooth; (*de alho*) clove; **~te do siso** wisdom tooth. **~tição** *f* teething; (*dentadura*) teeth. **~tífrico** *m* toothpaste. **~tista** *m/f* dentist
dentre =DE + ENTRE
dentro /'dẽtru/ *adv* inside; **lá ~** in there; **por ~** on the inside; **~ de** inside; (*tempo*) within
dentu|ça /dẽ'tusa/ *f* buck teeth. **~ço** *a* with buck teeth
denúncia /de'nũsia/ *f* (*à polícia etc*) report; (*na imprensa etc*) disclosure
denunciar /denũsi'ar/ *vt* (*à polícia etc*) report; (*na imprensa etc*) denounce
deparar /depa'rar/ *vi* **~ com** come across
departamento /departa'mẽtu/ *m* department
depauperar /depawpe'rar/ *vt* impoverish
depenar /depe'nar/ *vt* pluck ‹*aves*›; (*roubar*) fleece
depen|dência /depẽ'dẽsia/ *f* dependence; *pl* premises. **~dente** *a* dependent (**de** on) ● *m/f* dependant. **~der** *vi* depend (**de** on)
depi|lação /depila'sãw/ *f* depilation. **~lar** *vt* depilate. **~latório** *m* depilatory cream
deplo|rar /deplo'rar/ *vt* deplore. **~rável** (*pl* **~ráveis**) *a* deplorable
de|poente /depo'ẽtʃi/ *m/f* witness. **~poimento** *m* (*à polícia*) statement; (*na justiça*) *fig* testimony
depois /de'pojs/ *adv* after(wards); **~ de** after; **~ que** after
depor /de'por/ *vi* (*na polícia*) make a statement; (*na justiça*) give evidence, testify ● *vt* lay down ‹*armas*›; depose ‹*rei, presidente*›
depor|tação /deporta'sãw/ *f* deportation. **~tar** *vt* deport

deposi|tante /depozi'tãtʃi/ *m/f* depositor. **~tar** *vt* deposit; cast ‹*voto*›; place ‹*confiança*›

depósito /de'pɔzitu/ *m* deposit; (*armazém*) warehouse

depra|vação /deprava'sãw/ *f* depravity. **~vado** *a* depraved. **~var** *vt* deprave

depre|ciação /depresia'sãw/ *f* (*perda de valor*) depreciation; (*menosprezo*) deprecation. **~ciar** *vt* (*desvalorizar*) devalue; (*menosprezar*) deprecate. **~ciar-se** *vpr* ‹*bens*› depreciate; ‹*pessoa*› deprecate o.s.. **~ciativo** *a* deprecatory

depre|dação /depreda'sãw/ *f* depredation. **~dar** *vt* wreck

depressa /dʒi'prɛsa/ *adv* fast, quickly

depres|são /depre'sãw/ *f* depression. **~sivo** *a* depressive

depri|mente /depri'mẽtʃi/ *a* depressing. **~mido** *a* depressed. **~mir** *vt* depress. **~mir-se** *vpr* get depressed

depurar /depu'rar/ *vt* purify

depu|tação /deputa'sãw/ *f* deputation. **~tado** *m* deputy, MP, *Amer* congressman (*f* -woman). **~tar** *vt* delegate

deque /'dɛki/ *m* (sun)deck

deri|va /de'riva/ *f* **à ~va** adrift; **andar à ~va** drift. **~vação** *f* derivation. **~var** *vt* derive; (*desviar*) divert ● *vi*, **~var-se** *vpr* derive, be derived (**de** from); ‹*navio*› drift

dermatolo|gia /dermatolo'ʒia/ *f* dermatology. **~gista** *m/f* dermatologist

derradeiro /dexa'deru/ *a* last, final

derra|mamento /dexama'mẽtu/ *m* spill, spillage; **~mamento de sangue** bloodshed. **~mar** *vt* spill; shed ‹*lágrimas*›. **~mar-se** *vpr* spill. **~me** *m* spill, spillage; **~me cerebral** stroke

derra|pagem /dexa'paʒẽ/ *f* skidding; (*uma*) skid. **~par** *vi* skid

derreter /dexe'ter/ *vt* melt. **~-se** *vpr* melt

derro|ta /de'xɔta/ *f* defeat. **~tar** *vt* defeat. **~tismo** *m* defeatism. **~tista** *a & m/f* defeatist

derrubar /dexu'bar/ *vt* knock down; bring down ‹*governo*›

desaba|far /dʒizaba'far/ *vi* speak one's mind. **~fo** *m* outburst

desa|bamento /dʒizaba'mẽtu/ *m* collapse. **~bar** *vi* collapse; ‹*chuva*› pour down

desabotoar /dʒizaboto'ar/ *vt* unbutton

desabri|gado /dʒizabri'gadu/ *a* homeless. **~gar** *vt* make homeless

desabrochar /dʒizabro'ʃar/ *vi* blossom, bloom

desaca|tar /dʒizaka'tar/ *vt* defy. **~to** *m* (*de pessoa*) disrespect; (*da lei etc*) disregard

desacerto /dʒiza'sertu/ *m* mistake

desacompanhado /dʒizakõpa'ɲadu/ *a* unaccompanied

desaconse|lhar /dʒizakõse'ʎar/ *vt* advise against. **~lhável** (*pl* **~lháveis**) *a* inadvisable

desacor|dado /dʒizakor'dadu/ *a* unconscious. **~do** /o/ *m* disagreement

desacostu|mado /dʒizakostu'madu/ *a* unaccustomed. **~mar** *vt* **~mar alguém de** break sb of the habit of; **~mar-se de** get out of the habit of

desacreditar /dʒizakredʒi'tar/ *vt* discredit

desafeto /dʒiza'fɛtu/ *m* disaffection

desafi|ador /dʒizafia'dor/ *a* ‹*tarefa*› challenging; ‹*pessoa*› defiant. **~ar** *vt* challenge; (*fazer face a*) defy ‹*perigo, morte*›

desafi|nado /dʒizafi'nadu/ *a* out of tune. **~nar** *vi* (*cantando*) sing out of tune; (*tocando*) play out of tune ● *vt* put out of tune

desafio /dʒiza'fiu/ *m* challenge

desafivelar /dʒizafive'lar/ *vt* unbuckle

desafo|gar /dʒizafo'gar/ *vt* vent; (*desapertar*) relieve. **~gar-se** *vpr* give vent to one's feelings. **~go** /o/ *m* (*alívio*) relief

desafo|rado /dʒizafo'radu/ *a* cheeky. **~ro** /o/ *m* cheek; (*um*) liberty

desafortunado /dʒizafortu'nadu/ *a* unfortunate

desagra|dar /dʒizagra'dar/ *vt* displease. **~dável** (*pl* **~dáveis**) *a* unpleasant. **~do** *m* displeasure

desagravo *m* redress, amends

desagregar /dʒizagre'gar/ *vt* split up. **~-se** *vpr* split up

desaguar /dʒiza'gwar/ *vt* drain ● *vi* ‹*rio*› flow (**em** into)

desajeitado /dʒizaʒej'tadu/ *a* clumsy

desajuizado /dʒizaʒui'zadu/ *a* foolish

desajus|tado /dʒizaʒus'tadu/ *a* *Psic* maladjusted. **~te** *m* *Psic* maladjustment

d

desalen|tar /dʒizalẽ'tar/ *vt* dishearten. **~tar-se** *vpr* get disheartened. **~to** *m* discouragement

desali|nhado /dʒizali'ɲadu/ *a* untidy. **~nho** *m* untidiness

desalojar /dʒizalo'ʒar/ *vt* turn out ‹*inquilino*›; flush out ‹*inimigo, ladrões*›

desamarrar /dʒizama'xar/ *vt* untie ● *vi* cast off

desamarrotar /dʒizamaxo'tar/ *vt* smooth out

desamassar /dʒizama'sar/ *vt* smooth out

desambientado /dʒizãbiẽ'tadu/ *a* unsettled

desampa|rar /dʒizãpa'rar/ *vt* abandon. **~ro** *m* abandonment

desandar /dʒizã'dar/ *vi* ‹*molho*› separate; **~ a** start to

de|sanimar /dʒizani'mar/ *vt* discourage ● *vi* ‹*pessoa*› lose heart; ‹*fato*› be discouraging. **~sânimo** *m* discouragement

desapaixonado /dʒizapaʃo'nadu/ *a* dispassionate

desaparafusar /dʒizaparafu'zar/ *vt* unscrew

desapare|cer /dʒizapare'ser/ *vi* disappear. **~cimento** *m* disappearance

desapego /dʒiza'pegu/ *m* detachment; (*indiferença*) indifference

desapercebido /dʒizaperse'bidu/ *a* unnoticed

desapertar /dʒizaper'tar/ *vt* loosen

desapon|tamento /dʒizapõta'mẽtu/ *m* disappointment. **~tar** *vt* disappoint

desapropriar /dʒizapropri'ar/ *vt* expropriate

desapro|vação /dʒizaprova'sãw/ *f* disapproval. **~var** *vt* disapprove of

desaproveitado /dʒizaprovej-'tadu/ *a* wasted

desar|mamento /dʒizarma'mẽtu/ *m* disarmament. **~mar** *vt* disarm; take down ‹*barraca*›

desarran|jar /dʒizaxã'ʒar/ *vt* mess up; upset ‹*estômago*›. **~jo** *m* mess; (*do estômago*) upset

desarregaçar /dʒizaxega'sar/ *vt* roll down

desarru|mado /dʒizaxu'madu/ *a* untidy. **~mar** *vt* untidy; unpack ‹*mala*›

desarticular /dʒizartʃiku'lar/ *vt* dislocate

desarvorado /dʒizarvo'radu/ *a* disoriented, at a loss

desassociar /dʒizasosi'ar/ *vt* disassociate. **~-se** *vpr* disassociate o.s.

desas|trado /dʒizas'tradu/ *a* accident-prone. **~tre** *m* disaster. **~troso** /o/ *a* disastrous

desatar /dʒiza'tar/ *vt* untie; **~ a chorar** dissolve in tears

desatarraxar /dʒizataxa'ʃar/ *vt* unscrew

desaten|cioso /dʒizatẽsi'ozu/ *a* inattentive. **~to** *a* oblivious (**a** to)

desati|nar /dʒizatʃi'nar/ *vt* bewilder ● *vi* not think straight. **~no** *m* mental aberration, bewilderment; (*um*) folly

desativar /dʒizatʃi'var/ *vt* deactivate; shut down ‹*fábrica*›

desatrelar /dʒizatre'lar/ *vt* unhitch

desatualizado /dʒizatuali'zadu/ *a* out-of-date

desavença /dʒiza'vẽsa/ *f* dispute

desavergonhado /dʒizavergo'ɲadu/ *a* shameless

desbancar /dʒizbã'kar/ *vt* outdo

desbaratar /dʒizbara'tar/ *vt* (*desperdiçar*) waste

desbocado /dʒizbo'kadu/ *a* outspoken

desbotar /dʒizbo'tar/ *vt/i* fade

desbra|vador /dʒizbrava'dor/ *m* explorer. **~var** *vt* explore

desbun|dante /dʒizbũ'dãtʃi/ *a* [!] mind-blowing. **~dar** *vt* [!] blow the mind of ● *vi* [!] flip, freak out. **~de** *m* [!] knockout

descabido /dʒiska'bidu/ *a* inappropriate

descafeinado /dʒiskafej'nadu/ *a* decaffeinated

descalabro /dʒiska'labru/ *m* debacle

descalço /dʒis'kawsu/ *a* barefoot

descambar /dʒiskã'bar/ *vi* deteriorate, degenerate

descan|sar /dʒiskã'sar/ *vt/i* rest. **~so** *m* rest; (*de prato, copo*) mat

descapotável /dʒiskapu'tavɛɫ/ *a & m* *Port* convertible

desca|rado /dʒiska'radu/ *a* blatant. **~ramento** *m* cheek

descarga /dʒis'karga/ *f Eletr* discharge; (*da privada*) flush; **dar ~** flush (the toilet)

descarregar /dʒiskaxe'gar/ *vt* unload ‹*mercadorias*›; discharge ‹*poluentes*›; vent ‹*raiva*› ● *vi* ‹*bateria*› go flat; **~ em**

cima de alguém take it out on sb

descarrilhar /dʒiskaxi'ʎar/ *vt/i* derail

descar|tar /dʒiskar'tar/ *vt* discard. **~tável** (*pl* **~táveis**) *a* disposable

descascar /dʒiskas'kar/ *vt* peel ‹*frutas, batatas*›; shell ‹*nozes*› ● *vi* ‹*pessoa, pele*› peel

descaso /dʒis'kazu/ *m* indifference

descen|dência /desẽ'dẽsia/ *f* descent. **~dente** *a* descended ● *m/f* descendant. **~der** *vi* descend (**de** from)

descentralizar /dʒisẽtrali'zar/ *vt* decentralize

des|cer /de'ser/ *vi* go down; ‹*avião*› descend; (*do ônibus, trem*) get off; (*do carro*) get out ● *vt* go down ‹*escada, ladeira*›; scroll down ‹*página*›. **~cida** *f* descent

desclassificar /dʒisklasifi'kar/ *vt* disqualify

desco|berta /dʒisko'bɛrta/ *f* discovery. **~berto** /ɛ/ *a* uncovered; ‹*conta*› overdrawn; **a ~berto** overdrawn. **~bridor** *m* discoverer. **~brimento** *m* discovery. **~brir** *vt* discover; (*expor*) uncover

> *i* **Descobrimentos** The term *Descobrimentos* refers to the Age of Discovery in the 15th and 16th centuries, during which the Portuguese engaged in extensive maritime travels in search of new trade routes with the New World. Significant events include the route charted round Africa to India by Vasco da Gama in 1498, and the discovery of Brazil by Pedro Álvares Cabral in 1500.

descolar /dʒisko'lar/ *vt* unstick; ! (*dar*) give; (*arranjar*) get hold of, rustle up; *Port* ‹*avião*› take off

descom|por /dʒiskõ'por/ *vt* (*censurar*) scold. **~-se** *vpr* ‹*pessoa*› lose one's composure. **~postura** *f* (*estado*) loss of composure; (*censura*) talking-to

descomprometido /dʒiskõprome'tʃidu/ *a* free

descomu|nal /dʒiskomu'naw/ (*pl* **~nais**) *a* extraordinary; (*grande*) huge

desconcentrar /dʒiskõsẽ'trar/ *vt* distract

desconcer|tante /dʒiskõser'tãtʃi/ *a* disconcerting. **~tar** *vt* disconcert

desconexo /dʒisko'nɛksu/ *a* incoherent

desconfi|ado /dʒiskõfi'adu/ *a* suspicious. **~ança** *f* mistrust. **~ar** *vi* suspect

desconfor|tável /dʒiskõfor'tavew/ (*pl* **~táveis**) *a* uncomfortable. **~to** /o/ *m* discomfort

descongelar /dʒiskõʒe'lar/ *vt* defrost ‹*geladeira*›; thaw ‹*comida*›

descongestio|nante /dʒiskõʒestʃio'nãtʃi/ *a & m* decongestant. **~nar** *vt* decongest

desconhe|cer /dʒiskoɲe'ser/ *vt* not know. **~cido** *a* unknown ● *m* stranger

desconsiderar /dʒiskõside'rar/ *vt* ignore

desconsolado /dʒiskõso'ladu/ *a* disconsolate

descontar /dʒiskõ'tar/ *vt* deduct; (*não levar em conta*) discount

desconten|tamento /dʒiskõtẽta'mẽtu/ *m* discontent. **~te** *a* discontent

descontinuado /dʒiskõti'nwadu/ *a* discontinued

desconto /dʒis'kõtu/ *m* discount; **dar um ~** *fig* make allowances

descontra|ção /dʒiskõtra'sãw/ *f* informality. **~ído** *a* informal, casual. **~ir** *vt* relax. **~ir-se** *vpr* relax

descontro|lar-se /dʒiskõtro'larsi/ *vpr* ‹*pessoa*› lose control; ‹*coisa*› go out of control. **~le** /o/ *m* lack of control

desconversar /dʒiskõver'sar/ *vi* change the subject

descortesia /dʒiskorte'zia/ *f* rudeness

descostu|rar /dʒiskostu'rar/ *vt* unrip. **~rar-se** *vpr* come undone

descrédito /dʒis'krɛdʒitu/ *m* discredit

descren|ça /dʒis'krẽsa/ *f* disbelief. **~te** *a* sceptical, disbelieving

des|crever /dʒiskre'ver/ *vt* describe. **~crição** *f* description. **~critivo** *a* descriptive

descui|dado /dʒiskui'dadu/ *a* careless. **~dar** *vt* neglect. **~do** *m* carelessness; (*um*) oversight

descul|pa /dʒis'kuwpa/ *f* excuse; **pedir ~pas** apologize. **~par** *vt* excuse; **~pe!** sorry!. **~par-se** *vpr* apologize. **~pável** (*pl* **~páveis**) *a* excusable

> **desde** /'dezdʒi/ ● *prep*
>
> ····➤ since; **moro aqui ~ 2008** I have lived here since 2008
>
> ····➤ (*em expressões*) **~ ... até ...** from ... to ...; **~ junho até agosto** from June to August; **a loja vende tudo, ~ roupas até livros** the shop sells

d

everything, from clothes to books; **~ que** as long as; **~ que você me informe** as long as you let me know

des|dém /dez'dẽj/ *m* disdain. **~denhar** *vt* disdain. **~denhoso** /o/ *a* disdainful

desdentado /dʒizdẽ'tadu/ *a* toothless

desdita /dʒiz'dʒita/ *f* unhappiness

desdizer /dʒizdʒi'zer/ *vt* take back, withdraw ● *vi* take back what one said

desdo|bramento /dʒizdobra'mẽtu/ *m* implication. **~brar** *vt* (*abrir*) unfold; break down ‹*dados, contas*›. **~brar-se** *vpr* unfold; (*empenhar-se*) go to a lot of trouble, bend over backwards

dese|jar /deze'ʒar/ *vt* want; (*apaixonadamente*) desire; **~jar algo a alguém** wish sb sth. **~jável** (*pl* **~jáveis**) *a* desirable. **~jo** /e/ *m* wish; (*forte*) desire. **~joso** /o/ *a* desirous

deselegante /dʒizele'gãtʃi/ *a* inelegant

desemaranhar /dʒizemara'ɲar/ *vt* untangle

desembara|çado /dʒizĩbara'sadu/ *a* ‹*pessoa*› confident, nonchalant. **~çar-se** *vpr* rid o.s. (**de** of). **~ço** *m* confidence, ease

desembar|car /dʒizĩbar'kar/ *vt/i* disembark. **~que** *m* disembarkation; (*seção do aeroporto*) arrivals

desembocar /dʒizĩbo'kar/ *vi* flow

desembol|sar /dʒizĩbow'sar/ *vt* spend, pay out. **~so** /o/ *m* expenditure

desembrulhar /dʒizĩbru'ʎar/ *vt* unwrap

desembuchar /dʒizĩbu'ʃar/ *vi* [!](*desabafar*) get things off one's chest; (*falar logo*) spit it out

desempacotar /dʒizĩpako'tar/ *vt* unpack

desempatar /dʒizĩpa'tar/ *vt* decide ‹*jogo*›

desempe|nhar /dʒizĩpe'ɲar/ *vt* perform; play ‹*papel*›. **~nho** *m* performance

desempre|gado /dʒizĩpre'gadu/ *a* unemployed. **~go** /e/ *m* unemployment

desencadear /dʒizĩkadʒi'ar/ *vt* set off, trigger

desencaminhar /dʒizĩkami'ɲar/ *vt* lead astray; embezzle ‹*dinheiro*›

desencantar /dʒizĩkã'tar/ *vt* disenchant

desencon|trar-se /dʒizĩkõ'trarsi/ *vpr* miss each other, fail to meet. **~tro** *m* failure to meet

desencorajar /dʒizĩkora'ʒar/ *vt* discourage

desenferrujar /dʒizĩfexu'ʒar/ *vt* derust ‹*metal*›; stretch ‹*pernas*›; brush up ‹*língua*›

desenfreado /dʒizĩfri'adu/ *a* unbridled

desenganar /dʒizĩga'nar/ *vt* disabuse; declare incurable ‹*doente*›

desengonçado /dʒizĩgõ'sadu/ *a* ‹*pessoa*› ungainly

desengre|nado /dʒizĩgre'nadu/ *a* ‹*carro*› in neutral. **~nar** *vt* put in neutral ‹*carro*›; (*tecn*) disengage

dese|nhar /deze'ɲar/ *vt* draw. **~nhista** *m/f* drawer; (*industrial*) designer. **~nho** /e/ *m* drawing

desenlace /dʒizĩ'lasi/ *m* dénouement, outcome

desenrascar-se /dizẽxaʃ'karsi/ *vpr* *Port* to get by

desenredar /dʒizĩxe'dar/ *vt* unravel

desenrolar /dʒizĩxo'lar/ *vt* unroll ‹*rolo*›

desenten|der /dʒizĩtẽ'der/ *vt* misunderstand. **~der-se** *vpr* (*não se dar bem*) not get on. **~dimento** *m* misunderstanding

desenterrar /dʒizĩte'xar/ *vt* dig up ‹*cadáver*›; unearth ‹*informação*›

desentortar /dʒizĩtor'tar/ *vt* straighten out

desentupir /dʒizĩtu'pir/ *vt* unblock

desenvol|to /dʒizĩ'vowtu/ *a* casual, nonchalant. **~tura** *f* casualness, nonchalance; **com ~tura** nonchalantly. **~ver** *vt* develop. **~ver-se** *vpr* develop. **~vimento** *m* development

desequi|librado *a* unbalanced. **~librar** *vt* unbalance. **~librar-se** *vpr* become unbalanced. **~líbrio** *m* imbalance

deser|ção /dezer'sãw/ *f* desertion. **~tar** *vt/i* desert. **~to** /ɛ/ *a* deserted; **ilha ~ta** desert island ● *m* desert. **~tor** *m* deserter

desespe|rado /dʒizispe'radu/ *a* desperate. **~rador** *a* hopeless. **~rar** *vt* (*desesperançar*) make despair ● *vi*, **~rar-se** *vpr* despair. **~ro** /e/ *m* despair

desestabilizar /dʒizistabili'zar/ *vt* destabilize

desestimular /dʒizistʃimu'lar/ *vt* discourage

desfal|car /dʒisfaw'kar/ *vt* embezzle. **~que** *m* embezzlement

desfa|lecer /dʒisfale'ser/ *vt* (*desmaiar*) faint. **~lecimento** *m* faint

desfavor /dʒisfa'vor/ *m* disfavour

desfavo|rável /dʒisfavo'ravew/ (*pl* **~ráveis**) *a* unfavourable. **~recer** *vt* be unfavourable to; treat less favourably ‹*minorias etc*›

desfazer /dʒisfa'zer/ *vt* undo; unpack ‹*mala*›; strip ‹*cama*›; break ‹*contrato*›; clear up ‹*mistério*›. **~-se** *vpr* come undone; ‹*casamento*› break up; ‹*sonhos*› crumble; **~-se em lágrimas** dissolve into tears

desfe|char /dʒisfe'ʃar/ *vt* throw ‹*murro, olhar*›. **~cho** /e/ *m* outcome, dénouement

desfeita /dʒis'fejta/ *f* slight, insult

desferir /dʒisfe'rir/ *vt* give ‹*pontapé*›; launch ‹*ataque*›; fire ‹*flecha*›

desfiar /dʒisfi'ar/ *vt* pick the meat off ‹*frango*›. **~-se** *vpr* ‹*tecido*› fray

desfigurar /dʒisfigu'rar/ *vt* disfigure; *fig* distort

desfi|ladeiro /dʒisfila'deru/ *m* pass. **~lar** *vi* parade. **~le** *m* parade; **~le de modas** fashion show

desflorestamento /dʒisfloresta'mẽtu/ *m* deforestation

desforra /dʒis'fɔxa/ *f* revenge

desfraldar /dʒisfraw'dar/ *vt* unfurl

desfrutar /dʒisfru'tar/ *vt* enjoy

desgas|tante /dʒizgas'tãtʃi/ *a* wearing, stressful. **~tar** *vt* wear out. **~te** *m* (*de máquina etc*) wear and tear; (*de pessoa*) stress and strain

desgosto /dʒiz'gostu/ *m* sorrow

desgovernar-se /dʒizgover'narsi/ *vpr* go out of control

desgraça /dʒiz'grasa/ *f* misfortune. **~do** *a* wretched ● *m* wretch

desgravar /dʒizgra'var/ *vt* erase

desgrenhado /dʒizgre'ɲadu/ *a* unkempt

desgrudar /dʒizgru'dar/ *vt* unstick. **~-se** *vpr* ‹*pessoa*› tear o.s. away

desidra|tação /dʒizidrata'sãw/ *f* dehydration. **~tar** *vt* dehydrate

desig|nação /dezigna'sãw/ *f* designation. **~nar** *vt* designate

desi|gual /dʒizi'gwaw/ (*pl* **~guais**) *a* unequal; ‹*terreno*› uneven. **~gualdade** *f* inequality; (*de terreno*) unevenness

desilu|dir /dʒizilu'dʒir/ *vt* disillusion. **~são** *f* disillusionment

desinfe|tante /dʒizĩfe'tãtʃi/ *a & m* disinfectant. **~tar** *vt* disinfect

desinibido /dʒizini'bidu/ *a* uninhibited

desintegrar-se /dʒizĩte'grarsi/ *vpr* disintegrate

desinteres|sado /dʒizĩtere'sadu/ *a* uninterested. **~sante** *a* uninteresting. **~sar-se** *vpr* lose interest (**de** in). **~se** /e/ *m* disinterest

d

desintoxicação /dʒizĩtoksika'sãw/ *f* rehabilitation; **clínica de ~** rehabilitation centre

desis|tência /dezis'tẽsia/ *f* giving up. **~tir** *vt/i* **~tir (de)** give up

desle|al /dʒizle'aw/ (*pl* **~ais**) *a* disloyal. **~aldade** *f* disloyalty

deslei|xado /dʒizle'ʃadu/ *a* sloppy; (*no vestir*) scruffy. **~xo** *m* carelessness; (*no vestir*) scruffiness

desli|gado /dʒizli'gadu/ *a* ‹*luz, TV*› off; ‹*pessoa*› absent-minded. **~gar** *vt* turn off ‹*luz, TV, motor*›; hang up, put down ‹*telefone*› ● *vi* (*ao telefonar*) hang up, put the phone down

deslindar /dʒizlĩ'dar/ *vt* clear up, solve

desli|zante /dʒizli'zãtʃi/ *a* slippery; ‹*inflação*› creeping. **~zar** *vi* slip. **~zar-se** *vpr* creep. **~ze** *m* slip; *fig* (*erro*) slip-up

deslo|cado /dʒizlo'kadu/ *a* ‹*membro*› dislocated; *fig* out of place. **~calizar** /dʒizlokali'zar/ *vt Port* ‹*fábricas, empresas*› relocate. **~car** /dʒizlo'kar/ *vt* move; *Med* dislocate ‹*fábricas, empresas*› relocate. **~car-se** *vpr* move

deslum|brado /dʒizlũ'bradu/ *a fig* starry-eyed. **~bramento** *m fig* wonderment. **~brante** *a* dazzling. **~brar** *vt* dazzle. **~brar-se** *vpr fig* be dazzled

desmai|ado /dʒizmaj'adu/ *a* unconscious. **~ar** *vi* faint. **~o** *m* faint

desman|cha-prazeres /dʒizmãʃapra'zeris/ *m/f invar* spoilsport. **~char** *vt* break up; break off ‹*noivado*›; shatter ‹*sonhos*›. **~char-se** *vpr* break up; (*no ar, na água, em lágrimas*) dissolve

desmantelar /dʒizmãte'lar/ *vt* dismantle

desmarcar /dʒizmar'kar/ *vt* cancel ‹*encontro*›

desmascarar /dʒizmaske'rar/ *vt* unmask

desma|tamento /dʒizmata'mẽtu/ *m* deforestation. **~tar** *vt* clear (of forest)

desmedido /dʒizme'didu/ *a* excessive

desmemoriado /dʒizmemori'adu/ *a* forgetful

desmen|tido /dʒizmẽ'tʃidu/ *m* denial. **~tir** *vt* deny

d

desmiolado /dʒizmio'ladu/ *a* brainless

desmontar /dʒizmõ'tar/ *vt* dismantle

desmorali|zante /dʒizmorali'zãtʃi/ *a* demoralizing. **~zar** *vt* demoralize

desmoro|namento /dʒizmorona'mẽtu/ *m* collapse. **~nar** *vt* destroy. **~nar-se** *vpr* collapse

desnatar /dʒizna'tar/ *vi* skim ‹*leite*›

desnecessário /dʒiznese'sariu/ *a* unnecessary

desní|vel /dʒiz'nivew/ (*pl* **~veis**) *m* difference in height

desnortear /dʒiznortʃi'ar/ *vt* disorientate, *Amer* disorient

desnutrição /dʒiznutri'sãw/ *f* malnutrition

desobe|decer /dʒizobede'ser/ *vt/i* **~decer (a)** disobey. **~diência** *f* disobedience. **~diente** *a* disobedient

desobrigar /dʒizobri'gar/ *vt* release (**de** from)

desobstruir /dʒizobistru'ir/ *vt* unblock; empty ‹*casa*›

desocupado /dʒizoku'padu/ *a* unoccupied

desodorante /dʒizodo'rãtʃi/ *m*, *Port* **desodorizante** /dʒizoduri'zãtʃi/ *m* deodorant

deso|lação /dezola'sãw/ *f* desolation. **~lado** *a* ‹*lugar*› desolate; ‹*pessoa*› desolated. **~lar** *vt* desolate

desones|tidade /dʒizonestʃi'dadʒi/ *f* dishonesty. **~to** /ɛ/ *a* dishonest

deson|ra /dʒi'zõxa/ *f* dishonour. **~rar** *vt* dishonour. **~roso** /o/ *a* dishonourable

desor|deiro /dʒizor'deru/ *a* troublemaking ● *m* troublemaker. **~dem** *f* disorder. **~denado** *a* disorganized; ‹*vida*› disordered. **~denar** *vt* disorganize

desorgani|zação /dʒizorganiza'sãw/ *f* disorganization. **~zar** *vt* disorganize. **~zar-se** *vpr* get disorganized

desorientar /dʒizoriẽ'tar/ *vt* disorientate; *Amer* disorient

desossar /dʒizo'sar/ *vt* bone

deso|va /dʒi'zɔva/ *f* roe. **~var** *vi* spawn

despa|chado /dʒispa'ʃadu/ *a* efficient. **~chante** *m/f* (*de mercadorias*) shipping agent; (*de documentos*) documentation agent. **~char** *vt* deal with; dispatch, forward ‹*mercadorias*›. **~cho** *m* dispatch

desparafusar /dʒisparafu'zar/ *vt* unscrew

despedaçar /dʒispeda'sar/ *vt* (*rasgar*) tear to pieces; (*quebrar*) smash. **~-se** *vpr* ‹*vidro, vaso*› smash; ‹*papel, tecido*› tear

despe|dida /dʒispe'dʒida/ *f* farewell; **~dida de solteiro** stag night, *Amer* bachelor party. **~dir** *vt* dismiss; sack ‹*empregado*›. **~dir-se** *vpr* say goodbye (**de** to)

despedimento /diʃpidi'mẽtu/ *m Port* dismissal

despei|tado /dʒispej'tadu/ *a* spiteful. **~to** *m* spite; **a ~to de** despite, in spite of

despe|jar /dʒispe'ʒar/ *vt* pour out ‹*líquido*›; empty ‹*recipiente*›; evict ‹*inquilino*›. **~jo** /e/ *m* (*de inquilino*) eviction

despencar /dʒispẽ'kar/ *vi* plummet

despender /dʒispẽ'der/ *vt* spend ‹*dinheiro*›

despensa /dʒis'pẽsa/ *f* pantry, larder

despentear /dʒispẽtʃi'ar/ *vt* mess up ‹*cabelo*›; mess up the hair of ‹*pessoa*›

despercebido /dʒisperse'bidu/ *a* unnoticed

desper|diçar /dʒisperdʒi'sar/ *vt* waste. **~dício** *m* waste

desper|tador /dʒisperta'dor/ *m* alarm clock. **~tar** *vt* rouse ‹*pessoa*›; *fig* arouse ‹*interesse, suspeitas etc*› ● *vi* awake

despesa /dʒis'peza/ *f* expense

des|pido /des'pidu/ *a* bare, stripped (**de** of). **~pir** *vt* strip (**de** of); strip off ‹*roupa*›. **~pir-se** *vpr* strip (off), get undressed

despo|jar /dʒispo'ʒar/ *vt* strip (**de** of). **~jar-se** *vpr* divest o.s. (**de** of). **~jo** /o/ *m* spoils, booty; **~jos mortais** mortal remains

despontar /dʒispõ'tar/ *vi* emerge

despor|tista /diʃpur'tiʃta/ *Port m/f* sportsman (*f*-woman). **~tivo** *Port a* sporting. **~to** /o/ *Port m* sport; **carro de ~to** sports car

déspota /'dɛspota/ *m/f* despot

despótico /des'pɔtʃiku/ *a* despotic

despovoar /dʒispovo'ar/ *vt* depopulate

desprender /dʒisprẽ'der/ *vt* detach; (*da parede*) take down. **~-se** *vpr* come off; *fig* detach o.s.

despreocupado /dʒisprioku'padu/ *a* unconcerned

despreparado /dʒisprepa'radu/ *a* unprepared

desprestigiar /dʒisprestʃiʒi'ar/ *vt* discredit

despretensioso /dʒispretẽsi'ozu/ *a* unpretentious

desprevenido /dʒispreve'nidu/ *a* off one's guard, unprepared; **apanhar ~** catch unawares

despre|zar /dʒispre'zar/ *vt* despise; (*ignorar*) ignore. **~zível** (*pl* **~zíveis**) *a* despicable. **~zo** /e/ *m* contempt

desproporção /dʒispropor'sãw/ *f* disproportion

desproporcio|nado /dʒisproporsio'nadu/ *a* disproportionate. **~nal** (*pl* **~nais**) *a* disproportional

despropositado /dʒispropozi'tadu/ *a* (*absurdo*) preposterous

desprovido /dʒispro'vidu/ *a* **~ de** without

desqualificar /dʒiskwalifi'kar/ *vt* disqualify

desqui|tar-se /dʒiski'tarsi/ *vpr* (legally) separate. **~te** *m* (legal) separation

desrespei|tar /dʒizxespej'tar/ *vt* not respect; (*ignorar*) disregard. **~to** *m* disrespect. **~toso** /o/ *a* disrespectful

dessa(s), **desse(s)** = **de + essa(s), esse(s)**

desta = **de + esta**

desta|camento /dʒistaka'mẽtu/ *m* detachment. **~car** *vt* detach; (*ressaltar*) bring out, make stand out. **~car-se** *vpr* (*desprender-se*) come off; ‹*corredor*› break away; (*sobressair*) stand out (**sobre** against). **~cável** (*pl* **~cáveis**) *a* detachable; ‹*caderno*› pull-out

destam|pado /dʒistã'padu/ *a* (*panela*) uncovered. **~par** *vt* remove the lid of

destapar /dʒista'par/ *vt* uncover

destaque /dʒis'taki/ *m* prominence; (*coisa, pessoa*) highlight; (*do noticiário*) headline

destas, **deste** = **de + estas, este**

destemido /dʒiste'midu/ *a* intrepid, courageous

desterrar /dʒiste'xar/ *vt* (*exilar*) exile

destes = **de + estes**

destilar /desti'lar/ *vt* distil. **~ia** *f* distillery

desti|nado /destʃi'nadu/ *a* (*fadado*) destined. **~nar** *vt* intend, mean (**para** for). **~natário** *m* addressee. **~no** *m* (*de viagem*) destination; (*sorte*) fate

destituir /destʃitu'ir/ *vt* remove

desto|ante /dʒisto'ãtʃi/ *a* ‹*sons*› discordant; ‹*cores*› clashing. **~ar** *vi* **~ar de** clash with

destrancar /dʒistrã'kar/ *vt* unlock

destreza /des'treza/ *f* skill

destrinchar /dʒistrĩ'ʃar/ *vt* (*expor*) dissect; (*resolver*) sort out

destro /'destru/ *a* skilful

destro|çar /dʒistro'sar/ *vt* wreck. **~ços** *m pl* wreckage

destronar /dʒistro'nar/ *vt* depose

destroncar /dʒistrõ'kar/ *vt* rick

destru|ição /dʒistrui'sãw/ *f* destruction. **~idor** *a* destructive ● *m* destroyer. **~ir** *vt* destroy

desumano /dʒizu'manu/ *a* inhuman; (*cruel*) inhumane

desunião /dʒizuni'ãw/ *f* disunity

desu|sado /dʒizu'zadu/ *a* disused. **~so** *m* disuse

desvairado /dʒizvaj'radu/ *a* delirious, raving

desvalori|zação /dʒizvaloriza'sãw/ *f* devaluation. **~zar** *vt* devalue

desvanta|gem /dʒizvã'taʒẽ/ *f* disadvantage. **~joso** /o/ *a* disadvantageous

desve|lar /dʒizve'lar/ *vt* unveil; uncover ‹*segredo*›. **~lar-se** *vpr* go to a lot of trouble. **~lo** /e/ *m* great care

desvencilhar /dʒizvẽsi'ʎar/ *vt* extricate, free

desvendar /dʒizvẽ'dar/ *vt* reveal ‹*segredo*›; solve ‹*mistério*›

desventura /dʒizvẽ'tura/ *f* misfortune; (*infelicidade*) unhappiness

desviar /dʒizvi'ar/ *vt* divert ‹*trânsito, rio, atenção, dinheiro*›; avert ‹*golpe, suspeitas, olhos*›. **~-se** *vpr* deviate; ‹*do tema*› digress

desvincular /dʒizvĩku'lar/ *vt* free

desvio /dʒiz'viu/ *m* diversion; (*do trânsito*) diversion, *Amer* detour; (*linha ferroviária*) siding

desvirtuar /dʒizvirtu'ar/ *vt* misrepresent ‹*verdade*›

deta|lhado /deta'ʎadu/ *a* detailed. **~lhar** *vt* detail. **~lhe** *m* detail

detec|tar /detek'tar/ *vt* detect. **~tor** *m* detector

de|tenção /detẽ'sãw/ *f* (*prisão*) detention. **~tentor** *m* holder. **~ter** *vt* (*ter*) hold; (*prender*) detain

detergente /deter'ʒẽtʃi/ *m* detergent

d

deterio|ração /deteriora'sãw/ *f* deterioration. **~rar** *vt* damage. **~rar-se** *vpr* deteriorate

determi|nação /determina'sãw/ *f* determination. **~nado** *a* (*certo*) certain; (*resoluto*) determined. **~nar** *vt* determine

d

detestar /detes'tar/ *vt* hate

detetive /dete'tʃivi/ *m* detective

detido /de'tʃidu/; *pp de* ▶ DETER ● *a* thorough ● *m* detainee

detonar /deto'nar/ *vt* detonate; [!] (*criticar*) pull to pieces ● *vi* detonate

detrás /de'traʃ/ *adv* behind ● *prep* **~ de** behind

detrito /de'tritu/ *m* detritus

deturpar /detur'par/ *vt* misrepresent, distort

deus /dews/ *m* (*f* **deusa**) god (*f* goddess). **~-dará** *m* **ao ~-dará** at the mercy of chance

devagar /dʒiva'gar/ *adv* slowly

deva|near /devani'ar/ *vi* daydream. **~neio** *m* daydream

devas|sar /deva'sar/ *vt* expose. **~sidão** *f* debauchery. **~so** *a* debauched

devastar /devas'tar/ *vt* devastate

devedor /deve'dor/ *a* debit ● *m* debtor

dever /de'ver/ ● *vt*

····➤ (*seguido de substantivo*) owe; **devo R$5/uma explicação para você** I owe you R$5/an explanation (*seguido de infinitivo: obrigação*) must; **você deve estudar!** you must study!; **ela já deve estar em casa** she must be at home by now; **não deve ser fácil!** it can't be easy (*seguido de infinitivo: conselho, crítica*) should; **você não devia sair assim!** you shouldn't go out like that!; **você deveria ter vindo mais cedo** you should have come earlier

● *vpr*

····➤ **~se a algo** be due to sth; **isso se deve à falta de recursos** that's due to a lack of funds

● *m*

····➤ duty; **cumprir o ~** do one's duty

····➤ (*em expressões*) **como deve ser: uma carta como deve ser** a proper letter; **coma como deve ser** eat properly

de|vido /devi'do/ *a* due (**a** to); **~voção** *f* devotion

de|volução /devolu'sãw/ *f* return. **~volver** *vt* return

devorar /devo'rar/ *vt* devour

devo|tar /devo'tar/ *vt* devote. **~tar-se** *vpr* devote o.s. (**a** to). **~to** /ɔ/ *a* devout

dez /dɛs/ *a* & *m* ten

dezanove /dza'nɔv/ *Port a* & *m* nineteen

dezas|seis /dza'sejʃ/ *Port a* & *m* sixteen. **~sete** /ɛ/ *Port a* & *m* seventeen

dezembro /de'zẽbru/ *m* December

deze|na /de'zena/ *f* ten; **uma ~ (de)** about ten. **~nove** /ɔ/ *a* & *m* nineteen

dezes|seis /dʒize'sejs/ *a* & *m* sixteen. **~sete** /ɛ/ *a* & *m* seventeen

dezoito /dʒi'zojtu/ *a* & *m* eighteen

dia /'dʒia/ *m* day; **de ~** by day; **(no) ~ 20 de julho** (on) July 20th; **~ de folga** day off; **~ útil** working day. **o ~ a ~** *m* everyday life

dia|bete /dʒia'bɛtʃi/ *f* diabetes. **~bético** *a* & *m* diabetic

dia|bo /dʒi'abu/ *m* devil. **~bólico** *a* diabolical, devilish. **~brete** /e/ *m* little devil. **~brura** *f* (*de criança*) bit of mischief; *pl* mischief

diadema /dʒia'dema/ *m* tiara

diafragma /dʒia'fragima/ *m* diaphragm

diag|nosticar /dʒiagnostʃi'kar/ *vt* diagnose. **~nóstico** *m* diagnosis ● *a* diagnostic

diago|nal /dʒiago'naw/ (*pl* **~nais**) *a* & *f* diagonal

diagra|ma /dʒia'grama/ *m* diagram. **~mação** *f* design. **~mador** *m* designer. **~mar** *vt* design ‹*livro, revista*›

dia|lética /dʒia'lɛtʃika/ *f* dialectics. **~leto** /ɛ/ *m* dialect

dialogar /dʒialo'gar/ *vi* talk; *Pol* hold talks

diálogo /dʒi'alogu/ *m* dialogue

diamante /dʒia'mãtʃi/ *m* diamond

diâmetro /dʒi'ametru/ *m* diameter

dian|te /dʒi'ãtʃi/ *adv* **de ... em ~te** from ... on(wards); **~te de** (*enfrentando*) faced with; (*perante*) before. **~teira** *f* lead. **~teiro** *a* front

diapasão /dʒiapa'zãw/ *m* tuning fork

diapositivo /dʒiapozi'tʃivu/ *m* transparency

diá|ria /dʒi'aria/ *f* daily rate. **~rio** *a* daily

diarista /dʒia'rista/ *m/f* day labourer; (*faxineira*) daily (help)

diarreia /dʒia'xɛja/ *f* diarrhoea
dica /'dʒika/ *f* tip, hint
dicção /dʒik'sãw/ *f* diction
dicionário /dʒisio'nariu/ *m* dictionary
didáti|ca /dʒi'datʃika/ *f* teaching methodology. **~co** *a* teaching; ‹*livro*› educational; ‹*estilo*› didactic
die|ta /dʒi'ɛta/ *f* diet; **de ~ta** on a diet. **~tista** *m/f* dietician
difa|mação /dʒifama'sãw/ *f* defamation. **~mar** *vt* defame. **~matório** *a* defamatory
diferen|ça /dʒife'rẽsa/ *f* difference. **~cial** (*pl* **~ciais**) *a & f* differential. **~ciar** *vt* differentiate. **~ciar-se** *vpr* differ. **~te** *a* different
dife|rimento /dʒiferi'mẽtu/ *m* deferment. **~rir** *vt* defer ● *vi* differ
difí|cil /dʒi'fisiw/ (*pl* **~ceis**) *a* difficult; (*improvável*) unlikely
dificilmente /dʒifisiw'mẽtʃi/ *adv* **~ poderá fazê-lo** he's unlikely to be able to do it
dificul|dade /dʒifikuw'dadʒi/ *f* difficulty. **~tar** *vt* make difficult
difteria /dʒifte'ria/ *f* diphtheria
difun|dir /dʒifũ'dʒir/ *vt* spread; (*pela rádio*) broadcast; diffuse ‹*luz, calor*›. **~dir-se** *vpr* spread
difu|são /dʒifu'zãw/ *f* diffusion. **~so** *a* diffuse
dige|rir /dʒiʒe'rir/ *vt* digest. **~rível** (*pl* **~ríveis**) *a* digestible
diges|tão /dʒiʒes'tãw/ *f* digestion. **~tivo** *a* digestive
digi|tal /dʒiʒi'taw/ (*pl* **~tais**) *a* digital; **impressão ~tal** fingerprint. **~tar** *vt* key
dígito /'dʒiʒitu/ *m* digit
digladiar /dʒigladʒi'ar/ *vi* do battle
dig|nar-se /dʒig'narsi/ *vpr* deign (**de** to). **~nidade** *f* dignity. **~nificar** *vt* dignify. **~no** *a* worthy (**de** of); (*decoroso*) dignified
digressão /digrə'sãw/ *f Port* (*de concerto, volta de bicicleta*) tour
dilace|rante /dʒilase'rãtʃi/ *a* ‹*dor*› excruciating. **~rar** *vt* tear to pieces
dilapidar /dʒilapi'dar/ *vt* squander
dilatar /dʒila'tar/ *vt* expand; *Med* dilate. **~-se** *vpr* expand; *Med* dilate
dilema /dʒi'lema/ *m* dilemma
diletante /dʒile'tãtʃi/ *a & m/f* dilettante
dili|gência /dʒili'ʒẽsia/ *f* diligence; (*carruagem*) stagecoach. **~gente** *a* diligent, hard-working
diluir /dʒilu'ir/ *vt* dilute
dilúvio /dʒi'luviu/ *m* deluge
dimen|são /dʒimẽ'sãw/ *f* dimension. **~sionar** *vt* size up
diminu|ição /dʒiminui'sãw/ *f* reduction. **~ir** *vt* reduce ● *vi* lessen; ‹*carro, motorista*› slow down. **~tivo** *a & m* diminutive. **~to** *a* minute
Dinamarca /dʒina'marka/ *f* Denmark
dinamar|quês /dʒinamar'kes/ (*f* **~quesa**) *a* Danish ● *m* Dane
dinâmi|ca /dʒi'namika/ *f* dynamics. **~co** *a* dynamic
dina|mismo /dʒina'mizmu/ *m* dynamism. **~mite** *f* dynamite
dínamo /'dʒinamu/ *m* dynamo
dinastia /dʒinas'tʃia/ *f* dynasty
dinda /'dʒĩda/ *f* [!] godmother
dinheiro /dʒi'ɲeru/ *m* money
dinossauro /dʒino'sawru/ *m* dinosaur
diocese /dʒio'sɛzi/ *f* diocese
dióxido /dʒi'ɔksidu/ *m* dioxide; **~ de carbono** carbon dioxide
diplo|ma /dʒi'ploma/ *m* diploma. **~macia** *f* diplomacy. **~mar-se** *vpr* take one's diploma. **~mata** *m/f* diplomat ● *a* diplomatic. **~mático** *a* diplomatic
direção /dʒire'sãw/ *f* (*sentido*) direction; (*de empresa*) management; (*condução de carro*) driving; (*manuseio do volante*) steering
direi|ta /dʒi'rejta/ *f* right. **~tinho** *adv* exactly right. **~tista** *a* right-wing ● *m/f* right-winger, rightist. **~to** *a* right; (*ereto*) straight ● *adv* properly ● *m* right
dire|tas /dʒi'rɛtas/ *f pl* direct (presidential) elections. **~to** *a* direct ● *adv* directly. **~tor** *m* director; (*de escola*) head teacher; (*de jornal*) editor; **~tor-gerente** managing director. **~toria** *f* (*diretores*) board of directors; (*sala*) boardroom. **~tório** *m* directory. **~triz** *f* directive
diri|gente /dʒiri'ʒẽtʃi/ *a* leading ● *m/f* leader. **~gir** *vt* direct; manage ‹*empresa*›; drive ‹*carro*›. **~gir-se** *vpr* (*ir*) make one's way; **~gir-se a** (*falar com*) address
dis|cagem /dʒis'kaʒẽ/ *f* dialling; **~cagem rápida** speed dialling. **~car** *vt/i* dial
discente /dʒi'sẽtʃi/ *a* **corpo ~** student body
discer|nimento /dʒiserni'mẽtu/ *m* discernment. **~nir** *vt* discern

discipli|na /dʒisi'plina/ *f* discipline. **~nador** *a* disciplinary. **~nar** *vt* discipline

discípulo /dʒi'sipulu/ *m* disciple

disco-jóquei /dʒisk'ʒɔkej/ *m* disc jockey

disco /'dʒisku/ *m* disc; (*de música*) record; (*no atletismo*) discus ● *f* [!] disco; **~ flexível/rígido** floppy/hard disk; **~ laser** CD, compact disc; **~ voador** flying saucer

d

discor|dante /dʒiskor'dãtʃi/ *a* conflicting. **~dar** *vi* disagree (**de** with)

discote|ca /dʒisko'tɛka/ *f* discotheque. **~cário** *m* DJ

discre|pância /dʒiskre'pãsia/ *f* discrepancy. **~pante** *a* inconsistent. **~par** *vi* diverge (**de** from)

dis|creto /dʒis'krɛtu/ *a* discreet. **~crição** *f* discretion

discrimi|nação /dʒiskrimina'sãw/ *f* discrimination; (*descrição*) description. **~nar** *vt* discriminate. **~natório** *a* discriminatory

discur|sar /dʒiskur'sar/ *vi* speak. **~so** *m* speech

discussão /dʒisku'sãw/ *f* discussion; (*briga*) argument

discu|tir /dʒisku'tʃir/ *vt/i* discuss; (*brigar*) argue. **~tível** (*pl* **~tíveis**) *a* debatable

disenteria /dʒizẽte'ria/ *f* dysentery

disfar|çar /dʒisfar'sar/ *vt* disguise. **~çar-se** *vpr* disguise o.s.. **~ce** *m* disguise

dis|lético /dʒiz'lɛtʃiku/ *a & m* dyslexic. **~lexia** *f* dyslexia. **~léxico** *a & m* dyslexic

dispa|rada /dʒispa'rada/ *f* bolt. **~rado** *adv* **o melhor ~rado** the best by a long way. **~rar** *vt* fire ‹*arma*› ● *vi* (*com arma*) fire; ‹*preços, inflação*› shoot up; ‹*corredor*› surge ahead

disparate /dʒispa'ratʃi/ *m* piece of nonsense; *pl* nonsense

dis|pêndio /dʒis'pẽdʒiu/ *m* expenditure. **~pendioso** /o/ *a* costly

dispen|sa /dʒis'pẽsa/ *f* exemption. **~sar** *vt* (*distribuir*) dispense; (*isentar*) exempt (**de** from); (*prescindir de*) dispense with. **~sável** (*pl* **~sáveis**) *a* dispensable

dispersar /dʒisper'sar/ *vt* disperse; waste ‹*energias*› ● *vi*, **~-se** *vpr* disperse

disperso /dʒis'pɛrsu/ *a* scattered

dispo|nibilidade /dʒisponibili'dadʒi/ *f* availability. **~nível** (*pl* **~níveis**) *a* available

dis|por /dʒis'por/ *vt* arrange ● *vi* **~por de** have at one's disposal. **~por-se** *vpr* form up ● *m* **ao seu ~por** at your disposal. **~posição** *f* (*vontade*) willingness; (*arranjo*) arrangement; (*de espírito*) frame of mind; (*de testamento etc*) provision; **à ~posição de alguém** at sb's disposal. **~positivo** *m* device. **~posto** *a* prepared, willing (**a** to)

dispu|ta /dʒis'puta/ *f* dispute. **~tar** *vt* dispute; (*tentar ganhar*) compete for

disquete /dʒis'ketʃi/ *m* diskette, floppy (disk)

dissabores /dʒisa'boris/ *m pl* troubles

disseminar /dʒisemi'nar/ *vt* disseminate

dissertação /dʒiserta'sãw/ *f* dissertation, lecture

dissi|dência /dʒisi'dẽsia/ *f* dissidence. **~dente** *a & m* dissident

dissídio /dʒi'sidʒiu/ *m* dispute

dissimular /dʒisimu'lar/ *vt* hide ● *vi* dissimulate

dissipar /dʒisi'par/ *vt* clear ‹*nevoeiro*›; dispel ‹*dúvidas, suspeitas, ilusões*›; dissipate ‹*fortuna*›. **~-se** *vpr* ‹*nevoeiro*› clear; ‹*dúvidas etc*› be dispelled

disso = **de** + **isso**

dissolu|ção /dʒisolu'sãw/ *f* dissolution. **~to** *a* dissolute

dissolver /dʒisow'ver/ *vt* dissolve. **~-se** *vpr* dissolve

dissuadir /dʒisua'dʒir/ *vt* dissuade (**de** from)

distância /dʒis'tãsia/ *f* distance

distan|ciar /dʒistãsi'ar/ *vt* distance. **~ciar-se** *vpr* distance o.s.. **~te** *a* distant

disten|der /dʒistẽ'der/ *vt* stretch ‹*pernas*›; relax ‹*músculo*›. **~der-se** *vpr* relax. **~são** *f Med* pull; **~são muscular** pulled muscle

distin|ção /dʒistʃĩ'sãw/ *f* distinction. **~guir** *vt* distinguish (**de** from). **~guir-se** *vpr* distinguish o.s.. **~tivo** *a* distinctive ● *m* badge. **~to** *a* distinct; ‹*senhor*› distinguished

disto = **de** + **isto**

distor|ção /dʒistor'sãw/ *f* distortion. **~cer** *vt* distort

distra|ção /dʒistra'sãw/ *f* distraction. **~ído** *a* absent-minded. **~ir** *vt* distract; (*divertir*) amuse. **~ir-se** *vpr* be distracted; (*divertir-se*) amuse o.s.

distribu|ição /dʒistribui'sãw/ *f* distribution. **~idor** *m* distributor. **~idora** *f* distributor, distribution company. **~ir**

vt distribute

distrito /dʒis'tritu/ *m* district

distúrbio /dʒis'turbiu/ *m* trouble

di|tado /dʒi'tadu/ *m* dictation; (*provérbio*) saying. **~tador** *m* dictator. **~tadura** *f* dictatorship. **~tame** *m* dictate. **~tar** *vt* dictate. **~tatorial** (*pl* **~tatoriais**) *a* dictatorial

dito /'dʒitu/ *a* **~ e feito** no sooner said than done ● *m* remark

ditongo /dʒi'tõgu/ *m* diphthong

DIU /'dʒiu/ *m* IUD, coil

diurno /dʒi'urnu/ *a* day

divã /dʒi'vã/ *m* couch

divagar /dʒiva'gar/ *vi* digress

diver|gência /dʒiver'ʒẽsia/ *a* divergence. **~gente** *a* divergent. **~gir** *vi* diverge (**de** from). **~são** *f* diversion; (*divertimento*) amusement. **~sidade** *f* diversity. **~sificar** *vt/i* diversify. **~so** /ɛ/ *a* (*diferente*) diverse; *pl* (*vários*) several. **~tido** *a* (*engraçado*) funny; (*que se curte*) enjoyable. **~timento** *m* enjoyment, fun; (*um*) amusement. **~tir** *vt* amuse. **~tir-se** *vpr* enjoy o.s., have fun

dívida /'dʒivida/ *f* debt; **~ externa** foreign debt

divi|dendo /dʒivi'dẽdu/ *m* dividend. **~dido** *a* ‹*pessoa*› torn. **~dir** *vt* divide; (*compartilhar*) share. **~dir-se** *vpr* be divided

divindade /dʒivĩ'dadʒi/ *f* divinity

divino /dʒi'vinu/ *a* divine

divi|sa /dʒi'viza/ *f* (*lema*) motto; (*galão*) stripes; (*fronteira*) border; *pl* foreign currency. **~são** *f* division. **~sória** *f* partition

divorci|ado /dʒivorsi'adu/ *a* divorced ● *m* divorcé (*f* divorcée). **~ar** *vt* divorce. **~ar-se** *vpr* get divorced; **~ar-se de** divorce

divórcio /dʒi'vɔrsiu/ *m* divorce

divul|gado /dʒivuw'gadu/ *a* widespread. **~gar** *vt* spread; publish ‹*notícia*›; divulge ‹*segredo*›. **~gar-se** *vpr* be spread

dizer /dʒi'zer/ *vt* say; **~ a alguém que** tell sb that; **~ para alguém fazer** tell sb to do ● *vi* **~ com** go with. **~-se** *vpr* claim to be ● *m* saying

dizimar /dʒizi'mar/ *vt* decimate

do ▶ DE + O

dó /dɔ/ *m* pity; **dar ~** be pitiful; **ter ~ de** feel sorry for

do|ação /doa'sãw/ *f* donation. **~ador** *m* donor. **~ar** *vt* donate

do|bra /'dɔbra/ *f* fold; (*de calça*) turn-up, *Amer* cuff. **~bradiça** *f* hinge. **~bradiço** *a* pliable. **~brado** *a* (*duplo*) double. **~brar** *vt* (*duplicar*) double; (*fazer dobra em*) fold; (*curvar*) bend; go round ‹*esquina*›; ring ‹*sinos*›; *Port* dub ‹*filme*› ● *vi* double; ‹*sinos*› ring. **~brar-se** *vpr* bend. **~bro** *m* double

doca /'dɔka/ *f* dock

doce /'dosi/ *a* sweet; ‹*água*› fresh ● *m* sweet; **~ de leite** fudge

docente /do'sẽtʃi/ *a* teaching; **corpo ~** teaching staff, *Amer* faculty

dó|cil /'dɔsiw/ (*pl* **~ceis**) *a* docile

documen|tação /dokumẽta'sãw/ *f* documentation. **~tar** *vt* document. **~tário** *a & m* documentary. **~to** *m* document

doçura /do'sura/ *f* sweetness

dodói /do'dɔj/ ! *m* **ter ~** have a pain ● *a* poorly, ill

doen|ça /do'ẽsa/ *f* illness; (*infecciosa*) *fig* disease; **~ da vaca louca** mad cow disease. **~te** *a* ill. **~tio** *a* ‹*criança, aspecto*› sickly; ‹*interesse, curiosidade*› morbid

doer /do'er/ *vi* hurt; ‹*cabeça, músculo*› ache

dog|ma /'dɔgima/ *m* dogma. **~mático** *a* dogmatic

doido /'dojdu/ *a* crazy

dois /dojs/ *a & m* (*f* **duas**) two

dólar /'dɔlar/ *m* dollar

dolo|rido /dolo'ridu/ *a* sore. **~roso** /o/ *a* painful

dom /dõ/ *m* gift

do|mador /doma'dor/ *m* tamer. **~mar** *vt* tame

doméstica /do'mɛstʃika/ *f* housemaid

domesticar /domestʃi'kar/ *vt* domesticate

doméstico /do'mɛstʃiku/ *a* domestic

domi|ciliar /domisili'ar/ *a* home. **~cílio** *m* home

domi|nação /domina'sãw/ *f* domination. **~nador** *a* domineering. **~nante** *a* dominant. **~nar** *vt* dominate; have a command of ‹*língua*›. **~nar-se** *vpr* control o.s.

domin|go /do'mĩgu/ *m* Sunday. **~gueiro** *a* Sunday

domini|cal /domini'kaw/ (*pl* **~cais**) *a* Sunday. **~cano** *a & m* Dominican

domínio /do'miniu/ *m* command

dona /'dona/ *f* owner; **D~** (*com nome*) Miss. **~ de casa** housewife

d
e

donativo /dona'tʃivu/ *m* donation
donde /'dõdʒi/ *adv* from where; (*motivo*) from whence
dono /'donu/ *m* owner
donut /'donut/ *m* doughnut
donzela /dõ'zɛla/ *f* maiden
dopar /do'par/ *vt* drug
dor /dor/ *f* pain; (*menos aguda*) ache; **~ de cabeça** headache
dor|mente /dor'mẽtʃi/ *a* numb ● *m* sleeper. **~mida** *f* sleep. **~minhoco** /o/ *m* sleepyhead. **~mir** *vi* sleep. **~mitar** *vi* doze. **~mitório** *m* bedroom; (*comunitário*) dormitory
dorso /'dorsu/ *m* back; (*de livro*) spine
dos = **de** + **os**
do|sagem /do'zaʒẽ/ *f* dosage. **~sar** *vt* moderate. **~se** /ɔ/ *f* dose; (*de uísque etc*) shot, measure
dossiê /dosi'e/ *m* file
do|tação /dota'sãw/ *f* endowment. **~tado** *a* gifted; **~tado de** endowed with. **~tar** *vt* endow (**de** with). **~te** /ɔ/ *m* (*de noiva*) dowry; (*dom*) endowment
dou|rado /do'radu/ *a* (*de cor*) golden; (*revestido de ouro*) gilded, gilt ● *m* gilt. **~rar** *vt* gild
dou|to /'dotu/ *a* learned. **~tor** *m* doctor. **~torado** *m* doctorate, PhD. **~trina** *f* doctrine. **~trinar** *vt* indoctrinate
doutoramento /dotora'mẽtu/ *m* PhD
doze /'dozi/ *a* & *m* twelve
dragão /dra'gãw/ *m* dragon
dragar /dra'gar/ *vt* dredge
drágea /'draʒia/ *f* lozenge
dra|ma /'drama/ *m* drama. **~malhão** *m* melodrama. **~mático** *a* dramatic. **~matizar** *vt* dramatize. **~maturgo** *m* dramatist, playwright
drapeado /drapi'adu/ *a* draped
drástico /'drastʃiku/ *a* drastic
dre|nagem /dre'naʒẽ/ *f* drainage. **~nar** *vt* drain. **~no** /ɛ/ *m* drain
driblar /dri'blar/ *vt* (*em futebol*) dribble round, beat; *fig* get round
drinque /'drĩki/ *m* drink
drive /'drajvi/ *m* disk drive
dro|ga /'drɔga/ *f* drug; [!] (*coisa sem valor*) dead loss; (*coisa chata*) drag ● *int* damn. **~gado** *a* on drugs ● *m* drug addict. **~gar** *vt* drug. **~gar-se** *vpr* take drugs. **~garia** *f* dispensing chemist's, pharmacy
duas /'duas/ ▶ DOIS
dúbio /'dubiu/ *a* dubious
dub|lagem /du'blaʒẽ/ *f* dubbing. **~lar** *vt* dub ‹*filme*›; mime ‹*música*›. **~lê** *m* double
ducentésimo /dusẽ'tɛzimu/ *a* two-hundredth
ducha /'duʃa/ *f* shower
duche /'duʃe/ *m Port* shower
ducto /'duktu/ *m* duct
duelo /du'ɛlu/ *m* duel
duende /du'ẽdʒi/ *m* elf
dueto /du'etu/ *m* duet
duna /'duna/ *f* dune
duodécimo /duo'dɛsimu/ *a* twelfth
duodeno /duo'dɛnu/ *m* duodenum
dupla /'dupla/ *f* pair, duo; ‹*no tênis*› doubles
duplex /du'plɛks/ *a invar* two-floor ● *m invar* two-floor apartment, *Amer* duplex
dupli|car /dupli'kar/ *vt/i* double. **~cidade** *f* duplicity. **~cata** *f* duplicate
duplo /'duplu/ *a* double
duque /'duki/ *m* duke. **~sa** /e/ *f* duchess
du|ração /dura'sãw/ *f* duration. **~radouro** *a* lasting. **~rante** *prep* during. **~rar** *vi* last. **~rável** (*pl* **~ráveis**) *a* durable
durex® /du'rɛks/ *m invar* Sellotape®
du|reza /du'reza/ *f* hardness. **~ro** *a* hard; [!] (*sem dinheiro*) hard up, broke
dúvida /'duvida/ *f* doubt; (*pergunta*) query
duvi|dar /duvi'dar/ *vt/i* doubt. **~doso** /o/ *a* doubtful
duzentos /du'zẽtus/ *a* & *m* two hundred
dúzia /'duzia/ *f* dozen
DVD /deve'de/ *m* DVD; **gravador de ~** DVD burner; **leitor de ~** DVD player

Ee

e /i/ *conj* and
ébano /'ɛbanu/ *m* ebony
ébrio /'ɛbriu/ *a* drunk ● *m* drunkard
ebulição /ebuli'sãw/ *f* boiling
eclesiástico /eklezi'astʃiku/ *a* ecclesiastical
eclético /e'klɛtʃiku/ *a* eclectic

eclip|sar /eklip'sar/ *vt* eclipse. **~se** *m* eclipse

eclodir /eklo'dʒir/ *vi* emerge; (*estourar*) break out; ‹*flor*› open

eco /'ɛku/ *m* echo; **ter ~** have repercussions. **~ar** *vt/i* echo

ecografia /ekogra'fia/ *f* ultrasound (scan)

eco|logia /ekolo'ʒia/ *f* ecology. **~lógico** /eko'lɔʒiku/ *a* ecological; **grupo ~lógico** environmental group. **~logista** *m/f* ecologist

eco|nomia /ekono'mia/ *f* economy; (*ciência*) economics; *pl* (*dinheiro poupado*) savings. **~nômico** *a* economic; (*rentável, barato*) economical. **~nomista** *m/f* economist. **~nomizar** *vt* save ● *vi* economize

ecoponto /ɛkɔ'põtu/ *m Port* recycling point

ecossistema /ekosiʃ'tema/ *m* ecosystem

écran /ɛ'krã/ *Port m* screen

eczema /ek'zɛma/ *m* eczema

edição /edʒi'sãw/ *f* edition; (*de filmes*) editing

edificante /edʒifi'kãtʃi/ *a* edifying

edifício /edʒi'fisiu/ *m* building

Edimburgo /edʒĩ'burgu/ *f* Edinburgh

edi|tal /edʒi'taw/ (*pl* **~tais**) *m* announcement. **~tar** *vt* publish; *Comput* edit. **~to** *m* edict. **~tor** *m* publisher. **~tora** *f* publishing company. **~torial** (*pl* **~toriais**) *a* publishing ● *m* editorial

edredom /edre'dõ/ *m*, *Port* **edredão** /edre'dãw/ *m* quilt

educa|ção /eduka'sãw/ *f* (*ensino*) education; (*polidez*) good manners; **é falta de ~ção** it's rude. **~cional** (*pl* **~cionais**) *a* education

edu|cado /edu'kadu/ *a* polite. **~car** *vt* educate. **~cativo** *a* educational

EEB /ee'be/ *f* BSE

efeito /e'fejtu/ *m* effect; **fazer ~** have an effect; **para todos os ~s** to all intents and purposes; **~ colateral** side effect; **~ estufa** greenhouse effect

efêmero /e'fẽmeru/ *a* ephemeral

efeminado /efemi'nadu/ *a* effeminate

efervescente /eferve'sẽtʃi/ *a* effervescent

efe|tivar /efetʃi'var/ *vt* bring into effect; (*contratar*) make a permanent member of staff. **~tivo** *a* real, effective; ‹*cargo, empregado*› permanent. **~tuar** *vt* carry out, effect

efi|cácia /efi'kasia/ *f* effectiveness. **~caz** *a* effective

efici|ência /efisi'ẽsia/ *f* efficiency. **~ente** *a* efficient

efígie /e'fiʒi/ *f* effigy

Egeu /e'ʒew/ *a & m* Aegean

égide /'ɛʒidʒi/ *f* aegis

egípcio /e'ʒipsiu/ *a & m* Egyptian

Egito /e'ʒitu/ *m* Egypt

ego /'ɛgu/ *m* ego. **~cêntrico** *a* self-centred, egocentric. **~ísmo** *m* selfishness. **~ísta** *a* selfish ● *m/f* egoist ● *m* (*de rádio etc*) earplug

égua /'ɛgwa/ *f* mare

eis /ejs/ *adv* (*aqui está*) here is/are; (*isso é*) that is

eixo /'ejʃu/ *m* axle; *Mat* (*entre cidades*) axis; **pôr nos ~s** set straight

ela /'ɛla/ ● *pron*

····➤ (*pessoa*) she; **~ e Catarina são primas** she and Catarina are cousins; (*complemento, em comparações*) her; **é para ~** it's for her; **você é mais alto do que ~** you're taller than her; (*coisa*) it; **~ mesma** (she) herself

elaborar /elabo'rar/ *vt* (*fazer*) make, produce; (*desenvolver*) work out

elasticidade /elastʃisi'dadʒi/ *f* (*de coisa*) elasticity; (*de pessoa*) suppleness

elástico /e'lastʃiku/ *a* elastic ● *m* (*de borracha*) elastic band; (*de calcinha etc*) elastic

ele /'eli/ ● *pron*

····➤ (*pessoa*) he; **~ e José são primos** he and José are cousins; **~ é um rapaz simpático** he's a nice boy; (*complemento, em comparações*) him; **é para ~** it's for him; **você é mais alto do que ~** you're taller than him; (*coisa*) it; **~ mesmo** (he) himself

elefante /ele'fãtʃi/ *m* elephant

ele|gância /ele'gãsia/ *f* elegance. **~gante** *a* elegant

eleger /ele'ʒer/ *vt* elect. **~-se** *vpr* get elected

elegia /ele'ʒia/ *f* elegy

elei|ção /elej'sãw/ *f* election. **~to** *a* elected, elect; ‹*povo*› chosen. **~tor** *m* voter. **~torado** *m* electorate. **~toral** (*pl* **~torais**) *a* electoral

elemen|tar /elemẽ'tar/ *a* elementary. **~to** *m* element

elenco /e'lẽku/ *m* (*de filme, peça*) cast

eles /'elis/, **elas** /'ɛlas/ ● *pron*
····➤ (*sujeito*) they; (*complemento, em comparações*) them; **isto é para eles** this is for them
····➤ (*em expressões*) **agora é que são elas!** now comes the difficult part!; **elas por elas: o plano do governo deu elas por elas** the government's plan made no difference

e

eletri|cidade /eletrisi'dadʒi/ *f* electricity. **~cista** *m/f* electrician
elétrico /i'lɛktriku/ *Port m* tram, *Amer* streetcar ● *a* electric
eletri|ficar /eletrifi'kar/ *vt* electrify. **~zar** *vt* electrify
eletro /e'lɛtru/ *m* ECG. **~cutar** *vt* electrocute. **~do** /o/ *m* electrode. **~domésticos** *m pl* electrical appliances
eletrôni|ca /ele'tronika/ *f* electronics. **~co** *a* electronic
ele|vação /eleva'sãw/ *f* elevation; (*aumento*) rise. **~vado** *a* high; ‹*sentimento, estilo*› elevated. **~vador** *m* lift, *Amer* elevator. **~var** *vt* raise; (*promover*) elevate. **~var-se** *vpr* rise
elimi|nar /elimi'nar/ *vt* eliminate. **~natória** *f* heat. **~natório** *a* eliminatory
elipse /e'lipsi/ *f* ellipse
elíptico /e'liptʃiku/ *a* elliptical
eli|te /e'litʃi/ *f* elite. **~tismo** *m* elitism. **~tista** *a & m/f* elitist
elmo /'ɛwmu/ *m* helmet
elo /'ɛlu/ *m* link
elo|giar /eloʒi'ar/ *vt* praise; **~giar alguém por** compliment sb on. **~gio** *m* (*louvor*) praise; (*um*) compliment. **~gioso** /o/ *a* complimentary
elo|quência /elo'kwẽsia/ *f* eloquence. **~quente** *a* eloquent
eluci|dar /elusi'dar/ *vt* elucidate. **~dativo** *a* elucidatory
em /ẽj/ *prep* in; (*sobre*) on; **ela está no Eduardo** she's at Eduardo's (house); **de casa ~ casa** from house to house; **aumentar ~ 10%** increase by 10%
emagre|cer /emagre'ser/ *vi* lose weight, get thinner ● *vt* make thinner. **~cimento** *m* slimming
emanar /ema'nar/ *vi* emanate (**de** from)
emanci|pação /emãsipa'sãw/ *f* emancipation. **~par** *vt* emancipate. **~par-se** *vpr* become emancipated
emara|nhado /emara'ɲadu/ *a* tangled ● *m* tangle. **~nhar** *vt* tangle; (*envolver*) entangle. **~nhar-se** *vpr* get tangled up; (*envolver-se*) become entangled (**em** in)
embaçar /ĩba'sar/, *Port* **embaciar** /ĩbasi'ar/ *vt* steam up ‹*vidro*› ● *vi* ‹*vidro*› steam up; ‹*olhos*› grow misty
embainhar /ĩbaj'ɲar/ *vt* hem ‹*vestido, calça*›
embaixa|da /ĩba'ʃada/ *f* embassy. **~dor** *m* ambassador. **~triz** *f* ambassador; (*esposa*) ambassador's wife
embaixo /ĩ'baʃu/ *adv* underneath; (*em casa*) downstairs; **~ de** under
emba|lagem /ĩba'laʒẽ/ *f* packaging
emba|lar /ĩba'lar/ *vt* pack; (*move back and forth*) rock ‹*criança*›. **~lo** *m fig* excitement, thrill
embalsamar /ĩbawsa'mar/ *vt* embalm
embara|çar /ĩbara'sar/ *vt* embarrass. **~çar-se** *vpr* get embarrassed (**com** by). **~ço** *m* embarrassment. **~çoso** /o/ *a* embarrassing
embaralhar /ĩbara'ʎar/ *vt* muddle up; shuffle ‹*cartas*›. **~-se** *vpr* get muddled up
embar|cação /ĩbarka'sãw/ *f* vessel. **~cadouro** *m* wharf. **~car** *vt/i* board, embark
embar|gado /ĩbar'gadu/ *a* ‹*voz*› faltering. **~go** *m* embargo
embarque /ĩ'barki/ *m* boarding; (*seção do aeroporto*) departures
embasba|cado /ĩbazba'kadu/ *a* open-mouthed. **~car-se** *vpr* be left open-mouthed
embate /ĩ'batʃi/ *m* (*de carros etc*) crash; *fig* clash
embebedar /ĩbebe'dar/ *vt* make drunk. **~-se** *vpr* get drunk
embeber /ĩbe'ber/ *vt* soak; **~-se de** soak up; **~-se em** get absorbed in
embele|zador /ĩbeleza'dor/ *a* ‹*cirurgia*› cosmetic. **~zar** *vt* embellish; spruce up ‹*casa*›. **~zar-se** *vpr* make o.s. beautiful
embevecer /ĩbeve'ser/ *vt* captivate, engross. **~-se** *vpr* get engrossed, be captivated
emblema /ẽ'blema/ *m* emblem
embocadura /ĩboka'dura/ *f* (*de instrumento*) mouthpiece; (*de freio*) bit; (*de rio*) mouth; (*de rua*) entrance
êmbolo /'ẽbulu/ *m* piston
embolsar /ĩbow'sar/ *vt* pocket; (*reembolsar*) reimburse

embora /ĩ'bɔra/ *adv* away ● *conj* although

emborcar /ĩbor'kar/ *vi* overturn; ‹*barco*› capsize

emboscada /ĩbos'kada/ *f* ambush

embrai|agem /ẽbraj'aʒẽ/ *Port f* ▶ EMBREAGEM. **~ar** *Port vi* ▶ EMBREAR

embre|agem /ẽbri'aʒẽ/ *f* clutch. **~ar** *vi* let in the clutch

embria|gar /ẽbria'gar/ *vt* intoxicate. **~gar-se** *vpr* get drunk, become intoxicated. **~guez** /e/ *f* drunkenness; **~guez no volante** drunken driving

embri|ão /ẽbri'ãw/ *m* embryo. **~onário** *a* embryonic

embro|mação /ĩbroma'sãw/ *f* flannel. **~mar** *vt* flannel, string along; (*enganar*) con ● *vi* stall, drag one's feet

embru|lhada /ĩbru'ʎada/ *f* muddle. **~lhar** *vt* wrap up ‹*pacote*›; upset ‹*estômago*›; (*confundir*) muddle up. **~lhar-se** *vpr* ‹*pessoa*› get muddled up. **~lho** *m* parcel; *fig* mix-up

embur|rado /ĩbu'xadu/ *a* sulky. **~rar** *vi* sulk

embuste /ĩ'bustʃi/ *m* hoax, put-up job

embu|tido /ĩbu'tʃidu/ *a* built-in, fitted. **~tir** *vt* build in, fit

emen|da /e'mẽda/ *f* correction, improvement; (*de lei*) amendment. **~dar** *vt* correct; amend ‹*lei*›. **~dar-se** *vpr* mend one's ways

ementa /i'mẽta/ *Port f* menu

emer|gência /emer'ʒẽsia/ *f* emergency. **~gente** *a* emergent. **~gir** *vi* surface

emi|gração /emigra'sãw/ *f* emigration; (*de aves etc*) migration. **~grado** *a & m* émigré. **~grante** *a & m/f* emigrant. **~grar** *vi* emigrate; ‹*aves, animais*› migrate

emi|nência /emi'nẽsia/ *f* eminence. **~nente** *a* eminent

emis|são /emi'sãw/ *f* (*de ações etc*) issue; (*na rádio, TV*) transmission, broadcast; (*de som, gases*) emission. **~sário** *m* emissary. **~sor** *m* transmitter. **~sora** *f* (*de rádio*) radio station; (*de TV*) TV station

emitir /emi'tʃir/ *vt* issue ‹*ações, selos etc*›; emit ‹*sons*›; (*pela rádio, TV*) transmit, broadcast

emoção /emo'sãw/ *f* emotion; (*excitação*) excitement

emocio|nal /emosio'naw/ (*pl* **~nais**) *a* emotional. **~nante** *a* (*excitante*) exciting; (*comovente*) touching, emotional. **~nar** *vt* (*excitar*) excite; (*comover*) move, touch. **~nar-se** *vpr* get emotional

emoldurar /emowdu'rar/ *vt* frame

emotivo /emo'tʃivu/ *a* emotional

empacar /ĩpa'kar/ *vi* ‹*cavalo*› baulk; ‹*negociações etc*› grind to a halt; ‹*orador*› dry up

empacotar /ĩpako'tar/ *vt* pack up; (*pôr em pacotes*) packet

empa|da /ẽ'pada/ *f* pie. **~dão** *m* (large) pie

empalhar /ĩpa'ʎar/ *vt* stuff

empalidecer /ĩpalide'ser/ *vi* turn pale

empanar[1] /ẽpa'nar/ *vt* tarnish, dull

empanar[2] /ẽpa'nar/ *vt* cook in batter ‹*carne etc*›

empanturrar /ĩpãtu'xar/ *vt* stuff. **~-se** *vpr* stuff o.s. (**de** with)

empapar /ĩpa'par/ *vt* soak

empa|tar /ẽpa'tar/ *vt* draw ‹*jogo*› ● *vi* ‹*times*› draw; ‹*corredores*› tie. **~te** *m* (*em jogo*) draw; (*em corrida, votação*) tie; (*em xadrez*) *fig* stalemate

empatia /ẽpa'tʃia/ *f* empathy

empecilho /ẽpe'siʎu/ *m* hindrance

empenar /ẽpe'nar/ *vt/i* warp

empe|nhar /ĩpe'ɲar/ *vt* (*penhorar*) pawn; (*prometer*) pledge. **~nhar-se** *vpr* do one's utmost (**em** to). **~nho** /e/ *m* (*compromisso*) pledge; (*diligência*) effort, commitment

emperrar /ĩpe'xar/ *vt* make stick ● *vi* stick

emperti|gado /ĩpertʃi'gadu/ *a* upright. **~gar-se** *vpr* stand up straight

empilhar /ĩpi'ʎar/ *vt* pile up

empi|nado /ĩpi'nadu/ *a* erect; (*íngreme*) sheer, steep; ‹*nariz*› turned-up; *fig* stuck-up. **~nar** *vt* stand upright; fly ‹*pipa*›; tip up ‹*copo*›

empírico /ẽ'piriku/ *a* empirical

emplacar /ĩpla'kar/ *vt* notch up ‹*pontos, sucessos, anos*›; license ‹*carro*›

emplastro /ĩ'plastru/ *m* surgical plaster; **~ de nicotina** nicotine patch

empobre|cer /ĩpobre'ser/ *vt* impoverish. **~cimento** *m* impoverishment

empoderamento /ẽpodera'mẽtu/ *Port m* empowerment

empoleirar /ĩpole'rar/ *vt* perch. **~-se** *vpr* perch

empol|gação /ĩpowga'sãw/ *f* fascination. **~gante** *a* fascinating. **~gar** *vt* fascinate

e

empossar /ĩpo'sar/ *vt* swear in

empreen|dedor /ẽpriẽde'dor/ *a* enterprising ● *m* entrepreneur. **~der** *vt* undertake. **~dimento** *m* undertaking

empre|gada /ĩpre'gada/ *f* (*doméstica*) maid. **~gado** *m* employee. **~gador** *m* employer. **~gar** *vt* employ. **~gar-se** *vpr* get a job. **~gatício** *a* **vínculo ~gatício** contract of employment. **~go** /e/ *m* (*trabalho*) job; (*uso*) use

emprei|tada /ĩprej'tada/ *f* commission, contract; (*empreendimento*) venture. **~teira** *f* contractor, firm of contractors. **~teiro** *m* contractor

empre|sa /ĩ'preza/ *f* company. **~sa dot.com** dot-com. **~sariado** *m* business community. **~sarial** (*pl* **~sariais**) *a* business. **~sário** *m* businessman; (*de cantor etc*) manager

empres|tado /ĩpres'tadu/ *a* on loan; **pedir ~tado** (ask to) borrow; **tomar ~tado** borrow. **~tar** *vt* lend

empréstimo /ĩ'prɛstʃimu/ *m* loan

empur|rão /ĩpu'xãw/ *m* push. **~rar** *vt* push

emular /emu'lar/ *vt* emulate

enamorado /enamo'radu/ *a* (*apaixonado*) in love

encabeçar /ĩkabe'sar/ *vt* head

encabu|lado /ĩkabu'ladu/ *a* shy. **~lar** *vt* embarrass. **~lar-se** *vpr* be shy

encadear /ĩkade'ar/ *vt* chain *ou* link together

encader|nação /ĩkaderna'sãw/ *f* binding. **~nado** *a* bound; (*com capa dura*) hardback. **~nar** *vt* bind

encai|xar /ĩka'ʃar/ *vt/i* fit. **~xe** *m* (*cavidade*) socket; (*juntura*) joint

encalço /ĩ'kawsu/ *m* pursuit; **no ~ de** in pursuit of

encalhar /ĩka'ʎar/ *vi* ‹*barco*› run aground; *fig* get bogged down; ‹*mercadoria*› not sell; [!] (*ficar solteiro*) be left on the shelf

encaminhar /ĩkami'ɲar/ *vt* (*dirigir*) steer, direct; (*remeter*) pass on; set in motion ‹*processo*›. **~-se** *vpr* set out

encana|dor /ĩkana'dor/ *m* plumber. **~mento** *m* plumbing

encan|tador /ĩkãta'dor/ *a* enchanting. **~tamento** *m* enchantment. **~tar** *vt* enchant. **~to** *m* charm

encaraco|lado /ĩkarako'ladu/ *a* curly. **~lar** *vt* curl. **~lar-se** *vpr* curl up

encarar /ĩka'rar/ *vt* confront, face

encarcerar /ĩkarse'rar/ *vt* imprison

encardido /ĩkar'dʒidu/ *a* grimy

encarecidamente /ĩkaresida'mẽtʃi/ *adv* insistently

encargo /ĩ'kargu/ *m* task, responsibility

encar|nação /ĩkarna'sãw/ *f* (*do espírito*) incarnation; (*de um personagem*) embodiment. **~nar** *vt* embody; play ‹*papel*›

encarre|gado /ĩkaxe'gadu/ *a* in charge (**de** of) ● *m* person in charge; (*de operários*) foreman; **~gado de negócios** chargé d'affaires. **~gar** *vt* **~gar alguém de** put sb in charge of; **~gar-se de** undertake to

encarte /ĩ'kartʃi/ *m* insert

ence|nação /ĩsena'sãw/ *f* (*de peça*) production; (*fingimento*) play-acting. **~nar** *vt* put on ● *vi* put it on

ence|radeira /ĩsera'dera/ *f* floor polisher. **~rar** *vt* wax

encer|rado /ĩse'xadu/ *a* ‹*assunto*› closed. **~ramento** *m* close. **~rar** *vt* close. **~rar-se** *vpr* close

encharcar /ĩʃar'kar/ *vt* soak

en|chente /ẽ'ʃẽtʃi/ *f* flood. **~cher** *vt* fill; [!] annoy ● *vi* [!] be annoying. **~cher-se** *vpr* fill up; [!] (*fartar-se*) get fed up (**de** with)

enciclopédia /ẽsiklo'pɛdʒia/ *f* encyclopaedia

enco|berto /ĩko'bɛrtu/ *a* ‹*céu, tempo*› overcast. **~brir** *vt* cover up ● *vi* ‹*tempo*› become overcast

encolher /ĩko'ʎer/ *vt* shrug ‹*ombros*›; pull up ‹*pernas*›; shrink ‹*roupa*› ● *vi* ‹*roupa*› shrink. **~-se** *vpr* (*de medo*) shrink; (*de frio*) huddle; (*espremer-se*) squeeze up

encomen|da /ĩko'mẽda/ *f* order; **de** *ou* **sob ~da** to order. **~dar** *vt* order (**a** from)

encon|trão /ĩkõ'trãw/ *m* bump; (*empurrão*) shove. **~trar** *vt* (*achar*) find; (*ver*) meet; **~trar com** meet. **~trar-se** *vpr* (*ver-se*) meet; (*estar*) be. **~tro** *m* meeting; *Mil* encounter; **ir ao ~tro de** go to meet; *fig* meet; **ir de ~tro a** run into; *fig* go against

encorajar /ĩkora'ʒar/ *vt* encourage

encor|pado /ĩkor'padu/ *a* stocky; ‹*vinho*› full-bodied. **~par** *vt/i* fill out

encos|ta /ĩ'kɔsta/ *f* slope. **~tar** *vt* (*apoiar*) lean; park ‹*carro*›; leave on the latch ‹*porta*›; (*pôr de lado*) put aside ● *vi* ‹*carro*› pull in. **~tar-se** *vpr* lean. **~to** /o/ *m* back

encra|vado /ĩkra'vadu/ *a* ‹*unha, pelo*› ingrowing. **~var** *vt* stick

encren|ca /ĩ'krẽka/ *f* fix, jam; *pl* trouble. **~car** *vt* get into trouble ‹*pessoa*›; complicate ‹*situação*› ● *vi* ‹*situação*› get complicated; ‹*carro*› break down. **~car-se** *vpr* ‹*pessoa*› get into trouble. **~queiro** *m* troublemaker

encres|pado /ĩkres'padu/ *a* ‹*mar*› choppy. **~par** *vt* frizz ‹*cabelo*›. **~par-se** *vpr* ‹*cabelo*› go frizzy; ‹*mar*› get choppy

encruzilhada /ĩkruzi'ʎada/ *f* crossroads

encurralar /ĩkuxa'lar/ *vt* hem in

encurtar /ĩkur'tar/ *vt* shorten

endere|çar /ĩdere'sar/ *vt* address. **~ço** /e/ *m* address; *Comput* **~ço de e-mail** email address

endinheirado /ĩdʒiɲe'radu/ *a* well-off

endireitar /ĩdʒirej'tar/ *vt* straighten. **~-se** *vpr* straighten up

endivi|dado /ĩdʒivi'dadu/ *a* in debt. **~dar** *vt* put into debt. **~dar-se** *vpr* get into debt

endoidecer /ĩdojde'ser/ *vi* get mad

endos|sar /ĩdo'sar/ *vt* endorse. **~so** /o/ *m* endorsement

endurecer /ĩdure'ser/ *vt/i* harden

ener|gético /ener'ʒɛtʃiku/ *a* energy. **~gia** /ener'ʒia/ *f* energy; **~gia solar/ nuclear/eólica** solar/nuclear/wind power

enérgico /e'nɛrʒiku/ *a* vigorous; ‹*remédio, discurso*› powerful

enevoado /enevu'adu/ *a* (*com névoa*) misty; (*com nuvens*) cloudy

enfarte /ĩ'fartʃi/ *m* heart attack

ênfase /'ẽfazi/ *f* emphasis; **dar ~ a** emphasize

enfático /ẽ'fatʃiku/ *a* emphatic

enfatizar /ẽfatʃi'zar/ *vt* emphasize

enfei|tar /ĩfej'tar/ *vt* decorate. **~tar-se** *vpr* dress up. **~te** *m* decoration

enfeitiçar /ĩfejtʃi'sar/ *vt* bewitch

enfer|magem /ĩfer'maʒẽ/ *f* nursing. **~maria** *f* ward. **~meira** *f* nurse. **~meiro** *m* male nurse. **~midade** *f* illness. **~mo** *a* sick ● *m* patient

enferru|jado /ĩfexu'ʒadu/ *a* rusty. **~jar** *vt/i* rust

enfezado /ĩfe'zadu/ *a* bad-tempered

enfiar /ẽfi'ar/ *vt* put; slip on ‹*roupa*›; thread ‹*agulha*›; string ‹*pérolas*›

enfileirar /ĩfilej'rar/ *vt* line up. **~-se** *vpr* line up

enfim /ẽ'fĩ/ *adv* (*finalmente*) finally; (*resumindo*) anyway

enfo|car /ĩfo'kar/ *vt* tackle. **~que** *m* approach

enfor|camento /ĩforka'mẽtu/ *m* hanging. **~car** *vt* hang. **~car-se** *vpr* hang o.s.

enfraquecer /ĩfrake'ser/ *vt/i* weaken

enfrentar /ĩfrẽ'tar/ *vt* face

enfumaçado /ĩfuma'sadu/ *a* smoky

enfurecer /ĩfure'ser/ *vt* infuriate. **~se** *vpr* get furious

enga|jamento /ĩgaʒa'mẽtu/ *m* commitment. **~jado** *a* committed. **~jar-se** *vpr* get involved (**em** in)

engalfinhar-se /ĩgawfi'ɲarsi/ *vpr* grapple

enga|nado /ĩga'nadu/ *a* (*errado*) mistaken. **~nar** *vt* deceive; cheat on ‹*marido, esposa*›; stave off ‹*fome*›. **~nar-se** *vpr* be mistaken. **~no** *m* (*erro*) mistake; (*desonestidade*) deception

engarra|famento /ĩgaxafa'mẽtu/ *m* traffic jam. **~far** *vt* bottle ‹*vinho etc*›; block ‹*trânsito*›

engas|gar /ĩgaz'gar/ *vt* choke ● *vi* choke; ‹*motor*› backfire. **~go** *m* choking

engastar /ĩgaʃ'tar/ *vt* set ‹*joias*›

engatar /ĩga'tar/ *vt* hitch ‹*reboque etc*› (**a** to); engage ‹*marcha*›

engatinhar /ĩgatʃi'ɲar/ *vi* crawl; *fig* start out

engave|tamento /ĩgaveta'mẽtu/ *m* pile-up. **~tar** *vt* shelve

engelhar /ĩʒe'ʎar/ *vi* (*pele*) wrinkle

enge|nharia /ĩʒeɲa'ria/ *f* engineering. **~nheiro** *m* engineer. **~nho** /e/ *m* (*de pessoa*) ingenuity; (*de açúcar*) sugar mill; (*máquina*) device. **~nhoca** /ɔ/ *f* gadget. **~nhoso** *a* ingenious

engessar /ĩʒe'sar/ *vt* put in plaster

engodo /ĩ'godu/ *m* lure

engolir /ĩgo'lir/ *vt/i* swallow; **~ em seco** gulp

engomar /ĩgo'mar/ *vt* press; (*com goma*) starch

engonhar /ẽgo'ɲar/ *vi Port* faff about ou around

engordar /ĩgor'dar/ *vt* make fat; fatten ‹*animais*› ● *vi* ‹*pessoa*› put on weight; ‹*comida*› be fattening

engraçado /ĩgra'sadu/ *a* funny

engradado /ĩgra'dadu/ *m* crate

engravidar /ĩgravi'dar/ *vt* make pregnant ● *vi* get pregnant

engraxar /ĩgra'ʃar/ *vt* polish

engre|nado /ĩgre'nadu/ *a* ‹*carro*› in gear. **~nagem** *f* gear; *fig* mechanism. **~nar** *vt* put into gear ‹*carro*›; strike up ‹*conversa*›. **~nar-se** *vpr* mesh; *fig* ‹*pessoas*› get on

engrossar /ĩgro'sar/ *vt* thicken; raise ‹*voz*› ● *vi* thicken; ‹*pessoa*› turn nasty

enguia /ẽ'gia/ *f* eel

e

engui|çar /ẽgi'sar/ *vi* break down. **~ço** *m* breakdown

enig|ma /e'nigima/ *m* enigma. **~mático** *a* enigmatic

enjaular /ĩʒaw'lar/ *vt* cage

enjo|ar /ĩʒo'ar/ *vt* sicken ● *vi*, **~ar-se** *vpr* get sick (**de** of). **~ativo** *a* ‹*comida*› sickly; ‹*livro etc*› boring

enjoo /ĩ'ʒou/ *m* sickness

enlameado /ĩlami'adu/ *a* muddy

enlatado /ĩla'tadu/ *a* tinned, canned. **~s** *m pl* tinned foods

enle|var /ẽle'var/ *vt* enthral. **~vo** /e/ *m* rapture

enlouquecer /ĩloke'ser/ *vt* drive mad ● *vi* go mad

enluarado /ĩlua'radu/ *a* moonlit

enor|me /e'nɔrmi/ *a* enormous. **~midade** *f* enormity

enquadrar /ĩkwa'drar/ *vt* fit ● *vi*, **~-se** *vpr* fit in

enquanto /ĩ'kwãtu/ *conj* while; **~ isso** meanwhile; **por ~** for the time being

enquete /ã'kɛtʃi/ *f* survey

enraivecer /ĩxajve'ser/ *vt* enrage

enredo /ẽ'redu/ *m* plot

enrijecer /ĩxiʒe'ser/ *vt* stiffen. **~-se** *vpr* stiffen

enrique|cer /ĩxike'ser/ *vt* (*dar dinheiro a*) make rich; *fig* enrich ● *vi* get rich. **~cimento** *m* enrichment

enro|lado /ĩxo'ladu/ *a* complicated. **~lar** *vt* (*envolver*) roll up; (*complicar*) complicate; (*enganar*) cheat. **~lar-se** *vpr* (*envolver-se*) roll up; (*confundir-se*) get mixed up

enroscar /ĩxos'kar/ *vt* twist

enrouquecer /ĩxoke'ser/ *vi* go hoarse

enrugar /ĩxu'gar/ *vt* wrinkle ‹*pele, tecido*›; furrow ‹*testa*›

enrustido /ĩxus'tʃidu/ *a* repressed

ensaboar /ĩsabo'ar/ *vt* soap

ensai|ar /ĩsaj'ar/ *vt* (*provar*) try out; (*repetir*) rehearse. **~o** *m* (*prova*) test; (*repetição*) rehearsal; (*escrito*) essay

ensanguentado /ĩsãgwẽ'tadu/ *a* bloody, bloodstained

enseada /ĩsi'ada/ *f* inlet

ensebado /ĩse'badu/ *a* greasy

ensimesmado /ĩsimez'madu/ *a* lost in thought

ensi|nar /ẽsi'nar/ *vt/i* teach (**algo a alguém** sb sth); **~nar alguém a nadar** teach sb to swim. **~no** *m* teaching; (*em geral*) education

ensolarado /ĩsola'radu/ *a* sunny

enso|pado /ĩso'padu/ *a* soaked ● *m* stew. **~par** *vt* soak

ensurde|cedor /ĩsurdese'dor/ *a* deafening. **~cer** *vt* deafen ● *vi* go deaf

entabular /ĩtabu'lar/ *vt* open, start

entalar /ĩta'lar/ *vt* wedge, jam; (*em apertos*) get. **~-se** *vpr* get wedged, get jammed; (*em apertos*) get caught up

entalhar /ĩta'ʎar/ *vt* carve

entanto /ĩ'tãtu/ *m* **no ~** however

então /ĩ'tãw/ ● *adv*

····➤ (*aquela época*) **desde ~** since then; **fui no casamento do Pedro e não o vejo desde ~** I went to Pedro's wedding and I haven't seen him since

····➤ (*naquele tempo*) at that time; **~ era mais magro** I was thinner at that time

····➤ (*por isso*) so; **eles não vinham, ~ fui embora** they didn't come, so I left

● *int*

····➤ (*para animar*) **~, anime-se!** come on, cheer up!

····➤ (*para chamar a atenção*) **~, o que você pensa que está fazendo?!** hey, what do you think you're doing?!

(*em expressões*) **e ~?...** (*não dar importância*) so what?; (*para saber informação extra*) so, what happened then?

entardecer /ĩtarde'ser/ *m* sunset

ente /'ẽtʃi/ *m* being

entea|da /ẽtʃi'ada/ *f* stepdaughter. **~do** *m* stepson

entedi|ante /ĩtedʒi'ãtʃi/ *a* boring. **~ar** *vt* bore. **~ar-se** *vpr* get bored

enten|der /ĩtẽ'der/ *vt* understand; **dar a ~der** give to understand; **~der de futebol** know about football. **~der-se** *vpr* (*dar-se bem*) get on (**com** with). **~dimento** *m* understanding

enternecedor /ĩternese'dor/ *a* touching

enter|rar /ĩte'xar/ *vt* bury. **~ro** /e/ *m* burial; (*cerimônia*) funeral

entidade /ẽtʃi'dadʒi/ *f* entity; (*órgão*) body

entornar /ĩtor'nar/ *vt* tip over, spill

entorpe|cente /ĩtorpe'sẽtʃi/ *m* drug, narcotic. **~cer** *vt* numb

entortar /ĩtor'tar/ *vt* make crooked

entrada /ẽ'trada/ *f* entry; (*onde se entra*) entrance; (*bilhete*) ticket; (*prato*) starter; (*pagamento*) deposit; *pl* (*no cabelo*) receding hairline; **dar ~ a** enter; **~ proibida** no entry

entranhas /ĩ'traɲas/ *f pl* entrails

entrar /ẽ'trar/ *vi* go/come in; **~ com** enter ‹*dados*›; put in ‹*dinheiro*›; **~ em detalhes** go into details; **~ em vigor** come into force

entravar /ẽtra'var/ *vt* hamper

entre /'ẽtri/ *prep* between; (*em meio a*) among

entreaberto /ẽtria'bɛrtu/ *a* half-open

entrecortar /ẽtrikor'tar/ *vt* intersperse; (*cruzar*) intersect

entre|ga /ĩ'trɛga/ *f* delivery; (*rendição*) surrender; **~ga a domicílio** home delivery. **~gar** *vt* hand over; deliver ‹*mercadorias, cartas*›; hand in ‹*caderno, trabalho escolar*›. **~gar-se** *vpr* give o.s. up (**a** to). **~gue** *pp de* ▶ **ENTREGAR**

entrelaçar /ẽtrela'sar/ *vt* intertwine; clasp ‹*mãos*›

entrelinhas /ẽtri'liɲas/ *f pl* **ler nas ~** read between the lines

entremear /ẽtrimi'ar/ *vt* intersperse

entreolhar-se /ẽtrio'ʎarsi/ *vpr* look at one another

entretanto /ẽtre'tãtu/ *conj* however

entre|tenimento /ẽtreteni'mẽtu/ *m* entertainment. **~ter** *vt* entertain

entrever /ẽtre'ver/ *vt* glimpse

entrevis|ta /ẽtre'vista/ *f* interview. **~tador** *m* interviewer. **~tar** *vt* interview

entristecer /ĩtriste'ser/ *vt* sadden ● *vi* be saddened (**com** by)

entroncamento /ĩtrõka'mẽtu/ *m* junction

entrosar /ĩtro'zar/ *vt/i* integrate

entu|lhar /ĩtu'ʎar/ *vt* cram (**de** with). **~lho** *m* rubble

entupir /ĩtu'pir/ *vt* block. **~pir-se** *vpr* get blocked; (*de comida*) stuff o.s. (**de** with)

enturmar-se /ĩtur'marsi/ *vpr* mix in, fit in

entusias|mar /ĩtuziaz'mar/ *vt* fill with enthusiasm. **~mar-se** *vpr* get enthusiastic (**com** about). **~mo** *m* enthusiasm. **~ta** *m/f* enthusiast ● *a* enthusiastic

entusiástico /ĩtuzi'astʃiku/ *a* enthusiastic

enumerar /enume'rar/ *vt* enumerate

envelhecer /ĩveʎe'ser/ *vt/i* age

envelope /ẽve'lɔpi/ *m* envelope

envenenar /ĩvene'nar/ *vt* poison; [!] soup up ‹*carro*›

envergadura /ĩverga'dura/ *f* wingspan; *fig* scale

envergo|nhado /ĩvergo'ɲadu/ *a* ashamed; (*constrangido*) embarrassed. **~nhar** *vt* disgrace; (*constranger*) embarrass. **~nhar-se** *vpr* be ashamed; (*acanhar-se*) get embarrassed

envernizar /ĩverni'zar/ *vt* varnish

en|viado /ẽvi'adu/ *m* envoy. **~viar** *vt* send. **~vio** *m* (*ato*) sending; (*remessa*) consignment

envidraçar /ĩvidra'sar/ *vt* glaze

enviesado /ĩvie'zadu/ *a* (*não vertical*) slanting; (*torto*) crooked

envol|vente /ĩvow'vẽtʃi/ *a* compelling, gripping. **~ver** *vt* (*embrulhar*) wrap; (*enredar*) involve. **~ver-se** *vpr* (*enrolar-se*) wrap o.s.; (*enredar-se*) get involved. **~vimento** *m* involvement

enxada /ẽ'ʃada/ *f* hoe

enxaguar /ẽʃa'gwar/ *vt* rinse

enxame /ẽ'ʃami/ *m* swarm

enxaqueca /ẽʃa'keka/ *f* migraine

enxergar /ĩʃer'gar/ *vt/i* see

enxer|tar /ĩʃer'tar/ *vt* graft. **~to** /e/ *m* graft

enxofre /ẽ'ʃofri/ *m* sulphur

enxotar /ĩʃo'tar/ *vt* drive away

enxo|val /ẽʃo'vaw/ (*pl* **~vais**) *m* (*de noiva*) trousseau; (*de bebê*) layette

enxugar /ĩʃu'gar/ *vt* dry. **~se** *vpr* dry o.s.

enxurrada /ĩʃu'xada/ *f* torrent; *fig* flood

enxuto /ĩ'ʃutu/ *a* dry; ‹*corpo*› shapely

enzima /ẽ'zima/ *f* enzyme

epicentro /epi'sẽtru/ *m* epicentre

épico /'ɛpiku/ *a* epic

epidemia /epide'mia/ *f* epidemic

e

epi|lepsia /epilep'sia/ *f* epilepsy. **~léptico** *a & m* epileptic

epílogo /e'pilogu/ *m* epilogue

episódio /epi'zɔdʒiu/ *m* episode

epitáfio /epi'tafiu/ *m* epitaph

época /'ɛpoca/ *f* time; (*da história*) age, period; **fazer ~** make history; **móveis da ~** period furniture

epopeia /epo'pɛja/ *f* epic

equação /ekwa'sãw/ *f* equation

equador /ekwa'dor/ *m* equator; **o E~** Ecuador

equatori|al /ekwatori'aw/ (*pl* **~ais**) *a* equatorial. **~ano** *a & m* Ecuadorian

equilibrar /ekili'brar/ *vt* balance. **~-se** *vpr* balance

equilíbrio /eki'libriu/ *m* balance

equipa /e'kipa/ *Port f* team

equi|pamento /ekipa'mẽtu/ *m* equipment. **~par** *vt* equip

equiparar /ekipa'rar/ *vt* equate (**com** with). **~-se** *vpr* compare (**a** with)

equipe /e'kipi/ *f* team

equitação /ekita'sãw/ *f* riding

equiva|lência /ekiva'lẽsia/ *f* equivalence. **~lente** *a* equivalent. **~ler** *vi* be equivalent (**a** to)

equivo|cado /ekivo'kadu/ *a* mistaken. **~car-se** *vpr* make a mistake

equívoco /e'kivoku/ *a* equivocal ● *m* mistake

era /'ɛra/ *f* era

erário /e'rariu/ *m* exchequer

ereção /ere'sãw/ *f* erection

eremita /ere'mita/ *m/f* hermit

ereto /e'rɛtu/ *a* erect

erguer /er'ger/ *vt* raise; erect ‹*monumento etc*›. **~-se** *vpr* rise

eri|çado /eri'sadu/ *a* bristling. **~çar-se** *vpr* bristle

ermo /'ermu/ *a* deserted ● *m* wilderness

erosão /ero'zãw/ *f* erosion

erótico /e'rɔtʃiku/ *a* erotic

erotismo /ero'tʃizmu/ *m* eroticism

er|rado /e'xadu/ *a* wrong. **~rante** *a* wandering. **~rar** *vt* (*não fazer certo*) get wrong; miss ‹*alvo*› ● *vi* (*enganar-se*) be wrong; (*vaguear*) wander. **~ro** /e/ *m* mistake; **fazer um ~ro** make a mistake. **~rôneo** *a* erroneous

erudi|ção /erudʒi'sãw/ *f* learning. **~to** *a* learned; ‹*música*› classical ● *m* scholar

erupção /erup'sãw/ *f* (*vulcânica*) eruption; (*cutânea*) rash

erva /'ɛrva/ *f* herb; **~ daninha** weed. **~-doce** *f* aniseed

ervilha /er'viʎa/ *f* pea

esban|jador /izbãʒa'dor/ *a* extravagant ● *m* spendthrift. **~jar** *vt* squander; burst with ‹*saúde, imaginação, energia etc*›

esbar|rão /izba'xãw/ *m* bump. **~rar** *vi* **~rar com** ou **em** bump into ‹*pessoa*›; come up against ‹*problema*›

esbelto /iz'bɛwtu/ *a* svelte

esbo|çar /izbo'sar/ *vt* sketch ‹*desenho etc*›; outline ‹*plano etc*›; **~çar um sorriso** give a hint of a smile. **~ço** /o/ *m* (*desenho*) sketch; (*plano*) outline; (*de um sorriso*) hint

esbofetear /izbofetʃi'ar/ *vt* slap

esborrachar /izboxa'ʃar/ *vt* squash. **~-se** *vpr* crash

esbravejar /izbrave'ʒar/ *vi* rant, rail

esbuga|lhado /izbuga'ʎadu/ *a* ‹*olhos*› bulging. **~lhar-se** *vpr* ‹*olhos*› pop out

esbura|cado /izbura'kadu/ *a* full of holes. **~car** *vt* make holes in

escabroso /iska'brozu/ *a fig* difficult, tough

escada /is'kada/ *f* (*dentro de casa*) stairs; (*na rua*) steps; (*de mão*) ladder; **~ de incêndio** fire escape; **~ rolante** escalator. **~ria** *f* staircase

escafan|drista /iskafã'drista/ *m/f* diver. **~dro** *m* diving suit

escala /is'kala/ *f* scale; (*de navio*) port of call; (*de avião*) stopover; **fazer ~** stop over; **sem ~** ‹*voo*› non-stop

esca|lada /iska'lada/ *f fig* escalation. **~lão** *m* echelon, level. **~lar** *vt* (*subir a*) scale; (*designar*) select

escaldar /iskaw'dar/ *vt* scald; blanch ‹*vegetais*›

escalfar /iskaw'far/ *vt* poach

escalonar /iskalo'nar/ *vt* schedule ‹*pagamento*›

escama /is'kama/ *f* scale

escanca|rado /iskãka'radu/ *a* wide open. **~rar** *vt* open wide

escandalizar /iskãdali'zar/ *vt* scandalize. **~-se** *vpr* be scandalized

escândalo /is'kãdalu/ *m* (*vexame*) scandal; (*tumulto*) fuss, uproar; **fazer um ~** make a scene

escandaloso /iskãda'lozu/ *a* (*chocante*) scandalous; (*espalhafatoso*) outrageous, loud

Escandinávia /iskãdʒi'navia/ *f* Scandinavia

escandinavo /iskãdʒi'navu/ *a & m* Scandinavian

escanga|lhado /iskãga'ʎadu/ *a* broken. **~lhar** *vt* break up. **~lhar-se** *vpr* fall to pieces; **~lhar-se de rir** split one's sides laughing

escaninho /iska'niɲu/ *m* pigeonhole

escanteio /iskã'teju/ *m* corner

esca|pada /iska'pada/ *f* (*fuga*) escape; (*aventura*) escapade. **~pamento** *m* exhaust. **~par** *vi* **~par a** ou **de** (*livrar-se*) escape from; (*evitar*) escape; **~pou-lhe a palavra** the word slipped out; **o copo ~pou-me das mãos** the glass slipped out of my hands; **o nome me ~pa** the name escapes me; **~par de boa** have a narrow escape. **~patória** *f* way out; (*desculpa*) pretext. **~pe** *m* escape; (*de carro etc*) exhaust. **~pulir** *vi* escape (**de** from)

escaramuça /iskara'musa/ *f* skirmish

escaravelho /iskara'vɛʎu/ *m* beetle

escarcéu /iskar'sɛw/ *m* uproar, fuss

escarlate /iskar'latʃi/ *a* scarlet

escarnecer /iskarne'ser/ *vt* mock

escárnio /is'karniu/ *m* derision

escarpado /iskar'padu/ *a* steep

escarrado /iska'xadu/ *m* **ele é o pai ~** he's the spitting image of his father

escarro /is'kaxu/ *m* phlegm

escas|sear /iskasi'ar/ *vi* run short. **~sez** *f* shortage. **~so** *a* (*raro*) scarce; (*ralo*) scant

esca|vadeira /iskava'dera/ *f* digger. **~var** *vt* excavate

esclare|cer /isklare'ser/ *vt* explain ‹*fatos*›; enlighten ‹*pessoa*›. **~cer-se** *vpr* ‹*fato*› be explained; ‹*pessoa*› find out. **~cimento** *m* (*de pessoas*) enlightenment; (*de fatos*) explanation

esclerosado /isklero'zadu/ *a* senile

escoar /isko'ar/ *vt/i* drain

esco|cês /isko'ses/ *a* (*f* **~cesa**) Scottish ● *m* (*f* **~cesa**) Scot

Escócia /is'kɔsia/ *f* Scotland

esco|la /is'kɔla/ *f* school; **~la de samba** samba school. **~lar** *a* school ● *m/f* schoolchild. **~laridade** *f* schooling

> **escola de samba** *Escolas de samba* (samba schools) are local organizations in which people sing and dance to samba music, often in competition with other schools. The samba schools parade on floats once a year, during Carnival. The most famous parades take place in the Rio de Janeiro Carnival, in the Avenida Marquês de Sapucaí Sambadrome.

esco|lha /is'koʎa/ *f* choice. **~lher** *vt* choose

escol|ta /is'kɔwta/ *f* escort. **~tar** *vt* escort

escombros /is'kõbrus/ *m pl* debris

escon|de-esconde /iskõdʒis'kõdʒi/ *m* hide-and-seek. **~der** *vt* hide. **~der-se** *vpr* hide. **~derijo** *m* hiding place; (*de bandidos*) hideout. **~didas** *f pl* **às ~didas** secretly

esco|ra /is'kɔra/ *f* prop. **~rar** *vt* prop up. **~rar-se** *vpr* ‹*argumento etc*› be based (**em** on)

escore /is'kɔri/ *m* score

escória /is'kɔria/ *f* scum, dross

escori|ação /iskoria'sãw/ *f* graze, abrasion. **~ar** *vt* graze

escorpião /iskorpi'ãw/ *m* scorpion; **E~** Scorpio

escorredor /iskoxe'dor/ *m* drainer

escorrega /isko'xega/ *m* slide

escorre|gador /iskoxega'dor/ *m* slide. **~gão** *m* slip. **~gar** *vi* slip

escor|rer /isko'xer/ *vt* drain ● *vi* trickle. **~rido** *a* ‹*cabelo*› straight

escoteiro /isko'teru/ *m* boy scout

escotilha /isko'tʃiʎa/ *f* hatch

esco|va /is'kova/ *f* brush; **fazer ~va no cabelo** blow-dry one's hair; **~va de dentes** toothbrush. **~var** *vt* brush. **~vinha** *f* **cabelo à ~vinha** crew cut

escra|chado /iskra'ʃadu/ *a* [!] outspoken. **~char** *vt* [!] tell off

escra|vatura /iskrava'tura/ *f* slavery. **~vidão** *f* slavery. **~vizar** *vt* enslave. **~vo** *m* slave

escre|vente /iskre'vẽtʃi/ *m/f* clerk. **~ver** *vt/i* write

escri|ta /is'krita/ *f* writing; **~ta inteligente** *Telec* predictive text messaging. **~to** *pp de* ▶ ESCREVER ● *a* written; **por ~to** in writing. **~tor** *m* writer. **~tório** *m* office; (*numa casa*) study

escritu|ra /iskri'tura/ *f* (*a Bíblia*) scripture; (*contrato*) deed. **~ração** *f* bookkeeping. **~rar** *vt* keep, write up ‹*contas*›; draw up ‹*documento*›

e

escri|vaninha /iskriva'niɲa/ *f* bureau, writing desk. **~vão** *m* (*f* **~vã**) registrar

escrúpulo /is'krupulu/ *m* scruple

escrupuloso /iskrupu'lozu/ *a* scrupulous

escrutínio /iskru'tʃiniu/ *m* ballot

escu|dar /isku'dar/ *vt* shield. **~deria** *f* team. **~do** *m* shield; (*moeda*) escudo

escula|chado /iskula'ʃadu/ *a* [!] sloppy. **~char** *vt* [!] mess up ‹*coisa*›; tell off ‹*pessoa*›. **~cho** *m* [!](*bagunça*) mess; (*bronca*) telling-off

escul|pir /iskuw'pir/ *vt* sculpt. **~tor** *m* sculptor. **~tura** *f* sculpture. **~tural** (*pl* **~turais**) *a* statuesque

escuma /is'kuma/ *f* scum. **~deira** *f* skimmer

escuna /is'kuna/ *f* schooner

escu|ras /is'kuras/ *f pl* **às ~ras** in the dark. **~recer** *vt* darken ● *vi* get dark. **~ridão** *f* darkness. **~ro** *a* & *m* dark

escuso /is'kuzu/ *a* shady

escu|ta /is'kuta/ *f* listening; **estar à ~ta** be listening; **~ta telefônica** phone tapping. **~tar** *vt* (*perceber*) hear; (*prestar atenção a*) listen to ● *vi* (*poder ouvir*) hear; (*prestar atenção*) listen

esdrúxulo /iz'druʃulu/ *a* weird

esfacelar /isfase'lar/ *vt* wreck

esfalfar /isfaw'far/ *vt* wear out. **~-se** *vpr* get worn out

esfaquear /isfaki'ar/ *vt* stab

esfarelar /isfare'lar/ *vt* crumble. **~-se** *vpr* crumble

esfarrapado /isfaxa'padu/ *a* ragged; ‹*desculpa*› lame

es|fera /is'fɛra/ *f* sphere. **~férico** *a* spherical

esferográfi|co /isfero'grafiku/ *a* **caneta ~ca** ballpoint pen

esfiapar /isfia'par/ *vt* fray. **~-se** *vpr* fray

esfinge /is'fĩʒi/ *f* sphinx

esfolar /isfo'lar/ *vt* skin; *fig* overcharge

esfomeado /isfomi'adu/ *a* starving, famished

esfor|çar-se /isfor'sarsi/ *vpr* make an effort. **~ço** /o/ *m* effort; **fazer ~ço** make an effort

esfre|gaço /isfre'gasu/ *m* smear. **~gar** *vt* rub; (*para limpar*) scrub

esfriar /isfri'ar/ *vt* cool ● *vi* cool (down); (*sentir frio*) get cold

esfumaçado /isfuma'sadu/ *a* smoky

esfuziante /isfuzi'ãtʃi/ *a* irrepressible, exuberant

esganar /izga'nar/ *vt* throttle

esganiçado /izgani'sadu/ *a* shrill

esgarçar /izgar'sar/ *vt/i* fray

esgo|tado /izgo'tadu/ *a* exhausted; ‹*estoque, lotação*› sold out. **~tamento** *m* exhaustion; **~tamento nervoso** nervous breakdown. **~tar** *vt* exhaust; (*gastar*) use up. **~tar-se** *vpr* ‹*pessoa*› become exhausted; ‹*estoque, lotação*› sell out; ‹*recursos, provisões*› run out. **~to** /o/ *m* drain; (*de detritos*) sewer

esgri|ma /iz'grima/ *f* fencing. **~mir** *vt* brandish ● *vi* fence. **~mista** *m/f* fencer

esgrouvinhado /izgrovi'ɲadu/ *a* tousled, dishevelled

esgueirar-se /izge'rarsi/ *vpr* slip, sneak

esguelha /iz'geʎa/ *f* **de ~** askew; ‹*olhar*› askance

esgui|char /izgi'ʃar/ *vt/i* spurt, squirt. **~cho** *m* jet, spurt

esguio /iz'gio/ *a* slender

eslavo /iz'lavu/ *a* Slavic ● *m* Slav

esmaecer /izmaj'ser/ *vi* fade

esma|gador /izmaga'dor/ *a* ‹*vitória, maioria*› overwhelming; ‹*provas*› incontrovertible. **~gar** *vt* crush

esmalte /iz'mawtʃi/ *m* enamel; **~ de unhas** nail varnish

esmeralda /izme'rawda/ *f* emerald

esme|rar-se /izme'rarsi/ *vpr* take great care (**em** over). **~ro** /e/ *m* great care

esmigalhar /izmiga'ʎar/ *vt* crumble ‹*pão etc*›; shatter ‹*vidro, copo*›. **~-se** *vpr* ‹*pão etc*› crumble; ‹*vidro, copo*› shatter

esmiuçar /izmiu'sar/ *vt* examine in detail

esmo /'ezmu/ *m* **a ~** ‹*escolher*› at random; ‹*andar*› aimlessly; ‹*falar*› nonsense

esmola /iz'mɔla/ *f* donation; *pl* charity

esmorecer /izmore'ser/ *vi* flag

esmurrar /izmu'xar/ *vt* punch

esno|bar /izno'bar/ *vt* snub ● *vi* be snobbish. **~be** /iz'nɔbi/ *a* snobbish ● *m/f* snob. **~bismo** *m* snobbishness

esotérico /ezo'tɛriku/ *a* esoteric

espa|çar /ispa'sar/ *vt* space out; make less frequent ‹*visitas, consultas etc*›. **~cial** (*pl* **~ciais**) *a* space. **~ço** *m* space; (*cultural etc*) venue. **~çoso** /o/ *a* spacious

espada /is'pada/ *f* sword; *pl* (*naipe*) spades. **~chim** *m* swordsman

espádua /is'padua/ *f* shoulder blade

espaguete /ispa'gɛtʃi/ *m* spaghetti

espaire|cer /ispajre'ser/ *vt* amuse ● *vi* relax; (*dar uma volta*) go for a walk. **~cimento** *m* recreation

espaldar /ispaw'dar/ *m* back

espalhafato /ispaʎa'fatu/ *m* (*barulho*) fuss, uproar; (*de roupa etc*) extravagance. **~so** /o/ *a* (*barulhento*) noisy, rowdy; (*ostentoso*) extravagant

espalhar /ispa'ʎar/ *vt* scatter; spread ‹*notícia, terror etc*›; shed ‹*luz*›. **~-se** *vpr* spread; ‹*pessoas*› spread out

espa|nador /ispana'dor/ *m* feather duster. **~nar** *vt* dust

espan|camento /ispãka'mẽtu/ *m* beating. **~car** *vt* beat up

Espanha /is'paɲa/ *f* Spain

espa|nhol /ispa'ɲɔw/ (*pl* **~nhóis**) *a* (*f* **~nhola**) Spanish ● *m* (*f* **~nhola**) Spaniard; (*língua*) Spanish; **os ~nhóis** the Spanish

espan|talho /ispã'taʎu/ *m* scarecrow. **~tar** *vt* (*admirar*) amaze; (*assustar*) scare; (*afugentar*) drive away. **~tar-se** *vpr* (*admirar-se*) be amazed; (*assustar-se*) get scared. **~to** *m* (*susto*) fright; (*admiração*) amazement. **~toso** /o/ *a* amazing

esparadrapo /ispara'drapu/ *m* sticking plaster

espargo /is'pargu/ *Port m* asparagus

esparramar /ispaxa'mar/ *vt* scatter. **~-se** *vpr* be scattered, spread

espartano /ispar'tanu/ *a* spartan

espartilho /ispar'tʃiʎu/ *m* corset

espas|mo /is'pazmu/ *m* spasm. **~módico** *a* spasmodic

espatifar /ispatʃi'far/ *vt* smash. **~-se** *vpr* smash; ‹*carro, avião*› crash

especi|al /ispesi'aw/ (*pl* **~ais**) *a* special. **~alidade** *f* speciality. **~alista** *m/f* specialist

especiali|zado /ispesiali'zadu/ *a* specialized; ‹*mão de obra*› skilled. **~zar-se** *vpr* specialize (**em** in)

especiaria /ispesia'ria/ *f* spice

espécie /is'pɛsi/ *f* sort, kind; (*de animais*) species

especifi|cação /ispesifika'sãw/ *f* specification. **~car** *vt* specify

específico /ispe'sifiku/ *a* specific

espécime /is'pesimi/ *m* specimen

espectador /ispekta'dor/ *m* (*de TV*) viewer; (*de jogo, espetáculo*) spectator; (*de acidente etc*) onlooker

espectro /is'pɛktru/ *m* (*fantasma*) spectre; (*de cores*) spectrum

especu|lação /ispekula'sãw/ *f* speculation. **~lador** *m* speculator. **~lar** *vi* speculate (**sobre** on). **~lativo** *a* speculative

espe|lhar /ispe'ʎar/ *vt* mirror. **~lhar-se** *vpr* be mirrored. **~lho** /e/ *m* mirror; **~lho retrovisor** rear-view mirror

espelunca /ispe'lũka/ *f* [!] dive [!]

espera /is'pɛra/ *f* wait; **à ~ de** waiting for

esperan|ça /ispe'rãsa/ *f* hope. **~çoso** /o/ *a* hopeful

esperar /ispe'rar/ *vt* (*aguardar*) wait for; (*desejar*) hope for; (*contar com*) expect ● *vi* wait (**por** for); **fazer alguém ~** keep sb waiting; **espero que ele venha** I hope (that) he comes; **espero que sim/não** I hope so/not

esperma /is'pɛrma/ *m* sperm

espernear /isperni'ar/ *vi* kick; *fig* (*reclamar*) kick up

esper|talhão /isperta'ʎãw/ *m* (*f* **~talhona**) wise guy. **~teza** /e/ *f* cleverness; (*uma*) clever move. **~to** /e/ *a* clever

espes|so /is'pesu/ *a* thick. **~sura** *f* thickness

espe|tacular /ispetaku'lar/ *a* spectacular. **~táculo** *m* (*no teatro etc*) show; (*cena impressionante*) spectacle. **~taculoso** /o/ *a* spectacular

espe|tar /ispe'tar/ *vt* (*cravar*) stick; (*furar*) skewer. **~tar-se** *vpr* (*cravar-se*) stick; (*ferir-se*) prick o.s.. **~tinho** *m* skewer; (*de carne etc*) kebab. **~to** /e/ *m* spit

espevitado /ispevi'tadu/ *a* cheeky

espezinhar /ispezi'ɲar/ *vt* walk all over

espi|a /is'pia/ *m/f* spy. **~ão** *m* (*f* **~ã**) spy. **~ada** *f* peep. **~ar** *vt* (*observar*) spy on; (*aguardar*) watch for ● *vi* peer, peep

espicaçar /ispika'sar/ *vt* goad ‹*pessoa*›; excite ‹*imaginação, curiosidade*›

espichar /ispi'ʃar/ *vt* stretch ● *vi* shoot up. **~-se** *vpr* stretch out

espiga /is'piga/ *f* (*de trigo etc*) ear; (*de milho*) cob

espina|fração /ispinafra'sãw/ *f* [!] telling-off. **~frar** *vt* [!] tell off. **~fre** *m* spinach

espingarda /ispĩ'garda/ *f* rifle, shotgun

e

e

espinha /is'piɲa/ *f* (*de peixe*) bone; (*na pele*) spot; **~ dorsal** spine

espinho /is'piɲu/ *m* thorn. **~so** /o/ *a* thorny; *fig* difficult, tough

espio|nagem /ispio'naʒẽ/ *f* espionage, spying. **~nar** *vt* spy on ● *vi* spy

espi|ral /ispi'raw/ (*pl* **~rais**) *a* & *f* spiral

espírita /is'pirita/ *a* & *m/f* spiritualist

espiritismo /ispiri'tʃizmu/ *m* spiritualism

espírito /is'piritu/ *m* spirit; (*graça*) wit

espiritu|al /ispiritu'aw/ (*pl* **~ais**) *a* spiritual. **~oso** /o/ *a* witty

espir|rar /ispi'xar/ *vt* spurt ● *vi* ‹*pessoa*› sneeze; ‹*lama, tinta etc*› spatter; ‹*fogo, lenha, fritura etc*› spit. **~ro** *m* sneeze

esplêndido /is'plẽdʒidu/ *a* splendid

esplendor /isplẽ'dor/ *m* splendour

espoleta /ispo'leta/ *f* fuse

espoliar /ispoli'ar/ *vt* plunder, pillage

espólio /is'pɔliu/ *m* (*herdado*) estate; (*roubado*) spoils

espon|ja /is'põʒa/ *f* sponge. **~joso** /o/ *a* spongy

espon|taneidade /ispõtanej'dadʒi/ *f* spontaneity. **~tâneo** *a* spontaneous

espora /is'pɔra/ *f* spur

esporádico /ispo'radʒiku/ *a* sporadic

esporear /ispori'ar/ *vt* spur on

espor|te /is'pɔrtʃi/ *m* sport ● *a invar* ‹*roupa*› casual; **carro ~te** sports car. **~tista** *m/f* sportsman (*f* -woman). **~tiva** *f* sense of humour. **~tivo** *a* sporting

espo|sa /is'poza/ *f* wife. **~so** *m* husband

espregui|çadeira /ispregisa'dera/ *f* (*tipo cadeira*) deckchair; (*tipo cama*) sun lounger. **~çar-se** *vpr* stretch

esprei|ta /is'prejta/ *f* **ficar à ~ta** lie in wait. **~tar** *vt* stalk ‹*caça, vítima*›; spy on ‹*vizinhos, inimigos etc*›; look out for ‹*ocasião*› ● *vi* peep, spy

espre|medor /ispreme'dor/ *m* squeezer. **~mer** *vt* squeeze; wring out ‹*roupa*›; squash ‹*pessoa*›. **~mer-se** *vpr* squeeze up

espu|ma /is'puma/ *f* foam; **~ma de borracha** foam rubber. **~mante** *a* ‹*vinho*› sparkling. **~mar** *vi* foam, froth

espúrio /is'puriu/ *a* spurious

esqua|dra /is'kwadra/ *f* squad; **~dra de polícia** *Port* police station. **~drão** *m* squadron. **~dria** *f* doors and windows. **~drinhar** *vt* explore. **~dro** *m* set square

esqualidez /iskwali'des/ *f* squalor

esquálido /is'kwalidu/ *a* squalid

esquartejar /iskwarte'ʒar/ *vt* chop up

esque|cer /iske'ser/ *vt/i* forget; **~cer-se de** forget. **~cido** *a* forgotten; (*com memória fraca*) forgetful. **~cimento** *m* oblivion; (*memória fraca*) forgetfulness

esque|lético /iske'lɛtʃiku/ *a* skinny, skeleton-like. **~leto** /e/ *m* skeleton

esque|ma /is'kema/ *m* outline, draft; (*operação*) scheme; **~ma de segurança** security operation. **~mático** *a* schematic

esquentar /iskẽ'tar/ *vt* warm up; **~ a cabeça** ! get worked up ● *vi* warm up; ‹*roupa*› be warm. **~-se** *vpr* get annoyed

esquer|da /is'kerda/ *f* left; **à ~da** (*posição*) on the left; (*direção*) to the left. **~dista** *a* left-wing ● *m/f* left-winger. **~do** /e/ *a* left

esqui /is'ki/ *m* ski; (*esporte*) skiing; **~ aquático** water skiing. **~ador** *m* skier. **~ar** *vi* ski

esquilo /is'kilu/ *m* squirrel

esquina /is'kina/ *f* corner

esquisi|tice /iskizi'tʃisi/ *f* strangeness; (*uma*) strange thing. **~to** *a* strange

esqui|var-se /iski'varsi/ *vpr* dodge out of the way; **~var-se de** dodge. **~vo** *a* elusive; ‹*pessoa*› aloof, antisocial

esquizo|frenia /iskizofre'nia/ *f* schizophrenia. **~frênico** *a* & *m* schizophrenic

es|sa /'ɛsa/ *pron* that (one); **~sa é boa** that's a good one; **~sa não** come off it; **por ~sas e outras** for these and other reasons. **~se** /e/ *a* that; *pl* those; ! (*este*) this; *pl* these ● *pron* that one; *pl* those; ! (*este*) this one; *pl* these

essência /e'sẽsia/ *f* essence

essenci|al /esẽsi'aw/ (*pl* **~ais**) *a* essential; **o ~al** what is essential

estabele|cer /istabele'ser/ *vt* establish. **~cer-se** *vpr* establish o.s.. **~cimento** *m* establishment

estabili|dade /istabili'dadʒi/ *f* stability. **~zar** *vt* stabilize. **~zar-se** *vpr* stabilize

estábulo /is'tabulu/ *m* cowshed

estaca /is'taka/ *f* stake; (*de barraca*) peg; **voltar à ~ zero** go back to square one

estação /ista'sãw/ *f* (*do ano*) season; (*ferroviária etc*) station; **~ balneária** seaside resort

estacar /ista'kar/ *vi* stop short

estacio|namento /istasiona'mẽtu/ *m* (*ação*) parking; (*lugar*) car park, *Amer* parking lot. **~nar** *vt/i* park

estada /is'tada/ *f*, **estadia** /ista'dʒia/ *f* stay

estádio /is'tadʒiu/ *m* stadium

esta|dista /ista'dʒista/ *m/f* statesman (*f*-woman). **~do** *m* state; **~do civil** marital status; **~do de espírito** state of mind; **Estados Unidos da América** United States of America. **Estado-Maior** *m* Staff. **~dual** (*pl* **~duais**) *a* state

esta|fa /is'tafa/ *f* exhaustion. **~fante** *a* exhausting. **~far** *vt* tire out. **~far-se** *vpr* get tired out

estagi|ar /istaʒi'ar/ *vi* do a traineeship. **~ário** *m* trainee

estágio /is'taʒiu/ *m* traineeship

estag|nado /istagi'nadu/ *a* stagnant. **~nar** *vi* stagnate

estalagem /ista'laʒẽ/ *f* inn

estalar /ista'lar/ *vt* (*quebrar*) crack; (*fazer barulho com*) click ● *vi* crack

estaleiro /ista'leru/ *m* shipyard

estalo /is'talu/ *m* crack; (*de dedos, língua*) click; **me deu um ~** it clicked (in my mind)

estam|pa /is'tãpa/ *f* print. **~pado** *a* ‹*tecido*› patterned ● *m* (*desenho*) pattern; (*tecido*) print. **~par** *vt* print

estampido /istã'pidu/ *m* bang

estancar /istã'kar/ *vt* staunch. **~-se** *vpr* dry up

estância /is'tãsia/ *f* **~ hidromineral** spa

estandarte /istã'dartʃi/ *m* banner

estanho /is'taɲu/ *m* tin

estanque /is'tãki/ *a* watertight

estante /is'tãtʃi/ *f* bookcase

estapafúrdio /istapa'furdʒiu/ *a* weird, odd

estar /is'tar/ ● *vi*

····➤ (*com lugar*) be; **a Lúcia está em casa** is Lúcia at home?

····➤ (*achar-se*) **~ doente/cansado** be ill/tired

····➤ (*aparência*) look; **você está muito bonita!** you look very pretty!

····➤ **~ em** (*consistir em*) lie in; **o êxito do grupo está na sua originalidade** the group's success lies in their originality

····➤ **~ a** *Port* (*seguido de infinitivo*) **estavam a jogar** they were playing

● *v aux*

····➤ (*com gerúndio*) **eles estão brincando** they're playing; **está fazendo 40ºC em São Paulo** it's 40ºC in São Paulo

····➤ (*com particípio*) **o arroz está cozido** the rice is cooked; **está aberto** it's open

● *v imp*

····➤ (*com temperatura*) **está frio/calor** it's cold/hot

····➤ (*em expressões*) **está bem?** (*de acordo?*) OK?; **você me empresta, está bem?** you'll lend it to me, won't you?; **~ a** *Port* (*com data*) **estamos a dois de junho** it's the second of June; (*com preço*) **a quanto está a banana?** how much are the bananas?; **~ com** (*apoiar*) be rooting for; **força, estou contigo!** go for it! I'm rooting for you; (*doença*) have; **estou com gripe** I've got the flu; **~ de partida** be leaving soon; **estou de partida para Londres** I'm leaving for London soon; **~ em** (*com data*) **estamos em três de abril** it's the third of April; **~ numa de** be into; **ultimamente ela está numa de ouvir rock** she's been into rock music lately; **estar sem: estou sem dinheiro** I haven't got any money; **está sem comer há três dias** she hasn't eaten for three days; **estou!, está lá!** *Port* (*ao telefone*) hello!; **não ~ para** not to be in the mood for; **não estou para brincadeiras** I'm not in the mood for jokes

! Quando o verbo **estar** é parte integrante de uma frase como por exemplo **estar acostumado**, **estar com pressa**, **estar de acordo**, **estar de pé**, pesquise pelo adjetivo ou substantivo que o acompanha.

estardalhaço /istarda'ʎasu/ *m* (*barulho*) fuss; (*ostentação*) extravagance

estarre|cedor /istaxese'dor/ *a* horrifying. **~cer** *vt* horrify. **~cer-se** *vpr* be horrified

esta|tal /ista'taw/ (*pl* **~tais**) *a* state-owned ● *f* state company

estate|lado /istate'ladu/ *a* sprawling. **~lar** *vt* knock down. **~lar-se** *vpr* go sprawling

estático /is'tatʃiku/ *a* static

estatísti|ca /ista'tʃistʃika/ *f* statistics. **~co** *a* statistical

estati|zação /istatʃiza'sãw/ *f* nationalization. **~zar** *vt* nationalize

e

estátua /is'tatua/ *f* statue

estatueta /istatu'eta/ *f* statuette

estatura /ista'tura/ *f* stature

estatuto /ista'tutu/ *m* statute

está|vel /is'tavew/ (*pl* **~veis**) *a* stable

este[1] /'ɛstʃi/ *a invar & m* east

este[2] /'estʃi/ *a* this; *pl* these ● *pron* this one; *pl* these; (*mencionado por último*) the latter

e

esteio /is'teju/ *m* prop; *fig* mainstay

esteira /is'tera/ *f* (*tapete*) mat; (*rastro*) wake

estelionato /istelio'natu/ *m* fraud

estender /istẽ'der/ *vt* (*desdobrar*) spread out; (*alongar*) stretch; (*ampliar*) extend; hold out ‹*mão*›; hang out ‹*roupa*›; roll out ‹*massa*›; draw out ‹*conversa*›. **~-se** *vpr* (*deitar-se*) stretch out; (*ir longe*) stretch, extend; **~-se sobre** dwell on

esteno|datilógrafo /istenodatʃi'lɔgrafu/ *m* shorthand typist. **~grafia** *f* shorthand

estepe /is'tɛpi/ *m* spare wheel

esterco /is'terku/ *m* dung

estéreo /is'tɛriu/ *a invar* stereo

estere|otipado /isteriotʃi'padu/ *a* stereotypical. **~ótipo** *m* stereotype

esté|ril /is'tɛriw/ (*pl* **~reis**) *a* sterile

esterili|dade /isterili'dadʒi/ *f* sterility. **~zar** *vt* sterilize

esterli|no /ister'lino/ *a* **libra ~na** pound sterling

esteroide /iste'rɔjdʒi/ *m* steroid

estética /is'tɛtʃika/ *f* aesthetics

esteticista /istetʃi'sista/ *m/f* beautician

estético /is'tɛtʃiku/ *a* aesthetic

estetoscópio /istetos'kɔpiu/ *m* stethoscope

estiagem /istʃi'aʒẽ/ *f* dry spell

estibordo /istʃi'bɔrdu/ *m* starboard

esti|cada /istʃi'kada/ *f* **dar uma ~cada** go on. **~car** *vt* stretch ● *vi* [!] go on. **~car-se** *vpr* stretch out

estigma /is'tʃigima/ *m* stigma. **~tizar** *vt* brand (**de** as)

estilha|çar /istʃiʎa'sar/ *vt* shatter. **~çar-se** *vpr* shatter. **~ço** *m* shard, fragment

estilingue /istʃi'lĩgi/ *m* catapult

estilis|mo /istʃi'lizmu/ *m* fashion design. **~ta** *m/f* fashion designer

esti|lístico /istʃi'listʃiku/ *a* stylistic. **~lizar** *vt* stylize. **~lo** *m* style; **~lo de vida** lifestyle

esti|ma /es'tʃima/ *f* esteem. **~mação** *f* estimation; **cachorro de ~mação** pet dog. **~mado** *a* esteemed; **Estimado Senhor** Dear Sir. **~mar** *vt* value ‹*bens, joias etc*› (**em** at); estimate ‹*valor, preço etc*› (**em** at); think highly of ‹*pessoa*›. **~mativa** *f* estimate

estimu|lante /istʃimu'lãtʃi/ *a* stimulating ● *m* stimulant. **~lar** *vt* stimulate; (*incentivar*) encourage

estímulo /is'tʃimulu/ *m* stimulus; (*incentivo*) incentive

estio /is'tʃiu/ *m* summer

estipu|lação /istʃipula'sãw/ *f* stipulation. **~lar** *vt* stipulate

estirar /istʃi'rar/ *vt* stretch. **~-se** *vpr* stretch

estirpe /is'tʃirpi/ *f* stock, line

estivador /istʃiva'dor/ *m* docker

estocada /isto'kada/ *f* thrust

estocar /isto'kar/ *vt* stock ● *vi* stock up

Estocolmo /isto'kɔwmu/ *f* Stockholm

esto|far /isto'far/ *vt* upholster ‹*móveis*›. **~fo** /o/ *m* upholstery

estoico /is'tɔjku/ *a & m* stoic

estojo /is'toʒu/ *m* case

estômago /is'tomagu/ *m* stomach

Estônia /is'tonia/ *f* Estonia

estonte|ante /istõtʃi'ãtʃi/ *a* stunning, mind-boggling. **~ar** *vt* stun

estopim /isto'pĩ/ *m* fuse; *fig* flashpoint

estoque /is'tɔki/ *m* stock

estore /is'tɔri/ *m* blind

estória /is'tɔria/ *f* story

estor|var /istor'var/ *vt* hinder; obstruct ‹*entrada, trânsito*›. **~vo** /o/ *m* hindrance

estou|rado /isto'radu/ *a* ‹*pessoa*› explosive. **~rar** *vi* ‹*bomba, escândalo, pessoa*› blow up; ‹*pneu*› burst; ‹*guerra*› break out; ‹*moda, cantor etc*› make it big. **~ro** *m* (*de bomba, moda etc*) explosion; (*de pessoa*) outburst; (*de pneu*) blowout; (*de guerra*) outbreak

estrábico /is'trabiku/ *a* ‹*olhos*› squinty; ‹*pessoa*› squint-eyed

estrabismo /istra'bizmu/ *m* squint

estraçalhar /istrasa'ʎar/ *vt* tear to pieces

estrada /is'trada/ *f* road; **~ de ferro** railway, *Amer* railroad; **~ de rodagem** highway; **~ de terra** dirt road

estrado /is'tradu/ *m* podium; (*de cama*) base

estragão /istra'gãw/ *m* tarragon

estraga-prazeres /istragapra'zeris/ *m/f invar* spoilsport

estra|gar /istra'gar/ *vt* (*tornar desagradável*) spoil; (*acabar com*) ruin ● *vi* (*quebrar*) break; (*apodrecer*) go off. **~go** *m* damage; *pl* damage; (*da guerra, do tempo*) ravages

estrangeiro /istrã'ʒeru/ *a* foreign ● *m* foreigner; **do ~** from abroad; **para o/no ~** abroad

estrangular /istrãgu'lar/ *vt* strangle

estra|nhar /istra'ɲar/ *vt* (*achar estranho*) find strange; (*não se adaptar a*) find it hard to get used to; (*não se sentir à vontade com*) be shy with; **~nhar que** find it strange that; **estou te ~nhando** that's not like you; **não é de se ~nhar** it's not surprising. **~nheza** /e/ *f* (*esquisitice*) strangeness; (*surpresa*) surprise. **~nho** *a* strange ● *m* stranger

estratagema /istrata'ʒema/ *m* stratagem

estraté|gia /istra'tɛʒia/ *f* strategy. **~gico** *a* strategic

estrato /is'tratu/ *m* (*camada*) stratum; (*nuvem*) stratus. **~sfera** *f* stratosphere

estre|ante /istri'ãtʃi/ *a* new ● *m/f* newcomer. **~ar** *vt* premiere ‹*peça, filme*›; embark on ‹*carreira*›; wear for the first time ‹*roupa*› ● *vi* ‹*pessoa*› make one's debut; ‹*filme, peça*› open

estrebaria /istreba'ria/ *f* stable

estreia /is'trɛja/ *f* (*de pessoa*) debut; (*de filme, peça*) premiere

estrei|tar /istrej'tar/ *vt* narrow; take in ‹*vestido*›; make closer ‹*relações, laços*› ● *vi* narrow. **~tar-se** *vpr* ‹*relações*› become closer. **~to** *a* narrow; ‹*relações, laços*› close; ‹*saia*› straight ● *m* strait

estre|la /is'trela/ *f* star. **~lado** *a* ‹*céu*› starry; ‹*ovo*› fried; **~lado por** ‹*filme etc*› starring. **~la-do-mar** (*pl* **~las-do-mar**) *f* starfish. **~lar** *vt* fry ‹*ovo*›; star in ‹*filme, peça*›. **~lato** *m* stardom. **~lismo** *m* star quality

estreme|cer /istreme'ser/ *vt* shake; strain ‹*relações, amizade*› ● *vi* shudder; ‹*relações, amizade*› become strained. **~cimento** *m* shudder; (*de relações, amizade*) strain

estrepar-se /istre'parsi/ *vpr* [!] come a cropper

estrépito /is'trɛpitu/ *m* noise; **com ~** noisily

estrepitoso /istrepi'tozu/ *a* noisy; ‹*sucesso etc*› resounding

estres|sante /istre'sãtʃi/ *a* stressful. **~sar** *vt* stress. **~se** /ɛ/ *m* stress

estria /is'tria/ *f* streak; (*no corpo*) stretch mark

estribeira /istri'bera/ *f* stirrup; **perder as ~s** lose control

estribilho /istri'biʎu/ *m* chorus

estribo /is'tribu/ *m* stirrup

estridente /istri'dẽtʃi/ *a* strident

estripulia /istripu'lia/ *f* antic

estrito /is'tritu/ *a* strict

estrofe /is'trɔfi/ *f* stanza, verse

estrógeno /is'trɔʒenu/ *m* oestrogen

estrogonofe /istrogo'nɔfi/ *m* stroganoff

estron|do /is'trõdu/ *m* crash. **~doso** /o/ *a* loud; ‹*aplausos*› thunderous; ‹*sucesso, fracasso*› resounding

estropiar /istropi'ar/ *vt* cripple ‹*pessoa*›; mangle ‹*palavras*›

estrume /is'trumi/ *m* manure

estrutu|ra /istru'tura/ *f* structure. **~ral** (*pl* **~rais**) *a* structural. **~rar** *vt* structure

estuário /istu'ariu/ *m* estuary

estudan|te /istu'dãtʃi/ *m/f* student. **~til** (*pl* **~tis**) *a* student

estudar /istu'dar/ *vt/i* study

estúdio /is'tudʒiu/ *m* studio

estu|dioso /istudʒi'ozu/ *a* studious ● *m* scholar. **~do** *m* study

estufa /is'tufa/ *f* (*para plantas*) greenhouse; (*de aquecimento*) stove. **~do** *m* stew

estupefato /istupe'fatu/ *a* dumbfounded

estupendo /iste'pẽdu/ *a* stupendous

estupidez /istupi'des/ *f* (*grosseria*) rudeness; (*uma*) rude thing; (*burrice*) stupidity; (*uma*) stupid thing

estúpido /is'tupidu/ *a* (*grosso*) rude, coarse; (*burro*) stupid ● *m* lout

estupor /istu'por/ *m* stupor

estu|prador /istupra'dor/ *m* rapist. **~prar** *vt* rape. **~pro** *m* rape

esturricar /istuxi'kar/ *vt* parch

esvair-se /izva'irsi/ *vpr* fade; **~ em sangue** bleed to death

esvaziar /izvazi'ar/ *vt* empty. **~-se** *vpr* empty

esverdeado /izverdʒi'adu/ *a* greenish

e

e

esvoa|çante /izvoa'sãtʃi/ *a* ‹*cabelo*› flyaway. **~çar** *vi* flutter

eta /'eta/ *int* what a

etapa /e'tapa/ *f* stage; (*de corrida, turnê etc*) leg

etário /e'tariu/ *a* age

éter /'ɛter/ *m* ether

etéreo /e'tɛriu/ *a* ethereal

eter|nidade /eterni'dadʒi/ *f* eternity. **~no** /ɛ/ *a* eternal

éti|ca /'ɛtʃika/ *f* ethics. **~co** *a* ethical

etimo|logia /etʃimolo'ʒia/ *f* etymology. **~lógico** *a* etymological

etíope /e'tʃiopi/ *a* & *m/f* Ethiopian

Etiópia /etʃi'ɔpia/ *f* Ethiopia

etique|ta /etʃi'keta/ *f* (*rótulo*) label; (*bons modos*) etiquette. **~tar** *vt* label

étnico /'ɛtʃiniku/ *a* ethnic

eu /ew/ *pron* I ● *m* self; **mais alto do que ~** taller than me; **sou ~** it's me

EUA *m pl* USA

eucalipto /ewka'liptu/ *m* eucalyptus

eufemismo /ewfe'mizmu/ *m* euphemism

euforia /ewfo'ria/ *f* euphoria

euro /'ewru/ *m* euro

Europa /ew'rɔpa/ *f* Europe

euro|peu /ewro'pew/ *a* & *m* (*f* **~peia**) European

eutanásia /ewta'nazia/ *f* euthanasia

evacu|ação /evakua'sãw/ *f* evacuation. **~ar** *vt* evacuate

evadir /eva'dʒir/ *vt* evade. **~-se** *vpr* escape (**de** from)

evan|gelho /evã'ʒɛʎu/ *m* gospel

evaporar /evapo'rar/ *vt* evaporate. **~-se** *vpr* evaporate

eva|são /eva'zãw/ *f* escape; (*fiscal etc*) evasion; **~ fiscal** tax evasion; **~são escolar** truancy. **~siva** *f* excuse. **~sivo** *a* evasive

even|to /e'vẽtu/ *m* event. **~tual** (*pl* **~tuais**) *a* possible. **~tualidade** *f* eventuality

evidência /evi'dẽsia/ *f* evidence

eviden|ciar /evidẽsi'ar/ *vt* show up. **~ciar-se** *vpr* show up. **~te** *a* obvious, evident

evi|tar /evi'tar/ *vt* avoid; **~tar de beber** avoid drinking. **~tável** (*pl* **~táveis**) *a* avoidable

evocar /evo'kar/ *vt* call to mind, evoke ‹*passado etc*›; call up ‹*espíritos etc*›

evolu|ção /evolu'sãw/ *f* evolution. **~ir** *vi* evolve

exacerbar /ezaser'bar/ *vt* exacerbate

exage|rado /ezaʒe'radu/ *a* over the top. **~rar** *vt* (*atribuir proporções irreais a*) exaggerate; (*fazer em excesso*) overdo ● *vi* (*ao falar*) exaggerate; (*exceder-se*) overdo it. **~ro** /e/ *m* exaggeration

exa|lação /ezala'sãw/ *f* fume; (*agradável*) scent. **~lar** *vt* give off ‹*perfume etc*›

exal|tação /ezawta'sãw/ *f* (*excitação*) agitation; (*engrandecimento*) exaltation. **~tar** *vt* (*excitar*) agitate; (*enfurecer*) infuriate; (*louvar*) exalt. **~tar-se** *vpr* (*excitar-se*) get agitated; (*enfurecer-se*) get furious

exa|me /e'zami/ *m* examination; (*na escola*) exam(ination); **~me de sangue** blood test. **~minar** *vt* examine

exaspe|ração /ezaspera'sãw/ *f* exasperation. **~rar** *vt* exasperate. **~rar-se** *vpr* get exasperated

exa|tidão /ezatʃi'dãw/ *f* exactness. **~to** *a* exact

exaurir /ezaw'rir/ *vt* exhaust. **~-se** *vpr* become exhausted

exaus|tivo /ezaws'tʃivu/ *a* ‹*estudo*› exhaustive; ‹*trabalho*› exhausting. **~to** *a* exhausted

exceção /ese'sãw/ *f* exception; **abrir ~** make an exception; **com ~ de** with the exception of

exce|dente /ese'dẽtʃi/ *a* & *m* excess, surplus. **~der** *vt* exceed. **~der-se** *vpr* overdo it

exce|lência /ese'lẽsia/ *f* excellence; (*tratamento*) excellency. **~lente** *a* excellent

excentricidade /esẽtrisi'dadʒi/ *f* eccentricity

excêntrico /e'sẽtriku/ *a* & *m* eccentric

excep|cional /esepsjo'naw/ (*pl* **~cionais**) *a* exceptional; (*deficiente*) handicapped

exces|sivo /ese'sivu/ *a* excessive. **~so** /ɛ/ *m* excess; **~so de bagagem** excess baggage; **~so de velocidade** speeding

exce|to /e'sɛtu/ *prep* except. **~tuar** *vt* except

exci|tação /esita'sãw/ *f* excitement. **~tante** *a* exciting. **~tar** *vt* excite. **~tar-se** *vpr* get excited

excla|mação /isklama'sãw/ *f* exclamation. **~mar** *vt/i* exclaim

exclu|ir /isklu'ir/ *vt* exclude. **~são** *f* exclusion; **com ~são de** with the exclusion of. **~sividade** *f* exclusive rights; **com ~sividade** exclusively. **~sivo** *a* exclusive. **~so** *a* excluded

excomungar /iskomũ'gar/ *vt* excommunicate

excremento /iskre'mẽtu/ *m* excrement

excur|são /iskur'sãw/ *f* excursion; (*a pé*) hike, walk. **~sionista** *m/f* day tripper; (*a pé*) hiker, walker

execu|ção /ezeku'sãw/ *f* execution. **~tante** *m/f* performer. **~tar** *vt* carry out ‹*ordem, plano etc*›; perform ‹*papel, música*›; execute ‹*preso, criminoso etc*›. **~tivo** *a & m* executive

exem|plar /ezẽ'plar/ *a* exemplary ● *m* (*de espécie*) example; (*de livro, jornal etc*) copy. **~plificar** *vt* exemplify

exemplo /e'zẽplu/ *m* example; **a ~ de** following the example of; **por ~** for example; **dar o ~** set an example

exequí|vel /eze'kwivew/ (*pl* **~veis**) *a* feasible

exer|cer /ezer'ser/ *vt* exercise; exert ‹*pressão, influência*›; carry on ‹*profissão*›. **~cício** *m* exercise; *Mil* drill; (*de profissão*) practice; (*financeiro*) financial year. **~citar** *vt* exercise; practise ‹*ofício*›. **~citar-se** *vpr* train

exército /e'zɛrsitu/ *m* army

exibição /ezibi'sãw/ *f* (*de filme, passaporte etc*) showing; (*de talento, força, ostentação*) show

exibicionis|mo /ezibisio'nizmu/ *m* exhibitionism. **~ta** *a & m/f* exhibitionist

exi|bido /ezi'bidu/ *a* ‹*pessoa*› pretentious ● *m* show-off. **~bir** *vt* show; (*ostentar*) show off. **~bir-se** *vpr* (*ostentar-se*) show off

exi|gência /ezi'ʒẽsia/ *f* demand. **~gente** *a* demanding. **~gir** *vt* demand

exíguo /e'zigwu/ *a* (*muito pequeno*) tiny; (*escasso*) minimal

exi|lado /ezi'lado/ *a* exiled ● *m* exile. **~lar** *vt* exile. **~lar-se** *vpr* go into exile

exílio /e'ziliu/ *m* exile

exímio /e'zimiu/ *a* distinguished

eximir /ezi'mir/ *vt* exempt (**de** from); **~-se de** get out of

exis|tência /ezis'tẽsia/ *f* existence. **~tencial** (*pl* **~tenciais**) *a* existential. **~tente** *a* existing. **~tir** *vi* exist

êxito /'ezitu/ *m* success; (*música, filme etc*) hit; **ter ~** succeed

êxodo /'ezodu/ *m* exodus

exonerar /ezone'rar/ *vt* (*de cargo*) dismiss, sack. **~-se** *vpr* resign

exorbitante /ezorbi'tãtʃi/ *a* exorbitant

exor|cismo /ezor'sizmu/ *m* exorcism. **~cista** *m/f* exorcist. **~cizar** *vt* exorcize

exótico /e'zɔtʃiku/ *a* exotic

expan|dir /ispã'dʒir/ *vt* spread. **~dir-se** *vpr* spread; ‹*pessoa*› open up; **~dir-se sobre** expand upon. **~são** *f* expansion. **~sivo** *a* expansive, open

expatri|ado /ispatri'ado/ *a & m* expatriate. **~ar-se** *vpr* leave one's country

expectativa /ispekta'tʃiva/ *f* expectation; **na ~ de** expecting; **estar na ~** wait to see what happens; **~ de vida** life expectancy

expedição /espedʒi'sãw/ *f* (*de encomendas, cartas*) dispatch; (*de passaporte, diploma etc*) issue; (*viagem*) expedition

expediente /ispedʒi'ẽtʃi/ *a* ‹*pessoa*› resourceful ● *m* (*horário*) working hours; (*meios*) expedient; **meio ~** part-time

expe|dir /ispe'dʒir/ *vt* dispatch ‹*encomendas, cartas*›; issue ‹*passaporte, diploma*›. **~dito** *a* prompt, quick

expelir /ispe'lir/ *vt* expel

experi|ência /isperi'ẽsia/ *f* experience; (*teste, tentativa*) experiment. **~ente** *a* experienced

experimen|tação /isperimẽta'sãw/ *f* experimentation. **~tado** *a* experienced. **~tar** *vt* (*provar*) try out; try on ‹*roupa*›; try ‹*comida*›; (*sentir, viver*) experience. **~to** *m* experiment

expi|ar /espi'ar/ *vt* atone for. **~atório** *a* **bode ~atório** scapegoat

expi|ração /espira'sãw/ *f* (*vencimento*) expiry; (*de ar*) exhalation. **~rar** *vt* exhale ● *vi* (*morrer, vencer*) expire; (*expelir ar*) breath out, exhale

expli|cação /isplika'sãw/ *f* explanation. **~car** *vt* explain. **~car-se** *vpr* explain o.s.. **~cável** (*pl* **~cáveis**) *a* explainable

explicitar /isplisi'tar/ *vt* set out

explícito /is'plisitu/ *a* explicit

explodir /isplo'dʒir/ *vt* explode ● *vi* explode; ‹*ator etc*› make it big

explo|ração /isplora'sãw/ *f* (*uso, abuso*) exploitation; (*pesquisa*) exploration. **~rar** *vt* (*tirar proveito de*) exploit; (*esquadrinhar*) explore

e

explo|são /isplo'zãw/ *f* explosion. **~sivo** *a & m* explosive

expor /es'por/ *vt* (*sujeitar, arriscar*) expose (**a** to); display ‹*mercadorias*›; exhibit ‹*obras de arte*›; (*explicar*) expound; **~ a vida** risk one's life. **~-se** *vpr* expose o.s. (**a** to)

expor|tação /isporta'sãw/ *f* export. **~tador** *a* exporting ● *m* exporter. **~tadora** *f* export company. **~tar** *vt* export

exposi|ção /ispozi'sãw/ *f* (*de arte etc*) exhibition; (*de mercadorias*) display; (*de filme fotográfico*) exposure; (*explicação*) exposition. **~tor** *m* exhibitor

exposto /is'postu/ *a* exposed (**a** to); ‹*mercadoria, obra de arte*› on display

expres|são /ispre'sãw/ *f* expression. **~sar** *vt* express. **~sar-se** *vpr* express o.s.. **~sivo** *a* expressive; ‹*número, quantia*› significant. **~so** /ɛ/ *a & m* express

exprimir /ispri'mir/ *vt* express. **~-se** *vpr* express o.s.

expropriar /ispropri'ar/ *vt* expropriate

expul|são /ispuw'sãw/ *f* expulsion; (*de jogador*) sending off. **~sar** *vt* (*de escola, partido, país etc*) expel; (*de clube, bar, festa etc*) throw out; (*de jogo*) send off. **~so** *pp de* ▶ **EXPULSAR**

expur|gar /ispur'gar/ *vt* purge; expurgate ‹*livro*›. **~go** *m* purge

êxtase /'estazi/ *f* ecstasy

extasiado /istazi'adu/ *a* ecstatic

exten|são /istẽ'sãw/ *f* extension; (*tamanho, alcance, duração*) extent; (*de terreno*) expanse; **~são (de arquivo)** *Comput* (file) extension. **~sivo** *a* extensive. **~so** *a* extensive; **por ~so** in full

extenu|ante /istenu'ãtʃi/ *a* wearing, tiring. **~ar** *vt* tire out. **~ar-se** *vpr* tire o.s. out

exterior /isteri'or/ *a* outside, exterior; ‹*aparência*› outward; ‹*relações, comércio etc*› foreign ● *m* outside, exterior; (*de pessoa*) exterior; **o ~** (*outros países*) abroad; **para o/no ~** abroad

exter|minar /istermi'nar/ *vt* exterminate. **~mínio** *m* extermination

exter|nar /ister'nar/ *vt* show. **~na** /ɛ/ *f* location shot. **~no** /ɛ/ *a* external; ‹*dívida etc*› foreign ● *m* day pupil

extin|ção /istʃĩ'sãw/ *f* extinction. **~guir** *vt* extinguish ‹*fogo*›; wipe out ‹*dívida, animal, povo*›. **~guir-se** *vpr* ‹*fogo, luz*› go out; ‹*animal, planta*› become extinct. **~to** *a* extinct; ‹*organização, pessoa*› defunct. **~tor** *m* fire extinguisher

extirpar /istʃir'par/ *vt* remove ‹*tumor etc*›; uproot ‹*ervas daninhas*›; eradicate ‹*abusos*›

extor|quir /istor'kir/ *vt* extort. **~são** *f* extortion

extra /'ɛstra/ *a & m/f* extra; **horas ~s** overtime

extração /istra'sãw/ *f* extraction; (*da loteria*) draw

extraconju|gal /estrakõʒu'gaw/ (*pl* **~gais**) *a* extramarital

extracurricular /estrakuxiku'lar/ *a* extracurricular

extradi|ção /istradʒi'sãw/ *f* extradition. **~tar** *vt* extradite

extrair /istra'ir/ *vt* extract; draw ‹*números da loteria*›

extrajudici|al /estraʒudʒisi'aw/ (*pl* **~ais**) *a* out-of-court. **~almente** *adv* out of court

extraordinário /istraordʒi'nariu/ *a* extraordinary

extrapolar /istrapo'lar/ *vt* (*exceder*) overstep; (*calcular*) extrapolate ● *vi* overstep the mark, go too far

extrasensori|al /estrasẽsori'aw/ (*pl* **~ais**) *a* extrasensory

extraterrestre /estrate'xestri/ *a & m* extraterrestrial

extrato /is'trato/ *m* extract; (*de conta*) statement

extrava|gância /istrava'gãsia/ *f* extravagance. **~gante** *a* extravagant

extravasar /istrava'zar/ *vt* release, let out ‹*emoções, sentimentos*› ● *vi* overflow

extra|viado /istravi'adu/ *a* lost. **~viar** *vt* lose, mislay ‹*papéis, carta*›; lead astray ‹*pessoa*›; embezzle ‹*dinheiro*›. **~viar-se** *vpr* go astray; ‹*carta*› get lost. **~vio** *m* (*perda*) misplacement; (*de dinheiro*) embezzlement

extre|midade /estremi'dadʒi/ *f* end; (*do corpo*) extremity. **~mismo** *m* extremism. **~mista** *a & m/f* extremist. **~mo** /e/ *a & m* extreme; **o Extremo Oriente** the Far East. **~moso** /o/ *a* doting

extrovertido /istrover'tʃido/ *a & m* extrovert

exube|rância /ezube'rãsia/ *f* exuberance. **~rante** *a* exuberant

exultar /ezuw'tar/ *vi* exult

exumar /ezu'mar/ *vt* exhume ‹*cadáver*›; dig up ‹*documentos etc*›

Ff

fã /fã/ *m/f* fan

fábrica /ˈfabrika/ *f* factory

fabri|cação /fabrikaˈsãw/ *f* manufacture. **~cante** *m/f* manufacturer. **~car** *vt* manufacture; (*inventar*) fabricate

fábula /ˈfabula/ *f* fable; [!] (*dinheirão*) fortune

fabuloso /fabuˈlozu/ *a* fabulous

faca /ˈfaka/ *f* knife. **~da** *f* knife blow; **dar uma ~da em** *fig* get some money off

façanha /faˈsaɲa/ *f* feat

facção /fakˈsãw/ *f* faction

face /ˈfasi/ *f* face; (*do rosto*) cheek. **~ta** /e/ *f* facet

fachada /faˈʃada/ *f* facade

facho /ˈfaʃu/ *m* beam

faci|al /fasiˈaw/ (*pl* **~ais**) *a* facial

fá|cil /ˈfasiw/ (*pl* **~ceis**) *a* easy; ‹*pessoa*› easy-going

facili|dade /fasiliˈdadʒi/ *f* ease; (*talento*) facility. **~tar** *vt* facilitate

facilitismo /faciliˈtiʒmu/ *m* **o ~ na educação** falling education standards

fã-clube /fãˈklubi/ *m* fan club

fac-símile /fakˈsimili/ *m* facsimile; (*fax*) fax

fact- *Port* ▶ **fat-**

facul|dade /fakuwˈdadʒi/ *f* (*mental etc*) faculty; (*escola*) university, *Amer* college; **fazer ~dade** go to university. **~tativo** *a* optional

fada /ˈfada/ *f* fairy. **~do** *a* destined, doomed. **~-madrinha** (*pl* **~s-madrinhas**) *f* fairy godmother

fadiga /faˈdʒiga/ *f* fatigue

fa|dista /faˈdʒista/ *m/f* fado singer. **~do** *m* fado

> *i*
> **fado** *Fado*, literally meaning 'fate', is a traditional Portuguese style of song dating back to the early 19th century. The songs have a melancholy, plaintive style, and are associated with the Portuguese concept of *saudade* (longing). There are two types of *fado*: Lisbon *fado* is traditionally sung by a woman accompanied by two or three guitarists, whereas Coimbra *fado* is performed by a male soloist.

fagote /faˈgɔtʃi/ *m* bassoon

fagulha /faˈguʎa/ *f* spark

faia /ˈfaja/ *f* beech

faisão /fajˈzãw/ *m* pheasant

faísca /faˈiska/ *f* spark

fais|cante /fajsˈkãtʃi/ *a* sparkling. **~car** *vi* spark; (*cintilar*) sparkle

faixa /ˈfaʃa/ *f* strip; (*cinto*) sash; (*em karatê, judô*) belt; (*da estrada*) lane; (*de ônibus*) bus lane; (*para pedestres*) zebra crossing, *Amer* crosswalk; (*atadura*) bandage; (*de disco*) track; **~ etária** age group

fajuto /faˈʒutu/ *a* [!] fake

fala /ˈfala/ *f* speech

fala-barato /ˈfalaˈbaratu/ *m/f invar Port* ▶ **TAGARELA**

falácia /faˈlasia/ *f* fallacy

fa|lado /faˈladu/ *a* ‹*língua*› spoken; ‹*caso, pessoa*› talked about. **~lante** *a* talkative. **~lar** *vt/i* speak; (*dizer*) say; **~lar com** talk to; **~lar de** ou **em** talk about; **por ~lar em** speaking of; **sem ~lar em** not to mention; **~lou!** [!] OK!. **~latório** *m* (*boatos*) talk; (*som de vozes*) talking

falaz /faˈlas/ *a* fallacious

falcão /fawˈkãw/ *m* falcon

falcatrua /fawkaˈtrua/ *f* swindle

fale|cer /faleˈser/ *vi* die, pass away. **~cido** *a & m* deceased. **~cimento** *m* death

falência /faˈlẽsia/ *f* bankruptcy; **ir à ~** go bankrupt

falésia /faˈlɛzia/ *f* cliff

fa|lha /ˈfaʎa/ *f* fault; (*omissão*) failure. **~lhar** *vi* fail. **~lho** *a* faulty

fálico /ˈfaliku/ *a* phallic

fa|lido /faˈlidu/ *a & m* bankrupt. **~lir** *vi* go bankrupt. **~lível** (*pl* **~líveis**) *a* fallible

falo /ˈfalu/ *m* phallus

fal|sário /fawˈsariu/ *m* forger. **~sear** *vt* falsify. **~sete** *m* falsetto. **~sidade** *f* falseness; (*mentira*) falsehood

falsifi|cação /fawsifikaˈsãw/ *f* forgery. **~cador** *m* forger. **~car** *vt* falsify; forge ‹*documentos, notas*›

falso /ˈfawsu/ *a* false

fal|ta /ˈfawta/ *f* lack; (*em futebol*) foul; **em ~ta** at fault; **por ~ta de** for lack of; **sem ~ta** without fail; **fazer ~ta** be needed; **sentir a ~ta de** miss. **~tar** *vi* be missing; ‹*aluno*› be absent; **~tam dois dias para** it's two days until; **me ~ta ...** I don't have ...; **~tar a** miss ‹*aula etc*›; break ‹*palavra, promessa*›. **~to** *a* short (**de** of)

fa|ma /'fama/ *f* reputation; (*celebridade*) fame. **~migerado** *a* notorious

família /fa'milia/ *f* family

famili|ar /famili'ar/ *a* familiar; (*de família*) family. **~aridade** *f* familiarity. **~arizar** *vt* familiarize. **~arizar-se** *vpr* familiarize o.s.

faminto /fa'mĩtu/ *a* starving

famoso /fa'mozu/ *a* famous

fanático /fa'natʃiku/ *a* fanatical ● *m* fanatic

fanatismo /fana'tʃizmu/ *m* fanaticism

fanfarrão /fãfa'xãw/ *m* braggart

fanhoso /fa'ɲozu/ *a* nasal; **ser ~** talk through one's nose

fanta|sia /fãta'zia/ *f* (*faculdade*) imagination; (*devaneio*) fantasy; (*roupa*) fancy dress. **~siar** *vt* dream up ● *vi* fantasize. **~siar-se** *vpr* dress up (**de** as). **~sioso** /o/ *a* fanciful; ‹*pessoa*› imaginative. **~sista** *a* imaginative

fantasma /fã'tazma/ *m* ghost. **~górico** *a* ghostly

fantástico /fã'tastʃiku/ *a* fantastic

fantoche /fã'tɔʃi/ *m* puppet

faqueiro /fa'keru/ *m* canteen of cutlery

fara|ó /fara'ɔ/ *m* pharaoh. **~ônico** *a fig* of epic proportions

farda /'farda/ *f* uniform. **~do** *a* uniformed

fardo /'fardu/ *m fig* burden

fare|jador /fareʒa'dor/ *a* **cão ~jador** sniffer dog. **~jar** *vt* sniff out ● *vi* sniff

farelo /fa'rɛlu/ *m* bran; (*de pão*) crumb; (*de madeira*) sawdust

farfalhar /farfa'ʎar/ *vi* rustle

farináceo /fari'nasiu/ *a* starchy. **~s** *m pl* starchy foods

farin|ge /fa'rĩʒi/ *f* pharynx. **~gite** *f* pharyngitis

farinha /fa'riɲa/ *f* flour; **~ de rosca** breadcrumbs

far|macêutico /farma'sewtʃiku/ *a* pharmaceutical ● *m* (*pessoa*) pharmacist. **~mácia** *f* (*loja*) chemist's, *Amer* pharmacy; (*ciência*) pharmacy

faro /'faru/ *f* sense of smell; *fig* nose

faroeste /faro'ɛstʃi/ *m* (*filme*) western; (*região*) wild west

faro|fa /fa'rɔfa/ *f* fried manioc flour. **~feiro** *m* [!] day tripper

fa|rol /fa'rɔw/ (*pl* **~róis**) *m* (*de carro*) headlight; (*de trânsito*) traffic light; (*à beira-mar*) lighthouse; **~rol alto** full beam; **~rol baixo** dipped beam. **~roleiro** *a* boastful ● *m* big-head. **~rolete** /e/ *m*, *Port* **~rolim** *m* sidelight; (*traseiro*) tail light

farpa /'farpa/ *f* splinter; (*de metal*) *fig* barb. **~do** *a* **arame ~do** barbed wire

farra /'faxa/ *f* [!] partying; **cair na ~** go out and party

farrapo /fa'xapu/ *m* rag

far|rear /faxi'ar/ *vi* [!] party. **~rista** *m/f* [!] raver [!]

far|sa /'farsa/ *f* (*peça*) farce; (*fingimento*) pretence. **~sante** *m/f* (*brincalhão*) joker; (*pessoa sem seriedade*) unreliable character

far|tar /far'tar/ *vt* satiate. **~tar-se** *vpr* (*saciar-se*) gorge o.s. (**de** with); (*cansar*) tire (**de** of). **~to** *a* (*abundante*) plentiful; (*cansado*) fed up (**de** with). **~tura** *f* abundance

fascículo /fa'sikulu/ *m* instalment

fasci|nação /fasina'sãw/ *f* fascination. **~nante** *a* fascinating. **~nar** *vt* fascinate

fascínio /fa'siniu/ *m* fascination

fas|cismo /fa'sizmu/ *m* fascism. **~cista** *a* & *m/f* fascist

fase /'fazi/ *f* phase

fa|tal /fa'taw/ (*pl* **~tais**) *a* fatal. **~talismo** *m* fatalism. **~talista** *a* fatalistic ● *m/f* fatalist. **~talmente** *adv* inevitably

fatia /fa'tʃia/ *f* slice

fatídico /fa'tʃidʒiku/ *a* fateful

fati|gante /fatʃi'gãtʃi/ *a* tiring. **~gar** *vt* tire, fatigue

> *i*
> **Fátima** Fátima is a town in central Portugal famous for its Marian shrine, the Basilica of Our Lady of Fátima. The shrine was built to commemorate the reported apparition of the Virgin Mary to three shepherds in 1917, and it attracts millions of Catholic pilgrims every year.

fato[1] /'fatu/ *m* fact; **de ~** as a matter of fact, in fact; **~ consumado** fait accompli

fato[2] /'fatu/ *Port m* suit

fator /fa'tor/ *m* factor

fátuo /'fatuu/ *a* fatuous

fatu|ra /fa'tura/ *f* invoice. **~ramento** *m* turnover. **~rar** *vt* invoice for ‹*encomenda*›; make ‹*dinheiro*›; *fig* (*emplacar*) notch up ● *vi* [!] rake it in [!]

fauna /'fawna/ *f* fauna

fava /'fava/ *f* broad bean; **mandar alguém às ~s** tell sb where to get off

favela /fa'vɛla/ *f* shanty town. **~do** *m* shanty-dweller

favela *Favelas* are Brazilian shanty towns, characterized by precarious housing, very little infrastructure and a lack of official recognition. The houses in the *favelas* are known as *barracos*, and many have no running water or sanitation. The most famous shanty towns in Brazil are in Rio de Janeiro, such as the *Favela da Rocinha*, which is home to sixty thousand people.

favo /'favu/ *m* honeycomb

favor /fa'vor/ *m* favour; **a ~ de** in favour of; **por ~** please; **faça ~** please

favo|rável /favo'ravew/ (*pl* **~ráveis**) *a* favourable. **~recer** *vt* favour. **~ritismo** *m* favouritism. **~rito** *a & m* favourite

faxi|na /fa'ʃina/ *f* clean-up. **~neiro** *m* cleaner

fazen|da /fa'zẽda/ *f* (*de café, gado etc*) farm; (*tecido*) fabric, material; (*pública*) treasury. **~deiro** *m* farmer

fazer /fa'zer/ ● *vt*

····➤ (*produzir, preparar*) make; **~ uma blusa** make a blouse; **~ muito ruído** make a lot of noise; **~ um café** make a coffee; **~ uma pergunta** ask a question

····➤ (*realizar*) to do; **~ um exame/lição de casa** do an exam/some homework

····➤ (*praticar*) do; **~ ginástica/judô** do gymnastics/judo

····➤ (*favor*) to do; **você me faria um favor?** can you do me a favour?

····➤ (*comentário, promessa, esforço*) make; **você precisa ~ um esforço** you have to make an effort

····➤ (*amor*) make; **faça amor, não faça guerra** make love not war

····➤ (*anos*) be; **ela faz 20 anos em março** she'll be 20 in March

····➤ (*profissão*) do; **o que você faz? Sou piloto** what do you do? I'm a pilot

····➤ (*obrigar*) make; **~ alguém rir** make sb laugh; **você me faz vir aqui todos os dias** you make me come here everyday

● *vi*

····➤ (*com tempo atmosférico*) **faz frio/calor** it's cold/hot

····➤ (*em expressões*) **~ bem/mal** (*ao agir*) be right/wrong; (*à saúde*) **fumar faz mal à saúde** smoking is bad for you; **o exercício faz bem** exercise is good for you; **~ de conta que** pretend; **ela fez de conta que não me viu** she pretended she hadn't seen me; **não faz mal** (*não importa*) it doesn't matter

● *vpr*

····➤ **~-se de** (*fingir*) pretend; **ele se fez de burro** he pretended not to understand

faz-tudo /fas'tudu/ *m/f invar* jack of all trades

fé /fɛ/ *f* faith

fe|bre /'fɛbri/ *f* fever; **~bre amarela** yellow fever; **~bre do feno** hay fever. **~bril** (*pl* **~bris**) *a* feverish

fe|chado /fe'ʃadu/ *a* closed; ‹*curva*› sharp; ‹*sinal*› red; ‹*torneira*› off; ‹*tempo*› overcast; ‹*cara*› stern; ‹*pessoa*› reserved. **~chadura** *f* lock. **~chamento** *m* closure. **~char** *vt* close, shut; turn off ‹*torneira*›; do up ‹*calça, casaco*›; close ‹*negócio*› ● *vi* close, shut; ‹*sinal*› go red; ‹*tempo*› cloud over; **~char à chave** lock; **~char a cara** frown. **~cho** /e/ *m* fastener; **~cho ecler** zip

fécula /'fɛkula/ *f* starch

fecun|dar /fekũ'dar/ *vt* fertilize. **~do** *a* fertile

feder /fe'der/ *vi* stink

fede|ração /federa'sãw/ *f* federation. **~ral** (*pl* **~rais**) *a* federal; [!] huge. **~rativo** *a* federal

fedor /fe'dor/ *m* stink, stench. **~ento** *a* stinking

feérico /feɛriku/ *a* magical

feições /fej'sõjs/ *f pl* features

fei|jão /fe'ʒãw/ *m* bean; (*coletivo*) beans. **~joada** *f* bean stew. **~joeiro** *m* bean plant

feijoada *Feijoada* is Brazil's most typical dish, and is traditionally made with black beans, pork meat and pork trimmings, such as the ear, feet, and tail. It is often served with sautéed greens, orange and *farofa*, toasted manioc flour. The dish dates back to the colonial period when African slaves had to make use of the parts of the pig that had been discarded by their owners. Portugal also has its own version of *feijoada*, made with pork, kidney beans, *chouriço* (cured sausage) and cabbage.

feio /'feju/ *a* ugly; ‹*palavra, situação, tempo*› nasty; ‹*olhar*› dirty. **~so** /o/ *a* plain

fei|ra /'fera/ *f* market; (*industrial*) trade fair. **~rante** *m/f* market trader

feiti|çaria /fejtʃi'sera/ *f* magic. **~ceira** *f* witch. **~ceiro** *m* wizard ● *a* bewitching. **~ço** *m* spell

fei|tio /fej'tʃiu/ *m* (*de pessoa*) make-up. **~to** *pp de* ▶ FAZER ● *m* (*ato*) deed; (*proeza*) feat ● *conj* like; **bem ~to por ele** (it) serves him right. **~tura** *f* making

feiura /fej'ura/ *f* ugliness

feixe /'feʃi/ *m* bundle

fel /fɛw/ *m* gall; *fig* bitterness

felicidade /felisi'dadʒi/ *f* happiness

felici|tações /felisita'sõjs/ *f pl* congratulations. **~tar** *vt* congratulate (**por** on)

felino /fe'linu/ *a* feline

feliz /fe'lis/ *a* happy. **~ardo** *a* lucky. **~mente** *adv* fortunately

fel|pa /'fewpa/ *f* (*de pano*) nap; (*penugem*) down, fluff. **~pudo** *a* fluffy

feltro /'fewtru/ *m* felt

fêmea /'femia/ *a & f* female

femi|nil /femi'niw/ (*pl* **~nis**) *a* feminine. **~nilidade** *f* femininity. **~nino** *a* female; ‹*palavra*› feminine. **~nismo** *m* feminism. **~nista** *a & m/f* feminist

fêmur /'femur/ *m* femur

fen|da /'fẽda/ *f* crack. **~der** *vt/i* split, crack

feno /'fenu/ *m* hay

fenome|nal /fenome'naw/ (*pl* **~nais**) *a* phenomenal

fenômeno /fe'nomenu/ *m* phenomenon

fera /'fɛra/ *f* wild beast; **ficar uma ~** get really angry; **ser ~ em** [!] be brilliant at

féretro /'fɛretru/ *m* coffin

feriado /feri'adu/ *m* public holiday

férias /'fɛrias/ *f pl* holiday(s), *Amer* vacation; **de ~** on holiday; **tirar ~** take a holiday

feri|da /fe'rida/ *f* injury; (*com arma*) wound. **~do** *a* injured; *Mil* wounded ● *m* injured person; **os ~dos** the injured; *Mil* the wounded. **~r** *vt* injure; (*com arma*) wound; (*magoar*) hurt

fermen|tar /fermẽ'tar/ *vt/i* ferment. **~to** *m* yeast; *fig* ferment; **~to em pó** baking powder

fe|rocidade /ferosi'dadʒi/ *f* ferocity. **~roz** *a* ferocious

fer|rado /fe'xadu/ *a* **estou ~rado** [!] I've had it [!]; **~rado no sono** fast asleep. **~radura** *f* horseshoe. **~ragem** *f* ironwork; *pl* hardware. **~ramenta** *f* tool; (*coletivo*) tools. **~rão** *m* (*de abelha*) sting. **~rar** *vt* brand ‹*gado*›; shoe ‹*cavalo*›. **~rar-se** *vpr* [!] come a cropper. **~reiro** *m* blacksmith. **~renho** *a* ‹*partidário etc*› staunch; ‹*vontade*› iron

férreo /'fɛxiu/ *a* iron

ferro /'fɛxu/ *m* iron. **~lho** /o/ *m* bolt. **~-velho** (*pl* **~s-velhos**) *m* (*pessoa*) scrap-metal dealer; (*lugar*) scrap-metal yard. **~via** *f* railway, *Amer* railroad. **~viário** *a* railway ● *m* railway worker

ferrugem /fe'xuʒẽ/ *f* rust

fér|til /'fɛrtʃiw/ (*pl* **~teis**) *a* fertile

fertili|dade /fertʃili'dadʒi/ *f* fertility. **~zante** *m* fertilizer. **~zar** *vt* fertilize

fer|vente /fer'vẽtʃi/ *a* boiling. **~ver** *vi* boil; (*de raiva*) seethe. **~vilhar** *vi* bubble; **~vilhar de** swarm with. **~vor** *m* fervour. **~vura** *f* boiling

fes|ta /'fɛsta/ *f* party; (*religiosa*) festival. **~tejar** *vt/i* celebrate; (*acolher*) fete. **~tejo** /e/ *m* celebration. **~tim** *m* feast. **~tival** (*pl* **~tivais**) *m* festival. **~tividade** *f* festivity. **~tivo** *a* festive

festa Every town in Portugal has its own patron saint, and festivals, called *festas*, are held nationwide during the summer months to celebrate the local saint's day. The festivals consist of colourful processions through the town, coupled with music, street food and much revelry. One of the most famous festivals is the *Festa de Santo António* in Lisbon during which a mass wedding is held at Lisbon Cathedral in honour of St Anthony, the saint of marriages.

festas juninas *Festas juninas* are festivals that take place in Brazil over the month of June in honour of various saints: St Anthony on the 13th, St John on the 24th, and St Peter and St Paul on the 29th. During these festivals, various typical dishes are served, such as roasted sweet potato, popcorn, rice pudding, corn bread, and *quentão*, a hot drink made with wine, sugar, cloves and cinnamon. The festivities often include lighting bonfires, releasing hot-air balloons and dancing to *música caipira*, Brazilian country music.

feti|che /fe'tʃiʃi/ *m* fetish. **~chismo** *m* fetishism. **~chista** *m/f* fetishist ● *a* fetishistic

fétido /'fɛtʃidu/ *a* fetid

feto[1] /'fɛtu/ *m* (*no útero*) foetus

feto[2] /'fɛtu/ *Port m* (*planta*) fern

feu|dal /few'daw/ (*pl* **~dais**) *a* feudal. **~dalismo** *m* feudalism

fevereiro /feve'reru/ *m* February

fezes /'fɛzis/ *f pl* faeces

fiação /fia'sãw/ *f Eletr* wiring; (*fábrica*) mill

fia|do /fi'adu/ *a* ‹*conversa*› idle ● *adv* ‹*comprar*› on credit. **~dor** *m* guarantor

fiambre /fi'ãbri/ *m* cooked ham

fiança /fi'ãsa/ *f* surety; *Jurid* bail

fiapo /fi'apu/ *m* thread

fiar /fi'ar/ *vt* spin ‹*lã etc*›

fiasco /fi'asku/ *m* fiasco

fibra /'fibra/ *f* fibre

ficar /fi'kar/ ● *vi*

····➤ (*estar situado*) be; **onde fica a casa deles?** where is their home?

····➤ (*permanecer*) stay; **~ em casa** stay at home

····➤ (*restar*) be left (over); **~am apenas 3 concorrentes** there were just 3 contestants left

····➤ (*tornar-se*) **~ rico/doente/velho/gordo** get rich/ill/old/fat; **~ careca/cego** go bald/blind

····➤ **~ com** (*guardar*) **~ com o troco** keep the change

····➤ **~ de** (*prometer*) **ele ficou de me ajudar** he promised to help me; (*concordar*) **ficamos do nos encontrar na terça-feira** we agreed to meet on Tuesday

····➤ **~ por** (*custar*) **este vestido ficou por R$30** this dress cost me R$30

····➤ **~ sem**; (*perder*) lose; **ela ficou sem o emprego** she lost her job; (*esgotar-se*) run out of; **fiquei sem açúcar** I ran out of sugar

····➤ (*em expressões*) **~ bem/mal:** ‹*roupa*› **a camisa fica bem em você** the shirt suits you; **~ para trás: ande, não fique para trás** come on, don't get left behind

fic|ção /fik'sãw/ *f* fiction; **~ção científica** science fiction. **~cionista** *m/f* fiction writer

fi|cha /'fiʃa/ *f* (*de telefone*) token; (*de jogo*) chip; (*da caixa*) ticket; (*de fichário*) file card; (*na polícia*) record; *Port* (*tomada*) plug. **~chário** *m*, *Port* **~cheiro** *m* file; (*móvel*) filing cabinet

fictício /fik'tʃisiu/ *a* fictitious

fidalgo /fi'dalgu/ *m* nobleman

fide|digno /fide'dʒignu/ *a* trustworthy. **~lidade** *f* fidelity

fiduciário /fidusi'ariu/ *a* fiduciary ● *m* trustee

fi|el /fi'ɛw/ (*pl* **~éis**) *a* faithful ● *m* **os ~éis** (*na igreja*) the congregation

figa /'figa/ *f* talisman

fígado /'figadu/ *f* liver

fi|go /'figu/ *m* fig. **~gueira** *f* fig tree

figu|ra /fi'gura/ *f* figure; (*carta de jogo*) face card; [!] (*pessoa*) character; **fazer (má) ~ra** make a (bad) impression. **~rado** *a* figurative. **~rante** *m/f* extra. **~rão** *m* big shot. **~rar** *vi* appear, figure. **~rativo** *a* figurative. **~rinha** *f* sticker. **~rino** *m* fashion plate; (*de filme, peça*) costume design; *fig* model; **como manda o ~rino** as it should be

fila /'fila/ *f* line; (*de espera*) queue, *Amer* line; (*fileira*) row; **fazer ~** queue up, *Amer* stand in line; **~ indiana** single file

filamento /fila'mẽtu/ *m* filament

filante /fi'lãtʃi/ *m/f* [!] sponger

filan|tropia /filãtro'pia/ *f* philanthropy. **~trópico** *a* philanthropic. **~tropo** /o/ *m* philanthropist

filão /fi'lãw/ *m* (*de ouro*) seam; *fig* money-spinner

filar /fi'lar/ *vt* [!] sponge [!], cadge [!]

filar|mônica /filar'monika/ *f* philharmonic (orchestra). **~mônico** *a* philharmonic

filate|lia /filate'lia/ *f* philately. **~lista** *m/f* philatelist

filé /fi'lɛ/ *m* fillet

fileira /fi'lera/ *f* row

filete /fi'lɛtʃi/ *m* fillet

fi|lha /'fiʎa/ *f* daughter. **~lho** *m* son; **~lho da puta** (*vulg*) bastard, *Amer* son of a bitch; **~lho de criação** foster child; **~lho único** only child ● *pl* (*crianças*) children. **~lhote** *m* (*de cão*) pup; (*de lobo etc*) cub; *pl* young

fili|ação /filia'sãw/ *f* affiliation. **~al** (*pl* **~ais**) *a* filial ● *f* branch

Filipinas /fili'pinas/ *f pl* Philippines

filipino /fili'pinu/ *a & m* Filipino

fil|madora /fiwma'dora/ *f* camcorder. **~magem** *f* filming. **~mar** *vt/i* film. **~me** *m* film

fi|lologia /filolo'ʒia/ *f* philology. **~lólogo** *m* philologist

filo|sofar /filozo'far/ *vi* philosophize. **~sofia** *f* philosophy. **~sófico** *a* philosophical

filósofo /fi'lɔzofu/ *m* philosopher

fil|trar /fiw'trar/ *vt* filter. **~tro** *m* filter

fim /fĩ/ *m* end; **a ~ de** (*para*) in order to; **estar a ~ de** fancy; **por ~** finally; **sem ~** endless; **ter ~** come to an end; **~ de semana** weekend

f

fi|nado /fi'nadu/ *a & m* deceased, departed. **~nal** (*pl* **~nais**) *a* final ● *m* end ● *f* final. **~nalista** *m/f* finalist. **~nalizar** *vt/i* finish

finan|ças /fi'nãsas/ *f pl* finances. **~ceiro** *a* financial ● *m* financier. **~ciamento** *m* financing; (*um*) loan. **~ciar** *vt* finance. **~cista** *m/f* financier

fincar /fĩ'kar/ *vt* plant; **~ o pé** *fig* dig one's heels in

findar /fĩ'dar/ *vt/i* end

fineza /fi'neza/ *f* finesse; (*favor*) kindness

fin|gido /fĩ'ʒidu/ *a* feigned; ‹*pessoa*› insincere. **~gimento** *m* pretence. **~gir** *vt* pretend; feign ‹*doença etc*› ● *vi* pretend; **~gir-se de** pretend to be

fi|ninho /fi'niɲu/ *adv* **sair de ~ninho** slip away. **~no** *a* (*não grosso*) thin; ‹*areia, pó etc*› fine; (*refinado*) refined. **~nório** *a* crafty. **~nura** *f* thinness; fineness

finito /fi'nitu/ *a* finite

finlan|dês /fĩlã'des/ *a* (*f* **~desa**) Finnish ● *m* (*f* **~desa**) Finn; (*língua*) Finnish

Finlândia /fĩ'lãdʒia/ *f* Finland

fio /'fiu/ *m* thread; (*elétrico*) wire; (*de sangue, água*) trickle; (*de luz, esperança*) glimmer; (*de navalha etc*) edge; **horas a ~** hours on end

fir|ma /'firma/ *f* firm; (*assinatura*) signature. **~mamento** *m* firmament. **~mar** *vt* fix; (*basear*) base ● *vi* settle. **~mar-se** *vpr* be based (**em** on). **~me** *a* firm; ‹*tempo*› settled ● *adv* firmly. **~meza** *f* firmness

fis|cal /fis'kaw/ (*pl* **~cais**) *m* inspector. **~calização** *f* inspection. **~calizar** *vt* inspect. **~co** *m* inland revenue, *Amer* internal revenue service

fis|gada /fiz'gada/ *f* stabbing pain. **~gar** *vt* hook

físi|ca /'fizika/ *f* physics. **~co** *a* physical ● *m* (*pessoa*) physicist; (*corpo*) physique

fisio|nomia /fiziono'mia/ *f* face. **~nomista** *m/f* **ser ~nomista** have a good memory for faces. **~terapeuta** *m/f* physiotherapist. **~terapia** *f* physiotherapy

fissura /fi'sura/ *f* fissure; [!] craving. **~do** *a* **~do em** [!] mad about

fita /'fita/ *f* tape; [!] (*encenação*) play-acting; **fazer ~** [!] put on an act; **~ adesiva** *Port* adhesive tape; **~ métrica** tape measure

fitar /fi'tar/ *vt* stare at

FIV *abr f* (= **fertilização in vitro**) IVF

fivela /fi'vɛla/ *f* buckle

fi|xador /fiksa'dor/ *m* (*de cabelo*) setting lotion; (*de fotos*) fixative. **~xar** *vt* fix; stick up ‹*cartaz*›. **~xo** *a* fixed

flácido /'flasidu/ *a* flabby

flagelo /fla'ʒɛlu/ *m* scourge

fla|grante /fla'grãtʃi/ *a* flagrant; **apanhar em ~grante (delito)** catch in the act. **~grar** *vt* catch

flame|jante /flame'ʒãtʃi/ *a* blazing. **~jar** *vi* blaze

flamengo /fla'mẽgu/ *a* Flemish ● *m* Fleming; (*língua*) Flemish

flamingo /fla'mĩgu/ *m* flamingo

flâmula /'flamula/ *f* pennant

flanco /'flãku/ *m* flank

flanela /fla'nɛla/ *f* flannel

flanquear /flãki'ar/ *vt* flank

flash /flɛʃ/ *m invar* flash

flau|ta /'flawta/ *f* flute. **~tista** *m/f* flautist

flecha /'flɛʃa/ *f* arrow

fler|tar /fler'tar/ *vi* flirt. **~te** *m* flirtation

fleuma /'flewma/ *f* phlegm

flex /flɛks/ *m invar* ‹*carro*› flexible-fuel car (car designed to run on petrol and ethanol)

fle|xão /flek'sãw/ *f* press-up, *Amer* push-up; *Ling* inflection. **~xibilidade** *f* flexibility. **~xionar** *vt/i* flex ‹*perna, braço*›; *Ling* inflect. **~xível** (*pl* **~xíveis**) *a* flexible

fliperama /flipe'rama/ *m* pinball machine

floco /'flɔku/ *m* flake

flor /flor/ *f* flower; **a fina ~** the cream; **à ~ da pele** *fig* on edge

flo|ra /'flɔra/ *f* flora. **~reado** *a* full of flowers; *fig* florid. **~reio** *m* clever turn of phrase. **~rescer** *vi* flower. **~resta** /ɛ/ *f* forest. **~restal** (*pl* **~restais**) *a* forest. **~rido** *a* in flower; *fig* florid. **~rir** *vi* flower

flotilha /flo'tʃiʎa/ *f* flotilla

flu|ência /flu'ẽsia/ *f* fluency. **~ente** *a* fluent

flui|dez /flui'des/ *f* fluidity. **~do** *a* & *m* fluid

fluir /flu'ir/ *vi* flow

fluminense /flumi'nẽsi/ *a* & *m* (person) from Rio de Janeiro state

fluorescente /fluore'sẽtʃi/ *a* fluorescent

flutu|ação /flutua'sãw/ *f* fluctuation. **~ante** *a* floating. **~ar** *vi* float; ‹*bandeira*› flutter; (*hesitar*) waver

fluvi|al /fluvi'aw/ (*pl* **~ais**) *a* river

fluxo /'fluksu/ *m* flow. **~grama** *m* flow chart

fobia /fo'bia/ *f* phobia

foca /'fɔka/ *f* seal

focalizar /fokali'zar/ *vt* focus on

focinho /fo'siɲu/ *m* snout

foco /'fɔku/ *m* focus; *fig* centre

fofo /'fofu/ *a* soft; ‹*pessoa*› cuddly

fofo|ca /fo'fɔka/ *f* piece of gossip; *pl* gossip. **~car** *vi* gossip. **~queiro** *m* gossip ● *a* gossipy

fo|gão /fo'gãw/ *m* stove; (*de cozinhar*) cooker. **~go** /o/ *m* fire; **tem ~go?** have you got a light?; **ser ~go** [!] (*ser chato*) be a pain in the neck; (*ser incrível*) be amazing; **~gos de artifício** fireworks. **~goso** /o/ *a* fiery. **~gueira** *f* bonfire. **~guete** /e/ *m* rocket

foice /'fojsi/ *f* scythe

fol|clore /fow'klɔri/ *m* folklore. **~clórico** *a* folk

fole /'fɔli/ *m* bellows

fôlego /'folegu/ *m* breath; *fig* stamina

fol|ga /'fɔwga/ *f* rest, break; [!] (*cara de pau*) cheek. **~gado** *a* ‹*roupa*› full, loose; ‹*vida*› leisurely; [!] (*atrevido*) cheeky. **~gar** *vt* loosen ● *vi* have time off

fo|lha /'foʎa/ *f* leaf; (*de papel*) sheet; **novo em ~lha** brand new; **~lha de pagamento** payroll. **~lhagem** *f* foliage. **~lhear** *vt* leaf through. **~lheto** /e/ *m* pamphlet. **~lhinha** *f* tear-off calendar. **~lhudo** *a* leafy

folhado /fo'ʎadu/ *m* (*massa*) puff pastry

foli|a /fo'lia/ *f* revelry. **~ão** *m* (*f* **~ona**) reveller

folículo /fo'likulu/ *m* follicle

fome /'fomi/ *f* hunger; **estar com ~** be hungry

fomentar /fomẽ'tar/ *vt* foment

fone /'foni/ *m* (*do telefone*) receiver; (*de rádio etc*) headphones

fonema /fo'nema/ *m* phoneme

fonéti|ca /fo'nɛtʃika/ *f* phonetics. **~co** *a* phonetic

fonologia /fonolo'ʒia/ *f* phonology

fonte /'fõtʃi/ *f* (*de água*) spring; *fig* source

fora /'fɔra/ *adv* outside; (*não em casa*) out; (*viajando*) away ● *prep* except; **dar um ~** drop a clanger; **dar um ~ em alguém** cut sb dead; chuck ‹*namorado*›; **por ~** on the outside. **~ de lei** *m/f invar* outlaw

foragido /fora'ʒidu/ *a* at large, on the run ● *m* fugitive

forasteiro /foras'teru/ *m* outsider

forca /'forka/ *f* gallows

for|ça /'forsa/ *f* (*vigor*) strength; (*violência*) force; (*elétrica*) power; **dar uma ~ça a alguém** help sb out; **fazer ~ça** make an effort; **~ças armadas** armed forces. **~çar** *vt* force. **~ça-tarefa** (*pl* **~ças-tarefa**) *f* task force

fórceps /'fɔrseps/ *m invar* forceps

forçoso /for'sozu/ *a* forced

for|ja /'fɔrʒa/ *f* forge. **~jar** *vt* forge

forma[1] /'fɔrma/ *f* form; (*contorno*) shape; (*maneira*) way; **de qualquer ~** anyway; **manter a ~** keep fit

forma[2] /'forma/ *f* mould; (*de cozinha*) baking tin

for|mação /forma'sãw/ *f* formation; (*educação*) education; (*profissionalizante*) training. **~mado** *m* graduate. **~mal** (*pl* **~mais**) *a* formal. **~malidade** *f* formality. **~malizar** *vt* formalize. **~mar** *vt* form; (*educar*) educate. **~mar-se** *vpr* be formed; ‹*estudante*› graduate. **~mato** *m* format. **~matura** *f* graduation

formatar /forma'tar/ *vt Comput* format

formidá|vel /formi'davew/ (*pl* **~veis**) *a* formidable; (*muito bom*) tremendous

formi|ga /for'miga/ *f* ant. **~gamento** *m* pins and needles. **~gar** *vi* swarm (**de** with); ‹*perna, mão etc*› tingle. **~gueiro** *m* ants' nest

formosura /formo'zura/ *f* beauty

fórmula /'fɔrmula/ *f* formula

formu|lação /formula'sãw/ *f* formulation. **~lar** *vt* formulate. **~lário** *m* form

fornalha /for'naʎa/ *f* furnace

forne|cedor /fornese'dor/ *m* supplier. **~cer** *vt* supply; **~cer algo a alguém** supply sb with sth. **~cimento** *m* supply

forno /'fornu/ *m* oven; (*para louça etc*) kiln

foro /'foru/ *m* forum

forra /'fɔxa/ *f* **ir à ~** get one's own back

for|ragem /fo'xaʒẽ/ *f* fodder. **~rar** *vt* line ‹*roupa, caixa etc*›; cover ‹*sofá etc*›; carpet ‹*assoalho, sala etc*›. **~ro** /o/ *m* (*de roupa, caixa etc*) lining; (*de sofá etc*) cover; (*carpete*) (fitted) carpet

forró /fo'xɔ/ *m* type of Brazilian dance

fortale|cer /fortale'ser/ *vt* strengthen. **~cimento** *m* strengthening. **~za** /e/ *f* fortress

for|te /'fɔrtʃi/ *a* strong; ‹*golpe*› hard; ‹*chuva*› heavy; ‹*físico*› muscular ● *adv* strongly; ‹*bater, chover*› hard ● *m* (*militar*) fort; (*habilidade*) strong point, forte. **~tificação** *f* fortification. **~tificar** *vt* fortify

fortu|ito /for'tuitu/ *a* chance. **~na** *f* fortune

fosco /'fosku/ *a* dull; ‹*vidro*› frosted

fosfato /fos'fatu/ *m* phosphate

fósforo /'fɔsforu/ *m* match; (*elemento químico*) phosphor

fossa /'fɔsa/ *f* pit; **na ~** *fig* miserable, depressed

fós|sil /'fɔsiw/ (*pl* **~seis**) *m* fossil

fosso /'fosu/ *m* ditch; (*de castelo*) moat

foto /'fɔtu/ *f* photo. **~cópia** *f* photocopy. **~copiadora** *f* photocopier. **~copiar** *vt* photocopy. **~gênico** *a* photogenic. **~grafar** *vt* photograph. **~grafia** *f* photography. **~gráfico** *a* photographic

fotógrafo /fo'tɔgrafu/ *m* photographer

foz /fɔs/ *f* mouth

fração /fra'sãw/ *f* fraction

fracas|sado /fraka'sadu/ *a* failed ● *m* failure. **~sar** *vi* fail. **~so** *m* failure

fracionar /frasio'nar/ *vt* break up

fraco /'fraku/ *a* weak; ‹*luz, som*› faint; ‹*medíocre*› poor ● *m* weakness, weak spot

frade /'fradʒi/ *m* friar

fragata /fra'gata/ *f* frigate

frá|gil /'fraʒiw/ (*pl* **~geis**) *a* fragile; ‹*pessoa*› frail

fragilidade /fraʒili'dadʒi/ *f* fragility; (*de pessoa*) frailty

fragmen|tar /fragmẽ'tar/ *vt* fragment. **~tar-se** *vpr* fragment. **~to** *m* fragment

fra|grância /fra'grãsia/ *f* fragrance. **~grante** *a* fragrant

fralda /'frawda/ *f* nappy, *Amer* diaper

framboesa /frãbo'eza/ *f* raspberry

França /'frãsa/ *f* France

fran|cês /frã'ses/ *a* (*f* **~cesa**) French ● *m* (*f* **~cesa**) Frenchman (*f* -woman); (*língua*) French; **os ~ceses** the French

franco /'frãku/ *a* (*honesto*) frank; (*óbvio*) clear; (*gratuito*) free ● *m* franc. **~-atirador** (*pl* **~atiradores**) *m* sniper; *fig* maverick

frangalho /frã'gaʎu/ *m* tatter

frango /'frãgu/ *m* chicken

franja /'frãʒa/ *f* fringe; (*do cabelo*) fringe, *Amer* bangs

fran|quear /frãki'ar/ *vt* frank ‹*carta*›. **~queza** /e/ *f* frankness. **~quia** *f* (*de cartas*) franking; *Jurid* franchise

fran|zino /frã'zinu/ *a* skinny. **~zir** *vt* gather ‹*tecido*›; wrinkle ‹*testa*›

fraque /'fraki/ *m* morning suit

fraqueza /fra'keza/ *f* weakness; (*de luz, som*) faintness

frasco /'frasku/ *m* bottle

frase /'frazi/ *f* (*oração*) sentence; (*locução*) phrase. **~ado** *m* phrasing

frasqueira /fras'kera/ *f* vanity case

frater|nal /frater'naw/ (*pl* **~nais**) *a* fraternal. **~nidade** *f* fraternity. **~nizar** *vi* fraternize. **~no** *a* fraternal

fratu|ra /fra'tura/ *f* fracture. **~rar** *vt* fracture. **~rar-se** *vpr* fracture

frau|dar /fraw'dar/ *vt* defraud. **~de** *f* fraud. **~dulento** *a* fraudulent

frear /fri'ar/ *vt/i* brake

freezer /'frizer/ *m* freezer

fre|guês /fre'ges/ *m* (*f* **~guesa**) customer. **~guesia** *f* (*de loja etc*) clientele; (*paróquia*) parish

frei /frej/ *m* brother

freio /'freju/ *m* brake; (*de cavalo*) bit

freira /'frera/ *f* nun

freixo /'freʃu/ *m* ash

fremir /fre'mir/ *vi* shake

frêmito /'fremitu/ *m* wave

frenesi /frene'zi/ *m* frenzy

frenético /fre'nɛtʃiku/ *a* frantic

frente /ˈfrẽtʃi/ *f* front; **em ~ a** ou **de** in front of; **para a ~** forward; **pela ~** ahead; **fazer ~ a** face

frequência /freˈkwẽsia/ *f* frequency; (*assiduidade*) attendance; **com muita ~** often

frequen|tador /frekwẽtaˈdor/ *m* regular visitor (**de** to). **~tar** *vt* frequent; (*cursar*) attend. **~te** *a* frequent

fres|cão /fresˈkãw/ *m* air-conditioned coach. **~co** /e/ *a* ‹*comida etc*› fresh; ‹*vento, água, quarto*› cool; 🅘 (*afetado*) affected; (*exigente*) fussy. **~cobol** *m* kind of racquetball. **~cor** *m* freshness. **~cura** *f* 🅘 (*afetação*) affectation; (*ser exigente*) fussiness; (*coisa sem importância*) trifle

fresta /ˈfrɛsta/ *f* slit

fre|tar /freˈtar/ *vt* charter ‹*avião*›; hire ‹*caminhão*›. **~te** /ɛ/ *m* freight; (*aluguel de avião*) charter; (*de caminhão*) hire

frevo /ˈfrevu/ *m* type of Brazilian dance

fria /ˈfria/ *f* 🅘 difficult situation, spot. **~gem** *f* chill

fric|ção /frikˈsãw/ *f* friction. **~cionar** *vt* rub

fri|eira /friˈera/ *f* chilblain. **~eza** /e/ *f* coldness

frigideira /friʒiˈdera/ *f* frying pan

frígido /ˈfriʒidu/ *a* frigid

frigorífico /frigoˈrifiku/ *m* cold store, refrigerator, fridge

frincha /ˈfrĩʃa/ *f* chink

frio /ˈfriu/ *a & m* cold; **estar com ~** be cold. **~rento** *a* sensitive to the cold

frisar /friˈzar/ *vt* (*enfatizar*) stress; crimp ‹*cabelo*›

friso /ˈfrizu/ *m* frieze

fri|tada /friˈtada/ *f* fry-up. **~tar** *vt* fry. **~tas** *f pl* chips, *Amer* French fries. **~to** *a* fried; **está ~to** 🅘 he's had it 🅘. **~tura** *f* fried food

frivolidade /frivoliˈdadʒi/ *f* frivolity. **frívolo** *a* frivolous

fronha /ˈfroɲa/ *f* pillowcase

fronte /ˈfrõtʃi/ *f* forehead, brow

frontei|ra /frõˈtera/ *f* border. **~riço** *a* border

frota /ˈfrɔta/ *f* fleet

frou|xidão /froʃiˈdãw/ *f* looseness; (*moral*) laxity. **~xo** *a* loose; ‹*regulamento*› lax; ‹*pessoa*› lackadaisical

fru|gal /fruˈgaw/ (*pl* **~gais**) *a* frugal. **~galidade** *f* frugality

frus|tração /frustraˈsãw/ *f* frustration. **~trante** *a* frustrating. **~trar** *vt* frustrate

fru|ta /ˈfruta/ *f* fruit. **~ta-do-conde** (*pl* **~tas-do-conde**) *f* sweetsop; **~ta-pão** (*pl* **~tas-pão**) *f* breadfruit. **~teira** *f* fruit bowl. **~tífero** *a fig* fruitful. **~to** *m* fruit

fubá /fuˈba/ *m* maize flour

fu|çar /fuˈsar/ *vi* nose around. **~ças** *f pl* 🅘 face, chops 🅘

fu|ga /ˈfuga/ *f* escape. **~gaz** *a* fleeting. **~gida** *f* escape. **~gir** *vi* run away; (*soltar-se*) escape; **~gir a** avoid. **~gitivo** *a & m* fugitive

fulano /fuˈlanu/ *m* whatever his name is

fuleiro /fuˈleru/ *a* downmarket, cheap and cheerful

fulgor /fuwˈgor/ *m* brightness; *fig* splendour

fuligem /fuˈliʒẽ/ *f* soot

fulmi|nante /fuwmiˈnãtʃi/ *a* devastating. **~nar** *vt* strike down; *fig* devastate; **~nado por um raio** struck by lightning ● *vi* (*criticar*) rail

fulo /ˈfulu/ *a Port* furious

fu|maça /fuˈmasa/ *f* smoke. **~maceira** *f* cloud of smoke. **~mante**, *Port* **~mador** *m* smoker. **~mar** *vt/i* smoke. **~mê** *a invar* smoked. **~megar** *vi* smoke. **~mo** /ˈfumu/ *m* (*tabaco*) tobacco; *Port* (*fumaça*) smoke; (*fumar*) smoking; **~mo passivo** passive smoking

função /fũˈsãw/ *f* function; **em ~ de** as a result of; **fazer as funções de** function as

funcho /ˈfũʃu/ *m* fennel

funcio|nal /fũsioˈnaw/ (*pl* **~nais**) *a* functional. **~nalismo** *m* civil service. **~namento** *m* working. **~nar** *vi* work. **~nário** *m* employee; **~nário público** civil servant

fun|dação /fũdaˈsãw/ *f* foundation. **~dador** *m* founder ● *a* founding

fundamen|tal /fũdamẽˈtaw/ (*pl* **~tais**) *a* fundamental. **~tar** *vt* (*basear*) base; (*justificar*) substantiate. **~to** *m* foundation

fun|dar /fũˈdar/ *vt* (*criar*) found; (*basear*) base. **~dar-se** *vpr* be based (**em** on). **~dear** *vi* drop anchor, anchor. **~dilho** *m* seat

fundir /fũˈdʒir/ *vt* melt ‹*ouro, ferro*›; cast ‹*sino, estátua*›; (*juntar*) merge. **~-se** *vpr* ‹*ouro, ferro*› melt; (*juntar-se*) merge

fundo /ˈfũdu/ *a* deep ● *m* (*parte de baixo*) bottom; (*parte de trás*) back;

f

(*de quadro, foto*) background; (*de dinheiro*) fund; **no ~** basically. **~s** *m pl* (*da casa etc*) back; (*recursos*) funds

fúnebre /'funebri/ *a* funereal

funerário /fune'rariu/ *a* funeral

funesto /fu'nɛstu/ *a* fatal

fungar /fũ'gar/ *vt/i* sniff

fungo /'fũgu/ *m* fungus

fu|nil /fu'niw/ (*pl* **~nis**) *m* funnel. **~nilaria** *f* panel beating; (*oficina*) body shop

furacão /fura'kãw/ *m* hurricane

furado /fu'radu/ *a* **papo ~** 🄸 hot air

furão /fu'rãw/ *m* (*animal*) ferret

furar /fu'rar/ *vt* pierce ‹*orelha etc*›; puncture ‹*pneu*›; make a hole in ‹*roupa etc*›; jump ‹*fila*›; break ‹*greve*› ● *vi* ‹*roupa etc*› go into a hole; ‹*pneu*› puncture; 🄸 ‹*programa*› fall through

fur|gão /fur'gãw/ *m* van. **~goneta** /e/ *Port f* van

fúria /'furia/ *f* fury

furioso /furi'ozu/ *a* furious

furo /'furu/ *m* hole; (*de pneu*) puncture; (*jornalístico*) scoop; 🄸 (*gafe*) blunder, faux pas; **dar um ~** put one's foot in it

furor /fu'ror/ *m* furore

fur|ta-cor /furta'kor/ *a invar* iridescent. **~tar** *vt* steal. **~tivo** *a* furtive. **~to** *m* theft

furúnculo /fu'rũkulu/ *m* boil

fusão /fu'zãw/ *f* fusion; (*de empresas*) merger

fusca /'fuska/ *f* VW beetle

fuselagem /fuze'laʒẽ/ *f* fuselage

fusí|vel /fu'zivew/ (*pl* **~veis**) *m* fuse

fuso /'fuzu/ *m* spindle; **~ horário** time zone

fustigar /fustʃi'gar/ *vt* lash; *fig* (*com palavras*) lash out at

futebol /futʃi'bɔw/ *m* football. **~ístico** *a* football

fú|til /'futʃiw/ (*pl* **~teis**) *a* frivolous, inane

futilidade /futʃili'dadʒi/ *f* frivolity, inanity; (*uma*) frivolous thing

futu|rismo /futu'rizmu/ *m* futurism. **~rista** *a & m* futurist. **~rístico** *a* futuristic. **~ro** *a & m* future

fu|zil /fu'ziw/ (*pl* **~zis**) *m* rifle. **~zilamento** *m* shooting. **~zilar** *vt* shoot ● *vi* flash. **~zileiro** *m* rifleman; **~zileiro naval** marine

fuzuê /fuzu'e/ *m* commotion

Gg

gabarito /gaba'ritu/ *m* calibre

gabar-se /ga'barsi/ *vpr* boast (**de** of)

gabinete /gabi'netʃi/ *m* (*em casa*) study; (*escritório*) office; (*ministros*) cabinet

gado /'gadu/ *m* livestock; (*bovino*) cattle

gaélico /ga'ɛliku/ *a & m* Gaelic

gafanhoto /gafa'ɲotu/ *m* (*pequeno*) grasshopper; (*grande*) locust

gafe /'gafi/ *f* faux pas, gaffe

gafieira /gafi'era/ *f* dance; (*salão*) dance hall

gagá /ga'ga/ *a* 🄸 senile

ga|go /'gagu/ *a* stuttering ● *m* stutterer. **~gueira** *f* stutter. **~guejar** *vi* stutter

gaiato /gaj'atu/ *a* funny

gaiola /gaj'ɔla/ *f* cage

gaita /'gajta/ *f* **~ de foles** bagpipes

gaivota /gaj'vɔta/ *f* seagull

gajo /'gaʒu/ *m Port* guy, bloke

gala /'gala/ *f* **festa de ~** gala; **roupa de ~** formal dress

galã /ga'lã/ *m* leading man

galan|tear /galãtʃi'ar/ *vt* woo. **~teio** *m* wooing; (*um*) courtesy

galão /ga'lãw/ *m* (*enfeite*) braid; *Mil* stripe; (*medida*) gallon; *Port* (*café*) white coffee

galáxia /ga'laksia/ *f* galaxy

galé /ga'lɛ/ *f* galley

galego /ga'legu/ *a & m* Galician

galera /ga'lɛra/ *f* 🄸 crowd

galeria /gale'ria/ *f* gallery

Gales /'galis/ *m* **País de G~** Wales

ga|lês /ga'les/ *a* (*f* **~lesa**) Welsh ● *m* (*f* **~lesa**) Welshman (*f* -woman); (*língua*) Welsh

galeto /ga'letu/ *m* spring chicken

galgar /gaw'gar/ *vt* (*transpor*) jump over; climb ‹*escada*›

galgo /'gawgu/ *m* greyhound

galheteiro /gaʎe'teru/ *m* cruet stand

galho /'gaʎu/ *m* branch; **quebrar um ~** 🄸 help out

galináceos /gali'nasius/ *m pl* poultry

gali|nha /ga'liɲa/ *f* chicken. **~nheiro** *m* chicken coop

galo /'galu/ *m* cock; (*inchação*) bump

galocha /ga'lɔʃa/ *f* Wellington boot

galo|pante /galo'pãtʃi/ *a* galloping. **~par** *vi* gallop. **~pe** /ɔ/ *m* gallop

galpão /gaw'pãw/ *m* shed

galvanizar /gawvani'zar/ *vt* galvanize

gama /'gama/ *f* (*musical*) scale; *fig* range

gamado /ga'madu/ *a* besotted (**por** with)

gamão /ga'mãw/ *m* backgammon

gamar /ga'mar/ *vi* fall in love (**por** with)

gana /'gana/ *f* desire

ganância /ga'nãsia/ *f* greed

ganancioso /ganãsi'ozu/ *a* greedy

gancho /'gãʃu/ *m* hook

gangorra /gã'goxa/ *f* see-saw

gangrena /gã'grena/ *f* gangrene

gangue /'gãgi/ *m* gang

ga|nhador /gaɲa'dor/ *m* winner ● *a* winning. **~nhar** *vt* win ‹*corrida, prêmio*›; earn ‹*salário*›; get ‹*presente*›; gain ‹*vantagem, tempo, amigo*› ● *vi* win; **~nhar a vida** earn a living. **~nha-pão** *m* livelihood. **~nho** *m* gain; *pl* (*no jogo*) winnings

ga|nido *m* squeal; (*de cachorro*) yelp. **~nir** *vi* squeal; ‹*cachorro*› yelp

ganso /'gãsu/ *m* goose

gara|gem /ga'raʒẽ/ *f* garage. **~gista** *m/f* garage attendant

garanhão /gara'ɲãw/ *m* stallion

garan|tia /garã'tʃia/ *f* guarantee. **~tir** *vt* guarantee

garatujar /garatu'ʒar/ *vt* scribble

gar|bo /'garbu/ *m* grace. **~boso** *a* graceful

garça /'garsa/ *f* heron

gar|çom /gar'sõ/ *m* waiter. **~çonete** /ɛ/ *f* waitress

gar|fada /gar'fada/ *f* forkful. **~fo** *m* fork

gargalhada /garga'ʎada/ *f* gale of laughter; **rir às ~s** roar with laughter

gargalo /gar'galu/ *m* bottleneck; **tomar no ~** drink out of the bottle

garganta /gar'gãta/ *f* throat

gargare|jar /gargare'ʒar/ *vi* gargle. **~jo** /e/ *m* gargle

gari /ga'ri/ *m/f* (*lixeiro*) dustman, *Amer* garbage collector; (*varredor de rua*) roadsweeper, *Amer* streetsweeper

garim|par /garĩ'par/ *vi* prospect. **~peiro** *m* prospector. **~po** *m* mine

garo|a /ga'roa/ *f* drizzle. **~ar** *vi* drizzle

garo|ta /ga'rota/ *f* girl. **~to** /o/ *m* boy; *Port* (*café*) coffee with milk

garoupa /ga'ropa/ *f* grouper

garra /'gaxa/ *f* claw; *fig* drive, determination; *pl* (*poder*) clutches

garra|fa /ga'xafa/ *f* bottle. **~fada** *f* blow with a bottle. **~fão** *m* flagon

garrancho /ga'xãʃu/ *m* scrawl

garrido /ga'xidu/ *a* (*alegre*) lively

garupa /ga'rupa/ *f* (*de animal*) rump; (*de moto*) pillion seat

gás /gas/ *m* gas; *pl* (*intestinais*) wind, *Amer* gas; **~ lacrimogêneo** tear gas

gasóleo /ga'zɔliu/ *m* diesel oil

gasolina /gazo'lina/ *f* petrol

gaso|sa /ga'zɔza/ *f* fizzy lemonade, *Amer* soda. **~so** *a* gaseous; ‹*bebida*› fizzy

gáspea /'gaspia/ *f* upper

gas|tador /gasta'dor/ *a & m* spendthrift. **~tar** *vt* spend ‹*dinheiro, tempo*›; use up ‹*energia*›; wear out ‹*roupa, sapatos*›. **~to** *m* expense; *pl* spending, expenditure; **dar para o ~to** do

gastrenterite /gastrẽte'ritʃi/ *f* gastroenteritis

gástrico /'gastriku/ *a* gastric

gastrite /gas'tritʃi/ *f* gastritis

gastronomia /gastrono'mia/ *f* gastronomy

ga|ta /'gata/ *f* cat; [!] sexy woman. **~tão** *m* [!] hunk [!]

gatilho /ga'tʃiʎu/ *m* trigger

ga|tinha /ga'tʃiɲa/ *f* [!] sexy woman. **~to** *m* cat; [!] hunk [!]; **fazer alguém de ~to-sapato** treat sb like a doormat

gatuno /ga'tunu/ *m* crook ● *a* crooked

gaúcho /ga'uʃu/ *a & m* (person) from Rio Grande do Sul

gaveta /ga'veta/ *f* drawer

gavião /gavi'ãw/ *m* hawk

gaze /'gazi/ *f* gauze

gazela /ga'zɛla/ *f* gazelle

gazeta /ga'zeta/ *f* gazette

geada /ʒi'ada/ *f* frost

ge|ladeira /ʒela'dera/ *f* fridge. **~lado** *a* frozen; (*muito frio*) freezing ● *m Port* ice cream. **~lar** *vt/i* freeze

gelati|na /ʒela'tʃina/ *f* (*sobremesa*) jelly; (*pó*) gelatine. **~noso** /o/ *a* gooey

geleia /ʒe'lɛja/ *f* jam

ge|leira /ʒe'lera/ *f* glacier. **~lo** /e/ *m* ice

gema /'ʒema/ *f* (*de ovo*) yolk; (*pedra*) gem; **carioca da ~** carioca born and bred. **~da** *f* egg yolk whisked with sugar

gêmeo /'ʒemiu/ *a & m* twin; **Gêmeos** (*signo*) Gemini

ge|mer /ʒe'mer/ *vi* moan, groan. **~mido** *m* moan, groan

gene /'ʒɛni/ *m* gene. **~alogia** *f* genealogy. **~alógico** *a* genealogical; **árvore ~alógica** family tree

Genebra /ʒe'nɛbra/ *f* Geneva

gene|ral /ʒene'raw/ (*pl* **~rais**) *m* general. **~ralidade** *f* generality. **~ralização** *f* generalization. **~ralizar** *vt/i* generalize. **~ralizar-se** *vpr* become generalized

g

genérico /ʒe'nɛriku/ *a* generic

gênero /'ʒeneru/ *m* type, kind; (*gramatical*) gender; (*literário*) genre; *pl* goods; **~s alimentícios** foodstuffs; **ela não faz o meu ~** she's not my type

gene|rosidade /ʒenerozi'dadʒi/ *f* generosity. **~roso** /o/ *a* generous

genéti|ca /ʒe'nɛtʃika/ *f* genetics. **~co** *a* genetic

gengibre /ʒẽ'ʒibri/ *m* ginger

gengiva /ʒẽ'ʒiva/ *f* gum

geni|al /ʒeni'aw/ (*pl* **~ais**) *a* brilliant

gênio /'ʒeniu/ *m* genius; (*temperamento*) temperament

genioso /ʒeni'ozu/ *a* temperamental

geni|tal /ʒeni'taw/ (*pl* **~tais**) *a* genital

genitivo /ʒeni'tʃivu/ *a & m* genitive

genocídio /ʒeno'sidʒiu/ *m* genocide

genro /'ʒẽxu/ *m* son-in-law

gente /'ʒẽtʃi/ *f* people; ! folks; **a ~** (*sujeito*) we; (*objeto*) us ● *interj* ! gosh

gen|til /ʒẽ'tʃiw/ (*pl* **~tis**) *a* kind. **~tileza** /e/ *f* kindness

genuíno /ʒenu'inu/ *a* genuine

geo|grafia /ʒeogra'fia/ *f* geography. **~gráfico** *a* geographical

geógrafo /ʒe'ɔgrafu/ *m* geographer

geo|logia /ʒeolo'ʒia/ *f* geology. **~lógico** *a* geological

geólogo /ʒe'ɔlogu/ *m* geologist

geo|metria /ʒeome'tria/ *f* geometry. **~métrico** *a* geometrical. **~político** *a* geopolitical

Geórgia /ʒi'ɔrʒia/ *f* Georgia

georgiano /ʒiorʒi'anu/ *a & m* Georgian

gera|ção /ʒera'sãw/ *f* generation. **~dor** *m* generator

ge|ral /ʒe'raw/ (*pl* **~rais**) *a* general ● *f* (*limpeza*) spring clean; **em ~ral** in general

gerânio /ʒe'raniu/ *m* geranium

gerar /ʒe'rar/ *vt* create; generate ‹*eletricidade*›

gerência /ʒe'rẽsia/ *f* management

gerenci|ador /ʒerẽsia'dor/ *m* manager. **~al** (*pl* **~ais**) *a* management. **~ar** *vt* manage

gerente /ʒe'rẽtʃi/ *m* manager ● *a* managing

gergelim /ʒerʒe'lĩ/ *m* sesame

geri|atria /ʒeria'tria/ *f* geriatrics. **~átrico** *a* geriatric

geringonça /ʒerĩ'gõsa/ *f* contraption

gerir /ʒe'rir/ *vt* manage

germânico /ʒer'maniku/ *a* Germanic

ger|me /'ʒɛrmi/ *m* germ; **~me de trigo** wheatgerm. **~minar** *vi* germinate

gerúndio /ʒe'rũdʒiu/ *m* gerund

gesso /'ʒesu/ *m* plaster

ges|tação /ʒesta'sãw/ *f* gestation. **~tante** *f* pregnant woman

gestão /ʒes'tãw/ *f* management

ges|ticular /ʒestʃiku'lar/ *vi* gesticulate. **~to** *m* gesture

gibi /ʒi'bi/ *m* ! comic

Gibraltar /ʒibraw'tar/ *f* Gibraltar

gigan|te /ʒi'gãtʃi/ *a & m* giant. **~tesco** /e/ *a* gigantic

gilete /ʒi'lɛtʃi/ *f* razor blade ● *a & m/f* ! bisexual

gim /ʒĩ/ *m* gin

ginásio /ʒi'naziu/ *m* (*escola*) secondary school; (*de ginástica*) gymnasium

ginasta /ʒi'nasta/ *m/f* gymnast

ginásti|ca /ʒi'nastʃika/ *f* gymnastics; (*aeróbica*) aerobics. **~co** *a* gymnastic

ginecolo|gia /ʒinekolo'ʒia/ *f* gynaecology. **~gista** *m/f* gynaecologist

gingar /ʒĩ'gar/ *vi* sway

gira-discos /ʒira'diʃkuʃ/ *m invar Port* record player

girafa /ʒi'rafa/ *f* giraffe

gi|rar /ʒi'rar/ *vt/i* spin, revolve. **~rassol** (*pl* **~rassóis**) *m* sunflower. **~ratório** *a* revolving

gíria /'ʒiria/ *f* slang; (*uma ~*) slang expression

giro /'ʒiru/ *m* spin, turn ● *a Port* ! nice, cute

giz /ʒis/ *m* chalk

gla|cê /gla'se/ *m* icing. **~cial** (*pl* **~ciais**) *a* icy

glamour /gla'mur/ *m* glamour. **~oso** /o/ *a* glamorous

glândula /'glãdula/ *f* gland

glandular /glãdu'lar/ *a* glandular

glicerina /glise'rina/ *f* glycerine

glicose /gli'kɔzi/ *f* glucose

glo|bal /glo'baw/ (*pl* **~bais**) *a* (*mundial*) global; ‹*preço etc*› overall. **~bo** /o/ *m* globe; **~bo ocular** eyeball

globalização /globaliza'sãw/ *f* globalization

globalizar /globali'zar/ *vt* globalize

glóbulo /'glɔbulu/ *m* globule; (*do sangue*) corpuscle

glória /'glɔria/ *f* glory

glori|ficar /glorifi'kar/ *vt* glorify. **~oso** /o/ *a* glorious

glossário /glo'sariu/ *m* glossary

glu|tão /glu'tãw/ *m* (*f* **~tona**) glutton ● *a* (*f* **~tona**) greedy

gnomo /gi'nomu/ *m* gnome

godê /go'de/ *a* flared

goela /go'ɛla/ *f* gullet

gogó /go'gɔ/ *m* [!] Adam's apple

goia|ba /goj'aba/ *f* guava. **~bada** *f* guava jelly. **~beira** *f* guava tree

gol /'gow/ (*pl* **~s**) *m* goal

gola /'gɔla/ *f* collar

gole /'gɔli/ *m* mouthful

go|lear /goli'ar/ *vt* thrash. **~leiro** *m* goalkeeper

golfe /'gowfi/ *m* golf

golfinho /gow'fiɲu/ *m* dolphin

golfista /gow'fista/ *m/f* golfer

golo /'golu/ *m Port* goal

golpe /'gɔwpi/ *m* blow; (*manobra*) trick; **~ (de estado)** coup (d'état); **~ de mestre** masterstroke; **~ de vento** gust of wind; **~ de vista** glance. **~ar** *vt* hit

goma /'goma/ *f* gum; (*para roupa*) starch

gomo /'gomu/ *m* segment

gôndola /'gõdola/ *f* rack

gongo /'gõgu/ *m* gong

gonorreia /gono'xɛja/ *f* gonorrhea

gonzo /'gõzu/ *m* hinge

googar /gu'gar/ *vt* google

gorar /go'rar/ *vi* go wrong, fail

gor|do /'gordu/ *a* fat. **~ducho** *a* plump

gordu|ra /gor'dura/ *f* fat. **~rento** *a* greasy. **~roso** /u/ *a* fatty; ‹*pele*› greasy, oily

gorgolejar /gorgole'ʒar/ *vi* gurgle

gorila /go'rila/ *m* gorilla

gor|jear /gorʒi'ar/ *vi* twitter. **~jeio** *m* twittering

gorjeta /gor'ʒeta/ *f* tip

gorro /'goxu/ *m* hat

gos|ma /'gɔzma/ *f* slime. **~mento** *a* slimy

gos|tar /gos'tar/ *vi* **~tar de** like. **~to** /o/ *m* taste; (*prazer*) pleasure; **para o meu ~to** for my taste; **ter ~to de** taste of. **~toso** *a* nice; ‹*comida*› nice, tasty; [!] ‹*pessoa*› gorgeous

go|ta /'gota/ *f* drop; (*que cai*) drip; (*doença*) gout; **foi a ~ta d'água** *fig* it was the last straw. **~teira** *f* (*buraco*) leak; (*cano*) gutter. **~tejar** *vi* drip; ‹*telhado*› leak ● *vt* drip

gótico /'gɔtʃiku/ *a* Gothic

gotícula /go'tʃicula/ *f* droplet

gourmet /gur'me/ *a* gourmet; **loja ~** delicatessen

gover|nador /governa'dor/ *m* governor. **~namental** (*pl* **~namentais**) *a* government. **~nanta** *f* housekeeper. **~nante** *a* ruling ● *m/f* ruler. **~nar** *vt* govern. **~nista** *a* government ● *m/f* government supporter. **~no** /e/ *m* government

go|zação /goza'sãw/ *f* joking; (*uma*) send-up. **~zado** *a* funny. **~zar** *vt* **~zar (de)** enjoy; [!] (*zombar de*) make fun of ● *vi* (*ter orgasmo*) come. **~zo** *m* (*prazer*) enjoyment; (*posse*) possession; (*orgasmo*) orgasm; **ser um ~zo** be funny

Grã-Bretanha /grãbre'taɲa/ *f* Great Britain

graça /'grasa/ *f* grace; (*piada*) joke; (*humor*) humour, funny side; *Jurid* pardon; **de ~** for nothing; **sem ~** (*enfadonho*) dull; (*não engraçado*) unfunny; (*envergonhado*) embarrassed; **ser uma ~** be lovely; **ter ~** be funny; **não tem ~ sair sozinho** it's no fun to go out alone; **~s a** thanks to

grace|jar /grase'ʒar/ *vi* joke. **~jo** /e/ *m* joke

graci|nha /gra'siɲa/ *f* **ser uma ~nha** be sweet. **~oso** /o/ *a* gracious

grada|ção /grada'sãw/ *f* gradation. **~tivo** *a* gradual

grade /'gradʒi/ *f* grille, grating; (*cerca*) railings; **atrás das ~s** behind bars. **~ado** *a* ‹*janela*› barred

g

grado /'gradu/ *m* **de bom/mau ~** willingly/unwillingly

gradu|ação /gradua'sãw/ *f* graduation; *Mil* rank; (*variação*) gradation. **~ado** *a* ‹*escala*› graduated; ‹*estudante*› graduate; ‹*militar*› high-ranking; (*eminente*) respected. **~al** (*pl* **~ais**) *a* gradual. **~ar** *vt* graduate ‹*escala*›; (*ordenar*) grade; (*regular*) regulate. **~ar-se** *vpr* ‹*estudante*› graduate

grafia /gra'fia/ *f* spelling

gráfi|ca /'grafika/ *f* (*arte*) graphics; (*oficina*) print shop. **~co** *a* graphic ● *m* (*pessoa*) printer; (*diagrama*) graph; *pl* (*de computador*) graphics

g

grã-fino /grã'finu/ [!] *a* posh, upper-class ● *m* posh person

grafite /gra'fitʃi/ *f* (*mineral*) graphite; (*de lápis*) lead; (*pichação*) piece of graffiti

grafiteiro /grafi'teru/ *m* graffitist

grafiti /gra'fiti/ *m Port* ▶ **grafite**

gra|fologia /grafolo'ʒia/ *f* graphology. **~fólogo** *m* graphologist

grama[1] /'grama/ *m* gramme

grama[2] /'grama/ *f* grass. **~do** *m* lawn; (*campo de futebol*) field

gramática /gra'matʃika/ *f* grammar

gramati|cal /gramatʃi'kaw/ (*pl* **~cais**) *a* grammatical

gram|peador /grãpia'dor/ *m* stapler. **~pear** *vt* staple ‹*papéis etc*›; tap ‹*telefone*›. **~po** *m* (*de cabelo*) hair clip; (*para papéis etc*) staple; (*ferramenta*) clamp

grana /'grana/ *f* [!] cash

granada /gra'nada/ *f* (*projétil*) grenade; (*pedra*) garnet

gran|dalhão /grãda'ʎãw/ *a* (*f* **~dalhona**) enormous. **~dão** *a* (*f* **~dona**) huge. **~de** *a* big; *fig* ‹*escritor, amor etc*› great. **~deza** /e/ *f* greatness; (*tamanho*) magnitude. **~dioso** /o/ *a* grand

granel /gra'nɛw/ *m* **a ~** in bulk

granito /gra'nitu/ *m* granite

granizo /gra'nizu/ *m* hail

gran|ja /'grãʒa/ *f* farm. **~jear** *vt* win, gain

granulado /granu'ladu/ *a* granulated

grânulo /'granulu/ *m* granule

grão /grãw/ (*pl* **~s**) *m* grain; (*de café*) bean. **~-de-bico** (*pl* **~s-de-bico**) *m* chickpea

grasnar /graz'nar/ *vi* ‹*pato*› quack; ‹*rã*› croak; ‹*corvo*› caw

grati|dão /gratʃi'dãw/ *f* gratitude. **~ficação** *f* (*dinheiro a mais*) gratuity; (*recompensa*) gratification. **~ficante** *a* gratifying. **~ficar** *vt* (*dar dinheiro a*) give a gratuity to; (*recompensar*) gratify

gratinado /gratʃi'nadu/ *a & m* gratin

grátis /'gratʃis/ *adv* free

grato /'gratu/ *a* grateful

gratuito /gra'tuito/ *a* (*de graça*) free; (*sem motivo*) gratuitous

grau /graw/ *m* degree; **escola de 1°/2° ~** primary/secondary school

graúdo /gra'udu/ *a* big; (*importante*) important

gra|vação /grava'sãw/ *f* (*de som*) recording; (*de desenhos etc*) engraving. **~vador** *m* (*pessoa*) engraver; (*máquina*) tape recorder. **~vadora** *f* record company. **~var** *vt* record ‹*música, disco*›; (*fixar na memória*) memorize; (*estampar*) engrave

gravata /gra'vata/ *f* tie; (*golpe*) stranglehold; **~ borboleta** bow tie

grave /'gravi/ *a* serious; ‹*voz, som*› deep; ‹*acento*› grave

grávida /'gravida/ *a* pregnant

gravidade /gravi'dadʒi/ *f* gravity

gravidez /gravi'des/ *f* pregnancy

gravura /gra'vura/ *f* engraving; (*em livro*) illustration

graxa /'graʃa/ *f* (*de sapatos*) polish; (*de lubrificar*) grease

Grécia /'grɛsia/ *f* Greece

grego /'gregu/ *a & m* Greek

grei /grej/ *f* flock

gre|lha /'grɛʎa/ *f* grill. **~lhado** *a* grilled ● *m* grill. **~lhar** *vt* grill

grêmio /'gremiu/ *m* guild, association

grená /gre'na/ *a & m* dark red

gre|ta /'greta/ *f* crack. **~tar** *vt/i* crack

gre|ve /'grɛvi/ *f* strike; **entrar em ~ve** go on strike; **~ve de fome** hunger strike. **~vista** *m/f* striker

gri|fado /gri'fadu/ *a* in italics. **~far** *vt* italicize

griffe /'grifi/ *f* label, line

gri|lado /gri'ladu/ *a* [!] hung up. **~lar** *vt* [!] bug. **~lar-se** *vpr* [!] get hung up (**com** about)

grilhão /gri'ʎãw/ *m* fetter

grilo /'grilu/ *m* (*bicho*) cricket; [!] (*preocupação*) hang-up; (*problema*) hassle; (*barulho*) squeak

grinalda /gri'nawda/ *f* garland

gringo /'grĩgu/ [!] *a* foreign ● *m* foreigner

gri|pado /gri'padu/ *a* **estar/ficar ~pado** have/get the flu. **~par-se** *vpr* get the flu. **~pe** /'gripi/ *f* flu, influenza; **~pe das aves** bird flu; **~pe suína** swine flu

grisalho /gri'zaʎu/ *a* grey

gri|tante /gri'tãtʃi/ *a* ‹*erro*› glaring, gross; ‹*cor*› loud, garish. **~tar** *vt/i* shout; (*de medo*) scream. **~taria** *f* shouting. **~to** *m* shout; (*de medo*) scream; **aos ~tos** in a loud voice; **no ~to** [!] by force

grogue /'grɔgi/ *a* groggy

grosa /'grɔza/ *f* gross

groselha /gro'zɛʎa/ *f* (*vermelha*) redcurrant; (*espinhosa*) gooseberry; **~ negra** blackcurrant

gros|seiro /gro'seru/ *a* rude; (*tosco, malfeito*) rough. **~seria** *f* rudeness; (*uma*) rude thing. **~so** /o/ *a* thick; ‹*voz*› deep; [!] ‹*pessoa, atitude*› rude. **~sura** *f* thickness; [!] (*grosseria*) rudeness

grotesco /gro'tesku/ *a* grotesque

grua /'grua/ *f* crane

gru|dado /gru'dadu/ *a* stuck; *fig* very attached (**em** to). **~dar** *vt/i* stick. **~de** *m* glue. **~dento** *a* sticky

gru|nhido /gru'ɲidu/ *m* grunt. **~nhir** *vi* grunt

grupo /'grupu/ *m* group

gruta /'gruta/ *f* cave

guaraná /gwara'na/ *m* guarana

> **guaraná** *Guaraná* is a common plant native to the Amazon Basin. The term is used to refer to the small fruit of the *guaraná* plant, but also to soft drinks made with guaraná extract, which are very popular in Brazil. *Guaraná* is also used as a stimulant in herbal supplements due to its high caffeine content.

guarani /gwara'ni/ *a & m/f* Guarani

guarda /'gwarda/ *f* guard ● *m/f* guard; (*policial*) policeman (*f*-woman); **~ costeira** coastguard. **~-chuva** *m* umbrella; **~-costas** *m invar* bodyguard; **~-florestal** (*pl* **~s-florestais**) *m/f* forest ranger; **~-louça** *m* china cupboard; **~-noturno** (*pl* **~s-noturnos**) *m* night watchman. **~dor** *m* parking attendant. **~napo** *m* napkin, serviette

guardar /gwar'dar/ *vt* (*pôr no lugar*) put away; (*conservar*) keep; (*vigiar*) guard; (*não esquecer*) remember; **~-se de** guard against

guarda|-redes /'gwarda-'xedʃ/ *m invar Port* goalkeeper. **~-roupa** *m* wardrobe; **~-sol** (*pl* **~-sóis**) *m* sunshade

guardi|ão /gwardʒi'ãw/ (*pl* **~ães** ou **~ões**) *m* (*f* **~ã**) guardian

guarita /gwa'rita/ *f* sentry box

guar|necer /gwarne'ser/ *vt* (*fortificar*) garrison; (*munir*) equip; (*enfeitar*) garnish. **~nição** *f Mil* garrison; (*enfeite*) garnish

Guatemala /gwate'mala/ *f* Guatemala

guatemalteco /gwatemal'tɛku/ *a & m* Guatemalan

gude /'gudʒi/ *m* **bola de ~** marble

guelra /'gɛwxa/ *f* gill

guer|ra /'gɛxa/ *f* war. **~reiro** *m* warrior ● *a* warlike. **~rilha** *f* guerrilla war. **~rilheiro** *a & m* guerrilla

gueto /'getu/ *m* ghetto

gugar /gu'gar/ *vt* ▶ **googar**

guia /'gia/ *m/f* guide ● *m* guide(book) ● *f* delivery note

Guiana /gi'ana/ *f* Guyana

guianense /gia'nẽsi/ *a & m/f* Guyanan

guiar /gi'ar/ *vt* guide; drive ‹*veículo*› ● *vi* drive. **~-se** *vpr* be guided

guichê /gi'ʃe/ *m* window

guidom /gi'dõ/, *Port* **guidão** /gi'dãw/ *m* handlebars

guilhotina /giʎo'tʃina/ *f* guillotine

guimba /'gĩba/ *f* butt

guinada /gi'nada/ *f* change of direction; **dar uma ~** change direction

guinchar[1] /gĩ'ʃar/ *vi* squeal; ‹*freios*› screech

guinchar[2] /gĩ'ʃar/ *vt* tow ‹*carro*›; (*içar*) winch

guincho[1] /'gĩʃu/ *m* squeal; (*de freios*) screech

guincho[2] /'gĩʃu/ *m* (*máquina*) winch; (*veículo*) tow truck

guin|dar /gĩ'dar/ *vt* hoist. **~daste** *m* crane

Guiné /gi'nɛ/ *f* Guinea

gui|sado /gi'zadu/ *m* stew. **~sar** *vt* stew

guitar|ra /gi'taxa/ *f* (electric) guitar. **~rista** *m/f* guitarist

guizo /'gizu/ *m* bell

gu|la /'gula/ *f* greed. **~lodice** *f* greed. **~loseima** *f* delicacy. **~loso** /o/ *a* greedy

gume /'gumi/ *m* cutting edge

guri /gu'ri/ *m* boy. **~a** *f* girl

guru /gu'ru/ *m* guru

gutu|ral /gutu'raw/ (*pl* **~rais**) *a* guttural

Hh

há|bil /'abiw/ (*pl* **~beis**) *a* clever, skilful
habili|dade /abili'dadʒi/ *f* skill; **ter ~dade com** be good with. **~doso** /o/ *a* skilful. **~tação** *f* qualification. **~tar** *vt* qualify
habi|tação /abita'sãw/ *f* housing; (*casa*) dwelling. **~tacional** (*pl* **~tacionais**) *a* housing. **~tante** *m/f* inhabitant. **~tar** *vt* inhabit ● *vi* live. **~tável** (*pl* **~táveis**) *a* habitable
hábito /'abitu/ *m* habit
h
habitu|al /abitu'aw/ (*pl* **~ais**) *a* habitual. **~ar** *vt* accustom (**a** to). **~ar-se** *vpr* get accustomed (**a** to)
hacker /'akɛr/ *m/f BR* hacker
hacking *m BR* hacking
hadoque /a'dɔki/ *m* haddock
Haia /'aja/ *f* the Hague
Haiti /aj'tʃi/ *m* Haiti
haitiano /ajtʃi'anu/ *a & m* Haitian
hálito /'alitu/ *m* breath
halitose /ali'tɔzi/ *f* halitosis
hall /xɔw/ (*pl* **~s**) *m* hall; (*de hotel*) foyer
halogênio /alo'ʒenju/ *m* halogen
halte|re /aw'tɛri/ *m* dumb-bell. **~rofilismo** *m* weightlifting. **~rofilista** *m/f* weightlifter
hambúrguer /ã'burger/ *m* hamburger
hangar /ã'gar/ *m* hangar
haras /'aras/ *m invar* stud farm
hardware /'xarduɛr/ *m* hardware
harmo|nia /armo'nia/ *f* harmony. **~nioso** /o/ *a* harmonious. **~nizar** *vt* harmonize; (*conciliar*) reconcile. **~nizar-se** *vpr* (*combinar*) tone in; (*concordar*) coincide
har|pa /'arpa/ *f* harp. **~pista** *m/f* harpist
haste /'astʃi/ *m* pole; (*de planta*) stem, stalk. **~ar** *vt* hoist, raise
Havaí /ava'i/ *m* Hawaii
havaiano /avaj'anu/ *a & m* Hawaiian
haver /a'ver/ *m* credit; *pl* possessions ● *vt auxiliar* **havia sido** it had been; (*impessoal*) **há** there is/are; **ele trabalha aqui há anos** he's been working here for years; **ela morreu há vinte anos (atrás)** she died twenty years ago
haxixe /a'ʃiʃi/ *m* hashish
he|braico /e'brajku/ *a & m* Hebrew. **~breu** *a & m* (*f* **~breia**) Hebrew
hectare /ek'tari/ *m* hectare
hediondo /edʒi'õdu/ *a* hideous
hein /ẽj/ *int* eh
hélice /'ɛlisi/ *f* propeller
helicóptero /eli'kɔpteru/ *m* helicopter
hélio /'ɛliu/ *m* helium
heliporto /eli'portu/ *m* heliport
hem /ẽj/ *int* eh
hematoma /ema'toma/ *m* bruise
hemisfério /emis'fɛriu/ *m* hemisphere; **Hemisfério Norte/Sul** Northern/Southern Hemisphere
hemo|filia /emofi'lia/ *f* haemophilia. **~fílico** *a & m* haemophiliac. **~globina** *f* haemoglobin. **~grama** *m* blood count
hemor|ragia /emoxa'ʒia/ *f* haemorrhage. **~roidas** *f pl* haemorrhoids
henê /e'ne/ *m* henna
hepatite /epa'tʃitʃi/ *f* hepatitis
hera /'ɛra/ *f* ivy
heráldi|ca /e'rawdʒika/ *f* heraldry. **~co** *a* heraldic
herança /e'rãsa/ *f* inheritance; (*de um povo etc*) heritage
her|bicida /erbi'sida/ *m* weedkiller. **~bívoro** *a* herbivorous ● *m* herbivore
her|dar /er'dar/ *vt* inherit. **~deiro** *m* heir
hereditário /eredʒi'tariu/ *a* hereditary
here|ge /e'rɛʒi/ *m/f* heretic. **~sia** *f* heresy
herético /e'rɛtʃiku/ *a* heretical
hermético /er'mɛtʃiku/ *a* airtight; *fig* obscure
hérnia /'ɛrnia/ *f* hernia
her|ói /e'rɔj/ *m* hero. **~oico** *a* heroic
hero|ína /ero'ina/ *f* (*mulher*) heroine; (*droga*) heroin. **~ísmo** *m* heroism
herpes /'ɛrpis/ *m invar* herpes. **~-zoster** *m* shingles
hesi|tação /ezita'sãw/ *f* hesitation. **~tante** *a* hesitant. **~tar** *vi* hesitate
hetero|doxo /etero'dɔksu/ *a* unorthodox. **~gêneo** *a* heterogeneous
heterossexu|al /eteroseksu'aw/ (*pl* **~ais**) *a & m* heterosexual
hexago|nal /eksago'naw/ (*pl* **~nais**) *a* hexagonal
hexágono /ek'sagonu/ *m* hexagon
hiato /i'atu/ *m* hiatus
hiber|nação /iberna'sãw/ *f* hibernation. **~nar** *vi* hibernate

híbrido /'ibridu/ *a & m* hybrid; **carro ~** hybrid car

hidrante /i'drãtʃi/ *m* fire hydrant

hidra|tante /idra'tãtʃi/ *a* moisturising ● *m* moisturizer. **~tar** *vt* moisturize ‹*pele*›. **~to** *m* **~to de carbono** carbohydrate

hidráuli|ca /i'drawlika/ *f* hydraulics. **~co** *a* hydraulic

hidrelétri|ca /idre'lɛtrika/ *f* hydroelectric power station. **~co** *a* hydroelectric

hidro|avião /idroavi'ãw/ *m* seaplane. **~carboneto** /e/ *m* hydrocarbon

hidrófilo /i'drɔfilu/ *a* absorbent; **algodão ~** cotton wool, *Amer* absorbent cotton

hidrofobia /idrofo'bia/ *f* rabies

hidro|gênio /idro'ʒeniu/ *m* hydrogen. **~massagem** *f* **banheira de ~massagem** jacuzzi. **~via** *f* waterway

hiena /i'ena/ *f* hyena

hierarquia /ierar'kia/ *f* hierarchy

hieróglifo /ie'rɔglifu/ *m* hieroglyphic

hífen /'ifẽ/ *m* hyphen

higi|ene /iʒi'eni/ *f* hygiene. **~ênico** *a* hygienic

hilari|ante /ilari'ãtʃi/ *a* hilarious. **~dade** *f* hilarity

Himalaia /ima'laja/ *m* Himalayas

hin|di /ĩ'dʒi/ *m* Hindi. **~du** *a & m/f* Hindu. **~duísmo** *m* Hinduism. **~duísta** *a & m/f* Hindu

hino /'inu/ *m* hymn; **~ nacional** national anthem

hipermercado /ipermer'kadu/ *m* hypermarket

hipersensí|vel /iperse͂'sivew/ (*pl* **~veis**) *a* hypersensitive

hipertensão /iperte͂'sãw/ *f* hypertension

hípico /'ipiku/ *a* horse riding

hipismo /i'pizmu/ *m* horse riding; (*corridas*) horse racing

hip|nose /ipi'nɔzi/ *f* hypnosis. **~nótico** *a* hypnotic. **~notismo** *m* hypnotism. **~notizador** *m* hypnotist. **~notizar** *vt* hypnotize

hipnoterapia /ipnotera'pia/ *f* hypnotherapy

hipocondríaco /ipokõ'driaku/ *a & m* hypochondriac

hipocrisia /ipokri'zia/ *f* hypocrisy

hipócrita /i'pɔkrita/ *m/f* hypocrite ● *a* hypocritical

hipódromo /i'pɔdromu/ *m* race course, *Amer* race track

hipopótamo /ipo'pɔtamu/ *m* hippopotamus

hipote|ca /ipo'tɛka/ *f* mortgage. **~car** *vt* mortgage. **~cário** *a* mortgage

hipotermia /ipoter'mia/ *f* hypothermia

hipótese /i'pɔtezi/ *f* hypothesis; **na ~ de** in the event of; **na pior das ~s** at worst

hipotético /ipo'tɛtʃiku/ *a* hypothetical

hirto /'irtu/ *a* rigid, stiff

hispânico /is'paniku/ *a* Hispanic

histamina /ista'mina/ *f* histamine

his|terectomia /isterekto'mia/ *f* hysterectomy. **~teria** *f* hysteria. **~térico** *a* hysterical. **~terismo** *m* hysteria

his|tória /is'tɔria/ *f* (*do passado*) history; (*conto*) story; *pl* (*amolação*) trouble. **~toriador** *m* historian. **~tórico** *a* historical; (*marcante*) historic ● *m* history

hoje /'oʒi/ *adv* today; **~ em dia** nowadays; **~ de manhã** this morning; **~ à noite** tonight

Holanda /o'lãda/ *f* Holland

holan|dês /olã'des/ *a* (*f* **~desa**) Dutch ● *m* (*f* **~desa**) Dutchman (*f* -woman); (*língua*) Dutch; **os ~deses** the Dutch

holding /'xɔwdʒĩ/ (*pl* **~s**) *f* holding company

holerite /ole'ritʃi/ *m* pay slip

holo|causto /olo'kawstu/ *m* holocaust. **~fote** /ɔ/ *m* spotlight. **~grama** *m* hologram

homem /'omẽ/ *m* man; **~ de negócios** businessman. **~-rã** (*pl* **homens-rã**) *m* frogman

homena|gear /omenaʒi'ar/ *vt* pay tribute to. **~gem** *f* tribute; **em ~gem a** in honour of

homeo|pata /omio'pata/ *m/f* homoeopath. **~patia** *f* homoeopathy. **~pático** *a* homoeopathic

homérico /o'mɛriku/ *a* (*estrondoso*) booming; (*extraordinário*) phenomenal

homi|cida /omi'sida/ *a* homicidal ● *m/f* murderer. **~cídio** *m* homicide; **~cídio involuntário** manslaughter

homo|geneizado /omoʒenej'zadu/ *a* ‹*leite*› homogenized. **~gêneo** *a* homogeneous

homologar /omolo'gar/ *vt* ratify

homólogo /o'mɔlogu/ *m* opposite number ● *a* equivalent

h

homônimo /o'monimu/ *m* (*xará*) namesake; (*vocábulo*) homonym

homossexu|al /omoseksu'aw/ (*pl* **~ais**) *a & m* homosexual. **~alismo** *m* homosexuality

Honduras /õ'duras/ *f* Honduras

hondurenho /õdu'reɲu/ *a & m* Honduran

hones|tidade /onestʃi'dadʒi/ *f* honesty. **~to** /ɛ/ *a* honest

hono|rário /ono'rariu/ *a* honorary. **~rários** *m pl* fees. **~rífico** *a* honorific

hon|ra /'õxa/ *f* honour. **~radez** *f* honesty, integrity. **~rado** *a* honourable. **~rar** *vt* honour. **~roso** /o/ *a* honourable

h

hóquei /'ɔkej/ *m* (field) hockey; **~ sobre gelo** ice hockey; **~ sobre patins** roller hockey

hora /'ɔra/ *f* (*unidade de tempo*) hour; (*ocasião*) time; **que ~s são?** what's the time?; **a que ~s?** at what time?; **às três ~s** at three o'clock; **dizer as ~s** tell the time; **tem ~s?** do you have the time?; **em cima da ~** at the last minute; **na ~** (*naquele momento*) at the time; (*no ato*) on the spot; (*a tempo*) on time; **está na ~ de ir** it's time to go; **na ~ H** (*no momento certo*) at just the right moment; (*no momento crítico*) at the crucial moment; **meia ~** half an hour; **toda ~** all the time; **fazer ~** kill time; **marcar ~** make an appointment; **perder a ~** lose track of time; **não tenho ~** my time is my own; **não vejo a ~ de ir** I can't wait to go; **~s extras** overtime; **~s vagas** spare time

horário /o'rariu/ *a* hourly; **km ~s** km per hour ● *m* (*hora*) time; (*tabela*) timetable; (*de trabalho etc*) hours; **~ nobre** prime time

horda /'ɔrda/ *f* horde

horista /o'rista/ *a* paid by the hour ● *m/f* worker paid by the hour

horizon|tal /orizõ'taw/ (*pl* **~tais**) *a & f* horizontal. **~te** *m* horizon

hor|monal /ormo'naw/ (*pl* **~monais**) *a* hormonal. **~mônio** *m* hormone

horóscopo /o'rɔskopu/ *m* horoscope

horrendo /o'xẽdu/ *a* horrid

horripi|lante /oxipi'lãtʃi/ *a* horrifying. **~lar** *vt* horrify

horrí|vel /o'xivew/ (*pl* **~veis**) *a* horrible, awful

horror /o'xor/ *m* horror (**a** of); (*coisa horrorosa*) horrible thing; **ser um ~** be awful; **que ~!** how awful!

horro|rizar /oxori'zar/ *vt/i* horrify. **~rizar-se** *vpr* be horrified. **~roso** /o/ *a* horrible

horta /'ɔrta/ *f* vegetable plot; **~ comercial** market garden, *Amer* truck farm. **~liça** *f* vegetable

hortelã /orte'lã/ *f* mint; **~-pimenta** peppermint

horti|cultor /ortʃikuw'tor/ *m* horticulturalist. **~cultura** *f* horticulture. **~frutigranjeiros** *m pl* fruit and vegetables. **~granjeiros** *m pl* vegetables

horto /'ortu/ *m* market garden; (*viveiro*) nursery

hospe|dagem /ospe'daʒẽ/ *f* accommodation. **~dar** *vt* put up. **~dar-se** *vpr* stay

hóspede /'ɔspidʒi/ *m/f* guest

hospedei|ra /ospe'dera/ *f* landlady; **~ra de bordo** *Port* flight attendant. **~ro** *m* landlord

hospício /os'pisiu/ *m* (*de loucos*) asylum

hospi|tal /ospi'taw/ (*pl* **~tais**) *m* hospital. **~talar** *a* hospital. **~taleiro** *a* hospitable. **~talidade** *f* hospitality. **~talizar** *vt* hospitalize

hóstia /'ɔstʃia/ *f* Host, Communion wafer

hos|til /os'tʃiw/ (*pl* **~tis**) *a* hostile. **~tilidade** *f* hostility. **~tilizar** *vt* antagonize

ho|tel /o'tɛw/ (*pl* **~téis**) *m* hotel. **~teleiro** *a* hotel ● *m* hotelier

huma|nidade /umani'dadʒi/ *f* humanity. **~nismo** *m* humanism. **~nista** *a & m/f* humanist. **~nitário** *a & m* humanitarian. **~nizar** *vt* humanize. **~no** *a* human; (*compassivo*) humane. **~nos** *m pl* humans

húmido /'umidu/ *a Port* humid

humil|dade /umiw'dadʒi/ *f* humility. **~de** *a* humble

humi|lhação /umiʎa'sãw/ *f* humiliation. **~lhante** *a* humiliating. **~lhar** *vt* humiliate

humor /u'mor/ *m* humour; (*disposição do espírito*) mood; **de bom/mau ~** in a good/bad mood

humo|rismo /umo'rizmu/ *m* humour. **~rista** *m/f* (*no palco*) comedian; (*escritor*) humorist. **~rístico** *a* humorous

húngaro /'ũgaru/ *a & m* Hungarian

Hungria /ũ'gria/ *f* Hungary

hurra /'uxa/ *int* hurrah ● *m* cheer

Ii

ia|te /i'atʃi/ *m* yacht. **~tismo** *m* yachting. **~tista** *m/f* yachtsman (*f*-woman)
ibérico /i'bɛriku/ *a & m* Iberian
ibope /i'bɔpi/ *m* **dar ~** [!] be popular
içar /i'sar/ *vt* hoist
iceberg /ajs'bɛrgi/ (*pl* **~s**) *m* iceberg
ícone /'ikoni/ *m* icon
iconoclasta /ikono'klasta/ *m/f* iconoclast ● *a* iconoclastic
icterícia /ikte'risia/ *f* jaundice
ida /'ida/ *f* going; **na ~** on the way there; **~ e volta** return, *Amer* round trip
idade /i'dadʒi/ *f* age; **meia ~** middle age; **homem de meia ~** middle-aged man; **senhor de ~** elderly man; **Idade Média** Middle Ages
ide|al /ide'aw/ (*pl* **~ais**) *a & m* ideal. **~alismo** *m* idealism. **~alista** *m/f* idealist ● *a* idealistic. **~alizar** *vt* (*criar*) devise; (*sublimar*) idealize. **~ar** *vt* devise. **~ário** *m* ideas
ideia /i'dɛja/ *f* idea; **mudar de ~** change one's mind
idem /'idẽ/ *adv* ditto
idêntico /i'dẽtʃiku/ *a* identical
identi|dade /idẽtʃi'dadʒi/ *f* identity. **~ficar** *vt* identify. **~ficar-se** *vpr* identify (**com** with)
ideo|logia /ideolo'ʒia/ *f* ideology. **~lógico** *a* ideological
idílico /i'dʒiliku/ *a* idyllic
idílio /i'dʒiliu/ *m* idyll
idio|ma /idʒi'oma/ *m* language. **~mático** *a* idiomatic
idio|ta /idʒi'ɔta/ *m/f* idiot ● *a* idiotic. **~tice** *f* stupidity; (*uma*) stupid thing
idola|trar /idola'trar/ *vt* idolize. **~tria** *f* idolatry
ídolo /'idulu/ *m* idol
idôneo /i'doniu/ *a* suitable
idoso /i'dozu/ *a* elderly
Iêmen /i'emẽ/ *m* Yemen
iemenita /ieme'nita/ *a & m/f* Yemeni
iene /i'ɛni/ *m* yen
iglu /i'glu/ *m* igloo
ignição /igni'sãw/ *f* ignition
ignomínia /igno'minia/ *f* ignominy
igno|rância /igno'rãsia/ *f* ignorance. **~rante** *a* ignorant. **~rar** *vt* (*desconsiderar*) ignore; (*desconhecer*) not know
igreja /i'greʒa/ *f* church
igu|al /i'gwaw/ (*pl* **~ais**) *a* equal; (*em aparência*) identical; (*liso*) even ● *m/f* equal; **por ~al** equally. **~alar** *vt* equal; level ‹*terreno*›; **~alar(-se) a** be equal to. **~aldade** *f* equality. **~alitário** *a* egalitarian. **~almente** *adv* equally; (*como resposta*) the same to you. **~alzinho** *a* exactly the same (**a** as)
iguaria /igwa'ria/ *f* delicacy
iídiche /i'idiʃi/ *m* Yiddish
ile|gal /ile'gaw/ (*pl* **~gais**) *a* illegal. **~galidade** *f* illegality
ilegítimo /ile'ʒitʃimu/ *a* illegitimate
ilegí|vel /ile'ʒivew/ (*pl* **~veis**) *a* illegible
ileso /i'lɛzu/ *a* unhurt
iletrado /ile'tradu/ *a & m* illiterate
ilha /'iʎa/ *f* island
ilharga /i'ʎarga/ *f* side
ilhéu /i'ʎɛw/ *m* (*f* **ilhoa**) islander
ilhós /i'ʎɔs/ *m invar* eyelet
ilhota /i'ʎɔta/ *f* small island
ilícito /i'lisitu/ *a* illicit
ilimitado /ilimi'tadu/ *a* unlimited
ilógico /i'lɔʒiku/ *a* illogical
iludir /ilu'dʒir/ *vt* delude. **~-se** *vpr* delude o.s.
ilumi|nação /ilumina'sãw/ *f* lighting; (*inspiração*) enlightenment. **~nar** *vt* light up, illuminate; (*inspirar*) enlighten
ilu|são /ilu'zãw/ *f* illusion; (*sonho*) delusion. **~sionista** *m/f* illusionist. **~sório** *a* illusory
ilus|tração /ilustra'sãw/ *f* illustration; (*erudição*) learning. **~trador** *m* illustrator. **~trar** *vt* illustrate. **~trativo** *a* illustrative. **~tre** *a* illustrious; **~tríssimo senhor** Dear Sir
ímã /'imã/ *m* magnet
imaculado /imaku'ladu/ *a* immaculate
imagem /i'maʒẽ/ *f* image; (*da TV*) picture
imagi|nação /imaʒina'sãw/ *f* imagination. **~nar** *vt* imagine. **~nário** *a* imaginary. **~nativo** *a* imaginative. **~nável** (*pl* **~náveis**) *a* imaginable. **~noso** /o/ *a* imaginative
imatu|ridade /imaturi'dadʒi/ *f* immaturity. **~ro** *a* immature
imbatí|vel /ĩba'tʃivew/ (*pl* **~veis**) *a* unbeatable

imbe|cil /ĩbe'siw/ (*pl* **~cis**) *a* stupid ● *m/f* imbecile

imberbe /ĩ'berbi/ *a* (*sem barba*) beardless

imbricar /ĩbri'kar/ *vt* overlap. **~-se** *vpr* overlap

imedia|ções /imedʒia'sõjs/ *f pl* vicinity. **~tamente** *adv* immediately. **~to** *a* immediate

imemori|al /imemori'aw/ (*pl* **~ais**) *a* immemorial

imen|sidão /imẽsi'dãw/ *f* vastness. **~so** *a* immense

imergir /imer'ʒir/ *vt* immerse

imi|gração /imigra'sãw/ *f* immigration. **~grante** *a & m/f* immigrant. **~grar** *vi* immigrate

i

imi|nência /imi'nẽsia/ *f* imminence. **~nente** *a* imminent

imiscuir-se /imisku'irsi/ *vpr* interfere

imi|tação /imita'sãw/ *f* imitation. **~tador** *m* imitator. **~tar** *vt* imitate

imobili|ária /imobili'aria/ *f* estate agent's, *Amer* realtor. **~ário** *a* property. **~dade** *f* immobility. **~zar** *vt* immobilize

imo|ral /imo'raw/ (*pl* **~rais**) *a* immoral. **~ralidade** *f* immorality

imor|tal /imor'taw/ (*pl* **~tais**) *a* immortal ● *m/f* member of the Brazilian Academy of Letters. **~talidade** *f* immortality. **~talizar** *vt* immortalize

imó|vel /i'mɔvew/ (*pl* **~veis**) *a* motionless, immobile ● *m* building, property; *pl* property, *Amer* real estate

impaci|ência /ĩpasi'ẽsia/ *f* impatience. **~entar-se** *vpr* get impatient. **~ente** *a* impatient

impacto /ĩ'paktu/, *Port* **impacte** /ĩ'paktʃi/ *m* impact

impagá|vel /ĩpa'gavew/ (*pl* **~veis**) *a* priceless

ímpar /'ĩpar/ *a* unique; ‹*número*› odd

imparci|al /ĩparsi'aw/ (*pl* **~ais**) *a* impartial. **~alidade** *f* impartiality

impasse /ĩ'pasi/ *m* impasse

impassí|vel /ĩpa'sivew/ (*pl* **~veis**) *a* impassive

impecá|vel /ĩpe'kavew/ (*pl* **~veis**) *a* impeccable

impe|dido /ĩpe'dʒidu/ *a* ‹*rua*› blocked; *Port* (*ocupado*) engaged, *Amer* busy; (*no futebol*) offside. **~dimento** *m* prevention; (*estorvo*) obstruction; (*no futebol*) offside position. **~dir** *vt* stop; (*estorvar*) hinder; block ‹*rua*›; **~dir alguém de ir** ou **que alguém vá** stop sb going

impelir /ĩpe'lir/ *vt* drive

impenetrá|vel /ĩpene'travew/ (*pl* **~veis**) *a* impenetrable

impensá|vel /ĩpẽ'savew/ (*pl* **~veis**) *a* unthinkable

impe|rador /ĩpera'dor/ *m* emperor. **~rar** *vi* reign, rule. **~rativo** *a & m* imperative. **~ratriz** *f* empress

imperceptí|vel /ĩpersep'tʃivew/ (*pl* **~veis**) *a* imperceptible

imperdí|vel /ĩper'dʒivew/ (*pl* **~veis**) *a* unmissable

imperdoá|vel /ĩperdo'avew/ (*pl* **~veis**) *a* unforgivable

imperfei|ção /ĩperfej'sãw/ *f* imperfection. **~to** *a & m* imperfect

imperi|al /ĩperi'aw/ (*pl* **~ais**) *a* imperial ● *f Port* (*de cerveja*) glass of draught beer. **~alismo** *m* imperialism. **~alista** *a & m/f* imperialist

império /ĩ'pɛriu/ *m* empire

imperioso /ĩperi'ozu/ *a* imperious; ‹*necessidade*› pressing

imperme|abilizar /ĩpermiabili'zar/ *vt* waterproof. **~ável** (*pl* **~áveis**) *a* waterproof; *fig* impervious (**a** to) ● *m* raincoat

imperti|nência /ĩpertʃi'nẽsia/ *f* impertinence. **~nente** *a* impertinent

impesso|al /ĩpeso'aw/ (*pl* **~ais**) *a* impersonal

ímpeto /'ĩpetu/ *m* (*vontade*) urge, impulse; (*de emoção*) surge; (*movimento*) start; (*na física*) impetus

impetuo|sidade /ĩpetuozi'dadʒi/ *f* impetuosity. **~so** /o/ *a* impetuous

impiedoso /ĩpie'dozu/ *a* merciless

impingir /ĩpĩ'ʒir/ *vt* foist (**a** on)

implacá|vel /ĩpla'kavew/ (*pl* **~veis**) *a* implacable

implan|tar /ĩplã'tar/ *vt* introduce; (*no corpo*) implant. **~te** *m* implant

implemen|tar /ĩplemẽ'tar/ *vt* implement. **~to** *m* implement

impli|cação /ĩplika'sãw/ *f* implication. **~cância** *f* (*ato*) harassment; (*antipatia*) grudge; **estar de ~cância com** have it in for. **~cante** *a* troublesome ● *m/f* troublemaker. **~car** *vt* (*comprometer*) implicate; **~car (em)** (*dar a entender*) imply; (*acarretar, exigir*) involve; **~car com** (*provocar*) pick on; (*antipatizar*) not get on with

implícito /ĩ'plisitu/ *a* implicit

implorar /ĩplo'rar/ *vt* plead for (**a** from)

imponente /ĩpo'nẽtʃi/ *a* imposing

impopular /ĩpopu'lar/ *a* unpopular

impor /ĩ'por/ *vt* impose (**a** on); command ‹*respeito*›. **~-se** *vpr* assert o.s.

impor|tação /ĩporta'sãw/ *f* import. **~tador** *m* importer. **~tadora** *f* import company. **~tados** *m pl* imported goods. **~tância** *f* importance; (*quantia*) amount; **ter ~tância** be important. **~tante** *a* important. **~tar** *vt* import ‹*mercadorias*›; **~tar em** (*montar a*) amount to; (*resultar em*) lead to ● *vi* matter; **~tar-se (com)** mind

importu|nar /ĩportu'nar/ *vt* bother. **~no** *a* annoying

imposição /ĩpozi'sãw/ *f* imposition

impossibili|dade /ĩposibili'dadʒi/ *f* impossibility. **~tar** *vt* make impossible; **~tar alguém de ir, ~tar a alguém ir** prevent sb from going, make it impossible for sb to go

impossí|vel /ĩpo'sivew/ (*pl* **~veis**) *a* impossible

impos|to /ĩ'postu/ *m* tax; **~to de renda** income tax; **~to sobre o valor acrescentado** *Port* VAT. **~tor** *m* impostor. **~tura** *f* deception

impo|tência /ĩpo'tẽsia/ *f* impotence. **~tente** *a* impotent

impreci|são /ĩpresi'zãw/ *f* imprecision. **~so** *a* imprecise

impregnar /ĩpreg'nar/ *vt* impregnate

imprensa /ĩ'prẽsa/ *f* press; **~ marrom** gutter press

imprescindí|vel /ĩpresĩ'dʒivew/ (*pl* **~veis**) *a* essential

impres|são /ĩpre'sãw/ *f* impression; (*no prelo*) printing; **~são digital** fingerprint. **~sionante** *a* (*imponente*) impressive; (*comovente*) striking. **~sionar** *vt* (*causar admiração*) impress; (*comover*) make an impression on. **~sionar-se** *vpr* be impressed (**com** by). **~sionável** (*pl* **~sionáveis**) *a* impressionable. **~sionismo** *m* Impressionism. **~sionista** *a & m/f* Impressionist. **~so** *a* printed ● *m* printed sheet; *pl* printed matter. **~sor** *m* printer. **~sora** *f* printer

impresta|vel /ĩpres'tavew/ (*pl* **~veis**) *a* useless

impre|visível /ĩprevi'zivew/ (*pl* **~visíveis**) *a* unpredictable. **~visto** *a* unforeseen ● *m* unforeseen circumstance

imprimir /ĩpri'mir/ *vt* print

impropério /ĩpro'pɛriu/ *m* term of abuse; *pl* abuse

impróprio /ĩ'prɔpriu/ *a* improper; (*inadequado*) unsuitable (**para** for)

imprová|vel /ĩpro'vavew/ (*pl* **~veis**) *a* unlikely

improvi|sação /ĩproviza'sãw/ *f* improvisation. **~sar** *vt/i* improvise. **~so** *m* **de ~so** on the spur of the moment

impru|dência /ĩpru'dẽsia/ *f* recklessness. **~dente** *a* reckless

impul|sionar /ĩpuwsio'nar/ *vt* drive. **~sivo** *a* impulsive. **~so** *m* impulse

impu|ne /ĩ'puni/ *a* unpunished. **~nidade** *f* impunity

impu|reza /ĩpu'reza/ *f* impurity. **~ro** *a* impure

imun|dície /imũ'dʒisi/ *f* filth. **~do** *a* filthy

imu|ne /i'muni/ *a* immune (**a** to). **~nidade** *f* immunity. **~nizar** *vt* immunize

inabalá|vel /inaba'lavew/ (*pl* **~veis**) *a* unshakeable

iná|bil /i'nabiw/ (*pl* **~beis**) *a* (*desafeitado*) clumsy

inabitado /inabi'tadu/ *a* uninhabited

inacabado /inaka'badu/ *a* unfinished

inaceitá|vel /inasej'tavew/ (*pl* **~veis**) *a* unacceptable

inacessí|vel /inase'sivew/ (*pl* **~veis**) *a* inaccessible

inacreditá|vel /inakredʒi'tavew/ (*pl* **~veis**) *a* unbelievable

inadequado /inade'kwadu/ *a* unsuitable

inadmissí|vel /inadʒimi'sivew/ (*pl* **~veis**) *a* inadmissible

inadvertência /inadʒiver'tẽsia/ *f* oversight

inalar /ina'lar/ *vt* inhale

inalcançá|vel /inawkã'savew/ (*pl* **~veis**) *a* unattainable

inalterá|vel /inawte'ravew/ (*pl* **~veis**) *a* unchangeable

inanição /inani'sãw/ *f* starvation

inanimado /inani'madu/ *a* inanimate

inapto /i'naptu/ *a* (*incapaz*) unfit

inati|vidade /inatʃivi'dadʒi/ *f* inactivity. **~vo** *a* inactive

inato /i'natu/ *a* innate

inaudito /inaw'dʒitu/ *a* unheard of

inaugu|ração /inawgura'sãw/ *f* inauguration. **~ral** (*pl* **~rais**) *a* inaugural. **~rar** *vt* inaugurate

incabí|vel /ĩka'bivew/ (*pl* **~veis**) *a* inappropriate
incalculá|vel /ĩkawku'lavew/ (*pl* **~veis**) *a* incalculable
incandescente /ĩkãde'sẽtʃi/ *a* red-hot
incansá|vel /ĩkã'savew/ (*pl* **~veis**) *a* tireless
incapaci|tado /ĩkapasi'tadu/ *a* ‹*pessoa*› disabled. **~tar** *vt* incapacitate
incauto /ĩ'kawtu/ *a* reckless
incendi|ar /ĩsẽdʒi'ar/ *vt* set alight. **~ar-se** *vpr* catch fire. **~ário** *a* incendiary; *fig* ‹*discurso*› inflammatory ● *m* arsonist; *fig* agitator
incêndio /ĩ'sẽdʒiu/ *m* fire
incenso /ĩ'sẽsu/ *m* incense
incenti|var /ĩsẽtʃi'var/ *vt* encourage. **~vo** *m* incentive
incer|teza /ĩser'teza/ *f* uncertainty. **~to** /ɛ/ *a* uncertain
inces|to /ĩ'sɛstu/ *m* incest. **~tuoso** /o/ *a* incestuous
in|chação /ĩʃa'sãw/ *f* swelling. **~char** *vt/i* swell
inci|dência /ĩsi'dẽsia/ *f* incidence. **~dente** *m* incident. **~dir** *vi* **~dir em** ‹*luz*› shine on; ‹*imposto*› be payable on
incineradora /ĩsinera'dora/ *f* incinerator
incinerar /ĩsine'rar/ *vt* incinerate
inci|são /ĩsi'zãw/ *f* incision. **~sivo** *a* incisive
incitar /ĩsi'tar/ *vt* incite
incli|nação /ĩklina'sãw/ *f* (*do chão*) incline; (*da cabeça*) nod; (*propensão*) inclination. **~nado** *a* ‹*chão*› sloping; ‹*edifício*› leaning; (*propenso*) inclined (**a** to). **~nar** *vt* tilt; nod ‹*cabeça*› ● *vi* ‹*chão*› slope; ‹*edifício*› lean; (*tender*) incline (**para** towards). **~nar-se** *vpr* lean
inclu|ir /ĩklu'ir/ *vt* include. **~são** *f* inclusion. **~sive** *prep* including ● *adv* inclusive; (*até*) even. **~so** *a* included
incoe|rência /ĩkoe'rẽsia/ *f* (*falta de nexo*) incoherence; (*inconsequência*) inconsistency. **~rente** *a* (*sem nexo*) incoherent; (*inconsequente*) inconsistent
incógni|ta /ĩ'kɔgnita/ *f* unknown. **~to** *adv* incognito
incolor /ĩko'lor/ *a* colourless
incólume /ĩ'kɔlumi/ *a* unscathed
incomodar /ĩkomo'dar/ *vt* bother ● *vi* be a nuisance. **~-se** *vpr* (*dar-se ao trabalho*) bother (**em** to); **~-se (com)** be bothered (by), mind
incômodo /ĩ'komodu/ *a* (*desagradável*) tiresome; (*sem conforto*) uncomfortable ● *m* nuisance
incompa|rável /ĩkõpa'ravew/ (*pl* **~ráveis**) *a* incomparable. **~tível** (*pl* **~tíveis**) *a* incompatible
incompe|tência /ĩkõpe'tẽsia/ *f* incompetence. **~tente** *a* incompetent
incompleto /ĩkõ'plɛtu/ *a* incomplete
incompreensí|vel /ĩkõpriẽ'sivew/ (*pl* **~veis**) *a* incomprehensible
inconcebí|vel /ĩkõse'bivew/ (*pl* **~veis**) *a* inconceivable
incondicio|nal /ĩkõdʒisio'naw/ (*pl* **~nais**) *a* unconditional; ‹*fã, partidário*› firm
inconformado /ĩkõfor'madu/ *a* unreconciled (**com** to)
inconfundí|vel /ĩkõfũ'dʒivew/ (*pl* **~veis**) *a* unmistakeable
inconsciente /ĩkõsi'ẽtʃi/ *a* & *m* unconscious
inconsequente /ĩkõse'kwẽtʃi/ *a* inconsistent
incons|tância /ĩkõs'tãsia/ *f* changeability. **~tante** *a* changeable
inconstitucio|nal /ĩkõstʃitusio'naw/ (*pl* **~nais**) *a* unconstitutional
incontestá|vel /ĩkõtes'tavew/ (*pl* **~veis**) *a* indisputable
incontornável /ĩkõtor'navɛw/ *a* unavoidable
inconveniente /ĩkõveni'ẽtʃi/ *a* (*difícil*) inconvenient; (*desagradável*) annoying, tiresome; (*indecente*) unseemly ● *m* drawback
incorporar /ĩkorpo'rar/ *vt* incorporate
incorrer /ĩko'xer/ *vi* **~ em** ‹*multa etc*› incur
incorrigí|vel /ĩkoxi'ʒivew/ (*pl* **~veis**) *a* incorrigible
incrédulo /ĩ'krɛdulu/ *a* incredulous
incremen|tado /ĩkremẽ'tadu/ *a* [!] stylish. **~tar** *vt* build up; [!] jazz up. **~to** *m* development, growth
incriminar /ĩkrimi'nar/ *vt* incriminate
incrí|vel /ĩ'krivew/ (*pl* **~veis**) *a* incredible
incu|bação /ĩkuba'sãw/ *f* incubation. **~badora** *f* incubator. **~bar** *vt/i* incubate
inculto /ĩ'kuwtu/ *a* ‹*pessoa*› uneducated; ‹*terreno*› uncultivated
incum|bência /ĩkũ'bẽsia/ *f* task. **~bir** *vt* **~bir alguém de algo/de ir** assign sb sth/to go ● *vi* **~bir a** be up to; **~bir-se de** take on

incurá|vel /ĩku'ravew/ (*pl* **~veis**) *a* incurable

incursão /ĩkur'sãw/ *f* incursion

incutir /ĩku'tʃir/ *vt* instil (**em** in)

indagar /ĩda'gar/ *vt* inquire (into)

inde|cência /ĩde'sẽsia/ *f* indecency. **~cente** *a* indecent

indecifrá|vel /ĩdesi'fravew/ (*pl* **~veis**) *a* indecipherable

indeciso /ĩde'sizu/ *a* undecided

indecoroso /ĩdeko'rozu/ *a* indecorous

indefi|nido /ĩdefi'nidu/ *a* indefinite. **~nível** (*pl* **~níveis**) *a* indefinable

indelé|vel /ĩde'lɛvew/ (*pl* **~veis**) *a* indelible

indelica|deza /ĩdelika'deza/ *f* impoliteness; (*uma*) impolite thing. **~do** *a* impolite

indeni|zação /ĩdeniza'sãw/ *f* compensation. **~zar** *vt* compensate

indepen|dência /ĩdepẽ'dẽsia/ *f* independence. **~dente** *a* independent

indescrití|vel /ĩdʒiskri'tʃivew/ (*pl* **~veis**) *a* indescribable

indesculpá|vel /ĩdʒiskuw'pavew/ (*pl* **~veis**) *a* inexcusable

indesejá|vel /ĩdeze'ʒavew/ (*pl* **~veis**) *a* undesirable

indestrutí|vel /ĩdʒistru'tʃivew/ (*pl* **~veis**) *a* indestructible

indeterminado /ĩdetermi'nadu/ *a* indeterminate

indevido /ĩde'vidu/ *a* undue

indexar /ĩdek'sar/ *vt* index; index-link ‹*salário, preços*›

Índia /'ĩdʒia/ *f* India

indiano /ĩdʒi'anu/ *a & m* Indian

indi|cação /ĩdʒika'sãw/ *f* indication; (*do caminho*) directions; (*nomeação*) nomination; (*recomendação*) recommendation. **~cador** *m* indicator; (*dedo*) index finger ● *a* indicative (**de** of). **~car** *vt* indicate; (*para cargo, prêmio*) nominate (**para** for); (*recomendar*) recommend. **~cativo** *a & m* indicative

índice /'ĩdʒisi/ *m* (*taxa*) rate; (*em livro etc*) index; **~ de audiência** ratings

indiciar /ĩdʒisi'ar/ *vt* charge

indício /ĩ'dʒisiu/ *m* sign, indication; (*de crime*) clue

indife|rença /ĩdʒife'rẽsa/ *f* indifference. **~rente** *a* indifferent

indígena /ĩ'dʒiʒena/ *a* indigenous, native ● *m/f* native

indiges|tão /ĩdʒiʒes'tãw/ *f* indigestion. **~to** *a* indigestible; *fig* heavy going

indig|nação /ĩdʒigna'sãw/ *f* indignation. **~nado** *a* indignant. **~nar** *vt* make indignant. **~nar-se** *vpr* get indignant (**com** about)

indig|nidade /ĩdʒigni'dadʒi/ *f* indignity. **~no** *a* ‹*pessoa*› unworthy; ‹*ato*› despicable

índio /'ĩdʒiu/ *a & m* Indian

indire|ta /ĩdʒi'rɛta/ *f* hint. **~to** /ɛ/ *a* indirect

indis|creto /ĩdʒis'krɛtu/ *a* indiscreet. **~crição** *f* indiscretion

indiscriminado /ĩdʒiskrimi-'nadu/ *a* indiscriminate

indiscutí|vel /ĩdʒisku'tʃivew/ (*pl* **~veis**) *a* unquestionable

indispensá|vel /ĩdʒispẽ'savew/ (*pl* **~veis**) *a* indispensable

indisponí|vel /ĩdʒispo'nivew/ (*pl* **~veis**) *a* unavailable

indis|por /ĩdʒis'por/ *vt* upset; **~por alguém contra** turn sb against. **~por-se** *vpr* fall out (**com** with). **~posição** *f* indisposition. **~posto** *a* (*doente*) indisposed

indistinto /ĩdʒis'tʃĩtu/ *a* indistinct

individu|al /ĩdʒividu'aw/ (*pl* **~ais**) *a* individual. **~alidade** *f* individuality. **~alismo** *m* individualism. **~alista** *a & m/f* individualist

indivíduo /ĩdʒi'viduu/ *m* individual

indizí|vel /ĩdʒi'zivew/ (*pl* **~veis**) *a* unspeakable

índole /'ĩdoli/ *f* nature

indo|lência /ĩdo'lẽsia/ *f* indolence. **~lente** *a* indolent

indolor /ĩdo'lor/ *a* painless

Indonésia /ĩdo'nɛzia/ *f* Indonesia

indonésio /ĩdo'nɛziu/ *a & m* Indonesian

indubitá|vel /ĩdubi'tavew/ (*pl* **~veis**) *a* undoubted

indul|gência /ĩduw'ʒẽsia/ *f* indulgence. **~gente** *a* indulgent

indulto /ĩ'duwtu/ *m* pardon

indumentária /ĩdumẽ'taria/ *f* outfit

indústria /ĩ'dustria/ *f* industry

industri|al /ĩdustri'aw/ (*pl* **~ais**) *a* industrial ● *m/f* industrialist. **~alizado** *a* ‹*país*› industrialized; ‹*mercadoria*› manufactured; ‹*comida*› processed. **~alizar** *vt* industrialize ‹*país, agricultura*

i

etc›; process ‹*comida, lixo etc*›. **~oso** /o/ *a* industrious
induzir /ĩdu'zir/ *vt* (*persuadir*) induce; (*inferir*) infer (**de** from); **~ em erro** lead astray, mislead sb
inebriante /inebri'ãtʃi/ *a* intoxicating
inédito /i'nɛdʒitu/ *a* unheard-of, unprecedented; (*não publicado*) unpublished
ineficaz /inefi'kas/ *a* ineffective
inefici|ência /inefisi'ẽsia/ *f* inefficiency. **~ente** *a* inefficient
inegá|vel /ine'gavew/ (*pl* **~veis**) *a* undeniable
inépcia /i'nɛpsia/ *f* ineptitude
inepto /i'nɛptu/ *a* inept
inequívoco /ine'kivoku/ *a* unmistakeable
inércia /i'nɛrsia/ *f* inertia
inerente /ine'rẽtʃi/ *a* inherent (**a** in)
inerte /i'nɛrtʃi/ *a* inert
inesgotá|vel /inezgo'tavew/ (*pl* **~veis**) *a* inexhaustible
inesperado /inespe'radu/ *a* unexpected
inesquecí|vel /ineske'sivew/ (*pl* **~veis**) *a* unforgettable
inevitá|vel /inevi'tavew/ (*pl* **~veis**) *a* inevitable
inexato /ine'zatu/ *a* inaccurate
inexis|tência /inezis'tẽsia/ *f* lack. **~tente** *a* non-existent
inexperi|ência /inisperi'ẽsia/ *f* inexperience. **~ente** *a* inexperienced
inexpressivo /inespre'sivu/ *a* expressionless
infalí|vel /ĩfa'livew/ (*pl* **~veis**) *a* infallible
infame /ĩ'fami/ *a* despicable; (*péssimo*) dreadful
infâmia /ĩ'famia/ *f* disgrace
infância /ĩ'fãsia/ *f* childhood
infantaria /ĩfãta'ria/ *f* infantry
infan|til /ĩfã'tʃiw/ *a* ‹*roupa, livro*› children's; (*bobo*) childish. **~tilidade** *f* childishness; (*uma*) childish thing
infarto /ĩ'fartu/ *m* heart attack
infec|ção /ĩfek'sãw/ *f* infection. **~cionar** *vt* infect. **~cioso** *a* infectious
infeliz /ĩfe'lis/ *a* (*não contente*) unhappy; (*inconveniente*) unfortunate; (*desgraçado*) wretched ● *m* (*desgraçado*) wretch. **~mente** *adv* unfortunately
inferi|or /ĩferi'or/ *a* lower; (*em qualidade*) inferior (**a** to). **~oridade** *f* inferiority
inferir /ĩfe'rir/ *vt* infer
infer|nal /ĩfer'naw/ (*pl* **~nais**) *a* infernal. **~nizar** *vt* **~nizar a vida dele** make his life hell. **~no** /ɛ/ *m* hell
infér|til /ĩ'fɛrtʃiw/ (*pl* **~teis**) *a* infertile
infertilidade /ĩfertʃili'dadʒi/ *f* infertility
infestar /ĩfes'tar/ *vt* infest
infetar /ĩfe'tar/ *vt* infect
infidelidade /ĩfideli'dadʒi/ *f* infidelity
infi|el /ĩfi'ɛw/ (*pl* **~éis**) *a* unfaithful
infiltrar /ĩfiw'trar/ *vt* infiltrate; **~-se em** infiltrate
ínfimo /'ĩfimu/ *a* lowest; (*muito pequeno*) tiny
infindá|vel /ĩfĩ'davew/ (*pl* **~veis**) *a* unending
infinidade /ĩfini'dadʒi/ *f* infinity; **uma ~ de** an infinite number of
infini|tesimal /ĩfinitezi'maw/ (*pl* **~tesimais**) *a* infinitesimal. **~tivo** *a & m* infinitive. **~to** *a* infinite ● *m* infinity
infla|ção /ĩfla'sãw/ *f* inflation. **~cionar** *vt* inflate. **~cionário** *a* inflationary. **~cionista** *a & m/f* inflationist
infla|mação /ĩflama'sãw/ *f* inflammation. **~mar** *vt* inflame. **~mar-se** *vpr* become inflamed. **~matório** *a* inflammatory. **~mável** (*pl* **~máveis**) *a* inflammable
in|flar *vt* inflate. **~flar-se** *vpr* inflate. **~flável** (*pl* **~fláveis**) *a* inflatable
infle|xibilidade /ĩfleksibili'dadʒi/ *f* inflexibility. **~xível** (*pl* **~xíveis**) *a* inflexible
infligir /ĩfli'ʒir/ *vt* inflict (**a** on)
influência /ĩflu'ẽsia/ *f* influence
influen|ciar /ĩfluẽsi'ar/ *vt* **~ciar (em)** influence. **~ciar-se** *vpr* be influenced. **~ciável** (*pl* **~ciáveis**) *a* open to influence. **~te** *a* influential
influir /ĩflu'ir/ *vi* **~ em** ou **sobre** influence
informação /ĩforma'sãw/ *f* information; (*uma*) a piece of information; *Mil* intelligence; *pl* information
infor|mal /ĩfor'maw/ (*pl* **~mais**) *a* informal. **~malidade** *f* informality
infor|mar /ĩfor'mar/ *vt* inform. **~mar-se** *vpr* find out (**de** about). **~mática**/ ĩfoʁ'matʃika/ *f* information technology; **especialista em ~mática** IT specialist. **~mativo** *a* informative. **~matizar** *vt* computerize. **~me** *m Mil*

i

piece of intelligence

informático /ĩfor'matʃiku/ *a* computer ● *m Port* IT specialist

informatização /ĩformatʃiza'sãw/ *f* computerization

infortúnio /ĩfor'tuniu/ *m* misfortune

infração /ĩfra'sãw/ *f* infringement

infraestrutura /ĩfraistru'tura/ *f* infrastructure

infrator /ĩfra'tor/ *m* offender

infravermelho /ĩfraver'meʎu/ *a* infrared

infringir /ĩfrĩ'ʒir/ *vt* infringe

infrutífero /ĩfru'tʃiferu/ *a* fruitless

infundado /ĩfũ'dadu/ *a* unfounded

infundir /ĩfũ'dʒir/ *vt* (*insuflar*) infuse; (*incutir*) instil

infusão /ĩfu'zãw/ *f* infusion

ingenuidade /ĩʒenui'dadʒi/ *f* naivety

ingênuo /ĩ'ʒenuu/ *a* naive

ingerir /ĩʒe'rir/ *vt* ingest; (*engolir*) swallow

Inglaterra /ĩgla'tɛxa/ *f* England

in|glês /ĩ'gles/ *a* (*f* **~glesa**) English ● *m* (*f* **~glesa**) Englishman (*f* -woman); (*língua*) English; **os ~gleses** the English

ingra|tidão /ĩgratʃi'dãw/ *f* ingratitude. **~to** *a* ungrateful

ingrediente /ĩgredʒi'ẽtʃi/ *m* ingredient

íngreme /'ĩgrimi/ *a* steep

ingres|sar /ĩgre'sar/ *vi* **~sar em** join. **~so** *m* entry; (*bilhete*) ticket

inhame /i'ɲami/ *m* yam

ini|bição /inibi'sãw/ *f* inhibition. **~bir** *vt* inhibit

inici|ado /inisi'adu/ *m* initiate. **~al** (*pl* **~ais**) *a* & *f* initial. **~ar** *vt* (*começar*) begin; (*em ciência, seita etc*) initiate (**em** into) ● *vi* begin. **~ativa** *f* initiative

início /i'nisiu/ *m* beginning

iniguala|vel /inigwa'lavew/ (*pl* **~veis**) *a* unparalleled

inimaginá|vel /inimaʒi'navew/ (*pl* **~veis**) *a* unimaginable

inimi|go /ini'migu/ *a* & *m* enemy. **~zade** *f* enmity

ininterrupto /inĩte'xuptu/ *a* continuous

inje|ção /ĩʒe'sãw/ *f* injection. **~tado** *a* ‹*olhos*› bloodshot. **~tar** *vt* inject. **~tável** (*pl* **~táveis**) *a* ‹*droga*› intravenous

injúria /ĩ'ʒuria/ *f* insult

injuriar /ĩʒuri'ar/ *vt* insult

injus|tiça /ĩʒus'tʃisa/ *f* injustice. **~tiçado** *a* wronged. **~to** *a* unfair, unjust

ino|cência /ino'sẽsia/ *f* innocence. **~centar** *vt* clear (**de** of). **~cente** *a* innocent

inocular /inoku'lar/ *vt* inoculate

inócuo /i'nɔkuu/ *a* harmless

inodoro /ino'dɔru/ *a* odourless

inofensivo /inofẽ'sivu/ *a* harmless

inoportuno /inopor'tunu/ *a* inopportune

inorgânico /inor'ganiku/ *a* inorganic

inóspito /i'nɔspitu/ *a* inhospitable

ino|vação /inova'sãw/ *f* innovation. **~var** *vt/i* innovate

inoxidá|vel /inoksi'davew/ (*pl* **~veis**) *a* ‹*aço*› stainless

inquérito /ĩ'kɛritu/ *m* inquiry

inquie|tação /ĩkieta'sãw/ *f* concern. **~tador, ~tante** *a* worrying. **~tar** *vt* worry. **~tar-se** *vpr* worry. **~to** /ɛ/ *a* uneasy

inquili|nato /ĩkili'natu/ *m* tenancy. **~no** *m* tenant

inquirir /ĩki'rir/ *vt* cross-examine ‹*testemunha*›

Inquisição /ĩkizi'sãw/ *f* **a ~** the Inquisition

insaciá|vel /ĩsasi'avew/ (*pl* **~veis**) *a* insatiable

insalubre /ĩsa'lubri/ *a* unhealthy

insatis|fação /ĩsatʃisfa'sãw/ *f* dissatisfaction. **~fatório** *a* unsatisfactory. **~feito** *a* dissatisfied

ins|crever /ĩskre'ver/ *vt* (*registrar*) register; (*gravar*) inscribe. **~crever-se** *vpr* register; (*em escola etc*) enrol. **~crição** *f* (*registro*) registration; (*em clube, escola*) enrolment; (*em monumento etc*) inscription

insegu|rança /ĩsegu'rãsa/ *f* insecurity. **~ro** *a* insecure

insemi|nação /ĩsemina'sãw/ *f* insemination. **~nar** *vt* inseminate

insen|satez /ĩsẽsa'tes/ *f* folly. **~sato** *a* foolish. **~sibilidade** *f* insensitivity. **~sível** (*pl* **~síveis**) *a* insensitive

insepará|vel /ĩsepa'ravew/ (*pl* **~veis**) *a* inseparable

inserção /ĩser'sãw/ *f* insertion

inserir /ĩse'rir/ *vt* insert; enter ‹*dados*›

inse|ticida /ĩsetʃi'sida/ *m* insecticide. **~to** /ɛ/ *m* insect

insígnia /ĩ'signia/ *f* insignia

insignifi|cância /ĩsignifi'kãsia/ *f* insignificance. **~cante** *a* insignificant

i

insincero /ĩsĩ'sɛru/ *a* insincere

insinu|ante /ĩsinu'ãtʃi/ *a* suggestive. **~ar** *vt/i* insinuate

insípido /ĩ'sipidu/ *a* insipid

insis|tência /ĩsis'tẽsia/ *f* insistence. **~tente** *a* insistent. **~tir** *vt/i* insist (**em** on)

insolação /ĩsola'sãw/ *f* sunstroke

inso|lência /ĩso'lẽsia/ *f* insolence. **~lente** *a* insolent

insólito /ĩ'sɔlitu/ *a* unusual

insolú|vel /ĩso'luvew/ (*pl* **~veis**) *a* insoluble

insone /ĩ'sɔni/ *a* ‹*noite*› sleepless; ‹*pessoa*› insomniac ● *m/f* insomniac

insônia /ĩ'sonia/ *f* insomnia

insosso /ĩ'sosu/ *a* bland; (*sem sabor*) tasteless; (*sem sal*) unsalted

inspe|ção /ĩspe'sãw/ *f* inspection. **~cionar** *vt* inspect. **~tor** *m* inspector

inspi|ração /ĩspira'sãw/ *f* inspiration. **~rar** *vt* inspire. **~rar-se** *vpr* take inspiration (**em** from)

instabilidade /ĩstabili'dadʒi/ *f* instability

insta|lação /ĩstala'sãw/ *f* installation. **~lar** *vt* install. **~lar-se** *vpr* install o.s.

instan|tâneo /ĩstã'taniu/ *a* instant. **~te** *m* instant

instaurar /ĩstaw'rar/ *vt* set up

instá|vel /ĩ'stavew/ (*pl* **~veis**) *a* unstable; ‹*tempo*› unsettled

insti|gação /ĩstʃiga'sãw/ *f* instigation. **~gante** *a* stimulating. **~gar** *vt* incite

instin|tivo /ĩstʃĩ'tʃivu/ *a* instinctive. **~to** *m* instinct

institu|cional /ĩstʃitusio'naw/ (*pl* **~cionais**) *a* institutional. **~ição** *f* institution. **~ir** *vt* set up; set ‹*prazo*›. **~to** *m* institute

instru|ção /ĩstru'sãw/ *f* instruction. **~ir** *vt* instruct; train ‹*recrutas*›; (*informar*) advise (**sobre** of)

instrumen|tal /ĩstrumẽ'taw/ (*pl* **~tais**) *a* instrumental. **~tista** *m/f* instrumentalist. **~to** *m* instrument

instru|tivo /ĩstru'tʃivu/ *a* instructive. **~tor** *m* instructor

insubstituí|vel /ĩsubistʃitu'ivew/ (*pl* **~veis**) *a* irreplaceable

insucesso /ĩsu'sesu/ *m* failure

insufici|ência /ĩsufisi'ẽsia/ *f* insufficiency; (*dos órgãos*) failure. **~ente** *a* insufficient

insulina /ĩsu'lina/ *f* insulin

insul|tar /ĩsuw'tar/ *vt* insult. **~to** *m* insult

insuperá|vel /ĩsupe'ravew/ (*pl* **~veis**) *a* ‹*problema*› insurmountable; ‹*qualidade*› unsurpassed

insuportá|vel /ĩsupor'tavew/ (*pl* **~veis**) *a* unbearable

insur|gente /ĩsur'ʒẽtʃi/ *a & m/f* insurgent. **~gir-se** *vpr* rise up, revolt. **~reição** *f* insurrection

intato /ĩ'tatu/ *a* intact

íntegra /'ĩtegra/ *f* full text; **na ~** in full

inte|gração /ĩtegra'sãw/ *f* integration. **~gral** (*pl* **~grais**) *a* whole; **arroz/pão ~gral** brown rice/bread. **~grante** *a* integral ● *m/f* member. **~grar** *vt* make up, form; **~grar-se em** become a part of. **~gridade** *f* integrity

íntegro /'ĩtegru/ *a* honest

intei|ramente /ĩtera'mẽtʃi/ *adv* completely. **~rar** *vt* (*informar*) fill in, inform (**de** about). **~rar-se** *vpr* find out (**de** about). **~riço** *a* in one piece. **~ro** *a* whole

intelec|to /ĩte'lɛktu/ *m* intellect. **~tual** (*pl* **~tuais**) *a & m/f* intellectual

inteli|gência /ĩteli'ʒẽsia/ *f* intelligence. **~gente** *a* clever, intelligent. **~gível** (*pl* **~gíveis**) *a* intelligible

intem|périe /ĩtẽ'pɛri/ *f* bad weather. **~pestivo** *a* ill-timed

inten|ção /ĩtẽ'sãw/ *f* intention; **segundas ~ções** ulterior motives

intencio|nado /ĩtẽsio'nadu/ *a* **bem ~nado** well-meaning. **~nal** (*pl* **~nais**) *a* intentional. **~nar** *vt* intend

inten|sidade /ĩtẽsi'dadʒi/ *f* intensity. **~sificar** *vt* intensify. **~sificar-se** *vpr* intensify. **~sivo** *a* intensive. **~so** *a* intense

intento /ĩ'tẽtu/ *m* intention

intera|ção /ĩtera'sãw/ *f* interaction. **~gir** *vi* interact. **~tivo** *a* interactive

inter|calar /ĩterka'lar/ *vt* insert. **~câmbio** *m* exchange. **~ceptar** *vt* intercept

intercontinen|tal /ĩterkõtʃinẽ'taw/ (*pl* **~tais**) *a* intercontinental

interdepen|dência /ĩterdepẽ'dẽsia/ *f* interdependence. **~dente** *a* interdependent

interdi|ção /ĩterdʒi'sãw/ *f* closure; *Jurid* injunction. **~tar** *vt* close ‹*rua etc*›; (*proibir*) ban

interes|sante /ĩtere'sãtʃi/ *a* interesting. **~sar** *vt* interest ● *vi* be relevant. **~sar-se** *vpr* be interested (**em** ou **por** in). **~se** /e/ *m* interest; (*próprio*) self-interest. **~seiro** *a* self-seeking

interestadu|al /ĩteristadu'aw/ (*pl* **~ais**) *a* interstate

interface /ĩter'fasi/ *f* interface

interfe|rência /ĩterfe'rẽsia/ *f* interference. **~rir** *vi* interfere

interfone /ĩter'fɔni/ *m* intercom

ínterim /'ĩterĩ/ *m* interim; **nesse ~** in the interim

interino /ĩte'rinu/ *a* temporary

interior /ĩteri'or/ *a* inner; (*dentro do país*) internal, domestic ● *m* inside; (*do país*) country, interior

inter|jeição /ĩterʒej'sãw/ *f* interjection. **~ligar** *vt* interconnect. **~locutor** *m* interlocutor. **~mediário** *a & m* intermediary

intermédio /ĩter'mɛdʒiu/ *m* **por ~ de** through

interminá|vel /ĩtermi'navew/ (*pl* **~veis**) *a* interminable

internacio|nal /ĩternasio'naw/ (*pl* **~nais**) *a* international

inter|nar /ĩter'nar/ *vt* intern ‹*preso*›; admit to hospital ‹*doente*›. **~nato** *m* boarding school

internauta /ĩter'nawta/ *m/f Comput* netsurfer

Internet /ĩter'nɛt/ *f* Internet

interno /ĩ'tɛrnu/ *a* internal

interpelar /ĩterpe'lar/ *vt* question

interpor /ĩter'por/ *vt* interpose. **~-se** *vpr* intervene

interpre|tação /ĩterpreta'sãw/ *f* interpretation. **~tar** *vt* interpret; perform ‹*papel, música*›. **intérprete** *m/f* (*de línguas*) interpreter; (*de teatro etc*) performer

interro|gação /ĩtexoga'sãw/ *f* interrogation. **~gar** *vt* interrogate, question. **~gativo** *a* interrogative. **~gatório** *m* interrogation

inter|romper /ĩtexõ'per/ *vt* interrupt. **~rupção** *f* interruption. **~ruptor** *m* switch

interurbano /ĩterur'banu/ *a* long-distance ● *m* trunk call

intervalo /ĩter'valu/ *m* interval

inter|venção /ĩtervẽ'sãw/ *f* intervention. **~vir** *vi* intervene

intesti|nal /ĩtestʃi'naw/ (*pl* **~nais**) *a* intestinal. **~no** *m* intestine

inti|mação /ĩtʃima'sãw/ *f* (*da justiça*) summons. **~mar** *vt* order; (*à justiça*) summon

intimidade /ĩtʃimi'dadʒi/ *f* intimacy; (*entre amigos*) closeness; (*vida íntima*) private life; **ter ~ com** be close to

intimidar /ĩtʃimi'dar/ *vt* intimidate. **~-se** *vpr* be intimidated

íntimo /'ĩtʃimu/ *a* intimate; ‹*amigo*› close; ‹*vida*› private ● *m* close friend

intitular /ĩtʃitu'lar/ *vt* entitle

intocá|vel /ĩto'kavew/ (*pl* **~veis**) *a* untouchable

intole|rância /ĩtole'rãsia/ *f* intolerance. **~rável** (*pl* **~ráveis**) *a* intolerable

intoxi|cação /ĩtoksika'sãw/ *f* poisoning; **~cação alimentar** food poisoning. **~car** *vt* poison

intragá|vel /ĩtra'gavew/ (*pl* **~veis**) *a* ‹*comida*› inedible; ‹*pessoa*› unbearable

intransigente /ĩtrãzi'ʒẽtʃi/ *a* uncompromising

intransi|tável /ĩtrãzi'tavew/ (*pl* **~táveis**) *a* impassable. **~tivo** *a* intransitive

intratá|vel /ĩtra'tavew/ (*pl* **~veis**) *a* ‹*pessoa*› difficult

intrauterino /ĩtraute'rinu/ *a* **dispositivo ~** intrauterine device, IUD

intrépido /ĩ'trɛpidu/ *a* intrepid

intri|ga /ĩ'triga/ *f* intrigue; (*enredo*) plot. **~gante** *a* intriguing. **~gar** *vt* intrigue

intrincado /ĩtrĩ'kadu/ *a* intricate

intrínseco /ĩ'trĩsiku/ *a* intrinsic

introdu|ção /ĩtrodu'sãw/ *f* introduction. **~tório** *a* introductory. **~zir** *vt* introduce

introme|ter-se /ĩtrome'tersi/ *vpr* interfere. **~tido** *a* interfering ● *m* busybody

introspec|ção /ĩtrospek'sãw/ *f* introspection. **~tivo** *a* introspective

introvertido /ĩtrover'tʃidu/ *a* introverted ● *m* introvert

intruso /ĩ'truzu/ *a* intrusive ● *m* intruder

intu|ição /ĩtui'sãw/ *f* intuition. **~ir** *vt* intuit. **~itivo** *a* intuitive. **~ito** *m* purpose

inumano /inu'manu/ *a* inhuman

inumerá|vel /inume'ravew/ (*pl* **~veis**) *a* innumerable

inúmero /i'numeru/ *a* countless

inun|dação /inũda'sãw/ *f* flood. **~dar** *vt/i* flood

i

inusitado /inuzi'tadu/ *a* unusual
inú|til /i'nutʃiw/ (*pl* **~teis**) *a* useless
inutilizar /inutʃili'zar/ *vt* render useless; damage ‹*aparelho*›; thwart ‹*esforços*›
inutilmente /inutʃiw'mẽtʃi/ *adv* in vain
invadir /ĩva'dʒir/ *vt* invade
invali|dar /ĩvali'dar/ *vt* invalidate; disable ‹*pessoa*›. **~dez** /e/ *f* disability
inválido /ĩ'validu/ *a & m* invalid
invariá|vel /ĩvari'avew/ (*pl* **~veis**) *a* invariable
inva|são /ĩva'zãw/ *f* invasion. **~sor** *m* invader ● *a* invading
inve|ja /ĩ'vɛʒa/ *f* envy. **~jar** *vt* envy. **~jável** (*pl* **~jáveis**) *a* enviable. **~joso** /o/ *a* envious

i

inven|ção /ĩvẽ'sãw/ *f* invention. **~tar** *vt* invent. **~tário** *m* inventory. **~tivo** *a* inventive. **~tor** *m* inventor
inver|nar /ĩver'nar/ *vi* winter, spend the winter. **~no** /ɛ/ *m* winter
inverossí|mil /ĩvero'simiw/ (*pl* **~meis**) *a* improbable
inver|são /ĩver'sãw/ *f* inversion. **~so** *a* inverse; ‹*ordem*› reverse ● *m* reverse. **~ter** *vt* reverse; (*colocar de cabeça para baixo*) invert
invertebrado /ĩverte'bradu/ *a & m* invertebrate
invés /ĩ'vɛs/ *m* **ao ~ de** instead of
investida /ĩves'tʃida/ *f* attack
investidura /ĩvestʃi'dura/ *f* investiture
investi|gação /ĩvestʃiga'sãw/ *f* investigation. **~gar** *vt* investigate
inves|timento /ĩvestʃi'mẽtu/ *m* investment. **~tir** *vt/i* invest; **~tir contra** attack
inveterado /ĩvete'radu/ *a* inveterate
inviá|vel /ĩvi'avew/ (*pl* **~veis**) *a* impracticable
invicto /ĩ'viktu/ *a* unbeaten
invisí|vel /ĩvi'zivew/ (*pl* **~veis**) *a* invisible
invocar /ĩvo'kar/ *vt* invoke; Ⓘ pester
invólucro /ĩ'vɔlukru/ *m* covering
involuntário /ĩvolũ'tariu/ *a* involuntary
invulnerá|vel /ĩvuwne'ravew/ (*pl* **~veis**) *a* invulnerable
iodo /i'odu/ *m* iodine
ioga /i'ɔga/ *f* yoga
iogurte /io'gurtʃi/ *m* yoghurt

ir /ir/ ● *vi*

····➤ (*deslocar-se*) go; **vamos para Paris** we are going to Paris; **~ de carro/trem...** go by car/train...; **como vão as coisas em casa?** how are things at home?

····➤ (*estar*) be; **~ bem vestido** be well dressed

····➤ (*começar*) **vai fazendo sua lição de casa** start doing your homework

····➤ (*em expressões*) **~ com** (*combinar roupa*) go with; **essa camisa não vai com o casaco** that shirt doesn't go with that coat; **~ dar em** (*ruas*) lead to; **esta rua vai dar no banco** this street leads to the bank; **~ de:** (*vestido*) **ele foi de palhaço/de azul** he was dressed as a clown/in blue; **~ para:** (*profissão ou área de estudos*) **ele vai para medicina** he is going to study medicine; **~ indo, como vai a sua mãe? Vai indo** how's your mother? Not so bad; **já vou!** coming!; **vamos...?** shall we...?

● *v aux*

····➤ (*seguido de infinitivo*) **vamos vender a casa** we are going to sell our house; **você vai gostar** you're going to like it; (*em ordens*) **vai pôr a mesa!** go and lay the table!; **vá falar com o seu pai!** go and talk to your father!

● *vpr*

····➤ **~se** (*partir*) go; **fui-me embora** I left; (*morrer*) **ele se foi** he died

ira /'ira/ *f* wrath
Irã /i'rã/ *m* Iran
iraniano /irani'anu/ *a & m* Iranian
Irão /i'rãw/ *m Port* Iran
Iraque /i'raki/ *m* Iraq
iraquiano /iraki'anu/ *a & m* Iraqi
Irlanda /ir'lãda/ *f* Ireland
irlan|dês /irlã'des/ *a* (*f* **~desa**) Irish ● *m* (*f* **~desa**) Irishman (*f* -woman); (*língua*) Irish; **os ~deses** the Irish
irmã /ir'mã/ *f* sister
irmandade /irmã'dadʒi/ *f* (*associação*) brotherhood
irmão /ir'mãw/ (*pl* **~s**) *m* brother
ironia /iro'nia/ *f* irony
irônico /i'roniku/ *a* ironic
IRPF *abr m* (= **Imposto de Renda de Pessoa Física**) income tax
irracio|nal /ixasio'naw/ (*pl* **~nais**) *a* irrational

irradiar /ixadʒi'ar/ *vt* radiate; (*pelo rádio*) broadcast ● *vi* shine. **~-se** *vpr* spread, radiate

irre|al /ixe'aw/ (*pl* **~ais**) *a* unreal

irreconhecí|vel /ixekoɲe'sivew/ (*pl* **~veis**) *a* unrecognizable

irrecuperá|vel /ixekupe'ravew/ (*pl* **~veis**) *a* irretrievable

irrefletido /ixefle'tʃidu/ *a* rash

irregu|lar /ixegu'lar/ *a* irregular; (*inconstante*) erratic. **~laridade** *f* irregularity

irrelevante /ixele'vãtʃi/ *a* irrelevant

irrepará|vel /ixepa'ravew/ (*pl* **~veis**) *a* irreparable

irrepreensí|vel /ixeprië'sivew/ (*pl* **~veis**) *a* irreproachable

irrequieto /ixeki'ɛtu/ *a* restless

irresistí|vel /ixezis'tʃivew/ (*pl* **~veis**) *a* irresistible

irresoluto /ixezo'lutu/ *a* ‹*questão*› unresolved; ‹*pessoa*› indecisive

irresponsá|vel /ixespõ'savew/ (*pl* **~veis**) *a* irresponsible

irreverente /ixeve'rẽtʃi/ *a* irreverent

irri|gação /ixiga'sãw/ *f* irrigation. **~gar** *vt* irrigate

irrisório /ixi'zɔriu/ *a* derisory

irri|tação /ixita'sãw/ *f* irritation. **~tadiço** *a* irritable. **~tante** *a* irritating. **~tar** *vt* irritate. **~tar-se** *vpr* get irritated

irromper /ixõ'per/ *vi* **~ em** burst into

IRS /ir'jɛs/ *abr m* (*Port* = **Imposto sobre o Rendimento das Pessoas Singulares**) income tax

isca /'iska/ *f* bait

isen|ção /izẽ'sãw/ *f* exemption. **~tar** *vt* exempt. **~to** *a* exempt

Islã /iz'lã/ *m* Islam

islâmico /iz'lamiku/ *a* Islamic

isla|mismo /izla'mizmu/ *m* Islam. **~mita** *a & m/f* Muslim

islan|dês /izlã'des/ *a* (*f* **~desa**) Icelandic ● *m* (*f* **~desa**) Icelander; (*língua*) Icelandic

Islândia /iz'lãdʒia/ *f* Iceland

iso|lamento /izola'mẽtu/ *m* isolation; *Eletr* insulation. **~lante** *a* insulating. **~lar** *vt* isolate; *Eletr* insulate ● *vi* (*contra azar*) touch wood, *Amer* knock on wood

isopor /izo'por/ *m* polystyrene

isqueiro /is'keru/ *m* lighter

Israel /izxa'ɛw/ *m* Israel

israe|lense /izraj'lẽsi/ *a & m/f* Israeli. **~lita** *a & m/f* Israelite

---

isso /'isu/ ● *pron*

····➤ that; **o que é ~?** what's that?

····➤ (*em expressões*) **~!** (*aprovação*) Well done!; **nem por ~** not really; **para ~** in order to; **quer passar? Para ~ você terá que estudar** do you want to pass? You'll have to study in order to do that; **por ~** so; **ganhei na loteria, por ~ vou viajar muito** I won the lottery, so I am going to travel a lot

---

isto /'istu/ *pron* this; **~ é** that is

Itália /i'talia/ *f* Italy

italiano /itali'anu/ *a & m* Italian

itálico /i'taliku/ *a & m* italic

item /'itẽ/ *m* item

itine|rante /itʃine'rãtʃi/ *a* itinerant. **~rário** *m* itinerary

Iugoslávia /iugoz'lavia/ *f* Yugoslavia

iugoslavo /iugoz'lavu/ *a & m* Yugoslavian

IVA /'iva/ *abr m* VAT

Jj

já /ʒa/ *adv* already; (*agora*) right away ● *conj* on the other hand; **desde ~** from now on; **~ não** no longer; **~ que** since; **~, ~** in no time

jabuticaba /ʒabutʃi'kaba/ *f* jaboticaba

jaca /'ʒaka/ *f* jack fruit

jacaré /ʒaka'rɛ/ *m* alligator

jacinto /ʒa'sĩtu/ *m* hyacinth

jactância /ʒak'tãsia/ *f* boasting

jade /'ʒadʒi/ *m* jade

jaguar /ʒagu'ar/ *m* jaguar

jagunço /ʒa'gũsu/ *m* hired gunman

Jamaica /ʒa'majka/ *f* Jamaica

jamaicano /ʒamaj'kanu/ *a & m* Jamaican

jamais /ʒa'majs/ *adv* never

jamanta /ʒa'mãta/ *f* juggernaut

janeiro /ʒa'neru/ *m* January

janela /ʒa'nɛla/ *f* window; **~ de oportunidade** window of opportunity

jangada /ʒã'gada/ *f* (fishing) raft

janta /'ʒãta/ *f* [!] dinner

jantar /ʒã'tar/ *m* dinner ● *vi* have dinner ● *vt* have for dinner

Japão /ʒa'pãw/ *m* Japan

i j

japo|na /ʒa'pɔna/ *f* pea jacket ● *m/f* [!] Japanese. **~nês** *a & m* (*f* **~nesa**) Japanese

jaqueira /ʒa'kera/ *f* jackfruit tree

jaqueta /ʒa'keta/ *f* jacket

jarda /'ʒarda/ *f* yard

jar|dim /ʒar'dʒĩ/ *m* garden. **~dim de infância** (*pl* **~dins de infância**) *f* kindergarten

jardim-escola /ʒardʒĩʃ'kɔla/ *m* (*pl* **jardins-escola**) *Port* nursery school

jardi|nagem /ʒardʒi'naʒẽ/ *f* gardening. **~nar** *vi* garden. **~neira** *f* (*calça*) dungarees; (*vestido*) pinafore dress, *Amer* jumper; (*ônibus*) open-sided bus; (*para flores*) flower stand. **~neiro** *m* gardener

jargão /ʒar'gãw/ *m* jargon

jar|ra /'ʒaxa/ *f* pot. **~ro** *m* jug

jasmim /ʒaz'mĩ/ *m* jasmine

j

jato /'ʒatu/ *m* jet

jaula /'ʒawla/ *f* cage

ja|zer /ʒa'zer/ *vi* lie. **~zida** *f* deposit. **~zigo** *m* family grave

jazz /dʒaz/ *m* jazz. **~ista** *m/f* jazz artist. **~ístico** *a* jazzy

jeans /dʒĩ:z/ *mpl* jeans

jeca /'ʒɛka/ *m/f* country bumpkin ● *a* countrified; (*cafona*) tacky. **~-tatu** *m/f* country bumpkin

jei|tão /ʒej'tãw/ *m* [!] individual style. **~tinho** *m* knack. **~to** *m* way; (*de pessoa*) manner; (*habilidade*) skill; **de qualquer ~to** anyway; **de ~to nenhum** no way; **pelo ~to** by the looks of things; **sem ~to** awkward; **dar um ~to** find a way; **dar um ~to em** (*arrumar*) tidy up; (*consertar*) fix; (*torcer*) twist ‹*pé etc*›; **ter ~to de** look like; **ter** ou **levar ~to para** be good at; **tomar ~to** pull one's socks up. **~toso** /o/ *a* skilful; (*de aparência*) elegant

je|juar /ʒeʒu'ar/ *vi* fast. **~jum** *m* fast

Jeová /ʒio'va/ *m* **testemunha de ~** Jehovah's witness

jérsei /'ʒersej/ *m* jersey

jesuíta /ʒezu'ita/ *a & m/f* Jesuit

Jesus /ʒe'zus/ *m* Jesus

jiboia /ʒi'bɔja/ *f* boa constrictor

jiboiar /ʒiboj'ar/ *vi* have a rest to let one's dinner go down

jiló /ʒi'lɔ/ *m* okra

jipe /'ʒipi/ *m* jeep

jiu-jítsu /ʒiu'ʒitsu/ *m* jiu-jitsu

joa|lheiro /ʒoa'ʎeru/ *m* jeweller. **~lheria** *f* jeweller's (shop)

joaninha /ʒoa'niɲa/ *f* ladybird, *Amer* ladybug; (*alfinete*) safety pin

joão-ninguém /ʒoãwnĩ'gẽj/ (*pl* **joões-ninguém**) *m* nobody

jocoso /ʒo'kozu/ *a* jocular

joe|lhada /ʒoe'ʎada/ *f* blow with the knee. **~lheira** *f* kneepad. **~lho** /e/ *m* knee; **de ~lhos** kneeling

jo|gada /ʒo'gada/ *f* move. **~gado** *a* ‹*pessoa*› flat out; ‹*papéis, roupa etc*› lying around. **~gador** *m* player; (*no cassino etc*) gambler. **~gar** *vt* play; (*atirar*) throw; (*arriscar no jogo*) gamble ● *vi* play; (*no cassino etc*) gamble; (*balançar*) toss; **~gar fora** throw away. **~gatina** *f* gambling

jogging /'ʒɔgĩ/ *m* (*cooper*) jogging; (*roupa*) track suit

jogo /'ʒogu/ *m* (*partida*) game; (*ação de jogar*) play; (*jogatina*) gambling; (*conjunto*) set; **em ~** at stake; **~ de cintura** *fig* flexibility, room to manoeuvre; **~ de luz** lighting effects; **~ do bicho** illegal numbers game; **Jogos Olímpicos** Olympic Games. **~ da velha** *m* noughts and crosses

joguete /ʒo'getʃi/ *m* plaything

joia /'ʒɔja/ *f* jewel; (*propina*) entry fee ● *a* [!] great

joio /'ʒoju/ *m* chaff; **separar o ~ do trigo** separate the wheat from the chaff

jóquei /'ʒɔkej/ *m* (*pessoa*) jockey; (*lugar*) race course

Jordânia /ʒor'dania/ *f* Jordan

jordaniano /ʒordani'anu/ *a & m* Jordanian

jor|nada /ʒor'nada/ *f* (*viagem*) journey; **~nada de trabalho** working day. **~nal** (*pl* **~nais**) *m* newspaper; (*na TV*) news

jorna|leco /ʒorna'lɛku/ *m* rag, scandal sheet. **~leiro** *m* (*vendedor*) newsagent, *Amer* newsdealer; (*entregador*) paper boy. **~lismo** *m* journalism. **~lista** *m/f* journalist. **~lístico** *a* journalistic

jor|rar /ʒo'xar/ *vi* gush, spurt. **~ro** /'ʒoxu/ *m* spurt

jota /'ʒɔta/ *m* (letter) J

jovem /'ʒɔvẽ/ *a* young; (*criado por jovens*) youth ● *m/f* young man (*f*-woman); *pl* young people

jovi|al /ʒovi'aw/ (*pl* **~ais**) *a* jovial

juba /'ʒuba/ *f* mane

jubileu /ʒubi'lew/ *m* jubilee

júbilo /'ʒubilu/ *m* joy

ju|daico /ʒu'dajku/ *a* Jewish. **~daísmo** *m* Judaism. **~deu** *a* (*f* **~dia**) Jewish ● *m* (*f* **~dia**) Jew. **~diação** *f* ill-treatment; (*uma*) terrible thing. **~diar** *vi* **~diar de** ill-treat

judici|al /ʒudʒisi'aw/ (*pl* **~ais**) *a* judicial. **~ário** *a* judicial ● *m* judiciary. **~oso** /o/ *a* judicious

judô /ʒu'do/ *m* judo

judoca /ʒu'dɔka/ *m/f* judo player

jugo /'ʒugu/ *m* yoke

juiz /ʒu'is/ *m* (*f* **juíza**) judge; (*em jogos*) referee

juizado /ʒui'zadu/ *m* court

juízo /ʒu'izu/ *m* judgement; (*tino*) sense; (*tribunal*) court; **perder o ~** lose one's head; **ter ~** be sensible; **tomar** ou **criar ~** come to one's senses

jujuba /ʒu'ʒuba/ *f* (*bala*) fruit jelly

jul|gamento /ʒuwga'mẽtu/ *m* judgement. **~gar** *vt* judge; pass judgement on ‹*réu*›; (*imaginar*) think. **~gar-se** *vpr* consider o.s.

julho /'ʒuʎu/ *m* July

jumento /ʒu'mẽtu/ *m* donkey

junção /ʒũ'sãw/ *f* join; (*ação*) joining

junco /'ʒũku/ *m* reed

junho /'ʒuɲu/ *m* June

juni|no /ʒu'ninu/ *a* **festa ~na** St John's Day festival

júnior /'ʒunior/ *a & m* junior

jun|ta /'ʒũta/ *f* board; *Pol* junta. **~tar** *vt* (*acrescentar*) add; (*uma coisa a outra*) join; (*uma coisa com outra*) combine; save up ‹*dinheiro*›; gather up ‹*papéis, lixo etc*› ● *vi* gather. **~tar-se** *vpr* join together; ‹*multidão*› gather; ‹*casal*› live together; **~tar-se a** join. **~to** *a* together ● *adv* together; **~to a** next to; **~to com** together with

ju|ra /'ʒura/ *f* vow. **~rado** *m* juror. **~ramentado** *a* accredited. **~ramento** *m* oath. **~rar** *vt/i* swear; **~ra?** [!] really?

júri /'ʒuri/ *m* jury

jurídico /ʒu'ridʒiku/ *a* legal

juris|consulto /ʒuriskõ'suwtu/ *m* legal advisor. **~dição** *f* jurisdiction. **~prudência** *f* jurisprudence. **~ta** *m/f* jurist

juros /'ʒurus/ *m pl* interest

jus /ʒus/ *m* **fazer ~ a** live up to

jusante /ʒu'zãtʃi/ *f* **a ~** downstream

justamente /ʒusta'mẽtʃi/ *adv* exactly; (*com justiça*) fairly

justapor /ʒusta'por/ *vt* juxtapose

justi|ça /ʒus'tʃisa/ *f* (*perante a lei*) justice; (*para com outros*) fairness; (*tribunal*) court. **~ceiro** *a* fair-minded ● *m* vigilante

justifi|cação /ʒustʃifika'sãw/ *f* justification. **~car** *vt* justify. **~cativa** *f* justification. **~cável** (*pl* **~cáveis**) *a* justifiable

justo /'ʒustu/ *a* fair; (*apertado*) tight ● *adv* just

juve|nil /ʒuve'niw/ (*pl* **~nis**) *a* youthful; (*para jovens*) for young people; ‹*time, torneio*› junior ● *m* junior championship

juventude /ʒuvẽ'tudʒi/ *f* youth

Kk

karaokê /karao'ke/ *m* karaoke

karatê /kara'te/ *m* karate

karateca /kara'tɛka/ *m/f* karate expert

kart /'kartʃi/ (*pl* **~s**) *m* go-kart

ketchup /ke'tʃupi/ *m* ketchup

kickboxing /kikbɔksĩŋ/ *m* kickboxing

kilowatt /kilo'wɔt/ *m* kilowatt

kispo® /'kiʃpu/ *m Port* anorak

kit /'kitʃi/ (*pl* **~s**) *m* kit

kitchenette /kitʃe'nɛtʃi/ *f* bedsitter

kiwi /ki'vi/ *m* kiwi

Kuwait /ku'wajtʃi/ *m* Kuwait

kuwaitiano /kuwajtʃi'anu/ *a & m* Kuwaiti

Ll

lá /la/ ● *adv*

····➤ there; **até ~** ‹*ir*› there; ‹*esperar etc*› until then; **por ~** (*naquela direção*) that way; (*naquele lugar*) around there; **~ fora** outside; **sei ~** how should I know?

lã /lã/ *f* wool

labareda /laba'reda/ *f* flame

lábia /'labia/ *f* flannel; **ter ~** have the gift of the gab

lábio /'labio/ *m* lip

labirinto /labi'rĩtu/ *m* labyrinth

laboral /labo'raw/ *a Port* labour; **horário ~** working hours

laboratório /labora'tɔriu/ *m* laboratory
laborioso /labori'ozu/ *a* hard-working
labu|ta /la'buta/ *f* drudgery. **~tar** *vi* slog
laca /'laka/ *f* lacquer
laçada /la'sada/ *f* slip knot
lacaio /la'kaju/ *m* lackey
la|çar /la'sar/ *vt* lasso ‹*boi*›. **~ço** *m* bow; (*de vaqueiro*) lasso; (*vínculo*) tie
lacônico /la'koniku/ *a* laconic
lacraia /la'kraja/ *f* centipede
la|crar /la'krar/ *vt* seal. **~cre** *m* (*substância*) sealing wax; (*fechamento*) seal
lacri|mejar /lakrime'ʒar/ *vi* water. **~mogêneo** *a* ‹*gás*› tear; ‹*filme*› tear-jerking. **~moso** /o/ *a* tearful
lácteo /'laktʃiu/ *a* milk; **Via Láctea** Milky Way
lacticínio /laktʃi'siniu/ *m* ▶ LATICÍNIO
lacuna /la'kuna/ *f* gap
ladainha /lada'iɲa/ *f* litany
la|dear /ladʒi'ar/ *vt* flank; sidestep ‹*dificuldade*›. **~deira** *f* slope
lado /'ladu/ *m* side; **o ~ de cá/lá** this/that side; **ao ~ de** beside; **~ a ~** side by side; **para este ~** this way; **por outro ~** on the other hand
la|drão /la'drãw/ *m* (*f* **~dra**) thief; (*tubo*) overflow pipe ● *a* thieving
ladrar /la'drar/ *vi* bark
ladri|lhar /ladri'ʎar/ *vt* tile. **~lho** *m* tile
ladroagem /ladro'aʒẽ/ *f* stealing
lagar|ta /la'garta/ *f* caterpillar; (*numa roda*) caterpillar track. **~tear** *vi* bask in the sun. **~tixa** *f* gecko. **~to** *m* lizard
lago /'lagu/ *m* lake
lagoa /la'goa/ *f* lagoon
lagos|ta /la'gosta/ *f* lobster. **~tim** *m* crayfish, *Amer* crawfish
lágrima /'lagrima/ *f* tear
laia /'laja/ *f* kind
laico /'lajku/ *adj* ‹*pessoa*› lay; ‹*ensino*› secular
laivos /'lajvus/ *m pl* traces
laje /'laʒi/ *m* flagstone. **~ar** *vt* pave
lajota /la'ʒɔta/ *f* small paving stone
lama /'lama/ *f* mud. **~çal** (*pl* **~çais**) *m* bog. **~cento** *a* muddy
lamba|da /lã'bada/ *f* lambada. **~teria** *f* lambada club
lam|ber /lã'ber/ *vt* lick. **~bida** *f* lick
lambreta /lã'breta/ *f* moped
lambris /lã'bris/ *m pl* panelling
lambuzar /lãbu'zar/ *vt* smear. **~-se** *vpr* get sticky
lamen|tar /lamẽ'tar/ *vt* (*lastimar*) lament; (*sentir*) be sorry; **~tar-se de** lament. **~tável** (*pl* **~táveis**) *a* lamentable. **~to** *m* lament
lâmina /'lamina/ *f* blade; (*de persiana*) slat
laminar /lami'nar/ *vt* laminate
lâmpada /'lãpada/ *f* light bulb; (*abajur*) lamp; **~ compacta** energy-saving lightbulb
lampe|jar /lãpe'ʒar/ *vi* flash. **~jo** /e/ *m* flash
lampião /lãpi'ãw/ *m* lantern
lamúria /la'muria/ *f* moaning
lamuriar-se /lamuri'arsi/ *vpr* moan (**de** about)
lan|ça /'lãsa/ *f* spear. **~çamento** *m* (*de navio, foguete, produto*) launch; (*de filme, disco*) release; (*novo produto*) new line; (*novo filme, disco*) release; (*novo livro*) new title; (*em livro comercial*) entry. **~çar** *vt* (*atirar*) throw; launch ‹*navio, foguete, novo produto, livro*›; release ‹*filme, disco*›; (*em livro comercial*) enter; (*em leilão*) bid; **~çar mão de** make use of. **~ce** *m* (*num filme, jogo*) bit, moment; (*episódio*) episode; (*questão*) matter; (*jogada*) move; (*em leilão*) bid; (*de escada*) flight; (*de casas*) row
lancha /'lãʃa/ *f* launch
lan|char /lã'ʃar/ *vi* have a snack ● *vt* have a snack of. **~che** *m* snack. **~chonete** /ɛ/ *f* snack bar
lancinante /lãsi'nãtʃi/ *a* ‹*dor*› shooting; ‹*grito*› piercing
lânguido /'lãgidu/ *a* languid
lan house *m* internet cafe
lantejoula /lãte'ʒola/ *f* sequin
lanter|na /lã'tɛrna/ *f* lantern; (*de bolso*) torch, *Amer* flashlight. **~nagem** *f* panel beating; (*oficina*) body shop. **~ninha** *m/f* usher; (*f* usherette)
lanugem /la'nuʒẽ/ *f* down
lapela /la'pɛla/ *f* lapel
lapidar /lapi'dar/ *vt* cut ‹*pedra preciosa*›; *fig* polish
lápide /'lapidʒi/ *f* tombstone
lápis /'lapis/ *m invar* pencil
lapiseira /lapi'zera/ *f* propelling pencil; (*caixa*) pencil box
Lapônia /la'ponia/ *f* Lapland
lapso /'lapsu/ *m* lapse
laptop /lap'tɔp/ *m* laptop

la|quê /la'ke/ *m* lacquer. **~quear** *vt* lacquer

lar /lar/ *m* home

laran|ja /la'rãʒa/ *f* orange ● *a invar* orange. **~jada** *f* orangeade. **~jeira** *f* orange tree

lareira /la'rera/ *f* hearth, fireplace

lar|gada /lar'gada/ *f* start; **dar a ~gada** start off. **~gar** *vt* (*soltar*) let go of; give up ‹*estudos, emprego etc*›; **~gar de fumar** give up smoking. **~go** *a* wide; ‹*roupa*› loose ● *m* (*praça*) square; **ao ~go** (*no alto-mar*) out at sea. **~gura** *f* width

larin|ge /la'rĩʒi/ *f* larynx. **~gite** *f* laryngitis

larva /'larva/ *f* larva

lasanha /la'zaɲa/ *f* lasagne

las|ca /'laska/ *f* chip. **~car** *vt/i* chip; **de ~car** 🅸 awful

lástima /'lastʃima/ *f* shame

lastro /'lastru/ *m* ballast

la|ta /'lata/ *f* (*material*) tin; (*recipiente*) tin, *Amer* can; **~ta de lixo** dustbin, *Amer* trash can. **~tão** *m* brass

late|jante /late'ʒãtʃi/ *a* throbbing. **~jar** *vi* throb

latente /la'tẽtʃi/ *a* latent

late|ral /late'raw/ (*pl* **~rais**) *a* side, lateral

laticínio /latʃi'siniu/ *m* dairy product

latido /la'tʃidu/ *m* bark

lati|fundiário /latʃifũdʒi'ariu/ *a* landowning ● *m* landowner. **~fúndio** *m* estate

latim /la'tʃĩ/ *m* Latin

latino /la'tʃinu/ *a & m* Latin. **~-americano** *a & m* Latin American

latir /la'tʃir/ *vi* bark

latitude /latʃi'tudʒi/ *f* latitude

lauda /'lawda/ *f* side

laudo /'lawdu/ *m* report, findings

lava /'lava/ *f* lava

lava|bo /la'vabu/ *m* toilet. **~dora** *f* washing machine. **~gem** *f* washing; **~gem a seco** dry cleaning; **~gem cerebral** brainwashing

lavanda /la'vãda/ *f* lavender

lavanderia /lavãde'ria/ *f* laundry

lavar /la'var/ *vt* wash; **~ a seco** dry-clean. **~-se** *vpr* wash

lavatório /lava'tɔriu/ *m Port* washbasin

lavoura /la'vora/ *f* (*agricultura*) farming; (*terreno*) field

lav|rador /lavra'dor/ *m* farmhand. **~rar** *vt* work; draw up ‹*documento*›

laxante /la'ʃãtʃi/ *a & m* laxative

lazer /la'zer/ *m* leisure

le|al /le'aw/ (*pl* **~ais**) *a* loyal. **~aldade** *f* loyalty

leão /le'ãw/ *m* lion; **Leão** (*signo*) Leo. **~ de chácara** (*pl* **leões de chácara**) *m* bouncer

lebre /'lɛbri/ *f* hare

lecionar /lesio'nar/ *vt/i* teach

le|gação /lega'sãw/ *f* legation. **~gado** *m* (*pessoa*) legate; (*herança*) legacy

le|gal /le'gaw/ (*pl* **~gais**) *a* legal; 🅸 good; ‹*pessoa*› nice; **tá ~gal** OK. **~galidade** *f* legality. **~galizar** *vt* legalize

legar /le'gar/ *vt* bequeath

legenda /le'ʒẽda/ *f* (*de quadro*) caption; (*de filme*) subtitle; (*inscrição*) inscription

legi|ão /leʒi'ãw/ *f* legion. **~onário** *m* (*romano*) legionary; (*da legião estrangeira*) legionnaire

legis|lação /leʒizla'sãw/ *f* legislation. **~lador** *m* legislator. **~lar** *vi* legislate. **~lativo** *a* legislative ● *m* legislature. **~latura** *f* legislature. **~ta** *m/f* legal expert

legiti|mar /leʒitʃi'mar/ *vt* legitimize. **~midade** *f* legitimacy

legítimo /le'ʒitʃimu/ *a* legitimate

legí|vel /le'ʒivew/ (*pl* **~veis**) *a* legible

légua /'lɛgwa/ *f* league

legume /le'gumi/ *m* vegetable

lei /lej/ *f* law

leigo /'lejgu/ *a* lay ● *m* layman

lei|lão /lej'lãw/ *m* auction. **~loar** *vt* auction. **~loeiro** *m* auctioneer

leitão /lej'tãw/ *m* sucking pig

lei|te /'lejtʃi/ *m* milk; **~te condensado/desnatado** condensed/skimmed milk. **~teira** *f* (*jarro*) milk jug; (*panela*) milk saucepan. **~teiro** *m* milkman ● *a* ‹*vaca*› dairy

leito /'lejtu/ *m* bed

leitor /lej'tor/ *m* reader

leitoso /lej'tozu/ *a* milky

leitura /lej'tura/ *f* (*ação*) reading; (*material*) reading matter

lema /'lema/ *m* motto

lem|brança /lẽ'brãsa/ *f* memory; (*presente*) souvenir. **~brar** *vt/i* remember; **~brar-se de** remember; **~brar algo a alguém** remind sb of sth. **~brete** /e/ *m* reminder

leme /'lemi/ *m* rudder

len|ço /'lẽsu/ (*pl* **lençóis**) *m* (*para o nariz*) handkerchief; (*para vestir*) scarf. **~çol** /ɔ/ *m* sheet

len|da /'lẽda/ *f* legend. **~dário** *a* legendary

lenha /'leɲa/ *f* firewood; (*uma*) log. **~dor** *m* woodcutter

lente /'lẽtʃi/ *f* lens; **~ de contato** contact lens

lentidão /lẽtʃi'dãw/ *f* slowness

lentilha /lẽ'tʃiʎa/ *f* lentil

lento /'lẽtu/ *a* slow

leoa /le'oa/ *f* lioness

leopardo /lio'pardu/ *m* leopard

le|pra /'lɛpra/ *f* leprosy. **~proso** /o/ *a* leprous ● *m* leper

leque /'lɛki/ *m* fan; *fig* array

ler /ler/ *vt/i* read

LER *abr f* (= **lesão por esforço repetitivo**) RSI

ler|deza /ler'deza/ *f* sluggishness. **~do** /ɛ/ *a* sluggish

le|são /le'zãw/ *f* lesion, injury; **~são por esforço repetitivo** repetitive strain injury. **~sar** *vt* damage

l

lésbi|ca /'lɛzbika/ *f* lesbian. **~co** *a* lesbian

lesionado /lezjo'nadu/ *a* injured

lesionar /lezio'nar/ *vt* injure

lesma /'lezma/ *f* slug

leste /'lɛstʃi/ *m* east

le|tal /le'taw/ (*pl* **~tais**) *a* lethal

le|tão /le'tãw/ *a & m* (*f* **~tã**) Latvian

letargia /letar'ʒia/ *f* lethargy

letivo /le'tʃivu/ *a* **ano ~** academic year

Letônia /le'tonia/ *f* Latvia

letra /'letra/ *f* letter; (*de música*) lyrics, words; (*caligrafia*) writing; **Letras** Modern Languages; **ao pé da ~** literally; **com todas as ~s** in no uncertain terms; **tirar de ~** take in one's stride; **~ de forma** block letter

letreiro /le'treru/ *m* sign

leucemia /lewse'mia/ *f* leukaemia

leva /ɛ/ *f* batch

levado /le'vadu/ *a* naughty

levan|tamento /levãta'mẽtu/ *m* (*enquete*) survey; (*rebelião*) uprising; **~tamento de pesos** weightlifting. **~tar** *vt* raise; lift ‹*peso*› ● *vi* get up. **~tar-se** *vpr* get up; (*revoltar-se*) rise up

levante /le'vãtʃi/ *m* east

levar /le'var/ *vt* take; lead ‹*vida*›; get ‹*tapa, susto etc*› ● *vi* lead (**a** to)

leve /'lɛvi/ *a* light; (*não grave*) slight; **de ~** lightly

levedura /leve'dura/ *f* yeast

leveza /le'veza/ *f* lightness

levi|andade /leviã'dadʒi/ *f* frivolity. **~ano** *a* frivolous

levitar /levi'tar/ *vi* levitate

lexi|cal /leksi'kaw/ (*pl* **~cais**) *a* lexical

léxico /'leksiku/ *m* lexicon

lexicografia /leksikogra'fia/ *f* lexicography

lhe /ʎi/ *pron* (*a ele*) to him; (*a ela*) to her; (*a você*) to you. **~s** *pron* to them; (*a vocês*) to you

liba|nês /liba'nes/ *a & m* (*f* **~nesa**) Lebanese

Líbano /'libanu/ *m* Lebanon

libélula /li'bɛlula/ *f* dragonfly

libe|ração /libera'sãw/ *f* release. **~ral** (*pl* **~rais**) *a & m* liberal. **~ralismo** *m* liberalism. **~ralizar** *vt* liberalize. **~rar** *vt* release

liberdade /liber'dadʒi/ *f* freedom; **pôr em ~** set free; **~ condicional** probation

líbero /'liberu/ *m* sweeper

liber|tação /liberta'sãw/ *f* liberation. **~tar** *vt* free

Líbia /'libia/ *f* Libya

libi|dinoso /libidʒi'nozu/ *a* lecherous. **~do** *f* libido

líbio /'libiu/ *a & m* Libyan

li|bra /'libra/ *f* pound; **Libra** (*signo*) Libra. **~briano** *a & m* Libran

lição /li'sãw/ *f* lesson

licen|ça /li'sẽsa/ *f* leave; (*documento*) licence; **com ~ça** excuse me; **de ~ça** on leave; **sob ~ça** under licence. **~ciar** *vt* (*autorizar*) license; (*dar férias a*) give leave to. **~ciar-se** *vpr* (*tirar férias*) take leave; (*formar-se*) graduate. **~ciatura** *f* degree. **~cioso** /o/ *a* licentious

licenciado /lisẽsi'adu/ *m* graduate

liceu /li'sew/ *m Port* secondary school, *Amer* high school

licor /li'kor/ *m* liqueur

lida /'lida/ *f* slog, grind; (*leitura*) read

lidar /li'dar/ *vt/i* **~ com** deal with

lide /'lidʒi/ *f* (*trabalho*) work

líder /'lider/ *m/f* leader

lide|rança /lide'rãsa/ *f* (*de partido etc*) leadership; (*em corrida, jogo etc*) lead. **~rar** *vt* lead

lido /'lidu/ *a* well-read

liga /'liga/ *f* (*aliança*) league; (*tira*) garter; (*presilha*) suspender; (*de metais*) alloy

li|gação /liga'sãw/ *f* connection; (*telefônica*) call; (*amorosa*) liaison. **~gada** *f* call, ring. **~gado** *a* ‹*luz*, *TV*› on; **~gado em** attached to ‹*pessoa*›; hooked on ‹*droga*›. **~gamento** *m* ligament. **~gar** *vt* join, connect; switch on ‹*luz*, *TV etc*›; start up ‹*carro*›; bind ‹*amigos*› ● *vi* ring up, call; **~gar para** (*telefonar*) ring, call; (*dar importância*) care about; (*dar atenção*) pay attention to. **~gar-se** *vpr* join

ligeiro /li'ʒeru/ *a* light; ‹*ferida*, *melhora*› slight; (*ágil*) nimble

lilás /li'las/ *m* lilac ● *a invar* mauve

lima[1] /'lima/ *f* (*ferramenta*) file

lima[2] /'lima/ *f* (*fruta*) lime

limão /li'mãw/ *m* lime; (*amarelo*) lemon

limar /li'mar/ *vt* file

limeira /li'mera/ *f* lime tree

limiar /limi'ar/ *m* threshold

limi|tação /limita'sãw/ *f* limitation. **~tar** *vt* limit. **~tar-se** *vpr* limit o.s.; **~tar(-se) com** border on. **~te** *m* limit; (*de terreno*) boundary; **passar dos ~tes** go too far; **~te de velocidade** speed limit

limo|eiro /limo'eiru/ *m* lemon tree. **~nada** *f* lemonade

lim|pador /lĩpa'dor/ *m* **~pador de para-brisas** windscreen wiper. **~par** *vt* clean; wipe ‹*lágrimas*, *suor*›; *fig* clean up ‹*cidade*, *organização*›. **~peza** /e/ *f* (*ato*) cleaning; (*qualidade*) cleanness; *fig* clean-up; **~peza pública** sanitation. **~po** *a* clean; ‹*céu*, *consciência*› clear; ‹*lucro*› net, clear; *fig* pure; **passar a ~po** write up ‹*trabalho*›; *fig* sort out ‹*vida*›; **tirar a ~po** get to the bottom of ‹*caso*›

limusine /limu'zini/ *f* limousine

lince /'lĩsi/ *m* lynx

lindo /'lĩdu/ *a* beautiful

linear /lini'ar/ *a* linear

lingote /lĩ'gɔtʃi/ *m* ingot

língua /'lĩgwa/ *f* (*na boca*) tongue; (*idioma*) language; **~ materna** mother tongue

linguado /lĩ'gwadu/ *m* sole

lingua|gem /lĩ'gwaʒẽ/ *f* language. **~jar** *m* speech, dialect

lingueta /lĩ'gweta/ *f* bolt

linguiça /lĩ'gwisa/ *f* pork sausage

lin|guista /lĩ'gwiʃta/ *m/f* linguist. **~guística** *f* linguistics. **~guístico** *a* linguistic

linha /'liɲa/ *f* line; (*fio*) thread; **perder a ~** lose one's cool; **~ aérea** airline; **~ de fogo** firing line; **~ de montagem** assembly line. **~gem** *f* lineage

linho /'liɲu/ *m* linen; (*planta*) flax

link /lɪŋk/ *m Comput* link, hyperlink

linóleo /li'nɔliu/ *m* lino(leum)

lipoaspiração /lipoaspira'sãw/ *f* liposuction

liqui|dação /likida'sãw/ *f* liquidation; (*de loja*) clearance sale; (*de conta*) settlement. **~dar** *vt* liquidate; settle ‹*conta*›; pay off ‹*dívida*›; sell off, clear ‹*mercadorias*›

liquidificador /likwidʒifika'dor/ *m* liquidizer

líquido /'likidu/ *a* liquid; ‹*lucro*, *salário*› net ● *m* liquid

líri|ca /'lirika/ *f Mus* lyrics; (*poesia*) lyric poetry. **~co** *a* lyrical; ‹*poesia*› lyric

lírio /'liriu/ *m* lily

Lisboa /liz'boa/ *f* Lisbon

Lisboa – O Grande Terremoto *i*

The 1755 Lisbon earthquake, also known as the Great Lisbon Earthquake, took place on Saturday 1 November 1755. The earthquake was followed by fires and a tsunami, which caused near-total destruction of Lisbon and adjoining areas. Estimates place the death toll in Lisbon alone between 10,000 and 100,000 people, making it one of the deadliest earthquakes in history.

lisboeta /lizbo'eta/ *a* & *m/f* (person) from Lisbon

liso /'lizu/ *a* smooth; (*sem desenho*) plain; ‹*cabelo*› straight; [!] (*duro*) broke

lison|ja /li'zõʒa/ *f* flattery. **~jear** *vt* flatter

lista /'lista/ *f* list; (*listra*) stripe; **~ telefônica** telephone directory

listra /'listra/ *f* stripe. **~do** *a* striped, stripey

lite|ral /lite'raw/ (*pl* **~rais**) *a* literal. **~rário** *a* literary. **~ratura** *f* literature

litígio /li'tʃiʒiu/ *m* dispute; *Jurid* lawsuit

lito|ral /lito'raw/ (*pl* **~rais**) *m* coastline. **~râneo** *a* coastal

litro /'litru/ *m* litre

Lituânia /litu'ania/ *f* Lithuania

lituano /litu'anu/ *a* & *m* Lithuanian

living /'livĩ/ (*pl* **~s**) *m* living room

livrar /li'vrar/ *vt* free; (*salvar*) save. **~-se** *vpr* escape; **~-se de** get rid of

livraria /livra'ria/ *f* bookshop

livre /'livri/ *a* free; **~ de impostos** tax-free. **~-arbítrio** *m* free will

liv|reiro /li'vreru/ *m* bookseller. **~ro** *m* book; **~ro de consulta** reference book; **~ro de cozinha** cookery book; **~ro de texto** textbook; **~ro eletrônico** e-book

li|xa /'liʃa/ *f* (*de unhas*) emery board; (*para madeira etc*) sandpaper. **~xar** *vt* sand ‹*madeira*›; file ‹*unhas*›; **estou me ~xando** [!] I couldn't care less

li|xeira /li'ʃeira/ *f* dustbin, *Amer* garbage can. **~xeiro** *m* dustman, *Amer* garbage collector. **~xo** *m* rubbish, *Amer* garbage; (*atômico*) waste

lobisomem /lobi'zomẽ/ *m* werewolf

lobo /'lobu/ *m* wolf. **~-marinho** (*pl* **~s-marinhos**) *m* sea lion

lóbulo /'lɔbulu/ *m* lobe

lo|cação /loka'sãw/ *f* (*de imóvel*) lease; (*de carro*) rental. **~cador** *m* (*de casa*) landlord. **~cadora** *f* rental company; (*de vídeos*) video shop

l

lo|cal /lo'kaw/ (*pl* **~cais**) *a* local ● *m* site; (*de um acidente etc*) scene. **~calidade** *f* locality. **~calização** *f* location. **~calizar** *vt* locate. **~calizar-se** *vpr* (*orientar-se*) get one's bearings

loção /lo'sãw/ *f* lotion; **~ após-barba** aftershave lotion

locatário /loka'tariu/ *m* (*de imóvel*) tenant; (*de carro etc*) hirer

locomo|tiva /lokomo'tʃiva/ *f* locomotive. **~ver-se** *vpr* get around

locu|ção /loku'sãw/ *f* phrase. **~tor** *m* announcer

lodo /'lodu/ *m* mud. **~so** /o/ *a* muddy

logaritmo /loga'ritʃimu/ *m* logarithm

lógi|ca /'lɔʒika/ *f* logic. **~co** *a* logical

logo /'lɔgu/ *adv* (*em seguida*) straightaway; (*em breve*) soon; (*justamente*) just; **~ mais** later; **~ antes/depois** just before/straight after; **~ que** as soon as; **até ~** goodbye

logotipo /logo'tʃipu/ *m* logo

logradouro /logra'doru/ *m* public place

loiro /'lojru/ *a* ▶ LOURO

lo|ja /'lɔja/ *f* shop, *Amer* store; **~ja de departamentos** department store; **~ja maçônica** Masonic lodge. **~jista** *m/f* shopkeeper

lom|bada /lõ'bada/ *f* (*de livro*) spine; (*na rua*) speed bump. **~binho** *m* tenderloin. **~bo** *m* back; (*carne*) loin

lona /'lona/ *f* canvas

Londres /'lõdris/ *f* London

londrino /lõ'drinu/ *a* London ● *m* Londoner

longa-metragem /lõgame'traʒẽ/ (*pl* **longas-metragens**) *m* feature film

longe /'lõʒi/ *adv* far, a long way; **de ~** from a distance; (*por muito*) by far; **~ disso** far from it

longevidade /lõʒevi'dadʒi/ *f* longevity

longínquo /lõ'ʒĩkwu/ *a* distant

longitude /lõʒi'tudʒi/ *f* longitude

longo /'lõgu/ *a* long ● *m* long dress; **ao ~ de** along; (*durante*) through, over

lontra /'lõtra/ *f* otter

lorde /'lɔrdʒi/ *m* lord

lorota /lo'rɔta/ *f* [!] fib

losango /lo'zãgu/ *m* diamond

lo|tação /lota'sãw/ *f* capacity; (*ônibus*) bus; **~tação esgotada** full house. **~tado** *a* crowded; ‹*teatro, ônibus*› full. **~tar** *vt* fill ● *vi* fill up

lote /'lɔtʃi/ *m* (*quinhão*) portion; (*de terreno*) plot, *Amer* lot; (*em leilão*) lot; (*porção de coisas*) batch

loteria /lote'ria/ *f* lottery

louça /'losa/ *f* china; (*pratos etc*) crockery; **lavar a ~** wash up, *Amer* do the dishes

lou|co /'loku/ *a* mad, crazy ● *m* madman; **estou ~co para ir** [!] I'm dying to go. **~cura** *f* madness; (*uma*) crazy thing

louro /'loru/ *a* blond ● *m* laurel; (*condimento*) bay leaf

lou|var /lo'var/ *vt* praise. **~vável** (*pl* **~váveis**) *a* praiseworthy. **~vor** /o/ *m* praise

lua /'lua/ *f* moon. **~ de mel** *f* honeymoon

lu|ar /lu'ar/ *m* moonlight. **~arento** *a* moonlit

lubrifi|cação /lubrifika'sãw/ *f* lubrication. **~cante** *a* lubricating ● *m* lubricant. **~car** *vt* lubricate

lucidez /lusi'des/ *f* lucidity

lúcido /'lusidu/ *a* lucid

lu|crar /lu'krar/ *vi* profit (**com** by). **~cratividade** *f* profitability. **~crativo** *a* profitable, lucrative. **~cro** *m* profit

ludibriar /ludʒibri'ar/ *vt* cheat

lúdico /'ludʒiku/ *a* playful

lugar /lu'gar/ *m* place; (*espaço*) room; **em ~ de** in place of; **em primeiro ~** in the first place; **em algum ~** somewhere; **em todo ~** everywhere; **dar ~ a** give rise to; **ter ~** take place

lugarejo /luga'reʒu/ *m* village

lúgubre /'lugubri/ *a* gloomy, dismal

lula /'lula/ *f* squid

lume /'lumi/ *m* fire

luminária /lumi'naria/ *f* light, lamp; *pl* illuminations

luminoso /lumi'nozu/ *a* luminous; ‹*ideia*› brilliant

lunar /lu'nar/ *a* lunar ● *m* mole

lupa /'lupa/ *f* magnifying glass

lusco-fusco /lusku'fusku/ *m* twilight

lusitano /luzi'tanu/, **luso** /'luzu/ *a & m* Portuguese

lus|trar /lus'trar/ *vt* shine, polish. **~tre** *m* shine; *fig* lustre; (*luminária*) light, lamp. **~troso** /o/ *a* shiny

lu|ta /'luta/ *f* fight, struggle; **~ta livre** wrestling. **~tador** *m* fighter; (*de luta livre*) wrestler. **~tar** *vi* fight ● *vt* do ‹*judô etc*›

luto /'lutu/ *m* mourning

luva /'luva/ *f* glove

luxação /luʃa'sãw/ *f* dislocation

Luxemburgo /luʃẽ'burgu/ *m* Luxembourg

luxembur|guês /luʃẽbur'ges/ *a* (*f* **~guesa**) Luxembourg ● *m* (*f* **~guesa**) Luxembourger; (*língua*) Luxembourgish

luxo /'luʃu/ *m* luxury; **hotel de ~** luxury hotel; **cheio de ~** [!] fussy

luxuoso /luʃu'ozu/ *a* luxurious

luxúria /lu'ʃuria/ *f* lust

luxuriante /luʃuri'ãtʃi/ *a* lush

luz /lus/ *f* light; **à ~ de** by the light of ‹*velas etc*›; in the light of ‹*fatos etc*›; **dar à ~** give birth to

luzidio /luzi'dʒio/ *a* shiny

luzir /lu'zir/ *vi* shine

Mm

maca /'maka/ *f* stretcher

maçã /ma'sã/ *f* apple

macabro /ma'kabru/ *a* macabre

maca|cão /maka'kãw/ *m* (*de trabalho*) overalls, *Amer* coveralls; (*tipo de calça*) dungarees; (*roupa inteiriça*) jumpsuit; (*para bebê*) romper suit. **~co** *m* monkey; (*aparelho*) jack

maçada /ma'sada/ *f* bore

maçaneta /masa'neta/ *f* doorknob

maçante /ma'sãtʃi/ *a* boring

macar|rão /maka'xãw/ *m* pasta; (*espaguete*) spaghetti. **~ronada** *f* pasta with tomato sauce and cheese

macarrônico /maka'xoniku/ *a* broken

macete /ma'setʃi/ *m* trick

machado /ma'ʃadu/ *m* axe

ma|chão /ma'ʃãw/ *a* tough ● *m* tough guy. **~chismo** *m* machismo. **~chista** *a* chauvinistic ● *m* male chauvinist. **~cho** *a* male; ‹*homem*› macho ● *m* male

machu|cado /maʃu'kadu/ *m* injury; (*na pele*) sore patch. **~car** *vt/i* hurt. **~car-se** *vpr* hurt o.s.

maciço /ma'sisu/ *a* solid; ‹*dose etc*› massive ● *m* massif

macieira /masi'era/ *f* apple tree

maciez /masi'es/ *f* softness

macilento /masi'lẽtu/ *a* haggard

macio /ma'siu/ *a* soft; ‹*carne*› tender

maço /'masu/ *m* (*de cigarros*) packet; (*de notas*) bundle

ma|çom /ma'sõ/ *m* freemason. **~çonaria** *f* freemasonry

maconha /ma'koɲa/ *f* marijuana

maçônico /ma'soniku/ *a* Masonic

má-criação /makria'sãw/ *f* rudeness

macrobiótico /makrobi'ɔtʃiku/ *a* macrobiotic

macum|ba /ma'kũba/ *f* Afro-Brazilian cult; (*uma*) spell. **~beiro** *m* follower of macumba ● *a* macumba

madame /ma'dami/ *f* lady

madeira /ma'dera/ *f* wood ● *m* (*vinho*) Madeira; **~ de lei** hardwood

Madeira /ma'dera/ *f* Madeira

madeirense /made'rẽsi/ *a & m* Madeiran

madeixa /ma'deʃa/ *f* lock

madrasta /ma'drasta/ *f* stepmother

madrepérola /madre'pɛrola/ *f* mother of pearl

madressilva /madre'siwva/ *f* honeysuckle

Madri /ma'dri/ *f* Madrid

madrinha /ma'driɲa/ *f* (*de batismo*) godmother; (*de casamento*) bridesmaid

madru|gada /madru'gada/ *f* early morning. **~gador** *m* early riser. **~gar** *vi* get up early

maduro /ma'duru/ *a* ‹*fruta*› ripe; ‹*pessoa*› mature

mãe /mãj/ *f* mother. **~ de santo** (*pl* **~s de santo**) *f* macumba priestess

maes|tria /majs'tria/ *f* expertise. **~tro** *m* conductor

máfia /'mafia/ *f* mafia

magazine /maga'zini/ *m* department store

magia /ma'ʒia/ *f* magic

mági|ca /'maʒika/ *f* magic; (*uma*) magic trick. **~co** *a* magic ● *m* magician

magis|tério /maʒis'tɛriu/ *m* teaching; (*professores*) teachers. **~trado** *m* magistrate

magnânimo /mag'nanimu/ *a* magnanimous

magnata /mag'nata/ *m* magnate

magnésio /mag'nɛziu/ *m* magnesium

mag|nético /mag'nɛtʃiku/ *a* magnetic. **~netismo** *m* magnetism. **~netizar** *vt* magnetize; *fig* mesmerize

mag|nificência /magnifi'sẽsia/ *f* magnificence. **~nífico** *a* magnificent

magnitude /magni'tudʒi/ *f* magnitude

m

mago /'magu/ *m* magician; **os reis ~s** the Three Wise Men

mágoa /'magoa/ *f* sorrow

magoar /mago'ar/ *vt/i* hurt. **~-se** *vpr* be hurt

ma|gricela /magri'sɛla/ *a* skinny. **~gro** *a* thin; ‹*leite*› skimmed; ‹*carne*› lean; *fig* meagre

maio /'maju/ *m* May

maiô /ma'jo/ *m* swimsuit

maionese /majo'nɛzi/ *f* mayonnaise

maior /ma'jɔr/ *a* bigger; ‹*escritor, amor etc*› greater; **o ~ carro** the biggest car; **o ~ escritor** the greatest writer; **~ de idade** of age

Maiorca /ma'jɔrka/ *f* Majorca

maio|ria /majo'ria/ *f* majority; **a ~ria dos brasileiros** most Brazilians. **~ridade** *f* majority, adulthood

mais /majs/ ● *adv*

····➤ (*uso comparativo: com adjetivos*) more; **~ fácil** easier; **~ inteligente** more intelligent; **é ~ alta/elegante que eu** she's taller/slimmer than me

! Os adjetivos de uma sílaba formam o comparativo com o acréscimo *-er*: **mais devagar** *slower*, **mais rico** *richer*. Para formar o comparativo da maioria de adjetivos de duas ou mais sílabas, usa-se *more* + adjetivo: **mais caro** *more expensive*.

····➤ (*uso comparativo: com verbos*) **durar ~** last longer; **trabalhar ~** work harder; **~ de** more than; **você viajou ~ do que eu** you've travelled more than me; **~ de 2 semanas** more than 2 weeks; **gosto ~ de peixe** I like fish better

····➤ (*uso superlativo*) most; **a cidade ~ bonita do mundo** the most beautiful city in the world; **o ~ simpático de todos** the nicest of all; **a loja que vendeu ~ livros** the shop that sold most books

! Os adjetivos de uma sílaba formam o superlativo com o acréscimo *-est*: **a cidade mais fria** *the coldest city*, **a mulher mais rica** *the richest woman*. Para formar o superlativo da maioria de adjetivos de duas ou mais sílabas, usa-se *most* + adjetivo: **o mais inteligente** *the most intelligent*.

····➤ (*com pronomes*) else; **você tem ~ alguma coisa para me dizer?** have you got anything else to tell me?; **~ alguém?** anyone else?; **~ nada** nothing else; **~ ninguém** nobody else

····➤ (*em exclamações*) **que paisagem ~ bonita!** what lovely scenery!

····➤ (*em negativas*) **não sabemos ~ do que disseram no rádio** we only know what it said on the radio; **não foi ~ que uma coincidência** it was just a coincidence

● *prep*

····➤ *Mat* plus; **5 ~ 5 são 10** 5 plus 5 makes ten

····➤ (*em expressões*) **a ~** (*para além do necessário*) too much, too many; **há 2 cadeiras a ~** there are 2 chairs too many; (*de sobra*) spare; **eu tenho uma caneta a ~** I've got a spare pen; **~ nada** nothing else; **não tenho ~ nada para lhe dizer** I've got nothing else to tell you; **~ ou menos** more or less; **ela ganha ~ ou menos R$200 por dia** she earns around R$200 a day; **~ dia menos dia** one of these days; **ela vai emigrar, ~ dia menos dia** she's going to emigrate one of these days; **além do ~** what's more

maisena /maj'zɛna/ *f* cornflour, *Amer* cornstarch

maître /mɛtr/ *m* head waiter

maiúscula /ma'juskula/ *f* capital letter

majes|tade /maʒes'tadʒi/ *f* majesty. **~toso** *a* majestic

major /ma'jɔr/ *m* major

majoritário /maʒori'tariu/ *a* majority

mal /maw/ ● *adv*

····➤ (*imperfeitamente*) badly; **portar-se ~/falar ~** behave/speak badly; **cheirar ~** smell; **ela ouve muito ~** her hearing is very bad

····➤ (*erradamente*) wrong; **você escolheu ~** you made the wrong choice

····➤ (*quase não*) hardly; **eles ~ se falaram** they hardly spoke; (*quase nunca*) hardly ever; **~ os vemos** we hardly ever see them

····➤ (*doente*) **estar ~** be quite ill; **sentir-se ~** feel ill

● *m*

····➤ (*dano*) harm; **não lhe desejo nenhum ~** I don't wish you any harm

····➤ (*maldade*) **o bem e o ~** good and evil

····➤ (*doença*) illness; **tem um ~ incurável** he has an incurable illness

····➤ (*problema*) **esse foi um ~ menor** that was the least of my troubles

● *conj*

····➤ (*logo que*) as soon as; **~ chegaram** as soon as they arrived

····➤ (*em expressões*) **estar ~ de** (*dinheiro*) be short of; **não fazer por ~** mean no harm; **ele não faz por ~** he doesn't mean any harm

mala /'mala/ *f* suitcase; (*do carro*) boot, *Amer* trunk; **~ aérea** air courier

malabaris|mo /malaba'rizmu/ *m* juggling act. **~ta** *m/f* juggler

mal-agradecido /malagrade'sidu/ *a* ungrateful

malagueta /mala'geta/ *f* chilli pepper

malaio /ma'laju/ *a & m* Malay

Malaísia /mala'izia/ *f* Malaysia

malaísio /mala'iziu/ *a & m* Malaysian

malan|dragem /malã'draʒẽ/ *f* hustling; (*uma*) clever trick. **~dro** *a* cunning ● *m* hustler

malária /ma'laria/ *f* malaria

mal-assombrado /malasõ'bradu/ *a* haunted

Malavi /mala'vi/ *m* Malawi

malcriado /mawkri'adu/ *a* rude

mal|dade /maw'dadʒi/ *f* wickedness; (*uma*) wicked thing; **por ~dade** out of spite. **~dição** *f* curse. **~dito** *a* cursed, damned. **~doso** /o/ *a* wicked

maleá|vel /mali'avew/ (*pl* **~veis**) *a* malleable

maledicência /maledi'sẽsia/ *f* malicious gossip

maléfico /ma'lɛfiku/ *a* evil; (*prejudicial*) harmful

mal-encarado /malĩka'radu/ *a* shady, dubious ● *m* shady character

mal-entendido /malĩtẽ'dʒidu/ *m* misunderstanding

mal-estar /malis'tar/ *m* (*doença*) ailment; (*constrangimento*) discomfort

maleta /ma'leta/ *f* overnight bag

malévolo /ma'lɛvolu/ *a* malevolent

malfei|to /maw'fejtu/ *a* badly done; ‹*roupa etc*› badly made; *fig* wrongful. **~tor** *m* wrongdoer. **~toria** *f* wrongdoing

ma|lha /'maʎa/ *f* (*ponto*) stitch; (*tricô*) knitting; (*tecido*) jersey; (*casaco*) jumper, *Amer* sweater; (*para ginástica*) leotard; (*de rede*) mesh; **fazer ~lha** knit. **~lhado** *a* ‹*animal*› dappled; ‹*roque*› heavy. **~lhar** *vt* beat; thresh ‹*trigo etc*› ● *vi* [!] work out

mal-humorado /malumo'radu/ *a* in a bad mood, grumpy

malícia /ma'lisia/ *f* (*má índole*) malice; (*astúcia*) guile; (*humor*) innuendo

malicioso /malisi'ozu/ *a* (*mau*) malicious; (*astuto*) crafty; (*que põe malícia*) dirty-minded

maligno /ma'liginu/ *a* malignant

malmequer /mawme'ker/ *m* marigold

malnutrido /mawnu'tridu/ *a* malnourished

maloca /ma'lɔka/ *f* Indian village

malo|grar-se /malo'grarsi/ *vpr* go wrong, fail. **~gro** /o/ *m* failure

malpassado /mawpa'sadu/ *a* ‹*carne*› rare

Malta /'mawta/ *f* Malta

malte /'mawtʃi/ *m* malt

maltrapilho /mawtra'piʎu/ *a* scruffy

maltratar /mawtra'tar/ *vt* ill-treat, mistreat

malu|co /ma'luku/ *a* [!] mad, crazy [!] ● *m* madman. **~quice** *f* madness; (*uma*) crazy thing

malvado /maw'vadu/ *a* wicked

malver|sação /mawversa'sãw/ *f* mismanagement; (*de fundos*) misappropriation. **~sar** *vt* mismanage; misappropriate ‹*dinheiro*›

Malvinas /maw'vinas/ *f pl* Falklands

mamadeira /mama'dera/ *f* (baby's) bottle

mamãe /ma'mãj/ *f* mum

mamão /ma'mãw/ *m* papaya

ma|mar /ma'mar/ *vi* suckle. **~mata** *f* [!] fiddle

mamífero /ma'miferu/ *m* mammal

mamilo /ma'milu/ *m* nipple

mamoeiro /mamo'eru/ *m* papaya tree

mamografia /mamogra'fia/ *f* mammography

mamoplastia /mamoplaʃ'tʃia/ *f* breast surgery, mammoplasty

manada /ma'nada/ *f* herd

mananci|al /manãsi'aw/ (*pl* **~ais**) *m* spring; *fig* rich source

man|cada /mã'kada/ *f* blunder. **~car** *vi* limp. **~car-se** *vpr* [!] take the hint, get the message

man|cha /'mãʃa/ *f* stain; (*na pele*) mark. **~char** *vt* stain

m

Mancha /'mãʃa/ *f* **o canal da ~** the English Channel

manchete /mã'ʃɛtʃi/ *f* headline

manco /'mãku/ *a* lame ● *m* cripple

mandachuva /mãda'ʃuva/ *m* [!] bigwig; (*chefe*) boss

man|dado /mã'dadu/ *m* order; **~dado de busca** search warrant; **~dado de prisão** arrest warrant. **~damento** *m* commandment. **~dante** *m/f* person in charge. **~dão** *a* (*f* **~dona**) bossy. **~dar-se** *vpr* [!] take off. **~dato** *m* mandate

mandar /mã'dar/ ● *vt*

····➤ (*ordenar*) tell; **faça o que eu lhe mando** do what I tell you

····➤ (*enviar*) send; **mande a carta para mim pelo correio** send the letter to me by mail

····➤ (*atirar*) throw; **mande a bola** throw the ball

····➤ (*em expressões*) **~ fazer algo** have sth done; **vou ~ consertar o carro** I'm going to have the car repaired; **~ buscar/chamar alguém** send for sb; **mandei buscar o cozinheiro** I sent for the chef; **~ dizer** send word; **~ alguém às favas** tell sb to get lost

● *vi*

····➤ (*ser o chefe*) be in charge; **quem manda aqui?** who's in charge here?. **~dar-se**

● *vpr*

····➤ [!] take off

mandíbula /mã'dʒibula/ *f* (lower) jaw

mandioca /mãdʒi'ɔka/ *f* manioc

maneira /ma'nera/ *f* way; *pl* (*boas*) manners; **desta ~** in this way; **de qualquer ~** anyway

mane|jar /mane'ʒar/ *vt* handle; operate ‹*máquina*›. **~jável** (*pl* **~jáveis**) *a* manageable. **~jo** /e/ *m* handling

manequim /mane'kĩ/ *m* (*boneco*) dummy; (*medida*) size ● *m/f* mannequin, model

maneta /ma'neta/ *a* one-armed ● *m/f* person with one arm

manga[1] /'mãga/ *f* (*de roupa*) sleeve

manga[2] /'mãga/ *f* (*fruta*) mango

manganês /mãga'nes/ *m* manganese

mangue /'mãgi/ *m* mangrove swamp

mangueira[1] /mã'gera/ *f* (*tubo*) hose

mangueira[2] /mã'gera/ *f* (*árvore*) mango tree

manha /'maɲa/ *f* tantrum

manhã /ma'ɲã/ *f* morning; **de ~** in the morning

manhoso /ma'ɲozu/ *a* wilful

mania /ma'nia/ *f* (*moda*) craze; (*doença*) mania

maníaco /ma'niaku/ *a* manic ● *m* maniac. **~-depressivo** *a & m* manic depressive

manicômio /mani'komiu/ *m* lunatic asylum

manicura /mani'kura/ *f* manicure; (*pessoa*) manicurist

manifes|tação /manifesta'sãw/ *f* manifestation; (*passeata*) demonstration. **~tante** *m/f* demonstrator. **~tar** *vt* manifest, demonstrate. **~tar-se** *vpr* (*revelar-se*) manifest o.s.; (*exprimir-se*) express an opinion. **~to** /ɛ/ *a* manifest, clear ● *m* manifesto

manipular /manipu'lar/ *vt* manipulate

manjedoura /mãʒe'dora/ *f* manger

manjericão /mãʒeri'kãw/ *m* basil

mano|bra /ma'nɔbra/ *f* manoeuvre. **~brar** *vt* manoeuvre. **~brista** *m/f* parking valet

mansão /mã'sãw/ *f* mansion

man|sidão /mãsi'dãw/ *f* gentleness; (*do mar*) calm. **~sinho** *adv* **de ~sinho** (*devagar*) slowly; (*de leve*) gently; (*de fininho*) stealthily. **~so** *a* gentle; ‹*mar*› calm; ‹*animal*› tame

manta /'mãta/ *f* blanket; (*casaco*) cloak

mantei|ga /mã'tejga/ *f* butter. **~gueira** *f* butter dish

manter /mã'ter/ *vt* keep. **~-se** *vpr* keep; (*sustentar-se*) keep o.s.

mantimentos /mãtʃi'mẽtus/ *m pl* provisions

manto /'mãtu/ *m* mantle

manu|al /manu'aw/ (*pl* **~ais**) *a & m* manual. **~fatura** *f* manufacture; (*fábrica*) factory. **~faturar** *vt* manufacture

manuscrito /manus'kritu/ *a* handwritten ● *m* manuscript

manu|sear /manuzi'ar/ *vt* handle. **~seio** *m* handling

manutenção /manutẽ'sãw/ *f* maintenance; (*de prédio*) upkeep

mão /mãw/ (*pl* **~s**) *f* hand; (*do trânsito*) direction; (*de tinta*) coat; **abrir ~ de** give up; **aguentar a ~** hang on; **dar a ~ a alguém** hold sb's hand; (*cumprimentando*) shake sb's hand; **deixar alguém na ~** let sb down; **enfiar** ou **meter a ~ em** hit, slap; **lançar ~ de** make use of; **escrito à ~** written by hand; **ter à ~** have to hand; **de ~s dadas** hand in hand; **em segunda ~** second-hand; **fora de ~** out of the way; **~ única** one way. **~-de-obra** *f* labour

mapa /'mapa/ *m* map

maquete /ma'kɛtʃi/ *f* model

maqui|agem /maki'aʒẽ/ *f* make-up. **~ar** *vt* make up. **~ar-se** *vpr* put on make-up

maquiavélico /makia'vɛliku/ *a* Machiavellian

maqui|lagem, **~lar**, *Port* **~lhagem**, **~lhar** ▶ MAQUIAGEM

máquina /'makina/ *f* machine; (*ferroviária*) engine; **escrever à ~** type; **~ de costura** sewing machine; **~ de escrever** typewriter; **~ de lavar (roupa)** washing machine; **~ de lavar pratos** dishwasher; **~ fotográfica** camera

maqui|nação /makina'sãw/ *f* machination. **~nal** (*pl* **~nais**) *a* mechanical. **~nar** *vt/i* plot. **~nária** *f* machinery. **~nista** *m/f* (*ferroviário*) engine driver; (*de navio*) engineer

mar /mar/ *m* sea

maracu|já /maraku'ʒa/ *m* passion fruit. **~jazeiro** *m* passion fruit plant

marasmo /ma'razmu/ *f* stagnation

marato|na /mara'tona/ *f* marathon. **~nista** *m/f* marathon runner

maravi|lha /mara'viʎa/ *f* marvel; **às mil ~lhas** wonderfully. **~lhar** *vt* amaze. **~lhar-se** *vpr* marvel (**de** at). **~lhoso** /o/ *a* marvellous

mar|ca /'marka/ *f* (*sinal*) mark; (*de carro, máquina*) make; (*de cigarro, sabão etc*) brand; **~ca registrada** registered trademark. **~cação** /marka'sãw/ *f* marking; *Port* (*discagem*) dialling; **~ rápida** *Port Telec* speed dialling. **~cador** *m* marker; (*em livro*) bookmark; (*placar*) scoreboard; (*jogador*) scorer. **~cante** *a* outstanding. **~ca-passo** *m* pacemaker. **~car** *vt* mark; arrange ‹*hora, encontro, jantar etc*›; score ‹*gol, ponto*›; *Port* (*discar*) dial; ‹*relógio, termômetro*› show; brand ‹*gado*›; (*observar*) keep a close eye on; (*impressionar*) leave one's mark on; **~car época** make history; **~car hora** make an appointment; **~car o compasso** beat time; **~car os pontos** keep the score ● *vi* make one's mark

marce|naria /marsena'ria/ *f* cabinetmaking; (*oficina*) cabinet maker's workshop. **~neiro** *m* cabinetmaker

mar|cha /'marʃa/ *f* march; (*de carro*) gear; **pôr-se em ~cha** get going; **~cha à ré**, *Port* **~cha atrás** reverse. **~char** *vi* march

marci|al /marsi'aw/ (*pl* **~ais**) *a* martial. **~ano** *a & m* Martian

marco[1] /'marku/ *m* (*sinal*) landmark

marco[2] /'marku/ *m* (*moeda*) mark

março /'marsu/ *m* March

maré /ma'rɛ/ *f* tide

mare|chal /mare'ʃaw/ (*pl* **~chais**) *m* marshal

maresia /mare'zia/ *f* smell of the sea

marfim /mar'fĩ/ *m* ivory

margarida /marga'rida/ *f* daisy; (*para impressora*) daisy wheel

margarina /marga'rina/ *f* margarine

mar|gem /'marʒẽ/ *f* (*de rio*) bank; (*de lago*) shore; (*parte em branco*) *fig* margin. **~ginal** (*pl* **~ginais**) *a* marginal; (*delinquente*) delinquent ● *m/f* delinquent ● *f* (*rua*) riverside road. **~ginalidade** *f* delinquency. **~ginalizar** *vt* marginalize

marido /ma'ridu/ *m* husband

marimbondo /marĩ'bõdu/ *m* hornet

marina /ma'rina/ *f* marina

mari|nha /ma'riɲa/ *f* navy; **~nha mercante** merchant navy. **~nheiro** *m* sailor. **~nho** *a* marine
marionete /mario'nɛtʃi/ *f* puppet
mariposa /mari'poza/ *f* moth
mariscos /ma'riskus/ *m* seafood
mari|tal /mari'taw/ (*pl* **~tais**) *a* marital
marítimo /ma'ritʃimu/ *a* sea; ‹*cidade*› seaside
marmanjo /mar'mãʒu/ *m* grown-up
marme|lada /marme'lada/ *f* [!] fix. **~lo** /ɛ/ *m* quince
marmita /mar'mita/ *f* (*de soldado*) mess tin; (*de trabalhador*) lunch box
mármore /'marmori/ *m* marble
marmóreo /mar'mɔriu/ *a* marble
marquise /mar'kizi/ *f* awning
marreco /ma'xɛku/ *m* wild duck
Marrocos /ma'xɔkus/ *m* Morocco
marrom /ma'xõ/ *a* & *m* brown
marroquino /maxo'kinu/ *a* & *m* Moroccan
Marte /'martʃi/ *m* Mars
marte|lada /marte'lada/ *f* hammer blow. **~lar** *vt/i* hammer; **~lar em** *fig* go on and on about. **~lo** /ɛ/ *m* hammer
mártir /'martʃir/ *m/f* martyr
mar|tírio /mar'tʃiriu/ *m* martyrdom; *fig* torture. **~tirizar** *vt* martyr; *fig* torture
marujo /ma'ruʒu/ *m* sailor
mar|xismo /mark'sizmu/ *m* Marxism. **~xista** *a* & *m/f* Marxist
mas /mas/ *conj* but
mascar /mas'kar/ *vt* chew
máscara /'maskara/ *f* mask; (*tratamento facial*) face pack
mascarar /maska'rar/ *vt* mask
mascate /mas'katʃi/ *m* street vendor
mascavo /mas'kavu/ *a* **açúcar ~** brown sugar
mascote /mas'kɔtʃi/ *f* mascot
masculino /masku'linu/ *a* male; (*para homens*) men's; ‹*palavra*› masculine ● *m* masculine
másculo /'maskulu/ *a* masculine
masmorra /maz'moxa/ *f* dungeon
masoquis|mo /mazo'kizmu/ *m* masochism. **~ta** *m/f* masochist ● *a* masochistic
massa /'masa/ *f* mass; (*de pão*) dough; (*de torta, empada*) pastry; (*macarrão etc*) pasta; **cultura de ~** mass culture; **em ~** en masse; **as ~s** the masses
massa|crante /masa'krãtʃi/ *a* gruelling. **~crar** *vt* massacre; *fig* (*maçar*) wear out. **~cre** *m* massacre
massa|gear /masaʒi'ar/ *vt* massage. **~gem** *f* massage. **~gista** *m/f* masseur (*f* masseuse)
mastigar /mastʃi'gar/ *vt* chew; (*ponderar*) chew over
mastro /'mastru/ *m* mast; (*de bandeira*) flagpole
mastur|bação /masturba'sãw/ *f* masturbation. **~bar-se** *vpr* masturbate
mata /'mata/ *f* forest
mata-borrão /matabo'xãw/ *m* blotting paper
matadouro /mata'doru/ *m* slaughterhouse
mata|gal /mata'gaw/ (*pl* **~gais**) *m* thicket
mata-moscas /mata'moskas/ *m invar* fly spray
ma|tança /ma'tãsa/ *f* slaughter. **~tar** *vt* kill; satisfy ‹*fome*›; quench ‹*sede*›; guess ‹*charada*›; (*fazer nas coxas*) dash off; [!] skive off ‹*aula, serviço*› ● *vi* kill
mata-ratos /mata'xatus/ *m invar* rat poison
mate[1] /'matʃi/ *m* (*chá*) maté
mate[2] /'matʃi/ *a invar* matt
matemáti|ca /mate'matʃika/ *f* mathematics. **~co** *a* mathematical ● *m* mathematician
matéria /ma'tɛria/ *f* (*assunto, disciplina*) subject; (*no jornal*) article; (*substância*) matter; (*usada para fazer algo*) material; **em ~ de** in the way of
materi|al /materi'aw/ (*pl* **~ais**) *m* materials ● *a* material. **~alismo** *m* materialism. **~alista** *a* materialistic ● *m/f* materialist. **~alizar-se** *vpr* materialize
matéria-prima /matɛria'prima/ (*pl* **matérias-primas**) *f* raw material
mater|nal /mater'naw/ (*pl* **~nais**) *a* maternal. **~nidade** *f* maternity; (*clínica*) maternity hospital. **~no** /ɛ/ *a* maternal; **língua ~na** mother tongue
mati|nal /matʃi'naw/ (*pl* **~nais**) *a* morning. **~nê** *f* matinee
matiz /ma'tʃis/ *m* shade; (*político*) colouring; (*pontinha*) (*de ironia etc*) tinge
matizar /matʃi'zar/ *vt* tinge (**de** with)
mato /'matu/ *m* scrubland, bush
matraca /ma'traka/ *f* rattle; (*tagarela*) chatterbox
matreiro /ma'treru/ *a* cunning

matriar|ca /matri'arka/ *f* matriarch. **~cal** (*pl* **~cais**) *a* matriarchal

matrícula /ma'trikula/ *f* enrolment; (*taxa*) enrolment fee; *Port* (*de carro*) number plate, *Amer* license plate

matricular /matriku'lar/ *vt* enrol. **~-se** *vpr* enrol

matri|monial /matrimoni'aw/ (*pl* **~moniais**) *a* marriage. **~mônio** *m* marriage

matriz /ma'tris/ *f* matrix; (*útero*) womb; (*sede*) head office

maturidade /maturi'dadʒi/ *f* maturity

matutino /matu'tʃinu/ *a* morning ● *m* morning paper

matuto /ma'tutu/ *a* countrified ● *m* country bumpkin

mau /maw/ *a* (*f* **má**) bad. **~-caráter** *m invar* bad lot ● *a invar* no-good; **~-olhado** *m* evil eye

mausoléu /mawzo'lɛw/ *m* mausoleum

maus-tratos /maws'tratus/ *m pl* ill-treatment

maxilar /maksi'lar/ *m* jaw

máxima /'masima/ *f* maxim

maximizar /masimi'zar/ *vt* maximize; (*exagerar*) play up

máximo /'masimu/ *a* (*antes do substantivo*) utmost, greatest; (*depois do substantivo*) maximum ● *m* maximum; **o ~** [!] (*o melhor*) really something; **ao ~** to the maximum; **no ~** at most

maxixe /ma'ʃiʃi/ *m* gherkin

me /mi/ *pron* me; (*indireto*) (to) me; (*reflexivo*) myself

meada /mi'ada/ *f* skein; **perder o fio da ~** lose one's thread

meados /mi'adus/ *m pl* **~ de maio** mid-May

meandro /mi'ãdru/ *f* meander; *pl fig* twists and turns

mecâni|ca /me'kanika/ *f* mechanics. **~co** *a* mechanical ● *m* mechanic

meca|nismo /meka'nizmu/ *m* mechanism. **~nizar** *vt* mechanize

mecenas /me'sɛnas/ *m invar* patron

mecha /'mɛʃa/ *f* (*de vela*) wick; (*de bomba*) fuse; (*porção de cabelos*) lock; (*cabelo tingido*) highlight. **~do** *a* highlighted

meda|lha /me'daʎa/ *f* medal. **~lhão** *m* medallion; (*joia*) locket

média /'mɛdʒia/ *f* average; (*café*) white coffee; **em ~** on average

medi|ação /medʒia'sãw/ *f* mediation. **~ador** *m* mediator. **~ante** *prep* through, by. **~ar** *vi* mediate

medica|ção /medʒika'sãw/ *f* medication. **~mento** *m* medicine

medição /medʒi'sãw/ *f* measurement

medicar /medʒi'kar/ *vt* treat ● *vi* practise medicine. **~-se** *vpr* dose o.s. up

medici|na /medʒi'sina/ *f* medicine; **~na legal** forensic medicine. **~nal** (*pl* **~nais**) *a* medicinal

médico /'mɛdʒiku/ *m* doctor ● *a* medical. **~-legal** (*pl* **~-legais**) *a* forensic; **~-legista** (*pl* **~s-legistas**) *m/f* forensic scientist

medi|da /me'dʒida/ *f* measure; (*dimensão*) measurement; **à ~da que** as; **sob ~da** made to measure; **tirar as ~das de alguém** take sb's measurements. **~dor** *m* meter

medie|val /medʒie'vaw/ (*pl* **~vais**) *a* medieval

médio /'mɛdʒiu/ *a* (*típico*) average; ‹*tamanho, prazo*› medium; ‹*classe, dedo*› middle

medíocre /me'dʒiokri/ *a* mediocre

mediocridade /medʒiokri'dadʒi/ *f* mediocrity

medir /me'dʒir/ *vt* measure; weigh ‹*palavras*› ● *vi* measure. **~-se** *vpr* measure o.s.; **quanto você mede?** how tall are you?

medi|tação /medʒita'sãw/ *f* meditation. **~tar** *vi* meditate

mediterrâneo /medʒite'xaniu/ *a* Mediterranean ● *m* **o Mediterrâneo** the Mediterranean

médium /'mɛdʒiũ/ *m/f* medium

medo /'medu/ *m* fear; **ter ~ de** be afraid of; **com ~** afraid. **~nho** /o/ *a* frightful

medroso /me'drozu/ *a* fearful, timid

medula /me'dula/ *f* marrow

megalomania /megaloma'nia/ *f* megalomania

meia /'meja/ *f* (*comprida*) stocking; (*curta*) sock; (*seis*) six. **~-calça** (*pl* **~s-calças**) *f* tights, *Amer* pantihose; **~-idade** *f* middle age; **~-noite** *f* midnight; **~-volta** (*pl* **~s-voltas**) *f* about-turn

mei|go /'mejgu/ *a* sweet. **~guice** *f* sweetness

meio /'meju/ *a* half ● *adv* rather ● *m* (*centro*) middle; (*ambiente*) environment; (*recurso*) means; **~ litro**

m

half a litre; **dois meses e ~** two and a half months; **em ~ a** amid; **por ~ de** through; **o ~ ambiente** the environment; **os ~s de comunicação** the media; **~s de comunicação social** *Port* social media. **~-dia** *m* midday; **~-fio** *m* kerb; **~-termo** *m* (*acordo*) compromise

mel /mɛw/ *m* honey

mela|ço /me'lasu/ *m* molasses. **~do** *a* sticky ● *m* treacle

melancia /melã'sia/ *f* watermelon

melan|colia /melãko'lia/ *f* melancholy. **~cólico** *a* melancholic

melão /me'lãw/ *m* melon

melar /me'lar/ *vt* make sticky

melhor /me'ʎɔr/ *a & adv* better; **o ~** the best

melho|ra /me'ʎɔra/ *f* improvement; **~ras!** get well soon!. **~ramento** *m* improvement. **~rar** *vt* improve ● *vi* improve; ‹*doente*› get better

melin|drar /melĩ'drar/ *vt* hurt. **~drar-se** *vpr* be hurt. **~droso** /o/ *a* delicate; ‹*pessoa*› sensitive

melodi|a /melo'dʒia/ *f* melody. **~oso** /o/ *a* melodious

m

melodra|ma /melo'drama/ *m* melodrama. **~mático** *a* melodramatic

meloso /me'lozu/ *a* sickly sweet

melro /'mɛwxu/ *m* blackbird

membrana /mẽ'brana/ *f* membrane

membro /'mẽbru/ *m* member; (*braço, perna*) limb

memo|rando /memo'rãdu/ *m* memo. **~rável** (*pl* **~ráveis**) *a* memorable

memória /me'mɔria/ *f* memory; *pl* (*autobiografia*) memoirs

men|ção /mẽ'sãw/ *f* mention; **fazer ~ção de** mention. **~cionar** *vt* mention

mendi|cância /mẽdʒi'kãsia/ *f* begging. **~gar** *vi* beg. **~go** *m* beggar

menina /me'nina/ *f* girl; **a ~ dos olhos de alguém** the apple of sb's eye

meningite /menĩ'ʒitʃi/ *f* meningitis

meni|nice /meni'nisi/ *f* (*idade*) childhood. **~no** *m* boy

menopausa /meno'pawza/ *f* menopause

menor /me'nɔr/ *a* smaller ● *m/f* minor; **o|a ~** the smallest; (*mínimo*) the slightest, the least

menos /'menos/ *adv & pron* less ● *prep* except; **dois dias a ~** two days less; **a ~ que** unless; **ao** ou **pelo ~** at least; **o ~ bonito** the least pretty. **~prezar** *vt* look down upon. **~prezo** /e/ *m* disdain

mensa|geiro /mẽsa'ʒeru/ *m* messenger. **~gem** /mẽ'saʒẽ j̃/ *f* message; **~gem instantânea** *Telec* instant messaging. **~gem escrita** (*telec*) text message

men|sal /mẽ'saw/ (*pl* **~sais**) *a* monthly. **~salidade** *f* monthly payment. **~salmente** *adv* monthly

menstru|ação /mẽstrua'sãw/ *f* menstruation. **~ada** *a* **estar ~ada** be having one's period. **~al** (*pl* **~ais**) *a* menstrual. **~ar** *vi* menstruate

menta /'mẽta/ *f* mint

men|tal /mẽ'taw/ (*pl* **~tais**) *a* mental. **~talidade** *f* mentality. **~te** *f* mind

men|tir /mẽ'tʃir/ *vi* lie. **~tira** *f* lie. **~tiroso** /o/ *a* lying ● *m* liar

mentor /mẽ'tor/ *m* mentor

mercado /mer'kadu/ *m* market. **~ria** *f* commodity; *pl* goods

mercan|te /mer'kãtʃi/ *a* merchant. **~til** (*pl* **~tis**) *a* mercantile

mercê /mer'se/ *f* **à ~ de** at the mercy of

merce|aria /mersia'ria/ *f* grocer's. **~eiro** *m* grocer

mercenário /merse'nariu/ *a & m* mercenary

mercúrio /mer'kuriu/ *m* mercury; **Mercúrio** Mercury

merda /'mɛrda/ *f* (*vulgar*) shit

mere|cedor /merese'dor/ *a* deserving. **~cer** *vt* deserve ● *vi* be deserving. **~cimento** *m* merit

merenda /me'rẽda/ *f* packed lunch; **~ escolar** school dinner

mere|trício /mere'trisiu/ *m* prostitution. **~triz** *f* prostitute

mergu|lhador /merguʎa'dor/ *m* diver. **~lhar** *vt* dip (**em** into) ● *vi* (*na água*) dive; (*no trabalho*) bury o.s.. **~lho** *m* dive; (*esporte*) diving; (*banho de mar*) dip

meridi|ano /meridʒi'anu/ *m* meridian. **~onal** (*pl* **~onais**) *a* southern

mérito /'mɛritu/ *m* merit

merluza /mer'luza/ *f* hake

mero /'mɛru/ *a* mere

mês /mes/ (*pl* **meses**) *m* month

mesa /'meza/ *f* table; (*de trabalho*) desk; **~ de centro** coffee table; **~ de jantar** dining table; **~ telefônica** switchboard

mesada /me'zada/ *f* monthly allowance

mescla /'mɛskla/ *f* mixture, blend

mesmice /mez'misi/ *f* sameness

mesmo /'mezmu/ *a* same ● *adv* (*até*) even; (*justamente*) right; (*de verdade*) really; **você ~** you yourself; **hoje ~** this very day; **~ assim** even so; **~ que** even if; **dá no ~** it comes to the same thing; **fiquei na mesma** I'm none the wiser

mesqui|nharia /meskiɲa'ria/ *f* meanness; (*uma*) mean thing. **~nho** *a* mean

mesquita /mes'kita/ *f* mosque

Messias /me'sias/ *m* Messiah

mesti|çagem /mestʃi'saʒẽ/ *f* interbreeding. **~ço** *a* ‹*pessoa*› of mixed race; ‹*animal*› cross-bred ● *m* (*pessoa*) person of mixed race; (*animal*) mongrel

mes|trado /mes'tradu/ *m* master's degree. **~tre** /ɛ/ *m* (*f* **~tra**) master; mistress; (*de escola*) teacher ● *a* main; ‹*chave*› master. **~tre de obras** (*pl* **~tres de obras**) *m* foreman; **~tre-sala** (*pl* **~tres-salas**) *m* master of ceremonies (in carnival procession). **~tria** *f* expertise

meta /'mɛta/ *f* (*de corrida*) finishing post; (*gol*) *fig* goal

meta|bólico /meta'bɔliku/ *a* metabolic. **~bolismo** *m* metabolism

metade /me'tadʒi/ *f* half; **pela ~** halfway

metafísi|ca /meta'fizika/ *f* metaphysics. **~co** *a* metaphysical

metáfora /me'tafora/ *f* metaphor

metafórico /meta'fɔriku/ *a* metaphorical

me|tal /me'taw/ (*pl* **~tais**) *m* metal; *pl* (*numa orquestra*) brass. **~tálico** *a* metallic

meta|lurgia /metalur'ʒia/ *f* metallurgy. **~lúrgica** *f* metal works. **~lúrgico** *a* metallurgical ● *m* metalworker

metamorfose /metamor'fɔzi/ *f* metamorphosis

metano /me'tanu/ *m* methane

meteórico /mete'ɔriku/ *a* meteoric

meteoro /mete'ɔru/ *m* meteor. **~logia** *f* meteorology. **~lógico** *a* meteorological. **~logista** *m/f* (*cientista*) meteorologist; (*na TV*) weather forecaster

meter /me'ter/ *vt* put; **~ medo** be frightening. **~-se** *vpr* (*envolver-se*) get (**em** into); (*intrometer-se*) meddle (**em** in)

meticuloso /metʃiku'lozu/ *a* meticulous

metido /me'tʃidu/ *a* snobbish; **ele é ~ a perito** he thinks he's an expert

metódico /me'tɔdʒiku/ *a* methodical

metodista /meto'dʒista/ *a & m/f* Methodist

método /'mɛtodu/ *m* method

metra|lhadora /metraʎa'dora/ *f* machine gun. **~lhar** *vt* machine-gun

métri|co /'mɛtriku/ *a* metric; **fita ~ca** tape measure

metro[1] /'mɛtru/ *m* metre

metro[2] /'mɛtru/ *m Port* (*metropolitano*) underground, *Amer* subway

metrô /me'tro/ *m* underground, *Amer* subway

metrópole /me'trɔpoli/ *f* metropolis

metropolitano /metropoli'tanu/ *a* metropolitan ● *m Port* underground, *Amer* subway

meu /mew/ *a* (*f* **minha**) my ● *pron* (*f* **minha**) mine; **um amigo ~** a friend of mine; **fico na minha** [!] I keep myself to myself

mexer /me'ʃer/ *vt* move; (*com colher etc*) stir ● *vi* move; **~ com** (*comover*) affect, get to; (*brincar com*) tease; (*trabalhar com*) work with; **~ em** touch. **~-se** *vpr* move; (*apressar-se*) get a move on

mexeri|ca /meʃe'rika/ *f* tangerine. **~car** *vi* gossip. **~co** *m* piece of gossip; *pl* gossip. **~queiro** *a* gossiping ● *m* gossip

mexicano /meʃi'kanu/ *a & m* Mexican

México /'mɛʃiku/ *m* Mexico

mexido /me'ʃidu/ *a* **ovos ~s** scrambled eggs

mexilhão /meʃi'ʎãw/ *m* mussel

mi|ado /mi'adu/ *m* miaow. **~ar** *vi* miaow

micreiro /mi'krejru/ *m* PC hacker

micróbio /mi'krɔbiu/ *m* microbe

micro|cosmo /mikro'kɔzmu/ *m* microcosm. **~empresa** /e/ *f* small business. **~empresário** *m* small businessman. **~filme** *m* microfilm. **~fone** *m* microphone. **~-onda** *f* microwave. **(forno de) ~-ondas** *m* microwave (oven). **~-ônibus** *m invar* minibus. **~processador** *m* microprocessor

microrganismo /mikrorga'nizmu/ *m* microorganism

microscó|pico /mikros'kɔpiku/ *a* microscopic. **~pio** *m* microscope

mídia /'midʒia/ *f* media; **~ social** social media

migalha /mi'gaʎa/ *f* crumb

m

mi|gração /migra'sãw/ *f* migration. **~grar** *vi* migrate

mi|jar /mi'ʒar/ *vi* ! pee. **~jar-se** *vpr* wet o.s.. **~jo** *m* ! pee

mil /miw/ *a & m invar* thousand; **estar a ~** be on top form

mila|gre /mi'lagri/ *m* miracle. **~groso** /o/ *a* miraculous

milênio /mi'leniu/ *m* millennium

milésimo /mi'lɛzimu/ *a* thousandth

milha /'miʎa/ *f* mile

milhão /mi'ʎãw/ *m* million; **um ~ de dólares** a million dollars

milhar /mi'ʎar/ *m* thousand; **~es de vezes** thousands of times; **aos ~es** in their thousands

milho /'miʎo/ *m* maize, *Amer* corn

milico /mi'liku/ *m* ! military man; **os ~s** the military

mili|grama /mili'grama/ *m* milligram. **~litro** *m* millilitre. **milímetro** /e/ *m* millimetre

milionário /milio'nariu/ *a & m* millionaire

mili|tante /mili'tãtʃi/ *a & m* militant. **~tar** *a* military ● *m* soldier

m

mim /mĩ/ *pron* me

mimar /mi'mar/ *vt* spoil

mímica /'mimika/ *f* mime; (*brincadeira*) charades

mi|na /'mina/ *f* mine. **~nar** *vt* mine; *fig* (*prejudicar*) undermine

mindinho /mĩ'dʒiɲu/ *m* little finger, *Amer* pinkie

mineiro /mi'neru/ *a* mining; (*de MG*) from Minas Gerais ● *m* miner; (*de MG*) person from Minas Gerais

mine|ração /minera'sãw/ *f* mining. **~ral** (*pl* **~rais**) *a & m* mineral. **~rar** *vt/i* mine

minério /mi'nɛriu/ *m* ore

mingau /mĩ'gaw/ *m* porridge

míngua /'mĩgwa/ *f* lack

minguante /mĩ'gwãtʃi/ *a* **quarto ~** last quarter

minguar /mĩ'gwar/ *vi* dwindle

minha /'miɲa/ *a & pron* ▶ MEU

minhoca /mi'ɲɔka/ *f* worm

miniatura /minia'tura/ *f* miniature

mini|malista /minima'lista/ *a & m/f* minimalist. **~mizar** *vt* minimize; (*subestimar*) play down

mínimo /'minimu/ *a* (*muito pequeno*) tiny; (*mais baixo*) minimum ● *m* minimum; **a mínima ideia** the slightest idea; **no ~** at least

minissaia /mini'saja/ *f* miniskirt

minis|terial /ministeri'aw/ (*pl* **~teriais**) *a* ministerial. **~tério** *m* ministry; **Ministério do Interior** Home Office, *Amer* Department of the Interior

minis|trar /minis'trar/ *vt* administer. **~tro** *m* minister; **primeiro ~tro** prime minister

Minorca /mi'nɔrka/ *f* Menorca

mino|ritário /minori'tariu/ *a* minority. **~ria** *f* minority

minúcia /mi'nusia/ *f* detail

minucioso /minusi'ozu/ *a* thorough

minúscu|la /mi'nuskula/ *f* small letter. **~lo** *a* ‹*letra*› small; (*muito pequeno*) minuscule

minuta /mi'nuta/ *f* (*rascunho*) rough draft

minuto /mi'nutu/ *m* minute

miolo /mi'olu/ *f* (*de fruta*) flesh; (*de pão*) crumb; *pl* brains

míope /'miopi/ *a* short-sighted

miopia /mio'pia/ *f* myopia

mira /'mira/ *f* sight; **ter em ~** have one's sights on

mirabolante /mirabo'lãtʃi/ *a* amazing; ‹*ideias, plano*› grandiose

mi|ragem /mi'raʒẽ/ *f* mirage. **~rante** *m* lookout. **~rar** *vt* look at. **~rar-se** *vpr* look at o.s.

mirim /mi'rĩ/ *a* little

miscelânea /mise'lania/ *f* miscellany

miscigenação /misiʒena'sãw/ *f* interbreeding

miserá|vel /mize'ravew/ (*pl* **~veis**) *a* miserable

miséria /mi'zɛria/ *f* misery; (*pobreza*) poverty; **uma ~** (*pouco dinheiro*) a pittance; **chorar ~** claim poverty

miseri|córdia /mizeri'kɔrdʒia/ *f* mercy. **~cordioso** *a* merciful

misógino /mi'zɔʒinu/ *m* misogynist ● *a* misogynistic

miss /'misi/ *f* beauty queen

missa /'misa/ *f* mass

missão /mi'sãw/ *f* mission

mís|sil /'misiw/ (*pl* **~seis**) *m* missile; **~sil de longo alcance** long-range missile

missionário /misio'nariu/ *m* missionary

missiva /mi'siva/ *f* missive

mis|tério /mis'tɛriu/ *m* mystery. **~terioso** /o/ *a* mysterious. **~ticismo** *m* mysticism

místico /'mistʃiku/ *m* mystic ● *a* mystical

misto /'mistu/ *a* mixed ● *m* mix; **~ quente** toasted ham and cheese sandwich

mistu|ra /mis'tura/ *f* mixture. **~rar** *vt* mix; (*confundir*) mix up. **~rar-se** *vpr* mix (**com** with)

mítico /'mitʃiku/ *a* mythical

mito /'mitu/ *m* myth. **~logia** *f* mythology. **~lógico** *a* mythological

miudezas /miu'dezas/ *f pl* odds and ends

miúdo /mi'udu/ *a* tiny, minute; ‹*chuva*› fine; ‹*despesas*› minor ● *m* (*criança*) child, little one; *pl* (*de galinha*) giblets; **trocar em ~s** go into detail

mixaria /miʃa'ria/ *f* [!] (*soma irrisória*) pittance

mixórdia /mi'ʃɔrdʒia/ *f* muddle

MMS *abr m* (= **Serviço de Mensagens Multimédia**) MMS

mnemônico /ne'moniku/ *a* mnemonic

mobilar /mobi'lar/ *vt Port* furnish

mobília /mo'bilia/ *f* furniture

mobili|ar /mobili'ar/ *vt* furnish. **~ário** *m* furniture

mobili|dade /mobili'dadʒi/ *f* mobility. **~zar** *vt* mobilize

moça /'mosa/ *f* girl

moçambicano /mosãbi'kanu/ *a & m* Mozambican

Moçambique /mosã'biki/ *m* Mozambique

moção /mo'sãw/ *f* motion

mochila /mo'ʃila/ *f* rucksack

moço /'mosu/ *a* young ● *m* boy, lad

moda /'mɔda/ *f* fashion; **na ~** fashionable

modalidade /modali'dadʒi/ *f* (*esporte*) event

mode|lagem /mode'laʒẽ/ *f* modelling. **~lar** *vt* model (**a** on). **~lar-se** *vpr* model o.s. (**a** on). **~lo** /e/ *a* model ● *m* model

mode|ração /modera'sãw/ *f* moderation. **~rado** *a* moderate. **~rar** *vt* moderate; reduce ‹*velocidade, despesas*›. **~rar-se** *vpr* restrain oneself

moder|nidade /moderni'dadʒi/ *f* modernity. **~nismo** *m* modernism. **~nista** *a & m/f* modernist. **~nizar** *vt* modernize. **~no** /ɛ/ *a* modern

modess™ /'mɔdʒis/ *m invar* ™sanitary towel

modéstia /mo'dɛstʃia/ *f* modesty

modesto /mo'dɛstu/ *a* modest

módico /'mɔdʒiku/ *a* modest

modifi|cação /modʒifika'sãw/ *f* modification. **~car** *vt* modify

mo|dismo /mo'dʒizmu/ *m* idiom. **~dista** *f* dressmaker

modo /'mɔdu/ *m* way; *Ling* mood; *pl* (*maneiras*) manners

modular /modu'lar/ *vt* modulate ● *a* modular

módulo /'mɔdulu/ *m* module

moeda /mo'ɛda/ *f* (*peça de metal*) coin; (*dinheiro*) currency

mo|edor /moe'dor/ *m* **~edor de café** coffee grinder; **~edor de carne** mincer. **~er** *vt* grind ‹*café, trigo*›; squeeze ‹*cana*›; mince ‹*carne*›; (*bater*) beat

mo|fado /mo'fadu/ *a* mouldy. **~far** *vi* moulder. **~fo** /o/ *m* mould

mogno /'mɔgnu/ *m* mahogany

moinho /mo'iɲu/ *m* mill; **~ de vento** windmill

moisés /moj'zɛs/ *m invar* carrycot

moita /'mojta/ *f* bush

mola /'mɔla/ *f* spring

mol|dar /mow'dar/ *vt* mould; cast ‹*metal*›. **~de** /ɔ/ *m* mould; (*para costura etc*) pattern

moldu|ra /mow'dura/ *f* frame. **~rar** *vt* frame

mole /'mɔli/ *a* soft; ‹*pessoa*› listless; [!] (*fácil*) easy ● *adv* easily; **é ~?** [!] can you believe it?

molécula /mo'lɛkula/ *f* molecule

moleque /mo'lɛki/ *m* (*menino*) lad; (*de rua*) urchin; (*homem*) scoundrel

molestar /moles'tar/ *vt* bother

moléstia /mo'lɛstʃia/ *f* disease

moletom /mole'tõ/ *m* (*tecido*) knitted cotton; (*blusa*) sweatshirt

moleza /mo'leza/ *f* softness; (*de pessoa*) laziness; **viver na ~** lead a cushy life; **ser ~** be easy

mo|lhado /mo'ʎadu/ *a* wet. **~lhar** *vt* wet. **~lhar-se** *vpr* get wet

molho[1] /'mɔʎu/ *m* (*de chaves*) bunch; (*de palha*) sheaf

molho[2] /'moʎu/ *m* sauce; (*para salada*) dressing; **deixar de ~** leave in soak ‹*roupa*›; **~ inglês** Worcester sauce

molusco /mo'lusku/ *m* mollusc

m

momen|tâneo /momẽ'taniu/ *a* momentary. **~to** *m* moment; (*força*) momentum

Mônaco /'monaku/ *m* Monaco

monar|ca /mo'narka/ *m/f* monarch. **~quia** *f* monarchy. **~quista** *a & m/f* monarchist

monástico /mo'nastʃiku/ *a* monastic

monção /mõ'sãw/ *f* monsoon

mone|tário /mone'tariu/ *a* monetary. **~tarismo** *m* monetarism. **~tarista** *a & m/f* monetarist

monge /'mõʒi/ *m* monk

monitor /moni'tor/ *m* monitor; **~ de vídeo** VDU

monitorar /monito'rar/ *vt* monitor

mono|cromo /mono'krɔmu/ *a* monochrome. **~gamia** *f* monogamy

monógamo /mo'nɔgamu/ *a* monogamous

monograma /mono'grama/ *m* monogram

monólogo /mo'nɔlogu/ *m* monologue

mononucleose /mononukli'ɔzi/ *f* glandular fever

m

mono|pólio /mono'pɔliu/ *m* monopoly. **~polizar** *vt* monopolize

monossílabo /mono'silabu/ *a* monosyllabic ● *m* monosyllable

monotonia /monoto'nia/ *f* monotony

monótono /mo'nɔtonu/ *a* monotonous

monóxido /mo'nɔksidu/ *m* **~ de carbono** carbon monoxide

mons|tro /'mõstru/ *m* monster. **~truosidade** *f* monstrosity. **~truoso** /o/ *a* monstrous

monta|dor /mõta'dor/ *m* (*de cinema*) editor. **~dora** *f* assembly company. **~gem** *f* assembly; (*de filme*) editing; (*de peça teatral*) production

monta|nha /mõ'taɲa/ *f* mountain. **~nha-russa** (*pl* **~nhas-russas**) *f* roller coaster. **~nhismo** *m* mountaineering. **~nhoso** /o/ *a* mountainous

mon|tante /mõ'tãtʃi/ *m* amount ● *a* rising; **a ~tante** upstream. **~tão** *m* heap. **~tar** *vt* ride ‹*cavalo, bicicleta*›; assemble ‹*peças, máquina*›; put up ‹*barraca*›; set up ‹*empresa, escritório*›; mount ‹*guarda, diamante*›; put on ‹*espetáculo, peça*›; edit ‹*filme*›; **~tar a** amount to; **~tar em** (*subir em*) mount ● *vi* ride. **~taria** *f* mount. **~te** *m* heap; **um ~te de coisas** [!] loads of things; **o Monte Branco** Mont Blanc

Montevidéu /mõtʃivi'dɛw/ *f* Montevideo

montra /'mõtra/ *f Port* shop window

monumen|tal /monumẽ'taw/ (*pl* **~tais**) *a* monumental. **~to** *m* monument

mora|da /mo'rada/ *f* dwelling; *Port* address. **~dia** *f* dwelling. **~dor** *m* resident

mo|ral /mo'raw/ (*pl* **~rais**) *a* moral ● *f* (*ética*) morals; (*de uma história*) moral ● *m* (*ânimo*) morale; (*de pessoa*) moral sense. **~ralidade** *f* morality. **~ralista** *a* moralistic ● *m/f* moralist. **~ralizar** *vi* moralize

morango /mo'rãgu/ *m* strawberry

morar /mo'rar/ *vi* live

moratória /mora'tɔria/ *f* moratorium

mórbido /'mɔrbidu/ *a* morbid

morcego /mor'segu/ *m* bat

mor|daça /mor'dasa/ *f* gag; (*para cão*) muzzle. **~daz** *a* scathing. **~der** *vt/i* bite. **~dida** *f* bite

mordo|mia /mordo'mia/ *f* (*no emprego*) perk; (*de casa etc*) comfort. **~mo** /o/ *m* butler

more|na /mo'rena/ *f* brunette. **~no** *a* dark; (*bronzeado*) brown ● *m* dark person

morfina /mor'fina/ *f* morphine

moribundo /mori'bũdu/ *a* dying

moringa /mo'rĩga/ *f* water jug

morma|cento /morma'sẽtu/ *a* sultry. **~ço** *m* sultry weather

morno /'mornu/ *a* lukewarm

moro|sidade /morozi'dadʒi/ *f* slowness. **~so** /o/ *a* slow

morrer /mo'xer/ *vi* die; ‹*luz, dia, ardor, esperança etc*› fade; ‹*carro*› stall

morro /'moxu/ *m* hill; *fig* (*favela*) slum

mortadela /morta'dɛla/ *f* mortadella, salami

mor|tal /mor'taw/ (*pl* **~tais**) *a & m* mortal. **~talha** *f* shroud. **~talidade** *f* mortality. **~tandade** *f* slaughter. **~te** /ɔ/ *f* death. **~tífero** *a* deadly. **~tificar** *vt* mortify. **~to** /o/ *a* dead

mosaico /mo'zajku/ *m* mosaic

mosca /'moska/ *f* fly

Moscou /mos'ku/, *Port* **Moscovo** /moʃ'kovu/ *f* Moscow

mosquito /mos'kitu/ *m* mosquito

mostarda /mos'tarda/ *f* mustard

mosteiro /mos'teru/ *m* monastery

mos|tra /'mɔstra/ *f* display; **dar ~tras de** show signs of; **pôr à ~tra** show up. **~trador** *m* face, dial. **~trar** *vt* show. **~trar-se** *vpr* (*revelar-se*) show o.s. to be; (*exibir-se*) show off. **~truário** *m* display case

mo|tel /mo'tɛw/ (*pl* **~téis**) *m* motel

motim /mo'tʃĩ/ *m* riot; (*na marinha*) mutiny

moti|vação /motʃiva'sãw/ *f* motivation. **~var** *vt* (*incentivar*) motivate; (*provocar*) cause. **~vo** *m* (*razão*) reason; (*estímulo*) motive; (*na arte, música*) motif; **dar ~vo de** give cause for

moto /'mɔtu/ *f* motorbike. **~ca** /mo'tɔka/ *f* [!] motorbike

motoci|cleta /motosi'klɛta/ *f* motorcycle. **~clismo** *m* motorcycling. **~clista** *m/f* motorcyclist

motoqueiro /moto'keru/ *m* [!] biker

motor /mo'tor/ *m* (*de carro, avião etc*) engine; (*elétrico*) motor ● *a* (*f* **motriz**) ‹*força*› driving; *Anat* motor; **~ de arranque** starter motor; **~ de popa** outboard motor

moto|rista /moto'rista/ *m/f* driver. **~rizado** *a* motorized. **~rizar** *vt* motorize

mouse *m Comput* mouse

mousepad *m Comput* mousemat

movedi|ço /move'dʒisu/ *a* unstable, moving; **areia ~ça** quicksand

mó|vel /'mɔvew/ (*pl* **~veis**) *a* ‹*peça, parte*› moving; ‹*tropas*› mobile; ‹*festa*› movable ● *m* piece of furniture; *pl* furniture

mo|ver /mo'ver/ *vt* move; (*impulsionar*) *fig* drive. **~ver-se** *vpr* move. **~vido** *a* driven; **~vido a álcool** alcohol-powered

movimen|tação /movimẽta'sãw/ *f* bustle. **~tado** *a* ‹*rua, loja*› busy; ‹*música*› upbeat, lively; ‹*pessoa, sessão*› lively. **~tar** *vt* liven up. **~tar-se** *vpr* move. **~to** *m* movement; *Tecn* motion; (*na rua etc*) activity

MP3 *m* MP3 player

muam|ba /mu'ãba/ *f* contraband. **~beiro** *m* smuggler

muco /'muku/ *m* mucus

muçulmano /musuw'manu/ *a & m* Muslim

mu|da /'muda/ *f* (*planta*) seedling; **~da de roupa** change of clothes. **~dança** *f* change; (*de casa*) move; (*de carro*) transmission. **~dar** *vt/i* change; **~dar de assunto** change the subject; **~dar (de casa)** move (house); **~dar de cor** change colour; **~dar de ideia** change one's mind; **~dar de lugar** change places; **~dar de roupa** change (clothes). **~dar-se** *vpr* move

mu|dez /mu'des/ *f* silence. **~do** *a* silent; (*deficiente*) dumb; ‹*telefone*› dead ● *m* mute

mu|gido /mu'ʒidu/ *m* moo. **~gir** *vi* moo

muito /'mũitu/ *a* a lot of; *pl* many ● *pron* a lot ● *adv* (*com adjetivo, advérbio*) very; (*com verbo*) a lot; **~ maior** much bigger; **~ tempo** a long time

mula /'mula/ *f* mule

mulato /mu'latu/ *a & m* mulatto

muleta /mu'leta/ *f* crutch

mulher /mu'ʎɛr/ *f* woman; (*esposa*) wife

mulherengo /muʎe'rẽgu/ *a* womanizing ● *m* womanizer, ladies' man

mul|ta /'muwta/ *f* fine. **~tar** *vt* fine

multicolor /muwtʃiko'lor/ *a* multicoloured

multidão /muwtʃi'dãw/ *f* crowd

multinacio|nal /muwtʃinasio'naw/ (*pl* **~nais**) *a & f* multinational

multipli|cação /muwtʃiplika'sãw/ *f* multiplication. **~car** *vt* multiply. **~car-se** *vpr* multiply. **~cidade** *f* multiplicity

múltiplo /'muwtʃiplu/ *a & m* multiple

multirraci|al /muwtʃixasi'aw/ (*pl* **~ais**) *a* multiracial

múmia /'mumia/ *f* mummy

mun|dano /mũ'danu/ *a* ‹*prazeres etc*› worldly; ‹*vida, mulher*› society. **~dial** (*pl* **~diais**) *a* world ● *m* world championship. **~do** *m* world; **todo (o) ~do** everybody

munição /muni'sãw/ *f* ammunition

muni|cipal /munisi'paw/ (*pl* **~cipais**) *a* municipal. **~cípio** *m* (*lugar*) borough, community; (*prédio*) town hall; (*autoridade*) local authority

munir /mu'nir/ *vt* provide (**de** with). **~-se** *vpr* equip o.s. (**de** with)

mu|ral /mu'raw/ (*pl* **~rais**) *a & m* mural. **~ralha** *f* wall

mur|char /mur'ʃar/ *vi* ‹*planta*› wither, wilt; ‹*salada*› go limp; ‹*beleza*› fade ● *vt* wither, wilt ‹*planta*›. **~cho** *a* ‹*planta*› wilting; ‹*pessoa*› broken

mur|murar /murmu'rar/ *vi* murmur; (*queixar-se*) mutter ● *vt* murmur. **~múrio** *m* murmur

muro /'muru/ *m* wall

murro /'muxu/ *m* punch

m

musa /'muza/ *f* muse

muscu|lação /muskula'sãw/ *f* weight training. **~lar** *a* muscular. **~latura** *f* musculature

músculo /'muskulu/ *m* muscle

musculoso /musku'lozu/ *a* muscular

museu /mu'zew/ *m* museum

musgo /'muzgu/ *m* moss

música /'muzika/ *f* music; (*uma*) song; **~ de câmara** chamber music; **~ de fundo** background music; **~ clássica** ou **erudita** classical music

musi|cal /muzi'kaw/ (*pl* **~cais**) *a & m* musical. **~car** *vt* set to music

músico /'muziku/ *m* musician ● *a* musical

musse /'musi/ *f* mousse

mutilar /mutʃi'lar/ *vt* mutilate; maim ‹*pessoa*›

mutirão /mutʃi'rãw/ *m* joint effort

mútuo /'mutuu/ *a* mutual

muxoxo /mu'ʃoʃu/ *m* **fazer ~** tut

Nn

na = **em + a**

nabo /'nabu/ *m* turnip

nação /na'sãw/ *f* nation

nacio|nal /nasio'naw/ (*pl* **~nais**) *a* national; (*brasileiro*) home-produced. **~nalidade** *f* nationality. **~nalismo** *m* nationalism. **~nalista** *a & m/f* nationalist. **~nalizar** *vt* nationalize

naco /'naku/ *m* chunk

nada /'nada/ *pron* nothing ● *adv* not at all; **de ~** (*não há de quê*) don't mention it; **que ~!, ~ disso!** no way!

na|dadeira /nada'dera/ *f* (*de peixe*) fin; (*de mergulhador*) flipper. **~dador** *m* swimmer. **~dar** *vi* swim

nadador-salvador /nada'dorsawva'dor/ *m* (*pl* **nadadores-salvadores**) *Port* lifeguard

nádegas /'nadegas/ *f pl* buttocks

nado /'nadu/ *m* **~ borboleta** butterfly stroke; **~ de costas** backstroke; **~ de peito** breaststroke; **atravessar a ~** swim across

náilon /'najlõ/ *m* nylon

naipe /'najpi/ *m* (*em jogo de cartas*) suit

namo|rada /namo'rada/ *f* girlfriend. **~rado** *m* boyfriend. **~rador** *a* amorous ● *m* ladies' man. **~rar** *vt* (*ter relação com*) go out with; (*cobiçar*) eye up ● *vi* ‹*casal*› (*ter relação*) go out together; (*beijar-se etc*) kiss and cuddle; ‹*homem*› have a girlfriend; ‹*mulher*› have a boyfriend. **~ro** /o/ *m* relationship

nanar /na'nar/ *vi* (*col*) sleep

nanico /na'niku/ *a* tiny

nanotecnologia /nãnoteknolo'ʒia/ *f* nanotechnology

não /nãw/ *adv* not; (*resposta*) no ● *m* no. **~ alinhado** *a* non-aligned; **~ conformista** *a & m/f* nonconformist

naquela, **naquele**, **naquilo** = **em + aquela, aquele, aquilo**

narci|sismo /narsi'zizmu/ *m* narcissism. **~sista** *m/f* narcissist ● *a* narcissistic. **~so** *m* narcissus

narcótico /nar'kɔtʃiku/ *a & m* narcotic

narcotraficante /narkotrafi'kãntʃi/ *m/f* drug dealer

narcotráfico /narko'trafiku/ *m* drug trafficking

nari|gudo /nari'gudu/ *a* with a big nose; **ser ~gudo** have a big nose. **~na** *f* nostril

nariz /na'ris/ *m* nose

nar|ração /naxa'sãw/ *f* narration. **~rador** *m* narrator. **~rar** *vt* narrate. **~rativa** *f* narrative. **~rativo** *a* narrative

nas = **em + as**

na|sal /na'zaw/ (*pl* **~sais**) *a* nasal. **~salizar** *vt* nasalize

nas|cença /na'sẽsa/ *f* birth. **~cente** *a* nascent ● *f* source. **~cer** *vi* be born; ‹*dente, espinha*› grow; ‹*planta*› sprout; ‹*sol, lua*› rise; ‹*dia*› dawn; *fig* ‹*empresa, projeto etc*› come into being ● *m* **o ~cer do sol** sunrise. **~cimento** *m* birth

nata /'nata/ *f* cream

natação /nata'sãw/ *f* swimming

na|tal /na'taw/ (*pl* **~tais**) *a* ‹*país, terra*› native

Natal /na'taw/ *m* Christmas

nata|lício /nata'lisiu/ *a & m* birthday. **~lidade** *f* **índice de ~lidade** birth rate. **~lino** *a* Christmas

nati|vidade /natʃivi'dadʒi/ *f* nativity. **~vo** *a & m* native

nato /'natu/ *a* born

natu|ral /natu'raw/ (*pl* **~rais**) *a* natural; (*oriundo*) originating (**de** from) ● *m* native (**de** of)

natura|lidade /naturali'dadʒi/ *f* naturalness; **com ~lidade** matter-of-factly; **de ~lidade carioca** born in Rio de Janeiro. **~lismo** *m* naturalism. **~lista** *a & m/f* naturalist. **~lizar** *vt* naturalize. **~lizar-se** *vpr* become naturalized

natureza /natu'reza/ *f* nature; **~ morta** still life

naturis|mo /natu'rizmu/ *m* naturism. **~ta** *m/f* naturist

nau|fragar /nawfra'gar/ *vi* ‹*navio*› be wrecked; ‹*tripulação*› be shipwrecked; *fig* ‹*plano, casamento etc*› founder. **~frágio** *m* shipwreck; *fig* failure

náufrago /'nawfragu/ *m* castaway

náusea /'nawzia/ *f* nausea

nauseabundo /nawzia'bũdu/ *a* nauseating

náuti|ca /'nawtʃika/ *f* navigation. **~co** *a* nautical

na|val /na'vaw/ (*pl* **~vais**) *a* naval; **construção ~val** shipbuilding

navalha /na'vaʎa/ *f* razor. **~da** *f* cut with a razor

nave /'navi/ *f* nave; **~ espacial** spaceship

nave|gação /navega'sãw/ *f* navigation; (*tráfego*) shipping. **~gador** *m* navigator; *Comput* browser. **~gante** *m/f* seafarer. **~gar** *vt* navigate; sail ‹*mar*› ● *vi* sail; (*traçar o rumo*) navigate. **~gável** (*pl* **~gáveis**) *a* navigable

navio /na'viu/ *m* ship; **~ cargueiro** cargo ship; **~ de guerra** warship; **~ petroleiro** oil tanker

nazista /na'zista/, *Port* **nazi** /na'zi/ *a & m/f* Nazi

neblina /ne'blina/ *f* mist

nebulo|sa /nebu'lɔza/ *f* nebula. **~sidade** *f* cloud. **~so** /o/ *a* cloudy; *fig* obscure

neces|saire /nese'sɛr/ *m* toilet bag. **~sário** *a* necessary. **~sidade** *f* necessity; (*que se impõe*) need; (*pobreza*) need. **~sitado** *a* needy ● *m* person in need. **~sitar** *vt* require; (*tornar necessário*) necessitate; **~sitar de** need

necro|lógio /nekro'lɔʒiu/ *m* obituary column. **~tério** *m* mortuary, *Amer* morgue

nectarina /nekta'rina/ *f* nectarine

nefasto /ne'fastu/ *a* fatal

ne|gação /nega'sãw/ *f* denial; *Ling* negation; **ser uma ~gação em** be hopeless at. **~gar** *vt* deny; **~gar-se a** refuse to. **~gativa** *f* refusal; *Ling* negative. **~gativo** *a & m* negative

negli|gência /negli'ʒẽsia/ *f* negligence. **~genciar** *vt* neglect. **~gente** *a* negligent

negoci|ação /negosia'sãw/ *f* negotiation. **~ador** *m* negotiator. **~ante** *m/f* dealer (**de** in). **~ar** *vt/i* negotiate; **~ar em** deal in. **~ata** *f* shady deal. **~ável** (*pl* **~áveis**) *a* negotiable

negócio /ne'gɔsiu/ *m* deal; [!] (*coisa*) thing; *pl* business; **a** ou **de ~s** on business

negocista /nego'sista/ *m* wheeler-dealer ● *a* wheeler-dealing

ne|grito /ne'gritu/ *m* bold. **~gro** /e/ *a & m* black; (*de raça*) Negro

nela, **nele** = **em + ela, ele**

nem /nẽj/ *adv* not even ● *conj* **~ ... ~ ...** neither ... nor ...; **~ sempre** not always; **~ todos** not all; **~ que** not even if; **que ~** like; **~ eu** nor do I

nenê /ne'ne/, **neném** /ne'nẽj/ *m* baby

nenhum /ne'ɲũ/ *a* (*f* **nenhuma**) no ● *pron* (*f* **nenhuma**) not one; **~ dos dois** neither of them; **~ erro** no mistakes; **erro ~** no mistakes at all, not a single mistake; **~ lugar** nowhere

nenúfar /ne'nufar/ *m* water lily

neoconservador /neokõserva'dor/ *a* neoconservative

neologismo /neolo'ʒizmu/ *m* neologism

néon /'nɛõ/ *m* neon

neozelan|dês /neozelã'des/ *a* (*f* **~desa**) New Zealand ● *m* (*f* **~desa**) New Zealander

Nepal /ne'paw/ *m* Nepal

nervo /'nervu/ *m* nerve. **~sismo** *m* (*chateação*) annoyance; (*medo*) nervousness. **~so** /o/ *a* ‹*sistema, doença*› nervous; (*chateado*) annoyed; (*medroso*) nervous; **deixar alguém ~so** get on sb's nerves

nessa(s), **nesse(s)** = **em + essa(s), esse(s)**

nesta(s), **neste(s)** = **em + esta(s), este(s)**

ne|ta /'nɛta/ *f* granddaughter. **~to** /ɛ/ *m* grandson; *pl* grandchildren

neuro|logia /newrolo'ʒia/ *f* neurology. **~lógico** *a* neurological. **~logista** *m/f* neurologist

neu|rose /new'rɔzi/ *f* neurosis. **~rótico** *a* neurotic

neutrali|dade /newtrali'dadʒi/ *f* neutrality. **~zar** *vt* neutralize

neutrão /new'trãw/ *m Port* ▶ **NÊUTRON**

n

neutro /'newtru/ *a* neutral

nêutron /'newtrõ/ *m* neutron

ne|vada /ne'vada/ *f* snowfall. **~vado** *a* snow-covered. **~var** *vi* snow. **~vasca** *f* snowstorm. **~ve** /ɛ/ *f* snow

névoa /'nɛvoa/ *f* haze

nevoeiro /nevo'eru/ *m* fog

nexo /'nɛksu/ *m* connection; **sem ~** incoherent

Nicarágua /nika'ragwa/ *f* Nicaragua

nicaraguense /nikara'gwẽsi/ *a & m/f* Nicaraguan

nicho /'niʃu/ *m* niche

nicotina /niko'tʃina/ *f* nicotine

Níger /'niʒer/ *m* Niger

Nigéria /ni'ʒɛria/ *f* Nigeria

nigeriano /niʒeri'anu/ *a & m* Nigerian

Nilo /'nilu/ *m* Nile

ninar /ni'nar/ *vt* lull to sleep

ninfa /'nĩfa/ *f* nymph

ninguém /nĩ'gẽj/ *pron* no one, nobody

ninhada /ni'ɲada/ *f* brood

ninharia /niɲa'ria/ *f* trifle

ninho /'niɲu/ *m* nest

níquel /'nikew/ *m* nickel

nisei /ni'sej/ *a & m/f* Japanese Brazilian

nisso = **em + isso**

nisto = **em + isto**

nitidez /nitʃi'des/ *f* (*de imagem etc*) sharpness

nítido /'nitʃidu/ *a* ‹*imagem, foto*› sharp; ‹*diferença, melhora*› distinct, clear

nitrogênio /nitro'ʒeniu/ *m* nitrogen

ní|vel /'nivew/ (*pl* **~veis**) *m* level; **a ~vel de** in terms of

nivelamento /nivela'mẽtu/ *m* levelling

nivelar /nive'lar/ *vt* level

no = **em + o**

nó /nɔ/ *m* knot; **dar um ~** tie a knot; **~ dos dedos** knuckle; **um ~ na garganta** a lump in one's throat

nobre /'nɔbri/ *a* noble; ‹*bairro*› exclusive ● *m/f* noble. **~za** /e/ *f* nobility

noção /no'sãw/ *f* notion; *pl* (*rudimentos*) elements

nocaute /no'kawtʃi/ *m* knockout; **pôr alguém ~** knock sb out. **~ar** *vt* knock out

nocivo /no'sivu/ *a* harmful

nódoa /'nodoa/ *f Port* stain

nogueira /no'gera/ *f* (*árvore*) walnut tree

noi|tada /noj'tada/ *f* night. **~te** *f* night; (*antes de dormir*) evening; **à** ou **de ~te** at night; (*antes de dormir*) in the evening; **hoje à ~te** tonight; **ontem à ~te** last night; **boa ~te** (*ao chegar*) good evening; (*ao despedir-se*) good night; **~te em branco** ou **claro** sleepless night

noi|vado /noj'vadu/ *m* engagement. **~va** *f* fiancée; (*no casamento*) bride. **~vo** *m* fiancé; (*no casamento*) bridegroom; **os ~vos** the engaged couple; (*no casamento*) the bride and groom; **ficar ~vo** get engaged

no|jento /no'ʒẽtu/ *a* disgusting. **~jo** /o/ *m* disgust

nômade /'nomadʒi/ *m/f* nomad ● *a* nomadic

nome /'nomi/ *m* name; **de ~** by name; **em ~ de** in the name of; **~ comercial** trade name; **~ de batismo** Christian name; **~ de guerra** professional name

nome|ação /nomia'sãw/ *f* appointment. **~ar** *vt* (*para cargo*) appoint; (*chamar pelo nome*) name

nomi|nal /nomi'naw/ (*pl* **~nais**) *a* nominal

nonagésimo /nona'ʒɛzimu/ *a* ninetieth

nono /'nonu/ *a & m* ninth

nora /'nɔra/ *f* daughter-in-law

nordes|te /nor'dɛstʃi/ *m* north-east. **~tino** *a* north-eastern ● *m* person from the north-east (of Brazil)

nórdico /'nɔrdʒiku/ *a* Nordic

nor|ma /'nɔrma/ *f* norm. **~mal** (*pl* **~mais**) *a* normal

normali|dade /normali'dadʒi/ *f* normality. **~zar** *vt* bring back to normal; normalize ‹*relações diplomáticas*›. **~zar-se** *vpr* return to normal

noroeste /noro'ɛstʃi/ *a & m* north-west

norte /'nɔrtʃi/ *a & m* north. **~-africano** *a & m* North African; **~-americano** *a & m* North American; **~-coreano** *a & m* North Korean

nortista /nor'tʃista/ *a* Northern ● *m/f* Northerner

Noruega /noru'ɛga/ *f* Norway

norue|guês /norue'ges/ *a & m* (*f* **~guesa**) Norwegian

nos[1] = **em + os**

nos[2] /nus/ *pron* us; (*indireto*) (to) us; (*reflexivo*) ourselves

nós /nɔs/ *pron* we; (*depois de preposição*) us

nos|sa /'nɔsa/ *int* gosh. **~so** /ɔ/ *a* our ● *pron* ours

nos|talgia /nostaw'ʒia/ *f* nostalgia. **~tálgico** *a* nostalgic

nota /'nɔta/ *f* note; (*na escola etc*) mark; (*conta*) bill; **custar uma ~ (preta)** [!] cost a bomb; **tomar ~** take note (**de** of); **~ fiscal** receipt

no|tação /nota'sãw/ *f* notation. **~tar** *vt* notice, note; **fazer ~tar** point out. **~tável** (*pl* **~táveis**) *a & m/f* notable

notícia /no'tʃisia/ *f* piece of news; *pl* news

notici|ar /notʃi'sjar/ *vt* report. **~ário** *m* (*na TV*) news; (*em jornal*) news section. **~arista** *m/f* (*na TV*) newsreader; (*em jornal*) news reporter. **~oso** /o/ *a* **agência ~osa** news agency

notifi|cação /notʃifika'sãw/ *f* notification. **~car** *vt* notify

notívago /no'tʃivagu/ *a* nocturnal ● *m* night person

notório /no'tɔriu/ *a* well-known

noturno /no'turnu/ *a* night; ‹*animal*› nocturnal

nova /'nɔva/ *f* piece of news. **~mente** *adv* again

novato /no'vatu/ *m* novice

nove /'nɔvi/ *a & m* nine. **~centos** *a & m* nine hundred

novela /no'vɛla/ *f* (*na TV*) soap opera; (*livro*) novella

novembro /no'vẽbru/ *m* November

noventa /no'vẽta/ *a & m* ninety

noviço /no'visu/ *m* novice

novidade /novi'dadʒi/ *f* novelty; (*notícia*) piece of news; *pl* (*notícias*) news

novilho /no'viʎu/ *m* calf

novo /'novu/ *a* new; (*jovem*) young; **de ~** again; **~ em folha** brand new

noz /nɔs/ *f* walnut; **~ moscada** nutmeg

nu /nu/ *a* (*f* **~a**) ‹*corpo, pessoa*› naked; ‹*braço, parede, quarto*› bare ● *m* nude; **~ em pelo** stark naked; **a verdade ~a e crua** the plain truth

nuança /nu'ãsa/ *f* nuance

nu|blado /nu'bladu/ *a* cloudy. **~blar** *vt* cloud. **~blar-se** *vpr* cloud over

nuca /'nuka/ *f* nape of the neck

nuclear /nukli'ar/ *a* nuclear

núcleo /'nukliu/ *m* nucleus

nu|dez /nu'des/ *f* nakedness; (*na TV etc*) nudity; (*da parede etc*) bareness. **~dismo** *m* nudism. **~dista** *m/f* nudist

nulo /'nulu/ *a* void

num, numa(s) = em + um, uma(s)

nume|ral /nume'raw/ (*pl* **~rais**) *a & m* numeral. **~rar** *vt* number

numérico /nu'mɛriku/ *a* numerical

número /'numeru/ *m* number; (*de jornal, revista*) issue; (*de sapatos*) size; (*espetáculo*) act; **fazer ~** make up the numbers

numeroso /nume'rozu/ *a* numerous

nunca /'nũka/ *adv* never; **~ mais** never again

nuns = em + uns

nupci|al /nupsi'aw/ (*pl* **~ais**) *a* bridal

núpcias /'nupsias/ *f pl* marriage

nu|trição /nutri'sãw/ *f* nutrition. **~trir** *vt* nourish; *fig* harbour ‹*ódio, esperança*›. **~tritivo** *a* nourishing; ‹*valor*› nutritional

nuvem /'nuvẽ/ *f* cloud

Oo

o /u/ ● *artigo*

····➤ the; **~ trem** the train; **~ vizinho ao lado** the next-door neighbour; **~ João está em casa** João is at home

! O artigo é omitido em inglês com nomes próprios, ou com parentes: **o vovô já chegou** *granddad has arrived*; **onde está o Carlos?** *where's Carlos?*

····➤ (*com partes do corpo, roupa*) **lavei ~ cabelo** I washed my hair; **~ sapato está desamarrado** your shoe is undone

! Em português, utiliza-se em geral o artigo para se referir a partes do corpo, enquanto no inglês usa-se o pronome possessivo.

····➤ (*com adjetivo*) **~ interessante...** what's interesting...; **~ difícil é...** the difficult thing is...

····➤ (*com substantivo abstrato*) **~ amor** love; **~ sucesso** success; **~ conhecimento** knowledge

····➤ (*com substantivo usado em sentido geral*) **na prisão** in jail; **no hospital** in hospital

! Observe que o artigo não é traduzido com substantivos abstratos ou substantivos usados em sentido geral: **ele está no hospital** *he's in hospital*.

n o

● *pron*

····➤ (*ele*) him; **eu ~ vi no sábado à tarde** I saw him on Saturday afternoon

····➤ (*coisa*) it; **onde é que você ~ guarda** where do you keep it?

····➤ (*você*) you; **eu ~ avisei?** I told you so!

····➤ **~ de** (*com características, procedência*) the one with/from; **~ de barba** the one with the beard; **~ do Rio** the one from Rio; **~ que** (*pessoa*) the one; **~ que eu vi era mais alto** the one I saw was taller; (*quem quer que*) whoever; **~ que chegar primeiro faz o café** whoever gets there first has to make the coffee; **~ que** (*como*) what; **nem imagina ~ que foi aquilo** you can't imagine what it was like; **~ que** (*referindo-se a toda a frase anterior*) which; **ele disse que era professor, ~ que não é verdade** he said he was a teacher, which isn't true

ó /ɔ/ *int* [I] look

ô /o/ *int* oh

oásis /o'azis/ *m invar* oasis

oba /'oba/ *int* great

obcecar /obise'kar/ *vt* obsess

obe|decer /obede'ser/ *vt* **~decer a** obey. **~diência** *f* obedience. **~diente** *a* obedient

obe|sidade /obezi'dadʒi/ *f* obesity. **~so** /e/ *a* obese

óbito /'ɔbitu/ *m* death

obituário /obitu'ariu/ *m* obituary

obje|ção /obiʒe'sãw/ *f* objection. **~tar** *vt/i* object (**a** to)

objeti|va /obiʒe'tʃiva/ *f* lens. **~vidade** *f* objectivity. **~vo** *a & m* objective

objeto /obi'ʒɛtu/ *m* object

objetor /obʒɛ'toɾ/ *m* objector; **~ de consciência** conscientious objector

oblíquo /o'blikwu/ *a* oblique; ‹*olhar*› sidelong

obliterar /oblite'rar/ *vt* obliterate

oblongo /o'blõgu/ *a* oblong

obo|é /obo'ɛ/ *m* oboe. **~ísta** *m/f* oboist

obra /'ɔbra/ *f* work; **em ~s** being renovated; **~ de arte** work of art; **~ de caridade** charity. **~-prima** (*pl* **~s-primas**) *f* masterpiece

obri|gação /obriga'sãw/ *f* obligation; (*título*) bond. **~gado** *int* thank you; (*não querendo*) no thank you. **~gar** *vt* force, oblige (**a** to). **~gar-se** *vpr* undertake (**a** to). **~gatório** *a* obligatory, compulsory

obsce|nidade /obiseni'dadʒi/ *f* obscenity. **~no** /e/ *a* obscene

obscu|ridade /obiskuri'dadʒi/ *f* obscurity. **~ro** *a* obscure

obséquio /obi'sɛkiu/ *m* favour

obsequioso /obiseki'ozu/ *a* obsequious

obser|vação /obiserva'sãw/ *f* observation. **~vador** *a* observant ● *m* observer. **~vância** *f* observance. **~var** *vt* observe. **~vatório** *m* observatory

obses|são /obise'sãw/ *f* obsession. **~sivo** *a* obsessive

obsoleto /obiso'letu/ *a* obsolete

obstáculo /obis'takulu/ *m* obstacle

obstar /obis'tar/ *vt* stand in the way (**a** of)

obs|tetra /obis'tɛtra/ *m/f* obstetrician. **~tetrícia** *f* obstetrics. **~tétrico** *a* obstetric

obsti|nação /obistina'sãw/ *f* obstinacy. **~nado** *a* obstinate. **~nar-se** *vpr* insist (**em** on)

obstru|ção /obistru'sãw/ *f* obstruction. **~ir** *vt* obstruct

ob|tenção /obitẽ'sãw/ *f* obtaining. **~ter** *vt* obtain

obtu|ração /obitura'sãw/ *f* filling. **~rador** *m* shutter. **~rar** *vt* fill ‹*dente*›

obtuso /obi'tuzu/ *a* obtuse

óbvio /'ɔbviu/ *a* obvious

ocasi|ão /okazi'ãw/ *f* occasion; (*oportunidade*) opportunity; (*compra*) bargain. **~onal** (*pl* **~onais**) *a* chance. **~onar** *vt* cause

Oceania /osia'nia/ *f* Oceania

oce|ânico /osi'aniku/ *a* ocean. **~ano** *m* ocean

ociden|tal /osidẽ'taw/ (*pl* **~tais**) *a* western ● *m/f* Westerner. **~te** *m* West

ócio /'ɔsiu/ *m* (*lazer*) leisure; (*falta de trabalho*) idleness

ocioso /osi'ozu/ *a* idle ● *m* idler

oco /'oku/ *a* hollow; ‹*cabeça*› empty

ocor|rência /oko'xẽsia/ *f* occurrence. **~rer** *vi* occur (**a** to)

ocu|lar /oku'lar/ *a* **testemunha ~lar** eye witness. **~lista** *m/f* optician

óculos /'ɔkulus/ *m pl* glasses; **~ de sol** sunglasses

ocul|tar /okuw'tar/ *vt* conceal. **~to** *a* hidden; (*sobrenatural*) occult

ocu|pação /okupa'sãw/ *f* occupation. **~pado** *a* ‹*pessoa*› busy; ‹*cadeira*› taken; ‹*telefone*› engaged, *Amer* busy. **~par** *vt* occupy; take up ‹*tempo, espaço*›; hold ‹*cargo*›. **~par-se** *vpr* keep busy; **~par-se com** ou **de** be involved with ‹*política, literatura etc*›; take care of ‹*cliente, doente, problema*›; occupy one's time with ‹*leitura, palavras cruzadas etc*›

ocupacional /okupasio'naw/ *a* occupational; **terapia ~** occupational therapy

odiar /odʒi'ar/ *vt* hate

ódio /'ɔdʒiu/ *m* hatred, hate; (*raiva*) anger

odioso /odʒi'ozu/ *a* hateful

odontologia /odõtolo'ʒia/ *f* dentistry

odor /o'dor/ *m* odour

oeste /o'ɛstʃi/ *a & m* west

ofe|gante /ofe'gãtʃi/ *a* panting. **~gar** *vi* pant

ofen|der /ofẽ'der/ *vt* offend. **~der-se** *vpr* take offence. **~sa** *f* insult. **~siva** *f* offensive. **~sivo** *a* offensive

ofere|cer /ofere'ser/ *vt* offer. **~cer-se** *vpr* ‹*pessoa*› offer o.s. (**como** as); ‹*ocasião*› arise; **~cer-se para ajudar** offer to help. **~cimento** *m* offer

oferenda /ofe'rẽda/ *f* offering

oferta /o'fɛrta/ *f* offer; **em ~** on offer; **a ~ e a demanda** supply and demand

offline /of'lajni/ *a & adv Comput* offline

ofici|al /ofisi'aw/ (*pl* **~ais**) *a* official ● *m* officer. **~alizar** *vt* make official. **~ar** *vi* officiate

oficina /ofi'sina/ *f* workshop; (*para carros*) garage, *Amer* shop

ofício /o'fisiu/ *m* (*profissão*) trade; (*na igreja*) service

oficioso /ofisi'ozu/ *a* unofficial

ofus|cante /ofus'kãtʃi/ *a* dazzling. **~car** *vt* dazzle ‹*pessoa*›; obscure ‹*sol etc*›; *fig* (*eclipsar*) outshine

OGM /oʒe'ɛm/ *m Biol* GMO

oi /oj/ *int* (*cumprimento*) hi; (*resposta*) yes?

oi|tavo /oi'tavu/ *a & m* eighth. **~tenta** *a & m* eighty. **~to** *a & m* eight. **~tocentos** *a & m* eight hundred

olá /o'la/ *int* hello

olaria /ola'ria/ *f* pottery

óleo /'ɔliu/ *m* oil

oleo|duto /oliu'dutu/ *m* oil pipeline. **~so** /o/ *a* oily

olfato /ow'fatu/ *m* sense of smell

olhada /o'ʎada/ *f* look; **dar uma ~** have a look

olhar /o'ʎar/ *vt* look at; (*assistir*) watch ● *vi* look ● *m* look; **~ para** look at; **~ por** look after; **e olhe lá** [!] and that's pushing it

olheiras /o'ʎeras/ *f pl* dark rings under one's eyes

olho /'oʎu/ *m* eye; **a ~ nu** with the naked eye; **custar os ~s da cara** cost a fortune; **ficar de ~** keep an eye out; **ficar de ~ em** keep an eye on; **pôr alguém no ~ da rua** throw sb out; **não pregar o ~** not sleep a wink; **~ gordo** ou **grande** envy; **~ mágico** peephole; **~ roxo** black eye

Olimpíada /olĩ'piada/ *f* Olympic Games

olímpico /o'lĩpiku/ *a* ‹*jogos, vila*› Olympic; *fig* blithe

oliveira /oli'vera/ *f* olive tree

olmo /'owmu/ *m* elm

om|breira /õ'brera/ *f* (*para roupa*) shoulder pad; **~bro** *m* shoulder; **dar de ~bros** shrug one's shoulders

omelete /ome'lɛtʃi/, *Port* **omeleta** /ome'leta/ *f* omelette

omis|são /omi'sãw/ *f* omission. **~so** *a* negligent, remiss

omitir /omi'tʃir/ *vt* omit

omni- *Port* ▶ **oni-**

omoplata /omo'plata/ *f* shoulder blade

onça[1] /'õsa/ *f* (*peso*) ounce

onça[2] /'õsa/ *f* (*animal*) jaguar

onda /'õda/ *f* wave. **pegar ~** [!] surf

onde /'õdʒi/ *adv* where; **por ~?** which way?; **~ quer que** wherever

ondu|lação /õdula'sãw/ *f* undulation; (*do cabelo*) wave. **~lado** *a* wavy. **~lante** *a* undulating. **~lar** *vt* wave ‹*cabelo*› ● *vi* undulate

onerar /one'rar/ *vt* burden

ONG /'õgi/ *abr f* (= **Organização Não Governamental**) NGO

ônibus /'onibus/ *m invar* bus; **~ espacial** space shuttle

onipotente /onipo'tẽtʃi/ *a* omnipotent

onírico /o'niriku/ *a* dreamlike

onisciente /onisi'ẽtʃi/ *a* omniscient

online /õ'lajni/ *a & adv Comput* online

onomatopeia /onomato'pɛja/ *f* onomatopoeia

ontem /'õtẽ/ *adv* yesterday

onze /'õzi/ *a & m* eleven

opaco /o'paku/ *a* opaque

opala /o'pala/ *f* opal

opção /opi'sãw/ *f* option

ópera /'ɔpera/ *f* opera

ope|ração /opera'sãw/ *f* operation; (*bancária etc*) transaction. **~rador** *m* operator. **~rar** *vt* operate; operate on ‹*doente*›; work ‹*milagre*› ● *vi* operate. **~rar-se** *vpr* (*acontecer*) come about; (*fazer operação*) have an operation. **~rário** *a* working ● *m* worker

opereta /ope'reta/ *f* operetta

opinar /opi'nar/ *vt* think ● *vi* express one's opinion

opinião /opini'ãw/ *f* opinion; **na minha ~** in my opinion; **~ pública** public opinion

ópio /'ɔpiu/ *m* opium

opor /o'por/ *vt* put up ‹*resistência, argumento*›; (*pôr em contraste*) contrast (**a** with); **~-se a** (*não aprovar*) oppose; (*ser diferente*) contrast with

oportu|nidade /oportuni'dadʒi/ *f* opportunity. **~nista** *a & m/f* opportunist. **~no** *a* opportune

oposi|ção /opozi'sãw/ *f* opposition (**a** to). **~cionista** *a* opposition ● *m/f* opposition politician

oposto /o'postu/ *a & m* opposite

O

opres|são /opre'sãw/ *f* oppression; (*no peito*) tightness. **~sivo** *a* oppressive. **~sor** *m* oppressor

oprimir /opri'mir/ *vt* oppress; (*com trabalho*) weigh down ● *vi* be oppressive

optar /opi'tar/ *vi* opt (**por** for); **~ por ir** opt to go

óptica, **óptico** ▶ **ótica**, **ótico**

opu|lência /opu'lẽsia/ *f* opulence. **~lento** *a* opulent

ora /'ɔra/ *adv & conj* now ● *int* come; **~ essa!** come now! **~ ..., ~ ...** first ..., then...

oração /ora'sãw/ *f* (*prece*) prayer; (*discurso*) oration; (*frase*) clause

oráculo /o'rakulu/ *m* oracle

orador /ora'dor/ *m* orator

oral /o'raw/ (*pl* **orais**) *a & f* oral

orar /o'rar/ *vi* pray

órbita /'ɔrbita/ *f* orbit; (*do olho*) socket

orçamen|tário /orsamẽ'tariu/ *a* budgetary. **~to** *m* (*plano financeiro*) budget; (*previsão dos custos*) estimate

orçar /or'sar/ *vt* estimate (**em** at)

ordeiro /or'deru/ *a* orderly

ordem /'ɔrdẽ/ *f* order; **por ~ alfabética** in alphabetical order; **~ de pagamento** banker's draft; **~ do dia** agenda

orde|nação /ordena'sãw/ *f* ordering; (*de padre*) ordination. **~nado** *a* ordered ● *m* wages. **~nar** *vt* order; put in order ‹*papéis, livros etc*›; ordain ‹*padre*›

ordenhar /orde'ɲar/ *vt* milk

ordinário /ordʒi'nariu/ *a* (*normal*) ordinary; (*grosseiro*) vulgar; (*de má qualidade*) inferior; (*sem caráter*) rough

ore|lha /o'reʎa/ *f* ear. **~lhão** *m* phone booth. **~lhudo** *a* with big ears; **ser ~lhudo** have big ears

orfanato /orfa'natu/ *m* orphanage

ór|fão /'ɔrfãw/ (*pl* **~fãos**) *a & m* (*f* **~fã**) orphan

orgânico /or'ganiku/ *a* organic

orga|nismo /orga'nizmu/ *m* organism; (*do Estado etc*) institution; **~ geneticamente modificado** GMO. **~nista** *m/f* organist

organi|zação /organiza'sãw/ *f* organization. **~zador** *a* organizing ● *m* organizer. **~zar** *vt* organize

órgão /'ɔrgãw/ (*pl* **~s**) *m* organ; (*do Estado etc*) body

orgasmo /or'gazmu/ *m* orgasm

orgia /or'ʒia/ *f* orgy

orgu|lhar /orgu'ʎar/ *vt* make proud. **~lhar-se** *vpr* be proud (**de** of). **~lho** *m* pride. **~lhoso** /o/ *a* proud

orien|tação /oriẽta'sãw/ *f* orientation; (*direção*) direction; (*vocacional etc*) guidance. **~tador** *m* advisor. **~tal** (*pl* **~tais**) *a* eastern; (*da Asia*) oriental. **~tar** *vt* direct; (*aconselhar*) advise; (*situar*) position. **~tar-se** *vpr* get one's bearings; **~tar-se por** be guided by. **~te** *m* east; **Oriente Médio** Middle East; **Extremo Oriente** Far East

orifício /ori'fisiu/ *m* opening; (*no corpo*) orifice

origem /o'riʒẽ/ *f* origin; **dar ~ a** give rise to; **ter ~** originate

origi|nal /oriʒi'naw/ (*pl* **~nais**) *a & m* original. **~nalidade** *f* originality. **~nar** *vt* give rise to. **~nar-se** *vpr* originate. **~nário** *a* ‹*planta, animal*› native (**de** to); ‹*pessoa*› originating (**de** from)

oriundo /o'rjũdu/ *a* originating (**de** from)

orla /'ɔrla/ *f* border; **~ marítima** seafront

ornamen|tação /ornamẽta'sãw/ *f* ornamentation. **~tal** (*pl* **~tais**) *a* ornamental. **~tar** *vt* decorate. **~to** *m* ornament

orques|tra /or'kɛstra/ *f* orchestra. **~tra sinfônica** symphony orchestra. **~tral** (*pl* **~trais**) *a* orchestral. **~trar** *vt* orchestrate

orquídea /or'kidʒia/ *f* orchid

ortodoxo /orto'dɔksu/ *a* orthodox

orto|grafia /ortogra'fia/ *f* spelling, orthography. **~gráfico** *a* orthographic

orto|pedia /ortope'dʒia/ *f* orthopaedics. **~pédico** *a* orthopaedic. **~pedista** *m/f* orthopaedic surgeon

orvalho /or'vaʎu/ *m* dew

os /us/, **as** /as/ ● *artigo*

····➤ the; **os livros que comprei ontem** the books I bought yesterday

● *pron*

····➤ them; **eu os/as vi no cinema** I saw them at the cinema; **os/as de** (*características, procedência*) the ones with/from; **os de branco** the ones in white; **as de Salvador** the ones from Salvador; **os da minha avó** my grandmother's ▶ **o**

oscilar /osi'lar/ *vi* oscillate

ósseo /'ɔsiu/ *a* bone

os|so /'osu/ *m* bone. **~sudo** *a* bony

ostensivo /ostẽ'sivu/ *a* ostensible

osten|tação /ostẽta'sãw/ *f* ostentation. **~tar** *vt* show off. **~toso** *a* showy, ostentatious

osteopata /ostʃio'pata/ *m/f* osteopath

ostra /'ostra/ *f* oyster

ostracismo /ostra'sizmu/ *m* ostracism

otário /o'tariu/ *m* [!] fool

óti|ca /'ɔtʃika/ *f* (*ciência*) optics; (*loja*) optician's; (*ponto de vista*) viewpoint. **~co** *a* optical

otimis|mo /otʃi'mizmu/ *m* optimism. **~ta** *m/f* optimist ● *a* optimistic

otimizar /otʃimi'zar/ *vt* optimize

ótimo /'otʃimu/ *a* excellent

otorrino /oto'xinu/ *m* ear, nose and throat specialist

ou /o/ *conj* or; **~ ... ~ ...** either ... or ...; **~ seja** in other words

ouriço /o'risu/ *m* hedgehog. **~-do-mar** (*pl* **~s-do-mar**) *m* sea urchin

ouri|ves /o'rivis/ *m/f invar* jeweller. **~vesaria** *f* (*loja*) jeweller's

ouro /'oru/ *m* gold; *pl* (*naipe*) diamonds; **de ~** golden

ou|sadia /oza'dʒia/ *f* daring; (*uma*) daring step. **~sado** *a* daring. **~sar** *vt/i* dare

outdoor /'awtdor/ (*pl* **~s**) *m* billboard

outo|nal /oto'naw/ (*pl* **~nais**) *a* autumnal. **~no** /o/ *m* autumn, *Amer* fall

outorgar /otor'gar/ *vt* grant

ou|trem /o'trẽj/ *pron* (*outro*) someone else; (*outros*) others. **~tro** *a* other ● *pron* (*um*) another (one); *pl* others; **~tra coisa** something else; **~tro dia** the other day; **no ~tro dia** the next day; **~tra vez** again. **~tro copo** another glass. **~trora** *adv* once upon a time. **~trossim** *adv* equally

outubro /o'tubru/ *m* October

ou|vido /o'vidu/ *m* ear; **de ~vido** by ear; **dar ~vidos a** listen to. **~vinte** *m/f* listener. **~vir** *vt* hear; (*atentamente*) listen to ● *vi* hear; **~vir dizer que** hear that; **~vir falar de** hear of

ovação /ova'sãw/ *f* ovation

oval /o'vaw/ (*pl* **ovais**) *a* & *f* oval

ovário /o'variu/ *m* ovary

ovelha /o'veʎa/ *f* sheep

overdose /over'dɔzi/ *f* overdose

óvni /'ɔvni/ *m* UFO

ovo /'ovu/ *m* egg; **~ cozido/frito/mexido/pochê** boiled/fried/scrambled/poached egg

oxi|genar /oksiʒe'nar/ *vt* bleach ‹*cabelo*›. **~gênio** *m* oxygen

ozônio /o'zoniu/ *m* ozone; **camada de ~** ozone layer

ozono /o'zonu/ *m Port* ▶ **ozônio** /o'zonju/

Pp

pá /pa/ *f* spade; (*de hélice*) blade; (*de moinho*) sail ● *m Port* [!] mate

pacato /pa'katu/ *a* quiet

pachorra /pa'ʃoxa/ *f Port* [!] patience; **não tenho ~** I can't be bothered

paci|ência /pasi'ẽsia/ *f* patience. **~ente** *a* & *m/f* patient

pacificar /pasifi'kar/ *vt* pacify

pacífico /pa'sifiku/ *a* peaceful; **Oceano Pacífico** Pacific Ocean; **ponto ~** undisputed point

pacifis|mo /pasi'fizmu/ *m* pacifism. **~ta** *a* & *m/f* pacifist

paço /'pasu/ *m* palace

pacote /pa'kɔtʃi/ *m* (*de biscoitos etc*) packet; (*mandado pelo correio*) parcel; (*econômico, turístico, software*) package

pacto /'paktu/ *m* pact

pactuar /paktu'ar/ *vi* **~ com** collude with

padaria /pada'ria/ *f* baker's (shop), bakery

padecer /pade'ser/ *vt/i* suffer

padeiro /pa'deru/ *m* baker

padiola /padʒi'ɔla/ *f* stretcher

padrão /pa'drãw/ *m* standard; (*desenho*) pattern

padrasto /pa'drastu/ *m* stepfather

padre /'padri/ *m* priest

padrinho /pa'driɲu/ *m* (*de batismo*) godfather; (*de casamento*) best man

padroeiro /padro'eru/ *m* patron saint

padronizar /padroni'zar/ *vt* standardize

paga /'paga/ *f* pay. **~mento** *m* payment

pa|gão /pa'gãw/ (*pl* **~gãos**) *a & m* (*f* **~gã**) pagan

pagar /pa'gar/ *vt* pay for ‹*compra, erro etc*›; pay ‹*dívida, conta, empregado etc*›; pay back ‹*empréstimo*›; repay ‹*gentileza etc*› ● *vi* pay; **eu pago para ver** I'll believe it when I see it

página /'paʒina/ *f* page; **~ web** web page

pago /'pagu/ *a* paid ● *pp de* ▶ **PAGAR**

P

pagode /pa'gɔdʒi/ *m* (*torre*) pagoda; 🅘 singalong

pai /paj/ *m* father; *pl* (*pai e mãe*) parents. **~ de santo** (*pl* **~s-de-santo**) *m* macumba priest

pai|nel /paj'nɛw/ (*pl* **~néis**) *m* panel; (*de carro*) dashboard

paio /'paju/ *m* pork sausage

pairar /paj'rar/ *vi* hover

país /pa'is/ *m* country; **P~ de Gales** Wales; **P~es Baixos** Netherlands

paisa|gem /paj'zaʒẽ/ *f* landscape. **~gista** *m/f* landscape gardener

paisana /paj'zana/ *f* **à ~** ‹*policial*› in plain clothes; ‹*soldado*› in civilian clothes

paixão /pa'ʃãw/ *f* passion

pala /'pala/ *f* (*de boné*) peak; (*de automóvel*) sun visor

palácio /pa'lasiu/ *m* palace

> *i* **Palácio do Planalto** The *Palácio do Planalto* is the main working office of the President of Brazil. It is the seat of the government and the President's official residence, and it also houses important government offices, such as the *Casa Civil* (Chief of Staff) and the *Gabinete de Segurança Institucional* (Office for Institutional Security).

paladar /pala'dar/ *m* palate, taste

palanque /pa'lãki/ *m* stand

palavra /pa'lavra/ *f* word; **pedir a ~** ask to speak; **ter ~** be reliable; **tomar a ~** start to speak; **sem ~** ‹*pessoa*› unreliable; **~ de ordem** watchword; **~s cruzadas** crossword

palavra-chave /palavra'ʃavi/ *f* (*pl* **palavras-chave**) password

palavrão /pala'vrãw/ *m* swear word

palco /'pawku/ *m* stage

palestino /pales'tʃinu/ *a & m* Palestinian

palestra /pa'lɛstra/ *f* lecture

paleta /pa'leta/ *f* palette

paletó /pale'tɔ/ *m* jacket

palha /'paʎa/ *f* straw

palha|çada /paʎa'sada/ *f* joke. **~ço** *m* clown

palhinha /pa'ʎĩɲa/ *f Port* (*para bebidas*) straw

paliativo /palia'tʃivu/ *a & m* palliative

palidez /pali'des/ *f* paleness

pálido /'palidu/ *a* pale

pali|tar /pali'tar/ *vt* pick ● *vi* pick one's teeth. **~teiro** *m* toothpick holder. **~to** *m* (*para dentes*) toothpick; (*de fósforo*) matchstick; (*pessoa magra*) beanpole

pal|ma /'pawma/ *f* palm; *pl* (*aplauso*) clapping; **bater ~mas** clap. **~meira** *f* palm tree. **~mito** *m* palm heart. **~mo** *m* span; **~mo a ~mo** inch by inch

palpá|vel /paw'pavew/ (*pl* **~veis**) *a* palpable

pálpebra /'pawpebra/ *f* eyelid

palpi|tação /pawpita'sãw/ *f* palpitation. **~tante** *a fig* thrilling. **~tar** *vi* ‹*coração*› flutter; ‹*pessoa*› tremble; (*dar palpite*) stick one's oar in. **~te** *m* (*pressentimento*) hunch; (*no jogo etc*) tip; **dar ~te** stick one's oar in

panaceia /pana'sɛja/ *f* panacea

panaché /pana'ʃɛ/ *m Port* (*bebida*) shandy

Panamá /pana'ma/ *m* Panama

panamenho /pana'meɲu/ *a & m* Panamanian

pan-americano /panameri'kanu/ *a* Pan-American

pança /'pãsa/ *f* paunch

pancada /pã'kada/ *f* blow; **~ d'água** downpour. **~ria** *f* fight, punch-up

pâncreas /'pãkrias/ *m invar* pancreas

pançudo /pã'sudu/ *a* paunchy

panda /'pãda/ *m* panda

pandarecos /pãda'rɛkus/ *m pl* **aos** ou **em ~** battered

pandeiro /pã'deru/ *m* tambourine

pandemônio /pãde'moniu/ *m* pandemonium

pane /'pani/ *f* breakdown

panela /pa'nɛla/ *f* saucepan; **~ de pressão** pressure cooker

panfleto /pã'fletu/ *m* pamphlet

pânico /'paniku/ *m* panic; **em ~** in a panic; **entrar em ~** panic

panifica|ção /panifika'sãw/ *f* bakery. **~dora** *f* bakery

pano /'panu/ *m* cloth; **~ de fundo** backdrop; **~ de pó** duster; **~ de pratos** tea towel

pano|rama /pano'rama/ *m* panorama. **~râmico** *a* panoramic

panqueca /pã'kɛka/ *f* pancake

panta|nal /pãta'naw/ (*pl* **~nais**) *m* marshland

> **Pantanal** The *Pantanal* is a tropical wetland located within the states of Mato Gross and Mato Grosso do Sul, covering an area of 250 thousand square kilometres. Much of the floodplains are submerged during the rainy season, forming a unique ecosystem which has been designated a UNESCO World Heritage Site, and one of Brazil's most important sites of national heritage. The area is home to hundreds of species of mammals, fish, birds and reptiles, including caimans, capybaras, and piranhas.

pântano /'pãtanu/ *m* marsh

pantanoso /pãta'nozu/ *a* marshy

pantera /pã'tɛra/ *f* panther

pantufa /pã'tufa/ *f* slipper

pão /pãw/ (*pl* **pães**) *m* bread; **~ de forma** sliced loaf; **~ integral** brown bread. **~ de ló** *m* sponge cake; **~-duro** (*pl* **pães-duros**) [I] *a* stingy, tight-fisted ● *m/f* skinflint. **~zinho** *m* bread roll

> **Pão de Açúcar** The *Pão de Açúcar* is a mountain situated at the mouth of Guanabara Bay in Rio de Janeiro. The summit stands at 395 meters above sea level, and is one of the city's most famous landmarks. A cable car (*Bondinho do Pão de Açúcar*) runs tourists up to the top, from which they can view Botafogo Bay, Leme Beach and the vast Atlantic Ocean.

papa /'papa/ *f* (*de nenem*) food; (*arroz etc*) mush

Papa /'papa/ *m* Pope

papagaio /papa'gaju/ *m* parrot

papai /pa'paj/ *m* dad, daddy; **Papai Noel** Father Christmas

papão /pa'pãw/ *m Port* bogeyman

papar /pa'par/ *vt/i* [I] eat

papari|car /papari'kar/ *vt* pamper. **~cos** *m pl* pampering

pa|pel /pa'pɛw/ (*pl* **~péis**) *m* (*de escrever etc*) paper; (*um*) piece of paper; (*numa peça, filme*) part; *fig* (*função*) role; **de ~pel passado** officially; **~pel de alumínio** aluminium foil; **~pel higiênico** toilet paper. **~pelada** *f* paperwork. **~pelão** *m* cardboard. **~pelaria** *f* stationer's (shop). **~pelzinho** *m* scrap of paper

papo /'papu/ *f* [I] (*conversa*) talk; (*do rosto*) double chin; **bater um ~** [I] have a chat; **~ furado** idle talk

papoula /pa'pola/ *f* poppy

páprica /'paprika/ *f* paprika

paque|ra /pa'kɛra/ *f* [I] pick-up. **~rador** *a* flirtatious ● *m* flirt. **~rar** *vt* flirt with ‹*pessoa*›; eye up ‹*vestido, carro etc*› ● *vi* flirt

paquista|nês /pakista'nes/ *a & m* (*f* **~nesa**) Pakistani

Paquistão /pakis'tãw/ *m* Pakistan

par /par/ *a* even ● *m* pair; (*parceiro*) partner; **a ~ de** up to date with ‹*notícias etc*›; **sem ~** unequalled

para /'para/ ● *prep*

····➤ (*uso, finalidade*) for; **é ~ você** it's for you; **muito útil ~ a chuva** very useful for the rain; **muito complicado ~ mim** too complicated for me; **~ que você quer?** what do you want it for?; **detergente ~ máquina** machine detergent

····➤ (*direção*) **~ sul/norte** towards south/north; **foi ~ a cama** she went to bed; **vai ~ casa!** go home!

P

····➤ (*com destino a*) **~ São Paulo** to São Paulo; **o voo ~ Salvador** the flight to Salvador

····➤ (*seguido de infinitivo*) **vieram ~ ficar** they've come to stay

····➤ (*tempo futuro*) **~ a próxima semana** for next week; **preciso disto ~ segunda** I need it for Monday; **são cinco ~ as dez** it's five to ten

····➤ (*lugar impreciso*) **estava (lá) ~ Recife** he was somewhere in Recife

····➤ (*em expressões*) **~ com** to; **foi muito simpático ~ com ela** he was very nice to her; ,**~ isso: foi ~ isso que você me chamou?** you called me here just for that?; **~ mim** (*opinião*) for me; **~ mim, ele é o melhor jogador** he is the best player for me; **~ que** so (that); **ela trabalhou muito ~ que ficasse tudo pronto na hora** she worked hard so (that) everything would be ready in time; **~ si** to yourself; **dizer algo ~ si próprio** say sth to o.s.

para|benizar /parabeni'zar/ *vt* congratulate (**por** on). **~béns** *m pl* congratulations

parábola /pa'rabola/ *f* (*conto*) parable; (*curva*) parabola

parabóli|co /para'bɔliku/ *a* **antena ~ca** satellite dish

para|brisa /para'briza/ *m* windscreen, *Amer* windshield. **~choque** *m* bumper

para|da /pa'rada/ *f* stop; (*interrupção*) stoppage; (*militar*) parade; ! (*coisa difícil*) ordeal, challenge; **~da cardíaca** cardiac arrest. **~deiro** *m* whereabouts

paradisíaco /paradʒi'ziaku/ *a* idyllic

parado /pa'radu/ *a* ‹*trânsito, carro*› at a standstill, stopped; *fig* ‹*pessoa*› dull; **ficar ~** ‹*pessoa*› stand still; ‹*trânsito*› stop; (*deixar de trabalhar*) stop work

parado|xal /paradok'saw/ (*pl* **~xais**) *a* paradoxical. **~xo** /ɔ/ *m* paradox

parafina /para'fina/ *f* paraffin

paráfrase /pa'rafrazi/ *f* paraphrase

parafrasear /parafrazi'ar/ *vt* paraphrase

parafuso /para'fuzu/ *f* screw; **entrar em ~** get into a state

para|gem /pa'raʒẽ/ *f Port* (*parada*) stop; **nestas ~gens** in these parts

parágrafo /pa'ragrafu/ *m* paragraph

Paraguai /para'gwaj/ *m* Paraguay

paraguaio /para'gwaju/ *a & m* Paraguayan

paraíso /para'izu/ *m* paradise

para-lama /para'lama/ *m* (*de carro*) wing, *Amer* fender; (*de bicicleta*) mudguard

parale|la /para'lɛla/ *f* parallel; *pl* (*aparelho*) parallel bars. **~lepípedo** *m* paving stone. **~lo** /ɛ/ *a & m* parallel

para|lisar /parali'zar/ *vt* paralyse; bring to a halt ‹*fábrica, produção*›. **~lisar-se** *vpr* become paralysed; ‹*fábrica, produção*› grind to a halt. **~lisia** *f* paralysis. **~lítico** *a & m* paralytic. **~médico** *m* paramedic

paranoi|a /para'nɔja/ *f* paranoia. **~co** *a* paranoid

parapeito /para'pejtu/ *m* (*muro*) parapet; (*da janela*) window sill

paraque|das /para'kɛdas/ *m invar* parachute. **~dista** *m/f* parachutist; (*militar*) paratrooper

parar /pa'rar/ *vt/i* stop; **~ de fumar** stop smoking; **ir ~** end up

para-raios /para'xajus/ *m invar* lightning conductor

parasita /para'zita/ *a & m/f* parasite

parceiro /par'seru/ *m* partner

parce|la /par'sɛla/ *f* (*de terreno*) plot; (*prestação*) instalment. **~lar** *vt* spread ‹*pagamento*›

parceria /parse'ria/ *f* partnership

parci|al /parsi'aw/ (*pl* **~ais**) *a* partial; (*partidário*) biased. **~alidade** *f* bias

parco /'parku/ *a* frugal; ‹*recursos*› scant

par|dal /par'daw/ (*pl* **~dais**) *m* sparrow. **~do** *a* ‹*papel*› brown; ‹*pessoa*› mulatto

pare|cer /pare'ser/ *vi* (*ter aparência de*) seem; (*ter semelhança com*) be like; **~cer-se com** look like, resemble ● *m* opinion. **~cido** *a* similar (**com** to)

parede /pa'redʒi/ *f* wall

paren|te /pa'rẽtʃi/ *m/f* relative, relation. **~tesco** /e/ *m* relationship

parêntese /pa'rẽtʃizi/ *f* parenthesis; *pl* (*sinais*) brackets, parentheses

paridade /pari'dadʒi/ *f* parity

parir /pa'rir/ *vt* give birth to ● *vi* give birth

parlamen|tar /parlamẽ'tar/ *a* parliamentary ● *m/f* member of parliament. **~tarismo** *m* parliamentary system. **~to** *m* parliament

parmesão /parme'zãw/ *a & m* **(queijo) ~** Parmesan (cheese)

paródia /pa'rɔdʒia/ *f* parody

parodiar /parodʒi'ar/ *vt* parody

paróquia /pa'rɔkia/ *f* parish

parque /'parki/ *m* park. **~ temático** *m* theme park

parquímetro /par'kimetru/ *m* parking meter

parte /'partʃi/ *f* part; (*quinhão*) share; (*num litígio, contrato*) party; **a maior ~ de** most of; **à ~** (*de lado*) aside; (*separadamente*) separately; **um erro da sua ~** a mistake on your part; **em ~** in part; **em alguma ~** somewhere; **por toda ~** everywhere; **por ~ do pai** on one's father's side; **fazer ~ de** be part of; **tomar ~ em** take part in

parteira /par'tera/ *f* midwife

partici|pação /partʃisipa'sãw/ *f* participation; (*numa empresa, nos lucros*) share. **~pante** *a* participating ● *m/f* participant. **~par** *vi* take part (**de** ou **em** in)

particípio /partʃi'sipiu/ *m* participle

partícula /par'tʃikula/ *f* particle

particu|lar /partʃiku'lar/ *a* private; (*especial*) unusual ● *m* (*pessoa*) private individual; *pl* (*detalhes*) particulars; **em ~lar** (*especialmente*) in particular; (*a sós*) in private. **~laridade** *f* peculiarity

partida /par'tʃida/ *f* (*saída*) departure; (*de corrida*) start; (*de futebol, xadrez etc*) match; **dar ~ em** start up

par|tidário /partʃi'dariu/ *a* partisan ● *m* supporter. **~tido** *a* broken ● *m* (*político*) party; (*casamento, par*) match; **tirar ~tido de** benefit from; **tomar o ~tido de** side with. **~tilha** *f* division. **~tir** *vi* (*sair*) depart; ‹*corredor*› start; **a ~tir de ...** from ... onwards; **~tir para** [!] resort to; **~tir para outra** do something different, change direction ● *vt* break. **~tir-se** *vpr* break. **~titura** *f* score

partilhar /parti'ʎar/ *vt/i Port* share

parto /'partu/ *m* birth

parvo /'parvu/ *a Port* stupid

Páscoa /'paskoa/ *f* Easter

pas|mar /paz'mar/ *vt* amaze. **~mar-se** *vpr* be amazed (**com** at). **~mo** *a* amazed ● *m* amazement

passa /'pasa/ *f* raisin

pas|sada /pa'sada/ *f* **dar uma ~sada em** call in at. **~sadeira** *f* (*mulher*) woman who irons; *Port* (*faixa*) zebra crossing, *Amer* crosswalk. **~sado** *a* ‹*ano, mês, semana*› last; ‹*tempo, particípio etc*› past; ‹*fruta, comida*› off; **são duas horas ~sadas** it's gone two o'clock; **bem/mal ~sado** well done/rare ● *m* past

passa|geiro /pasa'ʒeru/ *m* passenger ● *a* passing. **~gem** *f* passage; (*bilhete*) ticket; **de ~gem** in passing; **estar de ~gem** be passing through; **~gem de ida e volta** return ticket, *Amer* round trip ticket

passaporte /pasa'pɔrtʃi/ *m* passport

passar /pa'sar/ *vt* pass; spend ‹*tempo*›; cross ‹*ponte, rio*›; (*a ferro*) iron ‹*roupa etc*›; (*aplicar*) put on ‹*creme, batom etc*› ● *vi* pass; ‹*dor, medo, chuva etc*› go; (*ser aceitável*) be passable; **passou a beber muito** he started to drink a lot; **passei dos 30 anos** I'm over thirty; **não passa de um boato** it's nothing more than a rumour; **~ sem** do without; **~ por** go through; go along ‹*rua*›; (*ser considerado*) be taken for; **fazer-se ~ por** pass o.s. off as; **~ por cima de** *fig* overlook ● *m* passing. **~-se** *vpr* happen

passarela /pasa'rɛla/ *f* (*sobre rua*) footbridge; (*para desfile de moda*) catwalk

pássaro /'pasaru/ *m* bird

passatempo /pasa'tẽpu/ *m* pastime

passe /'pasi/ *m* pass

pas|sear /pasi'ar/ *vi* go out and about; (*viajar*) travel around ● *vt* take for a walk. **~seata** *f* protest march. **~seio** *m* outing; (*volta a pé*) walk; (*volta de carro*) drive; **dar um ~seio** (*a pé*) go for a walk; (*de carro*) go for a drive

passio|nal /pasio'naw/ (*pl* **~nais**) *a* **crime ~nal** crime of passion

passista /pa'sista/ *m/f* dancer

passí|vel /pa'sivew/ (*pl* **~veis**) *a* **~vel de** subject to

passi|vidade /pasivi'dadʒi/ *f* passivity. **~vo** *a* passive ● *m Com* liabilities; *Ling* passive

passo /'pasu/ *m* step; (*velocidade*) pace; (*barulho*) footstep; **~ a ~** step by step; **a dois ~s de** a stone's throw from; **dar um ~** take a step

pasta /'pasta/ *f* (*matéria*) paste; (*bolsa*) briefcase; (*fichário*) folder; **ministro sem ~** minister without portfolio; **~ de dentes** toothpaste

pas|tagem /pas'taʒẽ/ *f* pasture. **~tar** *vi* graze

pas|tel /pas'tɛw/ (*pl* **~téis**) *m* (*para comer*) samosa; *Port* (*doce*) pastry; *Port* (*pastéis*) pastries; (*para desenhar*) pastel. **~telão** *m* (*comédia*) slapstick. **~telaria** *f* (*loja*) samosa vendor; *Port* pastry shop

P

> **pastelaria** You can't go very far in Portugal without coming across a *pastelaria*. These are shops or cafes serving a huge variety of cakes and pastries, many of which originated in Portuguese convents. The fillings are often rich in egg yolk, left over after the nuns had used the whites to starch their habits.

pasteurizado /pastewri'zadu/ *a* pasteurized

pastilha /pas'tʃiʎa/ *f* pastille

pas|to /'pastu/ *m* (*erva*) fodder, feed; (*lugar*) pasture. **~tor** *m* (*de gado*) shepherd; (*clérigo*) vicar; **~tor alemão** (*cachorro*) Alsatian. **~toral** (*pl* **~torais**) *a* pastoral

pata /'pata/ *f* paw. **~da** *f* kick

patamar /pata'mar/ *m* landing; *fig* level

patê /pa'te/ *m* pâté

patente /pa'tẽtʃi/ *a* obvious ● *f Mil* rank; (*de invenção*) patent. **~ar** *vt* patent ‹*produto, invenção*›

pater|nal /pater'naw/ (*pl* **~nais**) *a* paternal. **~nidade** *f* paternity. **~no** /ɛ/ *a* paternal

pate|ta /pa'tɛta/ *a* daft, silly ● *m/f* fool. **~tice** *f* stupidity; (*uma*) silly thing

patético /pa'tɛtʃiku/ *a* pathetic

patíbulo /pa'tʃibulu/ *m* gallows

pati|faria /patʃifa'ria/ *f* roguishness; (*uma*) dirty trick. **~fe** *m* scoundrel

patim /pa'tʃĩ/ *m* skate; **~ de rodas** roller skate

pati|nação /patʃina'sãw/ *f* skating; (*rinque*) skating rink. **~nador** *m* skater. **~nar** *vi* skate; ‹*carro*› skid. **~nete** /ɛ/ *m* skateboard

pátio /'patʃiu/ *m* courtyard; (*de escola*) playground

pato /'patu/ *m* duck

pato|logia /patolo'ʒia/ *f* pathology. **~lógico** *a* pathological. **~logista** *m/f* pathologist

patrão /pa'trãw/ *m* boss

pátria /'patria/ *f* homeland

patriar|ca /patri'arka/ *m* patriarch. **~cal** (*pl* **~cais**) *a* patriarchal

patrimônio /patri'moniu/ *m* (*bens*) estate, property; *fig* (*herança*) heritage

patri|ota /patri'ɔta/ *m/f* patriot. **~ótico** *a* patriotic. **~otismo** *m* patriotism

patroa /pa'troa/ *f* boss; [!] (*esposa*) missus, wife

patro|cinador /patrosina'dor/ *m* sponsor. **~cinar** *vt* sponsor. **~cínio** *m* sponsorship

patru|lha /pa'truʎa/ *f* patrol. **~lhar** *vt/i* patrol

pau /paw/ *m* stick; [!] (*cruzeiro*) cruzeiro; (*chulo*) (*pênis*) prick; *pl* (*naipe*) clubs; **a meio ~** at half mast; **rachar ~** [!] (*brigar*) row, fight like cat and dog. **~lada** *f* blow with a stick

paulista /paw'lista/ *a & m/f* (person) from (the state of) São Paulo. **~no** *a & m* (person) from (the city of) São Paulo

pausa /'pawza/ *f* pause. **~do** *a* slow

pauta /'pawta/ *f* (*em papel*) lines; (*de música*) stave; *fig* (*de discussão etc*) agenda. **~do** *a* ‹*papel*› lined

pavão /pa'vãw/ *m* peacock

pavilhão /pavi'ʎãw/ *m* pavilion; (*no jardim*) summer house

pavimen|tar /pavimẽ'tar/ *vt* pave. **~to** *m* floor; (*de rua etc*) surface

pavio /pa'viu/ *m* wick

pavor /pa'vor/ *m* terror; **ter ~ de** be terrified of. **~oso** /o/ *a* dreadful

paz /pas/ *f* peace; **fazer as ~es** make up

pé /pɛ/ *m* foot; (*planta*) plant; (*de móvel*) leg; **a ~** on foot; **ao ~ da letra** literally; **estar de ~** ‹*festa etc*› be on; **ficar de ~** stand up; **em ~** standing (up); **em ~ de igualdade** on an equal footing; **~ de atleta** athlete's foot. **~ de meia** nest egg; **~ de pato** flipper; **~ de vento** gust of wind

peão /pi'ãw/ *m Port* (*pedestre*) pedestrian; (*no xadrez*) pawn

peça /'pɛsa/ *f* piece; (*de máquina, carro etc*) part; (*teatral*) play; **pregar uma ~ em** play a trick on; **~ de reposição** spare part; **~ de vestuário** item of clothing

pe|cado /pe'kadu/ *m* sin. **~cador** *m* sinner. **~caminoso** /o/ *a* sinful. **~car** *vi* (*contra a religião*) sin; *fig* fall down

pechin|cha /pe'ʃĩʃa/ *f* bargain. **~char** *vi* bargain, haggle

peçonhento /peso'ɲẽtu/ *a* **animais ~s** vermin

pecu|ária /peku'aria/ *f* livestock farming. **~ário** *a* livestock. **~arista** *m/f* livestock farmer

peculi|ar /pekuli'ar/ *a* peculiar. **~aridade** *f* peculiarity

pecúlio /pe'kuliu/ *m* savings

pedaço /pe'dasu/ *m* piece; **aos ~s** in pieces; **cair aos ~s** fall to pieces

pedágio /pe'daʒiu/ *m* toll; (*cabine*) tollbooth

peda|gogia /pedago'ʒia/ *f* education. **~gógico** *a* educational. **~gogo** /o/ *m* educationalist

pe|dal /pe'daw/ (*pl* **~dais**) *m* pedal. **~dalar** *vt/i* pedal

pedante /pe'dãtʃi/ *a* pretentious ● *m/f* pseud

pederneira /peder'nera/ *f* flint

pedes|tal /pedes'taw/ (*pl* **~tais**) *m* pedestal

pedestre /pe'dɛstri/ *a & m/f* pedestrian

pedia|tra /pedʒi'atra/ *m/f* paediatrician. **~tria** *f* paediatrics

pedicuro /pedʒi'kuru/ *m* chiropodist, *Amer* podiatrist

pe|dido /pe'dʒidu/ *m* request; (*encomenda*) order; **a ~dido de** at the request of; **~dido de demissão** resignation; **~dido de desculpa** apology. **~dir** *vt* ask for; (*num restaurante etc*) order; **~dir algo a alguém** ask sb for sth; **~dir para algém ir** ask sb to go; **~dir desculpa** apologize; **~dir em casamento** propose to ● *vi* ask; (*num restaurante etc*) order

pedinte /pe'dʒĩtʃi/ *m/f* beggar

pedra /'pɛdra/ stone; **~ de gelo** ice cube; **chuva de ~** hail; **~ pomes** pumice stone

pedregoso /pedre'gozu/ *a* stony

pedreiro /pe'dreru/ *m* builder

pegada /pe'gada/ *f* footprint; (*de goleiro*) save; **~ ecológica** carbon footprint

pegajoso /pega'ʒozu/ *a* sticky

pegar /pe'gar/ *vt* get; catch ‹*bola, doença, ladrão, ônibus*›; (*segurar*) get hold of; pick up ‹*emissora, hábito, mania*›; **~ bem/mal** go down well/badly; **~ fogo** catch fire; **pega essa rua** take that street; **~ em** grab; **~ no sono** get to sleep ● *vi* (*aderir*) stick; ‹*doença*› be catching; ‹*moda*› catch on; ‹*carro, motor*› start; ‹*mentira, desculpa*› stick. **~-se** *vpr* come to blows

pego /'pɛgu/; *pp de* ▶ PEGAR

pei|dar /pej'dar/ *vi* (*chulo*) fart. **~do** *m* (*chulo*) fart

pei|to /'pejtu/ *m* chest; (*seio*) breast; *fig* (*coragem*) guts. **~toril** (*pl* **~toris**) *m* window sill. **~tudo** *a* ‹*mulher*› busty; *fig* (*corajoso*) gutsy

pei|xaria /pe'ʃaria/ *f* fishmonger's. **~xe** *m* fish; **Peixes** (*signo*) Pisces. **~xeiro** *m* fishmonger

pela = **por + a**

pelado /pe'ladu/ *a* (*nu*) naked, in the nude

pelan|ca /pe'lãka/ *f* roll of fat; *pl* flab. **~cudo** *a* flabby

pelar /pe'lar/ *vt* peel ‹*fruta, batata*›; skin ‹*animal*›; [!] (*tomar dinheiro de*) fleece

pelas = **por + as**

pele /'pɛli/ *f* skin; (*como roupa*) fur. **~teiro** *m* furrier. **~teria** *f* furrier's

pelica /pe'lika/ *f* **luvas de ~** kid gloves

pelicano /peli'kanu/ *m* pelican

película /pe'likula/ *f* skin

pelo[1] /'pelu/ *m* hair; (*de animal*) coat; **nu em ~** stark naked; **montar em ~** ride bareback

pelo[2] = **por + o**

pelos = **por + os**

pelotão /pelo'tãw/ *m* platoon

pelúcia /pe'lusia/ *f* **bicho de ~** soft toy, fluffy animal

peludo /pe'ludu/ *a* hairy

pen /'pɛn/ *f Port* memory stick

pena[1] /'pena/ *f* (*de ave*) feather; (*de caneta*) nib

pena[2] /'pena/ *f* (*castigo*) penalty; (*de amor etc*) pang; **é uma ~ que** it's a pity that; **que ~!** what a pity! **dar ~** be upsetting; **estar com** ou **ter ~ de** feel sorry for; **(não) vale a ~** it's (not) worth it; **vale a ~ tentar** it's worth trying; **~ de morte** death penalty

penada /pe'nada/ *f* stroke of the pen

pe|nal /pe'naw/ (*pl* **~nais**) *a* penal. **~nalidade** *f* penalty. **~nalizar** *vt* penalize

pênalti /'penawtʃi/ *m* penalty

penar /pe'nar/ *vi* suffer

pen|dente /pẽ'dẽtʃi/ *a* hanging; *fig* (*causa*) pending. **~der** *vi* hang; (*inclinar-se*) slope; (*tender*) be inclined (**a** to). **~dor** *m* inclination

pen drive *m* memory stick

pêndulo /'pẽdulu/ *m* pendulum

pendu|rado /pẽdu'radu/ *a* hanging; [!] (*por fazer, pagar*) outstanding. **~rar** *vt* hang (up); [!] put on the slate ‹*compra*› ● *vi* [!] pay later. **~ricalho** *m* pendant

penedo /pe'nedu/ *m* rock

penei|ra /pe'nera/ *f* sieve. **~rar** *vt* sieve, sift ● *vi* drizzle

pene|tra /pe'nɛtra/ *m/f* [!] gatecrasher. **~tração** *f* penetration; *fig* perspicacity. **~trante** *a* ‹*som, olhar*› piercing; ‹*dor*›

P

sharp; ‹*ferida*› deep; ‹*frio*› biting; ‹*análise, espírito*› incisive, perceptive. **~trar** *vt* penetrate ● *vi* **~trar em** enter ‹*casa*›; *fig* penetrate

penhasco /pe'ɲasku/ *m* cliff

penhoar /peɲo'ar/ *m* dressing gown

penhor /pe'ɲor/ *m* pledge; **casa de ~es** pawnshop

penicilina /penisi'lina/ *f* penicillin

penico /pe'niku/ *m* potty

península /pe'nĩsula/ *f* peninsula

pênis /'penis/ *m invar* penis

penitência /peni'tẽsia/ *f* (*arrependimento*) penitence; (*expiação*) penance

penitenciá|ria /penitẽsi'aria/ *f* prison. **~rio** *a* prison ● *m* prisoner

penoso /pe'nozu/ *a* ‹*experiência, tarefa, assunto*› painful; ‹*trabalho, viagem*› hard, difficult

pensa|dor /pẽsa'dor/ *m* thinker. **~mento** *m* thought

pensão /pẽ'sãw/ *f* (*renda*) pension; (*hotel*) guest house; **~ (alimentícia)** (*paga por ex-marido*) alimony; **~ completa** full board

pen|sar /pẽ'sar/ *vt/i* think (**em** of ou about). **~sativo** *a* thoughtful, pensive

pên|sil /'pẽsiw/ (*pl* **~seis**) *a* **ponte ~sil** suspension bridge

penso /'pẽsu/ *m* (*curativo*) dressing

pentágono /pẽ'tagonu/ *m* pentagon

pentatlo /pẽ'tatlu/ *m* pentathlon

pente /'pẽtʃi/ *m* comb. **~adeira** *f* dressing table. **~ado** *m* hairstyle, hairdo. **~ar** *vt* comb. **~ar-se** *vpr* do one's hair; (*com pente*) comb one's hair

Pentecostes /pẽte'kɔstʃis/ *m* Whitsun

pente-fino /pẽtʃi'finu/ *m* **passar a ~** go over with a fine-tooth comb

pente|lhar /pẽte'ʎar/ *vt* [!] bother. **~lho** /e/ *m* pubic hair; [!] (*pessoa inconveniente*) pain (in the neck)

penugem /pe'nuʒẽ/ *f* down

penúltimo /pe'nuwtʃimu/ *a* last but one, penultimate

penumbra /pe'nũbra/ *f* half-light

penúria /pe'nuria/ *f* penury, extreme poverty

pepino /pe'pinu/ *m* cucumber

pepita /pe'pita/ *f* nugget

peque|nez /peke'nes/ *f* smallness; *fig* pettiness. **~nininho** *a* tiny. **~no** /e/ *a* small; (*mesquinho*) petty

pequeno-almoço /pikenwaw'mosu/ *m* (*pl* **pequenos-almoços**) *Port* breakfast

Pequim /pe'kĩ/ *f* Peking, Beijing

pequinês /peki'nes/ *m* Pekinese

pera /'pera/ *f* pear

perambular /perãbu'lar/ *vi* wander

perante /pe'rãtʃi/ *prep* before

percalço /per'kawsu/ *m* pitfall

perceber /perse'ber/ *vt* realize; *Port* (*entender*) understand; (*psiqu*) perceive

percen|tagem /persẽ'taʒẽ/ *f* percentage. **~tual** (*pl* **~tuais**) *a & m* percentage

percep|ção /persep'sãw/ *f* perception. **~tível** (*pl* **~tíveis**) *a* perceptible

percevejo /perse'veʒu/ *m* (*bicho*) bedbug; (*tachinha*) drawing pin, *Amer* thumbtack

per|correr /perko'xer/ *vt* cross; cover ‹*distância*›; (*viajar por*) travel through. **~curso** *m* journey

percus|são /perku'sãw/ *f* percussion. **~sionista** *m/f* percussionist

percutir /perku'tʃir/ *vt* strike

perda /'perda/ *f* loss; **~ de tempo** waste of time

perdão /per'dãw/ *f* pardon

perder /per'der/ *vt* lose; (*não chegar a ver, pegar*) miss ‹*ônibus, programa na TV etc*›; waste ‹*tempo*›; **~ algo de vista** lose sight of sth ● *vi* lose. **~-se** *vpr* get lost; **~-se de alguém** lose sb

perdiz /per'dʒis/ *f* partridge

perdoar /perdo'ar/ *vt* forgive (**algo a alguém** sb for sth)

perdulário /perdu'lariu/ *a & m* spendthrift

perdurar /perdu'rar/ *vi* endure; ‹*coisa ruim*› persist

pere|cer /pere'ser/ *vi* perish. **~cível** (*pl* **~cíveis**) *a* perishable

peregri|nação /peregrina'sãw/ *f* peregrination; (*romaria*) pilgrimage. **~nar** *vi* roam; (*por motivos religiosos*) go on a pilgrimage. **~no** *m* pilgrim

pereira /pe'rera/ *f* pear tree

peremptório /perẽp'tɔriu/ *a* peremptory

perene /pe'reni/ *a* perennial

perereca /pere'rɛka/ *f* tree frog

perfazer /perfa'zer/ *vt* make up

perfeccionis|mo /perfeksio'nizmu/ *m* perfectionism. **~ta** *a & m/f* perfectionist

perfei|ção /perfej'sãw/ *f* perfection. **~to** *a & m* perfect

per|fil /per'fiw/ (*pl* **~fis**) *m* profile. **~filar** *vt* line up. **~filar-se** *vpr* line up

perfu|mado /perfu'madu/ *a* ‹*flor, ar*› fragrant; ‹*sabonete etc*› scented; ‹*pessoa*› with perfume on. **~mar** *vt* perfume. **~mar-se** *vpr* put perfume on. **~maria** *f* perfumery; [!] trimmings, frills. **~me** *m* perfume

perfu|rador /perfura'dor/ *m* punch. **~rar** *vt* punch ‹*papel, bilhete*›; drill through ‹*chão*›; perforate ‹*úlcera, pulmão etc*›. **~ratriz** *f* drill

pergaminho /perga'miɲu/ *m* parchment

pergun|ta /per'gũta/ *f* question; **fazer uma ~ta** ask a question. **~tar** *vt/i* ask; **~tar algo a alguém** ask sb sth; **~tar por** ask after

perícia /pe'risia/ *f* (*mestria*) expertise; (*inspeção*) investigation; (*peritos*) experts

perici|al /perisi'aw/ (*pl* **~ais**) *a* expert

pericli|tante /perikli'tãtʃi/ *a* precarious. **~tar** *vi* be at risk

peri|feria /perife'ria/ *f* periphery; (*da cidade*) outskirts. **~férico** *a & m* peripheral

perigo /pe'rigu/ *m* danger. **~so** /o/ *a* dangerous

perímetro /pe'rimetru/ *m* perimeter

periódico /peri'ɔdʒiku/ *a* periodic ● *m* periodical

período /pe'riodu/ *m* period; **trabalhar meio ~** work part-time

peripécias /peri'pɛsias/ *f pl* ups and downs, vicissitudes

periquito /peri'kitu/ *m* parakeet; (*de estimação*) budgerigar

periscópio /peris'kɔpiu/ *m* periscope

perito /pe'ritu/ *a & m* expert (**em** at)

per|jurar /perʒu'rar/ *vi* commit perjury. **~júrio** *m* perjury. **~juro** *m* perjurer

perma|necer /permane'ser/ *vi* remain. **~nência** *f* permanence; (*estadia*) stay. **~nente** *a* permanent ● *f* perm

permeá|vel /permi'avew/ (*pl* **~veis**) *a* permeable

permis|são /permi'sãw/ *f* permission. **~sível** (*pl* **~síveis**) *a* permissible. **~sivo** *a* permissive

permitir /permi'tʃir/ *vt* allow, permit; **~ a alguém ir** allow sb to go

permutar /permu'tar/ *vt* exchange

perna /'pɛrna/ *f* leg

pernicioso /pernisi'ozu/ *a* pernicious

per|nil /per'niw/ (*pl* **~nis**) *m* leg

pernilongo /perni'lõgu/ *m* (large) mosquito

pernoi|tar /pernoj'tar/ *vi* spend the night. **~te** *m* overnight stay

pérola /'pɛrola/ *f* pearl

perpendicular /perpẽdʒiku'lar/ *a* perpendicular

perpetrar /perpe'trar/ *vt* perpetrate

perpetu|ar /perpetu'ar/ *vt* perpetuate. **~idade** *f* perpetuity

perpétu|o /per'pɛtuu/ *a* perpetual; **prisão ~a** life imprisonment

perple|xidade /perpleksi'dadʒi/ *f* puzzlement. **~xo** /ɛ/ *a* puzzled

persa /'pɛrsa/ *a & m/f* Persian

perse|guição /persegi'sãw/ *f* pursuit; (*de minorias etc*) persecution. **~guidor** *m* pursuer; (*de minorias etc*) persecutor. **~guir** *vt* pursue; persecute ‹*minoria, seita etc*›

perseve|rança /perseve'rãsa/ *f* perseverance. **~rante** *a* persevering. **~rar** *vi* persevere

persiana /persi'ana/ *f* blind

pérsico /'pɛrsiku/ *a* **Golfo Pérsico** Persian Gulf

persignar-se /persig'narsi/ *vt* cross o.s.

persis|tência /persis'tẽsia/ *f* persistence. **~tente** *a* persistent. **~tir** *vi* persist

perso|nagem /perso'naʒẽ/ *m/f* (*pessoa famosa*) personality; (*em livro, filme etc*) character. **~nalidade** *f* personality. **~nalizar** *vt* personalize. **~nificar** *vt* personify

perspectiva /perspek'tʃiva/ *f* (*na arte, ponto de vista*) perspective; (*possibilidade*) prospect

perspi|cácia /perspi'kasia/ *f* insight, perceptiveness. **~caz** *a* perceptive

persua|dir /persua'dʒir/ *vt* persuade (**alguém a** s.o. to). **~são** *f* persuasion. **~sivo** *a* persuasive

perten|cente /pertẽ'sẽtʃi/ *a* belonging (**a** to); (*que tem a ver com*) pertaining (**a** to). **~cer** *vi* belong (**a** to); (*referir-se*) pertain (**a** to). **~ces** *m pl* belongings

perto /'pɛrtu/ *adv* near (**de** to); **aqui ~** near here, nearby; **de ~** closely; ‹*ver*› close up

pertur|bação /perturba'sãw/ *f* disturbance; (*do espírito*) anxiety. **~bado**

a ‹*pessoa*› unsettled, troubled. **~bar** *vt* disturb. **~bar-se** *vpr* get upset, be perturbed

peru /pe'ru/ *m* turkey

Peru /pe'ru/ *m* Peru

perua /pe'rua/ *f* (*carro grande*) estate car, *Amer* station wagon; (*caminhonete*) van; (*para escolares etc*) minibus; [!] (*mulher*) brassy woman

peruano /peru'ano/ *a & m* Peruvian

peruca /pe'ruka/ *f* wig

perver|são /perver'sãw/ *f* perversion. **~so** *a* perverse. **~ter** *vt* pervert

pesadelo /peza'delu/ *m* nightmare

pesado /pe'zadu/ *a* heavy; ‹*estilo, livro*› heavy going ● *adv* heavily

pêsames /'pezamis/ *m pl* condolences

pesar[1] /pe'zar/ *vt* weigh; *fig* (*avaliar*) weigh up ● *vi* weigh; (*influir*) carry weight; **~ sobre** ‹*ameaça etc*› hang over. **~-se** *vpr* weigh o.s.

pesar[2] /pe'zar/ *m* sorrow. **~oso** /o/ *a* sorry, sorrowful

pes|ca /'pɛska/ *f* fishing; **ir à ~ca** go fishing. **~cador** *m* fisherman. **~car** *vt* catch; (*retirar da água*) fish out ● *vi* fish; [!] (*entender*) understand; (*cochilar*) nod off; **~car de** [!] know all about

pescoço /pes'kosu/ *m* neck

peseta /pe'zeta/ *f* peseta

peso /'pezu/ *m* weight; **de ~** *fig* ‹*pessoa*› influential; ‹*livro, argumento*› authoritative

pesqueiro /pes'keru/ *a* fishing

pesqui|sa /pes'kiza/ *f* research; (*uma*) study; *pl* research; **~sa de mercado** market research. **~sador** *m* researcher. **~sar** *vt/i* research

pêssego /'pesigu/ *m* peach

pessegueiro /pesi'geru/ *m* peach tree

pessimis|mo /pesi'mizmu/ *m* pessimism. **~ta** *a* pessimistic ● *m/f* pessimist

péssimo /'pɛsimu/ *a* terrible, awful

pesso|a /pe'soa/ *f* person; *pl* people; **em ~a** in person. **~al** (*pl* **~ais**) *a* personal ● *m* staff; [!] folks

pesta|na /pes'tana/ *f* eyelash; **tirar uma ~na** [!] have a nap. **~nejar** *vi* blink; **sem ~nejar** *fig* without batting an eyelid

pes|te /'pɛstʃi/ *f* (*doença*) plague; (*criança etc*) pest. **~ticida** *m* pesticide

pétala /'pɛtala/ *f* petal

peteca /pe'tɛka/ *f* kind of shuttlecock; (*jogo*) kind of badminton played with the hand

peteleco /pete'lɛku/ *m* flick

petição /petʃi'sãw/ *f* petition

petisco /pe'tʃisku/ *m* savoury, titbit

petrificar /petrifi'kar/ *vt* petrify; (*de surpresa*) stun. **~-se** *vpr* be petrified; (*de surpresa*) be stunned

petroleiro /petro'leru/ *a* oil ● *m* oil tanker

petróleo /pe'trɔliu/ *m* oil, petroleum; **~ bruto** crude oil

petrolífero /petro'liferu/ *a* oil-producing

petroquími|ca /petro'kimika/ *f* petrochemicals. **~co** *a* petrochemical

petu|lância /petu'lãsia/ *f* cheek. **~lante** *a* cheeky

peúga /pi'uga/ *f Port* sock

pevide /pe'vidʒi/ *f Port* pip

pia /'pia/ *f* (*do banheiro*) washbasin; (*da cozinha*) sink; **~ batismal** font

piada /pi'ada/ *f* joke

pia|nista /pia'nista/ *m/f* pianist. **~no** *m* piano; **~no de cauda** grand piano

piar /pi'ar/ *vi* ‹*pinto*› cheep; ‹*coruja*› hoot

picada /pi'kada/ *f* (*de agulha, alfinete etc*) prick; (*de abelha, vespa*) sting; (*de mosquito, cobra*) bite; (*de heroína*) shot; (*de avião*) nosedive; **o fim da ~** *fig* the limit

picadeiro /pika'deru/ *m* ring

picante /pi'kãtʃi/ *a* ‹*comida*› hot, spicy; ‹*piada*› risqué; ‹*filme, livro*› raunchy

pica-pau /pika'paw/ *m* woodpecker

picar /pi'kar/ *vt* (*com agulha, alfinete etc*) prick; ‹*abelha, vespa, urtiga*› sting; ‹*mosquito, cobra*› bite; ‹*pássaro*› peck; chop ‹*carne, alho etc*›; shred ‹*papel*› ● *vi* ‹*peixe*› bite; ‹*lã, cobertor*› prickle

picareta /pika'reta/ *f* pickaxe

pi|chação /piʃa'sãw/ *f* piece of graffiti; *pl* graffiti. **~char** *vt* spray with graffiti ‹*muro, prédio*›; spray ‹*grafite, desenho*›. **~che** *m* pitch

picles /'piklis/ *m pl* pickles

pico /'piku/ *m* peak; **20 anos e ~** *Port* just over 20

picolé /piko'lɛ/ *m* ice lolly

pico|tar /piko'tar/ *vt* perforate. **~te** /ɔ/ *m* perforations

pie|dade /pie'dadʒi/ *f* (*religiosidade*) piety; (*compaixão*) pity. **~doso** /o/ *a* merciful, compassionate

pie|gas /pi'ɛgas/ *a invar ‹filme, livro›* sentimental, schmaltzy; *‹pessoa›* soppy. **~guice** *f* sentimentality

piercing *m* piercing

pifar /pi'far/ *vi* [!] break down, go wrong

pigar|rear /pigaxi'ar/ *vi* clear one's throat. **~ro** *m* frog in the throat

pigmento /pig'mẽtu/ *m* pigment

pig|meu /pig'mew/ *a & m* (*f* **~meia**) pygmy

pijama /pi'ʒama/ *m* pyjamas

pilantra /pi'lãtra/ *m/f* [!] crook

pilão /pi'lãw/ *m* (*na cozinha*) pestle; (*na construção*) ram

pilar /pi'lar/ *m* pillar

pilastra /pi'lastra/ *f* pillar

pileque /pi'lɛki/ *m* drinking session; **tomar um ~** get drunk

pilha /'piʎa/ *f* (*monte*) pile; (*elétrica*) battery

pilhar /pi'ʎar/ *vt* pillage

pilhéria /pi'ʎɛria/ *f* joke

pilotar /pilo'tar/ *vt* fly, pilot *‹avião›*; drive *‹carro›*

pilotis /pilo'tʃis/ *m pl* pillars

piloto /pi'lotu/ *m* pilot; (*de carro*) driver; (*de gás*) pilot light ● *a invar* pilot

pílula /'pilula/ *f* pill

pimen|ta /pi'mẽta/ *f* pepper; **~ta-de-Caiena** cayenne pepper. **~ta-do-reino** *f* black pepper; **~ta-malagueta** (*pl* **~tas-malagueta**) *f* chilli pepper. **~tão** *m* (bell) pepper. **~teira** *f* pepper pot

PIN /'pin/ *m* PIN (number)

pinacoteca /pinako'tɛka/ *f* art gallery

pin|ça /'pĩsa/ (*para tirar pelos*) tweezers; (*para segurar*) tongs; (*de siri etc*) pincer. **~çar** *vt* pluck *‹sobrancelhas›*

pin|cel /pĩ'sɛw/ (*pl* **~céis**) *m* brush. **~celada** *f* brush stroke. **~celar** *vt* paint

pin|ga /'pĩga/ *f* Brazilian rum. **~gado** *a ‹café›* with a dash of milk. **~gar** *vi* drip; (*começar a chover*) spit (with rain) ● *vt* drip. **~gente** *m* pendant. **~go** *m* drop; (*no i*) dot

pingue-pongue /pĩgi'põgi/ *m* table tennis

pinguim /pĩ'gwĩ/ *m* penguin

pi|nha /'piɲa/ *f* pine cone. **~nheiro** *f* pine tree. **~nho** *m* pine

pino /'pinu/ *m* pin; (*para trancar carro*) lock; **a ~** upright; **bater ~** *‹carro›* knock

pin|ta /'pĩta/ *f* (*sinal*) mole; [!] (*aparência*) look. **~tar** *vt* paint; dye *‹cabelo›*; put make-up on *‹rosto, olhos›* ● *vi* paint; [!] *‹pessoa›* show up; *‹problema, oportunidade›* crop up. **~tar-se** *vpr* put on make-up

pintarroxo /pĩta'xoʃu/ *m* robin

pinto /'pĩtu/ *m* chick

pin|tor /pĩ'tor/ *m* painter. **~tura** *f* painting

pio[1] /'piu/ *m* (*de pinto*) cheep; (*de coruja*) hoot

pio[2] /'piu/ *a* pious

piolho /pi'oʎu/ *m* louse

pioneiro /pio'neru/ *m* pioneer ● *a* pioneering

pior /pi'ɔr/ *a & adv* worse; **o ~** the worst

pio|ra /pi'ɔra/ *f* worsening. **~rar** *vt* make worse, worsen ● *vi* get worse, worsen

pipa /'pipa/ *f* (*que voa*) kite; (*de vinho*) cask

pipilar /pipi'lar/ *vi* chirp

pipo|ca /pi'pɔka/ *f* popcorn. **~car** *vi* spring up. **~queiro** *m* popcorn seller

pique /'piki/ *m* (*disposição*) energy; **a ~** vertically; **ir a ~** *‹navio›* sink

piquenique /piki'niki/ *m* picnic

pique|te /pi'ketʃi/ *m* picket. **~teiro** *m* picket

pirado /pi'radu/ *a* [!] crazy

pirâmide /pi'ramidʒi/ *f* pyramid

piranha /pi'raɲa/ *f* piranha; [!] (*mulher*) maneater

pirar /pi'rar/ *vi* [!] flip out [!], go mad [!]

pirata /pi'rata/ *a & m/f* pirate; **~ informático** *Port* hacker. **~ria** *f* piracy; **~ria informática** *Port* hacking

pírcingue /'pirsinge/ *m Port* piercing; **~ de corpo** body piercing

pires /'piris/ *m invar* saucer

pirilampo /piri'lãpu/ *m* glow-worm

Pirineus /piri'news/ *m pl* Pyrenees

pirra|ça /pi'xasa/ *f* spiteful act; **fazer ~ça** be spiteful. **~cento** *a* spiteful

pirueta /piru'eta/ *f* pirouette

pirulito /piru'litu/ *m* lollipop

pi|sada /pi'zada/ *f* step; (*rastro*) footprint. **~sar** *vt* tread on; tread *‹uvas, palco›*; (*esmagar*) trample on ● *vi* step; **~sar em** step on; (*entrar*) set foot in

pis|cadela /piska'dɛla/ *f* wink. **~ca-pisca** *m* indicator. **~car** *vi* (*com o olho*) wink; (*pestanejar*) blink; *‹estrela, luz›* twinkle; *‹motorista›* indicate ● *m* **num ~car de olhos** in a flash

P

piscicultura /pisikuw'tura/ *f* fish farming; (*lugar*) fish farm

piscina /pi'sina/ *f* swimming pool

piso /'pizu/ *m* floor

pisotear /pizotʃi'ar/ *vt* trample

pista /'pista/ *f* track; (*da estrada*) carriageway; (*para aviões*) runway; (*de circo*) ring; (*dica*) clue; **~ de dança** dance floor

pistache /pis'taʃi/ *m*, **pistacho** /pis'taʃu/ *m* pistachio (nut)

pisto|la /pis'tɔla/ *f* pistol; (*para pintar*) spray gun. **~lão** *m* influential contact. **~leiro** *m* gunman

pitada /pi'tada/ *f* pinch

piteira /pi'tera/ *f* cigarette holder

pitoresco /pito'resku/ *a* picturesque

pitu /pi'tu/ *m* crayfish

pivete /pi'vɛtʃi/ *m/f* child thief

pivô /pi'vo/ *m* pivot

pixaim /piʃa'ĩ/ *a* frizzy

pizza /'pitsa/ *f* pizza. **~ria** *f* pizzeria

placa /'plaka/ *f* plate; (*de carro*) number plate, *Amer* license plate; (*comemorativa*) plaque; (*em computador*) board; **~ de sinalização** road sign

placar /pla'kar/ *m* scoreboard; (*escore*) scoreline

plácido /'plasidu/ *a* placid

plagi|ário /plaʒi'ariu/ *m* plagiarist. **~ar** *vt* plagiarize

plágio /'plaʒiu/ *m* plagiarism

P

plaina /'plajna/ *f* plane

planador /plana'dor/ *m* glider

planalto /pla'nawtu/ *m* plateau

planar /pla'nar/ *vi* glide

planeamento, **planear** *Port* ▶ PLANEJAMENTO

plane|jamento /planeʒa'mẽtu/ *m* planning; **~jamento familiar** family planning. **~jar** *vt* plan

planeta /pla'neta/ *m* planet

planície /pla'nisi/ *f* plain

planificar /planifi'kar/ *vt* (*programar*) plan (out)

planilha /pla'niʎa/ *f* spreadsheet

plano /'planu/ *a* flat ● *m* plan; (*superfície, nível*) plane; **primeiro ~** foreground

planta /'plãta/ *f* plant; (*do pé*) sole; (*de edifício*) ground plan. **~ção** *f* (*ato*) planting; (*terreno*) plantation. **~do** *a* **deixar alguém ~do** [!] keep sb waiting around

plantão /plã'tãw/ *m* duty; (*noturno*) night duty; **estar de ~** be on duty

plantar /plã'tar/ *vt* plant

plas|ma /'plazma/ *m* plasma. **~mar** *vt* mould, shape

plásti|ca /'plastʃika/ *f* facelift. **~co** *a & m* plastic

plataforma /plata'fɔrma/ *f* platform

plátano /'platanu/ *m* plane tree

plateia /pla'tɛja/ *f* audience; (*parte do teatro*) stalls, *Amer* orchestra

platina /pla'tʃina/ *f* platinum. **~dos** *m pl* points

platônico /pla'toniku/ *a* platonic

plausí|vel /plaw'zivew/ (*pl* **~veis**) *a* plausible

ple|be /'plɛbi/ *f* common people. **~beu** *a* (*f* **~beia**) plebeian ● *m* (*f* **~beia**) commoner. **~biscito** *m* plebiscite

plei|tear /plejtʃi'ar/ *vt* contest. **~to** *m* (*litígio*) case; (*eleitoral*) contest

ple|namente /plena'mẽtʃi/ *adv* fully. **~nário** *a* plenary ● *m* plenary assembly. **~no** /e/ *a* full; **em ~no verão** in the middle of summer

plissado /pli'sadu/ *a* pleated

pluma /'pluma/ *f* feather. **~gem** *f* plumage

plu|ral /plu'raw/ (*pl* **~rais**) *a & m* plural

plutónio /plu'toniu/ *m* plutonium

pluvi|al /pluvi'aw/ (*pl* **~ais**) *a* rain

pneu /pi'new/ *m* tyre. **~mático** *a* pneumatic ● *m* tyre

pneumonia /pineumo'nia/ *f* pneumonia

pó /pɔ/ *m* powder; (*poeira*) dust; **leite em ~** powdered milk; **~ de arroz** (face) powder

pobre /'pɔbri/ *a* poor ● *m/f* poor man (*f* woman); **os ~s** the poor. **~za** /e/ *f* poverty

poça /'posa/ *f* pool; (*deixada pela chuva*) puddle

poção /po'sãw/ *f* potion

pocilga /po'siwga/ *f* pigsty

poço /'posu/ *f* (*de água, petróleo*) well; (*de mina, elevador*) shaft

podar /po'dar/ *vt* prune

podcast *m* podcast

poder /po'der/ ● *v aux*

····➤ (*capacidade*) can, to be able to; **posso escolher São Paulo ou Porto Alegre** I can choose São Paulo or Porto Alegre; **não podia acreditar**

I couldn't believe it; **desde então, ele não pode andar** he hasn't been able to walk since then

····➤ (*permissão*) can, may; **posso sair?** can ou may I go out?

! Há duas traduções possíveis de **poder** quando se pede permissão para fazer algo: *may* e *can*. No entanto, observe que **may** é mais formal do que **can**: **posso entrar?** may I come in?, can I come in? (*probabilidade*) may, could, might; **isso pode ou não ser verdade** that may or may not be true

! **could** e **might** exprimem uma probabilidade menor do que **may**

● *m*

····➤ power; **tomar o ~** seize power; **~ de compra** purchasing power; **~ executivo/legislativo** executive/legislative power; **plenos ~es** full authority

····➤ (*em expressões*) **não ~ com alguém** dislike sb; **não posso com ele!** I can't stand him!; **não ~ mais** be exhausted; **querer é ~** where there's a will, there's a way

pode|rio /pode'riu/ *m* might. **~roso** /o/ *a* powerful

pódio /'pɔdʒiu/ *m* podium

podre /'podri/ *a* rotten; ⓘ (*cansado*) exhausted; (*doente*) grotty; **~ de rico** filthy rich. **~s** *m pl* faults

poei|ra /po'era/ *f* dust. **~rento** *a* dusty

poe|ma /po'ema/ *m* poem. **~sia** *f* (*arte*) poetry; (*poema*) poem. **~ta** *m* poet

poético /po'ɛtʃiku/ *a* poetic

poetisa /poe'tʃiza/ *f* poetess

pois /pojs/ *conj* as, since; **~ é** that's right; **~ não** of course; **~ não?** can I help you?; **~ sim** certainly not

polaco /pu'laku/ *Port a* Polish ● *m* Pole; (*língua*) Polish

polar /po'lar/ *a* polar

polarizar /polari'zar/ *vt* polarize. **~-se** *vpr* polarize

pole|gada /pole'gada/ *f* inch. **~gar** *m* thumb

poleiro /po'leru/ *m* perch

polêmi|ca /po'lemika/ *f* controversy, debate. **~co** *a* controversial

pólen /'pɔlẽ/ *m* pollen

polícia /po'lisia/ *f* police ● *m/f* policeman (*f*-woman)

polici|al /polisi'aw/ (*pl* **~ais**) *a* ‹*carro, inquérito etc*› police; ‹*romance, filme*› detective ● *m/f* policeman (*f*-woman). **~amento** *m* policing. **~ar** *vt* police

poli|dez /poli'des/ *f* politeness. **~do** *a* polite

poli|gamia /poliga'mia/ *f* polygamy. **~glota** *a & m/f* polyglot

Polinésia /poli'nɛzia/ *f* Polynesia

polinésio /poli'nɛziu/ *a & m* Polynesian

pólio /'pɔliu/ *f* polio

polir /po'lir/ *vt* polish

polissílabo /poli'silabu/ *m* polysyllable

políti|ca /po'litʃika/ *f* politics; (*uma*) policy. **~co** *a* political ● *m* politician

polo[1] /'pɔlu/ *m* pole

polo[2] /'pɔlu/ *m* (*jogo*) polo; **~ aquático** water polo

polo|nês /polo'nes/ *a* (*f* **~nesa**) Polish ● *m* (*f* **~nesa**) Pole; (*língua*) Polish

Polônia /po'lonia/ *f* Poland

polpa /'powpa/ *f* pulp

poltrona /pow'trona/ *f* armchair

polu|ente /polu'ẽtʃi/ *a & m* pollutant. **~ição** *f* pollution. **~ir** *vt* pollute

polvilhar /powvi'ʎar/ *vt* sprinkle

polvo /'powvu/ *m* octopus

pólvora /'pɔwvora/ *f* gunpowder

polvorosa /powvo'rɔza/ *f* uproar; **em ~** in uproar; ‹*pessoa*› in a flap

pomada /po'mada/ *f* ointment

pomar /po'mar/ *m* orchard

pom|ba /'põba/ *f* dove. **~bo** *m* pigeon

pomo de Adão /pomudʃia'dãw/ *m* Adam's apple

pom|pa /'põpa/ *f* pomp. **~poso** /o/ *a* pompous

ponche /'põʃi/ *m* punch

ponderar /põde'rar/ *vt/i* ponder

pônei /'ponej/ *m* pony

ponta /'põta/ *f* end; (*de faca, prego*) point; (*de nariz, dedo, língua*) tip; (*de sapato*) toe; *Cine, Teat* (*papel curto*) walk-on part; (*no campo de futebol*) wing; (*jogador*) winger; **na ~ dos pés** on tiptoe; **uma ~ de** a touch of ‹*ironia etc*›; **aguentar as ~s** ⓘ hold on. **~-cabeça** /e/ *f* **de ~-cabeça** upside down

pontada /põ'tada/ *f* (*dor*) twinge

pontapé /põta'pɛ/ *m* kick; **~ inicial** kick-off

pontaria /põta'ria/ *f* aim; **fazer ~** take aim

P

ponte /'põtʃi/ *f* bridge; **~ aérea** shuttle; (*em tempo de guerra*) airlift; **~ de safena** heart bypass; **~ pênsil** suspension bridge

> **ponte** If a public holiday falls on a Thursday or a Tuesday, it's common for people in Portugal or Brazil to take a day off in between. In Portugal, this practice is called *fazer ponte* (literally "make a bridge") between the holiday and the weekend, and is a very common way of extending holiday celebrations.

ponteiro /põ'teru/ *m* pointer; (*de relógio*) hand

pontiagudo /põtʃia'gudu/ *a* sharp

pontilhado /põtʃi'ʎadu/ *a* dotted

ponto /'põtu/ *m* point; (*de costura, tricô*) stitch; (*no final de uma frase*) full stop, *Amer* period; (*sinalzinho, no i*) dot; (*de ônibus*) stop; (*no teatro*) prompter; **a ~ de** on the point of; **ao ~** ‹*carne*› medium; **até certo ~** to a certain extent; **às duas em ~** at exactly two o'clock; **dormir no ~** [!] miss the boat; **entregar os ~s** [!] give up; **fazer ~** [!] hang out; **dois ~s** colon; **~ de exclamação/interrogação** exclamation/question mark; **~ de reciclagem** recycling point; **~ de táxi** taxi rank, *Amer* taxi stand; **~ de vista** point of view; **~ morto** neutral. **~ e vírgula** *m* semicolon

pontu|ação /põtua'sãw/ *f* punctuation. **~al** (*pl* **~ais**) *a* punctual. **~alidade** *f* punctuality. **~ar** *vt* punctuate

pontudo /põ'tudu/ *a* pointed

popa /'popa/ *f* stern

popu|lação /popula'sãw/ *f* population. **~lacional** (*pl* **~lacionais**) *a* population. **~lar** *a* popular. **~laridade** *f* popularity. **~larizar** *vt* popularize. **~larizar-se** *vpr* become popular

pôquer /'poker/ *m* poker

> **por** /por/ ● *prep*
>
> ····➤ (*lugar*) **circular pela direita** drive on the right; **passar pelo centro de Brasília** go through the centre of Brasilia; **viajar pelo Brasil** travel round Brazil; **você passa ~ uma farmácia?** are you going past a chemist's?; **passo pela sua casa amanhã** I'll drop in tomorrow
>
> ····➤ (*durante*) for; **só ~ uns dias** only for a few days; (*tempo aproximado*) about; **~ volta de 8 horas** about 8
>
> ····➤ (*causa*) **foi despedido ~ ser preguiçoso** he was sacked for being lazy; **~ inveja/ciúme/hábito** out of jealousy/envy/habit; **faria qualquer coisa ~ você** I'll do anything for you; **trabalhar ~ dinheiro** work for money
>
> ····➤ (*agente*) by; **assinado/escrito/pintado ~** signed/written/painted by
>
> ····➤ (*para com*) for; **sentir carinho ~ alguém** to feel affection for sb
>
> ····➤ (*não feito*) **~ lavar** not yet washed; **tive de deixar o trabalho ~ acabar** I had to leave the work unfinished
>
> ····➤ (*substituição*) **ela irá ~ mim** she'll go instead of me
>
> ····➤ (*preço*) for; **comprei ~ mil euros** I bought it for a thousand euros
>
> ····➤ (*com verbos como agarrar, pegar*) by; **segurei-o pelo braço** I grabbed him by the arm
>
> ····➤ (*em expressões*) **~ isso** so; **~ mim** (*no que me diz respeito*) as far as I'm concerned; **~ mais que** however much

pôr /por/ *vt* put; put on ‹*roupa, chapéu, óculos*›; lay ‹*mesa, ovos*› ● *m* **o ~ do sol** sunset. **~-se** *vpr* ‹*sol*› set; **~-se a** start to; **~-se a caminho** set off

porão /po'rãw/ *m* (*de prédio*) basement; (*de casa*) cellar; (*de navio*) hold

porca /'pɔrka/ *f* (*de parafuso*) nut; (*animal*) sow

porção /por'sãw/ *f* portion; **uma ~ de** (*muitos*) a lot of

porcaria /porka'ria/ *f* (*sujeira*) filth; (*coisa malfeita*) piece of trash; *pl* trash

porcelana /porse'lana/ *f* china

porcentagem /porsẽ'taʒẽ/ *f* percentage

porco /'porku/ *a* filthy ● *m* (*animal*) pig; (*carne*) pork. **~-espinho** (*pl* **~s-espinhos**) *m* porcupine

porém /po'rẽj/ *conj* however

pormenor /porme'nɔr/ *m* detail

por|nô /por'no/ *a* porn ● *m* porn film. **~nografia** *f* pornography. **~nográfico** *a* pornographic

poro /'pɔru/ *m* pore. **~so** /o/ *a* porous

por|quanto /por'kwãtu/ *conj* since. **~que** /por'ki/ *conj* because; *Port* (*por quê?*) why. **~quê** /por'ke/ *adv Port* why ● *m* reason why

porquinho|-da-índia /porkiɲuda'ĩdʒia/ (*pl* **~s-da-índia**) *m* guinea pig

porrada /po'xada/ *f* [!] beating

porre /'pɔxi/ *m* [!] drinking session, booze-up [!]; **de ~** drunk; **tomar um ~** get drunk

porta /'pɔrta/ *f* door

porta-aviões /pɔrtavi'õjs/ *m invar* aircraft carrier

porta-bagagens /pɔrtaba'gaʒãjʃ/ *m Port* ▶ PORTA-MALAS

porta|-chaves /pɔrta'ʃavis/ *m invar* keyholder ou key-ring. **~-joias** *m invar* jewellery box; **~-lápis** *m invar* pencil holder; **~-luvas** *m invar* glove compartment; **~-malas** *m invar* boot, *Amer* trunk; **~-níqueis** *m invar* purse

portador /porta'dor/ *m* bearer

portagem /por'taʒẽ/ *f Port* toll

portanto /por'tãtu/ *conj* therefore

portão /por'tãw/ *m* gate

portar /por'tar/ *vt* carry. **~-se** *vpr* behave

porta|-retrato /pɔrtaxe'tratu/ *m* photo frame. **~-revistas** *m invar* magazine rack

portaria /porta'ria/ *f* (*entrada*) entrance; (*decreto*) decree

portá|til (*pl* **~teis**) *a* portable

portátil /pur'tatiɫ/ *m Port* laptop

porta|-toalhas /pɔrtato'aʎas/ *m invar* towel rail. **~-voz** *m/f* spokesman (*f* -woman)

porte /'pɔrtʃi/ *m* (*frete*) carriage; (*de cartas etc*) postage; (*de pessoa*) bearing; (*dimensão*) scale; **de grande/pequeno ~** large-/small-scale

porteiro /por'teru/ *m* doorman; **~ eletrônico** entryphone

porto /'portu/ *m* port; **o P~** Oporto. **~ de escala** *m* port of call; **P~ Rico** *m* Puerto Rico; **~-riquenho** /e/ *a & m* Puerto Rican; **~ USB** *m* USB port

portuário /portu'ariu/ *a* port ● *m* dock worker, docker

portuense /portu'ẽsi/ *a & m/f* (person) from Oporto

Portugal /portu'gaw/ *m* Portugal

portu|guês /portu'ges/ *a & m* (*f* **~guesa**) Portuguese

> *i* **Português** With over 250 million speakers, Portuguese is the sixth most widely spoken language in the world. The *CPLP* (*Comunidade dos Países de Língua Portuguesa*) comprises eight countries that have Portuguese as an official language: Angola, Brazil, Cape Verde, East Timor, Guinea-Bissau, Mozambique, Portugal, and São Tomé and Príncipe. African Portuguese-speaking countries are referred to as the *PALOP* (*Países Africanos de Língua Oficial Portuguesa*).

po|sar /po'zar/ *vi* pose. **~se** /o/ *f* pose; (*de filme*) exposure

pós-datar /pɔzda'tar/ *vt* post-date

pós-escrito /pɔzis'kritu/ *m* postscript

pós-gradua|ção /pɔzgradua'sãw/ *f* postgraduation. **~do** *a & m* postgraduate

pós-guerra /pɔz'gɛxa/ *m* post-war period; **a Europa do ~** post-war Europe

posi|ção /pozi'sãw/ *f* position. **~cionar** *vt* position. **~tivo** *a & m* positive

posologia /pozolo'ʒia/ *f* dosage

pos|sante /po'sãtʃi/ *a* powerful. **~se** /ɔ/ *f* (*de casa etc*) possession, ownership; (*do presidente etc*) swearing in; *pl* (*pertences*) possessions; **tomar ~se** take office; **tomar ~se de** take possession of

posses|são /pose'sãw/ *f* possession. **~sivo** *a* possessive. **~so** /ɛ/ *a* possessed; (*com raiva*) furious

possibili|dade /posibili'dadʒi/ *f* possibility. **~tar** *vt* make possible

possí|vel /po'sivew/ (*pl* **~veis**) *a* possible; **fazer todo o ~vel** do one's best

possuir /posu'ir/ *vt* possess; (*ser dono de*) own

posta /'pɔsta/ *f* (*de peixe*) steak

pos|tal /pos'taw/ (*pl* **~tais**) *a* postal ● *m* postcard

postar /pos'tar/ *vt* place. **~-se** *vpr* position o.s.

poste /'pɔstʃi/ *m* post

pôster /'poster/ *m* poster

posteri|dade /posteri'dadʒi/ *f* posterity. **~or** *a* (*no tempo*) subsequent, later; (*no espaço*) rear. **~ormente** *adv* subsequently

postiço /pos'tʃisu/ *a* false

posto /'postu/ *m* post; **~ de gasolina**; petrol station, *Amer* gas station; **~ de saúde** health centre ● *pp de* ▶ PÔR. **~ que** although

póstumo /'pɔstumu/ *a* posthumous

postura /pos'tura/ *f* posture

potá|vel /po'tavew/ (*pl* **~veis**) *a* **água ~vel** drinking water

pote /'pɔtʃi/ *m* pot; (*de vidro*) jar

potência /po'tẽsia/ *f* power

P

poten|cial /potẽsi'aw/ (*pl* **~ciais**) *a & m* potential. **~te** *a* potent

potencializar /potẽsiali'zar/ *vt* ‹*vendas, crescimento*› boost

potenciar /putẽsi'ar/ *vt Port* ▶ POTENCIALIZAR

potro /'potru/ *m* foal

pouco /'poku/ *a & pron* little ● *adv* not much ● *m* **um ~** a little; **~ a ~** little by little; **aos ~s** gradually; **daqui a ~** shortly; **por ~** almost; **~ tempo** a short time

pou|pança /po'pãsa/ *f* saving; (*conta*) savings account. **~par** *vt* save; spare ‹*vida*›

pouquinho /po'kiɲu/ *m* **um ~ (de)** a little

pou|sada /po'zada/ *f* inn. **~sar** *vi* land. **~so** *m* landing

> **pousada** In the 1940s, the Portuguese government decided to create a series of hotels, called *pousadas*, in buildings of historic interest, such as convents, monasteries and castles. Although privately owned now, Portuguese *pousadas* still offer high-quality accommodation in very unique settings. In Brazil, a *pousada* is usually a guest house or a budget hotel.

po|vão /po'vãw/ *m* common people. **~vo** /o/ *m* people

P **povo|ação** /povoa'sãw/ *f* settlement. **~ar** *vt* populate

poxa /'poʃa/ *int* gosh

pra /pra/ *prep* [!] ▶ PARA

praça /'prasa/ *f* (*largo*) square; (*mercado*) market ● *m* (*soldado*) private

prado /'pradu/ *m* meadow

pra-frente /pra'frẽtʃi/ *a invar* [!] with it [!], modern

praga /'praga/ *f* curse; (*inseto, doença, pessoa*) pest

prag|mático /prag'matʃiku/ *a* pragmatic. **~matismo** *m* pragmatism

praguejar /prage'ʒar/ *vt/i* curse

praia /'praja/ *f* beach

pran|cha /'prãʃa/ *f* plank; (*de surfe*) board. **~cheta** /e/ *f* drawing board

pranto /'prãtu/ *m* weeping

pra|ta /'prata/ *f* silver. **~taria** *f* (*coisas de prata*) silverware. **~teado** *a* silver-plated; (*cor*) silver

prateleira /prate'lera/ *f* shelf

prática /'pratʃika/ *f* practice; **na ~** in practice

prati|cante /pratʃi'kãtʃi/ *a* practising ● *m/f* apprentice; (*de esporte etc*) player. **~car** *vt* practise; (*cometer, executar*) carry out ● *vi* practise. **~cável** (*pl* **~cáveis**) *a* practicable

prático /'pratʃiku/ *a* practical

prato /'pratu/ *m* (*objeto*) plate; (*comida*) dish; (*parte de uma refeição*) course; (*do toca-discos*) turntable; *pl* (*instrumento*) cymbals; **~ fundo** dish; **~ principal** main course

praxe /'praʃi/ *f* normal practice; **de ~** usually

> **praxe** The *código da praxe* refers to a set of rules and traditions to be followed by students at Portuguese universities. Thought to have originated at Portugal's oldest university in Coimbra, the traditions start in freshers' week in which the *caloiros* (freshers) are subjected to various initiation rites and practical jokes, such as being made to walk around town with cans attached to their feet.

prazer /pra'zer/ *m* pleasure; **muito ~ (em conhecê-lo)** pleased to meet you. **~oso** /o/ *a* pleasurable

prazo /'prazu/ *m* term, time; **a ~** ‹*compra etc*› on credit; **a curto/longo ~** in the short/long term; **último ~** deadline

preâmbulo /pri'ãbulu/ *m* preamble

precário /pre'kariu/ *a* precarious

precaução /prekaw'sãw/ *f* precaution

preca|ver-se /preka'versi/ *vpr* take precautions (**de** against). **~vido** *a* cautious

prece /'prɛsi/ *f* prayer

prece|dência /prese'dẽsia/ *f* precedence. **~dente** *a* preceding ● *m* precedent. **~der** *vt/i* precede

preceito /pre'sejtu/ *m* precept

precioso /presi'ozu/ *a* precious

precipício /presi'pisiu/ *m* precipice

precipi|tação /presipita'sãw/ *f* haste; (*chuva etc*) precipitation. **~tado** *a* ‹*fuga*› headlong; ‹*decisão, ato*› hasty, rash. **~tar** *vt* (*lançar*) throw; (*antecipar*) hasten. **~tar-se** *vpr* (*lançar-se*) throw o.s.; (*apressar-se*) rush; (*agir sem pensar*) act rashly

precisamente /presiza'mẽtʃi/ *adv* precisely

precisão /presi'zãw/ *f* precision, accuracy

preci|sar /presi'zar/ *vt* (*necessitar*) need; (*indicar com exatidão*) specify ● *vi* be necessary; **~sar de** need; **~so ir** I have to go; **~sa-se** wanted. **~so** *a* (*exato*) precise; (*necessário*) necessary

preço /'presu/ *m* price; **~ de custo** cost price; **~ fixo** set price

precoce /pre'kɔsi/ *a* ‹*fruto*› early; ‹*velhice, calvície etc*› premature; ‹*criança*› precocious

precon|cebido /prekõse'bidu/ *a* preconceived. **~ceito** *m* prejudice. **~ceituoso** *a* prejudiced

preconizar /prekoni'zar/ *vt* advocate

precursor /prekur'sor/ *m* forerunner

preda|dor /preda'dor/ *m* predator. **~tório** *a* predatory

predecessor /predese'sor/ *m* predecessor

predestinar /predestʃi'nar/ *vt* predestine

predeterminar /predetermi'nar/ *vt* predetermine

predição /predʒi'sãw/ *f* prediction

predile|ção /predʒile'sãw/ *f* preference. **~to** /ɛ/ *a* favourite

prédio /'prɛdʒiu/ *m* building

predis|por /predʒis'por/ *vt* prepare (**para** for); (*tornar parcial*) prejudice (**contra** against). **~por-se** *vpr* prepare o.s.. **~posto** *a* predisposed; (*contra*) prejudiced

predizer /predʒi'zer/ *vt* predict, foretell

predomi|nância /predomi'nãsia/ *f* predominance. **~nante** *a* predominant. **~nar** *vi* predominate

predomínio /predo'miniu/ *m* predominance

preencher /priẽ'ʃer/ *vt* fill; fill in, *Amer* fill out ‹*formulário*›; meet ‹*requisitos*›

pré|-escola /prɛis'kɔla/ *f* infant school, *Amer* preschool. **~-escolar** *a* preschool; **~-estreia** *f* preview; **~-fabricado** *a* prefabricated

prefácio /pre'fasiu/ *m* preface

prefei|to /pre'fejtu/ *m* mayor. **~tura** *f* prefecture; (*prédio*) town hall

prefe|rência /prefe'rẽsia/ *f* preference; (*direito no trânsito*) right of way; **de ~rência** preferably. **~rencial** (*pl* **~renciais**) *a* preferential; ‹*rua*› main. **~rido** *a* favourite. **~rir** *vt* prefer (**a** to). **~rível** (*pl* **~ríveis**) *a* preferable

prefixo /pre'fiksu/ *m* prefix

prega /'prɛga/ *f* pleat

pregador[1] /prega'dor/ *m* (*de roupa*) peg

pre|gador[2] /prega'dor/ *m* (*quem prega*) preacher. **~gão** *m* (*de vendedor*) cry; **o ~gão** (*na bolsa de valores*) trading; (*em leilão*) bidding

pregar[1] /pre'gar/ *vt* fix; (*com prego*) nail; sew on ‹*botão*›; **não ~ olho** not sleep a wink; **~ uma peça em** play a trick on; **~ um susto em alguém** give sb a fright

pregar[2] /pre'gar/ *vt/i* preach

prego /'prɛgu/ *m* nail

pregui|ça /pre'gisa/ *f* laziness; (*bicho*) sloth; **estou com ~ça de ir** I can't be bothered to go. **~çoso** *a* lazy

pré-histórico /prɛjs'tɔriku/ *a* prehistoric

preia-mar /preja'mar/ *f* high tide

prejudi|car /preʒudʒi'kar/ *vt* harm; damage ‹*saúde*›. **~car-se** *vpr* harm o.s.. **~cial** (*pl* **~ciais**) *a* harmful, damaging (**a** to)

prejuízo /preʒu'izu/ *m* damage; (*financeiro*) loss; **em ~ de** to the detriment of

prejulgar /preʒuw'gar/ *vt* prejudge

preliminar /prelimi'nar/ *a & m/f* preliminary

prelo /'prɛlu/ *m* printing press; **no ~** being printed

prelúdio /pre'ludʒiu/ *m* prelude

prematuro /prema'turu/ *a* premature

premeditar /premedʒi'tar/ *vt* premeditate

premente /pre'mẽtʃi/ *a* pressing

premi|ado /premi'adu/ *a* ‹*romance, atleta etc*› prizewinning; ‹*bilhete, número etc*› winning ● *m* prizewinner. **~ar** *vt* award a prize to ‹*romance, atleta etc*›; reward ‹*honestidade, mérito*›

prêmio /'premiu/ *m* prize; (*de seguro*) premium; **Grande Prêmio** (*de F1*) Grand Prix

premir /pre'mir/ *vt Port* press ‹*tecla*›

premissa /pre'misa/ *f* premiss

premonição /premoni'sãw/ *f* premonition

pré-na|tal /prɛna'taw/ (*pl* **~tais**) *a* antenatal, *Amer* prenatal

prenda /ˈprẽda/ *f Port* present; **~s domésticas** household chores. **~do** *a* domesticated

pren|dedor /prẽdeˈdor/ *m* clip; **~dedor de roupa** clothes peg. **~der** *vt* (*pregar*) fix; (*capturar*) arrest; (*atar*) tie up ‹*cachorro*›; tie back ‹*cabelo*›; (*restringir*) restrict; (*ligar afetivamente*) bind; **~der (a atenção de) alguém** grab sb ('s attention)

prenhe /ˈpreɲi/ *a* pregnant

prenome /preˈnomi/ *m* first name

pren|sa /ˈprẽsa/ *f* press. **~sar** *vt* press

preocu|pação /preokupaˈsãw/ *f* concern. **~pante** *a* worrying. **~par** *vt* worry. **~par-se** *vpr* worry (**com** about)

prepa|ração /preparaˈsãw/ *f* preparation. **~rado** *m* preparation. **~rar** *vt* prepare. **~rar-se** *vpr* prepare, get ready. **~rativos** *m pl* preparations. **~ro** *m* preparation; (*competência*) knowledge; **~ro físico** physical fitness

preponderar /prepõdeˈrar/ *vi* prevail (**sobre** over)

preposição /prepoziˈsãw/ *f* preposition

prerrogativa /prexogaˈtʃiva/ *f* prerogative

presa /ˈpreza/ *f* (*de caça*) prey; (*de cobra*) fang; (*de elefante*) tusk; **~ de guerra** spoils of war

prescin|dir /presĩˈdʒir/ *vi* **~dir de** dispense with. **~dível** (*pl* **~díveis**) *a* dispensable

pres|crever /preskreˈver/ *vt* prescribe. **~crição** *f* prescription; (*norma*) rule

presen|ça /preˈzẽsa/ *f* presence; **~ça de espírito** presence of mind. **~ciar** *vt* (*estar presente a*) be present at; (*testemunhar*) witness. **~te** *a* & *m* present. **~tear** *vt* **~tear alguém (com algo)** give sb (sth as) a present

presépio /preˈzɛpiu/ *m* crib

preser|vação /prezervaˈsãw/ *f* preservation. **~var** *vt* preserve, protect. **~vativo** *m* (*em comida*) preservative; (*camisinha*) condom

presi|dência /preziˈdẽsia/ *f* presidency; (*de uma reunião*) chair. **~dencial** (*pl* **~denciais**) *a* presidential. **~dencialismo** *m* presidential system. **~dente** *m* (*f* **~denta**) president; (*de uma reunião*) chairperson

presidiário /prezidʒiˈariu/ *m* convict

presídio /preˈzidʒiu/ *m* prison

presidir /preziˈdʒir/ *vi* preside (**a** over)

presilha /preˈziʎa/ *f* fastener; (*de cabelo*) slide

preso /ˈprezu/ *pp de* ▶ **PRENDER** ● *m* prisoner; **ficar ~** get stuck; ‹*saia, corda etc*› get caught

pressa /ˈprɛsa/ *f* hurry; **às ~s** in a hurry, hurriedly; **estar com** ou **ter ~** be in a hurry

presságio /preˈsaʒiu/ *m* omen

pressão /preˈsãw/ *f* pressure; **fazer ~ sobre** put pressure on; **~ arterial** blood pressure

pressen|timento /presẽtʃiˈmẽtu/ *m* premonition, feeling. **~tir** *vt* sense

pressionar /presioˈnar/ *vt* press ‹*botão*›; pressure ‹*pessoa*›

pressupor /presuˈpor/ *vt* ‹*pessoa*› presume; ‹*coisa*› presuppose

pressurizado /presuriˈzadu/ *a* pressurized

pres|tação /prestaˈsãw/ *f* repayment, instalment. **~tar** *vt* render ‹*contas, serviço*›; **não ~ta** he/it is no good; **~tar atenção** pay attention; **~tar juramento** take an oath ● *vi* be of use. **~tativo** *a* helpful. **~tável** (*pl* **~táveis**) *a* serviceable

prestes /ˈprɛstʃis/ *a invar* **~ a** about to

prestidigita|ção /prestʃidʒiʒitaˈsãw/ *f* conjuring. **~dor** *m* conjurer

pres|tigiar /prestʃiʒiˈar/ *vt* give prestige to. **~tígio** *m* prestige. **~tigioso** /o/ *a* prestigious

préstimo /ˈprɛstʃimu/ *m* merit

presumir /prezuˈmir/ *vt* presume

presun|ção /prezũˈsãw/ *f* presumption. **~çoso** /o/ *a* presumptuous

presunto /preˈzũtu/ *m* ham

pretendente /pretẽˈdẽtʃi/ *m/f* (*candidato*) candidate, applicant

preten|der /pretẽˈder/ *vt* intend. **~são** *f* pretension. **~sioso** /o/ *a* pretentious

preterir /preteˈrir/ *vt* disregard

pretérito /preˈtɛritu/ *m* preterite

pretexto /preˈtestu/ *m* pretext

preto /ˈpretu/ *a* & *m* black. **~ e branco** *a invar* black and white

prevalecer /prevaleˈser/ *vi* prevail

prevenção /prevẽˈsãw/ *f* (*impedimento*) prevention; (*parcialidade*) bias

prevenir /preveˈnir/ *vt* (*evitar*) prevent; (*avisar*) warn. **~-se** *vpr* take precautions

preventivo /prevẽˈtʃivu/ *a* preventive

prever /preˈver/ *vt* foresee, predict

P

previdência /previ'dẽsia/ *f* foresight; ~ **social** social security

prévio /'prɛviu/ *a* prior

previ|são /previ'zãw/ *f* prediction, forecast; **~são do tempo** weather forecast. **~sível** (*pl* **~síveis**) *a* predictable

pre|zado /pre'zadu/ *a* esteemed; **Prezado Senhor** Dear Sir. **~zar** *vt* think highly of. **~zar-se** *vpr* have self-respect

prima /'prima/ *f* cousin

primário /pri'mariu/ *a* primary; (*fundamental*) basic

primata /pri'mata/ *m* primate

primave|ra /prima'vɛra/ *f* spring; (*flor*) primrose. **~ril** (*pl* **~ris**) *a* spring

primazia /prima'zia/ *f* primacy

primei|ra /pri'mera/ *f* (*marcha*) first (gear); **de ~ra** first-rate; ‹*carne*› prime. **~ra-dama** (*pl* **~ras-damas**) *f* first lady. **~ranista** *m/f* first-year (student). **~ro** *a & adv* first; **no dia ~ro de maio** on the first of May; **em ~ro lugar** (*para começar*) in the first place; (*numa corrida, competição*) in first place; **~ro de tudo** first of all; **~ros socorros** first aid. **~ro-ministro** (*pl* **~ros-ministros**) *m* (*f* **~ra-ministra**) prime-minister

primitivo /primi'tʃivu/ *a* primitive

primo /'primu/ *m* cousin ● *a* **número ~** prime number. **~gênito** *a & m* firstborn

primor /pri'mor/ *m* perfection

primordi|al /primordʒi'aw/ (*pl* **~ais**) *a* (*primitivo*) primordial; (*fundamental*) fundamental

primoroso /primo'rozu/ *a* exquisite

princesa /prĩ'seza/ *f* princess

princi|pado /prĩsipi'adu/ *m* principality. **~pal** (*pl* **~pais**) *a* main ● *m* principal

príncipe /'prĩsipi/ *m* prince

principiante /prĩsipi'ãtʃi/ *m/f* beginner

princípio /prĩ'sipiu/ *m* (*início*) beginning; (*regra*) principle; **em ~** in principle; **por ~** on principle

priori|dade /priori'dadʒi/ *f* priority. **~tário** *a* priority

prisão /pri'zãw/ *f* (*ato de prender*) arrest; (*cadeia*) prison; (*encarceramento*) imprisonment; **~ perpétua** life imprisonment; **~ de ventre** constipation

prisioneiro /prizio'neru/ *m* prisoner

prisma /'prizma/ *m* prism

privação /priva'sãw/ *f* deprivation

privacidade /privasi'dadʒi/ *f* privacy

pri|vada /pri'vada/ *f* toilet. **~vado** *a* private; **~vado de** deprived of. **~var** *vt* deprive (**de** of). **~var-se** *vpr* deprive o.s. (**de** of)

privati|vo /priva'tʃivu/ *a* private. **~zar** *vt* privatize

privi|legiado /privileʒi'adu/ *a* privileged; ‹*tratamento*› preferential. **~legiar** *vt* favour. **~légio** *m* privilege

pro [!]= **para + o**

pró /prɔ/ *adv* for ● *m* **os ~s e os contras** the pros and cons

proa /'proa/ *f* bow, prow

proativo /prɔa'tivu/ *a* proactive

probabilidade /probabili'dadʒi/ *f* probability

proble|ma /pro'blema/ *m* problem. **~mático** *a* problematic

proce|dência /prose'dẽsia/ *f* origin. **~dente** *a* logical; **~dente de** coming from. **~der** *vi* proceed; (*comportar-se*) behave; (*na justiça*) take legal action; **~der de** come from. **~dimento** *m* procedure; (*comportamento*) behaviour; (*na justiça*) proceedings

proces|sador /prosesa'dor/ *m* processor; **~sador de texto** word processor. **~samento** *m* processing; (*na justiça*) prosecution; **~samento de dados** data processing. **~sar** *vt* process; (*por crime*) prosecute; (*por causa civil*) sue. **~so** /ɛ/ *m* process; (*criminal*) trial; (*civil*) lawsuit

procla|mação /proklama'sãw/ *f* proclamation. **~mar** *vt* proclaim

procri|ação /prokria'sãw/ *f* procreation. **~ar** *vt/i* procreate

procu|ra /pro'kura/ *f* search; (*de produto*) demand; **à ~ra de** in search of. **~ração** *f* power of attorney. **~rado** *a* sought after, in demand; **~rado pela polícia** wanted by the police. **~rador** *m* (*mandatário*) proxy; (*advogado*) public prosecutor. **~rar** *vt* look for; (*contatar*) get in touch with; (*ir visitar*) look up; **~rar saber** try to find out

prodígio /pro'dʒiʒiu/ *m* wonder; (*pessoa*) prodigy

prodigioso /prodʒiʒi'ozu/ *a* prodigious

pródigo /'prɔdigu/ *a* lavish, extravagant

produ|ção /produ'sãw/ *f* production. **~tividade** *f* productivity. **~tivo** *a* productive. **~to** *m* product; (*renda*) proceeds; **~to nacional bruto** gross national product; **~tos agrícolas** agricultural produce. **~tor** *m* producer ● *a* **país ~tor de trigo** wheat-producing country. **~zido** *a* [!] (*arrumado*) done up. **~zir** *vt* produce

proeminente /proemi'nẽtʃi/ *a* prominent

proeza /pro'eza/ *f* achievement

profa|nar /profa'nar/ *vt* desecrate. **~no** *a* profane

profecia /profe'sia/ *f* prophecy

proferir /profe'rir/ *vt* utter; give ‹*discurso, palestra*›; pass ‹*sentença*›

profes|sar /profe'sar/ *vt* profess. **~so** /ɛ/ *a* professed; ‹*político etc*› seasoned. **~sor** *m* teacher; **~sor catedrático** professor

pro|feta /pro'fɛta/ *m* prophet. **~fético** *a* prophetic. **~fetizar** *vt* prophesy

profissão /profi'sãw/ *f* profession

profissio|nal /profisio'naw/ (*pl* **~nais**) *a & m/f* professional. **~nalismo** *m* professionalism. **~nalizante** *a* vocational. **~nalizar-se** *vpr* ‹*esportista etc*› turn professional

profun|didade /profũdʒi'dadʒi/ *f* depth. **~do** *a* deep; ‹*sentimento etc*› profound

profusão /profu'zãw/ *f* profusion

prog|nosticar /prognostʃi'kar/ *vt* forecast. **~nóstico** *m* forecast; *Med* prognosis

progra|ma /pro'grama/ *m* programme; (*de computador*) program; (*diversão*) thing to do. **~mação** *f* programming. **~mador** *m* programmer. **~mar** *vt* plan; program ‹*computador etc*›. **~mável** (*pl* **~máveis**) *a* programmable

progredir /progre'dʒir/ *vi* progress

progres|são /progre'sãw/ *f* progression. **~sista** *a & m/f* progressive. **~sivo** *a* progressive. **~so** /ɛ/ *m* progress

proi|bição /proibi'sãw/ *f* ban (**de** on). **~bido** *a* forbidden. **~bir** *vt* forbid (**alguém de** sb to); ban ‹*livro, importações etc*›. **~bitivo** *a* prohibitive

proje|ção /proʒe'sãw/ *f* projection. **~tar** *vt* plan ‹*viagem, estrada etc*›; design ‹*casa, carro etc*›; project ‹*filme, luz*›

projé|til /pro'ʒɛtʃiw/ (*pl* **~teis**) *m* projectile

proje|tista /proʒe'tʃista/ *m/f* designer. **~to** /ɛ/ *m* project; (*de casa, carro*) design; **~to de lei** bill. **~tor** *m* projector

prol /prɔw/ *m* **em ~ de** on behalf of

prole /'prɔli/ *f* offspring. **~tariado** *m* proletariat. **~tário** *a & m* proletarian

prolife|ração /prolifera'sãw/ *f* proliferation. **~rar** *vi* proliferate

prolífico /pro'lifiku/ *a* prolific

prolixo /pro'liksu/ *a* verbose, long-winded

prólogo /'prɔlogu/ *m* prologue

prolon|gado /prolõ'gadu/ *a* prolonged. **~gar** *vt* prolong. **~gar-se** *vpr* go on

promessa /pro'mɛsa/ *f* promise

prome|tedor /promete'dor/ *a* promising. **~ter** *vt* promise ● *vi* (*dar esperança*) show promise; **~ter voltar** promise to return

promíscuo /pro'miskuu/ *a* promiscuous

promis|sor /promi'sor/ *a* promising. **~sória** *f* promissory note

promoção /promo'sãw/ *f* promotion

promontório /promõ'tɔriu/ *m* promontory

promo|tor /promo'tor/ *m* promoter; (*advogado*) prosecutor. **~ver** *vt* promote

promulgar /promuw'gar/ *vt* promulgate

prono|me /pro'nomi/ *m* pronoun. **~minal** (*pl* **~minais**) *a* pronominal

pron|tidão /prõtʃi'dãw/ *f* readiness; **com ~tidão** promptly; **estar de ~tidão** be at the ready. **~tificar** *vt* get ready. **~tificar-se** *vpr* volunteer (**a** to **para** for). **~to** *a* ready; (*rápido*) prompt ● *int* that's that. **~to-socorro** (*pl* **~tos-socorros**) *m* casualty department; *Port* (*reboque*) tow truck. **~tuário** *m* (*manual*) manual, handbook; (*médico*) notes; (*policial*) record, file

pronto-a-comer /prõtwaku'mer/ *m invar Port* take-away, *Amer* take-out

pronúncia /pro'nũsia/ *f* pronunciation

pronunci|ado /pronũsi'adu/ *a* pronounced. **~amento** *m* pronouncement. **~ar** *vt* pronounce

propagar /propa'gar/ *vt* propagate ‹*espécie*›; spread ‹*notícia, ideia, fé*›. **~-se** *vpr* spread; ‹*espécie*› propagate

propen|são /propẽ'sãw/ *f* propensity. **~so** *a* inclined (**a** to)

pro|piciar /propisi'ar/ *vt* provide. **~pício** *a* propitious

propina /pro'pina/ *f* bribe; *Port* (*escolar*) fee

propor /pro'por/ *vt* propose. **~-se** *vpr* set o.s. ‹*objetivo*›; **~-se a estudar** set out to study

proporção /propor'sãw/ *f* proportion

proporcio|nado /proporsio'nadu/ *a* proportionate (**a** to); **bem-~nado** well proportioned. **~nal** (*pl* **~nais**) *a* proportional. **~nar** *vt* provide

proposi|ção /propozi'sãw/ *f* proposition. **~tado** *a*, **~tal** (*pl* **~tais**) *a* intentional

propósito /pro'pɔzitu/ *m* intention; **a ~** by the way; **a ~ de** on the subject of; **chegar a ~** arrive at the right time; **de ~** on purpose

proposta /pro'pɔsta/ *f* proposal

propriamente /propria'mẽtʃi/ *adv* strictly; **a casa ~ dita** the house proper

proprie|dade /proprie'dadʒi/ *f* property; (*direito sobre bens*) ownership. **~tário** *m* owner; (*de casa alugada*) landlord

próprio /'prɔpriu/ *a* (*de si*) own; ‹*sentido*› literal; ‹*nome*› proper; **meu ~ carro** my own car; **um carro ~** a car of my own; **o ~ rei** the king himself; **~ a** peculiar to; **~ para** suited to

prorro|gação /proxoga'sãw/ *f* extension; (*de dívida*) deferment; (*em futebol etc*) extra time. **~gar** *vt* extend ‹*prazo*›; defer ‹*pagamento*›

pro|sa /'prɔza/ *f* prose. **~sador** *m* prose writer. **~saico** *a* prosaic

proscrever /proskre'ver/ *vt* proscribe

prospecto /pros'pɛktu/ *m* (*livro*) brochure; (*folheto*) leaflet

prospe|rar /prospe'rar/ *vi* prosper. **~ridade** *f* prosperity

próspero /'prɔsperu/ *a* prosperous

prosse|guimento /prosegi'mẽtu/ *m* continuation. **~guir** *vt* continue ● *vi* proceed, go on

prostitu|ição /prostʃitui'sãw/ *f* prostitution. **~ta** *f* prostitute

pros|tração /prostra'sãw/ *f* debility. **~trado** *a* prostrate. **~trar** *vt* prostrate; (*enfraquecer*) debilitate. **~trar-se** *vpr* prostrate o.s.

protago|nista /protago'nista/ *m/f* protagonist. **~nizar** *vt* be at the centre of ‹*acontecimento*›; feature in ‹*peça, filme*›

prote|ção /prote'sãw/ *f* protection. **~cionismo** *m* protectionism. **~cionista** *a & m/f* protectionist. **~ger** *vt* protect. **~gido** *m* protégé

proteína /prote'ina/ *f* protein

protelar /prote'lar/ *vt* put off

protes|tante /protes'tãtʃi/ *a & m/f* Protestant. **~tar** *vt/i* protest. **~to** /ɛ/ *m* protest

protetor /prote'tor/ *m* protector ● *a* protective

protocolo /proto'kɔlu/ *m* protocol; (*registro*) register

protótipo /pro'tɔtʃipu/ *m* prototype

protuberância /protube'rãsia/ *f* bulge

pro|va /'prɔva/ *f* (*que comprova*) proof; (*teste*) trial; (*exame*) exam; (*esportiva*) competition; (*de livro etc*) proof; *pl* (*na justiça*) evidence; **à ~va de bala** bulletproof; **pôr à ~va** put to the test. **~vado** *a* proven. **~var** *vt* try ‹*comida*›; try on ‹*roupa*›; try out ‹*carro, novo sistema etc*›; (*comprovar*) prove

prová|vel /pro'vavew/ (*pl* **~veis**) *a* probable

proveito /pro'vejtu/ *m* profit, advantage; **tirar ~ de** (*beneficiar-se*) profit from; (*explorar*) take advantage of. **~so** /o/ *a* useful

proveni|ência /proveni'ẽsia/ *f* origin. **~ente** *a* originating (**de** from)

proventos /pro'vẽtus/ *m pl* proceeds

prover /pro'ver/ *vt* provide (**de** with)

provérbio /pro'vɛrbiu/ *m* proverb

proveta /pro'veta/ *f* test tube; **bebê de ~** test-tube baby

provi|dência /provi'dẽsia/ *f* (*medida*) measure, step; (*divina*) providence; **tomar ~dências** take steps, take action. **~denciar** *vt* (*prover*) get hold of, provide; (*resolver*) see to, take care of ● *vi* take action

província /pro'vĩsia/ *f* province; (*longe da cidade*) provinces

provinci|al /provĩsi'aw/ (*pl* **~ais**) *a* provincial. **~ano** *a & m* provincial

provir /pro'vir/ *vi* come (**de** from); (*resultar*) be due (**de** to)

provi|são /provi'zãw/ *f* provision. **~sório** *a* provisional

provo|cação /provoka'sãw/ *f* provocation. **~cador, ~cante** *a* provocative. **~car** *vt* provoke; (*ocasionar*) cause

proximidade /prosimi'dadʒi/ *f* closeness; *pl* (*imediações*) vicinity

próximo /'prɔsimo/ *a* (*no tempo*) next; (*perto*) near, close (**de** to); ‹*parente*› close; ‹*futuro*› near ● *m* neighbour, fellow man

pru|dência /pru'dẽsia/ *f* prudence. **~dente** *a* prudent

prumo /'prumu/ *m* plumb line; **a ~** vertically

prurido /pru'ridu/ *m* itch

pseudônimo /pisew'donimu/ *m* pseudonym

psica|nálise /pisika'nalizi/ *f* psychoanalysis. **~nalista** *m/f* psychoanalyst

psi|cologia /pisikolo'ʒia/ *f* psychology. **~colcógico** *a* psychological. **~cólogo** *m* psychologist

psico|pata /pisiko'pata/ *m/f* psychopath. **~se** /ɔ/ *f* psychosis. **~terapeuta** *m/f* psychotherapist. **~terapia** *f* psychotherapy

psicótico /pisi'kɔtʃiku/ *a & m* psychotic

psique /pi'siki/ *f* psyche

psiqui|atra /pisiki'atra/ *m/f* psychiatrist. **~atria** *f* psychiatry. **~átrico** *a* psychiatric

psíquico /pi'sikiku/ *a* psychic

pua /'pua/ *f* bit

puberdade /puber'dadʒi/ *f* puberty

publi|cação /publika'sãw/ *f* publication. **~car** *vt* publish

publici|dade /publisi'dadʒi/ *f* publicity; (*reclame*) advertising. **~tário** *a* publicity; (*de reclame*) advertising ● *m* advertising executive

público /'publiku/ *a* public ● *m* public; (*plateia*) audience; **em ~** in public; **o grande ~** the general public

pudera /pu'dɛra/ *int* no wonder!

pudico /pu'dʒiku/ *a* prudish

pudim /pu'dʒĩ/ *m* pudding

pudor /pu'dor/ *m* modesty, shame

pue|ril /pue'riw/ (*pl* **~ris**) *a* puerile

pugilis|mo /puʒi'lizmu/ *m* boxing. **~ta** *m* boxer

pu|ído /pu'idu/ *a* worn through. **~ir** *vt* wear through

pujan|ça /pu'ʒãsa/ *f* power. **~te** *a* powerful; (*de saúde*) robust

pular /pu'lar/ *vt* jump (over); (*omitir*) skip ● *vi* jump; **~ de contente** jump for joy; **~ carnaval** celebrate Carnival; **~ corda** skip

pulga /'puwga/ *f* flea

pulmão /puw'mãw/ *m* lung

pulo /'pulu/ *m* jump; **dar um ~ em** drop by; **dar ~s** jump up and down

pulôver /pu'lover/ *m* pullover

púlpito /'puwpitu/ *m* pulpit

pul|sar /puw'sar/ *vi* pulsate. **~seira** *f* bracelet. **~so** *m* (*do braço*) wrist; (*batimento arterial*) pulse

pulular /pulu'lar/ *vi* swarm (**de** with)

pulveri|zador /puwveriza'dor/ *m* spray. **~zar** *vt* spray ‹*líquido*›; (*reduzir a pó*) *fig* pulverize

pun|gente /pũ'ʒẽtʃi/ *a* consuming. **~gir** *vt* afflict

pu|nhado /pu'ɲadu/ *m* handful. **~nhal** (*pl* **~nhais**) *m* dagger. **~nhalada** *f* stab wound. **~nho** *m* fist; (*de camisa etc*) cuff; (*de espada*) hilt

pu|nição /puni'sãw/ *f* punishment. **~nir** *vt* punish. **~nitivo** *a* punitive

pupila /pu'pila/ *f* pupil

purê /pu're/ *m* purée; **~ de batata** mashed potato

pureza /pu'reza/ *f* purity

pur|gante /pur'gãtʃi/ *a & m* purgative. **~gar** *vt* purge. **~gatório** *m* purgatory

purificar /purifi'kar/ *vt* purify

puritano /puri'tanu/ *a & m* puritan

puro /'puru/ *a* pure; ‹*aguardente*› neat; **~ e simples** pure and simple. **~-sangue** (*pl* **~s-sangues**) *a & m* thoroughbred

púrpura /'purpura/ *a* purple

purpurina /purpu'rina/ *f* glitter

purulento /puru'lẽtu/ *a* festering

pus /pus/ *m* pus

pusilânime /puzi'lanimi/ *a* faint-hearted

pústula /'pustula/ *f* pimple

puta /'puta/ *f* whore ● *a invar* [!] **um ~ carro** one hell of a car; **filho da ~** (*vulg*) bastard; **~ que (o) pariu!** (*chulo*) fucking hell!

puto /'putu/ *a* [!] furious

putrefazer /putrefa'zer/ *vi* putrefy

puxa /'puʃa/ *int* gosh

pu|xado /pu'ʃadu/ *a* [!] ‹*exame*› tough; ‹*trabalho*› hard; ‹*aluguel, preço*› steep. **~xador** *m* handle. **~xão** *m* pull, tug. **~xa-puxa** *m* toffee. **~xar** *vt* pull; strike up ‹*conversa*›; bring up ‹*assunto*›; **~xar de uma perna** limp; **~xar para** (*parecer com*) take after; **~xar por** (*exigir muito de*) push (hard). **~xa-saco** *m* [!] creep

Qq

QI /ke i/ *m* IQ

quadra /'kwadra/ *f* (*de tênis etc*) court; (*quarteirão*) block. **~do** *a & m* square

quadragésimo /kwadra'ʒɛzimu/ *a* fortieth

qua|dril /kwa'driw/ (*pl* **~dris**) *m* hip

quadrilha /kwa'driʎa/ *f* (*bando*) gang; (*dança*) square dance

quadrinho /kwa'driɲu/ *m* frame; **história em ~s** comic strip

quadro /'kwadru/ *m* picture; (*pintado*) painting; (*tabela*) table; (*pessoal*) staff; (*equipe*) team; (*de uma peça*) scene; **~ interativo** interactive whiteboard. **~-negro** (*pl* **~s-negros**) *m* blackboard

quadruplicar /kwadrupli'kar/ *vt/i* quadruple

quádruplo /'kwadruplu/ *a* quadruple. **~s** *m pl* (*crianças*) quads

qual /kwaw/ (*pl* **quais**) *pron* which (one); **o/a ~** (*coisa*) that, which; (*pessoa*) that, who; **~ é o seu nome?** what's your name?; **seja ~ for a decisão** whatever the decision may be

qualidade /kwali'dadʒi/ *f* quality; **na ~ de** in one's capacity as, as

qualifi|cação /kwalifika'sãw/ *f* qualification. **~car** *vt* qualify; (*descrever*) describe (**de** as). **~car-se** *vpr* qualify

qualitativo /kwalita'tʃivu/ *a* qualitative

> **qualquer** /kwaw'kɛr/ ● *a & pron*
>
> ····➤ (*não importa qual*) any; **pegue ~ ônibus que vai para o centro** catch any bus that goes downtown; **em ~ caso** in any case; **em ~ momento** at any time; **~ coisa/pessoa** anything/ any one; **~ uma serve** any of them will do; **~ um** (*qualquer pessoa*) **~ um pode se enganar** anyone can make a mistake; **~ um sabe isso** everybody knows that; (*entre dois*) either one; **qual dos dois livros devo levar? ~ um** which of the two books should I take?_either one
>
> ····➤ (*em expressões*) **~ dia** one of these days

quando /'kwãdu/ *adv & conj* when; **~ quer que** whenever; **~ de** at the time of; **~ muito** at most

quantia /kwã'tʃia/ *f* amount

quanti|dade /kwãtʃi'dadʒi/ *f* quantity; **uma ~dade de** a lot of; **em ~dade** in large amounts. **~ficar** *vt* quantify. **~tativo** *a* quantitative

quanto /'kwãtu/ *adv & pron* how much; *pl* how many; **~ tempo?** how long?; **~ mais barato melhor** the cheaper the better; **tão alto ~ eu** as tall as me; **~ ri!** how I laughed!; **~ a** as for; **~ antes** as soon as possible

quaren|ta /kwa'rẽta/ *a & m* forty. **~tão** *a & m* (*f* **~tona**) forty-year-old. **~tena** /e/ *f* quarantine

quaresma /kwa'rɛzma/ *f* Lent

quarta /'kwarta/ *f* (*dia*) Wednesday; (*marcha*) fourth (gear). **~ de final** (*pl* **~s de final**) *f* quarter final; **~-feira** (*pl* **~s-feiras**) *f* Wednesday

quartanista /kwarta'nista/ *m/f* fourth-year (student)

quarteirão /kwarte'rãw/ *m* block

quar|tel /kwar'tɛw/ (*pl* **~téis**) *m* barracks. **~tel-general** (*pl* **~téis-generais**) *m* headquarters

quarteto /kwar'tetu/ *m* quartet; **~ de cordas** string quartet

quarto /'kwartu/ *a* fourth ● *m* (*parte*) quarter; (*aposento*) bedroom; (*guarda*) watch; **são três e/menos um ~** *Port* it's quarter past/to three; **~ de banho** *Port* bathroom; **~ de hora** quarter of an hour; **~ de hóspedes** guest room

quartzo /'kwartzu/ *m* quartz

quase /'kwazi/ *adv* almost, nearly; **~ nada/nunca** hardly anything/ever

quatro /'kwatru/ *a & m* four; **de ~** (*no chão*) on all fours; **~ por ~** ‹*carro*› four-by-four. **~centos** *a & m* four hundred

> **que** /ki/ ● *pron rel*
>
> ····➤ (*pessoas, sujeito*) who, that; **o homem ~ esteve aqui ontem** the man who came here yesterday; (*pessoas, complemento*) whom, that; **o rapaz ~ você conheceu** the boy (whom) you met; (*coisas*) that, which; **o carro ~ está estacionado na praça** the car that is parked in the square
>
> **!** quando *que* é complemento, é frequentemente omitido: **a revista que lhe emprestei ontem** *the magazine (that/which) I lent you yesterday*
>
> ● *conj*
>
> ····➤ (*integrante*) that; **disse ~ viria esta semana** he said (that) he would come this week; (*em ordens*) **quero**

~ me deixem em paz! I want to be left alone!; (*em comparações*) than; **o meu irmão é mais alto do ~ eu** my brother is taller than me; (*resultado*) that; **estava tão cansada ~ adormeci** I was so tired (that) I fell asleep; (*causa*) **não saias ~ está a chover muito** don't go out because it's pouring

● *pron*

····➤ (*interrogativo*) what; **~ horas são?** what time is it?; **em ~ andar você mora?** what floor do you live on?; (*com escolha limitada*) which; **com ~ carro vamos hoje? o seu ou o meu?** which car shall we take today? yours or mine?; (*exclamação*) what; **~ casas tão bonitas!** what lovely houses!; **~ vida!** what a life!; **~ horror!** how dreadful!; **~ aborrecimento!** how annoying!

····➤ (*em expressões*) **~ tal?: que tal foi o filme?** how was the film?; **~ tal um café?** how about a coffee?

quê /ke/ *pron* what ● *m* **um ~** something; **não tem de ~** don't mention it

quebra /'kɛbra/ *f* break; (*de empresa, banco*) crash; (*de força*) cut; **de ~** in addition. **~-cabeça** *m* jigsaw (puzzle); *fig* puzzle. **~diço** *a* breakable. **~do** *a* broken; ‹*carro*› broken down. **~dos** *m pl* small change. **~-galho** *m* [!] stopgap; **~-mar** *m* breakwater; **~-molas** *m invar* speed bump; **~-nozes** *m invar* nutcrackers; **~-pau** *m* [!] row; **~-quebra** *m* riot

q

quebrar /ke'brar/ *vt* break ● *vi* break; ‹*carro etc*› break down; ‹*banco, empresa etc*› crash, go bust. **~-se** *vpr* break

queda /'kɛda/ *f* fall; **ter uma ~ por** have a soft spot for. **~ de braço** *f* arm wrestling

quei|jeira /ke'ʒera/ *f* cheese dish. **~jo** *m* cheese; **~jo prato** Cheddar. **~jo de minas** *m* Cheshire cheese

queima /'kejma/ *f* burning. **~da** *f* forest fire. **~do** *a* burnt; (*bronzeado*) tanned, brown; **cheiro de ~do** smell of burning

queimar /kej'mar/ *vt* burn; (*bronzear*) tan ● *vi* burn; ‹*lâmpada*› go; ‹*fusível*› blow. **~-se** *vpr* burn o.s.; (*bronzear-se*) go brown

queima-roupa /kejma'xopa/ *f* **à ~** point-blank

quei|xa /'keʃa/ *f* complaint. **~xar-se** *vpr* complain (**de** about)

queixo /'keʃu/ *m* chin; **bater o ~** shiver

queixoso /ke'ʃozu/ *a* plaintive ● *m* plaintiff

quem /kẽj/ *pron* who; (*a pessoa que*) anyone who, he who; **de ~ é este livro?** whose is this book?; **~ quer que** whoever; **seja ~ for** whoever it is; **~ falou isso fui eu** it was me who said that; **~ me dera (que) ...** I wish ..., if only ...

Quênia /'kenia/ *m* Kenya

queniano /keni'anu/ *a & m* Kenyan

quen|tão /kẽ'tãw/ *m* mulled wine. **~te** *a* hot; (*com calor agradável*) warm. **~tura** *f* heat

quepe /'kɛpi/ *m* cap

quer /kɛr/ *conj* **~ ... ~ ...** whether ... or ...

querer /ke'rer/ *vt/i* want; **quero ir** I want to go; **quero que você vá** I want you to go; **eu queria falar com o Sr X** I'd like to speak to Mr X; **vai ~ vir amanhã?** do you want to come tomorrow?; **vou ~ um cafezinho** I'd like a coffee; **se você quiser** if you want; **queira sentar** do sit down; **~ dizer** mean; **quer dizer** (*isto é*) that is to say, I mean

querido /ke'ridu/ *a* dear ● *m* darling

quermesse /ker'mɛsi/ *f* fête, fair

querosene /kero'zeni/ *m* kerosene

questão /kes'tãw/ *m* question; (*assunto*) matter; **em ~** in question; **fazer ~ de** really want to; **não faço ~ de ir** I don't mind not going

questio|nar /kestʃio'nar/ *vt/i* question. **~nário** *m* questionnaire. **~nável** (*pl* **~náveis**) *a* questionable

quiabo /ki'abu/ *m* okra

quibe /'kibi/ *m* savoury meatball

quicar /ki'kar/ *vt/i* bounce

quiche /'kiʃi/ *f* quiche

quie|to /ki'ɛtu/ *a* (*calado*) quiet; (*imóvel*) still. **~tude** *f* quiet

quilate /ki'latʃi/ *m* carat; *fig* calibre

quilha /'kiʎa/ *f* keel

quilo /'kilo/ *m* kilo. **~grama** *m* kilogram. **~metragem** *f* mileage. **~métrico** *a* mile-long

quilômetro /ki'lometru/ *m* kilometre

quimbanda /kĩ'bãda/ *m* Afro-Brazilian cult

qui|mera /ki'mɛra/ *f* fantasy. **~mérico** *a* fanciful

químí|ca /'kimika/ *f* chemistry. **~co** *a* chemical ● *m* chemist

quimioterapia /kimiotera'pia/ *f* chemotherapy

quimono /ki'mɔnu/ *m* kimono

quina /'kina/ *f* **de ~** edgeways

quindim /kĩ'dʒĩ/ *m* sweet made of coconut, sugar and egg yolks

quinhão /ki'ɲãw/ *m* share

quinhentos /ki'ɲẽtus/ *a & m* five hundred

quinina /ki'nina/ *f* quinine

quinquagésimo /kwĩkwa'ʒɛzimu/ *a* fiftieth

quinquilharias /kĩkiʎa'rias/ *f pl* knick-knacks

quinta[1] /'kĩta/ *f* (*fazenda*) farm

quinta[2] /'kĩta/ *f* (*dia*) Thursday. **~-feira** (*pl* **~s-feiras**) *f* Thursday

quin|tal /kĩ'taw/ (*pl* **~tais**) *m* back yard

quinteiro /kĩ'tajru/ *m Port* farmer

quinteto /kĩ'tetu/ *m* quintet

quin|to /'kĩtu/ *a & m* fifth. **quíntuplo** *a* fivefold. **quíntuplos** *m pl* (*crianças*) quins

quinze /'kĩzi/ *a & m* fifteen; **às dez e ~** at quarter past ten; **são ~ para as dez** it's quarter to ten. **~na** /e/ *f* fortnight. **~nal** (*pl* **~nais**) *a* fortnightly. **~nalmente** *adv* fortnightly

quiosque /ki'ɔski/ *m* (*banca*) kiosk; (*no jardim*) gazebo

quiro|mância /kiro'mãsia/ *f* palmistry. **~mante** *m/f* palmist

quisto /'kistu/ *m* cyst

quitan|da /ki'tãda/ *f* grocer's (shop). **~deiro** *m* grocer

qui|tar /ki'tar/ *vt* pay off ‹*dívida*›. **~te** *a* **estar ~te** be quits

quociente /kwosi'ẽtʃi/ *m* quotient

quórum /'kwɔrũ/ *m* quorum

Rr

rã /xã/ *f* frog

rabanete /xaba'netʃi/ *m* radish

rabear /xabi'ar/ *vi* ‹*caminhão*› jack-knife

rabino /xa'binu/ *m* rabbi

rabis|car /xabis'kar/ *vt* scribble ● *vi* (*escrever mal*) scribble; (*fazer desenhos*) doodle. **~co** *m* doodle

rabo /'xabu/ *m* (*de animal*) tail; **com o ~ do olho** out of the corner of one's eye. **~ de cavalo** (*pl* **~s de cavalo**) *m* pony tail

rabugento /xabu'ʒẽtu/ *a* grumpy

raça /'xasa/ *f* (*de homens*) race; (*de animais*) breed

ração /xa'sãw/ *f* (*de comida*) ration; (*para animal*) food

racha /'xaʃa/ *f* crack. **~dura** *f* crack

rachar /xa'ʃar/ *vt* (*dividir*) split; (*abrir fendas em*) crack; chop ‹*lenha*›; split ‹*despesas*› ● *vi* (*dividir-se*) split; (*apresentar fendas*) crack; (*ao pagar*) split the cost

raci|al /xasi'aw/ (*pl* **~ais**) *a* racial

racio|cinar /xasiosi'nar/ *vi* reason. **~cínio** *m* reasoning. **~nal** (*pl* **~nais**) *a* rational. **~nalizar** *vt* rationalize

racio|namento /xasiona'mẽtu/ *m* rationing. **~nar** *vt* ration

racis|mo /xa'sizmu/ *m* racism. **~ta** *a & m/f* racist

radar /xa'dar/ *m* radar; (*na estrada*) speed camera

radia|ção /xadʒia'sãw/ *f* radiation. **~dor** *m* radiator

radialista /radʒia'lista/ *m/f* radio announcer

radiante /xadʒi'ãtʃi/ *a* (*de alegria*) overjoyed

radi|cal /xadʒi'kaw/ (*pl* **~cais**) *a & m* radical. **~car-se** *vpr* settle

rádio[1] /'xadʒiu/ *m* radio ● *f* radio station

rádio[2] /'xadʒiu/ *m* (*elemento*) radium

radioati|vidade /xadioatʃivi'dadʒi/ *f* radioactivity. **~vo** *a* radioactive

radiodifusão /xadʒiodʒifu'zãw/ *f* broadcasting

radiogra|far /radʒiogra'far/ *vt* X-ray ‹*pulmões, osso etc*›; radio ‹*mensagem*›. **~fia** *f* X-ray

radiolo|gia /radʒiolo'ʒia/ *f* radiology. **~gista** *m/f* radiologist

radio|novela /xadʒiono'vɛla/ *f* radio serial. **~patrulha** *f* patrol car. **~táxi** *m* radio taxi. **~terapia** *f* radiotherapy, ray treatment

raia /'xaja/ *f* (*em corrida*) lane; (*peixe*) ray

rainha /xa'iɲa/ *f* queen. **~-mãe** *f* queen mother

raio /'xaju/ *m* (*de luz etc*) ray; (*de círculo*) radius; (*de roda*) spoke; (*relâmpago*) bolt of lightning; **~ de ação** range

rai|va /'xajva/ *f* rage; (*doença*) rabies; **estar com ~va** be furious (**de** with);

q r

ter ~va de alguém have it in for sb. **~voso** *a* furious; ‹*cachorro*› rabid

raiz /xa'iz/ *f* root; **~ quadrada/cúbica** square/cube root

rajada /xa'ʒada/ *f* (*de vento*) gust; (*de tiros*) burst

ra|lador /xala'dor/ *m* grater. **~lar** *vt* grate

ralé /xa'lɛ/ *f* rabble

ralhar /xa'ʎar/ *vi* scold

ralo[1] /'xalu/ *m* (*ralador*) grater; (*de escoamento*) drain

ralo[2] /'xalu/ *a* ‹*cabelo*› thinning; ‹*sopa, tecido*› thin; ‹*vegetação*› sparse; ‹*café*› weak

ra|mal /xa'maw/ (*pl* **~mais**) *m* (*telefone*) extension; (*de ferrovia*) branch line

ramalhete /xama'ʎetʃi/ *m* posy, bouquet

ramifi|cação /xamifika'sãw/ *f* branch. **~car-se** *vi* branch off

ramo /'xamu/ *m* branch; (*profissional etc*) field; (*buquê*) bunch; **Domingo de Ramos** Palm Sunday

rampa /'xãpa/ *f* ramp

rancor /xã'kor/ *m* resentment. **~oso** /o/ *a* resentful

rançoso /xã'sozu/ *a* rancid

ran|ger /xã'ʒer/ *vt* grind ‹*dentes*› ● *vi* creak. **~gido** *m* creak

ranhura /xa'ɲura/ *f* groove; (*para moedas*) slot

ranzinza /xã'zĩza/ *a* cantankerous

rapariga /xapa'riga/ *f Port* girl

rapaz /xa'pas/ *m* boy

r

rapé /xa'pɛ/ *m* snuff

rapel /ra'pɛw/ *m* abseiling

rapidez /xapi'des/ *f* speed

rápido /'xapidu/ *a* fast ● *adv* ‹*fazer*› quickly; ‹*andar*› fast

rapina /xa'pina/ *f* **ave de ~** bird of prey

rapo|sa /xa'poza/ *f* vixen. **~so** *m* fox

rapsódia /xap'sɔdʒia/ *f* rhapsody

rap|tar /xap'tar/ *vt* abduct, kidnap ‹*criança*›. **~to** *m* abduction, kidnapping (de criança)

raquete /xa'kɛtʃi/ *f*, *Port* **raqueta** /xa'keta/ *f* racquet

raquítico /xa'kitʃiku/ *a* puny

ra|ramente /xara'mẽtʃi/ *adv* rarely. **~ridade** *f* rarity. **~ro** *a* rare ● *adv* rarely

rascunho /xas'kuɲu/ *m* rough version, draft

ras|gado /xaz'gadu/ *a* torn; *fig* ‹*elogios etc*› effusive. **~gão** *m* tear. **~gar** *vt* tear; (*em pedaços*) tear up ● *vi*, **~gar-se** *vpr* tear. **~go** *m* tear; *fig* burst

raso /'xazu/ *a* ‹*água*› shallow; ‹*sapato*› flat; ‹*colher etc*› level

ras|pão /xas'pãw/ *m* graze; **atingir de ~pão** graze. **~par** *vt* shave ‹*cabeça, pelos*›; plane ‹*madeira*›; (*para limpar*) scrape; (*tocar de leve*) graze; **~par em** scrape

ras|teiro /xas'teru/ *a* ‹*planta*› creeping; ‹*animal*› crawling. **~tejante** *a* crawling; ‹*voz*› slurred. **~tejar** *vi* crawl

rasto /'xastu/ *m* ▶ RASTRO

ras|trear /xastri'ar/ *vt* track ‹*satélite etc*›; scan ‹*céu, corpo etc*›. **~tro** *m* trail

rasura /xa'zura/ *f* crossing-out

rasurar /xazu'rar/ *vt* to cross out

ratear[1] /xatʃi'ar/ *vi* ‹*motor*› miss

ra|tear[2] /xatʃi'ar/ *vt* share. **~teio** *m* sharing

ratifi|cação /xatʃifika'sãw/ *f* ratification. **~car** *vt* ratify

rato /'xatu/ *m* rat; (*camundongo*) mouse; *Port Comput* mouse. **~eira** *f* mousetrap

ravina /xa'vina/ *f* ravine

razão /xa'zãw/ *f* reason; (*proporção*) ratio ● *m* ledger; **à ~ de** at the rate of; **em ~ de** on account of; **ter ~** be right; **não ter ~** be wrong

razoá|vel /xazo'avew/ (*pl* **~veis**) *a* reasonable

ré[1] /xɛ/ *f* (*na justiça*) defendant

ré[2] /xɛ/ *f* (*marcha*) reverse; **dar ~** reverse

reabastecer /xeabaste'ser/ *vt/i* refuel

reabilitar /xeabili'tar/ *vt* rehabilitate

rea|ção /xea'sãw/ *f* reaction; **~ção em cadeia** chain reaction. **~cionário** *a & m* reactionary

readmitir /xeadʒimi'tʃir/ *vt* reinstate ‹*funcionário*›

reagir /xea'ʒir/ *vi* react; ‹*doente*› respond

reajus|tar /xeaʒus'tar/ *vt* readjust. **~te** *m* adjustment

re|al /xe'aw/ (*pl* **~ais**) *a* (*verdadeiro*) real; (*da realeza*) royal

real|çar /xeaw'sar/ *vt* highlight. **~ce** *m* prominence

realejo /xea'leʒu/ *m* barrel organ

realeza /xea'leza/ *f* royalty

realidade /xeali'dadʒi/ *f* reality

realimentação /xealimẽta'sãw/ *f* feedback

realis|mo /xea'lizmu/ *m* realism. **~ta** *a* realistic ● *m/f* realist

realização /'xealiza'sãw/ *f* (*de projeto*) implementation; (*de sonho, objetivo*) fulfilment; *Cine* direction

reali|zado /xeali'zadu/ *a* ‹*pessoa*› fulfilled. **~zar** *vt* (*fazer*) carry out; (*tornar real*) realize ‹*sonho, capital*›. **~zar-se** *vpr* ‹*sonho*› come true; ‹*pessoa*› fulfil o.s.; ‹*casamento, reunião etc*› take place

realizador /xializa'dor/ *m Port Cine* director

realmente /xeaw'mẽtʃi/ *adv* really

reaparecer /xeapare'ser/ *vi* reappear

reativar /xeatʃi'var/ *vt* reactivate

reaver /xea'ver/ *vt* get back

reavivar /xeavi'var/ *vt* revive

rebaixar /xeba'ʃar/ *vt* lower ‹*preço*›; *fig* demean ● *vi* ‹*preços*› drop. **~-se** *vpr* demean o.s.

rebanho /xe'baɲu/ *m* herd; (*fiéis*) flock

reba|te /xe'batʃi/ *m* alarm. **~ter** *vt* return ‹*bola*›; refute ‹*acusação*›; (*ao computador*) retype

rebelar-se /xebe'larsi/ *vpr* rebel

rebel|de /xe'bɛwdʒi/ *a* rebellious ● *m/f* rebel. **~dia** *f* rebelliousness

rebelião /xebeli'ãw/ *f* rebellion

reben|tar /xebẽ'tar/ *vt/i* ▶ ARREBENTAR. **~to** *m* (*de planta*) shoot; (*descendente*) offspring

rebite /xe'bitʃi/ *m* rivet

rebobinar /xebobi'nar/ *vt* rewind

rebo|cador /xeboka'dor/ *m* tug. **~car** *vt* (*tirar*) tow; (*cobrir com reboco*) plaster. **~co** /o/ *m* plaster

rebolar /xebo'lar/ *vi* swing one's hips

reboque /xe'bɔki/ *m* towing; (*veículo a* ~) trailer; (*com guindaste*) towtruck; **a ~** on tow

rebote /xe'bɔtʃi/ *m* (*esporte*) rebound

rebuçado /xebu'sadu/ *m Port* sweet, *Amer* candy

rebuliço /xebu'lisu/ *m* commotion

rebuscado /xebus'kadu/ *a* recherché

recado /xe'kadu/ *m* message

reca|ída /xeka'ida/ *f* relapse. **~ir** *vi* relapse; ‹*acento, culpa*› fall

recal|cado /xekaw'kadu/ *a* repressed. **~car** *vt* repress

recanto /xe'kãtu/ *m* nook, recess

recapitular /xekapitu'lar/ *vt* review ● *vi* recap

recarga /xe'karga/ *f* (*de caneta*) refill

recarregar /rekare'gar/ *vt* recharge ‹*bateria*›; top up ‹*crédito*›

reca|tado /xeka'tadu/ *a* reserved, withdrawn. **~to** *m* reserve

recear /xesi'ar/ *vt/i* fear (**por** for)

rece|ber /xese'ber/ *vt* receive; entertain ‹*convidados*› ● *vi* (*~ber salário*) get paid; (*~ber convidados*) entertain. **~bimento** *m* receipt

receio /xe'seju/ *m* fear

recei|ta /xe'sejta/ *f* (*de cozinha*) recipe; (*médica*) prescription; (*dinheiro*) revenue. **~tar** *vt* prescribe

recém|-casados /xesẽjka'zadus/ *m pl* newly-weds. **~-chegado** *m* newcomer; **~-nascido** *a* newborn ● *m* newborn child, baby

recenseamento /xesẽsja'mẽtu/ *m Port* ▶ CENSO

recente /xe'sẽtʃi/ *a* recent. **~mente** *adv* recently

receoso /xese'ozu/ *a* (*apreensivo*) afraid

recep|ção /xesep'sãw/ *f* reception; *Port* (*de carta*) receipt; **~ção de sinal** *Telec* reception. **~cionar** *vt* receive. **~cionista** *m/f* receptionist. **~táculo** *m* receptacle. **~tivo** *a* receptive. **~tor** *m* receiver

reces|são /xese'sãw/ *f* recession. **~so** /ɛ/ *m* recess

re|chear /xeʃi'ar/ *vt* stuff ‹*frango, assado*›; fill ‹*empada*›. **~cheio** *m* (*para frango etc*) stuffing; (*de empada etc*) filling

rechonchudo /xeʃõ'ʃudu/ *a* plump

recibo /xe'sibu/ *m* receipt

reciclagem /xesi'klaʒẽj/ *f* recycling

reciclar /xesik'lar/ *vt* recycle

recife /xe'sifi/ *m* reef

recinto /xe'sĩtu/ *m* enclosure

recipiente /xesipi'ẽtʃi/ *m* container

reciprocar /xesipro'kar/ *vt* reciprocate

recíproco /xe'siproku/ *a* reciprocal; ‹*sentimento*› mutual

reci|tal /xesi'taw/ (*pl* **~tais**) *m* recital. **~tar** *vt* recite

recla|mação /xeklama'sãw/ *f* complaint; (*no seguro*) claim. **~mar** *vt* claim ● *vi* complain (**de** about); (*no seguro*) claim. **~me** *m*, *Port* **~mo** *m* advertising

reclinar-se /xekli'narsi/ *vpr* recline

recluso /xe'kluzu/ *a* reclusive ● *m* recluse

r

recobrar /xeko'brar/ *vt* recover. **~-se** *vpr* recover

recolher /xeko'ʎer/ *vt* collect; (*retirar*) withdraw. **~-se** *vpr* retire

recomeçar /xekome'sar/ *vt/i* start again

recomen|dação /xekomẽda'sãw/ *f* recommendation. **~dar** *vt* recommend. **~dável** (*pl* **~dáveis**) *a* advisable

recompen|sa /xekõ'pẽsa/ *f* reward. **~sar** *vt* reward

reconcili|ação /xekõsilia'sãw/ *f* reconciliation. **~ar** *vt* reconcile. **~ar-se** *vpr* be reconciled

reconhe|cer /xekoɲe'ser/ *vt* recognize; (*admitir*) acknowledge; *Mil* reconnoitre; identify ‹*corpo*›. **~cimento** *m* recognition; (*gratidão*) gratitude; *Mil* reconnaissance; (*de corpo*) identification. **~cível** (*pl* **~cíveis**) *a* recognizable

reconsiderar /xekõside'rar/ *vt/i* reconsider

reconstituinte /xekõstʃitu'ĩtʃi/ *m* tonic

reconstituir /xekõstʃitu'ir/ *vt* reform; reconstruct ‹*crime, cena*›

reconstruir /xekõstru'ir/ *vt* rebuild

recor|dação /xekorda'sãw/ *f* recollection; (*objeto*) memento. **~dar** *vt* recollect; **~dar-se (de)** recall

recor|de /xe'kɔrdʒi/ *a invar & m* record. **~dista** *a* record-breaking ● *m/f* record holder

recorrer /xeko'xer/ *vi* **~ a** turn to ‹*médico, amigo*›; resort to ‹*violência, tática*›; **~ de** appeal against

recor|tar /xekor'tar/ *vt* cut out. **~te** /ɔ/ *m* cutting, *Amer* clipping

r

recostar /xekos'tar/ *vt* lean back. **~-se** *vpr* lean back

recreio /xe'kreju/ *m* recreation; (*na escola*) break

recriar /xekri'ar/ *vt* recreate

recriminação /xekrimina'sãw/ *f* recrimination

recrudescer /xekrude'ser/ *vi* intensify

recru|ta /xe'kruta/ *m/f* recruit. **~tamento** *m* recruitment. **~tar** *vt* recruit

recu|ar /xeku'ar/ *vi* move back; ‹*tropas*› retreat; (*no tempo*) go back; (*ceder*) back down; (*não cumprir*) back out (**de** of) ● *vt* move back. **~o** *m* retreat; *fig* (*de intento*) climbdown

recupe|ração /xekupera'sãw/ *f* recovery. **~rar** *vt* recover; make up ‹*atraso, tempo perdido*›. **~rar-se** *vpr* recover (**de** from)

recurso /xe'kursu/ *m* resort; (*coisa útil*) resource; (*na justiça*) appeal; *pl* resources

recu|sa /xe'kuza/ *f* refusal. **~sar** *vt* refuse; turn down ‹*convite, oferta*›. **~sar-se** *vpr* refuse (**a** to)

reda|ção /xeda'sãw/ *f* (*de livro, contrato*) draft; (*pessoal*) editorial staff; (*seção*) editorial department; (*na escola*) composition. **~tor** *m* editor

rede /'xedʒi/ *f* net; (*para deitar*) hammock; *fig* (*sistema*) network; **~ social** social network. **~ corporativa** *Comput* intranet

rédea /'xɛdʒia/ *f* rein

redemoinho /xedemo'iɲu/ *m* ▶ RODAMOINHO

reden|ção /xedẽ'sãw/ *f* redemption. **~tor** *a* redeeming ● *m* redeemer

redigir /xedʒi'ʒir/ *vt* draw up ‹*contrato*›; write ‹*artigo*›; edit ‹*dicionário*›

redimir /xedʒi'mir/ *vt* redeem

redobrar /xedo'brar/ *vt* redouble

redon|deza /xedõ'deza/ *f* roundness; *pl* vicinity. **~do** *a* round

redor /xe'dɔr/ *m* **ao** ou **em ~ de** around

redução /xedu'sãw/ *f* reduction

redun|dante /xedũ'dãtʃi/ *a* redundant. **~dar** *vi* **~dar em** develop into

redu|zido /xedu'zidu/ *a* limited; (*pequeno*) small. **~zir** *vt* reduce. **~zir-se** *vpr* (*ficar reduzido*) be reduced (**a** to); (*resumir-se*) come down (**a** to)

reeleger /xeele'ʒer/ *vt* re-elect

reeleição /xeelej'sãw/ *f* re-election

reembol|sar /xeẽbow'sar/ *vt* reimburse ‹*pessoa*›; refund ‹*dinheiro*›. **~so** /o/ *m* refund; **~so postal** cash on delivery

reencarnação /xeẽkarna'sãw/ *f* reincarnation

reentrância /xeẽ'trãsia/ *f* recess

reescalonar /xeeskalo'nar/ *vt* reschedule

reescrever /xeeskre'ver/ *vt* rewrite

refastelar-se /xefaste'larsi/ *vpr* stretch out

refazer /xefa'zer/ *vt* redo; rebuild ‹*vida*›. **~-se** *vpr* recover (**de** from)

refei|ção /xefej'sãw/ *f* meal. **~tório** *m* dining hall

refém /xe'fẽj/ *m* hostage

referência /xefe'rẽsia/ *f* reference; **com ~ a** with reference to

referendum /xefe'rẽdũ/ *m* referendum

refe|rente /xefe'rẽtʃi/ *a* **~rente a** regarding. **~rir** *vt* report. **~rir-se** *vpr* refer (**a** to)

refestelar-se /xefeste'larsi/ *vpr Port* ▶ REFASTELAR-SE

re|fil /xe'fiw/ (*pl* **~fis**) *m* refill

refi|nado /xefi'nadu/ *a* refined. **~namento** *m* refinement. **~nar** *vt* refine. **~naria** *f* refinery

refle|tido /xefle'tʃidu/ *a* ‹*decisão*› well-thought-out; ‹*pessoa*› thoughtful. **~tir** *vt/i* reflect. **~tir-se** *vpr* be reflected. **~xão** /ks/ *f* reflection. **~xivo** /ks/ *a* reflexive. **~xo** /ɛks/ *a* ‹*luz*› reflected; ‹*ação*› reflex ● *m* (*de luz etc*) reflection; (*físico*) reflex; (*no cabelo*) streak

refluxo /xe'fluksu/ *m* ebb

refo|gado /xefo'gadu/ *m* lightly fried mixture of onions and garlic. **~gar** *vt* fry lightly

refor|çar /xefor'sar/ *vt* reinforce. **~ço** /o/ *m* reinforcement

refor|ma /xe'fɔrma/ *f* (*da lei etc*) reform; (*na casa etc*) renovation; (*de militar*) discharge; (*pensão*) pension; **~ma ministerial** cabinet reshuffle. **~mado** *a* reformed; *Port* (*aposentado*) retired ● *m Port* pensioner. **~mar** *vt* reform ‹*lei, sistema etc*›; renovate ‹*casa, prédio*›; *Port* (*aposentar*) retire. **~mar-se** *vpr Port* (*aposentar-se*) retire; ‹*criminoso*› reform. **~matório** *m* reform school. **~mista** *a & m/f* reformist

refrão /xe'frãw/ *m* chorus

refratário /xefra'tariu/ *a* ‹*tigela etc*› ovenproof, heatproof

refrear /xefri'ar/ *vt* rein in ‹*cavalo*›; *fig* curb, keep in check ‹*paixões etc*›. **~-se** *vpr* restrain o.s.

refrega /xe'frɛga/ *f* clash, fight

refres|cante /xefres'kãtʃi/ *a* refreshing. **~car** *vt* freshen, cool ‹*ar*›; refresh ‹*pessoa, memória etc*› ● *vi* get cooler. **~car-se** *vpr* refresh o.s.. **~co** /e/ *m* (*bebida*) soft drink; *pl* refreshments

refrige|rado /xefriʒe'radu/ *a* cooled; ‹*casa etc*› air-conditioned; (*na geladeira*) refrigerated. **~rador** *m* refrigerator. **~rante** *m* soft drink. **~rar** *vt* keep cool; (*na geladeira*) refrigerate

refugi|ado /xefuʒi'adu/ *m* refugee. **~ar-se** *vpr* take refuge

refúgio /xe'fuʒiu/ *m* refuge

refugo /xe'fugu/ *m* waste, refuse

refutar /xefu'tar/ *vt* refute

regaço /xe'gasu/ *m* lap

regador /xega'dor/ *m* watering can

regalia /xega'lia/ *f* privilege

regar /xe'gar/ *vt* water

regata /xe'gata/ *f* regatta

regatear /xegatʃi'ar/ *vi* bargain, haggle

re|gência /xe'ʒẽsia/ *f* (*de verbo etc*) government. **~gente** *m/f* (*de orquestra*) conductor. **~ger** *vt* govern ● *vi* rule

regenerar /xeʒene'rar/ *vt* regenerate

região /xeʒi'ãw/ *f* region; (*de cidade etc*) area

regi|me /xe'ʒimi/ *m* regime; (*dieta*) diet; **fazer ~me** diet. **~mento** *m* (*militar*) regiment; (*regulamento*) regulations

régio /'xɛʒiu/ *a* regal

Regiões Autónomas (de Portugal) *i*
The autonomous regions of Portugal are the archipelagos of Madeira and the Azores. Together with mainland Portugal, these make up the Portuguese Republic. Each autonomous region has its own government and legislative assembly.

regio|nal /xeʒio'naw/ (*pl* **~nais**) *a* regional

registar /xeʒiʃ'tar/ *vt Port* ▶ **registrar** /xeʒiʃ'trar/

registo /xe'ʒiʃtu/ *m Port* ▶ **registro** /xe'ʒiʃ'tru/

regis|trador /xeʒistra'dor/ *a* **caixa ~tradora** cash register. **~trar** *vt* register; (*anotar*) record. **~tro** *m* (*lista*) register; (*de um fato, em banco de dados*) record; (*ato de ~trar*) registration

rego /'xegu/ *m* (*de arado*) furrow; (*de roda*) rut; (*para escoamento*) ditch

regozi|jar /xegozi'ʒar/ *vt* delight. **~jar-se** *vpr* be delighted. **~jo** *m* delight

regra /'xɛgra/ *f* rule; *pl* (*menstruações*) periods; **em ~** as a rule

regres|sar /xegre'sar/ *vi* return. **~sivo** *a* regressive; **contagem ~siva** countdown. **~so** /ɛ/ *m* return

régua /'xɛgwa/ *f* ruler

regu|lagem /xegu'laʒẽ/ *f* (*de carro*) tuning. **~lamento** *m* regulations. **~lar** *a* regular; ‹*estatura, qualidade etc*› average ● *vt* regulate; tune ‹*carro, motor*›; set ‹*relógio*›; **~lar-se por** go by, be guided by ● *vi* work. **~laridade** *f* regularity. **~larizar** *vt* regularize

r

regurgitar /xegurʒi'tar/ *vt* bring up
rei /xej/ *m* king. **~nado** *m* reign
reincidir /xeĩsi'dʒir/ *vi* ‹*criminoso*› reoffend
reino /'xejnu/ *m* kingdom; *fig* (*da fantasia etc*) realm; **Reino Unido** United Kingdom
reiterar /xejte'rar/ *vt* reiterate
reitor /xej'tor/ *m* chancellor, *Amer* president
reivindi|cação /xejvĩdʒika'sãw/ *f* demand. **~car** *vt* claim, demand
rejei|ção /xeʒej'sãw/ *f* rejection. **~tar** *vt* reject
rejuvenescer /xeʒuvene'ser/ *vt* rejuvenate ● *vi* be rejuvenated
relação /xela'sãw/ *f* relationship; (*relatório*) account; (*lista*) list; *pl* relations; **com** ou **em ~ a** in relation to, regarding
relacio|namento /xelasiona-'mẽtu/ *m* relationship. **~nar** *vt* relate (**com** to); (*listar*) list. **~nar-se** *vpr* relate (**com** to)
relações-públicas /xelasõjs'publikas/ *m/f invar* public relations person
relâmpago /xe'lãpagu/ *m* flash of lightning; *pl* lightning ● *a* lightning; **num ~** in a flash
relampejar /xelãpe'ʒar/ *vi* flash; **relampejou** there was a flash of lightning
relance /xe'lãsi/ *m* glance; **olhar de ~** glance (at)
rela|tar /xela'tar/ *vt* relate. **~tivo** *a* relative. **~to** *m* account. **~tório** *m* report
rela|xado /xela'ʃadu/ *a* relaxed; ‹*disciplina*› lax; ‹*pessoa*› lazy, complacent. **~xamento** *m* (*físico*) relaxation; (*de pessoa*) complacency. **~xante** *a* relaxing ● *m* tranquillizer. **~xar** *vt* relax ● *vi* (*descansar*) relax; (*tornar-se omisso*) get complacent. **~xar-se** *vpr* relax. **~xe** *m* relaxation
reles /'xɛlis/ *a invar* ‹*gente*› common; ‹*ação*› despicable
rele|vância /xele'vãsia/ *f* relevance. **~vante** *a* relevant. **~var** *vt* emphasize. **~vo** /e/ *m* relief; (*importância*) prominence
religi|ão /xeliʒi'ãw/ *f* religion. **~oso** /o/ *a* religious
relin|char /xelĩ'ʃar/ *vi* neigh. **~cho** *m* neighing
relíquia /xe'likia/ *f* relic
relógio /xe'lɔʒiu/ *m* clock; (*de pulso*) watch
relu|tância /xelu'tãsia/ *f* reluctance. **~tante** *a* reluctant. **~tar** *vi* be reluctant (**em** to)
reluzente /xelu'zẽtʃi/ *a* shining, gleaming
relva /'xɛwva/ *f* grass. **~do** *m* lawn
remador /xema'dor/ *m* rower
remanescente /xemane'sẽtʃi/ *a* remaining ● *m* remainder
remar /xe'mar/ *vt/i* row
rema|tar /xema'tar/ *vt* finish off. **~te** *m* finish; (*adorno*) finishing touch; (*de piada*) punch line
remediar /xemedʒi'ar/ *vt* remedy
remédio /xe'mɛdʒiu/ *m* (*contra doença*) medicine, drug; (*a problema etc*) remedy
remelento /xeme'lẽtu/ *a* bleary
remen|dar /xemẽ'dar/ *vt* mend; (*com pedaço de pano*) patch. **~do** *m* mend; (*pedaço de pano*) patch
remessa /xe'mɛsa/ *f* (*de mercadorias*) shipment; (*de dinheiro*) remittance
reme|tente /xeme'tẽtʃi/ *m/f* sender. **~ter** *vt* send ‹*mercadorias, dinheiro etc*›; refer ‹*leitor*› (**a** to)
remexer /xeme'ʃer/ *vt* shuffle ‹*papéis*›; stir up ‹*poeira, lama*›; wave ‹*braços*› ● *vi* rummage. **~-se** *vpr* move around
reminiscência /xemini'sẽsia/ *f* reminiscence
remir /xe'mir/ *vt* redeem. **~-se** *vpr* redeem o.s.
remissão /xemi'sãw/ *f* (*de pecados*) redemption; (*de doença, pena*) remission; (*num livro*) cross reference
remo /'xemu/ *m* oar; (*esporte*) rowing
remoção /xemo'sãw/ *f* removal
remoinho /xemo'iɲu/ *m Port* ▶ RODAMOINHO
remontar /xemõ'tar/ *vi* **~ a** ‹*coisa*› date back to; ‹*pessoa*› think back to
remorso /xe'mɔrsu/ *m* remorse
remo|to /xe'mɔtu/ *a* remote. **~ver** *vt* remove
remune|ração /xemunera'sãw/ *f* payment. **~rador** *a* profitable. **~rar** *vt* pay
rena /'xena/ *f* reindeer
re|nal /xe'naw/ (*pl* **~nais**) *a* renal, kidney
Renascença /xena'sẽsa/ *f* Renaissance
renas|cer /xena'ser/ *vi* be reborn. **~cimento** *m* rebirth
renda[1] /'xẽda/ *f* (*tecido*) lace

r

ren|da[2] /'xẽda/ *f* income; *Port* (*aluguel*) rent; **~der** bring in, yield ‹*lucro*›; earn ‹*juros*›; fetch ‹*preço*›; bring ‹*resultado*› ● *vi* ‹*investimento, trabalho, ação*› pay off; ‹*comida*› go a long way; ‹*produto comprado*› give value for money. **~der-se** *vpr* surrender. **~dição** *f* surrender. **~dimento** *m* (*renda*) income; (*de investimento, terreno*) yield; (*de motor etc*) output; (*de produto comprado*) value for money. **~doso** /o/ *a* profitable

rene|gado /xene'gadu/ *a & m* renegade. **~gar** *vt* renounce

renhido /xe'ɲidu/ *a* hard-fought

Reno /'xenu/ *m* Rhine

reno|mado /xeno'madu/ *a* renowned. **~me** /o/ *m* renown

reno|vação /xenova'sãw/ *f* renewal. **~var** *vt* renew

renque /'xẽki/ *m* row

ren|tabilidade /xẽtabili'dadʒi/ *f* profitability. **~tável** (*pl* **~táveis**) *a* profitable

rente /'xẽtʃi/ *adv* **~ a** close to ● *a* ‹*cabelo*› cropped

renúncia /xe'nũsia/ *f* renunciation (**a** of); (*a cargo*) resignation (**a** from)

renunciar /xenũsi'ar/ *vi* ‹*presidente etc*› resign; **~ a** give up; waive ‹*direito*›

reorganizar /xeorgani'zar/ *vt* reorganize

repa|ração /xepara'sãw/ *f* reparation; (*conserto*) repair. **~rar** *vt* (*consertar*) repair; make up for ‹*ofensa, injustiça, erro*›; make good ‹*danos, prejuízo*› ● *vi* **~rar (em)** notice. **~ro** *m* (*conserto*) repair

repar|tição /xepartʃi'sãw/ *f* division; (*seção do governo*) department. **~tir** *vt* divide up

repassar /xepa'sar/ *vt* revise ‹*matéria, lição*›

repatriar /xepatri'ar/ *vt* repatriate

repe|lente /xepe'lẽtʃi/ *a & m* repellent. **~lir** *vt* repel; reject ‹*ideia, proposta etc*›

repensar /xepẽ'sar/ *vt/i* rethink

repen|te /xe'pẽtʃi/ *m* **de ~te** suddenly; [!] (*talvez*) maybe. **~tino** *a* sudden

reper|cussão /xeperku'sãw/ *f* repercussion. **~cutir** *vi* ‹*som*› reverberate; *fig* (*ter efeito*) have repercussions

repertório /xeper'tɔriu/ *m* (*músico etc*) repertoire; (*lista*) list

repe|tição /xepetʃi'sãw/ *f* repetition. **~tido** *a* repeated; **~tidas vezes** repeatedly. **~tir** *vt* repeat ● *vi* (*ao comer*) have seconds. **~tir-se** *vpr* ‹*pessoa*› repeat o.s.; ‹*fato, acontecimento*› recur. **~titivo** *a* repetitive

repi|car /xepi'kar/ *vt/i* ring. **~que** *m* ring

replay /xe'plej/ (*pl* **~s**) *m* action replay

repleto /xe'plɛtu/ *a* full up

réplica /'xɛplika/ *f* reply; (*cópia*) replica

replicar /xepli'kar/ *vt* answer ● *vi* reply

repolho /xe'poʎu/ *m* cabbage

repor /xe'por/ *vt* (*num lugar*) put back; (*substituir*) replace

reportagem /xepor'taʒẽ/ *f* (*uma*) report; (*ato*) reporting

repórter /xe'pɔrter/ *m/f* reporter

reposição /xepozi'sãw/ *f* replacement

repou|sar /xepo'sar/ *vt/i* rest. **~so** *m* rest

repreen|der /xepriẽ'der/ *vt* rebuke, reprimand. **~são** *f* rebuke, reprimand. **~sível** (*pl* **~síveis**) *a* reprehensible

represa /xe'preza/ *f* dam

represália /xepre'zalia/ *f* reprisal

represen|tação /xeprezẽta'sãw/ *f* representation; (*espetáculo*) performance; (*ofício de ator*) acting. **~tante** *m/f* representative. **~tar** *vt* represent; (*no teatro*) perform ‹*peça*›; play ‹*papel, personagem*› ● *vi* ‹*ator*› act. **~tativo** *a* representative

repres|são /xepre'sãw/ *f* repression. **~sivo** *a* repressive

repri|mido /xepri'midu/ *a* repressed. **~mir** *vt* repress

reprise /xe'prizi/ *f* (*na TV*) repeat; (*de filme*) rerun

reprodu|ção /xeprodu'sãw/ *f* reproduction. **~zir** *vt* reproduce. **~zir-se** *vpr* (*multiplicar-se*) reproduce; (*repetir-se*) recur

repro|vação /xeprova'sãw/ *f* disapproval; (*em exame*) failure. **~var** *vt* (*rejeitar*) disapprove of; (*em exame*) fail; **ser ~vado** ‹*aluno*› fail

rép|til /'xɛptʃiw/ (*pl* **~teis**) *m* reptile

república /xe'publika/ *f* republic; (*de estudantes*) hall of residence

republicano /xepubli'kanu/ *a & m* republican

repudiar /xepudʒi'ar/ *vt* disown; repudiate ‹*esposa*›

repug|nância /xepug'nãsia/ *f* repugnance. **~nante** *a* repugnant

repul|sa /xe'puwsa/ *f* repulsion; (*recusa*) rejection. **~sivo** *a* repulsive

reputação /xeputa'sãw/ *f* reputation

requebrar /xeke'brar/ *vt* swing. **~-se** *vpr* sway

requeijão /xeke'ʒãw/ *m* cheese spread, cottage cheese

reque|rer /xeke'rer/ *vt* (*pedir*) apply for; (*exigir*) require. **~rimento** *m* application

requin|tado /xekĩ'tadu/ *a* refined. **~tar** *vt* refine. **~te** *m* refinement

requisi|ção /xekizi'sãw/ *f* requisition. **~tar** *vt* requisition. **~to** *m* requirement

rês /xes/ (*pl* **reses**) *m* head of cattle; *pl* cattle

rescindir /xesĩ'dʒir/ *vt* rescind

rés do chão /xɛzdu'ʃãw/ *m invar Port* ground floor, *Amer* first floor

rese|nha /xe'zeɲa/ *f* review. **~nhar** *vt* review

reser|va /xe'zɛrva/ *f* reserve; (*em hotel, avião etc, ressalva*) reservation. **~var** *vt* reserve. **~vatório** *m* reservoir. **~vista** *m/f* reservist

resfri|ado /xesfri'ado/ *a* **estar ~ado** have a cold ● *m* cold. **~ar** *vt* cool ● *vi* get cold; (*tornar-se morno*) cool down. **~ar-se** *vpr* catch a cold

resga|tar /xezga'tar/ *vt* (*salvar*) rescue; (*remir*) redeem. **~te** *m* (*salvamento*) rescue; (*pago por refém*) ransom; (*remissão*) redemption

resguardar /xezgwar'dar/ *vt* protect. **~-se** *vpr* protect o.s. (**de** from)

residência /xezi'dẽsia/ *f* residence

residen|cial /xezidẽsi'aw/ (*pl* **~ciais**) *a* ‹*bairro*› residential; ‹*telefone etc*› home. **~te** *a* & *m/f* resident

residir /xezi'dʒir/ *vi* reside

resíduo /xe'ziduu/ *m* residue

resig|nação /xezigna'sãw/ *f* resignation. **~nado** *a* resigned. **~nar-se** *vpr* resign o.s. (**com** to)

resiliente /xezili'ẽtʃi/ *a* resilient

resina /xe'zina/ *f* resin

resis|tência /xezis'tẽsia/ *f* resistance; (*de atleta, mental*) endurance; (*de material, objeto*) toughness. **~tente** *a* strong, tough; ‹*tecido, roupa*› hard-wearing; ‹*planta*› hardy; **~tente a** resistant to. **~tir** *vi* (*opor* **~***tência*) resist; (*aguentar*) ‹*pessoa*› hold out; ‹*objeto*› hold; **~tir a** (*combater*) resist; (*aguentar*) withstand; **~tir ao tempo** stand the test of time

resmun|gar /xezmũ'gar/ *vi* grumble. **~go** *m* grumbling

resolu|ção /xezolu'sãw/ *f* resolution; (*firmeza*) resolve; (*de problema*) solution. **~to** *a* resolute; **~to a** resolved to

resolver /xezow'ver/ *vt* (*esclarecer*) sort out; solve ‹*problema, enigma*›; (*decidir*) decide. **~-se** *vpr* make up one's mind (**a** to)

respaldo /xes'pawdu/ *m* (*de cadeira*) back; *fig* (*apoio*) backing

respetivo /xespe'tʃivu/ *a* respective

respei|tabilidade /xespejtabili'dadʒi/ *f* respectability. **~tador** *a* respectful. **~tar** *vt* respect. **~tável** (*pl* **~táveis**) *a* respectable. **~to** *m* respect (**por** for); **a ~to de** about; **a este ~to** in this respect; **com ~to a** with regard to; **dizer ~to a** concern. **~toso** /o/ *a* respectful

respin|gar /xespĩ'gar/ *vt/i* splash. **~go** *m* splash

respi|ração /xespira'sãw/ *f* breathing. **~rador** *m* respirator. **~rar** *vt/i* breathe. **~ratório** *a* respiratory. **~ro** *m* breath; (*descanso*) break, breather

resplande|cente /xesplãde'sẽtʃi/ *a* resplendent. **~cer** *vi* shine

resplendor /xesplẽ'dor/ *m* brilliance; *fig* glory

respon|dão /xespõ'dãw/ *a* (*f* **~dona**) cheeky. **~der** *vt/i* answer; (*com insolência*) answer back; **~der a** answer; **~der por** answer for, take responsibility for

responsabili|dade /xespõsabili'dadʒi/ *f* responsibility. **~zar** *vt* hold responsible (**por** for). **~zar-se** *vpr* take responsibility (**por** for)

responsá|vel /xespõ'savew/ (*pl* **~veis**) *a* responsible (**por** for)

resposta /xes'pɔsta/ *f* answer

resquício /xes'kisiu/ *m* vestige, remnant

ressabiado /xesabi'adu/ *a* wary, suspicious

ressaca /xe'saka/ *f* (*depois de beber*) hangover; (*do mar*) undertow

ressaltar /xesaw'tar/ *vt* emphasize ● *vi* stand out

ressalva /xe'sawva/ *f* reservation, proviso; (*proteção*) safeguard

ressarcir /xesar'sir/ *vt* refund

resse|cado /xese'kadu/ *a* ‹*terra*› parched; ‹*pele*› dry. **~car** *vt/i* dry up

ressen|tido /xesẽ'tʃidu/ *a* resentful. **~timento** *m* resentment. **~tir-se** *vpr*

~tir-se de (*ofender-se*) resent; (*ser influenciado*) show the effects of

ressequido /xese'kidu/ *a* ▶ RESSECADO

resso|ar /xeso'ar/ *vi* resound. **~nância** *f* resonance. **~nante** *a* resonant. **~nar** *vi Port* snore

ressurgimento /xesurʒi'mẽtu/ *m* resurgence

ressurreição /xesuxej'sãw/ *f* resurrection

ressuscitar /xesusi'tar/ *vt* revive

restabele|cer /xestabele'ser/ *vt* restore; restore to health ‹*doente*›. **~cer-se** *vpr* recover. **~cimento** *m* restoration; (*de doente*) recovery

res|tante /xes'tãtʃi/ *a* remaining ● *m* remainder. **~tar** *vi* remain; **~ta-me dizer que ...** it remains for me to say that

restau|ração /xestawra'sãw/ *f* restoration. **~rante** *m* restaurant. **~rar** *vt* restore

restitu|ição /xestʃitui'sãw/ *f* return, restitution. **~ir** *vt* (*devolver*) return; restore ‹*forma, força etc*›; reinstate ‹*funcionário*›

resto /'xɛstu/ *m* rest; *pl* (*de comida*) leftovers; (*de cadáver*) remains; **de ~** besides

restrição /xestri'sãw/ *f* restriction

restringir /xestrĩ'ʒir/ *vt* restrict

restrito /xes'tritu/ *a* restricted

resul|tado /xezuw'tadu/ *m* result. **~tante** *a* resulting (**de** from). **~tar** *vi* result (**de** from **em** in)

resu|mir /xezu'mir/ *vt* (*abreviar*) summarize; (*conter em poucas palavras*) sum up. **~mir-se** *vpr* (*ser expresso em poucas palavras*) be summed up; **~mir-se em** (*ser apenas*) come down to. **~mo** *m* summary; **em ~mo** briefly

resvalar /xezva'lar/ *vi* (*sem querer*) slip; (*deslizar*) slide

reta /'xɛta/ *f* (*linha*) straight line; (*de pista etc*) straight; **~ final** home straight

retaguarda /xeta'gwarda/ *f* rearguard

retalho /xe'taʎu/ *m* scrap; **a ~** *Port* retail

retaliação /xetalia'sãw/ *f* retaliation

retangular /xetãgu'lar/ *a* rectangular

retângulo /xe'tãgulu/ *m* rectangle

retar|dado /xetar'dadu/ *a* retarded ● *m* retard. **~dar** *vt* delay. **~datário** *m* latecomer

retenção /xetẽ'sãw/ *f* retention

reter /xe'ter/ *vt* keep ‹*pessoa*›; hold back ‹*águas, riso, lágrimas*›; (*na memória*) retain. **~-se** *vpr* restrain o.s.

rete|sado /xete'zadu/ *a* taut. **~sar** *vt* pull taut

reticência /xetʃi'sẽsia/ *f* reticence

reti|dão /xetʃi'dãw/ *f* rectitude. **~ficar** *vt* rectify

reti|rada /xetʃi'rada/ *f* (*de tropas*) retreat; (*de dinheiro*) withdrawal. **~rado** *a* secluded. **~rar** *vt* withdraw; (*afastar*) move away. **~rar-se** *vpr* ‹*tropas*› retreat; (*afastar-se*) withdraw; (*de uma atividade*) retire. **~ro** *m* retreat

reto /'xɛtu/ *a* ‹*linha etc*› straight; ‹*pessoa*› honest

retocar /xeto'kar/ *vt* touch up ‹*desenho, maquiagem etc*›; alter ‹*texto*›

reto|mada /xeto'mada/ *f* (*continuação*) resumption; (*reconquista*) retaking. **~mar** *vt* (*continuar com*) resume; (*conquistar de novo*) retake

retoque /xe'tɔki/ *m* finishing touch

retorcer /xetor'ser/ *vt* twist. **~-se** *vpr* writhe

retóri|ca /xe'tɔrika/ *f* rhetoric. **~co** *a* rhetorical

retor|nar /xetor'nar/ *vi* return. **~no** *m* return; (*na estrada*) turning place; **dar ~no** do a U-turn

retrair /xetra'ir/ *vt* retract, withdraw. **~-se** *vpr* (*recuar*) withdraw; (*encolher-se*) retract

retrasa|do /xetra'zadu/ *a* **a semana ~da** the week before last

retratar[1] /xetra'tar/ *vt* (*desdizer*) retract

retra|tar[2] /xetra'tar/ *vt* (*em quadro, livro*) portray, depict. **~to** *m* portrait; (*foto*) photo; (*representação*) portrayal; **~to falado** identikit picture

retribuir /xetribu'ir/ *vt* return ‹*favor, visita*›; repay ‹*gentileza*›

retroativo /xetroa'tʃivu/ *a* retroactive; ‹*pagamento*› backdated

retro|ceder /xetrose'der/ *vi* retreat; (*desistir*) back down. **~cesso** /ɛ/ *m* retreat; (*ao passado*) regression

retrógrado /xe'trɔgradu/ *a* retrograde

retrospe|tiva /xetrospe'tʃiva/ *f* retrospective. **~tivo** *a* retrospective. **~to** /ɛ/ *m* look back; **em ~to** in retrospect

retrovisor /xetrovi'zor/ *a & m* **(espelho) ~** rear-view mirror

retrucar /xetru'kar/ *vt/i* retort

retum|bante /xetũ'bãtʃi/ *a* resounding. **~bar** *vi* resound

réu /'xɛw/ *m* (*f* **ré**) defendant

reumatismo /xewma'tʃizmu/ *m* rheumatism

reu|nião /xeuni'ãw/ *f* meeting; (*descontraída*) get-together; (*de família*) reunion; **~nião de cúpula** summit meeting. **~nir** *vt* bring together ‹*pessoas*›; combine ‹*qualidades*›. **~nir-se** *vpr* meet; ‹*amigos, familiares*› get together; **~nir-se a** join

revanche /xe'vãʃi/ *f* revenge; (*jogo*) return match

reveillon /xeve'jõ/ (*pl* **~s**) *m* New Year's Eve

reve|lação /xevela'sãw/ *f* revelation; (*de fotos*) developing; (*novo talento*) promising newcomer. **~lar** *vt* reveal; develop ‹*filme, fotos*›. **~lar-se** *vpr* (*vir a ser*) turn out to be

revelia /xeve'lia/ *f* **à ~** by default; **à ~ de** without the knowledge of

reven|dedor /xevẽde'dor/ *m* dealer. **~der** *vt* resell

rever /xe'ver/ *vt* (*ver de novo*) see again; (*revisar*) revise; (*examinar*) check

reve|rência /xeve'resia/ *f* reverence; (*movimento do busto*) bow; (*dobrando os joelhos*) curtsey. **~rente** *a* reverent

reverso /xe'vɛrsu/ *m* reverse; **o ~ da medalha** the other side of the coin

revés /xe'vɛs/ (*pl* **reveses**) *m* setback

reves|timento /xevestʃi'mẽtu/ *m* covering. **~tir** *vt* cover

reve|zamento /xeveza'mẽtu/ *m* alternation. **~zar** *vt/i* alternate. **~zar-se** *vpr* alternate

revi|dar /xevi'dar/ *vt* return ‹*golpe, insulto*›; refute ‹*crítica*›; (*retrucar*) retort ● *vi* hit back. **~de** *m* response

revigorar /xevigo'rar/ *vt* strengthen ● *vi*. **~-se** *vpr* regain one's strength

revi|rar /xevi'rar/ *vt* turn out ‹*bolsos, gavetas*›; turn over ‹*terra*›; turn inside out ‹*roupa*›; roll ‹*olhos*›. **~rar-se** *vpr* toss and turn. **~ravolta** /ɔ/ *f* (*na política etc*) about-face, about-turn; (*da situação*) turnabout, dramatic change

revi|são /xevi'zãw/ *f* (*de lições etc*) revision; (*de máquina, motor*) overhaul; (*de carro*) service; **~são de provas** proofreading. **~sar** *vt* revise ‹*provas, lições*›; service ‹*carro*›. **~sor** *m* (*de bilhetes*) ticket inspector; **~sor de provas** proofreader

revis|ta /xe'vista/ *f* (*para ler*) magazine; (*teatral*) revue; (*de tropas etc*) review; **passar ~ta a** review. **~tar** *vt* search

reviver /xevi'ver/ *vt* relive ● *vi* revive

revogar /xevo'gar/ *vt* revoke ‹*lei*›; cancel ‹*ordem*›

revol|ta /xe'vɔwta/ *f* (*rebelião*) revolt; (*indignação*) disgust. **~tante** *a* disgusting. **~tar** *vt* disgust. **~tar-se** *vpr* (*rebelar-se*) revolt; (*indignar-se*) be disgusted. **~to** /o/ *a* ‹*casa, gaveta*› upside down; ‹*cabelo*› dishevelled; ‹*mar*› rough; ‹*mundo, região*› troubled; ‹*anos*› turbulent

revolu|ção /xevolu'sãw/ *f* revolution. **~cionar** *vt* revolutionize. **~cionário** *a & m* revolutionary

revolver /xevow'ver/ *vt* turn over ‹*terra*›; roll ‹*olhos*›; go through ‹*gavetas, arquivos*›

revólver /xe'vɔwver/ *m* revolver

re|za /'xɛza/ *f* prayer. **~zar** *vi* pray ● *vt* say ‹*missa, oração*›; (*dizer*) state

riacho /xi'aʃu/ *m* stream

ribalta /xi'bawta/ *f* footlights

ribanceira /xibã'sera/ *f* embankment

ribombar /xibõ'bar/ *vi* rumble

rico /'xiku/ *a* rich ● *m* rich man; **os ~s** the rich

ricochete /xiko'ʃetʃi/ *m* ricochet. **~ar** *vi* ricochet

ricota /xi'kɔta/ *f* curd cheese, ricotta

ridicularizar /xidʒikulari'zar/ *vt* ridicule

ridículo /xi'dʒikulu/ *a* ridiculous

ri|fa /'xifa/ *f* raffle. **~far** *vt* raffle

rifão /xi'fãw/ *m* saying

rifle /'xifli/ *m* rifle

rigidez /xiʒi'des/ *f* rigidity

rígido /'xiʒidu/ *a* rigid

rigor /xi'gor/ *m* severity; (*meticulosidade*) rigour; **vestido a ~** evening dress; **de ~** essential

rigoroso /xigo'rozu/ *a* strict; ‹*inverno, pena*› severe, harsh; ‹*lógica, estudo*› rigorous

rijo /'xiʒu/ *a* stiff; ‹*músculos*› firm

rim /xĩ/ *m* kidney; *pl* (*parte das costas*) small of the back

ri|ma /'xima/ *f* rhyme. **~mar** *vt/i* rhyme

rí|mel /'ximew/ (*pl* **~meis**) *m* mascara

ringue /'xĩgi/ *m* ring

rinoceronte /xinose'rõtʃi/ *m* rhinoceros

rinque /'xĩki/ *m* rink

rio /'xio/ *m* river
riqueza /xi'keza/ *f* wealth; (*qualidade*) richness; *pl* riches
rir /xir/ *vi* laugh (**de** at)
risada /xi'zada/ *f* laugh, laughter; **dar ~** laugh
ris|ca /'xiska/ *f* stroke; (*listra*) stripe; (*do cabelo*) parting; **à ~ca** to the letter. **~car** *vt* (*apagar*) cross out ‹*erro*›; strike ‹*fósforo*›; scratch ‹*mesa, carro etc*›; write off ‹*amigo*›
risco[1] /'xisku/ *m* (*na parede etc*) scratch; (*no papel*) line; (*esboço*) sketch
risco[2] *m* risk
riso /'xizu/ *m* laugh. **~nho** /o/ *a* smiling
ríspido /'xispidu/ *a* harsh
rítmico /'xitʃmiku/ *a* rhythmic
ritmo /'xitʃimu/ *m* rhythm
rito /'xitu/ *m* rite
ritu|al /xitu'aw/ (*pl* **~ais**) *a & m* ritual
ri|val /xi'vaw/ (*pl* **~vais**) *a & m/f* rival. **~validade** *f* rivalry. **~valizar** *vt* rival ● *vi* vie (**com** with)
rixa /'xiʃa/ *f* fight
roaming /'xõming/ *m Telec* roaming
robô /xo'bo/ *m* robot
robusto /xo'bustu/ *a* robust
roça /'xɔsa/ *f* (*campo*) country
rocambole /xokã'bɔli/ *m* roll
roçar /xo'sar/ *vt* graze; **~ em** brush against
ro|cha /'xɔʃa/ *f* rock. **~chedo** /e/ *m* cliff
roda /'xɔda/ *f* (*de carro etc*) wheel; (*de amigos etc*) circle; **~ dentada** cog. **~da** *f* round. **~do** *a* **saia ~da** full skirt. **~-gigante** (*pl* **~s-gigantes**) *f* big wheel, *Amer* Ferris wheel. **~moinho** *m* (*de vento*) whirlwind; (*na água*) whirlpool; *fig* whirl, swirl. **~pé** *m* skirting board, *Amer* baseboard
rodar /xo'dar/ *vt* (*fazer girar*) spin; (*viajar por*) go round; do ‹*quilometragem*›; shoot ‹*filme*›; run ‹*programa*› ● *vi* (*girar*) spin; (*de carro*) drive round
rodear /xodʒi'ar/ *vt* (*circundar*) surround; (*andar ao redor de*) go round
rodeio /xo'deju/ *m* (*ao falar*) circumlocution; (*de gado*) round-up; **falar sem ~s** talk straight
rodela /xo'dɛla/ *f* (*de limão etc*) slice; (*peça de metal*) washer
rodízio /xo'dʒiziu/ *m* rota
rodo /'xodu/ *m* rake
rodopiar /xodopi'ar/ *vi* spin round
rodovi|a /xodo'via/ *f* highway. **~ária** *f* bus station; **polícia ~ária** traffic police. **~ário** *a* road
ro|edor /xoe'dor/ *m* rodent. **~er** *vt* gnaw; bite ‹*unhas*›; *fig* eat away
rogar /xo'gar/ *vi* request
rojão /xo'ʒãw/ *m* rocket
rol /xɔw/ (*pl* **róis**) *m* roll
rolar /xo'lar/ *vt* roll ● *vi* roll; [!] (*acontecer*) happen
roldana /xow'dana/ *f* pulley
roleta /xo'leta/ *f* (*jogo*) roulette; (*borboleta*) turnstile
rolha /'xoʎa/ *f* cork
roliço /xo'lisu/ *a* ‹*objeto*› cylindrical; ‹*pessoa*› plump
rolo /'xolu/ *m* (*de filme, tecido etc*) roll; (*máquina, de cabelo*) roller; **~ compressor** steamroller; **~ de massa** rolling pin
Roma /'xoma/ *f* Rome
romã /xo'mã/ *f* pomegranate
roman|ce /xo'mãsi/ *m* (*livro*) novel; (*caso*) romance. **~cista** *m/f* novelist
romano /xo'manu/ *a & m* Roman
romântico /xo'mãtʃiku/ *a* romantic
romantismo /xomã'tʃizmu/ *m* (*amor*) romance; (*idealismo*) romanticism
romaria /xoma'ria/ *f* pilgrimage
rombo /'xõbu/ *m* hole
Romênia /xo'menia/ *f* Romania
romeno /xo'menu/ *a & m* Romanian
rom|per /xõ'per/ *vt* break; break off ‹*relações*› ● *vi* ‹*dia*› break; ‹*sol*› rise; **~per com** break up with. **~pimento** *m* break; (*de relações*) breaking off
ron|car /xõ'kar/ *vi* (*ao dormir*) snore; ‹*estômago*› rumble. **~co** *m* snoring; (*um*) snore; (*de motor*) roar
ron|da /'xõda/ *f* round, patrol. **~dar** *vt* (*patrulhar*) patrol; (*espreitar*) prowl around ● *vi* ‹*vigia etc*› patrol; ‹*animal, ladrão*› prowl around
ronronar /xõxo'nar/ *vi* purr
roque[1] /'xɔki/ *m* (*em xadrez*) rook
ro|que[2] /'xɔki/ *m* (*música*) rock. **~queiro** *m* rock musician
rosa /'xɔza/ *f* rose ● *a invar* pink. **~do** *a* rosy; ‹*vinho*› rosé
rosário /xo'zariu/ *m* rosary
rosbife /xoz'bifi/ *m* roast beef
rosca /'xoska/ *f* (*de parafuso*) thread; (*biscoito*) rusk; **farinha de ~** breadcrumbs

roseira /xo'zera/ *f* rose bush

roseta /xo'zeta/ *f* rosette

rosnar /xoz'nar/ *vi* ‹*cachorro*› growl; ‹*pessoa*› snarl

rosto /'xostu/ *m* face

rota /'xɔta/ *f* route

rota|ção /xota'sãw/ *f* rotation. **~tividade** *f* turnround. **~tivo** *a* rotating

rotei|rista /xote'rista/ *m/f* scriptwriter. **~ro** *m* (*de viagem*) itinerary; (*de filme, peça*) script; (*de discussão etc*) outline

roti|na /xo'tʃina/ *f* routine. **~neiro** *a* routine

rótula /'xɔtula/ *f* kneecap

rotular /xotu'lar/ *vt* label (**de** as)

rótulo /'xɔtulu/ *m* label

rou|bar /xo'bar/ *vt* steal ‹*dinheiro, carro etc*›; rob ‹*pessoa, loja etc*› ● *vi* steal; (*em jogo*) cheat. **~bo** *m* theft, robbery

rouco /'xoku/ *a* hoarse; ‹*voz*› gravelly

rou|pa /'xopa/ *f* clothes; (*uma*) outfit; **~pa de baixo** underwear; **~pa de cama** bedclothes. **~pão** *m* dressing gown

rouquidão /xoki'dãw/ *f* hoarseness

rouxi|nol /xoʃi'nɔw/ (*pl* **~nóis**) *m* nightingale

roxo /'xoʃu/ *a* purple

rua /'xua/ *f* street

rubéola /xu'bɛola/ *f* German measles

rubi /xu'bi/ *m* ruby

rude /'xudʒi/ *a* rude

rudimentos /xudʒi'mẽtus/ *m pl* rudiments, basics

ruela /xu'ɛla/ *f* backstreet

rufar /xu'far/ *vi* ‹*tambor*› roll ● *m* roll

ruga /'xuga/ *f* (*na pele*) wrinkle; (*na roupa*) crease

ru|gido /xu'ʒidu/ *m* roar. **~gir** *vi* roar

ruibarbo /xui'barbu/ *m* rhubarb

ruído /xu'idu/ *m* noise

ruidoso /xui'dozu/ *a* noisy

ruim /xu'ĩ/ *a* bad

ruína /xu'ina/ *f* ruin

ruivo /'xuivu/ *a* ‹*cabelo*› red; ‹*pessoa*› red-haired ● *m* redhead

rulê /xu'le/ *a* **gola ~** roll-neck

rum /xũ/ *m* rum

ru|mar /xu'mar/ *vi* head (**para** for). **~mo** *m* course; **~mo a** heading for; **sem ~mo** ‹*vida*› aimless; ‹*andar*› aimlessly

rumor /xu'mor/ *m* (*da rua, de vozes*) hum; (*do trânsito*) rumble; (*boato*) rumour

ru|ral /xu'raw/ (*pl* **~rais**) *a* rural

rusga /'xuzga/ *f* quarrel, disagreement

rush /xaʃ/ *m* rush hour

Rússia /'xusia/ *f* Russia

russo /'xusu/ *a & m* Russian

rústico /'xustʃiku/ *a* rustic

Ss

Saara /saa'ra/ *m* Sahara

sábado /'sabadu/ *m* Saturday

sabão /sa'bãw/ *m* soap; **~ em pó** soap powder

sabatina /saba'tʃina/ *f* test

sabedoria /sabedo'ria/ *f* wisdom

saber /sa'ber/ *vt/i* know (**de** about); (*descobrir*) find out (**de** about) ● *m* knowledge; **eu sei cantar** I know how to sing, I can sing; **sei lá** I've no idea; **que eu saiba** as far as I know

sabiá /sabi'a/ *m* thrush

sabi|chão /sabi'ʃãw/ *a & m* (*f* **~chona**) know-it-all

sábio /'sabiu/ *a* wise ● *m* wise man

sabone|te /sabo'netʃi/ *m* bar of soap. **~teira** *f* soap dish

sabor /sa'bor/ *m* flavour; **ao ~ de** at the mercy of

sabo|rear /sabori'ar/ *vt* savour. **~roso** *a* tasty

sabo|tador /sabota'dor/ *m* saboteur. **~tagem** *f* sabotage. **~tar** *vt* sabotage

saca /'saka/ *f* sack

sacada /sa'kada/ *f* balcony

sa|cal /sa'kaw/ (*pl* **~cais**) *a* [!] boring

saca|na /sa'kana/ [!] *a* (*desonesto*) devious; (*lascivo*) dirty-minded, naughty ● *m/f* rogue. **~nagem** *f* [!](*esperteza*) trickery; (*sexo*) sex; (*uma*) dirty trick. **~near** *vt* [!](*enganar*) do the dirty on; (*amolar*) take the mickey out of

sacar /sa'kar/ *vt/i* withdraw ‹*dinheiro*›; draw ‹*arma*›; (*em tênis, vôlei etc*) serve; [!] (*entender*) understand

saçaricar /sasari'kar/ *vi* play around

sacarina /saka'rina/ *f* saccharine

saca-rolhas /saka'xoʎas/ *m invar* corkscrew

sacer|dócio /saser'dɔsiu/ *m* priesthood. **~dote** /ɔ/ *m* priest. **~dotisa** *f* priestess

sachê /sa'ʃe/ *m* sachet
saciar /sasi'ar/ *vt* satisfy
saco /'saku/ *m* bag; **que ~!** [!] what a pain! **estar de ~ cheio (de)** [!] be fed up (with), be sick (of); **encher o ~ de alguém** [!] get on sb's nerves; **puxar o ~ de alguém** [!] suck up to sb; **~ de dormir** sleeping bag. **~la** /ɔ/ *f* bag. **~lão** *m* wholesale fruit and vegetable market. **~lejar** *vt* shake
sacramento /sakra'mẽtu/ *m* sacrament
sacri|ficar /sakrifi'kar/ *vt* sacrifice; have put down ‹*cachorro etc*›. **~fício** *m* sacrifice. **~légio** *m* sacrilege
sacrílego /sa'krilegu/ *a* sacrilegious
sacro /'sakru/ *a* ‹*música*› religious
sacrossanto /sakro'sãtu/ *a* sacrosanct
sacu|dida /saku'dʒida/ *f* shake. **~dir** *vt* shake
sádico /'sadʒiku/ *a* sadistic ● *m* sadist
sadio /sa'dʒiu/ *a* healthy
sadismo /sa'dʒizmu/ *m* sadism
safa|deza /safa'deza/ *f* (*desonestidade*) deviousness; (*libertinagem*) indecency; (*uma*) dirty trick. **~do** *a* (*desonesto*) devious; (*lascivo*) dirty-minded; (*esperto*) quick; ‹*criança*› naughty
safena /sa'fɛna/ *f* **ponte de ~** heart bypass. **~do** *m* bypass patient
safira /sa'fira/ *f* sapphire
safra /'safra/ *f* crop
sagitariano /saʒitari'anu/ *a & m* Sagittarian
Sagitário /saʒi'tariu/ *m* Sagittarius
sagrado /sa'gradu/ *a* sacred
saguão /sa'gwãw/ *m* (*de teatro, hotel*) foyer, *Amer* lobby; (*de estação, aeroporto*) concourse
saia /'saja/ *f* skirt. **~-calça** (*pl* **~s-calças**) *f* culottes
saída /sa'ida/ *f* (*partida*) departure; (*porta*) *fig* way out; **de ~** at the outset; **estar de ~** be on one's way out
sair /sa'ir/ *vi* (*de dentro*) go/come out; (*partir*) leave; (*desprender-se*) come off; ‹*mancha*› come out; (*resultar*) turn out; **~ mais barato** work out cheaper. **~-se** *vpr* fare; **~-se com** (*dizer*) come out with
sal /saw/ (*pl* **sais**) *m* salt; **~ de frutas** Epsom salts
sala /'sala/ *f* (*numa casa*) lounge; (*num lugar público*) hall; (*classe*) class; **fazer ~ a** entertain; **~ (de aula)** classroom; **~ de embarque** departure lounge; **~ de espera** waiting room; **~ de jantar** dining room; **~ de operação** operating theatre
sala|da /sa'lada/ *f* salad; *fig* jumble, mishmash; **~da de frutas** fruit salad. **~deira** *f* salad bowl
sala e quarto /sali'kwartu/ *m* two-room flat
sala|me /sa'lami/ *m* salami. **~minho** *m* pepperoni
salão /sa'lãw/ *m* hall; (*de cabeleireiro*) salon; (*de carros*) show; **~ de beleza** beauty salon
salari|al /salari'aw/ (*pl* **~ais**) *a* wage
salário /sa'lariu/ *m* salary
sal|dar /saw'dar/ *vt* settle. **~do** *m* balance
saleiro /sa'leru/ *m* salt cellar
sal|gadinhos /sawga'dʒiɲus/ *m pl* snacks. **~gado** *a* salty; ‹*preço*› exorbitant. **~gar** *vt* salt
salgueiro /saw'geru/ *m* willow; **~ chorão** weeping willow
saliência /sali'ẽsia/ *f* projection
salien|tar /saliẽ'tar/ *vt* (*deixar claro*) point out; (*acentuar*) highlight. **~tar-se** *vpr* distinguish o.s.. **~te** *a* prominent
saliva /sa'liva/ *f* saliva
salmão /saw'mãw/ *m* salmon
salmo /'sawmu/ *m* psalm
salmonela /sawmo'nɛla/ *f* salmonella
salmoura /saw'mora/ *f* brine
salpicar /sawpi'kar/ *vt* sprinkle; (*sem querer*) spatter
salsa /'sawsa/ *f* parsley
salsicha /saw'siʃa/ *f* sausage
saltar /saw'tar/ *vt* (*pular*) jump; (*omitir*) skip ● *vi* jump; **~ à vista** be obvious; **~ do ônibus** get off the bus
saltear /sawtʃi'ar/ *vt* sauté ‹*batatas etc*›
saltitar /sawtʃi'tar/ *vi* hop
salto /'sawtu/ *m* (*pulo*) jump; (*de sapato*) heel; **~ com vara** pole vault; **~ em altura** high jump; **~ em distância** long jump. **~-mortal** (*pl* **~s-mortais**) *m* somersault
salu|bre /sa'lubri/ *a* healthy. **~tar** *a* salutary
salva[1] /'sawva/ *f* (*de canhões*) salvo; (*bandeja*) salver; **~ de palmas** round of applause
salva[2] /'sawva/ *f* (*erva*) sage
salva|ção /sawva'sãw/ *f* salvation. **~dor** *m* saviour
salvaguar|da /sawva'gwarda/ *f* safeguard. **~dar** *vt* safeguard

sal|vamento /sawva'mẽtu/ *m* rescue; (*de navio*) salvage. **~var** *vt* save. **~var-se** *vpr* escape. **~va-vidas** *m invar* (*bóia*) lifebelt ● *m/f* (*pessoa*) lifeguard ● *a* **barco ~va-vidas** lifeboat. **~vo** *a* safe ● *prep* save; **a ~vo** safe

samambaia /samã'baja/ *f* fern

sam|ba /'sãba/ *m* samba. **~ba-canção** (*pl* **~bas-canção**) *m* slow samba ● *a invar* **cueca ~ba-canção** boxer shorts; **~ba-enredo** (*pl* **~bas-enredo**) *m* samba story. **~bar** *vi* samba. **~bista** *m/f* (*dançarino*) samba dancer; (*compositor*) composer of sambas. **~bódromo** *m* Carnival parade ground

samovar /samo'var/ *m* tea urn

sanar /sa'nar/ *vt* cure

san|ção /sã'sãw/ *f* sanction. **~cionar** *vt* sanction

sandália /sã'dalia/ *f* sandal

sandes /'sãdiʃ/ *f invar Port* sandwich

sanduíche /sãdu'iʃi/ *m* sandwich

sane|amento /sania'mẽtu/ *m* (*esgotos*) sanitation; (*de finanças*) rehabilitation. **~ar** *vt* set straight ‹*finanças*›

sanfona /sã'fona/ *f* (*instrumento*) accordion; (*tricô*) ribbing. **~do** *a* ‹*porta*› folding; ‹*pulôver*› ribbed

san|grar /sã'grar/ *vt/i* bleed. **~grento** *a* bloody; ‹*carne*› rare. **~gria** *f* bloodshed; (*de dinheiro*) extortion

sangue /'sãgi/ *m* blood; **~ pisado** bruise. **~-frio** *m* cool, coolness

sanguessuga /sãgi'suga/ *f* leech

sanguinário /sãgi'nariu/ *a* bloodthirsty

sanguíneo /sã'giniu/ *a* blood

sanidade /sani'dadʒi/ *f* sanity

sanitário /sani'tariu/ *a* sanitary. **~s** *m pl* toilets

san|tidade /sãtʃi'dadʒi/ *f* sanctity. **~tificar** *vt* sanctify. **~to** *a* holy; **todo ~to dia** every single day ● *m* saint. **~tuário** *m* sanctuary

são /sãw/ (*pl* **~s**) *a* (*f* **sã**) healthy; (*mentalmente*) sane; ‹*conselho*› sound

São /sãw/ *a* Saint

sapataria /sapata'ria/ *f* shoe shop

sapate|ado /sapatʃi'adu/ *m* tap dancing. **~ador** *m* tap dancer. **~ar** *vi* tap one's feet; (*dançar*) tap-dance

sapa|teiro /sapa'teru/ *m* shoemaker. **~tilha** *f* pump; **~tilha de balé** ballet shoe

sapato /sa'patu/ *m* shoe

sapeca /sa'pɛka/ *a* saucy

sa|pinho /sa'piɲu/ *m* thrush. **~po** *m* toad

saque[1] /'saki/ *m* (*do banco*) withdrawal; (*em tênis, vôlei etc*) serve

saque[2] /'saki/ *m* (*de loja etc*) looting. **~ar** *vt* loot

saraiva /sa'rajva/ *f* hail. **~da** *f* hailstorm; **uma ~da de** a hail of

sarampo /sa'rãpu/ *m* measles

sarar /sa'rar/ *vt* cure ● *vi* get better; ‹*ferida*› heal

sar|casmo /sar'kazmu/ *m* sarcasm. **~cástico** *a* sarcastic

sarda /'sarda/ *f* freckle

Sardenha /sar'deɲa/ *f* Sardinia

sardento /sar'dẽtu/ *a* freckled

sardinha /sar'dʒiɲa/ *f* sardine

sardônico /sar'doniku/ *a* sardonic

sargento /sar'ʒẽtu/ *m* sergeant

sarjeta /sar'ʒeta/ *f* gutter

Satanás /sata'nas/ *m* Satan

satânico /sa'taniku/ *a* satanic

satélite /sa'tɛlitʃi/ *a & m* satellite

sátira /'satʃira/ *f* satire

satírico /sa'tʃiriku/ *a* satirical

satirizar /satʃiri'zar/ *vt* satirize

satisfa|ção /satʃisfa'sãw/ *f* satisfaction; **dar ~ções a** answer to. **~tório** *a* satisfactory. **~zer** *vt* **~zer (a)** satisfy ● *vi* be satisfactory. **~zer-se** *vpr* be satisfied

satisfeito /satʃis'fejtu/ *a* satisfied; (*contente*) content; (*de comida*) full

saturar /satu'rar/ *vt* saturate

Saturno /sa'turnu/ *m* Saturn

saudação /sawda'sãw/ *f* greeting

saudade /saw'dadʒi/ *f* longing; (*lembrança*) nostalgia; **estar com ~s de** miss; **matar ~s** catch up

saudar /saw'dar/ *vt* greet

saudá|vel /saw'davew/ (*pl* **~veis**) *a* healthy

saúde /sa'udʒi/ *f* health ● *int* (*ao beber*) cheers; (*ao espirrar*) bless you

saudo|sismo /sawdo'zizmu/ *m* nostalgia. **~so** /o/ *a* longing; **estar ~so de** miss; **o nosso ~so amigo** our much-missed friend

sauna /'sawna/ *f* sauna

saxofo|ne /sakso'foni/ *m* saxophone. **~nista** *m/f* saxophonist

sazo|nado /sazo'nadu/ *a* seasoned. **~nal** (*pl* **~nais**) *a* seasonal

S

se /si/ ● *conj*

····➤ (*causa*) if; **~ chover, não vamos** if it rains, we won't go; **~ fosse rico, comprava uma moto** if I were rich, I'd buy a motorbike

! É mais correto dizer if I/he/she/it **were**, mas coloquialmente usa-se frequentemente **was**. (*dúvida*) whether; **não sei se vou ou se fico** I don't know whether to stay or go

! usa-se **whether** e não **if** antes de infinitivo e depois de preposições. (*desejo*) if; **se ao menos você tivesse me dito!** if only you had told me!

● *pron*

····➤ (*reflexo*) (ele) himself, (ela) herself; (*coisa*) itself; (*você*) yourself; (*vocês*) yourselves; (*eles, elas*) themselves; **ela ~ cortou** she's cut herself; **vocês ~ magoaram** you've hurt yourselves; **eles ~ lavaram** they've washed themselves; (*recíproco*) each other, one another; **eles ~ amam** they love each other; **eles ~ telefonam todos os dias** they phone each other every day

····➤ (*passivo*) **registaram-~ três mortos** three deaths were recorded (*sujeito indeterminado*) **fala-~ alemão** German is spoken

····➤ (*em expressões*) **~ bem que** although

sebo /'sebu/ *m* (*sujeira*) grease; (*livraria*) second-hand bookshop. **~so** /o/ *a* greasy; ‹*pessoa*› slimy

seca /'seka/ *f* drought. **~dor** *m* **~dor de cabelo** hairdryer. **~dora** *f* tumble dryer

seção /se'sãw/ *f* section; (*de loja*) department

secar /se'kar/ *vt/i* dry

sec|ção /sek'sãw/ *f* ▶ SEÇÃO. **~cionar** *vt* split up

seco /'seku/ *a* dry; ‹*resposta, tom*› curt; ‹*pessoa, caráter*› cold; ‹*barulho, pancada*› dull; **estar ~ por** I'm dying for

secretaria /sekreta'ria/ *f* (*de empresa*) general office; (*ministério*) department

secretá|ria /sekre'taria/ *f* secretary; **~ria eletrônica** ansaphone. **~rio** *m* secretary

secreto /se'krɛtu/ *a* secret

secular /seku'lar/ *a* (*não religioso*) secular; (*antigo*) age-old

século /'sɛkulu/ *m* century; *pl* (*muito tempo*) ages

secundário /sekũ'dariu/ *a* secondary

secura /se'kura/ *f* dryness; **estar com uma ~ de** be longing for/to

seda /'seda/ *f* silk

sedativo /seda'tʃivu/ *a* & *m* sedative

sede[1] /'sɛdʒi/ *f* headquarters; (*local do governo*) seat

sede[2] /'sedʒi/ *f* thirst (**de** for); **estar com ~** be thirsty

sedentário /sedẽ'tariu/ *a* sedentary

sedento /se'dẽtu/ *a* thirsty (**de** for)

sediar /sedʒi'ar/ *vt* host

sedimen|tar /sedʒimẽ'tar/ *vt* consolidate. **~to** *m* sediment

sedoso /se'dozu/ *a* silky

sedu|ção /sedu'sãw/ *f* seduction. **~tor** *a* seductive. **~zir** *vt* seduce

segmento /seg'mẽtu/ *m* segment

segredo /se'gredu/ *m* secret; (*de cofre etc*) combination

segregar /segre'gar/ *vt* segregate

segui|da /se'gida/ *f* **em ~da** (*imediatamente*) straight away; (*depois*) next; **cinco horas ~das** five hours running. **~do** *a* followed (**de** by). **~dor** *m* follower. **~mento** *m* continuation; **dar ~mento a** go on with

se|guinte /se'gĩtʃi/ *a* following; ‹*dia, semana etc*› next. **~guir** *vt/i* follow; (*continuar*) continue; **~guir em frente** (*ir embora*) go; (*indicação na rua*) go straight ahead. **~guir-se** *vpr* follow

segun|da /se'gũda/ *f* (*dia*) Monday; (*marcha*) second; **de ~da** second-rate; **~das intenções** ulterior motives; **de ~da mão** second-hand. **~da-feira** (*pl* **~das-feiras**) *f* Monday. **~do** *a* & *m* second ● *adv* secondly ● *prep* according to ● *conj* according to what

segu|rança /segu'rãsa/ *f* security; (*estado de seguro*) safety; (*certeza*) assurance ● *m/f* security guard. **~rar** *vt* hold. **~rar-se** *vpr* (*controlar-se*) control o.s.; **~rar-se em** hold on to; **fazer ~ro de** insure. **~ro** *a* secure; (*fora de perigo*) safe; (*com certeza*) sure ● *m* insurance; **estar no ~ro** be insured. **~ro-desemprego** *m* unemployment benefit

seio /'seju/ *m* breast, bosom; **no ~ de** within

seis /sejs/ *a* & *m* six. **~centos** *a* & *m* six hundred

seita /'sejta/ *f* sect

seixo /'sejʃu/ *m* pebble

sela /'sɛla/ *f* saddle

S

selar[1] /se'lar/ *vt* saddle ‹*cavalo*›

selar[2] /se'lar/ *vt* seal; (*franquear*) stamp

sele|ção /sele'sãw/ *f* selection; (*time*) team. **~cionar** *vt* select. **~to** /ɛ/ *a* select

selim /se'lĩ/ *m* saddle

selo /'selu/ *m* seal; (*postal*) stamp; (*de discos*) label

selva /'sɛwva/ *f* jungle. **~gem** *a* wild. **~geria** *f* savagery

sem /sẽj/ *prep* without; **~ eu saber** without me knowing; **ficar ~ dinheiro** run out of money

semáforo /se'maforu/ *m* (*na rua*) traffic lights; (*de ferrovia*) signal

sema|na /se'mana/ *f* week. **~nal** (*pl* **~nais**) *a* weekly. **~nalmente** *adv* weekly. **~nário** *m* weekly

semear /semi'ar/ *vt* sow

semelhan|ça /seme'ʎãsa/ *f* similarity. **~te** *a* similar; (*tal*) such

sêmen /'semẽ/ *m* semen

semente /se'mẽtʃi/ *f* seed; (*em fruta*) pip

semestre /se'mɛstri/ *m* six months; (*da faculdade etc*) term, *Amer* semester

semi|círculo /semi'sirkulu/ *m* semicircle. **~final** (*pl* **~finais**) *f* semi-final

seminário /semi'nariu/ *m* (*aula*) seminar; (*colégio religioso*) seminary

sem-número /sẽ'numeru/ *m* **um ~ de** innumerable

sempre /'sẽpri/ *adv* always; **como ~** as usual; **para ~** for ever; **~ que** whenever

sem|-terra /sẽ'tɛxa/ *m/f invar* landless labourer. **~-teto** *a* homeless ● *m/f* homeless person; **~-vergonha** *a invar* brazen ● *m/f invar* scoundrel

sena|do /se'nadu/ *m* senate. **~dor** *m* senator

S

senão /si'nãw/ *conj* otherwise; (*mas antes*) but rather ● *m* snag

senda /'sẽda/ *f* path

senha /'seɲa/ *f* (*palavra*) password; (*número*) code; (*sinal*) signal

senhor /se'ɲor/ *m* gentleman; (*homem idoso*) older man; (*tratamento*) sir ● *a* (*f* **~a**) mighty; **Senhor** (*com nome*) Mr; (*Deus*) Lord; **o ~** (*você*) you

senho|ra /se'ɲɔra/ *f* lady; (*mulher idosa*) older woman; (*tratamento*) madam; **Senhora** (*com nome*) Mrs; **a ~ra** (*você*) you; **nossa ~ra!** [I] gosh. **~ria** *f* **Vossa Senhoria** you. **~rita** *f* young lady; (*tratamento*) miss; **Senhorita** (*com nome*) Miss

se|nil (*pl* **~nis**) *a* senile. **~nilidade** *f* senility

sensação /sẽsa'sãw/ *f* sensation

sensacio|nal /sẽsasio'naw/ (*pl* **~nais**) *a* sensational. **~nalismo** *m* sensationalism. **~nalista** *a* sensationalist

sen|sato /sẽ'satu/ *a* sensible. **~sibilidade** *f* sensitivity. **~sível** (*pl* **~síveis**) *a* sensitive; (*que se pode sentir*) noticeable. **~so** *m* sense. **~sual** (*pl* **~suais**) *a* sensual

sen|tado /sẽ'tadu/ *a* sitting. **~tar** *vt/i* sit. **~tar-se** *vpr* sit down

sentença /sẽ'tẽsa/ *f* sentence

sentido /sẽ'tʃidu/ *m* sense; (*direção*) direction ● *a* hurt; **fazer** ou **ter ~** make sense

sentimen|tal /sẽtʃimẽ'taw/ (*pl* **~tais**) *a* sentimental; **vida ~tal** love life. **~to** *m* feeling

sentinela /sẽtʃi'nɛla/ *f* sentry

sentir /sẽ'tʃir/ *vt* feel; (*notar*) sense; smell ‹*cheiro*›; taste ‹*gosto*›; tell ‹*diferença*›; (*ficar magoado por*) be hurt by ● *vi* feel. **~-se** *vpr* feel; **sinto muito** I'm very sorry

sepa|ração /separa'sãw/ *f* separation. **~rado** *a* separate; ‹*casal*› separated. **~rar** *vt* separate. **~rar-se** *vpr* separate

séptico /'sɛptʃiku/ *a* septic

sepul|tar /sepuw'tar/ *vt* bury. **~tura** *f* grave

sequência /se'kwẽsia/ *f* sequence

sequer /se'kɛr/ *adv* **nem ~** not even

seques|trador /sekwestra'dor/ *m* kidnapper; (*de avião*) hijacker. **~trar** *vt* kidnap ‹*pessoa*›; hijack ‹*avião*›; sequestrate ‹*bens*›. **~tro** /ɛ/ *m* (*de pessoa*) kidnapping; (*de avião*) hijack; (*de bens*) sequestration

ser /ser/ ● *vi*

····➤ be; **é alta** she's tall; **sou de Porto Alegre** I'm from Porto Alegre; **2 e 2 são 4** two and two are four; **são três reais** it's three reais; **o banco é na praça** the bank is in the square; (*com as horas*) **são sete horas** it's seven o'clock; **~ de** (*material*) be made of; **é de alumínio** it's made of aluminium; (*lugar*) be from; **ele é do Brasil** he's from Brazil; (*grupo esportivo*) support; **é do Flamengo** she is a Flamengo supporter

● *v aux*

····➤ (*passiva*) to be; **ele será julgado segunda-feira** he will be tried on Monday

● *nm*

····➤ being; **um ~ humano** a human being; **um ~ vivo** a living being

····➤ (*em expressões*) **é que:** (*ênfase*) **é que não me apetece** I just don't feel like it; **seja como for, seja o que for, seja quem for** no matter how/what/who; **sou eu/é você etc** it's me/you etc

sereia /se'reja/ *f* mermaid
serenata /sere'nata/ *f* serenade
sereno /se'renu/ *a* serene; ‹*tempo*› fine
série /'sɛri/ *f* series; (*na escola*) grade; **fora de ~** [!] incredible
seriedade /serie'dadʒi/ *f* seriousness
serin|ga /se'rĩga/ *f* syringe. **~gueiro** *m* rubber tapper
sério /'sɛriu/ *a* serious; (*responsável*) responsible; **~?** really?; **falar ~** be serious; **levar a ~** take seriously
sermão /ser'mãw/ *m* sermon
seropositivo /sɛrɔpuzi'tivu/ *a Port* ▶ **soropositivo** /soropozi'tʃivu/
serpen|te /ser'pẽtʃi/ *f* serpent. **~tear** *vi* wind. **~tina** *f* streamer
serra[1] /'sɛxa/ *f* (*montanhas*) mountain range
serra[2] /'sɛxa/ *f* (*de serrar*) saw. **~gem** *f* sawdust. **~lheiro** *m* locksmith
serrano /se'xanu/ *a* mountain
serrar /se'xar/ *vt* saw
ser|tanejo /serta'neʒu/ *a* from the backwoods ● *m* backwoodsman. **~tão** *m* backwoods
servente /ser'vẽtʃi/ *m/f* labourer
Sérvia /'sɛrvia/ *f* Serbia
servi|çal /servi'saw/ (*pl* **~çais**) *a* helpful ● *m/f* servant. **~ço** *m* service; (*trabalho*) work; (*tarefa*) job; **estar de ~ço** be on duty. **~dor** *m* servant; *Comput* server. **~dor público** *m* civil servant
ser|vil /ser'viw/ (*pl* **~vis**) *a* servile
sérvio /'sɛrviu/ *a & m* Serbian
servir /ser'vir/ *vt* serve; serve as ● *vi* serve; (*ser adequado*) do; (*ser útil*) be of use; ‹*roupa, sapato etc*› fit; **~ como** ou **de** serve as; **para que serve isso?** what is this (used) for?. **~-se** *vpr* (*ao comer etc*) help o.s. (**de** to); **~-se de** make use of
sessão /se'sãw/ *f* session; (*no cinema*) showing, performance
sessenta /se'sẽta/ *a & m* sixty
seta /'sɛta/ *f* arrow; (*de carro*) indicator
sete /'sɛtʃi/ *a & m* seven. **~centos** *a & m* seven hundred
setembro /se'tẽbru/ *m* September
setenta /se'tẽta/ *a & m* seventy
sétimo /'sɛtʃimu/ *a* seventh
setor /se'tor/ *m* sector
setuagésimo /setua'ʒɛzimu/ *a* seventieth
seu /sew/ *a* (*f* **sua**) (*dele*) his; (*dela*) her; (*de coisa*) its; (*deles*) their; (*de você, de vocês*) your ● *pron* (*dele*) his; (*dela*) hers; (*deles*) theirs; (*de você, de vocês*) yours; **~ idiota!** you idiot!; **seu João** Mr John
seve|ridade /severi'dadʒi/ *f* severity. **~ro** /ɛ/ *a* severe
sexagésimo /seksa'ʒɛzimu/ *a* sixtieth
sexo /'sɛksu/ *m* sex; **fazer ~** have sex; **do mesmo ~** ‹*casais, pessoas*› same-sex
sex|ta /'sesta/ *f* Friday. **~ta-feira** (*pl* **~tas-feiras**) *f* Friday; **Sexta-feira Santa** Good Friday. **~to** /e/ *a & m* sixth
sexu|al /seksu'aw/ (*pl* **~ais**) *a* sexual; **vida ~al** sex life
sexy /'sɛksi/ *a invar* sexy
shopping /'ʃɔpĩ/ (*pl* **~s**) *m* shopping centre, *Amer* mall
short /'ʃɔrtʃi/ *m* (*pl* **~s**) shorts; **um ~** a pair of shorts
show /'ʃou/ (*pl* **~s**) *m* show; (*de música*) concert
si /si/ *pron* (*ele*) himself; (*ela*) herself; (*coisa*) itself; (*você*) yourself; (*eles*) themselves; (*vocês*) yourselves; (*qualquer pessoa*) oneself; **em ~** in itself; **fora de ~** beside o.s.; **cheio de ~** full of o.s.; **voltar a ~** come round
sibilar /sibi'lar/ *vi* hiss
SIDA /'sida/ *f Port* ▶ **AIDS**
side|ral /side'raw/ (*pl* **~rais**) *a* **espaço ~ral** outer space
siderurgia /siderur'ʒia/ *f* iron and steel industry
siderúrgi|ca /side'rurʒika/ *f* steelworks. **~co** *a* iron and steel ● *m* steelworker
sifão /si'fãw/ *m* syphon
sífilis /'sifilis/ *f* syphilis
sigilo /si'ʒilu/ *m* secrecy. **~so** /o/ *a* secret
sigla /'sigla/ *f* acronym
signatário /signa'tariu/ *m* signatory
signifi|cação /signifika'sãw/ *f* significance. **~cado** *m* meaning. **~car** *vt* mean. **~cativo** *a* significant
signo /'signu/ *m* sign
sílaba /'silaba/ *f* syllable
silenciar /silẽsi'ar/ *vt* silence

silêncio /si'lẽsiu/ *m* silence

silencioso /silẽsi'ozu/ *a* silent ● *m* silencer, *Amer* muffler

silhueta /siʎu'eta/ *f* silhouette

silício /si'lisiu/ *m* silicon

silicone /sili'kɔni/ *m* silicone

silo /'silu/ *m* silo

silvar /siw'var/ *vi* hiss

sil|vestre /siw'vɛstri/ *a* wild. **~vicultura** *f* forestry

sim /sĩ/ *adv* yes; **acho que ~** I think so

simbólico /sĩ'bɔliku/ *a* symbolic

simbo|lismo /sĩbo'lizmu/ *m* symbolism. **~lizar** *vt* symbolize

símbolo /'sĩbolu/ *m* symbol

si|metria /sime'tria/ *f* symmetry. **~métrico** *a* symmetrical

similar /simi'lar/ *a* similar

sim|patia /sĩpa'tʃia/ *f* (*qualidade*) pleasantness; (*afeto*) fondness (**por** for); (*compreensão, apoio*) sympathy; *pl* sympathies; **ter ~patia por** be fond of. **~pático** *a* nice

simpati|zante /sĩpatʃi'zãtʃi/ *a* sympathetic ● *m/f* sympathizer. **~zar** *vi* **~zar com** take a liking to ‹*pessoa*›; sympathize with ‹*ideias, partido etc*›

simples /'sĩplis/ *a invar* simple; (*único*) single ● *f* (*no tênis etc*) singles. **~mente** *adv* simply

simpli|cidade /sĩplisi'dadʒi/ *f* simplicity. **~ficar** *vt* simplify

simplório /sĩ'plɔriu/ *a* simple

simpósio /sĩ'pɔziu/ *m* symposium

simu|lação /simula'sãw/ *f* simulation. **~lar** *vt* simulate

simultâneo /simuw'taniu/ *a* simultaneous

S

sina /'sina/ *f* fate

sinagoga /sina'gɔga/ *f* synagogue

si|nal /si'naw/ (*pl* **~nais**) *m* sign; (*aviso, de rádio etc*) signal; (*de trânsito*) traffic light; (*no telefone*) tone; (*dinheiro*) deposit; (*na pele*) mole; **por ~nal** as a matter of fact; **~nal de pontuação** punctuation mark. **~naleira** *f* traffic lights. **~nalização** *f* (*na rua*) road signs. **~nalizar** *vt* signal; signpost ‹*rua, cidade*›

since|ridade /sĩseri'dadʒi/ *f* sincerity. **~ro** /ɛ/ *a* sincere

sincro|nia /sĩkro'nia/ *f* synchronization. **~nizar** *vt* synchronize

sindi|cal /sĩdʒi'kaw/ (*pl* **~cais**) *a* trade union. **~calismo** *m* trade unionism. **~calista** *m/f* trade unionist. **~calizar** *vt* unionize. **~cato** *m* trade union

síndico /'sĩdʒiku/ *m* house manager

síndrome /'sĩdromi/ *f* syndrome

sinergia /siner'ʒia/ *f* synergy

sineta /si'neta/ *f* bell

sin|fonia /sĩfo'nia/ *f* symphony. **~fônica** *f* symphony orchestra

Singapura /sĩga'pura/ *f* Singapore

singe|leza /sĩʒe'leza/ *f* simplicity. **~lo** /ɛ/ *a* simple

singu|lar /sĩgu'lar/ *a* singular; (*estranho*) peculiar. **~larizar** *vt* single out

sinis|trado /sinis'tradu/ *a* damaged. **~tro** *a* sinister ● *m* accident

sino /'sinu/ *m* bell

sinônimo /si'nonimu/ *a* synonymous ● *m* synonym

sintaxe /sĩ'taksi/ *f* syntax

síntese /'sĩtezi/ *f* synthesis

sin|tético /sĩ'tɛtʃiku/ *a* (*artificial*) synthetic; (*resumido*) concise. **~tetizar** *vt* summarize

sinto|ma /sĩ'toma/ *m* symptom. **~mático** *a* symptomatic

sintoni|zador /sĩtoniza'dor/ *m* tuner. **~zar** *vt* tune ‹*rádio, TV*›; tune in to ‹*emissora*› ● *vi* be in tune (**com** with)

sinuca /si'nuka/ *f* snooker

sinuoso /sinu'ozu/ *a* winding

sinusite /sinu'zitʃi/ *f* sinusitis

siri /si'ri/ *m* crab

Síria /'siria/ *f* Syria

sírio /'siriu/ *a & m* Syrian

siso /'sizu/ *m* good sense

siste|ma /sis'tema/ *m* system. **~mático** *a* systematic

sisudo /si'zudu/ *a* serious

site /sajt/ *m Comput* website

sítio /'sitʃiu/ *m* (*chácara*) farm; *Port* (*local*) place; **estado de ~** state of siege

situ|ação /situa'sãw/ *f* situation; (*no governo*) party in power. **~ar** *vt* situate. **~ar-se** *vpr* be situated; ‹*pessoa*› position o.s.

smoking /iz'mokĩ/ (*pl* **~s**) *m* dinner jacket, *Amer* tuxedo

só /sɔ/ *a* alone; (*sentindo solidão*) lonely ● *adv* only; **um ~ voto** one single vote; **~ um carro** only one car; **a ~s** alone; **imagina ~** just imagine; **~ que** except (that)

soalho /so'aʎu/ *m* floor

soar /so'ar/ *vt/i* sound

sob /'sobi/ *prep* under

sobera|nia /sobera'nia/ *f* sovereignty. **~no** *a & m* sovereign

soberbo /so'berbu/ *a* ‹*pessoa*› haughty; (*magnífico*) splendid

sobra /'sɔbra/ *f* surplus; *pl* leftovers; **tempo de ~** (*muito*) plenty of time; **ficar de ~** be left over; **ter algo de ~** (*sobrando*) have sth left over

sobraçar /sobra'sar/ *vt* carry under one's arm

sobrado /so'bradu/ *m* (*casa*) house; (*andar*) upper floor

sobrancelha /sobrã'seʎa/ *f* eyebrow

so|brar /so'brar/ *vi* be left; **~bram-me dois** I have two left

sobre /'sobri/ *prep* (*em cima de*) on; (*por cima de, acima de*) over; (*acerca de*) about

sobreaviso /sobria'vizu/ *m* **estar de ~** be on one's guard

sobrecapa /sobri'kapa/ *f* dust jacket

sobrecarregar /sobrikaxe'gar/ *vt* overload

sobreloja /sobri'lɔʒa/ *f* mezzanine

sobremesa /sobri'meza/ *f* dessert

sobrenatu|ral /sobrinatu'raw/ (*pl* **~rais**) *a* supernatural

sobrenome /sobri'nomi/ *m* surname

sobrepor /sobri'por/ *vt* superimpose

sobrepujar /sobripu'ʒar/ *vt* (*em altura*) tower over; (*em valor, número etc*) surpass; overwhelm ‹*adversário*›; overcome ‹*problemas*›

sobrescritar /sobriskri'tar/ *vt* address

sobressair /sobrisa'ir/ *vi* stand out. **~-se** *vpr* stand out

sobressalente /sobrisa'lẽtʃi/ *a* spare

sobressal|tar /sobrisaw'tar/ *vt* startle. **~tar-se** *vpr* be startled. **~to** *m* (*movimento*) start; (*susto*) fright

sobretaxa /sobri'taʃa/ *f* surcharge

sobretudo /sobri'tudu/ *adv* above all ● *m* overcoat

sobrevir /sobri'vir/ *vi* happen suddenly; (*seguir*) ensue; **~ a** follow

sobrevi|vência /sobrivi'vẽsia/ *f* survival. **~vente** *a* surviving ● *m/f* survivor. **~ver** *vt/i* **~ver (a)** survive

sobrevoar /sobrivo'ar/ *vt* fly over

sobri|nha /so'briɲa/ *f* niece. **~nho** *m* nephew

sóbrio /'sɔbriu/ *a* sober

socar /so'kar/ *vt* (*esmurrar*) punch; (*amassar*) crush

soci|al /sosi'aw/ (*pl* **~ais**) *a* social; **camisa ~al** dress shirt. **~alismo** *m* socialism. **~alista** *a & m/f* socialist. **~alite** /-a'lajtʃi/ *m/f* socialite. **~ável** (*pl* **~áveis**) *a* sociable

sociedade /sosie'dadʒi/ *f* society; (*parceria*) partnership; **~ anônima** limited company

sócio /'sɔsiu/ *m* (*de empresa*) partner; (*de clube*) member

socioeconômico /sosioeko'nomiku/ *a* socio-economic

soci|ologia /sosiolo'ʒia/ *f* sociology. **~ológico** *a* sociological. **~ólogo** *m* sociologist

soco /'soku/ *m* punch; **dar um ~ em** punch

socor|rer /soko'xer/ *vt* help. **~ro** *m* aid; **primeiros ~ros** first aid ● *int* help

soda /'sɔda/ *f* (*água*) soda water; **~ cáustica** caustic soda

sódio /'sɔdʒiu/ *m* sodium

sofá /so'fa/ *m* sofa. **~-cama** (*pl* **~s-camas**) *m* sofa bed

sofisticado /sofistʃi'kadu/ *a* sophisticated

so|fredor /sofre'dor/ *a* martyred. **~frer** *vt* suffer ‹*dor, derrota, danos etc*›; have ‹*acidente*›; undergo ‹*operação, mudança etc*› ● *vi* suffer; **~frer de** suffer from ‹*doença*›; have trouble with ‹*coração etc*›. **~frido** *a* long-suffering. **~frimento** *m* suffering. **~frível** (*pl* **~fríveis**) *a* passable

soft /'sɔftʃi/ (*pl* **~s**) *m* software package. **~ware** *m* software; (*um*) software package

so|gra /'sɔgra/ *f* mother-in-law. **~gro** /o/ *m* father-in-law. **~gros** /ɔ/ *m pl* in-laws

soja /'sɔʒa/ *f* soya, *Amer* soy

sol /sɔw/ (*pl* **sóis**) *m* sun; **faz ~** it's sunny

sola /'sɔla/ *f* sole. **~do** *a* ‹*bolo*› flat

solapar /sola'par/ *vt* undermine

solar[1] /so'lar/ *a* solar

solar[2] /so'lar/ *vt* sole ‹*sapato*› ● *vi* ‹*bolo*› go flat

solavanco /sola'vãku/ *m* jolt; **dar ~s** jolt

soldado /sow'dadu/ *m* soldier

sol|dadura /sowda'dura/ *f* weld. **~dar** *vt* weld

soldo /'sowdu/ *m* pay

soleira /so'lera/ *f* doorstep

sole|ne /so'leni/ *a* solemn. **~nidade** *f* (*cerimônia*) ceremony; (*qualidade*) solemnity

soletrar /sole'trar/ *vt* spell

solici|tação /solisita'sãw/ *f* request (**de** for); (*por escrito*) application (**de** for). **~tante** *m/f* applicant. **~tar** *vt* request; (*por escrito*) apply for

solícito /so'lisitu/ *a* helpful

solidão /soli'dãw/ *f* loneliness

soli|dariedade /solidarie'dadʒi/ *f* solidarity. **~dário** *a* supportive (**com** of)

soli|dez /soli'des/ *f* solidity. **~dificar** *vt* solidify. **~dificar-se** *vpr* solidify

sólido /'sɔlidu/ *a & m* solid

solista /so'lista/ *m/f* soloist

solitá|ria /soli'taria/ *f* (*verme*) tapeworm; (*cela*) solitary confinement. **~rio** *a* solitary

solo[1] /'sɔlu/ *m* (*terra*) soil; (*chão*) ground

solo[2] /'sɔlu/ *m* solo

soltar /sow'tar/ *vt* let go ‹*prisioneiros, animal etc*›; let loose ‹*cães*›; (*deixar de segurar*) let go of; loosen ‹*gravata, corda etc*›; let down ‹*cabelo*›; let out ‹*grito, suspiro etc*›; let off ‹*foguetes*›; tell ‹*piada*›; take off ‹*freio*›. **~-se** *vpr* ‹*peça, parafuso*› come loose; ‹*pessoa*› let o.s. go

soltei|ra /sow'tera/ *f* single woman. **~rão** *m* bachelor. **~ro** *a* single ● *m* single man. **~rona** *f* spinster

solto /'sowtu/ *a* (*livre*) free; ‹*cães*› loose; ‹*cabelo*› down; ‹*arroz*› fluffy; (*frouxo*) loose; (*à vontade*) relaxed; (*abandonado*) abandoned; **correr ~** run wild

solução /solu'sãw/ *f* solution

S **soluçar** /solu'sar/ *vi* (*ao chorar*) sob; (*engasgar*) hiccup

solucionar /solusio'nar/ *vt* solve

soluço /so'lusu/ *m* (*ao chorar*) sob; (*engasgo*) hiccup; **estar com ~s** have the hiccups

solú|vel /so'luvew/ (*pl* **~veis**) *a* soluble

solvente /sow'vẽtʃi/ *a & m* solvent

som /sõ/ *m* sound; (*aparelho*) stereo; **um ~** [!] (*música*) a bit of music

so|ma /'soma/ *f* sum. **~mar** *vt* add up ‹*números etc*›; (*ter como soma*) add up to

sombra /'sõbra/ *f* shadow; (*área abrigada do sol*) shade; **à ~ de** in the shade of; **sem ~ de dúvida** without a shadow of a doubt

sombre|ado /sõbri'adu/ *a* shady ● *m* shading. **~ar** *vt* shade

sombrinha /sõ'briɲa/ *f* parasol

sombrio /sõ'briu/ *a* gloomy

somente /so'mẽtʃi/ *adv* only

sonâmbulo /so'nãbulu/ *m* sleepwalker

sonante /so'nãtʃi/ *a* **moeda ~** hard cash

sonata /so'nata/ *f* sonata

son|da /'sõda/ *f* probe. **~dagem** *f* (*no mar*) sounding; (*de terreno*) survey; **~dagem de opinião** opinion poll. **~dar** *vt* probe; sound ‹*profundeza*›; *fig* sound out ‹*pessoas, opiniões etc*›

soneca /so'nɛka/ *f* nap; **tirar uma ~** have a nap

sone|gação /sonega'sãw/ *f* (*de impostos*) tax evasion. **~gador** *m* tax dodger. **~gar** *vt* withhold

soneto /so'netu/ *m* sonnet

so|nhador /soɲa'dor/ *a* dreamy ● *m* dreamer. **~nhar** *vt/i* dream (**com** about). **~nho** /'soɲu/ *m* dream; (*doce*) doughnut

sono /'sonu/ *m* sleep; **estar com ~** be sleepy; **pegar no ~** get to sleep. **~lento** *a* sleepy

sono|plastia /sonoplas'tʃia/ *f* sound effects. **~ridade** *f* sound quality. **~ro** /ɔ/ *a* sound; ‹*voz*› sonorous; ‹*consoante*› voiced

sonso /'sõsu/ *a* devious

sopa /'sopa/ *f* soup

sopapo /so'papu/ *m* slap; **dar um ~ em** slap

sopé /so'pɛ/ *m* foot

sopeira /so'pera/ *f* soup tureen

soprano /so'pranu/ *m/f* soprano

so|prar /so'prar/ *vt* blow ‹*folhas etc*›; blow up ‹*balão*›; blow out ‹*vela*› ● *vi* blow. **~pro** *m* blow; (*de vento*) puff; **instrumento de ~pro** wind instrument

soquete[1] /so'kɛtʃi/ *f* ankle sock

soquete[2] /so'ketʃi/ *m* socket

sordidez /sordʒi'des/ *f* sordidness; (*imundície*) squalor

sórdido /'sɔrdʒidu/ *a* (*reles*) sordid; (*imundo*) squalid

soro /'soru/ *m* (*remédio*) serum; (*de leite*) whey

soropositivo /soropozi'tʃivu/ *a* HIV-positive

sorrateiro /soxa'teru/ *a* crafty

sor|ridente /soxi'dẽtʃi/ *a* smiling. **~rir** *vi* smile. **~riso** *m* smile

sorte /'sɔrtʃi/ *f* luck; (*destino*) fate; **pessoa de ~** lucky person; **por ~** luckily; **ter** ou **dar ~** be lucky; **tive a ~ de conhecê-lo** I was lucky enough to meet him; **tirar a ~** draw lots; **trazer ~** bring good luck

sor|tear /sortʃi'ar/ *vt* draw for ‹*prêmio*›; select in a draw ‹*pessoa*›. **~teio** *m* draw

sorti|do /sor'tʃidu/ *a* assorted. **~mento** *m* assortment

sorumbático /sorũ'batʃiku/ *a* sombre, gloomy

sorver /sor'ver/ *vt* sip ‹*bebida*›

sósia /'sɔzia/ *m/f* double

soslaio /soz'laju/ *m* **de ~** sideways; ‹*olhar*› askance

sosse|gado /sose'gadu/ *a* ‹*vida*› quiet; **ficar ~gado** ‹*pessoa*› rest assured. **~gar** *vt* reassure ● *vi* rest. **~go** /e/ *m* peace

sótão /'sɔtãw/ (*pl* **~s**) *m* attic, loft

sotaque /so'taki/ *m* accent

soterrar /sote'xar/ *vt* bury

soutien /suti'ã/ (*pl* **~s**) *m Port* bra

sova|co /so'vaku/ *m* armpit. **~queira** *f* BO, body odour

soviético /sovi'ɛtʃiku/ *a & m* Soviet

sovi|na /so'vina/ *a* stingy, mean, *Amer* cheap ● *m/f* cheapskate. **~nice** *f* stinginess, meanness, *Amer* cheapness

sozinho /sɔ'ziɲu/ *a* (*sem ninguém*) alone, on one's own; (*por si próprio*) by o.s.; **falar ~** talk to o.s.

spam *m* (*em correio eletrônico*) spam

spray /is'prej/ (*pl* **~s**) *m* spray

squash /is'kwɛʃ/ *m* squash

stand /is'tãdʒi/ (*pl* **~s**) *m* stand

status /is'tatus/ *m* status

stripper /is'triper/ (*pl* **~s**) *m/f* stripper

striptease /istripi'tʃizi/ *m* striptease

sua /'sua/ *a & pron* ▶ **SEU**

su|ado /su'adu/ *a* ‹*pessoa, roupa*› sweaty; *fig* hard-earned. **~ar** *vt/i* sweat; **~ar por/para** *fig* work hard for/to; **~ar frio** come out in a cold sweat

sua|ve /su'avi/ *a* ‹*toque, subida*› gentle; ‹*gosto, cheiro, dor, inverno*› mild; ‹*música, voz*› soft; ‹*vinho*› smooth; ‹*trabalho*› light; ‹*prestações*› easy. **~vidade** *f* gentleness; mildness; softness; smoothness; ▶ **SUAVE**. **~vizar** *vt* soften; soothe ‹*dor, pessoa*›

subalterno /subaw'tɛrnu/ *a & m* subordinate

subconsciente /subikõsi'ẽtʃi/ *a & m* subconscious

subdesenvolvido /subidʒizĩvow'vidu/ *a* underdeveloped

súbdito /'subditu/ *m Port* ▶ **SÚDITO**

subdividir /subidʒivi'dʒir/ *vt* subdivide

subemprego /subĩ'pregu/ *m* menial job

subemprei|tar /subĩprej'tar/ *vt* subcontract. **~teiro** *m* subcontractor

subenten|der /subĩtẽ'der/ *vt* infer. **~dido** *a* implied ● *m* insinuation

subestimar /subestʃi'mar/ *vt* underestimate

su|bida /su'bida/ *f* (*ação*) ascent; (*ladeira*) incline; (*de preços etc*) *fig* rise. **~bir** *vi* go up; ‹*rio, águas*› rise ● *vt* go up, climb; **~bir em** climb ‹*árvore*›; get up onto ‹*mesa*›; get on ‹*ônibus*›

súbito /'subitu/ *a* sudden; **(de) ~** suddenly

subjacente /subiʒa'sẽtʃi/ *a* underlying

subjeti|vidade /subiʒetʃivi'dadʒi/ *f* subjectivity. **~vo** *a* subjective

subjugar /subiʒu'gar/ *vt* subjugate

subjuntivo /subiʒũ'tʃivu/ *a & m* subjunctive

sublevar-se /suble'varsi/ *vpr* rise up

sublime /su'blimi/ *a* sublime

subli|nhado /subli'ɲadu/ *m* underlining. **~nhar** *vt* underline

sublocar /sublo'kar/ *vt/i* sublet

submarino /subima'rinu/ *a* underwater ● *m* submarine

submer|gir /subimer'ʒir/ *vt* submerge. **~gir-se** *vpr* submerge. **~so** *a* submerged

submeter /subime'ter/ *vt* subject (**a** to); put down, subdue ‹*povo, rebeldes etc*›; submit ‹*projeto*›. **~-se** *vpr* (*render-se*) submit; **~-se a** (*sofrer*) undergo

submis|são /subimi'sãw/ *f* submission. **~so** *a* submissive

submundo /subi'mũdu/ *m* underworld

subnutrição /subinutri'sãw/ *f* malnutrition

subordi|nado /subordʒi'nadu/ *a & m* subordinate. **~nar** *vt* subordinate (**a** to)

subor|nar /subor'nar/ *vt* bribe. **~no** /o/ *m* bribe

subproduto /subipro'dutu/ *m* by-product

subs|crever /subiskre'ver/ *vt* sign ‹*carta etc*›; subscribe to ‹*opinião*›; subscribe ‹*dinheiro*› (**para** to). **~crever-se** *vpr* sign one's name. **~crição** *f* subscription. **~crito** *pp de* ▶ SUBSCREVER

subsequente /subise'kwẽtʃi/ *a* subsequent

subserviente /subiservi'ẽtʃi/ *a* subservient

subsidiar /subisidʒi'ar/ *vt* subsidize

subsidiá|ria /subisidʒi'aria/ *f* subsidiary. **~rio** *a* subsidiary

subsídio /subi'sidʒiu/ *m* subsidy

subsistência /subisis'tẽsia/ *f* subsistence

subsolo /subi'sɔlu/ *m* (*porão*) basement

substância /subis'tãsia/ *f* substance

substan|cial /subistãsi'aw/ (*pl* **~ciais**) *a* substantial. **~tivo** *m* noun

substitu|ição /subistʃitui'sãw/ *f* replacement; substitution. **~ir** *vt* (*pôr B no lugar de A*) replace (**A por B** A with B); (*usar B em vez de A*) substitute (**A por B** B for A). **~to** *a & m* substitute

subterfúgio /subiter'fuʒiu/ *m* subterfuge

subterrâneo /subite'xaniu/ *a* underground

sub|til /sub'til/ (*pl* **~tis**) *a Port* ▶ SUTIL

subtra|ção /subitra'sãw/ *f* subtraction. **~ir** *vt* subtract ‹*números*›; (*roubar*) steal

suburbano /subur'banu/ *a* suburban

subúrbio /su'burbiu/ *m* suburbs

subven|ção /subivẽ'sãw/ *f* grant, subsidy. **~cionar** *vt* subsidize

S

subver|são /subiver'sãw/ *f* subversion. **~sivo** *a & m* subversive

suca|ta /su'kata/ *f* scrap metal. **~tear** *vt* scrap

sucção /suk'sãw/ *f* suction

suce|der /suse'der/ *vi* (*acontecer*) happen ● *vt* **~der a** succeed ‹*rei etc*›; (*vir depois*) follow. **~der-se** *vpr* follow on from one another. **~dido** *a* **bem-~dido** successful

suces|são /suse'sãw/ *f* succession. **~sivo** *a* successive. **~so** /ɛ/ *m* success; (*música*) hit; **fazer** ou **ter ~so** be successful. **~sor** *m* successor

sucinto /su'sĩtu/ *a* succinct

suco /'suku/ *m* juice

suculento /suku'lẽtu/ *a* juicy

sucumbir /sukũ'bir/ *vi* succumb (**a** to)

sucur|sal /sukur'saw/ (*pl* **~sais**) *f* branch

Sudão /su'dãw/ *m* Sudan

sudário /su'dariu/ *m* shroud

sudeste /su'dɛstʃi/ *a & m* south-east; **o Sudeste Asiático** South East Asia

súdito /'sudʒitu/ *m* subject

sudoeste /sudo'ɛstʃi/ *a & m* southwest

Suécia /su'ɛsia/ *f* Sweden

sueco /su'ɛku/ *a & m* Swedish

suéter /su'ɛter/ *m/f* sweater

sufici|ência /sufisi'ẽsia/ *f* sufficiency. **~ente** *a* enough, sufficient; **o ~ente** enough

sufixo /su'fiksu/ *m* suffix

suflê /su'fle/ *m* soufflé

sufo|cante /sufo'kãtʃi/ *a* stifling. **~car** *vt* (*asfixiar*) suffocate; *fig* stifle ● *vi* suffocate. **~co** /o/ *m* hassle; **estar num ~co** be having a tough time

sufrágio /su'fraʒiu/ *m* suffrage

sugar /su'gar/ *vt* suck

sugerir /suʒe'rir/ *vt* suggest

suges|tão /suʒes'tãw/ *f* suggestion; **dar uma ~tão** make a suggestion. **~tivo** *a* suggestive

Suíça /su'isa/ *f* Switzerland

suíças /su'isas/ *f pl* sideburns

sui|cida /sui'sida/ *a* suicidal; **ataque ~** suicide bombing; **bombardeador ~** suicide bomber ● *m/f* suicide (victim). **~cidar-se** *vpr* commit suicide. **~cídio** *m* suicide

suíço /su'isu/ *a & m* Swiss

suíno /su'inu/ *a & m* pig

suíte /su'itʃi/ *f* suite

su|jar /su'ʒar/ *vt* dirty; *fig* sully ‹*reputação etc*› ● *vi*, **~-se** *vpr* get dirty; **~jar-se com alguém** queer one's pitch with sb. **~jeira** *f* dirt; (*uma*) dirty trick

sujei|tar /suʒej'tar/ *vt* subject (**a** to). **~tar-se** *vpr* subject o.s. (**a** to). **~to** *a* subject (**a** to) ● *m* (*de oração*) subject; (*pessoa*) person

su|jidade /suʒi'dadʒi/ *f Port* dirt. **~jo** *a* dirty

sul /suw/ *a invar & m* south. **~-africano** *a & m* South African; **~-americano** *a & m* South American; **~-coreano** *a & m* South Korean

sul|car /suw'kar/ *vt* furrow ‹*testa*›. **~co** *m* furrow

sulfúrico /suw'furiku/ *a* sulphuric

sulista /su'lista/ *a* southern ● *m/f* southerner

sultão /suw'tãw/ *m* sultan

sumário /su'mariu/ *a* ‹*justiça*› summary; ‹*roupa*› skimpy, brief

su|miço /su'misu/ *m* disappearance; **dar ~miço em** spirit away; **tomar chá de ~miço** disappear. **~mido** *a* ‹*cor, voz*› faint. **~mir** *vi* disappear; **ele anda ~mido** he's disappeared

sumo /'sumu/ *m Port* juice

sumptuoso /sũtu'ozu/ *a Port* ▶ SUNTUOSO

sunga /'sũga/ *f* swimming trunks

suntuoso /sũtu'ozu/ *a* sumptuous

suor /su'ɔr/ *m* sweat

superar /supe'rar/ *vt* overcome ‹*dificuldade etc*›; surpass ‹*expetativa, pessoa*›

superá|vel /supe'ravew/ (*pl* **~veis**) *a* surmountable. **~vit** (*pl* **~vits**) *m* surplus

superestimar /superestʃi'mar/ *vt* overestimate

superestrutura /superistru'tura/ *f* superstructure

superfici|al /superfisi'aw/ (*pl* **~ais**) *a* superficial

superfície /super'fisi/ *f* surface; (*medida*) area

supérfluo /su'pɛrfluu/ *a* superfluous

superintendência /superĩtẽ'dẽsia/ *f* bureau

superi|or /superi'or/ *a* (*de cima*) upper; ‹*ensino*› higher; ‹*número, temperatura etc*› greater (**a** than); (*melhor*) superior (**a** to) ● *m* superior. **~oridade** *f* superiority

superlativo /superla'tʃivu/ *a & m* superlative

superlota|ção /superlota'sãw/ *f* overcrowding. **~do** *a* overcrowded

supermercado /supermer'kadu/ *m* supermarket

superpotência /superpo'tẽsia/ *f* superpower

superpovoado /superpovo'adu/ *a* overpopulated

supersecreto /superse'krɛtu/ *a* top secret

supersensí|vel /supersẽ'sivew/ (*pl* **~veis**) *a* oversensitive

supersônico /super'soniku/ *a* supersonic

supersti|ção /superstʃi'sãw/ *f* superstition. **~cioso** /o/ *a* superstitious

supervi|são /supervi'zãw/ *f* supervision. **~sionar** *vt* supervise. **~sor** *m* supervisor

supetão /supe'tãw/ *m* **de ~** all of a sudden

suplantar /suplã'tar/ *vt* supplant

suplemen|tar /suplemẽ'tar/ *a* supplementary ● *vt* supplement. **~to** *m* supplement

suplente /su'plẽtʃi/ *a & m/f* substitute

supletivo /suple'tʃivu/ *a* supplementary; **ensino ~** adult education

súplica /'suplika/ *f* plea; **tom de ~** pleading tone

suplicar /supli'kar/ *vt* plead for; (*em juízo*) petition for

suplício /su'plisiu/ *m* torture; *fig* (*aflição*) torment

supor /su'por/ *vt* suppose

supor|tar /supor'tar/ *vt* (*sustentar*) support; (*tolerar*) stand, bear. **~tável** (*pl* **~táveis**) *a* bearable. **~te** /ɔ/ *m* support

suposição /supozi'sãw/ *f* supposition

supositório /supozi'tɔriu/ *m* suppository

supos|tamente /suposta'mẽtʃi/ *adv* supposedly. **~to** /o/ *a* supposed; **~to que** supposing that

supre|macia /suprema'sia/ *f* supremacy. **~mo** /e/ *a* supreme

supressão /supre'sãw/ *f* (*de lei, cargo, privilégio*) abolition; (*de jornal, informação, nomes*) suppression; (*de palavras, cláusula*) deletion

suprimento /supri'mẽtu/ *m* supply

suprimir /supri'mir/ *vt* abolish ‹*lei, cargo, privilégio*›; suppress ‹*jornal, informação, nomes*›; delete ‹*palavras, cláusula*›

suprir /su'prir/ *vt* provide for ‹*família, necessidades*›; make up for ‹*falta*›; make up ‹*quantia*›; supply ‹*o que falta*›; (*substituir*) take the place of; **~ alguém de** provide sb with; **~ A por B** substitute B for A

supurar /supu'rar/ *vi* turn septic

sur|dez /sur'des/ *f* deafness. **~do** *a* deaf; ‹*consoante*› voiceless ● *m* deaf person; **os ~dos** the deaf. **~do-mudo** (*pl* **~dos-mudos**) *a* deaf and dumb ● *m* deaf mute

sur|fe /'surfi/ *m* surfing. **~fista** *m/f* surfer

S

sur|gimento /surʒi'mẽtu/ *m* appearance. **~gir** *vi* arise; **~gir à mente** spring to mind

Suriname /suri'nami/ *m* Surinam

surpreen|dente /surpriẽ'dẽtʃi/ *a* surprising. **~der** *vt* surprise ● *vi* be surprising. **~der-se** *vpr* be surprised (**de** at)

surpre|sa /sur'preza/ *f* surprise; **de ~sa** by surprise. **~so** /e/ *a* surprised

sur|ra /'suxa/ *f* thrashing. **~rado** *a* ‹*roupa*› worn-out. **~rar** *vt* thrash ‹*pessoa*›; wear out ‹*roupa*›

surrealis|mo /suxea'lizmu/ *m* surrealism. **~ta** *a & m/f* surrealist

surtir /sur'tʃir/ *vt* produce; **~ efeito** be effective

surto /'surtu/ *m* outbreak

susce|tibilidade /susetʃibili-'dadʒi/ *f* (*de pessoa*) sensitivity. **~tível** (*pl* **~tíveis**) *a* ‹*pessoa*› touchy, sensitive; **~tível de** open to

suscitar /susi'tar/ *vt* cause; raise ‹*dúvida, suspeita*›

suspei|ta /sus'pejta/ *f* suspicion. **~tar** *vt/i* **~tar (de)** suspect. **~to** *a* suspicious; (*duvidoso*) suspect ● *m* suspect. **~toso** /o/ *a* suspicious

suspen|der /suspẽ'der/ *vt* suspend. **~são** *f* suspension. **~se** *m* suspense. **~so** *a* suspended. **~sórios** *m pl* braces, *Amer* suspenders

suspi|rar /suspi'rar/ *vi* sigh; **~rar por** long for. **~ro** *m* sigh; (*doce*) meringue

sussur|rar /susu'xar/ *vt/i* whisper. **~ro** *m* whisper

sustar /sus'tar/ *vt/i* stop

sustenido /suʃte'nidu/ *a Mús* sharp; **tecla ~** hash key

sustentabilidade /suʃtẽtabili'dadʒi/ *f* sustainability

susten|táculo /sustẽ'takulu/ *m* mainstay. **~tar** *vt* support; (*afirmar*) maintain. **~to** *m* support; (*ganha-pão*) livelihood

sustentável /suʃtẽ'tavɛw/ *a* sustainable

susto /'sustu/ *m* fright

sutiã /sutʃi'ã/ *m* bra

su|til /su'tʃiw/ (*pl* **~tis**) *a* subtle. **~tileza** /e/ *f* subtlety

sutu|ra /su'tura/ *f* suture. **~rar** *vt* suture

SUV *m* (*carro*) SUV

sweatshirt /swɛt'ʃarte/ *f Port* sweatshirt

Tt

tá /ta/ *int* [!] OK; ▶ **ESTAR**

taba|caria /tabaka'ria/ *f* tobacconist's. **~co** *m* tobacco

tabefe /ta'bɛfi/ *m* slap

tabe|la /ta'bɛla/ *f* table. **~lar** *vt* tabulate

tablado /ta'bladu/ *m* platform

tabu /ta'bu/ *a & m* taboo

tábua /'tabua/ *f* board; **~ de passar roupa** ironing board

tabuleiro /tabu'leru/ *m* (*de xadrez etc*) board

tabuleta /tabu'lɛta/ *f* (*letreiro*) sign

taça /'tasa/ *f* (*prêmio*) cup; (*de champanhe etc*) glass

ta|cada /ta'kada/ *f* shot; **de uma ~cada** in one go. **~car** *vt* hit ‹*bola*›; [!] throw

tacha /'taʃa/ *f* tack

tachar /ta'ʃar/ *vt* brand (**de** as)

tachinha /ta'ʃiɲa/ *f* drawing pin, *Amer* thumbtack

tácito /'tasitu/ *a* tacit

taciturno /tasi'turnu/ *a* taciturn

taco /'taku/ *m* (*de golfe*) club; (*de bilhar*) cue; (*de hóquei*) stick

tagare|la /taga'rɛla/ *a* chatty, talkative ● *m/f* chatterbox. **~lar** *vi* chatter

tailan|dês /tajlã'des/ *a & m* (*f* **~desa**) Thai

Tailândia /taj'lãdʒia/ *f* Thailand

tailleur /ta'jɛr/ (*pl* **~s**) *m* suit

Taiti /taj'tʃi/ *m* Tahiti

tal /taw/ (*pl* **tais**) *a* such; **que ~?** what do you think?; *Port* how are you?; **que ~ uma cerveja?** how about a beer?; **~ como** such as; **~ qual** just like; **um ~ de João** someone called John; **e ~** and so on

tala /'tala/ *f* splint

talão /ta'lãw/ *m* stub; **~ de cheques** chequebook

talco /'tawku/ *m* talc

talen|to /ta'lẽtu/ *m* talent. **~toso** /o/ *a* talented

talhar /ta'ʎar/ *vt* slice ‹*dedo, carne*›; carve ‹*pedra, imagem*›

talharim /taʎa'rĩ/ *m* tagliatelle

talher /ta'ʎɛr/ *m* set of cutlery; *pl* cutlery

talho /'taʎu/ *m Port* butcher's

talismã /taliz'mã/ *m* charm, talisman
talo /'talu/ *m* stalk
talvez /taw'ves/ *adv* perhaps; **~ ele venha amanhã** he may come tomorrow
tamanco /ta'mãku/ *m* clog
tamanho /ta'maɲu/ *m* size ● *adj* such
tâmara /'tamara/ *f* date
tamarindo /tama'rĩdu/ *m* tamarind
também /tã'bẽj/ *adv* also; **~ não** not ... either, neither
tam|bor /tã'bor/ *m* drum. **~borilar** *vi* ‹*dedos*› drum; ‹*chuva*› patter. **~borim** *m* tambourine
Tâmisa /'tamiza/ *m* Thames
tam|pa /'tãpa/ *f* lid. **~pão** *m* (*vaginal*) tampon. **~par** *vt* put the lid on ‹*recipiente*›; (*tapar*) cover. **~pinha** *f* top ● *m/f* [!] shorthouse
tampouco /tã'poku/ *adv* nor, neither
tanga /'tãga/ *f* G-string; (*avental*) loincloth
tangente /tã'ʒẽtʃi/ *f* tangent; **pela ~** *fig* narrowly
tangerina /tãʒe'rina/ *f* tangerine
tango /'tãgu/ *m* tango
tanque /'tãki/ *m* tank; (*para lavar roupa*) sink
tanto /'tãtu/ *a & pron* so much; *pl* so many ● *adv* so much; **~ ... como ...** both ... and ...; **~ (...) quanto** as much (...) as; **~ melhor** so much the better; **~ tempo** so long; **vinte e ~s anos** twenty odd years; **nem ~** not as much; **um ~ difícil** somewhat difficult; **~ que** to the extent that
Tanzânia /tã'zania/ *f* Tanzania
tão /tãw/ *adv* so; **~ grande quanto** as big as. **~ somente** *adv* solely
tapa /'tapa/ *m ou f* slap; **dar um ~ em** slap
tapar /ta'par/ *vt* (*cobrir*) cover; block ‹*luz, vista*›; cork ‹*garrafa*›
tapeçaria /tapesa'ria/ *f* (*pano*) tapestry; (*loja*) carpet shop
tape|tar /tape'tar/ *vt* carpet. **~te** /e/ *m* carpet; **~te de rato** *Port* (*comput*) mousemat
tapioca /tapi'ɔka/ *f* tapioca
tapume /ta'pumi/ *m* fence
taquicardia /takikar'dʒia/ *f* palpitations
taquigra|far /takigra'far/ *vt/i* write in shorthand. **~fia** *f* shorthand
tara /'tara/ *f* fetish. **~do** *a* sex-crazed; **ser ~do por** be crazy about ● *m* sex maniac
tar|dar /tar'dar/ *vi* (*atrasar*) be late; (*demorar muito*) be long ● *vt* delay; **~dar a responder** take a long time to answer, be a long time answering; **o mais ~dar** at the latest; **sem mais ~dar** without further delay. **~de** *adv* late; **~de da noite** late at night ● *f* afternoon; **hoje à ~de** this afternoon. **~dinha** *f* late afternoon. **~dio** *a* late
tarefa /ta'rɛfa/ *f* task, job
tarifa /ta'rifa/ *f* tariff; **~ de embarque** airport tax
tarimbado /tarĩ'badu/ *a* experienced
tarja /'tarʒa/ *f* strip
ta|rô /ta'ro/ *m* tarot. **~rólogo** *m* tarot reader
tartamu|dear /tartamudʒi'ar/ *vi* stammer. **~do** *a* stammering ● *m* stammerer
tártaro /'tartaru/ *m* tartar
tartaruga /tarta'ruga/ *f* (*bicho*) turtle; (*material*) tortoiseshell
tatear /tatʃi'ar/ *vt* feel ● *vi* feel one's way
táti|ca /'tatʃika/ *f* tactics. **~co** *a* tactical
tá|til /'tatʃiw/ (*pl* **~teis**) *a* tactile
tato /'tatu/ *m* (*sentido*) touch; (*diplomacia*) tact
tatu /ta'tu/ *m* armadillo
tatu|ador /tatua'dor/ *m* tattooist. **~agem** *f* tattoo. **~ar** *vt* tattoo
tauromaquia /tawroma'kia/ *f* bullfighting
taxa /'taʃa/ *f* (*a pagar*) charge; (*índice*) rate; **~ de câmbio** exchange rate; **~ de juros** interest rate; **~ rodoviária** road tax
taxar /ta'ʃar/ *vt* tax
taxativo /taʃa'tʃivu/ *a* firm, categorical
táxi /'taksi/ *m* taxi
taxiar /taksi'ar/ *vi* taxi
taxímetro /tak'simetru/ *m* taxi meter
taxista /tak'sista/ *m/f* taxi driver
tchã /tʃã/ *m* [!] special something
tchau /tʃaw/ *int* goodbye, bye
tcheco /'tʃɛku/ *a & m* Czech
Tchecoslováquia /tʃekoslo'vakia/ *f* Czechoslovakia
te /tʃi/ *pron* you; (*a ti*) to you
tear /tʃi'ar/ *m* loom
tea|tral /tʃia'traw/ (*pl* **~trais**) *a* theatrical; ‹*grupo*› theatre. **~tro** *m* theatre. **~trólogo** *m* playwright

tece|lagem /tese'laʒẽ/ *f* (*trabalho*) weaving; (*fábrica*) textile factory. **~lão** *m* (*f* **~lã**) weaver

te|cer /te'ser/ *vt/i* weave. **~cido** *m* cloth; (*no corpo*) tissue

te|cla /'tɛkla/ *f* key. **~cladista** *m/f* (*músico*) keyboard player; (*de computador*) keyboard operator. **~clado** *m* keyboard. **~clar** *vt* key (in)

técni|ca /'tɛknika/ *f* technique. **~co** *a* technical ● *m* specialist; (*de time*) manager; (*que mexe com máquinas*) technician

tecno|crata /tekno'krata/ *m/f* technocrat. **~logia** *f* technology. **~lógico** *a* technological

teco-teco /tɛku'tɛku/ *m* light aircraft

tédio /'tɛdʒiu/ *m* boredom

tedioso /tedʒi'ozu/ *a* boring, tedious

Teerã /tee'rã/ *f* Teheran

teia /'teja/ *f* web

tei|ma /'tejma/ *f* persistence. **~mar** *vi* insist; **~mar em ir** insist on going. **~mosia** *f* stubborness. **~moso** /o/ *a* stubborn; ‹*ruído*› insistent

teixo /'tejʃu/ *m* yew

Tejo /'teʒu/ *m* Tagus

tela /'tɛla/ *f* (*de cinema, TV etc*) screen; (*tecido, pintura*) canvas. **~ plana** *f* flat screen

telecoman|dado /telekomã'dadu/ *a* remote-controlled. **~do** *m* remote control

telecomunicação /telekomunika'sãw/ *f* telecommunication

teleférico /tele'fɛriku/ *m* cable car

telefo|nar /telefo'nar/ *vi* telephone; **~nar para alguém** phone sb. **~ne** /o/ *m* telephone; (*número*) phone number; **~ne celular** cell phone; **~ne sem fio** cordless phone. **~nema** /e/ *m* phone call. **~nia** *f* telephone technology

telefôni|co /tele'foniku/ *a* telephone; **cabine ~ca** phone box, *Amer* phone booth; **mesa ~ca** switchboard

telefonista /telefo'nista/ *m/f* (*da companhia telefônica*) operator; (*dentro de empresa etc*) telephonist

tele|grafar /telegra'far/ *vt/i* telegraph. **~gráfico** *a* telegraphic

telégrafo /te'lɛgrafu/ *m* telegraph

tele|grama /tele'grama/ *m* telegram. **~guiado** *a* remote-controlled

telejor|nal /teleʒor'naw/ (*pl* **~nais**) *m* television news

telemóvel /tele'mɔvew/ *m Port* mobile phone, *Amer* cell phone

tele|novela /teleno'vɛla/ *f* TV soap opera. **~objetiva** *f* telephoto lens

tele|patia /telepa'tʃia/ *f* telepathy. **~pático** *a* telepathic

telescó|pico /teles'kɔpiku/ *a* telescopic. **~pio** *m* telescope

telespectador /telespekta'dor/ *m* television viewer ● *a* viewing

teletrabalho /teletra'baʎu/ *m* teleworking

televi|são /televi'zãw/ *f* television; **~são a cabo** cable television; **~são digital** digital television. **~sionar** *vt* televise. **~sivo** *a* television. **~sor** *m* television set

telex /te'lɛks/ *m invar* telex

telha /'teʎa/ *f* tile. **~do** *m* roof

te|ma /'tema/ *m* theme. **~mático** *a* thematic

temer /te'mer/ *vt* fear ● *vi* be afraid; **~ por** fear for

teme|rário /teme'rariu/ *a* reckless. **~ridade** *f* recklessness. **~roso** /o/ *a* fearful

te|mido /te'midu/ *a* feared. **~mível** (*pl* **~míveis**) *a* fearsome. **~mor** *m* fear

tempão /tẽ'pãw/ *m* **um ~** a long time

temperado /tẽpe'radu/ *a* ‹*clima*› temperate ● *pp de* ▶ TEMPERAR

temperamen|tal /tẽperamẽ'taw/ (*pl* **~tais**) *a* temperamental. **~to** *m* temperament

temperar /tẽpe'rar/ *vt* season ‹*comida*›; temper ‹*aço*›

temperatura /tẽpera'tura/ *f* temperature

tempero /tẽ'peru/ *m* seasoning

tempestade /tẽpes'tadʒi/ *f* storm

templo /'tẽplu/ *m* temple

tempo /'tẽpu/ *m* (*período*) time; (*atmosférico*) weather; (*do verbo*) tense; (*de jogo*) half; **ao mesmo ~** at the same time; **nesse meio ~** in the meantime; **o ~ todo** all the time; **de todos os ~s** of all time; **quanto ~** how long; **muito/pouco ~** a long/short time; **~ integral** full time

tempo|rada /tẽpo'rada/ *f* (*sazão*) season; (*tempo*) while. **~ral** (*pl* **~rais**) *a* temporal ● *m* storm. **~rário** *a* temporary

te|nacidade /tenasi'dadʒi/ *f* tenacity. **~naz** *a* tenacious ● *f* tongs

tenção /tẽ'sãw/ *f* intention

t

tencionar /tẽsio'nar/ *vt* intend

tenda /'tẽda/ *f* tent

tendão /tẽ'dãw/ *m* tendon; **~ de Aquiles** Achilles tendon

tendência /tẽ'dẽsia/ *f* (*moda*) trend; (*propensão*) tendency

tendencioso /tẽdẽsi'ozu/ *a* tendentious

ten|der /tẽ'der/ *vi* tend (**para** towards); **~de a engordar** he tends to get fat; **o tempo ~de a ficar bom** the weather is improving

tenebroso /tene'brozu/ *a* dark; *fig* (*terrível*) dreadful

tenente /te'nẽtʃi/ *m/f* lieutenant

tênis /'tenis/ *m invar* (*jogo*) tennis; (*sapato*) trainer; **um ~** (*par*) a pair of trainers; **~ de mesa** table tennis

tenista /te'nista/ *m/f* tennis player

tenor /te'nor/ *m* tenor

tenro /'tẽxu/ *a* tender

ten|são /tẽ'sãw/ *f* tension; **~são (arterial)** blood pressure. **~so** *a* tense

tentação /tẽta'sãw/ *f* temptation

tentáculo /tẽ'taculu/ *m* tentacle

ten|tador /tẽta'dor/ *a* tempting. **~tar** *vt* try; (*seduzir*) tempt ● *vi* try. **~tativa** *f* attempt. **~tativo** *a* tentative

tênue /'tenui/ *a* faint

teo|logia /teolo'ʒia/ *f* theology. **~lógico** *a* theological

teólogo /te'ɔlogu/ *m* theologian

teor /te'ɔr/ *m* (*de gordura etc*) content; (*de carta, discurso*) drift

teo|rema /teo'rema/ *m* theorem. **~ria** *f* theory

teórico /te'ɔriku/ *a* theoretical

teorizar /teori'zar/ *vt* theorize

tépido /'tɛpidu/ *a* tepid

ter /ter/ ● *vt*

····➤ (*posse*) have got, have; **você tem irmãos?** have you got any brothers or sisters?, do you have any brothers or sisters?; **ele não tem dinheiro nenhum** he doesn't have any money

! **ter** pode ser traduzido como *have* ou *have got*, mas observe que *have got* é muito mais comum em inglês britânico.

····➤ (*idade, tamanho*) be; **a minha filha tem 10 anos** my daughter is ten; **tem três metros de comprimento** it's three metres long

····➤ (*doença, dor*) have; **~ dor de dente/pneumonia/febre** to have toothache/pneumonia/a temperature

····➤ (*sentir*) **~ medo** be scared; **~ frio** be cold; **~ ciúmes** be jealous

! Observe que **ter + substantivo** em geral é traduzido como *to be* **+ adjetivo** quando significa 'sentir': **tenho medo** *I'm scared.*

····➤ (*dar à luz*) **~ um bebê** have a baby

● *v aux*

····➤ (*estar obrigado a*) **~ que** *ou* **de fazer algo** have to do sth; **tiveram que ir embora imediatamente** they had to leave straight away; **você tem de dizer a ele** you must tell him

····➤ (*seguido de particípio*) **tenho dito muitas vezes...** I have often said...

····➤ (*em expressões*) **ir ~ com** (*encontrar-se*) meet up with; **fiquei de ir ~ com ele logo** I arranged to meet up with him later

tera|peuta /tera'pewta/ *m/f* therapist. **~pêutico** *a* therapeutic. **~pia** *f* therapy

terça /'tersa/ *f* Tuesday. **~-feira** (*pl* **~s-feiras**) *f* Tuesday; **Terça-Feira Gorda** Shrove Tuesday

tercei|ra /ter'sera/ *f* (*marcha*) third. **~ranista** *m/f* third-year. **~ro** *a* third ● *m* third party

terço /'tersu/ *m* third

ter|çol (*pl* **~çóis**) *m* stye

tergal /ter'gaw/ *m* Terylene

térmi|co /'tɛrmiku/ *a* thermal; **garrafa ~ca** Thermos® flask

termi|nal /termi'naw/ (*pl* **~nais**) *a & m* terminal; **~nal de vídeo** VDU. **~nante** *a* definite. **~nar** *vt* finish ● *vi* ‹*pessoa, coisa*› finish; ‹*coisa*› end; **~nar com alguém** (*cortar relação*) break up with sb

ter|minologia /terminolo'ʒia/ *f* terminology. **~mo** ¹ /'termu/ *m* term; **pôr ~mo a** put an end to; **meio ~mo** compromise

termo² /'termu/ *m Port* Thermos® (flask)

ter|mômetro /ter'mometru/ *m* thermometer. **~mostato** *m* thermostat

terno¹ /'tɛrnu/ *m* suit

ter|no²/ 'tɛrnu/ *a* tender. **~nura** *f* tenderness

terra /'tɛxa/ *f* land; (*solo, elétrico*) earth; (*chão*) ground; **a Terra** Earth; **por ~** on the ground; **~ natal** homeland

terraço /te'xasu/ *m* terrace

terra|cota /texa'kɔta/ *f* terracotta. **~moto** /texa'mɔtu/ *m Port* earthquake. **~plenagem** *f* earth moving

terreiro /te'xeru/ *m* meeting place for Afro-Brazilian cults

terremoto /texe'mɔtu/ *m* earthquake

terreno /te'xenu/ *a* earthly ● *m* ground; *Geog* terrain; (*um*) piece of land; **~ baldio** piece of waste ground

térreo /'tɛxiu/ *a* ground-floor; **(andar) ~** ground-floor, *Amer* first-floor

terrestre /te'xɛstri/ *a* ‹*animal*, *batalha*, *forças*› land; (*da Terra*) of the Earth, the Earth's; ‹*alegrias etc*› earthly

terrificante /texifi'kãtʃi/ *a* terrifying

terrina /te'xina/ *f* tureen

territori|al /texitori'aw/ (*pl* **~ais**) *a* territorial

território /texi'tɔriu/ *m* territory

terrí|vel /te'xivew/ (*pl* **~veis**) *a* terrible

terror /te'xor/ *m* terror; **filme de ~** horror film

terroris|mo /texo'rizmu/ *m* terrorism. **~ta** *a & m/f* terrorist

tese /'tɛzi/ *f* theory; (*escrita*) thesis

teso /'tezu/ *a* (*apertado*) taut; (*rígido*) stiff

tesoura /te'zora/ *f* scissors; **uma ~** a pair of scissors

tesou|reiro /tezo'reru/ *m* treasurer. **~ro** *m* treasure; (*do Estado*) treasury

testa /'tɛsta/ *f* forehead. **~ de ferro** (*pl* **~s-de-ferro**) *m* frontman

testamento /testa'mẽtu/ *m* will; (*na Bíblia*) testament

tes|tar /tes'tar/ *vt* test. **~te** /ɛ/ *m* test

testemu|nha /teste'muɲa/ *f* witness; **~nha ocular** eye witness. **~nhar** *vt* bear witness to ● *vi* testify. **~nho** *m* evidence, testimony

t

testículo /tes'tʃikulu/ *m* testicle

teta /'teta/ *f* teat

tétano /'tɛtanu/ *m* tetanus

teto /'tɛtu/ *m* ceiling; **~ solar** sun roof

tétrico /'tɛtriku/ *a* (*triste*) dismal; (*medonho*) horrible

teu /tew/ (*f* **tua**) *a* your ● *pron* yours

têx|til /'testʃiw/ (*pl* **~teis**) *m* textile

tex|to /'testu/ *m* text. **~tura** *f* texture

texugo /te'ʃugu/ *m* badger

tez /tes/ *f* complexion

ti /tʃi/ *pron* you

tia /'tʃia/ *f* aunt. **~-avó** (*pl* **~s-avós**) *f* great aunt

tiara /tʃi'ara/ *f* tiara

tíbia /'tʃibia/ *f* shin bone

ticar /tʃi'kar/ *vt* tick

tico /'tʃiku/ *m* **um ~ de** a little bit of

tiete /tʃi'ɛtʃi/ *m/f* fan

tifo /'tʃifu/ *m* typhoid

tigela /tʃi'ʒɛla/ *f* bowl; **de meia ~** small-time

tigre /'tʃigri/ *m* tiger. **~sa** /e/ *f* tigress

tijolo /tʃi'ʒolu/ *m* brick

til /tʃiw/ (*pl* **tis**) *m* tilde

tilintar /tʃilĩ'tar/ *vi* jingle ● *m* jingling

timão /tʃi'mãw/ *m* tiller

timbre /'tʃĩbri/ *m* (*insígnia*) crest; (*em papel*) heading; (*de som*) tone; (*de vogal*) quality

time /'tʃimi/ *m* team

timidez /tʃimi'des/ *f* shyness

tímido /'tʃimidu/ *a* shy

tímpano /'tʃĩpanu/ *m* (*tambor*) kettledrum; (*no ouvido*) eardrum

tina /'tʃina/ *f* vat

tingir /tʃĩ'ʒir/ *vt* dye ‹*tecido*, *cabelo*›; *fig* tinge

ti|nido /tʃi'nidu/ *m* tinkling. **~nir** *vi* tinkle; ‹*ouvidos*› ring; (*tremer*) tremble; **estar ~nindo** *fig* be in peak condition

tino /'tʃinu/ *m* sense, judgement; **ter ~ para** have a flair for

tin|ta /'tʃĩta/ *f* (*para pintar*) paint; (*para escrever*) ink; (*para tingir*) dye. **~teiro** *m* inkwell

tintim /tʃĩ'tʃĩ/ *m* **contar ~ por ~** give a blow-by-blow account of

tin|to /'tʃĩtu/ *a* dyed; ‹*vinho*› red. **~tura** *f* dye; *fig* tinge. **~turaria** *f* dry cleaner's

tio /'tʃiu/ *m* uncle; *pl* (*e tia*) uncle and aunt. **~-avô** (*pl* **~s-avôs**) *m* great uncle

típico /'tʃipiku/ *a* typical

tipo /'tʃipu/ *m* type

tipoia /tʃi'pɔja/ *f* sling

tique /'tʃiki/ *m* (*sinal*) tick; (*do rosto etc*) twitch

tíquete /'tʃiketʃi/ *m* ticket

tiquinho /tʃi'kiɲu/ *m* **um ~ de** a tiny bit of

tira /'tʃira/ *f* strip ● *m/f* [!] copper, *Amer* cop

tiracolo /tʃira'kɔlu/ *m* **a ~** ‹*bolsa*› over one's shoulder; ‹*pessoa*› in tow

tiragem /tʃi'raʒẽ/ *f* (*de jornal*) circulation

tira|-gosto /tʃira'gostu/ *m* snack. **~-manchas** *m invar* stain remover

ti|rania /tʃira'nia/ *f* tyranny. **~rânico** *a* tyrannical. **~rano** *m* tyrant

tirar /tʃi'rar/ *vt* (*afastar*) take away; (*de dentro*) take out; take off ‹*roupa, sapato, tampa*›; take ‹*foto, cópia, férias*›; clear ‹*mesa*›; get ‹*nota, diploma, salário*›; get out ‹*mancha*›

tiritar /tʃiri'tar/ *vi* shiver

tiro /'tʃiru/ *m* shot; **~ ao alvo** shooting; **é ~ e queda** ⊡ it can't fail. **~teio** *m* shoot-out

titânio /tʃi'taniu/ *m* titanium

títere /'tʃiteri/ *m* puppet

ti|tia /tʃi'tʃia/ *f* auntie. **~tio** *m* uncle

tititi /tʃitʃi'tʃi/ *m* ⊡ talk

titubear /tʃitubi'ar/ *vi* stagger, totter; *fig* (*hesitar*) waver

titular /tʃitu'lar/ *m/f* title holder; (*de time*) captain ● *vt* title

título /'tʃitulu/ *m* title; (*obrigação*) bond; **a ~ de** on the basis of; **a ~ pessoal** on a personal basis; **~ eleitoral** electoral register

toa /'toa/ *f* **à ~** (*sem rumo*) aimlessly; (*ao acaso*) at random; (*sem motivo*) without reason; (*em vão*) for nothing; (*desocupado*) at a loose end; (*de repente*) out of the blue

toada /to'ada/ *f* melody

toalete /toa'lɛtʃi/ *m* toilet

toalha /to'aʎa/ *f* towel; **~ de mesa** tablecloth

tobogã /tobo'gã/ *m* (*rampa*) slide; (*trenó*) toboggan

toca /'tɔka/ *f* burrow

toca|-discos /toka'dʒiskus/ *m invar* record player. **~-fitas** *m invar* tape player

tocaia /to'kaja/ *f* ambush

tocante /to'kãtʃi/ *a* (*enternecedor*) moving

tocar /to'kar/ *vt* touch; play ‹*piano, música, disco etc*›; ring ‹*campainha*› ● *vi* touch; ‹*pianista, música, disco etc*› play; **~ a** (*dizer respeito*) concern; **~ em** touch; touch on ‹*assunto*›; ‹*campainha, telefone, sino*› ring. **~-se** *vpr* touch; (*mancar-se*) take the hint

tocha /'tɔʃa/ *f* torch

toco /'toku/ *m* (*de árvore*) stump; (*de cigarro*) butt

toda /'toda/ *f* **a ~** at full speed

todavia /toda'via/ *conj* however

todo /'todu/ *a* all; (*cada*) every; *pl* all; **~ o dinheiro** all the money; **~ dia, ~s os dias** every day; **~s os alunos** all the pupils; **o dia ~** all day; **em ~ lugar** everywhere; **~ mundo, ~s** everyone; **~s nós** all of us; **ao ~** in all. **~-poderoso** *a* almighty

todo-o-terreno /todute'xenu/ *a & m Port Auto* four-by-four

tofe /'tɔfi/ *m* toffee

toga /'tɔga/ *f* gown; (*de romano*) toga

toicinho /toj'siɲu/ *m* bacon

toldo /'towdu/ *m* awning

tole|rância /tole'rãsia/ *f* tolerance. **~rante** *a* tolerant. **~rar** *vt* tolerate. **~rável** (*pl* **~ráveis**) *a* tolerable

to|lice /to'lisi/ *f* foolishness; (*uma*) foolish thing. **~lo** /o/ *a* foolish ● *m* fool

tom /tõ/ *m* tone; **~ de toque** *Telec* ringtone

to|mada /to'mada/ *f* (*conquista*) capture; (*elétrica*) plughole; (*de filme*) shot. **~mar** *vt* take; (*beber*) drink; **~mar café** have breakfast

tomara /to'mara/ *int* I hope so; **~ que** let's hope that. **~-que caia** *a invar* ‹*vestido*› strapless

tomate /to'matʃi/ *m* tomato

tom|bar /tõ'bar/ *vt* (*derrubar*) knock down; list ‹*edifício*› ● *vi* fall over. **~bo** *m* fall; **levar um ~bo** have a fall

tomilho /to'miʎu/ *m* thyme

tomo /'tomu/ *m* volume

tona /'tona/ *f* **trazer à ~** bring up; **vir à ~** emerge

tonalidade /tonali'dadʒi/ *f* (*de música*) key; (*de cor*) shade

to|nel /to'nɛw/ (*pl* **~néis**) *m* cask. **~nelada** *f* tonne

tôni|ca /'tonika/ *f* tonic; *fig* (*assunto*) keynote. **~co** *a & m* tonic

tonificar /tonifi'kar/ *vt* tone up

ton|tear /tõtʃi'ar/ *vt* **~tear alguém** make sb's head spin. **~teira** *f* dizziness. **~to** *a* (*zonzo*) dizzy; (*bobo*) stupid; (*atrapalhado*) flustered. **~tura** *f* dizziness

to|pada /to'pada/ *f* trip; **dar uma ~pada em** stub one's toe on. **~par** *vt* agree to, accept; **~par com** bump into ‹*pessoa*›; come across ‹*coisa*›

topázio /to'paziu/ *m* topaz

topete /to'pɛtʃi/ *m* quiff

tópico /'tɔpiku/ *a* topical ● *m* topic

topless /topi'lɛs/ *a invar & adv* topless

topo /'topu/ *m* top

t

topografia /topogra'fia/ *f* topography

topônimo /to'ponimu/ *m* place name

toque /'tɔki/ *m* touch; (*da campainha, do telefone*) ring; (*de instrumento*) playing; **dar um ~ em** ! have a word with

Tóquio /'tɔkiu/ *f* Tokyo

tora /'tɔra/ *f* log

toranja /to'rãʒa/ *f* grapefruit

tórax /'tɔraks/ *m invar* thorax

tor|ção /tor'sãw/ *f* (*do braço etc*) sprain. **~cedor** *m* supporter. **~cer** *vt* twist; (*machucar*) sprain; (*espremer*) wring ‹*roupa*›; (*centrifugar*) spin ‹*roupa*› ● *vi* (*gritar*) cheer (**por** for); (*desejar sucesso*) keep one's fingers crossed (**por** for **para que** that). **~cer-se** *vpr* twist about. **~cicolo** /ɔ/ *m* stiff neck. **~cida** *f* (*torção*) twist; (*torcedores*) supporters; (*gritaria*) cheering

tormen|ta /tor'mẽta/ *f* storm. **~to** *m* torment. **~toso** /o/ *a* stormy

tornado /tor'nadu/ *m* tornado

tornar /tor'nar/ *vt* make. **~-se** *vpr* become

torne|ado /torni'adu/ *a* **bem ~ado** shapely. **~ar** *vt* turn

torneio /tor'neju/ *m* tournament

torneira /tor'nera/ *f* tap, *Amer* faucet

torniquete /torni'ketʃi/ *m* (*para ferido*) tourniquet; *Port* (*de entrada*) turnstile

torno /'tornu/ *m* lathe; (*de ceramista*) wheel; **em ~ de** around

tornozelo /torno'zelu/ *m* ankle

toró /to'rɔ/ *m* downpour

torpe /'torpi/ *a* dirty

torpe|dear /torpedʒi'ar/ *vt* torpedo. **~do** /e/ *m* torpedo

torpor /tor'por/ *m* torpor

torra|da /to'xada/ *f* piece of toast; *pl* toast. **~deira** *f* toaster

torrão /to'xãw/ *m* (*de terra*) turf; (*de açúcar*) lump

torrar /to'xar/ *vt* toast ‹*pão*›; roast ‹*café*›; blow ‹*dinheiro*›; sell off ‹*mercadorias*›

torre /'toxi/ *f* tower; (*em xadrez*) rook; **~ de controle** control tower. **~ão** *m* turret

torrefação /toxefa'sãw/ *f* (*ação*) roasting; (*fábrica*) coffee-roasting plant

torren|cial /toxẽsi'aw/ (*pl* **~ciais**) *a* torrential. **~te** *f* torrent

torresmo /to'xezmu/ *m* crackling

tórrido /'tɔxidu/ *a* torrid

torrone /to'xoni/ *m* nougat

torso /'torsu/ *m* torso

torta /'tɔrta/ *f* pie, tart

tor|to /'tortu/ *a* crooked; **a ~ e a direito** left, right and centre. **~tuoso** *a* winding

tortu|ra /tor'tura/ *f* torture. **~rador** *m* torturer. **~rar** *vt* torture

to|sa /'tɔza/ *f* (*de cachorro*) clipping; (*de ovelhas*) shearing. **~são** *m* fleece. **~sar** *vt* clip ‹*cachorro*›; shear ‹*ovelhas*›; crop ‹*cabelo*›

tosco /'tosku/ *a* rough, coarse

tosquiar /toski'ar/ *vt* shear ‹*ovelha*›

tos|se /'tɔsi/ *f* cough; **~se de cachorro** whooping cough. **~sir** *vi* cough

tostão /tos'tãw/ *m* penny

tostar /tos'tar/ *vt* brown ‹*carne*›; tan ‹ *pele, pessoa*›. **~-se** *vpr* (*ao sol*) go brown

to|tal /to'taw/ (*pl* **~tais**) *a & m* total

totali|dade /totali'dadʒi/ *f* entirety. **~tário** *a* totalitarian. **~zar** *vt* total

touca /'toka/ *f* bonnet; (*de freira*) wimple; **~ de banho** bathing cap. **~dor** *m* dressing table

toupeira /to'pera/ *f* mole

tou|rada /to'rada/ *f* bullfight. **~reiro** *m* bullfighter. **~ro** *m* bull; **Touro** (*signo*) Taurus

tóxico /'tɔksiku/ *a* toxic ● *m* toxic substance

toxicômano /toksi'komanu/ *m* drug addict

toxina /tok'sina/ *f* toxin

traba|lhador /trabaʎa'dor/ *a* ‹*pessoa*› hard-working; ‹*classe*› working ● *m* worker. **~lhar** *vt* work ● *vi* work; (*numa peça, filme*) act. **~lheira** *f* big job. **~lhista** *a* labour. **~lho** *m* work; (*um*) job; (*na escola*) assignment; **dar-se o ~lho de** go to the trouble of; **~lho de parto** labour; **~lhos forçados** hard labour. **~lhoso** *a* laborious

traça /'trasa/ *f* moth

tração /tra'sãw/ *f* traction

tra|çar /tra'sar/ *vt* draw; draw up ‹*plano*›; set out ‹*ordens*›. **~ço** *m* stroke; (*entre frases*) dash; (*vestígio*) trace; (*característica*) trait; *pl* (*do rosto*) features

tradi|ção /tradʒi'sãw/ *f* tradition. **~cional** (*pl* **~cionais**) *a* traditional

tradu|ção /tradu'sãw/ *f* translation. **~tor** *m* translator. **~zir** *vt/i* translate (**de** from **para** into)

t

trafe|gar /trafe'gar/ *vi* run. **~gável** (*pl* **~gáveis**) *a* open to traffic

tráfego /'trafegu/ *m* traffic

trafi|cância /trafi'kãsia/ *f* trafficking. **~cante** /trafi'kãtʃi/ *m/f* trafficker; **~cante de droga** drug dealer; **~cante sexual** sex trafficker. **~car** *vt/i* traffic (**com** in)

tráfico /'trafiku/ *m* traffic

tra|gada /tra'gada/ *f* (*de bebida*) swallow; (*de cigarro*) drag. **~gar** *vt* swallow; inhale ‹*fumaça*›

tragédia /tra'ʒɛdʒia/ *f* tragedy

trágico /'traʒiku/ *a* tragic

trago /'tragu/ *m* (*de bebida*) swallow; (*de cigarro*) drag; **de um ~** in one go

trai|ção /traj'sãw/ *f* (*ato*) betrayal; (*deslealdade*) treachery; (*da pátria*) treason. **~çoeiro** *a* treacherous. **~dor** *a* treacherous ● *m* traitor

trailer /'trejler/ (*pl* **~s**) *m* (*de filme etc*) trailer; (*casa móvel*) caravan, *Amer* trailer

traineira /traj'nera/ *f* trawler

training /'trejnĩ/ (*pl* **~s**) *m* track suit

trair /tra'ir/ *vt* betray; be unfaithful to ‹*marido, mulher*›. **~-se** *vpr* give o.s. away

tra|jar /tra'ʒar/ *vt* wear. **~jar-se** *vpr* dress (**de** in). **~je** *m* outfit; **~je a rigor** evening dress; **~je espacial** space suit

traje|to /tra'ʒɛtu/ *m* (*percurso*) journey; (*caminho*) route. **~tória** *f* trajectory; *fig* course

tralha /'traʎa/ *f* (*trastes*) junk

tra|ma /'trama/ *f* plot. **~mar** *vt/i* plot

trambi|que /trã'biki/ *m* ! con. **~queiro** *m* ! con artist

tramitar /trami'tar/ *vi* be processed

trâmites /'tramitʃis/ *m pl* channels

tramoia /tra'mɔja/ *f* scheme

trampolim /trãpo'lĩ/ *m* (*de ginástica*) trampoline; (*de piscina*) *fig* springboard

tranca /'trãka/ *f* bolt; (*em carro*) lock

trança /'trãsa/ *f* (*de cabelo*) plait

tran|cafiar /trãkafi'ar/ *vt* lock up. **~car** *vt* lock; cancel ‹*matrícula*›

trançar /trã'sar/ *vt* plait ‹*cabelo*›; weave ‹*palha etc*›

tranco /'trãku/ *m* jolt; **aos ~s e barrancos** in fits and starts

tranqueira /trã'kera/ *f* junk

tranqui|lidade /trãkwili'dadʒi/ *f* tranquillity. **~lizador** *a* reassuring. **~lizante** *m* tranquillizer ● *a* reassuring. **~lizar** *vt* reassure. **~lizar-se** *vpr* be reassured. **~lo** *a* ‹*bairro, sono*› peaceful; ‹*pessoa, voz, mar*› calm; ‹*consciência*› clear; ‹*sucesso, lucro*› sure-fire ● *adv* with no trouble

transa /'trãza/ *f* ! (*negócio*) deal; (*caso*) affair. **~ção** *f* transaction. **~do** *a* ! ‹*roupa, pessoa, casa*› stylish; ‹*relação*› healthy

Transamazônica /tranzama'zonika/ *f* trans-Amazonian highway

transar /trã'zar/ ! *vt* set up; do ‹*drogas*› ● *vi* (*negociar*) deal; (*fazer sexo*) have sex

transatlântico /trãzat'lãtʃiku/ *a* transatlantic ● *m* liner

transbordar /trãzbor'dar/ *vi* overflow

transcen|dental /trãsẽdẽ'taw/ (*pl* **~dentais**) *a* transcendental. **~der** *vt/i* **~der (a)** transcend

trans|crever /trãskre'ver/ *vt* transcribe. **~crição** *f* transcription. **~crito** *a* transcribed ● *m* transcript

transe /'trãzi/ *m* trance

transeunte /trãzi'ũtʃi/ *m/f* passer-by

transfe|rência /trãsfe'rẽsia/ *f* transfer. **~ridor** *m* protractor. **~rir** *vt* transfer. **~rir-se** *vpr* transfer

transfor|mação /trãsforma'sãw/ *f* transformation. **~mador** *m* transformer. **~mar** *vt* transform. **~mar-se** *vpr* be transformed

trânsfuga /'trãsfuga/ *m/f* deserter; (*de um país*) defector

transfusão /trãsfu'zãw/ *f* transfusion

trans|gredir /trãzgre'dʒir/ *vt* infringe. **~gressão** *f* infringement

transi|ção /trãzi'sãw/ *f* transition. **~cional** (*pl* **~cionais**) *a* transitional

transi|gente /trãzi'ʒẽtʃi/ *a* open to compromise. **~gir** *vi* compromise

transis|tor /trãzis'tor/ *m* transistor. **~torizado** *a* transistorized

transi|tar /trãzi'tar/ *vi* pass. **~tável** (*pl* **~táveis**) *a* passable. **~tivo** *a* transitive

trânsito /'trãzitu/ *m* traffic; **em ~** in transit

transitório /trãzi'tɔriu/ *a* transitory

translúcido /trãz'lusidu/ *a* translucent

transmis|são /trãzmi'sãw/ *f* transmission. **~sor** *m* transmitter

transmitir /trãzmi'tʃir/ *vt* transmit ‹*programa, calor, doença*›; convey ‹*notícia, ordens*›; transfer ‹*herança, direito*›. **~-se** *vpr* ‹*doença*› be transmitted

transpa|recer /trãspare'ser/ *vi* be visible; *fig* ‹*emoção, verdade*› come out. **~rência** *f* transparency. **~rente** *a* transparent

transpi|ração /trãspira'sãw/ *f* perspiration. **~rar** *vt* exude ● *vi* (*suar*) perspire; ‹*notícia*› trickle through; ‹*verdade*› come out

transplan|tar /trãsplã'tar/ *vt* transplant. **~te** *m* transplant

transpor /trãs'por/ *vt* cross ‹*rio, fronteira*›; get over ‹*obstáculo, dificuldade*›; transpose ‹*letras, música*›

transpor|tadora /trãsporta'dora/ *f* transport company. **~tar** *vt* transport; (*em contas*) carry forward. **~te** *m* transport; **~te coletivo** public transport

transposto /trãs'postu/ *pp de* ▶ TRANSPOR

transtor|nar /trãstor'nar/ *vt* mess up ‹*papéis, casa*›; disrupt ‹*rotina, ambiente*›; disturb, upset ‹*pessoa*›. **~nar-se** *vpr* ‹*pessoa*› be rattled. **~no** /o/ *m* (*de casa, rotina*) disruption; (*de pessoa*) disturbance; (*contratempo*) upset; **~no obsessivo compulsivo** *Psic* obsessive-compulsive disorder

transver|sal /trãzver'saw/ (*pl* **~sais**) *a* **(rua) ~sal** cross street. **~so** /ɛ/ *a* transverse

transvi|ado /trãzvi'adu/ *a* wayward. **~ar** *vt* lead astray

trapa|ça /tra'pasa/ *f* swindle. **~cear** *vi* cheat. **~ceiro** *a* crooked ● *m* cheat

trapa|lhada /trapa'ʎada/ *f* bungle. **~lhão** *a* (*f* **~lhona**) *f* bungling ● *m* (*f* **~lhona**) bungler

trapézio /tra'pɛziu/ *m* trapeze

trapezista /trape'zista/ *m/f* trapeze artist

trapo /'trapu/ *m* rag

traqueia /tra'kɛja/ *f* windpipe, trachea

traquejo /tra'keʒu/ *m* knack

traquinas /tra'kinas/ *a invar* mischievous

trás /tras/ *adv* **de ~** from behind; **a roda de ~** the back wheel; **de ~ para frente** back to front; **para ~** backwards; **deixar para ~** leave behind; **por ~ de** behind

traseiro /tra'zeru/ *a* rear, back ● *m* bottom

trasladar /trazla'dar/ *vt* transport

traspas|sado /traspa'sadu/ *a* ‹*paletó*› double-breasted. **~sar** *vt* pierce

traste /'trastʃi/ *m* (*pessoa*) pain; (*coisa*) piece of junk

tra|tado /tra'tadu/ *m* (*pacto*) treaty; (*estudo*) treatise. **~tamento** *m* treatment; (*título*) title. **~tar** *vt* treat; negotiate ‹*preço, venda*› ● *vi* (*manter relações*) have dealings (**com** with); (*combinar*) negotiate (**com** with); **~tar de** deal with; **~tar alguém de** ou **por** address sb. as; **~tar de voltar** (*tentar*) seek to return; (*resolver*) decide to return; **~tar-se de** be a matter of. **~tável** (*pl* **~táveis**) *a* ‹*doença*› treatable; ‹*pessoa*› accommodating. **~tos** *m pl* **maus-~tos** ill-treatment

trator /tra'tor/ *m* tractor

trauma /'trawma/ *m* trauma. **~tizante** *a* traumatic. **~tizar** *vt* traumatize

tra|vão /tra'vãw/ *m Port* brake. **~var** *vt* lock ‹*rodas, músculos*›; stop ‹*carro*›; block ‹*passagem*›; strike up ‹*amizade, conversa*›; wage ‹*luta, combate*› ● *vi Port* brake

trave /'travi/ *f* beam, joist; (*do gol*) crossbar

traves|sa /tra'vɛsa/ *f* (*trave*) crossbar; (*rua*) side street; (*prato*) dish; (*pente*) slide. **~são** *m* dash. **~seiro** *m* pillow. **~sia** *f* crossing. **~so** /e/ *a* ‹*criança*› naughty. **~sura** *f* prank; *pl* mischief

travesti /traves'tʃi/ *m* transvestite; (*artista*) drag artist. **~do** *a* in drag

trazer /tra'zer/ *vt* bring; bear ‹*nome, ferida*›; wear ‹*barba, chapéu, cabelo curto*›

trecho /'treʃu/ *m* (*de livro etc*) passage; (*de rua etc*) stretch

treco /'trɛku/ *m* [!] (*coisa*) thing; (*ataque*) turn

trégua /'trɛgwa/ *f* truce; *fig* respite

trei|nador /trejna'dor/ *m* trainer. **~namento** *m* training. **~nar** *vt* train ‹*atleta, animal*›; practise ‹*língua etc*› ● *vi* ‹*atleta*› train; ‹*pianista, principiante*› practise. **~no** *m* training; (*um*) training session

trejeito /tre'ʒejtu/ *m* grimace

trela /'trɛla/ *f* lead, *Amer* leash

treliça /tre'lisa/ *f* trellis

trem /trẽj/ *m* train; **~ de aterrissagem** undercarriage; **~ de carga** goods train, *Amer* freight train

trema /'trema/ *m* dieresis

treme|deira /treme'dera/ *f* shiver. **~licar** *vi* tremble. **~luzir** *vi* glimmer, flicker

tremendo /tre'mẽdu/ *a* tremendous

tre|mer /tre'mer/ *vi* tremble; ‹*terra*› shake. **~mor** *m* tremor; (*tremedeira*)

t

shiver. **~mular** *vi* ‹*bandeira*› flutter; ‹*luz, estrela*› glimmer, flicker

trêmulo /'tremulu/ *a* trembling; ‹*luz*› flickering

trena /'trena/ *f* tape measure

trenó /tre'nɔ/ *m* sledge, *Amer* sled; (*puxado a cavalos etc*) sleigh

tre|padeira /trepa'dera/ *f* climbing plant. **~par** *vt* climb ● *vi* climb; (*chulo*) fuck

três /tres/ *a & m* three

tresloucado /trezlo'kadu/ *a* deranged

trevas /'trɛvas/ *f pl* darkness

trevo /'trevu/ *m* (*planta*) clover; (*rodoviário*) interchange

treze /'trezi/ *a & m* thirteen

trezentos /tre'zẽtus/ *a & m* three hundred

triagem /tri'aʒẽ/ *f* (*escolha*) selection; (*separação*) sorting; **fazer uma ~ de** sort

tri|angular /triãgu'lar/ *a* triangular. **~ângulo** *m* triangle

tri|bal /tri'baw/ (*pl* **~bais**) *a* tribal. **~bo** *f* tribe

tribu|na /tri'buna/ *f* rostrum. **~nal** (*pl* **~nais**) *m* court

tribu|tação /tributa'sãw/ *f* taxation. **~tar** *vt* tax. **~tário** *a* tax ● *m* tributary. **~to** *m* tribute

tri|cô /tri'ko/ *m* knitting; **artigos de ~cô** knitwear. **~cotar** *vt/i* knit

tridimensio|nal /tridʒimẽsio'naw/ (*pl* **~nais**) *a* three-dimensional

trigêmeo /tri'ʒemiu/ *m* triplet

trigésimo /tri'ʒɛzimu/ *a* thirtieth

tri|go /'trigu/ *m* wheat. **~gueiro** *a* dark

trilha /'triʎa/ *f* path; (*pista, de disco*) track; **~ sonora** soundtrack

trilhão /tri'ʎãw/ *m* billion, *Amer* trillion

trilho /'triʎu/ *m* track

trilogia /trilo'ʒia/ *f* trilogy

trimes|tral /trimes'traw/ (*pl* **~trais**) *a* quarterly. **~tre** /ɛ/ *m* quarter; (*do ano letivo*) term

trincar /trĩ'kar/ *vt/i* crack

trincheira /trĩ'ʃera/ *f* trench

trinco /'trĩku/ *m* latch

trindade /trĩ'dadʒi/ *f* trinity

trinta /'trĩta/ *a & m* thirty

trio /'triu/ *m* trio; **~ elétrico** music float

tripa /'tripa/ *f* gut

tripé /tri'pɛ/ *m* tripod

tripli|car /tripli'kar/ *vt/i*, **~-se** *vpr* treble. **~cata** *f* triplicate

triplo /'triplu/ *a & m* triple

tripu|lação /tripula'sãw/ *f* crew. **~lante** *m/f* crew member. **~lar** *vt* man

triste /'tristʃi/ *a* sad. **~za** /e/ *f* sadness; **é uma ~za** [!] it's pathetic

tritu|rador /tritura'dor/ *m* (*de papel*) shredder; **~rador de lixo** waste disposal unit. **~rar** *vt* shred ‹*legumes, papel*›; grind up ‹*lixo*›

triun|fal /triũ'faw/ (*pl* **~fais**) *a* triumphal. **~fante** *a* triumphant. **~far** *vi* triumph. **~fo** *m* triumph

trivi|al /trivi'aw/ (*pl* **~ais**) *a* trivial. **~alidade** *f* triviality; *pl* trivia

triz /tris/ *m* **por um ~** narrowly, by a hair's breadth; **não foi atropelado por um ~** he narrowly missed being knocked down

tro|ca /'trɔka/ *f* exchange; **em ~ca de** in exchange for. **~cadilho** *m* pun. **~cado** *m* change. **~cador** *m* conductor. **~car** *vt* (*dar e receber*) exchange (**por** for); change ‹*dinheiro, lençóis, lâmpada, lugares etc*›; (*transpor*) change round; (*confundir*) mix up; **~car de roupa/trem/lugar** change clothes/trains/places. **~car-se** *vpr* change. **~ca-troca** *m* swap. **~co** /o/ *m* change; **a ~co de quê?** what for?; **dar o ~co em alguém** pay sb back

troço /'trɔsu/ *m* [!](*coisa*) thing; (*ataque*) turn; **me deu um ~** I had a funny turn

troféu /tro'fɛw/ *m* trophy

trólebus /'trɔlebus/ *m invar* trolley bus

trom|ba /'trõba/ *f* (*de elefante*) trunk; (*cara amarrada*) long face. **~bada** *f* crash. **~ba-d'água** (*pl* **~bas-d'água**) *f* downpour. **~badinha** *m* bag snatcher. **~bar** *vi* **~bar com** crash into ‹*poste, carro*›; bump into ‹*pessoa*›

trombo|ne /trõ'bɔni/ *m* trombone. **~nista** *m/f* trombonist

trompa /'trõpa/ *f* French horn; **~ de Falópio** fallopian tube

trompe|te /trõ'pɛtʃi/ *m* trumpet. **~tista** *m/f* trumpeter

tron|co /'trõku/ *m* trunk. **~cudo** *a* stocky

trono /'tronu/ *m* throne

tropa /'trɔpa/ *f* troop; (*exército*) army; *pl* troops; **~ de choque** riot police

trope|ção /trope'sãw/ *m* trip; (*erro*) slip-up. **~çar** *vi* trip; (*errar*) slip up. **~ço** /e/ *m* stumbling block

trôpego /'tropegu/ *a* unsteady

tropi|cal /tropi'kaw/ (*pl* **~cais**) *a* tropical

trópico /'trɔpiku/ *m* tropic

tro|tar /tro'tar/ *vi* trot. **~te** /ɔ/ *m* (*de cavalo*) trot; (*de estudantes*) practical joke; (*mentira*) hoax

trouxa /'troʃa/ *f* (*de roupa etc*) bundle ● *m/f* [!] sucker [!] ● *a* [!] gullible

tro|vão /tro'vãw/ *m* clap of thunder; *pl* thunder. **~vejar** *vi* thunder. **~voada** *f* thunderstorm. **~voar** *vi* thunder

trucidar /trusi'dar/ *vt* slaughter

trucu|lência /truku'lẽsia/ *f* barbarity. **~lento** *a* (*cruel*) barbaric; (*brigão*) belligerent

trufa /'trufa/ *f* truffle

trunfo /'trũfu/ *m* trump; *fig* trump card

truque /'truki/ *m* trick

truta /'truta/ *f* trout

tu /tu/ *pron* you

tua /'tua/ ▶ TEU

tuba /'tuba/ *f* tuba

tubarão /tuba'rãw/ *m* shark

tubá|rio /tu'bariu/ *a* **gravidez ~ria** ectopic pregnancy

tuberculose /tubercu'lɔzi/ *f* tuberculosis

tubo /'tubu/ *m* tube; (*no corpo*) duct

tubulação /tubula'sãw/ *f* ducting

tucano /tu'kanu/ *m* toucan

tudo /'tudu/ ● *pron*

····➤ all; **é ~ por hoje** that's all for today; (*todas as coisas*) everything; **~ tinha ido** everything had gone

····➤ (*em expressões*) **dar/fazer ~ por ~** give one's all; **no fim de ~** after all; **por ~ e por nada** over the slightest thing; **dar ~ por** *ou* **para algo** (*desejar muito*) give one's all for sth

tufão /tu'fãw/ *m* typhoon

tulipa /tu'lipa/ *f* tulip

tumba /'tũba/ *f* tomb

tumor /tu'mor/ *m* tumour; **~ cerebral** brain tumour

túmulo /'tumulu/ *m* grave

tumul|to /tu'muwtu/ *m* commotion; (*motim*) riot. **~tuado** *a* disorderly, rowdy. **~tuar** *vt* disrupt ● *vi* cause a commotion. **~tuoso** *a* tumultuous

tú|nel /'tunew/ (*pl* **~neis**) *m* tunnel

túnica /'tunika/ *f* tunic

Tunísia /tu'nizia/ *f* Tunisia

tupiniquim /tupini'kĩ/ *a* Brazilian

turbante /tur'bãtʃi/ *m* turban

turbilhão /turbi'ʎãw/ *m* whirlwind

turbina /tur'bina/ *f* turbine

turbu|lência /turbu'lẽsia/ *f* turbulence. **~lento** *a* turbulent

turco /'turku/ *a & m* Turkish

turfa /'turfa/ *f* peat

turfe /'turfe/ *m* horse racing

turis|mo /tu'rizmu/ *m* tourism; **fazer ~mo** go sightseeing. **~ta** *m/f* tourist

turístico /tu'ristʃiku/ *a* ‹*ponto, indústria*› tourist; ‹*viagem*› sightseeing

turma /'turma/ *f* group; (*na escola*) class

turnê /tur'ne/ *f* tour

turno /'turnu/ *m* (*de trabalho*) shift; (*de competição, eleição*) round

turquesa /tur'keza/ *m/f & a invar* turquoise

Turquia /tur'kia/ *f* Turkey

turra /'tuxa/ *f* **às ~s com** at loggerheads with

tur|var /tur'var/ *vt* cloud. **~vo** *a* cloudy

tutano /tu'tanu/ *m* marrow

tutela /tu'tɛla/ *f* guardianship

tutor /tu'tor/ *m* guardian

tutu /tu'tu/ *m* (*vestido*) tutu; (*prato*) beans with bacon and manioc flour

TV /te've/ *f* TV

Uu

ubíquo /u'bikwu/ *a* ubiquitous

Ucrânia /u'krania/ *f* Ukraine

ucraniano /ukrani'anu/ *a & m* Ukrainian

ué /u'ɛ/ *int* hang on

ufa /'ufa/ *int* phew

ufanis|mo /ufa'nizmu/ *m* chauvinism. **~ta** *a & m/f* chauvinist

Uganda /u'gãda/ *m* Uganda

ui /ui/ *int* (*de dor*) ouch; (*de nojo*) ugh; (*de espanto*) oh

uísque /u'iski/ *m* whisky

ui|var /ui'var/ *vi* howl. **~vo** *m* howl

úlcera /'uwsera/ *f* ulcer

ulterior /uwteri'or/ *a* further

ulti|mamente /uwtʃima'mẽtʃi/ *adv* recently. **~mar** *vt* finalize. **~mato** *m* ultimatum

último /'uwtʃimu/ *a* last; ‹*moda, notícia etc*› latest; **em ~ caso** as a last resort; **nos ~s anos** in recent years; **por ~** last

ultra|jante /uwtra'ʒãtʃi/ *a* offensive. **~jar** *vt* offend. **~je** *m* outrage

ultraleve /uwtra'lɛvi/ *m* microlite

ultra|mar /uwtra'mar/ *m* overseas. **~marino** *a* overseas

ultrapas|sado /uwtrapa'sadu/ *a* outdated. **~sagem** *f* overtaking, *Amer* passing. **~sar** *vt* (*de carro*) overtake, *Amer* pass; (*ser superior a*) surpass; (*exceder*) exceed; (*extrapolar*) go beyond ● *vi* overtake, *Amer* pass

ultrassonografia /uwtrasonogra'fia/ *f* ultrasound scan

ultravioleta /uwtravio'leta/ *a* ultraviolet

ulu|lante /ulu'lãtʃi/ *a fig* blatant. **~lar** *vi* wail

um /ũ/ (*f* **uma**, *pl* **uns**, *f pl* **umas**)

● *artigo*

····➤ a, an (*antes de som vocálico*); **~ carro** a car; **uma maçã** an apple

! *a forma an emprega-se antes de uma vogal ou som vocálico;* **uma árvore** *a tree*; **um braço** *an arm*. **uns, umas** some; **preciso de uns sapatos novos** I need some new shoes; **já que você vai lá, compre umas bananas** get some bananas while you're there

● *a*

····➤ (*numeral*) one; **disse ~ quilo, não dois** I said one kilo, not two; (*aproximadamente*) about; **uns quinze dias** about a fortnight

● *pron*

····➤ one; (*plural*) some; **como não tinha gravata, emprestei-lhe uma** he didn't have a tie so I lent him one; **uns gostam, outros não** some like it, some don't

····➤ (*em expressões*) **~ ao outro, uma à outra** *etc* each other; **ajudaram-se uns aos outros** they helped each other; **~ a ~, ~ por ~** one by one; **verifiquei os itens da lista ~ a ~** I went through the things on the list one by one

umbanda /ũ'bãda/ *m* Afro-Brazilian cult

umbigo /ũ'bigu/ *m* navel

umbili|cal /ũbili'kaw/ (*pl* **~cais**) *a* umbilical

umedecer /umede'ser/ *vt* moisten. **~-se** *vpr* moisten

umidade /umi'dadʒi/ *f* moisture; (*desagradável*) damp; (*do ar*) humidity

úmido /'umidu/ *a* moist; ‹*parede, roupa etc*› damp; ‹*ar, clima*› humid

unânime /u'nanimi/ *a* unanimous

unanimidade /unanimi'dadʒi/ *f* unanimity

undécimo /ũ'dɛsimu/ *a* eleventh

unguento /ũ'gwẽtu/ *m* ointment

unha /'uɲa/ *f* nail; (*de animal, utensílio*) claw

união /uni'ãw/ *f* union; (*concórdia*) unity; (*ato de unir*) joining; **~ civil** (*entre pessoas do mesmo sexo*) civil partnership; **União Européia** European Union, EU

unicamente /unika'mẽtʃi/ *adv* only

único /'uniku/ *a* only; (*ímpar*) unique

uni|dade /uni'dadʒi/ *f* unit. **~do** *a* united; ‹*família*› close

unifi|cação /unifika'sãw/ *f* unification. **~car** *vt* unify

unifor|me /uni'fɔrmi/ *a* uniform; ‹*superfície*› even ● *m* uniform. **~midade** *f* uniformity. **~mizado** *a* ‹*policial etc*› uniformed; (*padronizado*) standardized. **~zar** *vt* (*padronizar*) standardize

unilate|ral /unilate'raw/ (*pl* **~rais**) *a* unilateral

unir /u'nir/ *vt* unite ‹*povo, nações, família etc*›; (*ligar, casar*) join; (*combinar*) combine (**a** ou **com** with). **~-se** *vpr* (*aliar-se*) unite (**a** with); (*juntar-se*) join together; (*combinar-se*) combine (**a** ou **com** with)

unissex /uni'sɛks/ *a invar* unisex

uníssono /u'nisonu/ *m* **em ~** in unison

univer|sal /univer'saw/ (*pl* **~sais**) *a* universal

universi|dade /universi'dadʒi/ *f* university. **~tário** *a* university ● *m* university student

universo /uni'vɛrsu/ *m* universe

untar /ũ'tar/ *vt* grease ‹*fôrma*›; spread ‹*pão*›; smear ‹*corpo*›

upa /'upa/ *int* (*incentivando*) ups-a-daisy; (*ao cair algo etc*) whoops

urânio /u'raniu/ *m* uranium

Urano /u'ranu/ *m* Uranus

urbanis|mo /urba'nizmu/ *m* town planning. **~ta** *m/f* town planner

urbani|zado /urbani'zadu/ *a* built-up. **~zar** *vt* urbanize

urbano /ur'banu/ *a* (*da cidade*) urban; (*refinado*) urbane

urdir /ur'dʒir/ *vt* weave; (*maquinar*) hatch

urdu /ur'du/ *m* Urdu

ur|gência /ur'ʒẽsia/ *f* urgency. **~gente** *a* urgent. **~gir** *vi* be urgent; ‹*tempo*› press; **~ge irmos** we must go urgently

uri|na /u'rina/ *f* urine. **~nar** *vt* pass ● *vi* urinate. **~nol** (*pl* **~nóis**) *m* (*penico*) chamber pot; (*em banheiro*) urinal

urna /'urna/ *f* (*para cinzas*) urn; (*para votos*) ballot box; *pl fig* polls

ur|rar /u'xar/ *vt/i* roar. **~ro** *m* roar

urso /'ursu/ *m* bear. **~-branco** (*pl* **~s-brancos**) *m* polar bear

urti|cária /urtʃi'karia/ *f* nettle rash. **~ga** *f* nettle

urubu /uru'bu/ *m* black vulture

Uruguai /uru'gwaj/ *m* Uruguay

uruguaio /uru'gwaju/ *a & m* Uruguayan

urze /'urzi/ *f* heather

usado /u'zadu/ *a* used; ‹*roupa*› worn; ‹*palavra*› common

usar /u'zar/ *vt* wear ‹*roupa, óculos, barba etc*›; **~ (de)** (*utilizar*) use

USB *a & m* USB; **porta ~** USB port

usina /u'zina/ *f* plant; **~ termonuclear** nuclear power station

uso /'uzu/ *m* use; (*de palavras, linguagem*) usage; (*praxe*) practice

usu|al /uzu'aw/ (*pl* **~ais**) *a* common. **~ário** *m* user. **~fruir** *vt* enjoy ‹*coisas boas*›; have the use of ‹*prédio, jardim etc*›. **~fruto** *m* use

usuário /uzu'arju/ *m Comput* user; **nome do ~** username

usurário /uzu'rariu/ *a* money-grubbing ● *m* moneylender

usurpar /uzur'par/ *vt* usurp

uten|sílio /utẽ'siliu/ *m* utensil. **~te** *m/f Port* user

útero /'uteru/ *m* uterus, womb

UTI /ute'i/ *f* intensive care unit

útil /'utʃiw/ (*pl* **úteis**) *a* useful; **dia ~** workday

utili|dade /utʃili'dadʒi/ *f* usefulness; (*uma*) utility. **~tário** *a* utilitarian. **~zar** *vt* (*empregar*) use; (*tornar útil*) utilize. **~zável** (*pl* **~záveis**) *a* usable

utilizador /utʃiliza'dor/ *m Port* ▶ **USUÁRIO**

utopia /uto'pia/ *f* Utopia

utópico /u'tɔpiku/ *a* Utopian

uva /'uva/ *f* grape

úvula /'uvula/ *f* uvula

Vv

vaca /'vaka/ *f* cow

vaci|lante /vasi'lãtʃi/ *a* wavering; ‹*luz*› flickering. **~lar** *vi* waver; ‹*luz*› flicker; [!] (*bobear*) slip up

vaci|na /va'sina/ *f* vaccine. **~nação** *f* vaccination. **~nar** *vt* vaccinate

vácuo /'vakuu/ *m* vacuum

va|diar /vadʒi'ar/ *vi* (*viver ocioso*) laze around; (*fazer cera*) mess about. **~dio** *a* idle ● *m* idler

vaga /'vaga/ *f* (*posto*) vacancy; (*para estacionar*) parking place

vagabun|dear /vagabũdʒi'ar/ *vi* (*perambular*) roam; (*vadiar*) laze around. **~do** *a* ‹*pessoa, vida*› idle; ‹*produto, objeto*› shoddy ● *m* tramp; (*pessoa vadia*) bum

vaga-lume /vaga'lumi/ *m* glow-worm

va|gão /va'gãw/ *m* (*de passageiros*) carriage, *Amer* car; (*de carga*) wagon. **~gão-leito** (*pl* **~gões-leitos**) *m* sleeping car; **~gão-restaurante** (*pl* **~gões-restaurantes**) *m* dining car

vagar[1] /va'gar/ *vi* ‹*pessoa*› wander about; ‹*barco*› drift

vagar[2] /va'gar/ *vi* ‹*cargo, apartamento*› become vacant

vagaroso /vaga'rozu/ *a* slow

vagem /'vaʒẽ/ *f* green bean

vagi|na /va'ʒina/ *f* vagina. **~nal** (*pl* **~nais**) *a* vaginal

vago[1] /'vagu/ *a* (*indefinido*) vague

vago[2] /'vagu/ *a* (*desocupado*) vacant; ‹*tempo*› spare

vaguear /vagi'ar/ *vi* roam

vai|a /'vaja/ *f* boo. **~ar** *vi* boo

vai|dade /vaj'dadʒi/ *f* vanity. **~doso** *a* vain

vaivém /vaj'vẽj/ *m* comings and goings, toing and froing

vala /'vala/ *f* ditch; **~ comum** mass grave

vale[1] /'vali/ *m* (*de rio etc*) valley

vale[2] /'vali/ *m* (*ficha*) voucher; **~ postal** postal order

valen|tão /valẽ'tãw/ *a* (*f* **~tona**) tough ● *m* tough guy. **~te** *a* brave. **~tia** *f* bravery; (*uma*) feat

valer /va'ler/ *vt* be worth ● *vi* be valid; **~ algo a alguém** earn sb sth; **~-se de**

avail o.s. of; **~ a pena** be worth it; **vale a pena tentar** it's worth trying; **mais vale desistir** it's better to give up; **vale tudo** anything goes; **fazer ~** enforce ‹*lei*›; stand up for ‹*direitos*›; **para ~** (*a sério*) for real; (*muito*) really

vale|-refeição /valirefej'sãw/ (*pl* **~s-refeição**) *m* luncheon voucher

valeta /va'leta/ *f* gutter

valete /va'lɛtʃi/ *m* jack

valia /va'lia/ *f* value

validar /vali'dar/ *vt* validate

válido /'validu/ *a* valid

valioso /vali'ozu/ *a* valuable

valise /va'lizi/ *f* travelling bag

valor /va'lor/ *m* value; (*valentia*) valour; *pl* (*títulos*) securities; **no ~ de** to the value of; **sem ~** worthless; **objetos de ~** valuables; **~ nominal** face value

valori|zação /valoriza'sãw/ *f* (*apreciação*) valuing; (*aumento no valor*) increase in value. **~zado** *a* highly valued. **~zar** *vt* (*apreciar*) value; (*aumentar o valor de*) increase the value of. **~zar-se** *vt* ‹*coisa*› increase in value; ‹*pessoa*› value o.s.

val|sa /'vawsa/ *f* waltz. **~sar** *vi* waltz

válvula /'vawvula/ *f* valve

vampiro /vã'piru/ *m* vampire

vandalismo /vãda'lizmu/ *m* vandalism

vândalo /'vãdalu/ *m* vandal

vangloriar-se /vãglori'arsi/ *vpr* brag (**de** about)

vanguarda /vã'gwarda/ *f* vanguard; (*de arte*) avant-garde

vanta|gem /vã'taʒẽ/ *f* advantage; **contar ~gem** boast; **levar ~gem** have the advantage (**a** over); **tirar ~gem de** take advantage of. **~joso** /o/ *a* advantageous

vão /vãw/ (*pl* **~s**) *a* (*f* **vã**) vain; **em ~** in vain ● *m* gap

vapor /va'por/ *m* (*fumaça*) steam; (*gás*) vapour; (*barco*) steamer; **máquina a ~** steam engine; **a todo ~** at full blast

vaporizar /vapori'zar/ *vt* vaporize; (*com spray*) spray

vaqueiro /va'keru/ *m* cowboy

vaquinha /va'kiɲa/ *f* collection, whip-round

vara /'vara/ *f* rod; **~ cível** civil district; **~ mágica** ou **de condão** magic wand

va|ral /va'raw/ (*pl* **~rais**) *m* washing line

varanda /va'rãda/ *f* veranda

varão /va'rãw/ *m* male

varar /va'rar/ *vt* (*furar*) pierce; (*passar por*) sweep through

varejão /vare'ʒão/ *m* wholesale store

varejeira /vare'ʒera/ *f* bluebottle

vare|jista /vare'ʒista/ *a* retail ● *m/f* retailer. **~jo** /e/ *m* retail trade; **vender a ~jo** sell retail

vari|ação /varia'sãw/ *f* variation. **~ado** *a* varied. **~ante** *a & f* variant. **~ar** *vt/i* vary; **para ~ar** for a change. **~ável** (*pl* **~áveis**) *a* variable; ‹*tempo*› changeable

varicela /vari'sɛla/ *f* chickenpox

variedade /varie'dadʒi/ *f* variety

varinha /va'rĩɲa/ *f* **~ de condão** magic wand; **~ mágica** *Port* (*utensílio culinário*) hand mixer

varíola /va'riola/ *f* smallpox

vários /'varius/ *a pl* several

variz /va'ris/ *f* varicose vein

varo|nil /varo'niw/ (*pl* **~nis**) *a* manly

var|rer /va'xer/ *vt* sweep; *fig* sweep away. **~rido** *a* **um doido ~rido** a raving lunatic

Varsóvia /var'sɔvia/ *f* Warsaw

vasculhar /vasku'ʎar/ *vt* search through

vasectomia /vazekto'mia/ *f* vasectomy

vaselina /vaze'lina/ *f* vaseline

vasilha /va'ziʎa/ *f* jug

vaso /'vazu/ *m* pot; (*para flores*) vase; **~ sanguíneo** blood vessel

vassoura /va'sora/ *f* broom

vas|tidão /vastʃi'dãw/ *f* vastness. **~to** *a* vast

vatapá /vata'pa/ *m* spicy North-Eastern dish

Vaticano /vatʃi'kanu/ *m* Vatican

vati|cinar /vatʃisi'nar/ *vt* prophesy. **~cínio** *m* prophecy

va|zamento /vaza'mẽtu/ *m* leak. **~zante** *f* ebb tide. **~zão** *m* outflow; **dar ~zão a** *fig* give vent to. **~zar** *vt/i* leak

vazio /va'ziu/ *a* empty ● *m* emptiness; (*um*) void

veado /vi'adu/ *m* deer

ve|dação /veda'sãw/ *f* (*de casa, janela*) insulation; (*em motor etc*) gasket. **~dar** *vt* seal ‹*recipiente, abertura*›; stanch ‹*sangue*›; seal off ‹*saída, área*›; **~dar algo (a alguém)** prohibit sth (for s.o.)

vedete /ve'dɛte/ *f* star

vee|mência /vee'mẽsia/ *f* vehemence. **~mente** *a* vehement

vege|tação /veʒeta'sãw/ *f* vegetation. **~tal** (*pl* **~tais**) *a & m* vegetable. **~tar** *vi* vegetate. **~tariano** *a & m* vegetarian

veia /'veja/ *f* vein

veicular /veiku'lar/ *vt* convey; place ‹*anúncios*›

veículo /ve'ikulu/ *m* vehicle; **~ utilitário desportivo** sports utility vehicle, SUV; (*de comunicação etc*) medium

vela[1] /'vɛla/ *f* (*de barco*) sail; (*esporte*) sailing

vela[2] /'vɛla/ *f* candle; (*em motor*) spark plug; **segurar a ~** [!] play gooseberry

velar[1] /ve'lar/ *vt* (*cobrir*) veil

velar[2] /ve'lar/ *vt* watch over ● *vi* keep vigil

veleidade /velej'dadʒi/ *f* whim

ve|leiro /ve'leru/ *m* sailing boat. **~lejar** *vi* sail

velhaco /ve'ʎaku/ *a* crooked ● *m* crook

ve|lharia /veʎa'ria/ *f* old thing. **~lhice** *f* old age. **~lho** /ɛ/ *a* old ● *m* old man. **~lhote** /ɔ/ *m* old man

velocidade /velosi'dadʒi/ *f* speed; *Port* (*marcha*) gear; **a toda ~** at full speed; **~ máxima** speed limit

velocímetro /velo'simetru/ *m* speedometer

velocista /velo'sista/ *m/f* sprinter

velório /ve'lɔriu/ *m* wake

veloz /ve'los/ *a* fast

veludo /ve'ludu/ *m* velvet; **~ cotelê** corduroy

ven|cedor /vẽse'dor/ *a* winning ● *m* winner. **~cer** *vt* win over ‹*adversário etc*›; win ‹*partida, corrida, batalha*› ● *vi* (*triunfar*) win; ‹*prestação, aluguel, dívida*› fall due; ‹*contrato, passaporte, prazo*› expire; ‹*apólice*› mature. **~cido** *a* **dar-se por ~cido** give in. **~cimento** *m* (*de dívida, aluguel*) due date; (*de contrato, prazo*) expiry date; (*de alimento, remédio etc*) best before date; (*salário*) payment; *pl*, earnings

venda[1] /'vẽda/ *f* sale; (*loja*) general store; **à ~** on sale; **pôr à ~** put up for sale

ven|da[2] /'vẽda/ *f* blindfold. **~dar** *vt* blindfold

venda|val /vẽda'vaw/ (*pl* **~vais**) *m* gale, storm

ven|dável /vẽ'davew/ (*pl* **~dáveis**) *a* saleable. **~dedor** *m* (*de loja*) shop assistant; (*em geral*) seller. **~der** *vt/i* sell; **estar ~dendo saúde** be bursting with health

vendeta /vẽ'deta/ *f* vendetta

veneno /ve'nenu/ *m* poison; (*de cobra etc, malignidade*) venom. **~so** /o/ *a* poisonous; (*maldoso*) venomous

vene|ração /venera'sãw/ *f* reverence; (*de Deus etc*) worship. **~rar** *vt* revere; worship ‹*Deus etc*›

vené|reo /ve'nɛriu/ *a* **doença ~rea** venereal disease

Veneza /ve'neza/ *f* Venice

veneziana /venezi'ana/ *f* shutter

Venezuela /venezu'ɛla/ *f* Venezuela

venezuelano /venezue'lanu/ *a & m* Venezuelan

venta /'vẽta/ *f* nostril

ven|tania /vẽta'nia/ *f* gale. **~tar** *vi* be windy. **~tarola** /ɔ/ *f* fan

venti|lação /vẽtʃila'sãw/ *f* ventilation. **~lador** *m* fan. **~lar** *vt* ventilate; air ‹*sala, roupa*›

ven|to /'vẽtu/ *m* wind; **de ~to em popa** smoothly. **~toinha** *f* (*cata-vento*) weather vane; *Port* (*ventilador*) fan. **~tosa** /ɔ/ *f* sucker. **~toso** /o/ *a* windy

ven|tre /'vẽtri/ *m* belly. **~tríloquo** *m* ventriloquist

Vênus /'venus/ *f* Venus

ver /ver/ *vt* see; watch ‹*televisão*›; (*resolver*) see to ● *vi* see; **ter a ~ com** have to do with; **vai ~ que ela não sabe** [!] I bet she doesn't know; **vê se você não volta tarde** see you don't get back late; **viu?** [!] right? ● *m* **a meu ~** in my view. **~-se** *vpr* (*no espelho etc*) see o.s.; (*em estado, condição*) find o.s.; (*um ao outro*) see each other

veracidade /verasi'dadʒi/ *f* truthfulness

vera|near /verani'ar/ *vi* spend the summer. **~neio** *m* summer holiday, *Amer* summer vacation. **~nista** *m/f* holidaymaker, *Amer* vacationer

verão /ve'rãw/ *m* summer

veraz /ve'ras/ *a* truthful

ver|bal /ver'baw/ (*pl* **~bais**) *a* verbal. **~bete** /e/ *m* entry. **~bo** *m* verb. **~borragia** *f* waffle. **~boso** /o/ *a* verbose

verbas /'vɛrbas/ *f pl* funds

verda|de /ver'dadʒi/ *f* truth; **de ~de** ‹*coisa*› real; ‹*fazer*› really; **na ~de** actually; **para falar a ~de** to tell the truth. **~deiro** *a* ‹*declaração, pessoa*› truthful; (*real*) true

verde /'verdʒi/ *a & m* green; **jogar ~ para colher maduro** fish for information. **~-abacate** *a invar* avocado; **~-amarelo** *a* yellow and green; (*brasileiro*) Brazilian; (*nacionalista*) nationalistic; **~-esmeralda** *a invar* emerald green. **~jar** *vi* turn green

verdu|ra /ver'dura/ *f* (*para comer*) greens; (*da natureza*) greenery. **~reiro** *m* greengrocer, *Amer* produce dealer

vereador /veria'dor/ *m* councillor

vereda /ve'reda/ *f* path

veredito /vere'dʒitu/ *m* verdict

vergar /ver'gar/ *vt/i* bend

vergo|nha /ver'goɲa/ *f* (*pudor*) shame; (*constrangimento*) embarrassment; (*timidez*) shyness; (*uma*) disgrace; **ter ~nha** be ashamed; be embarrassed; be shy; **cria** ou **tome ~nha na cara!** you should be ashamed of yourself!. **~nhoso** *a* shameful

verídico /ve'ridʒiku/ *a* true

verificar /verifi'kar/ *vt* check, verify ‹*fatos, dados etc*›; **~ que** ascertain that; **~ se** check that. **~-se** *vpr* ‹*previsão etc*› come true; ‹*acidente etc*› happen

verme /'vɛrmi/ *m* worm

verme|lhidão /vermeʎi'dãw/ *f* redness. **~lho** /e/ *a & m* red; **no ~lho** (*endividado*) in the red

vernáculo /ver'nakulu/ *a & m* vernacular

verniz /ver'nis/ *f* varnish; (*couro*) patent leather

veros|símil /vero'simiw/ (*pl* **~símeis**) *a* plausible. **~similhança** *f* plausibility

verruga /ve'xuga/ *f* wart

ver|sado /ver'sadu/ *a* well-versed (**em** in). **~são** *f* version. **~sar** *vi* **~sar sobre** concern. **~sátil** (*pl* **~sáteis**) *a* versatile. **~satilidade** *f* versatility. **~sículo** *m* (*da Bíblia*) verse. **~so** [1] /ɛ/ *m* verse

verso[2] /ɛ/ *m* (*de página*) reverse, other side; **vide ~** see over

vértebra /'vɛrtebra/ *f* vertebra

verte|brado /verte'bradu/ *a & m* vertebrate. **~bral** (*pl* **~brais**) *a* spinal

ver|tente /ver'tẽtʃi/ *f* slope. **~ter** *vt* (*derramar*) pour; shed ‹*lágrimas, sangue*›; (*traduzir*) render (**para** into)

verti|cal /vertʃi'kaw/ (*pl* **~cais**) *a & f* vertical. **~gem** *f* dizziness. **~ginoso** /o/ *a* dizzy

vesgo /'vezgu/ *a* cross-eyed

vesícula /ve'zikula/ *f* gall bladder

vespa /'vespa/ *f* wasp

véspera /'vɛspera/ *f* **a ~** the day before; **a ~ de** the eve of; **a ~ de Natal** Christmas Eve; **nas ~s de** on the eve of

vespertino /vesper'tʃinu/ *a* evening

ves|te /'vɛstʃi/ *f* robe. **~tiário** *m* (*para se trocar*) changing room; (*para guardar roupa*) cloakroom

vestibular /vestʃibu'lar/ *m* university entrance exam

> **vestibular** The *vestibular* is a highly competitive exam that is taken by any student wishing to apply to university in Brazil. Candidates are tested on various subjects, such as Portuguese Language, History, Geography, Maths, etc. The most popular courses, such as Medicine, Dentistry, and Engineering, have as many as 70 applicants per place, and students are selected for admission based on their overall *vestibular* grade.

vestíbulo /ves'tʃibulu/ *m* hall(way); (*do teatro*) foyer

vestido /ves'tʃidu/ *m* dress ● *a* dressed (**de** in)

vestígio /ves'tʃiʒiu/ *m* trace

ves|timenta /vestʃi'mẽta/ *f* (*de sacerdote*) vestments. **~tir** *vt* (*pôr*) put on; (*usar*) wear; (*pôr roupa em*) dress; (*dar roupa a*) clothe. **~tir-se** *vpr* dress; **~tir-se de branco/de padre** dress in white/as a priest. **~tuário** *m* clothing

vetar /ve'tar/ *vt* veto

veterano /vete'ranu/ *a & m* veteran

veterinário /veteri'nariu/ *a* veterinary ● *m* vet

veto /'vɛtu/ *m* veto

véu /vɛw/ *m* veil

vexa|me /ve'ʃami/ *m* disgrace; **dar um ~me** make a fool of o.s.. **~minoso** /o/ *a* disgraceful

vexar /ve'ʃar/ *vt* shame. **~-se** *vpr* be ashamed (**de** of)

vez /ves/ *f* (*ocasião*) time; (*turno*) turn; **às ~es** sometimes; **cada ~ mais** more and more; **de ~** for good; **desta ~** this time; **de ~ em quando** now and again, from time to time; **de uma ~** (*ao mesmo tempo*) at once; (*de um golpe*) in one go; **de uma ~ por todas** once and for all; **duas ~es** twice; **em ~ de** instead of; **fazer as ~es de** take the place of; **mais uma ~, outra ~** again; **muitas ~es** (*com muita frequência*) often; (*repetidamente*) many times; **raras ~es** seldom; **repetidas ~es** repeatedly; **uma ~** once; **uma ~ que** since

via /'via/ *f* (*estrada*) road; (*rumo, meio*) way; (*exemplar*) copy; *pl* (*trâmites*) channels ● *prep* via; **em ~s de** on the point of; **por ~ aérea/marítima** by air/sea; **por ~ das dúvidas** just in case; **por ~ de regra** as a rule; **Via Láctea** Milky Way

viabili|dade /viabili'dadʒi/ *f* feasibility. **~zar** *vt* make feasible

viação /via'sãw/ *f* (*transporte*) road transport; (*estradas*) road network; (*companhia*) bus company

viaduto /via'dutu/ *m* viaduct; (*rodoviário*) flyover, *Amer* overpass

via|gem /vi'aʒẽ/ *f* (*uma*) trip, journey; (*em geral*) travelling; *pl* (*de uma pessoa*) travels; (*em geral*) travel; **boa ~gem!** have a good trip! **~gem de negócios** business trip. **~jado** *a* well-travelled. **~jante** *a* travelling ● *m/f* traveller. **~jar** *vi* travel; **estar ~jando** [!] (*com o pensamento longe*) be miles away

viário /vi'ariu/ *a* road; **anel ~** ring road

viatura /via'tura/ *f* vehicle

viá|vel /vi'avew/ (*pl* **~veis**) *a* feasible

víbora /'vibora/ *f* viper

vi|bração /vibra'sãw/ *f* vibration; *fig* thrill. **~brante** *a* vibrant. **~brar** *vt* shake ● *vi* vibrate; *fig* be thrilled (**com** by)

vice /'visi/ *m/f* deputy

vice-cam|peão /visikãpi'ãw/ *m* (*f* **~peã**) runner-up

vicejar /vise'ʒar/ *vi* flourish

vice-presiden|te /visiprezi'dẽtʃi/ *m* (*f* **~ta**) vice-president

vice-rei /visi'xej/ *m* viceroy

vice-versa /visi'vɛrsa/ *adv* vice versa

vici|ado /visi'adu/ *a* addicted (**em** to) ● *m* addict; **um ~ado em drogas** a drug addict. **~ar** *vt* (*falsificar*) tamper with; (*estragar*) ruin ● *vi* ‹*droga*› be addictive. **~ar-se** *vpr* get addicted (**em** to)

vício /'visiu/ *m* vice

vicioso /visi'ozu/ *a* **círculo ~** vicious circle

V

vicissitudes /visisi'tudʒis/ *f pl* ups and downs

viço /'visu/ *m* (*de plantas*) exuberance; (*de pessoa, pele*) freshness. **~so** /o/ *a* ‹*planta*› lush; ‹*pele, pessoa*› fresh

vida /'vida/ *f* life; **sem ~** lifeless; **dar ~ a** liven up

videira /vi'dera/ *f* vine

vidente /vi'dẽtʃi/ *m/f* clairvoyant

vídeo /'vidʒiu/ *m* video; (*tela*) screen

video|cassete /vidʒiuka'sɛtʃi/ *m* (*fita*) video tape; (*aparelho*) video, *Amer* VCR. **~clipe** *m* video. **~clube** *m* video club. **~game** *m* video game. **~teipe** *m* video tape

vidra|ça /vi'drasa/ *f* window pane. **~çaria** *f* (*fábrica*) glassworks; (*vidraças*) glazing. **~ceiro** *m* glazier

vi|drado /vi'dradu/ *a* glazed; **estar ~drado em** ou **por** [!] love. **~drar** *vt* glaze ● *vi* [!] fall in love (**em** ou **por** with). **~dro** *m* (*material*) glass; (*pote*) jar; (*janela*) window; **~dro fumê** tinted glass

viela /vi'ɛla/ *f* alley

Viena /vi'ɛna/ *f* Vienna

Vietnã /vietʃi'nã/ *m*, *Port* **Vietname** /viet'nam/ *m* Vietnam

vietnamita /vietna'mita/ *a & m/f* Vietnamese

viga /'viga/ *f* joist

vigarice /viga'risi/ *f* swindle

vigário /vi'gariu/ *m* vicar

vigarista /viga'rista/ *m/f* swindler, con artist

vi|gência /vi'ʒẽsia/ *f* (*qualidade*) force; (*tempo*) period in force. **~gente** *a* in force

vigésimo /vi'ʒɛzimu/ *a* twentieth

vigi|a /vi'ʒia/ *f* (*guarda*) watch; (*em navio*) porthole ● *m* night watchman. **~ar** *vt* (*observar*) watch; (*cuidar de*) watch over; (*como sentinela*) guard ● *vi* keep watch

vigi|lância /viʒi'lãsia/ *f* vigilance. **~lante** *a* vigilant

vigília /vi'ʒilia/ *f* vigil

vigor /vi'gor/ *m* vigour; **em ~** in force

vigo|rar /vigo'rar/ *vi* be in force. **~roso** *a* vigorous

VIH /veia'ga/ *abr m* (= **Vírus da Imunodeficiência Humana**) HIV

vil /viw/ (*pl* **vis**) *a* base, despicable

vila /'vila/ *f* (*cidadezinha*) small town; (*casa elegante*) villa; (*conjunto de casas*) housing estate; **~ olímpica** Olympic village

vi|lania /vila'nia/ *f* villainy. **~lão** *m* (*f* **~lã**) villain

vilarejo /vila'reʒu/ *m* village

vilipendiar /vilipẽdʒi'ar/ *vt* disparage

vime /'vimi/ *m* wicker

vina|gre /vi'nagri/ *m* vinegar. **~grete** /ɛ/ *m* vinaigrette

vin|car /vĩ'kar/ *vt* crease; line ‹*rosto*›. **~co** *m* crease; (*no rosto*) line

vincular /vĩku'lar/ *vt* bond, tie

vínculo /'vĩkulu/ *m* link, bond; **~ empregatício** contract of employment

vinda /'vĩda/ *f* coming; **dar as boas ~s a** welcome

vindicar /vĩdʒi'kar/ *vt* vindicate

vindima /vĩ'dʒima/ *f* vintage

vin|do /'vĩdu/ *pp e pres de* **vir**. **~douro** *a* coming

vin|gança /vĩ'gãsa/ *f* vengeance, revenge. **~gar** *vt* avenge ● *vi* ‹*flores*› thrive; ‹*criança*› survive; ‹*plano, empreendimento*› be successful. **~gar-se** *vpr* take one's revenge (**de** for **em** on). **~gativo** *a* vindictive

vinha /'viɲa/ *f* vineyard

vinhedo /vi'ɲedu/ *m* vineyard

vinheta /vi'ɲeta/ *f* (*na TV etc*) sequence

vinho /'viɲu/ *m* wine ● *a invar* maroon; **~ do Porto** port

> *i* **vinho verde** *Vinho verde* (literally 'green wine') is a light, slightly sparkling Portuguese wine originating from the Minho area in the north of the country. The 'green' in its name refers to its young age rather than to its colour, and it is available in white, red and rosé varieties.

vinícola /vi'nikola/ *a* wine-growing

vinicul|tor /vinikuw'tor/ *m* wine grower. **~tura** *f* wine growing

vinil /vi'niw/ *m* vinyl

vinte /'vĩtʃi/ *a & m* twenty. **~na** /e/ *f* score

viola /vi'ɔla/ *f* viola

violação /viola'sãw/ *f* violation

violão /vio'lãw/ *m* guitar

violar /vio'lar/ *vt* violate

vio|lência /vio'lẽsia/ *f* violence; (*uma*) act of violence. **~lentar** *vt* rape ‹*mulher*›. **~lento** *a* violent

violeta /vio'leta/ *f* violet ● *a invar* violet

violi|nista /violi'nista/ *m/f* violinist. **~no** *m* violin

violonce|lista /violõse'lista/ *m/f* cellist. **~lo** /ɛ/ *m* cello

vir /vir/ *vi* come; **o ano que vem** next year; **venho lendo os jornais** I have been reading the papers; **vem cá** come here; 🅸 listen; **isso não vem ao caso** that's irrelevant; **~ a ser** turn out to be; **~ com** give ‹*argumento etc*›

virabrequim /virabre'kĩ/ *m* crankshaft

viração /vira'sãw/ *f* breeze

vira-casaca /viraka'zaka/ *m/f* turncoat

vira|da /vi'rada/ *f* turn. **~do** *a* ‹*roupa*› inside out; (*de cabeça para baixo*) upside down; **~do para** facing

vira-lata /vira'lata/ *m* mongrel

virar /vi'rar/ *vt* turn; turn over ‹*disco, barco etc*›; turn inside out ‹*roupa*›; turn out ‹*bolsos*›; tip ‹*balde, água etc*› ● *vi* turn; ‹*barco*› turn over; (*tornar-se*) become; **vira e mexe** every so often. **~-se** *vpr* turn round; (*na vida*) get by, cope; **~-se para** turn to

viravolta /vira'vɔwta/ *f* about-turn

virgem /'virʒẽ/ *a* ‹*fita*› blank; ‹*floresta, noiva etc*› virgin ● *f* virgin; **Virgem** (*signo*) Virgo

virgindade /virʒĩ'dadʒi/ *f* virginity

vírgula /'virgula/ *f* comma; (*decimal*) point

vi|ril /vi'riw/ (*pl* **~ris**) *a* virile

virilha /vi'riʎa/ *f* groin

virilidade /virili'dadʒi/ *f* virility

virtu|al /virtu'aw/ (*pl* **~ais**) *a* virtual

virtude /vir'tudʒi/ *f* virtue

virtuo|sismo /virtuo'zizmu/ *m* virtuosity. **~so** /o/ *a* virtuous ● *m* virtuoso

virulento /viru'lẽtu/ *a* virulent

vírus /'virus/ *m invar* virus

visão /vi'zãw/ *f* vision; (*aspeto, ponto de vista*) view

visar /vi'zar/ *vt* aim at ‹*caça, alvo*›; **~ (a)** aim for ‹*objetivo*›; ‹*medida, ação*› be aimed at

vísceras /'viseras/ *f pl* innards

viscon|de /vis'kõdʒi/ *m* viscount. **~dessa** /e/ *f* viscountess

viscoso /vis'kozu/ *a* viscous

viseira /vi'zera/ *f* visor

visibilidade /vizibili'dadʒi/ *f* visibility

visionário /vizio'nariu/ *a & m* visionary

visi|ta /vi'zita/ *f* visit; (*visitante*) visitor; **fazer uma ~ta a alguém** pay s.o. a visit. **~tante** *a* visiting ● *m/f* visitor. **~tar** *vt* visit

visí|vel /vi'zivew/ (*pl* **~veis**) *a* visible

vislum|brar /vizlũ'brar/ *vt* (*entrever*) glimpse; (*imaginar*) envisage. **~bre** *m* glimpse

visom /vi'zõ/ *m* mink

visor /vi'zor/ *m* viewfinder

vis|ta /'vista/ *f* sight; (*dos olhos*) eyesight; (*panorama*) view; **à ~ta** (*visível*) in view; (*em dinheiro*) in cash; **à primeira ~ta** at first sight; **pôr à ~ta** put on show; **de ~ta** ‹*conhecer*› by sight; **em ~ta de** in view of; **ter em ~ta** have in view; **dar na ~ta** attract attention; **fazer ~ta** look nice; **fazer ~ta grossa** turn a blind eye (**a** to); **perder de ~ta** lose sight of; **a perder de ~ta** as far as the eye can see; **uma ~ta de olhos** a quick look. **~to** *a* seen ● *m* visa; **pelo ~to** by the looks of things; **~to que** seeing that

visto|ria /visto'ria/ *f* inspection. **~riar** *vt* inspect

vistoso /vis'tozu/ *a* eye-catching

visu|al /vizu'aw/ (*pl* **~ais**) *a* visual ● *m* look. **~alizar** *vt* visualize

vi|tal /vi'taw/ (*pl* **~tais**) *a* vital. **~talício** *a* for life. **~talidade** *f* vitality

vita|mina /vita'mina/ *f* vitamin; (*bebida*) liquidized fruit drink. **~minado** *a* with added vitamins. **~mínico** *a* vitamin

vitela /vi'tɛla/ *f* (*carne*) veal

viticultura /vitʃikuw'tura/ *f* viticulture

vítima /'vitʃima/ *f* victim

viti|mar /vitʃi'mar/ *vt* (*matar*) claim the life of; **ser ~mado por** fall victim to

vitória /vi'tɔria/ *f* victory

vitorioso /vitori'ozu/ *a* victorious

vi|tral /vi'traw/ (*pl* **~trais**) *m* stained glass window

vitrine /vi'trini/ *f* shop window

vitrola /vi'trɔla/ *f* jukebox

viú|va /vi'uva/ *f* widow. **~vo** *a* widowed ● *m* widower

viva /'viva/ *f* cheer ● *int* hurray; **~ a rainha** long live the queen

vivacidade /vivasi'dadʒi/ *f* vivacity

vivalma /vi'vawma/ *f* **não há ~ lá fora** there's not a soul outside

vivar /vi'var/ *vt/i* cheer

vivaz /vi'vas/ *a* lively, vivacious; ‹*planta*› hardy

viveiro /vi'veru/ *m* (*de plantas*) nursery; (*de peixes*) fishpond; (*de aves*) aviary; *fig* breeding ground

vivência /vi'vẽsia/ *f* experience

vivenda /vi'vẽda/ *f Port* detached house

viver /vi'ver/ *vt/i* live (**de** on); **ele vive reclamando** he's always complaining ● *m* life

víveres /'viveris/ *m pl* provisions

vívido /'vividu/ *a* vivid

vivissecção /vivisek'sãw/ *f* vivisection

vivo /'vivu/ *a* (*que vive*) living; (*animado*) lively; ‹*cor*› bright ● *m* **os ~s** the living; **ao ~** live; **estar ~** be alive; **dinheiro ~** cash

vizi|nhança /vizi'ɲãsa/ *f* neighbourhood. **~nho** *a* neighbouring ● *m* neighbour

vo|ador /voa'dor/ *a* flying. **~ar** *vi* fly; (*explodir*) blow up; **sair ~ando** rush off

vocabulário /vokabu'lariu/ *m* vocabulary

vocábulo /vo'kabulu/ *m* word

voca|ção /voka'sãw/ *f* vocation. **~cional** (*pl* **~cionais**) *a* vocational; **orientação ~cional** careers guidance

vo|cal /vo'kaw/ (*pl* **~cais**) *a* vocal

você /vo'se/ *pron* you. **~s** *pron* you

vociferar /vosife'rar/ *vi* shout abuse

vodca /'vɔdʒka/ *f* vodka

voga /'vɔga/ *f* (*moda*) vogue

vo|gal /vo'gaw/ (*pl* **~gais**) *f* vowel

volante /vo'lãtʃi/ *m* (*de carro*) steering wheel

volá|til /vo'latʃiw/ (*pl* **~teis**) *a* volatile

vôlei /'volej/ *m*, **voleibol** /'volej'bɔl/ *m* volleyball

volt /'vɔwtʃi/ (*pl* **~s**) *m* volt

volta /'vɔwta/ *f* (*retorno*) return; (*da pista*) lap; (*resposta*) response; **às ~s com** tied up with; **de ~** back; **em ~ de** around; **na ~** on the way back; **na ~ do correio** by return of post; **por ~ de** around; **dar a ~ ao mundo** go round the world; **dar a ~ por cima** make a comeback; **dar meia ~** turn round; **dar uma ~** (*a pé*) go for a walk; (*de carro*) go for a drive; **dar uma ~ em** turn round; **dar ~s** spin round; **ter ~** get a response; **~ e meia** every so often. **~do** *a* **~do para** geared towards

voltagem /vow'taʒẽ/ *f* voltage

voltar /vow'tar/ *vi* go/come back, return; **~ a si** come to; **~ a fazer** do again; **~ atrás** backtrack ● *vt* rewind ‹*fita*›. **~-se** *vpr* turn round; **~-se para/contra** turn to/against

volu|me /vo'lumi/ *m* volume. **~moso** *a* sizeable; ‹*som*› loud

voluntário /volũ'tariu/ *a & m* volunteer

volúpia /vo'lupia/ *f* sensuality, lust

voluptuoso /voluptu'ozu/ *a* sensual; ‹*mulher*› voluptuous

volú|vel /vo'luvew/ (*pl* **~veis**) *a* fickle
vomitar /vomi'tar/ *vt/i* vomit
vômito /'vomitu/ *m* vomit; *pl* vomiting
vontade /võ'tadʒi/ *f* will; **à ~** (*bem*) at ease; (*quanto quiser*) as much as one likes; **fique à ~** make yourself at home; **tem comida à ~** there's plenty of food; **estar com ~ de** feel like; **isso me dá ~ de chorar** it makes me feel like crying; **fazer a ~ de alguém** do what sb wants
voo /'vou/ *m* flight; **levantar ~** take off; **~ livre** hang-gliding
voraz /vo'ras/ *a* voracious
vos /vus/ *pron* you; (*a vocês*) to you
vós /vɔs/ *pron* you
vosso /'vɔsu/ *a* your ● *pron* yours
vo|tação /vota'sãw/ *f* vote. **~tante** *m/f* voter. **~tar** *vt* vote on ‹*lei etc*›; (*dedicar*) devote; (*prometer*) vow ● *vi* vote (**em** for)
voto /'vɔtu/ *m* (*em votação*) vote; (*promessa*) vow; *pl* (*desejos*) wishes
vo|vó /vo'vɔ/ *f* grandma. **~vô** *m* grandpa
voz /vɔs/ *f* voice; **dar ~ de prisão a alguém** place s.o. under arrest
vozerio /voze'riu/ *m* shouting
vul|cânico /vuw'kaniku/ *a* volcanic. **~cão** *m* volcano
vul|gar /vuw'gar/ *a* ordinary; (*baixo*) vulgar. **~garizar** *vt* popularize; (*tornar baixo*) vulgarize. **~go** *adv* commonly known as
vulne|rabilidade /vuwnerabili'dadʒi/ *f* vulnerability. **~rável** (*pl* **~ráveis**) *a* vulnerable
vul|to /'vuwtu/ *m* (*figura*) figure; (*tamanho*) bulk; (*importância*) importance; **de ~to** important. **~toso** /o/ *a* bulky

Ww

walkie-talkie /uɔki'tɔki/ (*pl* **~s**) *m* walkie-talkie
Walkman® /uɔk'mɛn/ *m invar* Walkman®
WAP /uap/ *a* (*telec*) WAP
watt /u'ɔtʃi/ (*pl* **~s**) *m* watt
web /uɛb/ *m* web, WWW
windsur|fe /uĩ'surfi/ *m* windsurfing. **~fista** *m/f* windsurfer

Xx

xadrez /ʃa'dres/ *m* (*jogo*) chess; (*desenho*) check; [!] (*prisão*) prison ● *a invar* check
xaile /'ʃajle/ *m* ▶ **xale**
xale /'ʃali/ *m* shawl
xampu /ʃã'pu/ *m* shampoo
xará /ʃa'ra/ *m/f* namesake
xarope /ʃa'rɔpi/ *m* syrup
xaxim /ʃa'ʃĩ/ *m* plant fibre
xenofobia /ʃenofo'bia/ *f* xenophobia
xenófobo /ʃe'nɔfobu/ *a* xenophobic ● *m* xenophobe
xepa /'ʃepa/ *f* scraps
xeque[1] /'ʃɛki/ *m* (*árabe*) sheikh
xeque[2] /'ʃɛki/ *m* (*no xadrez*) check. **~-mate** *m* checkmate
xere|ta /ʃe'reta/ [!] *a* nosy ● *m/f* nosy parker. **~tar** *vi* [!] nose around
xerez /ʃe'res/ *m* sherry
xerife /ʃe'rifi/ *m* sheriff
xerocar /ʃero'kar/ *vt* photocopy
xerox /ʃe'rɔks/ *m invar* photocopy
xexelento /ʃeʃe'lẽtu/ [!] *a* scruffy ● *m* scruff
xícara /'ʃikara/ *f* cup
xiita /ʃi'ita/ *a & m/f* Shiite
xilofone /ʃilo'foni/ *m* xylophone
xingar /ʃĩ'gar/ *vt* swear at ● *vi* swear
xis /ʃis/ *m invar* letter X; **o ~ do problema** the crux of the problem
xixi /ʃi'ʃi/ *m* [!] wee; **fazer ~** do a wee [!]
xô /ʃo/ *int* shoo
xucro /'ʃukru/ *a* ignorant

Zz

zagueiro /za'geru/ *m* full back
Zaire /'zajri/ *m* Zaire
Zâmbia /'zãbia/ *f* Zambia
zan|gado /zã'gadu/ *a* cross, annoyed. **~gar** *vt* annoy. **~gar-se** *vpr* get cross, get annoyed (**com** with)
zanzar /zã'zar/ *vi* wander
zarpar /zar'par/ *vi* set off; (*de navio*) set sail

zebra /'zebra/ *f* zebra; (*pessoa*) fool; (*resultado*) upset

ze|lador /zela'dor/ *m* caretaker, *Amer* janitor. **~lar** *vt* **~lar (por)** take care of. **~lo** /e/ *m* zeal; **~lo por** devotion to. **~loso** /o/ *a* zealous

zé-ninguém /zɛnĩ'gẽ/ *m* **ser um ~** to be a nobody

zero /'zɛru/ *m* zero; (*em escores*) nil. **~-quilômetro** *a invar* brand new

ziguezague /zigi'zagi/ *m* zigzag. **~ar** *vi* zigzag

Zimbábue /zĩ'babui/ *m* Zimbabwe

zinco /'zĩku/ *m* zinc

zíper /'ziper/ *m* zip, zipper

zodíaco /zo'dʒiaku/ *m* zodiac

zoeira /zo'era/ *f* din

zom|bador /zõba'dor/ *a* mocking. **~bar** *vi* **~bar (de)** mock. **~baria** *f* mockery

zona /'zona/ *f* (*área*) zone; (*de cidade*) district; (*desordem*) mess; (*tumulto*) commotion; (*bairro do meretrício*) red-light district

zonzo /'zõzu/ *a* dizzy

zoo /'zou/ *m* zoo

zoo|logia /zoolo'ʒia/ *f* zoology. **~lógico** *a* zoological

zoólogo /zo'ɔlogu/ *m* zoologist

zulu /zu'lu/ *a & m/f* Zulu

zum /zũ/ *m* zoom lens

zumbi /zũ'bi/ *m* zombie

zum|bido /zũ'bidu/ *m* buzz; (*no ouvido*) ringing. **~bir** *vi* buzz

zu|nido /zu'nidu/ *m* (*de vento, bala*) whistle; (*de inseto*) buzz. **~nir** *vi* ‹*vento, bala*› whistle; ‹*inseto*› buzz

zunzum /zũ'zũ/ *m* rumour

Zurique /zu'riki/ *f* Zurich

zurrar /zu'xar/ *vi* bray

Aa

a /ə/ *emphatic* /eɪ/

! before vowel or mute h **an** /ən/ *emphatic* /æn/ ● *indefinite article*

····➤ um(a); **~ pencil** um lápis; **~ pen** uma caneta

! When talking about what people do, **a** is not translated into Portuguese **she's a doctor** *ela é médica*

! **a** is not translated into Portuguese in the numbers **a hundred** and **a thousand**: **a hundred years ago** *há cem anos*; **there were a thousand people there** *havia mil pessoas lá*

····➤ per; **two pounds ~ metre** duas libras o metro; **sixty miles ~n hour** sessenta milhas por hora, (*P*) à hora; **once ~ year** uma vez por ano; **twice ~ year** duas vezes por ano

aback /ə'bæk/ *adv* **taken ~** desconcertado, (*P*) surpreendido

abandon /ə'bændən/ *vt* abandonar ● *n* abandono *m*. **~ed** *a* abandonado; ‹*behaviour*› livre, dissoluto

abate /ə'beɪt/ *vt/i* abater, abrandar, diminuir

abattoir /'æbətwɑ:(r)/ *n* matadouro *m*

abbey /'æbɪ/ *n* abadia *f*, mosteiro *m*

abbreviat|e /ə'bri:vɪeɪt/ *vt* abreviar. **~ion** /-'eɪʃn/ *n* abreviação *f*; (*short form*) abreviatura *f*

abdicat|e /'æbdɪkeɪt/ *vt/i* abdicar. **~ion** /-'keɪʃn/ *n* abdicação *f*

abdom|en /'æbdəmən/ *n* abdômen *m*, (*P*) abdómen *m*. **~inal** /-'dɒmɪnl/ *a* abdominal

abduct /æb'dʌkt/ *vt* raptar. **~ion** /-ʃn/ *n* rapto *m*

aberration /æbə'reɪʃn/ *n* aberração *f*

abeyance /ə'beɪəns/ *n* **in ~** ‹*matter*› em suspenso; ‹*custom*› em desuso

abhor /əb'hɔ:(r)/ *vt* (*pt* **abhorred**) abominar, ter horror a. **~rence** /-'hɒrəns/ *n* horror *m*. **~rent** /-'hɒrənt/ *a* abominável, execrável

abide /ə'baɪd/ *vt* (*pt* **abided**) suportar, tolerar; **~ by** ‹*promise*› manter; ‹*rules*› acatar

ability /ə'bɪlətɪ/ *n* capacidade *f* (**to do** para or de fazer); (*cleverness*) habilidade *f*, esperteza *f*

abject /'æbdʒekt/ *a* abjeto, (*P*) abjecto

ablaze /ə'bleɪz/ *a* em chamas; *fig* aceso, (*P*) excitado

abl|e /'eɪbl/ *a* (**er**, **est**) capaz (**to** de); **be ~e to** (*have power, opportunity*) ser capaz de, poder; (*know how to*) ser capaz de, saber. **~y** *adv* habilmente

abnormal /æb'nɔ:ml/ *a* anormal. **~ity** /-'mælətɪ/ *n* anormalidade *f*. **~ly** *adv* (*unusually*) excepcionalmente

aboard /ə'bɔ:d/ *adv* a bordo ● *prep* a bordo de

aboli|sh /ə'bɒlɪʃ/ *vt* abolir, extinguir. **~tion** /æbə'lɪʃn/ *n* abolição *f*, extinção *f*

abominable /ə'bɒmɪnəbl/ *a* abominável, detestável

abort /ə'bɔ:t/ *vt/i* (fazer) abortar. **~ive** *a* ‹*attempt etc*› abortado, malogrado

abortion /ə'bɔ:ʃn/ *n* aborto *m*; **have an ~** fazer um aborto, ter um aborto

abound /ə'baʊnd/ *vi* abundar (**in** em)

about /ə'baʊt/ *adv* (*approximately*) aproximadamente, cerca de; (*here and there*) aqui e ali; (*all round*) por todos os lados, em roda, em volta; (*in existence*) por aí; **~ here** por aqui; **be ~ to** estar prestes a; **he was ~ to eat** ia comer; **how** or **what ~ leaving?** e se nós fôssemos embora?; **know/talk ~** saber/falar sobre ● *prep* acerca de, sobre; (*round*) em torno de; (*somewhere in*) em, por. **~-face**, **~-turn** *ns* reviravolta *f*

above /ə'bʌv/ *adv* acima, por cima ● *prep* sobre; **he's not ~ lying** ele não é de mentir; **~ all** sobretudo. **~ board** *a* franco, honesto ● *adv* com lisura; **~-mentioned** *a* acima, supracitado

abrasive /ə'breɪsɪv/ *a* abrasivo; *fig* agressivo ● *n* abrasivo *m*

abreast /ə'brest/ *adv* lado a lado; **keep ~ of** manter-se a par de

abridge /ə'brɪdʒ/ *vt* abreviar

abroad /ə'brɔ:d/ *adv* no estrangeiro; (*far and wide*) por todo o lado; **go ~** ir para o estrangeiro

abrupt /ə'brʌpt/ *a* (*sudden, curt*) brusco; (*steep*) abrupto

abscess /'æbsɪs/ *n* abscesso *m*, (*P*) abcesso *m*

a

abscond /əb'skɒnd/ *vi* evadir-se, andar fugido

absen|t[1] /'æbsənt/ *a* ausente; ‹*look etc*› distraído. **~ce** *n* ausência *f*; (*lack*) falta *f*. **~t-minded** *a* distraído; **~t-mindedness** *n* distração *f*, (*P*) distracção *f*

absent[2] /əb'sent/ *v refl* **~ o.s.** ausentar-se

absentee /æbsen'tiː/ *n* ausente *mf*, (*P*) absentista *mf*

absolute /'æbsəluːt/ *a* absoluto; [!] ‹*coward etc*› autêntico, (*P*) verdadeiro. **~ly** *adv* absolutamente

absor|b /əb'sɔːb/ *vt* absorver. **~ption** *n* absorção *f*

absorbent /əb'sɔːbənt/ *a* absorvente; **~ cotton** *Amer* algodão hidrófilo *m*

abst|ain /əb'steɪn/ *vi* abster-se (**from** de). **~ention** /-'stenʃn/ *n* abstenção *f*

abstemious /əb'stiːmɪəs/ *a* abstêmio, (*P*) abstémio, sóbrio

abstinen|ce /'æbstɪnəns/ *n* abstinência *f*

abstract[1] /'æbstrækt/ *a* abstrato

abstract[2] /əb'strækt/ *vt* (*take out*) extrair; (*separate*) abstrair

absurd /əb'sɜːd/ *a* absurdo. **~ity** *n* absurdo *m*

abundan|t /ə'bʌndənt/ *a* abundante. **~ce** *n* abundância *f*

abuse[1] /ə'bjuːz/ *vt* (*misuse*) abusar de; (*ill-treat*) maltratar; (*insult*) injuriar, insultar

abus|e[2] /ə'bjuːs/ *n* (*wrong use*) abuso *m* (**of** de); (*insults*) insultos *mpl*. **~ive** *a* injurioso, ofensivo

abysmal /ə'bɪzməl/ *a* abismal; [!] (*bad*) abissal

abyss /ə'bɪs/ *n* abismo *m*

academic /ækə'demɪk/ *a* acadêmico, (*P*) académico, universitário; (*scholarly*) intelectual; *pej* acadêmico; (*P*) teórico ● *n* universitário

academy /ə'kædəmɪ/ *n* academia *f*

accelerat|e /ək'seləreɪt/ *vt* acelerar ● *vi* acelerar-se; *Auto* acelerar. **~ion** /-'reɪʃn/ *n* aceleração *f*

accelerator /ək'seləreɪtə(r)/ *n Auto* acelerador *m*

accent[1] /'æksənt/ *n* acento *m*; (*local pronunciation*) sotaque *m*

accent[2] /æk'sent/ *vt* acentuar

accept /ək'sept/ *vt* aceitar. **~able** *a* aceitável. **~ance** *n* aceitação *f*; (*approval*) aprovação *f*

access /'ækses/ *n* acesso *m* (**to** a). **~ible** /ək'sesəbl/ *a* acessível

accessory /ək'sesərɪ/ *a* acessório ● *n* acessório *m*; *Jur* (*person*) cúmplice *m*

accident /'æksɪdənt/ *n* acidente *m*, desastre *m*; (*chance*) acaso *m*. **~al** /-'dentl/ *a* acidental, fortuito. **~ally** /-'dentəlɪ/ *adv* acidentalmente, por acaso

acclaim /ə'kleɪm/ *vt* aclamar ● *n* aplauso *m*, aclamações *fpl*

acclimatiz|e /ə'klaɪmətaɪz/ *vt/i* aclimatar(-se)

accommodat|e /ə'kɒmədeɪt/ *vt* acomodar; (*lodge*) alojar; (*adapt*) adaptar; (*supply*) fornecer; (*oblige*) fazer a vontade de. **~ing** *a* obsequioso, amigo de fazer vontades. **~ion** /-'deɪʃn/ *n* acomodação *f*; (*rooms*) alojamento *m*, quarto *m*

accompan|y /ə'kʌmpənɪ/ *vt* acompanhar. **~iment** *n* acompanhamento *m*

accomplice /ə'kʌmplɪs/ *n* cúmplice *mf*

accomplish /ə'kʌmplɪʃ/ *vt* (*perform*) executar, realizar; (*achieve*) realizar, conseguir fazer. **~ed** *a* acabado. **~ment** *n* realização *f*; (*ability*) talento *m*, dote *m*

accord /ə'kɔːd/ *vi* concordar ● *vt* conceder ● *n* acordo *m*; **of one's own ~** por vontade própria, espontaneamente. **~ance** *n* **in ~ance with** em conformidade com, de acordo com

according /ə'kɔːdɪŋ/ *adv* **~ to** conforme. **~ly** *adv* (*therefore*) por conseguinte, por consequência; (*appropriately*) conformemente

accordion /ə'kɔːdɪən/ *n* acordeão *m*

accost /ə'kɒst/ *vt* abordar, abeirar-se de

account /ə'kaʊnt/ *n Comm* conta *f*; (*description*) relato *m*; (*importance*) importância *f* ● *vt* considerar; **~ for** dar contas de, explicar; **on ~ of** por causa de; **on no ~** em caso algum; **take into ~** ter or levar em conta. **~ number** *n* número *f* da conta, (*P*) número *m* de conta . **~able** /-əbl/ *a* responsável (**for** por)

accountant /ə'kaʊntənt/ *n* contador(a) *m/f*, (*P*) contabilista *mf*

accumulat|e /ə'kjuːmjʊleɪt/ *vt/i* acumular(-se). **~ion** /-'leɪʃn/ *n* acumulação *f*, acréscimo *m*

accura|te /'ækjərət/ *a* exato, preciso. **~cy** *n* exatidão *f*, precisão *f*

accus|e /ə'kjuːz/ *vt* acusar; **the ~ed** o acusado. **~ation** /ækjuː'zeɪʃn/ *n* acusação *f*

accustom /ə'kʌstəm/ *vt* acostumar, habituar; **get ~ed to** acostumar-se a, habituar-se a. **~ed** *a* acostumado, habituado

ace /eɪs/ *n* ás *m*

ache /eɪk/ *n* dor *f* ● *vi* doer; **my leg ~s** dói-me a perna, tenho dores na perna

achieve /ə'tʃiːv/ *vt* realizar, efetuar; ‹*success*› alcançar. **~ment** *n* realização *f*; ‹*feat*› feito *m*, façanha *f*, sucesso *m*

acid /'æsɪd/ *a* ácido; ‹*wine*› azedo; ‹*words*› áspero ● *n* ácido *m*. **~ity** /ə'sɪdətɪ/ *n* acidez *f*

acknowledge /ək'nɒlɪdʒ/ *vt* reconhecer; **~ (receipt of)** acusar a recepção de. **~ment** *n* reconhecimento *m*; (*letter etc*) acusação *f* de recebimento, (*P*) aviso *m* de recepção

acne /'æknɪ/ *n* acne *mf*

acorn /'eɪkɔːn/ *n* bolota *f*, glande *f*

acoustic /ə'kuːstɪk/ *a* acústico. **~s** *npl* acústica *f*

acquaint /ə'kweɪnt/ *vt* **~ sb with sth** pôr alguém a par de algo; **be ~ed with** ‹*person, fact*› conhecer. **~ance** *n* (*knowledge, person*) conhecimento *m*; (*person*) conhecido *m*

acqui|re /ə'kwaɪə(r)/ *vt* adquirir. **~sition** /ækwɪ'zɪʃn/ *n* aquisição *f*

acquit /ə'kwɪt/ *vt* (*pt* **acquitted**) absolver; **~ o.s. well** sair-se bem. **~tal** *n* absolvição *f*

acrid /'ækrɪd/ *a* acre

acrimon|ious /ækrɪ'məʊnɪəs/ *a* acrimonioso

acrobat /'ækrəbæt/ *n* acrobata *mf*. **~ic** /-'bætɪk/ *a* acrobático. **~ics** /-'bætɪks/ *npl* acrobacia *f*

acronym /'ækrənɪm/ *n* sigla *f*

across /ə'krɒs/ *adv & prep* (*side to side*) de lado a lado (de), de um lado para o outro (de); (*on the other side*) do outro lado (de); (*crosswise*) através (de), de través; **go** or **walk ~** atravessar; **swim ~** atravessar a nado

act /ækt/ *n* (*deed*) *Theatr* ato *m*; (*in variety show*) número *m*; (*decree*) lei *f* ● *vi* agir, atuar; *Theatr* representar; (*function*) funcionar; (*pretend*) fingir ● *vt* ‹*part, role*› desempenhar; **~ as** servir de. **~ing** *a* interino ● *n Theatr* desempenho *m*

action /'ækʃn/ *n* ação *f*; *Mil* combate *m*; **out of ~** fora de combate; *Techn* avariado; **take ~** agir, atuar

activ|e /'æktɪv/ *a* ativo; ‹*interest*› vivo; ‹*volcano*› em atividade. **~ity** /-'tɪvətɪ/ *n* atividade *f*

ac|tor /'æktə(r)/ *n* ator *m*. **~tress** *n* atriz *f*

actual /'æktʃʊəl/ *a* real, verdadeiro; ‹*example*› concreto; **the ~ pen which** a própria caneta que. **~ly** *adv* (*in fact*) na realidade

acupunctur|e /'ækjʊpʌŋktʃə(r)/ *n* acupuntura *f*, (*P*) acupunctura *f*. **~ist** *n* acupunturador *m*, (*P*) acupuncturista *mf*

acute /ə'kjuːt/ *a* agudo; ‹*mind*› perspicaz; ‹*emotion*› intenso, vivo; ‹*shortage*› grande. **~ly** *adv* vivamente

ad /æd/ *n* [!] anúncio *m*

AD *abbr* dC

adamant /'ædəmənt/ *a* inflexível

adapt /ə'dæpt/ *vt/i* adaptar(-se). **~ation** /ædæp'teɪʃn/ *n* adaptação *f*

adaptab|le /ə'dæptəbl/ *a* adaptável

add /æd/ *vt/i* acrescentar; **~ (up)** somar; **~ up to** (*total*) elevar-se a

adder /'ædə(r)/ *n* víbora *f*

addict /'ædɪkt/ *n* viciado *m*; **drug ~** viciado em droga, viciado da droga, (*P*) toxicodependente *mf*

addict|ed /ə'dɪktɪd/ *a* **be ~ed to** ‹*drink, drugs*› *also fig* ter o vício de. **~ion** /-ʃn/ *n Med* dependência *f*; *fig* vício *m*. **~ive** *a* que produz dependência

addition /ə'dɪʃn/ *n* adição *f*; **in ~** além disso; **in ~ to** além de. **~al** /-ʃənl/ *a* adicional, suplementar

address /ə'dres/ *n* endereço *m*; (*speech*) discurso *m* ● *vt* endereçar; (*speak to*) dirigir-se a

adequa|te /'ædɪkwət/ *a* adequado; (*satisfactory*) satisfatório

adhere /əd'hɪə(r)/ *vi* aderir (**to** a)

adhesive /əd'hiːsɪv/ *a & n* adesivo *m*; **~ plaster** esparadrapo *m*, (*P*) adesivo *m*

adjacent /ə'dʒeɪsnt/ *a* adjacente; contíguo (**to** a)

adjective /'ædʒektɪv/ *n* adjetivo *m*

adjoin /ə'dʒɔɪn/ *vt* confinar com, ficar contíguo a

adjourn /ə'dʒɜːn/ *vt* adiar ● *vi* suspender a sessão; **~ to** (*go*) passar a, ir para

adjudicate /ə'dʒuːdɪkeɪt/ *vt/i* julgar; (*award*) adjudicar

adjust /ə'dʒʌst/ *vt/i* (*alter*) ajustar, regular; (*arrange*) arranjar; **~ (o.s.) to** adaptar-se a. **~able** *a* regulável. **~ment** *n Techn* regulação *f*, afinação *f*; (*of person*) adaptação *f*

ad lib /æd'lɪb/ *vi* (*pt* **ad libbed**) [!] improvisar ● *adv* à vontade

a

administer /əd'mɪnɪstə(r)/ *vt* administrar
administrat|e /əd'mɪnɪstreɪt/ *vt* administrar, gerir. **~ion** /-'streɪʃn/ *n* administração *f*. **~or** *n* administrador *m*
admirable /'ædmərəbl/ *a* admirável
admiral /'ædmərəl/ *n* almirante *m*
admir|e /əd'maɪə(r)/ *vt* admirar. **~ation** /-mɪ'reɪʃn/ *n* admiração *f*. **~er** /-'maɪərə(r)/ *n* admirador *m*
admission /əd'mɪʃn/ *n* admissão *f*; (*to museum, theatre, etc*) ingresso *m*, (*P*) entrada *f*; (*confession*) confissão *f*
admit /əd'mɪt/ *vt* (*pt* **admitted**) (*let in*) admitir, permitir a entrada a; (*acknowledge*) reconhecer, admitir; **~ to** confessar. **~tance** *n* admissão *f*
admoni|sh /əd'mɒnɪʃ/ *vt* admoestar
adolescen|t /ædə'lesnt/ *a & n* adolescente *mf*. **~ce** *n* adolescência *f*
adopt /ə'dɒpt/ *vt* adotar; **~ed child** filho adotivo. **~ion** /-ʃn/ *n* adoção *f*
ador|e /ə'dɔ:(r)/ *vt* adorar. **~able** *a* adorável. **~ation** /ædə'reɪʃn/ *n* adoração *f*
adorn /ə'dɔ:n/ *vt* adornar, enfeitar
adrenalin /ə'drenəlɪn/ *n* adrenalina *f*
adrift /ə'drɪft/ *a & adv* à deriva
adult /'ædʌlt/ *a & n* adulto *m*. **~hood** *n* idade *f* adulta, (*P*) maioridade *f*
adulterat|e /ə'dʌltəreɪt/ *vt* adulterar
adulter|y /ə'dʌltərɪ/ *n* adultério *m*. **~er**, **~ess** *ns* adúlter/o, -a *mf*. **~ous** *a* adúltero
advance /əd'vɑ:ns/ *vt/i* avançar ● *n* avanço *m*; (*payment*) adiantamento *m* ● *a* ‹*payment, booking*› adiantado; **in ~** com antecedência. **~d** *a* avançado. **~ment** *n* promoção *f*, ascensão *f*
advantage /əd'vɑ:ntɪdʒ/ *n* vantagem *f*; **take ~ of** aproveitar-se de, tirar partido de; (*person*) explorar. **~ous** /ædvən'teɪdʒəs/ *a* vantajoso
adventur|e /əd'ventʃə(r)/ *n* aventura *f*. **~er** *n* aventureiro *m*, explorador *m*. **~ous** *a* aventuroso
adverb /'ædvɜ:b/ *n* advérbio *m*
adversary /'ædvəsərɪ/ *n* adversário *m*, antagonista *mf*
advers|e /'ædvɜ:s/ *a* (*contrary*) adverso; (*unfavourable*) desfavorável. **~ity** /əd'vɜ:sətɪ/ *n* adversidade *f*
advert /'ædvɜ:t/ *n* [!] anúncio *m*
advertise /'ædvətaɪz/ *vt/i* anunciar, fazer publicidade (de); (*sell*) pôr um anúncio (para); **~ for** procurar. **~r** /-ə(r)/ *n* anunciante *mf*
advertisement /əd'vɜ:tɪsmənt/ *n* anúncio *m*; (*advertising*) publicidade *f*
advice /əd'vaɪs/ *n* conselho(s) *mpl*; *Comm* aviso *m*
advis|e /əd'vaɪz/ *vt* aconselhar; (*inform*) avisar, informar; **~e against** desaconselhar. **~able** *a* aconselhável. **~er** *n* conselheiro *m*; (*in business*) consultor *m*. **~ory** *a* consultivo
advocate[1] /'ædvəkət/ *n Jur* advogado *m*; (*supporter*) defensor(a) *mf*
advocate[2] /'ædvəkeɪt/ *vt* advogar, defender
aerial /'eərɪəl/ *a* aéreo ● *n* antena *f*
aerobics /eə'rəʊbɪks/ *n* ginástica *f* aeróbica
aeroplane /'eərəpleɪn/ *n* avião *m*
aerosol /'eərəsɒl/ *n* aerossol *m*
aesthetic /i:s'θetɪk/ *a* estético
affair /ə'feə(r)/ *n* (*business*) negócio *m*; (*romance*) ligação *f*, aventura *f*; (*matter*) assunto *m*; **love ~** paixão *f*
affect /ə'fekt/ *vt* afetar. **~ation** /æfek'teɪʃn/ *n* afetação *f*. **~ed** *a* afetado, pretencioso
affection /ə'fekʃn/ *n* afeição *f*, afeto *m*
affectionate /ə'fekʃənət/ *a* afetuoso, carinhoso
affiliat|e /ə'fɪlɪeɪt/ *vt* afiliar; **~ed company** filial *f*. **~ion** /-'eɪʃn/ *n* afiliação *f*
affirm /ə'fɜ:m/ *vt* afirmar. **~ation** /æfə'meɪʃn/ *n* afirmação *f*
affirmative /ə'fɜ:mətɪv/ *a* afirmativo ● *n* afirmativa *f*
afflict /ə'flɪkt/ *vt* afligir. **~ion** /-ʃn/ *n* aflição *f*
affluen|t /'æfluənt/ *a* rico, afluente. **~ce** *n* riqueza *f*, afluência *f*
afford /ə'fɔ:d/ *vt* (*have money for*) permitir-se, ter meios (para); **can you ~ the time?** você teria tempo?; **I can't ~ a car** eu não posso comprar um carro; **we can't ~ to lose** não podemos perder
affront /ə'frʌnt/ *n* afronta *f* ● *vt* insultar
afloat /ə'fləʊt/ *adv & a* à tona, a flutuar; (*at sea*) no mar; ‹*business*› lançado, (*P*) sem dívidas
afraid /ə'freɪd/ *a* **be ~** ter medo (**of, to** de **that** que); (*be sorry*) lamentar, ter muita pena; **I'm ~ (that)** (*regret to say*) lamento or tenho muita pena de dizer que
Africa /'æfrɪkə/ *n* África *f*. **~n** *a & n* africano *m*

after /ɑːftə(r)/ *adv* depois ● *prep* depois de ● *conj* depois que; **~ all** afinal de contas; **~ doing** depois de fazer; **be ~** (*seek*) querer, pretender. **~-effect** *n* sequela *f*, efeito *m* retardado; (*of drug*) efeito *m* secundário

aftermath /'ɑːftəmæθ/ *n* consequências *fpl*

afternoon /ɑːftə'nuːn/ *n* tarde *f*

aftershave /'ɑːftəʃeɪv/ *n* loção *f* pós-barba, (*P*) loção *f* para a barba

afterthought /'ɑːftəθɔːt/ *n* reflexão *f* posterior; **as an ~** pensando melhor

afterwards /'ɑːftəwədz/ *adv* depois, mais tarde

again /ə'gen/ *adv* de novo, outra vez; (*on the other hand*) por outro lado; **then ~** além disso

against /ə'genst/ *prep* contra

age /eɪdʒ/ *n* idade *f*; (*period*) época *f*, idade *f*; **~s** ! (*very long time*) há séculos *mpl*; **of ~** *Jur* maior; **ten years of ~** com/de dez anos; **under ~** menor ● *vt/i* (*pres p* **ageing**) envelhecer. **~ group** *n* faixa etária *f*. **~less** *a* sempre jovem

aged[1] /eɪdʒd/ *a* **~ six** de seis anos de idade

aged[2] /'eɪdʒɪd/ *a* idoso, velho

agen|cy /'eɪdʒənsɪ/ *n* agência *f*; (*means*) intermédio *m*. **~t** *n* agente *mf*

agenda /ə'dʒendə/ *n* ordem *f* do dia

aggravat|e /'ægrəveɪt/ *vt* agravar; ! (*annoy*) irritar. **~ion** /-'veɪʃn/ *n* (*worsening*) agravamento *m*; (*exasperation*) irritação *f*; ! (*trouble*) aborrecimentos *mpl*

aggregate /'ægrɪgeɪt/ *vt/i* agregar(-se) ● /'ægrɪgət/ *a* total, global ● *n* (*total, mass, materials*) agregado *m*; **in the ~** no todo

aggress|ive /ə'gresɪv/ *a* agressivo; (*weapons*) ofensivo. **~ion** /-ʃn/ *n* agressão *f*. **~or** *n* agressor *m*

agil|e /'ædʒaɪl/ *a* ágil. **~ity** /ə'dʒɪlətɪ/ *n* agilidade *f*

agitat|e /'ædʒɪteɪt/ *vt* agitar. **~ion** /-'teɪʃn/ *n* agitação *f*

agnostic /æg'nɒstɪk/ *a & n* agnóstico *m*

ago /ə'gəʊ/ *adv* há; **a month ~** há um mês; **long ~** há muito tempo

agon|y /'ægənɪ/ *n* agonia *f*; (*mental*) angústia *f*. **~ize** *vi* atormentar-se, torturar-se

agree /ə'griː/ *vt/i* concordar; (*of figures*) acertar; **~ that** reconhecer que; **~ to do** concordar em or aceitar fazer; **~ to sth** concordar com alguma coisa; **seafood doesn't ~ with me** não me dou bem com mariscos. **~d** *a* ‹*time, place*› combinado; **be ~d** estar de acordo

agreeable /ə'griːəbl/ *a* agradável; **be ~ to** estar de acordo com

agreement /ə'griːmənt/ *n* acordo *m*; *Gramm* concordância *f*; (*contract*) contrato *m*; **in ~** de acordo

agricultur|e /'ægrɪkʌltʃə(r)/ *n* agricultura *f*. **~al** /-'kʌltʃərəl/ *a* agrícola

aground /ə'graʊnd/ *adv* **run ~** (*of ship*) encalhar

ahead /ə'hed/ *adv* à frente, adiante; (*in advance*) adiantado; **~ of sb** diante de alguém, à frente de alguém; **~ of time** antes da hora, adiantado; **straight ~** sempre em frente

aid /eɪd/ *vt* ajudar; **~ and abet** ser cúmplice de ● *n* ajuda *f*; **in ~ of** em auxílio de, a favor de

AIDS /eɪdz/ *n Med* AIDS *f*, (*P*) sida *m*. **~ awareness** *n* conscientização *f* sobre a AIDS, (*P*) consciencialização *f* sobre a SIDA; **~ virus** *n* vírus *m* da AIDS, (*P*) vírus *m* da SIDA

aim /eɪm/ *vt* ‹*gun*› apontar; ‹*efforts*› dirigir; (*send*) atirar (**at** para) ● *vi* visar ● *n* alvo *m*; **~ at** visar; **~ to** aspirar a, tencionar; **take ~** fazer pontaria. **~less** *a*, **~lessly** *adv* sem objetivo

air /eə(r)/ *n* ar *m*; **in the ~** ‹*rumour*› espalhado; ‹*plans*› no ar; **on the ~** *Radio* no ar ● *vt* arejar; ‹*views*› expor ● *a* ‹*base etc*› aéreo; **~ force** Força *f* Aérea; **~ hostess** aeromoça *f*, (*P*) hospedeira *f* de bordo; **~ raid** ataque *m* aéreo. **~-conditioned** *a* com ar condicionado; **~ conditioning** *n* condicionamento *m* do ar, (*P*) ar *m* condicionado; **~ strike** *n* ataque *m* aéreo

aircraft /'eəkrɑːft/ *n* (*pl invar*) avião *m*. **~ carrier** *n* porta-aviões *m*

airfield /'eəfiːld/ *n* campo *m* de aviação

airgun /'eəgʌn/ *n* espingarda *f* de pressão

airlift /'eəlɪft/ *n* ponte *f* aérea ● *vt* transportar em ponte aérea

airline /'eəlaɪn/ *n* linha *f* aérea

airmail /'eəmeɪl/ *n* correio *m* aéreo; **by ~** por avião

airport /'eəpɔːt/ *n* aeroporto *m*

airtight /'eətaɪt/ *a* hermético

airy /'eərɪ/ *a* (**-ier, -iest**) arejado; ‹*manner*› desenvolto

aisle /aɪl/ *n* (*of church*) nave *f* lateral; (*gangway*) coxia *f*

a

ajar /ə'dʒɑː(r)/ *adv & a* entreaberto

à la carte /ɑːlɑː'kɑːt/ *adv & a* à la carte, (*P*) à lista

alarm /ə'lɑːm/ *n* alarme *m*; (*clock*) campainha *f* ● *vt* alarmar. **~ clock** *n* despertador *m*. **~ing** *a* alarmante

alas /ə'læs/ *int* ai! ai de mim!

album /'ælbəm/ *n* álbum *m*

alcohol /'ælkəhɒl/ *n* álcool *m*. **~ic** /-'hɒlɪk/ *a* ‹*person, drink*› alcoólico ● *n* alcoólico *m*. **~ism** *n* alcoolismo *m*

alcove /'ælkəʊv/ *n* recesso *m*, alcova *f*

ale /eɪl/ *n* cerveja *f* inglesa

alert /ə'lɜːt/ *a* (*lively*) vivo; (*watchful*) vigilante ● *n* alerta *m*; **be on the ~** estar alerta ● *vt* alertar

algebra /'ældʒɪbrə/ *n* álgebra *f*

Algeria /æl'dʒɪərɪə/ *n* Argélia *f*

alias /'eɪlɪəs/ *n* (*pl* **-ases**) outro nome *m*, nome falso *m*, (*P*) pseudónimo *m* ● *adv* aliás

alibi /'ælɪbaɪ/ *n* (*pl* **-is**) álibi *m*, (*P*) alibi *m*

alien /'eɪlɪən/ *n & a* estrangeiro *m*; **~ to** (*contrary*) contrário a; (*differing*) alheio a, estranho a

alienat|e /'eɪlɪəneɪt/ *vt* alienar

alight[1] /ə'laɪt/ *vi* descer; (*bird*) pousar

alight[2] /ə'laɪt/ *a* (*on fire*) em chamas; (*lit up*) aceso

align /ə'laɪn/ *vt* alinhar. **~ment** *n* alinhamento *m*

alike /ə'laɪk/ *a* semelhante, parecido ● *adv* da mesma maneira; **look** or **be ~** parecer-se

alimony /'ælɪmənɪ/ *n* pensão *f* alimentar, (*P*) de alimentos

alive /ə'laɪv/ *a* vivo; **~ to** sensível a; **~ with** fervilhando de, (*P*) a fervilhar de

alkali /'ælkəlaɪ/ *n* (*pl* **-is**) álcali *m*, (*P*) alcali *m*

all /ɔːl/ ● *a*

····➤ (*with singular noun*) todo, toda; **~ the wine** o vinho todo; **~ my money** todo o meu dinheiro

····➤ (*with plural noun*) todos, todas; **~ the men** todos os homens; **~ the women** todas as mulheres

● *pron*

····➤ (*plural*) todos, todas; **~ are here** todos estão aqui; **are we ~ going?** vamos todos?

····➤ (*everything*) tudo; **~ she said was...** tudo o que ela disse foi...; **I ate ~ of it** Eu comi tudo

····➤ (*in phrases*) **~ in ~** de modo geral; **in ~** (*in total*) no total; **not at ~** (*in no way*) de modo algum; **it was not at ~ expensive** não foi nem um pouco caro; (*answer to 'thank you'*) de nada

● *adv*

····➤ (*completely*) completamente; **~ by myself** completamente só; **~ in white** todo de branco; (*in scores*) **two ~** dois a dois

····➤ (*in phrases*) **~ along** todo o tempo; **~ but** quase, todos menos; **~ in** (*exhausted*) esgotado; **~ over** (*in all parts of*) por todo; **I ache ~ over** dói-me o corpo inteiro; **~ the better/less/more/worse** *etc* tanto melhor/menos/mais/pior *etc*; **~ right** bem; (*as a response*) está bem.

~-in *a* tudo incluído; **~-out** *a* ‹*effort*› máximo; **~-round** *a* completo

allegation /ælɪ'geɪʃn/ *n* alegação *f*

allege /ə'ledʒ/ *vt* alegar

allegiance /ə'liːdʒəns/ *n* fidelidade *f*, lealdade *f*

allerg|y /'ælədʒɪ/ *n* alergia *f*. **~ic** /ə'lɜːdʒɪk/ *a* alérgico

alleviate /ə'liːvɪeɪt/ *vt* aliviar

alley /'ælɪ/ *n* (*pl* **-eys**) (*street*) viela *f*; (*for bowling*) pista *f*

alliance /ə'laɪəns/ *n* aliança *f*

allied /'ælaɪd/ *a* aliado

alligator /'ælɪgeɪtə(r)/ *n* jacaré *m*

allocat|e /'æləkeɪt/ *vt* (*share out*) distribuir; (*assign*) destinar. **~ion** /-'keɪʃn/ *n* atribuição *f*

allot /ə'lɒt/ *vt* (*pt* **allotted**) atribuir. **~ment** *n* atribuição *f*; (*share*) distribuição *f*; (*land*) horta *f* alugada

allow /ə'laʊ/ *vt* permitir; (*grant*) conceder, dar; (*reckon on*) contar com; (*agree*) admitir, reconhecer; **~ sb to** permitir a alguém (+ *inf*) or que (+ *subj*); **~ for** levar em conta

allowance /ə'laʊəns/ *n* (*for employees*) ajudas *fpl* de custo; (*monthly, for wife, child*) benefício *m*; (*tax*) desconto *m*; **make ~s for** (*person*) levar em consideração, ser indulgente para com; (*take into account*) atender a, levar em consideração

alloy /'ælɔɪ/ *n* liga *f*

allude /ə'luːd/ *vi* **~ to** aludir a

allure /ə'lʊə(r)/ *vt* seduzir, atrair

allusion /ə'luːʒn/ *n* alusão *f*

ally[1] /'ælaɪ/ *n* (*pl* **-lies**) aliado *m*

ally[2] /əˈlaɪ/ *vt* aliar; **~ oneself with/to** aliar-se com/a

almighty /ɔːlˈmaɪtɪ/ *a* todo-poderoso; [!] grande; formidável

almond /ˈɑːmənd/ *n* amêndoa *f*; **~ paste** maçapão *m*

almost /ˈɔːlməʊst/ *adv* quase

alone /əˈləʊn/ *a & adv* só; **leave ~** (*abstain from interfering with*) deixar em paz; **let ~** (*without considering*) sem or para não falar de

along /əˈlɒŋ/ *prep* ao longo de ● *adv* (*onward*) para diante; **all ~** durante todo o tempo; **~ with** com; **move ~, please** ande, por favor

alongside /əlɒŋˈsaɪd/ *adv Naut* atracado; **come ~** acostar ● *prep* ao lado de

aloof /əˈluːf/ *adv* à parte ● *a* distante

aloud /əˈlaʊd/ *adv* em voz alta

alphabet /ˈælfəbet/ *n* alfabeto *m*. **~ical** /-ˈbetɪkl/ *a* alfabético

alpine /ˈælpaɪn/ *a* alpino, alpestre

Alps /ælps/ *npl* **the ~** os Alpes *mpl*

Al-Qaeda /ˌælkæˈiːdə/ *pr n* Al-Qaeda *f*, (*P*) Alcaida *f*

already /ɔːlˈredɪ/ *adv* já

also /ˈɔlːsəʊ/ *adv* também

altar /ˈɔːltə(r)/ *n* altar *m*

alter /ˈɔːltə(r)/ *vt/i* alterar(-se), modificar(-se). **~ation** /-ˈreɪʃn/ *n* alteração *f*; (*to garment*) modificação *f*

alternate[1] /ɔːlˈtɜːnət/ *a* alternado

alternat|e[2] /ˈɔːltəneɪt/ *vt/i* alternar(-se); **~ing current** *Electr* corrente *f* alterna

alternative /ɔːlˈtɜːnətɪv/ *a* alternativo ● *n* alternativa *f*. **~ly** *adv* em alternativa; **or ~ly** ou então

although /ɔːlˈðəʊ/ *conj* embora, conquanto

altitude /ˈæltɪtjuːd/ *n* altitude *f*

altogether /ɔːltəˈgeðə(r)/ *adv* (*completely*) completamente; (*in total*) ao todo; (*on the whole*) de modo geral

aluminium /æljʊˈmɪnɪəm/ *Amer* **aluminum** /əˈluːmɪnəm/ *n* alumínio *m*

always /ˈɔːlweɪz/ *adv* sempre

am /æm/ ▶ BE

a.m. /eɪˈem/ *adv* da manhã

amass /əˈmæs/ *vt* amontoar, juntar

amateur /ˈæmətə(r)/ *n & a* amador *m*. **~ish** *a pej* de amador, (*P*) amadorístico

amaz|e /əˈmeɪz/ *vt* assombrar, espantar. **~ed** *a* assombrado. **~ement** *n* assombro *m*

Amazon /ˈæməzən/ *n* **the ~** o Amazonas

ambassador /æmˈbæsədə(r)/ *n* embaixador *m*

amber /ˈæmbə(r)/ *n* âmbar *m*; (*traffic light*) luz *f* amarela

ambigu|ous /æmˈbɪgjʊəs/ *a* ambíguo. **~ity** /-ˈgjuːətɪ/ *n* ambiguidade *f*

ambiti|on /æmˈbɪʃn/ *n* ambição *f*. **~ous** *a* ambicioso

ambivalen|t /æmˈbɪvələnt/ *a* ambivalente

amble /ˈæmbl/ *vi* caminhar sem pressa

ambulance /ˈæmbjʊləns/ *n* ambulância *f*

ambush /ˈæmbʊʃ/ *n* emboscada *f* ● *vt* fazer uma emboscada para, (*P*) fazer uma emboscada a

amend /əˈmend/ *vt* emendar, corrigir. **~ment** *n* (*to rule*) emenda *f*. **~s** *n* **make ~s for** reparar, compensar

amenities /əˈmiːnətɪz/ *npl* (*pleasant features*) atrativos *mpl*; (*facilities*) confortos *mpl*, comodidades *fpl*

America /əˈmerɪkə/ *n* América *f*. **~n** *a & n* americano *m*. **~nism** /-nɪzəm/ *n* americanismo *m*

> **American dream** O conceito de "sonho americano" baseia-se na ideia de que qualquer pessoa que vive nos Estados Unidos pode alcançar o sucesso se trabalhar arduamente. Para os imigrantes e para as minorias, o conceito inclui também liberdade e igualdade de direitos.

amiable /ˈeɪmɪəbl/ *a* amável

amicable /ˈæmɪkəbl/ *a* amigável, amigo

amid(st) /ˈəmɪd(st)/ *prep* entre, no meio de

amiss /əˈmɪs/ *a & adv* mal; **sth ~** qq coisa que não está bem; **take sth ~** levar qq coisa a mal

ammonia /əˈməʊnɪə/ *n* amoníaco *m*

ammunition /æmjʊˈnɪʃn/ *n* munições *fpl*

amnesia /æmˈniːzɪə/ *n* amnésia *f*

amnesty /ˈæmnəstɪ/ *n* anistia *f*, (*P*) amnistia *f*

among(st) /əˈmʌŋ(st)/ *prep* entre, no meio de; **~ ourselves** (aqui) entre nós

amoral /eɪˈmɒrəl/ *a* amoral

amorous /ˈæmərəs/ *a* amoroso

a

amount /ə'maʊnt/ *n* quantidade *f*; (*total*) montante *m*; (*sum of money*) quantia *f* ● *vi* ~ **to** elevar-se a; *fig* equivaler a

amp /æmp/ *n* ⓘ ampere *m*

amphibi|an /æm'fɪbɪən/ *n* anfíbio *m*. ~**ous** *a* anfíbio

ampl|e /'æmpl/ *a* (**-er**, **-est**) (*large, roomy*) amplo; (*enough*) suficiente, bastante

amplif|y /'æmplɪfaɪ/ *vt* ampliar, amplificar. ~**ier** *n* amplificador *m*

amputat|e /'æmpjʊteɪt/ *vt* amputar. ~**ion** /-'teɪʃn/ *n* amputação *f*

amus|e /ə'mju:z/ *vt* divertir. ~**ement** *n* divertimento *m*. ~**ing** *a* divertido

an /ən, æn/ ▶ **A**

anaem|ia /ə'ni:mɪə/ *n* anemia *f*. ~**ic** *a* anêmico, (*P*) anémico

anaesthetic /ænɪs'θetɪk/ *n* anestético *m*, (*P*) anestésico *m*; **give an ~ to** anestesiar

anaesthetist /ə'ni:sθətɪst/ *n* anestesista *mf*

anagram /'ænəgræm/ *n* anagrama *m*

analog(ue) /'ænəlɒg/ *a* análogo

analogy /ə'nælədʒɪ/ *n* analogia *f*

analys|e /'ænəlaɪz/ *vt* analisar. ~**t** /-ɪst/ *n* analista *mf*

analysis /ə'næləsɪs/ *n* (*pl* **-yses** /-əsi:z/) análise *f*

analytic(al) /ænə'lɪtɪk(l)/ *a* analítico

anarch|y /'ænəkɪ/ *n* anarquia *f*. ~**ist** *n* anarquista *mf*

anatom|y /ə'nætəmɪ/ *n* anatomia *f*. ~**ical** /ænə'tɒmɪkl/ *a* anatômico, (*P*) anatómico

ancest|or /'ænsestə(r)/ *n* antepassado *m*

ancestry /'ænsestrɪ/ *n* ascendência *f*, estirpe *f*

anchor /'æŋkə(r)/ *n* âncora *f* ● *vt/i* ancorar

ancient /'eɪnʃənt/ *a* antigo

and /ənd emphatic ænd/ *conj* e; **go ~ see** vá ver; **better ~ better/less ~ less** *etc* cada vez melhor/menos *etc*

anecdote /'ænɪkdəʊt/ *n* anedota *f*

angel /'eɪndʒl/ *n* anjo *m*. ~**ic** /æn'dʒelɪk/ *a* angélico, angelical

anger /'æŋgə(r)/ *n* cólera *f*, zanga *f* ● *vt* irritar

angle[1] /'æŋgl/ *n* ângulo *m*

angle[2] /'æŋgl/ *vi* (*fish*) pescar (à linha); **~ for** *fig* ‹*compliments, information*› andar à procura de. ~**r** /-ə(r)/ *n* pescador *m*

Anglo-Saxon /æŋgləʊ'sæksn/ *a & n* anglo-saxão *m*

angr|y /'æŋgrɪ/ *a* (**-ier**, **-iest**) zangado; **get ~y** zangar-se (**with** com)

anguish /'æŋgwɪʃ/ *n* angústia *f*

angular /'æŋgjʊlə(r)/ *a* angular; ‹*features*› › anguloso

animal /'ænɪml/ *a & n* animal *m*

animate[1] /'ænɪmət/ *a* animado

animat|e[2] /'ænɪmeɪt/ *vt* animar; **~ed cartoon** filme *m* de bonecos animados *or* (*P*) de desenhos animados. ~**ion** /-'meɪʃn/ *n* animação *f*

animosity /ænɪ'mɒsətɪ/ *n* animosidade *f*

aniseed /'ænɪsi:d/ *n* semente *f* de anis

ankle /'æŋkl/ *n* tornozelo *m*; **~ sock** meia *f* soquete

annex /ə'neks/ *vt* anexar

annexe /'æneks/ *n* anexo *m*

annihilate /ə'naɪəleɪt/ *vt* aniquilar

anniversary /ænɪ'vɜ:sərɪ/ *n* aniversário *m*

announce /ə'naʊns/ *vt* anunciar. ~**ment** *n* anúncio *m*. ~**r** /-ə(r)/ *n Radio, TV* locutor *m*

annoy /ə'nɔɪ/ *vt* irritar, aborrecer. ~**ance** *n* aborrecimento *m*. ~**ed** *a* aborrecido (**with** com); **get ~ed** aborrecer-se. ~**ing** *a* irritante

annual /'ænjʊəl/ *a* anual ● *n Bot* planta *f* anual; (*book*) anuário *m*

annul /ə'nʌl/ *vt* (*pt* **annulled**) anular

anomal|y /ə'nɒməlɪ/ *n* anomalia *f*

anonym|ous /ə'nɒnɪməs/ *a* anônimo, (*P*) anónimo

anorak /'ænəræk/ *n* anoraque *m*, anorak *m*

another /ə'nʌðə(r)/ *a & pron* (um) outro; **~ ten minutes** mais dez minutos; **to one ~** um ao outro, uns aos outros

answer /'ɑ:nsə(r)/ *n* resposta *f*; (*solution*) solução *f* ● *vt* responder a; ‹*prayer*› atender a ● *vi* responder; **~ the door** atender à porta; **~ back** retrucar, (*P*) responder torto; **~ for** responder por. **~ing machine** *n* secretária *f* eletrônica, (*P*) atendedor *m* de chamadas

ant /ænt/ *n* formiga *f*

antagonis|m /æn'tægənɪzəm/ *n* antagonismo *m*. ~**tic** /-'nɪstɪk/ *a* antagônico, (*P*) antagónico, hostil

antagonize /æn'tægənaɪz/ *vt* antagonizar, hostilizar

Antarctic /æn'tɑːktɪk/ *n* Antártico, (*P*) Antárctico *m* ● *a* antártico, (*P*) antárctico

antelope /'æntɪləʊp/ *n* antílope *m*

antenatal /æntɪ'neɪtl/ *a* pré-natal

antenna /æn'tenə/ *n* (*pl* **-ae** /-iː/) antena *f*

anthem /'ænθəm/ *n* cântico *m*; **national ~** hino *m* nacional

anthology /æn'θɒlədʒɪ/ *n* antologia *f*

anthropolog|y /ænθrə'pɒlədʒɪ/ *n* antropologia *f*. **~ist** *n* antropólogo *m*

anti- /æntɪ/ *pref* anti-

antibiotic /æntɪbaɪ'ɒtɪk/ *n* antibiótico *m*

antibody /'æntɪbɒdɪ/ *n* anticorpo *m*

anticipat|e /æn'tɪsɪpeɪt/ *vt* (*foresee, expect*) prever; (*forestall*) antecipar-se a. **~ion** /-'peɪʃn/ *n* antecipação *f*; (*expectation*) expectativa *f*; **in ~ion of** na previsão or expectativa de

anticlimax /æntɪ'klaɪmæks/ *n* anticlímax *m*; (*let-down*) decepção *f*; **it was an ~** não correspondeu à expectativa

anticlockwise /æntɪ'klɒkwaɪz/ *adv & a* no sentido contrário ao dos ponteiros do relógio

antics /'æntɪks/ *npl* (*of clown*) palhaçadas *fpl*; (*behaviour*) comportamento *m* bizarro

antidote /'æntɪdəʊt/ *n* antídoto *m*

antifreeze /'æntɪfriːz/ *n* anticongelante *m*

antipathy /æn'tɪpəθɪ/ *n* antipatia *f*

antiquated /'æntɪkweɪtɪd/ *a* antiquado

antique /æn'tiːk/ *a* antigo ● *n* antiguidade *f*; **~ dealer** antiquário *m*; **~ shop** loja *f* de antiguidades, (*P*) antiquário *m*

antiquity /æn'tɪkwətɪ/ *n* antiguidade *f*

antiseptic /æntɪ'septɪk/ *a & n* antisséptico *m*

antisocial /æntɪ'səʊʃl/ *a* antissocial; (*unsociable*) insociável

antlers /'æntləz/ *npl* chifres *mpl*, esgalhos *mpl*

antonym /'æntənɪm/ *n* antônimo *m*, (*P*) antónimo *m*

anus /'eɪnəs/ *n* ânus *m*

anvil /'ænvɪl/ *n* bigorna *f*

anxiety /æŋ'zaɪətɪ/ *n* ansiedade *f*; (*eagerness*) ânsia *f*

anxious /'æŋkʃəs/ *a* (*worried, eager*) ansioso (**to** de, por)

any /'enɪ/ *a & pron* qualquer, quaisquer; (*in neg and interr sentences*) algum, alguns; (*in neg sentences*) nenhum, nenhuns; (*every*) todo; **at ~ moment** a qualquer momento; **at ~ rate** de qualquer modo, em todo o caso; **in ~ case** em todo o caso; **have you ~ money/friends**? você tem (algum) dinheiro/(alguns) amigos?; **I don't have ~ time** não tenho nenhum tempo or tempo nenhum or tempo algum; **has she ~?** ela tem algum?; **she doesn't have ~** ela não tem nenhum ● *adv* (*at all*) de modo algum or nenhum; (*a little*) um pouco; **~ the less/ the worse** *etc* menos/pior *etc*

anybody /'enɪbɒdɪ/ *pron* qualquer pessoa; (*somebody*) alguém; (*after negative*) ninguém; **he didn't see ~** ele não viu ninguém

anyhow /'enɪhaʊ/ *adv* (*no matter how*) de qualquer modo; (*badly*) de qualquer maneira, ao acaso; (*in any case*) em todo o caso; **you can try, ~** em todo o caso, você pode tentar

anyone /'enɪwʌn/ *pron* = ANYBODY

anything /'enɪθɪŋ/ *pron* (*something*) alguma coisa; (*no matter what*) qualquer coisa; (*after negative*) nada; **~ you do** tudo o que você fizer; **he didn't say ~** não disse nada; **it is ~ but cheap** é tudo menos barato

anyway /'enɪweɪ/ *adv* de qualquer modo; (*in any case*) em todo o caso

anywhere /'enɪweə(r)/ *adv* (*somewhere*) em qualquer parte; (*after negative*) em parte alguma/nenhuma; **~ else** em qualquer outro lado; **~ you go** onde quer que você vá; **he doesn't go ~** ele não vai a lado nenhum

apart /ə'pɑːt/ *adv* à parte; (*separated*) separado; (*into pieces*) aos bocados; **~ from** à parte, além de; **ten metres ~** a dez metros de distância entre si; **come ~** desfazer-se; **keep ~** manter separado; **take ~** desmontar

apartment /ə'pɑːtmənt/ *n Amer* apartamento *m*; **~s** aposentos *mpl*

apath|y /'æpəθɪ/ *n* apatia *f*

ape /eɪp/ *n* macaco *m* ● *vt* macaquear

aperitif /ə'perətɪf/ *n* aperitivo *m*

apex /'eɪpeks/ *n* ápice *m*, cume *m*

apologetic /əpɒlə'dʒetɪk/ *a* ‹*tone etc*› apologético, de desculpas; **be ~** desculpar-se

apologize /ə'pɒlədʒaɪz/ *vi* desculpar-se (**for** de, por **to** junto de, perante) pedir desculpa (**for** por)

a

apology /ə'pɒlədʒɪ/ *n* desculpa *f*; (*defence of belief*) apologia *f*

apostle /ə'pɒsl/ *n* apóstolo *m*

apostrophe /ə'pɒstrəfɪ/ *n* apóstrofe *f*

appal /ə'pɔ:l/ *vt* (*pt* **-led**) estarrecer. **~ling** *a* estarrecedor

apparatus /æpə'reɪtəs/ *n* aparelho *m*

apparent /ə'pærənt/ *a* aparente. **~ly** *adv* aparentemente

apparition /æpə'rɪʃn/ *n* aparição *f*

appeal /ə'pi:l/ *vi Jur* apelar (**to** para); (*attract*) atrair (**to** a); (*for funds*) angariar ● *n* apelo *m*; (*attractiveness*) atrativo *m*; (*for funds*) angariação *f*; **~ to sb for sth** pedir algo a alguém. **~ing** *a* (*attractive*) atraente

appear /ə'pɪə(r)/ *vi* aparecer; (*seem*) parecer; (*in court, theatre*) apresentar-se. **~ance** *n* aparição *f*; (*aspect*) aparência *f*; (*in court*) comparecimento *m*, (*P*) comparência *f*

appease /ə'pi:z/ *vt* apaziguar

appendicitis /əpendɪ'saɪtɪs/ *n* apendicite *f*

appendix /ə'pendɪks/ *n* (*pl* **-ices** /-si:z/) (*of book*) apêndice *m*; (*pl* **-ixes** /-ksɪz/) *Anat* apêndice *m*

appetite /'æpɪtaɪt/ *n* apetite *m*

appetizer /'æpɪtaɪzə(r)/ *n* (*snack*) tira-gosto *m*, (*P*) aperitivo *m*; (*drink*) aperitivo *m*

appetizing /'æpɪtaɪzɪŋ/ *a* apetitoso

applau|d /ə'plɔ:d/ *vt/i* aplaudir. **~se** *n* aplauso(s) *m(pl)*

apple /'æpl/ *n* maçã *f*; **~ tree** macieira *f*

appliance /ə'plaɪəns/ *n* aparelho *m*, instrumento *m*, utensílio *m*; **household ~s** utensílios *mpl* domésticos

applicable /'æplɪkəbl/ *a* aplicável

applicant /'æplɪkənt/ *n* candidato *m* (**for** a)

application /æplɪ'keɪʃn/ *n* aplicação *f*; (*request*) pedido *m*; (*form*) formulário *m*; (*for job*) candidatura *f*

appl|y /ə'plaɪ/ *vt* aplicar ● *vi* **~y to** (*refer*) aplicar-se a; (*ask*) dirigir-se a; **~y for** ‹*job, grant*› candidatar-se a; **~y o.s. to** aplicar-se a. **~ied** *a* aplicado

appoint /ə'pɔɪnt/ *vt* (*to post*) nomear; ‹*time, date*› marcar. **well-~ed** *a* bem equipado, bem provido. **~ment** *n* nomeação *f*; (*meeting*) entrevista *f*; (*with friends*) encontro *m*; (*with doctor etc*) consulta *f*, (*P*) marcação *f*; (*job*) posto *m*

apprais|e /ə'preɪz/ *vt* avaliar. **~al** *n* avaliação *f*

appreciable /ə'pri:ʃəbl/ *a* apreciável

appreciat|e /ə'pri:ʃɪeɪt/ *vt* (*value*) apreciar; (*understand*) compreender; (*be grateful for*) estar/ficar grato por ● *vi* encarecer. **~ion** /-'eɪʃn/ *n* apreciação *f*; (*rise in value*) encarecimento *m*; (*gratitude*) reconhecimento *m*. **~ive** /ə'pri:ʃɪətɪv/ *a* apreciador; (*grateful*) reconhecido

apprehen|d /æprɪ'hend/ *vt* (*seize, understand*) apreender; (*dread*) recear. **~sion** *n* apreensão *f*

apprehensive /æprɪ'hensɪv/ *a* apreensivo

apprentice /ə'prentɪs/ *n* aprendiz, -a *mf* ● *vt* pôr como aprendiz (**to** de). **~ship** *n* aprendizagem *f*

approach /ə'prəʊtʃ/ *vt* aproximar; (*with request or offer*) abordar ● *vi* aproximar-se ● *n* aproximação *f*; **~ to** ‹*problem*› abordagem *f* de; ‹*place*› acesso *m* a; ‹*person*› diligência junto de. **~able** *a* acessível

appropriate[1] /ə'prəʊprɪət/ *a* apropriado, próprio

appropriate[2] /ə'prəʊprɪeɪt/ *vt* apropriar-se de

approval /ə'pru:vl/ *n* aprovação *f*; **on ~** *Comm* sob condição, à aprovação

approv|e /ə'pru:v/ *vt/i* aprovar; **~e of** aprovar

approximate[1] /ə'prɒksɪmət/ *a* aproximado. **~ly** *adv* aproximadamente

approximat|e[2] /ə'prɒksɪmeɪt/ *vt/i* aproximar(-se) de. **~ion** /-'meɪʃn/ *n* aproximação *f*

apricot /'eɪprɪkɒt/ *n* damasco *m*

April /'eɪprəl/ *n* Abril *m*; **~ Fool's Day** o primeiro de Abril, o dia das mentiras; **make an ~ fool of** pregar uma mentira em, (*P*) pregar uma mentira a

apron /'eɪprən/ *n* avental *m*

apt /æpt/ *a* apto; ‹*pupil*› dotado; **be ~ to** ser propenso a

aptitude /'æptɪtju:d/ *n* aptidão *f*, (*P*) aptitude *f*

aqualung /'ækwəlʌŋ/ *n* escafandro autônomo, (*P*) autónomo *m*

aquarium /ə'kweərɪəm/ *n* (*pl* **-ums**) aquário *m*

Aquarius /ə'kwɛərɪəs/ *n Astr* Aquário *m*

aquatic /ə'kwætɪk/ *a* aquático; ‹*sport*› náutico, aquático

Arab /'ærəb/ *a* & *n* árabe *mf*. **~ic** *a* & *n* *Lang* árabe *m*, arábico *m*; **~ic numerals** algarismos *mpl* árabes or arábicos

Arabian /ə'reɪbɪən/ *a* árabe
arable /'ærəbl/ *a* arável
arbitrary /'ɑ:bɪtrərɪ/ *a* arbitrário
arbitrat|e /'ɑ:bɪtreɪt/ *vi* arbitrar. **~ion** /-'treɪʃn/ *n* arbitragem *f*
arc /ɑ:k/ *n* arco *m*; **~ lamp** lâmpada *f* de arco; **~ welding** soldadura *f* a arco
arcade /ɑ:'keɪd/ *n* (*shop*) arcada *f*; **amusement ~** fliperama *m*
arch /ɑ:tʃ/ *n* arco *m*; (*vault*) abóbada *f* ● *vt/i* arquear(-se)
arch- /ɑ:tʃ/ *pref* arqui-
archaeolog|y /ɑ:kɪ'ɒlədʒɪ/ *n* arqueologia *f*. **~ical** /-ə'lɒdʒɪkl/ *a* arqueológico. **~ist** *n* arqueólogo *m*
archaic /ɑ:'keɪɪk/ *a* arcaico
archbishop /ɑ:tʃ'bɪʃəp/ *n* arcebispo *m*
archer /'ɑ:tʃə(r)/ *n* arqueiro *m*. **~y** *n* tiro *m* ao arco
archetype /'ɑ:kɪtaɪp/ *n* arquétipo *m*
architect /'ɑ:kɪtekt/ *n* arquiteto *m*
architectur|e /'ɑ:kɪtektʃə(r)/ *n* arquitetura *f*. **~al** /-'tektʃərəl/ *a* arquitetônico, (*P*) arquitetónico
archiv|es /'ɑ:kaɪvz/ *npl* arquivo *m*
archway /'ɑ:tʃweɪ/ *n* arcada *f*
Arctic /'ɑ:ktɪk/ *n* ártico *m* ● *a* ártico; **~ weather** tempo *m* glacial
ardent /'ɑ:dnt/ *a* ardente
ardour /'ɑ:də(r)/ *n* ardor *m*
arduous /'ɑ:djʊəs/ *a* árduo
are /ə(r) emphatic ɑ:(r)/ ▶ BE
area /'eərɪə/ *n* área *f*
arena /ə'ri:nə/ *n* arena *f*
Argentin|a /ɑ:dʒən'ti:nə/ *n* Argentina *f*. **~ian** /-'tɪnɪən/ *a & n* argentino *m*
argu|e /'ɑ:gju:/ *vi* discutir; (*reason*) argumentar, arguir ● *vt* (*debate*) discutir; **~e that** alegar que
argument /'ɑ:gjʊmənt/ *n* (*dispute*) disputa *f*; (*reasoning*) argumento *m*. **~ative** /-'mentətɪv/ *a* que gosta de discutir, argumentativo
arid /'ærɪd/ *a* árido
Aries /'eəri:z/ *n Astr* áries *m*, Carneiro *m*
arise /ə'raɪz/ *vi* (*pt* **arose**, *pp* **arisen**) surgir; **~ from** resultar de
aristocracy /ærɪ'stɒkrəsɪ/ *n* aristocracia *f*
aristocrat /'ærɪstəkræt/ *n* aristocrata *mf*. **~ic** /-'krætɪk/ *a* aristocrático
arithmetic /ə'rɪθmətɪk/ *n* aritmética *f*
arm[1] /ɑ:m/ *n* braço *m*; **~ in ~** de braço dado
arm[2] /ɑ:m/ *vt* armar; **~ed robbery** assalto à mão armada *m* ● *n Mil* arma *f*
armament /'ɑ:məmənt/ *n* armamento *m*
armchair /'ɑ:mtʃeə(r)/ *n* cadeira *f* de braços, poltrona *f*
armour /'ɑ:mə(r)/ *n* armadura *f*; (*on tanks etc*) blindagem *f*. **~ed** *a* blindado
armpit /'ɑ:mpɪt/ *n* axila *f*, sovaco *m*
arms /ɑ:mz/ *npl* armas *fpl*; **coat of ~** brasão *m*
army /'ɑ:mɪ/ *n* exército *m*
aroma /ə'rəʊmə/ *n* aroma *m*. **~tic** /ærə'mætɪk/ *a* aromático
arose /ə'rəʊz/ ▶ ARISE
around /ə'raʊnd/ *adv* em redor, em volta; (*here and there*) por aí ● *prep* em redor de, em torno de, em volta de; (*approximately*) aproximadamente; **~ here** por aqui
arouse /ə'raʊz/ *vt* despertar; (*excite*) excitar
arrange /ə'reɪndʒ/ *vt* arranjar; ‹*time, date*› combinar; **~ to do sth** combinar fazer algo. **~ment** *n* arranjo *m*; (*agreement*) acordo *m*; **make ~ments (for)** (*plans*) tomar disposições (para); (*preparations*) fazer preparativos (para)
arrears /ə'rɪəz/ *npl* dívidas *fpl* em atraso, atrasos *mpl*; **in ~** em atraso
arrest /ə'rest/ *vt* (*by law*) deter, prender; ‹*process, movement*› deter ● *n* captura *f*; **under ~** sob prisão
arrival /ə'raɪvl/ *n* chegada *f*; **new ~** recém-chegado *m*
arrive /ə'raɪv/ *vi* chegar
arrogan|t /'ærəgənt/ *a* arrogante. **~ce** *n* arrogância *f*
arrow /'ærəʊ/ *n* flecha *f*, seta *f*
arson /'ɑ:sn/ *n* fogo *m* posto. **~ist** *n* incendiário *m*
art[1] /ɑ:t/ *n* arte *f*; **the ~s** *Univ* letras *fpl*; **fine ~s** belas-artes *fpl*; **~ gallery** museu *m* (de arte); (*private*) galeria *f* de arte
artery /'ɑ:tərɪ/ *n* artéria *f*
arthritis /ɑ:'θraɪtɪs/ *n* artrite *f*
artichoke /'ɑ:tɪtʃəʊk/ *n* alcachofra *f*; **Jerusalem ~** topinambo *m*
article /'ɑ:tɪkl/ *n* artigo *m*
articulate[1] /ɑ:'tɪkjʊlət/ *a* que se exprime com clareza; ‹*speech*› bem articulado
articulat|e[2] /ɑ:'tɪkjʊleɪt/ *vt/i* articular; **~ed lorry** camião *m* articulado
artificial /ɑ:tɪ'fɪʃl/ *a* artificial

a

artillery /ɑː'tɪlərɪ/ *n* artilharia *f*
artisan /ɑːtɪ'zæn/ *n* artífice *mf*, artesão *m*, artesã *f*
artist /'ɑːtɪst/ *n* artista *mf*. **~ic** /-'tɪstɪk/ *a* artístico
artiste /ɑː'tiːst/ *n* artista *mf*
as /əz emphatic æz/ *adv & conj* como; (*while*) enquanto; (*when*) quando; **~ a gift** de presente; **~ tall ~** tão alto quanto, (*P*) tão alto como; **~ if** como se; **~ much** tanto, tantos; **~ many** quanto, quantos; **~ soon ~** logo que; **~ well** (*also*) também; **~ well ~** (*in addition to*) assim como; **~ for, ~ to** quanto a; **~ from** a partir de ● *pron* que; **I ate the same ~ him** comi o mesmo que ele
asbestos /æz'bestəs/ *n* asbesto *m*, amianto *m*
ASBO, Asbo /'æzbəʊ/ *abbr* (*pl* **ASBOs, Asbos**) Ordem *f* de Comportamento Antissocial
ascend /ə'send/ *vt/i* subir; **~ the throne** ascender or subir ao trono
ascent /ə'sent/ *n* ascensão *f*; (*slope*) subida *f*, rampa *f*
ascertain /æsə'teɪn/ *vt* certificar-se de; **~ that** certificar-se de que
ash[1] /æʃ/ *n* **~(-tree)** freixo *m*
ash[2] /æʃ/ *n* cinza *f*; **A~ Wednesday** Quarta-feira *f* de Cinzas
ashamed /ə'ʃeɪmd/ *a* **be ~** ter vergonha, ficar envergonhado (**of** de, por)
ashore /ə'ʃɔː(r)/ *adv* em terra; **go ~** desembarcar
ashtray /'æʃtreɪ/ *n* cinzeiro *m*
Asia /'eɪʃə/ *n* Ásia *f*. **~n** *a & n* asiático *m*
aside /ə'saɪd/ *adv* de lado, de parte ● *n Theat* aparte *m*; **~ from** *Amer* à parte
ask /ɑːsk/ *vt/i* pedir; ‹*a question*› perguntar; (*invite*) convidar; **~ sb sth** pedir algo a alguém; **~ about** informar-se de; **~ after sb** pedir notícias de alguém, perguntar por alguém; **~ for** pedir; **~ sb in** mandar entrar alguém; **~ sb to do sth** pedir a alguém para fazer algo
askew /ə'skjuː/ *adv & a* de través, de esguelha
asleep /ə'sliːp/ *adv & a* adormecido; (*numb*) dormente; **fall ~** adormecer
asparagus /ə'spærəgəs/ *n* (*plant*) aspargo *m*, (*P*) espargo *m*; *Culin* aspargos *mpl*, (*P*) espargo *m*
aspect /'æspekt/ *n* aspecto *m*; (*direction*) exposição *f*
asphalt /'æsfælt/ *n* asfalto *m* ● *vt* asfaltar
asphyxiat|e /əs'fɪksɪeɪt/ *vt/i* asfixiar. **~ion** /-'eɪʃn/ *n* asfixia *f*
aspir|e /əs'paɪə(r)/ *vi* **~e to** aspirar a. **~ation** /æspə'reɪʃn/ *n* aspiração *f*
aspirin /'æsprɪn/ *n* aspirina *f*
ass /æs/ *n* burro *m*; **make an ~ of o.s.** fazer papel de palhaço, (*P*) fazer figura de parvo
assail /ə'seɪl/ *vt* assaltar, agredir. **~ant** *n* assaltante *mf*, agressor *m*
assassin /ə'sæsɪn/ *n* assassino *m*
assassinat|e /ə'sæsɪneɪt/ *vt* assassinar. **~ion** /-'eɪʃn/ *n* assassinato *m*
assault /ə'sɔːlt/ *n* assalto *m* ● *vt* assaltar, atacar
assemble /ə'sembl/ *vt* ‹*people*› reunir; (*fit together*) montar ● *vi* reunir-se
assembly /ə'semblɪ/ *n* assembleia *f*; **~ line** linha *f* de montagem
assent /ə'sent/ *n* assentimento *m* ● *vi* **~ to** consentir em
assert /ə'sɜːt/ *vt* afirmar; ‹*one's rights*› reivindicar; **~ o.s.** impor-se. **~ion** /-ʃn/ *n* asserção *f*. **~ive** *a* dogmático, peremptório
assess /ə'ses/ avaliar; ‹*payment*› estabelecer o montante de. **~ment** *n* avaliação *f*
asset /'æset/ *n* (*advantage*) vantagem *f*; **~s** *Comm* ativo *m*; (*possessions*) bens *mpl*
assign /ə'saɪn/ *vt* atribuir, destinar; *Jur* transmitir; **~ sb to** designar alguém para
assignment /ə'saɪnmənt/ *n* tarefa *f*, missão *f*; *Jur* transmissão *f*
assimilat|e /ə'sɪmɪleɪt/ *vt/i* assimilar(-se)
assist /ə'sɪst/ *vt/i* ajudar. **~ance** *n* ajuda *f*, assistência *f*
assistant /ə'sɪstənt/ *n* (*helper*) assistente *mf*, auxiliar *mf*; (*in shop*) ajudante *mf*, empregado *m* ● *a* adjunto
associat|e[1] /ə'səʊʃɪeɪt/ *vt* associar ● *vi* **~e with** conviver com. **~ion** /-'eɪʃn/ *n* associação *f*
associate[2] /ə'səʊʃɪət/ *a & n* associado *m*
assort|ed /ə'sɔːtɪd/ *a* variados; ‹*foods*› sortidos. **~ment** *n* sortimento *m*, (*P*) sortido *m*
assume /ə'sjuːm/ *vt* assumir; (*presume*) supor, presumir
assumption /ə'sʌmpʃn/ *n* suposição *f*
assurance /ə'ʃʊərəns/ *n* certeza *f*, garantia *f*; (*insurance*) seguro *m*; (*self-*

confidence) segurança *f*, confiança *f*

assure /ə'ʃʊə(r)/ *vt* assegurar. **~d** *a* certo, garantido; **rest ~d that** ficar certo que

asterisk /'æstərɪsk/ *n* asterisco *m*

asthma /'æsmə/ *n* asma *f*

astonish /ə'stɒnɪʃ/ *vt* espantar. **~ment** *n* espanto *m*

astound /ə'staʊnd/ *vt* assombrar

astray /ə'streɪ/ *adv & a* **go ~** perder-se, extraviar-se; **lead ~** desencaminhar

astride /ə'straɪd/ *adv & prep* escarranchado (em)

astrolog|y /ə'strɒlədʒɪ/ *n* astrologia *f*. **~er** *n* astrólogo *m*

astronaut /'æstrənɔːt/ *n* astronauta *mf*

astronom|y /ə'strɒnəmɪ/ *n* astronomia *f*. **~er** *n* astrônomo *m*, (*P*) astrónomo *m*. **~ical** /æstrə'nɒmɪkl/ *a* astronômico, (*P*) astronómico

astute /ə'stjuːt/ *a* astuto, astucioso

asylum /ə'saɪləm/ *n* asilo *m*

at /ət *emphatic* æt/ ● *prep*

····▸ (*position*) em; (*at home*) em casa; (*at school*) na escola; (*at sea*) no mar; (*at the door*) à porta

! The preposition *em* often contracts with definite and indefinite articles *o*, *a* and *um*, *uma* to form *no*, *na* and *num*, *numa*

····▸ (*at someone's house*) na casa de; **~ Peter's** na casa do Pedro; (*at someone's business*) em; **~ the doctor's** no médico

····▸ (*time*) **~ two o'clock** às duas horas; **~ three years of age** aos três anos ; **~ night** à noite; **~ Christmas/Easter** no Natal/na Páscoa

····▸ (*price*) a; **~ £2.20 each** a duas libras e vinte cada

····▸ (*speed*) **~ 50 mph** a cinquenta milhas por hora

····▸ (*in email addresses=@*) arroba

····▸ (*in phrases*) **~ once** imediatamente; **~ the same time** ao mesmo tempo; **~ times** às vezes; **be good/bad ~ sth** ser bom/ruim em aco; **two ~ a time** dois de cada vez; **be angry/surprised ~ sb** estar brabo/surpreendido com alguém

ate /et/ ▶ EAT

atheis|t /'eɪθɪɪst/ *n* ateu *m*. **~m** /-zəm/ *n* ateísmo *m*

athlet|e /'æθliːt/ *n* atleta *mf*. **~ic** /-'letɪk/ *a* atlético. **~ics** /-'letɪks/ *n*(*pl*) atletismo *m*

Atlantic /ət'læntɪk/ *a* atlântico ● *n* **~ (Ocean)** Atlântico *m*

atlas /'ætləs/ *n* atlas *m*

atmospher|e /'ætməsfɪə(r)/ *n* atmosfera *f*

atom /'ætəm/ *n* átomo *m*. **~ic** /ə'tɒmɪk/ *a* atômico, (*P*) atómico; **~(ic) bomb** bomba *f* atômica, (*P*) atómica

atone /ə'təʊn/ *vi* **~ for** expiar

atrocious /ə'trəʊʃəs/ *a* atroz

atrocity /ə'trɒsətɪ/ *n* atrocidade *f*

attach /ə'tætʃ/ *vt/i* (*affix*) ligar(-se), prender(-se); (*join*) juntar(-se). **~ed** *a* ‹*document*› junto, anexo; **be ~ed to** (*like*) estar apegado a. **~ment** *n* ligação *f*; (*affection*) apego *m*; (*accessory*) acessório *m*; (*in email*) anexo *m*

attack /ə'tæk/ *n* ataque *m* ● *vt/i* atacar. **~er** *n* atacante *mf*

attain /ə'teɪn/ *vt* atingir. **~able** *a* atingível

attempt /ə'tempt/ *vt* tentar ● *n* tentativa *f*

attend /ə'tend/ *vt/i* atender (**to** a); (*escort*) acompanhar; (*look after*) tratar; ‹*meeting*› comparecer a; ‹*school*› frequentar. **~ance** *n* comparecimento *m*; (*times present*) frequência *f*; (*people*) assistência *f*

attendant /ə'tendənt/ *a* concomitante, que acompanha ● *n* empregado *m*; (*servant*) servidor *m*

attention /ə'tenʃn/ *n* atenção *f*; **~!** *Mil* sentido! **pay ~** prestar atenção (**to** a)

attentive /ə'tentɪv/ *a* atento; (*considerate*) atencioso

attic /'ætɪk/ *n* sótão *m*, água-furtada *f*

attitude /'ætɪtjuːd/ *n* atitude *f*

attorney /ə'tɜːnɪ/ *n* (*pl* **-eys**) procurador *m*; *Amer* advogado *m*

attract /ə'trækt/ *vt* atrair. **~ion** /-ʃn/ *n* atração *f*; (*charm*) atrativo *m*

attractive /ə'træktɪv/ *a* atraente

attribute[1] /ə'trɪbjuːt/ *vt* **~ to** atribuir a

attribute[2] /'ætrɪbjuːt/ *n* atributo *m*

aubergine /'əʊbəʒiːn/ *n* berinjela *f*

auburn /'ɔːbən/ *a* cor de acaju, castanho-avermelhado

auction /'ɔːkʃn/ *n* leilão *m* ● *vt* leiloar. **~eer** /-ə'nɪə(r)/ *n* leiloeiro *m*, (*P*) pregoeiro *m*

a

audaci|ous /ɔː'deɪʃəs/ *a* audacioso, audaz. **~ty** /-æsətɪ/ *n* audácia *f*
audible /'ɔːdəbl/ *a* audível
audience /'ɔːdɪəns/ *n* auditório *m*; *Theat, Radio* (*interview*) audiência *f*
audiovisual /ɔːdɪəʊ'vɪʒʊəl/ *a* audiovisual
audit /'ɔːdɪt/ *n* auditoria *f* ● *vt* fazer uma auditoria
audition /ɔː'dɪʃn/ *n* audição *f* ● *vt* dar/ fazer uma audição
auditor /'ɔːdɪtə(r)/ *n* perito-contador *m*, (*P*) perito-contabilista *m*
auditorium /ɔːdɪ'tɔːrɪəm/ *n* auditório *m*
augment /ɔːg'ment/ *vt/i* aumentar(-se)
August /'ɔːgəst/ *n* agosto *m*
aunt /ɑːnt/ *n* tia *f*
au pair /əʊ'peə(r)/ *n* au pair *f*
aura /'ɔːrə/ *n* aura *f*, emanação *f*
auspicious /ɔː'spɪʃəs/ *a* auspicioso
auster|e /ɔː'stɪə(r)/ *a* austero. **~ity** /-erətɪ/ *n* austeridade *f*
Australia /ɒ'streɪlɪə/ *n* Austrália *f*. **~n** *a & n* australiano *m*
Austria /'ɒstrɪə/ *n* Áustria *f*. **~n** *a & n* austríaco *m*
authentic /ɔː'θentɪk/ *a* autêntico. **~ity** /-ən'tɪsətɪ/ *n* autenticidade *f*
authenticate /ɔː'θentɪkeɪt/ *vt* autenticar
author /'ɔːθə(r)/ *n* autor *m*, autora *f*
authoritarian /ɔːθɒrɪ'teərɪən/ *a* autoritário
authorit|y /ɔː'θɒrətɪ/ *n* autoridade *f*; (*permission*) autorização *f*. **~ative** /-ɪtətɪv/ *a* (*trusted*) autorizado; (*manner*) autoritário
authoriz|e /'ɔːθəraɪz/ *vt* autorizar. **~ation** /-'zeɪʃn/ *n* autorização *f*
autistic /ɔː'tɪstɪk/ *a* autista, autístico
autobiography /ɔːtə'baɪɒgrəfɪ/ *n* autobiografia *f*
autograph /'ɔːtəgrɑːf/ *n* autógrafo *m* ● *vt* autografar
automat|e /'ɔːtəmeɪt/ *vt* automatizar. **~ion** /ɔːtə'meɪʃn/ *n* automação *f*
automatic /ɔːtə'mætɪk/ *a* automático ● *n* (*car*) automático *m*. **~ally** /-klɪ/ *adv* automaticamente
automobile /'ɔːtəməbiːl/ *n Amer* automóvel *m*
autonom|y /ɔː'tɒnəmɪ/ *n* autonomia *f*. **~ous** *a* autônomo, (*P*) autónomo
autopsy /'ɔːtɒpsɪ/ *n* autópsia *f*
autumn /'ɔːtəm/ *n* outono *m*. **~al** /-'tʌmnəl/ *a* outonal
auxiliary /ɔːg'zɪlɪərɪ/ *a & n* auxiliar *mf*; **~ verb** verbo *m* auxiliar
avail /ə'veɪl/ *vt* **~ o.s. of** servir-se de ● *vi* (*be of use*) valer ● *n* **of no ~** inútil; **to no ~** sem resultado, em vão
availab|le /ə'veɪləbl/ *a* disponível. **~ility** /-'bɪlətɪ/ *n* disponibilidade *f*
avalanche /'ævəlɑːnʃ/ *n* avalanche *f*
avaric|e /'ævərɪs/ *n* avareza *f*
avatar /'ævətɑː(r)/ *n* avatar *m*
avenge /ə'vendʒ/ *vt* vingar
avenue /'ævənjuː/ *n* avenida *f*; *fig* (*line of approach*) via *f*
average /'ævərɪdʒ/ *n* média *f* ● *a* médio ● *vt* tirar a média de; (*produce, do*) fazer em média ● *vi* **~ out at** dar de média, dar uma média de; **on ~** em média
avers|e /ə'vɜːs/ *a* **be ~e to** ser avesso a. **~ion** /-ʃn/ *n* aversão *f*, repugnância *f*
avert /ə'vɜːt/ *vt* (*turn away*) desviar; (*ward off*) evitar
aviary /'eɪvɪərɪ/ *n* aviário *m*
aviation /eɪvɪ'eɪʃn/ *n* aviação *f*
avid /'ævɪd/ *a* ávido
avocado /ævə'kɑːdəʊ/ *n* (*pl* **-s**) abacate *m*
avoid /ə'vɔɪd/ *vt* evitar. **~able** *a* que se pode evitar, evitável. **~ance** *n* evitação *f*
await /ə'weɪt/ *vt* aguardar
awake /ə'weɪk/ *vt/i* (*pt* **awoke**, *pp* **awoken**) acordar ● *a* **be ~** estar acordado
awaken /ə'weɪkən/ *vt/i* despertar. **~ing** *n* despertar *m*
award /ə'wɔːd/ *vt* atribuir, conferir; *Jur* adjudicar ● *n* recompensa *f*, prêmio *m*, (*P*) prémio *m*; ‹*scholarship*› bolsa *f*
aware /ə'weə(r)/ *a* ciente, cônscio; **be ~ of** estar consciente de or ter consciência de; **become ~ of** tomar consciência de; **make sb ~ of** sensibilizar alguém para. **~ness** *n* consciência *f*
away /ə'weɪ/ *adv* (*at a distance*) longe; (*to a distance*) para longe; (*absent*) fora; (*persistently*) sem parar; (*entirely*) completamente; **eight miles ~** a oito milhas (de distância); **four days ~** daí a quatro dias ● *a & n* **~ (match)** jogo *m* fora de casa
awe /ɔː/ *n* assombro *m*, admiração *f* reverente, terror *m* respeitoso. **~some** *a* assombroso

awful /ˈɔːfl/ *a* terrível. **~ly** *adv* muito, terrivelmente

awkward /ˈɔːkwəd/ *a* difícil; (*clumsy, difficult to use*) desajeitado, maljeitoso; (*inconvenient*) inconveniente; (*embarrassing*) embaraçoso; (*embarrassed*) embaraçado; **an ~ customer** [!] um freguês perigoso or intratável

awning /ˈɔːnɪŋ/ *n* toldo *m*

awoke, awoken /əˈwəʊk, əˈwəʊkən/ ▶ AWAKE

awry /əˈraɪ/ *adv* torto; **go ~** dar errado; **be ~** estar torto

axe /æks/ *n* machado *m* ● *vt* (*pres p* **axing**) (*reduce*) cortar; (*dismiss*) despedir

axis /ˈæksɪs/ *n* (*pl* **axes** /-iːz/) eixo *m*

axle /ˈæksl/ *n* eixo (de roda) *m*

Azores /əˈzɔːz/ *n* Açores *mpl*

Bb

BA *abbr* (= **Bachelor of Arts**) ▶ BACHELOR

baboon /bəˈbuːn/ *n* babuíno *m*

baby /ˈbeɪbɪ/ *n* bebê *m*, (*P*) bebé *m*; **~ carriage** *Amer* carrinho *m* de bebê, (*P*) bebé. **~sit** *vi* tomar conta de crianças; **~sitter** *n* baby-sitter *mf*, babá *f*

babyish /ˈbeɪbɪɪʃ/ *a* infantil

bachelor /ˈbætʃələ(r)/ *n* solteiro *m*; **B~ of Arts/Science** Bacharel *m* em Letras/Ciências

back /bæk/ *n* (*of person, hand, chair*) costas *fpl*; (*of animal*) dorso *m*; (*of car, train*) parte *f* traseira; (*of house, room*) fundo *m*; (*of coin*) reverso *m*; (*of page*) verso *m*; *Football* beque *m*; zagueiro *m*, (*P*) defesa *m*; **at the ~ of beyond** em casa do diabo, no fim do mundo ● *a* traseiro, posterior; ‹*taxes*› em atraso; **~ number** número *m* atrasado ● *adv* atrás, para trás; (*returned*) de volta ● *vt* (*support*) apoiar; ‹*horse*› apostar em; ‹*car*› (fazer) recuar ● *vi* recuar; **~ down** desistir (**from** de); **~ out** (*of an undertaking etc*) fugir (ao combinado *etc*); **~ up** *Auto* fazer marcha à ré, (*P*) atrás; *Comput* tirar um back-up de. **~up** *n* apoio *m*; *Comput* back-up *m*; *Amer* (*traffic jam*) engarrafamento *m* ● *a* de reserva; *Comput* backup

backache /ˈbækeɪk/ *n* dor *f* nas costas

backbiting /ˈbækbaɪtɪŋ/ *n* maledicência *f*

backbone /ˈbækbəʊn/ *n* espinha *f* dorsal

backdate /bækˈdeɪt/ *vt* antedatar

backer /ˈbækə(r)/ *n* (*of horse*) apostador *m*; (*of cause*) partidário *m*, apoiante *mf*; *Comm* patrocinador *m*, financiador *m*

backfire /bækˈfaɪə(r)/ *vi Auto* dar explosões no tubo de escape; *fig* sair o tiro pela culatra

background /ˈbækgraʊnd/ *n* (*of picture*) fundo *m*, segundo-plano *m*; (*context*) contexto *m*; (*environment*) meio *m*; (*experience*) formação *f*

backhand /ˈbækhænd/ *n Tennis* esquerda *f*. **~ed** *a* com as costas da mão; **~ed compliment** cumprimento *m* ambíguo

backing /ˈbækɪŋ/ *n* apoio *m*; *Comm* patrocínio *m*

backlash /ˈbæklæʃ/ *n fig* reação *f* violenta; repercussões *fpl*

backlog /ˈbæklɒg/ *n* acumulação *m* (de trabalho *etc*)

backside /ˈbæksaɪd/ *n* [!] (*buttocks*) traseiro *m*

backstage /bækˈsteɪdʒ/ *a & adv* por detrás dos bastidores

backstroke /ˈbækstrəʊk/ *n* nado *m* de costas

backtrack /ˈbæktræk/ *vi fig* voltar atrás

backward /ˈbækwəd/ *a* retrógrado; (*retarded*) atrasado; ‹*step, look, etc*› para trás

backwards /ˈbækwədz/ *adv* para trás; (*walk*) para trás; (*fall*) de costas, para trás; (*in reverse order*) de trás para diante, às avessas; **go ~ and forwards** ir e vir, andar para trás e para a frente; **know sth ~** saber algo de trás para a frente

backwater /ˈbækwɔːtə(r)/ *n pej* (*place*) lugar *m* atrasado

bacon /ˈbeɪkən/ *n* toucinho *m* defumado; (*in rashers*) bacon *m*

bacteria /bækˈtɪərɪə/ *npl* bactérias *fpl*

bad /bæd/ *a* (**worse**, **worst**) mau; ‹*accident*› grave; ‹*food*› estragado; (*ill*) doente; **feel ~** sentir-se mal; **~ language** palavrões *mpl*. **~-mannered** *a* mal-educado; **~-tempered** *a* mal-humorado. **~ly** *adv* mal; (*seriously*) gravemente; **want ~ly** (*desire*) desejar imensamente, ter grande vontade de; (*need*) precisar muito de

badge /bædʒ/ *n* emblema *m*; (*policeman's*) crachá *m*, (*P*) distintivo *m*

b

badger /ˈbædʒə(r)/ *n* texugo *m* ● *vt* atormentar; (*pester*) importunar

badminton /ˈbædmɪntən/ *n* badminton *m*

baffle /ˈbæfl/ *vt* atrapalhar, desconcertar

bag /bæg/ *n* saco *m*; (*handbag*) bolsa *f*, carteira *f*; **~s** (*luggage*) malas *fpl* ● *vt* (*pt* **bagged**) ensacar; 🅸 (*take*) embolsar

baggage /ˈbægɪdʒ/ *n* bagagem *f*

baggy /ˈbægɪ/ *a* ‹*clothes*› muito largo, bufante

bagpipes /ˈbægpaɪps/ *npl* gaita *f* de foles

Bahamas /bəˈhɑːməz/ *npl* **the ~** as Bahamas *fpl*

bail[1] /beɪl/ *n* fiança *f* ● *vt* pôr em liberdade sob fiança; **be out on ~** estar solto sob fiança

bail[2] /beɪl/ *vt* **~ (out)** *Naut* esgotar, tirar água de

bailiff /ˈbeɪlɪf/ *n* (*officer*) oficial *m* de diligências; (*of estate*) feitor *m*

bait /beɪt/ *n* isca *f* ● *vt* pôr isca; *fig* atormentar (com insultos); atazanar

bak|e /beɪk/ *vt/i* cozer (no forno); ‹*bread, cakes, etc*› assar; (*in the sun*) torrar. **~er** *n* padeiro *m*; (*of cakes*) doceiro *m*. **~ing** *n* cozedura *f*; (*batch*) fornada *f*; **~ing tin** forma *f*. **~ing powder** *n* fermento *m* em pó

bakery /ˈbeɪkərɪ/ *n* padaria *f*; (*cakes*) confeitaria *f*

balance /ˈbæləns/ *n* equilíbrio *m*; (*scales*) balança *f*; (*sum*) saldo *m*; *Comm* balanço *m*; **~ of power** equilíbrio *m* político; **~ of trade** balança *f* comercial ● *vt* equilibrar; (*weigh up*) pesar; ‹*budget*› equilibrar ● *vi* equilibrar-se. **~ sheet** *n* balanço *m*. **~d** *a* equilibrado

balcony /ˈbælkənɪ/ *n* balcão *m*; (*in a house*) varanda *f*

bald /bɔːld/ *a* (**-er**, **-est**) calvo, careca; ‹*tyre*› careca. **~ing** *a* **be ~ing** ficar calvo. **~ly** *adv* a nu e cru, (*P*) secamente. **~ness** *n* calvície *f*

bale[1] /beɪl/ *n* (*of straw*) fardo *m*; (*of cotton*) balote *m* ● *vt* enfardar

bale[2] /beɪl/ *vi* **~ out** saltar de paraquedas

balk /bɔːk/ *vt* frustrar, contrariar ● *vi* **~ at** assustar-se com, recuar perante

ball[1] /bɔːl/ *n* bola *f*

ball[2] /bɔːl/ *n* (*dance*) baile *m*

ballad /ˈbæləd/ *n* balada *f*

ballerina /bæləˈriːnə/ *n* bailarina *f*

ballet /ˈbæleɪ/ *n* balé *m*, (*P*) ballet *m*, bailado *m*

balloon /bəˈluːn/ *n* balão *m*

ballot /ˈbælət/ *n* escrutínio *m* ● *vt* (*members*) consultar por voto secreto ● *vi Pol* votar. **~ (paper)** *n* cédula *f* eleitoral, (*P*) boletim *m* de voto; **~ box** *n* urna *f*

ballroom /ˈbɔːlruːm/ *n* salão *m* de baile

balm /bɑːm/ *n* bálsamo *m*. **~y** *a* balsâmico; (*mild*) suave

bamboo /bæmˈbuː/ *n* bambu *m*

ban /bæn/ *vt* (*pt* **banned**) banir; **~ from** proibir de ● *n* proibição *f*

banal /bəˈnɑːl/ *a* banal. **~ity** /-ælətɪ/ *n* banalidade *f*

banana /bəˈnɑːnə/ *n* banana *f*

band /bænd/ *n* (*for fastening*) cinta *f*, faixa *f*; (*strip*) tira *f*, banda *f*; *Mus, Mil* banda *f*; *Mus* (*dance, jazz*) conjunto *m*; (*group*) bando *m* ● *vi* **~ together** juntar-se

bandage /ˈbændɪdʒ/ *n* atadura *f*, (*P*) ligadura *f* ● *vt* ligar

bandit /ˈbændɪt/ *n* bandido *m*

bandstand /ˈbændstænd/ *n* coreto *m*

bandwagon /ˈbændwægən/ *n* **climb on the ~** *fig* apanhar o trem, (*P*) o comboio

bang /bæŋ/ *n* (*blow*) pancada *f*; (*loud noise*) estouro *m*, estrondo *m*; (*of gun*) detonação *f* ● *vt/i* (*hit, shut*) bater ● *vi* explodir ● *int* pum; **~ in the middle** jogar no meio; **shut the door with a ~** bater (com) a porta

banger /ˈbæŋə(r)/ *n* (*firework*) bomba *f*; ☒ (*sausage*) salsicha *f*; **(old) ~** ☒ (*car*) calhambeque *m* 🅸

bangle /ˈbæŋgl/ *n* pulseira *f*, bracelete *m*

banish /ˈbænɪʃ/ *vt* banir, desterrar

banisters /ˈbænɪstəz/ *npl* corrimão *m*

banjo /ˈbændʒəʊ/ *n* (*pl* **-os**) banjo *m*

bank[1] /bæŋk/ *n* (*of river*) margem *f*; (*of earth*) talude *m*; (*of sand*) banco *m* ● *vt* amontoar ● *vi Aviat* inclinar-se numa curva

bank[2] /bæŋk/ *n Comm* banco *m*; **~ account** conta *f* bancária; **~ holiday** feriado *m* nacional; **~ rate** taxa *f* bancária ● *vt* depositar no banco; **~ on** contar com; **~ with** ter conta em

bank|er /ˈbæŋkə(r)/ *n* banqueiro *m*. **~ing** /-ɪŋ/ *n* operações *fpl* bancárias; (*career*) carreira *f* bancária, banca *f*

banknote /ˈbæŋknəʊt/ *n* nota *f* de banco

bankrupt /ˈbæŋkrʌpt/ *a & n* falido *m*; **go ~** falir ● *vt* levar à falência. **~cy** *n* falência *f*, bancarrota *f*

banner /ˈbænə(r)/ *n* bandeira *f*, estandarte *m*

banquet /ˈbæŋkwɪt/ *n* banquete *m*

banter /ˈbæntə(r)/ *n* gracejo *m*, brincadeira *f* ● *vi* gracejar, brincar

baptism /ˈbæptɪzəm/ *n* batismo *m*

Baptist /ˈbæptɪst/ *n* batista *mf*

baptize /bæpˈtaɪz/ *vt* batizar

bar /bɑː(r)/ *n* (*of chocolate*) tablette *f*, barra *f*; (*of metal, soap, sand etc*) barra *f*; (*of door, window*) tranca *f*; (*in pub*) bar *m*; (*counter*) balcão *m*, bar *m*; *Mus* barra *f* de compasso; *fig* (*obstacle*) barreira *f*; (*in law court*) teia *f*; **the B~** a advocacia *f*; **~ code** código *m* de barra; **behind ~s** na cadeia ● *vt* (*pt* **barred**) (*obstruct*) barrar; (*prohibit*) proibir (**from** de); (*exclude*) excluir; ‹*door, window*› trancar ● *prep* salvo, exceto; **~ none** sem exceção

Barbados /bɑːˈbeɪdɒs/ *n* Barbados *mpl*

barbarian /bɑːˈbeərɪən/ *n* bárbaro *m*

barbari|c /bɑːˈbærɪk/ *a* bárbaro. **~ty** /-ətɪ/ *n* barbaridade *f*

barbarous /ˈbɑːbərəs/ *a* bárbaro

barbecue /ˈbɑːbɪkjuː/ *n* (*grill*) churrasqueira *f*; (*occasion, food*) churrasco *m* ● *vt* assar

barbed /bɑːbd/ *a* **~ wire** arame *m* farpado

barber /ˈbɑːbə(r)/ *n* barbeiro *m*

bare /beə(r)/ *a* (**-er, -est**) nu; ‹*room*› vazio; (*mere*) mero ● *vt* pôr à mostra, pôr a nu, descobrir

bareback /ˈbeəbæk/ *adv* em pelo

barefaced /ˈbeəfeɪst/ *a* descarado

barefoot /ˈbeə(r)fʊt/ *adv* descalço

barely /ˈbeəlɪ/ *adv* apenas, mal

bargain /ˈbɑːgɪn/ *n* (*deal*) negócio *m*; (*good buy*) pechincha *f* ● *vi* negociar; (*haggle*) regatear; **~ for** esperar

barge /bɑːdʒ/ *n* barcaça *f* ● *vi* **~ in** interromper (despropositadamente); (*into room*) irromper

bark[1] /bɑːk/ *n* (*of tree*) casca *f*

bark[2] /bɑːk/ *n* (*of dog*) latido *m* ● *vi* latir; **his ~ is worse than his bite** cão que ladra não morde

barley /ˈbɑːlɪ/ *n* cevada *f*

barmaid /ˈbɑːmeɪd/ *n* empregada *f* de bar

barman /ˈbɑːmən/ *n* (*pl* **-men**) barman *m*, empregado *m* de bar

barmy /ˈbɑːmɪ/ *a* ☒ maluco [!]

barn /bɑːn/ *n* celeiro *m*

barometer /bəˈrɒmɪtə(r)/ *n* barômetro *m*, (*P*) barómetro *m*

baron /ˈbærən/ *n* barão *m*. **~ess** *n* baronesa *f*

barracks /ˈbærəks/ *n* quartel *m*, caserna *f*

barrage /ˈbærɑːʒ/ *n* barragem *f*; *fig* enxurrada *f*; *Mil* fogo *m* de barragem

barrel /ˈbærəl/ *n* (*of oil, wine*) barril *m*; (*of gun*) cano *m*

barren /ˈbærən/ *a* estéril; ‹*soil*› árido, estéril

barricade /bærɪˈkeɪd/ *n* barricada *f* ● *vt* barricar

barrier /ˈbærɪə(r)/ *n* barreira *f*; (*hindrance*) entrave *m*, barreira *f*

barrister /ˈbærɪstə(r)/ *n* advogado *m*

barrow /ˈbærəʊ/ *n* carrinho *m* de mão

barter /ˈbɑːtə(r)/ *n* troca *f* ● *vt* trocar

base /beɪs/ *n* base *f* ● *vt* basear (**on** em) ● *a* baixo, ignóbil. **~less** *a* infundado

baseball /ˈbeɪsbɔːl/ *n* beisebol *m*

basement /ˈbeɪsmənt/ *n* porão *m*, (*P*) cave *f*

bash /bæʃ/ *vt* bater com violência ● *n* pancada *f* forte; **have a ~ at** experimentar

bashful /ˈbæʃfl/ *a* tímido

basic /ˈbeɪsɪk/ *a* básico, elementar, fundamental. **~ally** *adv* basicamente, no fundo

basin /ˈbeɪsn/ *n* bacia *f*; (*for food*) tigela *f*; *Naut* ante-doca *f*; (*for washing*) pia *f*

basis /ˈbeɪsɪs/ *n* (*pl* **bases** /-siːz/) base *f*

bask /bɑːsk/ *vi* **~ in the sun** apanhar sol

basket /ˈbɑːskɪt/ *n* cesto *m*

basketball /ˈbɑːskɪtbɔːl/ *n* basquete(bol) *m*

Basque /bɑːsk/ *a & n* basco *m*

bass[1] /bæs/ *n* (*pl* **bass**) (*fish*) perca *f*

bass[2] /beɪs/ *a Mus* grave ● *n* (*pl* **basses**) *Mus* baixo *m*

bassoon /bəˈsuːn/ *n* fagote *m*

bastard /ˈbɑːstəd/ *n* (*illegitimate child*) bastardo *m*; ☒ *pej* safado *m* ☒; ☒ *not pej* cara *m* [!]

bat[1] /bæt/ *n Cricket* pá *f*; *Baseball* bastão *m*; *Table Tennis* rafuete *f* ● *vt/i* (*pt* **batted**) bater (em); **without ~ting an eyelid** sem pestanejar

b

bat[2] /bæt/ *n Zool* morcego *m*

batch /bætʃ/ *n* (*loaves*) fornada *f*; (*people*) monte *m*; (*goods*) remessa *f*; (*papers, letters etc*) batelada *f*, monte *m*

bath /bɑːθ/ *n* (*pl* **-s** /bɑːðz/) banho *m*; (*tub*) banheira *f*; **~s** (*washing*) banho *m* público; (*swimming*) piscina *f* ● *vt* dar banho a ● *vi* tomar banho

bathe /beɪð/ *vt* dar banho em; ‹*wound*› limpar ● *vi* tomar banho (de mar) ● *n* banho *m* (de mar). **~r** /-ə(r)/ *n* banhista *mf*

bathing /'beɪðɪŋ/ *n* banho *m* de mar. **~ costume/suit** *n* traje *m* de banho, (*P*) fato *m* de banho

bathrobe /'bɑːθrəʊb/ *n Amer* roupão *m*

bathroom /'bɑːθruːm/ *n* banheiro *m*, (*P*) casa *f* de banho

battalion /bə'tælɪən/ *n* batalhão *m*

batter /'bætə(r)/ *vt* bater, espancar, maltratar ● *n Culin* (*for cakes*) massa *f* de bolos; *Culin* (*for frying*) massa *f* de empanar. **~ed** *a* ‹*car, pan*› amassado; ‹*child, wife*› maltratado, espancado

battery /'bætərɪ/ *n Mil, Auto* bateria *f*; *Electr* pilha *f*

battle /'bætl/ *n* batalha *f*; *fig* luta *f* ● *vi* combater, batalhar, lutar

battlefield /'bætlfiːld/ *n* campo *m* de batalha

battleship /'bætlʃɪp/ *n* couraçado *m*

baulk /bɔːlk/ *vt/i* = BALK

bawl /bɔːl/ *vt/i* berrar

bay[1] /beɪ/ *n Bot* loureiro *m*

bay[2] /beɪ/ *n Geog* baía *f*; **~ window** janela *f* saliente

bay[3] /beɪ/ *n* (*bark*) latido *m* ● *vi* latir; **at ~** (*animal; also fig*) cercado, (*P*) em apuros; **keep at ~** manter à distância

bayonet /'beɪənɪt/ *n* baioneta *f*

bazaar /bə'zɑː(r)/ *n* bazar *m*

BC *abbr* (= **before Christ**) a C

bcc *abbr* (= **blind carbon copy**) Cco Com cópia oculta

be /biː/ ● *vi* (*pres* **am**, **are**, **is**, *pt* **was**, **were**, *pp* **been**);

! Portuguese has two verbs meaning **be**: *ser* and *estar*. As a general rule, *ser* is used to describe a permanent state or inherent characteristic, e.g. **I'm Brazilian** *sou brasileiro*, whereas *estar* is used to describe temporary states, e.g. **I'm tired** *estou cansado*.

····➤ (*identity or characteristic*) ser; **I'm Portuguese** sou português; **it's yellow** é amarelo

····➤ (*temporary state*) estar; **I'm angry/bored** estou brabo/entediado

····➤ (*situation*) ficar; **where's the town centre?** onde é que fica o centro?; **it's 10 minutes away** fica a 10 minutos

····➤ (*cost*) ser; **how much is it?** quanto é?; **it's £15** são 15 libras

····➤ (*feelings*) estar com; **I'm hungry/thirsty/sleepy** estou com fome/sede/sono; **I'm cold** estou com frio

····➤ (*health*) estar; **how are you?** como está?; **he's ill** ele está doente

····➤ (*age*) ter; **he's twenty** ele tem vinte anos

····➤ (*weather*) estar; **it's hot/cold** está calor/frio; **it's 30 degrees today** hoje estão 30 graus

····➤ (*become*) ficar; **he was disappointed** ficou desapontado

● *v aux*

····➤ (*in continuous tense*) **I am working** estou trabalhando, (*P*) estou a trabalhar; **She is leaving next week** ela vai embora na próxima semana

····➤ (*in passives*) **he was killed** ele foi morto; **the window has been fixed** a janela foi consertada

····➤ (*in tag questions*) **their house is lovely, isn't it?** a casa deles é linda, não é?

····➤ (*in short answers*) **are you a doctor? yes, I am** é médico? sim, sou.

····➤ (*with infinitive*) **she is to go immediately** ela tem que ir imediatamente; **they are to be married in August** eles vão casar em agosto

beach /biːtʃ/ *n* praia *f*

beacon /'biːkən/ *n* farol *m*; (*marker*) baliza *f*

bead /biːd/ *n* conta *f*; **~ of sweat** gota *f* de suor

beak /biːk/ *n* bico *m*

beam /biːm/ *n* (*of wood*) trave *f*, viga *f*; (*of light*) raio *m*; (*of torch*) feixe *m* de luz ● *vt/i* (*radiate*) irradiar; *fig* sorrir radiante. **~ing** *a* radiante

bean /biːn/ *n* feijão *m*; **broad ~** fava *f*; **coffee ~s** café *m* em grão; **runner ~** feijão *m* verde

bear[1] /beə(r)/ *n* urso *m*

bear[2] /beə(r)/ *vt/i* (*pt* **bore**, *pp* **borne**) sustentar, suportar; (*endure*) aguentar, suportar; ‹*child*› dar à luz; **~ in mind** ter em mente, lembrar; **~ left** virar à esquerda; **~ on** relacionar-se com, ter a ver com; **~ out** confirmar; **~ up!** coragem!. **~able** *a* tolerável, suportável. **~er** *n* portador *m*

beard /bɪəd/ *n* barba *f*. **~ed** *a* barbado, com barba

bearing /ˈbeərɪŋ/ *n* (*manner*) porte *m*; (*relevance*) relação *f*; *Naut* marcação *f*; **get one's ~s** orientar-se

beast /biːst/ *n* (*animal, person*) besta *f*, animal *m*; (*in fables*) fera *f*; **~ of burden** besta *f* de carga

beat /biːt/ *vt/i* (*pt* **beat**, *pp* **beaten**) bater; **~ about the bush** estar com rodeios; **~ a retreat** bater em retirada; **~ it** ☒ (*go away*) pôr-se a andar; **it ~s me** ! não consigo entender; **~ up** espancar ● *n Med* batimento *m*; *Mus* compasso *m*, ritmo *m*; (*of drum*) toque *m*; (*of policeman*) ronda *f*, (*P*) giro *m*. **~ing** *n* sova *f*

beautician /bjuːˈtɪʃn/ *n* esteticista *mf*

beautiful /ˈbjuːtɪfl/ *a* belo, lindo

beautify /ˈbjuːtɪfaɪ/ *vt* embelezar

beauty /ˈbjuːtɪ/ *n* beleza *f*; **~ parlour** instituto *m* de beleza; **~ spot** sinal *m* no rosto, mosca *f*; (*place*) local *m* pitoresco

beaver /ˈbiːvə(r)/ *n* castor *m*

became /bɪˈkeɪm/ ▶ BECOME

because /bɪˈkɒz/ *conj* porque ● *adv* **~ of** por causa de

beckon /ˈbekən/ *vt/i* **~ (to)** fazer sinal (para)

become /bɪˈkʌm/ *vt/i* (*pt* **became**, *pp* **become**) tornar-se; (*befit*) ficar bem a; **what has ~ of her?** que é feito dela?

becoming /bɪˈkʌmɪŋ/ *a* que fica bem, apropriado

bed /bed/ *n* cama *f*; (*layer*) camada *f*; (*of sea*) fundo *m*; (*of river*) leito *m*; (*of flowers*) canteiro *m*; **~ and breakfast (b & b)** quarto *m* com café da manhã, (*P*) com pequeno-almoço ● *vt/i* (*pt* **bedded**) **~ down** ir deitar-se; **~ in** plantar. **~sit(ter)** *n* ! misto *m* de quarto e sala; **go to ~** ir para cama; **in ~** na cama. **~ding** *n* roupa *f* de cama

> *i* **bed and breakfast** Os *bed and breakfast*, ou *B&B*, são casas particulares ou pequenos hotéis que oferecem alojamento e café da manhã aos hóspedes a preços normalmente baixos.

bedclothes /ˈbedkləʊðz/ *n* roupa *f* de cama

bedroom /ˈbedruːm/ *n* quarto *m* de dormir

b

bedside /ˈbedsaɪd/ *n* cabeceira *f*; **~ manner** (*doctor's*) modos *mpl* que inspiram confiança

bedspread /ˈbedspred/ *n* colcha *f*

bedtime /ˈbedtaɪm/ *n* hora *f* de deitar, hora *f* de ir para a cama

bee /biː/ *n* abelha *f*; **make a ~-line for** ir direto a

beech /biːtʃ/ *n* faia *f*

beef /biːf/ *n* carne *f* de vaca

beefburger /ˈbiːfbɜːgə(r)/ *n* hambúrguer *m*

beehive /ˈbiːhaɪv/ *n* colmeia *f*

been /biːn/ ▶ BE

beer /bɪə(r)/ *n* cerveja *f*

beet /biːt/ *n* beterraba *f*

beetle /ˈbiːtl/ *n* escaravelho *m*

beetroot /ˈbiːtruːt/ *n* (raiz de) beterraba *f*

before /bɪˈfɔː(r)/ *prep* (*time*) antes de; (*place*) em frente de ● *adv* antes; (*already*) já ● *conj* antes que; **~ leaving** antes de partir; **~ he leaves** antes que ele parta, antes de ele partir

beforehand /bɪˈfɔːhænd/ *adv* de antemão, antecipadamente

befriend /bɪˈfrend/ *vt* tornar-se amigo de; (*be helpful to*) auxiliar

beg /beg/ *vt/i* (*pt* **begged**) mendigar; (*entreat*) suplicar; **~ sb's pardon** pedir desculpa a alguém; **~ the question** fazer uma petição de princípio; **it's going ~ging** está sobrando, (*P*) a sobrar

began /bɪˈgæn/ ▶ BEGIN

beggar /ˈbegə(r)/ *n* mendigo *m*, pedinte *mf*; ! (*person*) cara *m* !

begin /bɪˈgɪn/ *vt/i* (*pt* **began**, *pp* **begun**, *pres p* **beginning**) começar, principiar. **~ner** *n* principiante *mf*. **~ning** *n* começo *m*, princípio *m*

begrudge /bɪˈgrʌdʒ/ *vt* ter inveja de; (*give*) dar de má vontade; **~ doing** fazer de má vontade or a contragosto

beguile /bɪˈgaɪl/ *vt* enganar

begun /bɪˈgʌn/ ▶ BEGIN

behalf /bɪˈhɑːf/ *n* **on ~ of** em nome de; (*in the interest of*) em favor de

behave /bɪˈheɪv/ *vi* portar-se; **~ (o.s.)** portar-se bem

behaviour /bɪˈheɪvjə(r)/ *n* conduta *f*, comportamento *m*

b

behead /bɪˈhed/ *vt* decapitar

behind /bɪˈhaɪnd/ *prep* atrás de ● *adv* atrás; (*late*) com atraso ● *n* [!] (*buttocks*) traseiro *m* [!]; **~ the times** antiquado, retrógrado; **leave ~** deixar para trás

beige /beɪʒ/ *a & n* bege *m*, (*P*) beige *m*

being /ˈbiːɪŋ/ *n* ser *m*; **bring into ~** criar; **come into ~** nascer, originar-se

belated /bɪˈleɪtɪd/ *a* tardio, atrasado

belch /beltʃ/ *vi* arrotar ● *vt* **~ out** ‹*smoke*› vomitar, lançar ● *n* arroto *m*

belfry /ˈbelfrɪ/ *n* campanário *m*

Belgi|um /ˈbeldʒəm/ *n* Bélgica *f*. **~an** *a & n* belga *mf*

belief /bɪˈliːf/ *n* crença *f*; (*trust*) confiança *f*; (*opinion*) convicção *f*

believ|e /bɪˈliːv/ *vt/i* acreditar; **~e in** acreditar em. **~able** *a* crível. **~er** /-ə(r)/ *n* crente *mf*

belittle /bɪˈlɪtl/ *vt* depreciar

bell /bel/ *n* sino *m*; (*small*) sineta *f*; (*on door, of phone*) campainha *f*; (*on cat, toy*) guizo *m*

bellow /ˈbeləʊ/ *vt/i* berrar, bramir; **~ out** rugir

belly /ˈbelɪ/ *n* barriga *f*, ventre *m*

belong /bɪˈlɒŋ/ *vi* **~ (to)** pertencer (a); ‹*club*› ser sócio (de)

belongings /bɪˈlɒŋɪŋz/ *npl* pertences *mpl*; **personal ~** objetos *mpl* de uso pessoal

beloved /bɪˈlʌvɪd/ *a & n* amado *m*

below /bɪˈləʊ/ *prep* abaixo de, debaixo de ● *adv* abaixo, em baixo; (*on page*) abaixo

belt /belt/ *n* cinto *m*; *Techn* correia *f*; *fig* zona *f* ● *vt* [✖] (*hit*) zurzir ● *vi* [✖] (*rush*) safar-se

bemused /bɪˈmjuːzd/ *a* estonteado, confuso; (*thoughtful*) pensativo

bench /bentʃ/ *n* banco *m*; (*seat, working-table*) bancada *f*; **the ~** *Jur* os magistrados (no tribunal)

bend /bend/ *vt/i* (*pt, pp* **bent**) curvar(-se); ‹*arm, leg*› dobrar; (*road, river*) fazer uma curva, virar ● *n* curva *f*; **~ over** debruçar-se or inclinar-se sobre

beneath /bɪˈniːθ/ *prep* abaixo de, debaixo de; *fig* abaixo de ● *adv* debaixo, em baixo

benefactor /ˈbenɪfæktə(r)/ *n* benfeitor *m*

beneficial /benɪˈfɪʃl/ *a* benéfico, proveitoso

beneficiary /benɪˈfɪʃərɪ/ *n* beneficiário *m*

benefit /ˈbenɪfɪt/ *n* (*advantage, performance*) benefício *m*; (*profit*) proveito *m*; (*allowance*) subsídio *m* ● *vt/i* (*pt* **benefited**, *pres p* **benefiting**) (*be useful to*) beneficiar (**by** de); (*do good to*) beneficiar, fazer bem a; (*receive benefit*) lucrar; ganhar (**by, from** com)

benevolen|t /bɪˈnevələnt/ *a* benevolente. **~ce** *n* benevolência *f*

bent /bent/ ▶ BEND *n* (*skill*) aptidão *f*; jeito *m* (**for** para); (*liking*) queda *f* (**for** para) ● *a* curvado; (*twisted*) torcido; [✖] (*dishonest*) desonesto; **~ on** decidido a

bequeath /bɪˈkwiːð/ *vt* legar

bereave|d /bɪˈriːvd/ *a* **the ~d wife/***etc* a esposa/*etc* do falecido; **the ~d family** a família enlutada. **~ment** *n* luto *m*

beret /ˈbereɪ/ *n* boina *f*

Bermuda /bəˈmjuːdə/ *n* Bermudas *fpl*

berry /ˈberɪ/ *n* baga *f*

berth /bɜːθ/ *n* (*in ship*) beliche *m*; (*in train*) couchette *f*; (*anchorage*) ancoradouro *m* ● *vi* atracar; **give a wide ~ to** passar ao largo, (*P*) de largo

beside /bɪˈsaɪd/ *prep* ao lado de, junto de; **~ o.s.** fora de si; **be ~ the point** não ter nada a ver com o assunto, não vir ao caso

besides /bɪˈsaɪdz/ *prep* além de; (*except*) fora, salvo ● *adv* além disso

besiege /bɪˈsiːdʒ/ *vt* sitiar, cercar; **~ with** assediar

best /best/ *a & n* **(the) ~** (o/a) melhor *mf* ● *adv* melhor; **~ man** padrinho *m* de casamento; **at (the) ~** na melhor das hipóteses; **do one's ~** fazer o (melhor) que se pode; **make the ~ of** tirar o melhor partido de; **the ~ part of** a maior parte de; **to the ~ of my knowledge** que eu saiba

bestseller /bestˈselə(r)/ *n* best-seller *m*

bet /bet/ *n* aposta *f* ● *vt/i* (*pt* **bet** *or* **betted**) apostar (**on** em)

betray /bɪˈtreɪ/ *vt* trair. **~al** *n* traição *f*

better /ˈbetə(r)/ *a & adv* melhor; **all the ~** tanto melhor; **~ off** (*richer*) mais rico; **he's ~ off at home** é melhor para ele ficar em casa; **I'd ~ go** é melhor ir-me embora; **get ~** melhorar ● *vt* melhorar ● *n* **our ~s** os nossos superiores *mpl*; **the ~ part of it** a maior parte disso; **get the ~ of sb** levar a melhor em relação a alguém

between /bɪˈtwiːn/ *prep* entre ● *adv* **in ~** no meio, no intervalo; **~ you and me** aqui entre nós

beverage /ˈbevərɪdʒ/ *n* bebida *f*

b

beware /bɪ'weə(r)/ *vi* acautelar-se (**of** com) tomar cuidado (**of** com)

bewilder /bɪ'wɪldə(r)/ *vt* desorientar. **~ment** *n* desorientação *f*, confusão *f*

bewitch /bɪ'wɪtʃ/ *vt* encantar, cativar

beyond /bɪ'jɒnd/ *prep* além de; (*doubt, reach*) fora de ● *adv* além; **it's ~ me** isso ultrapassa-me; **he lives ~ his means** ele vive acima dos seus meios

bias /'baɪəs/ *n* parcialidade *f*; *pej* (*prejudice*) preconceito *m*; *Sewing* viés *m* ● *vt* (*pt* **biased**) influenciar; **~ed against** de prevenção contra, (*P*) de pé atrás contra. **~ed** *a* parcial

bib /bɪb/ *n* babeiro *m*, babette *m*

Bible /'baɪbl/ *n* Bíblia *f*

biblical /'bɪblɪkl/ *a* bíblico

bibliography /bɪblɪ'ɒgrəfɪ/ *n* bibliografia *f*

biceps /'baɪseps/ *n* bíceps *m*

bicker /'bɪkə(r)/ *vi* questionar, discutir

bicycle /'baɪsɪkl/ *n* bicicleta *f* ● *vi* andar de bicicleta

bid /bɪd/ *n* oferta *f*, lance *m*; (*attempt*) tentativa *f* ● *vt/i* (*pt* **bid**, *pres p* **bidding**) fazer uma oferta, lançar, oferecer como lance. **~der** *n* licitante *mf*; **the highest ~der** quem dá or oferece mais

bide /baɪd/ *vt* **~ one's time** esperar pelo bom momento

big /bɪg/ *a* (**bigger**, **biggest**) grande; [x] (*generous*) generoso; **~ shot** [x] mandachuva *m* ● *adv* [!] em grande; **talk ~** gabar-se [!]; **think ~** [!] ter grandes planos. **~-headed** *a* pretensioso, convencido

bigam|y /'bɪgəmɪ/ *n* bigamia *f*. **~ist** *n* bígamo *m*. **~ous** *a* bígamo

bigot /'bɪgət/ *n* fanático *m*, intolerante *mf*. **~ed** *a* fanático, intolerante. **~ry** *n* fanatismo *m*, intolerância *f*

bigwig /'bɪgwɪg/ *n* [!] mandachuva *m*

bike /baɪk/ *n* [!] bicicleta *f*

bikini /bɪ'ki:nɪ/ *n* (*pl* **-is**) biquíni *m*

bile /baɪl/ *n* bílis *f*

bilingual /baɪ'lɪŋgwəl/ *a* bilíngue

bilious /'bɪlɪəs/ *a* bilioso

bill[1] /bɪl/ *n* (*invoice*) fatura *f*; (*in restaurant*) conta *f*; *Pol* projeto *m* de lei; *Amer* (*banknote*) nota *f* de banco; (*poster*) cartaz *m*; **~ of exchange** letra *f* de câmbio ● *vt* faturar; *Theatr* anunciar, pôr no programa; **~ sb for** apresentar a alguém a conta de

bill[2] /bɪl/ *n* (*of bird*) bico *m*

billiards /'bɪlɪədz/ *n* bilhar *m*

billion /'bɪlɪən/ *n* (10^9) mil milhões; (10^{12}) um milhão de milhões

bin /bɪn/ *n* (*for storage*) caixa *f*, lata *f*; (*for rubbish*) lata *f* do lixo, (*P*) caixote *m*

bind /baɪnd/ *vt* (*pt* **bound**) (*tie*) atar; ‹*book*› encadernar; *Jur* obrigar; (*cover the edge of*) debruar ● *n* [x] (*bore*) chatice *f* [x]; **be ~ing on** ser obrigatório para

binding /'baɪndɪŋ/ *n* encadernação *f*; (*braid*) debrum *m*

binge /bɪndʒ/ *n* [!] **go on a ~** cair na farra; (*overeat*) empanturrar-se. **~ drinking** *n*: consumo excessivo de álcool em pouco tempo

bingo /'bɪŋgəʊ/ *n* bingo *m* ● *int* acertei!

binoculars /bɪ'nɒkjʊləz/ *npl* binóculo *m*

biochemistry /baɪəʊ'kemɪstrɪ/ *n* bioquímica *f*

biodegradable /baɪəʊdɪ'greɪdəbl/ *a* biodegradável

biodiesel /'baɪəʊdi:zl/ *n* biodiesel *m*

biograph|y /baɪ'ɒgrəfɪ/ *n* biografia *f*. **~er** *n* biógrafo *m*

biolog|y /baɪ'ɒlədʒɪ/ *n* biologia *f*. **~ical** /-ə'lɒdʒɪkl/ *a* biológico. **~ist** *n* biólogo *m*

birch /bɜ:tʃ/ *n* (*tree*) bétula *f*

bird /bɜ:d/ *n* ave *f*, pássaro *m*; [x] (*girl*) garota *f* [!]; **~ sanctuary** refúgio *m* ornitológico. **~ flu** *n* gripe *f* aviária, (*P*) gripe *f* das aves; **~watcher** *n* ornitófilo *m*

Biro® /'baɪərəʊ/ *n* (*pl* **-os**) (caneta) esferográfica *f*, Bic® *f*

birth /bɜ:θ/ *n* nascimento *m*; **~ certificate** certidão *f* de nascimento; **~ control/rate** controle *m* /índice *m* de natalidade; **give ~ to** dar à luz. **~place** *n* lugar *m* de nascimento

birthday /'bɜ:θdeɪ/ *n* aniversário *m*, (*P*) dia *m* de anos; **his ~ is on 9 July** ele faz anos no dia 9 de julho

birthmark /'bɜ:θma:k/ *n* sinal *m*

biscuit /'bɪskɪt/ *n* biscoito *m*, bolacha *f*

bishop /'bɪʃəp/ *n* bispo *m*

bit[1] /bɪt/ *n* (*small piece, short time*) pedaço *m*, bocado *m*; (*of bridle*) freio *m*; (*of tool*) broca *f*; **a ~** um pouco

bit[2] /bɪt/ ▶ BITE

bitch /bɪtʃ/ *n* cadela *f*; [x] (*woman*) peste *f*; *fig* cadela *f* [x] ● *vt/i* [!] (*criticize*) malhar, (*P*) cortar (em) [!]; [!] (*grumble*) resmungar. **~y** *a* [!] maldoso

bite /baɪt/ *vt/i* (*pt* **bit**, *pp* **bitten**) morder; (*insect*) picar ● *n* mordida *f*; (*sting*) picada *f*; **have a ~ (to eat)** comer qualquer coisa

biting /ˈbaɪtɪŋ/ *a* cortante

bitter /ˈbɪtə(r)/ *a* amargo; (*weather*) glacial. **~ly** *adv* amargamente; **it's ~ly cold** está um frio de rachar. **~ness** *n* amargura *f*; (*resentment*) ressentimento *m*

bizarre /bɪˈzɑː(r)/ *a* bizarro

black /blæk/ *a* (**-er**, **-est**) negro, preto; **~ and blue** coberto de nódoas negras; **~ coffee** café *m* (sem leite); **~ eye** olho *m* negro; **~ ice** gelo *m* negro sobre o asfalto; **~ market** mercado *m* negro ● *n* negro *m*, preto *m*; **a ~** (*person*) um preto, um negro ● *vt* enegrecer; (*goods*) boicotar

blackberry /ˈblækbərɪ/ *n* amora *f* silvestre

blackbird /ˈblækbɜːd/ *n* melro *m*

blackboard /ˈblækbɔːd/ *n* quadro *m* preto

blackcurrant /ˈblækkʌrənt/ *n* groselha *f* negra

blacken /ˈblækən/ *vt/i* escurecer; **~ sb's name** difamar, denegrir

blacklist /ˈblæklɪst/ *n* lista *f* negra ● *vt* pôr na lista negra

blackmail /ˈblækmeɪl/ *n* chantagem *f* ● *vt* fazer chantagem. **~er** *n* chantagista *mf*

blackout /ˈblækaʊt/ *n* (*wartime*) blecaute *m*, (*P*) blackout *m*; *Med* desmaio *m*; *Electr* falta *f* de corrente; *Theatr* apagar *m* de luzes

bladder /ˈblædə(r)/ *n* bexiga *f*

blade /bleɪd/ *n* lâmina *f*; (*of oar, propeller*) pá *f*; (*of grass*) ervinha *f*, folhinha *f* de erva

blame /bleɪm/ *vt* culpar ● *n* culpa *f*; **be to ~** ser o culpado. **~less** *a* irrepreensível; (*innocent*) inocente

bland /blænd/ *a* (**-er**, **-est**) (*of manner*) suave; (*mild*) brando; (*insipid*) insípido

blank /blæŋk/ *a* ‹*space, cheque*› em branco; ‹*look*› vago; ‹*wall*› nu ● *n* espaço *m* em branco; (*cartridge*) cartucho *m* sem bala

blanket /ˈblæŋkɪt/ *n* cobertor *m*; *fig* manto *m* ● *vt* (*pt* **blanketed**) cobrir com cobertor; (*cover thickly*) encobrir, recobrir; **wet ~** desmancha-prazeres *mf*

blare /bleə(r)/ *vt/i* ressoar, atroar ● *n* clangor *m*; (*of horn*) buzinar *m*

blasé /ˈblɑːzeɪ/ *a* blasé

blasphem|y /ˈblæsfəmɪ/ *n* blasfêmia *f*, (*P*) blasfémia *f*

blast /blɑːst/ *n* (*gust*) rajada *f*; (*sound*) som *m*; (*explosion*) explosão *f* ● *vt* dinamitar; **~!** droga!, (*P*) raios!. **~ed** *a* maldito.

blatant /ˈbleɪtnt/ *a* flagrante; (*shameless*) descarado

blaze /bleɪz/ *n* chamas *fpl*; (*light*) clarão *m*; (*outburst*) explosão *f* ● *vi* arder; (*shine*) resplandecer, brilhar; **~ a trail** abrir o caminho, ser pioneiro

blazer /ˈbleɪzə(r)/ *n* blazer *m*

bleach /bliːtʃ/ *n* descolorante, descorante *m*; (*household*) água *f* sanitária, (*P*) lixívia ● *vt/i* branquear; ‹*hair*› oxigenar

bleak /bliːk/ *a* (**-er**, **-est**) ‹*place*› desolado; (*chilly*) frio; *fig* desanimador

bleary-eyed /ˈblɪərɪaɪd/ *a* com olhos injetados

bleat /bliːt/ *n* balido *m* ● *vi* balir

bleed /bliːd/ *vt/i* (*pt* **bled**) sangrar

bleep /bliːp/ *n* bip *m*. **~er** *n* bip *m*

blemish /ˈblemɪʃ/ *n* defeito *m*; (*on reputation*) mancha *f* ● *vt* manchar

blend /blend/ *vt/i* misturar(-se); (*go well together*) combinar-se ● *n* mistura *f*. **~er** *n Culin* liquidificador *m*

bless /bles/ *vt* abençoar; **be ~ed with** ter a felicidade de ter. **~ing** *n* benção *f*; (*thing one is glad of*) felicidade *f*; **it's a ~ing in disguise** há males que vêm para bem

blessed /ˈblesɪd/ *a* bem-aventurado; [!] (*cursed*) maldito

blew /bluː/ ▶ BLOW[1]

blight /blaɪt/ *n* doença *f* de plantas; *fig* influência *f* maligna ● *vt* arruinar, frustrar

blind /blaɪnd/ *a* cego; **~ alley** (*also fig*) beco *m* sem saída; **~ man/woman** cego *m* /cega *f* ● *vt* cegar ● *n* (*on window*) persiana *f*; (*deception*) ardil *m*; **be ~ to** não ver; **turn a ~ eye to** fingir não ver, fechar os olhos a. **~ly** *adv* às cegas. **~ness** *n* cegueira *f*

blindfold /ˈblaɪndfəʊld/ *a & adv* de olhos vendados ● *n* venda *f* ● *vt* vendar os olhos a

bling /blɪŋ/, **bling bling** /ˈblɪŋ blɪŋ/ *ns* [!] bling-bling *m*, estilo adotado principalmente por rappers, que se caracteriza pelo uso de muitas joias

blink /blɪŋk/ *vi* piscar

bliss /blɪs/ *n* felicidade *f*, beatitude *f*. **~ful** *a* felicíssimo

blister /ˈblɪstə(r)/ *n* bolha *f*, empola *f* ● *vi* empolar

blizzard /ˈblɪzəd/ *n* tempestade *f* de neve, nevasca *f*

bloated /ˈbləʊtɪd/ *a* inchado

blob /blɒb/ *n* pingo *m* grosso; (*stain*) mancha *f*

block /blɒk/ *n* bloco *m*; (*buildings*) quarteirão *m*; (*in pipe*) entupimento *m*; **~ (of flats)** prédio (de andares) *m*; **~ letters** maiúsculas *fpl* ● *vt* bloquear, obstruir; ‹*pipe*› entupir. **~age** *n* obstrução *f*

blockade /blɒˈkeɪd/ *n* bloqueio *m* ● *vt* bloquear

blog /blɒg/ *n* blogue *m*, (*P*) blog *m* ● *vi* blogar

blogger /ˈblɒgə(r)/ *n* blogueiro *m*, (*P*) bloguista *m*

bloke /bləʊk/ *n* [!] sujeito *m* [!]; cara *m* [!]

blond /blɒnd/ *a* & *n* louro *m*

blonde /blɒnd/ *a* & *n* loura *f*

blood /blʌd/ *n* sangue *m* ● *a* ‹*bank, donor, transfusion, etc*› de sangue; ‹*poisoning*› do sangue; ‹*group, vessel*› sanguíneo; **~ pressure** tensão *f* arterial; **~ test** exame *m* de sangue. **~-curdling** *a* horrendo

bloodhound /ˈblʌdhaʊnd/ *n* sabujo *m*

bloodshed /ˈblʌdʃed/ *n* derramamento *m* de sangue, carnificina *f*

bloodshot /ˈblʌdʃɒt/ *a* injetado de sangue

bloodstream /ˈblʌdstriːm/ *n* sangue *m*, fluxo *m* sanguíneo

bloodthirsty /ˈblʌdθɜːstɪ/ *a* sanguinário

bloody /ˈblʌdɪ/ *a* (**-ier**, **-iest**) ensanguentado; (*with much bloodshed*) sangrento; ⊠ grande; maldito ● *adv* ⊠ pra burro. **~-minded** *a* [!] do contra [!]; chato ⊠

bloom /bluːm/ *n* flor *f*; (*beauty*) frescura *f*, viço *m*; **in ~** em flor ● *vi* florir; *fig* vicejar

blossom /ˈblɒsəm/ *n* flor *f*; **in ~** em flor ● *vi* (*flower*) florir, desabrochar; (*develop, flourish*) florescer, desabrochar

blot /blɒt/ *n* mancha *f* ● *vt* (*pt* **blotted**) manchar; (*dry*) secar; **~ out** apagar; (*hide*) tapar, toldar

blotch /blɒtʃ/ *n* mancha *f*. **~y** *a* manchado

blouse /blaʊz/ *n* blusa *f*; (*in uniform*) blusão *m*

blow[1] /bləʊ/ *vt/i* (*pt* **blew**, *pp* **blown**) soprar; (*fuse*) fundir-se, queimar; ⊠ (*squander*) esbanjar; ‹*trumpet etc*› tocar; **~ a whistle** apitar; **~ one's nose** assoar o nariz; **~ out** ‹*candle*› apagar, soprar; **~ over** passar □ **~ away**, **~ off** *vt* levar, soprar ● *vi* voar, ir pelos ares (fora) □ **~ up** *vt* (*explode*) explodir; ‹*tyre*› encher; ‹*photograph*› ampliar ● *vi* (*explode*) explodir. **~-dry** *vt* ‹*hair*› fazer um brushing ● *n* brushing *m*

blow[2] /bləʊ/ *n* pancada *f*; (*slap*) bofetada *f*; (*punch*) murro *m*; *fig* golpe *m*

blowlamp /ˈbləʊlæmp/ *n* maçarico *m*

blown /bləʊn/ ▶ BLOW[1]

blue /bluː/ *a* (**-er**, **-est**) azul; (*indecent*) indecente ● *n* azul *m*; **come out of the ~** ser inesperado. **~s** *n Mus* blues; **have the ~s** [!] estar deprimido

bluebell /ˈbluːbel/ *n* jacinto *m* dos bosques

bluebottle /ˈbluːbɒtl/ *n* mosca *f* varejeira

blueprint /ˈbluːprɪnt/ *n* cópia *f* fotográfica de planta; *fig* projeto *m*

bluff /blʌf/ *vi* blefar, (*P*) fazer bluff ● *vt* enganar (fingindo), blefar ● *n* blefe *m*, (*P*) bluff *m*

blunder /ˈblʌndə(r)/ *vi* cometer um erro crasso; (*move*) avançar às cegas or tateando ● *n* erro *m* crasso, (*P*) bronca *f*

blunt /blʌnt/ *a* (**-er**, **-est**) embotado; ‹*person*› direto ● *vt* embotar. **~ly** *adv* sem rodeios

blur /blɜː(r)/ *n* mancha *f* ● *vt* (*pt* **blurred**) (*smear*) manchar; (*make indistinct*) toldar

blurb /blɜːb/ *n* contracapa *f*, sinopse *f* de um livro

blurt /blɜːt/ *vt* **~ out** deixar escapar

blush /blʌʃ/ *vi* corar ● *n* rubor *m*, vermelhidão *f*

bluster /ˈblʌstə(r)/ *vi* (*wind*) soprar em rajadas; (*swagger*) andar com ar fanfarrão. **~y** *a* borrascoso

boar /bɔː(r)/ *n* varrão *m*; **wild ~** javali *m*

board /bɔːd/ *n* tábua *f*; (*for notices*) quadro *m*, (*P*) placard *m*; (*food*) pensão *f*; *Admin* conselho *m* ● *vt/i* cobrir com tábuas; ‹*aircraft, ship, train*› embarcar (em); ‹*bus, train*› subir (em); **full ~** pensão *f* completa; **half ~** meia-pensão *f*; **on ~** a bordo; **~ up** entaipar; **~ with** ser pensionista em casa de. **~er** *n* pensionista *mf*; (*at school*) interno *m*. **~ing card** *n* cartão *m* de embarque; **~ing school** *n* internato *m*

boast /bəʊst/ *vi* gabar-se ● *vt* orgulhar-se de ● *n* gabarolice *f*. **~ful** *a* vaidoso

b

boat /bəʊt/ *n* barco *m*; **in the same ~** nas mesmas circunstâncias

bob /bɒb/ *vt/i* (*pt* **bobbed**) (*curtsy*) inclinar-se; (*hair*) cortar pelos ombros, (*P*) cortar à Joãozinho; **~ (up and down)** andar para cima e para baixo

bobsleigh /'bɒbsleɪ/ *n* trenó *m*

bodily /'bɒdɪlɪ/ *a* corporal, físico ● *adv* (*in person*) fisicamente, em pessoa; (*lift*) em peso

body /'bɒdɪ/ *n* corpo *m*; (*organization*) organismo *m*; **in a ~** em massa; **the main ~ of** o grosso de. **~(work)** *n* (*of car*) carroçaria *f*; **~building** *n* body building *m*; **~ piercing** *n* piercing *m* no corpo, (*P*) píercingue *m* de corpo

bodyguard /'bɒdɪgɑːd/ *n* guarda-costas *m*; (*escort*) escolta *f*

bog /bɒg/ *n* pântano *m* ● *vt* **get ~ged down** atolar-se; *fig* ficar emperrado

bogus /'bəʊgəs/ *a* falso

boil[1] /bɔɪl/ *n Med* furúnculo *m*

boil[2] /bɔɪl/ *vt/i* ferver; **come to the ~** ferver; **~ down to** resumir-se a; **~ over** transbordar, (*P*) a ferver **~ing hot** fervendo; **~ing point** ponto *m* de ebulição

boiler /'bɔɪlə(r)/ *n* caldeira *f*.; **~ suit** macacão *m*, (*P*) fato *m* de macaco

boisterous /'bɔɪstərəs/ *a* turbulento; (*noisy and cheerful*) animado

bold /bəʊld/ *a* (**-er**, **-est**) ousado; (*of colours*) vivo. **~ness** *n* ousadia *f*

Bolivia /bə'lɪvɪə/ *n* Bolívia *f*. **~n** *a & n* boliviano *m*

bolster /'bəʊlstə(r)/ *n* travesseiro *m* ● *vt* sustentar; ajudar; **~ one's spirits** levantar o moral

bolt /bəʊlt/ *n* (*on door etc*) ferrolho *m*; (*for nut*) parafuso *m*; (*lightning*) relâmpago *m*; **~ upright** reto *or* (*P*) direito como um fuso ● *vt* aferrolhar; ‹*food*› engolir ● *vi* fugir, disparar

bomb /bɒm/ *n* bomba *f* ● *vt* bombardear. **~er** *n* (*aircraft*) bombardeiro *m*; (*person*) bombista *mf*

bombard /bɒm'bɑːd/ *vt* bombardear

bombastic /bɒm'bæstɪk/ *a* bombástico

bombshell /'bɒmʃel/ *n* granada *f*; *fig* bomba *f*

bond /bɒnd/ *n* (*agreement*) compromisso *m*; (*link*) laço *m*, vínculo *m*; *Comm* obrigação *f*; **in ~** em depósito na alfândega

bondage /'bɒndɪdʒ/ *n* escravidão *f*, servidão *f*

bone /bəʊn/ *n* osso *m*; (*of fish*) espinha *f*; **~ idle** preguiçoso ● *vt* desossar. **~ dry** a completamente seco, ressecado

bonfire /'bɒnfaɪə(r)/ *n* fogueira *f*

bonnet /'bɒnɪt/ *n* chapéu *m*; *Auto* capô *m* do motor, (*P*) capot *m*

bonus /'bəʊnəs/ *n* bônus *m*, (*P*) bónus *m*

bony /'bəʊnɪ/ *a* (**-ier**, **-iest**) ossudo; ‹*meat*, *fish*› cheio de ossos/de espinhas

boo /buː/ *int* fora ● *vt/i* vaiar ● *n* vaia *f*

boob /buːb/ *n* ☒ (*mistake*) asneira *f*; disparate *m* ● *vi* ☒ fazer asneira(s)

booby /'buːbɪ/ *n* **~ prize** prêmio *or* (*P*) prémio *m* de consolação; **~ trap** bomba *f* armadilhada

book /bʊk/ *n* livro *m*; **~s** *Comm* contas *fpl*, escrita *f*; **~ of matches** carteira *f* de fósforos; **~ of tickets** (*bus*, *tube*) caderneta *f* de módulos; **~ing office** bilheteria *f*, (*P*) bilheteira *f* ● *vt* (*enter*) averbar, registrar; *Comm* escriturar; (*reserve*) marcar, reservar; **be fully ~ed** ter a lotação esgotada

bookcase /'bʊkkeɪs/ *n* estante *f*

bookkeep|er /'bʊkkiːpə(r)/ *n* guarda-livros *m*. **~ing** *n* contabilidade *f*, escrituração *f*

booklet /'bʊklɪt/ *n* brochura *f*

bookmaker /'bʊkmeɪkə(r)/ *n* book (maker) *m*

bookmark /'bʊkmɑːk/ *n* marca *f* de livro, marcador *m* de página

bookseller /'bʊkselə(r)/ *n* livreiro *m*

bookshop /'bʊkʃɒp/ *n* livraria *f*

bookstall /'bʊkstɔːl/ *n* quiosque *m*

boom /buːm/ *vi* ribombar; (*of trade*) prosperar ● *n* (*sound*) ribombo *m*; *Comm* boom *m*, prosperidade *f*

boon /buːn/ *n* bênção *f*, vantagem *f*

boost /buːst/ *vt* desenvolver, promover; ‹*morale*› levantar; ‹*price*› aumentar ● *n* força *f* ⊡. **~er** *n Med* dose suplementar *f*; (*vaccine*) revacinação *f*, (*P*) reforço *m*

boot /buːt/ *n* bota *f*; *Auto* portamala *f*, bagageira ● *vt* **~ (up)** *Comput* dar carga em; **to ~** (*in addition*) ainda por cima

booth /buːð/ *n* barraca *f*; (*telephone*, *voting*) cabine *f*

booty /'buːtɪ/ *n* saque *m*, pilhagem *f*

booze /buːz/ *vi* ⊡ embebedar-se ⊡; encharcar-se ⊡ ● *n* ⊡ pinga *f* ⊡

border /'bɔːdə(r)/ *n* borda *f*, margem *f*; (*frontier*) fronteira *f*; (*garden bed*) canteiro *m* ● *vi* **~ on** confinar com;

(*be almost the same as*) atingir as raias de

borderline /ˈbɔːdəlaɪn/ *n* linha *f* divisória; **~ case** caso *m* limite

bore[1] /bɔː(r)/ ▶ BEAR[2]

bore[2] /bɔː(r)/ *vt/i Techn* furar, perfurar ● *n* (*of gun barrel*) calibre *m*

bore[3] /bɔː(r)/ *vt* aborrecer, entediar ● *n* maçante *m*; (*thing*) chatice *f*; **be ~d** aborrecer-se, maçar-se. **~dom** *n* tédio *m*. **boring** *a* tedioso, maçante

born /bɔːn/ *a* nascido; **be ~** nascer

borne /bɔːn/ ▶ BEAR[2]

borough /ˈbʌrə/ *n* município *m*

borrow /ˈbɒrəʊ/ *vt* pedir emprestado (**from** a)

bosom /ˈbʊzəm/ *n* peito *m*; (*woman's; also fig*) (*midst*) seio *m*; **~ friend** amigo íntimo *m*

boss /bɒs/ *n* [!] patrão *m*; patroa *f*; mandachuva *m* [!] ● *vt* mandar; **~ sb about** [!] mandar em alguém

bossy /ˈbɒsɪ/ *a* mandão, autoritário

botan|y /ˈbɒtənɪ/ *n* botânica *f*. **~ical** /bəˈtænɪkl/ *a* botânico. **~ist** /-ɪst/ *n* botânico *m*

botch /bɒtʃ/ *vt* atamancar; (*spoil*) estragar, escangalhar

both /bəʊθ/ *a & pron* ambos, os dois; **~ of us** nós dois; **~ the books** ambos os livros ● *adv* **~ ... and** não só ... mas também, tanto ... como

bother /ˈbɒðə(r)/ *vt/i* incomodar(-se) ● *n* (*inconvenience*) incômodo *m*, (*P*) incómodo *m*; trabalho *m*; (*effort*) custo *m*, trabalho *m*; (*worry*) preocupação *f*; **don't ~** não se incomode; **I can't be ~ed** não posso me dar o trabalho

bottle /ˈbɒtl/ *n* garrafa *f*; (*small*) frasco *m*; (*for baby*) mamadeira *f*, (*P*) biberão *m* ● *vt* engarrafar; **~ up** reprimir. **~ opener** *n* saca-rolhas *m*

bottleneck /ˈbɒtlnek/ *n* (*obstruction*) entrave *m*; (*traffic jam*) engarrafamento *m*

bottom /ˈbɒtəm/ *n* fundo *m*; (*of hill*) sopé *m*; (*buttocks*) traseiro *m* ● *a* inferior; (*last*) último; **from top to ~** de alto a baixo

bough /baʊ/ *n* ramo *m*

bought /bɔːt/ ▶ BUY

boulder /ˈbəʊldə(r)/ *n* pedregulho *m*

bounce /baʊns/ *vi* saltar; (*of person*) pular, dar pulos; [x] (*of cheque*) ser devolvido ● *vt* fazer saltar ● *n* (*of ball*) salto *m*, (*P*) ressalto *m*

bound[1] /baʊnd/ *vi* pular; (*move by jumping*) ir aos pulos ● *n* pulo *m*

bound[2] /baʊnd/ ▶ BIND ● *a* **be ~ for** ir com destino a, ir para; **be ~ to** (*obliged*) ser obrigado a; (*certain*) haver de; **she's ~ to like it** ela há de gostar disso

b

boundary /ˈbaʊndrɪ/ *n* limite *m*

bound|s /baʊndz/ *npl* limites *mpl*; **out of ~s** interdito; **~ed by** limitado por. **~less** *a* sem limites

bouquet /bʊˈkeɪ/ *n* ramo *m* de flores; (*wine*) aroma *m*

bout /baʊt/ *n* período *m*; *Med* ataque *m*; *Boxing* combate *m*

boutique /buːˈtiːk/ *n* boutique *f*

bow[1] /bəʊ/ *n* (*weapon*) *Mus* arco *m*; (*knot*) laço *m*. **~ tie** *n* gravata borboleta *f*, (*P*) laço *m*

bow[2] /baʊ/ *n* vênia *f*, (*P*) vénia *f* ● *vt/i* inclinar(-se), curvar-se

bow[3] /baʊ/ *n Naut* proa *f*

bowels /ˈbaʊəlz/ *npl* intestinos *mpl*; *fig* entranhas *fpl*

bowl[1] /bəʊl/ *n* (*basin*) bacia *f*; (*for food*) tigela *f*; (*of pipe*) fornilho *m*

bowl[2] /bəʊl/ *n* (*ball*) boliche *m*, (*P*) bola *f* de madeira ● *vt Cricket* lançar; **~ over** siderar, varar. **~ing** *n* boliche *m*, (*P*) bowling *m*. **~s** *npl* boliche *m*, (*P*) jogo *m* com bolas de madeira. **~ing alley** *n* pista *f*

bowler[1] /ˈbəʊlə(r)/ *n Cricket* lançador *m*

bowler[2] /ˈbəʊlə(r)/ *n* **~ (hat)** (chapéu de) coco *m*

box[1] /bɒks/ *n* caixa *f*; *Theatr* camarote *m*; **B~ing Day** feriado *m* no primeiro dia útil depois do Natal ● *vt* pôr dentro duma caixa; **~ in** fechar. **~ office** *n* bilheteria *f*, (*P*) bilheteira *f*

box[2] /bɒks/ *vt/i Sport* lutar boxe; **~ the ears of** esbofetear. **~er** *n* pugilista *m*, boxeur *m*. **~ing** *n* boxe *m*, pugilismo *m*

boy /bɔɪ/ *n* rapaz *m*. **~friend** *n* namorado *m*. **~ish** *a* de menino

boycott /ˈbɔɪkɒt/ *vt* boicotar ● *n* boicote *m*

bra /brɑː/ *n* soutien *m*

brace /breɪs/ *n* braçadeira *f*; (*dental*) aparelho *m*; (*tool*) berbequim *m*; (*of birds*) par *m* ● *vt* apoiar, firmar; **~ o.s.** concentrar as energias, fazer força; (*for blow*) preparar-se. **~s** *npl* (*for trousers*) suspensórios *mpl*

bracelet /ˈbreɪslɪt/ *n* bracelete *m*, pulseira *f*

bracing /ˈbreɪsɪŋ/ *a* tonificante, estimulante

b

bracket /ˈbrækɪt/ *n* suporte *m*; (*group*) grupo *m*; **age/income ~** faixa *f* etária/salarial; **round ~s** parênteses *mpl*; **square ~s** parênteses *mpl*, colchetes *mpl* ● *vt* (*pt* **bracketed**) pôr entre parênteses; (*put together*) pôr em pé de igualdade, agrupar

brag /bræg/ *vi* (*pt* **bragged**) gabar-se (**about** de)

braid /breɪd/ *n* galão *m*; (*of hair*) trança *f*

Braille /breɪl/ *n* braile *m*

brain /breɪn/ *n* cérebro *m*; miolos *mpl* [!]; *fig* inteligência *f*; **~s** *Culin* miolos *mpl*. **~less** *a* estúpido

brainwash /ˈbreɪnwɒʃ/ *vt* fazer uma lavagem cerebral

brainwave /ˈbreɪnweɪv/ *n* ideia *f* genial

brainy /ˈbreɪnɪ/ *a* (**-ier**, **-iest**) inteligente, esperto

braise /breɪz/ *vt Culin* estufar

brake /breɪk/ *n* travão *m* ● *vt/i* travar; **~ light** farol *m* do freio, (*P*) luz *f* de travagem

branch /brɑːntʃ/ *n* ramo *m*; (*of road*) ramificação *f*; (*of railway line*) ramal *m*; *Comm* sucursal *f*; (*of bank*) balcão *m* ● *vi* **~ (off)** bifurcar-se, ramificar-se

brand /brænd/ *n* marca *f*; **~ name** marca *f* de fábrica ● *vt* marcar; **~ sb as** tachar alguém de, (*P*) rotular alguém de. **~-new** *a* novo em folha

brandish /ˈbrændɪʃ/ *vt* brandir

brandy /ˈbrændɪ/ *n* aguardente *f*, conhaque *m*

brass /brɑːs/ *n* latão *m*; **the ~** *Mus* os metais *mpl*; **top ~** [✱] os chefões [!] ● *a* de cobre, de latão; **get down to ~ tacks** tratar das coisas sérias

brassiere /ˈbræsɪə(r)/ *n* soutien *m*

brat /bræt/ *n pej* fedelho *m*

bravado /brəˈvɑːdəʊ/ *n* bravata *f*

brave /breɪv/ *a* (**-er**, **-est**) bravo, valente ● *vt* arrostar. **~ry** /-ərɪ/ *n* bravura *f*

brawl /brɔːl/ *n* briga *f*, rixa *f*, desordem *f* ● *vi* brigar

brawn /brɔːn/ *n* força *f* muscular, músculo *m*. **~y** *a* musculoso

bray /breɪ/ *n* zurro *m* ● *vi* zurrar

brazen /ˈbreɪzn/ *a* descarado

Brazil /brəˈzɪl/ *n* Brasil *m*; **~ nut** castanha *f* do Pará. **~ian** *a & n* brasileiro *m*

breach /briːtʃ/ *n* quebra *f*; (*gap*) brecha *f* ● *vt* abrir uma brecha em; **~ of contract** quebra *f* de contrato; **~ of the peace** perturbação *f* da ordem pública; **~ of trust** abuso *m* de confiança

bread /bred/ *n* pão *m*. **~winner** *n* ganha-pão *m*

breadcrumbs /ˈbredkrʌmz/ *npl* migalhas *fpl*; *Culin* farinha *f* de rosca

breadth /bredθ/ *n* largura *f*; (*of mind, view*) abertura *f*

break /breɪk/ *vt* (*pt* **broke**, *pp* **broken**) partir, quebrar; ‹*vow, silence, etc*› quebrar; ‹*law*› transgredir; ‹*journey*› interromper; ‹*news*› dar; ‹*a record*› bater; **~ one's arm/leg** quebrar *or* (*P*) partir o braço/a perna ● *vi* partir-se, quebrar-se; ‹*voice, weather*› mudar; **~ in** forçar uma entrada; **~ out** rebentar ● *n* quebra *f*, ruptura *f*; (*interval*) intervalo *m*; [!] (*opportunity*) oportunidade *f*; chance *f* □ **~ down** *vt* analisar ● *vi* (*of person*) ir-se abaixo; (*of machine*) avariar-se. **~ off** *vt* quebrar ● *vi* desligar-se. **~ up** *vt/i* terminar ● *vi* (*of schools*) entrar em férias. **~able** *a* quebrável. **~age** *n* quebra *f*

breakdown /ˈbreɪkdaʊn/ *n Techn* avaria *f*, pane *f*; *Med* esgotamento *m* nervoso; (*of figures*) análise *f* ● *a Auto* de pronto-socorro; **~ van** pronto-socorro *m*

breaker /ˈbreɪkə(r)/ *n* vaga *f* de rebentação

breakfast /ˈbrekfəst/ *n* café *m* da manhã, (*P*) pequeno-almoço

breakthrough /ˈbreɪkθruː/ *n* descoberta *f* decisiva, avanço *m*

breakwater /ˈbreɪkwɔːtə(r)/ *n* quebra-mar *m*

breast /brest/ *n* peito *m*. **~feed** *vt* amamentar; **~stroke** *n* estilo *m* bruços

breath /breθ/ *n* respiração *f*; **bad ~** mau hálito *m*; **out of ~** sem fôlego; **under one's ~** num murmúrio, baixo. **~less** *a* ofegante

breath|e /briːð/ *vt/i* respirar; **~e in** inspirar; **~e out** expirar. **~ing** *n* respiração *f*. **~ing space** *n* pausa *f*

breather /ˈbriːðə(r)/ *n* pausa *f* de descanso, momento *m* para respirar

breathtaking /ˈbreθteɪkɪŋ/ *a* assombroso, arrebatador

bred /bred/ ▶ BREED

breed /briːd/ *vt* (*pt* **bred**) criar ● *vi* reproduzir-se ● *n* raça *f*. **~er** *n* criador *m*. **~ing** *n* criação *f*; *fig* educação *f*

breez|e /briːz/ *n* brisa *f*. **~y** *a* fresco

brevity /ˈbrevətɪ/ *n* brevidade *f*

brew /bruː/ *vt* ‹*beer*› fabricar; ‹*tea*› fazer; *fig* armar; tramar ● *vi* fermentar; ‹*tea*› preparar; *fig* armar-se; preparar-se

● *n* decocção *f*; (*tea*) infusão *f*. **~er** *n* cervejeiro *m*. **~ery** *n* cervejaria *f*

bribe /braɪb/ *n* suborno *m* ● *vt* subornar. **~ry** /-ərɪ/ *n* suborno *m*, corrupção *f*

brick /brɪk/ *n* tijolo *m*

bricklayer /'brɪkleɪə(r)/ *n* pedreiro *m*

bridal /'braɪdl/ *a* nupcial

bride /braɪd/ *n* noiva *f*

bridegroom /'braɪdgrʊm/ *n* noivo *m*

bridesmaid /'braɪdzmeɪd/ *n* dama *f* de honra, (*P*) de honor

bridge[1] /brɪdʒ/ *n* ponte *f*; (*of nose*) cana *f* ● *vt* **~ a gap** preencher uma lacuna

bridge[2] /brɪdʒ/ *n Cards* bridge *m*

bridle /'braɪdl/ *n* cabeçada *f*, freio *m* ● *vt* refrear

brief[1] /bri:f/ *a* (**-er**, **-est**) breve. **~s** *npl* (*men's*) cueca *f*, (*P*) slip *m*; (*women's*) calcinhas *fpl*, (*P*) cuecas *fpl*. **~ly** *adv* brevemente

brief[2] /bri:f/ *n Jur* sumário *m*; (*case*) causa *f*; (*instructions*) instruções *fpl* ● *vt* dar instruções a

briefcase /'bri:fkeɪs/ *n* pasta *f*

brigad|e /brɪ'geɪd/ *n* brigada *f*

bright /braɪt/ *a* (**-er**, **-est**) brilhante; (*of colour*) vivo; (*of light*) forte; ‹*room*› claro; (*cheerful*) alegre; (*clever*) inteligente. **~ness** *n* (*sheen*) brilho *m*; (*clarity*) claridade *f*; (*intelligence*) inteligência *f*

brighten /'braɪtn/ *vt* alegrar ● *vi* (*of weather*) clarear; (*of face*) animar-se, iluminar-se

brillian|t /'brɪljənt/ *a* brilhante. **~ce** *n* brilho *m*

brim /brɪm/ *n* borda *f*; (*of hat*) aba *f* ● *vi* (*pt* **brimmed**) **~ over** transbordar, cair por fora

bring /brɪŋ/ *vt* (*pt* **brought**) trazer; **~ about** causar; **~ back** trazer (de volta); (*call to mind*) relembrar; **~ down** trazer para baixo; ‹*bird, plane*› abater; (*prices*) baixar; **~ forward** adiantar, apresentar; **~ it off** ser bem sucedido (em alguém coisa); **~ out** (*take out*) tirar; (*show*) revelar; ‹*book*› publicar; **~ round** or **to** reanimar, fazer voltar a si; **~ to bear** ‹*pressure etc*› exercer; **~ up** educar; *Med* vomitar; ‹*question*› levantar

brink /brɪŋk/ *n* beira *f*, borda *f*

brisk /brɪsk/ *a* (**-er**, **-est**) ‹*pace, movement*› vivo, rápido; ‹*business, demand*› grande

bristl|e /'brɪsl/ *n* pelo *m*

Britain /'brɪtən/ *n* Grã-Bretanha *f*

British /'brɪtɪʃ/ *a* britânico; **the ~** o povo *m* britânico, os britânicos *mpl*

brittle /'brɪtl/ *a* frágil

broach /brəʊtʃ/ *vt* abordar, entabular, encetar

broad /brɔ:d/ *a* (**-er**, **-est**) largo; (*daylight*) pleno; **~band** banda *f* larga; **~ bean** fava *f*. **~-minded** *a* tolerante, liberal. **~ly** *adv* de modo geral

broadband /'brɔ:dbænd/ *n* banda larga *f*

broadcast /'brɔ:dkɑ:st/ *vt/i* (*pt* **broadcast**) transmitir, fazer uma transmissão; ‹*person*› cantar, falar *etc* na rádio or na TV ● *n* emissão *f*. **~ing** *a & n* (de) rádiodifusão *f*

broaden /'brɔ:dn/ *vt/i* alargar(-se)

broccoli /'brɒkəlɪ/ *n inv* brócolis *mpl*, (*P*) brócolos *mpl*

brochure /'brəʊʃə(r)/ *n* brochura *f*

broke /brəʊk/ ▶ **BREAK** *a* ⊠ depenado ⊠ liso, (*P*) ⊠ teso ⊠

broken /'brəʊkən/ *a* **~ English** inglês *m* estropeado. **~-hearted** *a* com o coração despedaçado

broker /'brəʊkə(r)/ *n* corretor *m*, broker *m*

bronchitis /brɒŋ'kaɪtɪs/ *n* bronquite *f*

bronze /brɒnz/ *n* bronze *m*

brooch /brəʊtʃ/ *n* broche *m*

brood /bru:d/ *n* ninhada *f* ● *vi* chocar; *fig* cismar. **~y** *a* (*hen*) choca; *fig* sorumbático

brook /brʊk/ *n* regato *m*, ribeiro *m*

broom /bru:m/ *n* vassoura *f*; *Bot* giesta *f*

broth /brɒθ/ *n* caldo *m*

brothel /'brɒθl/ *n* bordel *m*

brother /'brʌðə(r)/ *n* irmão *m*. **~-in-law** *n* (*pl* **~s-in-law**) cunhado *m*. **~hood** *n* irmandade *f*; fraternidade *f*. **~ly** *a* fraternal

brought /brɔ:t/ ▶ **BRING**

brow /braʊ/ *n* (*forehead*) testa *f*; (*of hill*) cume *m*; (*eyebrow*) sobrancelha *f*

brown /braʊn/ *a* (**-er**, **-est**) castanho ● *n* castanho *m* ● *vt/i* acastanhar; (*in the sun*) bronzear, tostar; ‹*meat*› alourar

browse /braʊz/ *vi* (*through book*) folhear; (*of animal*) pastar; (*in a shop*) olhar sem comprar. **~r** *n Comput* navegador *m*

bruise /bru:z/ *n* hematoma *m*, contusão *f* ● *vt* causar um hematoma. **~d** *a* coberto de hematomas, contuso; ‹*fruit*› machucado, (*P*) pisado

b

brunette /bru:'net/ *n* morena *f*

brunt /brʌnt/ *n* **the ~ of** o maior peso de, o pior de

brush /brʌʃ/ *n* escova *f*; (*painter's*) pincel *m*; (*skirmish*) escaramuça *f*; **~ against** roçar; **~ aside** não fazer caso de; **~ off** [!] (*reject*) mandar passear [!]; **~ up (on)** aperfeiçoar

brusque /bru:sk/ *a* brusco

Brussels /'brʌslz/ *n* Bruxelas *f*; **~ sprouts** couve-de-Bruxelas *f*

brutal /'bru:tl/ *a* brutal. **~ity** /-'tæləti/ *n* brutalidade *f*

brute /bru:t/ *n & a* (*animal, person*) bruto *m*; **by ~ force** por força bruta

BSc *abbr* (= **Bachelor of Science**) ▶ BACHELOR

BSE /'bi:ɛs'i:/ *n* EEB, encefalopatia espongiforme bovina

btw *abbr* (= **by the way**) a propósito; **Thursday, ~, is also the day that our new kitchen gets delivered** a propósito, quinta-feira é também o dia em que nos entregam a nova cozinha

bubb|le /'bʌbl/ *n* bolha *f*; (*of soap*) bola *f* de sabão ● *vi* borbulhar; **~le over** transbordar. **~le gum** *n* chiclete *m*, (*P*) pastilha *f* elástica. **~ly** *a* efervescente

buck[1] /bʌk/ *n* macho *m* ● *vi* dar galões, (*P*) corcovear □ **~ up** *vt/i* ☒ animar(-se); ☒ (*rush*) apressar-se; despachar-se

buck[2] /bʌk/ *n Amer* ☒ dólar *m*

buck[3] /bʌk/ *n* **pass the ~**☒ fazer o jogo do empurra [!]

bucket /'bʌkɪt/ *n* balde *m*

buckle /'bʌkl/ *n* fivela *f* ● *vt/i* afivelar(-se); (*bend*) torcer(-se), vergar; **~ down to** empenhar-se

bud /bʌd/ *n* botão *m*, rebento *m* ● *vi* (*pt* **budded**) rebentar; **in ~** em botão

Buddhis|t /'bʊdɪst/ *a & n* budista *mf*. **~m** /-zəm/ *n* budismo *m*

budding /'bʌdɪŋ/ *a* nascente, em botão, incipiente

budge /bʌdʒ/ *vt/i* mexer(-se)

budget /'bʌdʒɪt/ *n* orçamento *m* ● *vi* (*pt* **budgeted**) **~ for** prever no orçamento *m*

buff /bʌf/ *n* (*colour*) cor *f* de camurça; [!] fanático *m*; entusiasta *mf* ● *vt* polir

buffalo /'bʌfələʊ/ *n* (*pl* **-oes**) búfalo *m*; *Amer* bisão *m*

buffer /'bʌfə(r)/ *n* para-choque *m*

buffet[1] /'bʊfeɪ/ *n* (*meal, counter*) bufê *m*, (*P*) bufete *m*

buffet[2] /'bʌfɪt/ *vt* (*pt* **buffeted**) esbofetear

bug /bʌg/ *n* (*insect*) bicho *m*; (*bedbug*) percevejo *m*; ☒ (*germ*) vírus *m*; ☒ (*device*) microfone *m* de escuta; ☒ (*defect*) defeito *m* ● *vt* (*pt* **bugged**) grampear; *Amer* ☒ (*annoy*) chatear ☒

buggy /'bʌgɪ/ *n* (*for baby*) carrinho *m*

bugle /'bju:gl/ *n* clarim *m*

build /bɪld/ *vt/i* (*pt* **built**) construir, edificar ● *n* físico *m*, compleição *f* □ **~ up** *vt/i* criar; (*increase*) aumentar; (*accumulate*) acumular(-se). **~-up** *n* acumulação *f*; *fig* publicidade *f*. **~er** *n* construtor *m*, empreiteiro *m*; (*workman*) operário *m*

building /'bɪldɪŋ/ *n* edifício *m*, prédio *m*; **~ site** canteiro *m* de obras; **~ society** sociedade *f* de investimentos imobiliários

built /bɪlt/ ▶ BUILD. **~-in** *a* incorporado; **~-in wardrobe** armário *m* embutido na parede; **~-up** *a* urbanizado

bulb /bʌlb/ *n* bolbo *m*; *Electr* lâmpada *f*. **~ous** *a* bolboso

Bulgaria /bʌl'geərɪə/ *n* Bulgária *f*

bulg|e /bʌldʒ/ *n* bojo *m*, saliência *f* ● *vi* inchar; (*jut out*) fazer uma saliência. **~ing** *a* inchado; ‹*pocket etc*› cheio

bulk /bʌlk/ *n* quantidade *f*, volume *m*; **in ~** por grosso; (*loose*) a granel; **the ~ of** a maior parte de. **~y** *a* volumoso

bull /bʊl/ *n* touro *m*. **~seye** *n* (*of target*) centro *m* do alvo, mosca *f*

bulldog /'bʊldɒg/ *n* buldogue *m*

bulldoze /'bʊldəʊz/ *vt* terraplanar. **~r** /-ə(r)/ *n* bulldozer *m*

bullet /'bʊlɪt/ *n* bala *f*. **~proof** *a* à prova de balas; ‹*vehicle*› blindado

bulletin /'bʊlətɪn/ *n* boletim *m*

bullfight /'bʊlfaɪt/ *n* tourada *f*, corrida *f* de touros. **~er** *n* toureiro *m*. **~ing** *n* tauromaquia *f*

bullring /'bʊlrɪŋ/ *n* arena *f*, (*P*) praça *f* de touros

bully /'bʊlɪ/ *n* mandão *m*, pessoa *f* prepotente; *Schol* terror *m*, o mau ● *vt* intimidar; (*treat badly*) atormentar; (*coerce*) forçar (**into** a)

bum[1] /bʌm/ *n* ☒ (*buttocks*) traseiro *m*; bunda *f* ☒

bum[2] /bʌm/ *n Amer* ☒ vagabundo *m*

bump /bʌmp/ *n* choque *m*, embate *m*; (*swelling*) inchaço *m*; (*on head*) galo *m* ● *vt/i* bater, chocar; **~ into** bater em, chocar com; (*meet*) esbarrar com, encontrar. **~y** *a* ‹*surface*› irregular; ‹*ride*› aos solavancos

bumper /ˈbʌmpə(r)/ *n* para-choques *m inv* ● *a* excepcional

bun /bʌn/ *n* pãozinho *m* doce com passas; (*hair*) coque *m*

bunch /bʌntʃ/ *n* (*of flowers*) ramo *m*; (*of keys*) molho *m*; (*of people*) grupo *m*; (*of grapes*) cacho *m*

bundle /ˈbʌndl/ *n* molho *m* ● *vt* atar num molho; (*push*) despachar

bung /bʌŋ/ *n* batoque *m*, rolha *f* ● *vt* rolhar; ⊠ (*throw*) atirar; deitar; **~ up** entupir

bungalow /ˈbʌŋgələʊ/ *n* chalé *m*; (*outside Europe*) bungalô *m*, (*P*) bungalow *m*

bungle /ˈbʌŋgl/ *vt* fazer malfeito, estragar

bunion /ˈbʌnjən/ *n Med* joanete *m*

bunk /bʌŋk/ *n* (*in train*) couchette *f*; (*in ship*) beliche *m*. **~ beds** *npl* beliches *mpl*

bunker /ˈbʌŋkə(r)/ *n Mil* abrigo *m*, casamata *f*, bunker *m*; *Golf* obstáculo *m* em cova de areia

buoy /bɔɪ/ *n* boia *f* ● *vt* **~ up** animar

buoyan|t /ˈbɔɪənt/ *a* flutuante; *fig* alegre. **~cy** *n fig* alegria *f*; exuberância *f*

burden /ˈbɜːdn/ *n* fardo *m* ● *vt* carregar, sobrecarregar

bureau /ˈbjʊərəʊ/ *n* (*pl* **-eaux** /-əʊz/) (*desk*) secretária *f*; (*office*) seção *f*, (*P*) secção *f*

bureaucracy /bjʊəˈrɒkrəsɪ/ *n* burocracia *f*

bureaucrat /ˈbjʊərəkræt/ *n* burocrata *mf*. **~ic** /-ˈkrætɪk/ *a* burocrático

burger /ˈbɜːgə(r)/ *n* hambúrguer *m*

burglar /ˈbɜːglə(r)/ *n* ladrão *m*, assaltante *mf*. **~ alarm** *n* alarme *m* contra ladrões. **~ize** *vt Amer* assaltar. **~y** *n* assalto *m*

burgle /ˈbɜːgl/ *vt* assaltar

burial /ˈberɪəl/ *n* enterro *m*

burka, **burkha** /ˈbəːkə, ˈbʊrkɑ/ *n* burca *f*

burly /ˈbɜːlɪ/ *a* (**-ier**, **-iest**) robusto e corpulento, forte

Burm|a /ˈbɜːmə/ *n* Birmânia *f*. **~ese** /-ˈmiːz/ *a* & *n* birmanês *m*

burn /bɜːn/ *vt* (*pt* **burned** *or* **burnt**) queimar ● *vi* queimar(-se), arder ● *n* queimadura *f*; **~ down** reduzir a cinzas. **~er** *n* (*of stove*) bico *m* de gás

burnt /bɜːnt/ ▶ BURN

burp /bɜːp/ *n* ⓘ arroto *m* ● *vi* ⓘ arrotar

burrow /ˈbʌrəʊ/ *n* toca *f* ● *vi* cavar, fazer uma toca

burst /bɜːst/ *vt/i* (*pt* **burst**) arrebentar; **~ into** ‹*flames, room etc*› irromper em; **~ into tears** desatar num choro, desfazer-se em lágrimas; **~ out laughing** desatar a rir ● *n* estouro *m*, rebentar *m*; (*of anger, laughter*) explosão *f*; (*of firing*) rajada *f*; (*of energy*) acesso *m*

bury /ˈberɪ/ *vt* sepultar, enterrar; (*hide*) esconder; (*engross, thrust*) mergulhar

bus /bʌs/ *n* (*pl* **buses**) ônibus *m*, (*P*) autocarro *m*; **~ lane** faixa *f* de ônibus, (*P*) de autocarro. **~ stop** *n* paragem *f*

bush /bʊʃ/ *n* arbusto *m*; (*land*) mato *m*. **~y** *a* espesso

business /ˈbɪznɪs/ *n* (*trade, shop, affair*) negócio *m*; (*task*) função *f*; (*occupation*) ocupação *f*; **have no ~ to** não ter o direito de; **it's no ~ of yours** não é da sua conta; **mind your own ~** cuide da sua vida; **that's my ~** isso é meu problema. **~like** *a* eficiente, sistemático. **~man** *n* homem *m* de negócios, comerciante *m*

busker /ˈbʌskə(r)/ *n* músico *m* ambulante

bust[1] /bʌst/ *n* busto *m*

bust[2] /bʌst/ *vt/i* (*pt* **busted** *or* **bust**) ⊠ ▶ BURST, ▶ BREAK ● *a* falido; **go ~** falir. **~-up** *n* ⊠ discussão *f*, (*P*) bulha *f*

bustl|e /ˈbʌsl/ *vi* andar numa azáfama; (*hurry*) apressar-se ● *n* azáfama *f*. **~ing** *a* animado, movimentado

bus|y /ˈbɪzɪ/ *a* (**-ier**, **-iest**) ocupado; ‹*street*› movimentado; ‹*day*› atarefado ● *vt* **~y o.s. with** ocupar-se com. **~ily** *adv* ativamente, atarefadamente

busybody /ˈbɪzɪbɒdɪ/ *n* intrometido *m*, pessoa *f* abelhuda

but /bʌt/ *conj* mas ● *prep* exceto, (*P*) excepto, senão ● *adv* apenas, só; **all ~** todos menos; (*nearly*) quase, por pouco não; **~ for** sem, se não fosse; **last ~ one/two** penúltimo/antepenúltimo; **nobody ~** ninguém a não ser

butcher /ˈbʊtʃə(r)/ *n* açougueiro *m*, (*P*) homem *m* do talho; *fig* carrasco *m*; **the ~'s** açougue *m*, (*P*) talho *m* ● *vt* chacinar

butler /ˈbʌtlə(r)/ *n* mordomo *m*

butt /bʌt/ *n* (*of gun*) coronha *f*; (*of cigarette*) ponta *f*; (*target*) alvo *m* de troça, de ridículo *etc*; (*cask*) barril *m* ● *vt/i* dar cabeçada em; **~ in** interromper

butter /ˈbʌtə(r)/ *n* manteiga *f* ● *vt* pôr manteiga em

buttercup /ˈbʌtəkʌp/ *n* botão-de-ouro *m*

butterfly /ˈbʌtəflaɪ/ *n* borboleta *f*

buttock /ˈbʌtək/ *n* nádega *f*

button /ˈbʌtn/ *n* botão *m* ● *vt/i* abotoar(-se)

buttonhole /ˈbʌtnhəʊl/ *n* casa *f* de botão; (*in lapel*) botoeira *f* ● *vt fig* obrigar a ouvir

buttress /ˈbʌtrɪs/ *n* contraforte *m*; *fig* esteio *m* ● *vt* sustentar

buy /baɪ/ *vt* (*pt* **bought**) comprar (**from** a); ☒ (*believe*) engolir ⓘ ● *n* compra *f*. **~er** *n* comprador *m*

buzz /bʌz/ *n* zumbido *m* ● *vi* zumbir; **~ off** pôr-se a andar. **~er** *n* campainha *f*

by /baɪ/ *prep* (*near*) junto de, perto de; (*along, past, means*) por; (*according to*) conforme; (*before*) antes de; **~ accident/mistake** sem querer; **~ bike/car** *etc* de bicicleta/carro *etc*; **~ day/night** de dia/noite; **~ the kilo** por quilo; **~ land/sea/air** por terra/mar/ar; **~ now** a esta hora; **~ oneself** sozinho ● *adv* (*near*) perto; **~ and ~** muito em breve; **~ and large** no conjunto. **~-election** *n* eleição *f* suplementar; **~-product** *n* derivado *m*

bye(-bye) /ˈbaɪ(baɪ)/ *int* ⓘ adeus; adeusinho

bypass /ˈbaɪpɑːs/ *n* (estrada) secundária *f*, desvio *m*; *Med* by-pass *m*, ponte *f* de safena ● *vt* fazer um desvio; *fig* contornar

bystander /ˈbaɪstændə(r)/ *n* circunstante *mf*, espectador *m*

byte /baɪt/ *n* byte *m*

Cc

cab /kæb/ *n* táxi *m*; (*of lorry, train*) cabina *f*, cabine *f*

cabaret /ˈkæbəreɪ/ *n* variedades *fpl*, cabaré *m*

cabbage /ˈkæbɪdʒ/ *n* couve *f*, repolho *m*

cabin /ˈkæbɪn/ *n* cabana *f*; (*in plane*) cabina *f*; (*in ship*) camarote *m*

cabinet /ˈkæbɪnɪt/ *n* armário *m*; **C~** *Pol* gabinete *m*

cable /ˈkeɪbl/ *n* cabo *m* ● *n* funicular *m*, teleférico *m*; **~ railway** funicular *m*; **~ television** televisão *f* a cabo. **~ channel** *n* canal de tevê a cabo *f*, (*P*) canal de televisão por cabo *m*

cache /kæʃ/ *n* (esconderijo *m* de) tesouro *m*, armas *fpl*, provisões *fpl*

cackle /ˈkækl/ *n* cacarejo *m* ● *vi* cacarejar

cactus /ˈkæktəs/ *n* (*pl* **es** *or* **cacti** /-taɪ/) cacto *m*

caddie /ˈkædɪ/ *n Golf* caddie *m*

caddy /ˈkædɪ/ *n* lata *f* para o chá

cadet /kəˈdet/ *n* cadete *m*

cadge /kædʒ/ *vt/i* filar, (*P*) cravar

Caesarean /sɪˈzeərɪən/ *a* **~ (section)** cesariana *f*

cafe /ˈkæfeɪ/ *n* café *m*

cafeteria /kæfɪˈtɪərɪə/ *n* cafeteria *f*, restaurante *m* self-service

cafetière /kæfəˈtjeə(r)/ *n* cafeteira de pistão *f*

caffeine /ˈkæfiːn/ *n* cafeína *f*

cage /keɪdʒ/ *n* gaiola *f*

cagey /ˈkeɪdʒɪ/ *a* ⓘ (*secretive*) misterioso; reservado

cake /keɪk/ *n* bolo *m*; **a piece of ~** ⓘ canja *f* ⓘ. **~d** *a* empastado; **his shoes were ~d with mud** tinha os sapatos cobertos de lama

calamity /kəˈlæmətɪ/ *n* calamidade *f*

calcium /ˈkælsɪəm/ *n* cálcio *m*

calculat|e /ˈkælkjʊleɪt/ *vt/i* calcular; *Amer* (*suppose*) supor. **~ed** *a* ‹*action*› deliberado, calculado. **~ing** *a* calculista. **~ion** /-ˈleɪʃn/ *n* cálculo *m*. **~or** *n* calculador *m*, (*P*) máquina *f* de calcular

calendar /ˈkælɪndə(r)/ *n* calendário *m*

calf[1] /kɑːf/ *n* (*pl* **calves**) (*young cow or bull*) vitelo *m*, bezerro *m*; (*of other animals*) cria *f*

calf[2] /kɑːf/ *n* (*pl* **calves**) (*of leg*) barriga *f* da perna

calibre /ˈkælɪbə(r)/ *n* calibre *m*

call /kɔːl/ *vt/i* chamar; (*summon*) convocar; (*phone*) telefonar; **~ (in or round)** (*visit*) passar por casa de; **be ~ed** (*named*) chamar-se; **~ back** (*phone*) tornar a telefonar; (*visit*) voltar; **~ for** (*demand*) pedir, requerer; (*fetch*) ir buscar; **~ off** cancelar; **~ on** (*visit*) visitar, fazer uma visita a; **~ out (to)** chamar; **~ up** *Mil* mobilizar, recrutar; (*phone*) telefonar ● *n* chamada *f*; (*bird's cry*) canto *m*; (*shout*) brado *m*, grito *m*; **be on ~** estar de serviço. **~ centre** *n* central *f* telefônica, (*P*) telefónica. **~er** *n* visitante *f*, visita *f*; (*phone*) chamador *m*, (*P*) pessoa *f* que faz a chamada. **~ing** *n* vocação *f*

callous /ˈkæləs/ *a* insensível

calm /kɑːm/ *a* (**-er, -est**) calmo ● *n* calma *f* ● *vt/i* **~ (down)** acalmar(-se). **~ness** *n* calma *f*

calorie /ˈkælərɪ/ *n* caloria *f*

camcorder /ˈkæmkɔːdə(r)/ *n* câmera *f or* (*P*) câmara *f* de filmar

came /keɪm/ ▶ COME

camel /ˈkæml/ *n* camelo *m*

camera /ˈkæmərə/ *n* máquina *f* fotográfica; *Cine, TV* câmera *f*, (*P*) câmara. **~man** *n* (*pl* **-men**) operador *m*; **~phone** *n* celular com câmera *m*, (*P*) telemóvel com câmara *m*

camouflage /ˈkæməflɑːʒ/ *n* camuflagem *f* ● *vt* camuflar

camp[1] /kæmp/ *n* acampamento *m* ● *vi* acampar. **~ bed** *n* cama *f* de campanha. **~er** *n* campista *mf*; (*car*) autocaravana *f*. **~ing** *n* campismo *m*

camp[2] /kæmp/ *a* afetado, efeminado

campaign /kæmˈpeɪn/ *n* campanha *f* ● *vi* fazer campanha

campsite /ˈkæmpsaɪt/ *n* área *f* de camping, (*P*) parque *m* de campismo

campus /ˈkæmpəs/ *n* (*pl* **-puses** /-pəsɪz/) campus *m*, (*P*) cidade *f* universitária

can[1] /kæn/ *n* vasilha *f* de lata; (*for food*) lata *f* (de conserva) ● *vt* (*pt* **canned**) enlatar; **~ned music** música *f* em fita para locais públicos. **~ opener** *n* abridor *m* de latas, (*P*) abrelatas *m*

can[2] /kæn *unstressed* kən /(*pres* **can**, *pt* **could**) ● *v aux*

····➤ (*be able to*) poder, conseguir; **I ~'t do it** não consigo fazer isso; **I could if I had time** poderia se tivesse tempo; **she ~ help you** ela pode ajudá-lo

····➤ (*know how to*) saber; **I ~ speak English** sei falar inglês; **he ~ drive** ele sabe dirigir

····➤ (*be allowed to*) poder, ser permitido; **you ~'t park here** não é permitido estacionar aqui; **nobody ~ take pictures** ninguém pode tirar fotografias

····➤ (*in requests*) poder; **~ I have a glass of water, please?** podia me dar um copo de água, por favor?; **could you ring me tomorrow?** podia me telefonar amanhã?

····➤ (*with verbs of perception*); **I ~ hear you** eu consigo ouvir você; **~ they see us?** eles conseguem nos ver?

····➤ could (*possibility*); **we could have won** podíamos ter ganhado; **I could phone her now, if you want** poderia telefonar para ela agora, se você quiser

Canad|a /ˈkænədə/ *n* Canadá *m*. **~ian** /kəˈneɪdɪən/ *a & n* canadense *mf*, (*P*) canadiano m

canal /kəˈnæl/ *n* canal *m*

canary /kəˈneərɪ/ *n* canário *m*. **C~ Islands** *npl* as (Ilhas) Canárias

cancel /ˈkænsl/ *vt* (*pt* **cancelled**) cancelar; (*cross out*) riscar; ‹*stamps*› inutilizar □ **~ out** *vi fig* neutralizar-se mutuamente. **~lation** /-ˈleɪʃn/ *n* cancelamento *m*

cancer /ˈkænsə(r)/ *n* câncer *m*, cancro *m*; **C~** *Astrol* Caranguejo *m*, Câncer *m*. **~ous** *a* canceroso

candid /ˈkændɪd/ *a* franco

candida|te /ˈkændɪdeɪt/ *n* candidato *m*

candle /ˈkændl/ *n* vela *f*; (*in church*) vela *f*, círio *m*

candlestick /ˈkændlstɪk/ *n* castiçal *m*

candy /ˈkændɪ/ *n* bala *f*, (*P*) açúcar cândi; *Amer* (*sweet, sweets*) doce(s) *m*. **~ floss** *n* algodão-doce *m*

cane /keɪn/ *n* cana *f*; (*walking stick*) bengala *f*; (*for baskets*) verga *f*; *Schol* (*for punishment*) vergasta *f* ● *vt* vergastar

canine /ˈkeɪnaɪn/ *a & n* canino *m*

cannabis /ˈkænəbɪs/ *n* cânhamo *m*, maconha *f*

cannibal /ˈkænɪbl/ *n* canibal *mf*. **~ism** /-zəm/ *n* canibalismo *m*

cannon /ˈkænən/ *n inv* canhão *m*

cannot /ˈkænət/ (= **can not**) ▶ CAN[2]

canny /ˈkænɪ/ *a* (**-ier, -iest**) astuto, manhoso

canoe /kəˈnuː/ *n* canoa *f* ● *vi* andar de canoa

canon /ˈkænən/ *n* cônego *m*, (*P*) cónego *m*; (*rule*) cânone *m*

can't /kɑːnt/ (= **can not**) ▶ CAN[2]

canteen /kænˈtiːn/ *n* cantina *f*; (*flask*) cantil *m*; (*for cutlery*) estojo *m*

canter /ˈkæntə(r)/ *n* meio galope *m*, cânter *m* ● *vi* andar a meio galope

canvas /ˈkænvəs/ *n* lona *f*; (*for painting or tapestry*) tela *f*

canvass /ˈkænvəs/ *vt/i* angariar votos or fregueses

canyon /ˈkænjən/ *n* canhão *m*, (*P*) desfiladeiro *m*

C

cap /kæp/ *n* (*with peak*) boné *m*; (*without peak*) barrete *m*; (*of nurse*) touca *f*; (*of bottle, pen, tube, etc*) tampa *f*; *Mech* tampa *f*, tampão *m* ● *vt* (*pt* **capped**) ‹*bottle, pen, tube, etc*› tapar, tampar; (*rates*) impôr um limite a; (*outdo*) suplantar; *Sport* selecionar, (*P*) seleccionar; **~ped with** encimado de, coroado de

capab|le /'keɪpəbl/ *a* ‹*person*› capaz (**of** de); ‹*things, situations*› suscetível (**of** de). **~ility** /-'bɪlətɪ/ *n* capacidade *f*

capacity /kə'pæsətɪ/ *n* capacidade *f*; **in one's ~ as** na (sua) qualidade de

cape[1] /keɪp/ *n* (*cloak*) capa *f*

cape[2] /keɪp/ *n Geog* cabo *m*

caper[1] /'keɪpə(r)/ *vi* andar aos pinotes

caper[2] /'keɪpə(r)/ *n Culin* alcaparra *f*

capital /'kæpɪtl/ *a* capital; **~ (letter)** maiúscula *f* ● *n* (*town*) capital *f*; (*money*) capital *m*; **~ punishment** pena *f* de morte

capitalis|t /'kæpɪtəlɪst/ *a & n* capitalista *mf*. **~m** /-zəm/ *n* capitalismo *m*

Capitol O Capitólio, como é conhecida a sede do Congresso (*Congress*) dos Estados Unidos, é situado em Washington DC. Como está situado em *Capitol Hill*, a imprensa utiliza com frequência este termo para se referir ao Congresso dos Estados Unidos.

Capricorn /'kæprɪkɔ:n/ *n Astrol* Capricórnio *m*

capsicum /'kæpsɪkəm/ *n* pimento *m*

capsize /kæp'saɪz/ *vt/i* virar(-se)

capsule /'kæpsju:l/ *n* cápsula *f*

captain /'kæptɪn/ *n* capitão *m*; *Navy* capitão-de-mar-e-guerra *m* ● *vt* capitanear, comandar

caption /'kæpʃn/ *n* legenda *f*; (*heading*) título *m*

captivate /'kæptɪveɪt/ *vt* cativar

captiv|e /'kæptɪv/ *a & n* cativo *m*, prisioneiro *m*. **~ity** /-'tɪvətɪ/ *n* cativeiro *m*

captor /'kæptə(r)/ *n* captor *m*

capture /'kæptʃə(r)/ *vt* capturar; ‹*attention*› prender ● *n* captura *f*

car /kɑ:(r)/ *n* carro *m*; **~ ferry** barca *f* para carros; **~ phone** telefone *m* de carro. **~ park** *n* (parque *m* de) estacionamento *m*; **~ wash** *n* estação *f* de lavagem

carafe /kə'ræf/ *n* garrafa *f* para água ou vinho

caramel /'kærəmel/ *n* caramelo *m*

carat /'kærət/ *n* quilate *m*

caravan /'kærəvæn/ *n* caravana *f*, reboque *m*

carbohydrate /kɑ:bəʊ'haɪdreɪt/ *n* hidrato *m* de carbono

carbon /'kɑ:bən/ *n* carbono *m*; **~ copy** cópia *f* em papel carbono, (*P*) químico; **~ monoxide** óxido *m* de carbono; **~ paper** papel *m* carbono, (*P*) químico. **~ footprint** *n* pegada *f* de carbono, (*P*) pegada *f* ecológica ; **~ neutral** *a* carbono *m* neutro ; **~ offsetting** *n* compensação *f* de carbono

carburettor /kɑ:bjʊ'retə(r)/ *n* carburador *m*

carcass /'kɑ:kəs/ *n* carcaça *f*

card /kɑ:d/ *n* cartão *m*; (*postcard*) postal *m*; (*playing card*) carta *f*. **~ game(s)** *n*(*pl*) jogo(s) *m*(*pl*) de cartas; **~ index** *n* fichário *m*, (*P*) ficheiro *m*

cardboard /'kɑ:dbɔ:d/ *n* cartão *m*, papelão *m*

cardigan /'kɑ:dɪgən/ *n* casaco *m* de lã

cardinal /'kɑ:dɪnl/ *a* cardeal, principal; **~ number** numeral *m* cardinal ● *n Relig* cardeal *m*

care /keə(r)/ *n* cuidado *m*; (*concern*) interesse *m* ● *vi* **~ about** (*be interested*) estar interessado por; (*be worried*) estar preocupado com; **~ for** (*like*) gostar de; (*look after*) tomar conta de; **take ~** tomar cuidado; **take ~ of** cuidar de; (*deal with*) tratar de; **he couldn't ~ less** ele está pouco ligando, ele não dá a menor [!]

career /kə'rɪə(r)/ *n* carreira *f* ● *vi* ir a toda a velocidade, ir numa carreira

carefree /'keəfri:/ *a* despreocupado

careful /'keəfl/ *a* cuidadoso; (*cautious*) cauteloso; **~!** cuidado!

careless /'keəlɪs/ *a* descuidado (**about** com). **~ness** *n* descuido *m*, negligência *f*

caress /kə'res/ *n* carícia *f* ● *vt* acariciar

caretaker /'keəteɪkə(r)/ *n* zelador *m* duma casa vazia; (*janitor*) zelador *m*, (*P*) porteiro *m*

cargo /'kɑ:gəʊ/ *n* (*pl* **-oes**) carregamento *m*, carga *f*

Caribbean /kærɪ'bi:ən/ *a* caraíba; **the ~** as Caraíbas *fpl*

caricature /'kærɪkətjʊə(r)/ *n* caricatura *f* ● *vt* caricaturar

caring /'keərɪŋ/ *a* carinhoso, afetuoso

carnage /'kɑ:nɪdʒ/ *n* carnificina *f*

carnation /kɑ:'neɪʃn/ *n* cravo *m*

carnival /'kɑːnɪvl/ *n* carnaval *m*

carol /'kærəl/ *n* cântico or canto *m* de Natal *m*

carp[1] /kɑːp/ *n inv* carpa *f*

carp[2] /kɑːp/ *vi* **~ (at)** criticar

carpent|er /'kɑːpɪntə(r)/ *n* carpinteiro *m*. **~ry** *n* carpintaria *f*

carpet /'kɑːpɪt/ *n* tapete *m*; **with fitted ~s** (estar) atapetado; **be on the ~** [!] ser chamado à ordem ● *vt* (*pt* **carpeted**) atapetar

carriage /'kærɪdʒ/ *n* carruagem *f*; (*of goods*) frete *m*, transporte *m*; (*cost, bearing*) porte *m*

carrier /'kærɪə(r)/ *n* transportador *m*; (*company*) transportadora *f*; *Med* portador *m*; **~ (bag)** saco *m* de plástico

carrot /'kærət/ *n* cenoura *f*

carry /'kærɪ/ *vt/i* levar; ‹*goods*› transportar; (*involve*) acarretar; (*have for sale*) ter à venda; **be carried away** entusiasmar-se, deixar-se levar; **~ off** levar à força; ‹*prize*› incluir; **~ it off** sair-se bem (de); **~ on** continuar; [!] (*flirt*) flertar; [!] (*behave*) portar-se (mal); **~ out** executar; ‹*duty*› cumprir; **~ through** levar a cabo

cart /kɑːt/ *n* carroça *f*; carro *m* ● *vt* acarretar; [!] carregar com

carton /'kɑːtn/ *n* embalagem *f* de cartão or de plástico; (*of yogurt*) embalagem *f*, pote *m*; (*of milk*) pacote *m*

cartoon /kɑː'tuːn/ *n* desenho *m* humorístico, caricatura *f*; (*strip*) estória *f* em quadrinhos, (*P*) banda *f* desenhada; (*film*) desenhos *mpl* animados. **~ist** *n* caricaturista *mf*; (*of strip, film*) desenhador *m*

cartridge /'kɑːtrɪdʒ/ *n* cartucho *m*

carv|e /kɑːv/ *vt* esculpir, talhar; ‹*meat*› trinchar; **~ing knife** faca *f* de trinchar, trinchante *m*. **~ing** *n* obra *f* de talha; (*on tree trunk*) incisão *f*

case[1] /keɪs/ *n* caso *m*; *Jur* causa *f*, processo *m*; *Phil* argumentos *mpl*; **in any ~** em todo caso; **in ~ (of)** no caso (de); **in that ~** nesse caso

case[2] /keɪs/ *n* caixa *f*; (*crate*) caixa *f*, caixote *m*; (*for camera, jewels, spectacles, etc*) estojo *m*; (*suitcase*) mala *f*; (*for cigarettes*) cigarreira *f*

cash /kæʃ/ *n* dinheiro *m*, numerário *m*, cash *m*; **be short of ~** ter pouco dinheiro; **in ~** em dinheiro; **pay ~** pagar em dinheiro; **~ desk** caixa *f*; **~ dispenser** caixa *f* electrônica, (*P*) multibanco *m*; **~ register** caixa *f* registradora, (*P*) registradora *f* ● *vt* (*obtain money for*) cobrar, receber; (*give money for*) pagar; **~ a cheque** (*receive/give*) cobrar/descontar um cheque; **~ in** receber; **~ in (on)** aproveitar-se de. **~ flow** *n* cash-flow *m*

cashback /'kæʃbæk/ *n* cashback *m* possibilidade que o cliente tem de pagar acima do valor da compra com cartão de crédito e receber 'troco'

cashew /kæ'ʃuː/ *n* caju *m*

cashier /kæ'ʃɪə(r)/ *n* caixa *mf*

cashmere /kæʃ'mɪə(r)/ *n* caxemira *f*

casino /kə'siːnəʊ/ *n* (*pl* **-os**) casino *m*

casserole /'kæsərəʊl/ *n* caçarola *f*; (*stew*) estufado *m*

cassette /kə'set/ *n* cassette *f*; **~ player** gravador *m*. **~ recorder** *n* gravador *m*

cast /kɑːst/ *vt* (*pt* **cast**) lançar, arremessar; (*shed*) despojar-se de; (*vote*) dar; ‹*metal*› fundir; ‹*shadow*› projetar ● *n Theatr* elenco *m*; (*mould*) molde *m*; *Med* aparelho *m* de gesso. **~-iron** *a* de ferro fundido; *fig* muito forte; **~-offs** *npl* roupa *f* velha

castanets /kæstə'nets/ *npl* castanholas *fpl*

castaway /'kɑːstəweɪ/ *n* náufrago *m*

caste /kɑːst/ *n* casta *f*

castigate /'kæstɪgeɪt/ *vt* castigar

castle /'kɑːsl/ *n* castelo *m*; *Chess* torre *f*

castor /'kɑːstə(r)/ *n* roda *f* de pé de móvel; **~ sugar** açúcar *m* em pó

casual /'kæʒʊəl/ *a* (*chance*) ‹*meeting*› casual; (*careless, unmethodical*) descuidado; (*informal*) informal; **~ clothes** roupa *f* prática or de lazer; **~ work** trabalho *m* ocasional

casualty /'kæʒʊəltɪ/ *n* (*dead*) morto *m*; (*death*) morte *f*; (*injured*) ferido *m*; (*victim*) vítima *f*; *Mil* baixa *f*

cat /kæt/ *n* gato *m*. **~seyes®** *npl* reflectores *mpl*

catalogue /'kætəlɒg/ *n* catálogo *m* ● *vt* catalogar

Catalonia /kætə'ləʊnɪə/ *n* Catalunha *f*

catalyst /'kætəlɪst/ *n* catalisador *m*

catapult /'kætəpʌlt/ *n* (*child's*) atiradeira *f*, (*P*) fisga *f* ● *vt* catapultar

cataract /'kætərækt/ *f* (*waterfall & Med*) catarata *f*

catarrh /kə'tɑː(r)/ *n* catarro *m*

catastroph|e /kə'tæstrəfɪ/ *n* catástrofe *f*. **~ic** /kætəs'trɒfɪk/ *a* catastrófico

catch /kætʃ/ *vt* (*pt* **caught**) apanhar; (*grasp*) agarrar; (*hear*) perceber; **~ sb's eye** atrair a atenção de alguém; **~ sight of** avistar ● *vi* prender-se (**in** em); (*get stuck*) ficar preso; **~ fire** pegar fogo, (*P*) incendiar-se; **~ on** 🅘 pegar, tornar-se popular; **~ up (with)** pôr-se a par (com); ‹*work*› pôr em dia ● *n* apanha *f*; (*of fish*) pesca *f*; (*trick*) ratoeira *f*; (*snag*) problema *m*; (*on door*) trinco *m*; (*fastener*) fecho *m*. **~phrase** *n* clichê *m*

catching /'kætʃɪŋ/ *a* contagioso, infeccioso

catchy /'kætʃɪ/ *a* que pega fácil

categorical /kætɪ'gɒrɪkl/ *a* categórico

category /'kætɪgərɪ/ *n* categoria *f*

cater /'keɪtə(r)/ *vi* fornecer comida (para clubes, casamentos, etc); **~ for** (*pander to*) satisfazer; ‹*consumers*› dirigir-se a. **~er** *n* fornecedor *m*. **~ing** *n* catering *m*

caterpillar /'kætəpɪlə(r)/ *n* lagarta *f*

cathedral /kə'θi:drəl/ *n* catedral *f*

catholic /'kæθəlɪk/ *a* universal; (*eclectic*) eclético. **C~** *a* & *n* católico *m*. **~ism** /kə'θɒlɪsɪzəm/ *n* catolicismo *m*

cattle /'kætl/ *npl* gado *m*

catty /'kætɪ/ *a* (dissimuladamente) maldoso, com perfídia

caught /kɔ:t/ ▶ CATCH

cauliflower /'kɒlɪflaʊə(r)/ *n* couve-flor *f*

cause /kɔ:z/ *n* causa *f* ● *vt* causar; **~ sth to grow/move** *etc* fazer algo crescer/mexer *etc*

cauti|on /'kɔ:ʃn/ *n* cautela *f*; (*warning*) aviso *m* ● *vt* avisar. **~ous** /'kɔ:ʃəs/ *a* cauteloso

cavalry /'kævəlrɪ/ *n* cavalaria *f*

cave /keɪv/ *n* caverna *f*, gruta *f* ● *vi* **~ in** desabar, dar de si

caveman /'keɪvmæn/ *n* (*pl* **-men**) troglodita *m*, homem *m* das cavernas; *fig* (tipo) primário *m*

cavern /'kævən/ *n* caverna *f*

caviare /'kævɪɑ:(r)/ *n* caviar *m*

cavity /'kævətɪ/ *n* cavidade *f*

cc *abbr* (= **carbon copy**) cópia *f* com papel carbono, (*P*) cópia *f* carbono

CD /si:'di/ ▶ COMPACT DISC

cease /si:s/ *vt/i* cessar. **~fire** *n* cessar-fogo *m*. **~less** *a* incessante

cedar /'si:də(r)/ *n* cedro *m*

cedilla /sɪ'dɪlə/ *n* cedilha *f*

ceiling /'si:lɪŋ/ *n lit* & *fig* teto *m*

celebrat|e /'selɪbreɪt/ *vt/i* celebrar, festejar. **~ion** /-'breɪʃn/ *n* celebração *f*, festejo *m*

celebrated /'selɪbreɪtɪd/ *a* célebre

celebrity /sɪ'lebrətɪ/ *n* celebridade *f*

celery /'selərɪ/ *n* aipo *m*

celiba|te /'selɪbət/ *a* celibatário. **~cy** *n* celibato *m*

cell /sel/ *n* (*of prison, convent*) cela *f*; *Biol, Pol, Electr* célula *f*; **~ phone** celular *m*, (*P*) telemóvel

cellar /'selə(r)/ *n* porão *m*, cave *f*; (*for wine*) adega *f*, cave *f*

cell|o /'tʃeləʊ/ *n* (*pl* **-os**) violoncelo *m*. **~ist** *n* violoncelista *mf*

cellphone /'selfəʊn/ *n* celular *m*, (*P*) telemóvel *m*

cellular /'seljʊlə(r)/ *a* celular

Celt /kelt/ *n* celta *mf*. **~ic** *a* celta, céltico

cement /sɪ'ment/ *n* cimento *m* ● *vt* cimentar

cemetery /'semətrɪ/ *n* cemitério *m*

censor /'sensə(r)/ *n* censor *m* ● *vt* censurar. **~ship** *n* censura *f*

censure /'senʃə(r)/ *n* censura *f*, crítica *f* ● *vt* censurar, criticar

census /'sensəs/ *n* recenseamento *m*, censo *m*

cent /sent/ *n* cêntimo *m*

centenary /sen'ti:nərɪ/ *n* centenário *m*

centigrade /'sentɪgreɪd/ *a* centígrado

centimetre /'sentɪmi:tə(r)/ *n* centímetro *m*

central /'sentrəl/ *a* central; **~ heating** aquecimento *m* central. **~ize** *vt* centralizar

centre /'sentə(r)/ *n* centro *m* ● *vt* (*pt* **centred**) centrar ● *vi* **~ on** concentrar-se em, fixar-se em

century /'sentʃərɪ/ *n* século *m*

ceramic /sɪ'ræmɪk/ *a* ‹*object*› em cerâmica. **~s** *n* cerâmica *f*

cereal /'sɪərɪəl/ *n* cereal *m*

ceremonial /serɪ'məʊnɪəl/ *a* de cerimônia ● *n* cerimonial *m*

ceremon|y /'serɪmənɪ/ *n* cerimônia *f*, (*P*) cerimónia *f*. **~ious** /-'məʊnɪəs/ *a* cerimonioso

certain /'sə:tn/ *a* certo; **be ~** ter a certeza; **for ~** com certeza, ao certo; **make ~** confirmar, verificar. **~ly** *adv* com certeza, certamente. **~ty** *n* certeza *f*

certificate /sə'tɪfɪkət/ *n* certificado *m*; (*birth, marriage*) certidão *f*; (*health*) atestado *m*

certif|y /ˈsɜːtɪfaɪ/ *vt/i* certificar

chafe /tʃeɪf/ *vt/i* esfregar; (*make/become sore*) esfolar/ficar esfolado; *fig* irritar(-se)

chaffinch /ˈtʃæfɪntʃ/ *n* tentilhão *m*

chain /tʃeɪn/ *n* corrente *f*, cadeia *f*; (*series*) cadeia *f*; **~ store** loja *f* pertencente a uma cadeia ● *vt* acorrentar; **~ reaction** reação *f* em cadeia. **~-smoke** *vi* fumar cigarros um atrás do outro

chair /tʃeə(r)/ *n* cadeira *f*; (*position of chairman*) presidência *f*; *Univ* cátedra *f* ● *vt* presidir

chairman /ˈtʃeəmən/ *n* (*pl* **-men**) presidente *mf*

chalet /ˈʃæleɪ/ *n* chalé *m*

chalk /tʃɔːk/ *n* greda *f*, cal *f*; (*for writing*) giz *m* ● *vt* traçar com giz

challeng|e /ˈtʃælɪndʒ/ *n* desafio *m*; (*by sentry*) interpelação *f* ● *vt* desafiar; (*question the truth of*) contestar. **~er** *n* *Sport* pretendente (ao título) *mf*. **~ing** *a* estimulante, que constitui um desafio

chamber /ˈtʃeɪmbə(r)/ *n old use* aposento *m*; **~ music** música *f* de câmara; **C~ of Commerce** Câmara *f* de Comércio. **~maid** *n* arrumadeira *f*, (*P*) criada *f*

chamois /ˈʃæmɪ/ *n* **~(-leather)** camurça *f*

champagne /ʃæmˈpeɪn/ *n* champanhe *m*

champion /ˈtʃæmpɪən/ *n* campeão *m*, campeã *f* ● *vt* defender. **~ship** *n* campeonato *m*

chance /tʃɑːns/ *n* acaso *m*; (*luck*) sorte *f*; (*opportunity*) oportunidade *f*, chance *f*; (*likelihood*) hipótese *f*, probabilidade *f*; (*risk*) risco *m* ● *a* casual, fortuito ● *vi* calhar ● *vt* arriscar; **by ~** por acaso

chancellor /ˈtʃɑːnsələ(r)/ *n* chanceler *m*; **C~ of the Exchequer** Ministro *m* das Finanças

chancy /ˈtʃɑːnsɪ/ *a* arriscado

chandelier /ʃændəˈlɪə(r)/ *n* lustre *m*

change /tʃeɪndʒ/ *vt* mudar; (*exchange*) trocar ‹*clothes, house, trains, etc*› mudar de; **~ hands** (*ownership*) mudar de dono; **~ one's mind** mudar de ideia(s) ● *vi* mudar; (**~** *clothes*) mudar-se, mudar de roupa; **~ into** ‹*a butterfly etc*› transformar-se em; ‹*evening dress etc*› pôr; **~ over** passar, mudar (**to** para) ● *n* mudança *f*; (*money*) troco *m*; **a ~ of clothes** uma muda de roupa. **~able** *a* variável

channel /ˈtʃænl/ *n* canal *m* ● *vt* (*pt* **channelled**) canalizar; **the C~ Islands** as Ilhas do Canal da Mancha; **the (English) C~** o Canal da Mancha

chant /tʃɑːnt/ *n* cântico *m* ● *vt/i* cantar, entoar

chao|s /ˈkeɪɒs/ *n* caos *m*. **~tic** /-ˈɒtɪk/ *a* caótico

chap /tʃæp/ *n* [!] sujeito *m*; cara *m* [!], (*P*) tipo *m*

chapel /ˈtʃæpl/ *n* capela *f*

chaplain /ˈtʃæplɪn/ *n* capelão *m*

chapter /ˈtʃæptə(r)/ *n* capítulo *m*

character /ˈkærəktə(r)/ *n* caráter *m*, (*P*) carácter *m*; (*in novel, play*) personagem *m*; (*reputation*) fama *f*; (*eccentric person*) excêntrico *m*; (*letter*) caractere *m*, (*P*) carácter *m*. **~ize** *vt* caracterizar

characteristic /kærəktəˈrɪstɪk/ *a* característico ● *n* característica *f*

charade /ʃəˈrɑːd/ *n* charada *f*

charcoal /ˈtʃɑːkəʊl/ *n* carvão *m* de lenha

charge /tʃɑːdʒ/ *n* preço *m*; *Electr, Mil* carga *f*; *Jur* acusação *f*; (*task, custody*) cargo *m* ● *vt/i* ‹*price*› cobrar; ‹*enemy*› atacar; *Jur* incriminar; **be in ~ of** ter a cargo; **take ~ of** encarregar-se de

chariot /ˈtʃærɪət/ *n* carro *m* de guerra *or* triunfal

charisma /kəˈrɪzmə/ *n* carisma *m*. **~tic** /kærɪzˈmætɪk/ *a* carismático

charit|y /ˈtʃærətɪ/ *n* caridade *f*; (*society*) instituição *f* de caridade. **~able** *a* caridoso

charm /tʃɑːm/ *n* encanto *m*, charme *m*; (*spell*) feitiço *m*; (*talisman*) amuleto *m* ● *vt* encantar. **~ing** *a* encantador

chart /tʃɑːt/ *n Naut* carta *f*; (*table*) mapa *m*, gráfico *m*, tabela *f* ● *vt* fazer o mapa de

charter /ˈtʃɑːtə(r)/ *n* carta *f*; **~ (flight)** (voo) charter *m* ● *vt* fretar

chase /tʃeɪs/ *vt* perseguir ● *vi* [!] correr (**after** atrás de) ● *n* caça *f*, perseguição *f*; **~ away** *or* **off** afugentar, expulsar

chasm /ˈkæzm/ *n* abismo *m*

chassis /ˈʃæsɪ/ *n* chassi *m*

chaste /tʃeɪst/ *a* casto

chastise /tʃæsˈtaɪz/ *vt* castigar

chastity /ˈtʃæstətɪ/ *n* castidade *f*

chat /tʃæt/ *n* conversa *f*; **have a ~** bater um papo, (*P*) dar dois dedos de conversa ● *vi* (*pt* **chatted**) conversar, cavaquear. **~room** *n* sala *f* de chat. **~ty** *a* conversador

C

chatter /ˈtʃætə(r)/ *vi* tagarelar; **his teeth are ~ing** seus dentes estão tiritando ● *n* tagarelice *f*

chauffeur /ˈʃəʊfə(r)/ *n* motorista *m*, chofer (particular) *m*, chauffeur *m*

chauvinis|t /ˈʃəʊvɪnɪst/ *n* chauvinista *mf*; **male ~t** *pej* machista *m*. **~m** /-zəm/ *n* chauvinismo *m*

cheap /tʃiːp/ *a* (**-er**, **-est**) barato; ‹*fare, rate*› reduzido

cheapen /ˈtʃiːpən/ *vt* depreciar

cheat /tʃiːt/ *vt* enganar, trapacear ● *vi* (*at games*) roubar, (*P*) fazer batota; (*in exams*) copiar ● *n* intrujão *m*; (*at games*) trapaceiro *m*, (*P*) batoteiro *m*

check[1] /tʃek/ *vt/i* (*examine*) verificar; ‹*tickets*› revisar; (*restrain*) controlar, refrear; **~ in** assinar o registro *or* (*P*) registo; (*at airport*) fazer o check-in; **~ out** pagar a conta ● *n* verificação *f*; (*tickets*) controle *m*; (*curb*) freio *m*; *Chess* xeque *m*; *Amer* (*bill*) conta *f*; *Amer* (*cheque*) cheque *m*. **~-in** *n* check-in *m*; **~out** *n* caixa *f*; **~-up** *n* exame *m* médico, check-up *m*

check[2] /tʃek/ *n* (*pattern*) xadrez *m*. **~ed** *a* de xadrez

cheek /tʃiːk/ *n* face *f*; *fig* descaramento *m*. **~y** *a* descarado

cheer /tʃɪə(r)/ *n* alegria *f*; (*shout*) viva *m* ● *vt/i* aclamar, aplaudir; **~s!** à sua!, (*P*) vossa (saúde)!; (*thank you*) obrigado; **~ (up)** animar(-se). **~ful** *a* bem disposto; alegre

cheerio /tʃɪərɪˈəʊ/ *int* 🄸 até logo, (*P*) adeusinho 🄸

cheese /tʃiːz/ *n* queijo *m*

cheetah /ˈtʃiːtə/ *n* chita *f*, lobo-tigre *m*

chef /ʃef/ *n* cozinheiro-chefe *m*

chemical /ˈkemɪkl/ *a* químico ● *n* produto *m* químico

chemist /ˈkemɪst/ *n* farmacêutico *m*; (*scientist*) químico *m*. **~'s (shop)** *n* farmácia *f*. **~ry** *n* química *f*

cheque /tʃek/ *n* cheque *m*. **~book** *n* talão *m* de cheques, (*P*) livro *m* de cheques; **~ card** *n* cartão *m* de banco

cherish /ˈtʃerɪʃ/ *vt* estimar, querer; ‹*hope*› acalentar

cherry /ˈtʃerɪ/ *n* cereja *f*

chess /tʃes/ *n* jogo *m* de xadrez. **~board** *n* tabuleiro *m* de xadrez

chest /tʃest/ *n* peito *m*; (*for money, jewels*) cofre *m*; **~ of drawers** cômoda *f*, (*P*) cómoda *f*

chestnut /ˈtʃesnʌt/ *n* castanha *f*

chew /tʃuː/ *vt* mastigar. **~ing gum** *n* chiclete *m*, (*P*) pastilha *f* elástica

chic /ʃiːk/ *a* chique

chick /tʃɪk/ *n* pinto *m*

chicken /ˈtʃɪkɪn/ *n* galinha *f* ● *vi* **~ out** 🅇 acovardar-se. **~pox** *n* catapora *f*, (*P*) varicela *f*

chief /tʃiːf/ *n* chefe *m* ● *a* principal. **~ly** *adv* principalmente

child /tʃaɪld/ *n* (*pl* **children** /ˈtʃɪldrən/) criança *f*; (*son*) filho *m*; (*daughter*) filha *f*. **~hood** *n* infância *f*, meninice *f*. **~ish** *a* infantil; (*immature*) acriançado, pueril. **~less** *a* sem filhos. **~like** *a* infantil. **~minder** *n* babá *f* que cuida de crianças em sua própria casa, (*P*) ama

childbirth /ˈtʃaɪldbɜːθ/ *n* parto *m*

Chile /ˈtʃɪlɪ/ *n* Chile *m*. **~an** *a & n* chileno *m*

chill /tʃɪl/ *n* frio *m*; *Med* resfriado *m*, (*P*) constipação *f* ● *vt/i* arrefecer; *Culin* refrigerar. **~y** *a* frio; **be** or **feel ~y** ter frio

chilli /ˈtʃɪlɪ/ *n* (*pl* **-ies**) malagueta *f*

chime /tʃaɪm/ *n* carrilhão *m*; (*sound*) música *m* de carrilhão ● *vt/i* tocar

chimney /ˈtʃɪmnɪ/ *n* (*pl* **-eys**) chaminé *f*

chimpanzee /tʃɪmpænˈziː/ *n* chimpanzé *m*

chin /tʃɪn/ *n* queixo *m*

china /ˈtʃaɪnə/ *n* porcelana *f*; (*crockery*) louça *f*

Chin|a /ˈtʃaɪnə/ *n* China *f*. **~ese** /-ˈniːz/ *a & n* chinês *m*

chink[1] /tʃɪŋk/ *n* (*crack*) fenda *f*, fresta *f*

chink[2] /tʃɪŋk/ *n* tinir *m* ● *vt/i* (fazer) tinir

chip /tʃɪp/ *n* (*broken piece*) bocado *m*; *Culin* batata *f* frita em palitos; (*gambling*) ficha *f*; (*electronic*) chip *m*, circuito *m* integrado ● *vt/i* (*pt* **chipped**) lascar(-se)

chiropodist /kɪˈrɒpədɪst/ *n* calista *mf*

chirp /tʃɜːp/ *n* pipilar *m*; (*of cricket*) cricri *m* ● *vi* pipilar; ‹*cricket*› cantar, fazer cricri

chivalr|y /ˈʃɪvlrɪ/ *n* cavalheirismo *m*. **~ous** *a* cavalheiresco

chive /tʃaɪv/ *n* cebolinho *m*

chlorine /ˈklɔːriːn/ *n* cloro *m*

chocolate /ˈtʃɒklɪt/ *n* chocolate *m*

choice /tʃɔɪs/ *n* escolha *f* ● *a* escolhido, seleto, (*P*) selecionado

choir /ˈkwaɪə(r)/ *n* coro *m*

choirboy /ˈkwaɪəbɔɪ/ *n* menino *m* de coro, corista *m*, (*P*) coralista *m*

choke /tʃəʊk/ *vt/i* sufocar; (*on food*) engasgar(-se) ● *n* *Auto* afogador *m*, (*P*) botão *m* do ar 🄸

cholesterol /kə'lestərɒl/ *n* colesterol *m*

choose /tʃu:z/ *vt/i* (*pt* **chose**, *pp* **chosen**) escolher; (*prefer*) preferir; **~ to do** decidir fazer

choosy /'tʃu:zɪ/ *a* ⓘ exigente; difícil de contentar

chop /tʃɒp/ *vt/i* (*pt* **chopped**) cortar ● *n* ‹*wood*› machadada *f*; *Culin* costeleta *f*; **~ down** abater. **~per** *n* cutelo *m*; ⊠ (*helicopter*) helicóptero *m*

choppy /'tʃɒpɪ/ *a* ‹*sea*› picado

chopstick /'tʃɒpstɪk/ *n* fachis *m*, pauzinho *m*

choral /'kɔ:rəl/ *a* coral

chord /kɔ:d/ *n Mus* acorde *m*

chore /tʃɔ:(r)/ *n* trabalho *m*; (*unpleasant task*) tarefa *f* maçante; **household ~s** afazeres *mpl* domésticos

choreograph|er /kɒrɪ'ɒgrəfə(r)/ *n* coreógrafo *m*. **~y** *n* coreografia *f*

chorus /'kɔ:rəs/ *n* coro *m*; (*of song*) refrão *m*, estribilho *m*

chose, **chosen** /tʃəʊz, 'tʃəʊzn/ ▶ CHOOSE

Christ /kraɪst/ *n* Cristo *m*

christen /'krɪsn/ *vt* batizar. **~ing** *n* batismo *m*

Christian /'krɪstʃən/ *a & n* cristão *m*; **~ name** nome *m* de batismo. **~ity** /-stɪ'ænətɪ/ *n* cristandade *f*

Christmas /'krɪsməs/ *n* Natal *m* ● *a* do Natal; **~ card** cartão *m* de Boas Festas; **~ Day/Eve** dia *m* /véspera *f* de Natal; **~ tree** árvore *f* de Natal

chrome /krəʊm/ *n* cromo *m*

chromosome /'krəʊməsəʊm/ *n* cromossoma *m*

chronic /'krɒnɪk/ *a* crônico, (*P*) crónico

chronicle /'krɒnɪkl/ *n* crônica *f*, (*P*) crónica *f*

chronological /krɒnə'lɒdʒɪkl/ *a* cronológico

chrysanthemum /krɪ'sænθəməm/ *n* crisântemo *m*

chubby /'tʃʌbɪ/ *a* (**-ier**, **-iest**) gorducho, rechonchudo

chuck /tʃʌk/ *vt* ⓘ deitar; atirar; **~ out** ‹*person*› expulsar; ‹*thing*› jogar fora, (*P*) deitar fora

chuckle /'tʃʌkl/ *n* riso *m* abafado ● *vi* rir sozinho

chum /tʃʌm/ *n* ⓘ amigo *m* íntimo, camarada *mf*. **~my** *a* amigável

chunk /tʃʌŋk/ *n* (grande) bocado *m*, naco *m*

church /tʃɜ:tʃ/ *n* igreja *f*

churchyard /'tʃɜ:tʃja:d/ *n* cemitério *m*

churlish /'tʃɜ:lɪʃ/ *a* grosseiro, indelicado

churn /tʃɜ:n/ *n* batedeira *f*; (*milk can*) vasilha *f* de leite ● *vt* bater; **~ out** produzir em série

chutney /'tʃʌtnɪ/ *n* (*pl* **-eys**) chutney *m*

cider /'saɪdə(r)/ *n* sidra *f*, (*P*) cidra *f*

cigar /sɪ'gɑ:(r)/ *n* charuto *m*

cigarette /sɪgə'ret/ *n* cigarro *m*

cinema /'sɪnəmə/ *n* cinema *m*

cinnamon /'sɪnəmən/ *n* canela *f*

circle /'sɛ:kl/ *n* círculo *m*; *Theat* balcão *m* ● *vt* dar a volta a ● *vi* descrever círculos, voltear

circuit /'sɜ:kɪt/ *n* circuito *m*

circuitous /sɜ:'kju:ɪtəs/ *a* indireto, tortuoso

circular /'sɜ:kjʊlə(r)/ *a* circular

circulat|e /'sɜ:kjʊleɪt/ *vt/i* (fazer) circular. **~ion** /-'leɪʃn/ *n* circulação *f*; (*sales of newspaper*) tiragem *f*

circumcis|e /'sɜ:kəmsaɪz/ *vt* circuncidar. **~ion** /-'sɪʒn/ *n* circuncisão *f*

circumference /sə'kʌmfərəns/ *n* circunferência *f*

circumflex /'sɜ:kəmfleks/ *n* circunflexo *m*

circumstance /'sɜ:kəmstəns/ *n* circunstância *f*; **~s** (*means*) situação *f* econômica, (*P*) económica

circus /'sɜ:kəs/ *n* circo *m*

cistern /'sɪstən/ *n* reservatório *m*; (*of WC*) autoclismo *m*

cit|e /saɪt/ *vt* citar. **~ation** /-'teɪʃn/ *n* citação *f*

citizen /'sɪtɪzn/ *n* cidadão *m*, cidadã *f*; (*of town*) habitante *mf*. **~ship** *n* cidadania *f*

citrus /'sɪtrəs/ *n* **~ fruit** citrino *m*

city /'sɪtɪ/ *n* cidade *f*

> *i*
> **The City** Área situada dentro dos limites da antiga cidade de Londres. Atualmente, é o centro financeiro da capital, na qual muitas instituições financeiras têm as suas sedes centrais. Muitas vezes, quando se fala de *The City*, está se referindo a essas sedes e não à área da cidade propriamente dita.

civic /'sɪvɪk/ *a* cívico

civil /'sɪvl/ *a* civil; ‹*rights*› cívico; (*polite*) delicado; **~ servant** funcionário *m* público; **C~ Service** Administração *f* Pública; **~ war** guerra *f* civil.

C

~ **partnership** *n* união *m* civil entre homossexuais, (*P*) união *f* de facto entre pessoas do mesmo sexo. **~ity** /-ˈvɪlətɪ/ *n* civilidade *f*, cortesia *f*

civilian /sɪˈvɪlɪən/ *a & n* civil *mf*, paisano *m*

C

civiliz|e /ˈsɪvəlaɪz/ *vt* civilizar. **~ation** /-ˈzeɪʃn/ *n* civilização *f*

claim /kleɪm/ *vt* reclamar; (*assert*) pretender ● *vi* (*from insurance*) reclamar ● *n* reivindicação *f*; (*assertion*) afirmação *f*; (*right*) direito *m*; (*from insurance*) reclamação *f*

clairvoyant /kleəˈvɔɪənt/ *n* vidente *mf* ● *a* clarividente

clam /klæm/ *n* molusco *m*

clamber /ˈklæmbə(r)/ *vi* trepar

clammy /ˈklæmɪ/ *a* (**-ier**, **-iest**) úmido, (*P*) húmido e pegajoso

clamour /ˈklæmə(r)/ *n* clamor *m*, vociferação *f* ● *vi* ~ **for** exigir aos gritos

clamp /klæmp/ *n* grampo *m*; (*for car*) bloqueador *m* ● *vt* prender com grampo; ‹*a car*› bloquear; ~ **down on** apertar, suprimir; [!] cair em cima de [!]

clan /klæn/ *n* clã *m*

clang /klæŋ/ *n* tinir *m*

clap /klæp/ *vt/i* (*pt* **clapped**) aplaudir; (*put*) meter ● *n* aplauso *m*; (*of thunder*) ribombo *m*; ~ **one's hands** bater palmas

claret /ˈklærət/ *n* clarete *m*

clarif|y /ˈklærɪfaɪ/ *vt* esclarecer. **~ication** /-ɪˈkeɪʃn/ *n* esclarecimento *m*

clarinet /klærɪˈnet/ *n* clarinete *m*

clarity /ˈklærətɪ/ *n* claridade *f*

clash /klæʃ/ *n* choque *m*; (*sound*) estridor *m*; *fig* conflito *m* ● *vt/i* entrechocar(-se); (*of colours*) destoar

clasp /klɑːsp/ *n* (*fastener*) fecho *m*; (*hold, grip*) aperto *m* de mão ● *vt* apertar, serrar

class /klɑːs/ *n* classe *f* ● *vt* classificar

classic /ˈklæsɪk/ *a & n* clássico *m*. **~s** *npl* letras *fpl* clássicas, (*P*) estudos *mpl* clássicos. **~al** *a* clássico

classif|y /ˈklæsɪfaɪ/ *vt* classificar; **~ied advertisement** anúncio *m* classificado. **~ication** /-ɪˈkeɪʃn/ *n* classificação *f*

classroom /ˈklɑːsruːm/ *n* sala *f* de aulas

clatter /ˈklætə(r)/ *n* estardalhaço *m* ● *vi* fazer barulho

clause /klɔːz/ *n* cláusula *f*; *Gram* oração *f*

claustrophob|ia /klɔːstrəˈfəʊbɪə/ *n* claustrofobia *f*. **~ic** *a* claustrofóbico

claw /klɔː/ *n* garra *f*; (*of lobster*) tenaz *f*, pinça *f* ● *vt* (*seize*) agarrar; (*scratch*) arranhar; (*tear*) rasgar

clay /kleɪ/ *n* argila *f*, barro *m*

clean /kliːn/ *a* (**-er**, **-est**) limpo ● *adv* completamente ● *vt* limpar ● *vi* ~ **up** fazer a limpeza. **~er** *n* faxineira *f*, (*P*) mulher *f* da limpeza; (*of clothes*) empregado *m* da tinturaria

cleans|e /klenz/ *vt* limpar; *fig* purificar; **~ing cream** creme *m* de limpeza

clear /klɪə(r)/ *a* (**-er**, **-est**) claro; ‹*glass*› transparente; (*without obstacles*) livre; ‹*profit*› líquido; ‹*sky*› limpo; ~ **of** (*away from*) afastado de ● *adv* claramente ● *vt* ‹*snow, one's name, etc*› limpar; ‹*the table*› tirar; ‹*jump*› transpor; ‹*debt*› saldar; *Jur* absolver; (*through customs*) despachar; ~ **out** (*clean*) fazer a limpeza; ~ **up** (*tidy*) arrumar; ‹*mystery*› desvendar ● *vi* ‹*fog*› dissipar-se; ‹*sky*› limpar; ~ **off** or **out** [x] sair andando, zarpar; ~ **up** (*of weather*) clarear, limpar

clearance /ˈklɪərəns/ *n* autorização *f*; (*for ship*) despacho *m*; (*space*) espaço *m* livre; ~ **sale** liquidação *f*, saldos *mpl*

clearing /ˈklɪərɪŋ/ *n* clareira *f*

cleaver /ˈkliːvə(r)/ *n* cutelo *m*

clench /klentʃ/ *vt* ‹*teeth, fists*› cerrar; (*grasp*) agarrar

clergy /ˈklɜːdʒɪ/ *n* clero *m*. **~man** (*pl* **-men**) *n* clérigo *m*, sacerdote *m*

cleric /ˈklerɪk/ *n* clérigo *m*. **~al** *a Relig* clerical; (*of clerks*) de escritório

clerk /klɑːk/ *n* auxiliar *m* de escritório

clever /ˈklevə(r)/ *a* (**-er**, **-est**) esperto, inteligente; (*skilful*) hábil, habilidoso

cliché /ˈkliːʃeɪ/ *n* chavão *m*, lugar-comum *m*, clichê *m*

click /klɪk/ *n* estalido *m*, clique *m* ● *vi* dar um estalido; *Comput* clicar

client /ˈklaɪənt/ *n* cliente *mf*

cliff /klɪf/ *n* penhasco *m*. **~s** *npl* falésia *f*

climat|e /ˈklaɪmɪt/ *n* clima *m*. ~ **change** *n* alterações *f* climáticas

climax /ˈklaɪmæks/ *n* clímax *m*, ponto *m* culminante

climb /klaɪm/ *vt* ‹*stairs*› subir; ‹*tree, wall*› subir em, trepar em, (*P*) subir, trepar; ‹*mountain*› escalar ● *vi* subir, trepar ● *n* subida *f*; (*mountain*) escalada *f*; ~ **down** descer; *fig* dar a mão à palmatória *fig*. **~er** *n Sport* alpinista *mf*; (*plant*) trepadeira *f*

cling /klɪŋ/ *vi* (*pt* **clung**) ~ **(to)** agarrar-se (a); (*stick*) colar-se (a)

clinic /'klɪnɪk/ *n* clínica *f*

clinical /'klɪnɪkl/ *a* clínico

clink /klɪŋk/ *n* tinido *m* ● *vt/i* (fazer) tilintar

clip[1] /klɪp/ *n* (*for paper*) clipe *m*; (*for hair*) grampo *m*, (*P*) gancho *m*; (*for tube*) braçadeira *f* ● *vt* (*pt* **clipped**) prender

clip[2] /klɪp/ *vt* (*pt* **clipped**) cortar; (*trim*) aparar ● *n* tosquia *f*; [!] (*blow*) murro *m*. **~ping** *n* recorte *m*

cloak /kləʊk/ *n* capa *f*, manto *m*

cloakroom /'kləʊkru:m/ *n* vestiário *m*; (*toilet*) toalete *m*, (*P*) lavabo *m*

clock /klɒk/ *n* relógio *m* ● *vi* **~ in/out** marcar o ponto (à entrada/à saída); **~ up** [!] ‹*miles etc*› fazer

clockwise /'klɒkwaɪz/ *a & adv* no sentido dos ponteiros do relógio

clockwork /'klɒkwɜ:k/ *n* mecanismo *m*; **go like ~** ir às mil maravilhas

clog /klɒg/ *n* tamanco *m*, soco *m* ● *vt/i* (*pt* **clogged**) entupir(-se)

cloister /'klɔɪstə(r)/ *n* claustro *m*

close[1] /kləʊs/ *a* (**-er**, **-est**) próximo (**to** de); ‹*link*, *collaboration*› estreito; ‹*friend*› íntimo; ‹*weather*› abafado; **have a ~ shave** *fig* escapar por um triz ● *adv* perto; **~ at hand**, **~ by** muito perto; **~ together** (*crowded*) espremido. **~-up** *n* grande plano *m*. **~ly** *adv* de perto

close[2] /kləʊz/ *vt/i* fechar(-se); (*end*) terminar; (*of shop etc*) fechar ● *n* fim *m*; **~d shop** organização *f* que só admite trabalhadores sindicalizados

closet /'klɒzɪt/ *n* armário *m*

closure /'kləʊʒə(r)/ *n* encerramento *m*

clot /klɒt/ *n* coágulo *m* ● *vi* (*pt* **clotted**) coagular

cloth /klɒθ/ *n* pano *m*; (*tablecloth*) toalha *f* de mesa

cloth|e /kləʊð/ *vt* vestir. **~ing** *n* vestuário *m*, roupa *f*

clothes /kləʊðz/ *npl* roupa *f*, vestuário *m*. **~ line** *n* varal *m* para roupa

cloud /klaʊd/ *n* nuvem *f* ● *vt/i* toldar(-se). **~ computing** *n* computação *f* na nuvem. **~y** *a* nublado, toldado; ‹*liquid*› turvo

clout /klaʊt/ *n* cascudo *m*, (*P*) carolo *m*; [!] (*power*) poder *m* efectivo ● *vt* [!] bater

clove /kləʊv/ *n* cravo *m*; **~ of garlic** dente *m* de alho

clover /'kləʊvə(r)/ *n* trevo *m*

clown /klaʊn/ *n* palhaço *m* ● *vi* fazer palhaçadas

club /klʌb/ *n* clube *m*; (*weapon*) cacete *m*; **~s** *Cards* paus *mpl* ● *vt/i* (*pt* **clubbed**) dar bordoadas or cacetadas (em); **~ together** (*share costs*) cotizar-se

clue /klu:/ *n* indício *m*, pista *f*; (*in crossword*) definição *f*; **not have a ~** [!] não fazer a menor ideia

clump /klʌmp/ *n* maciço *m*, tufo *m*

clumsy /'klʌmzɪ/ *a* (**-ier**, **-iest**) desajeitado

clung /klʌŋ/ ▶ CLING

cluster /'klʌstə(r)/ *n* (pequeno) grupo *m*; *Bot* cacho *m* ● *vt/i* agrupar(-se)

clutch /klʌtʃ/ *vt* agarrar (em), apertar ● *vi* agarrar-se (**at** a) ● *n* *Auto* embreagem *f*, (*P*) embraiagem *f*. **~es** *npl* garras *fpl*

clutter /'klʌtə(r)/ *n* barafunda *f*, desordem *f* ● *vt* atravancar

coach /kəʊtʃ/ *n* ônibus *m*, (*P*) autocarro *m*, camioneta *f*; (*of train*) carruagem *f*; *Sport* treinador *m* ● *vt* (*tutor*) dar aulas a; *Sport* treinar

coal /kəʊl/ *n* carvão *m*

coalition /kəʊə'lɪʃn/ *n* coligação *f*

coarse /kɔ:s/ *a* (**-er**, **-est**) grosseiro

coast /kəʊst/ *n* costa *f* ● *vi* costear; (*cycle*) descer em roda-livre; (*car*) ir em ponto morto

coastguard /'kəʊstgɑ:d/ *n* polícia *f* marítima

coastline /'kəʊstlaɪn/ *n* litoral *m*

coat /kəʊt/ *n* casaco *m*; (*of animal*) pelo *m*; (*of paint*) camada *f*, demão *f*; **~ of arms** brasão *m* ● *vt* cobrir. **~ing** *n* camada *f*

coax /kəʊks/ *vt* levar com afagos ou lisonjas, convencer

cobble /'kɒbl/ *n* **~(-stone)** pedra de *f* calçada

cobweb /'kɒbweb/ *n* teia *f* de aranha

cocaine /kəʊ'keɪn/ *n* cocaína *f*

cock /kɒk/ *n* (*male bird*) macho *m*; (*rooster*) galo *m* ● *vt* ‹*gun*› engatilhar; ‹*ears*› fitar

cockerel /'kɒkərəl/ *n* frango *m*, galo *m* novo

cockney /'kɒknɪ/ *n* (*pl* **-eys**) (*person*) londrino *m*; (*dialect*) dialeto *m* do leste de Londres

cockpit /'kɒkpɪt/ *n* cabine *f*

cockroach /'kɒkrəʊtʃ/ *n* barata *f*

cocktail /'kɒkteɪl/ *n* cocktail *m*, coquetel *m*; **fruit ~** salada *f* de fruta

cocky /'kɒkɪ/ *a* (**-ier**, **-iest**) convencido [!]

C

cocoa /ˈkəʊkəʊ/ *n* cacau *m*
coconut /ˈkəʊkənʌt/ *n* coco *m*
cod /kɒd/ *n* (*pl invar*) bacalhau *m*; **~-liver oil** óleo *m* de fígado de bacalhau
code /kəʊd/ *n* código *m* ● *vt* codificar
coerc|e /kəʊˈɜːs/ *vt* coagir. **~ion** /-ʃn/ *n* coação *f*
coexist /kəʊɪgˈzɪst/ *vi* coexistir. **~ence** *n* coexistência *f*
coffee /ˈkɒfɪ/ *n* café *m*; **~ bar** café *m*. **~ table** *n* mesa *f* baixa
coffin /ˈkɒfɪn/ *n* caixão *m*
cogent /ˈkəʊdʒənt/ *a* convincente; (*relevant*) pertinente
cognac /ˈkɒnjæk/ *n* conhaque *m*
cohabit /kəʊˈhæbɪt/ *vi* coabitar
coherent /kəˈhɪərənt/ *a* coerente
coil /kɔɪl/ *vt/i* enrolar(-se) ● *n* rolo *m*; *Electr* bobina *f*; (*one ring*) espiral *f*; (*contraceptive*) dispositivo *m* intrauterino, DIU
coin /kɔɪn/ *n* moeda *f* ● *vt* cunhar
coincide /kəʊɪnˈsaɪd/ *vi* coincidir
coinciden|ce /kəʊˈɪnsɪdəns/ *n* coincidência *f*. **~tal** /-ˈdentl/ *a* que acontece por coincidência
colander /ˈkʌləndə(r)/ *n* peneira *f*, (*P*) coador *m*
cold /kəʊld/ *a* (**-er**, **-est**) frio; **be** or **feel ~** estar com frio; **it's ~** está frio; **~ cream** creme *m* para a pele ● *n* frio *m*; *Med* resfriado *m*, constipação *f*. **~-blooded** *a* ‹*person*› insensível; ‹*deed*› a sangue frio. **~ness** *n* frio *m*; (*of feeling*) frieza *f*
coleslaw /ˈkəʊlslɔː/ *n* salada *f* de repolho cru
colic /ˈkɒlɪk/ *n* cólica(s) *f*(*pl*)
collaborat|e /kəˈlæbəreɪt/ *vi* colaborar. **~ion** /-ˈreɪʃn/ *n* colaboração *f*. **~or** *n* colaborador *m*
collapse /kəˈlæps/ *vi* desabar; *Med* ter um colapso ● *n* colapso *m*
collapsible /kəˈlæpsəbl/ *a* desmontável, dobrável
collar /ˈkɒlə(r)/ *n* gola *f*; (*of shirt*) colarinho *m*; (*of dog*) coleira *f* ● *vt* [!] pôr a mão a. **~bone** *n* clavícula *f*
colleague /ˈkɒliːg/ *n* colega *mf*
collect /kəˈlekt/ *vt* (*gather*) juntar; (*fetch*) ir/vir buscar; ‹*money, rent*› cobrar; (*as hobby*) colecionar ● *vi* juntar-se; **call ~** *Amer* chamar a cobrar. **~ion** /-ʃn/ *n* coleção *f*, (*in church*) coleta *f*, (*of mail*) tiragem *f*; coleta *f*, (*P*) abertura *f*. **~or** *n* (*as hobby*) colecionador *m*
college /ˈkɒlɪdʒ/ *n* colégio *m*
collide /kəˈlaɪd/ *vi* colidir
colliery /ˈkɒlɪərɪ/ *n* mina *f* de carvão
collision /kəˈlɪʒn/ *n* colisão *f*, choque *m*; *fig* conflito *m*
colloquial /kəˈləʊkwɪəl/ *a* coloquial
colon /ˈkəʊlən/ *n Gram* dois pontos *mpl*; *Anat* cólon *m*
colonel /ˈkɜːnl/ *n* coronel *m*
colonize /ˈkɒlənaɪz/ *vt* colonizar
colon|y /ˈkɒlənɪ/ *n* colônia *f*, (*P*) colónia *f*. **~ial** /kəˈləʊnɪəl/ *a* & *n* colonial *mf*
colossal /kəˈlɒsl/ *a* colossal
colour /ˈkʌlə(r)/ *n* cor *f* ● *a* ‹*photo, TV, etc*› a cores; ‹*film*› colorido ● *vt* colorir, dar cor a ● *vi* (*blush*) corar. **~-blind** *a* daltônico, (*P*) daltónico. **~ful** *a* colorido. **~ing** *n* (*of skin*) cor *f*; (*in food*) corante *m*. **~less** *a* descolorido
coloured /ˈkʌləd/ *a* ‹*pencil, person*› de cor ● *n* pessoa *f* de cor
column /ˈkɒləm/ *n* coluna *f*
columnist /ˈkɒləmnɪst/ *n* colunista *mf*
coma /ˈkəʊmə/ *n* coma *m*
comb /kəʊm/ *n* pente *m* ● *vt* pentear; (*search*) vasculhar; **~ one's hair** pentear-se
combat /ˈkɒmbæt/ *n* combate *m* ● *vt* (*pt* **combated**) combater
combination /kɒmbɪˈneɪʃn/ *n* combinação *f*
combine /kəmˈbaɪn/ *vt/i* combinar(-se), juntar(-se), reunir(-se)
combustion /kəmˈbʌstʃən/ *n* combustão *f*
come /kʌm/ *vi* (*pt* **came**, *pp* **come**) vir; (*arrive*) chegar; (*occur*) suceder; **~ about** acontecer; **~ across** encontrar, dar com; **~ away** or **off** soltar-se; **~ back** voltar; **~ by** obter; **~ down** descer; ‹*price*› baixar; **~ from** vir de; **~ in** entrar; **~ into** ‹*money*› herdar; **~ off** (*succeed*) ter êxito; (*fare*) sair-se; **~ on!** vamos!; **~ out** sair; **~ round** (*after fainting*) voltar a si; (*be converted*) deixar-se convencer; **~ to** (*amount to*) montar a; **~ up** subir; ‹*seeds*› despontar; *fig* surgir; **~ up with** ‹*idea*› ter, vir com, propor. **~back** *n* regresso *m*; (*retort*) réplica *f*; **~down** *n* humilhação *f*
comedian /kəˈmiːdɪən/ *n* comediante *mf*
comedy /ˈkɒmədɪ/ *n* comédia *f*
comet /ˈkɒmɪt/ *n* cometa *m*

comfort /ˈkʌmfət/ *n* conforto *m* ● *vt* confortar, consolar. **~ food** *n* comida *f* de conforto; **~ zone** *n* zona *f* de conforto; **to be in/out of one's ~ zone** estar dentro/fora da sua zona de conforto. **~able** *a* confortável

comic /ˈkɒmɪk/ *a* cômico, (*P*) cómico ● *n* cômico *m*, (*P*) cómico *m*; (*periodical*) estórias *fpl* em quadrinhos, (*P*) revista *f* de banda desenhada; **~ strip** estória *f* em quadrinhos, (*P*) banda *f* desenhada

coming /ˈkʌmɪŋ/ *n* vinda *f*; **~s and goings** idas e vindas *fpl* ● *a* próximo

comma /ˈkɒmə/ *n* vírgula *f*

command /kəˈmɑːnd/ *n Mil* comando *m*; (*order*) ordem *f*; (*mastery*) domínio *m* ● *vt* comandar; ‹*respect*› inspirar, impor. **~er** *n* comandante *m*

commemorat|e /kəˈmeməreɪt/ *vt* comemorar. **~ion** /ˈ-reɪʃn/ *n* comemoração *f*. **~ive** *a* comemorativo

commence /kəˈmens/ *vt/i* começar

commend /kəˈmend/ *vt* louvar; (*entrust*) confiar. **~able** *a* louvável. **~ation** /kɒmenˈdeɪʃn/ *n* louvor *m*

comment /ˈkɒment/ *n* comentário *m* ● *vi* comentar; **~ on** comentar, fazer comentários

commentary /ˈkɒməntrɪ/ *n* comentário *m*; *Radio, TV* relato *m*

commentat|e /ˈkɒmənteɪt/ *vi* fazer um relato. **~or** *n Radio, TV* comentarista *mf*, (*P*) comentador *m*

commerce /ˈkɒmɜːs/ *n* comércio *m*

commercial /kəˈmɜːʃl/ *a* comercial ● *n* publicidade (comercial) *f*. **~ize** *vt* comercializar

commiserat|e /kəˈmɪzəreɪt/ *vi* **~ with** compadecer-se de. **~ion** /-ˈreɪʃn/ *n* comiseração *f*, pesar *m*

commission /kəˈmɪʃn/ *n* comissão *f*; (*order for work*) encomenda *f* ● *vt* encomendar; *Mil* nomear; **~ to do** encarregar de fazer; **out of ~** fora de serviço ativo. **~er** *n* comissário *m*; *Police* chefe *m*

commit /kəˈmɪt/ *vt* (*pt* **committed**) cometer; (*entrust*) confiar; **~ o.s.** comprometer-se, empenhar-se; **~ suicide** suicidar-se; **~ to memory** decorar. **~ment** *n* compromisso *m*

committee /kəˈmɪtɪ/ *n* comissão *f*, comitê *m*, (*P*) comité *m*

commodity /kəˈmɒdətɪ/ *n* artigo *m*, mercadoria *f*

common /ˈkɒmən/ *a* (**-er, -est**) comum; (*usual*) usual, corrente; *pej* (*ill-bred*) ordinário; **~ law** direito *m* consuetudinário; **C~ Market** Mercado *m* Comum; **~ sense** bom senso *m*, senso *m* comum ● *n* prado *m* público, (*P*) baldio *m*; **House of C~s** Câmara *f* dos Comuns; **in ~** em comum. **~ room** *n* sala *f* comum. **~ly** *adv* mais comum

commoner /ˈkɒmənə(r)/ *n* plebeu *m*

commonplace /ˈkɒmənpleɪs/ *a* banal ● *n* lugar-comum *m*

> **i**
>
> **Commonwealth** A associação das antigas colônias e territórios que formavam o Império Britânico. De dois em dois anos, celebra-se um encontro de cúpula dos respectivos chefes de governo. Entre os países-membros existem inúmeros vínculos culturais, educativos e desportivos. Nos Estados Unidos, o termo *Commonwealth* emprega-se oficialmente quando se refere ao conjunto de quatro estados: Kentucky, Massachusetts, Pensilvânia e Virgínia.

commotion /kəˈməʊʃn/ *n* agitação *f*, confusão *f*, barulheira *f*

communal /ˈkɒmjʊnl/ *a* (*of a commune*) comunal; (*shared*) comum

commune /ˈkɒmjuːn/ *n* comuna *f*

communicat|e /kəˈmjuːnɪkeɪt/ *vt/i* comunicar. **~ion** /-ˈkeɪʃn/ *n* comunicação *f*; **~ion cord** sinal *m* de alarme. **~ive** /-ətɪv/ *a* comunicativo

communion /kəˈmjuːnɪən/ *n* comunhão *f*

communis|t /ˈkɒmjʊnɪst/ *n* comunista *mf* ● *a* comunista. **~m** /-zəm/ *n* comunismo *m*

community /kəˈmjuːnətɪ/ *n* comunidade *f*; **~ centre** centro *m* comunitário

commute /kəˈmjuːt/ *vi* viajar diariamente para o trabalho. **~r** /-ə(r)/ *n* pessoa *f* que viaja diariamente para o trabalho

compact[1] /kəmˈpækt/ *a* compacto. **~ disc** *n* cd *m*

compact[2] /ˈkɒmpækt/ *n* estojo *m* de pó-de-arroz, (*P*) caixa *f*

companion /kəmˈpænɪən/ *n* companheiro *m*. **~ship** *n* companhia *f*, convívio *m*

company /ˈkʌmpənɪ/ *n* companhia *f*; (*guests*) visitas *fpl*; **keep sb ~** fazer companhia a alguém

comparable /ˈkɒmpərəbl/ *a* comparável

C

compar|e /kəm'peə(r)/ *vt/i* comparar(-se) (**to, with** com). **~ative** /-'pærətɪv/ *a* comparativo; ‹*comfort etc*› relativo

comparison /kəm'pærɪsn/ *n* comparação *f*

compartment /kəm'pɑːtmənt/ *n* compartimento *m*

compass /'kʌmpəs/ *n* bússola *f*; **~es** compasso *m*

compassion /kəm'pæʃn/ *n* compaixão *f*. **~ate** *a* compassivo

compatib|le /kəm'pætəbl/ *a* compatível. **~ility** /-'bɪlətɪ/ *n* compatibilidade *f*

compel /kəm'pel/ *vt* (*pt* **compelled**) compelir, forçar. **~ling** *a* irresistível, convincente

compensat|e /'kɒmpənseɪt/ *vt/i* compensar. **~ion** /-'seɪʃn/ *n* compensação *f*; (*financial*) indenização *f*, (*P*) indemnização *f*

compete /kəm'piːt/ *vi* competir; **~ with** rivalizar com

competen|t /'kɒmpɪtənt/ *a* competente. **~ce** *n* competência *f*

competition /kɒmpə'tɪʃn/ *n* competição *f*; *Comm* concorrência *f*

competitive /kəm'petɪtɪv/ *a* ‹*sport, prices*› competitivo; **~ examination** concurso *m*

competitor /kəm'petɪtə(r)/ *n* competidor *m*, concorrente *mf*

compile /kəm'paɪl/ *vt* compilar, coligir. **~r** /-ə(r)/ *n* compilador *m*

complacen|t /kəm'pleɪsnt/ *a* satisfeito consigo mesmo, (*P*) complacente. **~cy** *n* (auto-)satisfação *f*, (*P*) complacência *f*

complain /kəm'pleɪn/ *vi* queixar-se (**about** de)

complaint /kəm'pleɪnt/ *n* queixa *f*; (*in shop*) reclamação *f*; *Med* doença *f*, achaque *m*

complement /'kɒmplɪmənt/ *n* complemento *m* ● *vt* completar, complementar. **~ary** /-'mentrɪ/ *a* complementar

complet|e /kəm'pliːt/ *a* completo; (*finished*) acabado; (*downright*) perfeito ● *vt* completar; ‹*a form*› preencher. **~ely** *adv* completamente. **~ion** /-ʃn/ *n* conclusão *f*, feitura *f*, realização *f*

complex /'kɒmpleks/ *a* complexo ● *n* complexo *m*. **~ity** /kəm'pleksətɪ/ *n* complexidade *f*

complexion /kəm'plekʃn/ *n* cor *f* da tez, tez *f*; *fig* caráter *m*, (*P*) carácter *m*, aspecto *m*

compliance /kəm'plaɪəns/ *n* docilidade *f*; (*agreement*) conformidade *f*; **in ~ with** em conformidade com

complicat|e /'kɒmplɪkeɪt/ *vt* complicar. **~ed** *a* complicado. **~ion** /-'keɪʃn/ *n* complicação *f*

compliment /'kɒmplɪmənt/ *n* cumprimento *m*, elogio *m* ● *vt* /'kɒmplɪment/ cumprimentar, elogiar

complimentary /kɒmplɪ'mentrɪ/ *a* amável, elogioso; **~ copy** oferta *f*; **~ ticket** bilhete *m* grátis

comply /kəm'plaɪ/ *vi* **~ with** agir em conformidade com

component /kəm'pəʊnənt/ *n* componente *m*; (*of machine*) peça *f* ● *a* componente, constituinte

compose /kəm'pəʊz/ *vt* compor; **~ o.s.** acalmar-se, dominar-se. **~d** *a* calmo, senhor de si. **~r** /-ə(r)/ *n* compositor *m*

composition /kɒmpə'zɪʃn/ *n* composição *f*

compost /'kɒmpɒst/ *n* húmus *m*, adubo *m*

composure /kəm'pəʊʒə(r)/ *n* calma *f*, domínio *m* de si mesmo

compound /'kɒmpaʊnd/ *n* composto *m*; (*enclosure*) cercado *m*, recinto *m* ● *a* composto; **~ fracture** fratura *f* exposta

comprehen|d /kɒmprɪ'hend/ *vt* compreender. **~sion** *n* compreensão *f*

comprehensive /kɒmprɪ'hensɪv/ *a* compreensivo, vasto; (*insurance*) contra todos os riscos; **~ school** escola *f* de ensino secundário técnico e acadêmico or (*P*) académico

compress /kəm'pres/ *vt* comprimir. **~ion** /-ʃn/ *n* compressão *f*

comprise /kəm'praɪz/ *vt* compreender, abranger

compromise /'kɒmprəmaɪz/ *n* compromisso *m* ● *vt* comprometer ● *vi* chegar a um meio-termo

compulsion /kəm'pʌlʃn/ *n* (*constraint*) coação *f*; *Psych* desejo *m* irresistível, compulsão *f*

compulsive /kəm'pʌlsɪv/ *a* *Psych* compulsivo; ‹*liar, smoker etc*› inveterado

compulsory /kəm'pʌlsərɪ/ *a* obrigatório, compulsório

computer /kəm'pjuːtə(r)/ *n* computador *m*; **~ science** informática *f*. **~ize** *vt* computerizar

comrade /ˈkɒmreɪd/ *n* camarada *mf*

con[1] /kɒn/ *vt* (*pt* **conned**) ☒ enganar ● *n* ☒ intrujice *f*; vigarice *f*; burla *f*; **~ man** ☒ intrujão *m*, vigarista *m*, burlão *m*

con[2] /kɒn/ ▶ PRO[1]

concave /ˈkɒŋkeɪv/ *a* côncavo

conceal /kənˈsiːl/ *vt* ocultar, esconder

concede /kənˈsiːd/ *vt* conceder, admitir; (*in a game etc*) ceder, dar-se por vencido

conceit /kənˈsiːt/ *n* presunção *f*. **~ed** *a* presunçoso, presumido, cheio de si

conceivabl|e /kənˈsiːvəbl/ *a* concebível

conceive /kənˈsiːv/ *vt/i* conceber

concentrat|e /ˈkɒnsntreɪt/ *vt/i* concentrar(-se). **~ion** /-ˈtreɪʃn/ *n* concentração *f*

concept /ˈkɒnsept/ *n* conceito *m*

conception /kənˈsepʃn/ *n* concepção *f*

concern /kənˈsɜːn/ *n* (*worry*) preocupação *f*; (*business*) negócio *m* ● *vt* dizer respeito a, respeitar; **~ o.s. with, be ~ed with** interessar-se por, ocupar-se de; (*regard*) dizer respeito a; **it's no ~ of mine** não me diz respeito. **~ing** *prep* sobre, respeitante a

concerned /kənˈsɜːnd/ *a* inquieto; preocupado (**about** com)

concert /ˈkɒnsət/ *n* concerto *m*

concession /kənˈseʃn/ *n* concessão *f*

conclu|de /kənˈkluːd/ *vt* concluir ● *vi* terminar. **~sion** *n* conclusão *f*

conclusive /kənˈkluːsɪv/ *a* conclusivo

concoct /kənˈkɒkt/ *vt* preparar por mistura; *fig* (*invent*) fabricar. **~ion** /-ʃn/ *n* mistura *f*; *fig* invenção *f*; mentira *f*

concrete /ˈkɒŋkriːt/ *n* concreto *m*, (*P*) cimento *m* ● *a* concreto ● *vt* concretar, (*P*) cimentar

concur /kənˈkɜː(r)/ *vi* (*pt* **concurred**) concordar; (*of circumstances*) concorrer

concussion /kənˈkʌʃn/ *n* comoção *f* cerebral

condemn /kənˈdem/ *vt* condenar. **~ation** /kɒndemˈneɪʃn/ *n* condenação *f*

condens|e /kənˈdens/ *vt/i* condensar(-se). **~ation** /kɒndenˈseɪʃn/ *n* condensação *f*

condescend /kɒndɪˈsend/ *vi* condescender; (*lower o.s.*) rebaixar-se

condition /kənˈdɪʃn/ *n* condição *f*; **on ~ that** com a condição de que ● *vt* condicionar. **~al** *a* condicional. **~er** *n* (*for hair*) condicionador *m*, creme *m* rinse

condolences /kənˈdəʊlənsɪz/ *npl* condolências *fpl*, pêsames *mpl*, sentimentos *mpl*

condom /ˈkɒndəm/ *n* preservativo *m*

condone /kənˈdəʊn/ *vt* desculpar, fechar os olhos a

conducive /kənˈdjuːsɪv/ *a* **be ~ to** contribuir para, ser propício a

conduct[1] /kənˈdʌkt/ *vt* conduzir, dirigir; ‹*orchestra*› reger

conduct[2] /ˈkɒndʌkt/ *n* conduta *f*

conductor /kənˈdʌktə(r)/ *n* maestro *m*; *Electr* (*of bus*) condutor *m*

cone /kəʊn/ *n* cone *m*; *Bot* pinha *f*; (*for ice cream*) casquinha *f*, (*P*) cone *m*

confectioner /kənˈfekʃnə(r)/ *n* confeiteiro *m*, (*P*) pasteleiro *m*. **~y** *n* confeitaria *f*, (*P*) pastelaria *f*

conference /ˈkɒnfərəns/ *n* conferência *f*; **in ~** em reunião *f*

confess /kənˈfes/ *vt/i* confessar; *Relig* confessar(-se). **~ion** /-ʃn/ *n* confissão *f*

confetti /kənˈfetɪ/ *n* confetes *mpl*, (*P*) confetti *mpl*

confide /kənˈfaɪd/ *vt* confiar ● *vi* **~ in** confiar em

confiden|t /ˈkɒnfɪdənt/ *a* confiante, confiado. **~ce** *n* confiança *f*; (*boldness*) confiança *f* em si; (*secret*) confidência *f*; **~ce trick** vigarice *f*; **in ~ce** em confidência

confidential /kɒnfɪˈdenʃl/ *a* confidencial

confine /kənˈfaɪn/ *vt* fechar; (*limit*) limitar (**to** a). **~ment** *n* detenção *f*; *Med* parto *m*

confirm /kənˈfɜːm/ *vt* confirmar. **~ation** /kɒnfəˈmeɪʃn/ *n* confirmação *f*. **~ed** *a* (*bachelor*) inveterado

confiscat|e /ˈkɒnfɪskeɪt/ *vt* confiscar. **~ion** /-ˈkeɪʃn/ *n* confiscação *f*

conflict[1] /ˈkɒnflɪkt/ *n* conflito *m*

conflict[2] /kənˈflɪkt/ *vi* estar em contradição. **~ing** *a* contraditório

conform /kənˈfɔːm/ *vt/i* conformar(-se)

confront /kənˈfrʌnt/ *vt* confrontar, defrontar, enfrentar; **~ with** confrontar-se com. **~ation** /kɒnfrʌnˈteɪʃn/ *n* confrontação *f*

confus|e /kənˈfjuːz/ *vt* confundir. **~ed** *a* confuso. **~ing** *a* que faz confusão. **~ion** /-ʒn/ *n* confusão *f*

congeal /kənˈdʒiːl/ *vt/i* congelar, solidificar

congenial /kənˈdʒiːnɪəl/ *a* (*agreeable*) simpático

C

congest|ed /kən'dʒestɪd/ *a* congestionado. **~ion** /-tʃn/ *n* (*traffic*) congestionamento *m*; *Med* congestão *f*

congratulat|e /kən'grætjʊleɪt/ *vt* felicitar; dar os parabéns (**on** por). **~ions** /-'leɪʃnz/ *npl* felicitações *fpl*, parabéns *mpl*

congregat|e /'kɒŋgrɪgeɪt/ *vi* reunir-se. **~ion** /-'geɪʃn/ *n* (*in church*) congregação *f*, fiéis *mpl*

congress /'kɒŋgres/ *n* congresso *m*; **C~** *Amer* Congresso *m*

> **Congress** O Congresso é o órgão legislativo dos Estados Unidos. Reúne-se no Capitólio (*Capitol*) e é composto por duas câmaras: o Senado e a Câmara de Representantes. O Congresso é renovado de dois em dois anos, e a sua função é elaborar leis que devem ser aprovadas, primeiro pelas duas câmaras e posteriormente pelo Presidente.

conjecture /kən'dʒektʃə(r)/ *n* conjectura *f*, (*P*) conjetura *f* ● *vt/i* conjecturar, (*P*) conjeturar

conjugat|e /'kɒndʒʊgeɪt/ *vt* conjugar. **~ion** /-'geɪʃn/ *n* conjugação *f*

conjunction /kən'dʒʌŋkʃn/ *n* conjunção *f*

conjur|e /'kʌndʒə(r)/ *vi* fazer truques mágicos ● *vt* **~e up** fazer aparecer. **~or** *n* mágico *m*, prestidigitador *m*

connect /kə'nekt/ *vt/i* ligar(-se); (*of train*) fazer ligação. **~ed** *a* ligado; **be ~ed with** estar relacionado com

connection /kə'nekʃn/ *n* relação *f*; *Rail* (*phone call*) ligação *f*; *Electr* contacto *m*

connectivity /kɒnek'tɪvəti/ *n* conectividade *f*

connoisseur /kɒnə'sɜː(r)/ *n* conhecedor *m*, apreciador *m*

conquer /'kɒŋkə(r)/ *vt* vencer; ‹*country*› conquistar. **~or** *n* conquistador *m*

conquest /'kɒŋkwest/ *n* conquista *f*

conscience /'kɒnʃəns/ *n* consciência *f*

conscientious /kɒnʃɪ'enʃəs/ *a* consciencioso

conscious /'kɒnʃəs/ *a* consciente. **~ness** *n* consciência *f*

conscript[1] /kən'skrɪpt/ *vt* recrutar. **~ion** /-ʃn/ *n* serviço *m* militar obrigatório

conscript[2] /'kɒnskrɪpt/ *n* recruta *m*

consecrate /'kɒnsɪkreɪt/ *vt* consagrar

consecutive /kən'sekjʊtɪv/ *a* consecutivo, seguido

consensus /kən'sensəs/ *n* consenso *m*

consent /kən'sent/ *vi* consentir (**to** em) ● *n* consentimento *m*

consequence /'kɒnsɪkwəns/ *n* consequência *f*

consequent /'kɒnsɪkwənt/ *a* resultante (**on, upon** de). **~ly** *adv* por consequência, por conseguinte

conservation /kɒnsə'veɪʃn/ *n* conservação *f*

conservative /kən'sɜːvətɪv/ *a* conservador; (*estimate*) moderado. ● **C~** *a & n* conservador *m*

conservatory /kən'sɜːvətrɪ/ *n* (*greenhouse*) estufa *f*; (*house extension*) jardim *m* de inverno

conserve /kən'sɜːv/ *vt* conservar

consider /kən'sɪdə(r)/ *vt* considerar; (*allow for*) levar em consideração. **~ation** /-'reɪʃn/ *n* consideração *f*. **~ing** *prep* em vista de, tendo em conta

considerabl|e /kən'sɪdərəbl/ *a* considerável; (*much*) muito

considerate /kən'sɪdərət/ *a* atencioso, delicado

consign /kən'saɪn/ *vt* consignar. **~ment** *n* consignação *f*

consist /kən'sɪst/ *vi* consistir (**of**, em)

consisten|t /kən'sɪstənt/ *a* (*unchanging*) constante; (*not contradictory*) coerente; **~t with** conforme com. **~cy** *n* consistência *f*; *fig* coerência *f*. **~tly** *adv* regularmente

consol|e /kən'səʊl/ *vt* consolar. **~ation** /kɒnsə'leɪʃn/ *n* consolação *f*; **~ation prize** prêmio *m* or (*P*) prémio *m* de consolação

consolidat|e /kən'sɒlɪdeɪt/ *vt/i* consolidar(-se). **~ion** /-'deɪʃn/ *n* consolidação *f*

consonant /'kɒnsənənt/ *n* consoante *f*

conspicuous /kən'spɪkjʊəs/ *a* conspícuo, visível; (*striking*) notável; **make o.s. ~** fazer-se notar, chamar a atenção

conspira|cy /kən'spɪrəsɪ/ *n* conspiração *f*. **~cy theory** *n* teoria *f* da conspiração

conspire /kən'spaɪə(r)/ *vi* conspirar

constable /'kʌnstəbl/ *n* polícia *m*

constant /'kɒnstənt/ *a* constante. **~ly** *adv* constantemente

constellation /kɒnstə'leɪʃn/ *n* constelação *f*

constipation /kɒnstɪ'peɪʃn/ *n* prisão *f* de ventre

constituency /kən'stɪtjʊənsɪ/ *n* (*pl* **-cies**) círculo *m* eleitoral

constituent /kən'stɪtjʊənt/ *a & n* constituinte *m*

constitut|e /'kɒnstɪtju:t/ *vt* constituir. **~ion** /-'tju:ʃn/ *n* constituição *f*. **~ional** /-'tju:ʃənl/ *a* constitucional

constrain /kən'streɪn/ *vt* constranger

constraint /kən'streɪnt/ *n* constrangimento *m*

constrict /kən'strɪkt/ *vt* constringir, apertar

construct /kən'strʌkt/ *vt* construir. **~ion** /-ʃn/ *n* construção *f*; **under ~ion** em construção

constructive /kən'strʌktɪv/ *a* construtivo

consul /'kɒnsl/ *n* cônsul *m*

consulate /'kɒnsjʊlət/ *n* consulado *m*

consult /kən'sʌlt/ *vt* consultar. **~ation** /kɒnsl'teɪʃn/ *n* consulta *f*

consultant /kən'sʌltənt/ *n* consultor *m*; *Med* especialista *mf*

consume /kən'sju:m/ *vt* consumir. **~r** /-ə(r)/ *n* consumidor *m*

consumption /kən'sʌmpʃn/ *n* consumo *m*

contact /'kɒntækt/ *n* contato *m*, (*P*) contacto *m*; ‹*person*› relação *f*; **~ lenses** lentes *fpl* de contato *or* (*P*) contacto ● *vt* contactar

contagious /kən'teɪdʒəs/ *a* contagioso

contain /kən'teɪn/ *vt* conter; **~ o.s.** conter-se. **~er** *n* recipiente *m*; (*for transport*) contentor *m*

contaminat|e /kən'tæmɪneɪt/ *vt* contaminar. **~ion** /-'neɪʃn/ *n* contaminação *f*

contemplat|e /'kɒntempleɪt/ *vt* contemplar; (*intend*) ter em vista; (*consider*) esperar, pensar em. **~ion** /-'pleɪʃn/ *n* contemplação *f*

contemporary /kən'temprərɪ/ *a & n* contemporâneo *m*

contempt /kən'tempt/ *n* desprezo *m*. **~ible** *a* desprezível. **~uous** /-tʃʊəs/ *a* desdenhoso

contend /kən'tend/ *vt* afirmar, sustentar ● *vi* **~ with** lutar contra. **~er** *n* adversário *m*, contendor *m*

content[1] /kən'tent/ *a* satisfeito, contente ● *vt* contentar. **~ed** *a* satisfeito, contente. **~ment** *n* contentamento *m*, satisfação *f*

content[2] /'kɒntent/ *n* conteúdo *m*; **(table of) ~s** índice *m*

contention /kən'tenʃn/ *n* disputa *f*, contenda *f*; (*assertion*) argumento *m*

contest[1] /'kɒntest/ *n* competição *f*; (*struggle*) luta *f*

contest[2] /kən'test/ *vt* contestar; (*compete for*) disputar. **~ant** *n* concorrente *mf*

context /'kɒntekst/ *n* contexto *m*

continent /'kɒntɪnənt/ *n* continente *m*; **the C~** a Europa (continental) *f*. **~al** /-'nentl/ *a* continental; (*of mainland Europe*) europeu; **~al breakfast** café *m* da manhã europeu, (*P*) pequeno-almoço *m* europeu; **~al quilt** edredom *m*, (*P*) edredão *m*

contingen|t /kən'tɪndʒənt/ *a & n* contingente *m*. **~cy** *n* contingência *f*; **~cy plan** plano *m* de emergência

continual /kən'tɪnjʊəl/ *a* contínuo. **~ly** *adv* continuamente

continu|e /kən'tɪnju:/ *vt/i* continuar. **~ation** /-tɪnjʊ'eɪʃn/ *n* continuação *f*

continuity /kɒntɪ'nju:ətɪ/ *n* continuidade *f*

continuous /kən'tɪnjʊəs/ *a* contínuo. **~ly** *adv* continuamente

contort /kən'tɔ:t/ *vt* contorcer; *fig* distorcer. **~ion** /-ʃn/ *n* contorção *f*

contour /'kɒntʊə(r)/ *n* contorno *m*

contraband /'kɒntrəbænd/ *n* contrabando *m*

contraception /kɒntrə'sepʃn/ *n* contracepção *f*

contraceptive /kɒntrə'septɪv/ *a & n* contraceptivo *m*

contract[1] /'kɒntrækt/ *n* contrato *m*

contract[2] /kən'trækt/ *vt/i* contrair(-se); (*make a contract*) contratar. **~ion** /-ʃn/ *n* contração *f*

contractor /kən'træktə(r)/ *n* empreiteiro *m*; (*firm*) firma *f* empreiteira de serviços, (*P*) recrutadora *f* de mão-de-obra temporária

contradict /kɒntrə'dɪkt/ *vt* contradizer. **~ion** /-ʃn/ *n* contradição *f*. **~ory** *a* contraditório

contrary[1] /'kɒntrərɪ/ *a & n* (*opposite*) contrário *m* ● *adv* **~ to** contrariamente a; **on the ~** ao *or* pelo contrário

contrary[2] /kən'treərɪ/ *a* (*perverse*) do contra, embirrento

contrast[1] /'kɒntrɑ:st/ *n* contraste *m*

contrast[2] /kən'trɑ:st/ *vt/i* contrastar. **~ing** *a* contrastante

C

C

contraven|e /kɒntrə'vi:n/ *vt* infringir. **~tion** /'-venʃn/ *n* contravenção *f*

contribut|e /kən'trɪbju:t/ *vt/i* contribuir (**to** para); (*to newspaper etc*) colaborar (**to** em). **~ion** /kɒntrɪ'bju:ʃn/ *n* contribuição *f*. **~or** /-'trɪbju:tə(r)/ *n* contribuinte *mf*; (*to newspaper*) colaborador *m*

contrivance /kən'traɪvəns/ *n* (*invention*) engenho *m*; (*device*) engenhoca *f*; (*trick*) maquinação *f*

control /kən'trəʊl/ *vt* (*pt* **controlled**) (*check, restrain*) controlar; ‹*firm etc*› dirigir ● *n* controle *m*; (*management*) direção *f*; **~s** (*of car, plane*) comandos *mpl*; (*knobs*) botões *mpl*; **be in ~ of** dirigir; **under ~** sob controle

controversial /kɒntrə'vɜ:ʃl/ *a* controverso, discutível

controversy /'kɒntrəvɜ:sɪ/ *n* controvérsia *f*

convalesce /kɒnvə'les/ *vi* convalescer. **~nce** *n* convalescença *f*

convene /kən'vi:n/ *vt* convocar ● *vi* reunir-se

convenience /kən'vi:nɪəns/ *n* conveniência *f*; **~s** (*appliances*) comodidades *fpl*; (*lavatory*) privada *f*, (*P*) casa *f* de banho; **at your ~** quando (e como) lhe convier; **~ foods** alimentos *mpl* semiprontos

convenient /kən'vi:nɪənt/ *a* conveniente; **be ~ for** convir a. **~ly** *adv* sem inconveniente; (*situated*) bem; (*arrive*) a propósito

convent /'kɒnvənt/ *n* convento *m*; **~ school** colégio *m* de freiras

convention /kən'venʃn/ *n* convenção *f*; (*custom*) uso *m*, costume *m*. **~al** *a* convencional

converge /kən'vɜ:dʒ/ *vi* convergir

conversation /kɒnvə'seɪʃn/ *n* conversa *f*. **~al** *a* de conversa, coloquial

converse[1] /kən'vɜ:s/ *vi* conversar

converse[2] /'kɒnvɜ:s/ *a & n* inverso *m*. **~ly** /kən'vɜ:slɪ/ *adv* ao invés, inversamente

conver|t[1] /kən'vɜ:t/ *vt* converter; (*house*) transformar. **~sion** /-ʃn/ *n* conversão *f*; ‹*house*› transformação *f*. **~tible** *a* convertível, conversível ● *n Auto* conversível *m*

convert[2] /'kɒnvɜ:t/ *n* convertido *m*, converso *m*

convex /'kɒnveks/ *a* convexo

convey /kən'veɪ/ *vt* transmitir; ‹*goods*› transportar; ‹*idea, feeling*› comunicar; **~or belt** tapete *m* rolante, correia *f* transportadora

convict[1] /kən'vɪkt/ *vt* declarar culpado. **~ion** /-ʃn/ *n* condenação *f*; (*opinion*) convicção *f*

convict[2] /'kɒnvɪkt/ *n* condenado *m*

convinc|e /kən'vɪns/ *vt* convencer. **~ing** *a* convincente

convoy /'kɒnvɔɪ/ *n* escolta *f*

convuls|e /kən'vʌls/ *vt* convulsionar; *fig* abalar; **be ~ed with laughter** torcer-se de riso

coo /ku:/ *vi* (*pt* **cooed**) arrulhar ● *n* arrulho *m*

cook /kʊk/ *vt/i* cozinhar; **~ up** [!] cozinhar *fig*, fabricar ● *n* cozinheira *f*, cozinheiro *m*

cooker /'kʊkə(r)/ *n* fogão *m*

cookery /'kʊkərɪ/ *n* cozinha *f*; **~ book** livro *m* de culinária

cookie /'kʊkɪ/ *n Amer* biscoito *m*

cool /ku:l/ *a* (**-er**, **-est**) fresco; (*calm*) calmo; (*unfriendly*) frio ● *n* frescura *f*; ⊠ (*composure*) sangue-frio *m* ● *vt/i* arrefecer. **~ box** *n* geladeira *f* portátil. **in the ~** no fresco. **~ly** /'ku:llɪ/ *adv* calmamente; *fig* friamente. **~ness** *n* frescura *f*; *fig* frieza *f*

coop /ku:p/ *n* galinheiro *m* ● *vt* **~ up** engaiolar, fechar

co-operat|e /kəʊ'ɒpəreɪt/ *vi* cooperar. **~ion** /-'reɪʃn/ *n* cooperação *f*

cooperative /kəʊ'ɒpərətɪv/ *a* cooperativo ● *n* cooperativa *f*

coordinat|e /kəʊ'ɔ:dɪneɪt/ *vt* coordenar. **~ion** /-'neɪʃn/ *n* coordenação *f*

cop /kɒp/ *n* ⊠ porco *m* ⊠, (*P*) chui *m* ⊠

cope /kəʊp/ *vi* aguentar-se, arranjar-se; **~ with** poder com, dar conta de

copious /'kəʊpɪəs/ *a* copioso

copper[1] /'kɒpə(r)/ *n* cobre *m* ● *a* de cobre

copper[2] /'kɒpə(r)/ *n* ⊠ porco *m* ⊠, (*P*) chui *m* ⊠

coppice /'kɒpɪs/, **copse** /kɒps/ *ns* mata *f* de corte

copulat|e /'kɒpjʊleɪt/ *vi* copular

copy /'kɒpɪ/ *n* cópia *f*; (*of book*) exemplar *m*; (*of newspaper*) número *m* ● *vt/i* copiar

copyright /'kɒpɪraɪt/ *n* direitos *mpl* autorais, (*P*) direitos *npl* de autor

coral /'kɒrəl/ *n* coral *m*

cord /kɔ:d/ *n* cordão *m*; *Electr* fio *m*

cordial /ˈkɔːdɪəl/ *a & n* cordial *m*
cordon /ˈkɔːdn/ *n* cordão *m* ● *vt* **~ off** fechar (com um cordão de isolamento)
corduroy /ˈkɔːdərɔɪ/ *n* veludo *m* cotelé
core /kɔː(r)/ *n* âmago *m*; (*of apple, pear*) coração *m*
cork /kɔːk/ *n* cortiça *f*; (*for bottle*) rolha *f* ● *vt* rolhar
corkscrew /ˈkɔːkskruː/ *n* saca-rolhas *m*
corn[1] /kɔːn/ *n* trigo *m*; *Amer* (*maize*) milho *m*; (*seed*) grão *m*; **~ on the cob** espiga *f* de milho, cozinhada inteira
corn[2] /kɔːn/ *n* (*hard skin*) calo *m*
corner /ˈkɔːnə(r)/ *n* canto *m*; (*of street*) esquina *f*; (*bend in road*) curva *f* ● *vt* encurralar; (*market*) monopolizar ● *vi* dar uma curva, virar
cornet /ˈkɔːnɪt/ *n Mus* cornetim *m*; (*for ice cream*) casquinha *f*, (*P*) cone *m*
cornflakes /ˈkɔːnfleɪks/ *npl* cornflakes *mpl*, cereais *mpl*
cornflour /ˈkɔːnflaʊə(r)/ *n* fécula *f* de milho, maisena *f*
corny /ˈkɔːnɪ/ *a* [!] batido, (*P*) estafado
coronation /kɒrəˈneɪʃn/ *n* coroação *f*
coroner /ˈkɒrənə(r)/ *n* magistrado *m* que investiga os casos de morte suspeita
corporal[1] /ˈkɔːpərəl/ *n Mil* cabo *m*
corporal[2] /ˈkɔːpərəl/ *a* **~ punishment** castigo *m* corporal
corporate /ˈkɔːpərət/ *a* coletivo; (*body*) corporativo
corporation /kɔːpəˈreɪʃn/ *n* corporação *f*; (*of town*) municipalidade *f*
corps /kɔː(r)/ *n* (*pl* **corps** /kɔːz/) corpo *m*
corpse /kɔːps/ *n* cadáver *m*
correct /kəˈrekt/ *a* correto; **the ~ time** a hora certa; **you are ~** você tem razão ● *vt* corrigir. **~ion** /-ʃn/ *n* correção *f*, emenda *f*
correlat|e /ˈkɒrəleɪt/ *vt/i* correlacionar(-se). **~ion** /-ˈleɪʃn/ *n* correlação *f*
correspond /kɒrɪˈspɒnd/ *vi* corresponder (**to, with** a). **~ence** *n* correspondência *f*. **~ent** *n* correspondente *mf*. **~ing** *a* correspondente
corridor /ˈkɒrɪdɔː(r)/ *n* corredor *m*
corro|de /kəˈrəʊd/ *vt/i* corroer(-se). **~sion** *n* corrosão *f*
corrugated /ˈkɒrəgeɪtɪd/ *a* corrugado; **~ cardboard** cartão *m* canelado; **~ iron** chapa *f* ondulada
corrupt /kəˈrʌpt/ *a* corrupto ● *vt* corromper. **~ion** /-ʃn/ *n* corrupção *f*
corset /ˈkɔːsɪt/ *n* espartilho *m*; (*elasticated*) cinta *f* elástica
Corsica /ˈkɔːsɪkə/ *n* Córsega *f*
cosmetic /kɒzˈmetɪk/ *n* cosmético *m* ● *a* cosmético; *fig* superficial
cosmonaut /ˈkɒzmənɔːt/ *n* cosmonauta *mf*
cosmopolitan /kɒzməˈpɒlɪtən/ *a & n* cosmopolita *mf*
cosset /ˈkɒsɪt/ *vt* (*pt* **cosseted**) proteger
cost /kɒst/ *vt* (*pt* **cost**) custar; (*pt* **costed**) fixar o preço de ● *n* custo *m*; **~s** *Jur* custos *mpl*; **at all ~s** custe o que custar; **to one's ~** à sua custa; **~ of living** custo *m* de vida
costly /ˈkɒstlɪ/ *a* (**-ier**, **-iest**) caro ● *a* caro; (*valuable*) precioso
costume /ˈkɒstjuːm/ *n* traje *m*
cos|y /ˈkəʊzɪ/ *a* (**-ier**, **-iest**) confortável, íntimo ● *n* abafador *m* (do bule do chá)
cot /kɒt/ *n* cama *f* de bêbê, (*P*) de bebé, berço *m*
cottage /ˈkɒtɪdʒ/ *n* pequena casa *f* de campo; **~ cheese** requeijão *m*, ricota *f*; **~ industry** artesanato *m*; **~ pie** empada *f* de carne picada
cotton /ˈkɒtn/ *n* algodão *m*; (*thread*) fio *m*, linha *f*; **~ wool** algodão *m* hidrófilo
couch /kaʊtʃ/ *n* divã *m*
couchette /kuːˈʃet/ *n* couchette *f*
cough /kɒf/ *vi* tossir ● *n* tosse *f*
could /kʊd, kəd/ *pt of* ▶ CAN[2]
council /ˈkaʊnsl/ *n* conselho *m*; **~ house** casa *f* de bairro popular
councillor /ˈkaʊnsələ(r)/ *n* vereador *m*
counsel /ˈka.ʊnsl/ *n* conselho *m*; (*pl invar*) *Jur* advogado *m*. **~lor** *n* conselheiro *m*
count[1] /kaʊnt/ *vt/i* contar; **~ on** contar com ● *n* conta *f*. **~down** *n* (*rocket*) contagem *f* regressiva *or* (*P*) decrescente
count[2] /kaʊnt/ *n* (*nobleman*) conde *m*
counter[1] /ˈkaʊntə(r)/ *n* (*in shop*) balcão *m*; (*in game*) ficha *f*, (*P*) tento *m*
counter[2] /ˈkaʊntə(r)/ *adv* **~ to** contrário a; **~ to** (*in the opposite direction*) em sentido contrário a ● *a* oposto ● *vt* opor; ‹*blow*› aparar ● *vi* ripostar
counter- /ˈkaʊntə(r)/ *pref* contra-
counteract /kaʊntərˈækt/ *vt* neutralizar, frustrar

C

counter-attack /ˈkaʊntərətæk/ *n* contra-ataque *m* ● *vt/i* contra-atacar

counterbalance /ˈkaʊntəbæləns/ *n* contrapeso *m* ● *vt* contrabalançar

counterfeit /ˈkaʊntəfɪt/ *a* falsificado, falso ● *n* falsificação *f* ● *vt* falsificar

counterfoil /ˈkaʊntəfɔɪl/ *n* talão *m*, canhoto *m*

counterpart /ˈkaʊntəpɑːt/ *n* equivalente *m*; (*person*) homólogo *m*

counterproductive /ˈkaʊntəprədʌktɪv/ *a* contraproducente

countersign /ˈkaʊntəsaɪn/ *vt* subscrever documento já assinado; ‹*cheque*› contrassinar

countess /ˈkaʊntɪs/ *n* condessa *f*

countless /ˈkaʊntlɪs/ *a* sem conta, incontável, inúmero

country /ˈkʌntrɪ/ *n* país *m*; (*homeland*) pátria *f*; (*countryside*) campo *m*

countryside /ˈkʌntrɪsaɪd/ *n* campo *m*

county /ˈkaʊntɪ/ *n* condado *m*

coup /kuː/ *n* **~ (d'état)** golpe *m* (de estado)

couple /ˈkʌpl/ *n* par *m*, casal *m*; **a ~ of** um par de ● *vt/i* unir(-se), ligar(-se); *Techn* acoplar

coupon /ˈkuːpɒn/ *n* cupão *m*

courage /ˈkʌrɪdʒ/ *n* coragem *f*. **~ous** /kəˈreɪdʒəs/ *a* corajoso

courgette /kʊəˈʒet/ *n* abobrinha *f*

courier /ˈkʊrɪə(r)/ *n* correio *m*; (*for tourists*) guia *mf*; (*for parcels, mail*) estafeta *m*

course /kɔːs/ *n* curso *m*; (*series*) série *f*; *Culin* prato *m*; (*for golf*) campo *m*; *fig* caminho *m*; **in due ~** na altura devida, oportunamente; **in the ~ of** durante; **of ~** está claro, com certeza

court /kɔːt/ *n* (*of monarch*) corte *f*; (*courtyard*) pátio *m*; *Tennis* court *m*; quadra *f*, (*P*) campo *m*; *Jur* tribunal *m* ● *vt* cortejar; (*danger*) provocar; **~ martial** (*pl* **courts martial**) conselho *m* de guerra

courteous /ˈkɜːtɪəs/ *a* cortês, delicado

courtesy /ˈkɜːtəsɪ/ *n* cortesia *f*

courtyard /ˈkɔːtjɑːd/ *n* pátio *m*

cousin /ˈkʌzn/ *n* primo *m*; **first/second ~** primo *m* em primeiro/segundo grau

cove /kəʊv/ *n* angra *f*, enseada *f*

cover /ˈkʌvə(r)/ *vt/i* cobrir; **~ up** tapar; *fig* encobrir ● *n* cobertura *f*; (*for bed*) colcha *f*; (*for book, furniture*) capa *f*; (*lid*) tampa *f*; (*shelter*) abrigo *m*; **~ charge** serviço *m*; **take ~** abrigar-se; **under separate ~** em separado. **~ing** *n* cobertura *f*; **~ing letter** carta (que acompanha um documento) *f*. **~-up** *n fig* encobrimento *m*

coverage /ˈkʌvərɪdʒ/ *n* (*of events*) reportagem *f*, cobertura *f*

covet /ˈkʌvɪt/ *vt* cobiçar

cow /kaʊ/ *n* vaca *f*

coward /ˈkaʊəd/ *n* covarde *mf*. **~ly** *a* covarde

cowardice /ˈkaʊədɪs/ *n* covardia *f*

cowboy /ˈkaʊbɔɪ/ *n* cowboy *m*, vaqueiro *m*

cower /ˈkaʊə(r)/ *vi* encolher-se (de medo)

cowshed /ˈkaʊʃed/ *n* estábulo *m*

coy /kɔɪ/ *a* (**-er**, **-est**) (falsamente) tímido

crab /kræb/ *n* caranguejo *m*

crack /kræk/ *n* fenda *f*; (*in glass*) rachadura *f*; (*noise*) estalo *m*; ☒ (*joke*) piada *f*; (*drug*) crack *m* ● *a* [!] de elite ● *vt/i* estalar; ‹*nut*› quebrar, (*P*) partir; ‹*joke*› contar; ‹*problem*› resolver; ‹*voice*› mudar; **~ down on** [!] cair em cima de, arrochar; **get ~ing** [!] pôr mãos à obra

cracker /ˈkrækə(r)/ *n* busca-pé *m*, bomba *f* de estalo; *Culin* bolacha *f* de água e sal

crackers /ˈkrækəz/ *a* ☒ desmiolado; maluco [!]

crackle /ˈkrækl/ *vi* crepitar ● *n* crepitação *f*

cradle /ˈkreɪdl/ *n* berço *m* ● *vt* embalar

craft[1] /krɑːft/ *n* ofício *m*; (*technique*) arte *f*; (*cunning*) manha *f*, astúcia *f*

craft[2] /krɑːft/ *n* (*invar*) (*boat*) embarcação *f*

craftsman /ˈkrɑːftsmən/ *n* (*pl* **-men**) artífice *mf*. **~ship** *n* arte *f*

crafty /ˈkrɑːftɪ/ *a* (**-ier**, **-iest**) manhoso, astucioso

crag /kræg/ *n* penhasco *m*. **~gy** *a* escarpado, íngreme

cram /kræm/ *vt* (*pt* **crammed**) **~ (for an exam)** decorar, (*P*) empinar; **~ into/with** entulhar com

cramp /kræmp/ *n* cãibra *f* ● *vt* restringir, tolher. **~ed** *a* apertado

crane /kreɪn/ *n* grua *f*; (*bird*) grou *m* ● *vt* ‹*neck*› esticar

crank[1] /kræŋk/ *n Techn* manivela *f*. **~shaft** *n Techn* cambota *f*

crank[2] /kræŋk/ *n* excêntrico *m*. **~y** *a* excêntrico

crash /kræʃ/ *n* acidente *m*; (*noise*) estrondo *m*; *Comm* falência *f*; (*financial*) colapso *m*, crash *m* ● *vt/i* (*fall/strike*) cair/ bater com estrondo; ‹*two cars*› chocar, bater; *Comm* abrir falência; ‹*plane*› cair; ~ **out** [!] (*go to sleep*) apagar, (*P*) apagar-se; (*be out of competition, race*) ser eliminado, (*P*) cair de sono ● *a* ‹*course, programme*› intensivo. ~ **helmet** *n* capacete *m*; ~**-land** *vi* fazer uma aterrissagem forçada, (*P*) uma aterragem forçada

crate /kreɪt/ *n* engradado *m*

crater /ˈkreɪtə(r)/ *n* cratera *f*

crav|e /kreɪv/ *vt/i* ~**e (for)** ansiar por. ~**ing** *n* desejo *m* irresistível, ânsia *f*

crawl /krɔːl/ *vi* rastejar; (*of baby*) engatinhar, (*P*) andar de gatas; (*of car*) mover-se lentamente ● *n* rastejo *m*; (*swimming*) crawl *m*; **be ~ing with** fervilhar de, estar cheio de

crayfish /ˈkreɪfɪʃ/ *n* (*pl invar*) lagostim *m*

crayon /ˈkreɪən/ *n* crayon *m*, lápis *m* de pastel

craze /kreɪz/ *n* moda *f*, febre *f*

craz|y /ˈkreɪzɪ/ *a* (**-ier**, **-iest**) doido; louco (**about** por). ~**iness** *n* loucura *f*

creak /kriːk/ *n* rangido *m* ● *vi* ranger

cream /kriːm/ *n* (*milk fat; also fig*) nata *f*; (*cosmetic*) *Culin* creme *m* ● *a* creme *invar* ● *vt* desnatar; ~ **cheese** queijo-creme *m*. ~**y** *a* cremoso

crease /kriːs/ *n* vinco *m* ● *vt/i* amarrotar(-se)

creat|e /kriːˈeɪt/ *vt* criar. ~**ion** /-ʃn/ *n* criação *f*. ~**ive** *a* criador, criativo. ~**or** *n* criador *m*

creature /ˈkriːtʃə(r)/ *n* criatura *f*

crèche /kreɪʃ/ *n* creche *f*

credentials /krɪˈdenʃlz/ *npl* credenciais *fpl*; (*of competence etc*) referências *fpl*

credib|le /ˈkredəbl/ *a* crível, verossímil. ~**ility** /-ˈbɪlətɪ/ *n* credibilidade *f*

credit /ˈkredɪt/ *n* crédito *m*; (*honour*) honra *f*; ~**s** (*cinema*) créditos *mpl*; ~ **card** cartão *m* de crédito ● *vt* (*pt* **credited**) acreditar em; *Comm* creditar; ~ **sb with** atribuir a alguém. ~**or** *n* credor *m*

creditable /ˈkredɪtəbl/ *a* louvável, honroso

creed /kriːd/ *n* credo *m*

creek /kriːk/ *n* enseada *f* estreita; **be up the** ~ ⊠ estar frito ⊠

creep /kriːp/ *vi* (*pt* **crept**) rastejar; (*move stealthily*) mover-se furtivamente ● *n* ⊠ cara *m* nojento, (*P*) tipo *m* nojento; **give sb the ~s** dar arrepios a alguém. ~**er** *n* (planta *f*) trepadeira *f*. ~**y** *a* arrepiante

cremat|e /krɪˈmeɪt/ *vt* cremar. ~**ion** /-ʃn/ *n* cremação *f*

crematorium /krəməˈtɔːrɪəm/ *n* (*pl* **-ia**) crematório *m*

crêpe /kreɪp/ *n* crepe *m*; ~ **paper** papel *m* crepom, (*P*) plissado

crept /krept/ ▶ CREEP

crescent /ˈkresnt/ *n* crescente *m*; (*street*) rua *f* em semicírculo

cress /kres/ *n* agrião *m*

crest /krest/ *n* (*of bird, hill*) crista *f*; (*on coat of arms*) timbre *m*

crevasse /krɪˈvæs/ *n* fenda(em geleira) *f*

crevice /ˈkrevɪs/ *n* racha *f*, fenda *f*

crew[1] /kruː/ ▶ CROW

crew[2] /kruː/ *n* tripulação *f*; (*gang*) bando *m*. ~ **cut** *n* corte *m* à escovinha; ~ **neck** *n* gola *f* redonda e um pouco subida, meia gola

crib[1] /krɪb/ *n* berço *m*; (*Christmas*) presépio *m*

crib[2] /krɪb/ *vt/i* (*pt* **cribbed**) [!] colar, (*P*) ⊠ cabular ⊠ ● *n* cópia *f*, plágio *m*; (*translation*) burro *m* ⊠

cricket[1] /ˈkrɪkɪt/ *n* críquete *m*. ~**er** *n* jogador *m* de críquete

cricket[2] /ˈkrɪkɪt/ *n* (*insect*) grilo *m*

crime /kraɪm/ *n* crime *m*; (*minor*) delito *m*; (*collectively*) criminalidade *f*

criminal /ˈkrɪmɪnl/ *a* & *n* criminoso *m*

crimson /ˈkrɪmzn/ *a* & *n* carmesim *m*

cring|e /krɪndʒ/ *vi* encolher-se

crinkle /ˈkrɪŋkl/ *vt/i* enrugar(-se) ● *n* vinco *m*, ruga *f*

cripple /ˈkrɪpl/ *n* aleijado *m*, coxo *m* ● *vt* estropiar; *fig* paralisar

crisis /ˈkraɪsɪs/ *n* (*pl* **crises** /-siːz/) crise *f*

crisp /krɪsp/ *a* (**-er**, **est**) *Culin* crocante; ‹*air*› fresco; ‹*manners, reply*› decidido. ~**s** *npl* batatas *fpl* fritas redondas

criterion /kraɪˈtɪərɪən/ *n* (*pl* **-ia**) critério *m*

critic /ˈkrɪtɪk/ *n* crítico *m*. ~**al** *a* crítico. ~**ally** *adv* de forma crítica; (*ill*) gravemente

criticism /ˈkrɪtɪsɪzəm/ *n* crítica *f*

criticize /ˈkrɪtɪsaɪz/ *vt/i* criticar

croak /krəʊk/ *n* (*frog*) coaxar *m*; (*raven*) crocitar *m*, crocito *m* ● *vi* (*frog*) coaxar; (*raven*) crocitar

crochet /ˈkrəʊʃeɪ/ *n* crochê *m* ● *vt* fazer em crochê

crockery /'krɒkərɪ/ *n* louça *f*

crocodile /'krɒkədaɪl/ *n* crocodilo *m*

crocus /'krəʊkəs/ *n* (*pl* **-uses** /-sɪz/) croco *m*

crony /'krəʊnɪ/ *n* camarada *mf*, amigão *m*, parceiro *m*

crook /krʊk/ *n* [!] (*criminal*) vigarista *mf*; (*stick*) cajado *m*

crooked /'krʊkɪd/ *a* torcido; (*winding*) tortuoso; (*askew*) torto; [!] (*dishonest*) desonesto

crop /krɒp/ *n* colheita *f*; *fig* quantidade *f*; (*haircut*) corte *m* rente ● *vt* (*pt* **cropped**) cortar ● *vi* **~ up** aparecer, surgir

croquet /'krəʊkeɪ/ *n* croquet *m*, croqué *m*

cross /krɒs/ *n* cruz *f* ● *vt/i* cruzar; ‹*cheque*› cruzar, (*P*) barrar; (*oppose*) contrariar; (*of paths*) cruzar-se ● *a* zangado; **~ off** or **out** riscar; **~ o.s.** benzer-se; **~ sb's mind** passar pela cabeça or pelo espírito de alguém, ocorrer a alguém; **talk at ~ purposes** falar sem se entender. **~-country** *a & adv* a corta-mato; **~-examine** *vt* fazer o contrainterrogatório (de testemunhas); **~-eyed** *a* vesgo, estrábico; **~-fire** *n* fogo *m* cruzado; **~-section** *n* corte *m* transversal; *fig* grupo or sector *m* representativo *m*

crossbar /'krɒsbɑ:(r)/ *n* barra *f* transversal *f*; (*of bicycle*) travessão *m*

crossing /'krɒsɪŋ/ *n* cruzamento *m*; (*by boat*) travessia *f*; (*on road*) passagem *f*

crossroads /'krɒsrəʊdz/ *n* encruzilhada *f*, cruzamento *m*

crossword /'krɒswɜ:d/ *n* palavras *fpl* cruzadas

crotch /krɒtʃ/ *n* entrepernas *fpl*

crouch /kraʊtʃ/ *vi* agachar-se

crow /krəʊ/ *n* corvo *m*; **as the ~ flies** em linha reta ● *vi* (*cock*) cantar; cantar; *fig* rejubilar-se (**over** com)

crowbar /'krəʊbɑ:(r)/ *n* alavanca *f*, pé-de-cabra *m*

crowd /kraʊd/ *n* multidão *f* ● *vi* afluir ● *vt* encher; **~ into** apinhar-se em. **~ed** *a* cheio, apinhado

crown /kraʊn/ *n* coroa *f*; (*of hill*) topo *m*, cume *m* ● *vt* coroar; ‹*tooth*› pôr uma coroa em

crucial /'kru:ʃl/ *a* crucial

crucifix /'kru:sɪfɪks/ *n* crucifixo *m*

crucif|y /'kru:sɪfaɪ/ *vt* crucificar. **~ixion** /-'fɪkʃn/ *n* crucificação *f*

crude /kru:d/ *a* (**-er**, **-est**) (*raw*) bruto; (*rough, vulgar*) grosseiro; **~ oil** petróleo *m* bruto

cruel /krʊəl/ *a* (**crueller**, **cruellest**) cruel. **~ty** *n* crueldade *f*

cruis|e /kru:z/ *n* cruzeiro *m* ● *vi* cruzar; (*of tourists*) fazer um cruzeiro; (*of car*) ir a velocidade de cruzeiro; **~ing speed** velocidade *f* de cruzeiro. **~er** *n* cruzador *m*

crumb /krʌm/ *n* migalha *f*, farelo *m*

crumble /'krʌmbl/ *vt/i* desfazer(-se); ‹*bread*› esmigalhar(-se); (*collapse*) desmoronar-se

crumple /'krʌmpl/ *vt/i* amarrotar(-se)

crunch /krʌntʃ/ *vt* trincar; (*under one's feet*) fazer ranger

crusade /kru:'seɪd/ *n* cruzada *f*. **~r** /-ə(r)/ *n* cruzado *m*; *fig* militante *mf*

crush /krʌʃ/ *vt* esmagar; ‹*clothes, papers*› amassar, amarrotar ● *n* aperto *m*; **a ~ on** [✱] uma paixonite *or* (*P*) paixoneta por

crust /krʌst/ *n* côdea *f*, crosta *f*. **~y** *a* crocante

crutch /krʌtʃ/ *n* muleta *f*; (*crotch*) entrepernas *fpl*

crux /krʌks/ *n* (*pl* **cruxes**) o ponto crucial

cry /kraɪ/ *n* grito *m*; **a far ~ from** muito diferente de ● *vi* (*weep*) chorar; (*call out*) gritar

crypt /krɪpt/ *n* cripta *f*

cryptic /'krɪptɪk/ *a* críptico, enigmático

crystal /'krɪstl/ *n* cristal *m*. **~lize** *vt/i* cristalizar(-se)

cub /kʌb/ *n* cria *f*, filhote *m*; **C~ (Scout)** lobito *m*

Cuba /'kju:bə/ *n* Cuba *f*

cubbyhole /'kʌbɪhəʊl/ *n* cochicho *m*; (*snug place*) cantinho *m*

cub|e /kju:b/ *n* cubo *m*. **~ic** *a* cúbico

cubicle /'kju:bɪkl/ *n* cubículo *m*, compartimento *m*; (*at swimming pool*) cabine *f*

cuckoo /'kʊku:/ *n* cuco *m*

cucumber /'kju:kʌmbə(r)/ *n* pepino *m*

cuddl|e /'kʌdl/ *vt/i* abraçar com carinho; (*nestle*) aninhar(-se) ● *n* abracinho *m*, festinha *f*. **~y** *a* fofo, aconchegante

cue[1] /kju:/ *n* *Theat* deixa *f*; (*hint*) sugestão *f*, sinal *m*

cue[2] /kju:/ *n* (*billiards*) taco *m*

cuff /kʌf/ *n* punho *m*; (*blow*) sopapo *m*; **off the ~** de improviso ● *vt* dar um sopapo. **~link** *n* botão *m* de punho

cul-de-sac /'kʌldəsæk/ *n* (*pl* **culs-de-sac**) beco *m* sem saída

culinary /'kʌlɪnərɪ/ *a* culinário

cull /kʌl/ *vt* (*select*) escolher; (*kill*) abater seletivamente ● *n* abate *m*

culminat|e /'kʌlmɪneɪt/ *vi* **~e in** acabar em. **~ion** /-'neɪʃn/ *n* auge *m*, ponto *m* culminante

culprit /'kʌlprɪt/ *n* culpado *m*

cult /kʌlt/ *n* culto *m*

cultivat|e /'kʌltɪveɪt/ *vt* cultivar. **~ion** /-'veɪʃn/ *n* cultivo *m*, cultivação *f*

cultural /'kʌltʃərəl/ *a* cultural

culture /'kʌltʃə(r)/ *n* cultura *f*. **~d** *a* culto

cumbersome /'kʌmbəsəm/ *a* (*unwieldy*) pesado; incômodo, (*P*) incómodo

cumulative /'kju:mjʊlətɪv/ *a* cumulativo

cunning /'kʌnɪŋ/ *a* astuto, manhoso ● *n* astúcia *f*, manha *f*

cup /kʌp/ *n* xícara *f*, (*P*) chávena *f*; (*prize*) taça *f*; **C~ Final** Final de Campeonato *f*

cupboard /'kʌbəd/ *n* armário *m*

curable /'kjʊərəbl/ *a* curável

curator /kjʊə'reɪtə(r)/ *n* (*museum*) conservador *m*; *Jur* curador *m*

curb /kɜ:b/ *n* freio *m* ● *vt* refrear; (*price increase etc*) sustar

curdle /'kɜ:dl/ *vt/i* coalhar

cure /kjʊə(r)/ *vt* curar ● *n* cura *f*

curfew /'kɜ:fju:/ *n* toque *m* de recolher, recolher *m* obrigatório

curio /'kjʊərɪəʊ/ *n* (*pl* **-os**) curiosidade *f*

curi|ous /'kjʊərɪəs/ *a* curioso. **~osity** /-'ɒsətɪ/ *n* curiosidade *f*

curl /kɜ:l/ *vt/i* encaracolar(-se) ● *n* caracol *m*; **~ up** enroscar(-se)

curler /'kɜ:lə(r)/ *n* rolo *m*

curly /'kɜ:lɪ/ *a* (**-ier**, **-iest**) encaracolado, crespo

currant /'kʌrənt/ *n* passa *f* de Corinto

currency /'kʌrənsɪ/ *n* moeda *f* corrente; (*general use*) circulação *f*; **foreign ~** moeda *f* estrangeira

current /'kʌrənt/ *a* (*common*) corrente; ‹*event, price, etc*› atual; **~ account** conta *f* corrente; **~ affairs** atualidades *fpl* ● *n* corrente *f*. **~ly** *adv* atualmente

curriculum /kə'rɪkjʊləm/ *n* (*pl* **-la**) currículo *m*, programa *m* de estudos. **~ vitae** *n* curriculum vitae *m*

curry[1] /'kʌrɪ/ *n* caril *m*

curry[2] /'kʌrɪ/ *vt* **~ favour with** procurar agradar a

curse /kɜ:s/ *n* maldição *f*, praga *f*; (*bad language*) palavrão *m* ● *vt* amaldiçoar, praguejar contra ● *vi* praguejar; (*swear*) dizer palavrões

C

cursor /'kɜ:sə(r)/ *n* cursor *m*

cursory /'kɜ:sərɪ/ *a* apressado, superficial; **a ~ look** uma olhada superficial

curt /kɜ:t/ *a* brusco

curtail /kɜ:'teɪl/ *vt* abreviar; ‹*expenses etc*› reduzir

curtain /'kɜ:tn/ *n* cortina *f*; *Theat* pano *m*

curtsy /'kɜ:tsɪ/ *n* reverência *f* ● *vi* fazer uma reverência

curve /kɜ:v/ *n* curva *f* ● *vt/i* curvar(-se); (*of road*) fazer uma curva

cushion /'kʊʃn/ *n* almofada *f* ● *vt* ‹*a blow*› amortecer; *fig* proteger

cushy /'kʊʃɪ/ *a* (**-ier**, **-iest**) [!] fácil; agradável; **~ job** sinecura *f*, tacho *m fig*

custard /'kʌstəd/ *n* creme *m*

custodian /kʌ'stəʊdɪən/ *n* guarda *m*

custody /'kʌstədɪ/ *n* (*safe keeping*) custódia *f*; *Jur* detenção *f*; (*of child*) tutela *f*

custom /'kʌstəm/ *n* costume *m*; *Comm* freguesia *f*, clientela *f*. **~ary** *a* habitual

customer /'kʌstəmə(r)/ *n* freguês *m*, cliente *mf*

customs /'kʌstəmz/ *npl* alfândega *f* ● *a* alfandegário; **~ clearance** desembaraço *m* alfandegário; **~ officer** funcionário *m* da alfândega

cut /kʌt/ *vt/i* (*pt* **cut**, *pres p* **cutting**) cortar; ‹*prices etc*› reduzir; **~ back** or **down (on)** reduzir; **~ in** intrometer-se; *Auto* cortar; **~ off** cortar; *fig* isolar; **~ out** recortar; (*leave out*) suprimir; **~ short** encurtar, (*P*) atalhar ● *n* corte *m*, golpe *m*; (*of clothes, hair*) corte *m*; (*piece*) pedaço *m*; (*prices etc*) redução *f*, corte *m*; [x] (*share*) comissão *f*, (*P*) talhada *f* [x]. **~back** *n* corte *m*; **~-out** *n* figura *f* para recortar; **~-price** *a* a preço(s) reduzido(s)

cute /kju:t/ *a* (**-er**, **-est**) [!] (*clever*) esperto; (*attractive*) bonito, (*P*) giro [!]

cutlery /'kʌtlərɪ/ *n* talheres *mpl*

cutlet /'kʌtlɪt/ *n* costeleta *f*

cutting /'kʌtɪŋ/ *a* cortante ● *n* (*from newspaper*) recorte *m*; (*plant*) estaca *f*; **~ edge** gume *m*

CV *abbr* ▶ CURRICULUM VITAE

cybercafe /'saɪbəkæfeɪ/ *n* lan house *f*, (*P*) cibercafé *m*

cyberspace /'saɪbəspeɪs/ *n* ciberespaço *m*

cybersquatter /'saɪbəskwɒtə(r)/ *n*: pessoa que compra nome de domínio de marca famosa para vendê-lo depois com lucro; (*P*) ciberespeculador/a *mf*

cyberterrorism /'saɪbəterərɪzəm/ *n* terrorismo *m* cibernético, (*P*) ciberterrorismo *m*

cycl|e /'saɪkl/ *n* ciclo *m*; (*bicycle*) bicicleta *f* ● *vi* andar de bicicleta; **~ lane** ciclovia *f*. **~ing** *n* ciclismo *m*. **~ist** *n* ciclista *mf*

cyclone /'saɪkləʊn/ *n* ciclone *m*

cylind|er /'sɪlɪndə(r)/ *n* cilindro *m*. **~rical** *a* cilíndrico

cymbals /'sɪmblz/ *npl Mus* pratos *mpl*

cynic /'sɪnɪk/ *n* cínico *m*. **~al** *a* cínico. **~ism** /-sɪzəm/ *n* cinismo *m*

Cypr|us /'saɪprəs/ *n* Chipre *m*. **~iot** /'sɪprɪət/ *a & n* cipriota *mf*

cyst /sɪst/ *n* quisto *m*

Czech /tʃek/ *a & n* tcheco *m*, (*P*) checo *m*

Dd

dab /dæb/ *vt* (*pt* **dabbed**) aplicar levemente ● *n* **a ~ of** uma aplicaçãozinha de; **~ sth on** aplicar qq coisa em gestos leves

dabble /'dæbl/ *vi* **~ in** interessar-se por, fazer um pouco de (como amador)

dad /dæd/ *n* [!] paizinho *m* [!]. **~dy** *n* (*children's use*) papai *m*, (*P*) papá *m*. **~dy-long-legs** *n* pernilongo *m*

daffodil /'dæfədɪl/ *n* narciso *m*

daft /dɑːft/ *a* (**-er**, **-est**) doido, maluco

dagger /'dægə(r)/ *n* punhal *m*; **at ~s drawn** prestes a lutar (**with** com)

> *i*
>
> **Dáil Éireann** É o nome da câmara baixa do Parlamento da República da Irlanda. Pronuncia-se /'ɛːr(ə)n, 'eːrʲən/ e é formada por 166 representantes ou deputados, normalmente conhecidos por *TDs*, que representam 41 circunscrições. São eleitos através do sistema de representação proporcional. De acordo com a Constituição, deve haver um deputado por cada 20.000 ou 30.000 pessoas.

daily /'deɪlɪ/ *a* diário, cotidiano, quotidiano ● *adv* diariamente, todos os dias ● *n* (*newspaper*) diário *m*; [!] (*charwoman*) faxineira *f*, (*P*) mulher *f* a dias

dainty /'deɪntɪ/ *a* (**-ier**, **-iest**) delicado; (*pretty, neat*) gracioso

dairy /'deərɪ/ *n* leiteria *f*, (*P*) leitaria; **~ products** laticínios *mpl*

daisy /'deɪzɪ/ *n* margarida *f*

dam /dæm/ *n* barragem *f*, represa *f* ● *vt* (*pt* **dammed**) represar

damag|e /'dæmɪdʒ/ *n* estrago(s) *mpl*; **~es** *Jur* perdas *fpl* e danos *mpl* ● *vt* estragar, danificar

dame /deɪm/ *n old use* dama *f*; *Amer* [x] mulher *f*

damn /dæm/ *vt Relig* condenar ao inferno; (*swear at*) amaldiçoar, maldizer; *fig* (*condemn*) condenar; **I'll be ~ed if** que um raio me atinja se ● *int* raios!, bolas! ● *n* **not care a ~** [!] estar pouco ligando [!], (*P*) estar-se marimbando [!] ● *a* [!] do diabo [!], danado ● *adv* [!] muitíssimo. **~ation** /-'neɪʃn/ *n* danação *f*, condenação *f*

damp /dæmp/ *n* umidade *f*, (*P*) humidade *f* ● *a* (**-er**, **-est**) úmido, (*P*) húmido ● *vt* umedecer, (*P*) humedecer. **~en** *vt* = DAMP. **~ness** *n* umidade *f*, (*P*) humidade *f*

dance /dɑːns/ *vt/i* dançar ● *n* dança *f*; **~ hall** sala *f* de baile. **~r** /-ə(r)/ *n* dançarino *m*; (*professional*) bailarino *m*

dandelion /'dændɪlaɪən/ *n* dente-de-leão *m*

dandruff /'dændrʌf/ *n* caspa *f*

Dane /deɪn/ *n* dinamarquês *m*

danger /'deɪndʒə(r)/ *n* perigo *m*; **be in ~ of** correr o risco de. **~ous** *a* perigoso

dangle /'dæŋgl/ *vi* oscilar, pender ● *vt* ter or trazer dependurado; (*hold*) balançar; *fig* ‹*hopes, etc*› acenar com

Danish /'deɪnɪʃ/ *a* dinamarquês ● *n Lang* dinamarquês *m*

dare /deə(r)/ *vt* **~ to do** ousar fazer; **~ sb to do** desafiar alguém a fazer; **I ~ say** creio ● *n* desafio *m*

daredevil /'deədevl/ *n* louco *m*, temerário *m*

daring /'deərɪŋ/ *a* audacioso ● *n* audácia *f*

dark /dɑːk/ *a* (**-er**, **-est**) escuro, sombrio; (*gloomy*) sombrio; (*of colour*) escuro; (*of skin*) moreno; **~ horse** concorrente *mf* que é uma incógnita ● *n* escuridão *f*, escuro *m*; (*nightfall*) anoitecer *m*, cair *m* da noite; **be in the ~ about** *fig* ignorar. **~room** *n* câmara *f* escura. **~ness** *n* escuridão *f*

darken /'dɑːkən/ *vt/i* escurecer

darling /'dɑːlɪŋ/ *a & n* querido *m*

darn /dɑːn/ *vt* serzir, remendar

dart /dɑːt/ *n* dardo *m*, flecha *f*; **~s** (*game*) jogo *m* de dardos ● *vi* lançar-se

dartboard /'dɑːtbɔːd/ *n* alvo *m*

dash /dæʃ/ *vi* precipitar-se; **~ off** partir a toda a velocidade; (*letter*) escrever à pressa ● *vt* arremessar; ‹*hopes*› destruir ● *n* corrida *f*; (*stroke*) travessão *m*; (*Morse*) traço *m*; **a ~ of** um pouco de

dashboard /'dæʃbɔːd/ *n* painel *m* de instrumentos, quadro *m* de bordo

data /'deɪtə/ *npl* dados *mpl*; **~ capture** aquisição *f* de informações, recolha *f* de dados; **~ processing** processamento *m* or tratamento *m* de dados. **~base** *n* base *f* de dados

date[1] /deɪt/ *n* data *f*; [!] encontro *m* marcado ● *vt/i* datar; [!] andar com; **out of ~** desatualizado; **to ~** até à data; **up to ~** ‹*style*› moderno; ‹*information etc*› em dia. **~d** *a* antiquado

date[2] /deɪt/ *n* (*fruit*) tâmara *f*

daub /dɔːb/ *vt* borrar, pintar toscamente

daughter /'dɔːtə(r)/ *n* filha *f*. **~-in-law** *n* (*pl* **~s-in-law**) nora *f*

daunt /dɔːnt/ *vt* assustar, intimidar, desencorajar

dawdle /'dɔːdl/ *vi* perder tempo

dawn /dɔːn/ *n* madrugada *f* ● *vi* madrugar, amanhecer; **~ on** *fig* fazer-se luz no espírito de, começar a perceber

day /deɪ/ *n* dia *m*; (*period*) época *f*, tempo *m*; **the ~ before** a véspera. **~dream** *n* devaneio *m* ● *vi* devanear

daybreak /'deɪbreɪk/ *n* romper *m* do dia, aurora *f*, amanhecer *m*

daylight /'deɪlaɪt/ *n* luz *f* do dia; **~ robbery** roubar descaradamente

daytime /'deɪtaɪm/ *n* dia *m*, dia *m* claro

daze /deɪz/ *vt* aturdir ● *n* **in a ~** aturdido

dazzle /'dæzl/ *vt* deslumbrar; (*with headlights*) ofuscar

dead /ded/ *a* morto; (*numb*) dormente; **~ end** beco *m* sem saída; **in the ~ centre** bem no meio ● *adv* completamente, de todo; **stop ~** estacar ● *n* **the ~** os mortos; **in the ~ of the night** a horas mortas, na calada da noite. **~-pan** *a* inexpressivo

deaden /'dedn/ *vt* ‹*sound, blow*› amortecer; ‹*pain*› aliviar

deadline /'dedlaɪn/ *n* prazo *m* final

deadlock /'dedlɒk/ *n* impasse *m*

deadly /'dedlɪ/ *a* (**-ier, -iest**) mortal; ‹*weapon*› mortífero

deaf /def/ *a* (**-er, -est**) surdo; **turn a ~ ear** fingir que não ouve; **~ mute** surdo-mudo *m*. **~ness** *n* surdez *f*

d

deafen /'defn/ *vt* ensurdecer. **~ing** *a* ensurdecedor

deal /diːl/ *vt* (*pt* **dealt**) distribuir; ‹*a blow, cards*› dar ● *vi* negociar ● *n* negócio *m*; *Cards* vez de dar *f*; **a great ~** muito (**of** de); **~ in** negociar em; **~ with** ‹*person*› tratar (com); ‹*affair*› tratar de. **~er** *n* comerciante *m*; (*agent*) concessionário *m*; representante *m*

dealt /delt/ ▶ DEAL

dean /diːn/ *n* decano *m*

dear /dɪə(r)/ *a* (**-er, -est**) (*cherished*) caro, querido; (*expensive*) caro ● *n* amor *m* ● *adv* caro ● *int* **oh ~!** meu Deus!. **~ly** *adv* (*very much*) muito; ‹*pay*› caro

dearth /dɜːθ/ *n* escassez *f*

death /deθ/ *n* morte *f*; **~ certificate** certidão *f* de óbito; **~ penalty** pena *f* de morte; **~ rate** taxa *f* de mortalidade. **~ trap** *n* lugar *m* perigoso, ratoeira *f*. **~ly** *a* de morte, mortal

debase /dɪ'beɪs/ *vt* degradar

debat|e /dɪ'beɪt/ *n* debate *m* ● *vt* debater. **~able** *a* discutível

debauchery /dɪ'bɔːtʃərɪ/ *n* deboche *m*, devassidão *f*

debit /'debɪt/ *n* débito *m* ● *vt* (*pt* **debited**) debitar

debris /'deɪbriː/ *n* destroços *mpl*

debt /det/ *n* dívida *f*; **in ~** endividado. **~or** *n* devedor *m*

debut /'deɪbjuː/ *n* (*of actor, play etc*) estreia *f*

decade /'dekeɪd/ *n* década *f*

decaden|t /'dekədənt/ *a* decadente. **~ce** *n* decadência *f*

decaffeinated /diː'kæfiːɪneɪtɪd/ *a* sem cafeína

decapitate /dɪ'kæpɪteɪt/ *vt* decapitar

decay /dɪ'keɪ/ *vi* apodrecer, estragar-se; ‹*food*› *fig* deteriorar-se; (*building*) degradar-se ● *n* apodrecimento *m*; (*of tooth*) cárie *f*; *fig* declínio *m*; decadência *f*

deceased /dɪ'siːst/ *a & n* falecido *m*, defunto *m*

deceit /dɪ'siːt/ *n* engano *m*. **~ful** *a* enganador

d

deceive /dɪ'siːv/ *vt* enganar, iludir

December /dɪ'sembə(r)/ *n* dezembro *m*

decen|t /'diːsnt/ *a* decente; [!] (*good*) (bastante) bom; [!] (*likeable*) simpático. **~cy** *n* decência *f*

decentralize /diː'sentrəlaɪz/ *vt* descentralizar

decept|ive /dɪ'septɪv/ *a* enganador, ilusório. **~ion** /-ʃn/ *n* engano *m*

decide /dɪ'saɪd/ *vt/i* decidir; **~ on** decidir-se por; **~ to do** decidir fazer. **~d** /-ɪd/ *a* decidido; (*clear*) definido, nítido. **~dly** /-ɪdlɪ/ *adv* decididamente

decimal /'desɪml/ *a* decimal ● *n* (fração *f*,) decimal *m*; **~ point** vírgula *f* decimal

decipher /dɪ'saɪfə(r)/ *vt* decifrar

decision /dɪ'sɪʒn/ *n* decisão *f*

decisive /dɪ'saɪsɪv/ *a* decisivo; ‹*manner*› decidido

deck /dek/ *n* convés *m*; (*of cards*) baralho *m*. **~chair** *n* espreguiçadeira *f*

declar|e /dɪ'kleə(r)/ *vt* declarar. **~ation** /deklə'reɪʃn/ *n* declaração *f*

decline /dɪ'klaɪn/ *vt* (*refuse*) declinar, recusar delicadamente; *Gram* declinar ● *vi* (*deteriorate*) declinar; (*fall*) baixar ● *n* declínio *m*; (*fall*) abaixamento *m*

decode /diː'kəʊd/ *vt* descodificar

decompos|e /diːkəm'pəʊz/ *vt/i* decompor(-se). **~ition** /-ɒmpə'zɪʃn/ *n* decomposição *f*

décor /'deɪkɔː(r)/ *n* decoração *f*

decorat|e /'dekəreɪt/ *vt* decorar, enfeitar; (*paint*) pintar; (*paper*) pôr papel em. **~ion** /-'reɪʃn/ *n* decoração *f*; (*medal etc*) condecoração *f*. **~ive** /-ətɪv/ *a* decorativo

decoy[1] /'diːkɔɪ/ *n* chamariz *m*, engodo *m*; (*trap*) armadilha *f*

decoy[2] /dɪ'kɔɪ/ *vt* atrair, apanhar

decrease[1] /diː'kriːs/ *vt/i* diminuir

decrease[2] /'diːkriːs/ *n* diminuição *f*

decrepit /dɪ'krepɪt/ *a* decrépito

dedicat|e /'dedɪkeɪt/ *vt* dedicar. **~ed** *a* dedicado. **~ion** /-'keɪʃn/ *n* dedicação *f*; (*in book*) dedicatória *f*

deduce /dɪ'djuːs/ *vt* deduzir

deduct /dɪ'dʌkt/ *vt* deduzir; (*from pay*) descontar

deduction /dɪ'dʌkʃn/ *n* dedução *f*; (*from pay*) desconto *m*

deed /diːd/ *n* ato *m*; *Jur* contrato *m*

deep /diːp/ *a* (**-er**, **-est**) profundo; **take a ~ breath** respirar fundo ● *adv* profundamente. **~ freeze** *n* congelador *m* ● **~-freeze** *vt* congelar

deepen /'diːpən/ *vt/i* aprofundar(-se); ‹*mystery, night*› adensar-se

deer /dɪə(r)/ *n* (*pl invar*) veado *m*

deface /dɪ'feɪs/ *vt* danificar, degradar

default /dɪ'fɔːlt/ *vi* faltar ● *n* **by ~** à revelia; **win by ~** *Sport* ganhar por não comparecimento, (*P*) comparência ● *n* *Comput* default *m*

defeat /dɪ'fiːt/ *vt* derrotar; (*thwart*) malograr ● *n* derrota *f*; (*of plan, etc*) malogro *m*

defect[1] /'diːfekt/ *n* defeito *m*. **~ive** /dɪ'fektɪv/ *a* defeituoso

defect[2] /dɪ'fekt/ *vi* desertar. **~ion** *n* defecção *m*. **~or** *n* trânsfuga *mf*, dissidente *mf*; (*political*) asilado *m* político

defence /dɪ'fens/ *n* defesa *f*. **~less** *a* indefeso

defend /dɪ'fend/ *vt* defender. **~ant** *n Jur* réu *m*, acusado *m*. **~er** *n* advogado *m* de defesa, defensor *m*

defensive /dɪ'fensɪv/ *a* defensivo ● *n* **on the ~** na defensiva *f*; ‹*person, sport*› na retranca *f* [!]

defer /dɪ'fɜː(r)/ *vt* (*pt* **deferred**) adiar, diferir ● *vi* **~ to** ceder, deferir

deferen|ce /'defərəns/ *n* deferência *f*. **~tial** /-'renʃl/ *a* deferente

defian|ce /dɪ'faɪəns/ *n* desafio *m*; **in ~ of** sem respeito por. **~t** *a* de desafio

deficien|t /dɪ'fɪʃnt/ *a* deficiente; **be ~t in** ter falta de. **~cy** *n* deficiência *f*

deficit /'defɪsɪt/ *n* déficit *m*

define /dɪ'faɪn/ *vt* definir

definite /'defɪnɪt/ *a* definido; (*clear*) categórico, claro; (*certain*) certo; **~ly** decididamente; (*clearly*) claramente

definition /defɪ'nɪʃn/ *n* definição *f*

definitive /dɪ'fɪnətɪv/ *a* definitivo

deflat|e /dɪ'fleɪt/ *vt* esvaziar; (*person*) desemproar, desinchar. **~ion** /-ʃn/ *n* esvaziamento *m*; *Econ* deflação *f*

deflect /dɪ'flekt/ *vt/i* desviar(-se)

deform /dɪ'fɔːm/ *vt* deformar. **~ed** *a* deformado, disforme. **~ity** *n* deformidade *f*

defraud /dɪ'frɔːd/ *vt* defraudar

defrost /diː'frɒst/ *vt* descongelar

deft /deft/ *a* (**-er**, **-est**) hábil

defuse /diː'fjuːz/ *vt* ‹*a bomb*› desativar; ‹*a situation*› acalmar

defy /dɪ'faɪ/ *vt* desafiar; (*attempts*) resistir a; (*the law*) desobedecer a;

(*public opinion*) opor-se a

degrad|e /dɪ'greɪd/ *vt* degradar

degree /dɪ'gri:/ *n* grau *m*; *Univ* diploma *m*; **to a ~** ao mais alto grau, muito

dehydrate /di:'haɪdreɪt/ *vt/i* desidratar(-se)

de-ice /di:'aɪs/ *vt* descongelar, degelar; (*windscreen*) tirar o gelo de

deign /deɪn/ *vt* **~ to do** dignar-se (a) fazer

deity /'di:ɪtɪ/ *n* divindade *f*

dejected /dɪ'dʒektɪd/ *a* abatido

delay /dɪ'leɪ/ *vt* atrasar; (*postpone*) retardar ● *vi* atrasar-se ● *n* atraso *m*, demora *f*

delegate[1] /'delɪgət/ *n* delegado *m*

delegat|e[2] /'delɪgeɪt/ *vt* delegar. **~ion** /-'geɪʃn/ *n* delegação *f*

delet|e /dɪ'li:t/ *vt* riscar. **~ion** /-ʃn/ *n* rasura *f*

deliberate[1] /dɪ'lɪbərət/ *a* deliberado; (*steps etc*) compassado

deliberat|e[2] /dɪ'lɪbəreɪt/ *vt/i* deliberar

delica|te /'delɪkət/ *a* delicado. **~cy** *n* delicadeza *f*; ‹*food*› guloseima *f*; iguaria *f*, (*P*) acepipe *m*

delicatessen /delɪkə'tesn/ *n* (*shop*) mercearias *fpl* finas

delicious /dɪ'lɪʃəs/ *a* delicioso

delight /dɪ'laɪt/ *n* grande prazer *m*, delícia *f*; (*thing*) delícia *f*, encanto *m* ● *vt* deliciar ● *vi* **~ in** deliciar-se com. **~ed** *a* deliciado, encantado. **~ful** *a* delicioso, encantador

delinquen|t /dɪ'lɪŋkwənt/ *a & n* delinquente *mf*

deliri|ous /dɪ'lɪrɪəs/ *a* delirante; **be ~ous** delirar. **~um** /-əm/ *n* delírio *m*

deliver /dɪ'lɪvə(r)/ *vt* entregar; ‹*letters*› distribuir; (*free*) libertar; *Med* fazer o parto. **~y** *n* entrega *f*; (*letters*) distribuição *f*; *Med* parto *m*

delu|de /dɪ'lu:d/ *vt* enganar; **~de o.s.** ter ilusões. **~sion** /-ʒn/ *n* ilusão *f*

deluge /'delju:dʒ/ *n* dilúvio *m* ● *vt* inundar

de luxe /dɪ'lʌks/ *a* de luxo

delve /delv/ *vi* **~ into** pesquisar, rebuscar

demand /dɪ'mɑ:nd/ *vt* exigir; (*ask to be told*) perguntar ● *n* exigência *f*; *Comm* procura *f*; (*claim*) reivindicação *f*; **in ~** procurado. **~ing** *a* exigente; ‹*work*› puxado, custoso

demeanour /dɪ'mi:nə(r)/ *n* comportamento *m*, conduta *f*

demented /dɪ'mentɪd/ *a* louco, demente; **become ~** enlouquecer

demo /'deməʊ/ *n* (*pl* **-os**) [!] manifestação *f*, (*P*) manif *f*

democracy /dɪ'mɒkrəsɪ/ *n* democracia *f*

democrat /'deməkræt/ *n* democrata *mf*. **~ic** /-'krætɪk/ *a* democrático

demoli|sh /dɪ'mɒlɪʃ/ *vt* demolir. **~tion** /demə'lɪʃn/ *n* demolição *f*

demon /'di:mən/ *n* demônio *m*, (*P*) demónio *m*

demonstrat|e /'demənstreɪt/ *vt* demonstrar ● *vi Pol* fazer uma manifestação, manifestar-se. **~ion** /-'streɪʃn/ *n* demonstração *f*; *Pol* manifestação *f*. **~or** *n Pol* manifestante *mf*

demonstrative /dɪ'mɒnstrətɪv/ *a* demonstrativo

demoralize /dɪ'mɒrəlaɪz/ *vt* desmoralizar

demote /dɪ'məʊt/ *vt* fazer baixar de posto, despromover, rebaixar

demure /dɪ'mjʊə(r)/ *a* recatado, modesto

den /den/ *n* antro *m*, covil *m*; (*room*) cantinho *m*, recanto *m*

denial /dɪ'naɪəl/ *n* negação *f*; (*refusal*) recusa *f*; (*statement*) desmentido *m*

denim /'denɪm/ *n* brim *m*; **~s** (*jeans*) jeans *mpl*, (*P*) calças *f* de ganga

Denmark /'denmɑ:k/ *n* Dinamarca *f*

denomination /dɪnɒmɪ'neɪʃn/ *n* denominação *f*; *Relig* confissão *f*, seita *f*; (*money*) valor *m*

denote /dɪ'nəʊt/ *vt* denotar

denounce /dɪ'naʊns/ *vt* denunciar

dens|e /dens/ *a* (**-er**, **-est**) denso; [!] ‹*person*› obtuso. **~ity** *n* densidade *f*

dent /dent/ *n* mossa *f*, depressão *f* ● *vt* dentear

dental /'dentl/ *a* dentário, dental

dentist /'dentɪst/ *n* dentista *mf*. **~ry** *n* odontologia *f*

denture /'dentʃə(r)/ *n* dentadura (postiça) *f*

deny /dɪ'naɪ/ *vt* negar; ‹*rumour*› desmentir; (*disown*) renegar; (*refuse*) recusar

deodorant /di:'əʊdərənt/ *n & a* desodorante *m*, (*P*) desodorizante *m*

d

depart /dɪ'pɑ:t/ *vi* partir; **~ from** (*deviate*) afastar-se de, desviar-se de

department /dɪ'pɑ:tmənt/ *n* departamento *m*; (*in shop, office*) seção *f*, (*P*) secção *f*; (*government*) repartição *f*; **~ store** loja *f* de departamentos, (*P*) grande armazém *m*

departure /dɪ'pɑ:tʃə(r)/ *n* partida *f*; **a ~ from** ‹*custom, diet etc*› uma mudança de; **a new ~** uma nova orientação

depend /dɪ'pend/ *vi* **~ on** depender de; (*trust*) contar com. **~able** *a* de confiança. **~ence** *n* dependência *f*. **~ent (on)** *a* dependente (de)

dependant /dɪ'pendənt/ *n* dependente *mf*

depict /dɪ'pɪkt/ *vt* descrever; (*in pictures*) representar

deplor|e /dɪ'plɔ:(r)/ *vt* deplorar. **~able** *a* deplorável

deport /dɪ'pɔ:t/ *vt* deportar. **~ation** /di:pɔ:'teɪʃn/ *n* deportação *f*

depose /dɪ'pəʊz/ *vt* depor

deposit /dɪ'pɒzɪt/ *vt* (*pt* **deposited**) depositar ● *n* depósito *m*; **~ account** conta *f* de depósito a prazo

depot /'depəʊ/ *n Mil* depósito *m*; (*buses*) garagem *f*; *Amer* (*station*) rodoviária *f*; estação *f* de trem, (*P*) de comboio

deprav|e /dɪ'preɪv/ *vt* depravar

depreciat|e /dɪ'pri:ʃɪeɪt/ *vt/i* depreciar(-se). **~ion** /-'eɪʃn/ *n* depreciação *f*

depress /dɪ'pres/ *vt* deprimir; (*press down*) carregar em. **~ion** /-ʃn/ *n* depressão *f*

deprivation /deprɪ'veɪʃn/ *n* privação *f*

deprive /dɪ'praɪv/ *vt* **~ of** privar de. **~d** *a* privado; (*underprivileged*) deserdado (da sorte), destituído; ‹*child*› carente

depth /depθ/ *n* profundidade *f*; **be out of one's ~** perder pé, (*P*) não ter pé; *fig* ficar desnorteado, estar perdido; **in the ~(s) of** no mais fundo de, nas profundezas de

deputy /'depjʊtɪ/ *n* (*pl* **-ies**) delegado *m* ● *a* adjunto; **~ chairman** vice-presidente *m*

derail /dɪ'reɪl/ *vt* descarrilhar; **be ~ed** descarrilhar. **~ment** *n* descarrilhamento *m*

deranged /dɪ'reɪndʒd/ *a* ‹*mind*› transtornado, louco

derelict /'derəlɪkt/ *a* abandonado

derivative /dɪ'rɪvətɪv/ *a* derivado; ‹*work*› pouco original ● *n* derivado *m*

deriv|e /dɪ'raɪv/ *vt* **~e from** tirar de ● *vi* **~e from** derivar de. **~ation** /derɪ'veɪʃn/ *n* derivação *f*

derogatory /dɪ'rɒgətrɪ/ *a* pejorativo; ‹*remark*› depreciativo

derv /dɜ:v/ *n* gasóleo *m*

descend /dɪ'send/ *vt/i* descer, descender; **be ~ed from** descender de. **~ant** *n* descendente *mf*

descent /dɪ'sent/ *n* descida *f*; (*lineage*) descendência *f*, origem *f*

descri|be /dɪs'kraɪb/ *vt* descrever. **~ption** /-'krɪpʃn/ *n* descrição *f*. **~ptive** /-'krɪptɪv/ *a* descritivo

desecrat|e /'desɪkreɪt/ *vt* profanar

desert[1] /'dezət/ *a* & *n* deserto *m*; **~ island** ilha *f* deserta

desert[2] /dɪ'zɜ:t/ *vt/i* desertar. **~ed** *a* abandonado. **~er** *n* desertor *m*. **~ion** /-ʃn/ *n* deserção *f*

deserv|e /dɪ'zɜ:v/ *vt* merecer. **~edly** /dɪ'zɜ:vɪdlɪ/ *adv* merecidamente, a justo título. **~ing** *a* ‹*person*› merecedor; ‹*action*› meritório

design /dɪ'zaɪn/ *n* desenho *m*; (*artistic*) design *m*; (*style of dress*) modelo *m*; (*pattern*) padrão *m*, motivo *m* ● *vt* desenhar; (*devise*) conceber. **~er** *n* desenhador *m*; (*of dresses*) costureiro *m*; (*of machine*) inventor *m*

designat|e /'dezɪgneɪt/ *vt* designar. **~ion** /'-neɪʃn/ *n* designação *f*

desir|e /dɪ'zaɪə(r)/ *n* desejo *m* ● *vt* desejar. **~able** *a* desejável, atraente

desk /desk/ *n* secretária *f*; (*of pupil*) carteira *f*; (*in hotel*) recepção *f*; (*in bank*) caixa *f*

desolat|e /'desələt/ *a* desolado. **~ion** /-'leɪʃn/ *n* desolação *f*

despair /dɪ'speə(r)/ *n* desespero *m* ● *vi* desesperar (**of** de)

desperate /'despərət/ *a* desesperado; (*criminal*) capaz de tudo; **be ~ for** ter uma vontade doida de

desperation /despə'reɪʃn/ *n* desespero *m*

despicable /dɪ'spɪkəbl/ *a* desprezível

despise /dɪ'spaɪz/ *vt* desprezar

despite /dɪ'spaɪt/ *prep* apesar de, a despeito de, mau grado

desponden|t /dɪ'spɒndənt/ *a* desanimado

dessert /dɪ'zɜ:t/ *n* sobremesa *f*. **~ spoon** *n* colher *f* de sobremesa

destination /destɪ'neɪʃn/ *n* destino *m*, destinação *f*

destiny /'destɪnɪ/ *n* destino *m*
destitute /'destɪtju:t/ *a* destituído, indigente
destr|oy /dɪ'strɔɪ/ *vt* destruir. **~uction** /-'strʌkʃn/ *n* destruição *f*. **~uctive** *a* destrutivo, destruidor
detach /dɪ'tætʃ/ *vt* separar, arrancar. **~able** *a* separável; ‹*lining etc*› solto. **~ed** *a* separado; (*impartial*) imparcial; (*unemotional*) desprendido; **~ed house** casa *f* sem parede-meia com outra
detachment /dɪ'tætʃmənt/ *n* separação *f*; (*indifference*) desprendimento *m*; *Mil* destacamento *m*; (*impartiality*) imparcialidade *f*
detail /'di:teɪl/ *n* pormenor *m*, detalhe *m* ● *vt* detalhar; ‹*troops*› destacar. **~ed** *a* detalhado
detain /dɪ'teɪn/ *vt* reter; (*in prison*) deter. **~ee** /di:teɪ'ni:/ *n* detido *m*
detect /dɪ'tekt/ *vt* detectar. **~ion** /-ʃn/ *n* detecção *f*
detective /dɪ'tektɪv/ *n* detetive *m*; **~ story** romance *m* policial
detention /dɪ'tenʃn/ *n* detenção *f*; **be given a ~** (*school*) ficar de castigo na escola
deter /dɪ'tɜ:(r)/ *vt* (*pt* **deterred**) dissuadir; (*hinder*) impedir
detergent /dɪ'tɜ:dʒənt/ *a* & *n* detergente *m*
deteriorat|e /dɪ'tɪərɪəreɪt/ *vi* deteriorar(-se). **~ion** /-'reɪʃn/ *n* deterioração *f*
determin|e /dɪ'tɜ:mɪn/ *vt* determinar; **~e to do** decidir fazer. **~ation** /-'neɪʃn/ *n* determinação *f*. **~ed** *a* determinado; **~ed to do** decidido a fazer
deterrent /dɪ'terənt/ *n* dissuasivo *m*
detest /dɪ'test/ *vt* detestar. **~able** *a* detestável
detonat|e /'detəneɪt/ *vt/i* detonar. **~or** *n* espoleta *f*, detonador *m*
detour /'di:tʊə(r)/ *n* desvio *m*
detract /dɪ'trækt/ *vi* **~ from** depreciar, menosprezar
detriment /'detrɪmənt/ *n* detrimento *m*. **~al** /-'mentl/ *a* prejudicial
devalu|e /di:'vælju:/ *vt* desvalorizar. **~ation** /-'eɪʃn/ *n* desvalorização *f*
devastat|e /'devəsteɪt/ *vi* devastar; *fig* (*overwhelm*) arrasar. **~ing** *a* devastador; (*criticism*) de arrasar
develop /dɪ'veləp/ *vt/i* (*pt* **developed**) desenvolver(-se); (*get*) contrair; (*build on*) urbanizar; (*film*) revelar; **~ into** tornar-se; **~ing country** país *m* em vias de desenvolvimento. **~ment** *n* desenvolvimento *m*; (*film*) revelação *f*; (*of land*) urbanização *f*
deviat|e /'di:vɪeɪt/ *vi* desviar-se. **~ion** /-'eɪʃn/ *n* desvio *m*
device /dɪ'vaɪs/ *n* dispositivo *m*; (*scheme*) processo *m*; **left to one's own ~s** entregue a si mesmo
devil /'devl/ *n* diabo *m*
devious /'di:vɪəs/ *a* tortuoso; *fig* ‹*means*› escuso; *fig* ‹*person*› pouco franco
devise /dɪ'vaɪz/ *vt* imaginar, inventar
devoid /dɪ'vɔɪd/ *a* **~ of** desprovido de, destituído de
devot|e /dɪ'vəʊt/ *vt* dedicar, devotar. **~ed** *a* dedicado, devotado. **~ion** /-ʃn/ *n* devoção *f*
devotee /devə'ti:/ *n* **~ of** adepto *m* de, entusiasta *mf* de
devour /dɪ'vaʊə(r)/ *vt* devorar
devout /dɪ'vaʊt/ *a* devota; ‹*prayer*› fervoroso
dew /dju:/ *n* orvalho *m*
dext|erity /dek'sterətɪ/ *n* destreza *f*, jeito *m*. **~rous** /'dekstrəs/ *a* destro, hábil
diabet|es /daɪə'bi:tiz/ *n* diabetes *f*. **~ic** /-'betɪk/ *a* diabético
diabolical /daɪə'bɒlɪkl/ *a* diabólico
diagnose /'daɪəgnəʊz/ *vt* diagnosticar
diagnosis /daɪəg'nəʊsɪs/ *n* (*pl* **-oses** /-si:z/) diagnóstico *m*
diagonal /daɪ'ægənl/ *a* & *n* diagonal *f*
diagram /'daɪəgræm/ *n* diagrama *m*, esquema *m*
dial /'daɪəl/ *n* mostrador *m* ● *vt* (*pt* **dialled**) ‹*number*› marcar, discar; **~ling code** código *m* de discagem; **~ling tone** sinal *m* de discar
dialect /'daɪəlekt/ *n* dialeto *m*
dialogue /'daɪəlɒg/ *n* diálogo *m*
diameter /daɪ'æmɪtə(r)/ *n* diâmetro *m*
diamond /'daɪəmənd/ *n* diamante *m*, brilhante *m*; (*shape*) losango *m*; **~s** *Cards* ouros *mpl*
diaper /'daɪəpə(r)/ *n Amer* fralda *f*
diarrhoea /daɪə'rɪə/ *n* diarreia *f*
diary /'daɪərɪ/ *n* agenda *f*; (*record*) diário *m*
dice /daɪs/ *n* (*pl invar*) dado *m*
dictat|e /dɪk'teɪt/ *vt/i* ditar. **~ion** /-ʃn/ *n* ditado *m*
dictator /dɪk'teɪtə(r)/ *n* ditador *m*. **~ship** *n* ditadura *f*

d

dictionary /'dɪkʃənrɪ/ *n* dicionário *m*

did /dɪd/ ▶ DO

diddle /'dɪdl/ *vt* [!] trapacear; enganar

didn't /'dɪdnt/ (= **did not**) ▶ DO

die /daɪ/ *vi* (*pres p* **dying**) morrer; **be dying to** estar doido para; **~ down** diminuir, baixar; **~ out** desaparecer, extinguir-se

diesel /'di:zl/ *n* diesel *m*; **~ engine** motor *m* a diesel

diet /'daɪət/ *n* dieta *f* ● *vi* fazer dieta, estar de dieta

differ /'dɪfə(r)/ *vi* diferir; (*disagree*) discordar

differen|t /'dɪfrənt/ *a* diferente. **~ce** *n* diferença *f*; (*disagreement*) desacordo *m*. **~ly** *adv* diferentemente

differentiate /dɪfə'renʃɪeɪt/ *vt/i* diferençar(-se), diferenciar(-se)

difficult /'dɪfɪkəlt/ *a* difícil. **~y** *n* dificuldade *f*

diffiden|t /'dɪfɪdənt/ *a* acanhado, inseguro. **~ce** *n* acanhamento *m*, insegurança *f*

diffuse[1] /dɪ'fju:s/ *a* difuso

diffus|e[2] /dɪ'fju:z/ *vt* difundir

dig /dɪg/ *vt/i* (*pt* **dug**, *pres p* **digging**) cavar; (*thrust*) espetar ● *n* (*with elbow*) cotovelada *f*; (*with finger*) cutucada *f*, (*P*) espetadela *f*; (*remark*) ferroada *f*; *Archaeol* excavação *f*; **~s** [!] quarto *m* alugado; **~ up** desenterrar

digest /dɪ'dʒest/ *vt/i* digerir. **~ible** *a* digerível, digestível. **~ion** /-ʃn/ *n* digestão *f*

digit /'dɪdʒɪt/ *n* dígito *m*

digital /'dɪdʒɪtl/ *a* digital; **~ clock** relógio *m* digital. **~ camera** *n* câmera *f* digital, (*P*) câmara *f* digital; **~ television** *n* televisão *f* ou TV digital

dignif|y /'dɪgnɪfaɪ/ *vt* dignificar. **~ied** *a* digno

dignitary /'dɪgnɪtərɪ/ *n* dignitário *m*

dignity /'dɪgnətɪ/ *n* dignidade *f*

digress /daɪ'gres/ *vi* digressar, divagar; **~ from** desviar-se de. **~ion** /-ʃn/ *n* digressão *f*

dilapidated /dɪ'læpɪdeɪtɪd/ *a* ‹*house*› arruinado, degradado; ‹*car*› estragado

dilat|e /daɪ'leɪt/ *vt/i* dilatar(-se)

dilemma /dɪ'lemə/ *n* dilema *m*

diligen|t /'dɪlɪdʒənt/ *a* diligente, aplicado. **~ce** *n* diligência *f*, aplicação *f*

dilute /daɪ'lju:t/ *vt* diluir ● *a* diluído

dim /dɪm/ *a* (**dimmer**, **dimmest**) (*weak*) fraco; (*dark*) sombrio; (*indistinct*) vago; [!] (*stupid*) burro [!] ● *vt/i* (*pt* **dimmed**) ‹*light*› baixar. **~ly** *adv* (*shine*) fracamente; (*remember*) vagamente

dime /daɪm/ *n Amer* moeda *f* de dez centavos

dimension /daɪ'menʃn/ *n* dimensão *f*

diminish /dɪ'mɪnɪʃ/ *vt/i* diminuir

diminutive /dɪ'mɪnjʊtɪv/ *a* diminuto ● *n* diminutivo *m*

dimple /'dɪmpl/ *n* covinha *f*

din /dɪn/ *n* barulheira *f*, (*P*) chinfrim *m*

dine /daɪn/ *vi* jantar. **~r** /-ə(r)/ *n* (*person*) comensal *m*; *Rail* vagão-restaurante *m*; *Amer* (*restaurant*) lanchonete *f*

dinghy /'dɪŋgɪ/ *n* (*pl* **-ghies**) bote *m*; (*inflatable*) bote *m* de borracha, (*P*) barco *m* de borracha

dingy /'dɪndʒɪ/ *a* (**-ier**, **-iest**) com ar sujo, esquálido

dining room /'daɪnɪŋru:m/ *n* sala *f* de jantar

dinner /'dɪnə(r)/ *n* jantar *m*; (*lunch*) almoço *m*. **~ jacket** *n* smoking *m*

dinosaur /'daɪnəsɔ:(r)/ *n* dinossauro *m*

dip /dɪp/ *vt/i* (*pt* **dipped**) mergulhar; (*lower*) baixar ● *n* mergulho *m*; (*bathe*) banho *m* rápido, mergulho *m*; (*slope*) descida *f*; *Culin* molho *m*; **~ into** ‹*book*› folhear; **~ one's headlights** baixar para médios

diploma /dɪ'pləʊmə/ *n* diploma *m*

diplomacy /dɪ'pləʊməsɪ/ *n* diplomacia *f*

diplomat /'dɪpləmæt/ *n* diplomata *mf*. **~ic** /-'mætɪk/ *a* diplomático

dire /daɪə(r)/ *a* (**-er**, **-est**) terrível; ‹*need, poverty*› extremo

direct /dɪ'rekt/ *a* direto ● *adv* diretamente ● *vt* dirigir; **~ sb to** indicar a alguém o caminho para

direction /dɪ'rekʃn/ *n* direção *f*, sentido *m*; **~s** instruções *fpl*; **~s for use** modo *m* de emprego

directly /dɪ'rektlɪ/ *adv* diretamente; (*at once*) imediatamente, logo

director /dɪ'rektə(r)/ *n* diretor *m*

directory /dɪ'rektərɪ/ *n* **(telephone) ~** lista *f* telefônica *or* (*P*) telefónica

dirt /dɜ:t/ *n* sujeira, sujidade *f*; **~ cheap** [!] baratíssimo

dirty /'dɜ:tɪ/ *a* (**-ier**, **-iest**) sujo; ‹*word*› obsceno ● *vt/i* sujar(-se); **~ trick** golpe *m* baixo, (*P*) boa partida *f*

disability /dɪsə'bɪlətɪ/ *n* deficiência *f*

disable /dɪs'eɪbl/ *vt* incapacitar. **~d** *a* inválido, deficiente

disadvantage /dɪsəd'vɑːntɪdʒ/ *n* desvantagem *f*

disagree /dɪsə'griː/ *vi* discordar (**with** de); **~ with** ‹*food, climate*› não fazer bem. **~ment** *n* desacordo *m*; (*quarrel*) desentendimento *m*

disagreeable /dɪsə'griːəbl/ *a* desagradável

disappear /dɪsə'pɪə(r)/ *vi* desaparecer. **~ance** *n* desaparecimento *m*

disappoint /dɪsə'pɔɪnt/ *vt* desapontar, decepcionar. **~ment** *n* desapontamento *m*, decepção *f*

disapprov|e /dɪsə'pruːv/ *vi* **~e (of)** desaprovar. **~al** *n* desaprovação *f*

disarm /dɪ'sɑːm/ *vt/i* desarmar. **~ament** *n* desarmamento *m*

disast|er /dɪ'zɑːstə(r)/ *n* desastre *m*. **~rous** *a* desastroso

disband /dɪs'bænd/ *vt/i* debandar; ‹*troops*› dispersar

disbelief /dɪsbɪ'liːf/ *n* incredulidade *f*

disc /dɪsk/ *n* disco *m*; **~ jockey** disc(o) jockey *m*

discard /dɪs'kɑːd/ *vt* pôr de lado, descartar(-se) de; ‹*old clothes etc*› desfazer-se de

discern /dɪ'sɜːn/ *vt* discernir. **~ible** *a* perceptível. **~ing** *a* perspicaz. **~ment** *n* discernimento *m*, perspicácia *f*

discharge[1] /dɪs'tʃɑːdʒ/ *vt* descarregar; (*dismiss*) despedir, mandar embora; ‹*duty*› cumprir; ‹*liquid*› vazar, (*P*) deitar; ‹*patient*› dar alta a; ‹*prisoner*› absolver, pôr em liberdade; ‹*pus*› purgar, (*P*) deitar

discharge[2] /'dɪstʃɑːdʒ/ *n* descarga *f*; (*dismissal*) despedimento *m*; (*of patient*) alta *f*; (*of prisoner*) absolvição *f*; *Med* secreção *f*

disciple /dɪ'saɪpl/ *n* discípulo *m*

disciplin|e /'dɪsɪplɪn/ *n* disciplina *f* ● *vt* disciplinar; (*punish*) castigar. **~ary** *a* disciplinar

disclaim /dɪs'kleɪm/ *vt Jur* repudiar; (*deny*) negar. **~er** *n* desmentido *m*

disclos|e /dɪs'kləʊz/ *vt* revelar. **~ure** /-ʒə(r)/ *n* revelação *f*

disco /'dɪskəʊ/ *n* (*pl* **-os**) 🅸 discoteca *f*

discolour /dɪs'kʌlə(r)/ *vt/i* descolorir(-se); (*in sunlight*) desbotar(-se)

discomfort /dɪs'kʌmfət/ *n* mal-estar *m*; (*lack of comfort*) desconforto *m*

disconcert /dɪskən'sɜːt/ *vt* desconcertar. **~ing** *a* desconcertante

disconnect /dɪskə'nekt/ *vt* desligar

discontent /dɪskən'tent/ *n* descontentamento *m*. **~ed** *a* descontente

discontinue /dɪskən'tɪnjuː/ *vt* descontinuar, suspender

discord /'dɪskɔːd/ *n* discórdia *f*

discount[1] /'dɪskaʊnt/ *n* desconto *m*

discount[2] /dɪs'kaʊnt/ *vt* descontar; (*disregard*) dar o desconto a

discourage /dɪs'kʌrɪdʒ/ *vt* desencorajar

discourte|ous /dɪs'kɜːtɪəs/ *a* indelicado

discover /dɪs'kʌvə(r)/ *vt* descobrir. **~y** *n* descoberta *f*; (*of island etc*) descobrimento *m*

discredit /dɪs'kredɪt/ *vt* (*pt* **discredited**) desacreditar ● *n* descrédito *m*

discreet /dɪ'skriːt/ *a* discreto

discrepancy /dɪ'skrepənsɪ/ *n* discrepância *f*

discretion /dɪ'skreʃn/ *n* discrição *f*; (*prudence*) prudência *f*

discriminat|e /dɪs'krɪmɪneɪt/ *vt/i* discriminar; **~e against** tomar partido contra, fazer discriminação contra. **~ing** *a* discriminador; (*having good taste*) com discernimento. **~ion** /-'neɪʃn/ *n* discernimento *m*; (*bias*) discriminação *f*

discus /'dɪskəs/ *n* disco *m*

discuss /dɪ'skʌs/ *vt* discutir. **~ion** /-ʃn/ *n* discussão *f*

disdain /dɪs'deɪn/ *n* desdém *m* ● *vt* desdenhar. **~ful** *a* desdenhoso

disease /dɪ'ziːz/ *n* doença *f*. **~d** *a* ‹*plant*› atacado por doença; ‹*person, animal*› doente

disembark /dɪsɪm'bɑːk/ *vt/i* desembarcar

disenchant /dɪsɪn'tʃɑːnt/ *vt* desencantar. **~ment** *n* desencantamento *m*

disengage /dɪsɪn'geɪdʒ/ *vt* desprender, soltar; *Mech* desengatar

disentangle /dɪsɪn'tæŋgl/ *vt* desembaraçar, desenredar

disfigure /dɪs'fɪgə(r)/ *vt* desfigurar

disgrace /dɪs'greɪs/ *n* vergonha *f*; (*disfavour*) desgraça *f* ● *vt* desonrar. **~ful** *a* vergonhoso

disgruntled /dɪs'grʌntld/ *a* descontente

d

disguise /dɪs'gaɪz/ *vt* disfarçar ● *n* disfarce *m*; **in ~** disfarçado

disgust /dɪs'gʌst/ *n* repugnância *f* ● *vt* repugnar. **~ing** *a* repugnante

dish /dɪʃ/ *n* prato *m* ● *vt* **~ out** [!] distribuir; **~ up** servir; **the ~es** (*crockery*) a louça *f*

d

dishcloth /'dɪʃklɒθ/ *n* pano *m* de prato

dishearten /dɪs'hɑ:tn/ *vt* desencorajar, desalentar

dishonest /dɪs'ɒnɪst/ *a* desonesto. **~y** *n* desonestidade *f*

dishonour /dɪs'ɒnə(r)/ *n* desonra *f* ● *vt* desonrar. **~able** *a* desonroso

dishwasher /'dɪʃwɒʃə(r)/ *n* lavadora *f* de pratos, (*P*) máquina *f* de lavar a louça

disillusion /dɪsɪ'lu:ʒn/ *vt* desiludir. **~ment** *n* desilusão *f*

disinfect /dɪsɪn'fekt/ *vt* desinfetar, (*P*) desinfectar. **~ant** *n* desinfetante *m*, (*P*) desinfectante *m*

disinherit /dɪsɪn'herɪt/ *vt* deserdar

disintegrate /dɪs'ɪntɪgreɪt/ *vt/i* desintegrar(-se)

disinterested /dɪs'ɪntrəstɪd/ *a* desinteressado

disjointed /dɪs'dʒɔɪntɪd/ *a* ‹*talk*› descosido, desconexo

disk /dɪsk/ *n Comput* disco *m Amer* ▶ DISC; **~ drive** unidade *f* de disco

dislike /dɪs'laɪk/ *n* aversão *f*, antipatia *f* ● *vt* não gostar de, antipatizar com

dislocat|e /'dɪsləkeɪt/ *vt* ‹*limb*› deslocar

dislodge /dɪs'lɒdʒ/ *vt* desalojar

disloyal /dɪs'lɔɪəl/ *a* desleal. **~ty** *n* deslealdade *f*

dismal /'dɪzməl/ *a* tristonho

dismantle /dɪs'mæntl/ *vt* desmantelar

dismay /dɪs'meɪ/ *n* consternação *f* ● *vt* consternar

dismiss /dɪs'mɪs/ *vt* despedir; (*from mind*) afastar, pôr de lado. **~al** *n* despedimento *m*

dismount /dɪs'maʊnt/ *vi* desmontar

disobedien|t /dɪsə'bi:dɪənt/ *a* desobediente. **~ce** *n* desobediência *f*

disobey /dɪsə'beɪ/ *vt/i* desobedecer (a)

disorder /dɪs'ɔ:də(r)/ *n* desordem *f*; *Med* perturbações *fpl*, disfunção *f*. **~ly** *a* desordenado; (*riotous*) desordeiro

disown /dɪs'əʊn/ *vt* repudiar

disparaging /dɪ'spærɪdʒɪŋ/ *a* depreciativo

dispatch /dɪ'spætʃ/ *vt* despachar ● *n* despacho *m*

dispel /dɪs'pel/ *vt* (*pt* **dispelled**) dissipar

dispensary /dɪ'spensərɪ/ *n* dispensário *m*, farmácia *f*

dispense /dɪ'spens/ *vt* dispensar ● *vi* **~ with** dispensar, passar sem. **~r** /-ə(r)/ *n* (*container*) distribuidor *m*

dispers|e /dɪ'spɜ:s/ *vt/i* dispersar(-se)

dispirited /dɪ'spɪrɪtɪd/ *a* desanimado

display /dɪ'spleɪ/ *vt* exibir, mostrar; ‹*feeling*› manifestar, dar mostras de ● *n* exposição *f*; (*of computer*) apresentação *f* visual; *Comm* objetos *mpl* expostos

displeas|e /dɪs'pli:z/ *vt* desagradar a; **~ed with** descontente com. **~ure** /-'pleʒə(r)/ *n* desagrado *m*

disposable /dɪ'spəʊzəbl/ *a* descartável

dispos|e /dɪ'spəʊz/ *vt* dispor ● *vi* **~e of** desfazer-se de; **well ~ed towards** bem disposto para com. **~al** *n* (*of waste*) eliminação *f*; **at sb's ~al** à disposição de alguém

disposition /dɪspə'zɪʃn/ *n* disposição *f*; (*character*) índole *f*

disproportionate /dɪsprə'pɔ:ʃənət/ *a* desproporcionado

disprove /dɪs'pru:v/ *vt* refutar

dispute /dɪ'spju:t/ *vt* contestar; (*fight for, quarrel*) disputar ● *n* disputa *f*; (*industrial*) *Pol* conflito *m*; **in ~** em questão

disqualif|y /dɪs'kwɒlɪfaɪ/ *vt* tornar inapto; *Sport* desqualificar; **~y from driving** apreender a carteira de motorista, (*P*) a carta de conduçâo. **~ication** /-ɪ'keɪʃn/ *n* desqualificação *f*

disregard /dɪsrɪ'gɑ:d/ *vt* não fazer caso de ● *n* indiferença *f* (**for** por)

disrepair /dɪsrɪ'peə(r)/ *n* mau estado *m*, abandono *m*, degradação *f*

disreputable /dɪs'repjʊtəbl/ *a* pouco recomendável; (*in appearance*) com mau aspecto; (*in reputation*) vergonhoso, de má fama

disrepute /dɪsrɪ'pju:t/ *n* descrédito *m*

disrespect /dɪsrɪ'spekt/ *n* falta *f* de respeito. **~ful** *a* desrespeitoso, irreverente

disrupt /dɪs'rʌpt/ *vt* perturbar; ‹*plans*› transtornar; (*break up*) dividir. **~ion** /-ʃn/ *n* perturbação *f*. **~ive** *a* perturbador

dissatisf|ied /dɪ'sætɪsfaɪd/ *a* descontente. **~action** /dɪsætɪs'fækʃn/ *n* descontentamento *m*

dissect /dɪ'sekt/ *vt* dissecar. **~ion** /-ʃn/ *n* dissecação *f*
dissent /dɪ'sent/ *vi* dissentir, discordar ● *n* dissensão *f*, desacordo *m*
dissertation /dɪsə'teɪʃn/ *n* dissertação *f*
disservice /dɪs'sɜːvɪs/ *n* **do sb a ~** prejudicar alguém
dissident /'dɪsɪdənt/ *a & n* dissidente *mf*
dissimilar /dɪ'sɪmɪlə(r)/ *a* diferente
dissociate /dɪ'səʊʃɪeɪt/ *vt* dissociar, desassociar
dissolve /dɪ'zɒlv/ *vt/i* dissolver(-se)
dissuade /dɪ'sweɪd/ *vt* dissuadir
distance /'dɪstəns/ *n* distância *f*; **from a ~** de longe; **in the ~** ao longe, à distância
distant /'dɪstənt/ *a* distante; ‹*relative*› afastado
distil /dɪ'stɪl/ *vt* (*pt* **distilled**) destilar
distillery /dɪ'stɪlərɪ/ *n* destilaria *f*
distinct /dɪ'stɪŋkt/ *a* distinto; (*marked*) claro, nítido. **~ion** /-ʃn/ *n* distinção *f*. **~ive** *a* distintivo, característico. **~ly** *adv* distintamente; (*markedly*) claramente
distinguish /dɪ'stɪŋgwɪʃ/ *vt/i* distinguir. **~ed** *a* distinto
distort /dɪ'stɔːt/ *vt* distorcer; (*misrepresent*) deturpar. **~ion** /-ʃn/ *n* distorção *f*; (*misrepresentation*) deturpação *f*
distract /dɪ'strækt/ *vt* distrair. **~ed** *a* (*distraught*) desesperado, fora de si. **~ing** *a* enlouquecedor. **~ion** /-ʃn/ *n* distração *f*
distraught /dɪ'strɔːt/ *a* desesperado, fora de si
distress /dɪ'stres/ *n* (*physical*) dor *f*; (*anguish*) aflição *f*; (*poverty*) miséria *f*; (*danger*) perigo *m* ● *vt* afligir. **~ing** *a* aflitivo, doloroso
distribut|e /dɪ'strɪbjuːt/ *vt* distribuir. **~ion** /-'bjuːʃn/ *n* distribuição *f*. **~or** *n* distribuidor *m*
district /'dɪstrɪkt/ *n* região *f*; (*of town*) zona *f*
distrust /dɪs'trʌst/ *n* desconfiança *f* ● *vt* desconfiar de
disturb /dɪ'stɜːb/ *vt* perturbar; (*move*) desarrumar; (*bother*) incomodar. **~ance** *n* (*noise, disorder*) distúrbio *m*. **~ed** *a* perturbado. **~ing** *a* perturbador
disused /dɪs'juːzd/ *a* fora de uso, desusado, em desuso
ditch /dɪtʃ/ *n* fosso *m* ● *vt* ☒ (*abandon*) abandonar; largar
dither /'dɪðə(r)/ *vi* hesitar
ditto /'dɪtəʊ/ *adv* idem
div|e /daɪv/ *vi* mergulhar; (*rush*) precipitar-se ● *n* mergulho *m*; (*of plane*) picada *f*; ☒ (*place*) espelunca *f*. **~er** *n* mergulhador *m*. **~ing board** *n* prancha *f* de saltos
diverge /daɪ'vɜːdʒ/ *vi* divergir
diverse /daɪ'vɜːs/ *a* diverso
diversify /daɪ'vɜːsɪfaɪ/ *vt* diversificar
diversity /daɪ'vɜːsətɪ/ *n* diversidade *f*
diver|t /daɪ'vɜːt/ *vt* desviar; (*entertain*) divertir. **~sion** /-ʃn/ *n* diversão *f*; (*traffic*) desvio *m*
divide /dɪ'vaɪd/ *vt/i* dividir(-se); **~ in two** (*branch, river, road*) bifurcar-se
dividend /'dɪvɪdend/ *n* dividendo *m*
divine /dɪ'vaɪn/ *a* divino
divinity /dɪ'vɪnətɪ/ *n* divindade *f*; *Theology* teologia *f*
division /dɪ'vɪʒn/ *n* divisão *f*
divorce /dɪ'vɔːs/ *n* divórcio *m* ● *vt/i* divorciar(-se) de. **~d** *a* divorciado
divorcee /dɪvɔː'siː/ *n* divorciado *m*
divulge /daɪ'vʌldʒ/ *vt* divulgar
DIY *abbr* ▶ DO-IT-YOURSELF
dizz|y /'dɪzɪ/ *a* (**-ier, -iest**) tonto; **be** or **feel ~y** ter tonturas, sentir-se tonto. **~iness** *n* tontura *f*, vertigem *f*

do /duː: *unstressed* də/ (*pres* **do**, *3rd person sing.* **does**, *pt* **did**, *pp* **done**) ● *vt*

····➤ (*carry out*) fazer; **she's ~ing her homework** ela está fazendo os deveres; **what are you ~ing?** o que você está fazendo?; **~ something!** faça alguma coisa!; **~ the washing-up** lavar a louça; **~ the cleaning** fazer a faxina

····➤ (*as job*) **what does she ~?** o que ela faz?

····➤ (*arrange*) **~ one's hair** pentear-se; **~ one's make-up** maquiar-se

····➤ (*cheat*) enganar; **this isn't a genuine antique, you've been done** esta antiguidade é falsa, você foi enganado

● *vi*

····➤ (*get on*) ir; **how are they ~ing at school?** como eles vão na escola?; **how are you ~ing?** como vai?

····➤ (*with as or adverb*) fazer; **~ as they ~** faça como eles; **he can ~ as**

d

he likes ele pode fazer do jeito que gosta; **you did well** você fez bem

····➤ (*be suitable*) servir; **this will ~** isso serve

····➤ (*be sufficient*) bastar; **one bottle of water will ~** uma garrafa de água basta; **will £20 ~?** £20 chegam?

····➤ (*in phrases*) **that does it!** chega!; **well done!** muito bem!

● *v aux*

····➤ (*in questions and negatives*) **~ you see?** vê?; **I ~ not smoke** não fumo; **Mary didn't phone** a Mary não telefonou; **Don't ~ that!** não faça isso!

····➤ (*in tag questions*) **you like chocolate, don't you?** você gosta de chocolate, não gosta?; **he lives in London, doesn't he?** ele mora em Londres, não mora?

····➤ (*as verb substitute*) **you speak Portuguese better than I ~** você fala português melhor do que eu

····➤ (*in short answers*) **does he work there? yes, he does/no, he doesn't** ele trabalha ali? sim, trabalha/não, não trabalha

····➤ (*for emphasis*) **I ~ like her** gosto mesmo dela

● *n* (*pl* **dos**, *or* **do's**)

····➤ festa *f*; *npl* **dos and don'ts** regras a seguir

□ **~ away with** ● *vt* eliminar. **~ in** ● *vt* (*kill* ⊠) matar, liquidar. **~ up** ● *vt* (*fasten*) ‹*shoelaces*› amarrar; ‹*buttons, coat, zip*› fechar; ‹*house*› renovar. **~ without** ● *vt* passar sem. **~ with:** ● *vt* (*need*) **I could ~ with a cup of tea** me cairia bem uma xícara de chá; **it could ~ with a wash** precisa de uma lavagem; (*connected with*) **it's to ~ with** tem a ver com; **it's nothing to ~ with** não tem nada a ver com

docile /ˈdəʊsaɪl/ *a* dócil

dock[1] /dɒk/ *n* doca *f* ● *vt* levar à doca ● *vi* entrar na doca. **~er** *n* estivador *m*

dock[2] /dɒk/ *n Jur* banco *m* dos réus

dockyard /ˈdɒkjɑːd/ *n* estaleiro *m*

doctor /ˈdɒktə(r)/ *n* médico *m*, doutor *m*; *Univ* doutor *m* ● *vt* (*cat*) capar; *fig* adulterar; falsificar

doctorate /ˈdɒktərət/ *n* doutorado *m*, (*P*) doutoramento *m*

doctrine /ˈdɒktrɪn/ *n* doutrina *f*

document /ˈdɒkjʊmənt/ *n* documento *m* ● *vt* documentar. **~ary** /-ˈmentrɪ/ *a* documental ● *n* documentário *m*

dodge /dɒdʒ/ *vt/i* esquivar(-se), furtar(-se) a ● *n* ⊡ truque *m*

dodgy /ˈdɒdʒɪ/ *a* (**-ier, -iest**) ⊡ delicado; difícil; embaraçoso; arriscado

does /dʌz/ ▶ DO

doesn't /ˈdʌznt/ (= **does not**) ▶ DO

dog /dɒg/ *n* cão *m* ● *vt* (*pt* **dogged**) ir no encalço de, perseguir. **~-eared** *a* com os cantos dobrados

dogged /ˈdɒgɪd/ *a* obstinado, persistente

dogma /ˈdɒgmə/ *n* dogma *m*. **~tic** /-ˈmætɪk/ *a* dogmático

dogsbody /ˈdɒgzbɒdɪ/ *n* ⊡ pau-para-toda-obra *m* ⊡; factótum *m*

do-it-yourself *a* faça-você-mesmo

doldrums /ˈdɒldrəmz/ *npl* **be in the ~** estar com a neura; ‹*business*› estar parado

dole /dəʊl/ *vt* **~ out** distribuir ● *n* ⊡ auxílio *m* de desemprego; **on the ~** ⊡ desempregado (titular de auxílio)

doll /dɒl/ *n* boneca *f* ● *vt/i* **~ up** ⊡ embonecar(-se)

dollar /ˈdɒlə(r)/ *n* dólar *m*

dolphin /ˈdɒlfɪn/ *n* golfinho *m*

domain /dəʊˈmeɪn/ *n* domínio *m*

dome /dəʊm/ *n* cúpula *f*; (*vault*) abóbada *f*

domestic /dəˈmestɪk/ *a* (*of home, animal, flights*) doméstico; ‹*trade*› interno; ‹*news*› nacional. **~ated** /-keɪtɪd/ *a* ‹*animal*› domesticado; ‹*person*› que gosta de trabalhos caseiros

dominant /ˈdɒmɪnənt/ *a* dominante

dominat|e /ˈdɒmɪneɪt/ *vt/i* dominar. **~ion** /-ˈneɪʃn/ *n* dominação *f*, domínio *m*

domineer /dɒmɪˈnɪə(r)/ *vi* **~ over** mandar (em), ser autocrático (para com). **~ing** *a* mandão, autocrático

domino /ˈdɒmɪnəʊ/ *n* (*pl* **-oes**) dominó *m*

donat|e /dəʊˈneɪt/ *vt* fazer doação de, doar, dar. **~ion** /-ʃn/ *n* donativo *m*

done /dʌn/ ▶ DO

donkey /ˈdɒŋkɪ/ *n* burro *m*

donor /ˈdəʊnə(r)/ *n* (*of blood*) doador *m*, (*P*) dador *m*

don't /dəʊnt/ (= **do not**) ▶ DO

doodle /ˈduːdl/ *vi* rabiscar

doom /duːm/ *n* ruína *f*; (*fate*) destino *m*; **be ~ed to** ser/estar condenado a; **~ed (to failure)** condenado ao fracasso

door /dɔː(r)/ *n* porta *f*

doorman /'dɔːmən/ *n* (*pl* **-men**) porteiro *m*

doormat /'dɔːmæt/ *n* capacho *m*

doorstep /'dɔːstep/ *n* degrau *m* da porta

doorway /'dɔːweɪ/ *n* vão *m* da porta, (*P*) entrada *f*

dope /dəʊp/ *n* [!] droga *f*; [x] (*idiot*) imbecil *mf* ● *vt* dopar, drogar

dormant /'dɔːmənt/ *a* dormente; (*inactive*) inativo; (*latent*) latente

dormitory /'dɔːmɪtrɪ/ *n* dormitório *m*; *Amer Univ* residência *f*

dos|e /dəʊs/ *n* dose *f* ● *vt* medicar. **~age** *n* dosagem *f*; (*on label*) posologia *f*

dot /dɒt/ *n* ponto *m*; **on the ~** no momento preciso ● *vt* **be ~ted with** estar pejado de; **~ted line** linha *f* pontilhada

dot-com /dɒt'kɒm/ *n* empresa *f* dot. com

dote /dəʊt/ *vi* **~ on** ser louco por

double /'dʌbl/ *a* duplo; ‹*room, bed*› de casal; **~ chin** papada *f*; **~ Dutch** algaraviada *f*, fala *f* incompreensível; **~ glazing** (janela *f* de) vidro *m* duplo ● *adv* duas vezes mais ● *n* dobro *m*; **~s** *Tennis* dupla *f*, (*P*) pares *mpl*; **at the ~** a passo acelerado ● *vt/i* dobrar, duplicar; (*fold*) dobrar em dois. **~ bass** *n* contrabaixo *m*; **~-cross** *vt* enganar; **~-decker** *n* ônibus *m*, (*P*) autocarro *m* de dois andares. **doubly** *adv* duplamente

doubt /daʊt/ *n* dúvida *f* ● *vt* duvidar de; **~ if** or **that** duvidar que. **~ful** *a* duvidoso; (*hesitant*) que tem dúvidas. **~less** *adv* sem dúvida, indubitavelmente

dough /dəʊ/ *n* massa *f*

doughnut /'dəʊnʌt/ *n* sonho *m*, (*P*) bola *f* de Berlim

dove /dʌv/ *n* pomba *f*

dowdy /'daʊdɪ/ *a* (**-ier, -iest**) sem graça, sem gosto

down[1] /daʊn/ *n* (*feathers, hair*) penugem *f*

down[2] /daʊn/ *adv* (*to lower place*) abaixo, para baixo; (*in lower place*) em baixo; **be ~** ‹*level, price*› descer; ‹*sun*› estar posto; **come** or **go ~** descer; **~ under** na Austrália; **~ with** abaixo ● *prep* por (+*n*) (*n*+) abaixo; **~ the hill/street** *etc* pelo monte/pela rua *etc* abaixo ● *vt* [!] (*knock down*) jogar *or* (*P*) atirar abaixo; [!] (*drink*) esvaziar. **~-and-out** *n* marginal *m*; **~hearted** *a* desencorajado, desanimado; **~-to-earth** *a* terra-a-terra *invar*

downcast /'daʊnkɑːst/ *a* abatido, deprimido, desmoralizado

downfall /daʊn'fɔːl/ *n* queda *f*, ruína *f*

downhill /daʊn'hɪl/ *adv* **go ~** descer; *fig* ir abaixo ● *a* /'daʊnhɪl/ *a* descer, descendente

> **i**
>
> **Downing Street** É uma rua no bairro londrino de Westminster. O número 10 é a residência oficial do Primeiro-Ministro, e o número 11, a do *Chancellor of the Exchequer* (Ministro da Economia e Finanças). Os jornalistas costumam utilizar as expressões *Downing Street* ou *Number 10* para se referir ao Primeiro-Ministro e ao Governo.

download /daʊn'ləʊd/ *vt Comput* baixar

downpour /'daʊnpɔː(r)/ *n* aguaceiro *m* forte, (*P*) chuvada *f*

downright /'daʊnraɪt/ *a* franco; (*utter*) autêntico, verdadeiro ● *adv* positivamente

downstairs /daʊn'steəz/ *adv* (*at/to*) em/para baixo, no/para o andar de baixo ● /'daʊnsteəz/ *a* ‹*flat etc*› de baixo, do andar de baixo

downstream /'daʊnstriːm/ *adv* rio abaixo

downtown /'daʊntaʊn/ *a & adv* (de, em, para) o centro da cidade; **~ Boston** o centro de Boston

downtrodden /'daʊntrɒdn/ *a* espezinhado, oprimido

downward /'daʊnwəd/ *a* descendente. **~(s)** *adv* para baixo

dowry /'daʊərɪ/ *n* dote *m*

doze /dəʊz/ *vi* dormitar; **~ off** cochilar ● *n* soneca *f*, cochilo *m*

dozen /'dʌzn/ *n* dúzia *f*; **~s of** [!] dezenas de, dúzias de

Dr *abbr* (= **Doctor**) Dr

drab /dræb/ *a* insípido; (*of colour*) morto, apagado

draft[1] /drɑːft/ *n* rascunho *m*; *Comm* ordem *f* de pagamento ● *vt* fazer o rascunho de; (*draw up*) redigir; **the ~** *Amer Mil* recrutamento *m*

draft[2] /drɑːft/ *n Amer* = DRAUGHT

drag /dræg/ *vt/i* (*pt* **dragged**) arrastar(-se); ‹*river*› dragar; (*pull away*) arrancar ● *n* [!] (*task*) chatice *f* ⊠; [!] (*person*) estorvo *m*; ⊠ (*clothes*) travesti *m*

dragon /ˈdrægən/ *n* dragão *m*

dragonfly /ˈdrægənflaɪ/ *n* libélula *f*

drain /dreɪn/ *vt* drenar; ‹*vegetables*› escorrer; ‹*glass, tank*› esvaziar; (*use up*) esgotar ● *vi* ~ **(off)** escoar-se ● *n* cano *m*; **~(pipe)** cano *m* de esgoto. **~s** *npl* (*sewers*) esgotos *mpl*. **~age** *n* drenagem *f*. **~ing board** *n* escorredouro *m*

drama /ˈdrɑːmə/ *n* arte *f* dramática; (*play, event*) drama *m*. **~tic** /drəˈmætɪk/ *a* dramático. **~tist** /ˈdræmətɪst/ *n* dramaturgo *m*. **~tize** /ˈdræmətaɪz/ *vt* dramatizar

drank /dræŋk/ ▶ DRINK

drape /dreɪp/ *vt* ~ **round/over** dispor (tecido) em pregas à volta de or sobre. **~s** *npl Amer* cortinas *fpl*

drastic /ˈdræstɪk/ *a* drástico, violento

draught /drɑːft/ *n* corrente *f* de ar; *Naut* calado *m*; **~s** (*game*) (jogo *m* das) damas *fpl*; ~ **beer** chope *m*, (*P*) cerveja à caneca, imperial *f* [!]. **~y** *a* com correntes de ar, ventoso

draw /drɔː/ *vt* (*pt* **drew**, *pp* **drawn**) puxar; (*attract*) atrair; ‹*picture*› desenhar; (*in lottery*) tirar à sorte; ‹*line*› traçar; (*open curtains*) abrir; (*close curtains*) fechar ● *vi* desenhar; *Sport* empatar; (*come*) vir ● *n Sport* empate *m*; (*lottery*) sorteio *m*; ~ **back** recuar; ~ **in** (*of days*) diminuir; ~ **near** aproximar-se; ~ **out** ‹*money*› levantar; ~ **up** deter-se, parar; ‹*document*› redigir; ‹*chair*› aproximar, chegar

drawback /ˈdrɔːbæk/ *n* inconveniente *m*, desvantagem *f*

drawer /drɔː(r)/ *n* gaveta *f*

drawing /ˈdrɔːɪŋ/ *n* desenho *m*. ~ **board** *n* prancheta *f*; ~ **pin** *n* percevejo *m*

drawl /drɔːl/ *n* fala *f* arrastada

drawn /drɔːn/ ▶ DRAW

dread /dred/ *n* terror *m* ● *vt* temer

dreadful /ˈdredfl/ *a* medonho, terrível

dream /driːm/ *n* sonho *m* ● *vt/i* (*pt* **dreamed**, *or* **dreamt**) sonhar (**of** com) ● *a* (*ideal*) dos seus sonhos; ~ **up** imaginar. **~er** *n* sonhador *m*. **~y** *a* sonhador; ‹*music*› romântico

dreary /ˈdrɪərɪ/ *a* (**-ier**, **-iest**) tristonho; (*boring*) aborrecido

dredge /dredʒ/ *n* draga *f* ● *vt/i* dragar. **~r** /-ə(r)/ *n* draga *f*; (*for sugar*) polvilhador *m*

dregs /dregz/ *npl* depósito *m*, sedimento *m*; *fig* escória *f*

drench /drentʃ/ *vt* encharcar

dress /dres/ *n* vestido *m*; (*clothing*) roupa *f* ● *vt/i* vestir(-se); ‹*food*› temperar; ‹*wound*› fazer curativo, (*P*) pensar, (*P*) tratar; ~ **rehearsal** ensaio *m* geral; ~ **up as** fantasiar-se de; **get ~ed** vestir-se

dresser /ˈdresə(r)/ *n* (*furniture*) guarda-louça *m*

dressing /ˈdresɪŋ/ *n* (*sauce*) tempero *m*; (*bandage*) curativo *m*, (*P*) penso *m*. ~ **gown** *n* roupão *m*; ~ **room** *n Sport* vestiário *m*; *Theat* camarim *m*; **~-table** *n* toucador *m*

dressmak|er /ˈdresmeɪkə(r)/ *n* costureira *f*, modista *f*. **~ing** *n* costura *f*

dressy /ˈdresɪ/ *a* (**-ier**, **-iest**) elegante, chique *invar*

drew /druː/ ▶ DRAW

dribble /ˈdrɪbl/ *vi* pingar; ‹*person*› babar-se; ‹*football*› driblar

dried /draɪd/ *a* ‹*fruit etc*› seco

drier /ˈdraɪə(r)/ *n* secador *m*

drift /drɪft/ *vi* ir à deriva; (*pile up*) amontoar-se ● *n* força *f* da corrente; (*pile*) monte *m*; (*of events*) rumo *m*; (*meaning*) sentido *m*. **~er** *n* pessoa *f* sem rumo

drill /drɪl/ *n* (*tool*) broca *f*; (*training*) exercício *m*, treino *m*; (*routine procedure*) exercícios *mpl* ● *vt* furar, perfurar; (*train*) treinar; ‹*tooth*› abrir ● *vi* treinar-se

drink /drɪŋk/ *vt/i* (*pt* **drank**, *pp* **drunk**) beber ● *n* bebida *f*; **a ~ of water** um copo de água; **~ing water** água *f* potável. **~able** *a* potável; (*palatable*) bebível. **~er** *n* bebedor *m*

drip /drɪp/ *vi* (*pt* **dripped**) pingar ● *n* pingar *m*; ⊠ (*person*) banana *mf* [!]. **~-dry** *vt* deixar escorrer ● *a* que não precisa passar

drive /draɪv/ *vt* (*pt* **drove**, *pp* **driven** /ˈdrɪvn/) empurrar, impelir, levar; ‹*car, animal*› dirigir, conduzir, (*P*) guiar; ‹*machine*› acionar; ~ **at** chegar a; ~ **in** (*force in*) enterrar; ~ **mad** (fazer) enlouquecer, pôr fora de si ● *vi* dirigir, conduzir, (*P*) guiar; ~ **away** ‹*car*› partir ● *n* passeio *m* de carro; (*private road*) entrada *f* para veículos; *fig* energia *f*; *Psych* drive *m*, compulsão *f*, impulso *m*; (*campaign*) campanha *f*. **~-in** *n* ‹*bank, cinema etc*› banco *m*, cinema *etc* em que se é atendido no carro, drive-in *m*

drivel /'drɪvl/ *n* baboseira *f*, bobagem *f*

driver /'draɪvə(r)/ *n* condutor *m*; (*of taxi, bus*) chofer *m*, motorista *mf*

driving /'draɪvɪŋ/ *n* condução *f*. **~ licence** *n* carteira *f* de motorista, (*P*) carta *f* de condução; **~ school** *n* auto-escola *f*, (*P*) escola *f* de condução; **~ test** *n* exame *m* de motorista *or* (*P*) de condução

drizzle /'drɪzl/ *n* chuvisco *m* ● *vi* chuviscar

drone /drəʊn/ *n* zumbido *m*; (*male bee*) zangão *m* ● *vi* zumbir; *fig* falar monotonamente

drool /dru:l/ *vi* babar(-se)

droop /dru:p/ *vi* pender, curvar-se

drop /drɒp/ *n* gota *f*; (*fall*) queda *f*; (*distance*) altura *f* de queda ● *vt/i* (*pt* **dropped**) (deixar) cair; (*fall, lower*) baixar; **~ (off)** (*person from car*) deixar, largar; **~ a line** escrever duas linhas (**to** a); **~ in** passar por (**on** em casa de); **~ off** (*doze*) adormecer; **~ out** (*withdraw*) retirar-se; (*of student*) abandonar. **~out** *n* marginal *mf*, marginalizado *m*

droppings /'drɒpɪŋz/ *npl* excrementos *mpl* de animal; (*of birds*) cocô, (*P*) cocó *m* [!]; porcaria *f* [!]

drought /draʊt/ *n* seca *f*

drove /drəʊv/ ▶ DRIVE

drown /draʊn/ *vt/i* afogar(-se)

drowsy /'draʊzɪ/ *a* sonolento; **be** or **feel ~** ter vontade de dormir

drudge /drʌdʒ/ *n* mouro *m* de trabalho. **~ry** /-ərɪ/ *n* trabalho *m* penoso e monótono, estafa *f*

drug /drʌg/ *n* droga *f*; *Med* medicamento *m*, remédio *m* ● *vt* (*pt* **drugged**) drogar; **~ addict** drogado *m*, tóxico-dependente *m*

drugstore /'drʌgstɔ:(r)/ *n Amer* farmácia *f* que vende também sorvetes etc, (*P*) drogaria *f*

drum /drʌm/ *n Mus* tambor *m*; (*for oil*) barril *m*, tambor *m*; **~s** *Mus* bateria *f* ● *vi* (*pt* **drummed**) tocar tambor; (*with one's fingers*) tamborilar ● *vt* **~ into sb** fazer entrar na cabeça de alguém; **~ up** ‹*support*› conseguir obter; ‹*business*› criar. **~mer** *n* tambor *m*; (*in pop group etc*) baterista *m*, (*P*) bateria *m*

drunk /drʌŋk/ ▶ DRINK *a* embriagado, bêbedo; **get ~** embebedar-se, embriagar-se ● *n* bêbedo *m*. **~ard** *n* alcoólico *m*, bêbedo *m*. **~en** *a* embriagado, bêbedo; (*habitually*) bêbedo

dry /draɪ/ *a* (**drier**, **driest**) seco; ‹*day*› sem chuva; **be** or **feel ~** ter sede ● *vt/i* secar; **~ up** ‹*dishes*› secar a louça; (*of supplies*) esgotar-se. **~-clean** *vt* limpar a seco; **~-cleaner's** *n* (loja de) lavagem *f* a seco, lavanderia *f*. **~ness** *n* secura *f*

dual /'dju:əl/ *a* duplo; **~ carriageway** estrada *f* dividida por faixa central

d

dub /dʌb/ *vt* (*pt* **dubbed**) ‹*film*› dobrar; ‹*nickname*› apelidar de

dubious /'dju:bɪəs/ *a* duvidoso; ‹*character, compliment*› dúbio; **feel ~ about** ter dúvidas quanto a

duchess /'dʌtʃɪs/ *n* duquesa *f*

duck /dʌk/ *n* pato *m* ● *vi* abaixar-se rapidamente ● *vt* ‹*head*› baixar; ‹*person*› batizar, pregar uma amona em. **~ling** *n* patinho *m*

duct /dʌkt/ *n* canal *m*, tubo *m*

dud /dʌd/ *a* [x] (*thing*) que não presta ou não funciona; [x] (*coin*) falso; [x] (*cheque*) sem fundos, (*P*) careca [x]

due /dju:/ *a* devido; (*expected*) esperado; **~ to** devido a, por causa de; **in ~ course** no tempo devido ● *adv* **~ east** /*etc* exatamente, /*etc* ● *n* devido *m*; **~s** direitos *mpl*; (*of club*) cota *f*

duel /'dju:əl/ *n* duelo *m*

duet /dju:'et/ *n* dueto *m*

dug /dʌg/ ▶ DIG

duke /dju:k/ *n* duque *m*

dull /dʌl/ *a* (**-er**, **-est**) (*boring*) enfadonho; ‹*colour*› morto; ‹*mirror*› embaçado; ‹*weather*› encoberto; ‹*sound*› surdo; (*stupid*) burro

duly /'dju:lɪ/ *adv* devidamente; (*in due time*) no tempo devido

dumb /dʌm/ *a* (**-er**, **-est**) mudo; [!] (*stupid*) bronco [!]; burro [!]

dumbfound /dʌm'faʊnd/ *vt* pasmar

dummy /'dʌmɪ/ *n* imitação *f*, coisa *f* simulada; (*of tailor*) manequim *m*; (*of baby*) chupeta *f*

dump /dʌmp/ *vt* ‹*rubbish*› jogar fora; (*put down*) deixar cair; [!] (*abandon*) largar ● *n* monte *m* de lixo; (*tip*) lixeira *f*; *Mil* depósito *m*; [!] buraco *m*

dunce /dʌns/ *n* burro *m*; **~'s cap** orelhas *fpl* de burro

dune /dju:n/ *n* duna *f*

dung /dʌŋ/ *n* esterco *m*; (*manure*) estrume *m*

dungarees /dʌŋgə'ri:z/ *npl* macacão *m*, (*P*) fato *m* de macaco

dungeon /'dʌndʒən/ *n* calabouço *m*, masmorra *f*

dupe /djuːp/ *vt* enganar ● *n* trouxa *m*
duplicate[1] /ˈdjuːplɪkət/ *n* duplicado *m* ● *a* idêntico
duplicate[2] /ˈdjuːplɪkeɪt/ *vt* duplicar, fazer em duplicado; (*on machine*) fotocopiar
duplicity /djuːˈplɪsətɪ/ *n* duplicidade *f*
durable /ˈdjʊərəbl/ *a* resistente; (*enduring*) duradouro, durável
duration /djʊˈreɪʃn/ *n* duração *f*
duress /djʊˈres/ *n* **under ~** sob coação *f*
during /ˈdjʊərɪŋ/ *prep* durante
dusk /dʌsk/ *n* crepúsculo *m*, anoitecer *m*
dust /dʌst/ *n* pó *m*, poeira *f* ● *vt* limpar o pó de; (*sprinkle*) polvilhar
dustbin /ˈdʌstbɪn/ *n* lata *f* do lixo, (*P*) caixote *m*
duster /ˈdʌstə(r)/ *n* pano *m* do pó
dustman /ˈdʌstmən/ *n* (*pl* **-men**) lixeiro *m*, (*P*) homem *m* do lixo
dusty /ˈdʌstɪ/ *a* (**-ier**, **-iest**) poeirento, empoeirado
Dutch /dʌtʃ/ *a* holandês; **go ~** pagar cada um a sua despesa ● *n Lang* holandês *m*. **~man** *n* holandês *m*
dutiful /ˈdjuːtɪfl/ *a* cumpridor; (*showing respect*) respeitador
dut|y /ˈdjuːtɪ/ *n* dever *m*; (*tax*) impostos *mpl*; **~ies** (*of official etc*) funções *fpl*; **off ~y** de folga; **on ~y** de serviço. **~y-free** *a* isento de impostos; **~y-free shop** free shop *m*
duvet /ˈdjuːveɪ/ *n* edredom *m*, (*P*) edredão *m* de penas
DVD *abbr* (= **Digital Versatile Disc**) DVD *m*. **~ burner** *n* gravador *m* de DVD; **~ player** *n* leitor *m* de DVD
dwarf /dwɔːf/ *n* (*pl* **-fs**) anão *m*
dwell /dwel/ *vi* (*pt* **dwelt**) morar; **~ on** alongar-se sobre. **~ing** *n* habitação *f*
dwindle /ˈdwɪndl/ *vi* diminuir, reduzir-se
dye /daɪ/ *vt* (*pres p* **dyeing**) tingir ● *n* tinta *f*
dying /ˈdaɪɪŋ/ ▶ DIE
dynamic /daɪˈnæmɪk/ *a* dinâmico
dynamite /ˈdaɪnəmaɪt/ *n* dinamite *f* ● *vt* dinamitar
dynamo /ˈdaɪnəməʊ/ *n* (*pl* **-os**) dínamo *m*
dysentery /ˈdɪsəntrɪ/ *n* disenteria *f*
dyslex|ia /dɪsˈleksɪə/ *n* dislexia *f*. **~ic** *a* disléxico

Ee

each /iːtʃ/ *a & pron* cada; **~ one** cada um; **~ other** um ao outro, uns aos outros; **they like ~ other** gostam um do outro/uns dos outros; **know/love/** *etc* **~ other** conhecer-se/amar-se/ *etc*
eager /ˈiːɡə(r)/ *a* ansioso (**to** por) desejoso (**for** de); ‹*supporter*› entusiástico; **be ~ to** ter vontade de. **~ly** *adv* com impaciência, ansiosamente; (*keenly*) com entusiasmo. **~ness** *n* ansiedade *f*, desejo *m*; (*keenness*) entusiasmo *m*
eagle /ˈiːɡl/ *n* águia *f*
ear /ɪə(r)/ *n* ouvido *m*; (*external part*) orelha *f*. **~drum** *n* tímpano *m*; **~ring** *n* brinco *m*
earache /ˈɪəreɪk/ *n* dor *f* de ouvidos
earl /ɜːl/ *n* conde *m*
early /ˈɜːlɪ/ (**-ier**, **-iest**) *adv* cedo ● *a* primeiro; ‹*hour*› matinal; ‹*fruit*› temporão; ‹*retirement*› antecipado; **have an ~ dinner** jantar cedo; **in ~ summer** no princípio do verão
earmark /ˈɪəmɑːk/ *vt* destinar; reservar (**for** para)
earn /ɜːn/ *vt* ganhar; (*deserve*) merecer
earnest /ˈɜːnɪst/ *a* sério; **in ~** a sério
earnings /ˈɜːnɪŋz/ *npl* salário *m*; (*profits*) ganhos *mpl*, lucros *mpl*
earshot /ˈɪəʃɒt/ *n* **within ~** ao alcance da voz
earth /ɜːθ/ *n* terra *f* ● *vt Electr* ligar à terra; **why on ~?** por que diabo?, porque cargas d'água?. **~ly** *a* terrestre, terreno
earthenware /ˈɜːθənweə(r)/ *n* louça *f* de barro, faiança *f*
earthquake /ˈɜːθkweɪk/ *n* tremor *m* de terra, terremoto *m*, (*P*) terramoto *m*
earthy /ˈɜːθɪ/ *a* terroso, térreo; (*coarse*) grosseiro
ease /iːz/ *n* facilidade *f*; (*comfort*) bem-estar *m*; **at ~** à vontade; *Mil* descansar; **ill at ~** pouco à vontade; **with ~** facilmente ● *vt/i* (*from pain, anxiety*) acalmar(-se); (*slow down*) afrouxar; (*slide*) deslizar; **~ in/out** fazer entrar/sair com cuidado
easel /ˈiːzl/ *n* cavalete *m*
east /iːst/ *n* este *m*, leste *m*, oriente *m*; **the E~** o Oriente ● *a* este, (de) leste, oriental ● *adv* a/para leste; **~ of** para

o leste de. **~erly** *a* oriental, leste, a/de leste. **~ward** *a*, **~ward(s)** *adv* para leste

Easter /ˈiːstə(r)/ *n* Páscoa *f*; **~ egg** ovo *m* de Páscoa

eastern /ˈiːstən/ *a* oriental, leste

easy /ˈiːzɪ/ *a* (**-ier**, **-iest**) fácil; (*relaxed*) natural, descontraído; **take it ~** levar as coisas com calma; **~ chair** poltrona *f*. **~-going** *a* bonacheirão. **easily** *adv* facilmente

eat /iːt/ *vt/i* (*pt* **ate**, *pp* **eaten**) comer; **~ into** corroer. **~able** *a* comestível

eaves /iːvz/ *npl* beiral *m*

eavesdrop /ˈiːvzdrɒp/ *vi* (*pt* **-dropped**) escutar por detrás da porta

ebb /eb/ *n* vazante *f*, baixa-mar *m* ● *vi* vazar; *fig* declinar

e-book /ˈiːbʊk/ *n* livro *m* eletrônico, (*P*) eletrónico

EC /iːˈsiː/ *abbr* (= **European Commission**) CE *f*

eccentric /ɪkˈsentrɪk/ *a & n* excêntrico *m*. **~ity** /eksenˈtrɪsətɪ/ *n* excentricidade *f*

ecclesiastical /ɪkliːzɪˈæstɪkl/ *a* eclesiástico

echo /ˈekəʊ/ *n* (*pl* **-oes**) eco *m* ● *vt/i* (*pt* **echoed**, *pres p* **echoing**) ecoar; *fig* repetir

eclipse /ɪˈklɪps/ *n* eclipse *m* ● *vt* eclipsar

ecolog|y /iːˈkɒlədʒɪ/ *n* ecologia *f*. **~ical** /iːkəˈlɒdʒɪkl/ *a* ecológico

e-commerce /ˈiːkɒmɜːs/ *n* comércio *m* eletrônico *or* (*P*) eletrónico

economic /iːkəˈnɒmɪk/ *a* econômico, (*P*) económico; (*profitable*) rentável. **~al** *a* econômico, (*P*) económico. **~s** *n* economia *f* política

economist /ɪˈkɒnəmɪst/ *n* economista *mf*

econom|y /ɪˈkɒnəmɪ/ *n* economia *f*. **~ize** *vt/i* economizar

ecstasy /ˈekstəsɪ/ *n* êxtase *m*

ecstatic /ɪkˈstætɪk/ *a* extático

eczema /ˈɛksɪmə/ *n* eczema *m*

edge /edʒ/ *n* borda *f*, beira *f*; (*of town*) periferia *f*, limite *m*; (*of knife*) fio *m* ● *vt* debruar ● *vi* (*move*) avançar pouco a pouco

edgy /ˈedʒɪ/ *a* irritadiço, nervoso

edible /ˈedɪbl/ *a* comestível

edifice /ˈedɪfɪs/ *n* edifício *m*

i **Edinburgh Festival** É o evento cultural mais importante da Grã-Bretanha, que se celebra em agosto, na capital da Escócia desde 1947. O festival atrai um grande número de visitantes e um aspecto muito relevante do evento são os espetáculos que não formam parte do programa oficial, e aos quais se dá o nome de *the Fringe*.

edit /ˈedɪt/ *vt* (*pt* **edited**) ‹*newspaper*› dirigir; ‹*text*› editar

edition /ɪˈdɪʃn/ *n* edição *f*

editor /ˈedɪtə(r)/ *n* (*of newspaper*) diretor *m*; (*P*) diretor *m*; editor *m* responsável; (*of text*) organizador *m* de texto; **the ~ (in chief)** redator-chefe *m*. **~ial** /edɪˈtɔːrɪəl/ *a & n* editorial *m*

e

educat|e /ˈedʒʊkeɪt/ *vt* instruir; ‹*mind, public*› educar. **~ed** *a* instruído; educado. **~ion** /-ˈkeɪʃn/ *n* educação *f*; (*schooling*) ensino *m*. **~ional** /-ˈkeɪʃənl/ *a* educativo, pedagógico

eel /iːl/ *n* enguia *f*

eerie /ˈɪərɪ/ *a* (**-ier**, **-iest**) arrepiante, misterioso

effect /ɪˈfekt/ *n* efeito *m* ● *vt* efetuar; **come into ~** entrar em vigor; **in ~** na realidade; **take ~** ter efeito

effective /ɪˈfektɪv/ *a* eficaz, eficiente; (*striking*) sensacional; (*actual*) efetivo. **~ly** *adv* (*efficiently*) eficazmente; (*strikingly*) de forma sensacional; (*actually*) efetivamente. **~ness** *n* eficácia *f*

effeminate /ɪˈfemɪnət/ *a* efeminado, afeminado

effervescent /efəˈvesnt/ *a* efervescente

efficien|t /ɪˈfɪʃnt/ *a* eficiente, eficaz. **~cy** *n* eficiência *f*. **~tly** *adv* eficientemente

effort /ˈefət/ *n* esforço *m*. **~less** *a* fácil, sem esforço

e.g. /iːˈdʒiː/ *abbr* por ex

egg[1] /eg/ *n* ovo *m*. **~plant** *n* beringela *f*

egg[2] /eg/ *vt* **~ on** [!] incitar

eggshell /ˈegʃel/ *n* casca *f* de ovo

ego /ˈegəʊ/ *n* (*pl* **-os**) ego *m*, eu *m*. **~ism** *n* egoísmo *m*. **~ist** *n* egoísta *mf*. **~tism** *n* egotismo *m*. **~tist** *n* egotista *mf*

Egypt /ˈiːdʒɪpt/ *n* Egito *m*. **~ian** /ɪˈdʒɪpʃn/ *a & n* egípcio *m*

eh /eɪ/ *int* [!] hã?

eiderdown /ˈaɪdədaʊn/ *n* edredão *m*, edredom *m*

eight /eɪt/ *a & n* oito *m*. **~h** *a & n* oitavo *m*

eighteen /eɪˈtiːn/ *a & n* dezoito *m*. **~th** *a & n* décimo oitavo *m*

eight|y /'eɪtɪ/ *a & n* oitenta *m*. **~ieth** *a & n* octogésimo *m*

either /'aɪðə(r)/ *a & pron* um e outro; (*with negative*) nem um nem outro; (*each*) cada ● *adv* também não ● *conj* **~ ... or** ou ... ou; (*with negative*) nem ... nem

ejaculate /ɪ'dʒækjʊleɪt/ *vt/i* ejacular; (*exclaim*) exclamar

eject /ɪ'dʒekt/ *vt* expelir; (*expel*) expulsar, despejar, ejetar

e

elaborate[1] /ɪ'læbərət/ *a* elaborado, rebuscado, minucioso

elaborate[2] /ɪ'læbəreɪt/ *vt* elaborar ● *vi* entrar em pormenores; **~ on** estender-se sobre

elapse /ɪ'læps/ *vi* decorrer

elastic /ɪ'læstɪk/ *a & n* elástico *m*; **~ band** elástico *m*

elat|ed /ɪ'leɪtɪd/ *a* radiante, exultante. **~ion** *n* exultação *f*

elbow /'elbəʊ/ *n* cotovelo *m*

elder[1] /'eldə(r)/ *a* mais velho. **~s** *npl* pessoas *fpl* mais velhas

elder[2] /'eldə(r)/ *n* (*tree*) sabugueiro *m*

elderly /'eldəlɪ/ *a* idoso; **the ~** as pessoas de idade

eldest /'eldɪst/ *a & n* o mais velho *m*

elect /ɪ'lekt/ *vt* eleger ● *a* eleito. **~ion** /-kʃn/ *n* eleição *f*

electric /ɪ'lektrɪk/ *a* elétrico

electrician /ɪlek'trɪʃn/ *n* eletricista *m*

electricity /ɪlek'trɪsətɪ/ *n* eletricidade *f*

electrify /ɪ'lektrɪfaɪ/ *vt* eletrificar; *fig* (*excite*) eletrizar

electrocute /ɪ'lektrəkju:t/ *vt* eletrocutar

electronic /ɪlek'trɒnɪk/ *a* eletrônico, (*P*) electrónico. **~s** *n* eletrônica *f*, (*P*) eletrónica *f*

elegan|t /'elɪgənt/ *a* elegante. **~ce** *n* elegância *f*

element /'elɪmənt/ *n* elemento *m*; (*of heater etc*) resistência *f*. **~ary** /-'mentrɪ/ *a* elementar; (*school*) primário

elephant /'elɪfənt/ *n* elefante *m*

elevat|e /'elɪveɪt/ *vt* elevar. **~ion** /-'veɪʃn/ *n* elevação *f*

elevator /'elɪveɪtə(r)/ *n Amer* (*lift*) elevador *m*; ascensor *m*

eleven /ɪ'levn/ *a & n* onze *m*. **~th** *a & n* décimo primeiro *m*; **at the ~th hour** à última hora

eligible /'elɪdʒəbl/ *a* (*for office*) idôneo, (*P*) idóneo (**for** para); (*desirable*) aceitável; **be ~ for** (*entitled to*) ter direito a

eliminat|e /ɪ'lɪmɪneɪt/ *vt* eliminar

elite /eɪ'li:t/ *n* elite *f*

elm /elm/ *n* olmo *m*, ulmeiro *m*

elocution /elə'kju:ʃn/ *n* elocução *f*

elope /ɪ'ləʊp/ *vi* fugir

eloquen|t /'eləkwənt/ *a* eloquente. **~ce** *n* eloquência *f*

else /els/ *adv* mais; **everybody ~** todos os outros; **nobody ~** mais ninguém; **nothing ~** nada mais; **or ~** ou então, senão; **somewhere ~** noutro lado qualquer. **~where** *adv* noutro lado

elusive /ɪ'lu:sɪv/ *a* ‹*person*› esquivo, difícil de apanhar; ‹*answer*› evasivo

emaciated /ɪ'meɪʃɪeɪtɪd/ *a* emaciado, macilento

email /'i:meɪl/ *n* correio *m* eletrônico, (*P*) eletrónico, e-mail *m*; **~ address** endereço *m* de e-mail

embankment /ɪm'bæŋkmənt/ *n* (*of river*) dique *m*; (*of railway*) terrapleno *m*; talude *m*, (*P*) aterro *m*

embargo /ɪm'bɑ:gəʊ/ *n* (*pl* **-oes**) embargo *m*

embark /ɪm'bɑ:k/ *vt/i* embarcar; **~ on** ‹*business etc*› embarcar em, meter-se em [!]; ‹*journey*› começar

embarrass /ɪm'bærəs/ *vt* embaraçar, confundir. **~ment** *n* embaraço *m*, atrapalhação *f*

embassy /'embəsɪ/ *n* embaixada *f*

embellish /ɪm'belɪʃ/ *vt* embelezar, enfeitar

embezzle /ɪm'bezl/ *vt* desviar (fundos). **~ment** *n* desfalque *m*

emblem /'embləm/ *n* emblema *m*

embod|y /ɪm'bɒdɪ/ *vt* encarnar; (*include*) incorporar, incluir. **~iment** *n* personificação *f*

embrace /ɪm'breɪs/ *vt/i* abraçar(-se); ‹*offer, opportunity*› acolher ● *n* abraço *m*

embroider /ɪm'brɔɪdə(r)/ *vt* bordar. **~y** *n* bordado *m*

embryo /'embrɪəʊ/ *n* (*pl* **-os**) embrião *m*

emerald /'emərəld/ *n* esmeralda *f*

emerge /ɪ'mɜ:dʒ/ *vi* emergir, surgir

emergency /ɪ'mɜ:dʒənsɪ/ *n* emergência *f*; (*urgent case*) urgência *f*; **~ exit** saída *f* de emergência; **in an ~** em caso de urgência

emigrant /'emɪgrənt/ *n* emigrante *mf*

emigrat|e /'emɪgreɪt/ *vi* emigrar. **~ion** /-'greɪʃn/ *n* emigração *f*

eminen|t /'emɪnənt/ *a* eminente

emi|t /ɪ'mɪt/ *vt* (*pt* **emitted**) emitir. **~ssion** /-ʃn/ *n* emissão *f*

emotion /ɪ'məʊʃn/ *n* emoção *f*. **~al** *a* ‹*person, shock*› emotivo; ‹*speech, scene*› emocionante

emperor /'empərə(r)/ *n* imperador *m*

emphasis /'emfəsɪs/ *n* ênfase *f*; **lay ~ on** pôr em relevo

emphasize /'emfəsaɪz/ *vt* enfatizar, sublinhar; ‹*syllable, word*› acentuar

emphatic /ɪm'fætɪk/ *a* enfático; ‹*manner*› enérgico

empire /'empaɪə(r)/ *n* império *m*

employ /ɪm'plɔɪ/ *vt* empregar. **~ee** /emplɔɪ'i:/ *n* empregado *m*. **~er** *n* patrão *m*. **~ment** *n* emprego *m*; **~ment agency** agência *f* de emprego

empower /ɪm'paʊə(r)/ *vt* autorizar (**to do** a fazer)

empress /'emprɪs/ *n* imperatriz *f*

empt|y /'emptɪ/ *a* vazio; ‹*promise*› falso; **on an ~y stomach** com o estômago vazio, em jejum ● *vt/i* esvaziar(-se). **~iness** *n* vazio *m*

emulsion /ɪ'mʌlʃn/ *n* emulsão *f*

enable /ɪ'neɪbl/ *vt* **~ sb to do** permitir a alguém fazer

enact /ɪ'nækt/ *vt Jur* decretar; *Theat* representar

enamel /ɪ'næml/ *n* esmalte *m* ● *vt* (*pt* **enamelled**) esmaltar

enchant /ɪn'tʃɑ:nt/ *vt* encantar. **~ing** *a* encantador. **~ment** *n* encantamento *m*

encircle /ɪn's3:kl/ *vt* cercar, rodear

enclose /ɪn'kləʊz/ *vt* (*land*) cercar; (*with letter*) enviar incluso/junto. **~d** *a* ‹*space*› fechado; (*with letter*) anexo, incluso, junto

enclosure /ɪn'kləʊʒə(r)/ *n* cercado *m*, recinto *m*; (*with letter*) documento *m* anexo

encore /ɒŋ'kɔ:(r)/ *int & n* bis *m*

encounter /ɪn'kaʊntə(r)/ *vt* encontrar, deparar com ● *n* encontro *m*

encourage /ɪn'kʌrɪdʒ/ *vt* encorajar. **~ment** *n* encorajamento *m*

encroach /ɪn'krəʊtʃ/ *vi* **~ on** ‹*land*› invadir; ‹*time*› abusar de

encycloped|ia /ɪnsaɪklə'pi:dɪə/ *n* enciclopédia *f*. **~ic** *a* enciclopédico

end /end/ *n* fim *m*; (*farthest part*) extremo *m*, ponta *f*; **in the ~** por fim; **no ~ of** [!] muito, enorme, imenso; **on ~** (*upright*) em pé; (*consecutive*) a fio, de seguida ● *vt/i* acabar, terminar; **~ up** (*arrive finally*) ir parar (**in** a/em); **~ up doing** acabar por fazer

endanger /ɪn'deɪndʒə(r)/ *vt* pôr em perigo

endeavour /ɪn'devə(r)/ *n* esforço *m* ● *vi* esforçar-se (**to** por)

ending /'endɪŋ/ *n* fim *m*; (*of word*) terminação *f*

endless /'endlɪs/ *a* interminável; ‹*times*› sem conta; ‹*patience*› infinito

endorse /ɪn'dɔ:s/ *vt* ‹*document*› endossar; ‹*action*› aprovar. **~ment** *n Auto* averbamento *m*

endow /ɪn'daʊ/ *vt* doar. **~ment** *n* doação *f*

endur|e /ɪn'djʊə(r)/ *vt* suportar ● *vi* durar. **~ance** *n* resistência *f*

enemy /'enəmɪ/ *n & a* inimigo *m*

energetic /enə'dʒetɪk/ *a* enérgico

energy /'enədʒɪ/ *n* energia *f*

enforce /ɪn'fɔ:s/ *vt* aplicar

engage /ɪn'geɪdʒ/ *vt* (*staff*) contratar; *Mech* engrenar ● *vi* **~ in** envolver-se em, lançar-se em. **~d** *a* noivo; (*busy*) ocupado. **~ment** *n* noivado *m*; (*undertaking, appointment*) compromisso *m*; *Mil* combate *m*

engine /'endʒɪn/ *n* motor *m*; (*of train*) locomotiva *f*

engineer /endʒɪ'nɪə(r)/ *n* engenheiro *m* ● *vt* engenhar. **~ing** *n* engenharia *f*

England /'ɪŋglənd/ *n* Inglaterra *f*

English /'ɪŋglɪʃ/ *a* inglês ● *n Lang* inglês *m*; **the ~** os ingleses *mpl*. **~man** *n* inglês *m*. **~woman** *n* inglesa *f*

engrav|e /ɪn'greɪv/ *vt* gravar. **~ing** *n* gravura *f*

engrossed /ɪn'grəʊst/ *a* absorto (**in** em)

engulf /ɪn'gʌlf/ *vt* engolfar, tragar

enhance /ɪn'hɑ:ns/ *vt* aumentar; (*heighten*) realçar

enigma /ɪ'nɪgmə/ *n* enigma *m*. **~tic** /enɪg'mætɪk/ *a* enigmático

enjoy /ɪn'dʒɔɪ/ *vt* gostar de; (*benefit from*) gozar de; **~ o.s.** divertir-se. **~able** *a* agradável. **~ment** *n* prazer *m*

enlarge /ɪn'lɑ:dʒ/ *vt/i* aumentar; **~ upon** alargar-se sobre. **~ment** *n* ampliação *f*

enlighten /ɪn'laɪtn/ *vt* esclarecer. **~ment** *n* esclarecimento *m*, elucidação *f*

enlist /ɪn'lɪst/ *vt* recrutar; *fig* aliciar; granjear ● *vi* alistar-se

enliven /ɪn'laɪvn/ *vt* animar

enmity /'enmətɪ/ *n* inimizade *f*

enormous /ɪ'nɔːməs/ *a* enorme

enough /ɪ'nʌf/ *a* bastante *m*, suficiente *m* ● *adv & n* bastante *m*, suficiente *m* ● *int* basta!, chega!

enquir|e /ɪn'kwaɪə(r)/ *vt/i* perguntar, indagar; **~e about** informar-se de, pedir informações sobre. **~y** *n* pedido *m* de informações

enrage /ɪn'reɪdʒ/ *vt* enfurecer, enraivecer

enrich /ɪn'rɪtʃ/ *vt* enriquecer

enrol /ɪn'rəʊl/ *vt/i* (*pt* **enrolled**) inscrever(-se); *Schol* matricular(-se). **~ment** *n* inscrição *f*; *Schol* matrícula *f*

ensemble /ɒn'sɒmbl/ *n* conjunto *m*

ensu|e /ɪn'sjuː/ *vi* seguir-se. **~ing** *a* decorrente

ensure /ɪn'ʃʊə(r)/ *vt* assegurar; **~ that** assegurar-se de que

entail /ɪn'teɪl/ *vt* acarretar

entangle /ɪn'tæŋgl/ *vt* emaranhar, enredar

enter /'entə(r)/ *vt* ‹*room, club etc*› entrar em; (*register*) registar; ‹*data*› entrar com ● *vi* entrar (**into** em); **~ for** inscrever-se em

enterprise /'entəpraɪz/ *n* empresa *f*, empreendimento *m*; *fig* iniciativa *f*

enterprising /'entəpraɪzɪŋ/ *a* empreendedor

entertain /entə'teɪn/ *vt* entreter; ‹*guests*› receber; ‹*ideas*› alimentar, nutrir. **~er** *n* artista *mf*. **~ment** *n* entretenimento *m*; (*performance*) espetáculo *m*

enthral /ɪn'θrɔːl/ *vt* (*pt* **enthralled**) fascinar

enthuse /ɪn'θjuːz/ *vi* **~ over** entusiasmar-se por

enthusias|m /ɪn'θjuːzɪæzm/ *n* entusiasmo *m*. **~t** *n* entusiasta *mf*. **~tic** /-'æstɪk/ *a* entusiástico

entice /ɪn'taɪs/ *vt* atrair; **~ to do** induzir a fazer. **~ment** *n* tentação *f*, engodo *m*

entire /ɪn'taɪə(r)/ *a* inteiro. **~ly** *adv* inteiramente

entirety /ɪn'taɪərətɪ/ *n* **in its ~** por inteiro, na (sua) totalidade

entitle /ɪn'taɪtl/ *vt* dar direito. **~d** *a* ‹*book*› intitulado; **be ~d to sth** ter direito a algo. **~ment** *n* direito *m*

entrance /'entrəns/ *n* entrada *f* (**to** para); (*right to enter*) admissão *f*

entrant /'entrənt/ *n Sport* concorrente *mf*; (*in exam*) candidato *m*

entreat /ɪn'triːt/ *vt* rogar, suplicar. **~y** *n* rogo *m*, súplica *f*

entrust /ɪn'trʌst/ *vt* confiar

entry /'entrɪ/ *n* entrada *f*; (*on list*) item *m*; (*in dictionary*) verbete *m*; **~ form** ficha *f* de inscrição, (*P*) boletim *m* de inscrição; **no ~** entrada proibida

envelop /ɪn'veləp/ *vt* (*pt* **enveloped**) envolver

envelope /'envələʊp/ *n* envelope *m*, sobrescrito *m*

enviable /'envɪəbl/ *a* invejável

envious /'envɪəs/ *a* invejoso; **be ~ of** ter inveja de

environment /ɪn'vaɪərənmənt/ *n* meio *m*; (*ecological*) meio ambiente *m*. **~al** /-'mentl/ *a* do meio; (*ecological*) do ambiente

envisage /ɪn'vɪzɪdʒ/ *vt* encarar; (*foresee*) prever

envoy /'envɔɪ/ *n* enviado *m*

envy /'envɪ/ *n* inveja *f* ● *vt* invejar, ter inveja de

epic /'epɪk/ *n* epopeia ● *a* épico

epidemic /epɪ'demɪk/ *n* epidemia *f*

epilep|sy /'epɪlepsɪ/ *n* epilepsia *f*. **~tic** /-'leptɪk/ *a & n* epiléptico *m*, (*P*) epilético *m*

episode /'epɪsəʊd/ *n* episódio *m*

epitom|e /ɪ'pɪtəmɪ/ *n* (*summary*) epítome *m*; (*embodiment*) modelo *m*. **~ize** *vt fig* representar; encarnar; (*summarize*) resumir

epoch /'iːpɒk/ *n* época *f*. **~-making** *a* que marca uma época

equal /'iːkwəl/ *a & n* igual *m*; **~ to** (*task*) à altura de ● *vt* (*pt* **equalled**) igualar, ser igual a. **~ity** /iː'kwɒlətɪ/ *n* igualdade *f*. **~ly** *adv* igualmente; (*similarly*) de igual modo

equalize /'iːkwəlaɪz/ *vt/i* igualar; *Sport* empatar

equate /ɪ'kweɪt/ *vt* equacionar (**with** com); (*treat as equal*) equiparar (**with** a)

equation /ɪ'kweɪʒn/ *n* equação *f*

equator /ɪ'kweɪtə(r)/ *n* equador *m*

equilibrium /iːkwɪ'lɪbrɪəm/ *n* equilíbrio *m*

equip /ɪ'kwɪp/ *vt* (*pt* **equipped**) equipar (**with** com); munir (**with** de). **~ment** *n* equipamento *m*

equitable /'ekwɪtəbl/ *a* equitativo

equity /'ekwətɪ/ *n* equidade *f*

equivalent /ɪ'kwɪvələnt/ *a & n* equivalente *m*

era /ˈɪərə/ *n* era *f*, época *f*
eradicate /ɪˈrædɪkeɪt/ *vt* erradicar, suprimir
erase /ɪˈreɪz/ *vt* apagar. **~r** /-ə(r)/ *n* borracha (de apagar) *f*
erect /ɪˈrekt/ *a* ereto ● *vt* erigir. **~ion** /-ʃn/ *n* ereção *f*; (*building*) construção *f*, edifício *m*
ero|de /ɪˈrəʊd/ *vt* corroer. **~sion** /ɪˈrəʊʒn/ *n* erosão *f*
erotic /ɪˈrɒtɪk/ *a* erótico
err /ɜː(r)/ *vi* (*pt* **erred**) errar
errand /ˈerənd/ *n* recado *m*
erratic /ɪˈrætɪk/ *a* errático, irregular; ‹*person*› variável, imprevisível
erroneous /ɪˈrəʊnɪəs/ *a* errôneo, (*P*) erróneo, errado
error /ˈerə(r)/ *n* erro *m*
erupt /ɪˈrʌpt/ *vi* ‹*war, fire*› irromper; ‹*volcano*› entrar em erupção. **~ion** /-ʃn/ *n* erupção *f*
escalat|e /ˈeskəleɪt/ *vt/i* intensificar(-se); (*of prices*) subir em espiral
escalator /ˈeskəleɪtə(r)/ *n* escada *f* rolante
escape /ɪˈskeɪp/ *vi* escapar-se ● *vt* escapar a ● *n* fuga *f*; (*of prisoner*) evasão *f*, fuga *f*; **~ from sb** escapar de alguém; **~ to** fugir para; **have a lucky** or **narrow ~** escapar por um triz
escapism /ɪˈskeɪpɪzəm/ *n* escapismo *m*
escort[1] /ˈeskɔːt/ *n* escolta *f*; (*of woman*) cavalheiro *m*, acompanhante *m*
escort[2] /ɪˈskɔːt/ *vt* escoltar; (*accompany*) acompanhar
Eskimo /ˈeskɪməʊ/ *n* (*pl* **-os**) esquimó *mf*
especial /ɪˈspeʃl/ *a* especial. **~ly** *adv* especialmente
espionage /ˈespɪənɑːʒ/ *n* espionagem *f*
espresso /eˈspressəʊ/ *n* (*pl* **-os**) (*coffee*) expresso *m*, (*P*) bica *f*
essay /ˈeseɪ/ *n* ensaio *m*; *Schol* redação *f*
essence /ˈesns/ *n* essência *f*
essential /ɪˈsenʃl/ *a* essencial ● *n* **the ~s** o essencial *m*. **~ly** *adv* essencialmente
establish /ɪˈstæblɪʃ/ *vt* estabelecer; ‹*business, state*› fundar; (*prove*) provar, apurar. **~ment** *n* estabelecimento *m*; (*institution*) instituição *f*; **the E~ment** o Establishment *m*, a classe *f* dirigente
estate /ɪˈsteɪt/ *n* propriedade *f*; (*possessions*) bens *mpl*; (*inheritance*) herança *f*; **~ agent** agente *m* imobiliário; **(housing) ~** conjunto *m* habitacional; **~ car** perua *f*, (*P*) carrinha *f*
esteem /ɪˈstiːm/ *vt* estimar ● *n* estima *f*
estimate[1] /ˈestɪmət/ *n* cálculo *m*, avaliação *f*; *Comm* orçamento *m*, estimativa *f*
estimat|e[2] /ˈestɪmeɪt/ *vt* calcular, estimar. **~ion** /-ˈmeɪʃn/ *n* opinião *f*
estuary /ˈestʃʊərɪ/ *n* estuário *m*
etc *abbr* (= **et cetera**) etc
eternal /ɪˈtɜːnl/ *a* eterno
eternity /ɪˈtɜːnətɪ/ *n* eternidade *f*
ethic /ˈeθɪk/ *n* ética *f*; **~s** ética *f*. **~al** *a* ético
ethnic /ˈeθnɪk/ *a* étnico
etiquette /ˈetɪket/ *n* etiqueta *f*
eulogy /ˈjuːlədʒɪ/ *n* elogio *m* (fúnebre)
euphemism /ˈjuːfəmɪzəm/ *n* eufemismo *m*
euro /ˈjʊərəʊ/ *n* euro *m*
Europe /ˈjʊərəp/ *n* Europa *f*. **E~an** /-ˈpɪən/ *a & n* europeu *m*; **E~an Union** União Europeia
evacuat|e /ɪˈvækjʊeɪt/ *vt* evacuar. **~ion** /-ˈeɪʃn/ *n* evacuação *f*
evade /ɪˈveɪd/ *vt* evadir
evaluate /ɪˈvæljʊeɪt/ *vt* avaliar
evangelical /iːvænˈdʒelɪkl/ *a* evangélico
evaporat|e /ɪˈvæpəreɪt/ *vt/i* evaporar(-se); **~ed milk** leite *m* evaporado. **~ion** /-ˈreɪʃn/ *n* evaporação *f*
evasion /ɪˈveɪʒn/ *n* evasão *f*
evasive /ɪˈveɪsɪv/ *a* evasivo
eve /iːv/ *n* véspera *f*
even /ˈiːvn/ *a* regular; ‹*surface*› liso, plano; ‹*amounts*› igual; ‹*number*› par; **get ~ with** ajustar contas com ● *vt/i* **~ up** igualar(-se), acertar ● *adv* mesmo; **~ better** ainda melhor. **~ly** *adv* uniformemente
evening /ˈiːvnɪŋ/ *n* entardecer *m*, anoitecer *m*; (*whole evening*) serão *m*; **~ class** aula *f* à noite (para adultos); **~ dress** traje *m* de cerimônia *or* (*P*) cerimónia or de rigor; (*woman's*) vestido *m* de noite
event /ɪˈvent/ *n* acontecimento *m*; **in the ~ of** no caso de. **~ful** *a* movimentado, memorável
eventual /ɪˈventʃʊəl/ *a* final. **~ly** *adv* por fim; (*in future*) eventualmente
ever /ˈevə(r)/ *adv* jamais; (*at all times*) sempre; **do you ~ go?** você já foi alguma vez?, costumas ir?; **the best I ~ saw** o melhor que já vi; **~ so** ▶

muitíssimo, tão; **hardly ~** quase nunca. **~ since** *adv* desde então ● *prep* desde ● *conj* desde que

evergreen /'evəgri:n/ *n* sempre-verde *f*, planta *f* de folhas persistentes ● *a* persistente

everlasting /'evəlɑ:stɪŋ/ *a* eterno

every /'evrɪ/ *a* cada; **~ now and then** de vez em quando, volta e meia; **~ one** cada um; **~ other day** dia sim dia não, de dois em dois dias; **~ three days** de três em três dias

e

everybody /'evrɪbɒdɪ/ *pron* todo o mundo, todos

everyday /'evrɪdeɪ/ *a* cotidiano, (*P*) quotidiano, diário; (*common*) do dia a dia, vulgar

everyone /'evrɪwʌn/ *pron* todo o mundo, todos

everything /'evrɪθɪŋ/ *pron* tudo

everywhere /'evrɪweə(r)/ *adv* (*position*) em todo lugar, em toda parte; (*direction*) a todo lugar, a toda parte

evict /ɪ'vɪkt/ *vt* expulsar, despejar. **~ion** /-ʃn/ *n* despejo *m*

evidence /'evɪdəns/ *n* evidência *f*; (*proof*) prova *f*; (*testimony*) testemunho *m*, depoimento *m*; **~ of** sinal de; **give ~** testemunhar; **in ~** em evidência

evident /'evɪdənt/ *a* evidente. **~ly** *adv* evidentemente

evil /'i:vl/ *a* mau ● *n* mal *m*

evo|ke /ɪ'vəʊk/ *vt* evocar. **~cative** /ɪ'vɒkətɪv/ *a* evocativo

evolution /i:və'lu:ʃn/ *n* evolução *f*

evolve /ɪ'vɒlv/ *vi* evolucionar, evoluir ● *vt* desenvolver, produzir

ex- /eks/ *pref* ex-

exact /ɪg'zækt/ *a* exato ● *vt* exigir (**from** de). **~ing** *a* exigente; ‹*task*› difícil. **~ly** *adv* exatamente

exaggerat|e /ɪg'zædʒəreɪt/ *vt/i* exagerar. **~ion** /-'reɪʃn/ *n* exagero *m*

exam /ɪg'zæm/ *n* [!] exame *m*

examination /ɪgzæmɪ'neɪʃn/ *n* exame *m*; *Jur* interrogatório *m*

examine /ɪg'zæmɪn/ *vt* examinar; ‹*witness etc*› interrogar. **~r** /-ə(r)/ *n* examinador *m*

example /ɪg'zɑ:mpl/ *n* exemplo *m*; **for ~** por exemplo; **make an ~ of** castigar para servir de exemplo

exasperat|e /ɪg'zæspəreɪt/ *vt* exasperar. **~ion** /-'reɪʃn/ *n* exaspero *m*

excavat|e /'ekskəveɪt/ *vt* escavar; (*uncover*) desenterrar. **~ion** /-'veɪʃn/ *n* escavação *f*

exceed /ɪk'si:d/ *vt* exceder; ‹*speed limit*› ultrapassar, exceder

excel /ɪk'sel/ *vi* (*pt* **excelled**) distinguir-se ● *vt* superar, ultrapassar

excellen|t /'eksələnt/ *a* excelente. **~ce** *n* excelência *f*

except /ɪk'sept/ *prep* exceto, fora; **~ for** a não ser, menos, salvo ● *vt* excetuar. **~ion** /-ʃn/ *n* exceção *f*; **take ~ion to** (*object to*) achar inaceitável; (*be offended by*) achar ofensivo

exceptional /ɪk'sepʃənl/ *a* excepcional, (*P*) excecional

excerpt /'eksɜ:pt/ *n* trecho *m*, excerto *m*

excess[1] /ɪk'ses/ *n* excesso *m*

excess[2] /'ekses/ *a* excedente, em excesso; **~ fare** excesso *m*, suplemento *m*; **~ luggage** excesso *m* de peso

excessive /ɪk'sesɪv/ *a* excessivo

exchange /ɪks'tʃeɪndʒ/ *vt* trocar ● *n* troca *f*; (*of currency*) câmbio *m*; **(telephone) ~** central *f* telefônica, (*P*) telefónica; **~ rate** taxa *f* de câmbio

excit|e /ɪk'saɪt/ *vt* excitar; (*rouse*) despertar; (*enthuse*) entusiasmar. **~able** *a* excitável. **~ed** *a* excitado; **get ~ed** excitar-se, entusiasmar-se. **~ement** *n* excitação *f*. **~ing** *a* excitante, emocionante

exclaim /ɪk'skleɪm/ *vi* exclamar

exclamation /eksklə'meɪʃn/ *n* exclamação *f*; **~ mark** ponto *m* de exclamação

exclu|de /ɪk'sklu:d/ *vt* excluir. **~ding** *prep* excluído. **~sion** /ɪk'sklu:ʒn/ *n* exclusão *f*

exclusive /ɪk'sklu:sɪv/ *a* ‹*rights etc*› exclusivo; ‹*club etc*› seleto; ‹*news item*› (em) exclusivo; **~ of** sem incluir. **~ly** *adv* exclusivamente

excruciating /ɪk'skru:ʃɪeɪtɪŋ/ *a* excruciante, atroz

excursion /ɪk'skɜ:ʃn/ *n* excursão *f*

excus|e[1] /ɪk'skju:z/ *vt* desculpar; **~e me!** desculpe!, com licença! **~e from** (*exempt*) dispensar de. **~able** *a* desculpável

excuse[2] /ɪk'skju:s/ *n* desculpa *f*

ex-directory /eksdɪ'rektərɪ/ *a* que não vem no anuário *or* (*P*) na lista

execute /'eksɪkju:t/ *vt* executar

execution /eksɪ'kju:ʃn/ *n* execução *f*

executive /ɪg'zekjʊtɪv/ *a & n* executivo *m*

exemplary /ɪg'zemplərɪ/ *a* exemplar

exemplify /ɪg'zemplɪfaɪ/ *vt* exemplificar, ilustrar

exempt /ɪg'zempt/ *a* isento (**from** de) ● *vt* dispensar, eximir. **~ion** /-ʃn/ *n* isenção *f*

exercise /'eksəsaɪz/ *n* exercício *m* ● *vt* ‹*powers, restraint etc*› exercer; ‹*dog*› levar para passear ● *vi* fazer exercício; **~ book** caderno *m* (de exercícios)

exert /ɪg'zɜ:t/ *vt* empregar, exercer; **~ o.s.** esforçar-se, fazer um esforço. **~ion** /-ʃn/ *n* esforço *m*

exhaust /ɪg'zɔ:st/ *vt* esgotar ● *n Auto* (tubo de) escape *m*. **~ed** *a* esgotado, exausto. **~ion** /-stʃən/ *n* esgotamento *m*, exaustão *f*

exhaustive /ɪg'zɔ:stɪv/ *a* exaustivo, completo

exhibit /ɪg'zɪbɪt/ *vt* exibir, mostrar; ‹*thing, collection*› expor ● *n* objeto *m*, exposto

exhibition /eksɪ'bɪʃn/ *n* exposição *f*; (*act of showing*) demonstração *f*

exhilarat|e /ɪg'zɪləreɪt/ *vt* regozijar; (*invigorate*) animar, estimular. **~ion** /-'reɪʃn/ *n* animação *f*, alegria *f*

exile /'eksaɪl/ *n* exílio *m*; (*person*) exilado *m* ● *vt* exilar, desterrar

exist /ɪg'zɪst/ *vi* existir. **~ence** *n* existência *f*; **be in ~ence** existir

exit /'eksɪt/ *n* saída *f*

exorbitant /ɪg'zɔ:bɪtənt/ *a* exorbitante

exotic /ɪg'zɒtɪk/ *a* exótico

expan|d /ɪk'spænd/ *vt/i* expandir(-se); (*extend*) estender(-se), alargar(-se); ‹*gas, liquid, metal*› dilatar(-se). **~sion** *n* expansão *f*; (*extension*) alargamento *m*; (*of gas etc*) dilatação *f*

expanse /ɪk'spæns/ *n* extensão *f*

expatriate /eks'pætrɪət/ *a & n* expatriado *m*

expect /ɪk'spekt/ *vt* esperar; (*suppose*) crer, supor; (*require*) contar com, esperar; ‹*baby*› esperar; **~ to do** contar fazer. **~ation** /ekspek'teɪʃn/ *n* expectativa *f*

expectan|t /ɪk'spektənt/ *a* **~t mother** gestante *f*. **~cy** *n* expectativa *f*

expedient /ɪk'spi:dɪənt/ *a* oportuno ● *n* expediente *m*

expedition /ekspɪ'dɪʃn/ *n* expedição *f*

expel /ɪk'spel/ *vt* (*pt* **expelled**) expulsar; ‹*gas, poison etc*› expelir

expend /ɪk'spend/ *vt* despender

expenditure /ɪk'spendɪtʃə(r)/ *n* despesa *f*, gasto *m*

expense /ɪk'spens/ *n* despesa *f*; (*cost*) custo *m*; **at sb's ~** à custa de alguém; **at the ~ of** *fig* à custa de

expensive /ɪk'spensɪv/ *a* caro, dispendioso; ‹*tastes, habits*› de luxo

experience /ɪk'spɪərɪəns/ *n* experiência *f* ● *vt* experimentar; (*feel*) sentir. **~d** *a* experiente

experiment /ɪk'sperɪmənt/ *n* experiência *f* ● *vi* /ɪk'sperɪment/ fazer uma experiência. **~al** /-'mentl/ *a* experimental

expert /'ekspɜ:t/ *a & n* perito *m*

expertise /ekspɜ:'ti:z/ *n* perícia *f*, competência *f*

expir|e /ɪk'spaɪə(r)/ *vi* expirar. **~y** *n* fim *m* de prazo, expiração *f*

expl|ain /ɪk'spleɪn/ *vt* explicar. **~anation** /eksplə'neɪʃn/ *n* explicação *f*. **~anatory** /ɪk'splæ-nətrɪ/ *a* explicativo

explicit /ɪk'splɪsɪt/ *a* explícito

explo|de /ɪk'spləʊd/ *vt/i* (fazer) explodir. **~sion** /ɪk'spləʊʒn/ *n* explosão *f*. **~sive** *a & n* explosivo *m*

exploit[1] /'eksplɔɪt/ *n* façanha *f*

exploit[2] /ɪk'splɔɪt/ *vt* explorar. **~ation** /eksplɔɪ'teɪʃn/ *n* exploração *f*

explor|e /ɪk'splɔ:(r)/ *vt* explorar; *fig* examinar. **~ation** /eksplə'reɪʃn/ *n* exploração *f*. **~er** *n* explorador *m*

export[1] /ɪk'spɔ:t/ *vt* exportar. **~er** *n* exportador *m*

export[2] /'ekspɔ:t/ *n* exportação *f*

expos|e /ɪk'spəʊz/ *vt* expor; (*disclose*) revelar; (*unmask*) desmascarar. **~ure** /-ʒə(r)/ *n* exposição *f*; (*cold*) frio *m*

express[1] /ɪk'spres/ *a* expresso, categórico ● *adv* (por) expresso ● *n* (*train*) rápido *m*, expresso *m*. **~ly** *adv* expressamente

express[2] /ɪk'spres/ *vt* exprimir. **~ion** /-ʃn/ *n* expressão *f*. **~ive** *a* expressivo

expulsion /ɪk'spʌlʃn/ *n* expulsão *f*

exquisite /'ekskwɪzɪt/ *a* requintado

exten|d /ɪk'stend/ *vt* (*stretch*) estender; (*enlarge*) aumentar, ampliar; (*prolong*) prolongar; (*grant*) oferecer ● *vi* (*stretch*) estender-se; (*in time*) prolongar-se. **~sion** /ɪk'stenʃn/ *n* (*incl phone*) extensão *f*; (*of deadline*) prorrogação *f*; (*building*) anexo *m*

extensive /ɪk'stensɪv/ *a* extenso; ‹*damage, study*› vasto. **~ly** *adv* muito

e

extent /ɪk'stent/ *n* extensão *f*; (*degree*) medida *f*; **to some ~** até certo ponto, em certa medida; **to such an ~ that** a tal ponto que

exterior /ɪk'stɪərɪə(r)/ *a & n* exterior *m*

exterminat|e /ɪk'stɜːmɪneɪt/ *vt* exterminar. **~ion** /-'neɪʃn/ *n* exterminação *f*, extermínio *m*

external /ɪk'stɜːnl/ *a* externo. **~ly** *adv* exteriormente

extinct /ɪk'stɪŋkt/ *a* extinto. **~ion** /-ʃn/ *n* extinção *f*

extinguish /ɪk'stɪŋgwɪʃ/ *vt* extinguir, apagar. **~er** *n* extintor *m*

extort /ɪk'stɔːt/ *vt* extorquir (**from** a). **~ion** /-ʃn/ *n* extorsão *f*

extortionate /ɪk'stɔːʃənət/ *a* exorbitante

extra /'ekstrə/ *a* extra, adicional; **~ strong** extra-forte; **~ time** *Football* prorrogação *f*, (*P*) prolongamento *m* ● *adv* extra, excepcionalmente, (*P*) excecionalmente ● *n* extra *m*; *Cine, Theat* extra *mf*, figurante *mf*

extra- /'ekstrə/ *pref* extra-

extract[1] /ɪk'strækt/ *vt* extrair; ‹*promise, tooth*› arrancar; *fig* obter. **~ion** /-ʃn/ *n* extração *f*; (*descent*) origem *f*

extract[2] /'ekstrækt/ *n* extrato *m*

extraordinary /ɪk'strɔːdnrɪ/ *a* extraordinário

extravagan|t /ɪk'strævəgənt/ *a* extravagante; (*wasteful*) esbanjador. **~ce** *n* extravagância *f*; (*wastefulness*) esbanjamento *m*

extrem|e /ɪk'striːm/ *a & n* extremo *m*. **~ely** *adv* extremamente. **~ist** *n* extremista *mf*

extricate /'ekstrɪkeɪt/ *vt* desembaraçar, livrar

extrovert /'ekstrəvɜːt/ *n* extrovertido *m*

exuberan|t /ɪg'zjuːbərənt/ *a* exuberante

exude /ɪg'zjuːd/ *vt* ‹*charm etc*› destilar; ressumar, (*P*) transpirar

exult /ɪg'zʌlt/ *vi* exultar

eye /aɪ/ *n* olho *m* ● *vt* (*pt* **eyed**, *pres p* **eyeing**) olhar; **keep an ~ on** vigiar; **see ~ to ~** concordar inteiramente. **~-opener** *n* revelação *f*; **~shadow** *n* sombra *f*

eyeball /'aɪbɔːl/ *n* globo *m* ocular

eyebrow /'aɪbraʊ/ *n* sobrancelha *f*

eyelash /'aɪlæʃ/ *n* pestana *f*

eyelid /'aɪlɪd/ *n* pálpebra *f*

eyesight /'aɪsaɪt/ *n* vista *f*

eyesore /'aɪsɔː(r)/ *n* monstruosidade *f*, horror *m*

eyewitness /'aɪwɪtnɪs/ *n* testemunha *f* ocular

Ff

fable /'feɪbl/ *n* fábula *f*

fabric /'fæbrɪk/ *n* tecido *m*; (*structure*) edifício *m*

fabricat|e /'fæbrɪkeɪt/ *vt* fabricar; (*invent*) urdir, inventar. **~ion** /-'keɪʃn/ *n* fabrico *m*; (*invention*) invenção *f*

fabulous /'fæbjʊləs/ *a* fabuloso

face /feɪs/ *n* face *f*, cara *f*, rosto *m*; (*expression*) face *f*; (*grimace*) careta *f*; (*of clock*) mostrador *m*; **~ to ~** cara a cara, frente a frente; **in the ~ of** em vista de; **on the ~ of it** a julgar pelas aparências; **pull ~s** fazer caretas ● *vt* (*look towards*) encarar; (*confront*) enfrentar ● *vi* (*be opposite*) estar de frente para; **~ up to** enfrentar. **~cloth** *n* toalha *f* de rosto; **~lift** *n* cirurgia *f* plástica do rosto; **~ pack** *n* máscara de beleza *f*

faceless /'feɪslɪs/ *a fig* anônimo, (*P*) anónimo

facet /'fæsɪt/ *n* faceta *f*

facetious /fə'siːʃəs/ *a* faceto; *pej* [!] engraçadinho [!] *pej*

facial /'feɪʃl/ *a* facial

facile /'fæsaɪl/ *a* fácil; (*superficial*) superficial

facilitate /fə'sɪlɪteɪt/ *vt* facilitar

facilit|y /fə'sɪlətɪ/ *n* facilidade *f*; **~ies** (*means*) facilidades *fpl*; (*installations*) instalações *fpl*

facsimile /fæk'sɪməlɪ/ *n* facsímile *m*

fact /fækt/ *n* fato *m*, (*P*) facto *m*; **in ~, as a matter of ~** na realidade

faction /'fækʃn/ *n* facção *f*, (*P*) fação *f*

factor /'fæktə(r)/ *n* fator *m*

factory /'fæktərɪ/ *n* fábrica *f*

factual /'fæktʃʊəl/ *a* concreto, real

faculty /'fækltɪ/ *n* faculdade *f*

fad /fæd/ *n* capricho *m*, mania *f*; (*craze*) moda *f*

fade /feɪd/ *vt/i* ‹*colour*› desbotar; ‹*sound*› diminuir; (*disappear*) apagar(-se)

faff /fæf/ *vi* enrolar 'ele ficou enrolando o dia todo', (*P*) engonhar 'esteve aí só a engonhar todo o dia'

fag /fæg/ *n* [!] (*chore*) estafa *f*; [x] (*cigarette*) cigarro *m*

fail /feɪl/ *vt/i* falhar; (*in an examination*) reprovar; (*omit, neglect*) deixar de; *Comm* falir ● *n* **without ~** sem falta

failing /'feɪlɪŋ/ *n* deficiência *f* ● *prep* na falta de, à falta de

failure /'feɪljə(r)/ *n* fracasso *m*, (*P*) falhanço *m*; (*of engine*) falha *f*; (*of electricity*) falta *f*; (*person*) fracassado *m*

faint /feɪnt/ *a* (**-er, -est**) (*indistinct*) apagado; (*weak*) fraco; (*giddy*) tonto ● *vi* desmaiar ● *n* desmaio *m*. **~ness** *n* debilidade *f*; (*indistinctness*) apagado *m*

fair[1] /feə(r)/ *n* feira *f*. **~ground** *n* parque *m* de diversões, (*P*) largo *m* de feira

fair[2] /feə(r)/ *a* (**-er, -est**) ‹*hair*› louro; ‹*weather*› bom; (*of moderate quality*) razoável; (*just*) justo; **~ play** jogo *m* limpo, fair play *m*. **~ly** *adv* razoavelmente. **~ness** *n* justiça *f*. **~ trade** *n* comércio *m* justo

fairy /'feərɪ/ *n* fada *f*; **~ story, ~ tale** conto *m* de fadas

faith /feɪθ/ *n* fé *f*; (*religion*) religião *f*; (*loyalty*) lealdade *f*; **in good ~** de boa fé

faithful /'feɪθfl/ *a* fiel ● *adv* fielmente; **yours ~ly** atenciosamente. **~ness** *n* fidelidade *f*

fake /feɪk/ *n* ‹*thing*› imitação *f*; ‹*person*› impostor *m* ● *a* falsificado ● *vt* falsificar; (*pretend*) simular, fingir

falcon /'fɔlkən/ *n* falcão *m*

fall /fɔ:l/ *vi* (*pt* **fell**, *pp* **fallen**) cair; **~ back** bater em retirada; **~ back on** recorrer a; **~ behind** atrasar-se (**with** em); **~ down** or **off** cair; **~ flat** falhar, não resultar; **~ flat on one's face** estatelar-se; **~ for** ‹*a trick*› cair em, deixar-se levar por; [!] ‹*a person*› apaixonar-se por, ficar caído por [!]; **~ in** ‹*roof*› ruir; *Mil* alinhar-se, pôr-se em forma; **~ out** brigar, (*P*) zangar-se (**with** com); **~ through** (*of plans*) falhar ● *n* quedas *f*; *Amer* (*autumn*) outono *m*. **~s** *npl* (*waterfall*) queda-d'água *f*, cataratas *fpl*. **~out** *n* poeira *f* radioativa

fallac|y /'fæləsɪ/ *n* falácia *f*, engano *m*

fallen /'fɔ:lən/ ▶ FALL

fallible /'fæləbl/ *a* falível

false /fɔ:ls/ *a* falso; **~ teeth** dentadura *f*. **~ly** *adv* falsamente

falsehood /'fɔ:lshʊd/ *n* falsidade *f*, mentira *f*

falsify /'fɔ:lsɪfaɪ/ *vt* (*pt* **-fied**) falsificar; ‹*a story*› deturpar

falter /'fɔ:ltə(r)/ *vi* vacilar; (*of the voice*) hesitar

fame /feɪm/ *n* fama *f*

familiar /fə'mɪlɪə(r)/ *a* familiar; (*intimate*) íntimo; **be ~ with** estar familiarizado com

familiarity /fəmɪlɪ'ærɪtɪ/ *n* familiaridade *f*

familiarize /fə'mɪlɪəraɪz/ *vt* familiarizar (**with/to** com); (*make well known*) tornar conhecido

family /'fæməlɪ/ *n* família *f*; **~ doctor** médico *m* da familia; **~ tree** árvore *f* genealógica

famine /'fæmɪn/ *n* fome *f*

famished /'fæmɪʃt/ *a* esfomeado, faminto; **be ~** [!] estar morrendo de fome, (*P*) estar a morrer de fome

famous /'feɪməs/ *a* famoso

fan[1] /fæn/ *n* (*in the hand*) leque *m*; (*mechanical*) ventilador *m*, (*P*) ventoinha *f* ● *vt* (*pt* **fanned**) abanar; ‹*a fire*› *also fig* atiçar ● *vi* **~ out** abrir-se em leque; **~ belt** correia *f* da ventoinha

fan[2] /fæn/ *n* [!] fã *mf*; **~ mail** correio *m* de fãs

fanatic /fə'nætɪk/ *n* fanático *m*. **~al** *a* fanático. **~ism** /-sɪzəm/ *n* fanatismo *m*

fanciful /'fænsɪfl/ *a* fantasioso, fantasista

fancy /'fænsɪ/ *n* fantasia *f*; (*liking*) gosto *m*; **it took my ~** gostei disso, (*P*) deu-me no gosto; **a passing ~** um entusiasmo passageiro; **~ dress** traje *m* fantasia ● *a* extravagante, fantástico; (*of buttons etc*) de fantasia; (*of prices*) exorbitante ● *vt* imaginar; [!] (*like*) gostar de; [!] (*want*) apetecer

fanfare /'fænfeə(r)/ *n* fanfarra *f*

fang /fæŋ/ *n* presa *f*, dente *m* canino

fantastic /fæn'tæstɪk/ *a* fantástico

fantas|y /'fæntəsɪ/ *n* fantasia *f*. **~ize** *vt* fantasiar, imaginar

far /fɑ:(r)/ *adv* longe; (*much, very*) muito ● *a* distante, longínquo; (*end, side*) outro; **~ away, ~ off** ao longe; **as ~ as** (*up to*) até; **as ~ as I know** tanto quanto saiba; **the F~ East** o Extremo-Oriente *m*. **~-fetched** *a* forçado; (*unconvincing*) pouco plausível; **~-reaching** *a* de grande alcance

farc|e /fɑ:s/ *n* farsa *f*. **~ical** *a* de farsa; ridículo

fare /feə(r)/ *n* preço *m* da passagem; (*in taxi*) tarifa *f*, preço *m* da corrida; (*passenger*) passageiro *m*; (*food*) comida *f* ● *vi* (*get on*) dar-se

farewell /feə'wel/ *int & n* adeus *m*

farm /fɑːm/ *n* quinta *f*, fazenda *f* ● *vt* cultivar ● *vi* ser fazendeiro, (*P*) lavrador; **~ out** (*of work*) delegar a tarefeiros. **~er** *n* fazendeiro *m*, (*P*) lavrador *m*. **~ing** *n* agricultura *f*, lavoura *f*

farmhouse /'fɑːmhaʊs/ *n* casa *f* da fazenda, (*P*) quinta

farmyard /'fɑːmjɑːd/ *n* quintal de fazenda *m*, (*P*) pátio *m* de quinta

farth|er /'fɑːðə(r)/ *adv* mais longe ● *a* mais distante. **~est** *adv* mais longe ● *a* o mais distante

f

fascinat|e /'fæsɪneɪt/ *vt* fascinar. **~ion** /-'neɪʃn/ *n* fascínio *m*, fascinação *f*

fascis|t /'fæʃɪst/ *n* fascista *mf*. **~m** /-zəm/ *n* fascismo *m*

fashion /'fæʃn/ *n* moda *f*; (*manner*) maneira *f* ● *vt* amoldar, (*P*) moldar. **~able** *a* na moda

fast[1] /fɑːst/ *a* (**-er**, **-est**) rápido; (*colour*) fixo, que não desbota ● *adv* depressa; (*firmly*) firmemente; **be ~** (*of clock*) adiantar-se, estar adiantado; **~ asleep** profundamente adormecido, ferrado no sono. **~ food** *n* fast-food *f*

fast[2] /fɑːst/ *vi* jejuar ● *n* jejum *m*

fasten /'fɑːsn/ *vt/i* prender; ‹*door, window*› fechar(-se); ‹*seat-belt*› apertar. **~er ~ing** *ns* fecho *m*

fastidious /fə'stɪdɪəs/ *a* exigente

fat /fæt/ *n* gordura *f* ● *a* (**fatter**, **fattest**) gordo

fatal /'feɪtl/ *a* fatal; **~ injuries** ferimentos *mpl* mortais. **~ity** /fə'tælətɪ/ *n* fatalidade *f*. **~ly** *adv* fatalmente, mortalmente

fate /feɪt/ *n* (*destiny*) destino *m*; (*one's lot*) destino *m*, sorte *f*. **~ful** *a* fatídico

father /'fɑːðə(r)/ *n* pai *m* ● *vt* gerar. **~-in-law** *n* (*pl* **~s-in-law**) sogro *m*. **~ly** *a* paternal

fathom /'fæðəm/ *n* braça *f* ● *vt* **~ (out)** (*comprehend*) compreender

fatigue /fə'tiːg/ *n* fadiga *f* ● *vt* fatigar

fatten /'fætn/ *vt/i* engordar. **~ing** *a* que engorda

fatty /'fætɪ/ *a* (**-ier**, **-iest**) gorduroso; ‹*tissue*› adiposo

fault /fɔːlt/ *n* defeito *m*, falha *f*; (*blame*) falta *f*, culpa *f*; *Geol* falha *f*; **at ~** culpado; **it's your ~** é culpa sua. **~less** *a* impecável. **~y** *a* defeituoso

favour /'feɪvə(r)/ *n* favor *m* ● *vt* favorecer; (*prefer*) preferir; **do sb a ~** fazer um favor a alguém. **~able** *a* favorável

favourit|e /'feɪvərɪt/ *a & n* favorito *m*. **~ism** /-ɪzəm/ *n* favoritismo *m*

fawn[1] /fɔːn/ *n* cervo *m* novo ● *a* (*colour*) castanho claro

fawn[2] /fɔːn/ *vi* **~ on** adular, bajular

fax /fæks/ *n* fax *m*, fac-símile *m*; **~ machine** fax *m* ● *vt* mandar um fax

fear /fɪə(r)/ *n* medo *m*, receio *m*, temor *m*; (*likelihood*) perigo *m* ● *vt* recear, ter medo de. **for ~ of/that** com medo de/que. **~ful** *a* (*terrible*) medonho; (*timid*) medroso, receoso. **~less** *a* destemido, intrépido

feasib|le /'fiːzəbl/ *a* factível, praticável; (*likely*) plausível. **~ility** /-'bɪlətɪ/ *n* possibilidade *f*; (*plausibility*) plausibilidade *f*

feast /fiːst/ *n* festim *m*; *Relig also fig* festa *f* ● *vt/i* festejar; (*eat and drink*) banquetear-se; **~ on** regalar-se com

feat /fiːt/ *n* feito *m*, façanha *f*

feather /'feðə(r)/ *n* pena *f*, pluma *f*

feature /'fiːtʃə(r)/ *n* feição *f*, traço *m*; (*quality*) característica *f*; (*film*) longa-metragem *f*; (*article*) artigo *m* em destaque ● *vt* representar; ‹*film*› ter como protagonista ● *vi* figurar

February /'februərɪ/ *n* fevereiro *m*

fed /fed/ ▶ FEED ● *a* **be ~ up** estar farto [!](with de)

federa|l /'fedərəl/ *a* federal. **~tion** /-'reɪʃn/ *n* federação *f*

fee /fiː/ *n* preço *m*; **~(s)** (*of doctor, lawyer etc*) honorários *mpl*; (*member's subscription*) quota *f*; (*P*) *Univ* propinas *fpl*; (*enrolment/registration*) matrícula *f*; **school ~s** mensalidades *fpl* escolares

feeble /'fiːbl/ *a* (**-er**, **-est**) débil, fraco

feed /fiːd/ *vt* (*pt* **fed**) alimentar, dar de comer a; (*suckle*) alimentar; (*supply*) alimentar, abastecer ● *vi* alimentar-se ● *n* comida *f*; (*breastfeeding*) amamentação *f*; *Mech* alimentação *f*

feedback /'fiːdbæk/ *n* reação *f*; *Electr* regeneração *f*, (*P*) feedback *m*

feel /fiːl/ *vt* (*pt* **felt**) sentir; (*touch*) apalpar, tatear ● *vi* (*tired, lonely etc*) sentir-se; **~ hot/thirsty** ter calor/sede; **~ as if** ter a impressão (de) que; **~ like** ter vontade de

feeling /'fiːlɪŋ/ *n* sentimento *m*; (*physical*) sensação *f*

feet /fiːt/ ▶ FOOT

feign /feɪn/ *vt* fingir

feline /'fiːlaɪn/ *a* felino

fell[1] /fel/ *vt* abater, derrubar
fell[2] /fel/ ▶ FALL
fellow /ˈfeləʊ/ *n* companheiro *m*, camarada *m*; (*of society, college*) membro *m*; [!] cara *m*, (*P*) tipo *m* [!]
felt[1] /felt/ *n* feltro *m*
felt[2] /felt/ ▶ FEEL
female /ˈfiːmeɪl/ *a* ‹*animal etc*› fêmea *f*; ‹*voice, sex etc*› feminino ● *n* mulher *f*; (*animal*) fêmea *f*
feminin|e /ˈfemənɪn/ *a* & *n* feminino *m*. **~ity** /-ˈnɪnətɪ/ *n* feminilidade *f*
feminist /ˈfemɪnɪst/ *n* feminista *mf*
fenc|e /fens/ *n* tapume *m*, cerca *f* ● *vt* cercar ● *vi* esgrimir. **~er** *n* esgrimista *mf*. **~ing** *n* esgrima *f*; (*fences*) tapume *m*
fend /fend/ *vi* **~ for o.s.** defender-se, virar-se [!], governar-se ● *vt* **~ off** defender-se de
fender /ˈfendə(r)/ *n* guarda-fogo *m*; *Amer* (*mudguard*) para-lama *m*, (*P*) guarda-lamas *m*
fennel /ˈfenl/ *n* (*herb*) funcho *m*, erva-doce *f*
ferment[1] /fəˈment/ *vt/i* fermentar; (*excite*) excitar
ferment[2] /ˈfɜːment/ *n* fermento *m*; *fig* efervescência *f*
fern /fɜːn/ *n* feto *m*
feroc|ious /fəˈrəʊʃəs/ *a* feroz. **~ity** /-ˈrɒsətɪ/ *n* ferocidade *f*
ferry /ˈferɪ/ *n* barco *m* de travessia, ferry(-boat) *m* ● *vt* transportar
fertil|e /ˈfɜːtaɪl/ *a* fértil, fecundo. **~ity** /fəˈtɪlətɪ/ *n* fertilidade *f*, fecundidade *f*. **~ize** /-əlaɪz/ *vt* fertilizar, fecundar
fertilizer /ˈfɜːtəlaɪzə(r)/ *n* adubo *m*, fertilizante *m*
fervent /ˈfɜːvənt/ *a* fervoroso
fervour /ˈfɜːvə(r)/ *n* fervor *m*, ardor *m*
fester /ˈfestə(r)/ *vt/i* infectar; *fig* envenenar
festival /ˈfestɪvl/ *n* festival *m*; *Relig* festa *f*
festiv|e /ˈfestɪv/ *a* festivo; **~e season** período *m* das festas. **~ity** /fesˈtɪvətɪ/ *n* festividade *f*, regozijo *m*; **~ities** festas *fpl*, festividades *fpl*
festoon /feˈstuːn/ *vt* engrinaldar (**with** de **or** com)
fetch /fetʃ/ *vt* (*go for*) ir buscar; (*bring*) trazer; (*be sold for*) vender-se por, render
fetching /ˈfetʃɪŋ/ *a* atraente
fête /feɪt/ *n* festa or feira *f* de caridade ao ar livre *f* ● *vt* festejar
fetish /ˈfetɪʃ/ *n* fetiche *m*, ídolo *m*; (*obsession*) mania *f*
feud /fjuːd/ *n* discórdia *f*, inimizade *f*. **~al** *a* feudal
fever /ˈfiːvə(r)/ *n* febre *f*. **~ish** *a* febril
few /fjuː/ *a* & *n* poucos *mpl*; **~ books** poucos livros; **they are ~** são poucos. **a ~** *a* & *n* alguns *mpl*; **a good ~, quite a ~** bastantes
fiancé /fɪˈanseɪ/ *n* noivo *m*. **~e** *n* noiva *f*
fiasco /fɪˈæskəʊ/ *n* (*pl* **-os**) fiasco *m*
fib /fɪb/ *n* lorota *f*, cascata *f*, peta *f*, mentira *f* ● *vi* (*pt* **fibbed**) mentir
fibre /ˈfaɪbə(r)/ *n* fibra *f*
fibreglass /ˈfaɪbəglɑːs/ *n* fibra *f* de vidro
fickle /ˈfɪkl/ *a* leviano, inconstante
fiction /ˈfɪkʃn/ *n* ficção *f*; **(works of) ~** romances *mpl*, obras *fpl* de ficção. **~al** *a* de ficção, fictício
fictitious /fɪkˈtɪʃəs/ *a* fictício
fiddle /ˈfɪdl/ *n* [!] violino *m*; [✖] (*swindle*) trapaça *f*, (*P*) aldrabice *f* ● *vi* [✖] trapacear [✖], (*P*) aldrabar ● *vt* [✖] (*falsify*) falsificar, cozinhar [✖]; **~ with** [!] brincar com, remexer em, (*P*) estar a brincar com, estar a (re)mexer em
fidelity /fɪˈdelətɪ/ *n* fidelidade *f*
fidget /ˈfɪdʒɪt/ *vi* (*pt* **fidgeted**) estar irrequieto, remexer-se; **~ with** remexer em. **~y** *a* irrequieto; (*impatient*) impaciente
field /fiːld/ *n* campo *m*; **F~ Marshal** marechal de campo *m* ● *vt/i* *Cricket* (estar pronto para) apanhar ou interceptar or (*P*) intercetar a bola
fieldwork /ˈfiːldwɜːk/ *n* trabalho *m* de campo; *Mil* fortificação *f* de campanha
fiend /fiːnd/ *n* diabo *m*, demônio *m*, (*P*) demónio *m*. **~ish** *a* diabólico
fierce /fɪəs/ *a* (**-er**, **-est**) feroz; ‹*storm, attack*› violento; ‹*heat*› intenso, abrasador. **~ness** *n* ferocidade *f*; (*of storm, attack*) violência *f*; (*of heat*) intensidade *f*
fiery /ˈfaɪərɪ/ *a* (**-ier**, **-iest**) ardente; ‹*temper, speech*› inflamado
fifteen /fɪfˈtiːn/ *a* & *n* quinze *m*. **~th** *a* & *n* décimo quinto *m*
fifth /fɪfθ/ *a* & *n* quinto *m*
fift|y /ˈfɪftɪ/ *a* & *n* cinquenta *m*. **~y-~y** *a* meias. **~ieth** *a* & *n* quinquagésimo *m*
fig /fɪg/ *n* figo *m*
fight /faɪt/ *vi* (*pt* **fought**) lutar, combater; **~ over sth** lutar por algo; **~ shy of** esquivar-se de, fugir de ● *vt*

f

lutar contra, combater ● *n* luta *f*; (*quarrel, brawl*) briga *f*. **~er** *n* lutador *m*; *Mil* combatente *mf*; (*plane*) caça *m*. **~ing** *n* combate *m*

figurative /ˈfɪgjərətɪv/ *a* figurado

figure /ˈfɪgə(r)/ *n* (*number*) algarismo *m*; (*diagram, body*) figura *f*; **~ of speech** figura *f* de retórica ● *vt* imaginar, supor; **~ out** compreender ● *vi* (*appear*) figurar (**in** em). **~head** *n* figura *f* de proa; *pej* (*person*) testa de ferro *m*; chefe *m* nominal

f

fil|e[1] /faɪl/ *n* (*tool*) lixa *f*, lima *f* ● *vt* lixar, limar

fil|e[2] /faɪl/ *n* fichário *m*, (*P*) dossier *m*; (*box, drawer*) fichário *m*, (*P*) ficheiro *m*; *Comput* arquivo *m*; (*line*) fila *f*; **(in) single ~e** (em) fila indiana ● *vt* arquivar ● *vi* **~e (past)** desfilar, marchar em fila; **~e in/out** entrar/sair em fila; **~ing cabinet** fichário *m*, (*P*) ficheiro *m*. **~ extension** *n* *Comput* extensão *f* de arquivo justo

fill /fɪl/ *vt/i* encher(-se); ‹*vacancy*› preencher ● *n* **eat one's ~** comer o que quiser; **have one's ~** estar farto; **~ in** ‹*form*› preencher; **~ out** (*get fat*) engordar; **~ up** encher até cima; *Auto* encher o tanque, (*P*) atestar o depósito

fillet /ˈfɪlɪt/ *n* (*meat, fish*) filé *m*, (*P*) filete *m* ● *vt* (*pt* **filleted**) ‹*meat, fish*› cortar em filés, (*P*) filetes

filling /ˈfɪlɪŋ/ *n* recheio *m*; (*of tooth*) obturação *f*, (*P*) chumbo *m*; **~ station** posto *m* de gasolina

film /fɪlm/ *n* filme *m*; **~ star** estrela or vedete *f* de cinema, astro *m* ● *vt/i* filmar

filter /ˈfɪltə(r)/ *n* filtro *m*; **~ coffee** café *m* de filtro ● *vt/i* filtrar(-se)

filth /fɪlθ/ *n* imundície *f*; *fig* obscenidade *f*. **~y** *a* imundo; *fig* obsceno

fin /fɪn/ *n* barbatana *f*

final /ˈfaɪnl/ *a* final; (*conclusive*) decisivo ● *n* *Sport* final *f*. **~s** *npl* (*exams*) finais *fpl*. **~ist** *n* finalista *mf*. **~ly** *adv* finalmente, por fim; (*once and for all*) definitivamente

finale /fɪˈnɑːlɪ/ *n* final *m*

finalize /ˈfaɪnəlaɪz/ *vt* finalizar

financ|e /ˈfaɪnæns/ *n* finança(s) *f* ● *a* financeiro ● *vt* financiar

financial /faɪˈnænʃl/ *a* financeiro

find /faɪnd/ *vt* (*pt* **found**) ‹*sth lost*› achar, encontrar; (*think*) achar; (*discover*) descobrir; *Jur* declarar ● *n* achado *m* □ **~ out** *vt* apurar, descobrir ● *vi* informar-se (**about** sobre)

fine[1] /faɪn/ *n* multa *f* ● *vt* multar

fine[2] /faɪn/ *a* (**-er**, **-est**) fino; (*splendid*) belo, lindo; **~ arts** belas artes *fpl*; **~ weather** bom tempo ● *adv* (muito) bem; (*small*) fino, fininho

finesse /fɪˈnes/ *n* finura *f*, sutileza *f*, (*P*) subtileza *f*

finger /ˈfɪŋgə(r)/ *n* dedo *m* ● *vt* apalpar. **~nail** *n* unha *f*

fingerprint /ˈfɪŋgəprɪnt/ *n* impressão *f* digital

fingertip /ˈfɪŋgətɪp/ *n* ponta *f* do dedo

finicky /ˈfɪnɪkɪ/ *a* meticuloso, miudinho

finish /ˈfɪnɪʃ/ *vt/i* acabar, terminar ● *n* fim *m*; (*of race*) chegada *f*; (*on wood, clothes*) acabamento *m*; **~ doing** acabar de fazer; **~ up doing** acabar por fazer; **~ up in** ir parar a, acabar em

finite /ˈfaɪnaɪt/ *a* finito

Fin|land /ˈfɪnlənd/ *n* Finlândia *f*. **~n** *n* finlandês *m*. **~nish** *a & n* *Lang* finlandês *m*

fir /fɜː(r)/ *n* abeto *m*

fire /ˈfaɪə(r)/ *n* fogo *m*; (*conflagration*) incêndio *m*; (*heater*) aquecedor *m*; **on ~** em chamas; **set ~ to** pôr fogo a/em; **~ brigade** bombeiros *mpl*; **~ station** quartel *m* dos bombeiros **~ alarm** *n* alarme *m* de incêndio; **~ engine** *n* carro *m* de bombeiro; **~ escape** *n* saída *f* de incêndio; **~ extinguisher** *n* extintor *m* de incêndio ● *vt* ‹*bullet, gun, etc*› disparar; (*dismiss*) despedir; *fig* (*stimulate*) inflamar ● *vi* atirar; fazer fogo (**at** sobre)

firearm /ˈfaɪərɑːm/ *n* arma *f* de fogo

fireman /ˈfaɪəmən/ *n* (*pl* **-men**) bombeiro *m*

fireplace /ˈfaɪəpleɪs/ *n* chaminé *f*, lareira *f*

firewood /ˈfaɪəwʊd/ *n* lenha *f*

firework /ˈfaɪəwɜːk/ *n* fogo *m* de artifício

firing squad /ˈfaɪərɪŋskwɒd/ *n* pelotão *m* de execução

firm[1] /fɜːm/ *n* firma *f* comercial

firm[2] /fɜːm/ *a* (**-er**, **-est**) firme; (*belief*) firme, inabalável

first /fɜːst/ *a & n* primeiro *m*; *Auto* primeira *f*; **~ name** nome *m* próprio; **for the ~ time** pela primeira vez; **~ aid** primeiros socorros *mpl* ● *adv* primeiro, em primeiro lugar; **at ~** a princípio, no início; **~ of all** antes de mais nada. **~-class** *a* de primeira classe; **~-rate** *a* excelente. **~ly** *adv* primeiramente, em primeiro lugar

fish /fɪʃ/ *n* (*pl usually invar*) peixe *m* ● *vt/i* pescar; **~ out** ! tirar. **~ing** *n* pesca *f*; **go ~ing** ir pescar, (*P*) ir à pesca. **~y** *a* de peixe; *fig* (*dubious*) suspeito

fisherman /'fɪʃəmən/ *n* (*pl* **-men**) pescador *m*

fishmonger /'fɪʃmʌŋgə(r)/ *n* dono *m* /empregado *m* de peixaria; **~'s (shop)** peixaria *f*

fission /'fɪʃn/ *n* fissão *f*, cisão *f*

fist /fɪst/ *n* punho *m*, mão *f* fechada, (*P*) punho *m*

fit[1] /fɪt/ *n* acesso *m*, ataque *m*; (*of generosity*) rasgo *m*

fit[2] /fɪt/ *a* (**fitter**, **fittest**) de boa saúde, em forma; (*proper*) próprio; (*good enough*) em condições; (*able*) capaz ● *vt/i* (*pt* **fitted**) assentar, ficar bem (a); (*into space*) caber; (*match*) ajustar-se (a); (*install*) instalar; **~ out** equipar; **~ted carpet** carpete *m*, (*P*) alcatifa *f* ● *n* **be a good ~** assentar bem; **be a tight ~** estar justo. **~ness** *n* saúde *f*, (*P*) condição *f* física

fitting /'fɪtɪŋ/ *a* apropriado ● *n* (*clothes*) prova *f*; **~s** (*fixtures*) instalações *fpl*; (*fitments*) mobiliário *m*; **~ room** cabine *f* (de provas)

five /faɪv/ *a & n* cinco *m*

fix /fɪks/ *vt* fixar; (*mend, prepare*) arranjar ● *n* **in a ~** em apuros, (*P*) numa alhada; **~ sb up with sth** conseguir algo para alguém. **~ed** *a* fixo

fixation /fɪk'seɪʃn/ *n* fixação *f*; (*obsession*) obsessão *f*

fixture /'fɪkstʃə(r)/ *n* equipamento *m*, instalação *f*; *Sport* (data *f* marcada para) competição *f*

fizz /fɪz/ *vi* efervescer, borbulhar ● *n* efervescência *f*. **~y** *a* gasoso

fizzle /'fɪzl/ *vi* **~ out** ‹*plan etc*› acabar em nada or (*P*) em águas de bacalhau [!]

flab /flæb/ *n* [!] gordura *f*; banha *f* [!]. **~by** *a* flácido

flabbergasted /'flæbəgɑːstɪd/ *a* [!] espantado; pasmado [!]

flag[1] /flæg/ *n* bandeira *f* ● *vt* (*pt* **flagged**) fazer sinal; **~ down** fazer sinal para parar. **~pole** *n* mastro *m* (de bandeira)

flag[2] /flæg/ *vi* (*pt* **flagged**) (*droop*) cair, pender, tombar; (*of person*) esmorecer

flagrant /'fleɪgrənt/ *a* flagrante

flagstone /'flægstəʊn/ *n* laje *f*

flair /fleə(r)/ *n* jeito *m*, habilidade *f*

flak|e /fleɪk/ *n* floco *m*; (*paint*) lasca *f* ● *vi* descamar-se, lascar-se. **~y** *a* ‹*paint*› descamado, lascado

flamboyant /flæm'bɔɪənt/ *a* flamejante; (*showy*) flamante, vistoso; (*of manner*) extravagante

flame /fleɪm/ *n* chama *f*, labareda *f* ● *vi* flamejar; **burst into ~s** incendiar-se

flamingo /flə'mɪŋgəʊ/ *n* (*pl* **-os**) flamingo *m*

flammable /'flæməbl/ *a* inflamável

flan /flæn/ *n* torta *f*, (*P*) tarte *f*

flank /flæŋk/ *n* flanco *m* ● *vt* flanquear

flannel /'flænl/ *n* flanela *f*; (*for face*) toalha *f* de rosto

flap /flæp/ *vi* (*pt* **flapped**) bater ● *vt* **~ its wings** bater as asas ● *n* (*of table, pocket*) aba *f*; ⊠ (*panic*) pânico *m*

flare /fleə(r)/ *vi* **~ up** irromper em chamas; (*of war*) rebentar; *fig* (*of person*) enfurecer-se ● *n* chamejar *m*; (*dazzling light*) clarão *m*; (*signal*) foguete *m* de sinalização. **~d** *a* ‹*skirt*› evasê

flash /flæʃ/ *vi* brilhar subitamente; (*on and off*) piscar; *Auto* fazer sinal com o pisca-pisca; **~ past** passar como uma bala, (*P*) passar como um bólide ● *vt* fazer brilhar; (*send*) lançar, dardejar; (*flaunt*) fazer alarde de, ostentar ● *n* clarão *m*, lampejo *m*; *Photo* flash *m*

flashback /'flæʃbæk/ *n* cena *f* retrospectiva *or* (*P*) retrospetiva, flashback *m*

flashlight /'flæʃlaɪt/ *n* lanterna *f* elétrica

flashy /'flæʃɪ/ *a* espalhafatoso, que dá nas vistas

flask /flɑːsk/ *n* frasco *m*; (*vacuum flask*) garrafa *f* térmica, (*P*) termo *m*

flat /flæt/ *a* (**flatter**, **flattest**) plano, chato; ‹*tyre*› arriado, vazio, furado; (*battery*) fraco; ‹*refusal*› categórico; ‹*fare, rate*› fixo; (*monotonous*) monótono; *Mus* bemol; (*out of tune*) desafinado; **~ out** (*drive*) em alta velocidade; (*work*) a dar tudo por tudo ● *n* apartamento *m*; [!] (*tyre*) furo *m* no pneu; *Mus* bemol *m*. **~ly** *adv* categoricamente

flatter /'flætə(r)/ *vt* lisonjear, adular. **~ing** *a* lisonjeiro, adulador. **~y** *n* lisonja *f*

flaunt /flɔːnt/ *vt/i* pavonear(-se), ostentar

flavour /'fleɪvə(r)/ *n* sabor *m* (**of** a) ● *vt* dar sabor a, temperar. **~ing** *n* aroma *m* sintético; (*seasoning*) tempero *m*

flaw /flɔː/ *n* falha *f*, imperfeição *f*. **~less** *a* perfeito

flea /fliː/ *n* pulga *f*

fled /fled/ ▶ FLEE

flee /fliː/ *vi* (*pt* **fled**) fugir ● *vt* fugir de

fleece /fliːs/ *n* lã *f* de carneiro, velo *m* ● *vt fig* esfolar; roubar

fleet /fliːt/ *n* (*of warships*) esquadra *f*; (*of merchant ships, vehicles*) frota *f*

fleeting /ˈfliːtɪŋ/ *a* curto, fugaz

Flemish /ˈflemɪʃ/ *a* & *n Lang* flamengo *m*

flesh /fleʃ/ *n* carne *f*; (*of fruit*) polpa *f*

flew /fluː/ ▶ FLY²

flex¹ /fleks/ *vt* flexionar

flex² /fleks/ *n Electr* fio *f* flexível

flexib|le /ˈfleksəbl/ *a* flexível. **~ility** /-ˈbɪlətɪ/ *n* flexibilidade *f*

flick /flɪk/ *n* (*light blow*) safanão *m*; (*with fingertip*) piparote *m* ● *vt* dar um safanão em; (*with fingertip*) dar um piparote a; **~ through** folhear

flicker /ˈflɪkə(r)/ *vi* vacilar, oscilar, tremular ● *n* oscilação *f*, tremular *m*; (*light*) luz *f* trémula

flier /ˈflaɪə(r)/ *n* = FLYER

flight¹ /flaɪt/ *n* (*flying*) voo *m*; **~ of stairs** lance *m* de escada

flight² /flaɪt/ *n* (*fleeing*) fuga *f*; **put to ~** pôr em fuga; **take ~** pôr-se em fuga

flimsy /ˈflɪmzɪ/ *a* (**-ier**, **-iest**) ‹*material*› fino; ‹*object*› frágil; ‹*excuse etc*› fraco, esfarrapado

flinch /flɪntʃ/ *vi* (*wince*) retrair-se; (*draw back*) recuar; (*hesitate*) hesitar

fling /flɪŋ/ *vt/i* (*pt* **flung**) atirar(-se), arremessar(-se); (*rush*) precipitar-se

flint /flɪnt/ *n* sílex *m*; (*for lighter*) pedra *f*

flip /flɪp/ *vt* (*pt* **flipped**) fazer girar com o dedo e o polegar ● *n* pancadinha *f*; **~ through** folhear

flippant /ˈflɪpənt/ *a* irreverente, petulante

flirt /flɜːt/ *vt* namoriscar, flertar, (*P*) flartar ● *n* namorador *m*, namoradeira *f*. **~ation** /-ˈteɪʃn/ *n* namorico *m*, flerte *m*, (*P*) flirt *m*. **~atious** *a* namorador *m*, namoradeira *f*

flit /flɪt/ *vi* (*pt* **flitted**) esvoaçar

float /fləʊt/ *vt/i* (fazer) flutuar; (*company*) lançar ● *n* boia *f*; (*low cart*) carro *m* alegórico

flock /flɒk/ *n* (*of sheep; congregation*) rebanho *m*; (*of birds*) bando *m*; (*crowd*) multidão *f* ● *vi* afluir, juntar-se

flog /flɒg/ *vt* (*pt* **flogged**) açoitar; ☒ (*sell*) vender

flood /flʌd/ *n* inundação *f*, cheia *f*; (*of tears*) dilúvio *m*, rio *m* ● *vt* inundar, alagar ● *vi* estar inundado; ‹*river*› transbordar; *fig* ‹*people*› afluir

floodlight /ˈflʌdlaɪt/ *n* projetor *m*, holofote *m* ● *vt* (*pt* **floodlit**) iluminar

floor /flɔː(r)/ *n* chão *m*, soalho *m*; (*for dancing*) pista *f*; (*storey*) andar *m* ● *vt* assoalhar; (*baffle*) desconcertar, embatucar

flop /flɒp/ *vi* (*pt* **flopped**) (*drop*) (deixar-se) cair; (*move helplessly*) debater-se; ☒ (*fail*) ser um fiasco ● *n* ☒ fiasco *m*. **~py** *a* mole, tombado; **~py (disk)** disquete *m*

floral /ˈflɒːrəl/ *a* floral

florid /ˈflɒrɪd/ *a* florido

florist /ˈflɒrɪst/ *n* florista *mf*

flounder /ˈflaʊndə(r)/ *vi* esbracejar, debater-se; *fig* meter os pés pelas mãos

flour /ˈflaʊə(r)/ *n* farinha *f*

flourish /ˈflʌrɪʃ/ *vi* florescer, prosperar ● *vt* brandir ● *n* floreado *m*; (*movement*) gesto *m* elegante

flout /flaʊt/ *vt* escarnecer (de)

flow /fləʊ/ *vi* correr, fluir; (*traffic*) mover-se; (*hang loosely*) flutuar; (*gush*) jorrar ● *n* corrente *f*; (*of tide; also fig*) enchente *f*; **~ into** (*of river*) desaguar em; **~ chart** organograma *m*

flower /ˈflaʊə(r)/ *n* flor *f* ● *vi* florir, florescer. **~ bed** *n* canteiro *m*. **~y** *a* florido

flown /fləʊn/ ▶ FLY²

flu /fluː/ *n* [!] gripe *f*

fluctuat|e /ˈflʌktʃʊeɪt/ *vi* flutuar, oscilar. **~ion** /-ˈeɪʃn/ *n* flutuação *f*, oscilação *f*

fluen|t /ˈfluːənt/ *a* fluente; **be ~t (in a language)** falar correntemente (uma língua). **~cy** *n* fluência *f*. **~tly** *adv* fluentemente

fluff /flʌf/ *n* cotão *m*; (*down*) penugem *f* ● *vt* [!] (*bungle*) estender-se em ☒; executar mal. **~y** *a* penugento, fofo

fluid /ˈfluːɪd/ *a* & *n* fluido *m*

fluke /fluːk/ *n* bambúrrio *m* [!]; golpe *m* de sorte

flung /flʌŋ/ ▶ FLING

flunk /flʌŋk/ *vt/i Amer* [!] levar pau [!], (*P*) chumbar [!]

fluorescent /flʊəˈresnt/ *a* fluorescente

fluoride /ˈflʊəraɪd/ *n* flúor *m*

flush¹ /flʌʃ/ *vi* corar, ruborizar-se ● *vt* lavar com água, (*P*) lavar a jorros de água; **~ the toilet** dar descarga, (*P*) puxar o autoclismo ● *n* rubor *m*, vermelhidão *f*; *fig* excitação *f*; (*of water*) jorro *m* ● *a* **~ with** ao nível de, rente a

flush² /flʌʃ/ *vt* **~ out** desalojar

fluster /ˈflʌstə(r)/ *vt* atarantar, perturbar, enervar

flute /fluːt/ *n* flauta *f*

flutter /ˈflʌtə(r)/ *vi* esvoaçar; ‹*wings*› bater; ‹*heart*› palpitar ● *vt* bater; **~ one's eyelashes** pestanejar ● *n* (*of wings*) batimento *m*; *fig* agitação *f*

flux /flʌks/ *n* **in a state of ~** em mudança *f* contínua

fly[1] /flaɪ/ *n* mosca *f*

fly[2] /flaɪ/ *vi* (*pt* **flew**, *pp* **flown**) voar; ‹*passengers*› ir de/viajar de avião; (*rush*) correr ● *vt* pilotar; ‹*passengers, goods*› transportar por avião; ‹*flag*› hastear, (*P*) arvorar ● *n* (*of trousers*) braguilha *f*

flyer /ˈflaɪə(r)/ *n* aviador *m*; *Amer* (*circular*) prospecto *m*, (*P*) prospeto *m*

flying /ˈflaɪɪŋ/ *a* voador; **with ~ colours** com grande êxito, esplendidamente; **~ saucer** disco *m* voador; **~ start** bom arranque *m*; **~ visit** visita *f* de médico

flyover /ˈflaɪəʊvə(r)/ *n* viaduto *m*

foal /fəʊl/ *n* potro *m*

foam /fəʊm/ *n* espuma *f* ● *vi* espumar

fob /fɒb/ *vt* (*pt* **fobbed**) **~ off** iludir, entreter com artifícios; **~ off on** impingir a

focus /ˈfəʊkəs/ *n* (*pl* **-cuses** *or* **-ci**) /-saɪ/ foco *m*; **in ~** focado, em foco; **out of ~** desfocado ● *vt/i* (*pt* **focused**) focar

fodder /ˈfɒdə(r)/ *n* forragem *f*

foetus /ˈfiːtəs/ *n* (*pl* **-tuses**) feto *m*

fog /fɒg/ *n* nevoeiro *m* ● *vt/i* (*pt* **fogged**) enevoar(-se). **~horn** *n* sereia *f* de nevoeiro. **~gy** *a* enevoado, brumoso; **it is ~gy** está nevoento *or* (*P*) de nevoeiro

foible /ˈfɔɪbl/ *n* fraqueza *f*, ponto *m* fraco

foil[1] /fɔɪl/ *n* papel *m* de alumínio; *fig* contraste *m*

foil[2] /fɔɪl/ *vt* frustrar

fold /fəʊld/ *vt/i* dobrar(-se); (*arms*) cruzar; [!] (*fail*) falir ● *n* dobra *f*. **~er** *n* pasta *f*; (*leaflet*) prospecto *m or* (*P*) prospeto *m* (desdobrável) *m*. **~ing** *a* dobrável, dobradiço

foliage /ˈfəʊlɪɪdʒ/ *n* folhagem *f*

folk /fəʊk/ *n* povo *m*; **~s** (*family, people*) gente *f* [!], pessoal *m* [!] ● *a* folclórico, popular. **~lore** *n* folclore *m*

follow /ˈfɒləʊ/ *vt/i* seguir; **it ~s that** quer dizer que; **~ suit** ‹*cards*› servir o naipe jogado; *fig* seguir o exemplo, fazer o mesmo; **~ up** (*letter etc*) dar seguimento a. **~er** *n* partidário *m*, seguidor *m*. **~ing** *n* partidários *mpl* ● *a* seguinte ● *prep* em seguimento a

folly /ˈfɒlɪ/ *n* loucura *f*

fond /fɒnd/ *a* **-er -est** carinhoso; (*hope*) caro; **be ~ of** gostar de, ser amigo de. **~ness** *n* (*for people*) afeição *f*; (*for thing*) gosto *m*

fondle /ˈfɒndl/ *vt* acariciar

font /fɒnt/ *n* pia *f* batismal

food /fuːd/ *n* alimentação *f*, comida *f*; (*nutrient*) alimento *m* ● *a* alimentar; **~ poisoning** envenenamento *m* alimentar

fool /fuːl/ *n* idiota *mf*, parvo *m* ● *vt* enganar ● *vi* **~ around** andar sem fazer nada

foolhardy /ˈfuːlhɑːdɪ/ *a* imprudente, atrevido

foolish /ˈfuːlɪʃ/ *a* idiota, parvo. **~ness** *n* idiotice *f*, parvoice *f*

foolproof /ˈfuːlpruːf/ *a* infalível

foot /fʊt/ *n* (*pl* **feet**) (*of person, bed, stairs*) pé *m*; (*of animal*) pata *f*; (*measure*) pé *m* (= 30,48 cm); **on ~** a pé; **on** or **to one's feet** de pé; **put one's ~ in it** cometer uma gafe; **to be under sb's feet** atrapalhar alguém ● *vt* **~ the bill** pagar a conta. **~bridge** *n* passarela *f*

football /ˈfʊtbɔːl/ *n* bola *f* de futebol; (*game*) futebol *m*; **~ pools** loteria *f* esportiva, (*P*) totobola *m*. **~er** *n* futebolista *mf*, jogador *m* de futebol

foothills /ˈfʊthɪlz/ *npl* contrafortes *mpl*

foothold /ˈfʊthəʊld/ *n* ponto *m* de apoio

footing /ˈfʊtɪŋ/ *n* **firm ~** apoio *m* seguro; **on an equal ~** em pé de igualdade

footlights /ˈfʊtlaɪts/ *npl* ribalta *f*

footnote /ˈfʊtnəʊt/ *n* nota *f* de rodapé

footpath /ˈfʊtpɑːθ/ *n* (*pavement*) calçada *f*, (*P*) passeio *m*; (*in open country*) atalho *m*, caminho *m*

footprint /ˈfʊtprɪnt/ *n* pegada *f*

footstep /ˈfʊtstep/ *n* passo *m*

footwear /ˈfʊtweə(r)/ *n* calçado *m*

for *unstressed* /fə(r) *emphatic* fɔː(r)/ ● *prep*

····➤ (*expressing purpose*) para; **~ me** para mim; **music ~ dancing** música para dançar; **what is it ~?** para que serve isto?; **what have you got ~ a cold?** o que tem para gripe?

····➤ (*on behalf of, in place of*) por; **I did it ~ you** fiz isso por si; **I took her classes ~ her** fiquei com as turmas dela; **I'm speaking ~ everyone in this department** falo por todos neste departamento

····➤ (*expressing worth*) no valor de; **a check/bill ~ ten euros** um cheque/ uma conta no valor de dez euros

····➤ (*expressing reason*) por; **famous ~ its wine** famoso pelo seu vinho; **he was sentenced to death ~ murder** ele foi condenado à morte por homicídio; **~ fear/love of** por medo/ amor de

! the preposition *por* often contracts with the definite articles o and *a* to form *pelo, pela*

····➤ (*expressing direction*) para; **the train ~ Oxford** o trem para Oxford

····➤ (*with a time period that is still continuing*) há; **I've been waiting ~ two hours** estou esperando há duas horas; **I haven't seen him ~ ten years** há dez anos que não o vejo; (*with a time period that has ended*) durante; **I waited ~ two hours** esperei durante duas horas; (*with a future time period*) durante; **I'm going to Paris ~ six weeks** vou para Paris por seis semanas; **he'll be away ~ a few weeks** ele vai ficar fora durante algumas semanas

····➤ (*with distances*) durante; **I drove ~ 50 kilometres** dirigi durante 50 quilômetros

● *conj*

····➤ porque, visto que; **he's not coming, ~ he has no money** ele não vem, porque não tem dinheiro

forbade /fə'bæd/ ▶ FORBID

forbid /fə'bɪd/ *vt* (*pt* **forbade**, *pp* **forbidden**) proibir; **you are ~den to smoke** você está proibido de fumar, (*P*) estás proibido de fumar. **~ding** *a* severo, intimidante

force /fɔːs/ *n* força *f*; **come into ~** entrar em vigor; **the ~s** as Forças Armadas ● *vt* forçar; **~ into** fazer entrar à força; **~ on** impor a. **~d** *a* forçado. **~ful** *a* enérgico

force-feed /'fɔːsfiːd/ *vt* (*pt* **-fed**) alimentar à força

forceps /'fɔːseps/ *n* ; *pl invar* fórceps *m*

forcibl|e /'fɔːsəbl/ *a* convincente; (*done by force*) à força. **~y** *adv* à força

ford /fɔːd/ *n* vau *m* ● *vt* passar a vau, vadear

fore /fɔː(r)/ *a* dianteiro ● *n* **to the ~** em evidência

forearm /'fɔːrɑːm/ *n* antebraço *m*

forecast /'fɔːkɑːst/ *vt* (*pt* **forecast**) prever ● *n* previsão *f*; **weather ~** boletim *m* meteorológico, previsão *f* do tempo

forefinger /'fɔːfɪŋgə(r)/ *n* (dedo) indicador *m*

foregone /'fɔːgɒn/ *a* **~ conclusion** resultado *m* previsto

foreground /'fɔːgraʊnd/ *n* primeiro plano *m*

forehead /'fɒrɪd/ *n* testa *f*

foreign /'fɒrən/ *a* estrangeiro; ‹*trade*› externo; ‹*travel*› ao/no estrangeiro; **F~ Office** Ministério *m* dos Negócios Estrangeiros. **~er** *n* estrangeiro *m*

foreman /'fɔːmən/ *n* (*pl* **foremen**) contramestre *m*; (*of jury*) primeiro jurado *m*

foremost /'fɔːməʊst/ *a* principal, primeiro ● *adv* **first and ~** antes de mais nada, em primeiro lugar

forename /'fɔːneɪm/ *n* prenome *m*

forerunner /'fɔːrʌnə(r)/ *n* precursor *m*

foresee /fɔː'siː/ *vt* (*pt* **-saw**, *pp* **-seen**) prever. **~able** *a* previsível

foresight /'fɔːsaɪt/ *n* previsão *f*, previdência *f*

forest /'fɒrɪst/ *n* floresta *f*

forestry /'fɒrɪstrɪ/ *n* silvicultura *f*

forever /fə'revə(r)/ *adv* (*endlessly*) constantemente, para sempre

foreword /'fɔːwɜːd/ *n* prefácio *m*

forfeit /'fɔːfɪt/ *n* penalidade *f*, preço *m*; (*in game*) prenda *f* ● *vt* perder

forgave /fə'geɪv/ ▶ FORGIVE

forge[1] /fɔːdʒ/ *vi* **~ ahead** tomar a dianteira, avançar

forge[2] /fɔːdʒ/ *n* forja *f* ● *vt* ‹*metal, friendship*› forjar; (*counterfeit*) falsificar, forjar. **~r** /-ə(r)/ *n* falsificador *m*, forjador *m*. **~ry** /-ərɪ/ *n* falsificação *f*

forget /fə'get/ *vt/i* (*pt* **forgot**, *pp* **forgotten**) esquecer; **~ o.s.** portar-se com menos dignidade, esquecer-se de quem é. **~-me-not** *n* miosótis *m*. **~ful** *a* esquecido. **~fulness** *n* esquecimento *m*

forgive /fə'gɪv/ *vt* (*pt* **forgave**, *pp* **forgiven**) perdoar (**sb for sth** algo a alguém). **~ness** *n* perdão *m*

forgo /fɔː'gəʊ/ *vt* (*pt* **forwent**, *pp* **forgone**) renunciar a

fork /fɔːk/ *n* garfo *m*; (*for digging etc*) forquilha *f*; (*in road*) bifurcação *f* ● *vi* bifurcar; **~ out** [!] desembolsar. **~lift truck** *n* empilhadeira *f*

forlorn /fə'lɔ:n/ *a* abandonado, desolado

form /fɔ:m/ *n* forma *f*; (*document*) impresso *m*, formulário *m*; *Schol* classe *f* ● *vt/i* formar(-se)

formal /'fɔ:ml/ *a* formal; ‹*dress*› de cerimônia *or* (*P*) cerimónia. **~ity** /-'mælətɪ/ *n* formalidade *f*

format /'fɔ:mæt/ *n* formato *m* ● *vt* (*pl* **formatted**) ‹*disk*› formatar

formation /fɔ:'meɪʃn/ *n* formação *f*

former /'fɔ:mə(r)/ *a* antigo; (*first of two*) primeiro; **the ~** aquele. **~ly** *adv* antigamente

formidable /'fɔ:mɪdəbl/ *a* formidável, tremendo

formula /'fɔ:mjʊlə/ *n* (*pl* **-ae** /-i:/; *or* **-as**) fórmula *f*

formulate /'fɔ:mjʊleɪt/ *vt* formular

forsake /fə'seɪk/ *vt* (*pt* **forsook**, *pp* **forsaken**) abandonar

fort /fɔ:t/ *n Mil* forte *m*

forth /fɔ:θ/ *adv* adiante, para a frente; **and so ~** e assim por diante, etcetera; **go back and ~** andar de trás para diante

forthcoming /fɔ:θ'kʌmɪŋ/ *a* que está para vir, próximo; (*communicative*) comunicativo, receptivo, (*P*) recetivo; ‹*book*› no prelo

forthright /'fɔ:θraɪt/ *a* franco, direto

fortif|y /'fɔ:tɪfaɪ/ *vt* fortificar. **~ication** /-ɪ'keɪʃn/ *n* fortificação *f*

fortitude /'fɔ:tɪtju:d/ *n* fortitude *f*, fortaleza *f*

fortnight /'fɔ:tnaɪt/ *n* quinze dias *mpl*, (*P*) quinzena *f*. **~ly** *a* quinzenal ● *adv* de quinze em quinze dias

fortress /'fɔ:trɪs/ *n* fortaleza *f*

fortunate /'fɔ:tʃənət/ *a* feliz, afortunado; **be ~** ter sorte. **~ly** *adv* felizmente

fortune /'fɔ:tʃən/ *n* sorte *f*; (*wealth*) fortuna *f*; **have the good ~ to** ter a sorte de. **~ teller** *n* cartomante *mf*

fort|y /'fɔ:tɪ/ *a & n* quarenta *m*. **~ieth** *a & n* quadragésimo *m*

forum /'fɔ:rəm/ *n* fórum *m*, foro *m*

forward /'fɔ:wəd/ *a* (*in front*) dianteiro; (*towards the front*) para a frente; (*advanced*) adiantado; (*pert*) atrevido ● *n Sport* atacante *m*, (*P*) avançado *m* ● *adv* **~(s)** para a frente, para diante; **come ~** apresentar-se; **go ~** avançar ● *vt* ‹*letter*› remeter; ‹*goods*› expedir; *fig* (*help*) favorecer

fossil /'fɒsl/ *a & n* fóssil *m*

foster /'fɒstə(r)/ *vt* fomentar; ‹*child*› criar. **~-child** *n* filho *m* adotivo; **~-mother** *n* mãe *f* adotiva

fought /fɔ:t/ ▶ FIGHT

foul /faʊl/ *a* (**-er**, **-est**) infecto; ‹*language*› obsceno; ‹*weather*› mau; **~ play** jogo *m* desleal; (*crime*) crime *m* ● *n Football* falta *f* ● *vt* sujar, emporcalhar. **~-mouthed** *a* de linguagem obscena

found[1] /faʊnd/ ▶ FEEL

found[2] /faʊnd/ *vt* fundar. **~ation** /-'deɪʃn/ *n* fundação *f*; (*basis*) fundamento *m*. **~ations** *npl* (*of building*) alicerces *mpl*

founder[1] /'faʊndə(r)/ *n* fundador *m*

founder[2] /'faʊndə(r)/ *vi* afundar-se

foundry /'faʊndrɪ/ *n* fundição *f*

fountain /'faʊntɪn/ *n* fonte *f*. **~ pen** *n* caneta-tinteiro *f*, (*P*) caneta *f* de tinta permanente

four /fɔ:(r)/ *a & n* quatro *m*. **~th** *a & n* quarto *m*

fourteen /fɔ:'ti:n/ *a & n* catorze *m*. **~th** *a & n* décimo quarto *m*

fowl /faʊl/ *n* ave *f* de capoeira

fox /fɒks/ *n* raposa *f* ● *vt* ⓘ deixar perplexo; enganar; **be ~ed** ficar perplexo

foyer /'fɔɪeɪ/ *n* foyer *m*

fraction /'frækʃn/ *n* fração *f*; (*small bit*) bocadinho *m*, partícula *f*

fracture /'fræktʃə(r)/ *n* fratura *f* ● *vt/i* fraturar(-se)

fragile /'frædʒaɪl/ *a* frágil

fragment /'frægmənt/ *n* fragmento *m*

fragran|t /'freɪgrənt/ *a* fragrante, perfumado. **~ce** *n* fragrância *f*, perfume *m*

frail /freɪl/ *a* (**-er**, **-est**) frágil

frame /freɪm/ *n Techn* (*of spectacles*) armação *f*; (*of picture*) moldura *f*; (*of window*) caixilho *m*; (*body*) corpo *m*, (*P*) estrutura *f* ● *vt* colocar a armação em; ‹*picture*› emoldurar; *fig* formular; ⊠ incriminar falsamente; tramar; **~ of mind** estado *m* de espírito

framework /'freɪmwɜ:k/ *n* estrutura *f*; (*context*) quadro *m*, esquema *m*

France /frɑ:ns/ *n* França *f*

franchise /'fræntʃaɪz/ *n Pol* direito *m* de voto; *Comm* concessão *f*, franchise *f*

frank[1] /fræŋk/ *a* franco

frank[2] /fræŋk/ *vt* franquear

frantic /'fræntɪk/ *a* frenético

fraternal /frə'tɜ:nl/ *a* fraternal

f

fraud /frɔːd/ *n* fraude *f*; (*person*) impostor *m*. **~ulent** /'frɔːdjʊlənt/ *a* fraudulento

fraught /frɔːt/ *a* **~ with** cheio de

fray[1] /freɪ/ *n* rixa *f*

fray[2] /freɪ/ *vt/i* desfiar(-se), puir, esgarçar(-se)

freak /friːk/ *n* aberração *f*, anomalia *f* ● *a* anormal; **~ of nature** aborto *m* da natureza. **~ish** *a* anormal

freckle /'frekl/ *n* sarda *f*

f

free /friː/ *a* (**freer**, **freest**) livre; (*gratis*) grátis; (*lavish*) liberal ● *vt* (*pt* **freed**) libertar (**from** de); (*rid*) livrar (**of** de); **~ of charge** grátis, de graça; **a ~ hand** carta *f* branca. **~lance** *a* independente, free-lance; **~-range** *a* ‹*egg*› de galinha criada ao ar livre. **~ly** *adv* livremente

freedom /'friːdəm/ *n* liberdade *f*

freez|e /friːz/ *vt/i* (*pt* **froze**, *pp* **frozen**) gelar; *Culin, Finance* congelar(-se) ● *n* gelo *m*; *Culin, Finance* congelamento *m*. **~er** *n* congelador *m*. **~ing** *a* gélido, glacial; **below ~ing** abaixo de zero

freight /freɪt/ *n* frete *m*

French /frentʃ/ *a* francês; **~ window** porta *f* envidraçada ● *n Lang* francês *m*; **the ~** os franceses. **~man** *n* francês *m*; **~woman** *n* francesa *f*

frenz|y /'frenzɪ/ *n* frenesi *m*

frequen|t[1] /'friːkwənt/ *a* frequente. **~cy** *n* frequência *f*. **~tly** *adv* frequentemente

frequent[2] /frɪ'kwent/ *vt* frequentar

fresh /freʃ/ *a* (**-er**, **-est**) fresco; (*different, additional*) novo; [!] (*cheeky*) descarado; atrevido. **~ness** *n* frescura *f*

fret /fret/ *vt/i* (*pt* **fretted**) ralar(-se). **~ful** *a* rabugento

friction /'frɪkʃn/ *n* fricção *f*

Friday /'fraɪdɪ/ *n* sexta-feira *f*; **Good ~** Sexta-Feira *f* Santa

fridge /frɪdʒ/ *n* [!] geladeira *f*, (*P*) frigorífico *m*

fried /fraɪd/ ▶ **FRY** ● *a* frito

friend /frend/ *n* amigo *m*. **~ship** *n* amizade *f*

friendl|y /'frendlɪ/ *a* (**-ier**, **-iest**) amigável, amigo, simpático. **~iness** *n* simpatia *f*, gentileza *f*

fright /fraɪt/ *n* medo *m*, susto *m*; **give sb a ~** pregar um susto em alguém. **~ful** *a* medonho, assustador

frighten /'fraɪtn/ *vt* assustar; **~ off** afugentar. **~ed** *a* assustado; **be ~ed (of)** ter medo (de)

frigid /'frɪdʒɪd/ *a* frígido. **~ity** /-'dʒɪdətɪ/ *n* frigidez *f*, frieza *f*; *Psych* frigidez *f*

frill /frɪl/ *n* babado *m*, (*P*) folho *m*

fringe /frɪndʒ/ *n* franja *f*; (*of area*) borda *f*; (*of society*) margem *f*; **~ benefits** (*work*) regalias *fpl* extras; **~ theatre** teatro *m* alternativo, teatro *m* de vanguarda

frisk /frɪsk/ *vi* pular, brincar ● *vt* revistar

fritter[1] /'frɪtə(r)/ *n* bolinho *m* frito, (*P*) frito *m*

fritter[2] /'frɪtə(r)/ *vt* **~ away** desperdiçar

frivol|ous /'frɪvələs/ *a* frívolo. **~ity** /-'vɒlətɪ/ *n* frivolidade *f*

fro /frəʊ/ (= **to and fro**) ▶ **TO**

frock /frɒk/ *n* vestido *m*

frog /frɒg/ *n* rã *f*

frolic /'frɒlɪk/ *vi* (*pt* **frolicked**) brincar, fazer travessuras ● *n* brincadeira *f*, travessura *f*

from /frəm emphatic frɒm/ *prep* de; (*with time, prices etc*) de, a partir de; (*according to*) por, a julgar por

front /frʌnt/ *n Meteo, Mil, Pol* (*of car, train*) frente *f*; (*of shirt*) peitilho *m*; (*of building; also fig*) fachada *f*; (*promenade*) calçada à beira-mar *f* ● *a* da frente; (*first*) primeiro; **in ~ (of)** em frente (de); **~ door** porta *f* da rua; **~-wheel drive** tração *f* dianteira

frontier /'frʌntɪə(r)/ *n* fronteira *f*

frost /frɒst/ *n* gelo *m*, temperatura *f* abaixo de zero; (*on ground, plants etc*) geada *f* ● *vt/i* cobrir(-se) de geada. **~bite** *n* queimadura *f* de frio; **~bitten** *a* queimado pelo frio. **~ed** *a* ‹*glass*› fosco. **~y** *a* glacial

froth /frɒθ/ *n* espuma *f* ● *vi* espumar, fazer espuma. **~y** *a* espumoso

frown /fraʊn/ *vi* franzir as sobrancelhas ● *n* franzir *m* de sobrancelhas; **~ on** desaprovar

froze, **frozen** /frəuz, 'frəuzn/ ▶ **FREEZE**

froze, frozen /frəʊz, 'frəʊzn/ ▶ **FREEZE**

frugal /'fruːgl/ *a* poupado; ‹*meal*› frugal

fruit /fruːt/ *n* fruto *m*; (*collectively*) fruta *f*; **~ machine** caça-níqueis *mpl*, (*P*) máquina *f* de jogo; **~ salad** salada *f* de frutas. **~y** *a* que tem gosto or cheiro de fruta

fruit|ful /'fruːtfl/ *a* frutífero, produtivo. **~less** *a* infrutífero

fruition /fruː'ɪʃn/ *n* **come to ~** realizar-se

frustrat|e /frʌ'streɪt/ *vt* frustrar. **~ion** /-ʃn/ *n* frustração *f*

fry /fraɪ/ *vt/i* (*pt* **fried**) fritar. **~ing pan** *n* frigideira *f*

fudge /fʌdʒ/ *n Culin* doce *m* de leite, (*P*) doce *m* acaramelado ● *vt/i* ~ **(the issue)** lançar a confusão

fuel /'fju:əl/ *n* combustível *m*; (*for car*) carburante *m* ● *vt* (*pt* **fuelled**) abastecer de combustível; *fig* atear

fugitive /'fju:dʒətɪv/ *a & n* fugitivo *m*

fulfil /fʊl'fɪl/ *vt* (*pt* **fulfilled**) cumprir, realizar; ‹*condition*› satisfazer; ~ **o.s.** realizar-se. **~ment** *n* realização *f*; (*of condition*) satisfação *f*

full /fʊl/ *a* (**-er**, **-est**) cheio; ‹*meal*› completo; ‹*price*› total, por inteiro; ‹*skirt*› rodado; ~ **moon** lua *f* cheia; ~ **stop** ponto *m* final; **at ~ speed** a toda velocidade; **to the ~** ao máximo; **be ~ up** [!] (*after eating*) estar cheio [!] ● *adv* **in ~** integralmente. **~-scale** *a* em grande; **~-size** *a* em tamanho natural; **~-time** *a & adv* a tempo integral, full-time. **~y** *adv* completamente

fumble /'fʌmbl/ *vi* tatear; (*in the dark*) andar tateando; ~ **with** estar atrapalhado com, andar às voltas com

fume /fju:m/ *vi* defumar, (*P*) deitar fumo, fumegar; (*with anger*) ferver. **~s** *npl* gases *mpl*

fun /fʌn/ *n* divertimento *m*; **for ~** de brincadeira; **make ~ of** zombar de, fazer troça de. **~fair** *n* parque *m* de diversões, (*P*) feira *f* de diversões, (*P*) feira *f* popular

function /'fʌŋkʃn/ *n* função *f* ● *vi* funcionar. **~al** *a* funcional

fund /fʌnd/ *n* fundos *mpl* ● *vt* financiar

fundamental /fʌndə'mentl/ *a* fundamental

funeral /'fju:nərəl/ *n* enterro *m*, funeral *m* ● *a* fúnebre

fungus /'fʌŋgəs/ *n* (*pl* **-gi** /-gaɪ/) fungo *m*

funnel /'fʌnl/ *n* funil *m*; (*of ship*) chaminé *f*

funn|y /'fʌnɪ/ *a* (**-ier**, **-iest**) engraçado, divertido; (*odd*) esquisito. **~ily** *adv* comicamente; (*oddly*) estranhamente; **~ily enough** por incrível que pareça

fur /fɜ:(r)/ *n* pelo *m*; (*for clothing*) pele *f*; (*in kettle*) depósito *m*, crosta *f*; ~ **coat** casaco *m* de pele

furious /'fjʊərɪəs/ *a* furioso

furnace /'fɜ:nɪs/ *n* fornalha *f*

furnish /'fɜ:nɪʃ/ *vt* mobiliar, (*P*) mobilar; (*supply*) prover (**with** de). **~ings** *npl* mobiliário *m* e equipamento *m*

furniture /'fɜ:nɪtʃə(r)/ *n* mobília *f*

furry /'fɜ:rɪ/ *a* (**-ier**, **-iest**) peludo; ‹*toy*› de pelúcia, (*P*) de peluche

furth|er /'fɜ:ðə(r)/ *a* mais distante; (*additional*) adicional, suplementar ● *adv* mais longe; (*more*) mais ● *vt* promover; **~er education** ensino *m* supletivo, cursos *mpl* livres, (*P*) educação *f* superior. **~est** *a* o mais distante ● *adv* mais longe

furthermore /fɜ:ðə'mɔ:(r)/ *adv* além disso

fury /'fjʊərɪ/ *n* fúria *f*, furor *m*

fuse[1] /fju:z/ *vt/i* fundir(-se); *fig* amalgamar ● *n* fusível *m*; **the lights ~d** os fusíveis queimaram

fuse[2] /fju:z/ *n* (*of bomb*) espoleta *f*

fuselage /'fju:zəlɑ:ʒ/ *n* fuselagem *f*

fuss /fʌs/ *n* história(s) *f(pl)*, escarcéu *m* ● *vi* preocupar-se com ninharias; **make a ~ of** ligar demasiado para *or* (*P*) a, criar caso com, fazer um espalhafato com. **~y** *a* exigente, complicado

futile /'fju:taɪl/ *a* fútil

future /'fju:tʃə(r)/ *a & n* futuro *m*; **in ~** no futuro, de agora em diante

futuristic /fju:tʃə'rɪstɪk/ *a* futurista, futurístico

fuzz /fʌz/ *n* penugem *f*; (*hair*) cabelo *m* frisado

fuzzy /'fʌzɪ/ *a* ‹*hair*› frisado; ‹*photo*› pouco nítido, desfocado

Gg

gabble /'gæbl/ *vt/i* tagarelar, falar, ler muito depressa ● *n* tagarelice *f*, algaravia *f*

gable /'geɪbl/ *n* empena *f*, oitão *m*

gadget /'gædʒɪt/ *n* pequeno utensílio *m*; (*fitting*) dispositivo *m*; (*device*) engenhoca *f* [!]

Gaelic /'geɪlɪk/ *n* galês *m*

gag /gæg/ *n* mordaça *f*; (*joke*) gag *m*, piada *f* ● *vt* (*pt* **gagged**) amordaçar

gaiety /'geɪətɪ/ *n* alegria *f*

gaily /'geɪlɪ/ *adv* alegremente

gain /geɪn/ *vt* ganhar ● *vi* (*of clock*) adiantar-se; ~ **weight** aumentar de peso; ~ **on** (*get closer to*) aproximar-se de ● *n* ganho *m*; (*increase*) aumento *m*

gait /geɪt/ *n* (modo de) andar *m*

gala /'gɑːlə/ *n* gala *m*; *Sport* festival *m*
galaxy /'gæləksɪ/ *n* galáxia *f*
gale /geɪl/ *n* vento *m* forte
gallant /'gælənt/ *a* galhardo, valente; (*chivalrous*) galante, cortês. **~ry** *n* galhardia *f*, valentia *f*; (*chivalry*) galanteria *f*, cortesia *f*
gallery /'gælərɪ/ *n* galeria *f*
galley /'gælɪ/ *n* (*pl* **-eys**) galera *f*; (*ship's kitchen*) cozinha *f*
gallon /'gælən/ *n* galão *m* = 4,546 litros, Amer = 3.785 litros
gallop /'gæləp/ *n* galope *m* ● *vi* (*pt* **galloped**) galopar
gallows /'gæləʊz/ *npl* forca *f*
galore /gə'lɔː(r)/ *adv* a beça, em abundância
gambl|e /'gæmbl/ *vt/i* jogar ● *n* jogo (de azar) *m*; *fig* risco *m*; **~e on** apostar em. **~er** *n* jogador *m*
game /geɪm/ *n* jogo *m*; *Football* desafio *m*; (*animals*) caça *f* ● *a* bravo; **~ for** pronto para
gamekeeper /'geɪmkiːpə(r)/ *n* guarda-florestal *m*
gammon /'gæmən/ *n* presunto *m* defumado
gang /gæng/ *n* bando *m*, gang *m*; (*of workmen*) turma *f*, (*P*) grupo *m* ● *vi* **~ up** ligar-se (**on** contra)
gangling /'gæŋglɪŋ/ *a* desengonçado
gangrene /'gæŋgriːn/ *n* gangrena *f*
gangster /'gæŋstə(r)/ *n* gângster *m*, bandido *m*
gangway /'gæŋweɪ/ *n* passagem *f*; (*aisle*) coxia *f*; (*on ship*) portaló *m*; (*from ship to shore*) passadiço *m*
gaol /dʒeɪl/ *n & vt* = JAIL
gap /gæp/ *n* abertura *f*, brecha *f*; (*in time*) intervalo *m*; (*deficiency*) lacuna *f*
gap|e /geɪp/ *vi* ficar boquiaberto or embasbacado. **~ing** *a* escancarado

> *i*
> **gap year** Na Grã-Bretanha, é o período de tempo entre o final dos estudos no ensino secundário e a entrada na universidade. Muitos estudantes dedicam este período a obter experiência laboral relacionada com as suas futuras carreiras profissionais. Outros realizam atividades não-relacionadas com os estudos, e para alguns é uma oportunidade para poupar dinheiro ou viajar.

garage /'gærɑːʒ/ *n* garagem *f*; (*service station*) posto *m* de gasolina, (*P*) estação *f* de serviço ● *vt* pôr na garagem
garbage /'gɑːbɪdʒ/ *n* lixo *m*; **~ can** *Amer* lata *f* do lixo, (*P*) caixote *m* do lixo
garden /'gɑːdn/ *n* jardim *m* ● *vi* jardinar. **~er** *n* jardineiro *m*. **~ing** *n* jardinagem *f*
gargle /'gɑːgl/ *vi* gargarejar ● *n* gargarejo *m*
garish /'geərɪʃ/ *a* berrante, espalhafatoso
garland /'gɑːlənd/ *n* grinalda *f*
garlic /'gɑːlɪk/ *n* alho *m*
garment /'gɑːmənt/ *n* peça *f* de vestuário, roupa *f*
garnish /'gɑːnɪʃ/ *vt* enfeitar, guarnecer ● *n* guarnição *f*
garrison /'gærɪsn/ *n* guarnição *f* ● *vt* guarnecer
garrulous /'gærələs/ *a* tagarela
garter /'gɑːtə(r)/ *n* liga *f*
gas /gæs/ *n* (*pl* **gases**) gás *m*; *Med* anestésico *m*; *Amer* [!] (*petrol*) gasolina *f* ● *vt* (*pt* **gassed**) asfixiar; *Mil* gasear ● *vi* [!] fazer conversa fiada; **~ fire** aquecedor *m* a gás; **~ mask** máscara *f* antigás; **~ meter** medidor *m* or (*P*) contador *m* do gás
gash /gæʃ/ *n* corte *m*, lanho *m* ● *vt* cortar
gasket /'gæskɪt/ *n* junta *f*
gasoline /'gæsəliːn/ *n Amer* gasolina *f*
gasp /gɑːsp/ *vi* arfar, arquejar; *fig* (*with rage, surprise*) ficar sem ar ● *n* arquejo *m*
gastric /'gæstrɪk/ *a* gástrico
gastronomy /gæ'strɒnəmɪ/ *n* gastronomia *f*
gate /geɪt/ *n* portão *m*; (*of wood*) cancela *f*; (*barrier*) barreira *f*; (*airport*) porta *f*
gatecrash /'geɪtkræʃ/ *vt/i* entrar (numa festa) sem convite
gateway /'geɪtweɪ/ *n* (porta de) entrada *f*
gather /'gæðə(r)/ *vt* reunir, juntar; (*pick up, collect*) apanhar; (*amass, pile up*) acumular, juntar; (*conclude*) deduzir; ‹*cloth*› franzir ● *vi* reunir-se; (*pile up*) acumular-se; **~ speed** ganhar velocidade. **~ing** *n* reunião *f*
gaudy /'gɔːdɪ/ *a* (**-ier**, **-iest**) (*bright*) berrante; (*showy*) espalhafatoso
gauge /geɪdʒ/ *n* medida *f* padrão; (*device*) indicador *m*; (*railway*) bitola *f* ● *vt* medir, avaliar

gaunt /gɔːnt/ *a* emagrecido, macilento; (*grim*) lúgubre, desolado

gauze /gɔːz/ *n* gaze *f*

gave /geɪv/ ▶ GIVE

gawky /ˈgɔːkɪ/ *a* (**-ier**, **-iest**) desajeitado

gay /geɪ/ *a* (**-er**, **-est**) alegre; [!] (*homosexual*) homossexual; gay

gaze /geɪz/ *vi* ~ **(at)** olhar fixamente (para) ● *n* contemplação *f*

GB *abbr* ▶ GREAT BRITAIN

gear /gɪə(r)/ *n* equipamento *m*; *Techn* engrenagem *f*; *Auto* velocidade *f*; **in ~** engrenado; **out of ~** em ponto morto ● *vt* equipar; (*adapt*) adaptar

gearbox /ˈgɪəbɒks/ *n* caixa *f* de mudança, caixa *f* de transmissão, (*P*) caixa *f* de velocidades

geese /giːs/ ▶ GOOSE

gel /dʒel/ *n* geleia *f*

gelatine /ˈdʒelətiːn/ *n* gelatina *f*

gem /dʒem/ *n* gema *f*, pedra *f* preciosa

Gemini /ˈdʒemɪnaɪ/ *n Astr* Gêmeos *mpl*, (*P*) Gémeos *mpl*

gender /ˈdʒendə(r)/ *n* gênero *m*, (*P*) género *m*

gene /dʒiːn/ *n* gene *m*

genealogy /dʒiːnɪˈælədʒɪ/ *n* genealogia *f*

general /ˈdʒenrəl/ *a* geral; **~ election** eleições *fpl* legislativas; **in ~** em geral ● *n* general *m*. **~ practitioner** *n* clínico-geral *m*, (*P*) médico *m* de família. **~ly** *adv* geralmente

generaliz|e /ˈdʒenrəlaɪz/ *vt/i* generalizar. **~ation** /-ˈzeɪʃn/ *n* generalização *f*

generate /ˈdʒenəreɪt/ *vt* gerar, produzir

generation /dʒenəˈreɪʃn/ *n* geração *f*

generator /ˈdʒenəreɪtə(r)/ *n* gerador *m*

gener|ous /ˈdʒenərəs/ *a* generoso; (*plentiful*) abundante. **~osity** /-ˈrɒsətɪ/ *n* generosidade *f*

genetic /dʒɪˈnetɪk/ *a* genético. **~s** *n* genética *f*

genial /ˈdʒiːnɪəl/ *a* agradável

genius /ˈdʒiːnɪəs/ *n* (*pl* **-uses**) gênio *m*, (*P*) génio *m*

genocide /ˈdʒenəsaɪd/ *n* genocídio *m*

gent /dʒent/ *n* **the G~s** [!] banheiros *mpl* de homens, (*P*) lavabos *mpl* para homens

genteel /dʒenˈtiːl/ *a* elegante, fino, refinado

gentl|e /ˈdʒentl/ *a* (**er**, **est**) brando, suave. **~eness** *n* brandura *f*, suavidade *f*. **~y** *adv* brandamente, suavemente

gentleman /ˈdʒentlmən/ *n* (*pl* **-men**) senhor *m*; (*well-bred*) cavalheiro *m*

genuine /ˈdʒenjʊɪn/ *a* genuíno, verdadeiro; (*belief*) sincero

geograph|y /dʒɪˈɒgrəfɪ/ *n* geografia *f*. **~ical** /dʒɪəˈgræfɪkl/ *a* geográfico

geolog|y /dʒɪˈɒlədʒɪ/ *n* geologia *f*. **~ical** /dʒɪəˈlɒdʒɪkl/ *a* geológico. **~ist** *n* geólogo *m*

geometr|y /dʒɪˈɒmətrɪ/ *n* geometria *f*. **~ic(al)** /dʒɪəˈmetrɪk(l)/ *a* geométrico

geranium /dʒəˈreɪnɪəm/ *n* gerânio *m*

geriatric /dʒerɪˈætrɪk/ *a* geriátrico

germ /dʒɜːm/ *n* germe *m*, micróbio *m*

German /ˈdʒɜːmən/ *a & n* alemão *m*, alemã *f*; *Lang* alemão *m*; **G~ measles** rubéola *f*. **G~ic** /dʒəˈmænɪk/ *a* germânico. **G~y** *n* Alemanha *f*

germinate /ˈdʒɜːmɪneɪt/ *vi* germinar

gesticulate /dʒeˈstɪkjʊleɪt/ *vi* gesticular

gesture /ˈdʒestʃə(r)/ *n* gesto *m*

get /get/ ● *vt* (*pt* **got**, *pp* **got**, **gotten** *US pres p* **getting**)

····▸ (*receive*) receber; **we got a letter** recebemos uma carta

····▸ (*obtain, achieve*) conseguir, obter; **I got a job in São Paulo** consegui um emprego em São Paulo; **he ~s good grades** ele tem boas notas

····▸ (*buy*) comprar; **~ sb a present** comprar um presente para alguém

····▸ (*fetch*) ir buscar; **go and ~ a chair** vá buscar uma cadeira

····▸ (*travel by*) apanhar; **we can ~ the bus** podemos pegar o ônibus

····▸ (*understand*) perceber; **I don't ~ it** não percebo

····▸ (*experience*) ter; **~ a surprise** ter uma surpresa; **~ a shock** ter um choque

····▸ ‹*illness*› pegar, apanhar; **~ the flu/a cold** pegar uma gripe

····▸ (*cause to be done*) **~ the TV repaired** mandar arrumar a televisão; **~ one's hair cut** (ir) cortar o cabelo

····▸ (*ask or persuade*) **~ sb to do sth** fazer com que alguém faça algo; **he got his sister to help him with the homework** ele convenceu a irmã a ajudá-lo no trabalho de casa

● *vi*

····➤ (*become*) tornar-se, ficar; **he is getting old** está ficando velho; **he got rich** ficou rico

····➤ (*into state/condition*) **~ married** casar-se; **~ hurt** ficar ferido; **~ better/ worse** melhorar/piorar

····➤ (*arrive*) chegar; **~ to the airport** chegar ao aeroporto

□ **~ about** ● *vi* (*person*) deslocar-se. **~ along** ● *vi* (*progress*) **how is she getting along?** como ela está progredindo?. **~ along with** ● *vi* dar-se bem com. **~ at** ● *vt* (*have access to*) alcançar; (*criticize*) criticar; (*mean*) querer dizer, insinuar; **what are you getting at?** o que você está insinuando?. **~ away** ● *vi* escapar. **~ back** ● *vi* voltar ● *vt* recuperar. **~ by** ● *vi* safar-se. **~ down** ● *vt/i* descer. **~ in** ● *vi* (*enter*) entrar; ‹*bus, train*› chegar. **~ into** ● *vt* (*dress*) vestir. **~ off** ● *vi* (*from bus, train, horse*) descer ● *vt* (*remove*) remover; ‹*bus, train, horse*› descer de. **~ on** ● *vi* ‹*bus*› subir; (*be on good terms*) **~ on well with sb** dar-se bem com alguém; (*make progress*) **how are you getting on?** como você está indo?. **~ out** ● *vi* sair. **~ over** ● *vt* ‹*illness*› recuperar. **~ round** ● *vt* ‹*rule*› contornar; ‹*person*› convencer. **~ through** ● *vi* (*on the phone*) estabelecer contato. **~ up** ● *vi* levantar-se

g

getaway /'getəweɪ/ *n* fuga *f*

get-up *n* [!] apresentação *f*

ghastly /'gɑ:stlɪ/ *a* (**-ier**, **-iest**) horrível; (*pale*) lívido

gherkin /'gɜ:kɪn/ *n* pepino *m* pequeno para conservas, cornichão *m*

ghetto /'getəʊ/ *n* (*pl* **-os**) gueto *m*, ghetto *m*

ghost /gəʊst/ *n* fantasma *m*, espectro *m*. **~ly** *a* fantasmagórico, espectral

giant /'dʒaɪənt/ *a & n* gigante *m*

gibberish /'dʒɪbərɪʃ/ *n* algaravia *f*, linguagem *f* incompreensível

giblets /'dʒɪblɪts/ *npl* miúdos *mpl*, miudezas *fpl*

giddy /'gɪdɪ/ *a* (**-ier**, **-iest**) estonteante, vertiginoso; **be** or **feel ~** ter tonturas or vertigens

gift /gɪft/ *n* presente *m*, dádiva *f*; (*ability*) dom *m*, dote *m*. **~-wrap** *vt* (*pt* **-wrapped**) fazer um embrulho de presente

gifted /'gɪftɪd/ *a* dotado

gig /gɪg/ *n* [!] show *m*; sessão *f* de jazz etc

gigantic /dʒaɪ'gæntɪk/ *a* gigantesco

giggle /'gɪgl/ *vi* dar risadinhas nervosas ● *n* risinho *m* nervoso

gild /gɪld/ *vt* dourar

gilt /gɪlt/ *a & n* dourado *m*. **~-edged** *a* de toda a confiança

gimmick /'gɪmɪk/ *n* truque *m*, artifício *m*

gin /dʒɪn/ *n* gin *m*, genebra *f*

ginger /'dʒɪndʒə(r)/ *n* gengibre *m* ● *a* louro-avermelhado, ruivo; **~ ale**, **~ beer** cerveja *f* de gengibre, (*P*) ginger ale *m*

gingerbread /'dʒɪndʒəbred/ *n* pão *m* de gengibre

gingerly /'dʒɪndʒəlɪ/ *adv* cautelosamente

gipsy /'dʒɪpsɪ/ *n* = GYPSY

giraffe /dʒɪ'rɑ:f/ *n* girafa *f*

girder /'gɜ:də(r)/ *n* trave *f*, viga *f*

girl /gɜ:l/ *n* (*child*) menina *f*; (*young woman*) moça *f*, (*P*) rapariga *f*. **~friend** *n* amiga *f*; (*of boy*) namorada *f*

gist /dʒɪst/ *n* essencial *m*

give /gɪv/ *vt/i* (*pt* **gave**, *pp* **given**) dar; (*bend, yield*) ceder; **~ away** dar; ‹*secret*› revelar, trair; **~ back** devolver; **~ in** dar-se por vencido, render-se; **~ off** emitir; **~ way** ceder; ‹*traffic*› dar prioridade; (*collapse*) dar de si □ **~ out** *vt* anunciar ● *vi* esgotar-se. **~ up** *vt/i* desistir (de), renunciar (a); **~ o.s. up** entregar-se

given /'gɪvn/ ▶ GIVE *a* dado; **~ name** nome *m* de batismo

glacier /'glæsɪə(r)/ *n* glaciar *m*, geleira *f*

glad /glæd/ *a* contente. **~ly** *adv* com (todo o) prazer

glam|our /'glæmə(r)/ *n* fascinação *f*, encanto *m*, (*P*) glamour *m*. **~orize** *vt* tornar fascinante. **~orous** *a* fascinante, sedutor, glamoroso

glance /glɑ:ns/ *n* relance *m*, olhar *m*; **at first ~** à primeira vista ● *vi* **~ at** dar uma olhada a

gland /glænd/ *n* glândula *f*

glar|e /gleə(r)/ *vi* brilhar intensamente, faiscar ● *n* luz *f* crua; *fig* olhar *m* feroz; **~e at** olhar ferozmente para. **~ing** *a* brilhante; (*obvious*) flagrante

glass /glɑ:s/ *n* vidro *m*; (*vessel, its contents*) copo *m*; (*mirror*) espelho *m*; **~es** óculos *mpl*. **~y** *a* vítreo

glaze /gleɪz/ *vt* ‹*door etc*› envidraçar; ‹*pottery*› vidrar ● *n* vidrado *m*

gleam /gli:m/ *n* raio *m* de luz frouxa; *fig* vislumbre *m* ● *vi* luzir, brilhar
glee /gli:/ *n* alegria *f*
glib /glɪb/ *a* que tem a palavra fácil, verboso
glide /glaɪd/ *vi* deslizar; ‹*bird, plane*› planar. **~r** /-ə(r)/ *n* planador *m*
glimmer /ˈglɪmə(r)/ *n* luz *f* trêmula *or* (*P*) trémula, ténue ● *vi* tremular
glimpse /glɪmps/ *n* vislumbre *m*; **catch a ~ of** entrever, ver de relance
glint /glɪnt/ *n* brilho *m*, reflexo *m* ● *vi* brilhar, cintilar
glisten /ˈglɪsn/ *vi* reluzir
glitter /ˈglɪtə(r)/ *vi* luzir, resplandecer ● *n* esplendor *m*, cintilação *f*
gloat /gləʊt/ *vi* **~ over** ter um prazer maligno em, exultar com
global /ˈgləʊbl/ *a* global
globalization /gləʊbəlaɪˈzeɪʃən, *Amer* -lɪˈz-/ *n* globalização *f*
globe /gləʊb/ *n* globo *m*
gloom /glu:m/ *n* obscuridade *f*; *fig* tristeza *f*. **~y** *a* sombrio; (*sad*) triste; (*pessimistic*) pessimista
glorif|y /ˈglɔ:rɪfaɪ/ *vt* glorificar; **a ~ied waitress/***etc* pouco mais que uma garçonete/*etc*, (*P*) empregada-de-mesa/*etc*
glorious /ˈglɔ:rɪəs/ *a* glorioso
glory /ˈglɔ:rɪ/ *n* glória *f*; (*beauty*) esplendor *m* ● *vi* **~ in** orgulhar-se de
gloss /glɒs/ *n* brilho *m* ● *a* brilhante ● *vt* **~ over** minimizar, encobrir. **~y** *a* brilhante
glossary /ˈglɒsərɪ/ *n* (*pl* **-ries**) glossário *m*
glove /glʌv/ *n* luva *f*; **~ compartment** porta-luvas *m*
glow /gləʊ/ *vi* arder; ‹*person*› resplandecer ● *n* brasa *f*. **~ing** *a fig* entusiástico
glucose /ˈglu:kəʊs/ *n* glucose *f*
glue /glu:/ *n* cola *f* ● *vt* (*pres p* **gluing**) colar
glum /glʌm/ *a* (**glummer**, **glummest**) sorumbático; (*dejected*) abatido
glut /glʌt/ *n* superabundância *f*
glutton /ˈglʌtn/ *n* glutão *m*. **~ous** *a* glutão. **~y** *n* gula *f*
GMO /dʒi:ɛmˈəʊ/ *n* OGM *m*, organismo *m* geneticamente modificado
gnash /næʃ/ *vt* **~ one's teeth** ranger os dentes
gnat /næt/ *n* mosquito *m*
gnaw /nɔ:/ *vt/i* roer

go /gəʊ/ ● *vi* (*3rd person sing pres. tense* **goes**, *pt* **went**, *pp* **gone**)

····➤ ir; **~ to school/town/the cinema** ir à escola/à cidade/ao cinema; **~ shopping/swimming/riding** ir às compras/nadar/andar a cavalo; **~ for a walk** sair para um passeio; **~ for a nap** tirar uma soneca

····➤ (*leave*) ir; **I must be ~ing** tenho de ir

····➤ (*vanish*) ir-se, desaparecer; **the money's gone** o dinheiro acabou; **my bike's gone** a minha bicicleta desapareceu; **my headache is gone** a minha dor de cabeça desapareceu

····➤ (*work, function*) funcionar; **is the car ~ing?** o carro funciona?

····➤ (*become*) ficar; **~ blind** ficar cego; **~ pale/red** ficar pálido/corado

····➤ (*turn out, progress*) ir correr; **how's it ~ing?** como vai tudo?; **how did the exam ~?** como correu o exame?

····➤ (*match*) combinar; **the two colours don't ~ [together]** as duas cores não combinam

····➤ (*in future tenses*) **be ~ing to** ir (+ *inf*); **it's ~ing to rain** vai chover; **I'm not ~ing to do it** não vou fazer isso

● *n* (*pl* **goes**)

····➤ (*turn*) vez *f*; **it's your ~** é a sua vez

····➤ (*try*) tentativa *f*; **have a ~ at doing sth** fazer uma tentativa de aco

····➤ (*energy*) dinamismo *m*; **Mary's always got plenty of ~** a Mary sempre foi muito dinâmica

····➤ (*in phrases*) **on the ~** em grande atividade; **make a ~ of sth** tornar aco um sucesso.

~-ahead *n* luz *f* verde ● *a* dinâmico; **~-between** *n* intermediário

□ **~ across** ● *vi* ir para diante. **~ away** ● *vi* ir embora. **~ back** ● *vi* voltar. **~ back on** ● *vi* voltar atrás com; (*return*) voltar. **~ by** ● *vi* (*pass*) passar. **~ down** ● *vi* descer; ‹*sun*› pôr-se; ‹*ship*› afundar. **~ for** ● *vt* ir buscar; (*like*) gostar de; (*attack*) atacar. **~ in** ● *vi* entrar. **~ in for** ● *vt* ‹*exam*› apresentar-se a. **~ off** ● *vi* ir embora; (*explode*) arrebentar; (*sound*) soar; (*decay*) estragar. **~ on** ● *vi* continuar; (*happen*) acontecer. **~ out** ● *vi* sair; ‹*light*› apagar. **~ over** ● *vt*

g

(*check*) verificar, examinar. **~ round** ● *vi* (*be enough*) chegar. **~ through** ● *vt* (*check*) verificar, examinar. **~ under** ● *vi* ir abaixo. **~ up** ● *vi* subir. **~ without** ● *vt* passar sem

goal /gəʊl/ *n* meta *f*; (*area*) baliza *f*; (*score*) gol *m*, (*P*) golo *m*. **~post** *n* trave *f*

goalkeeper /ˈgəʊlkiːpə(r)/ *n* goleiro *m*, (*P*) guarda-redes *m*

goat /gəʊt/ *n* cabra *f*

gobble /ˈgɒbl/ *vt* comer com sofreguidão, devorar

god /gɒd/ *n* deus *m*. **~-daughter** *n* afilhada *f*. **~dess** *n* deusa *f*. **~father** *n* padrinho *m*. **~ly** *a* devoto. **~mother** *n* madrinha *f*; **~son** *n* afilhado *m*

g

God /gɒd/ *n* Deus *m*

godsend /ˈgɒdsend/ *n* achado *m*, dádiva *f* do céu

goggles /ˈgɒglz/ *npl* óculos *mpl* de proteção

going /ˈgəʊɪŋ/ *n* **it is slow/hard ~** é demorado/difícil ● *a* ‹*price, rate*› corrente; atual. **~s-on** *npl* acontecimentos *mpl* estranhos

gold /gəʊld/ *n* ouro *m* ● *a* de/em ouro. **~ mine** *n* mina *f* de ouro

golden /ˈgəʊldən/ *a* de ouro; (*like gold*) dourado; (*opportunity*) único; **~ wedding** bodas *fpl* de ouro

goldfish /ˈgəʊldfɪʃ/ *n* peixe *m* dourado/vermelho

goldsmith /ˈgəʊldsmɪθ/ *n* ourives *m inv*

golf /gɒlf/ *n* golfe *m*; **~ club** clube *m* de golfe, associação *f* de golfe; (*stick*) taco *m*. **~ course** *n* campo *m* de golfe. **~er** *n* jogador *m* de golfe

gone /gɒn/ ▶ GO *a* ido, passado; **~ six o'clock** depois das seis

gong /gɒŋ/ *n* gongo *m*

good /gʊd/ *a* (**better, best**) bom; **as ~ as** praticamente; **G~ Friday** Sexta-feira *f* Santa; **~ name** bom nome *m* ● *n* bem *m*; **for ~** para sempre; **it is no ~** não adianta; **it is no ~ shouting/*etc*** não adianta gritar/*etc*. **~ afternoon** *int* boa(s) tarde(s); **~ evening/night** *int* boa(s) noite(s); **~-looking** *a* bonito; **~ morning** *int* bom dia

goodbye /gʊdˈbaɪ/ *int & n* adeus *m*

goodness /ˈgʊdnɪs/ *n* bondade *f*; **my ~!** meu Deus!

goods /gʊdz/ *npl Comm* mercadorias *fpl*; **~ train** trem *m* de carga, (*P*) comboio *m* de mercadorias

goodwill /gʊdˈwɪl/ *n* boa vontade *f*

goose /guːs/ *n* (*pl* **geese**) ganso *m*. **~flesh**, **~-pimples** *ns* pele *f* de galinha

gooseberry /ˈgʊzbərɪ/ *n* (*fruit*) groselha *f*; (*bush*) groselheira *f*

gore[2] /gɔː(r)/ *vt* perfurar

gorge /gɔːdʒ/ *n* desfiladeiro *m*, garganta *f* ● *vt* **~ o.s.** empanturrar-se

gorgeous /ˈgɔːdʒəs/ *a* magnífico, maravilhoso

gorilla /gəˈrɪlə/ *n* gorila *m*

gormless /ˈgɔːmlɪs/ *a* ☒ estúpido

gorse /gɔːs/ *n* giesta *f*, tojo *m*, urze *f*

gory /ˈgɔːrɪ/ *a* (**-ier, -iest**) sangrento

gosh /gɒʃ/ *int* puxa!, (*P*) caramba!

gospel /ˈgɒspl/ *n* evangelho *m*

gossip /ˈgɒsɪp/ *n* bisbilhotice *f*, fofoca *f*; (*person*) bisbilhoteiro *m*, fofoqueiro *m* ● *vi* (*pt* **gossiped**) bisbilhotar

got /gɒt/ ▶ GET; **have ~** ter; **have ~ to do** ter que fazer, (*P*) ter de fazer

Gothic /ˈgɒθɪk/ *a* gótico

gourmet /ˈgʊəmeɪ/ *n* gastrônomo *m*, (*P*) gastrónomo *m*, gourmet *m*

govern /ˈgʌvn/ *vt/i* governar. **~ess** *n* preceptora *f*. **~or** *n* governador *m*; (*of school, hospital etc*) diretor *m*

government /ˈgʌvənmənt/ *n* governo *m*

gown /gaʊn/ *n* vestido *m*; (*of judge, teacher*) toga *f*

GP *abbr* ▶ GENERAL PRACTITIONER

grab /græb/ *vt* (*pt* **grabbed**) agarrar, apanhar

grace /greɪs/ *n* graça *f* ● *vt* honrar; (*adorn*) ornar; **say ~** dar graças. **~ful** *a* gracioso

gracious /ˈgreɪʃəs/ *a* gracioso; (*kind*) amável, afável

grade /greɪd/ *n* categoria *f*; (*of goods*) classe *f*, qualidade *f*; (*on scale*) grau *m*; (*school mark*) nota *f* ● *vt* classificar

gradient /ˈgreɪdɪənt/ *n* gradiente *m*, declive *m*

gradual /ˈgrædʒʊəl/ *a* gradual, progressivo. **~ly** *adv* gradualmente

graduate[1] /ˈgrædʒʊət/ *n* diplomado *m*, graduado *m*, licenciado *m*

graduat|e[2] /ˈgrædʒʊeɪt/ *vt/i* formar(-se). **~ion** /-ˈeɪʃn/ *n* colação *f* de grau, (*P*) formatura *f*

graffiti /grəˈfiːtiː/ *npl* graffiti *mpl*

graft /grɑːft/ *n Med, Bot* enxerto *m*; (*work*) batalha *f* ● *vt* enxertar; (*work*) batalhar

grain /greɪn/ *n* grão *m*; (*collectively*) cereais *mpl*; (*in wood*) veio *m*; **against the ~** *fig* contra a maneira de ser

gram /græm/ *n* grama *m*

gramm|ar /ˈgræmə(r)/ *n* gramática *f*. **~atical** /grəˈmætɪkl/ *a* gramatical

grand /grænd/ *a* (**-er**, **-est**) grandioso, magnífico; ‹*duke, master*› grão; **~ piano** piano *m* de cauda

grand|child /ˈgrændtʃaɪld/ *n* (*pl* **-children**) neto *m*. **~daughter** *n* neta *f*. **~father** *n* avô *m*. **~mother** *n* avó *f*. **~parents** *npl* avós *mpl*. **~son** *n* neto *m*

grandeur /ˈgrændʒə(r)/ *n* grandeza *f*

grandiose /ˈgrændɪəʊs/ *a* grandioso

grandstand /ˈgrændstænd/ *n* tribuna *f* principal

granite /ˈgrænɪt/ *n* granito *m*

grant /grɑːnt/ *vt* conceder; ‹*a request*› ceder a; (*admit*) admitir (**that** que) ● *n* subsídio *m*; *Univ* bolsa *f*; **take for ~ed** dar por garantido, contar com

grape /greɪp/ *n* uva *f*

grapefruit /ˈgreɪpfruːt/ *n inv* grapefruit *m*, toranja *f*

graph /grɑːf/ *n* gráfico *m*

graphic /ˈgræfɪk/ *a* gráfico; *fig* vívido. **~s** *npl Comput* gráficos *mpl*

grapple /ˈgræpl/ *vi* **~ with** estar engalfinhado com; *fig* estar às voltas com

grasp /grɑːsp/ *vt* agarrar; (*understand*) compreender ● *n* domínio *m*; (*reach*) alcance *m*; *fig* (*understanding*) compreensão *f*

grasping /ˈgrɑːspɪŋ/ *a* ganancioso

grass /grɑːs/ *n* erva *f*; (*lawn*) grama *f*, (*P*) relva *f*; (*pasture*) pastagem *f*; ⊠ (*informer*) delator *m* ● *vt* cobrir com grama, (*P*) relva; ⊠ (*betray*) delatar; **~ roots** *Pol* bases *fpl*. **~y** *a* coberto de erva

grasshopper /ˈgrɑːshɒpə(r)/ *n* gafanhoto *m*

grate[1] /greɪt/ *n* (*fireplace*) lareira *f*; (*frame*) grelha *f*

grate[2] /greɪt/ *vt* ralar ● *vi* ranger; **~ one's teeth** ranger os dentes. **~r** /-ə(r)/ *n* ralador *m*

grateful /ˈgreɪtfl/ *a* grato, agradecido

gratify /ˈgrætɪfaɪ/ *vt* (*pt* **-fied**) contentar, satisfazer. **~ing** *a* gratificante

gratis /ˈgreɪtɪs/ *a & adv* grátis (*invar*), de graça

gratitude /ˈgrætɪtjuːd/ *n* gratidão *f*, reconhecimento *m*

gratuitous /grəˈtjuːɪtəs/ *a* gratuito; (*uncalled-for*) sem motivo

gratuity /grəˈtjuːətɪ/ *n* gratificação *f*, gorjeta *f*

grave[1] /greɪv/ *n* cova *f*, sepultura *f*, túmulo *m*

grave[2] /greɪv/ *a* (**-er**, **-est**) grave, sério

grave[3] /grɑːv/ *a* **~ accent** acento *m* grave

gravel /ˈgrævl/ *n* cascalho *m* miúdo, saibro *m*

gravestone /ˈgreɪvstəʊn/ *n* lápide *f*, campa *f*

graveyard /ˈgreɪvjɑːd/ *n* cemitério *m*

gravity /ˈgrævətɪ/ *n* gravidade *f*

gravy /ˈgreɪvɪ/ *n* molho (de carne) *m*

graze[1] /greɪz/ *vt/i* pastar

graze[2] /greɪz/ *vt* roçar; (*scrape*) esfolar ● *n* esfoladura *f*, (*P*) esfoladela *f*

greas|e /griːs/ *n* gordura *f* ● *vt* engordurar; *Culin* untar; *Mech* lubrificar; **~e-proof paper** papel *m* vegetal. **~y** *a* gorduroso

great /greɪt/ *a* (**-er**, **-est**) grande; [!] (*splendid*) esplêndido. **~-grandfather** *n* bisavô *m*; **~-grandmother** *n* bisavó *f*. **~ly** *adv* grandemente, muito. **~ness** *n* grandeza *f*

Great Britain /greɪtˈbrɪtən/ *n* Grã-Bretanha *f*

Greece /griːs/ *n* Grécia *f*

greed /griːd/ *n* cobiça *f*, ganância *f*; (*for food*) gula *f*. **~y** *a* cobiçoso, ganancioso; (*for food*) guloso

Greek /griːk/ *a & n* grego *m*

green /griːn/ *a* (**-er**, **-est**) verde ● *n* verde *m*; (*grass*) gramado *m*, (*P*) relvado *m*; **~s** hortaliças *fpl*; **~ belt** zona *f* verde, paisagem *f* protegida; **~ light** luz *f* verde. **~ery** *n* verdura *f*

> *i*
> **green card** Nos Estados Unidos, é o documento oficial que qualquer pessoa que não seja cidadão norte-americano deve obter para morar e trabalhar neste país. No Reino Unido, é o documento que se deve obter da companhia de seguros para que a cobertura de uma apólice continue em vigor quando se conduz um veículo no estrangeiro.

greengrocer /ˈgriːngrəʊsə(r)/ *n* quitandeiro *m*, (*P*) vendedor *m* de hortaliças

greenhouse /ˈgriːnhaʊs/ *n* estufa *f*; **~ effect** efeito estufa, (*P*) efeito de estufa

Greenland /ˈgriːnlənd/ *n* Groenlândia *f*, (*P*) Gronelândia *f*

greet /griːt/ *vt* acolher. **~ing** *n* saudação *f*; (*welcome*) acolhimento *m*. **~ings** *npl* cumprimentos *mpl*; (*Christmas etc*) votos *mpl*, desejos *mpl*

grenade /grɪˈneɪd/ *n* granada *f*

grew /gruː/ ▶ GROW

grey /greɪ/ *a* (**-er**, **-est**) cinzento; ‹*hair*› grisalho ● *n* cinzento *m*

greyhound /ˈgreɪhaʊnd/ *n* galgo *m*

grid /grɪd/ *n* (*grating*) gradeamento *m*, grade *f*; *Electr* rede *f*

grief /griːf/ *n* dor *f*; **come to ~** acabar mal

grievance /ˈgriːvns/ *n* razão *f* de queixa

grieve /griːv/ *vt* sofrer, afligir ● *vi* sofrer; **~ for** chorar por

grill /grɪl/ *n* grelha *f*; (*food*) grelhado *m*; (*place*) grill *m* ● *vt* grelhar; (*question*) submeter a interrogatório cerrado, apertar com perguntas ● *vi* grelhar

grille /grɪl/ *n* grade *f*; (*of car*) grelha *f*

grim /grɪm/ *a* (**grimmer**, **grimmest**) sinistro; (*without mercy*) implacável

grimace /grɪˈmeɪs/ *n* careta *f* ● *vi* fazer careta(s)

grim|e /graɪm/ *n* sujeira *f*. **~y** *a* encardido, sujo

grin /grɪn/ *vi* (*pt* **grinned**) sorrir abertamente, dar um sorriso largo ● *n* sorriso *m* aberto

grind /graɪnd/ *vt* (*pt* **ground**) triturar; ‹*coffee*› moer; (*sharpen*) amolar, afiar; **~ one's teeth** ranger os dentes; **~ to a halt** parar freando, (*P*) travar lentamente

grip /grɪp/ *vt* (*pt* **gripped**) agarrar; (*interest*) prender ● *n* (*of hands*) aperto *m*; (*control*) controle *m*, domínio *m*; **come to ~s with** fazer face a. **~ping** *a* apaixonante

grisly /ˈgrɪzlɪ/ *a* (**-ier**, **-iest**) macabro, horrível

gristle /ˈgrɪsl/ *n* cartilagem *f*

grit /grɪt/ *n* areia *f*, grão *m* de areia; *fig* (*pluck*) coragem *f*; fortaleza *f* ● *vt* (*pt* **gritted**) ‹*road*› jogar *or* (*P*) deitar areia em; ‹*teeth*› cerrar

groan /grəʊn/ *vi* gemer ● *n* gemido *m*

grocer /ˈgrəʊsə(r)/ *n* dono/a *m/f* de mercearia. **~ies** *npl* artigos *mpl* de mercearia. **~y** *n* (*shop*) mercearia *f*

groggy /ˈgrɒgɪ/ *a* (**-ier**, **-iest**) grogue, fraco das pernas

groin /grɔɪn/ *n* virilha *f*

groom /gruːm/ *n* noivo *m*; (*for horses*) moço *m* de estrebaria ● *vt* ‹*horse*› tratar de; *fig* preparar

groove /gruːv/ *n* ranhura *f*; (*for door, window*) calha *f*; (*in record*) estria *f*; *fig* rotina *f*

grope /grəʊp/ *vi* tatear; **~ for** procurar às cegas

gross /grəʊs/ *a* (**-er**, **-est**) (*vulgar*) grosseiro; (*flagrant*) flagrante; (*of error*) crasso; (*of weight, figure etc*) bruto ● *n* (*pl invar*) grosa *f*. **~ly** *adv* grosseiramente; (*very*) extremamente

grotesque /grəʊˈtesk/ *a* grotesco

grotty /ˈgrɒtɪ/ *a* ☒ sórdido

grouch /graʊtʃ/ *vi* [!] ralhar. **~y** *a* [!] rabugento

ground[1] /graʊnd/ *n* chão *m*, solo *m*; (*area*) terreno *m*; (*reason*) razão *f*, motivo *m*; **~s** jardins *mpl*; (*of coffee*) borra(s) *f* (*pl*); **~ floor** térreo *m*, (*P*) rés do chão *m* ● *vt/i* *Naut* encalhar; ‹*plane*› reter em terra. **~less** *a* infundado, sem fundamento

ground[2] /graʊnd/ ▶ GRIND

grounding /ˈgraʊndɪŋ/ *n* bases *fpl*, conhecimentos *mpl* básicos

groundsheet /ˈgraʊndʃiːt/ *n* impermeável *m* para o chão

groundwork /ˈgraʊndwɜːk/ *n* trabalhos *mpl* de base or preliminares

group /gruːp/ *n* grupo *m* ● *vt/i* agrupar(-se)

grouse[1] /graʊs/ *n* (*pl invar*) galo *m* silvestre

grouse[2] /graʊs/ *vi* [!] (*grumble*) resmungar; [!] (*complain*) queixar-se

grovel /ˈgrɒvl/ *vi* (*pt* **grovelled**) humilhar-se; *fig* rebaixar-se

grow /grəʊ/ *vi* (*pt* **grew**, *pp* **grown**) crescer; (*become*) tornar-se; **~ old** envelhecer; **~ up** crescer, tornar-se adulto ● *vt* cultivar

growl /graʊl/ *vi* rosnar ● *n* rosnadela *f*

grown /grəʊn/ *a* **~ man** homem feito. **~-up** *a* adulto ● *n* pessoa *f* adulta

growth /grəʊθ/ *n* crescimento *m*; (*increase*) aumento *m*; *Med* tumor *m*

grub /grʌb/ *n* larva *f*; ☒ (*food*) boia *f*; rango *m*, (*P*) comida *f*

grubby /ˈgrʌbɪ/ *a* (**-ier**, **-iest**) sujo, porco

grudge /grʌdʒ/ *vt* dar/reconhecer de má vontade; **~ doing** fazer de má vontade; **~ sb sth** dar algo a alguém de má vontade ● *n* má vontade *f*; **have**

a ~ against ter ressentimento contra. **grudgingly** *adv* relutantemente

gruelling /ˈgruːəlɪŋ/ *a* estafante, extenuante

gruesome /ˈgruːsəm/ *a* macabro

gruff /grʌf/ *a* (**-er**, **-est**) carrancudo, rude

grumble /ˈgrʌmbl/ *vi* resmungar (**at** contra, por)

grumpy /ˈgrʌmpɪ/ *a* (**-ier**, **-iest**) mal-humorado, rabugento

grunt /grʌnt/ *vi* grunhir ● *n* grunhido *m*

guarantee /gærənˈtiː/ *n* garantia *f* ● *vt* garantir

guard /gɑːd/ *vt* guardar, proteger ● *vi* **~ against** precaver-se contra ● *n* guarda *f*; (*person*) guarda *m*; (*on train*) condutor *m*. **~ian** *n* guardião *m*, defensor *m*; (*of orphan*) tutor *m*

guarded /ˈgɑːdɪd/ *a* cauteloso, circunspeto, (*P*) circunspecto

guerrilla /gəˈrɪlə/ *n* guerrilheiro *m*; **~ warfare** guerrilha *f*, guerra *f* de guerrilhas

guess /ges/ *vt/i* adivinhar; (*suppose*) supor ● *n* suposição *f*, conjetura *f*

guesswork /ˈgeswɜːk/ *n* suposição *f*, conjetura(s) *f(pl)*

guest /gest/ *n* convidado *m*; (*in hotel*) hóspede *mf*. **~ house** *n* pensão *f*

guidance /ˈgaɪdns/ *n* orientação *f*, direção *f*, (*P*) direcção *f*

guide /gaɪd/ *n* guia *mf* ● *vt* guiar; **~d missile** míssil *m* guiado; (*remote-control*) míssil *m* teleguiado. **~ dog** *n* cão *m* de cego, cão-guia *m*; **~lines** *npl* diretrizes *fpl*

Guide /gaɪd/ *n* Guia *f*

guidebook /ˈgaɪdbʊk/ *n* guia *m* (turístico)

guilt /gɪlt/ *n* culpa *f*. **~y** *a* culpado

guinea pig /ˈgɪnɪpɪg/ *n* cobaia *f*, porquinho-da-Índia *m*

guitar /gɪˈtɑː(r)/ *n* guitarra *f*, violão *m*, (*P*) viola *f*. **~ist** *n* guitarrista *mf*, tocador *m* de violão, (*P*) de viola

gulf /gʌlf/ *n* golfo *m*; (*hollow*) abismo *m*

gull /gʌl/ *n* gaivota *f*

gullible /ˈgʌləbl/ *a* crédulo

gully /ˈgʌlɪ/ *n* barranco *m*; (*drain*) sarjeta *f*

gulp /gʌlp/ *vt* engolir, devorar ● *vi* engolir em seco ● *n* trago *m*

gum[1] /gʌm/ *n Anat* gengiva *f*

gum[2] /gʌm/ *n* goma *f*; (*chewing gum*) chiclete *m*; goma *f* elástica, (*P*) pastilha *f* elástica ● *vt* (*pt* **gummed**) colar

gun /gʌn/ *n* (*pistol*) pistola *f*; (*rifle*) espingarda *f*; (*cannon*) canhão *m* ● *vt* (*pt* **gunned**) **~ down** abater a tiro

gunfire /ˈgʌnfaɪə(r)/ *n* tiroteio *m*

gunman /ˈgʌnmən/ *n* (*pl* **-men**) bandido *m* armado, atirador *m*

gunpowder /ˈgʌnpaʊdə(r)/ *n* pólvora *f*

gunshot /ˈgʌnʃɒt/ *n* tiro *m*

gurgle /ˈgɜːgl/ *n* gorgolejo *m* ● *vi* gorgolejar

gush /gʌʃ/ *vi* jorrar ● *n* jorro *m*. **~ing** *a* efusivo, derretido

gust /gʌst/ *n* (*of wind*) rajada *f*; (*of smoke*) nuvem *f*. **~y** *a* ventoso

gusto /ˈgʌstəʊ/ *n* gosto *m*, entusiasmo *m*

gut /gʌt/ *n* tripa *f*; **~s** (*belly*) barriga *f*; [!] (*courage*) coragem *f* ● *vt* (*pt* **gutted**) estripar; ‹*fish*› limpar; ‹*fire*› destruir o interior de

gutter /ˈgʌtə(r)/ *n* calha *f*, canaleta *f*; (*in street*) sarjeta *f*, valeta *f*

guy /gaɪ/ *n* [!] (*man*) cara *m*, (*P*) tipo *m* [!]

guzzle /ˈgʌzl/ *vt/i* comer/beber com sofreguidão, encher-se (de)

gym /dʒɪm/ *n* [!] (*gymnasium*) ginásio *m*; [!] (*gymnastics*) ginástica *f*

gym|nasium /dʒɪmˈneɪzɪəm/ *n* ginásio *m*. **~nast** /ˈdʒɪmnæst/ *n* ginasta *mf*. **~nastics** /-ˈnæstɪks/ *npl* ginástica *f*

gynaecolog|y /gaɪnɪˈkɒlədʒɪ/ *n* ginecologia *f*. **~ist** *n* ginecologista *mf*

gypsy /ˈdʒɪpsɪ/ *n* cigano *m*

Hh

haberdashery /ˈhæbədæʃərɪ/ *n* armarinho *m*, (*P*) retrosaria *f*

habit /ˈhæbɪt/ *n* hábito *m*, costume *m*; (*costume*) hábito *m*; **be in/get into the ~ of** ter/apanhar o hábito de

habit|able /ˈhæbɪtəbl/ *a* habitável. **~ation** /-ˈteɪʃn/ *n* habitação *f*

habitat /ˈhæbɪtæt/ *n* habitat *m*

habitual /həˈbɪtʃʊəl/ *a* habitual, costumeiro; ‹*smoker, liar*› inveterado. **~ly** *adv* habitualmente

hack[1] /hæk/ *n* (*horse*) cavalo *m* de aluguel *or* (*P*) aluguer; (*writer*) escrevinhador *m pej*. **~er** *n Comput* micreiro *m*, hacker *m*, (*P*) pirata *m* informático

hack² /hæk/ *vt* cortar, despedaçar; **~ to pieces** cortar em pedaços

hackneyed /'hæknɪd/ *a* banal, batido

had /hæd/ ▶ HAVE

haddock /'hædək/ *n* (*invar*) hadoque *m*, eglefim *m*; **smoked ~** hadoque *m* fumado

haemorrhage /'hemərɪdʒ/ *n* hemorragia *f*

haemorrhoids /'hemərɔɪdz/ *npl* hemorroidas *fpl*

haggard /'hægəd/ *a* desfigurado, com o rosto desfeito, magro e macilento

h

haggle /'hægl/ *vi* **~ (over)** regatear

hail¹ /heɪl/ *vt* saudar; ‹*taxi*› fazer sinal para, chamar ● *vi* **~ from** vir de

hail² /heɪl/ *n* granizo *m*, (*P*) saraiva *f*, (*P*) chuva de pedra *f* ● *vi* chover granizo, (*P*) saraivar

hailstone /'heɪlstəʊn/ *n* pedra *f* de granizo

hair /heə(r)/ *n* (*on head*) cabelo(s) *m(pl)*; (*on body*) pêlos *mpl*; (*single strand*) cabelo *m*; (*of animal*) pêlo *m*. **~do** *n* [!] penteado *m*; **~dryer** *n* secador *m* de cabelo; **~-raising** *a* horripilante, de pôr os cabelos em pé; **~style** *n* estilo *m* de penteado

hairbrush /'heəbrʌʃ/ *n* escova *f* para o cabelo

haircut /'heəkʌt/ *n* corte *m* de cabelo

hairdresser /'heədresə(r)/ *n* cabeleireiro *m*, cabeleireira *f*

hairpin /'heəpɪn/ *n* grampo *m*, (*P*) gancho *m* para o cabelo; **~ bend** curva *f* fechada, quase em V

hairy /'heərɪ/ *a* (**-ier**, **-iest**) peludo, cabeludo; [✱] (*terrifying*) de pôr os cabelos em pé; horripilante

hake /heɪk/ *n* (*pl invar*) abrótea *f*

half /hɑːf/ *n* (*pl* **halves** /hɑːvz/) metade *f*, meio *m*; **go halves** dividir as despesas ● *a* meio; **~ a dozen** meia dúzia; **~ an hour** meia hora ● *adv* ao meio. **~-caste** *n* mestiço *m*; **~-hearted** *a* sem grande entusiasmo; **~-term** *n* férias *fpl* no meio do trimestre; **~-time** *n* meio-tempo *m*; **~-way** *a & adv* a meio caminho; **~-wit** *n* idiota *mf*

halibut /'hælɪbət/ *n* (*pl invar*) halibute *m*

hall /hɔːl/ *n* sala *f*; (*entrance*) vestíbulo *m*, entrada *f*; (*mansion*) solar *m*; **~ of residence** residência *f* de estudantes

hallmark /'hɔːlmɑːk/ *n* (*on gold etc*) marca *f* do contraste; *fig* cunho *m*; selo *m*

hallo /hə'ləʊ/ *int & n* (*greeting, surprise*) olá; (*on phone*) está

Halloween /hæləʊ'iːn/ *n* véspera *f* do Dia de Todos os Santos *or* (*P*) Dia das Bruxas

hallucination /həluːsɪ'neɪʃn/ *n* alucinação *f*

halo /'heɪləʊ/ *n* (*pl* **-oes**) halo *m*, auréola *f*

halt /hɔːlt/ *n* parada *f*, (*P*) paragem *f* ● *vt* deter, fazer parar ● *vi* fazer alto, parar

halve /hɑːv/ *vt* dividir ao meio; ‹*time etc*› reduzir à metade

ham /hæm/ *n* presunto *m*

hamburger /'hæmbɜːgə(r)/ *n* hambúrguer *m*

hammer /'hæmə(r)/ *n* martelo *m* ● *vt/i* martelar; *fig* bater com força

hammock /'hæmək/ *n* rede (de dormir) *f*

hamper¹ /'hæmpə(r)/ *n* cesto *m*, (*P*) cabaz *m*

hamper² /'hæmpə(r)/ *vt* dificultar, atrapalhar

hamster /'hæmstə(r)/ *n* hamster *m*

hand /hænd/ *n* mão *f*; (*of clock*) ponteiro *m*; (*writing*) letra *f*; (*worker*) trabalhador *m*; *Cards* mão *f*; (*measure*) palmo *m*; **(helping) ~** ajuda *f*, mão *f*; **at ~** à mão; **on the one ~... on the other ~** por um lado ... por outro; **out of ~** incontrolável; **to ~** à mão ● *vt* dar, entregar; **~ in** or **over** entregar; **~ out** distribuir. **~-baggage** *n* bagagem *f* de mão; **~-out** *n* impresso *m*, folheto *m*; (*money*) esmola *f*, donativo *m*

handbag /'hændbæg/ *n* carteira *f*, bolsa de mão *f*, mala de mão *f*

handbook /'hændbʊk/ *n* manual *m*

handbrake /'hændbreɪk/ *n* freio *m* de mão, (*P*) travão *m* de mão

handcuffs /'hændkʌfs/ *npl* algemas *fpl*

handful /'hændfʊl/ *n* mão-cheia *f*, punhado *m*; (*a few*) punhado *m*; (*difficult task*) mão de obra *f*; **she's a ~** [!] ela é danada

handicap /'hændɪkæp/ *n* (*in competition*) handicap *m*; (*disadvantage*) desvantagem *f* ● *vt* (*pt* **handicapped**) prejudicar. **~ped** *a* deficiente; **mentally ~ped** deficiente mental

handicraft /'hændɪkrɑːft/ *n* artesanato *m*, trabalho *m* manual

handiwork /'hændɪwɜːk/ *n* obra *f*, trabalho *m*

handkerchief /ˈhæŋkətʃɪf/ *n* lenço *m*

handle /ˈhændl/ *n* (*of door etc*) maçaneta *f*, puxador *m*; (*of cup etc*) asa *f*; (*of implement*) cabo *m*; (*of pan etc*) alça *f*, (*P*) pega *f* ● *vt* (*touch*) manusear, tocar; (*operate with hands*) manejar; (*deal in*) negociar em; (*deal with*) tratar de; ‹*person*› lidar com; **fly off the ~** [!] perder as estribeiras

handlebar /ˈhændlbɑː(r)/ *n* guidão *m*, (*P*) guiador *m*

handmade /ˈhændmeɪd/ *a* feito à mão

handshake /ˈhændʃeɪk/ *n* aperto *m* de mão

handsome /ˈhænsəm/ *a* bonito; *fig* generoso

handwriting /ˈhændraɪtɪŋ/ *n* letra *f*, caligrafia *f*

handy /ˈhændɪ/ *a* (**-ier**, **-iest**) (*convenient, useful*) útil, prático; ‹*person*› jeitoso; (*near*) à mão

handyman /ˈhændɪmæn/ *n* (*pl* **-men**) faz-tudo *m*

hang /hæŋ/ *vt* (*pt* **hung**) pendurar, suspender; ‹*head*› baixar (*pt* **hanged**) ‹*criminal*› enforcar; **~ on to** (*hold tightly*) agarrar-se a; **~ up** ‹*phone*› desligar ● *vi* estar dependurado, pender; ‹*criminal*› ser enforcado; **~ about** andar por aí; **~ back** hesitar; **~ on** (*wait*) aguardar; **~ out** [✱] (*live*) morar ● *n* **get the ~ of** [!] pegar o jeito de, (*P*) apanhar. **~-gliding** *n* asa-delta *f*; **~-up** *n* [✱] complexo *m*

hangar /ˈhæŋə(r)/ *n* hangar *m*

hanger /ˈhæŋə(r)/ *n* (*for clothes*) cabide *m*. **~-on** *n* parasita *mf*

hangover /ˈhæŋəʊvə(r)/ *n* (*from drinking*) ressaca *f*

hanker /ˈhæŋkə(r)/ *vi* **~ after** ansiar por, suspirar por

happen /ˈhæpən/ *vi* acontecer, suceder; **he ~s to be out** por acaso ele não está. **~ing** *n* acontecimento *m*

happ|y /ˈhæpɪ/ *a* (**-ier**, **-iest**) feliz; **be ~y with** estar contente com. **~y-go-lucky** *a* despreocupado. **~ily** *adv* com satisfação; **she smiled ~ily** ela sorriu feliz; (*fortunately*) felizmente. **~iness** *n* felicidade *f*

harass /ˈhærəs/ *vt* amofinar, atormentar, perseguir. **~ment** *n* amofinação *f*, perseguição *f*; **sexual ~ment** assédio *m* sexual

harbour /ˈhɑːbə(r)/ *n* porto *m*; (*shelter*) abrigo *m* ● *vt* abrigar, dar asilo a; *fig* (*in the mind*) ocultar; obrigar

hard /hɑːd/ *a* (**-er**, **-est**) duro; (*difficult*) difícil; **~-boiled egg** ovo *m* cozido; **~ disk** disco *m* rígido, (*P*) duro; **~ of hearing** meio surdo; **~ shoulder** acostamento *m*, (*P*) berma *f* alcatroada; **~ water** água *f* dura ● *adv* muito, intensamente; (*look*) fixamente; (*pull*) com força; (*think*) a fundo, a sério; **~ by** muito perto; **~ up** [✱] sem dinheiro, teso [✱], liso [✱]. **~back** *n* livro *m* encadernado.

hardboard /ˈhɑːdbɔːd/ *n* madeira *f* compensada, madeira *f* prensada

harden /ˈhɑːdn/ *vt/i* endurecer. **~ed** *a* (*callous*) calejado; (*robust*) enrijado

hardly /ˈhɑːdlɪ/ *adv* mal, dificilmente, a custo; **~ ever** quase nunca

h

hardship /ˈhɑːdʃɪp/ *n* provação *f*, adversidade *f*; (*suffering*) sofrimento *m*; (*financial*) privação *f*

hardware /ˈhɑːdweə(r)/ *n* ferragens *fpl*; *Comput* hardware *m*

hardy /ˈhɑːdɪ/ *a* (**-ier**, **-iest**) resistente

hare /heə(r)/ *n* lebre *f*

harm /hɑːm/ *n* mal *m*; **out of ~'s way** a salvo; **there's no ~ in** não há mal em ● *vt* prejudicar, fazer mal a. **~ful** *a* prejudicial, nocivo. **~less** *a* inofensivo

harmonica /hɑːˈmɒnɪkə/ *n* gaita *f* de boca, (*P*) beiços

harmon|y /ˈhɑːmənɪ/ *n* harmonia *f*. **~ious** /-ˈməʊnɪəs/ *a* harmonioso. **~ize** *vt/i* harmonizar(-se)

harness /ˈhɑːnɪs/ *n* arreios *mpl* ● *vt* arrear; *fig* (*use*) aproveitar; utilizar

harp /hɑːp/ *n* harpa *f* ● *vi* **~ on (about)** repisar

harpsichord /ˈhɑːpsɪkɔːd/ *n* cravo *m*

harrowing /ˈhærəʊɪŋ/ *a* dilacerante, lancinante

harsh /hɑːʃ/ *a* (**-er**, **-est**) duro, severo; ‹*texture, voice*› áspero; ‹*light*› cru; ‹*colour*› gritante; ‹*climate*› rigoroso. **~ness** *n* dureza *f*

harvest /ˈhɑːvɪst/ *n* colheita *f*, ceifa *f* ● *vt* colher, ceifar

has /hæz/ ▶ HAVE

hash /hæʃ/ *n* picadinho *m*, carne *f* cozida; *fig* (*jumble*) bagunça *f*; **make a ~ of** fazer uma bagunça de. **~ key** *n* tecla *f* sustenido, (*P*) tecla *f* cardinal

hashish /ˈhæʃɪʃ/ *n* haxixe *m*

hassle /ˈhæsl/ *n* [!] (*quarrel*) discussão *f*; [!] (*struggle*) dificuldade *f* ● *vt* [!] aborrecer

haste /heɪst/ *n* pressa *f*; **make ~** apressar-se

hasten /'heɪsn/ *vt/i* apressar(-se)

hast|y /'heɪstɪ/ *a* (**-ier**, **-iest**) apressado; (*too quick*) precipitado

hat /hæt/ *n* chapéu *m*

hatch[1] /hætʃ/ *n* (*for food*) postigo *m*; *Naut* escotilha *f*

hatch[2] /hætʃ/ *vt/i* chocar; ‹*a plot etc*› tramar, urdir

hatchback /'hætʃbæk/ *n* carro *m* de três ou cinco portas

hate /heɪt/ *n* ódio *m* ● *vt* odiar, detestar. **~ful** *a* odioso, detestável

hatred /'heɪtrɪd/ *n* ódio *m*

h

haughty /'hɔːtɪ/ *a* (**-ier**, **-iest**) altivo, soberbo, arrogante

haul /hɔːl/ *vt* arrastar, puxar; ‹*goods*› transportar em camião ● *n* (*booty*) presa *f*; (*fish caught*) apanha *f*; (*distance*) percurso *m*. **~age** *n* transporte *m* de cargas

haunt /hɔːnt/ *vt* rondar, frequentar; ‹*ghost*› assombrar; ‹*thought*› obcecar ● *n* lugar *m* favorito; **~ed house** casa *f* mal-assombrada

have /hæv *unstressed* həv, əv/ ● *vt* (*3 sing pres* **has**, *pt and pp* **had**)

····➤ (*possess*) ter; **I ~ (got) a car** tenho um carro; **they ~ (got) problems** eles têm problemas

····➤ (*do sth*) (*have a try*) tentar; **~ a bath** tomar banho; **~ a meal** comer uma refeição; **~ a walk** dar um passeio

····➤ (*take, esp. in restaurant, shop*) **I'll ~ the soup** vou querer a sopa; **I'll ~ the red dress** vou levar o vestido vermelho

····➤ (*receive*) receber; **I had a letter from her** recebi uma carta dela

····➤ (*have sth done*) mandar fazer; **we had the house painted** mandamos pintar a casa; **~ one's hair cut** cortar o cabelo

● *v aux*

····➤ (*in perfect tenses*) ter; **~ done** ter feito; **I ~ seen him** eu o vi

····➤ (*in tag questions*) **you've seen her, ~n't you?** você a viu, não viu?; **you ~n't seen her, have you?** você não a viu, viu?

····➤ (*in short answers*) **'you've never met him' -'yes, I ~'** 'você nunca o conheceu'- 'sim, conheci'

····➤ (*must*) **~ to** ter de; **I ~ to go** tenho de ir; **you don't ~ to do it** você não tem que fazer isso

□ **have on** ● *vt* (*be wearing*) ter vestido; **~ sb on** gozar com alguém. **have out** ● *vt* ‹*tooth, tonsils*› extrair; **~ it out with sb** pôr a coisa em pratos limpos com alguém

havoc /'hævək/ *n* estragos *mpl*; **play ~ with** causar estragos em

hawk[1] /hɔːk/ *n* falcão *m*

hawk[2] /hɔːk/ *vt* vender de porta em porta. **~er** *n* vendedor *m* ambulante

hawthorn /'hɔːθɔːn/ *n* pilriteiro *m*, estripeiro *m*

hay /heɪ/ *n* feno *m*; **~ fever** febre *f* do feno

haystack /'heɪstæk/ *n* palheiro *m*

hazard /'hæzəd/ *n* risco *m*; **~ warning lights** pisca-alerta *m* ● *vt* arriscar. **~ous** *a* arriscado

haze /heɪz/ *n* bruma *f*, neblina *f*, cerração *f*

hazel /'heɪzl/ *n* aveleira *f*. **~-nut** *n* avelã *f*

hazy /'heɪzɪ/ *a* (**-ier**, **-iest**) brumoso, encoberto; *fig* (*vague*) vago

he /hiː/ *pron* ele ● *n* macho *m*

head /hed/ *n* cabeça *f*; (*chief*) chefe *m*; (*of beer*) espuma *f*; **~ first** de cabeça; **~s or tails** cara ou coroa?; **~ waiter** chefe *m* de garçons, (*P*) empregados de mesa ● *a* principal ● *vt* encabeçar, estar à frente de ● *vi* **~ for** dirigir-se para. **~-dress** *n* toucador *m*; **~-on** *a* frontal ● *adv* de frente. **~er** *n Football* cabeçada *f*

headache /'hedeɪk/ *n* dor *f* de cabeça

heading /'hedɪŋ/ *n* cabeçalho *m*, título *m*; (*subject category*) rubrica *f*

headlamp /'hedlæmp/ *n* farol *m*

headland /'hedlənd/ *n* promontório *m*

headlight /'hedlaɪt/ *n* farol *m*

headline /'hedlaɪn/ *n* título *m*, cabeçalho *m*

headlong /'hedlɒŋ/ *a* de cabeça; (*rash*) precipitado ● *adv* de cabeça; (*rashly*) precipitadamente

head|master /hed'mɑːstə(r)/ *n* diretor *m*. **~mistress** *n* diretora *f*

headphone /'hedfəʊn/ *n* fone *m* de cabeça, (*P*) auscultador *m*

headquarters /hed'kwɔːtəz/ *npl* sede *f*; *Mil* quartel *m* general

headrest /'hedrest/ *n* apoio *m* para a cabeça

headroom /ˈhedruːm/ *n Auto* espaço *m* para a cabeça; (*bridge*) limite *m* de altura, altura *f* máxima

headstrong /ˈhedstrɒŋ/ *a* teimoso

headway /ˈhedweɪ/ *n* progresso *m*; **make ~** fazer progressos

heady /ˈhedɪ/ *a* (**-ier**, **-iest**) empolgante

heal /hiːl/ *vt/i* curar(-se), sarar; ‹*wound*› cicatrizar

health /helθ/ *n* saúde *f*; **~ centre** posto *m* de saúde, (*P*) centro *m* de saúde; **~ foods** alimentos *mpl* naturais. **~y** *a* saudável, sadio

heap /hiːp/ *n* monte *m*, pilha *f* ● *vt* amontoar, empilhar; **~s of money** [!] dinheiro aos montes [!]

hear /hɪə(r)/ *vt/i* (*pt* **heard** /hɜːd/) ouvir; **~, hear!** apoiado! **~ from** ter notícias de; **~ of** or **about** ouvir falar de; **I won't ~ of it** nem quero ouvir falar nisso. **~ing** *n* ouvido *m*, audição *f*; *Jur* audiência *f*. **~ing-aid** *n* aparelho *m* de audição, (*P*) aparelho *m* auditivo

hearsay /ˈhɪəseɪ/ *n* boato *m*; **it's only ~** é só por ouvir dizer

hearse /hɜːs/ *n* carro *m* funerário

heart /hɑːt/ *n* coração *m*; **~s** *Cards* copas *fpl*; **at ~** no fundo; **by ~** de cor; **~ attack** ataque *m* de coração; **lose ~** perder a coragem, desanimar. **~-beat** *n* pulsação *f*, batida *f*; **~-breaking** *a* de partir o coração; **~-broken** *a* com o coração partido, desfeito; **~-to-heart** *a* com o coração nas mãos

heartburn /ˈhaːtbɜːn/ *n* azia *f*

hearten /ˈhɑːtn/ *vt* animar, encorajar

heartfelt /ˈhɑːtfelt/ *a* sincero, sentido

hearth /hɑːθ/ *n* lareira *f*

heartless /ˈhɑːtlɪs/ *a* insensível, desalmado, cruel

heart|y /ˈhɑːtɪ/ *a* (**-ier**, **-iest**) caloroso; ‹*meal*› abundante. **~ily** *adv* calorosamente; ‹*eat, laugh*› com vontade

heat /hiːt/ *n* calor *m*; *fig* ardor *m*; (*contest*) eliminatória *f* ● *vt/i* aquecer. **~stroke** *n* insolação *f*. **~wave** *n* onda *f* de calor. **~er** *n* aquecedor *m*. **~ing** *n* aquecimento *m*

heated /ˈhiːtɪd/ *a fig* acalorado; aceso

heathen /ˈhiːðn/ *n* pagão *m*, pagã *f*

heather /ˈheðə(r)/ *n* urze *f*

heave /hiːv/ *vt/i* (*lift*) içar; ‹*a sigh*› soltar; (*retch*) ter náuseas; [!] (*throw*) atirar

heaven /ˈhevn/ *n* céu *m*. **~ly** *a* celestial; [!] divino

heav|y /ˈhevɪ/ *a* (**-ier**, **-iest**) pesado; ‹*blow, rain*› forte; ‹*cold, drinker*› grande; ‹*traffic*› intenso. **~ily** *adv* pesadamente; ‹*drink, smoke etc*› desalmadamente

heavyweight /ˈhevɪweɪt/ *n Boxing* peso-pesado *m*

Hebrew /ˈhiːbruː/ *a* hebreu, hebraico ● *n Lang* hebreu *m*

heckle /ˈhekl/ *vt* interromper, interpelar

hectic /ˈhektɪk/ *a* muito agitado, febril

hedge /hedʒ/ *n* sebe *f* ● *vt* cercar ● *vi* (*in answering*) usar de evasivas; **~ one's bets** *fig* resguardar-se

hedgehog /ˈhedʒhɒg/ *n* ouriço-cacheiro *m*

heed /hiːd/ *vt* prestar atenção a, escutar ● *n* **pay ~ to** prestar atenção a, dar ouvidos a

heel /hiːl/ *n* calcanhar *m*; (*of shoe*) salto *m*; [✖] canalha *m*

hefty /ˈheftɪ/ *a* (**-ier**, **-iest**) robusto e corpulento

height /haɪt/ *n* altura *f*; (*of mountain, plane*) altitude *f*; *fig* auge *m*; cúmulo *m*

heighten /ˈhaɪtn/ *vt/i* aumentar, elevar(-se)

heir /eə(r)/ *n* herdeiro *m*. **~ess** *n* herdeira *f*

heirloom /ˈeəluːm/ *n* peça *f* de família, (*P*) relíquia *f* de família

held /held/ ▶ **HOLD**[1]

helicopter /ˈhelɪkɒptə(r)/ *n* helicóptero *m*

hell /hel/ *n* inferno *m*; **for the ~ of it** só por gozo. **~ish** *a* infernal

hello /həˈləʊ/ *int & n* = **HALLO**

helm /helm/ *n* leme *m*

helmet /ˈhelmɪt/ *n* capacete *m*

help /help/ *vt/i* ajudar ● *n* ajuda *f*; **home ~** empregada *f*, faxineira *f*, (*P*) mulher *f* a dias; **~ o.s. to** servir-se de; **he cannot ~ laughing** ele não pode conter o riso; **it can't be ~ed** não há remédio. **~er** *n* ajudante *mf*. **~ful** *a* útil; (*serviceable*) de grande ajuda. **~less** *a* impotente

helping /ˈhelpɪŋ/ *n* porção *f*, dose *f*

hem /hem/ *n* bainha *f* ● *vt* (*pt* **hemmed**) fazer a bainha; **~ in** cercar, encurralar

hemisphere /ˈhemɪsfɪə(r)/ *n* hemisfério *m*

hemp /hemp/ *n* cânhamo *m*

hen /hen/ *n* galinha *f*

h

hence /hens/ *adv* (*from now*) a partir desta altura; (*for this reason*) daí, por isso; **a week ~** daqui a uma semana. **~forth** *adv* de agora em diante, doravante

henpecked /'henpekt/ *a* mandado, (*P*) dominado pela mulher

her /hɜ:(r)/ *pron* a (a ela); (*after prep*) ela; **(to) ~** lhe; **I know ~** conheço-a ● *a* seu(s), sua(s), dela

herald /'herəld/ *vt* anunciar

heraldry /'herəldrɪ/ *n* heráldica *f*

herb /hɜ:b/ *n* erva *f* culinária or medicinal

herd /hɜ:d/ *n* manada *f*; (*of pigs*) vara *f* ● *vi* **~ together** juntar-se em rebanho

h

here /hɪə(r)/ *adv* aqui ● *int* tome; aqui está; **to/from ~** para aqui/daqui

hereafter /hɪər'ɑ:ftə(r)/ *adv* de/para o futuro, daqui em diante ● *n* **the ~** a vida de além-túmulo, (*P*) a vida *f* para além da morte

hereby /hɪə'baɪ/ *adv Jur* pelo presente ato ou decreto, etc

hereditary /hɪ'redɪtrɪ/ *a* hereditário

here|sy /'herəsɪ/ *n* heresia *f*. **~tic** *n* herege *mf*. **~tical** /hɪ'retɪkl/ *a* herético

heritage /'herɪtɪdʒ/ *n* herança *f*, patrimônio *m*, (*P*) património *m*

hermit /'hɜ:mɪt/ *n* eremita *m*

hernia /'hɜ:nɪə/ *n* hérnia *f*

hero /'hɪərəʊ/ *n* (*pl* **-oes**) herói *m*

heroic /hɪ'rəʊɪk/ *a* heroico

heroin /'herəʊɪn/ *n* heroína *f*

heroine /'herəʊɪn/ *n* heroína *f*

heroism /'herəʊɪzəm/ *n* heroísmo *m*

heron /'herən/ *n* garça *f*

herring /'herɪŋ/ *n* arenque *m*

hers /hɜ:z/ *poss pron* o(s) seu(s), a(s) sua(s), o(s) dela, a(s) dela; **it is ~** é (o) dela or o seu

herself /hɜ:'self/ *pron* ela mesma/própria; (*reflexive*) se; **by ~** sozinha; **for ~** para si mesma/própria; **to ~** a/para si mesma/própria; **Mary ~ said so** foi a própria Maria que o disse

hesitant /'hezɪtənt/ *a* hesitante

hesitat|e /'hezɪteɪt/ *vt* hesitar. **~ion** /-'teɪʃn/ *n* hesitação *f*

heterosexual /hetərəʊ'seksjʊəl/ *a & n* heterossexual *mf*

hexagon /'heksəgən/ *n* hexágono *m*. **~al** /-'ægənl/ *a* hexagonal

hey /heɪ/ *int* eh, olá

heyday /'heɪdeɪ/ *n* auge *m*, apogeu *m*

hi /haɪ/ *int* olá, viva

hibernat|e /'haɪbəneɪt/ *vi* hibernar. **~ion** /-'neɪʃn/ *n* hibernação *f*

hiccup /'hɪkʌp/ *n* soluço *m* ● *vi* soluçar, estar com soluços

hide[1] /haɪd/ *vt/i* (*pt* **hid**, *pp* **hidden**) esconder(-se) (**from** de). **~-and-seek** *n* (*game*) esconde-esconde *m*, (*P*) jogo *m* das escondidas; **~-out** *n* [!] esconderijo *m*

hide[2] /haɪd/ *n* pele *f*, couro *m*

hideous /'hɪdɪəs/ *a* horrendo, medonho

hiding /'haɪdɪŋ/ *n* [!] (*thrashing*) sova *f*; surra *f*; **go into ~** esconder-se

hierarchy /'haɪərɑ:kɪ/ *n* hierarquia *f*

hi-fi /haɪ'faɪ/ *a & n* (de) alta fidelidade *f*

high /haɪ/ *a* (**-er**, **-est**) alto; ‹*price, number*› elevado; ‹*voice, pitch*› agudo; **~ chair** cadeira *f* alta para crianças; **~ jump** salto *m* em altura; **~-rise building** edifício *m* alto, (*P*) torre *f*; **~ school** escola *f* secundária; **in the ~ season** em plena estação; **~ spot** ponto *m* culminante; **~ street** rua *f* principal; **~ tide** maré *f* alta; **~er education** ensino *m* superior ● *n* alta *f* ● *adv* alto; **two metres ~** com dois metros de altura. **~-handed** *a* autoritário, prepotente; **~-speed** *a* ultrarápido

highbrow /'haɪbraʊ/ *a & n* [!] intelectual *m*

highlight /'haɪlaɪt/ *n fig* ponto *m* alto ● *vt* salientar, pôr em relevo, realçar

highly /'haɪlɪ/ *adv* altamente, extremamente; **speak ~ of** falar bem de. **~-strung** *a* muito sensível, nervoso, tenso

Highness /'haɪnɪs/ *n* Alteza *f*

> *i*
> **high school** Nos Estados Unidos, é o último ciclo de ensino secundário, geralmente frequentado por alunos de idades entre os 14 e os 18 anos. Na Grã-Bretanha, alguns colégios de ensino secundário também se chamam *high schools*.

highway /'haɪweɪ/ *n* estrada *f*, rodovia *f*; **H~ Code** Código *m* Nacional de Trânsito

hijab /hɪ'dʒɑ:b/ *n* hijab *m*

hijack /'haɪdʒæk/ *vt* sequestrar ● *n* sequestro *m*. **~er** *n* (*of plane*) pirata (do ar) *m*

hike /haɪk/ *n* caminhada no campo *f* ● *vi* fazer uma caminhada. **~r** /-ə(r)/ *n* excursionista *mf*, caminhante *mf*

hilarious /hɪ'leərɪəs/ *a* divertido, desopilante

hill /hɪl/ *n* colina *f*, monte *m*; (*slope*) ladeira *f*, subida *f*. **~y** *a* acidentado

hillside /'hɪlsaɪd/ *n* encosta *f*, vertente *f*

him /hɪm/ *pron* o (a ele); (*after prep*) ele; **(to) ~** lhe; **I know ~** conheço-o

himself /hɪm'self/ *pron* ele mesmo/próprio; (*reflexive*) se; **by ~** sozinho; **for ~** para si mesmo/próprio; **to ~** a/para si mesmo/próprio; **Peter ~ saw it** foi o próprio Pedro que o viu

hind /haɪnd/ *a* traseiro, posterior

hind|er /'hɪndə(r)/ *vt* empatar, estorvar; (*prevent*) impedir. **~rance** *n* estorvo *m*

hindsight /'haɪndsaɪt/ *n* **with ~** em retrospecto, (*P*) em retrospetiva

Hindu /hɪn'duː/ *n & a* hindu *mf*. **~ism** /-ɪzəm/ *n* hinduísmo *m*

hinge /hɪndʒ/ *n* dobradiça *f* ● *vi* **~ on** depender de

hint /hɪnt/ *n* insinuação *f*, indireta *f*; (*advice*) sugestão *f*; dica *f* [!] ● *vt* dar a entender, insinuar ● *vi* **~ at** fazer alusão a

hip /hɪp/ *n* quadril *m*, anca *f*

hippie /'hɪpɪ/ *n* hippie *mf*

hippopotamus /hɪpə'pɒtəməs/ *n* (*pl* **-muses**) hipopótamo *m*

hire /'haɪə(r)/ *vt* alugar; ‹*person*› contratar ● *n* aluguel *m*, (*P*) aluguer *m*

his /hɪz/ *a* seu(s), sua(s), dele ● *poss pron* o(s) seu(s), a(s) sua(s), o(s) dele, a(s) dele; **it is ~** é (o) dele *or* o seu

Hispanic /hɪs'pænɪk/ *a* hispânico

hiss /hɪs/ *n* silvo *m*; (*for disapproval*) assobio *m*, vaia *f* ● *vt/i* sibilar; (*for disapproval*) assobiar, vaiar

historian /hɪ'stɔːrɪən/ *n* historiador *m*

histor|y /'hɪstərɪ/ *n* história *f*. **~ic(al)** /hɪ'stɒrɪk(l)/ *a* histórico

hit /hɪt/ *vt* (*pt* **hit**, *pres p* **hitting**) atingir, bater em; (*knock against, collide with*) chocar com, ir de encontro a; (*strike a target*) acertar em; (*find*) descobrir; (*affect*) atingir; **~ it off** dar-se bem (**with**com) ● *vi* **~ on** dar com ● *n* pancada *f*; *fig* (*success*) sucesso *m*. **~-and-run** *a* (*driver*) que foge depois do desastre; **~-or-miss** *a* ao acaso

hitch /hɪtʃ/ *vt* atar, prender; (*to a hook*) enganchar; **~ up** puxar para cima; **~ a lift, ~-hike** viajar de carona *or* (*P*) boleia ● *n* sacão *m*; (*snag*) problema *m*. **~-hiker** *n* o que viaja de carona, boleia

HIV *abbr* (= **human immunodeficiency virus**) HIV *m*, (*P*) VIH *m*; **~-positive** soropositivo, (*P*) seropositivo; **to be ~-positive/negative** ser soropositivo/soronegativo, (*P*) ser seropositivo/seronegativo, ter um resultado positivo/negativo no teste de VIH

hive /haɪv/ *n* colmeia *f* ● *vt* **~ off** separar e tornar independente

hoard /hɔːd/ *vt* juntar, açambarcar ● *n* provisão *f*; (*of valuables*) tesouro *m*

hoarding /'hɔːdɪŋ/ *n* tapume *m*, outdoor *m*

hoarse /hɔːs/ *a* (**-er, -est**) rouco. **~ness** *n* rouquidão *f*

hoax /həʊks/ *n* (*malicious*) logro *m*, embuste *m*; (*humorous*) trote *m* ● *vt* (*malicious*) enganar, lograr; passar um trote, pregar uma peça em

h

hob /hɒb/ *n* placa *f* de aquecimento (do fogão)

hobble /'hɒbl/ *vi* coxear ● *vt* pear

hobby /'hɒbɪ/ *n* passatempo *m* favorito. **~ horse** *n fig* tópico *m* favorito

hockey /'hɒkɪ/ *n* hóquei *m*

hoe /həʊ/ *n* enxada *f* ● *vt* trabalhar com enxada

hog /hɒg/ *n* porco *m*; (*greedy person*) glutão *m* ● *vt* (*pt* **hogged**) [!] açambarcar

hoist /hɔɪst/ *vt* içar ● *n* guindaste *m*, (*P*) monta-cargas *m*

hold[1] /həʊld/ *vt* (*pt* **held**) segurar; (*contain*) levar; (*possess*) ter, possuir; (*occupy*) ocupar; (*keep, maintain*) conservar, manter; (*affirm*) manter; **~ on to** guardar; (*cling to*) agarrar-se a; **~ one's breath** suster a respiração; **~ one's tongue** calar-se; **~ the line** não desligar; **~ up** (*support*) sustentar; (*delay*) demorar; (*rob*) assaltar ● *vi* (*of rope etc*) aguentar(-se); **~ back** reter; **~ on** [!] esperar; **~ out** resistir; **~ with** aguentar ● *n* (*influence*) domínio *m*; **get ~ of** pôr as mãos em; *fig* apanhar. **~-up** *n* atraso *m*; *Auto* engarrafamento *m*; (*robbery*) assalto *m*. **~er** *n* detentor *m*; (*of post, title etc*) titular *mf*; (*for object*) suporte *m*

hold[2] /həʊld/ *n* (*of ship, plane*) porão *m*

holdall /'həʊldɔːl/ *n* saco *m* de viagem

holding /'həʊldɪŋ/ *n* (*land*) propriedade *f*; *Comm* ações *fpl*, valores *mpl*, holding *m*

hole /həʊl/ *n* buraco *m* ● *vt* abrir buraco(s) em, esburacar

holiday /'hɒlədeɪ/ *n* férias *fpl*; (*day off; public*) feriado *m* ● *vi* passar férias.

~maker *n* pessoa *f* em férias; (*in summer*) veranista *mf*, (*P*) veraneante *mf*

holiness /'həʊlɪnɪs/ *n* santidade *f*

Holland /'hɒlənd/ *n* Holanda *f*

hollow /'hɒləʊ/ *a* oco, vazio; *fig* falso; ‹*cheeks*› fundo; ‹*sound*› surdo ● *n* (*in the ground*) cavidade *f*; (*in the hand*) cova *f*

holly /'hɒlɪ/ *n* azevinho *m*

holster /'həʊlstə(r)/ *n* coldre *m*

holy /'həʊlɪ/ *a* (**-ier**, **-iest**) santo, sagrado; ‹*water*› benta; **H~ Ghost, H~ Spirit** Espírito *m* Santo

homage /'hɒmɪdʒ/ *n* homenagem *f*; **pay ~ to** prestar homenagem a

home /həʊm/ *n* casa *f*, lar *m*; (*institution*) lar *m*, asilo *m*; (*country*) país *m* natal ● *a* caseiro, doméstico; (*of family*) de família; *Pol* nacional, interno; ‹*football match*› em casa; **H~ Office** Ministério *m* do Interior; **~ town** cidade *f* or terra *f* natal; **~ truth** dura verdade *f*, verdade(s) *f(pl)* amarga(s) ● *adv* **(at) ~** em casa; **come/go ~** vir/ir para casa; **make oneself at ~** não fazer cerimônia or (*P*) cerimónia. **~-made** *a* caseiro. **~less** *a* sem casa, desabrigado

homeland /'həʊmlænd/ *n* pátria *f*

homely /'həʊmlɪ/ *a* (**-ier**, **-iest**) (*simple*) simples; *Amer* (*ugly*) sem graça

homesick /'həʊmsɪk/ *a* **be ~** ter saudades (de casa)

homework /'həʊmwɜːk/ *n* trabalho *m* de casa, dever *m* de casa

homicide /'hɒmɪsaɪd/ *n* homicídio *m*; (*person*) homicida *mf*

homoeopath|y /həʊmɪ'ɒpəθɪ/ *n* homeopatia *f*. **~ic** *a* homeopático

homosexual /hɒmə'sekʃʊəl/ *a* & *n* homossexual *mf*

honest /'ɒnɪst/ *a* honesto; (*frank*) franco. **~y** *n* honestidade *f*

honey /'hʌnɪ/ *n* mel *m*; [!] (*darling*) querido *m*; querida *f*; meu bem *m*

honeycomb /'hʌnɪkəʊm/ *n* favo *m* de mel

honeymoon /'hʌnɪmuːn/ *n* lua *f* de mel

honorary /'ɒnərərɪ/ *a* honorário

honour /'ɒnə(r)/ *n* honra *f* ● *vt* honrar. **~able** *a* honrado, honroso

hood /hʊd/ *n* capuz *m*; (*car roof*) capota *f*, (*P*) tejadilho *m*; *Amer* (*bonnet*) capô *m*, (*P*) capot *m*

hoodie /'hʊdi/ *n* moletom *m* com capuz, (*P*) sweatshirt *f* com capuz

hoodwink /'hʊdwɪŋk/ *vt* enganar

hoof /huːf/ *n* (*pl* **-fs**) casco *m*

hook /hʊk/ *n* gancho *m*; (*on garment*) colchete *m*; (*for fishing*) anzol *m* ● *vt* enganchar; ‹*fish*› apanhar, pescar; **off the ~** livre de dificuldades; ‹*phone*› desligado

hooked /hʊkt/ *a* **be ~ on** [x] ter o vício de, estar viciado em

hookey /'hʊkɪ/ *n* **play ~** *Amer* [x] fazer gazeta

hooligan /'huːlɪgən/ *n* desordeiro *m*

hoop /huːp/ *n* arco *m*; (*of cask*) cinta *f*

hooray /huː'reɪ/ *int* & *n* = HURRAH

hoot /huːt/ *n* (*of owl*) pio *m* de mocho; (*of horn*) buzinada *f*; (*jeer*) apupo *m* ● *vi* (*of owl*) piar; (*of horn*) buzinar; (*jeer*) apupar. **~er** *n* buzina *f*; (*of factory*) sirene *f*

Hoover® /'huːvə(r)/ *n* aspirador de pó *m*, (*P*) aspirador *m* ● *vt* passar o aspirador

hop[1] /hɒp/ *vi* (*pt* **hopped**) saltar num pé só, (*P*) ao pé coxinho; **~ in** [!] subir, saltar [!]; **~ it** [x] pôr-se a andar [!]; **~ out** [!] descer, saltar [!] ● *n* salto *m*

hop[2] /hɒp/ *n* (*plant*) lúpulo *m*; **~s** espigas *fpl* de lúpulo

hope /həʊp/ *n* esperança *f* ● *vt/i* esperar; **~ for** esperar (ter). **~ful** *a* esperançoso; (*promising*) promissor; **be ~ful (that)** ter esperança (que), confiar (em que). **~fully** *adv* esperançosamente; (*it is hoped that*) é de esperar que. **~less** *a* desesperado, sem esperança; (*incompetent*) incapaz

horde /hɔːd/ *n* horda *f*

horizon /hə'raɪzn/ *n* horizonte *m*

horizontal /hɒrɪ'zɒntl/ *a* horizontal

hormone /'hɔːməʊn/ *n* hormônio *m*, (*P*) hormona *f*

horn /hɔːn/ *n* chifre *m*, corno *m*; (*of car*) buzina *f*; *Mus* trompa *f*. **~y** *a* caloso, calejado

hornet /'hɔːnɪt/ *n* vespão *m*

horoscope /'hɒrəskəʊp/ *n* horóscopo *m*

horrible /'hɒrəbl/ *a* horrível, horroroso

horrid /'hɒrɪd/ *a* horrível, horripilante

horrific /hə'rɪfɪk/ *a* horrífico

horr|or /'hɒrə(r)/ *n* horror *m* ● *a* (*film etc*) de terror. **~ify** *vt* horrorizar, horripilar

horse /hɔːs/ *n* cavalo *m*. **~ chestnut** *n* castanha-da-Índia *f*; **~ racing** *n* corrida *f* de cavalos, hipismo *m*; **~radish** *n* rábano *m*

horseback /'hɔːsbæk/ *n* **on ~** a cavalo

horseplay /'hɔːspleɪ/ *n* brincadeira *f* grosseira, abrutalhada *f*

horsepower /'hɔːspaʊə(r)/ *n* cavalo-vapor *m*

horseshoe /'hɔːsʃuː/ *n* ferradura *f*

horticultur|e /'hɔːtɪkʌltʃə(r)/ *n* horticultura *f*

hose /həʊz/ *n* **~(-pipe)** mangueira *f* ● *vt* regar com a mangueira

hospice /'hɒspɪs/ *n* hospício *m*; (*for travellers*) hospedaria *f*

hospit|able /hə'spɪtəbl/ *a* hospitaleiro. **~ality** /-'tælətɪ/ *n* hospitalidade *f*

hospital /'hɒspɪtl/ *n* hospital *m*

host[1] /həʊst/ *n* anfitrião *m*, dono *m* da casa. **~ess** *n* anfitriã *f*, dona *f* da casa

host[2] /həʊst/ *n* **a ~ of** uma multidão de, um grande número de

host[3] /həʊst/ *n Relig* hóstia *f*

hostage /'hɒstɪdʒ/ *n* refém *m*

hostel /'hɒstl/ *n* residência *f* de estudantes *etc*, pousada *f*

hostil|e /'hɒstaɪl/ *a* hostil. **~ity** /hɒ'stɪlətɪ/ *n* hostilidade *f*

hot /hɒt/ *a* (**hotter**, **hottest**) quente; *Culin* picante; **be** or **feel ~** estar com or ter calor; **it is ~** está or faz calor; **~ dog** cachorro-quente *m*; **~ line** linha direta *f* esp entre chefes de estado; **~-water bottle** saco *m* de água quente ● *vt/i* (*pt* **hotted**) **~ up** [I] aquecer

hotbed /'hɒtbed/ *n fig* foco *m*

hotel /həʊ'tel/ *n* hotel *m*

hound /haʊnd/ *n* cão *m* de caça e de corrida, sabujo *m* ● *vt* acossar, perseguir

hour /'aʊə(r)/ *n* hora *f*. **~ly** *adv* de hora em hora ● *a* de hora em hora; **~ly pay** retribuição *f* horária; **paid ~ly** pago por hora

house[1] /haʊs/ *n* (*pl* **~s** /'haʊzɪz/) casa *f*; *Pol* câmara *f*; **on the ~** por conta da casa. **~-warming** *n* inauguração *f* da casa

house[2] /haʊz/ *vt* alojar; (*store*) arrecadar, guardar

houseboat /'haʊsbəʊt/ *n* casa *f* flutuante

household /'haʊshəʊld/ *n* família *f*, agregado *m* familiar. **~er** *n* ocupante *mf*; (*owner*) proprietário *m*

housekeep|er /'haʊskiːpə(r)/ *n* governanta *f*. **~ing** *n* (*work*) tarefas *fpl* domésticas

housewife /'haʊswaɪf/ *n* (*pl* **-wives**) dona *f* de casa

housework /'haʊswɜːk/ *n* tarefas *fpl* domésticas

housing /'haʊzɪŋ/ *n* alojamento *m*; **~ estate** zona *f* residencial

hovel /'hɒvl/ *n* casebre *m*, tugúrio *m*

hover /'hɒvə(r)/ *vi* pairar; (*linger*) deixar-se ficar, demorar-se

hovercraft /'hɒvəkrɑːft/ *n* (*invar*) aerobarco *m*, hovercraft *m*

how /haʊ/ *adv* como; **~ long/old is...?** que comprimento/idade tem...?; **~ far?** a que distância?; **~ many?** quantos?; **~ much?** quanto?; **~ often?** com que frequência; **~ pretty it is** como é lindo; **~ about a walk?** e se fôssemos dar uma volta?; **~ are you?** como vai?; **~ do you do?** muito prazer!; **and ~!** oh se é!

however /haʊ'evə(r)/ *adv* de qualquer maneira; (*though*) contudo, no entanto, todavia; **~ small it may be** por menor que seja

howl /haʊl/ *n* uivo *m* ● *vi* uivar

hub /hʌb/ *n* cubo *m* da roda; *fig* centro *m*. **~cap** *n* calota *f*, (*P*) tampão *m* da roda

hubbub /'hʌbʌb/ *n* chinfrim *m*

huddle /'hʌdl/ *vt/i* apinhar(-se); **~ together** aconchegar-se

huff /hʌf/ *n* **in a ~** com raiva, zangado

hug /hʌg/ *vt* (*pt* **hugged**) abraçar, apertar nos braços; (*keep close to*) chegar-se a ● *n* abraço *m*

huge /hjuːdʒ/ *a* enorme

hull /hʌl/ *n* (*of ship*) casco *m*

hullo /hə'ləʊ/ *int & n* = HALLO

hum /hʌm/ *vt/i* (*pt* **hummed**) cantar com a boca fechada; (*of insect, engine*) zumbir ● *n* zumbido *m*

human /'hjuːmən/ *a* humano ● *n* **~ (being)** ser *m* humano

humane /hjuː'meɪn/ *a* humano, compassivo

humanitarian /hjuːmænɪ'teərɪən/ *a* humanitário

humanity /hjuː'mænətɪ/ *n* humanidade *f*

humbl|e /'hʌmbl/ *a* (**-er**, **-est**) humilde ● *vt* humilhar

humdrum /'hʌmdrʌm/ *a* monótono, rotineiro

humid /'hjuːmɪd/ *a* úmido, (*P*) húmido. **~ity** /-'mɪdətɪ/ *n* umidade *f*, (*P*) humidade *f*

humiliat|e /hjuː'mɪlɪeɪt/ *vt* humilhar. **~ion** /-'eɪʃn/ *n* humilhação *f*

humility /hjuːˈmɪlətɪ/ *n* humildade *f*

hum|our /ˈhjuːmə(r)/ *n* humor *m* ● *vt* fazer a vontade de. **~orous** *a* humorístico; ‹*person*› divertido, espirituoso

hump /hʌmp/ *n* corcova *f*; (*of the back*) corcunda *f* ● *vt* corcovar, arquear; **the ~** ☒ a neura [!]

hunch[1] /hʌntʃ/ *vt* curvar; **~ed up** curvado

hunch[2] /hʌntʃ/ *n* [!] palpite *m*

hunchback /ˈhʌntʃbæk/ *n* corcunda *mf*

hundred /ˈhʌndrəd/ *a* cem ● *n* centena *f*, cento *m*; **~s of** centenas de. **~th** *a & n* centésimo *m*

hundredweight /ˈhʌndrədweɪt/ *n* quintal *m* (= 50,8 kg, *Amer* = 45,36 kg)

hung /hʌŋ/ ▶ HANG

Hungar|y /ˈhʌŋgərɪ/ *n* Hungria *f*. **~ian** /-ˈgeərɪən/ *a & n* húngaro *m*

hunger /ˈhʌŋgə(r)/ *n* fome *f* ● *vi* **~ for** ter fome de; *fig* desejar vivamente, ansiar por

hungr|y /ˈhʌŋgrɪ/ *a* (**ier**, **-iest**) esfomeado, faminto; **be ~y** ter fome, estar com fome

hunk /hʌŋk/ *n* grande naco *m*

hunt /hʌnt/ *vt/i* caçar ● *n* caça *f*; **~ for** andar à caça de, andar à procura de. **~er** *n* caçador *m*. **~ing** *n* caça *f*, caçada *f*

hurdle /ˈhɜːdl/ *n* obstáculo *m*

hurl /hɜːl/ *vt* arremessar, lançar com força

hurrah, **hurray** /hʊˈrɑː, hʊˈreɪ/ *int & n* hurra *m*, viva *m*

hurricane /ˈhʌrɪkən/ *n* furacão *m*

hurried /ˈhʌrɪd/ *a* apressado. **~ly** *adv* apressadamente, às pressas

hurry /ˈhʌrɪ/ *vt/i* apressar(-se), despachar(-se) ● *n* pressa *f*; **be in a ~** estar com or ter pressa; **do sth in a ~** fazer algo à pressa; **~ up!** ande logo, (*P*) despache-se

hurt /hɜːt/ *vt* (*pt* **hurt**) fazer mal a; (*injure, offend*) magoar, ferir ● *vi* doer ● *a* magoado, ferido ● *n* mal *m*; ‹*feelings*› mágoa *f*. **~ful** *a* prejudicial; ‹*remark etc*› que magoa

hurtle /ˈhɜːtl/ *vi* despenhar-se; (*move rapidly*) precipitar-se ● *vt* arremessar

husband /ˈhʌzbənd/ *n* marido *m*, esposo *m*

hush /hʌʃ/ *vt* (fazer) calar; **~ up** abafar, encobrir ● *vi* calar-se; **~!** silêncio! ● *n* silêncio *m*. **~-hush** *a* [!] muito em segredo

husky /ˈhʌskɪ/ *a* (**-ier**, **-iest**) (*hoarse*) rouco, enrouquecido; (*burly*) corpulento ● *n* cão *m* esquimó

hustle /ˈhʌsl/ *vt* empurrar, dar encontrões a ● *n* empurrão *m*; **~ and bustle** grande movimento *m*, azáfama *f*

hut /hʌt/ *n* cabana *f*, barraca *f* de madeira

hutch /hʌtʃ/ *n* coelheira *f*

hybrid /ˈhaɪbrɪd/ *a & n* híbrido *m*. **~ car** *n* carro *m* híbrido

hydraulic /haɪˈdrɔːlɪk/ *a* hidráulico

hydroelectric /haɪdrəʊɪˈlektrɪk/ *a* hidrelétrico, (*P*) hidroelétrico

hydrogen /ˈhaɪdrədʒən/ *n* hidrogênio *m*, (*P*) hidrogénio *m*

hygiene /ˈhaɪdʒiːn/ *n* higiene *f*

hygienic /haɪˈdʒiːnɪk/ *a* higiênico, (*P*) higiénico

hymn /hɪm/ *n* hino *m*, cântico *m*

hyper- /ˈhaɪpə(r)/ *pref* hiper-

hypermarket /ˈhaɪpəmɑːkɪt/ *n* hipermercado *m*

hyphen /ˈhaɪfn/ *n* hífen *m*, traço de união *m*. **~ate** *vt* hifenizar

hypno|sis /hɪpˈnəʊsɪs/ *n* hipnose *f*. **~tic** /-ˈnɒtɪk/ *a* hipnótico

hypnot|ize /ˈhɪpnətaɪz/ *vt* hipnotizar. **~ism** /-ɪzəm/ *n* hipnotismo *m*

hypochondriac /haɪpəˈkɒndrɪæk/ *n* hipocondríaco *m*

hypocrisy /hɪˈpɒkrəsɪ/ *n* hipocrisia *f*

hypocrit|e /ˈhɪpəkrɪt/ *n* hipócrita *mf*. **~ical** /-ˈkrɪtɪkl/ *a* hipócrita

hypodermic /haɪpəˈdɜːmɪk/ *a* hipodérmico ● *n* seringa *f*

hypothe|sis /haɪˈpɒθəsɪs/ *n* (*pl* **-theses** /-siːz/) hipótese *f*. **~tical** /-əˈθetɪkl/ *a* hipotético

hyster|ia /hɪˈstɪərɪə/ *n* histeria *f*. **~ical** /hɪˈsterɪkl/ *a* histérico

Ii

I /aɪ/ *pron* eu

Iberian /aɪˈbiːrɪən/ *a* ibérico ● *n* ibero *m*

ice /aɪs/ *n* gelo *m*; **~ hockey** hóquei *m* sobre o gelo; **~ lolly** picolé *m* ● *vt/i* gelar; ‹*cake*› cobrir com glacê *or* (*P*) glace ● *vi* **~ up** gelar. **~box** *n Amer* geladeira *f*, (*P*) frigorífico *m*; **~ (cream)** *n* sorvete *m*, (*P*) gelado *m*; **~ cube** *n* cubo *m* or pedra *f* de gelo; ~ **pack** *n* saco *m* de gelo; ~ **rink** *n* rinque *m* de patinação, (*P*) patinagem *f* no gelo; ~ **skating** *n* patinação *f*, (*P*) patinagem *f* no gelo

iceberg /'aɪsbɜ:g/ *n* iceberg *m*; *fig* pedaço *m* de gelo

Iceland /'aɪslənd/ *n* Islândia *f*

icicle /'aɪsɪkl/ *n* pingente *m* de gelo

icing /'aɪsɪŋ/ *n Culin* cobertura *f* de açúcar, glacê *m*, (*P*) glace *m*

icy /'aɪsɪ/ *a* (**-ier**, **-iest**) gelado, gélido, glacial; ‹*road*› com gelo

idea /aɪ'dɪə/ *n* ideia *f*

ideal /aɪ'dɪəl/ *a & n* ideal *m*. **~ize** *vt* idealizar. **~ly** *adv* idealmente

idealis|t /aɪ'dɪəlɪst/ *n* idealista *mf*. **~m** /-zəm/ *n* idealismo *m*. **~tic** /-'lɪstɪk/ *a* idealista

identical /aɪ'dentɪkl/ *a* idêntico

identif|y /aɪ'dentɪfaɪ/ *vt* identificar ● *vi* **~y with** identificar-se com. **~ication** /-ɪ'keɪʃn/ *n* identificação *f*

identity /aɪ'dentətɪ/ *n* identidade *f*; ~ **card** carteira *f* de identidade, (*P*) bilhete *m* de identidade

ideolog|y /aɪdɪ'ɒlədʒɪ/ *n* ideologia *f*. **~ical** *a* /-ɪə'lɒdʒɪkl/ ideológico

idiom /'ɪdɪəm/ *n* idioma *m*; (*phrase*) expressão *f* idiomática. **~atic** /-'mætɪk/ *a* idiomático

idiosyncrasy /ɪdɪə'sɪŋkrəsɪ/ *n* idiossincrasia *f*, peculiaridade *f*

idiot /'ɪdɪət/ *n* idiota *mf*. **~ic** /-'ɒtɪk/ *a* idiota

idl|e /'aɪdl/ *a* (**-er**, **-est**) (*not active; lazy*) ocioso; (*unemployed*) sem trabalho; (*of machines*) parado; *fig* (*useless*) inútil ● *vt/i* (*of engine*) estar em ponto morto. **~eness** *n* ociosidade *f*

idol /'aɪdl/ *n* ídolo *m*. **~ize** *vt* idolatrar

idyllic /ɪ'dɪlɪk/ *a* idílico

i.e. *abbr* isto é, quer dizer

if /ɪf/ *conj* se

igloo /'ɪglu:/ *n* iglu *m*

ignite /ɪg'naɪt/ *vt/i* inflamar(-se), acender; (*catch fire*) pegar fogo; (*set fire to*) atear fogo a

ignition /ɪg'nɪʃn/ *n Auto* ignição *f*; ~ **(key)** chave *f* de ignição

ignoran|t /'ɪgnərənt/ *a* ignorante; **be ~t of** ignorar. **~ce** *n* ignorância *f*

ignore /ɪg'nɔ:(r)/ *vt* não fazer caso de, passar por cima de; ‹*person in the street etc*› fingir não ver

ill /ɪl/ *a* (*sick*) doente; ~ **at ease** pouco à vontade; ~ **will** má vontade *f*, animosidade *f* ● *adv* mal ● *n* mal *m*. **~-advised** *a* pouco aconselhável; **~-bred** *a* mal-educado; **~-fated** *a* malfadado; **~-treat** *vt* maltratar

illegal /ɪ'li:gl/ *a* ilegal

illegible /ɪ'ledʒəbl/ *a* ilegível

illegitima|te /ɪlɪ'dʒɪtɪmət/ *a* ilegítimo. **~cy** *n* ilegitimidade *f*

illitera|te /ɪ'lɪtərət/ *a* analfabeto; (*uneducated*) iletrado. **~cy** *n* analfabetismo *m*

illness /'ɪlnɪs/ *n* doença *f*

illogical /ɪ'lɒdʒɪkl/ *a* ilógico

illuminat|e /ɪ'lu:mɪneɪt/ *vt* iluminar; (*explain*) esclarecer. **~ion** /-'neɪʃn/ *n* iluminação *f*. **~ions** *npl* luminárias *fpl*

illusion /ɪ'lu:ʒn/ *n* ilusão *f*

illusory /ɪ'lu:sərɪ/ *a* ilusório

illustrat|e /'ɪləstreɪt/ *vt* ilustrar. **~ion** /-'streɪʃn/ *n* ilustração *f*

illustrious /ɪ'lʌstrɪəs/ *a* ilustre

image /'ɪmɪdʒ/ *n* imagem *f*; **(public)** ~ imagem *f* pública

imaginary /ɪ'mædʒɪnərɪ/ *a* imaginário

imaginat|ion /ɪmædʒɪ'neɪʃn/ *n* imaginação *f*. **~ive** /ɪ'mædʒɪnətɪv/ *a* imaginativo

imagin|e /ɪ'mædʒɪn/ *vt* imaginar. **~able** *a* imaginável

imbalance /ɪm'bæləns/ *n* desequilíbrio *m*

imbecile /'ɪmbəsi:l/ *a & n* imbecil *mf*

imitat|e /'ɪmɪteɪt/ *vt* imitar. **~ion** /-'teɪʃn/ *n* imitação *f*

immaculate /ɪ'mækjʊlət/ *a* imaculado; (*impeccable*) impecável

immaterial /ɪmə'tɪərɪəl/ *a* (*of no importance*) irrelevante; **that's ~ to me** para mim tanto faz

immature /ɪmə'tjʊə(r)/ *a* imaturo

immediate /ɪ'mi:dɪət/ *a* imediato. **~ly** *adv* imediatamente ● *conj* logo que, assim que

immens|e /ɪ'mens/ *a* imenso

immers|e /ɪ'mɜ:s/ *vt* mergulhar, imergir; **be ~ed in** *fig* estar imerso em. **~ion** /-ʃn/ *n* imersão *f*; **~ion heater** aquecedor *m* de água elétrico

immigr|ate /'ɪmɪgreɪt/ *vi* imigrar. **~ant** *n & a* imigrante *mf*, imigrado *m*. **~ation** /-'greɪʃn/ *n* imigração *f*

imminen|t /'ɪmɪnənt/ *a* iminente

immobil|e /ɪ'məʊbaɪl/ *a* imóvel. **~ize** /-əlaɪz/ *vt* imobilizar

immoral /ɪ'mɒrəl/ *a* imoral. **~ity** /ɪmə'rælətɪ/ *n* imoralidade *f*

immortal /ɪ'mɔːtl/ *a* imortal. **~ity** /-'tælətɪ/ *n* imortalidade *f*. **~ize** *vt* imortalizar

immun|e /ɪ'mjuːn/ *a* imune; imunizado (**from** contra). **~ity** *n* imunidade *f*

imp /ɪmp/ *n* diabrete *m*

impact /'ɪmpækt/ *n* impacto *m*

impair /ɪm'peə(r)/ *vt* deteriorar; (*damage*) prejudicar

impart /ɪm'pɑːt/ *vt* comunicar; transmitir (**to** a)

impartial /ɪm'pɑːʃl/ *a* imparcial. **~ity** /-ʃɪ'ælətɪ/ *n* imparcialidade *f*

i

impassable /ɪm'pɑːsəbl/ *a* ‹*road, river*› impraticável, intransitável; ‹*barrier etc*› intransponível

impatien|t /ɪm'peɪʃənt/ *a* impaciente. **~ce** *n* impaciência *f*

impeccable /ɪm'pekəbl/ *a* impecável

impede /ɪm'piːd/ *vt* impedir, estorvar

impediment /ɪm'pedɪmənt/ *n* impedimento *m*, obstáculo *m*; **(speech) ~** defeito (na fala) *m*

impel /ɪm'pel/ *vt* (*pt* **impelled**) impelir; forçar (**to do** a fazer)

impending /ɪm'pendɪŋ/ *a* iminente

impenetrable /ɪm'penɪtrəbl/ *a* impenetrável

imperative /ɪm'perətɪv/ *a* imperativo; ‹*need etc*› imperioso ● *n* imperativo *m*

imperceptible /ɪmpə'septəbl/ *a* imperceptível, (*P*) imperceptível

imperfect /ɪm'pɜːfɪkt/ *a* imperfeito. **~ion** /-ə'fekʃn/ *n* imperfeição *f*

imperial /ɪm'pɪərɪəl/ *a* imperial; (*of measures*) legal *na GB*. **~ism** /-lɪzəm/ *n* imperialismo *m*

impersonal /ɪm'pɜːsənl/ *a* impessoal

impersonat|e /ɪm'pɜːsəneɪt/ *vt* fazer-se passar por; *Theat* fazer or representar (o papel) de. **~ion** /-'neɪʃn/ *n* imitação *f*

impetuous /ɪm'petʃʊəs/ *a* impetuoso

impetus /'ɪmpɪtəs/ *n* ímpeto *m*

impinge /ɪm'pɪndʒ/ *vi* **~ on** afetar; (*encroach*) infringir

implacable /ɪm'plækəbl/ *a* implacável

implant /ɪm'plɑːnt/ *vt* implantar

implement[1] /'ɪmplɪmənt/ *n* instrumento *m*, utensílio *m*

implement[2] /'ɪmplɪment/ *vt* implementar, executar

implicit /ɪm'plɪsɪt/ *a* implícito; (*unquestioning*) absoluto, incondicional

implore /ɪm'plɔː(r)/ *vt* implorar, suplicar, rogar

imply /ɪm'plaɪ/ *vt* implicar; (*hint*) sugerir, dar a entender, insinuar

impolite /ɪmpə'laɪt/ *a* indelicado, incorreto

import[1] /ɪm'pɔːt/ *vt* importar. **~er** *n* importador *m*

import[2] /'ɪmpɔːt/ *n* importação *f*; (*meaning*) significado *m*; (*importance*) importância *f*

importan|t /ɪm'pɔːtnt/ *a* importante. **~ce** *n* importância *f*

impos|e /ɪm'pəʊz/ *vt* impôr; (*inflict*) infligir ● *vi* **~e on** abusar de. **~ition** /-ə'zɪʃn/ *n* imposição *f*; (*unfair burden*) abuso *m*

imposing /ɪm'pəʊzɪŋ/ *a* imponente

impossib|le /ɪm'pɒsəbl/ *a* impossível. **~ility** /-'bɪlətɪ/ *n* impossibilidade *f*

impostor /ɪm'pɒstə(r)/ *n* impostor *m*

impoten|t /'ɪmpətənt/ *a* impotente. **~ce** *n* impotência *f*

impoverish /ɪm'pɒvərɪʃ/ *vt* empobrecer

impracticable /ɪm'præktɪkəbl/ *a* impraticável

impractical /ɪm'præktɪkl/ *a* pouco prático

imprecise /ɪmprɪ'saɪs/ *a* impreciso

impregnate /'ɪmpregneɪt/ *vt* impregnar (**with** de)

impresario /ɪmprɪ'sɑːrɪəʊ/ *n* (*pl* **-os**) empresário *m*

impress /ɪm'pres/ *vt* impressionar, causar impressão a; (*imprint*) imprimir; **~ sth on sb** inculcar algo em alguém

impression /ɪm'preʃn/ *n* impressão *f*. **~able** *a* impressionável. **~ist** *n* impressionista *mf*

impressive /ɪm'presɪv/ *a* impressionante, imponente

imprint[1] /'ɪmprɪnt/ *n* impressão *f*, marca *f*

imprint[2] /ɪm'prɪnt/ *vt* imprimir

imprison /ɪm'prɪzn/ *vt* prender, aprisionar. **~ment** *n* aprisionamento *m*, prisão *f*

improbab|le /ɪm'prɒbəbl/ *a* improvável

impromptu /ɪm'prɒmptju:/ *a & adv* de improviso ● *n* impromptu *m*

improper /ɪm'prɒpə(r)/ *a* impróprio; (*indecent*) indecente, pouco decente; (*wrong*) incorreto

improve /ɪm'pru:v/ *vt/i* melhorar; **~ on** aperfeiçoar. **~ment** *n* melhoria *f*; (*in house etc*) melhoramento *m*; (*in health*) melhoras *fpl*

improvis|e /'ɪmprəvaɪz/ *vt/i* improvisar. **~ation** /-'zeɪʃn/ *n* improvisação *f*

imprudent /ɪm'pru:dnt/ *a* imprudente

impuden|t /'ɪmpjʊdənt/ *a* descarado, insolente. **~ce** *n* descaramento *m*, insolência *f*

impulse /'ɪmpʌls/ *n* impulso *m*

impulsive /ɪm'pʌlsɪv/ *a* impulsivo

impur|e /ɪm'pjʊə(r)/ *a* impuro. **~ity** *n* impureza *f*

in /ɪn/ *prep* em, dentro de; **~ Lisbon/English** em Lisboa/inglês; **~ winter** no inverno; **~ an hour** (*at end of, within*) numa hora; **~ the rain** na/à chuva; **~ doing** ao fazer; **~ the evening** à tardinha; **the best ~** o melhor em ● *adv* dentro; (*at home*) em casa; (*in fashion*) na moda; **we are ~ for** vamos ter ● *n* **the ~s and outs** meandros *mpl*. **~-laws** *npl* [!] sogros *mpl*; **~patient** *n* doente *m* internado

inability /ɪnə'bɪlətɪ/ *n* incapacidade *f* (**to do** para fazer)

inaccessible /ɪnæk'sesəbl/ *a* inacessível

inaccura|te /ɪn'ækjərət/ *a* inexato. **~cy** *n* inexatidão *f*, falta *f* de rigor

inaction /ɪn'ækʃn/ *n* inação *f*

inactiv|e /ɪn'æktɪv/ *a* inativo. **~ity** /-'tɪvətɪ/ *n* inação *f*

inadequa|te /ɪn'ædɪkwət/ *a* inadequado, impróprio; (*insufficient*) insuficiente. **~cy** *n* inadequação *f*; (*insufficiency*) insuficiência *f*

inadvertently /ɪnəd'vɜ:təntlɪ/ *adv* inadvertidamente; (*unintentionally*) sem querer, sem ser por mal

inadvisable /ɪnəd'vaɪzəbl/ *a* desaconselhável, não aconselhável

inane /ɪ'neɪn/ *a* tolo, oco

inanimate /ɪn'ænɪmət/ *a* inanimado

inappropriate /ɪnə'prəʊprɪət/ *a* impróprio, inadequado

inarticulate /ɪnɑ:'tɪkjʊlət/ *a* inarticulado; (*of person*) incapaz de se exprimir claramente

inattentive /ɪnə'tentɪv/ *a* desatento

inaugural /ɪ'nɔ:gjʊrəl/ *a* inaugural

inaugurat|e /ɪ'nɔ:gjʊreɪt/ *vt* inaugurar. **~ion** /-'reɪʃn/ *n* inauguração *f*

inauspicious /ɪnɔ:'spɪʃəs/ *a* pouco auspicioso

inborn /ɪn'bɔ:n/ *a* inato

inbox /'ɪnbɒks/ *n* caixa *f* de entrada

inbred /ɪn'bred/ *a* inato, congênito, (*P*) congénito

incalculable /ɪn'kælkjʊləbl/ *a* incalculável

incapable /ɪn'keɪpəbl/ *a* incapaz

incendiary /ɪn'sendɪərɪ/ *a* incendiário ● *n* bomba *f* incendiária

incense[1] /'ɪnsens/ *n* incenso *m*

incense[2] /ɪn'sens/ *vt* exasperar, enfurecer

incentive /ɪn'sentɪv/ *n* incentivo, estímulo

incessant /ɪn'sesənt/ *a* incessante. **~ly** *adv* incessantemente, sem cessar

incest /'ɪnsest/ *n* incesto *m*. **~uous** /ɪn'sestjʊəs/ *a* incestuoso

inch /ɪntʃ/ *n* polegada *f* (= 2,54 cm) ● *vt/i* avançar palmo a palmo or pouco a pouco; **within an ~ of** a um passo de

incidence /'ɪnsɪdəns/ *n* incidência *f*; (*rate*) percentagem *f*

incident /'ɪnsɪdənt/ *n* incidente *m*

incidental /ɪnsɪ'dentl/ *a* incidental, acessório; (*casual*) acidental; ‹*expenses*› eventuais; ‹*music*› de cena, incidental. **~ly** *adv* incidentalmente; (*by the way*) a propósito

incinerat|e /ɪn'sɪnəreɪt/ *vt* incinerar. **~or** *n* incinerador *m*

incision /ɪn'sɪʒn/ *n* incisão *f*

incisive /ɪn'saɪsɪv/ *a* incisivo

incite /ɪn'saɪt/ *vt* incitar, instigar. **~ment** *n* incitamento *m*

inclination /ɪnklɪ'neɪʃn/ *n* inclinação *f*, tendência *f*

incline[1] /ɪn'klaɪn/ *vt/i* inclinar(-se); **be ~d to** inclinar-se para; (*have tendency*) ter tendência para

incline[2] /'ɪnklaɪn/ *n* inclinação *f*, declive *m*

inclu|de /ɪn'klu:d/ *vt* incluir; (*in letter*) enviar junto or em anexo. **~ding** *prep* inclusive. **~sion** *n* inclusão *f*

inclusive /ɪn'klu:sɪv/ *a & adv* inclusive; **be ~ of** incluir

i

incognito /ɪnkɒg'ni:təʊ/ *a & adv* incógnito

incoherent /ɪnkə'hɪərənt/ *a* incoerente

income /'ɪŋkʌm/ *n* rendimento *m*; **~ tax** imposto sobre a renda, (*P*) imposto sobre o rendimento

incoming /'ɪnkʌmɪŋ/ *a* ‹*tide*› enchente; ‹*tenant etc*› novo

incomparable /ɪn'kɒmpərəbl/ *a* incomparável

incompatible /ɪnkəm'pætəbl/ *a* incompatível

incompeten|t /ɪn'kɒmpɪtənt/ *a* incompetente. **~ce** *n* incompetência *f*

incomplete /ɪnkəm'pli:t/ *a* incompleto

incomprehensible /ɪnkɒmprɪ-'hensəbl/ *a* incompreensível

inconceivable /ɪnkən'si:vəbl/ *a* inconcebível

inconclusive /ɪnkən'klu:sɪv/ *a* inconcludente

incongruous /ɪn'kɒŋgrʊəs/ *a* incongruente; (*absurd*) absurdo

inconsiderate /ɪnkən'sɪdərət/ *a* impensado, inconsiderado; (*lacking in regard*) pouco atencioso, sem consideração (pelos sentimentos *etc* de outrem)

inconsisten|t /ɪnkən'sɪstənt/ *a* incoerente; (*at variance*) contraditório; **~t with** incompatível com. **~cy** *n* incoerência *f*

inconspicuous /ɪnkən'spɪkjʊəs/ *a* que não dá nas vistas, que não chama a atenção

incontinen|t /ɪn'kɒntɪnənt/ *a* incontinente. **~ce** *n* incontinência *f*

inconvenien|t /ɪnkən'vi:nɪənt/ *a* inconveniente, incômodo, (*P*) incómodo. **~ce** *n* inconveniência *f*; (*drawback*) inconveniente *m* ● *vt* incomodar

incorporate /ɪn'kɔ:pəreɪt/ *vt* incorporar; (*include*) incluir

incorrect /ɪnkə'rekt/ *a* incorreto

incorrigible /ɪn'kɒrɪdʒəbl/ *a* incorrigível

increas|e[1] /ɪn'kri:s/ *vt/i* aumentar. **~ing** *a* crescente. **~ingly** *adv* cada vez mais

increase[2] /'ɪnkri:s/ *n* aumento *m*; **on the ~** aumentando, crescendo, (*P*) em crescimento, em alta

incredible /ɪn'kredəbl/ *a* incrível

incredulous /ɪn'kredjʊləs/ *a* incrédulo

incriminat|e /ɪn'krɪmɪneɪt/ *vt* incriminar

incubat|e /'ɪnkjʊbeɪt/ *vt* incubar. **~ion** /-'beɪʃn/ *n* incubação *f*. **~or** *n* incubadora *f*

incur /ɪn'kɜ:r/ *vt* (*pt* **incurred**) ‹*displeasure, expense etc*› incorrer em; ‹*debts*› contrair

incurable /ɪn'kjʊərəbl/ *a* incurável, que não tem cura

indebted /ɪn'detɪd/ *a* **~ to sb** em dívida (para) com alguém (**for** por)

indecen|t /ɪn'di:snt/ *a* indecente. **~t assault** *n* atentado *m* contra o pudor. **~cy** *n* indecência *f*

indecision /ɪndɪ'sɪʒn/ *n* indecisão *f*

indecisive /ɪndɪ'saɪsɪv/ *a* inconcludente, não decisivo; (*hesitating*) indeciso

indeed /ɪn'di:d/ *adv* realmente, deveras, mesmo; (*in fact*) de fato, (*P*) facto; **very much ~** muitíssimo

indefinite /ɪn'defɪnət/ *a* indefinido; (*time*) indeterminado. **~ly** *adv* indefinidamente

indent /ɪn'dent/ *vt* ‹*notch*› recortar; *Typ* entrar. **~ation** /-'teɪʃn/ *n* recorte *m*; *Typ* entrada *f*

independen|t /ɪndɪ'pendənt/ *a* independente. **~ce** *n* independência *f*

indescribable /ɪndɪ'skraɪbəbl/ *a* indescritível

indestructible /ɪndɪ'strʌktəbl/ *a* indestrutível

indeterminate /ɪndɪ'tɜ:mɪnət/ *a* indeterminado

index /'ɪndeks/ *n* (*pl* **indexes**) (*in book*) índice *m*; (*in library*) catálogo *m* ● *vt* indexar; **~ card** ficha (de fichário), (*P*) ficheiro *f*; **~ finger** index *m*, (dedo) indicador *m*. **~-linked** *a* ligado ao índice de inflação

India /'ɪndɪə/ *n* Índia *f*. **~n** *a & n* (*of India*) indiano (*m*); (*American*) índio (*m*)

indicat|e /'ɪndɪkeɪt/ *vt* indicar. **~ion** /-'keɪʃn/ *n* indicação *f*. **~or** *n* indicador *m*; *Auto* pisca-pisca *m*; (*board*) quadro *m*

indicative /ɪn'dɪkətɪv/ *a & n* indicativo *m*

indict /ɪn'daɪt/ *vt* acusar. **~ment** *n* acusação *f*

indifferen|t /ɪn'dɪfrənt/ *a* indiferente; (*not good*) medíocre. **~ce** *n* indiferença *f*

indigenous /ɪn'dɪdʒɪnəs/ *a* indígena; natural; nativo (**to** de)

i

indigest|ion /ɪndɪ'dʒestʃən/ *n* indigestão *f*. **~ible** /-təbl/ *a* indigesto

indign|ant /ɪn'dɪgnənt/ *a* indignado. **~ation** /-'neɪʃn/ *n* indignação *f*

indirect /ɪndɪ'rekt/ *a* indireto. **~ly** *adv* indiretamente

indiscr|eet /ɪndɪ'skri:t/ *a* indiscreto; (*not wary*) imprudente. **~etion** /-'eʃn/ *n* indiscrição *f*; (*action, remark etc*) deslize *m*

indiscriminate /ɪndɪ'skrɪmɪnət/ *a* que tem falta de discernimento; (*random*) indiscriminado. **~ly** *adv* sem discernimento; (*at random*) indiscriminadamente, ao acaso

indispensable /ɪndɪ'spensəbl/ *a* indispensável

indispos|ed /ɪndɪ'spəʊzd/ *a* indisposto

indisputable /ɪndɪ'spju:təbl/ *a* indisputável, incontestável

indistinct /ɪndɪ'stɪŋkt/ *a* indistinto

indistinguishable /ɪndɪ'stɪŋgwɪʃ-əbl/ *a* indistinguível, imperceptível; (*identical*) indiferenciável

individual /ɪndɪ'vɪdʒʊəl/ *a* individual ● *n* indivíduo *m*. **~ity** /-'æləti/ *n* individualidade *f*. **~ly** *adv* individualmente

indivisible /ɪndɪ'vɪzəbl/ *a* indivisível

indoctrinat|e /ɪn'dɒktrɪneɪt/ *vt* (en) doutrinar

indolen|t /'ɪndələnt/ *a* indolente. **~ce** *n* indolência *f*

indoor /'ɪndɔ:(r)/ *a* (de) interior, interno; (*under cover*) coberto; ‹*games*› de salão. **~s** /ɪn'dɔ:z/ *adv* dentro de casa, no interior

induce /ɪn'dju:s/ *vt* induzir, levar; (*cause*) causar, provocar

indulge /ɪn'dʌldʒ/ *vt* satisfazer; (*spoil*) fazer a(s) vontade(s) de ● *vi* **~ in** entregar-se a

indulgen|t /ɪn'dʌldʒənt/ *a* indulgente. **~ce** *n* (*leniency*) indulgência *f*; (*desire*) satisfação *f*

industrial /ɪn'dʌstrɪəl/ *a* industrial; ‹*unrest etc*› trabalhista; ‹*action*› reivindicativo; **~ estate** zona *f* industrial. **~ist** *n* industrial *m*. **~ized** *a* industrializado

industrious /ɪn'dʌstrɪəs/ *a* trabalhador, aplicado

industry /'ɪndəstrɪ/ *n* indústria *f*; (*zeal*) aplicação *f*, diligência *f*, zelo *m*

inebriated /ɪ'ni:brɪeɪtɪd/ *a* embriagado, ébrio

inedible /ɪ'nedɪbl/ *a* não comestível

ineffective /ɪnɪ'fektɪv/ *a* ineficaz; ‹*person*› ineficiente, incapaz

ineffectual /ɪnɪ'fektʃʊəl/ *a* ineficaz, improfícuo

inefficien|t /ɪnɪ'fɪʃnt/ *a* ineficiente. **~cy** *n* ineficiência *f*

ineligible /ɪn'elɪdʒəbl/ *a* inelegível; (*undesirable*) indesejável; **be ~ for** não ter direito a

inept /ɪ'nept/ *a* inepto

inequality /ɪnɪ'kwɒlətɪ/ *n* desigualdade *f*

inevitable /ɪn'evɪtəbl/ *a* inevitável, fatal

inexcusable /ɪnɪk'skju:zəbl/ *a* indesculpável, imperdoável

inexhaustible /ɪnɪg'zɔ:stəbl/ *a* inesgotável, inexaurível

inexpensive /ɪnɪk'spensɪv/ *a* barato, em conta

inexperience /ɪnɪk'spɪərɪəns/ *n* inexperiência *f*, falta *f* de experiência. **~d** *a* inexperiente

inexplicable /ɪn'eksplɪkəbl/ *a* inexplicável

infallib|le /ɪn'fæləbl/ *a* infalível

infam|ous /'ɪnfəməs/ *a* infame. **~y** *n* infâmia *f*

infan|t /'ɪnfənt/ *n* bebê *m*, (*P*) bebé *m*; (*child*) criança *f*. **~cy** *n* infância *f*; (*babyhood*) primeira infância *f*

infantile /'ɪnfəntaɪl/ *a* infantil

infantry /'ɪnfəntrɪ/ *n* infantaria *f*

infatuat|ed /ɪn'fætʃʊeɪtɪd/ *a* **~ed with** cego or perdido por. **~ion** /-'eɪʃn/ *n* cegueira *f*, paixão *f*

infect /ɪn'fekt/ *vt* infetar, (*P*) infectar; **~ sb with** contagiar or contaminar alguém com. **~ion** /-ʃn/ *n* infecção *f*, (*P*) infeção *f*, contágio *m*. **~ious** /-ʃəs/ *a* infeccioso, contagioso

infer /ɪn'fɜ:(r)/ *vt* (*pt* **inferred**) inferir, deduzir. **~ence** /'ɪnfərəns/ *n* inferência *f*

inferior /ɪn'fɪərɪə(r)/ *a* inferior; ‹*work etc*› de qualidade inferior ● *n* inferior *mf*; (*in rank*) subalterno *m*. **~ity** /-'ɒrətɪ/ *n* inferioridade *f*

infernal /ɪn'fɜ:nl/ *a* infernal

infertil|e /ɪn'fɜ:taɪl/ *a* infértil, estéril. **~ity** /-ə'tɪlətɪ/ *n* infertilidade *f*, esterilidade *f*

infest /ɪn'fest/ *vt* infestar (**with** de). **~ation** *n* infestação *f*

i

infidelity /ɪnfɪ'delətɪ/ *n* infidelidade *f*
infiltrat|e /'ɪnfɪltreɪt/ *vt/i* infiltrar(-se). **~ion** /-'treɪʃn/ *n* infiltração *f*
infinite /'ɪnfɪnət/ *a & n* infinito *m*. **~ly** *adv* infinitamente
infinitive /ɪn'fɪnətɪv/ *n* infinitivo *m*
infinity /ɪn'fɪnətɪ/ *n* infinidade *f*, infinito *m*
infirm /ɪn'fɜːm/ *a* débil, fraco
inflam|e /ɪn'fleɪm/ *vt* inflamar. **~mable** /-æməbl/ *a* inflamável. **~mation** /-ə'meɪʃn/ *n* inflamação *f*
inflate /ɪn'fleɪt/ *vt* ‹*balloon etc*› encher de ar; ‹*prices*› causar inflação de
inflation /ɪn'fleɪʃn/ *n* inflação *f*. **~ary** *a* inflacionário
inflection /ɪn'flekʃn/ *n* inflexão *f*; *Gram* flexão *f*, desinência *f*
inflexible /ɪn'fleksəbl/ *a* inflexível
inflict /ɪn'flɪkt/ *vt* infligir; impor (**on** a)
influence /'ɪnflʊəns/ *n* influência *f* ● *vt* influenciar, influir sobre
influential /ɪnflʊ'enʃl/ *a* influente
influenza /ɪnflʊ'enzə/ *n* gripe *f*
influx /'ɪnflʌks/ *n* afluência *f*, influxo *m*
inform /ɪn'fɔːm/ *vt* informar; **~ against** or **on** denunciar; **keep ~ed** manter ao corrente or a par. **~ant** *n* informante *mf*. **~er** *n* delator *m*, denunciante *mf*
informal /ɪn'fɔːml/ *a* informal; (*simple*) simples; sem cerimônia; (*P*) cerimónia; (*unofficial*) oficioso; (*colloquial*) familiar; ‹*dress*› de passeio, à vontade; ‹*dinner, gathering*› íntimo. **~ity** /-'mælətɪ/ *n* informalidade *f*; (*simplicity*) simplicidade *f*; (*intimacy*) intimidade *f*. **~ly** *adv* informalmente, sem cerimônia, (*P*) cerimónia, à vontade
information /ɪnfə'meɪʃn/ *n* informação *f*; (*facts, data*) informações *fpl*; **~ technology** tecnologia *f* de informação
informative /ɪn'fɔːmətɪv/ *a* informativo
infrared /ɪnfrə'red/ *a* infravermelho
infrequent /ɪn'friːkwənt/ *a* pouco frequente. **~ly** *adv* raramente
infringe /ɪn'frɪndʒ/ *vt* infringir; **~ on** transgredir; ‹*rights*› violar. **~ment** *n* infração *f*; (*rights*) violação *f*
infuriat|e /ɪn'fjʊərɪeɪt/ *vt* enfurecer, enraivecer. **~ing** *a* enfurecedor, de enfurecer, de dar raiva
infus|e /ɪn'fjuːz/ *vt* infundir, incutir; ‹*herbs, tea*› pôr de infusão. **~ion** /-ʒn/ *n* infusão *f*
ingen|ious /ɪn'dʒiːnɪəs/ *a* engenhoso, bem pensado. **~uity** /-ɪ'njuːətɪ/ *n* engenho *m*, habilidade *f*, imaginação *f*
ingenuous /ɪn'dʒenjʊəs/ *a* cândido, ingênuo, (*P*) ingénuo
ingrained /ɪn'greɪnd/ *a* arraigado, enraizado; ‹*dirt*› entranhado
ingratiate /ɪn'greɪʃɪeɪt/ *vt* **~ o.s. with** insinuar-se junto de, cair nas or ganhar as boas graças de
ingratitude /ɪn'grætɪtjuːd/ *n* ingratidão *f*
ingredient /ɪn'griːdɪənt/ *n* ingrediente *m*
inhabit /ɪn'hæbɪt/ *vt* habitar. **~able** *a* habitável. **~ant** *n* habitante *mf*
inhale /ɪn'heɪl/ *vt* inalar, aspirar. **~r** /-ə(r)/ *n* inalador *m*
inherent /ɪn'hɪərənt/ *a* inerente. **~ly** *adv* inerentemente, em si
inherit /ɪn'herɪt/ *vt* herdar (**from** de). **~ance** *n* herança *f*
inhibit /ɪn'hɪbɪt/ *vt* inibir; (*prevent*) impedir; **be ~ed** ser (um) inibido. **~ion** /-'bɪʃn/ *n* inibição *f*
inhospitable /ɪn'hɒspɪtəbl/ *a* inóspito; (*of person*) inospitaleiro, pouco/nada hospitaleiro
inhuman /ɪn'hjuːmən/ *a* desumano
inhumane /ɪnhjuː'meɪn/ *a* inumano, cruel
inimitable /ɪ'nɪmɪtəbl/ *a* inimitável
initial /ɪ'nɪʃl/ *a & n* inicial *f* ● *vt* (*pt* **initialled**) assinar com as iniciais, rubricar. **~ly** *adv* inicialmente
initiat|e /ɪ'nɪʃɪeɪt/ *vt* iniciar (**into** em); ‹*scheme*› lançar. **~ion** /-'eɪʃn/ *n* iniciação *f*; (*start*) início *m*
initiative /ɪ'nɪʃətɪv/ *n* iniciativa *f*
inject /ɪn'dʒekt/ *vt* injetar; *fig* insuflar. **~ion** /-ʃn/ *n* injeção *f*
injure /'ɪndʒə(r)/ *vt* (*harm*) fazer mal a, prejudicar, lesar; (*hurt*) ferir
injury /'ɪndʒərɪ/ *n* ferimento *m*, lesão *f*; (*wrong*) mal *m*
injustice /ɪn'dʒʌstɪs/ *n* injustiça *f*
ink /ɪŋk/ *n* tinta *f*
inkling /'ɪŋklɪŋ/ *n* ideia *f*, suspeita *f*
inlaid /ɪn'leɪd/ ▶ HIRE
inland /'ɪnlənd/ *a* interior ● /ɪn'lænd/ *adv* no interior, para o interior; **the I~ Revenue** o Fisco, a Receita Federal
inlay[1] /ɪn'leɪ/ *vt* (*pt* **inlaid**) embutir, incrustar

inlay[2] /ˈɪnleɪ/ *n* incrustação *f*, obturação *f*

inlet /ˈɪnlet/ *n* braço *m* de mar, enseada *f*; *Techn* admissão *f*

inmate /ˈɪnmeɪt/ *n* residente *mf*; (*in hospital*) internado *m*; (*in prison*) presidiário *m*

inn /ɪn/ *n* estalagem *f*

innate /ɪˈneɪt/ *a* inato

inner /ˈɪnə(r)/ *a* interior, interno; *fig* íntimo; **~ city** centro *m* da cidade. **~most** *a* mais profundo, mais íntimo. **~ tube** *n* câmara *f* de ar

innings /ˈɪnɪŋz/ *n Cricket* vez *f* de bater; *Pol* período *m* no poder

innocen|t /ˈɪnəsnt/ *a* & *n* inocente *mf*. **~ce** *n* inocência *f*

innocuous /ɪˈnɒkjʊəs/ *a* inócuo, inofensivo

innovat|e /ˈɪnəveɪt/ *vi* inovar. **~ion** /-ˈveɪʃn/ *n* inovação *f*. **~or** *n* inovador *m*

innuendo /ɪnjuːˈendəʊ/ *n* (*pl* **-oes**) insinuação *f*, indireta *f*

innumerable /ɪˈnjuːmərəbl/ *a* inumerável

inoculat|e /ɪˈnɒkjʊleɪt/ *vt* inocular. **~ion** /-ˈleɪʃn/ *n* inoculação *f*, vacina *f*

inoffensive /ɪnəˈfensɪv/ *a* inofensivo

inopportune /ɪnˈɒpətjuːn/ *a* inoportuno

inordinate /ɪˈnɔːdɪnət/ *a* excessivo, desmedido. **~ly** *adv* excessivamente, desmedidamente

input /ˈɪnpʊt/ *n* (*data*) dados *mpl*; *Electr* (*power*) energia *f*; (*computer process*) entrada *f*, dados *mpl*

inquest /ˈɪnkwest/ *n* inquérito *m*

inquir|e /ɪnˈkwaɪə(r)/ *vi* informar-se ● *vt* perguntar, indagar, inquirir; **~e about** procurar informações sobre, indagar; **~e into** inquirir, indagar. **~ing** *a* ‹*look*› interrogativo; ‹*mind*› inquisitivo. **~y** *n* (*question*) pergunta *f*; *Jur* inquérito *m*; (*investigation*) investigação *f*

inquisition /ɪnkwɪˈzɪʃn/ *n* inquisição *f*

inquisitive /ɪnˈkwɪzətɪv/ *a* curioso, inquisitivo; (*prying*) intrometido, bisbilhoteiro

insan|e /ɪnˈseɪn/ *a* louco, doido. **~ity** /ɪnˈsænətɪ/ *n* loucura *f*, demência *f*

insanitary /ɪnˈsænɪtrɪ/ *a* insalubre, anti-higiênico, (*P*) anti-higiénico

insatiable /ɪnˈseɪʃəbl/ *a* insaciável

inscri|be /ɪnˈskraɪb/ *vt* inscrever; ‹*book*› dedicar. **~ption** /-ɪpʃn/ *n* inscrição *f*; (*in book*) dedicatória *f*

inscrutable /ɪnˈskruːtəbl/ *a* impenetrável, misterioso

insect /ˈɪnsekt/ *n* inseto *m*

insecur|e /ɪnsɪˈkjʊə(r)/ *a* (*not firm*) inseguro, mal seguro; (*unsafe*) *Psych* inseguro. **~ity** *n* insegurança *f*, falta *f* de segurança

insensitive /ɪnˈsensətɪv/ *a* insensível

inseparable /ɪnˈseprəbl/ *a* inseparável

insert[1] /ɪnˈsɜːt/ *vt* inserir; ‹*key*› meter, colocar; (*add*) pôr, inserir. **~ion** /-ʃn/ *n* inserção *f*

insert[2] /ˈɪnsɜːt/ *n* coisa *f* inserida, enxerto *m*

inside /ɪnˈsaɪd/ *n* interior *m*; **~s** [!] tripas *fpl* [!]; **~ out** de dentro para fora, do avesso; (*thoroughly*) por dentro e por fora, a fundo ● *a* interior, interno ● *adv* no interior, dentro, por dentro ● *prep* dentro de; (*of time*) em menos de

insight /ˈɪnsaɪt/ *n* penetração *f*, perspicácia *f*; (*glimpse*) vislumbre *m*

insignificant /ɪnsɪgˈnɪfɪkənt/ *a* insignificante

insincer|e /ɪnsɪnˈsɪə(r)/ *a* insincero. **~ity** /-ˈserətɪ/ *n* insinceridade *f*, falta *f* de sinceridade

insinuat|e /ɪnˈsɪnjʊeɪt/ *vt* insinuar. **~ion** /-ˈeɪʃn/ *n* (*act*) insinuação *f*; (*hint*) indireta *f*, insinuação *f*

insipid /ɪnˈsɪpɪd/ *a* insípido, sem sabor

insist /ɪnˈsɪst/ *vt/i* **~ (on/that)** insistir (em/em que)

insisten|t /ɪnˈsɪstənt/ *a* insistente. **~ce** *n* insistência *f*

insolen|t /ˈɪnsələnt/ *a* insolente. **~ce** *n* insolência *f*

insoluble /ɪnˈsɒljʊbl/ *a* insolúvel

insolvent /ɪnˈsɒlvənt/ *a* insolvente

insomnia /ɪnˈsɒmnɪə/ *n* insônia *f*, (*P*) insónia *f*

inspect /ɪnˈspekt/ *vt* inspecionar, examinar; ‹*tickets*› fiscalizar; ‹*passport*› controlar; ‹*troops*› passar revista a. **~ion** /-ʃn/ *n* inspeção *f*, exame *m*; ‹*ticket*› fiscalização *f*; ‹*troops*› revista *f*. **~or** *n* inspetor *m*; (*on train*) fiscal *m*

inspir|e /ɪnˈspaɪə(r)/ *vt* inspirar. **~ation** /-əˈreɪʃn/ *n* inspiração *f*

instability /ɪnstəˈbɪlətɪ/ *n* instabilidade *f*

install /ɪnˈstɔːl/ *vt* instalar; ‹*heater etc*› montar, instalar. **~ation** /-əˈleɪʃn/ *n* instalação *f*

instalment /ɪnˈstɔːlmənt/ *n* prestação *f*; (*of serial*) episódio *m*

instance /ˈɪnstəns/ *n* exemplo *m*, caso *m*; **for ~** por exemplo; **in the first ~** em primeiro lugar

instant /ˈɪnstənt/ *a* imediato; ‹*food*› instantâneo ● *n* instante *m*. **~ messaging** *n* mensagem *f* instantânea. **~ly** *adv* imediatamente, logo

instantaneous /ɪnstənˈteɪnɪəs/ *a* instantâneo

instead /ɪnˈsted/ *adv* em vez disso, em lugar disso; **~ of** em vez de, em lugar de

instigat|e /ˈɪnstɪgeɪt/ *vt* instigar, incitar. **~ion** /-ˈgeɪʃn/ *n* instigação *f*. **~or** *n* instigador *m*

instil /ɪnˈstɪl/ *vt* (*pt* **instilled**) instilar, insuflar

instinct /ˈɪnstɪŋkt/ *n* instinto *m*. **~ive** /ɪnˈstɪŋktɪv/ *a* instintivo

i

institut|e /ˈɪnstɪtjuːt/ *n* instituto *m* ● *vt* instituir; ‹*legal proceedings*› intentar; ‹*inquiry*› ordenar. **~ion** /-ˈtjuːʃn/ *n* instituição *f*; (*school*) estabelecimento *m* de ensino; (*hospital*) estabelecimento *m* hospitalar

instruct /ɪnˈstrʌkt/ *vt* instruir; (*order*) mandar, ordenar; ‹*a solicitor etc*› dar instruções a; **~ sb in sth** ensinar algo a alguém. **~ion** /-ʃn/ *n* instrução *f*. **~ions** /-ʃnz/ *npl* instruções *fpl*, modo *m* de emprego; (*orders*) ordens *fpl*. **~ive** *a* instrutivo. **~or** *n* instrutor *m*

instrument /ˈɪnstrʊmənt/ *n* instrumento *m*; **~ panel** painel *m* de instrumentos

instrumental /ɪnstrʊˈmentl/ *a* instrumental; **be ~ in** ter um papel decisivo em. **~ist** *n* instrumentalista *mf*

insubordinat|e /ɪnsəˈbɔːdɪnət/ *a* insubordinado. **~ion** /-ˈneɪʃn/ *n* insubordinação *f*

insufferable /ɪnˈsʌfrəbl/ *a* intolerável, insuportável

insufficient /ɪnsəˈfɪʃnt/ *a* insuficiente

insular /ˈɪnsjʊlə(r)/ *a* insular; *fig* (*narrow-minded*) bitolado, limitado, (*P*) tacanho

insulat|e /ˈɪnsjʊleɪt/ *vt* isolar; **~ing tape** fita *f* isolante. **~ion** /-ˈleɪʃn/ *n* isolamento *m*

insulin /ˈɪnsjʊlɪn/ *n* insulina *f*

insult[1] /ɪnˈsʌlt/ *vt* insultar, injuriar. **~ing** *a* insultante, injurioso

insult[2] /ˈɪnsʌlt/ *n* insulto *m*, injúria *f*

insur|e /ɪnˈʃʊə(r)/ *vt* segurar, pôr no seguro; *Amer* ▶ ENSURE. **~ance** *n* seguro *m*; **~ance policy** apólice *f* de seguro

insurmountable /ɪnsəˈmaʊntəbl/ *a* insuperável

intact /ɪnˈtækt/ *a* intato, (*P*) intacto

intake /ˈɪnteɪk/ *n* admissão *f*; *Techn* admissão *f*, entrada *f*; (*of food*) ingestão *f*

intangible /ɪnˈtændʒəbl/ *a* intangível

integral /ˈɪntɪgrəl/ *a* integral; **be an ~ part of** ser parte integrante de

integrat|e /ˈɪntɪgreɪt/ *vt/i* integrar(-se); **~ed circuit** circuito *m* integrado. **~ion** /-ˈgreɪʃn/ *n* integração *f*

integrity /ɪnˈtegrətɪ/ *n* integridade *f*

intellect /ˈɪntəlekt/ *n* intelecto *m*, inteligência *f*. **~ual** /-ˈlektʃʊəl/ *a & n* intelectual *mf*

intelligen|t /ɪnˈtelɪdʒənt/ *a* inteligente. **~ce** *n* inteligência *f*; *Mil* informações *fpl*

intelligible /ɪnˈtelɪdʒəbl/ *a* inteligível

intend /ɪnˈtend/ *vt* tencionar; (*destine*) reservar, destinar. **~ed** *a* intencional, propositado

intens|e /ɪnˈtens/ *a* intenso; ‹*person*› emotivo. **~ely** *adv* intensamente; (*very*) extremamente. **~ity** *n* intensidade *f*

intensif|y /ɪnˈtensɪfaɪ/ *vt* intensificar. **~ication** /-ɪˈkeɪʃn/ *n* intensificação *f*

intensive /ɪnˈtensɪv/ *a* intensivo; **~ care** tratamento *m* intensivo

intent /ɪnˈtent/ *n* intento *m*, desígnio *m*, propósito *m* ● *a* atento, concentrado; **~ on** absorto em; (*intending to*) decidido a. **~ly** *adv* atentamente

intention /ɪnˈtenʃn/ *n* intenção *f*. **~al** *a* intencional. **~ally** *adv* de propósito

inter /ɪnˈtɜː(r)/ *vt* (*pt* **interred**) enterrar

inter- /ˈɪntə(r)/ *pref* inter-

interact /ɪntəˈrækt/ *vi* agir uns sobre os outros. **~ion** /-ʃn/ *n* interação *f*

intercede /ɪntəˈsiːd/ *vi* interceder

intercept /ɪntəˈsept/ *vt* interceptar, (*P*) intercetar

interchange[1] /ɪntəˈtʃeɪndʒ/ *vt* permutar, trocar. **~able** *a* permutável

interchange[2] /ˈɪntətʃeɪndʒ/ *n* permuta *f*, intercâmbio *m*; (*road junction*) trevo *m* de trânsito, (*P*) nó *m*

intercom /ˈɪntəkɒm/ *n* interfone *m*, (*P*) intercomunicador *m*

interconnected /ɪntəkəˈnektɪd/ *a* ‹*facts, events etc*› ligado

intercourse /ˈɪntəkɔːs/ *n* (*sexual*) relações *fpl* sexuais

interest /ˈɪntrəst/ *n* interesse *m*; (*legal share*) título *m*; (*in finance*) juro(s) *m(pl)*; **rate of ~** taxa *f* de juros ● *vt* interessar. **~ed** *a* interessado; **be ~ed in** interessar-se por. **~ing** *a* interessante

interface /'ɪntəfeɪs/ *n* interface *f*

interfer|e /ɪntə'fɪə(r)/ *vi* interferir; intrometer-se (**in** em); (*meddle, hinder*) interferir (**with** com); (*tamper*) mexer indevidamente (**with** em). **~ence** *n* interferência *f*

interim /'ɪntərɪm/ *n* **in the ~** nesse/neste ínterim *m*, (*P*) interim *m* ● *a* interino, provisório

interior /ɪn'tɪərɪə(r)/ *a & n* interior *m*

interjection /ɪntə'dʒekʃn/ *n* interjeição *f*

interlock /ɪntə'lɒk/ *vt/i* entrelaçar; ‹*pieces of puzzle etc*› encaixar(-se); *Mech* ‹*wheels*› engrenar, engatar

intermarr|iage /ɪntə'mærɪdʒ/ *n* casamento *m* entre membros de diferentes famílias, raças etc; (*between near relations*) casamento *m* consanguíneo. **~y** *vi* ligar-se por casamento

intermediary /ɪntə'mi:dɪərɪ/ *a & n* intermediário *m*

intermediate /ɪntə'mi:dɪət/ *a* intermédio, intermediário

interminable /ɪn'tɜ:mɪnəbl/ *a* interminável, infindável

intermission /ɪntə'mɪʃn/ *n* intervalo *m*

intermittent /ɪntə'mɪtnt/ *a* intermitente. **~ly** *adv* intermitentemente

intern /ɪn'tɜ:n/ *vt* internar. **~ment** *n* internamento *m*

internal /ɪn'tɜ:nl/ *a* interno, interior; *Amer* **the ~ Revenue** a Receita Federal, (*P*) o Fisco. **~ly** *adv* internamente, interiormente

international /ɪntə'næʃnəl/ *a & n* internacional *mf*

Internet /'ɪntənet/ *n* Internet *f*. **~ cafe** *n* lan house *f*, (*P*) cibercafé *m*

interpret /ɪn'tɜ:prɪt/ *vt/i* interpretar. **~ation** /-'teɪʃn/ *n* interpretação *f*. **~er** *n* intérprete *mf*

interrogat|e /ɪn'terəgeɪt/ *vt* interrogar. **~ion** /-'geɪʃn/ *n* interrogação *f*; (*by police etc*) interrogatório *m*

interrogative /ɪntə'rɒgətɪv/ *a* interrogativo ● *n* (*pronoun*) pronome *m* interrogativo

interrupt /ɪntə'rʌpt/ *vt* interromper. **~ion** /-ʃn/ *n* interrupção *f*

intersect /ɪntə'sekt/ *vt/i* intersetar(-se), (*P*) intersectar(-se); ‹*roads*› cruzar-se. **~ion** /-ʃn/ *n* intersecção *f*, (*P*) interseção *f*; (*crossroads*) cruzamento *m*

intersperse /ɪntə'spɜ:s/ *vt* entremear, intercalar; (*scatter*) espalhar

interval /'ɪntəvl/ *n* intervalo *m*; **at ~s** a intervalos

interven|e /ɪntə'vi:n/ *vi* (*interfere*) intervir; (*of time*) decorrer; (*occur*) sobrevir, intervir. **~tion** /-'venʃn/ *n* intervenção *f*

interview /'ɪntəvju:/ *n* entrevista *f* ● *vt* entrevistar. **~ee** *n* entrevistado *m*. **~er** *n* entrevistador *m*

intestin|e /ɪn'testɪn/ *n* intestino *m*. **~al** *a* intestinal

intima|te[1] /'ɪntɪmət/ *a* íntimo; (*detailed*) profundo. **~cy** *n* intimidade *f*. **~tely** *adv* intimamente

intimate[2] /'ɪntɪmeɪt/ *vt* (*announce*) dar a conhecer, fazer saber; (*imply*) dar a entender

intimidat|e /ɪn'tɪmɪdeɪt/ *vt* intimidar. **~ion** /-'deɪʃn/ *n* intimidação *f*

into /'ɪntə emphatic 'ɪntʊ/ *prep* para dentro de; **divide ~ three** dividir em três; **~ pieces** aos/em bocados; **translate ~** traduzir para

intolerable /ɪn'tɒlərəbl/ *a* intolerável, insuportável

intoleran|t /ɪn'tɒlərənt/ *a* intolerante. **~ce** *n* intolerância *f*

intonation /ɪntə'neɪʃn/ *n* entonação *f*, entoação *f*, inflexão *f*

intoxicat|ed /ɪn'tɒksɪkeɪtɪd/ *a* embriagado, etilizado. **~ion** /-'keɪʃn/ *n* embriaguez *f*

intranet /'ɪntrənet/ *n* rede *f* corporativa

intransigent /ɪn'trænsɪdʒənt/ *a* intransigente

intransitive /ɪn'trænsətɪv/ *a* ‹*verb*› intransitivo

intravenous /ɪntrə'vi:nəs/ *a* intravenoso

intrepid /ɪn'trepɪd/ *a* intrépido, arrojado

intrica|te /'ɪntrɪkət/ *a* intrincado, complexo. **~cy** *n* complexidade *f*

intrigu|e /ɪn'tri:g/ *vt/i* intrigar ● *n* intriga *f*. **~ing** *a* intrigante, curioso

intrinsic /ɪn'trɪnsɪk/ *a* intrínseco. **~ally** /-klɪ/ *adv* intrinsecamente

introduce /ɪntrə'dju:s/ *vt* ‹*programme, question*› apresentar; (*bring in, insert*) introduzir; (*initiate*) iniciar; **~ sb to sb** ‹*person*› apresentar alguém a alguém

introduct|ion /ɪntrə'dʌkʃn/ *n* introdução *f*; (*of/to person*) apresentação *f*. **~ory** /-tərɪ/ *a* introdutório, de introdução; ‹*letter, words*› de apresentação
introspective /ɪntrə'spektɪv/ *a* introspectivo, (*P*) introspetivo
introvert /'ɪntrəvɜːt/ *n & a* introvertido *m*
intru|de /ɪn'truːd/ *vi* intrometer-se, ser a mais. **~der** *n* intruso *m*. **~sion** *n* intrusão *f*. **~sive** *a* intruso
intuit|ion /ɪntjuː'ɪʃn/ *n* intuição *f*. **~ive** /ɪn'tjuːɪtɪv/ *a* intuitivo
inundate /'ɪnʌndeɪt/ *vt* inundar (**with** de)
invade /ɪn'veɪd/ *vt* invadir. **~r** /-ə(r)/ *n* invasor *m*

i

invalid[1] /'ɪnvəlɪd/ *n* inválido *m*
invalid[2] /ɪn'vælɪd/ *a* inválido. **~ate** *vt* invalidar
invaluable /ɪn'væljʊəbl/ *a* inestimável
invariabl|e /ɪn'veərɪəbl/ *a* invariável. **~y** *adv* invariavelmente
invasion /ɪn'veɪʒn/ *n* invasão *f*
invent /ɪn'vent/ *vt* inventar. **~ion** *n* invenção *f*. **~ive** *a* inventivo. **~or** *n* inventor *m*
inventory /'ɪnvəntrɪ/ *n* inventário *m*
inver|t /ɪn'vɜːt/ *vt* inverter. **~ted commas** *npl* aspas *fpl*. **~sion** *n* inversão *f*
invest /ɪn'vest/ *vt* investir; ‹*time, effort*› dedicar ● *vi* fazer um investimento; **~ in** 🅸 (*buy*) gastar dinheiro em. **~ment** *n* investimento *m*. **~or** *n* investidor *m*, financiador *m*
investigat|e /ɪn'vestɪgeɪt/ *vt* investigar. **~ion** /-'geɪʃn/ *n* investigação *f*; **under ~ion** em estudo. **~or** *n* investigador *m*
invidious /ɪn'vɪdɪəs/ *a* antipático, odioso
invigorate /ɪn'vɪgəreɪt/ *vt* revigorar; (*encourage*) estimular
invincible /ɪn'vɪnsəbl/ *a* invencível
invisible /ɪn'vɪzəbl/ *a* invisível
invit|e /ɪn'vaɪt/ *vt* convidar; (*bring on*) pedir, provocar. **~ation** /ɪnvɪ'teɪʃn/ *n* convite *m*. **~ing** *a* (*tempting*) tentador; (*pleasant*) acolhedor, convidativo
invoice /'ɪnvɔɪs/ *n* fatura *f* ● *vt* faturar
involuntary /ɪn'vɒləntrɪ/ *a* involuntário
involve /ɪn'vɒlv/ *vt* implicar, envolver; **~d in** implicado em. **~d** *a* (*complex*) complicado; (*at stake*) em jogo; (*emotionally*) envolvido. **~ment** *n* envolvimento *m*, participação *f*
invulnerable /ɪn'vʌlnərəbl/ *a* invulnerável
inward /'ɪnwəd/ *a* interior; ‹*thought etc*› íntimo. **~(s)** *adv* para dentro, para o interior. **~ly** *adv* interiormente, intimamente
iodine /'aɪədiːn/ *n* iodo *m*; (*antiseptic*) tintura *f* de iodo
IOU /aɪəʊ'juː/ *n*, *abbr* vale *m*
IQ /aɪ'kjuː/ *abbr* (= **intelligence quotient**) QI *m*, (quociente *m* de inteligência)
Iran /ɪ'rɑːn/ *n* Irã *m*, (*P*) Irão
Iraq /ɪ'rɑːk/ *n* Iraque *m*
irascible /ɪ'ræsəbl/ *a* irascível
irate /aɪ'reɪt/ *a* irado, enraivecido
Ireland /'aɪələnd/ *n* Irlanda *f*
iris /'aɪərɪs/ *n Anat, Bot* íris *f*
Irish /'aɪərɪʃ/ *a & n* (*language*) irlandês *m*. **~man** *n* irlandês *m*. **~woman** *n* irlandesa *f*
iron /'aɪən/ *n* ferro *m*; (*appliance*) ferro *m* de engomar ● *a* de ferro ● *vt* passar a ferro; **~ out** fazer desaparecer; *fig* aplanar, resolver. **~ing** *n* **do the ~ing** passar a roupa. **~ing board** *n* tábua *f* de passar roupa, (*P*) tábua *f* de engomar
ironic(al) /aɪ'rɒnɪk(l)/ *a* irônico, (*P*) irónico
ironmonger /'aɪənmʌŋgə(r)/ *n* ferreiro *m*, (*P*) ferrageiro *m*. **~'s** *n* (*shop*) loja *f* de ferragens
irony /'aɪərənɪ/ *n* ironia *f*
irrational /ɪ'ræʃənl/ *a* irracional; ‹*person*› ilógico, que não raciocina
irreconcilable /ɪrekən'saɪləbl/ *a* irreconciliável
irrefutable /ɪrɪ'fjuːtəbl/ *a* irrefutável
irregular /ɪ'regjʊlə(r)/ *a* irregular. **~ity** /-'lærətɪ/ *n* irregularidade *f*
irrelevant /ɪ'reləvənt/ *a* irrelevante, que não é pertinente
irreparable /ɪ'repərəbl/ *a* irreparável, irremediável
irreplaceable /ɪrɪ'pleɪsəbl/ *a* insubstituível
irresistible /ɪrɪ'zɪstəbl/ *a* irresistível
irresolute /ɪ'rezəluːt/ *a* irresoluto
irrespective /ɪrɪ'spektɪv/ *a* **~ of** sem levar em conta, independente de
irresponsible /ɪrɪ'spɒnsəbl/ *a* irresponsável
irreverent /ɪ'revərənt/ *a* irreverente

irreversible /ɪrɪ'vɜːsəbl/ *a* irreversível; ‹*decision*› irrevogável

irrigat|e /'ɪrɪgeɪt/ *vt* irrigar. **~ion** /-'geɪʃn/ *n* irrigação *f*

irritable /'ɪrɪtəbl/ *a* irritável, irascível

irritat|e /'ɪrɪteɪt/ *vt* irritar. **~ion** /-'teɪʃn/ *n* irritação *f*

is /ɪz/ ▶ BE

Islam /'ɪzlɑːm/ *n* Islã *m*, (*P*) Islão. **~ic** /ɪz'læmɪk/ *a* islâmico

island /'aɪlənd/ *n* ilha *f*; **traffic ~** abrigo *m* de pedestres, (*P*) placa *f* de refúgio

isolat|e /'aɪsəleɪt/ *vt* isolar. **~ion** /-'leɪʃn/ *n* isolamento *m*

Israel /'ɪzreɪl/ *n* Israel *m*. **~i** /ɪz'reɪlɪ/ *a & n* israelense *mf*, (*P*) israelita *mf*

issue /'ɪʃuː/ *n* questão *f*; (*outcome*) resultado *m*; (*of magazine etc*) número *m*; (*of stamps, money etc*) emissão *f*; **at ~** em questão; **take ~ with** entrar em discussão com, discutir com ● *vt* distribuir, dar; ‹*stamps, money etc*› emitir; ‹*orders*› dar ● *vi* **~ from** sair de

it /ɪt/ ● *pron*

····► (*subject*) ele, ela; **'Where's the book/chair?' – '~'s in the kitchen'** 'onde está o livro/a cadeira?' – '(ele/ela) está na cozinha'

····► (*object*) o, a; **~'s my book and I want it** o livro é meu e eu quero; **that's my pen, give ~ to me** essa caneta é minha, me dê(!)

····► (*with preposition*) **we talked a lot about ~** falamos muito sobre isso; **Elliott went to ~** o Elliott foi lá

····► (*non-specific*) isto, isso, aquilo; **that's ~** é isso; **take ~** leve isso

····► (*impersonal*) **~ is cold** está frio; **~ is raining** está chovendo; **~ will snow** vai nevar; **~ is the 6th of May today** hoje é seis de maio; **who is ~?** quem é?

italic /ɪ'tælɪk/ *a* itálico. **~s** *npl* itálico *m*

Ital|y /'ɪtəlɪ/ *n* Itália *f*. **~ian** /ɪ'tælɪən/ *a & n* (*person*) *Lang* italiano *m*

itch /ɪtʃ/ *n* coceira *f*, (*P*) comichão *f*; *fig* (*desire*) desejo *m* ardente ● *vi* coçar, sentir comichão, comichar; **my arm ~es** estou com coceira *or* (*P*) comichão no braço; **I am ~ing to** estou morto por [!]. **~y** *a* que dá coceira *or* (*P*) comichão

item /'aɪtəm/ *n* item *m*, artigo *m*; (*on programme*) número *m*; (*on agenda*) ponto *m*; **news ~** notícia *f*. **~ize** /-aɪz/ *vt* discriminar, especificar

itinerant /aɪ'tɪnərənt/ *a* itinerante; ‹*musician, actor*› ambulante

itinerary /aɪ'tɪnərərɪ/ *n* itinerário *m*

its /ɪts/ *a* seu, sua, seus, suas

it's /ɪts/ (= **it is, it has**) ▶ BE, ▶ HAVE

itself /ɪt'self/ *pron* ele mesmo, ele próprio, ela mesma, ela própria; (*reflexive*) se; (*after prep*) si mesmo, si próprio, si mesma, si própria; **by ~** sozinho, por si

IVF *abbr* (= **in vitro fertilization**) FIV *f*

ivory /'aɪvərɪ/ *n* marfim *m*

ivy /'aɪvɪ/ *n* hera *f*

i

The Ivy League O grupo de universidades mais antigas e conceituadas dos Estados Unidos. Situadas no nordeste do país, compõem a *Ivy League* as universidades de Harvard, Yale, Columbia, Cornell, Dartmouth College, Brown, Princeton e Pennsylvania. O termo provém da hera que cresce nos edifícios antigos destas universidades.

Jj

jab /dʒæb/ *vt* (*pt* **jabbed**) espetar ● *n* espetadela *f*; [!] (*injection*) picada *f*, (*P*) injeção *f*

jabber /'dʒæbə(r)/ *vi* tagarelar; (*indistinctly*) falar confusamente ● *n* tagarelice *f*; (*indistinct speech*) algaravia *f*; (*indistinct voices*) algaraviada *f*

jack /dʒæk/ *n Techn* macaco *m*; *Cards* valete *m*; **the Union J~** a bandeira *f* inglesa ● *vt* **~ up** levantar com macaco

jacket /'dʒækɪt/ *n* casaco (curto) *m*; (*of book*) sobrecapa *f*; (*of potato*) casca *f*

jackpot /'dʒækpɒt/ *n* sorte *f* grande; **hit the ~** ganhar a sorte grande

Jacuzzi® /dʒə'kuːziː/ *n* jacuzzi *m*, banheira *f* de hidromassagem

jade /dʒeɪd/ *n* (*stone*) jade *m*

jaded /'dʒeɪdɪd/ *a* (*tired*) estafado; (*bored*) enfastiado

jagged /'dʒægɪd/ *a* recortado, denteado; (*sharp*) pontiagudo

jail /dʒeɪl/ *n* prisão *f* ● *vt* prender, colocar na cadeia. **~er** *n* carcereiro *m*, (*P*) guarda *mf* prisional

jam[1] /dʒæm/ *n* geleia *f*, compota *f*, (*P*) geleia

jam[2] /dʒæm/ *vt/i* (*pt* **jammed**) (*wedge*) entalar; (*become wedged*) entalar-se; (*crowd*) apinhar(-se); *Mech* bloquear; *Radio* provocar interferências em; **~ one's brakes on** [!] pôr o pé no freio, (*P*) no travão subitamente, apertar o freio subitamente ● *n* (*crush*) aperto *m*; (*traffic*) engarrafamento *m*; [!] (*difficulty*) apuro *m*; aperto *m*. **~-packed** *a* [!] abarrotado (**with** de)

Jamaica /dʒəˈmeɪkə/ *n* Jamaica *f*

jangle /ˈdʒæŋgl/ *n* som *m* estridente ● *vi* retinir

janitor /ˈdʒænɪtə(r)/ *n* porteiro *m*; (*caretaker*) zelador *m*

January /ˈdʒænjʊərɪ/ *n* janeiro *m*

Japan /dʒəˈpæn/ *n* Japão *m*. **~ese** /dʒæpəˈniːz/ *a* & *n* japonês *m*

jar[1] /dʒɑː(r)/ *n* pote *m*. **jam-~** *n* frasco *m* de geleia

jar[2] /dʒɑː(r)/ *vt/i* (*pt* **jarred**) ressoar; bater ruidosamente (**against** contra); (*of colours*) destoar; (*disagree*) discordar (**with** de) ● *n* (*shock*) choque *m*. **~ring** *a* dissonante

jargon /ˈdʒɑːgən/ *n* jargão *m*, gíria *f* profissional

jaundice /ˈdʒɔːndɪs/ *n* icterícia *f*

jaunt /dʒɔːnt/ *n* (*trip*) passeata *f*

jaunty /ˈdʒɔːntɪ/ *a* (**-ier, -iest**) (*cheerful*) alegre, jovial; (*sprightly*) desenvolto

javelin /ˈdʒævlɪn/ *n* dardo *m*

jaw /dʒɔː/ *n* maxilar *m*, mandíbula *f*

jazz /dʒæz/ *n* jazz *m* ● *vt* **~ up** animar. **~y** *a* [!] espalhafatoso

jealous /ˈdʒeləs/ *a* ciumento; (*envious*) invejoso. **~y** *n* ciúme *m*; (*envy*) inveja *f*

jeans /dʒiːnz/ *npl* (blue-)jeans *mpl*, calça *f* de zuarte, (*P*) calças *fpl* de ganga

jeep /dʒiːp/ *n* jipe *m*

jeer /dʒɪə(r)/ *vt/i* **~ at** (*laugh*) fazer troça de; (*scorn*) escarnecer de; (*boo*) vaiar ● *n* (*mockery*) troça *f*; (*booing*) vaia *f*

jelly /ˈdʒelɪ/ *n* gelatina *f*

jellyfish /ˈdʒelɪfɪʃ/ *n* água-viva *f*

jeopard|y /ˈdʒepədɪ/ *n* perigo *m*. **~ize** *vt* comprometer, pôr em perigo

jerk /dʒɜːk/ *n* solavanco *m*, (*P*) safanão *m*; [x] (*fool*) idiota *mf* ● *vt/i* sacudir; (*move jerkily*) mover (-se) aos solavancos, (*P*) mover (-se) aos sacões. **~y** *a* sacudido

jersey /ˈdʒɜːzɪ/ *n* (*pl* **-eys**) camisola *f*, pulôver *m*, suéter *m*; (*fabric*) jérsei *m*, (*P*) malha *f*

jest /dʒest/ *n* gracejo *m*, graça *f* ● *vi* gracejar, brincar

Jesus /ˈdʒiːzəs/ *n* Jesus *m*

jet[1] /dʒet/ *n* azeviche *m*. **~-black** *a* negro de azeviche

jet[2] /dʒet/ *n* jato *m*; (*plane*) (avião a) jato *m*; **~ lag** cansaço *m* provocado pela diferença de fuso horário. **~-propelled** *a* de propulsão a jato

jetty /ˈdʒetɪ/ *n* (*breakwater*) quebra-mar *m*; (*landing stage*) desembarcadouro *m*, cais *m*

Jew /dʒuː/ *n* judeu *m*

jewel /ˈdʒuːəl/ *n* joia *f*. **~ler** *n* joalheiro *m*; **~ler's (shop)** joalheria *f*, (*P*) joalharia *f*. **~lery** *n* joias *fpl*

Jewish /ˈdʒuːɪʃ/ *a* judeu

jib /dʒɪb/ *vi* (*pt* **jibbed**) recusar-se a avançar; (*of a horse*) empacar; **~ at** opor-se a, ter relutância em ● *n* (*sail*) bujarrona *f*

jig /dʒɪg/ *n* jiga *f*

jiggle /ˈdʒɪgl/ *vt* (*rock*) balançar; (*jerk*) sacolejar, (*P*) sacudir

jigsaw /ˈdʒɪgsɔː/ *n* **~(-puzzle)** puzzle *m*, quebra-cabeça *m*, (*P*) quebra-cabeças *m*

jilt /dʒɪlt/ *vt* deixar; abandonar; dar um fora em [!]; (*P*) mandar passear [!]

jingle /ˈdʒɪŋgl/ *vt/i* tilintar, tinir ● *n* tilintar *m*, tinido *m*; (*advertising etc*) música *f* de anúncio

jinx /dʒɪŋks/ *n* [!] pessoa or coisa *f* azarenta *f*; *fig* (*spell*) azar *m*

jitter|s /ˈdʒɪtəz/ *npl* **the ~s** [!] nervos *mpl*. **~y** /-ərɪ/ *a* **be ~y** [!] estar nervoso, ter os nervos à flor da pele [!]

job /dʒɒb/ *n* trabalho *m*; (*post*) emprego *m*; **have a ~ doing** ter dificuldade em fazer; **it is a good ~ that** felizmente que. **~less** *a* desempregado

jobcentre /ˈdʒɒbsentə(r)/ *n* posto *m* de desemprego, (*P*) centro *m* de emprego

jockey /ˈdʒɒkɪ/ *n* (*pl* **-eys**) jóquei *m*

jocular /ˈdʒɒkjʊlə(r)/ *a* jocoso, galhofeiro, brincalhão

jog /dʒɒg/ *vt* (*pt* **jogged**) dar um leve empurrão em, tocar em; (*memory*) refrescar ● *vi Sport* fazer jogging. **~ging** *n* jogging *m*

join /dʒɔɪn/ *vt* juntar, unir; (*become member*) fazer-se sócio de, entrar para; **~ sb** juntar-se a alguém ● *vi* (*of roads*) juntar-se, entroncar-se; (*of rivers*) confluir; **~ up** alistar-se ● *n* junção *f*, junta *f* □ **~ in** *vt/i* participar (em)

joiner /ˈdʒɔɪnə(r)/ *n* marceneiro *m*

joint /dʒɔɪnt/ *a* comum, conjunto; (*effort*) conjunto; **~ author** coautor *m* ● *n* junta *f*, junção *f*; *Anat* articulação *f*; *Culin* quarto *m*; (*roast meat*) carne *f* assada; ☒ (*place*) espelunca *f*. **~ly** *adv* conjuntamente

jok|e /dʒəʊk/ *n* piada *f*, gracejo *m* ● *vi* gracejar. **~er** *n* brincalhão *m*; *Cards* curinga *f* de baralho, (*P*) diabo *m*. **~ingly** *adv* na brincadeira

joll|y /'dʒɒlɪ/ *a* (**-ier**, **-iest**) alegre, bem-disposto ● *adv* [!] muito

jolt /dʒəʊlt/ *vt* sacudir, sacolejar ● *vi* ir aos solavancos ● *n* solavanco *m*; (*shock*) choque *m*, sobressalto *m*

jostle /'dʒɒsl/ *vt* dar um encontrão or encontrões em, empurrar ● *vi* empurrar, acotovelar-se

jot /dʒɒt/ *n* **(not a) ~** nada ● *vt* (*pt* **jotted**) **~ (down)** apontar, tomar nota de. **~ter** *n* (*pad*) bloco *m* de notas

journal /'dʒɜːnl/ *n* diário *m*; (*newspaper*) jornal *m*; (*periodical*) periódico *m*, revista *f*. **~ism** *n* jornalismo *m*. **~ist** *n* jornalista *mf*

journey /'dʒɜːnɪ/ *n* (*pl* **-eys**) viagem *f*; (*distance*) trajeto *m* ● *vi* viajar

jovial /'dʒəʊvɪəl/ *a* jovial

joy /dʒɔɪ/ *n* alegria *f*. **~ride** *n* passeio *m* em carro roubado. **~ful**, **~ous** *adjs* alegre

jubil|ant /'dʒuːbɪlənt/ *a* cheio de alegria, jubiloso. **~ation** /-'leɪʃn/ *n* júbilo *m*, regozijo *m*

jubilee /'dʒuːbɪliː/ *n* jubileu *m*

Judaism /'dʒuːdeɪɪzəm/ *n* Judaísmo *m*

judder /'dʒʌdə(r)/ *vi* trepidar, vibrar ● *n* trepidação *f*, vibração *f*

judge /dʒʌdʒ/ *n* juiz *m* ● *vt* julgar. **~ment** *n* (*judging*) julgamento *m*, juízo *m*; (*opinion*) juízo *m*; (*decision*) julgamento *m*

judic|iary /dʒuː'dɪʃərɪ/ *n* magistratura *f*; (*system*) judiciário *m*. **~ial** *a* judiciário

judicious /dʒuː'dɪʃəs/ *a* judicioso

judo /'dʒuːdəʊ/ *n* judô *m*, (*P*) judo *m*

jug /dʒʌg/ *n* (*tall*) jarro *m*; (*round*) botija *f*. **milk-~** *n* leiteira *f*

juggle /'dʒʌgl/ *vt/i* fazer malabarismos (**with** com). **~r** /-ə(r)/ *n* malabarista *mf*

juic|e /dʒuːs/ *n* suco *m*, (*P*) sumo *m*. **~y** *a* suculento; [!] ‹*story etc*› picante

jukebox /'dʒuːkbɒks/ *n* juke-box *m*, (*P*) máquina *f* de música

July /dʒuː'laɪ/ *n* julho *m*

jumble /'dʒʌmbl/ *vt* misturar ● *n* mistura *f*; **~ sale** venda *f* de caridade de objetos usados

jumbo /'dʒʌmbəʊ/ *a* **~ jet** (avião) jumbo *m*

jump /dʒʌmp/ *vt/i* saltar; (*start*) sobressaltar(-se); (*of prices etc*) subir repentinamente; **~ at** aceitar imediatamente; **~ the gun** agir prematuramente; **~ the queue** furar a fila; **~ to conclusions** tirar conclusões apressadas ● *n* salto *m*; (*start*) sobressalto *m*; (*of prices*) alta *f*

jumper /'dʒʌmpə(r)/ *n* pulôver *m*, suéter *m*, (*P*) camisola *f* de lã

jumpy /'dʒʌmpɪ/ *a* nervoso

junction /'dʒʌŋkʃn/ *n* junção *f*; (*of roads etc*) entroncamento *m*

June /dʒuːn/ *n* junho *m*

jungle /'dʒʌŋgl/ *n* selva *f*, floresta *f*

junior /'dʒuːnɪə(r)/ *a* júnior; (*in age*) mais novo (**to** que); (*in rank*) subalterno; ‹*school*› primária; **~ to** (*in rank*) abaixo de ● *n* o mais novo *m*; *Sport* júnior *mf*

junk /dʒʌŋk/ *n* ferro-velho *m*, velharias *fpl*; (*rubbish*) lixo *m*; **~ food** comida *f* sem valor nutritivo, comida *f* de plástico; **~ mail** material *m* impresso, enviado por correio, sem ter sido solicitado; **~ shop** loja *f* de ferro-velho, bricabraque *m*

junkie /'dʒʌŋkɪ/ *n* ☒ drogado *m*

jurisdiction /dʒʊərɪs'dɪkʃn/ *n* jurisdição *f*

juror /'dʒʊərə(r)/ *n* jurado *m*

jury /'dʒʊərɪ/ *n* júri *m*

just /dʒʌst/ *a* justo ● *adv* justamente, exatamente; (*only*) só; **~ listen!** escuta só! **~ as** assim como; (*with time*) assim que; **he has ~ left** ele acabou de sair; **~ as tall as** exatamente tão alto quanto; **~ as well that** ainda bem que; **~ before** um momento antes (de). **~ly** *adv* com justiça, justamente

justice /'dʒʌstɪs/ *n* justiça *f*; **J~ of the Peace** juiz *m* de paz

justifiabl|e /'dʒʌstɪfaɪəbl/ *a* justificável. **~y** *adv* com razão, justificadamente

justif|y /'dʒʌstɪfaɪ/ *vt* justificar. **~ication** /-ɪ'keɪʃn/ *n* justificação *f*

jut /dʒʌt/ *vi* (*pt* **jutted**) **~ out** fazer saliência, sobressair

juvenile /'dʒuːvənaɪl/ *a* (*youthful*) juvenil; (*childish*) pueril, infantil; (*delinquent*) jovem; (*court*) de menores ● *n* jovem *mf*

Kk

kaleidoscope /kə'laɪdəskəʊp/ *n* caleidoscópio *m*

kangaroo /kæŋgə'ru:/ *n* canguru *m*

karate /kə'rɑ:tɪ/ *n* karatê *m*, karaté *m*

kebab /kə'bæb/ *n* churrasquinho *m*, espetinho *m*

keel /ki:l/ *n* quilha *f* ● *vi* ~ **over** virar-se

keen /ki:n/ *a* (**-er**, **-est**) (*sharp*) agudo; (*eager*) entusiástico; (*of appetite*) devorador; (*of intelligence*) vivo; (*of wind*) cortante. **~ly** *adv* vivamente; (*eagerly*) com entusiasmo. **~ness** *n* vivacidade *f*; (*enthusiasm*) entusiasmo *m*

keep /ki:p/ (*pt* **kept**) *vt* guardar; ‹*family*› sustentar; ‹*animals*› ter, criar; (*celebrate*) festejar; (*conceal*) esconder; (*delay*) demorar; (*prevent*) impedir (**from** de); ‹*promise*› cumprir; ‹*shop*› ter; ~ **in/out** impedir de entrar/de sair; ~ **up** conservar; ~ **up (with)** acompanhar ● *vi* manter-se, conservar-se; (*remain*) ficar; ~ **(on)** continuar (**doing** fazendo *or* (*P*) a fazer) ● *n* sustento *m*; (*of castle*) torre *f* de menagem □ ~ **back** *vt* (*withhold*) reter ● *vi* manter-se afastado. **~er** *n* guarda *mf*

keeping /'ki:pɪŋ/ *n* guarda *f*, cuidado *m*; **in ~ with** em harmonia com, (*P*) de harmonia com

keepsake /'ki:pseɪk/ *n* (*thing*) lembrança *f*, recordação *f*

keg /keg/ *n* barril *m* pequeno

kennel /'kenl/ *n* casota (de cão) *f*. **~s** *npl* canil *m*

kept /kept/ ▶ KEEP

kerb /kɜ:b/ *n* meio fio *m*, (*P*) borda *f* do passeio

kernel /'kɜ:nl/ *n* (*of nut*) miolo *m*

kerosene /'kerəsi:n/ *n* (*paraffin*) querosene *m*, (*P*) petróleo *m*; (*aviation fuel*) gasolina *f*

ketchup /'ketʃəp/ *n* molho *m* de tomate, ketchup *m*

kettle /'ketl/ *n* chaleira *f*

key /ki:/ *n* chave *f*; (*of piano etc*) tecla *f*; *Mus* clave *f* ● *a* chave ● *vt* ~ **in** digitar, bater; **~ed up** tenso. **~ring** *n* chaveiro *m*, porta-chaves *m invar*

keyboard /'ki:bɔ:d/ *n* teclado *m*

keyhole /'ki:həʊl/ *n* buraco *m* da fechadura

khaki /'kɑ:kɪ/ *a & n* cáqui *invar m*, (*P*) caqui *invar m*

kick /kɪk/ *vt/i* dar um pontapé *or* pontapés (**a** em); ‹*ball*› chutar (em); (*of horse*) dar um coice *or* coices, escoicear; ~ **out** 🄸 pôr na rua; ~ **up** 🄸 ‹*fuss, racket*› fazer ● *n* pontapé *m*; (*of gun, horse*) coice *m*; 🄸 (*thrill*) excitação *f*; prazer *m*. **~-off** *n* chute *m* inicial, kick-off *m*

kid /kɪd/ *n* (*goat*) cabrito *m*; ☒ (*child*) garoto *m*; (*leather*) pelica *f* ● *vt/i* (*pt* **kidded**) 🄸 brincar (com)

kidnap /'kɪdnæp/ *vt* (*pt* **kidnapped**) raptar. **~ping** *n* rapto *m*

kidney /'kɪdnɪ/ *n* rim *m*

kill /kɪl/ *vt* matar; *fig* (*put an end to*) acabar com ● *n* matança *f*. **~er** *n* assassino *m*. **~ing** *n* matança *f*, massacre *m*; (*of game*) caçada *f* ● *a* 🄸 (*funny*) de morrer de rir; 🄸 (*exhausting*) de morte

killjoy /'kɪldʒɔɪ/ *n* desmancha-prazeres *mf*

kilo /'ki:ləʊ/ *n* (*pl* **-os**) quilo *m*

kilogram /'kɪləgræm/ *n* quilograma *m*

kilometre /'kɪləmi:tə(r)/ *n* quilômetro *m*, (*P*) quilómetro *m*

kilowatt /'kɪləwɒt/ *n* quilowatt *m*

kilt /kɪlt/ *n* kilt *m*, saiote *m* escocês, (*P*) saia *f* escocesa

kin /kɪn/ *n* família *f*, parentes *mpl*; **next of ~** os parentes mais próximos

kind[1] /kaɪnd/ *n* espécie *f*, gênero *m*, (*P*) género *m*, natureza *f*; **in ~** em gêneros *or* (*P*) géneros; *fig* (*in the same form*) na mesma moeda; ~ **of** 🄸 (*somewhat*) de certo modo, um pouco

kind[2] /kaɪnd/ *a* (**-er**, **-est**) (*good*) bom; (*friendly*) gentil, amável. **~-hearted** *a* bom, bondoso. **~ness** *n* bondade *f*

kindergarten /'kɪndəgɑ:tn/ *n* jardim de infância *m*, (*P*) infantário *m*

kindly /'kaɪndlɪ/ *a* (**-ier**, **-iest**) benévolo, bondoso ● *adv* bondosamente, gentilmente, com simpatia; ~ **wait** tenha a bondade de esperar

king /kɪŋ/ *n* rei *m*. **~-size(d)** *a* de tamanho grande

kingdom /'kɪŋdəm/ *n* reino *m*

kingfisher /'kɪŋfɪʃə(r)/ *n* pica-peixe *m*, martim-pescador *m*

kink /kɪŋk/ *n* (*in rope*) volta *f*, nó *m*; *fig* perversão *f*. **~y** *a* 🄸 excêntrico; pervertido; (*of hair*) encarapinhado

kiosk /'ki:ɒsk/ *n* quiosque *m*; **telephone ~** cabine telefônica, (*P*) telefónica

kip /kɪp/ *n* ☒ sono *m* ● *vi* (*pt* **kipped**) ☒ dormir

kipper /ˈkɪpə(r)/ *n* arenque *m* defumado

kiss /kɪs/ *n* beijo *m* ● *vt/i* beijar(-se)

kit /kɪt/ *n* equipamento *m*; (*set of tools*) ferramenta *f*; (*for assembly*) kit *m* ● *vt* (*pt* **kitted**) **~ out** equipar

kitchen /ˈkɪtʃɪn/ *n* cozinha *f*; **~ garden** horta *f*; **~ sink** pia *f*, (*P*) lava-louças *m*

kite /kaɪt/ *n* (*toy*) pipa *f*, (*P*) papagaio *m* de papel

kitten /ˈkɪtn/ *n* gatinho *m*

kitty /ˈkɪtɪ/ *n* (*fund*) fundo *m* comum, vaquinha *f*; *Cards* bolo *m*

knack /næk/ *n* jeito *m*

knapsack /ˈnæpsæk/ *n* mochila *f*

knead /ni:d/ *vt* amassar

knee /ni:/ *n* joelho *m*

kneecap /ˈni:kæp/ *n* rótula *f*

kneel /ni:l/ *vi* (*pt* **knelt**) **~ (down)** ajoelhar(-se)

knelt /nelt/ ▶ KNEEL

knew /nju:/ ▶ KNOW

knickers /ˈnɪkəz/ *npl* calcinhas (de senhora) *fpl*

knife /naɪf/ *n* (*pl* **knives**) faca *f* ● *vt* esfaquear, apunhalar

knight /naɪt/ *n* cavaleiro *m*; *Chess* cavalo *m*. **~hood** *n* grau *m* de cavaleiro

knit /nɪt/ *vt* (*pt* **knitted**, *or* **knit**) tricotar ● *vi* tricotar, fazer tricô; *fig* (*unite*) unir-se; (*of bones*) soldar-se; **~ one's brow** franzir as sobrancelhas. **~ting** *n* malha *f*, tricô *m*

knitwear /ˈnɪtweə(r)/ *n* roupa *f* de malha, malhas *fpl*

knob /nɒb/ *n* (*of door*) maçaneta *f*; (*of drawer*) puxador *m*; (*of radio, TV etc*) botão *m*; (*of butter*) noz *f*. **~bly** *a* nodoso

knock /nɒk/ *vt/i* bater (em); ☒ (*criticize*) desancar (em); **~ down** ‹*chair, pedestrian*› deitar no chão, derrubar; (*demolish*) jogar *or* (*P*) deitar abaixo; [!] (*reduce*) baixar, reduzir; (*at auction*) adjudicar (**to** a); **~ out** pôr fora de combate, eliminar; (*stun*) assombrar; **~ over** entornar; **~ up** ‹*meal etc*› arranjar às pressas □ **~ about** *vt* tratar mal ● *vi* (*wander*) andar a esmo. **~ off** *vt* [!] (*complete quickly*) despachar; ☒ (*steal*) roubar ● *vi* [!] parar de trabalhar; fechar a loja [!]. **~-down** *a* ‹*price*› muito baixo; **~-kneed** *a* de pernas de tesoura; **~out** *n* *Boxing* nocaute *m*, KO *m*. **~er** *n* aldrava *f*

knot /nɒt/ *n* nó *m* ● *vt* (*pt* **knotted**) atar com nó, dar nó or nós em

knotty /ˈnɒtɪ/ *a* (**-ier**, **-iest**) nodoso, cheio de nós; (*difficult*) complicado, espinhoso

know /nəʊ/ *vt/i* (*pt* **knew**, *pp* **known**) saber (**that** que); (*person, place*) conhecer; **~ about** ‹*cars etc*› saber sobre, saber de; **~ of** ter conhecimento de, ter ouvido falar de ● *n* **in the ~** [!] por dentro. **~-all** *n* sabe-tudo *m* [!]; **~-how** *n* know-how *m*, conhecimentos *mpl* técnicos, culturais etc. **~ingly** *adv* com ar conhecedor; (*consciously*) conscientemente

knowledge /ˈnɒlɪdʒ/ *n* conhecimento *m*; (*learning*) saber *m*. **~able** *a* conhecedor, entendido, versado

known /nəʊn/ ▶ KNOW *a* conhecido

knuckle /ˈnʌkl/ *n* nó *m* dos dedos ● *vi* **~ under** ceder, submeter-se

Koran /kəˈrɑ:n/ *n* Alcorão *m*, Corão *m*

Korea /kəˈrɪə/ *n* Coreia *f*

kosher /ˈkəʊʃə(r)/ *a* aprovado pela lei judaica; [!] como deve ser

kowtow /kaʊˈtaʊ/ *vi* prostrar-se (**to** diante de); (*act obsequiously*) bajular

L l

lab /læb/ *n* [!] laboratório *m*

label /ˈleɪbl/ *n* (*on bottle etc*) rótulo *m*; (*on clothes, luggage*) etiqueta *f* ● *vt* (*pt* **labelled**) rotular; etiquetar, pôr etiqueta em

laboratory /ləˈbɒrətrɪ/ *n* laboratório *m*

laborious /ləˈbɔ:rɪəs/ *a* laborioso, trabalhoso

labour /ˈleɪbə(r)/ *n* trabalho *m*, labuta *f*; (*workers*) mão de obra *f*; **in ~** em trabalho de parto ● *vi* trabalhar; (*try hard*) esforçar-se ● *vt* alongar-se sobre, insistir em. **~ed** *a* ‹*writing*› laborioso, sem espontaneidade; ‹*breathing, movement*› difícil. **~-saving** *a* que poupa trabalho

Labour /ˈleɪbə(r)/ *n* (*party*) Partido *m* Trabalhista, os trabalhistas ● *a* trabalhista

labourer /ˈleɪbərə(r)/ *n* trabalhador *m*; (*on farm*) trabalhador *m* rural

labyrinth /ˈlæbərɪnθ/ *n* labirinto *m*

lace /leɪs/ *n* renda *f*; (*of shoe*) cordão *m* de sapato, (*P*) atacador *m* ● *vt* atar; ‹*drink*› juntar um pouco (de aguardente, rum etc)

lack /læk/ *n* falta *f* ● *vt* faltar (a), não ter; **be ~ing** faltar; **be ~ing in** carecer de

laconic /lə'kɒnɪk/ *a* lacônico, (*P*) lacónico

lacquer /'lækə(r)/ *n* laca *f*

lad /læd/ *n* rapaz *m*, moço *m*

ladder /'lædə(r)/ *n* escada *f* de mão, (*P*) escadote *m*; (*in stocking*) fio *m* corrido, (*P*) malha *f* (caída) ● *vi* deixar correr um fio, (*P*) deixar cair uma malha ● *vt* fazer malhas em

laden /'leɪdn/ *a* carregado (**with** de)

ladle /'leɪdl/ *n* concha (de sopa) *f*

lady /'leɪdɪ/ *n* senhora *f*; (*title*) Lady *f*; **young ~** jovem *f*. **~-in-waiting** *n* dama *f* de companhia, (*P*) dama *f* de honor; **~like** *a* senhoril, elegante. **Ladies** *n* (*toilets*) toalete *m* das Senhoras, (*P*) lavabos *m* para Senhoras

ladybird /'leɪdɪbɜːd/ *n* joaninha *f*

lag[1] /læg/ *vi* (*pt* **lagged**) atrasar-se, ficar para trás ● *n* atraso *m*

lag[2] /læg/ *vt* (*pt* **lagged**) ‹*pipes etc*› revestir com isolante térmico

lager /'lɑːgə(r)/ *n* cerveja *f* leve e clara; "loura" *f* ⊠

lagoon /lə'guːn/ *n* lagoa *f*

laid /leɪd/ ▶ LAY[2]

lain /leɪn/ ▶ LIE[2]

lair /leə(r)/ *n* toca *f*, covil *m*

lake /leɪk/ *n* lago *m*

lamb /læm/ *n* cordeiro *m*, carneiro *m*; (*meat*) carneiro *m*, borrego *m*

lambswool /'læmzwʊl/ *n* lã *f*

lame /leɪm/ *a* (**-er**, **-est**) coxo; *fig* (*unconvincing*) fraco

lament /lə'ment/ *n* lamento *m*, lamentação *f* ● *vt/i* lamentar(-se) (de/por)

laminated /'læmɪneɪtɪd/ *a* laminado

lamp /læmp/ *n* lâmpada *f*

lamp post /'læmppəʊst/ *n* poste (do candeeiro) (de iluminação pública) *m*

lampshade /'læmpʃeɪd/ *n* abajur *m*, quebra-luz *m*

lance /lɑːns/ *n* lança *f* ● *vt* lancetar

land /lænd/ *n* terra *f*; (*country*) país *m*; (*plot*) terreno *m*; (*property*) terras *fpl* ● *a* de terra, terrestre; ‹*policy etc*› agrário ● *vt/i* desembarcar; *Aviat* aterrissar, (*P*) aterrar; (*fall*) ir parar (**on** em/a); [!] (*obtain*) arranjar; ‹*a blow*› aplicar, mandar. **~locked** *a* rodeado de terra

landing /'lændɪŋ/ *n* desembarque *m*; *Aviat* aterrissagem *f*, (*P*) aterragem *f*; (*top of stairs*) patamar *m*

land|lady /'lændleɪdɪ/ *n* (*of rented house*) senhoria *f*, proprietária *f*; (*who lets rooms*) dona *f* da casa; (*of boarding house*) dona *f* da pensão; (*of inn etc*) proprietária *f*, estalajadeira *f*. **~lord** *n* (*of rented house*) senhorio *m*, proprietário *m*; (*of inn etc*) proprietário *m*, estalajadeiro *m*

landmark /'lændmɑːk/ *n* (*conspicuous feature*) ponto *m* de referência; *fig* marco *m*

landscape /'lændskeɪp/ *n* paisagem *f* ● *vt* projetar paisagisticamente

landslide /'lændslaɪd/ *n* desabamento or desmoronamento *m* de terras *m*; *fig Pol* vitória *f* esmagadora

lane /leɪn/ *n* senda *f*, caminho *m*; (*in country*) estrada *f* pequena; (*in town*) viela *f*, ruela *f*; (*of road*) faixa *f*, pista *f*; (*of traffic*) fila *f*; *Aviat* corredor *m*; *Naut* rota *f*

language /'læŋgwɪdʒ/ *n* língua *f*; (*speech, style*) linguagem *f*; **bad ~** linguagem *f* grosseira; **~ lab** laboratório *m* de línguas

languid /'læŋgwɪd/ *a* lânguido

languish /'læŋgwɪʃ/ *vi* elanguescer

lank /læŋk/ *a* (*of hair*) escorrido, liso

lanky /'læŋkɪ/ *a* (**-ier**, **-iest**) desengonçado, escanifrado

lantern /'læntən/ *n* lanterna *f*

lap[1] /læp/ *n* colo *m*; *Sport* volta *f* completa. **~dog** *n* cãozinho *m* de estimação, cão *m* de colo

lap[2] /læp/ *vt* **~ up** beber lambendo ● *vi* marulhar

lapel /lə'pel/ *n* lapela *f*

lapse /læps/ *vi* decair, degenerar-se; (*expire*) caducar ● *n* lapso *m*; *Jur* prescrição *f*; **~ into** ‹*thought*› mergulhar em; ‹*bad habit*› adquirir

lard /lɑːd/ *n* banha *f* de porco

larder /'lɑːdə(r)/ *n* despensa *f*

large /lɑːdʒ/ *a* (**-er**, **-est**) grande; **at ~** à solta, em liberdade; **by and ~** em geral. **~ly** *adv* largamente, em grande parte. **~ness** *n* grandeza *f*

lark[1] /lɑːk/ *n* (*bird*) cotovia *f*

lark[2] /lɑːk/ *n* [!] pândega *f*, brincadeira *f* ● *vi* **~ about** [!] fazer travessuras, brincar

larva /'lɑːvə/ *n* (*pl* **-vae** /-viː/) larva *f*

laryngitis /lærɪn'dʒaɪtɪs/ *n* laringite *f*

larynx /'lærɪŋks/ *n* laringe *f*

laser /'leɪzə(r)/ *n* laser *m*; **~ printer** impressora *f* a laser

lash /læʃ/ *vt* chicotear, açoitar; ‹*rain*› fustigar ● *n* chicote *m*; (*stroke*) chicotada *f*; (*eyelash*) pestana *f*, cílio *m*; **~ out** atacar, atirar-se a; 🄸 (*spend*) esbanjar dinheiro em algo

lasso /læ'suː/ *n* (*pl* **-os**) laço *m* ● *vt* laçar

last[1] /lɑːst/ *a* último; **~ night** ontem à noite, a noite passada; **the ~ straw** a gota d'água ● *adv* no fim, em último lugar; (*most recently*) a última vez ● *n* último *m*; **at (long) ~** por fim, finalmente; **to the ~** até ao fim. **~-minute** *a* de última hora. **~ly** *adv* finalmente, em último lugar

last[2] /lɑːst/ *vt/i* durar, continuar. **~ing** *a* duradouro, durável

latch /lætʃ/ *n* trinco *m*

late /leɪt/ *a* (**-er**, **-est**) atrasado; (*recent*) recente; (*former*) antigo, ex-, anterior; ‹*hour, fruit etc*› tardio; (*deceased*) falecido ● *adv* tarde; **in ~ July** no fim de julho; **of ~** ultimamente; **at the ~st** o mais tardar. **~ness** *n* atraso *m*

lately /'leɪtlɪ/ *adv* nos últimos tempos, ultimamente

latent /'leɪtnt/ *a* latente

lateral /'lætərəl/ *a* lateral

lather /'lɑːðə(r)/ *n* espuma *f* de sabão ● *vt* ensaboar ● *vi* fazer espuma

Latin /'lætɪn/ *n Lang* latim *m* ● *a* latino. **~ America** *n* América *f* Latina; **~ American** *a* & *n* latino-americano *m*

latitude /'lætɪtjuːd/ *n* latitude *f*

latter /'lætə(r)/ *a* último, mais recente ● *n* **the ~** este, esta. **~ly** *adv* recentemente

laudable /'lɔːdəbl/ *a* louvável

laugh /lɑːf/ *vi* rir (**at** de); **~ off** disfarçar com uma piada ● *n* riso *m*. **~able** *a* irrisório, ridículo. **~ing stock** *n* objeto *m* de troça

laughter /'lɑːftə(r)/ *n* riso *m*, risada *f*

launch[1] /lɔːntʃ/ *vt* lançar ● *n* lançamento *m*; **~ into** lançar-se or meter-se em; **~ing pad** plataforma *f* de lançamento

launch[2] /lɔːntʃ/ *n* (*boat*) lancha *f*

launder /'lɔːndə(r)/ *vt* lavar e passar

launderette /lɔːn'dret/ *n* lavanderia or (*P*) lavandaria *f* automática

laundry /'lɔːndrɪ/ *n* lavanderia *f*; (*clothes*) roupa *f*, (*P*) lavandaria *f*; **do the ~** lavar a roupa

laurel /'lɒrəl/ *n* loureiro *m*, louro *m*

lava /'lɑːvə/ *n* lava *f*

lavatory /'lævətrɪ/ *n* privada *f*, (*P*) casa de banho *f*; (*room*) toalete *m*, (*P*) lavabo *m*

lavender /'lævəndə(r)/ *n* alfazema *f*, lavanda *f*

lavish /'lævɪʃ/ *a* pródigo; (*plentiful*) copioso, generoso; (*lush*) suntuoso, (*P*) sumptuoso ● *vt* ser pródigo em, encher de

law /lɔː/ *n* lei *f*; (*profession, study*) direito *m*; **~ and order** ordem *f* pública. **~-abiding** *a* cumpridor da lei, respeitador da lei. **~ful** *a* legal, legítimo. **~fully** *adv* legalmente, legitimamente. **~less** *a* sem lei; (*act*) ilegal; (*person*) rebelde

law court /'lɔːkɔːt/ *n* tribunal *m*

lawn /lɔːn/ *n* gramado *m*, (*P*) relvado *m*. **~ mower** *n* cortador *m* de grama, (*P*) máquina *f* de cortar a relva

lawsuit /'lɔːsuːt/ *n* processo *m*, ação *f* judicial

lawyer /'lɔːjə(r)/ *n* advogado *m*

lax /læks/ *a* negligente; (*discipline*) frouxo; ‹*morals*› relaxado. **~ity** *n* negligência *f*; (*of discipline*) frouxidão *f*; (*of morals*) relaxamento *m*

laxative /'læksətɪv/ *n* laxante *m*, laxativo *m*

lay[1] /leɪ/ *a* leigo; **~ opinion** opinião *f* de um leigo

lay[2] /leɪ/ *vt* (*pt* **laid**) pôr, colocar; ‹*trap*› preparar, pôr; ‹*eggs, table, siege*› pôr; ‹*plan*› fazer; **~ on** ‹*gas, water etc*› instalar, ligar; ‹*entertainment etc*› organizar, providenciar; ‹*food*› servir; **~ out** ‹*design*› traçar, planejar; (*spread out*) estender, espalhar; ‹*money*› gastar ● *vi* pôr (ovos); **~ aside** pôr de lado; **~ down** pousar; ‹*condition, law, rule*› impor; ‹*arms*› depor; ‹*one's life*› oferecer; ‹*policy*› ditar; **~ hold of** agarrar(-se a) □ **~ off** *vt* ‹*worker*› suspender do trabalho ● *vi* 🄸 parar; desistir. **~ up** *vt* (*store*) juntar; ‹*ship, car*› pôr fora de serviço

lay[3] /leɪ/ ▶ LIE[2]

layabout /'leɪəbaʊt/ *n* ☒ vadio *m*

lay-by /'leɪbaɪ/ *n* acostamento *m*, (*P*) berma *f*

layer /'leɪə(r)/ *n* camada *f*

layman /'leɪmən/ *n* (*pl* **-men**) leigo *m*

layout /'leɪaʊt/ *n* disposição *f*; *Typ* composição *f*

laze /leɪz/ *vi* descansar, vadiar

l

laz|y /ˈleɪzɪ/ *a* (**-ier**, **-iest**) preguiçoso. **~iness** *n* preguiça *f*. **~ybones** *n* [!] vadio *m*; vagabundo *m*

lead[1] /liːd/ *vt/i* (*pt* **led**) conduzir, guiar, levar; ‹*team etc*› chefiar, liderar; ‹*life*› levar; ‹*choir, band etc*› dirigir; **~ away** levar; **~ on** *fig* encorajar; **~ the way** ir na frente; **~ up to** conduzir a ● *n* (*distance*) avanço *m*; (*first place*) dianteira *f*; (*clue*) indício *m*, pista *f*; (*leash*) coleira *f*; *Electr* cabo *m*; *Theatr* papel *m* principal; (*example*) exemplo *m*; **in the ~** na frente

lead[2] /led/ *n* chumbo *m*; (*of pencil*) grafite *f*

leader /ˈliːdə(r)/ *n* chefe *m*, líder *m*; (*of country, club, union etc*) dirigente *mf*; *Pol* líder; (*of orchestra*) regente *mf*, maestro *m*; (*in newspaper*) editorial *m*. **~ship** *n* direção *f*, liderança *f*

leading /ˈliːdɪŋ/ *a* principal; **~ article** artigo *m* de fundo, editorial *m*

leaf /liːf/ *n* (*pl* **leaves**) folha *f*; (*flap of table*) aba *f* ● *vi* **~ through** folhear. **~y** *a* frondoso

leaflet /ˈliːflɪt/ *n* prospecto *m*, folheto *m* informativo

league /liːg/ *n* liga *f*; *Sport* campeonato *m* da Liga; **in ~ with** de coligação com, em conluio com

leak /liːk/ *n* (*escape*) fuga *f*; (*hole*) buraco *m* ● *vt/i* ‹*roof, container*› pingar; *Electr, Gas* ter um escapamento, (*P*) ter uma fuga; *Naut* fazer água; **~ (out)** *fig* (*divulge*) divulgar; *fig* (*become known*) transpirar, divulgar-se. **~y** *a* que tem um vazamento, (*P*) que tem uma fuga

lean[1] /liːn/ *a* (**-er**, **-est**) magro

lean[2] /liːn/ *vt/i* (*pt* **leaned**, *or* **leant** /lent/) encostar(-se); apoiar-se (**on** em); (*be slanting*) inclinar(-se); **~ back/forward** or **over** inclinar-se para trás/para a frente; **~ on** [!] pressionar

leaning /ˈliːnɪŋ/ *a* inclinado ● *n* inclinação *f*

leap /liːp/ *vt* (*pt* **leaped** *or* **leapt** /lept/) galgar, saltar por cima de; **~ year** ano *m* bissexto ● *vi* saltar ● *n* salto *m*, pulo *m*. **~frog** *n* eixo-badeixo *m*, (*P*) jogo *m* do eixo

learn /lɜːn/ *vt/i* (*pt* **learned** *or* **learnt**) aprender; (*be told*) vir a saber, ouvir dizer. **~er** *n* principiante *mf*, aprendiz *m*

learn|ed /ˈlɜːnɪd/ *a* erudito. **~ing** *n* saber *m*, erudição *f*

lease /liːs/ *n* arrendamento *m*, aluguel *m*, (*P*) aluguer *m* ● *vt* arrendar, (*P*) alugar

leash /liːʃ/ *n* coleira *f*

least /liːst/ *a* o menor ● *n* o mínino *m*, o menos *m* ● *adv* o menos; **at ~** pelo menos; **not in the ~** de maneira alguma

leather /ˈleðə(r)/ *n* couro *m*, cabedal *m*

leave /liːv/ *vt/i* (*pt* **left**) deixar; (*depart from*) sair/partir (de), ir-se (de); **be left (over)** restar, sobrar; **~ alone** deixar em paz, não tocar; **~ out** omitir ● *n* licença *f*, permissão *f*; **~ of absence** licença *f*; **on ~** *Mil* de licença; **take one's ~** despedir-se (**of** de)

Leban|on /ˈlebənən/ *n* Líbano *m*

lecherous /ˈletʃərəs/ *a* lascivo

lecture /ˈlektʃə(r)/ *n* conferência *f*; *Univ* aula *f* teórica; *fig* sermão *m* ● *vi* dar uma conferência; *Univ* dar aula(s) ● *vt* pregar um sermão a alguém [!]. **~r** /-ə(r)/ *n* conferente *mf*, conferencista *mf*; *Univ* professor *m*

led /led/ ▶ LEAD[1]

ledge /ledʒ/ *n* rebordo *m*, saliência *f*; (*of window*) peitoril *m*

ledger /ˈledʒə(r)/ *n* livro-mestre *m*, razão *m*

leech /liːtʃ/ *n* sanguessuga *f*

leek /liːk/ *n* alho-poró *m*, (*P*) alho-porro *m*

leer /lɪə(r)/ *vi* **~ (at)** olhar de modo malicioso or manhoso (para) ● *n* olhar *m* malicioso or manhoso

leeway /ˈliːweɪ/ *n* *Naut* deriva *f*; *fig* liberdade *f* de ação, margem *f* [!]

left[1] /left/ ▶ LEAVE; **~ luggage (office)** depósito *m* de bagagens. **~overs** *npl* restos *mpl*, sobras *fpl*

left[2] /left/ *a* esquerdo; *Pol* de esquerda ● *n* esquerda *f* ● *adv* à/para a esquerda. **~-hand** *a* da esquerda; (*position*) à esquerda; **~-handed** *a* canhoto; **~-wing** *a* *Pol* de esquerda

leg /leg/ *n* perna *f*; (*of table*) pé *m*, perna *f*; (*of journey*) etapa *f*; **pull sb's ~** brincar or mexer com alguém; **stretch one's ~s** esticar as pernas. **~room** *n* espaço *m* para as pernas

legacy /ˈlegəsɪ/ *n* legado *m*

legal /ˈliːgl/ *a* legal; ‹*affairs etc*› jurídico; **~ adviser** advogado *m*. **~ity** /liːˈgælətɪ/ *n* legalidade *f*. **~ly** *adv* legalmente

legalize /ˈliːgəlaɪz/ *vt* legalizar

legend /ˈledʒənd/ *n* lenda *f*. **~ary** /ˈledʒəndrɪ/ *a* lendário

leggings /ˈlegɪŋz/ *npl* perneiras *fpl*; (*women's*) legging *m*, (*P*) leggings *m*

legib|le /ˈledʒəbl/ *a* legível

legion /ˈliːdʒən/ *n* legião *f*

legislat|e /ˈledʒɪsleɪt/ *vi* legislar. **~ion** /-ˈleɪʃn/ *n* legislação *f*

legislat|ive /ˈledʒɪslətɪv/ *a* legislativo

legitima|te /lɪˈdʒɪtɪmət/ *a* legítimo. **~cy** *n* legitimidade *f*

leisure /ˈleʒə(r)/ *n* lazer *m*, tempo *m* livre; **at one's ~** ao bel prazer, (*P*) a seu belo prazer; **~ centre** centro *m* de lazer. **~ly** *a* pausado, compassado ● *adv* sem pressa, devagar

lemon /ˈlemən/ *n* limão *m*

lemonade /leməˈneɪd/ *n* limonada *f*

lend /lend/ *vt* (*pt* **lent**) emprestar; (*contribute*) dar; **~ a hand to** (*help*) ajudar; **~ itself to** prestar-se a. **~er** *n* pessoa *f* que empresta. **~ing** *n* empréstimo *m*

length /leŋθ/ *n* comprimento *m*; (*in time*) período *m*; (*of cloth*) corte *m*; **at ~** extensamente; (*at last*) por fim, finalmente. **~y** *a* longo, demorado

lengthen /ˈleŋθən/ *vt/i* alongar(-se)

lengthways /ˈleŋθweɪz/ *adv* ao comprido, em comprimento, longitudinalmente

lenien|t /ˈliːnɪənt/ *a* indulgente, clemente. **~cy** *n* indulgência *f*, clemência *f*

lens /lenz/ *n* (*of spectacles*) lente *f*; *Photo* objetiva *f*

lent /lent/ ▶ LEND

Lent /lent/ *n* Quaresma *f*

lentil /ˈlentl/ *n* lentilha *f*

Leo /ˈliːəʊ/ *n Astr* Leão *m*

leopard /ˈlepəd/ *n* leopardo *m*

leotard /ˈliːəʊtɑːd/ *n* collant(s) *m(pl)*, (*P*) maillot *m* de ginástica ou dança

leper /ˈlepə(r)/ *n* leproso *m*

leprosy /ˈleprəsɪ/ *n* lepra *f*

lesbian /ˈlezbɪən/ *a* lésbico ● *n* lésbica *f*

less /les/ *a* (*in number*) menor (**than** que) ● *n, adv & prep* menos; **~ and ~** cada vez menos

lessen /ˈlesn/ *vt/i* diminuir

lesser /ˈlesə(r)/ *a* menor; **to a ~ degree** em menor grau

lesson /ˈlesn/ *n* lição *f*

let /let/ *vt* (*pt* **let**, *pres p* **letting**) deixar, permitir; (*lease*) alugar, arrendar; **~ alone** deixar em paz; (*not to mention*) sem falar em, para não o falar em; **~ down** baixar; (*deflate*) esvaziar; (*disappoint*) desapontar; (*fail to help*) deixar na mão; **~ in** deixar entrar; **~ o.s. in for** ‹*task, trouble*› meter-se em; **~ off** ‹*gun*› disparar; ‹*firework*› soltar, (*P*) deitar; (*excuse*) desculpar; **~ out** deixar sair; **~ through** deixar passar; **~ up** [!] abrandar, diminuir ● *v aux* **~'s go** vamos; **~ him do it** que o faça ele; **~ me know** diga-me, avise-me ● *n* aluguel *m*, (*P*) aluguer *m* ● *vt/i* **~ go** soltar □ **~ on** [!] *vt* revelar (**that** que) ● *vi* descoser-se [!], (*P*) descair-se [!]. **~-down** *n* desapontamento *m*; **~-up** *n* [!] pausa *f*; trégua *f*

lethal /ˈliːθl/ *a* fatal, mortal

letharg|y /ˈleθədʒɪ/ *n* letargia *f*, apatia *f*. **~ic** /lɪˈθɑːdʒɪk/ *a* letárgico, apático

letter /ˈletə(r)/ *n* (*symbol*) letra *f*; (*message*) carta *f*. **~ bomb** *n* carta-bomba *f*; **~ box** *n* caixa *f* do correio. **~ing** *n* letras *fpl*

lettuce /ˈletɪs/ *n* alface *f*

leukaemia /luːˈkiːmɪə/ *n* leucemia *f*

level /ˈlevl/ *a* plano; (*on surface*) horizontal; (*in height*) no mesmo nível (**with** que) ● *n* nível *m*; **on the ~** [!] franco, sincero ● *vt* (*pt* **levelled**) nivelar; ‹*gun, missile*› apontar; ‹*accusation*› dirigir; **~ crossing** passagem *f* de nível. **~-headed** *a* equilibrado, sensato

lever /ˈliːvə(r)/ *n* alavanca *f* ● *vt* **~ up** levantar com alavanca

leverage /ˈliːvərɪdʒ/ *n* influência *f*

levy /ˈlevɪ/ *vt* ‹*tax*› cobrar ● *n* imposto *m*

lewd /luːd/ *a* (**-er**, **-est**) libidinoso, obsceno

liabilit|y /laɪəˈbɪlətɪ/ *n* responsabilidade *f*; [!] (*handicap*) desvantagem *f*; **~ies** dívidas *fpl*

liable /ˈlaɪəbl/ *a* **~ to do** suscetível de fazer; **~ to** ‹*illness etc*› suscetível a; ‹*fine*› sujeito a; **~ for** responsável por

liaise /lɪˈeɪz/ *vi* [!] servir de intermediário (**between** entre); fazer a ligação (**with** com)

liaison /lɪˈeɪzn/ *n* ligação *f*

liar /ˈlaɪə(r)/ *n* mentiroso *m*

libel /ˈlaɪbl/ *n* difamação *f* ● *vt* (*pt* **libelled**) difamar

liberal /ˈlɪbərəl/ *a* liberal. **~ly** *adv* liberalmente

Liberal /ˈlɪbərəl/ *a & n* liberal *mf*

liberat|e /ˈlɪbəreɪt/ *vt* libertar. **~ion** /-ˈreɪʃn/ *n* libertação *f*; (*of women*) emancipação *f*

libert|y /ˈlɪbətɪ/ *n* liberdade *f*; **at ~y to** livre de; **take ~ies** tomar liberdades

libido /lɪˈbiːdəʊ/ *n* (*pl* **-os**) libido *m*

Libra /ˈliːbrə/ *n Astr* Balança *f*, Libra *f*

l

librar|y /'laɪbrərɪ/ *n* biblioteca *f*. **~ian** /-'breərɪən/ *n* bibliotecário *m*

> **Library of Congress** A biblioteca nacional dos Estados Unidos, situada em Washington DC. Fundada pelo Congresso (*Congress*), alberga mais de 80 milhões de livros em 470 línguas, e outros objectos.

Libya /'lɪbɪə/ *n* Líbia *f*. **~n** *a & n* líbio *m*

lice /laɪs/ *n* ▶ LOUSE

licence /'laɪsns/ *n* licença *f*; (*for TV*) taxa *f*; (*for driving*) carteira *f*, (*P*) carta *f*; (*behaviour*) libertinagem *f*

license /'laɪsns/ *vt* dar licença para, autorizar ● *n Amer* ▶ LICENCE; **~ plate** placa *f* do carro, (*P*) placa *f* de matrícula, matrícula *f*

lick /lɪk/ *vt* lamber; ⊠ (*defeat*) bater 🄸; dar uma surra em 🄸 ● *n* lambidela *f*; **a ~ of paint** uma mão de pintura

lid /lɪd/ *n* tampa *f*

lie[1] /laɪ/ *n* mentira *f* ● *vi* (*pt* **lied**, *pres p* **lying**) mentir; **give the ~ to** desmentir

l **lie**[2] /laɪ/ *vi* (*pt* **lay**, *pp* **lain**, *pres p* **lying**) estar deitado; (*remain*) ficar; (*be situated*) estar, encontrar-se; (*in grave*) (*on ground*) jazer; **~ down** descansar; **~ in, have a ~-in** dormir até tarde; **~ low** 🄸 (*hide*) andar escondido

lieu /lu:/ *n* **in ~ of** em vez de

lieutenant /lef'tenənt/ *n Army* tenente *m*; *Navy* 1.° tenente *m*

life /laɪf/ *n* (*pl* **lives**) vida *f*; **~ cycle** ciclo *m* vital; **~ expectancy** probabilidade *f* de vida, (*P*) esperança *f* média de vida; **~ insurance** seguro *m* de vida. **~guard** *n* salva-vidas *m*; **~ jacket** *n* colete *m* salva-vidas; **~-size(d)** *a* (de) tamanho natural *invar*

lifebelt /'laɪfbelt/ *n* cinto *m* salva-vidas, (*P*) boia *f* de salvação

lifeboat /'laɪfbəʊt/ *n* barco *m* salva-vidas

lifeless /'laɪflɪs/ *a* sem vida

lifelike /'laɪflaɪk/ *a* natural, real; (*of portrait*) muito parecido

lifelong /'laɪflɔŋ/ *a* de toda a vida, perpétuo

lifestyle /'laɪfstaɪl/ *n* estilo *m* de vida

lifetime /'laɪftaɪm/ *n* vida *f*; **the chance of a ~** uma oportunidade única

lift /lɪft/ *vt/i* levantar(-se), erguer(-se); 🄸 (*steal*) roubar; surripiar 🄸; (*of fog*) levantar, dispersar-se ● *n* ascensor *m*, elevador *m*; **give a ~ to** dar carona, (*P*) boleia a 🄸. **~-off** *n* decolagem *f*, (*P*) descolagem *f*

ligament /'lɪgəmənt/ *n* ligamento *m*

light[1] /laɪt/ *n* luz *f*; (*lamp*) lâmpada *f*; (*on vehicle*) farol *m*; (*spark*) lume *m* ● a claro ● *vt* (*pt* **lit**, *or* **lighted**) (*ignite*) acender; (*illuminate*) iluminar; **bring to ~** trazer à luz, revelar; **come to ~** vir à luz; **~ up** iluminar(-se), acender(-se)

light[2] /laɪt/ *a & adv* (**-er**, **-est**) leve. **~-headed** *a* (*dizzy*) estonteado, tonto; (*frivolous*) leviano; **~-hearted** *a* alegre, despreocupado. **~ly** *adv* de leve, levemente, ligeiramente. **~ness** *n* leveza *f*

lighten[1] /'laɪtn/ *vt/i* iluminar(-se); (*make brighter*) clarear

lighten[2] /'laɪtn/ *vt/i* ‹*load etc*› aligeirar(-se), tornar mais leve

lighter /'laɪtə(r)/ *n* isqueiro *m*

lighthouse /'laɪthaʊs/ *n* farol *m*

lighting /'laɪtɪŋ/ *n* iluminação *f*

lightning /'laɪtnɪŋ/ *n* relâmpago *m*; (*thunderbolt*) raio *m* ● *a* muito rápido; **like ~** como um relâmpago

lightweight /'laɪtweɪt/ *a* leve

like[1] /laɪk/ *a* semelhante (a), parecido (com) ● *prep* como ● *conj* 🄸 como ● *n* igual *m*, coisa *f* parecida; **the ~s of you** gente como você(s). **~-minded** *a* da mesma opinião

like[2] /laɪk/ *vt* gostar (de); **I would ~** gostaria (de), queria; **if you ~** se quiser; **would you ~?** gostaria?, queria?. **~able** *a* simpático

like|ly /'laɪklɪ/ *a* (**-ier**, **-iest**) provável ● *adv* provavelmente; **he is ~ly to come** é provável que ele venha; **not ~ly!** 🄸 nem morto 🄸, nem por sonhos. **~lihood** *n* probabilidade *f*

liken /'laɪkn/ *vt* comparar (**to** com)

likeness /'laɪknɪs/ *n* semelhança *f*

likewise /'laɪkwaɪz/ *adv* também; (*in the same way*) da mesma maneira

liking /'laɪkɪŋ/ *n* gosto *m*, inclinação *f*; (*for person*) afeição *f*; **take a ~ to** (*thing*) tomar gosto por; (*person*) simpatizar com

lilac /'laɪlək/ *n* lilás *m* ● *a* lilás *invar*

lily /'lɪlɪ/ *n* lírio *m*, lis *m*; **~ of the valley** lírio-do-vale *m*

limb /lɪm/ *n* membro *m*

lime[1] /laɪm/ *n* cal *f*

lime[2] /laɪm/ *n* (*fruit*) limão *m*, (*P*) lima *f*

lime[3] /laɪm/ *n* **~(-tree)** tília *f*

limelight /'laɪmlaɪt/ *n* **be in the ~** estar em evidência

limit /'lɪmɪt/ *n* limite *m* ● *vt* limitar. **~ation** /-'teɪʃn/ *n* limitação *f*. **~ed company** *n* sociedade *f* anônima, (*P*) anónima de responsabilidade limitada

limousine /'lɪməzi:n/ *n* limusine *f*

limp[1] /lɪmp/ *vi* mancar, coxear ● *n* **have a ~** coxear

limp[2] /lɪmp/ *a* (**-er**, **-est**) mole, frouxo

line[1] /laɪn/ *n* linha *f*; (*string*) fio *m*; (*rope*) corda *f*; (*row*) fila *f*; (*of poem*) verso *m*; (*wrinkle*) ruga *f*; (*of business*) ramo *m*; (*of goods*) linha *f*; *Amer* (*queue*) fila *f*, (*P*) fila *f*; **in ~ with** de acordo com ● *vt* marcar com linhas; ‹*streets etc*› ladear, enfileirar-se ao longo de; **~d paper** papel *m* pautado; **~ up** alinhar(-se), enfileirar(-se); (*in queue*) pôr(-se) em fila, (*P*) fila. **~-up** *n* (*players*) formação *f*

line[2] /laɪn/ *vt* (*garment*) forrar (**with** de)

linear /'lɪnɪə(r)/ *a* linear

linen /'lɪnɪn/ *n* ‹*sheets etc*› roupa *f* (branca) de cama; (*material*) linho *m*

liner /'laɪnə(r)/ *n* navio *m* de linha regular, (*P*) paquete *m*

linesman /'laɪnzmən/ *n Football, Tennis* juiz *m* de linha

linger /'lɪŋgə(r)/ *vi* demorar-se, deixar-se ficar; (*of smells etc*) persistir

lingerie /'lænʒərɪ/ *n* roupa *f* de baixo/interior (de senhora), lingerie *f*

linguist /'lɪŋgwɪst/ *n* linguista *mf*

linguistic /lɪŋ'gwɪstɪk/ *a* linguístico. **~s** *n* linguística *f*

lining /'laɪnɪŋ/ *n* forro *m*

link /lɪŋk/ *n* laço *m*; (*of chain; also fig*) elo *m*; (*on web page*) link *m* ● *vt* unir, ligar; (*relate*) ligar; ‹*arm*› enfiar; **~ up** (*of roads*) juntar-se (**with** a)

lint /lɪnt/ *n Med* curativo *m* de fibra de algodão; (*fluff*) cotão *m*

lion /'laɪən/ *n* leão *m*. **~ess** *n* leoa *f*

lip /lɪp/ *n* lábio *m*, beiço *m*; (*edge*) borda *f*; (*of jug etc*) bico *m*; **pay ~-service to** fingir pena, admiração etc. **~-read** *vt/i* entender pelos movimentos dos lábios, ler lábios

lipstick /'lɪpstɪk/ *n* batom *m*, (*P*) bâton *m*

liqueur /lɪ'kjʊə(r)/ *n* licor *m*

liquid /'lɪkwɪd/ *n & a* líquido *m*. **~ize** *vt* liquidificar. **~izer** *n* liquidificador *m*

liquor /'lɪkə(r)/ *n* bebida *f* alcoólica

liquorice /'lɪkərɪs/ *n* alcaçuz *m*

Lisbon /'lɪzbən/ *n* Lisboa *f*

lisp /lɪsp/ *n* ceceio *m* ● *vi* cecear

list[1] /lɪst/ *n* lista *f* ● *vt* fazer uma lista de; (*enter*) pôr na lista

list[2] /lɪst/ *vi* (*of ship*) adernar ● *n* adernamento *m*

listen /'lɪsn/ *vi* escutar, prestar atenção; **~ to, ~ in (to)** escutar, pôr-se à escuta. **~er** *n* ouvinte *mf*

listless /'lɪstlɪs/ *a* sem energia, apático

lit /lɪt/ ▶ LIGHT[1]

literal /'lɪtərəl/ *a* literal. **~ly** *adv* literalmente

litera|te /'lɪtərət/ *a* alfabetizado. **~cy** *n* alfabetização *f*, instrução *f*

literature /'lɪtrətʃə(r)/ *n* literatura *f*; [!] (*leaflets etc*) folhetos *mpl*

lithe /laɪð/ *a* ágil, flexível

litigation /lɪtɪ'geɪʃn/ *n* litígio *m*

litre /'li:tə(r)/ *n* litro *m*

litter /'lɪtə(r)/ *n* lixo *m*; (*animals*) ninhada *f* ● *vt* cobrir de lixo; **~ed with** coberto de. **~ bin** *n* lata *f*, (*P*) caixote *m* do lixo

little /'lɪtl/ *a* pequeno; (*not much*) pouco ● *n* pouco *m* ● *adv* pouco, mal, nem; **a ~** um pouco (de); **he ~ knows** ele mal/nem sabe; **~ by ~** pouco a pouco

live[1] /laɪv/ *a* vivo; ‹*wire*› eletrizado; ‹*broadcast*› em direto, ao vivo

live[2] /lɪv/ *vt/i* viver; (*reside*) habitar, morar, viver; **~ down** fazer esquecer; **~ it up** cair na farra; **~ on** viver de; (*continue*) continuar a viver; **~ up to** mostrar-se à altura de; (*fulfil*) cumprir

livelihood /'laɪvlɪhʊd/ *n* modo *m* de vida

livel|y /'laɪvlɪ/ *a* (**-ier**, **-iest**) vivo, animado. **~iness** *n* vivacidade *f*, animação *f*

liven /'laɪvn/ *vt/i* **~ up** animar(-se)

liver /'lɪvə(r)/ *n* fígado *m*

livestock /'laɪvstɒk/ *n* gado *m*

livid /'lɪvɪd/ *a* lívido; [!] (*furious*) furioso

living /'lɪvɪŋ/ *a* vivo ● *n* vida *f*; (*livelihood*) modo *m* de vida, sustento *m*; **earn** or **make a ~** ganhar a vida; **standard of ~** nível *m* de vida. **~ room** *n* sala *f* de estar

lizard /'lɪzəd/ *n* lagarto *m*

load /ləʊd/ *n* carga *f*; (*of lorry, ship*) carga *f*, carregamento *m*; (*weight, strain*) peso *m*; **~s of** montes de [!] ● *vt* carregar. **~ed** *a* ‹*dice*› viciado; [*] (*rich*) cheio da nota, (*P*) podre de rico

loaf[1] /ləʊf/ *n* (*pl* **loaves**) pão *m*

loaf[2] /ləʊf/ *vi* vadiar. **~er** *n* preguiçoso *m*, vagabundo *m*

loan /ləʊn/ *n* empréstimo *m* ● *vt* emprestar; **on ~** emprestado

loath /ləʊθ/ *a* sem vontade de, pouco disposto a, relutante em

loath|e /ləʊð/ *vt* detestar. **~ing** *n* repugnância *f*, aversão *f*

lobby /ˈlɒbɪ/ *n* entrada *f*, vestíbulo *m*; *Pol* lobby *m*, grupo *m* de pressão ● *vt* fazer pressão sobre

lobster /ˈlɒbstə(r)/ *n* lagosta *f*

local /ˈləʊkl/ *a* local; ‹*shops etc*› do bairro ● *n* pessoa *f* do lugar; [!] (*pub*) taberna *f* /pub *m* do bairro; **~ government** administração *f* municipal. **~ly** *adv* localmente

locality /ləʊˈkælətɪ/ *n* localidade *f*; (*position*) lugar *m*

localization /ləʊkəˈlaɪzeɪʃn/ *n* localização *f*

locat|e /ləʊˈkeɪt/ *vt* localizar; (*situate*) situar. **~ion** /-ʃn/ *n* localização *f*. **on ~ion** (*cinema*) em external, (*P*) no exterior

lock[1] /lɒk/ *n* (*hair*) mecha *f* de cabelo

lock[2] /lɒk/ *n* (*on door etc*) fecho *m*, fechadura *f*; (*on canal*) comporta *f*; **under ~ and key** a sete chaves ● *vt/i* fechar à chave; *Auto* ‹*wheels*› imobilizar(-se); **~ in** fechar à chave, encerrar; **~ out** fechar a porta para deixar na rua, ficar trancado do lado de fora; **~ up** fechar a casa. **~out** *n* lockout *m*

locker /ˈlɒkə(r)/ *n* compartimento *m* com chave

locket /ˈlɒkɪt/ *n* medalhão *m*

locksmith /ˈlɒksmɪθ/ *n* serralheiro *m*, chaveiro *m*

locomotion /ləʊkəˈməʊʃn/ *n* locomoção *f*

locomotive /ˈləʊkəməʊtɪv/ *n* locomotiva *f*

locum /ˈləʊkəm/ *n Med* substituto *m*

locust /ˈləʊkəst/ *n* gafanhoto *m*

lodge /lɒdʒ/ *n* casa *f* do guarda numa propriedade; (*of porter*) portaria *f* ● *vt* alojar; ‹*money*› depositar; **~ a complaint** apresentar uma queixa ● *vi* estar alojado (**with** em casa de); (*become fixed*) alojar-se. **~r** /-ə(r)/ *n* hóspede *mf*

lodgings /ˈlɒdʒɪŋz/ *n* quarto *m* mobiliado; (*flat*) apartamento *m*

loft /lɒft/ *n* sótão *m*

lofty /ˈlɒftɪ/ *a* (**-ier**, **-iest**) elevado; (*haughty*) altivo

log /lɒg/ *n* tronco *m*, toro *m*; **sleep like a ~** dormir como uma pedra ● *vt* (*pt* **logged**) *Naut/Aviat* lançar no diário de bordo; **~ off** acabar de usar, terminar a sessão (de utilizador); **~ on** iniciar a sessão

loggerheads /ˈlɒgəhedz/ *npl* **at ~** às turras (**with** com)

logic /ˈlɒdʒɪk/ *a* lógico. **~al** *a* lógico. **~ally** *adv* logicamente

logistics /ləˈdʒɪstɪks/ *n* logística *f*

logo /ˈləʊgəʊ/ *n* (*pl* **-os**) [!] emblema *m*; logotipo *m*, (*P*) logótipo *m*

loiter /ˈlɔɪtə(r)/ *vi* andar vagarosamente; (*stand about*) rondar

loll /lɔl/ *vi* refestelar-se

loll|ipop /ˈlɒlɪpɒp/ *n* pirulito *m*, (*P*) chupa-chupa *m*. **~y** *n* [!] pirulito *m*; (*P*) chupa-chupa *m*; [x] (*money*) grana *f*, pasta *f*

London /ˈlʌndən/ *n* Londres

lone /ləʊn/ *a* solitário. **~r** /-ə(r)/ *n* solitário *m*. **~some** *a* solitário

lonely /ˈləʊnlɪ/ *a* (**-ier**, **-iest**) solitário; ‹*person*› só, solitário

long[1] /lɒŋ/ *a* (**-er**, **-est**) longo, comprido; **~ face** cara *f* triste; **~ jump** salto *m* em distância, (*P*) em comprimento; **~-playing record** LP *m*; **~ wave** ondas *fpl* longas; **so ~!** [!] até logo! ● *adv* muito tempo, longamente; **how ~ is...?** (*in size*) qual é o comprimento de...?; **how ~?** (*in time*) quanto tempo?; **he will not be ~** ele não vai demorar; **a ~ time** muito tempo; **a ~ way** longe; **as** or **so ~ as** contanto que, desde que; **~ ago** há muito tempo; **before ~** (*future*) daqui a pouco, dentro em pouco; (*past*) pouco (tempo) depois; **in the ~ run** no fim de contas; **~ before** muito (tempo) antes. **~-distance** *a* ‹*flight*› de longa distância; ‹*phone call*› interurbano; **~-range** *a* de longo alcance; ‹*forecast*› a longo prazo; **~-sighted** *a* que enxerga mal a distância, (*P*) hipermetrope; **~-standing** *a* de longa data; **~-suffering** *a* com paciência exemplar/de santo; **~-term** *a* a longo prazo; **~-winded** *a* prolixo

long[2] /lɒŋ/ *vi* **~ for** ansiar por, ter grande desejo de; **~ to** desejar. **~ing** *n* desejo *m* ardente

longevity /lɒnˈdʒevətɪ/ *n* longevidade *f*, vida *f* longa

longhand /ˈlɒŋhænd/ *n* escrita *f* à mão

longitude /ˈlɒndʒɪtjuːd/ *n* longitude *f*

loo /luː/ *n* [!] banheiro *m*, (*P*) casa *f* de banho

look /lʊk/ *vt/i* olhar; (*seem*) parecer; **~ after** tomar conta de, olhar por; **~ at** olhar para; **~ down on** desprezar; **~ for** procurar; **~ forward to** aguardar com impaciência; **~ in on** visitar; **~ into** examinar, investigar; **~ like** parecer-se com, ter ar de; **~ on** (*as spectator*) ver, assistir; (*regard as*) considerar; **~ out** ter cautela; **~ out for** procurar; (*watch*) estar à espreita de; **~ round** olhar em redor; **~ up** ‹*word*› procurar; (*visit*) ir ver; **~ up to** respeitar ● *n* olhar *m*; (*appearance*) ar *m*, aspecto *m*; **(good) ~s** beleza *f*. **~out** *n Mil* posto *m* de observação; (*watcher*) vigia *m*

loom[1] /luːm/ *n* tear *m*

loom[2] /luːm/ *vi* surgir indistintamente; *fig* ameaçar

loony /ˈluːnɪ/ *n & a* [✖] maluco *m* [!]; doido *m*

loop /luːp/ *n* laçada *f*; (*curve*) volta *f*, arco *m*; *Aviat* loop *m* ● *vt* dar uma laçada

loophole /ˈluːphəʊl/ *n* (*in rule*) saída *f*, furo *m*

loose /luːs/ *a* (**-er**, **-est**) ‹*knot etc*› frouxo; ‹*page etc*› solto; ‹*clothes*› folgado; (*not packed*) a granel; (*inexact*) vago; ‹*morals*› dissoluto, imoral; **at a ~ end** sem saber o que fazer, sem ocupação definida; **break ~** soltar-se. **~ly** *adv* sem apertar; (*roughly*) vagamente

loosen /ˈluːsn/ *vt* (*slacken*) soltar, desapertar; (*untie*) desfazer, desatar

loot /luːt/ *n* saque *m* ● *vt* pilhar, saquear. **~er** *n* assaltante *mf*, salteador *m*. **~ing** *n* pilhagem *f*, saque *m*

lop /lɒp/ *vt* (*pt* **lopped**) **~ off** cortar, podar

lopsided /lɒpˈsaɪdɪd/ *a* torto, inclinado para um lado

lord /lɔːd/ *n* senhor *m*; (*title*) lord *m*; **the ~** o Senhor; **the L~'s Prayer** o Pai-Nosso; **(good) L~**! meu Deus!

lorry /ˈlɒrɪ/ *n* caminhão *m*, camião *m*

lose /luːz/ *vt/i* (*pt* **lost**) perder; **get lost** perder-se; **get lost** [✖] vai passear! [!]. **~r** /-ə(r)/ *n* perdedor *m*

loss /lɒs/ *n* perda *f*; **be at a ~** estar perplexo; **at a ~ for words** sem saber o que dizer

lost /lɒst/ ▶ LOSE ● *a* perdido; **~ property** objetos *mpl* perdidos (e achados)

lot[1] /lɒt/ *n* sorte *f*; (*at auction, land*) lote *m*; **draw ~s** tirar à sorte

lot[2] /lɒt/ *n* **the ~** tudo; (*people*) todos *mpl*; **a ~ (of), ~s (of)** [!] uma porção (de), (*P*) um monte (de) [!]; **quite a ~ (of)** [!] uma boa porção (de), (*P*) montes (de) [!]

lotion /ˈləʊʃn/ *n* loção *f*

lottery /ˈlɒtərɪ/ *n* loteria *f*, (*P*) lotaria *f*

loud /laʊd/ *a* (**-er**, **-est**) alto, barulhento, ruidoso; (*of colours*) berrante ● *adv* alto; **out ~** em voz alta

loudspeaker /laʊdˈspiːkə(r)/ *n* alto-falante *m*, (*P*) altifalante *m*

lounge /laʊndʒ/ *vi* recostar-se preguiçosamente ● *n* sala *f*, salão *m*

louse /laʊs/ *n* (*pl* **lice**) piolho *m*

lousy /ˈlaʊzɪ/ *a* (**-ier**, **-iest**) piolhento; [✖] (*very bad*) péssimo

lout /laʊt/ *n* pessoa *f* grosseira, arruaceiro *m*

lovable /ˈlʌvəbl/ *a* amoroso, adorável

love /lʌv/ *n* amor *m*; *Tennis* zero *m*, nada *m* ● *vt* amar, estar apaixonado por; (*like greatly*) gostar muito de; **in ~** apaixonado (**with** por); **~ affair** aventura *f* amorosa; **she sends you her ~** ela lhe manda lembranças, (*P*) ela manda-lhe cumprimentos

lovely /ˈlʌvlɪ/ *a* (**-ier**, **-iest**) lindo; [!] (*delightful*) encantador; delicioso

lover /ˈlʌvə(r)/ *n* namorado *m*, apaixonado *m*; (*illicit*) amante *m*; (*devotee*) admirador *m*, apreciador *m*

lovesick /ˈlʌvsɪk/ *a* perdido de amor

loving /ˈlʌvɪŋ/ *a* amoroso, terno, extremoso

low /ləʊ/ *a* (**-er**, **-est**) baixo ● *adv* baixo ● *n* baixa *f*; (*low pressure*) área de baixa pressão *f*. **~-cut** *a* decotado; **~-down** *a* baixo, reles ● *n* [!] a verdade autêntica, (*P*) a verdade nua e crua; **~-fat** *a* de baixo teor de gordura; **~-key** *a fig* moderado; discreto

lower /ˈləʊə(r)/ *a & adv* ▶ LOW ● *vt* baixar; **~ o.s.** (re)baixar-se (**to** a)

lowlands /ˈləʊləndz/ *npl* planície(s) *f(pl)*

lowly /ˈləʊlɪ/ *a* (**-ier**, **-iest**) humilde, modesto

loyal /ˈlɔɪəl/ *a* leal. **~ly** *adv* lealmente

lozenge /ˈlɒzɪndʒ/ *n* (*shape*) losango *m*; (*tablet*) pastilha *f*

lubric|ate /ˈluːbrɪkeɪt/ *vt* lubrificar. **~ant** *n* lubrificante *m*. **~ation** /-ˈkeɪʃn/ *n* lubrificação *f*

lucid /ˈluːsɪd/ *a* lúcido. **~ity** /luː-ˈsɪdətɪ/ *n* lucidez *f*

luck /lʌk/ *n* sorte *f*; **bad ~** pouca sorte *f*; **for ~** para dar sorte; **good ~!** boa sorte

luck|y /ˈlʌkɪ/ *a* (**-ier**, **-iest**) sortudo, com sorte; ‹*event etc*› feliz; ‹*number etc*› que dá sorte. **~ily** *adv* felizmente

lucrative /ˈluːkrətɪv/ *a* lucrativo, rentável

ludicrous /ˈluːdɪkrəs/ *a* ridículo, absurdo

lug /lʌg/ *vt* (*pt* **lugged**) arrastar

luggage /ˈlʌgɪdʒ/ *n* bagagem *f*. **~ rack** *n* porta-bagagem *m*

lukewarm /ˈluːkwɔːm/ *a* morno; *fig* sem entusiasmo; indiferente

lull /lʌl/ *vt* (*send to sleep*) embalar; ‹*suspicions*› acalmar ● *n* calmaria *f*, (*P*) acalmia *f*

lullaby /ˈlʌləbaɪ/ *n* canção *f* de embalar

lumbago /lʌmˈbeɪgəʊ/ *n* lumbago *m*

lumber /ˈlʌmbə(r)/ *n* trastes *mpl* velhos; (*wood*) madeira *f* cortada ● *vt* **~ sb with** sobrecarregar alguém com

luminous /ˈluːmɪnəs/ *a* luminoso

lump /lʌmp/ *n* bocado *m*; (*swelling*) caroço *m*; (*in the throat*) nó *m*; (*in liquid*) grumo *m*; (*of sugar*) torrão *m* ● *vt* **~ together** amontoar, juntar indiscriminadamente; **~ sum** quantia *f* total; (*payment*) pagamento *m* feito de uma vez. **~y** *a* grumoso, encaroçado

lunacy /ˈluːnəsɪ/ *n* loucura *f*

lunar /ˈluːnə(r)/ *a* lunar

lunatic /ˈluːnətɪk/ *n* lunático *m*; **~ asylum** manicômio *m*, (*P*) manicómio *m*

lunch /lʌntʃ/ *n* almoço *m* ● *vi* almoçar. **~time** *n* hora *f* do almoço

luncheon /ˈlʌntʃən/ *n* (*formal*) almoço *m*; **~ meat** carne *f* enlatada, (*P*) carnes frias *fpl*; **~ voucher** senha *f* de almoço

lung /lʌŋ/ *n* pulmão *m*

lunge /lʌndʒ/ *n* mergulho *m*, movimento *m* súbito para a frente; (*thrust*) arremetida *f* ● *vi* mergulhar; arremessar-se (**at** para cima de, contra)

lurch[1] /lɜːtʃ/ *n* **leave sb in the ~** deixar alguém em apuros

lurch[2] /lɜːtʃ/ *vi* ir aos ziguezagues, dar guinadas; (*stagger*) cambalear

lure /lʊə(r)/ *vt* atrair, tentar ● *n* chamariz *m*, engodo *m*; **the ~ of the sea** a atração do mar

lurid /ˈlʊərɪd/ *a* berrante; *fig* (*sensational*) sensacional; *fig* (*shocking*) horrífico

lurk /lɜːk/ *vi* esconder-se à espreita; (*prowl*) rondar; (*be latent*) estar latente

luscious /ˈlʌʃəs/ *a* apetitoso; (*voluptuous*) desejável

lush /lʌʃ/ *a* viçoso, luxuriante

Lusitanian /lusɪˈteɪnɪən/ *a* & *n* lusitano *m*

lust /lʌst/ *n* luxúria *f*, sensualidade *f*; *fig* cobiça *f*; desejo *m* ardente ● *vi* **~ after** cobiçar, desejar ardentemente. **~ful** *a* sensual

lustre /ˈlʌstə(r)/ *n* lustre *m*; *fig* prestígio *m*

lusty /ˈlʌstɪ/ *a* (**-ier**, **-iest**) robusto

lute /luːt/ *n* alaúde *m*

Luxemburg /ˈlʌksəmbɜːg/ *n* Luxemburgo *m*

luxuriant /lʌgˈʒʊərɪənt/ *a* luxuriante

luxurious /lʌgˈʒʊərɪəs/ *a* luxuoso

luxury /ˈlʌkʃərɪ/ *n* luxo *m* ● *a* de luxo

lying /ˈlaɪɪŋ/ ▶ LIE[1], LIE[2]

lynch /lɪntʃ/ *vt* linchar

lyric /ˈlɪrɪk/ *a* lírico. **~s** *npl Mus* letra *f*. **~al** *a* lírico

Mm

MA *abbr* (= **Master of Arts**) ▶ MASTER

mac /mæk/ *n* [!] impermeável *m*; gabardine *f*

macabre /məˈkɑːbrə/ *a* macabro

macaroni /mækəˈrəʊnɪ/ *n* macarrão *m*

macaroon /mækəˈruːn/ *n* bolinho *m* seco de amêndoa ralada

machine /məˈʃiːn/ *n* máquina *f*, legível à máquina *f*, (*P*) legível por máquina *f* ● *vt* fazer à máquina; (*sewing*) coser à máquina. **~ gun** *n* metralhadora *f*; **~-readable** *a* em linguagem de máquina, legível à máquina, (*P*) legível por máquina

machinery /məˈʃiːnərɪ/ *n* maquinaria *f*; (*working parts; also fig*) mecanismo *m*

machinist /məˈʃiːnɪst/ *n* maquinista *m*

macho /ˈmætʃəʊ/ *a* machista

mackerel /ˈmækrəl/ *n* (*pl invar*) cavala *f*

mackintosh /ˈmækɪntɒʃ/ *n* impermeável *m*, gabardine *f*

mad /mæd/ *a* (**madder**, **maddest**) doido, louco; ‹*dog*› raivoso; [!] (*angry*) furioso [!]; **~ cow disease** doença *f* da vaca louca *or* (*P*) das vacas loucas; **be ~**

about ser doido por; **like ~** como (um) doido. **~ly** *adv* loucamente; (*frantically*) enlouquecidamente. **~ness** *n* loucura *f*

Madagascar /mædəˈgæskə(r)/ *n* Madagáscar *m*

madam /ˈmædəm/ *n* senhora *f*; **no, ~** não senhora

madden /ˈmædn/ *vt* endoidecer, enlouquecer; **it's ~ing** é de enlouquecer

made /meɪd/ ▶ MAKE; **~ to measure** feito sob medida, (*P*) à medida

Madeira /məˈdɪərə/ *n* Madeira *f*; (*wine*) Madeira *m*

madman /ˈmædmən/ *n* (*pl* **-men**) doido *m*

Mafia /ˈmæfɪə/ *n* Máfia *f*

magazine /mægəˈzi:n/ *n* revista *f*, magazine *m*; (*of gun*) carregador *m*

maggot /ˈmægət/ *n* larva *f*

magic /ˈmædʒɪk/ *n* magia *f* ● *a* mágico. **~al** *a* mágico

magician /məˈdʒɪʃn/ *n* (*conjuror*) mágico *m*, prestidigitador *m*; (*wizard*) feiticeiro *m*

magistrate /ˈmædʒɪstreɪt/ *n* magistrado *m*

magnanim|ous /mægˈnænɪməs/ *a* magnânimo. **~ity** /-əˈnɪmətɪ/ *n* magnanimidade *f*

magnet /ˈmægnɪt/ *n* ímã *m*, (*P*) íman *m*. **~ic** /-ˈnetɪk/ *a* magnético. **~ism** /-ɪzəm/ *n* magnetismo *m*

magnificen|t /mægˈnɪfɪsnt/ *a* magnífico. **~ce** *n* magnificência *f*

magnif|y /ˈmægnɪfaɪ/ *vt* aumentar; ‹*sound*› ampliar, amplificar; **~ying glass** lupa *f*. **~ication** /-ɪˈkeɪʃn/ *n* aumento *m*, ampliação *f*

magnitude /ˈmægnɪtju:d/ *n* magnitude *f*

magpie /ˈmægpaɪ/ *n* pega *f*

mahogany /məˈhɒgənɪ/ *n* mogno *m*

maid /meɪd/ *n* criada *f*, empregada *f*; **old ~** solteirona *f*

maiden /ˈmeɪdn/ *n old use* donzela *f* ● *a* ‹*aunt*› solteira; ‹*speech, voyage*› inaugural; **~ name** nome *m* de solteira

mail[1] /meɪl/ *n* correio *m*; (*letters*) correio *m*, correspondência *f* ● *a* postal ● *vt* postar, pôr no correio; (*send by mail*) mandar pelo correio. **~bag** *n* mala *f* postal; **~box** *n Amer* caixa *f* do correio; **~ing list** *n* lista *f* de endereços; **~ order** *n* encomenda *f* por correspondência, (*P*) por correio

mail[2] /meɪl/ *n* (*armour*) cota *f* de malha

mailman /ˈmeɪlmæn/ *n* (*pl* **-men**) *Amer* carteiro *m*

maim /meɪm/ *vt* mutilar, aleijar

main[1] /meɪn/ *a* principal ● *n* **in the ~** em geral, essencialmente; **~ road** estrada *f* principal. **~ly** *adv* principalmente, sobretudo

main[2] /meɪn/ *n* **(water/gas) ~** cano *m* de água/gás; **the ~s** *Electr* a rede *f* elétrica

mainland /ˈmeɪnlənd/ *n* continente *m*

mainstay /ˈmeɪnsteɪ/ *n fig* esteio *m*

mainstream /ˈmeɪnstri:m/ *n* tendência *f* dominante, linha *f* principal

maintain /meɪnˈteɪn/ *vt* manter, sustentar; ‹*rights*› defender, manter

maintenance /ˈmeɪntənəns/ *n* (*care, continuation*) manutenção *f*; (*allowance*) pensão *f*

maisonette /meɪzəˈnet/ *n* dúplex *m*

maize /meɪz/ *n* milho *m*

majestic /məˈdʒestɪk/ *a* majestoso

majesty /ˈmædʒəstɪ/ *n* majestade *f*

major /ˈmeɪdʒə(r)/ *a* maior; (*very important*) de vulto; **~ road** estrada *f* principal ● *n* major *m* ● *vi* **~ in** *Amer Univ* especializar-se em

m

majority /məˈdʒɒrətɪ/ *n* maioria *f*; (*age*) maioridade *f* ● *a* majoritário, (*P*) maioritário; **the ~ of people** a maioria or a maior parte das pessoas

make /meɪk/ *vt/i* (*pt* **made**) fazer; ‹*decision*› tomar; ‹*destination*› chegar a; (*cause to*) fazer (+ *inf*) or (com) que (+ *subj*); **you ~ me angry** você me aborrece, (*P*) tu aborreces-me; **be made of** ser feito de; **~ o.s. at home** estar à vontade/como em sua casa; **~ it** chegar; (*succeed*) triunfar; **I ~ it two o'clock** são duas pelo meu relógio; **~ as if to** fazer or fingir que; **~ believe** fingir; **~ do with** arranjar-se com, contentar-se com; **~ for** dirigir-se para; (*contribute to*) ajudar a; **~ off** fugir (**with** com); **~ out** avistar, distinguir; (*understand*) entender; ‹*claim*› pretender; ‹*a cheque*› passar, emitir; **~ over** ceder, transferir ● *n* (*brand*) marca *f*; **on the ~** ☒ oportunista □ **~ up** *vt* fazer, compor; ‹*story*› inventar; ‹*deficit*› suprir; **~ up one's mind** decidir-se; **~ up (one's face)** maquilar-se, (*P*) maquilhar-se ● *vi* fazer as pazes; **~ up for** compensar. **~-believe** *a* fingido ● *n* fantasia *f*; **~-up** *n* maquilagem *f*, (*P*) maquilhagem *f*; (*of object*) composição *f*; *Psych* maneira *f* de ser, natureza *f*

maker /ˈmeɪkə(r)/ *n* fabricante *mf*

makeshift /ˈmeɪkʃɪft/ *n* solução *f* temporária ● *a* provisório

making /ˈmeɪkɪŋ/ *n* **be the ~ of** fazer, ser a causa do sucesso de; **in the ~** em formação; **he has the ~s of** ele tem as qualidades essenciais de

maladjusted /mæləˈdʒʌstɪd/ *a* desajustado, inadaptado

malaise /mæˈleɪz/ *n* mal-estar *m*

malaria /məˈleərɪə/ *n* malária *f*

Malay /məˈleɪ/ *a & n* malaio *m*. **~sia** /-ʒə/ *n* Malásia *f*

male /meɪl/ *a* ‹*voice, sex*› masculino; *Biol, Techn* macho ● *n* (*human*) homem *m*, indivíduo *m* do sexo masculino; (*arrival*) macho *m*

malevolen|t /məˈlevələnt/ *a* malévolo

malfunction /mælˈfʌŋkʃn/ *n* mau funcionamento *m* ● *vi* funcionar mal

malice /ˈmælɪs/ *n* maldade *f*, malícia *f*; **bear sb ~** guardar rancor a alguém

malicious /məˈlɪʃəs/ *a* maldoso, malicioso

malign /məˈlaɪn/ *vt* caluniar, difamar

malignan|t /məˈlɪgnənt/ *a* ‹*tumour*› maligno; (*malevolent*) malévolo

m

mallet /ˈmælɪt/ *n* maço *m*

malnutrition /mælnjuːˈtrɪʃn/ *n* desnutrição *f*, subalimentação *f*, subnutrição *f*

malpractice /mælˈpræktɪs/ *n* abuso *m*; (*incompetence*) incompetência *f* profissional, negligência *f*

malt /mɔːlt/ *n* malte *m*

Malt|a /ˈmɔːltə/ *n* Malta *f*

maltreat /mælˈtriːt/ *vt* maltratar. **~ment** *n* mau(s) trato(s) *m(pl)*

mammal /ˈmæml/ *n* mamífero *m*

mammoth /ˈmæməθ/ *n* mamute *m* ● *a* gigantesco, colossal

man /mæn/ *n* (*pl* **men**) homem *m*; (*in sports team*) jogador *m*; *Chess* peça *f*; **~ in the street** o homem *m* da rua, (*P*) o cidadão *m* comum; **~ to man** de homem para homem ● *vt* (*pt* **manned**) prover de pessoal; *Mil* guarnecer; *Naut* guarnecer, equipar, tripular; (*be on duty at*) estar de serviço em. **~-hour** *n* hora *f* de trabalho per capita, homem-hora *m*; **~hunt** *n* caça *f* ao homem; **~-made** *a* artificial

manage /ˈmænɪdʒ/ *vt* ‹*household*› governar; ‹*tool*› manejar; ‹*boat, affair, crowd*› manobrar; ‹*shop*› dirigir, gerir; **I could ~ another drink** até que tomaria mais um drinque [!], (*P*) até tomava mais outra bebida [!]; **~ to do** conseguir fazer; **managing director** diretor *m* geral ● *vi* arranjar-se. **~able** *a* manejável; (*easily controlled*) controlável. **~ment** *n* gerência *f*, direção *f*

manager /ˈmænɪdʒə(r)/ *n* diretor *m*; (*of bank, shop*) gerente *m*; (*of actor*) empresário *m*, representante *m*; *Sport* treinador *m*. **~ess** /-ˈres/ *n* diretora *f*; gerente *f*. **~ial** /-ˈdʒɪərɪəl/ *a* diretivo, administrativo; **~ial staff** gestores *mpl*

mandate /ˈmændeɪt/ *n* mandato *m*

mandatory /ˈmændətrɪ/ *a* obrigatório

mane /meɪn/ *n* crina *f*; (*of lion*) juba *f*

mango /ˈmæŋgəʊ/ *n* (*pl* **-oes**) manga *f*

manhandle /ˈmænhændl/ *vt* mover à força de braço; (*treat roughly*) tratar com brutalidade

manhole /ˈmænhəʊl/ *n* poço *m* de inspeção

manhood /ˈmænhʊd/ *n* idade *f* adulta; (*quality*) virilidade *f*

mania /ˈmeɪnɪə/ *n* mania *f*. **~c** /-ɪæk/ *n* maníaco *m*

manicur|e /ˈmænɪkjʊə(r)/ *n* manicure *f* ● *vt* fazer, arranjar

manifest /ˈmænɪfest/ *a* manifesto ● *vt* manifestar. **~ation** /-ˈsteɪʃn/ *n* manifestação *f*

manifesto /mænɪˈfestəʊ/ *n* (*pl* **-os**) manifesto *m*

manipulat|e /məˈnɪpjʊleɪt/ *vt* manipular. **~ion** /-ˈleɪʃn/ *n* manipulação *f*

mankind /mænˈkaɪnd/ *n* humanidade *f*, gênero *m*, (*P*) género *m* humano, raça *f* humana

manly /ˈmænlɪ/ *a* viril, másculo

manner /ˈmænə(r)/ *n* maneira *f*, modo *m*; (*attitude*) modo(s) *m(pl)*; (*kind*) espécie *f*; **~s** maneiras *fpl*; **bad ~s** má-criação *f*, falta *f* de educação; **good ~s** (boa) educação *f*

mannerism /ˈmænərɪzəm/ *n* maneirismo *m*, afetação *f*

manoeuvre /məˈnuːvə(r)/ *n* manobra *f* ● *vt/i* manobrar

manor /ˈmænə(r)/ *n* solar *m*

manpower /ˈmænpaʊə(r)/ *n* mão de obra *f*

mansion /ˈmænʃn/ *n* mansão *f*

manslaughter /ˈmænslɔːtə(r)/ *n* homicídio *m* involuntário

mantelpiece /ˈmæntlpiːs/ *n* (*shelf*) consolo *m* da lareira, (*P*) prateleira *f* da chaminé

manual /ˈmænjʊəl/ *a* manual ● *n* manual *m*

manufacture /mænjʊˈfæktʃə(r)/ *vt* fabricar ● *n* fabrico *m*, fabricação *f*. **~r** /-ə(r)/ *n* fabricante *mf*

manure /məˈnjʊə(r)/ *n* estrume *m*

manuscript /ˈmænjʊskrɪpt/ *n* manuscrito *m*

many /ˈmenɪ/ *a* (**more**, **most**) muitos; **~ a man/tear/***etc* muitos homens/muitas lágrimas/*etc*; **~ of us/them/you** muitos de nós/deles/de vocês; **you may take as ~ as you want** você pode levar quantos quiser; **how ~?** quantos?; **one too ~** um a mais ● *n* muitos; (*many people*) muita gente *f*; **a great ~** muitíssimos

map /mæp/ *n* mapa *m* ● *vt* (*pt* **mapped**) fazer um mapa de, mapear; **~ out** planear em pormenor; ‹*route*› traçar

maple /ˈmeɪpl/ *n* bordo *m*

mar /mɑː(r)/ *vt* (*pt* **marred**) estragar; ‹*beauty*› desfigurar

marathon /ˈmærəθən/ *n* maratona *f*

marble /ˈmɑːbl/ *n* mármore *m*; (*for game*) bola *f* de gude, (*P*) berlinde *m*

march /mɑːtʃ/ *vi* marchar ● *vt* **~ off** fazer marchar, conduzir à força; **he was ~ed off to prison** levaram-no à força para a prisão ● *n* marcha *f*

March /mɑːtʃ/ *n* março *m*

mare /meə(r)/ *n* égua *f*

margarine /mɑːdʒəˈriːn/ *n* margarina *f*

margin /ˈmɑːdʒɪn/ *n* margem *f*. **~al** *a* marginal; **~al seat** *Pol* lugar *m* ganho com pequena maioria. **~ally** *adv* por uma pequena margem, muito pouco

marigold /ˈmærɪɡəʊld/ *n* cravo-de-defunto *m*, (*P*) malmequer *m*

marijuana /mærɪˈwɑːnə/ *n* maconha *f*, marijuana *f*

marina /məˈriːnə/ *n* marina *f*

marinade /mærɪˈneɪd/ *n* marinada *f*, vinha d'alho, escabeche *m* ● *vt* pôr em marinada, pôr em vinha d'alho

marine /məˈriːn/ *a* marinho; (*of ship, trade etc*) marítimo ● *n* ‹*shipping*› marinha *f*; ‹*sailor*› fuzileiro *m* naval

marital /ˈmærɪtl/ *a* marital, conjugal, matrimonial; **~ status** estado *m* civil

maritime /ˈmærɪtaɪm/ *a* marítimo

mark[1] /mɑːk/ *n* (*currency*) marco *m*

mark[2] /mɑːk/ *n* marca *f*; (*trace*) marca *f*, sinal *m*; (*stain*) mancha *f*; *Schol* nota *f*; (*target*) alvo *m*; **make one's ~** ganhar nome ● *vt* marcar; ‹*exam etc*› marcar, classificar; **~ out** marcar; **~ out for** escolher para, designar para; **~ time** marcar passo. **~er** *n* marcador *m*. **~ing** *n* marcas *fpl*, marcação *f*

marked /mɑːkt/ *a* marcado. **~ly** /-ɪdlɪ/ *adv* manifestamente, visivelmente

market /ˈmɑːkɪt/ *n* mercado *m*; **on the ~** à venda; **~ garden** horta *f* de legumes para venda; **~ research** pesquisa *f* de mercado ● *vt* vender; (*launch*) comercializar, lançar. **~place** *n* mercado *m*. **~ing** *n* marketing *m*

marksman /ˈmɑːksmən/ *n* (*pl* **-men**) atirador *m* especial

marmalade /ˈmɑːməleɪd/ *n* compota *f* de laranja, (*P*) geleia

maroon /məˈruːn/ *a* & *n* bordô *m*, (*P*) bordeaux *m*

marooned /məˈruːnd/ *a* abandonado em ilha, costa deserta etc; *fig* (*stranded*) encalhado *fig*

marquee /mɑːˈkiː/ *n* barraca or tenda *f* grande *f*; *Amer* (*awning*) toldo *m*

marriage /ˈmærɪdʒ/ *n* casamento *m*, matrimônio *m*, (*P*) matrimónio *m*; **~ certificate** certidão *f* de casamento. **~able** *a* casadouro

marrow /ˈmærəʊ/ *n* (*of bone*) tutano *m*, medula *f*; (*vegetable*) abóbora *f*; **chilled to the ~** gelado até aos ossos

marr|y /ˈmærɪ/ *vt* casar(-se) com; (*give or unite in marriage*) casar; **get ~ied** casar-se ● *vi* casar-se. **~ied** *a* casado; ‹*life*› de casado, conjugal

Mars /mɑːz/ *n* Marte *m*

marsh /mɑːʃ/ *n* pântano *m*. **~y** *a* pantanoso

marshal /ˈmɑːʃl/ *n* *Mil* marechal *m*; (*steward*) mestre *m* de cerimônias, (*P*) cerimónias ● *vt* (*pt* **marshalled**) dispor em ordem, ordenar; (*usher*) conduzir, escoltar

marshmallow /mɑːʃˈmæləʊ/ *n* marshmallow *m*

martial /ˈmɑːʃl/ *a* marcial; **~ law** lei *f* marcial

martyr /ˈmɑːtə(r)/ *n* mártir *mf* ● *vt* martirizar. **~dom** *n* martírio *m*

marvel /ˈmɑːvl/ *n* maravilha *f*, prodígio *m* ● *vi* (*pt* **marvelled**) (*feel wonder*) maravilhar-se (**at** com); (*be astonished*) pasmar (**at** com)

marvellous /ˈmɑːvələs/ *a* maravilhoso

Marxis|t /ˈmɑːksɪst/ *a* & *n* marxista *mf*. **~m** /-zəm/ *n* marxismo *m*

marzipan /ˈmɑːzɪpæn/ *n* maçapão *m*

mascara /mæ'skɑːrə/ *n* rímel *m*

mascot /'mæskət/ *n* mascote *f*

masculin|e /'mæskjʊlɪn/ *a* masculino ● *n* masculino *m*. **~ity** /-'lɪnətɪ/ *n* masculinidade *f*

mash /mæʃ/ *n* (*pulp*) papa *f* ● *vt* esmagar; **~ed potatoes** purê *m or* (*P*) puré *m* de batata(s)

mask /mɑːsk/ *n* máscara *f* ● *vt* mascarar

masochis|t /'mæsəkɪst/ *n* masoquista *mf*. **~m** /-zəm/ *n* masoquismo *m*

mason /'meɪsn/ *n* maçom *m*; (*building*) pedreiro *m*. **~ry** *n* maçonaria *f*, mação *m*; (*building*) alvenaria *f*

mass[1] /mæs/ *n Relig* missa *f*

mass[2] /mæs/ *n* massa *f*; (*heap*) montão *m*; **the ~es** as massas, a grande massa ● *vt/i* aglomerar(-se), reunir(-se) em massa. **~-produce** *vt* produzir em série/massa

massacre /'mæsəkə(r)/ *n* massacre *m* ● *vt* massacrar

massage /'mæsɑːʒ/ *n* massagem *f* ● *vt* massagear, fazer massagens em, (*P*) dar massagens a

masseu|r /mæ'sɜː(r)/ *n* massagista *m*. **~se** /mæ'sɜːz/ *n* massagista *f*

m

massive /'mæsɪv/ *a* (*heavy*) maciço; (*huge*) enorme

mast /mɑːst/ *n* mastro *m*; (*for radio etc*) antena *f*

master /'mɑːstə(r)/ *n* (*in school*) professor *m*, mestre *m*; (*expert*) mestre *m*; (*boss*) patrão *m*; (*owner*) dono *m*; **~** (*boy*) menino *m*; **M~ of Arts/***etc* Licenciado *m* em Letras/*etc* ● *vt* dominar. **~ key** *n* chave-mestra *f*; **~mind** *n* (*of scheme etc*) cérebro *m* ● *vt* planejar, dirigir; **~ stroke** *n* golpe *m* de mestre. **~y** *n* domínio *m* (**over** sobre); (*knowledge*) conhecimento *m*; (*skill*) pericia *f*

masterly /'mɑːstəlɪ/ *a* magistral

masterpiece /'mɑːstəpiːs/ *n* obra-prima *f*

masturbat|e /'mæstəbeɪt/ *vi* masturbar-se. **~ion** /-'beɪʃn/ *n* masturbação *f*

mat /mæt/ *n* tapete *m* pequeno; (*at door*) capacho *m*. **(table) ~** *n* (*of cloth*) paninho *m* de mesa; (*for hot dishes*) descanso *m* para pratos

match[1] /mætʃ/ *n* fósforo *m*

match[2] /mætʃ/ *n* (*contest*) competição *f*, torneio *m*; (*game*) partida *f*; (*equal*) par *m*, parceiro *m*, igual *mf*; *fig* (*marriage*) casamento *m*; (*marriage partner*) partido *m* ● *vt/i* (*set against*) contrapôr (**against** a); (*equal*) igualar; (*go with*) condizer; (*be alike*) ir com, emparceirar com; **her shoes ~ed her bag** os sapatos dela combinavam com a bolsa. **~ing** *a* condizente, a condizer

matchbox /'mætʃbɒks/ *n* caixa *f* de fósforos

mat|e[1] /meɪt/ *n* companheiro *m*, camarada *mf*; (*of birds, animals*) macho *m*, fêmea *f*; (*assistant*) ajudante *mf* ● *vt/i* acasalar(-se) (**with** com)

mate[2] /meɪt/ *n Chess* mate *m*, xeque-mate *m*

material /mə'tɪərɪəl/ *n* material *m*; (*fabric*) tecido *m*; (*equipment*) apetrechos *mpl* ● *a* material; (*significant*) importante

materialis|m /mə'tɪərɪəlɪzəm/ *n* materialismo *m*. **~tic** /-'lɪstɪk/ *a* materialista

materialize /mə'tɪərɪəlaɪz/ *vi* realizar-se, concretizar-se; (*appear*) aparecer

maternal /mə'tɜːnəl/ *a* maternal

maternity /mə'tɜːnətɪ/ *n* maternidade *f* ● *a* ‹*clothes*› de grávida; **~ hospital** maternidade *f*; **~ leave** licença *f* de maternidade

mathematic|s /mæθə'mætɪks/ *n* matemática *f*. **~al** *a* matemático. **~ian** /-ə'tɪʃn/ *n* matemático *m*

maths /mæθs/ *n* [!] matemática *f*

matinee /'mætɪneɪ/ *n* matinê *f*, (*P*) matinée *f*

matrimon|y /'mætrɪmənɪ/ *n* matrimônio *m*, (*P*) matrimónio *m*

matron /'meɪtrən/ *n* matrona *f*; (*in school*) inspetora *f*; (*former use*) (*senior nursing officer*) enfermeira-chefe *f*

matt /mæt/ *a* fosco, sem brilho, mate

matted /'mætɪd/ *a* emaranhado

matter /'mætə(r)/ *n* (*substance*) matéria *f*; (*affair*) assunto *m*, caso *m*, questão *f*; (*pus*) pus *m*; **as a ~ of fact** na verdade; **no ~ what happens** não importa o que acontecer; **what is the ~?** o que é que há?, (*P*) o que é que se passa?; **what is the ~ with you?** o que é que você tem? ● *vi* importar; **it does not ~** não importa. **~-of-fact** *a* prosaico, terra a terra

mattress /'mætrɪs/ *n* colchão *m*

matur|e /mə'tjʊə(r)/ *a* maduro, amadurecido ● *vt/i* amadurecer; *Comm* vencer-se. **~ity** *n* madureza *f*, maturidade *f*; *Comm* vencimento *m*

maul /mɔːl/ *vt* maltratar, atacar

Mauritius /məˈrɪʃəs/ *n* Ilha *f* Maurícia

mausoleum /mɔːsəˈlɪəm/ *n* mausoléu *m*

mauve /məʊv/ *a & n* lilás *m*

maxim /ˈmæksɪm/ *n* máxima *f*

maxim|um /ˈmæksɪməm/ *a & n* (*pl* **-ima**) máximo *m*. **~ize** *vt* aumentar ao máximo, maximizar

---

may /meɪ/ ● *v aux* (*pt* **might**)

····➤ (*possibility*) poder; **he ~ come** talvez ele venha; **he ~ have missed his train** ele pode ter perdido o trem; **it ~ rain** talvez chova

····➤ (*permission*) **you ~ leave** pode ir; **~ I smoke?** posso fumar?

····➤ (*wish*) **~ he be happy** que ele seja feliz; **~ the best man win!** que ganhe o melhor!

····➤ (*in phrases*) **I ~ as well go** bem que eu podia ir embora; **we ~ as well give up** bem que podíamos desistir

---

May /meɪ/ *n* maio. **M~ Day** *n* o primeiro de maio

maybe /ˈmeɪbiː/ *adv* talvez

mayhem /ˈmeɪhem/ *n* (*disorder*) distúrbios *mpl* violentos; (*havoc*) estragos *mpl*

mayonnaise /meɪəˈneɪz/ *n* maionese *f*

mayor /meə(r)/ *n* prefeito *m*. **~ess** *n* prefeita *f*; (*mayor's wife*) mulher *f* do prefeito

maze /meɪz/ *n* labirinto *m*

me /miː/ *pron* me; (*after prep*) mim; **with ~** comigo; **he knows ~** ele me conhece; **it's ~** sou eu

meadow /ˈmedəʊ/ *n* prado *m*, campina *f*

meagre /ˈmiːgə(r)/ *a* (*thin*) magro; (*scanty*) escasso

meal[1] /miːl/ *n* refeição *f*

meal[2] /miːl/ *n* (*grain*) farinha *f* grossa

mean[1] /miːn/ *a* (**-er, -est**) mesquinho; (*unkind*) mau

mean[2] /miːn/ *a* médio; **Greenwich ~ time** tempo *m* médio de Greenwich ● *n* média *f*

mean[3] /miːn/ *vt* (*pt* **meant**) (*intend*) tencionar or ter (a) intenção (**to** de); (*signify*) querer dizer, significar; (*entail*) dar em resultado, resultar provavelmente em; (*refer to*) referir-se a; **be meant for** destinar-se a; **I didn't ~ it** desculpe, foi sem querer; **he ~s what he says** ele está falando sério, (*P*) ele está a falar a sério

meaning /ˈmiːnɪŋ/ *n* sentido *m*, significado *m*. **~ful** *a* significativo. **~less** *a* sem sentido

means /miːnz/ *n* meio(s) *m(pl)* ● *npl* meios *mpl* pecuniários, recursos *mpl*; **by ~ of** por meio de, através de; **by all ~** com certeza; **by no ~** de modo nenhum

meant /ment/ ▶ MEAN[3]

mean|time /ˈmiːntaɪm/ *adv* **(in the) ~time** entretanto. **~while** /-waɪl/ *adv* entretanto

measles /ˈmiːzlz/ *n* sarampo *m*; **German ~** rubéola *f*

measly /ˈmiːzlɪ/ *a* ⊠ miserável; ínfimo

measure /ˈmeʒə(r)/ *n* medida *f* ● *vt/i* medir; **made to ~** feito sob medida; **~ up to** mostrar-se à altura de, (*P*) à medida. **~d** *a* medido, calculado. **~ment** *n* medida *f*

meat /miːt/ *n* carne *f*. **~y** *a* carnudo; *fig* (*substantial*) substancial

mechanic /mɪˈkænɪk/ *n* mecânico *m*

mechanic|al /mɪˈkænɪkl/ *a* mecânico. **~s** *n* mecânica *f* ● *npl* mecanismo *m*

mechan|ism /ˈmekənɪzəm/ *n* mecanismo *m*. **~ize** *vt* mecanizar

medal /ˈmedl/ *n* medalha *f*. **~list** *n* condecorado *m*; **be a gold ~list** ser medalha de ouro

medallion /mɪˈdælɪən/ *n* medalhão *m*

meddle /ˈmedl/ *vi* (*interfere*) imiscuir-se; intrometer-se (**in** em); (*tinker*) mexer (**with** em). **~some** *a* intrometido, abelhudo

media /ˈmiːdɪə/ ▶ MEDIUM *npl*; **the ~** a mídia, (*P*) os media *mpl*, os meios de comunicação social or de massa

mediat|e /ˈmiːdɪeɪt/ *vi* servir de intermediário, mediar. **~ion** /-ˈeɪʃn/ *n* mediação *f*. **~or** *n* mediador *m*, intermediário *m*

medical /ˈmedɪkl/ *a* médico ● *n* ⊡ (*examination*) exame *m* médico

medicat|ed /ˈmedɪkeɪtɪd/ *a* medicinal. **~ion** /-ˈkeɪʃn/ *n* medicamentação *f*, medicação *f*

medicinal /mɪˈdɪsɪnl/ *a* medicinal

medicine /ˈmedsn/ *n* medicina *f*; (*substance*) remédio *m*, medicamento *m*

medieval /medɪˈiːvl/ *a* medieval

mediocr|e /miːdɪˈəʊkə(r)/ *a* medíocre. **~ity** /-ˈɒkrətɪ/ *n* mediocridade *f*

meditat|e /ˈmedɪteɪt/ *vt/i* meditar. **~ion** /-ˈteɪʃn/ *n* meditação *f*

m

Mediterranean /medɪtə'reɪnɪən/ *a* mediterrâneo ● *n* **the M~** o Mediterrâneo

medium /'mi:dɪəm/ *n* (*pl* **media**) meio *m* (*pl* **mediums**) (*person*) médium *mf* ● *a* médio; **~ wave** *Radio* onda *f* média; **the happy ~** o meio-termo

medley /'medlɪ/ *n* (*pl* **-eys**) miscelânea *f*

meek /mi:k/ *a* (**-er**, **-est**) manso, submisso, sofrido

meet /mi:t/ *vt* (*pt* **met**) encontrar; (*intentionally*) encontrar-se com, ir ter com; (*at station etc*) ir esperar, ir buscar; (*make the acquaintance of*) conhecer; (*conform with*) ir ao encontro de, satisfazer; ‹*opponent, obligation etc*› fazer face a; ‹*bill, expenses*› pagar ● *vi* encontrar-se; (*get acquainted*) familiarizar-se; (*in session*) reunir-se; **~ with** encontrar; ‹*accident, misfortune*› sofrer, ter

meeting /'mi:tɪŋ/ *n* reunião *f*, encontro *m*; (*between two people*) encontro *m*. **~ place** *n* ponto *m* de encontro

megalomania /megələʊ'meɪnɪə/ *n* megalomania *f*, mania *f* de grandeza, (*P*) das grandezas

m

megaphone /'megəfəʊn/ *n* megafone *m*, porta-voz *m*

melancholy /'melənkɒlɪ/ *n* melancolia *f* ● *a* melancólico

mellow /'meləʊ/ *a* (**-er**, **-est**) ‹*fruit, person*› amadurecido, maduro; ‹*sound, colour*› quente, suave ● *vt/i* amadurecer; (*soften*) suavizar

melodious /mɪ'ləʊdɪəs/ *a* melodioso

melodrama /'melədrɑ:mə/ *n* melodrama *m*. **~tic** /-ə'mætɪk/ *a* melodramático

melod|y /'melədɪ/ *n* melodia *f*. **~ic** /mɪ'lɒdɪk/ *a* melódico

melon /'melən/ *n* melão *m*

melt /melt/ *vt/i* ‹*metals*› fundir(-se); ‹*butter, snow etc*› derreter(-se); (*fade away*) desvanecer(-se). **~ing pot** *n* cadinho *m*

member /'membə(r)/ *n* membro *m*; (*of club etc*) sócio *m*; **M~ of Parliament** deputado *m*. **~ship** *n* qualidade *f* de sócio; (*members*) número *m* de sócios; (*fee*) cota *f*; **~ship card** carteira *f*, (*P*) cartão *m* de sócio

memento /mɪ'mentəʊ/ *n* (*pl* **-oes**) lembrança *f*, recordação *f*

memo /'meməʊ/ *n* (*pl* **-os**) [I] nota *f*; apontamento *m*; lembrete *m*

memoir /'memwɑ:(r)/ *n* (*record, essay*) memória *f*, memorial *m*. **~s** *npl* memórias *fpl*

memorable /'memərəbl/ *a* memorável

memorandum /memə'rændəm/ *n* (*pl* **-da**, *or* **-dums**) nota *f*, lembrete *m*; (*diplomatic*) memorando *m*

memorial /mɪ'mɔ:rɪəl/ *n* monumento *m* comemorativo ● *a* comemorativo

memorize /'meməraɪz/ *vt* decorar, memorizar, aprender de cor

memory /'memərɪ/ *n* memória *f*; **from ~** de memória, de cor; **in ~ of** em memória de. **~ stick** *n* pente *m* de memória, (*P*) dispositivo *m* de memória externa or pen*f*

men /men/ ▶ MAN

menac|e /'menəs/ *n* ameaça *f*; (*nuisance*) praga *f*, chaga *f* ● *vt* ameaçar

mend /mend/ *vt* consertar, reparar; (*darn*) remendar; **~ one's ways** corrigir-se, emendar-se ● *n* conserto *m*; (*darn*) remendo *m*; **on the ~** melhorando

menial /'mi:nɪəl/ *a* humilde

meningitis /menɪn'dʒaɪtɪs/ *n* meningite *f*

menopause /'menəpɔ:z/ *n* menopausa *f*

menstruation /menstrʊ'eɪʃn/ *n* menstruação *f*

mental /'mentl/ *a* mental; ‹*hospital*› de doentes mentais, psiquiátrico

mentality /men'tælətɪ/ *n* mentalidade *f*

mention /'menʃn/ *vt* mencionar; **don't ~ it**! não tem de quê, de nada ● *n* menção *f*

menu /'menju:/ *n* (*pl* **-us**) menu *m*, (*P*) ementa *f*

merchandise /'mɜ:tʃəndaɪz/ *n* mercadorias *fpl* ● *vt/i* negociar

merchant /'mɜ:tʃənt/ *n* mercador *m* ● *a* ‹*ship, navy*› mercante; **~ bank** banco *m* comercial

merciful /'mɜ:sɪfl/ *a* misericordioso

merciless /'mɜ:sɪlɪs/ *a* impiedoso, sem dó

mercury /'mɜ:kjʊrɪ/ *n* mercúrio *m*

mercy /'mɜ:sɪ/ *n* piedade *f*, misericórdia *f*; **at the ~ of** à mercê de

mere /mɪə(r)/ *a* mero, simples. **~ly** *adv* meramente, simplesmente, apenas

merge /mɜ:dʒ/ *vt/i* fundir(-se), amalgamar(-se); *Comm* ‹*companies*› fundir(-se). **~r** /-ə(r)/ *n* fusão *f*

meringue /mə'ræŋ/ *n* merengue *m*, suspiro *m*

merit /'merɪt/ *n* mérito *m* ● *vt* (*pt* **merited**) merecer

mermaid /'mɜ:meɪd/ *n* sereia *f*

merriment /'merɪmənt/ *n* divertimento *m*, alegria *f*, folguedo *m*

merry /'merɪ/ *a* (**-ier**, **-iest**) alegre, divertido; **~ Christmas** Feliz Natal. **~-go-round** *n* carrossel *m*; **~making** *n* festa *f*, divertimento *m*

mesh /meʃ/ *n* malha *f*

mess /mes/ *n* (*disorder*) desordem *f*, trapalhada *f*; (*trouble*) embrulhada *f*, trapalhada *f*; (*dirt*) porcaria *f*; *Mil* (*place*) cantina *f*, messe *f*; *Mil* (*food*) rancho *m*; **make a ~ of** estragar ● *vt* **~ up** (*make untidy*) desarrumar; (*make dirty*) sujar; (*confuse*) atrapalhar, estragar ● *vi* **~ about** perder tempo; (*behave foolishly*) fazer asneiras; **~ about with** (*tinker with*) entreter-se com, andar às voltas com

message /'mesɪdʒ/ *n* mensagem *f*; (*informal*) recado *m*

messenger /'mesɪndʒə(r)/ *n* mensageiro *m*

Messiah /mɪ'saɪə/ *n* Messias *m*

messy /'mesɪ/ *a* (**-ier**, **-iest**) desarrumado, bagunçado; (*dirty*) sujo, porco

met /met/ ▶ MEET

metabolism /mɪ'tæbəlɪzm/ *n* metabolismo *m*

metal /'metl/ *n* metal *m* ● *a* de metal. **~lic** /mɪ'tælɪk/ *a* metálico; ‹*paint, colour*› metalizado

metaphor /'metəfə(r)/ *n* metáfora *f*. **~ical** /-'fɒrɪkl/ *a* metafôrico, (*P*) metafórico

meteor /'mi:tɪə(r)/ *n* meteoro *m*

meteorolog|y /mi:tɪə'rɒlədʒɪ/ *n* meteorologia *f*. **~ical** /-ə'lɒdʒɪkl/ *a* meteorológico

meter[1] /'mi:tə(r)/ *n* contador *m*

meter[2] /'mi:tə(r)/ *n Amer* ▶ METRE

method /'meθəd/ *n* método *m*

methodical /mɪ'θɒdɪkl/ *a* metódico

Methodist /'meθədɪst/ *n* metodista *mf*

methylated /'meθɪleɪtɪd/ *a* **~ spirit** álcool *m* metílico

meticulous /mɪ'tɪkjʊləs/ *a* meticuloso

metre /'mi:tə(r)/ *n* metro *m*

metric /'metrɪk/ *a* métrico

metropol|is /mə'trɒpəlɪs/ *n* metrópole *f*. **~itan** /metrə'pɒlɪtən/ *a* metropolitano

mettle /'metl/ *n* têmpera *f*, caráter *m*; (*spirit*) brio *m*

mew /mju:/ *n* miado *m* ● *vi* miar

Mexic|o /'meksɪkəʊ/ *n* México *m*. **~an** *a & n* mexicano *m*

miaow /mi:'aʊ/ *n & vi* = MEW

mice /maɪs/ ▶ MOUSE

mickey /'mɪkɪ/ *n* **take the ~ out of** ⊠ fazer troça de, gozar ⊡

micro- /'maɪkrəʊ/ *pref* micro-

microchip /'maɪkrəʊtʃɪp/ *n* microchip *m*

microfilm /'maɪkrəʊfɪlm/ *n* microfilme *m*

microlight /'maɪkrəʊlaɪt/ *n Aviat* ultraleve *m*

microphone /'maɪkrəfəʊn/ *n* microfone *m*

microscop|e /'maɪkrəskəʊp/ *n* microscópio *m*. **~ic** /-'skɒpɪk/ *a* microscópico

microwave /'maɪkrəʊweɪv/ *n* micro-onda *f*; **~ oven** forno *m* de micro-ondas, (*P*) micro-ondas *m*

mid /mɪd/ *a* meio; **in ~-air** no ar, em pleno voo; **in ~-March** em meados de março

midday /mɪd'deɪ/ *n* meio-dia *m*

middle /'mɪdl/ *a* médio, meio; (*quality*) médio, mediano; **M~ Ages** Idade *f* Média; **~ class** classe *f* média; **M~ East** Médio Oriente *m*; **~ name** segundo nome *m* ● *n* meio *m*; **in the ~ of** no meio de. **~-aged** *a* de meia idade; **~-class** *a* burguês

middleman /'mɪdlmæn/ *n* (*pl* **-men**) intermediário *m*

midge /mɪdʒ/ *n* mosquito *m*

midget /'mɪdʒɪt/ *n* anão *m* ● *a* minúsculo

Midlands /'mɪdləndz/ *npl* região *f* do centro da Inglaterra

midnight /'mɪdnaɪt/ *n* meia-noite *f*

midriff /'mɪdrɪf/ *n* diafragma *m*; (*abdomen*) ventre *m*

midst /mɪdst/ *n* **in the ~ of** no meio de

midsummer /mɪd'sʌmə(r)/ *n* pleno verão *m*; (*solstice*) solstício *m* do verão

midway /mɪd'weɪ/ *adv* a meio caminho

midwife /'mɪdwaɪf/ *n* (*pl* **-wives**) parteira *f*

m

might[1] /maɪt/ *n* potência *f*; (*strength*) força *f*. **~y** *a* poderoso; *fig* (*great*) imenso ● *adv* [!] muito

might[2] /maɪt/ ▶ MAY

migraine /'mi:greɪn/ *n* enxaqueca *f*

migrant /'maɪgrənt/ *a* migratório ● *n* (*person*) migrante *mf*, emigrante *mf*

migrat|e /maɪ'greɪt/ *vi* migrar. **~ion** /-ʃn/ *n* migração *f*

mike /maɪk/ *n* [!] microfone *m*

mild /maɪld/ *a* (**-er**, **-est**) brando, manso; ‹*illness, taste*› leve; ‹*climate*› temperado; ‹*weather*› ameno. **~ly** *adv* brandamente, mansamente; **to put it ~ly** para não dizer coisa pior. **~ness** *n* brandura *f*

mildew /'mɪldju:/ *n* bolor *m*, mofo *m*; (*in plants*) míldio *m*

mile /maɪl/ *n* milha *f* (=*1,6 km*); **~s too big**/*etc* [!] grande demais, (*P*) demasiado grande. **~age** *n* (*loosely*) quilometragem *f*

milestone /'maɪlstəʊn/ *n* marco *m* miliário; *fig* data *f* or acontecimento *m* importante, marco *m*

militant /'mɪlɪtənt/ *a* & *n* militante *mf*

m

military /'mɪlɪtrɪ/ *a* militar

milk /mɪlk/ *n* leite *m* ● *a* (*product*) lácteo ● *vt* ordenhar; *fig* (*exploit*) explorar. **~shake** *n* milk-shake *m*, batido *m*. **~y** *a* (*like milk*) leitoso; ‹*tea etc*› com muito leite; **M~y Way** Via *f* Láctea

milkman /'mɪlkmən/ *n* (*pl* **-men**) leiteiro *m*

mill /mɪl/ *n* moinho *m*; (*factory*) fábrica *f* ● *vt* moer ● *vi* **~ around** aglomerar-se; ‹*crowd*› apinhar-se. **pepper-~** *n* moedor *m* de pimenta

millennium /mɪ'lenɪəm/ *n* (*pl* **-iums**, *or* **-ia**) milênio *m*, (*P*) milénio *m*

millet /'mɪlɪt/ *n* painço *m*, milhete *m*

milligram /'mɪlɪgræm/ *n* miligrama *m*

millilitre /'mɪlɪli:tə(r)/ *n* mililitro *m*

millimetre /'mɪlɪmi:tə(r)/ *n* milímetro *m*

million /'mɪlɪən/ *n* milhão *m*; **a ~ pounds** um milhão de libras. **~aire** /-'neə(r)/ *n* milionário *m*

mime /maɪm/ *n* mímica *f*; (*actor*) mímico *m* ● *vt/i* exprimir por mímica, mimar

mimic /'mɪmɪk/ *vt* (*pt* **mimicked**) imitar ● *n* imitador *m*, parodiante *mf*

mince /mɪns/ *vt* picar ● *n* carne *f* moída, (*P*) carne *f* picada. **~ pie** *n* pastel *m* recheado com massa de passas, amêndoas, especiarias etc. **~r** *n* máquina *f* de moer

mincemeat /'mɪnsmi:t/ *n* massa *f* de passas, amêndoas, especiarias etc usada para recheio; **make ~ of** [!] arrasar, aniquilar

mind *n* espírito *m*, mente *f*; (*intellect*) intelecto *m*; (*sanity*) razão *f*; **to be out of one's ~** estar fora de si; **have a good ~ to** estar disposto a; **make up one's ~** decidir-se; **presence of ~** presença *f* de espírito; **to my ~** a meu ver ● *vt* (*look after*) tomar conta de, tratar de; (*heed*) prestar atenção a; (*object to*) importar-se com, incomodar-se com; **do you ~ if I smoke?** você se incomoda or (*P*) importa-se que eu fume?; **do you ~ helping me?** quer fazer o favor de me ajudar?; **never ~** não se importe, não tem importância; **~ful of** atento a, consciente de. **~less** *a* insensato

minder /'maɪndə(r)/ *n* pessoa *f* que toma conta de crianças *mf*; (*bodyguard*) guarda-costas *mf*

mine[1] /maɪn/ *poss pron* o(s) meu(s), a(s) minha(s); **it is ~** é (o) meu or (a) minha

min|e[2] /maɪn/ *n* mina *f* ● *vt* escavar, explorar; (*extract*) extrair; *Mil* minar. **~er** *n* mineiro *m*. **~ing** *n* exploração *f* mineira ● *a* mineiro

minefield /'maɪnfi:ld/ *n* campo *m* minado

mineral /'mɪnərəl/ *n* mineral *m*; (*soft drink*) bebida *f* gasosa; **~ water** água *f* mineral

minesweeper /'maɪnswi:pə(r)/ *n* caça-minas *m*

mingle /'mɪŋgl/ *vt/i* misturar(-se) (**with** com)

miniature /'mɪnɪtʃə(r)/ *n* miniatura *f* ● *a* miniatural

minibus /'mɪnɪbʌs/ *n* (*public*) micro-ônibus *m*, (*P*) autocarro *m* pequeno, miniautocarro *m*

minim|um /'mɪnɪməm/ *a* & *n* (*pl* **-ma**) mínimo *m*. **~al** *a* mínimo. **~ize** *vt* minimizar, dar pouca importância a

miniskirt /'mɪnɪskɜ:t/ *n* minissaia *f*

minist|er /'mɪnɪstə(r)/ *n* ministro *m*; *Relig* pastor *m*. **~erial** /-'stɪərɪəl/ *a* ministerial. **~ry** *n* ministério *m*

mink /mɪŋk/ *n* (*fur*) marta *f*, visão *m*

minor /'maɪnə(r)/ *a* & *n* menor *mf*

minority /maɪ'nɒrətɪ/ *n* minoria *f* ● *a* minoritário

mint[1] /mɪnt/ *n* **the M~** a Casa da Moeda; **a ~** uma fortuna; **in ~**

condition em perfeito estado, como novo, impecável ● *vt* cunhar

mint² /mɪnt/ *n* (*plant*) hortelã *f*; (*sweet*) pastilha *f* de hortelã

minus /ˈmaɪnəs/ *prep* menos; [!] (*without*) sem ● *n* menos *m*

minute¹ /ˈmɪnɪt/ *n* minuto *m*; **~s** (*of meeting*) ata *f*

minute² /maɪˈnjuːt/ *a* diminuto, minúsculo; (*detailed*) minucioso

mirac|le /ˈmɪrəkl/ *n* milagre *m*. **~ulous** /mɪˈrækjʊləs/ *a* milagroso, miraculoso

mirage /ˈmɪrɑːʒ/ *n* miragem *f*

mire /maɪə(r)/ *n* lodo *m*, lama *f*

mirror /ˈmɪrə(r)/ *n* espelho *m*; (*in car*) retrovisor *m* ● *vt* refletir, espelhar

mirth /mɜːθ/ *n* alegria *f*, hilaridade *f*

misadventure /mɪsədˈventʃə(r)/ *n* desgraça *f*; **death by ~** morte *f* acidental

misanthropist /mɪsˈænθrəpɪst/ *n* misantropo *m*

misapprehension /mɪsæprɪˈhenʃn/ *n* mal-entendido *m*

misbehav|e /mɪsbɪˈheɪv/ *vi* portar-se mal, proceder mal. **~iour** /-ˈheɪvɪə(r)/ *n* mau comportamento *m*, má conduta *f*

miscalculat|e /mɪsˈkælkjʊleɪt/ *vi* calcular mal, enganar-se. **~ion** /-ˈleɪʃn/ *n* erro *m* de cálculo

miscarr|y /mɪsˈkærɪ/ *vi* abortar (espontaneamente), ter um aborto (espontâneo); (*fail*) falhar, malograr-se. **~iage** /-ɪdʒ/ *n* aborto (espontâneo) *m*; **~iage of justice** erro *m* judiciário

miscellaneous /mɪsəˈleɪnɪəs/ *a* variado, diverso

mischief /ˈmɪstʃɪf/ *n* (*of children*) diabrura *f*, travessura *f*; (*harm*) mal *m*, dano *m*; **get into ~** fazer disparates; **make ~** criar or semear discórdias

mischievous /ˈmɪstʃɪvəs/ *a* endiabrado, travesso

misconception /mɪskənˈsepʃn/ *n* ideia *f* errada, (*P*) ideia *f*, falso conceito *m*

misconduct /mɪsˈkɒndʌkt/ *n* conduta *f* imprópria

misconstrue /mɪskənˈstruː/ *vt* interpretar mal

misdemeanour /mɪsdɪˈmiːnə(r)/ *n* delito *m*

miser /ˈmaɪzə(r)/ *n* avarento *m*, sovina *mf*. **~ly** *a* avarento, sovina

miserable /ˈmɪzrəbl/ *a* infeliz; (*wretched, mean*) desgraçado, miserável

misery /ˈmɪzərɪ/ *n* infelicidade *f*

misfire /mɪsˈfaɪə(r)/ *vi* ‹*plan, gun, engine*› falhar

misfit /ˈmɪsfɪt/ *n* inadaptado *m*

misfortune /mɪsˈfɔːtʃən/ *n* desgraça *f*, infelicidade *f*, pouca sorte *f*

misgiving(s) /mɪsˈgɪvɪŋ(z)/ *n(pl)* dúvida(s) *f(pl)*, receio(s) *m(pl)*

misguided /mɪsˈgaɪdɪd/ *a* (*mistaken*) desencaminhado; (*misled*) mal aconselhado, enganado

mishap /ˈmɪshæp/ *n* contratempo *m*, desastre *m*

misinform /mɪsɪnˈfɔːm/ *vt* informar mal

misinterpret /mɪsɪnˈtɜːprɪt/ *vt* interpretar mal

misjudge /mɪsˈdʒʌdʒ/ *vt* julgar mal

mislay /mɪsˈleɪ/ *vt* (*pt* **mislaid**) perder, extraviar

mislead /mɪsˈliːd/ *vt* (*pt* **misled**) induzir em erro, enganar. **~ing** *a* enganador

mismanage /mɪsˈmænɪdʒ/ *vt* dirigir mal. **~ment** *n* má gestão *f*, desgoverno *m*

misnomer /mɪsˈnəʊmə(r)/ *n* termo *m* impróprio

misogynist /mɪˈsɒdʒɪnɪst/ *n* misógino *m*

misprint /ˈmɪsprɪnt/ *n* erro *m* tipográfico

mispronounce /mɪsprəˈnaʊns/ *vt* pronunciar mal

misquote /mɪsˈkwəʊt/ *vt* citar incorretamente

misread /mɪsˈriːd/ *vt* (*pt* **misread** /-ˈred/) ler or interpretar mal

misrepresent /mɪsreprɪˈzent/ *vt* deturpar, desvirtuar

miss /mɪs/ *vt/i* ‹*chance, bus etc*› perder; ‹*target*› errar, falhar; (*notice the loss of*) dar pela falta de; (*regret the absence of*) sentir a falta de, ter saudades de; **he ~es her/Portugal** ele sente a falta or tem saudades dela/de Portugal/*etc*; **~ out** omitir; **~ the point** não compreender ● *n* falha *f*; **it was a near ~** foi or escapou por um triz

Miss /mɪs/ *n* (*pl* **Misses**) Senhorita *f*, (*P*) Menina *f*

missile /ˈmɪsaɪl/ *n* míssil *m*; (*object thrown*) projétil *m*

missing /ˈmɪsɪŋ/ *a* que falta; (*lost*) perdido; ‹*person*› desaparecido; **a book with a page ~** um livro com uma página a menos

mission /ˈmɪʃn/ *n* missão *f*

m

missionary /'mɪʃənrɪ/ *n* missionário *m*
misspell /mɪs'spel/ *vt* (*pt* **misspelt** *or* **misspelled**) escrever mal
mist /mɪst/ *n* neblina *f*, névoa *f*, bruma *f*; *fig* névoa *f* ● *vt/i* enevoar(-se); ‹*window*› embaçar(-se)
mistake /mɪ'steɪk/ *n* engano *m*, erro *m* ● *vt* (*pt* **mistook**, *pp* **mistaken**) compreender mal; (*choose wrongly*) enganar-se em; **~ for** confundir com, tomar por. **~n** /-ən/ *a* errado; **be ~n** enganar-se. **~nly** /-ənlɪ/ *adv* por engano
mistletoe /'mɪsltəʊ/ *n* visco *m*
mistreat /mɪs'tri:t/ *vt* maltratar
mistress /'mɪstrɪs/ *n* senhora *f*, dona *f*; (*teacher*) professora *f*; (*lover*) amante *f*
mistrust /mɪs'trʌst/ *vt* desconfiar de, duvidar de ● *n* desconfiança *f*
misty /'mɪstɪ/ *a* (**-ier**, **-iest**) enevoado, brumoso; ‹*window*› embaçado; (*indistinct*) indistinto
misunderstand /mɪsʌndə'stænd/ *vt* (*pt* **-stood**) compreender mal. **~ing** *n* mal-entendido *m*
misuse[1] /mɪs'ju:z/ *vt* empregar mal; ‹*power etc*› abusar de

misuse[2] /mɪs'ju:s/ *n* mau uso *m*; (*abuse*) abuso *m*; (*of funds*) desvio *m*
mitten /'mɪtn/ *n* luva *f* com uma única divisão entre o polegar e os dedos, mitene *f*
mix /mɪks/ *vt/i* misturar(-se); **~ with** associar-se com; **~ up** misturar bem; *fig* (*confuse*) confundir ● *n* mistura *f*. **~-up** *n* trapalhada *f*, confusão *f*. **~er** *n* *Culin* batedeira *f*
mixed /mɪkst/ *a* ‹*school etc*› misto; (*assorted*) sortido; **be ~ up** [!] estar confuso
mixed-race *a* ‹*couple, marriage*› mestiço
mixture /'mɪkstʃə(r)/ *n* mistura *f*; **cough ~** xarope *m* para a tosse
MMS *abbr* (= **Multimedia Messaging Service**) MMS *m*
moan /məʊn/ *n* gemido *m* ● *vi* gemer; (*complain*) queixar-se; lastimar-se (**about** de)
moat /məʊt/ *n* fosso *m*
mob /mɒb/ *n* multidão *f*; (*tumultuous*) turba *f*; [×] (*gang*) bando *m* ● *vt* (*pt* **mobbed**) cercar, assediar
mobil|e /'məʊbaɪl/ *a* móvel; **~e home** caravana *f*, trailer *m*; **~e phone** celular *m* ● *n* celular *m*, (*P*) telemóvel *m*; **don't forget to switch your ~ off** não se esquece de desligar o celular, (*P*) não te esqueças de desligar o telemóvel. **~ity** /-'bɪlətɪ/ *n* mobilidade *f*
mobiliz|e /'məʊbɪlaɪz/ *vt/i* mobilizar
mock /mɒk/ *vt/i* zombar de, gozar ● *a* falso. **~-up** *n* maqueta *f*
mockery /'mɒkərɪ/ *n* troça *f*, gozação *f*, (*P*) gozo *m*, (*P*) um gozo *m*; **a ~ of** uma gozação de
mode /məʊd/ *n* modo *m*; (*fashion*) moda *f*
model /'mɒdl/ *n* modelo *m* ● *a* modelo; (*exemplary*) exemplar; (*toy*) em miniatura ● *vt* (*pt* **modelled**) modelar; ‹*clothes*› apresentar ● *vi* ser *or* trabalhar como modelo
modem /'məʊdem/ *n* modem *m*
moderate[1] /'mɒdərət/ *a & n* moderado *m*. **~ly** *adv* moderadamente; **~ly good** sofrível
moderat|e[2] /'mɒdəreɪt/ *vt/i* moderar(-se). **~ion** /-'reɪʃn/ *n* moderação *f*; **in ~ion** com moderação
modern /'mɒdn/ *a* moderno; **~ languages** línguas *fpl* vivas *or* modernas. **~ize** *vt* modernizar
modest /'mɒdɪst/ *a* modesto. **~y** *n* modéstia *f*
modif|y /'mɒdɪfaɪ/ *vt* modificar. **~ication** /-ɪ'keɪʃn/ *n* modificação *f*
module /'mɒdju:l/ *n* módulo *m*
moist /mɔɪst/ *a* (**-er**, **-est**) úmido, (*P*) húmido. **~ure** /'mɔɪstʃə(r)/ *n* umidade *f*, (*P*) humidade *f*. **~urizer** /-tʃəraɪzə(r)/ *n* creme *m* hidratante
moisten /'mɔɪsn/ *vt/i* umedecer, (*P*) humedecer
mole[1] /məʊl/ *n* (*on skin*) sinal *m* na pele
mole[2] /məʊl/ *n* (*animal*) toupeira *f*
molecule /'mɒlɪkju:l/ *n* molécula *f*
molest /mə'lest/ *vt* meter-se com, molestar
mollycoddle /'mɒlɪkɒdl/ *vt* mimar
molten /'məʊltən/ *a* fundido
moment /'məʊmənt/ *n* momento *m*
momentar|y /'məʊməntrɪ/ *a* momentâneo. **~ily** /'məʊməntrəlɪ/ *adv* momentaneamente
momentous /mə'mentəs/ *a* grave, importante
momentum /mə'mentəm/ *n* ímpeto *m*, velocidade *f* adquirida
Monaco /'mɒnəkəʊ/ *n* Mônaco *m*, (*P*) Mónaco *m*

monarch /'mɒnək/ *n* monarca *mf*. **~y** *n* monarquia *f*

monast|ery /'mɒnəstrɪ/ *n* mosteiro *m*, convento *m*. **~ic** /mə-'næstɪk/ *a* monástico

Monday /'mʌndɪ/ *n* segunda-feira *f*

monetary /'mʌnɪtrɪ/ *a* monetário

money /'mʌnɪ/ *n* dinheiro *m*; **~ order** vale *m* postal. **~ box** *n* cofre *m*; **~lender** *n* agiota *mf*, usurário

mongrel /'mʌŋgrəl/ *n* (cão) vira-lata *m*, (*P*) rafeiro *m*

monitor /'mɒnɪtə(r)/ *n* chefe *m* de turma; *Techn* monitor *m* ● *vt* controlar; ‹*a broadcast*› monitorar or monitorizar (a transmissão)

monk /mʌŋk/ *n* monge *m*, frade *m*

monkey /'mʌŋkɪ/ *n* (*pl* **-eys**) macaco *m*. **~ nut** *n* amendoim *m*

mono /'mɒnəʊ/ *n* (*pl* **-os**) gravação *f* mono ● *a* mono *invar*

monogram /'mɒnəgræm/ *n* monograma *m*

monologue /'mɒnəlɒg/ *n* monólogo *m*

monopol|y /mə'nɒpəlɪ/ *n* monopólio *m*. **~ize** *vt* monopolizar

monosyllab|le /'mɒnəsɪləbl/ *n* monossílabo *m*. **~ic** /-'læbɪk/ *a* monossilábico

monotone /'mɒnətəʊn/ *n* tom *m* uniforme

monoton|ous /mə'nɒtənəs/ *a* monótono. **~y** *n* monotonia *f*

monsoon /mɒn'su:n/ *n* monção *f*

monst|er /'mɒnstə(r)/ *n* monstro *m*. **~rous** *a* monstruoso

monstrosity /mɒn'strɒsətɪ/ *n* monstruosidade *f*

month /mʌnθ/ *n* mês *m*

monthly /'mʌnθlɪ/ *a* mensal ● *adv* mensalmente ● *n* (*periodical*) revista *f* mensal

monument /'mɒnjʊmənt/ *n* monumento *m*. **~al** /-'mentl/ *a* monumental

moo /mu:/ *n* mugido *m* ● *vi* mugir

mood /mu:d/ *n* humor *m*, disposição *f*; **in a good/bad ~** de bom/mau humor. **~y** *a* de humor instável; (*sullen*) carrancudo

moon /mu:n/ *n* lua *f*

moon|light /'mu:nlaɪt/ *n* luar *m*. **~lit** *a* iluminado pela lua, enluarado

moonlighting /'mu:nlaɪtɪŋ/ *n* [!] segundo emprego *m*; esp à noite

moor[1] /mʊə(r)/ *n* charneca *f*

moor[2] /mʊə(r)/ *vt* amarrar, atracar

moose /mu:s/ (*pl invar*) *n* alce *m*

moot /mu:t/ *a* discutível ● *vt* levantar

mop /mɒp/ *n* esfregão *m* ● *vt* (*pt* **mopped**) **~ (up)** limpar; **~ of hair** trunfa *f*

mope /məʊp/ *vi* estar or andar abatido e triste

moped /'məʊped/ *n* moto *f* pequena, (*P*) motorizada *f*

moral /'mɒrəl/ *a* moral ● *n* moral *f*; **~s** moral *f*, bons costumes *mpl*

morale /mə'rɑ:l/ *n* moral *m*

morality /mə'rælətɪ/ *n* moralidade *f*

morbid /'mɔ:bɪd/ *a* mórbido

more /mɔ:(r)/ *a & adv* mais (**than** (do) que) ● *n* mais *m*; **some ~ tea/pens/** *etc* mais chá/canetas/*etc*; **there is no ~ bread** não há mais pão; **~ or less** mais ou menos

moreover /mɔ:'rəʊvə(r)/ *adv* além disso, de mais a mais

morgue /mɔ:g/ *n* morgue *f*, necrotério *m*

morning /'mɔ:nɪŋ/ *n* manhã *f*; **in the ~** de manhã

Morocc|o /mə'rɒkəʊ/ *n* Marrocos *m*

moron /'mɔ:rɒn/ *n* idiota *mf*

morose /mə'rəʊs/ *a* taciturno e insociável, carrancudo

morphine /'mɔ:fi:n/ *n* morfina *f*

morsel /'mɔ:sl/ *n* bocado (esp de comida) *m*

mortal /'mɔ:tl/ *a & n* mortal *mf*. **~ity** /mɔ:'tælətɪ/ *n* mortalidade *f*

mortar /'mɔ:tə(r)/ *n* argamassa *f*; (*bowl*) almofariz *m*; *Mil* morteiro *m*

mortgage /'mɔ:gɪdʒ/ *n* hipoteca *f* ● *vt* hipotecar

mortify /'mɔ:tɪfaɪ/ *vt* mortificar

mortuary /'mɔ:tʃərɪ/ *n* casa *f* mortuária

mosaic /məʊ'zeɪɪk/ *n* mosaico *m*

Moscow /'mɔskəʊ/ *n* Moscou *m*, (*P*) Moscovo *m*

mosque /mɒsk/ *n* mesquita *f*

mosquito /mə'ski:təʊ/ *n* (*pl* **-oes**) mosquito *m*

moss /mɒs/ *n* musgo *m*. **~y** *a* musgoso

most /məʊst/ *a* o mais, o maior; (*majority*) a maioria de, a maior parte

m

de; **for the ~ part** na maior parte, na grande maioria ● *n* mais *m*; (*majority*) a maioria, a maior parte, o máximo ● *adv* o mais; (*very*) muito; **at ~** no máximo; **make the ~ of** aproveitar ao máximo, tirar o melhor partido de. **~ly** *adv* sobretudo

motel /məʊ'tel/ *n* motel *m*

moth /mɒθ/ *n* mariposa *f*, (*P*) borboleta *f* noturna. **(clothes-)~** *n* traça *f*. **~ball** *n* bola *f* de naftalina

mother /'mʌðə(r)/ *n* mãe *f*; **M~'s Day** o Dia da(s) Mãe(s) ● *vt* tratar como a um filho. **~hood** *n* maternidade *f*. **~-in-law** *n* (*pl* **~s-in-law**) sogra *f*; **~-of-pearl** *n* madrepérola *f*; **~-to-be** *n* futura mãe *f*. **~ly** *a* maternal

motif /məʊ'tiːf/ *n* tema *m*

motion /'məʊʃn/ *n* movimento *m*; (*proposal*) moção *f* ● *vt/i* **~ (to) sb to** fazer sinal a alguém para. **~less** *a* imóvel

motivat|e /'məʊtɪveɪt/ *vt* motivar. **~ion** /-'veɪʃn/ *n* motivação *f*

motive /'məʊtɪv/ *n* motivo *m*

motor /'məʊtə(r)/ *n* motor *m*; (*car*) automóvel *m* ● *a Anat* motor; ‹*boat*› a motor ● *vi* ir de automóvel; **~ bike** ⓘ moto *f* ⓘ; **~ car** carro *m*; **~ cycle** motocicleta *f*; **~ cyclist** motociclista *mf*; **~ vehicle** veículo *m* automóvel. **~ing** *n* automobilismo *m*. **~ized** *a* motorizado

motorist /'məʊtərɪst/ *n* motorista *mf*, automobilista *mf*

motorway /'məʊtəweɪ/ *n* rodovia *f*, (*P*) autoestrada *f*

mottled /'mɒtld/ *a* sarapintado, pintalgado

motto /'mɒtəʊ/ *n* (*pl* **-oes**) divisa *f*, lema *m*

mould[1] /məʊld/ *n* (*container*) forma *f*, molde *m*; *Culin* forma *f* ● *vt* moldar. **~ing** *n Archit* moldura *f*

mould[2] /məʊld/ *n* (*fungi*) bolor *m*, mofo *m*. **~y** *a* bolorento

moult /məʊlt/ *vi* estar na muda

mound /maʊnd/ *n* monte *m* de terra or de pedras; (*small hill*) montículo *m*

mount /maʊnt/ *vt/i* montar ● *n* (*support*) suporte *m*; (*for gem etc*) engaste *m*; **~ up** aumentar, subir

mountain /'maʊntɪn/ *n* montanha *f*; **~ bike** mountain bike *f*, bicicleta *f* de montanha. **~ous** *a* montanhoso

mountaineer /maʊntɪ'nɪə(r)/ *n* alpinista *mf*. **~ing** *n* alpinismo *m*

mourn /mɔːn/ *vt/i* **~ (for)** chorar (a morte de); **~ (over)** sofrer (por). **~er** *n* pessoa *f* que acompanha o enterro. **~ing** *n* luto *m*; **in ~ing** de luto

mournful /'mɔːnfl/ *a* triste; (*sorrowful*) pesaroso

mouse /maʊs/ *n* (*pl* **mice**) camundongo *m*, (*P*) rato *m*. **~mat** *n* mousepad *m*, (*P*) tapete de rato *m*

mousetrap /'maʊstræp/ *n* ratoeira *f*

mousse /muːs/ *n* mousse *f*

moustache /mə'stɑːʃ/ *n* bigode *m*

mouth[1] /maʊθ/ *n* boca *f*

mouth[2] /maʊð/ *vt/i* declamar; (*silently*) articular sem som

mouthful /'maʊθfʊl/ *n* bocado *m*

mouthpiece /'maʊθpiːs/ *n Mus* bocal *m*, boquilha *f*; *fig* (*person*) porta-voz *mf*

mouthwash /'maʊθwɒʃ/ *n* líquido *m* para bochecho

movable /'muːvəbl/ *a* móvel

move /muːv/ *vt/i* mover(-se), mexer(-se), deslocar(-se); (*emotionally*) comover; (*incite*) convencer, levar a; (*act*) agir; (*propose*) propor; (*depart*) ir, partir; (*go forward*) avançar; **~ (out)** mudar-se, sair; **~ back** recuar; **~ forward** avançar; **~ in** mudar-se para; **~ on!** circulem!; **~ over, please** chegue-se para lá, por favor ● *n* movimento *m*; (*in game*) jogada *f*; (*player's turn*) vez *f*; (*house change*) mudança *f*; **on the ~** em marcha

movement /'muːvmənt/ *n* movimento *m*

movie /'muːvɪ/ *n Amer* filme *m*; **the ~s** o cinema

moving /'muːvɪŋ/ *a* (*touching*) comovente; (*movable*) móvil; (*in motion*) em movimento

mow /məʊ/ *vt* (*pp* **mowed**, *or* **mown**) ceifar; ‹*lawn*› cortar a grama, (*P*) relva; **~ down** ceifar. **~er** *n* (*for lawn*) máquina *f* de cortar a grama, (*P*) relva

MP *abbr* (= **Member of Parliament**) ▶ **MEMBER**

MP3 player *n* MP3 *m*

Mr /'mɪstə(r)/ *n* (*pl* **Messrs**) Senhor *m*; **~ Smith** o Sr Smith

Mrs /'mɪsɪz/ *n* Senhora *f*; **~ Smith** a Sra Smith; **Mr and ~ Smith** o Sr Smith e a mulher

Ms /mɪz/ *n* Senhora D. *f*

much /mʌtʃ/ (**more, most**) *a, adv & n* muito *m*; **very ~** muito, muitíssimo; **you may have as ~ as you need** você pode levar o que precisar; **~ of it** muito or grande parte dele; **so ~ the better/ worse** tanto melhor/pior; **how ~?**

quanto?; **not ~** não muito; **too ~** demasiado, demais; **he's not ~ of a gardener** não é lá grande jardineiro

muck /mʌk/ *n* estrume *m*; [!] (*dirt*) porcaria *f* ● *vi* **~ about** ☒ entreter-se, perder tempo; **~ in** ☒ ajudar, dar uma mão ● *vt* **~ up** ☒ estragar. **~y** *a* sujo

mucus /ˈmju:kəs/ *n* muco *m*

mud /mʌd/ *n* lama *f*. **~dy** *a* lamacento, enlameado

muddle /ˈmʌdl/ *vt* baralhar, atrapalhar, confundir ● *vi* **~ through** sair-se bem, desenrascar-se ☒ ● *n* desordem *f*; (*mix-up*) confusão *f*, trapalhada *f*

mudguard /ˈmʌdgɑ:d/ *n* para-lama *m*, (*P*) para-lamas *m*

muffle /ˈmʌfl/ *vt* abafar; **~ (up)** agasalhar(-se); **~d sounds** sons *mpl* abafados. **~r** /-ə(r)/ *n* cachecol *m*

mug /mʌg/ *n* caneca *f*; ☒ (*face*) cara *f*; ☒ (*fool*) trouxa *mf* [!] ● *vt* (*pt* **mugged**) assaltar, agredir. **~ger** *n* assaltante *mf*. **~ging** *n* assalto *m*

muggy /ˈmʌgɪ/ *a* abafado

mule /mju:l/ *n* mulo *m*; (*female*) mula *f*

mull /mʌl/ *vt* **~ over** ruminar; *fig* matutar em

multi- /ˈmʌltɪ/ *pref* mult(i)-

multicoloured /ˈmʌltɪkʌləd/ *a* multicolor

multinational /mʌltɪˈnæʃnəl/ *a & n* multinacional *f*

multiple /ˈmʌltɪpl/ *a & n* múltiplo *m*

multipl|y /ˈmʌltɪplaɪ/ *vt/i* multiplicar(-se). **~ication** /-ɪˈkeɪʃn/ *n* multiplicação *f*

multistorey /mʌltɪˈstɔ:rɪ/ *a* (*car park*) em vários níveis, de vários andares

multitude /ˈmʌltɪtju:d/ *n* multidão *f*

mum[1] /mʌm/ *a* **keep ~** [!] ficar calado

mum[2] /mʌm/ *n* [!] mamãe *f* [!], (*P*) mamã *f* [!]

mumble /ˈmʌmbl/ *vt/i* resmungar, resmonear

mummy[1] /ˈmʌmɪ/ *n* (*body*) múmia *f*

mummy[2] /ˈmʌmɪ/ *n* (*esp child's lang*) mamãe *f*, (*P*) mamã *f*, mãezinha *f* [!]

mumps /mʌmps/ *n* caxumba *f*, parotidite *f*, papeira *f*

munch /mʌntʃ/ *vt* mastigar

mundane /mʌnˈdeɪn/ *a* banal; (*worldly*) mundano

municipal /mju:ˈnɪsɪpl/ *a* municipal. **~ity** /-ˈpælətɪ/ *n* municipalidade *f*

munitions /mju:ˈnɪʃnz/ *npl* munições *fpl*

mural /ˈmjʊərəl/ *a & n* mural *m*

murder /ˈmɜ:də(r)/ *n* assassínio *m*, assassinato *m* ● *vt* assassinar. **~er** *n* assassino *m*, assassina *f*. **~ous** *a* assassino, sanguinário; (*of weapon*) mortífero

murky /ˈmɜ:kɪ/ *a* (**-ier**, **-iest**) escuro, sombrio

murmur /ˈmɜ:mə(r)/ *n* murmúrio *m* ● *vt/i* murmurar

muscle /ˈmʌsl/ *n* músculo *m* ● *vi* **~ in** [!] impor-se, intrometer-se

muscular /ˈmʌskjʊlə(r)/ *a* muscular; (*brawny*) musculoso

muse /mju:z/ *vi* meditar, cismar

museum /mju:ˈzɪəm/ *n* museu *m*

mush /mʌʃ/ *n* papa *f* de farinha de milho. **~y** *a* mole; (*sentimental*) piegas *inv*

mushroom /ˈmʌʃrʊm/ *n* cogumelo *m* ● *vi* pulular, multiplicar-se com rapidez

music /ˈmju:zɪk/ *n* música *f*. **~al** *a* musical ● *n* (*show*) comédia *f* musical, musical *m*. **~al box** *n* caixa *f* de música; **~ stand** *n* estante *f* de música

musician /mju:ˈzɪʃn/ *n* músico *m*

musk /mʌsk/ *n* almíscar *m*

Muslim /ˈmʊzlɪm/ *a & n* muçulmano *m*

mussel /ˈmʌsl/ *n* mexilhão *m*

must /mʌst/ *v aux* dever; **you ~ go** é necessário que você parta; **he ~ be old** ele deve ser velho; **I ~ have done it** eu devo tê-lo feito ● *n* **be a ~** [!] ser imprescindível

mustard /ˈmʌstəd/ *n* mostarda *f*

muster /ˈmʌstə(r)/ *vt/i* juntar(-se), reunir(-se); **pass ~** ser aceitável

musty /ˈmʌstɪ/ *a* (**-ier**, **-iest**) mofado, bolorento

mutation /mju:ˈteɪʃn/ *n* mutação *f*

mute /mju:t/ *a & n* mudo *m*

muted /ˈmju:tɪd/ *a* ‹*sound*› em surdina; ‹*colour*› suave

mutilat|e /ˈmju:tɪleɪt/ *vt* mutilar. **~ion** /-ˈleɪʃn/ *n* mutilação *f*

mutin|y /ˈmju:tɪnɪ/ *n* motim *f* ● *vi* amotinar-se. **~ous** *a* amotinado

mutter /ˈmʌtə(r)/ *vt/i* resmungar

mutton /ˈmʌtn/ *n* (carne de) carneiro *m*

mutual /ˈmju:tʃʊəl/ *a* mútuo; [!] (*common*) comum. **~ly** *adv* mutuamente

muzzle /ˈmʌzl/ *n* focinho *m*; (*device*) focinheira *f*, (*P*) açaime *m*; (*of gun*) boca *f*

● *vt* amordaçar; ‹*dog*› pôr focinheira(*P*) açaime em
my /maɪ/ *a* meu(s), minha(s)
myself /maɪˈself/ *pron* eu mesmo, eu próprio; (*reflexive*) me; (*after prep*) mim (próprio, mesmo); **by ~** sozinho
mysterious /mɪˈstɪərɪəs/ *a* misterioso
mystery /ˈmɪstərɪ/ *n* mistério *m*
mystic /ˈmɪstɪk/ *a & n* místico *m*. **~al** *a* místico. **~ism** /-sɪzəm/ *n* misticismo *m*
mystify /ˈmɪstɪfaɪ/ *vt* deixar perplexo
mystique /mɪˈstiːk/ *n* mística *f*
myth /mɪθ/ *n* mito *m*. **~ical** *a* mítico
mytholog|y /mɪˈθɒlədʒɪ/ *n* mitologia *f*. **~ical** /mɪθəˈlɒdʒɪkl/ *a* mitológico

Nn

nab /næb/ *vt* (*pt* **nabbed**) ⊠ apanhar em flagrante; apanhar com a boca na botija ⓘ; pilhar
nag /næg/ *vt/i* (*pt* **nagged**) implicar (com), criticar constantemente; (*pester*) apoquentar
nail /neɪl/ *n* prego *m*; (*of finger, toe*) unha *f*; **~ polish** esmalte *m*, (*P*) verniz *m* para as unhas; **hit the ~ on the head** acertar em cheio; **on the ~** sem demora ● *vt* pregar. **~ file** *n* lixa *f* de unhas
naïve /naɪˈiːv/ *a* ingênuo, (*P*) ingénuo
naked /ˈneɪkɪd/ *a* nu; **to the ~ eye** a olho nu, à vista desarmada. **~ness** *n* nudez *f*
name /neɪm/ *n* nome *m*; *fig* reputação *f*; fama *f* ● *vt* (*mention; appoint*) nomear; (*give a name to*) chamar, dar o nome de; ‹*a date*› marcar; **be ~d after** ter o nome de. **~less** *a* sem nome, anônimo, (*P*) anónimo
namely /ˈneɪmlɪ/ *adv* a saber
namesake /ˈneɪmseɪk/ *n* homônimo *m*, (*P*) homónimo *m*
nanny /ˈnænɪ/ *n* ama *f*, babá *f*
nap[1] /næp/ *n* soneca *f* ● *vi* (*pt* **napped**) dormitar, tirar um cochilo, fazer uma sesta; **catch ~ping** apanhar desprevenido
nap[2] /næp/ *n* (*of material*) felpa *f*
napkin /ˈnæpkɪn/ *n* guardanapo *m*; (*for baby*) fralda *f*
nappy /ˈnæpɪ/ *n* fralda *f*. **~ rash** *n* assadura *f*
narcotic /nɑːˈkɒtɪk/ *a & n* narcótico *m*
narrat|e /nəˈreɪt/ *vt* narrar. **~ion** /-ʃn/ *n* narrativa *f*. **~or** *n* narrador *m*
narrative /ˈnærətɪv/ *n* narrativa *f* ● *a* narrativo
narrow /ˈnærəʊ/ *a* (**-er**, **-est**) estreito; *fig* restrito ● *vt/i* estreitar(-se); (*limit*) limitar(-se). **~ly** *adv* (*only just*) por pouco; (*closely, carefully*) de perto, com cuidado. **~-minded** *a* a bitolado, de visão limitada
nasal /ˈneɪzl/ *a* nasal
nast|y /ˈnɑːstɪ/ *a* (**-ier**, **-iest**) (*malicious, of weather*) mau; (*unpleasant*) desagradável, intragável; (*rude*) grosseiro
nation /ˈneɪʃn/ *n* nação *f*. **~wide** *a* em todo o país, em escala or a nível nacional
national /ˈnæʃnəl/ *a* nacional ● *n* natural *mf*; **~ anthem** hino *m* nacional. **~ism** *n* nacionalismo *m*. **~ize** *vt* nacionalizar
nationality /næʃəˈnælətɪ/ *n* nacionalidade *f*

> **National Trust** Fundação britânica cujo objetivo é a conservação de lugares de interesse histórico ou de beleza natural. É financiada por doações e subvenções privadas. É a maior proprietária de terras da Grã-Bretanha. Na Escócia, é um organismo independente chamado *National Trust for Scotland*.

native /ˈneɪtɪv/ *n* natural *mf*, nativo *m* ● *a* nativo; (*country*) natal; (*inborn*) inato; **be a ~ of** ser natural de; **~ language** língua *f* materna; **~ speaker of Portuguese** falante *m* nativo de Português
Nativity /nəˈtɪvətɪ/ *n* **the ~** a Natividade *f*
natter /ˈnætə(r)/ *vi* fazer conversa fiada, falar à toa, tagarelar
natural /ˈnætʃrəl/ *a* natural; **~ history** história *f* natural. **~ist** *n* naturalista *mf*. **~ly** *adv* naturalmente; (*by nature*) por natureza
naturaliz|e /ˈnætʃrəlaɪz/ *vt/i* naturalizar(-se); ‹*animal, plant*› aclimatar(-se). **~ation** /-ˈzeɪʃn/ *n* naturalização *f*
nature /ˈneɪtʃə(r)/ *n* natureza *f*; (*kind*) gênero *m*, (*P*) género *m*; (*of person*) índole *f*
naughty /ˈnɔːtɪ/ *a* (**-ier**, **-iest**) ‹*child*› levado; (*indecent*) picante

nause|a /'nɔːsɪə/ *n* náusea *f*. **~ating, ~ous** *a* nauseabundo, repugnante

nautical /'nɔːtɪkl/ *a* náutico; **~ mile** milha *f* marítima

naval /'neɪvl/ *a* naval; ‹*officer*› de marinha

nave /neɪv/ *n* nave *f*

navel /'neɪvl/ *n* umbigo *m*

navigable /'nævɪgəbl/ *a* navegável

navigat|e /'nævɪgeɪt/ *vt* ‹*sea etc*› navegar; ‹*ship*› pilotar ● *vi* navegar. **~ion** /-'geɪʃn/ *n* navegação *f*. **~or** *n* navegador *m*

navy /'neɪvɪ/ *n* marinha *f* de guerra; **~ (blue)** azul-marinho *m invar*

near /nɪə(r)/ *adv* perto, quase; **~ to** perto de; **draw ~** aproximar(-se) (**to** de) ● *prep* perto de ● *a* próximo; **N~ East** Oriente *m* Próximo, (*P*) Próximo Oriente *m* ● *vt* aproximar-se de, chegar-se a. **~ by** *adv* perto, próximo. **~ness** *n* proximidade *f*

nearby /'nɪəbaɪ/ *a & adv* próximo, perto

nearly /'nɪəlɪ/ *adv* quase, por pouco; **not ~ as pretty/***etc* **as** longe de ser tão bonita/*etc* como

neat /niːt/ *a* (**-er, -est**) (bem) cuidado; ‹*room*› bem arrumado; ‹*spirits*› puro, sem gelo. **~ly** *adv* (*with care*) com cuidado; (*cleverly*) habilmente. **~ness** *n* aspecto *m* cuidado

necessar|y /'nesəsərɪ/ *a* necessário. **~ily** *adv* necessariamente

necessitate /nɪ'sesɪteɪt/ *vt* exigir, obrigar a, tornar necessário

necessity /nɪ'sesətɪ/ *n* necessidade *f*; (*thing*) coisa *f* indispensável, artigo *m* de primeira necessidade

neck /nek/ *n* pescoço *m*; (*of dress*) gola *f*; **~ and neck** emparelhados

necklace /'neklɪs/ *n* colar *m*

neckline /'neklaɪn/ *n* decote *m*

nectarine /'nektərɪn/ *n* pêssego *m*

née /neɪ/ *a* em solteira; **Ann Jones ~ Drewe** Ann Jones cujo nome de solteira era Drewe

need /niːd/ *n* necessidade *f* ● *vt* precisar de, necessitar de; **you ~ not come** não tem de or não precisa (de) vir. **~less** *a* inútil, desnecessário. **~lessly** *adv* inutilmente, sem necessidade

needle /'niːdl/ *a* agulha *f* ● *vt* [!] (*provoke*) provocar

needlework /'niːdlwɜːk/ *n* costura *f*; (*embroidery*) bordado *m*

needy /'niːdɪ/ *a* (**-ier, -iest**) necessitado, carenciado, carente

negation /nɪ'geɪʃn/ *n* negação *f*

negative /'negətɪv/ *a* negativo ● *n* negativa *f*, negação *f*; *Photo* negativo *m*; **in the ~** ‹*answer*› na negativa; *Gram* na forma negativa. **~ly** *adv* negativamente

neglect /nɪ'glekt/ *vt* descuidar; ‹*opportunity*› desprezar; ‹*family*› não cuidar de; ‹*duty*› não cumprir; **~ to** (*omit to*) esquecer-se de ● *n* falta *f* de cuidado(s), descuido *m*; **(state of) ~** abandono *m*. **~ful** *a* negligente

negligen|t /'neglɪdʒənt/ *a* negligente. **~ce** *n* negligência *f*, desleixo *m*

negligible /'neglɪdʒəbl/ *a* insignificante, ínfimo

negotiable /nɪ'gəʊʃəbl/ *a* negociável

negotiat|e /nɪ'gəʊʃɪeɪt/ *vt/i* negociar; ‹*obstacle*› transpor; ‹*difficulty*› vencer. **~ion** /-sɪ'eɪʃn/ *n* negociação *f*. **~or** *n* negociador *m*

Negro /'niːgrəʊ/ *a & n* (*pl* **oes**) negro *m*, preto *m*

neigh /neɪ/ *n* relincho *m* ● *vi* relinchar

neighbour /'neɪbə(r)/ *n* vizinho *m*. **~hood** *n* vizinhança *f*. **~ing** *a* vizinho. **~ly** *a* de boa vizinhança

neither /'naɪðə(r)/ *a & pron* nenhum(a) (de dois or duas), nem um nem outro, nem uma nem outra ● *adv* tampouco, também não ● *conj* nem; **~ big nor small** nem grande nem pequeno; **~ am I** nem eu

neocon /'niːəʊkɒn/ *a & n* neoconservador *mf*

neon /'niːɒn/ *n* néon *m*

nephew /'nevjuː/ *n* sobrinho *m*

nerve /nɜːv/ *n* nervo *m*; *fig* (*courage*) coragem *f*; [!] (*impudence*) descaramento *m*, (*P*) lata *f* [!]; **get on sb's nerves** irritar, dar nos nervos de alguém. **~-racking** *a* de arrasar os nervos, enervante

nervous /'nɜːvəs/ *a* nervoso; **be** or **feel ~** (*afraid*) ter receio/um certo medo; **~ breakdown** esgotamento *m* nervoso. **~ly** *adv* nervosamente. **~ness** *n* nervosismo *m*; (*fear*) receio *m*

nest /nest/ *n* ninho *m* ● *vi* aninhar-se, fazer or ter ninho. **~ egg** *n* pé-de-meia *m*

nestle /'nesl/ *vi* aninhar-se

net[1] /net/ *n* rede *f* ● *vt* (*pt* **netted**) apanhar na rede. **~ting** *n* rede *f*; **wire ~ting** rede *f* de arame

net[2] /net/ *a* ‹*weight etc*› líquido

Netherlands /'neðələndz/ *npl* **the ~** os Países Baixos

nettle /'netl/ *n* urtiga *f*

network /'netwɜːk/ *n* rede *f*, cadeia *f*

neuro|sis /njʊə'rəʊsɪs/ *n* (*pl* **-oses** /-siːz/) neurose *f*. **~tic** /-'rɒtɪk/ *a & n* neurótico *m*

neuter /'njuːtə(r)/ *a & n* neutro *m* ● *vt* castrar, capar

neutral /'njuːtrəl/ *a* neutro; **~ (gear)** ponto *m* morto. **~ity** /-'trælətɪ/ *n* neutralidade *f*

never /'nevə(r)/ *adv* nunca; [!] (*not*) não; **he ~ refuses** ele nunca recusa; **I ~ saw him** [!] nunca o vi; **~ mind** não faz mal, deixe para lá. **~-ending** *a* interminável

nevertheless /nevəðə'les/ *adv & conj* contudo, no entanto

new /njuː/ *a* (**-er, -est**) novo; **~ moon** lua *f* nova; **~ year** ano *m* novo; **N~ Year's Day** dia *m* de Ano Novo; **N~ Year's Eve** véspera *f* de Ano Novo; **N~ Zealand** Nova Zelândia *f*; **N~ Zealander** neozelandês *m*. **~born** *a* recém-nascido. **~ness** *n* novidade *f*

New Age *n* Nova Era *f*, o Movimento Nova Era *f*

newcomer /'njuːkʌmə(r)/ *n* recém-chegado *m*

newfangled /njuː'fæŋgld/ *a pej* moderno

newly /'njuːlɪ/ *adv* há pouco, recentemente. **~-weds** *npl* recém-casados *mpl*

news /njuːz/ *n* notícia(s) *f(pl)*; *Radio* noticiário *m*, notícia(s) *fpl*; *TV* telejornal *m*. **~caster, ~reader** *n* locutor *m*; **~flash** *n* notícia *f* de última hora

newsagent /'njuːzeɪdʒənt/ *n* jornaleiro *m*

newsletter /'njuːzletə(r)/ *n* boletim *m* informativo

newspaper /'njuːzpeɪpə(r)/ *n* jornal *m*

newsreel /'njuːzriːl/ *n* atualidades *fpl*

newt /njuːt/ *n* tritão *m*

next /nekst/ *a* próximo; (*adjoining*) pegado, ao lado, contíguo; (*following*) seguinte ● *adv* a seguir; **~ to** ao lado de; **~ to nothing** quase nada ● *n* seguinte *mf*; **~ of kin** parente *m* mais próximo. **~-door** *a* do lado

nib /nɪb/ *n* bico *m*, (*P*) aparo *m*

nibble /'nɪbl/ *vt* mordiscar, dar dentadinhas em

nice /naɪs/ *a* (**-er, -est**) agradável, bom; (*kind*) simpático, gentil; (*pretty*) bonito; (*respectable*) bem-educado; correto; (*subtle*) fino, subtil. **~ly** *adv* agradavelmente; (*well*) bem

nicety /'naɪsətɪ/ *n* sutileza *f*, (*P*) subtileza *f*

niche /nɪtʃ/ *n* nicho *m*; *fig* bom lugar *m*

nick /nɪk/ *n* corte *m*, chanfradura *f*; [x] (*prison*) cadeia *f* ● *vt* dar um corte em; [x] (*steal*) roubar, limpar [!]; [x] (*arrest*) apanhar; pôr a mão em [!]; **in good ~** [!] em boa forma, em bom estado; **in the ~ of time** mesmo a tempo

nickel /'nɪkl/ *n* níquel *m*; *Amer* moeda *f* de cinco cêntimos

nickname /'nɪkneɪm/ *n* apelido *m*, (*P*) alcunha *f*; (*short form*) diminutivo *m* ● *vt* apelidar de

nicotine /'nɪkətiːn/ *n* nicotina *f*

niece /niːs/ *n* sobrinha *f*

Nigeria /naɪ'dʒɪərɪə/ *n* Nigéria *f*. **~n** *a & n* nigeriano *m*

night /naɪt/ *n* noite *f*; **at ~** à/de noite; **by ~** de noite ● *a* de noite, noturno. **~cap** *n* (*drink*) bebida *f* tomada na hora de deitar; **~club** *n* boate *f*, (*P*) boîte *f*; **~dress, ~gown** *ns* camisola *f* de dormir, (*P*) camisa *f* de noite; **~life** *n* vida *f* noturna; **~ school** *n* escola *f* noturna; **~-time** *n* noite *f*

nightfall /'naɪtfɔːl/ *n* anoitecer *m*

nightingale /'naɪtɪŋgeɪl/ *n* rouxinol *m*

nightly /'naɪtlɪ/ *a* noturno ● *adv* de noite, à noite, todas as noites

nightmare /'naɪtmeə(r)/ *n* pesadelo *m*

nil /nɪl/ *n* nada *m*; *Sport* zero *m* ● *a* nulo

nimble /'nɪmbl/ *a* (**-er, -est**) ágil, ligeiro

nin|e /naɪn/ *a & n* nove *m*. **~th** *a & n* nono *m*

nineteen /naɪn'tiːn/ *a & n* dezenove *m*, (*P*) dezanove *m*. **~th** *a & n* décimo nono *m*

ninet|y /'naɪntɪ/ *a & n* noventa *m*. **~ieth** *a & n* nonagésimo *m*

nip /nɪp/ *vt/i* (*pt* **nipped**) apertar, beliscar; [!] (*rush*) ir correndo; ir num pulo [!]; **~ in the bud** cortar pela raiz ● *n* aperto *m*, beliscão *m*; (*drink*) gole *m*, trago *m*; **a ~ in the air** um frio cortante

nipple /'nɪpl/ *n* mamilo *m*

nippy /'nɪpɪ/ *a* (**-ier, -iest**) [!] (*quick*) rápido; [!] (*chilly*) cortante

nitrogen /'naɪtrədʒən/ *n* azoto *m*, nitrogênio *m*, (*P*) nitrogénio *m*

nitwit /ˈnɪtwɪt/ *n* [!] imbecil *m*

no /nəʊ/ *a* nenhum; **~ entry** entrada *f* proibida; **~ money/time/***etc* nenhum dinheiro/tempo/*etc*; **~ man's land** terra *f* de ninguém; **~ one** ▶ NOBODY ● *adv* não; **~ smoking** é proibido fumar; **~ way!** [!] de modo nenhum! ● *n* (*pl* **noes**) não *m*

nob|le /ˈnəʊbl/ *a* (**-er**, **-est**) nobre. **~ility** /-ˈbɪlətɪ/ *n* nobreza *f*

nobleman /ˈnəʊblmən/ *n* (*pl* **-men**) nobre *m*, fidalgo *m*

nobody /ˈnəʊbɒdɪ/ *pron* ninguém ● *n* nulidade *f*; **he knows ~** ele não conhece ninguém; **~ is there** não tem ninguém lá, (*P*) não está lá ninguém

no-brainer /nəʊˈbreɪnə(r)/ *n* trivialidade *f*

nocturnal /nɒkˈtɜːnl/ *a* noturno

nod /nɒd/ *vt/i* (*pt* **nodded**) **~ (one's head)** acenar (com) a cabeça; **~ (off)** cabecear ● *n* aceno *m* com a cabeça (para dizer que sim or para cumprimentar)

noise /nɔɪz/ *n* ruído *m*, barulho *m*. **~less** *a* silencioso

nois|y /ˈnɔɪzɪ/ *a* (**-ier**, **-iest**) ruidoso, barulhento

nomad /ˈnəʊmæd/ *n* nômada *mf*, (*P*) nómada *mf*. **~ic** /-ˈmædɪk/ *a* nômada, (*P*) nómada

nominal /ˈnɒmɪnl/ *a* nominal; ‹*fee, sum*› simbólico

nominat|e /ˈnɒmɪneɪt/ *vt* (*appoint*) nomear; (*put forward*) propor. **~ion** /-ˈneɪʃn/ *n* nomeação *f*

non- /nɒn/ *pref* não, sem, in-, a-, anti-, des-. **~-stick** *a* não-aderente

nonchalant /ˈnɒnʃələnt/ *a* indiferente, desinteressado

non-commissioned /nɒnkəˈmɪʃnd/ *a* **~ officer** sargento *m*, cabo *m*

non-committal /nɒnkəˈmɪtl/ *a* evasivo

nondescript /ˈnɒndɪskrɪpt/ *a* insignificante, medíocre, indefinível

none /nʌn/ *pron* (*person*) nenhum, ninguém; (*thing*) nenhum, nada; **~ of us** nenhum de nós; **I have ~** não tenho nenhum; **~ of that!** nada disso! ● *adv* **~ too** não muito; **he is ~ the happier** nem por isso ele é mais feliz; **~ the less** contudo, no entanto, apesar disso

nonentity /nɒˈnentətɪ/ *n* nulidade *f*, zero à *m* esquerda, João Ninguém *m*

non-existent /nɒnɪgˈzɪstənt/ *a* inexistente

nonplussed /nɒnˈplʌst/ *a* perplexo, pasmado

nonsens|e /ˈnɒnsns/ *n* absurdo *m*, disparate *m*. **~ical** /-ˈsensɪkl/ *a* absurdo, disparatado

non-smoker /nɒnˈsməʊkə(r)/ *n* nãofumante *m*, (*P*) nãofumador *m*

non-stop /nɒnˈstɒp/ *a* ininterrupto, contínuo; ‹*train*› direto; ‹*flight*› sem escala ● *adv* sem parar

noodles /ˈnuːdlz/ *npl* talharim *m*, (*P*) macarronete *m*

nook /nʊk/ *n* (re)canto *m*

noon /nuːn/ *n* meio-dia *m*

noose /nuːs/ *n* laço *m* corrediço

nor /nɔː(r)/ *conj & adv* nem, também não; **~ do I** nem eu

norm /nɔːm/ *n* norma *f*

normal /ˈnɔːml/ *a & n* normal *m*; **above/below ~** acima/abaixo do normal. **~ity** /nɔːˈmælətɪ/ *n* normalidade *f*. **~ly** *adv* normalmente

north /nɔːθ/ *n* norte *m* ● *a* norte, do norte; (*of country, people etc*) setentrional ● *adv* a, ao/para o norte; **N~ America** América *f* do Norte. **~erly** /ˈnɔːðəlɪ/ *a* do norte. **~ward(s)** *adv* para o norte. **N~ American** *a & n* norte-americano *m*; **~-east** *n* nordeste *m*; **~-west** *n* noroeste *m*

northern /ˈnɔːðən/ *a* do norte

Norw|ay /ˈnɔːweɪ/ *n* Noruega *f*. **~egian** /nɔːˈwiːdʒən/ *a & n* norueguês *m*

nose /nəʊz/ *n* nariz *m*; (*of animal*) focinho *m* ● *vi* **~ about** farejar; **pay through the ~** pagar um preço exorbitante

nosebleed /ˈnəʊzbliːd/ *n* hemorragia *f* nasal or pelo nariz

nosedive /ˈnəʊzdaɪv/ *n* voo *m* picado

nostalg|ia /nɒˈstældʒə/ *n* nostalgia *f*. **~ic** *a* nostálgico

nostril /ˈnɒstrəl/ *n* narina *f*; (*of horse*) venta *f* (*usually pl*)

nosy /ˈnəʊzɪ/ *a* (**-ier**, **-iest**) [!] bisbilhoteiro

not /nɒt/ ● *adv*

····▶ não; **~ at all** nada, de modo nenhum; (*reply to thanks*) de nada; **he is ~ at all bored** ele não está nem um pouco entediado; **~ yet** ainda não; **I suppose ~** creio que não

notable /ˈnəʊtəbl/ *a* notável ● *n* notabilidade *f*

n

notably /'nəʊtəblɪ/ *adv* notavelmente; (*particularly*) especialmente

notch /nɒtʃ/ *n* corte *m* em V ● *vt* marcar com cortes; **~ up** ‹*score etc*› marcar

note /nəʊt/ *n* nota *f*; (*banknote*) nota (de banco) *f*; (*short letter*) bilhete *m* ● *vt* notar

notebook /'nəʊtbʊk/ *n* livrinho *m* de notas, (*P*) bloco *m* de notas

noted /'nəʊtɪd/ *a* conhecido, famoso

notepaper /'nəʊtpeɪpə(r)/ *n* papel *m* de carta

noteworthy /'nəʊtwɜ:ðɪ/ *a* notável

nothing /'nʌθɪŋ/ *n* nada *m*; (*person*) nulidade *f*, zero *m*; **he eats ~** ele não come nada; **~ big**/*etc* nada (de) grande/*etc*; **~ else** nada mais; **~ much** pouca coisa; **for ~** (*free*) de graça; (*in vain*) em vão ● *adv* nada, de modo algum or nenhum, de maneira alguma or nenhuma

notice /'nəʊtɪs/ *n* anúncio *m*, notícia *f*; (*in street, on wall*) letreiro *m*; (*warning*) aviso *m*; (*attention*) atenção *f*; **(advance) ~** pré-aviso *m*; **at short ~** num prazo curto; **a week's ~** o prazo de uma semana; **hand in one's ~** pedir demissão; **take ~** reparar (**of** em); **take no ~** não fazer caso (**of** de) ● *vt* notar, reparar. **~board** *n* quadro *m* para afixar anúncios etc

n

noticeabl|e /'nəʊtɪsəbl/ *a* visível. **~y** *adv* visivelmente

notif|y /'nəʊtɪfaɪ/ *vt* participar, notificar. **~ication** /-ɪ'keɪʃn/ *n* participação *f*, notificação *f*

notion /'nəʊʃn/ *n* noção *f*

notor|ious /nəʊ'tɔ:rɪəs/ *a* notório. **~iety** /-ə'raɪətɪ/ *n* fama *f*

notwithstanding /nɒtwɪθ'stændɪŋ/ *prep* apesar de, não obstante ● *adv* mesmo assim, ainda assim ● *conj* embora, conquanto, apesar de (que)

nougat /'nu:gɑ:/ *n* nugá *m*, torrone *m*, (*P*) nogado *m*

nought /nɔ:t/ *n* zero *m*

noun /naʊn/ *n* substantivo *m*, nome *m*

nourish /'nʌrɪʃ/ *vt* alimentar, nutrir. **~ing** *a* alimentício, nutritivo. **~ment** *n* alimento *m*, sustento *m*

novel /'nɒvl/ *n* romance *m* ● *a* novo, original. **~ist** *n* romancista *mf*. **~ty** *n* novidade *f*

November /nəʊ'vembə(r)/ *n* novembro *m*

novice /'nɒvɪs/ *n* (*beginner*) noviço *m*, novato *m*; *Relig* noviço *m*

now /naʊ/ *adv* agora; **by ~** a estas horas, por esta altura; **from ~ on** de agora em diante; **~ and again, ~ and then** de vez em quando; **right ~** já ● *conj* **~ (that)** agora que

nowadays /'naʊədeɪz/ *adv* hoje em dia, presentemente, atualmente

nowhere /'nəʊweə(r)/ *adv* (*position*) em lugar nenhum, em lado nenhum; (*direction*) a lado nenhum, a parte alguma or nenhuma

nozzle /'nɒzl/ *n* bico *m*, bocal *m*; (*of hose*) agulheta *f*

nuance /'nju:ɑ:ns/ *n* nuance *f*, matiz *m*

nuclear /'nju:klɪə(r)/ *a* nuclear

nucleus /'nju:klɪəs/ *n* (*pl* **-lei** /-lɪaɪ/) núcleo *m*

nud|e /nju:d/ *a & n* nu *m*; **in the ~e** nu. **~ity** *n* nudez *f*

nudge /nʌdʒ/ *vt* tocar com o cotovelo, cutucar ● *n* ligeira cotovelada *f*, cutucada *f*

nudis|t /'nju:dɪst/ *n* nudista *mf*

nuisance /'nju:sns/ *n* aborrecimento *m*; chatice *f* ☒; (*person*) chato *m* ☒

null /nʌl/ *a* nulo; **~ and void** *Jur* írrito e nulo

numb /nʌm/ *a* entorpecido, dormente ● *vt* entorpecer, adormecer

number /'nʌmbə(r)/ *n* número *m*; (*numeral*) algarismo *m* ● *vt* numerar; (*amount to*) ser em número de; (*count*) contar, incluir. **~ plate** *n* chapa (do carro) *f*, (*P*) matrícula *f* (do carro)

numeral /'nju:mərəl/ *n* número *m*, algarismo *m*

numerate /'nju:mərət/ *a* que tem conhecimentos básicos de matemática

numerical /nju:'merɪkl/ *a* numérico

numerous /'nju:mərəs/ *a* numeroso

nun /nʌn/ *n* freira *f*, religiosa *f*

nurs|e /nɜ:s/ *n* enfermeira *f*, enfermeiro *m*; (*nanny*) ama(-seca) *f*, babá *f* ● *vt* cuidar de, tratar de; ‹*hopes etc*› alimentar, acalentar. **~ing** *n* enfermagem *f*; **~ing home** clínica *f* de repouso, (*P*) lar *m* de idosos

nursery /'nɜ:sərɪ/ *n* quarto *m* de crianças; (*for plants*) viveiro *m*; **(day) ~** creche *f*; **~ rhyme** poema or canção *f* infantil *m*; **~ school** jardim *m* de infância

nurture /'nɜ:tʃə(r)/ *vt* educar

nut /nʌt/ *n Bot* noz *f*; *Techn* porca *f* de parafuso

nutcrackers /'nʌtkrækəz/ *npl* quebra-nozes *m invar*

nutmeg /ˈnʌtmeg/ *n* noz-moscada *f*
nutrient /ˈnjuːtrɪənt/ *n* substância *f* nutritiva, nutriente *m*
nutrit|ion /njuːˈtrɪʃn/ *n* nutrição *f*. **~ious** *a* nutritivo
nutshell /ˈnʌtʃel/ *n* casca *f* de noz; **in a ~** em poucas palavras, em suma
nuzzle /ˈnʌzl/ *vt* esfregar com o focinho
nylon /ˈnaɪlɒn/ *n* nylon *m*; **~s** meias *fpl* de nylon

Oo

oak /əʊk/ *n* carvalho *m*
OAP *abbr* (= **old-age pensioner**) ▶ **OLD**
oar /ɔː(r)/ *n* remo *m*
oasis /əʊˈeɪsɪs/ *n* (*pl* **oases** /-siːz/) oásis *m*
oath /əʊθ/ *n* juramento *m*; (*swear word*) praga *f*
oatmeal /ˈəʊtmiːl/ *n* farinha *f* de aveia; (*porridge*) papa *f* de aveia
oats /əʊts/ *npl* aveia *f*
obedien|t /əˈbiːdɪənt/ *a* obediente. **~ce** *n* obediência *f*
obes|e /əʊˈbiːs/ *a* obeso. **~ity** *n* obesidade *f*
obey /əˈbeɪ/ *vt/i* obedecer (a)
obituary /əˈbɪtʃʊərɪ/ *n* necrológio *m*, (*P*) necrologia *f*
object[1] /ˈɒbdʒɪkt/ *n* objeto *m*; (*aim*) objetivo *m*; *Gram* complemento *m*
object[2] /əbˈdʒekt/ *vt/i* objetar (que); **~ to** opor-se a, discordar de. **~ion** /-ʃn/ *n* objeção *f*
objectionable /əbˈdʒekʃnəbl/ *a* censurável; (*unpleasant*) desagradável
objectiv|e /əbˈdʒektɪv/ *a* objetivo. **~ity** /-ˈtɪvətɪ/ *n* objetividade *f*
obligation /ɒblɪˈgeɪʃn/ *n* obrigação *f*; **be under an ~ to sb** dever favores a alguém
obligatory /əˈblɪgətrɪ/ *a* obrigatório
oblig|e /əˈblaɪdʒ/ *vt* obrigar; (*do a favour*) fazer um favor a, obsequiar. **~ed** *a* obrigado (**to** a); **~ed to sb** em dívida (para) com alguém. **~ing** *a* prestável, amável
oblique /əˈbliːk/ *a* oblíquo
obliterat|e /əˈblɪtəreɪt/ *vt* obliterar. **~ion** /-ˈreɪʃn/ *n* obliteração *f*
oblivion /əˈblɪvɪən/ *n* esquecimento *m*
oblivious /əˈblɪvɪəs/ *a* esquecido; sem consciência (**of/to** de)
oblong /ˈɒblɒŋ/ *a* oblongo, alongado ● *n* retângulo *m*
obnoxious /əbˈnɒkʃəs/ *a* ofensivo, detestável
oboe /ˈəʊbəʊ/ *n* oboé *m*
obscen|e /əbˈsiːn/ *a* obsceno. **~ity** /-ˈenətɪ/ *n* obscenidade *f*
obscur|e /əbˈskjʊə(r)/ *a* obscuro ● *vt* obscurecer; (*conceal*) encobrir. **~ity** *n* obscuridade *f*
obsequious /əbˈsiːkwɪəs/ *a* demasiado obsequioso, subserviente
observan|t /əbˈzɜːvənt/ *a* observador. **~ce** *n* observância *f*, cumprimento *m*
observatory /əbˈzɜːvətrɪ/ *n* observatório *m*
observ|e /əbˈzɜːv/ *vt* observar. **~ation** /ɒbzəˈveɪʃn/ *n* observação *f*; **keep under ~ation** vigiar. **~er** *n* observador *m*
obsess /əbˈses/ *vt* obcecar. **~ion** /-ʃn/ *n* obsessão *f*. **~ive** *a* obsessivo
obsessive-compulsive disorder *n* transtorno obsessivo-compulsivo *m*
obsolete /ˈɒbsəliːt/ *a* obsoleto, antiquado
obstacle /ˈɒbstəkl/ *n* obstáculo *m*
obstetric|s /əbˈstetrɪks/ *n* obstetrícia *f*. **~ian** /ɒbstɪˈtrɪʃn/ *n* obstetra *mf*
obstina|te /ˈɒbstɪnət/ *a* obstinado. **~cy** *n* obstinação *f*
obstruct /əbˈstrʌkt/ *vt* obstruir, bloquear; (*hinder*) estorvar, obstruir. **~ion** /-ʃn/ *n* obstrução *f*; (*thing*) obstáculo *m*
obtain /əbˈteɪn/ *vt* obter ● *vi* prevalecer, estar em vigor. **~able** *a* que se pode obter
obtrusive /əbˈtruːsɪv/ *a* importuno; ‹*thing*› demasiadamente em evidência; que dá muito na(s) vista(s) 🄿
obvious /ˈɒbvɪəs/ *a* óbvio, evidente. **~ly** *adv* obviamente
occasion /əˈkeɪʒn/ *n* ocasião *f*; (*event*) acontecimento *m* ● *vt* ocasionar; **on ~** de vez em quando, ocasionalmente
occasional /əˈkeɪʒənl/ *a* ocasional. **~ly** *adv* de vez em quando, ocasionalmente
occult /ɒˈkʌlt/ *a* oculto
occupation /ɒkjʊˈpeɪʃn/ *n* ocupação *f*. **~al** *a* profissional; ‹*therapy*› ocupacional
occup|y /ˈɒkjʊpaɪ/ *vt* ocupar. **~ant** **~ier** *ns* ocupante *mf*

occur /ə'kɜː(r)/ *vi* (*pt* **occurred**) ocorrer, acontecer, dar-se; (*arise*) apresentar-se, aparecer; **~ to sb** ocorrer a alguém

occurrence /ə'kʌrəns/ *n* acontecimento *m*, ocorrência *f*

ocean /'əʊʃn/ *n* oceano *m*

o'clock /ə'klɒk/ *adv* **it is one ~** é uma hora; **it is six ~** são seis horas

octagon /'ɒktəgən/ *n* octógono *m*. **~al** /-'tægənl/ *a* octogonal

October /ɒk'təʊbə(r)/ *n* outubro *m*

octopus /'ɒktəpəs/ *n* (*pl* **-puses**) polvo *m*

odd /ɒd/ *a* (**-er**, **-est**) estranho, singular; ‹*number*› ímpar; (*left over*) de sobra; (*not of set*) desemparelhado; (*occasional*) ocasional; **~ jobs** (*paid*) biscates *mpl*; (*in garden etc*) trabalhos *mpl* diversos; **twenty ~** vinte e tantos. **~ity** *n* singularidade *f*; (*thing*) curiosidade *f*. **~ly** *adv* de modo estranho

oddment /'ɒdmənt/ *n* resto *m*, artigo *m* avulso

odds /ɒdz/ *npl* probabilidades *fpl*; (*in betting*) ganhos *mpl* líquidos; **at ~** em desacordo; (*quarrelling*) de mal, brigado; **it makes no ~** não faz diferença; **~ and ends** artigos *mpl* avulsos, coisas *fpl* pequenas

odious /'əʊdɪəs/ *a* odioso

odour /'əʊdə(r)/ *n* odor *m*. **~less** *a* inodoro

> **of** /əv *emphatic* ɒv/ ● *prep*
>
> ····➤ de; **a friend ~ mine** um amigo meu; **the mother ~ the twins** a mãe dos gêmeos; **the fifth ~ June** (dia) cinco de junho; **take six ~ them** leve seis deles; **the works ~ Shakespeare** as obras de Shakespeare; **made ~ gold** (feito) de ouro
>
> **!** the preposition *de* often contracts with: definite articles *o* and *a* to form *do*, *da*; demonstrative pronouns *este*, *esse*, *aquele*, *isto*, *isso*, *aquilo* to form *deste*, *desse*, *daquele*, *disto*, *disso*, *daquilo*; personal pronouns *ele*, *ela* to form *dele*, *dela*.
>
> ····➤ (*on the part of*) da parte de; **it was nice ~ him/John** foi simpático da parte dele/da parte do John →For translations of expressions such as **of course** and **consist of** see entries **course** and **consist**

off /ɒf/ *adv* embora, fora; (*switched off*) apagado, desligado; (*taken off*) tirado, desligado; (*cancelled*) cancelado; ‹*food*› estragado; **be well ~** ser abastado ● *prep* (fora) de; (*distant from*) a alguma distância de; **be ~** (*depart*) ir-se embora, partir; **be better/worse ~** estar em melhor/pior situação; **a day ~** um dia de folga; **20% ~** redução de 20%; **on the ~ chance that** no caso de; **~ colour** indisposto, adoentado. **~ licence** *n* loja *f* de bebidas alcoólicas; **~load** *vt* descarregar; **~putting** *a* desconcertante; **~-stage** *adv* fora de cena; **~-white** *a* branco-sujo

offal /'ɒfl/ *n* miudezas *fpl*, fressura *f*

offence /ə'fens/ *n* (*feeling*) ofensa *f*; (*crime*) delito *m*, transgressão *f*; **give ~ to** ofender; **take ~** ofender-se (**at** com)

offend /ə'fend/ *vt* ofender; **be ~ed** ofender-se (**at** com). **~er** *n* delinquente *mf*

offensive /ə'fensɪv/ *a* ofensivo; (*disgusting*) repugnante ● *n* ofensiva *f*

offer /'ɒfə(r)/ *vt* (*pt* **offered**) oferecer ● *n* oferta *f*; **on ~** em promoção. **~ing** *n* oferenda *f*

offhand /ɒf'hænd/ *a* espontâneo; (*curt*) seco ● *adv* de improviso, sem pensar

office /'ɒfɪs/ *n* escritório *m*; (*post*) cargo *m*; (*branch*) filial *f*; **~ hours** horas *fpl* de expediente; **in ~** no poder; **take ~** assumir o cargo

officer /'ɒfɪsə(r)/ *n* oficial *m*; (*policeman*) agente *m*

official /ə'fɪʃl/ *a* oficial ● *n* funcionário *m*. **~ly** *adv* oficialmente

officiate /ə'fɪʃɪeɪt/ *vi Relig* oficiar; **~ as** presidir, exercer as funções de

officious /ə'fɪʃəs/ *a* intrometido

offing /'ɒfɪŋ/ *n* **in the ~** *fig* em perspectiva

> **i** **off-licence** No Reino Unido, toda e qualquer loja que tenha uma licença para vender bebidas alcoólicas que devem ser consumidas fora do local. Abrem quando os *pubs* estão fechados e também costumam vender bebidas não alcoólicas, tabaco, guloseimas, etc. Muitas vezes alugam copos para festas, etc.

offset /'ɒfset/ *vt* (*pt* **-set**, *pres p* **-setting**) compensar, contrabalançar

offshoot /'ɔfʃuːt/ *n* rebento *m*; *fig* efeito *m* secundário

offshore /'ɒfʃɔː(r)/ *a* ao largo da costa

offside /ɒf'saɪd/ *a & adv* offside, em impedimento, (*P*) fora de jogo

offspring /'ɒfsprɪŋ/ *n* (*pl invar*) descendência *f*, prole *f*

often /'ɒfn/ *adv* muitas vezes, frequentemente; **every so ~** de vez em quando; **how ~?** quantas vezes?

oh /əʊ/ *int* oh, ah

oil /ɔɪl/ *n* óleo *m*; (*petroleum*) petróleo *m*; **~ rig** plataforma *f* de poço de petróleo; **~ well** poço *m* de petróleo ● *vt* lubrificar. **~ painting** *n* pintura *f* a óleo. **~y** *a* oleoso; ‹*food*› gorduroso

oilfield /'ɔɪlfi:ld/ *n* campo *m* petrolífero

ointment /'ɔɪntmənt/ *n* pomada *f*

OK /əʊ'keɪ/ *a & adv* [!] (está) bem; (está) certo; (está) legal

old /əʊld/ *a* (**-er, -est**) velho; ‹*person*› velho, idoso; (*former*) antigo; **how ~ is he?** que idade tem ele?; **of ~** (d)antes, antigamente; **~ age** velhice *f*; **~-age pensioner** reformado *m*, aposentado *m*, pessoa *f* de terceira idade; **~ boy** antigo aluno *m*; **~ girl** antiga aluna *f*; **~ maid** solteirona *f*; **~ man** homem *m* idoso, velho *m*; **~ woman** mulher *f* idosa, velha *f*. **~-fashioned** *a* fora de moda

olive /'ɒlɪv/ *n* azeitona *f* ● *a* de azeitona; **~ oil** azeite *m*

Olympic /ə'lɪmpɪk/ *a* olímpico; **~ Games** Jogos *mpl* Olímpicos. **~s** *npl* Olimpíadas *fpl*

omelette /'ɒmlɪt/ *n* omelete *f*

omen /'əʊmən/ *n* agouro *m*

ominous /'ɒmɪnəs/ *a* agourento

omi|t /ə'mɪt/ *vt* (*pt* **omitted**) omitir. **~ssion** /-ʃn/ *n* omissão *f*

on /ɒn/ *prep* sobre, em cima de, de, em; **~ arrival** na chegada, ao chegar; **~ foot** a pé *etc*; **~ doing** ao fazer; **~ time** na hora, dentro do horário; **~ Tuesday** na terça-feira; **~ Tuesdays** às terças-feiras ● *adv* para diante, para a frente; (*switched on*) aceso, ligado; (*tap*) aberto; (*machine*) em funcionamento; (*put on*) posto; (*happening*) em curso; **walk/*etc*~** continuar a andar/*etc*; **be ~ at** *Film, TV* estar levando or passando, (*P*) estar a dar; **~ and off** de vez em quando; **~ and ~** sem parar

once /wʌns/ *adv* uma vez; (*formerly*) noutro(s) tempo(s) ● *conj* uma vez que, desde que; **all at ~** de repente; (*simultaneously*) todos ao mesmo tempo; **just this ~** só esta vez; **~ (and) for all** duma vez para sempre; **~ upon a time** era uma vez. **~-over** *n* [!] vista *f* de olhos

oncoming /'ɒnkʌmɪŋ/ *a* que se aproxima, próximo; **the ~ traffic** o trânsito que vem do sentido oposto, (*P*) no sentido contrário

one /wʌn/ *a* um(a); (*sole*) único ● *n* um(a) *mf* ● *pron* um(a) *mf*; (*impersonal*) se; **~ by ~** um a um; **a big/red/*etc*~** um grande/vermelho/*etc*; **this/that ~** este/esse; **~ another** um ao outro, uns aos outros. **~-sided** *a* parcial; **~-way** *a* ‹*street*› mão única, (*P*) via *f* de sentido único; ‹*ticket*› simples

oneself /wʌn'self/ *pron* si, si mesmo/próprio; (*reflexive*) se; **by ~** sozinho

onion /'ʌnɪən/ *n* cebola *f*

online /ɒn'laɪn/ *a* conectado *or* (*P*) ligado (à Internet), online

onlooker /'ɒnlʊkə(r)/ *n* espectador *m*, circunstante *mf*

only /'əʊnlɪ/ *a* único; **an ~ child** um filho único ● *adv* apenas, só, somente; **he ~ has six** ele só tem seis; **not ~ ... but also** não só ... mas também; **~ too** muito, mais que ● *conj* só que

onset /'ɒnset/ *n* começo *m*; (*attack*) ataque *m*

onslaught /'ɒnslɔ:t/ *n* ataque *m* violento, assalto *m*

onward(s) /'ɒnwəd(z)/ *adv* para a frente/diante

ooze /u:z/ *vt/i* escorrer, verter

opal /'əʊpl/ *n* opala *f*

opaque /əʊ'peɪk/ *a* opaco, tosco

open /'əʊpən/ *a* aberto; ‹*view*› aberto, amplo; (*free to all*) aberto ao público; (*attempt*) franco; **in the ~ air** ao ar livre; **keep an ~ house** receber muito, abrir a porta para todos; **~ secret** segredo *m* de polichinelo; **~ sea** mar *m* alto ● *vt/i* abrir(-se); (*of shop, play*) abrir; **~ on to** dar para; **~ out** or **up** abrir(-se). **~-heart** *a* (*of surgery*) de coração aberto; **~-minded** *a* que tem uma mente aberta; **~-plan** *a* sem divisórias. **~ness** *n* abertura *f*; (*frankness*) franqueza *f*

opener /'əʊpənə(r)/ *n* (*tins*) abridor *m* de latas, (*P*) abre-latas *m invar*; (*bottles*) saca-rolhas *m invar*

opening /'əʊpənɪŋ/ *n* abertura *f*; (*beginning*) começo *m*; (*opportunity*) oportunidade *f*; (*job*) vaga *f*

openly /'əʊpənlɪ/ *adv* abertamente

i **Open University** A universidade à distância na Grã-Bretanha, fundada em 1969. As aulas são lecionadas por correspondência, através de material impresso, material enviado

O

pela Internet e de programas de televisão emitidos pela BBC. Também há cursos de verão aos quais os alunos devem assistir presencialmente. Não se exige nenhuma qualificação acadêmica para entrar na *Open University*.

opera /ˈɒprə/ *n* ópera *f*. **~ glasses** *npl* binóculo (de teatro) *m*, (*P*) binóculos *mpl*. **~tic** /ɒpəˈrætɪk/ *a* de ópera, operático

operat|e /ˈɒpəreɪt/ *vt/i* operar; *Techn* (pôr a) funcionar; **~e on** *Med* operar. **~ingtheatre** *n Med* anfiteatro *m*, sala *f* de operações. **~ion** /-ˈreɪʃn/ *n* operação *f*; **in ~ion** em vigor; *Techn* em funcionamento. **~ional** /-ˈreɪʃənl/ *a* operacional. **~or** *n* operador *m*; (*telephonist*) telefonista *mf*

operative /ˈɒpərətɪv/ *a* (*surgical*) operatório; ‹*law etc*› em vigor

opinion /əˈpɪnɪən/ *n* opinião *f*, parecer *m*; **in my ~** a meu ver. **~ poll** *n* sondagem (de opinião) *f*. **~ated** /-eɪtɪd/ *a* dogmático, opinioso

opium /ˈəʊpɪəm/ *n* ópio *m*

Oporto /əˈpɔːtəʊ/ *n* Porto *m*

opponent /əˈpəʊnənt/ *n* adversário *m*, antagonista *mf*, oponente *mf*

opportune /ˈɒpətjuːn/ *a* oportuno

opportunity /ɒpəˈtjuːnətɪ/ *n* oportunidade *f*

oppos|e /əˈpəʊz/ *vt* opor-se a; **~ed to** oposto a. **~ing** *a* oposto

opposite /ˈɒpəzɪt/ *a & n* oposto *m*, contrário *m* ● *adv* em frente ● *prep* **~ (to)** em frente de/a

opposition /ɒpəˈzɪʃn/ *n* oposição *f*

oppress /əˈpres/ *vt* oprimir. **~ion** /-ʃn/ *n* opressão *f*. **~ive** *a* opressivo

opt /ɒpt/ *vi* **~ for** optar por; **~ out** recusar-se a participar (**of** de); **~ to do** escolher fazer

optical /ˈɒptɪkl/ *a* óptico; **~ illusion** ilusão óptica *f*

optician /ɒpˈtɪʃn/ *n* oculista *mf*

optimis|t /ˈɒptɪmɪst/ *n* otimista *mf*. **~m** /-zəm/ *n* otimismo *m*. **~tic** /-ˈmɪstɪk/ *a* otimista

optimum /ˈɒptɪməm/ *a & n* (*pl* **-ima**) ótimo *m*, (*P*) óptimo *m*

option /ˈɒpʃn/ *n* escolha *f*, opção *f*; **have no ~ (but)** não ter outro remédio (senão)

optional /ˈɒpʃənl/ *a* opcional, facultativo

opulen|t /ˈɒpjʊlənt/ *a* opulento. **~ce** *n* opulência *f*

or /ɔː(r)/ *conj* ou; (*with negative*) nem; **~ else** senão

oracle /ˈɒrəkl/ *n* oráculo *m*

oral /ˈɔːrəl/ *a* oral

orange /ˈɒrɪndʒ/ *n* laranja *f*; (*colour*) laranja *m*, cor *f* de laranja ● *a* de laranja; (*colour*) alaranjado, cor de laranja

orator /ˈɒrətə(r)/ *n* orador *m*. **~y** *n* oratória *f*

orbit /ˈɔːbɪt/ *n* órbita *f* ● *vt* (*pt* **orbited**) gravitar em torno de

orchard /ˈɔːtʃəd/ *n* pomar *m*

orchestra /ˈɔːkɪstrə/ *n* orquestra *f*. **~l** /-ˈkestrəl/ *a* orquestral

orchestrate /ˈɔːkɪstreɪt/ *vt* orquestrar

orchid /ˈɔːkɪd/ *n* orquídea *f*

ordain /ɔːˈdeɪn/ *vt* decretar; *Relig* ordenar

ordeal /ɔːˈdiːl/ *n* prova *f*, provação *f*

order /ˈɔːdə(r)/ *n* ordem *f*; *Comm* encomenda *f*; pedido *m* ● *vt* ordenar; ‹*goods etc*› encomendar; **in ~ that** para que; **in ~ to** para

orderly /ˈɔːdəlɪ/ *a* ordenado, em ordem; (*not unruly*) ordeiro ● *n Mil* ordenança *f*; *Med* servente *m* de hospital

ordinary /ˈɔːdɪnrɪ/ *a* normal, ordinário, vulgar; **out of the ~** fora do comum

ordination /ɔːdɪˈneɪʃn/ *n Relig* ordenação *f*

ore /ɔː(r)/ *n* minério *m*

organ /ˈɔːgən/ *n* órgão *m*. **~ist** *n* organista *mf*

organic /ɔːˈgænɪk/ *a* orgânico

organism /ˈɔːgənɪzəm/ *n* organismo *m*

organiz|e /ˈɔːgənaɪz/ *vt* organizar. **~ation** /-ˈzeɪʃn/ *n* organização *f*. **~er** *n* organizador *m*

orgasm /ˈɔːgæzəm/ *n* orgasmo *m*

orgy /ˈɔːdʒɪ/ *n* orgia *f*

Orient /ˈɔːrɪənt/ *n* **the ~** o Oriente *m*

orientat|e /ˈɔːrɪənteɪt/ *vt* orientar. **~ion** /-ˈteɪʃn/ *n* orientação *f*

origin /ˈɒrɪdʒɪn/ *n* origem *f*

original /əˈrɪdʒənl/ *a* original; (*not copied*) original. **~ity** /-ˈnælətɪ/ *n* originalidade *f*. **~ly** *adv* originalmente; (*in the beginning*) originariamente

originat|e /əˈrɪdʒəneɪt/ *vt/i* originar(-se); **~e from** provir de

ornament /ˈɔːnəmənt/ *n* ornamento *m*; (*object*) peça *f* decorativa. **~al**

/-ˈmentl/ *a* ornamental

ornate /ɔːˈneɪt/ *a* florido, floreado

ornitholog|y /ɔːnɪˈθɒlədʒɪ/ *n* ornitologia *f*

orphan /ˈɔːfn/ *n* órfã(o) *f*(*m*) ● *vt* deixar órfão. **~age** *n* orfanato *m*

orthodox /ˈɔːθədɒks/ *a* ortodoxo

orthopaedic /ɔːθəˈpiːdɪk/ *a* ortopédico

oscillate /ˈɒsɪleɪt/ *vi* oscilar, vacilar

ostensibl|e /ɒsˈtensəbl/ *a* aparente, pretenso. **~y** *adv* aparentemente, pretensamente

ostentati|on /ɒstenˈteɪʃn/ *n* ostentação *f*. **~ous** /-ˈteɪʃəs/ *a* ostentoso, ostensivo

osteopath /ˈɒstɪəpæθ/ *n* osteopata *mf*

ostracize /ˈɒstrəsaɪz/ *vt* pôr de lado, marginalizar

ostrich /ˈɒstrɪtʃ/ *n* avestruz *mf*

other /ˈʌðə(r)/ *a, n & pron* outro *m*; **(some) ~s** outros; **the ~ day** no outro dia; **the ~ one** o outro ● *adv* **~ than** diferente de, senão

otherwise /ˈʌðəwaɪz/ *adv* de outro modo ● *conj* senão, caso contrário

otter /ˈɒtə(r)/ *n* lontra *f*

ouch /aʊtʃ/ *int* ai!, ui!

ought /ɔːt/ *v aux* (*pt* **ought**) dever; **you ~ to stay** você devia ficar; **he ~ to succeed** ele deve vencer; **I ~ to have done it** eu devia tê-lo feito

ounce /aʊns/ *n* onça *f* (= 28,35 g)

our /ˈaʊə(r)/ *a* nosso(s), nossa(s)

ours /ˈaʊəz/ *poss pron* o(s) nosso(s), a(s) nossa(s)

ourselves /aʊəˈselvz/ *pron* nós mesmos/próprios; (*reflexive*) nos; **by ~** sozinhos

oust /aʊst/ *vt* expulsar, obrigar a sair

out /aʊt/ *adv* fora; (*of light, fire*) apagado; (*in blossom*) aberto, desabrochado, em flor; (*of tide*) baixo; **be ~** não estar em casa, estar fora (de casa); (*wrong*) enganar-se; **be ~ to** estar resolvido a; **run/***etc* **~** sair correndo *or* (*P*) a correr/*etc*; **~ of** fora de; (*without*) sem; **~ of pity/***etc* por pena/*etc*; **made ~ of** feito de or em; **take ~ of** tirar de; **5 ~ of 6** 5 (de) entre 6; **~ of date** fora de moda; (*not valid*) fora do prazo; **~ of doors** ao ar livre; **~ of one's mind** doido; **~ of order** quebrado, (*P*) avariado; **~ of place** deslocado; **~ of the way** afastado. **~-and-~** *a* completo, rematado; **~patient** *n* doente *mf* de consulta externa

outboard /ˈaʊtbɔːd/ *a* **~ motor** motor *m* de popa

outbox /ˈaʊtbɒks/ *n* caixa *f* de saída

outbreak /ˈaʊtbreɪk/ *n* (*of flu etc*) surto *m*, epidemia *f*; (*of war*) deflagração *f*

outburst /ˈaʊtbɜːst/ *n* explosão *f*

outcast /ˈaʊtkɑːst/ *n* pária *m*

outcome /ˈaʊtkʌm/ *n* resultado *m*

outcry /ˈaʊtkraɪ/ *n* clamor *m*; (*protest*) protesto *m*

outdated /aʊtˈdeɪtɪd/ *a* fora da moda, ultrapassado

outdo /aʊtˈduː/ *vt* (*pt* **-did**, *pp* **-done**) ultrapassar, superar

outdoor /ˈaʊtdɔː(r)/ *a* ao ar livre. **~s** /-ˈdɔːz/ *adv* fora de casa, ao ar livre

outer /ˈaʊtə(r)/ *a* exterior; **~ space** espaço (cósmico) *m*

outfit /ˈaʊtfɪt/ *n* equipamento *m*; (*clothes*) roupa *f*

outgoing /ˈaʊtgəʊɪŋ/ *a* que vai sair; (*of minister etc*) demissionário; *fig* sociável. **~s** *npl* despesas *fpl*

outgrow /aʊtˈgrəʊ/ *vt* (*pt* **-grew**, *pp* **-grown**) crescer mais do que; ‹*clothes*› já não caber em

outing /ˈaʊtɪŋ/ *n* saída *f*, passeio *m*

outlandish /aʊtˈlændɪʃ/ *a* exótico, estranho

outlaw /ˈaʊtlɔː/ *n* fora da lei *mf*, bandido *m* ● *vt* banir, proscrever

outlay /ˈaʊtleɪ/ *n* despesa(s) *f*(*pl*)

outlet /ˈaʊtlet/ *n* saída *f*, escoadouro *m*; (*for goods*) mercado *m*, saída *f*; (*for feelings*) escape *m*, vazão *m*; *Electr* tomada *f*

outline /ˈaʊtlaɪn/ *n* contorno *m*; (*summary*) plano *m* geral, esquema *m*, esboço *m* ● *vt* contornar; (*summarize*) descrever em linhas gerais

outlive /aʊtˈlɪv/ *vt* sobreviver a

outlook /ˈaʊtlʊk/ *n* (*view*) vista *f*; (*mental attitude*) visão *f*; (*future prospects*) perspectiva(s) *f*(*pl*), (*P*) perspetiva(s) *f*(*pl*)

outlying /ˈaʊtlaɪɪŋ/ *a* afastado, remoto

outnumber /aʊtˈnʌmbə(r)/ *vt* ultrapassar em número

outpost /ˈaʊtpəʊst/ *n* posto *m* avançado

output /ˈaʊtpʊt/ *n* rendimento *m*; (*of computer*) saída *f*, output *m*

outrage /'aʊtreɪdʒ/ *n* atrocidade *f*, crime *m*; (*scandal*) escândalo *m* ● *vt* ultrajar

outrageous /aʊt'reɪdʒəs/ *a* (*shocking*) escandaloso; (*very cruel*) atroz

outright /'aʊtraɪt/ *adv* completamente; (*at once*) imediatamente; (*frankly*) abertamente ● *a* completo; (*refusal*) claro

outset /'aʊtset/ *n* início *m*, começo *m*, princípio *m*

outside[1] /aʊt'saɪd/ *n* exterior *m* ● *adv* (lá) (por) fora ● *prep* (para) fora de, além de; (*in front of*) diante de; **at the ~** no máximo

outside[2] /'aʊtsaɪd/ *a* exterior

outsider /aʊt'saɪdə(r)/ *n* estranho *m*; (*in race*) cavalo *m* com poucas probabilidades de vencer, azarão *m*

outsize /'aʊtsaɪz/ *a* tamanho extra *invar*

outskirts /'aʊtskɜːts/ *npl* arredores *mpl*, subúrbios *mpl*, arrabaldes *mpl*

outspoken /aʊt'spəʊkn/ *a* franco

outstanding /aʊt'stændɪŋ/ *a* saliente, proeminente; ‹*debt*› por saldar; (*very good*) notável, destacado

outstretched /aʊt'stretʃt/ *a* ‹*arm*› estendido, esticado

outward /'aʊtwəd/ *a* para o exterior; ‹*sign etc*› exterior; ‹*journey*› de ida. **~ly** *adv* exteriormente. **~s** *adv* para o exterior

outwit /aʊt'wɪt/ *vt* (*pt* **-witted**) ser mais esperto que, enganar

oval /'əʊvl/ *n & a* oval *m*

> *i*
>
> **Oval Office** O Salão Oval é o escritório oficial do Presidente dos Estados Unidos, situado na ala oeste da Casa Branca. A forma oval foi exigida por George Washington para ter contato visual com todos os presentes durante as reuniões. A princípio, o presidente queria que todas as divisões da Casa Branca fossem ovais, mas logo percebeu que este desenho era pouco prático.

ovary /'əʊvərɪ/ *n* ovário *m*

ovation /əʊ'veɪʃn/ *n* ovação *f*

oven /'ʌvn/ *n* forno *m*

over /'əʊvə(r)/ *prep* sobre, acima de, por cima de; (*across*) de para o/do outro lado de; (*during*) durante, em; (*more than*) mais de ● *adv* por cima; (*too*) demais, demasiadamente; (*ended*) acabado; **the film is ~** o filme já acabou; **jump/***etc***~** saltar/*etc* por cima; **he has some ~** ele tem uns de sobra; **all ~ the country** em/por todo o país; **all ~ the table** por toda a mesa; **~ and above** (*besides, in addition to*) (para) além de; **~ and ~** repetidas vezes; **~ there** ali, lá, acolá

over- /'əʊvə(r)/ *pref* sobre-, super-; (*excessively*) demais, demasiado

overall[1] /'əʊvərɔːl/ *n* bata *f*; **~s** macacão *m*, (*P*) fato-macaco *m*

overall[2] /'əʊvərɔːl/ *a* global; ‹*length etc*› total ● *adv* globalmente

overbalance /əʊvə'bæləns/ *vt/i* (fazer) perder o equilíbrio

overbearing /əʊvə'beərɪŋ/ *a* autoritário, despótico; (*arrogant*) arrogante

overboard /'əʊvəbɔːd/ *adv* (pela) borda fora

overcast /əʊvə'kɑːst/ *a* encoberto, nublado

overcharge /əʊvə'tʃɑːdʒ/ *vt* **~ sb (for)** cobrar demais a alguém (por)

overcoat /'əʊvəkəʊt/ *n* casacão *m*; (*for men*) sobretudo *m*

overcome /əʊvə'kʌm/ *vt* (*pt* **-came**, *pp* **-come**) superar, vencer; **~ by** sucumbindo a, dominado or vencido por

overcrowded /əʊvə'kraʊdɪd/ *a* apinhado, superlotado; ‹*country*› superpovoado

overdo /əʊvə'duː/ *vt* (*pt* **-did**, *pp* **-done**) exagerar, levar longe demais; **~ne** *Culin* cozinhado demais

overdose /'əʊvədəʊs/ *n* dose *f* excessiva, (*P*) overdose *f*

overdraft /'əʊvədrɑːft/ *n* saldo *m* negativo

overdraw /əʊvə'drɔː/ *vt* (*pt* **-drew**, *pp* **-drawn**) sacar a descoberto, (*P*) ter a conta a descoberto

overdue /əʊvə'djuː/ *a* em atraso, atrasado; (*belated*) tardio

overestimate /əʊvər'estɪmeɪt/ *vt* sobrestimar, atribuir valor excessivo a

overexpose /əʊvərɪk'spəʊz/ *vt* expor demais

overflow[1] /əʊvə'fləʊ/ *vt/i* extravasar; transbordar (**with** de)

overflow[2] /'əʊvəfləʊ/ *n* (*outlet*) descarga *f*; (*excess*) excesso *m*

overgrown /əʊvə'grəʊn/ *a* que cresceu demais; ‹*garden etc*› invadido pela vegetação

overhang /əʊvə'hæŋ/ *vt* (*pt* **-hung**) estar sobranceiro a, pairar sobre ● *vi* projetar-se ● *n* saliência *f*

overhaul[1] /əʊvə'hɔ:l/ *vt* fazer uma revisão em

overhaul[2] /'əʊvəhɔ:l/ *n* revisão *f*

overhead[1] /əʊvə'hed/ *adv* em or por cima, ao or no alto

overhead[2] /'əʊvəhed/ *a* aéreo. **~s** *npl* despesas *fpl* gerais

overhear /əʊvə'hɪə(r)/ *vt* (*pt* **-heard**) (*eavesdrop*) ouvir sem conhecimento do falante; (*hear by chance*) ouvir por acaso

overjoyed /əʊvə'dʒɔɪd/ *a* radiante, felicíssimo

overlap /əʊvə'læp/ *vt/i* (*pt* **-lapped**) sobrepor(-se) parcialmente; *fig* coincidir

overleaf /əʊvə'li:f/ *adv* no verso

overload /əʊvə'ləʊd/ *vt* sobrecarregar

overlook /əʊvə'lʊk/ *vt* deixar passar; (*of window*) dar para; (*of building*) dominar

overnight /əʊvə'naɪt/ *adv* durante a noite; *fig* dum dia para o outro ● *a* ‹*train*› da noite; ‹*stay, journey, etc*› de noite, noturno; *fig* súbito

overpass /əʊvə'pɑ:s/ *n* passagem *f* superior

overpay /əʊvə'peɪ/ *vt* (*pt* **-paid**) pagar em excesso

overpower /əʊvə'paʊə(r)/ *vt* dominar, subjugar; *fig* esmagar. **~ing** *a* esmagador; ‹*heat*› sufocante, insuportável

overpriced /əʊvə'praɪst/ *a* muito caro

overrid|e /əʊvə'raɪd/ *vt* (*pt* **-rode**, *pp* **-ridden**) prevalecer sobre, passar por cima de. **~ing** *a* primordial, preponderante; (*importance*) maior

overripe /'əʊvəraɪp/ *a* demasiado maduro

overrule /əʊvə'ru:l/ *vt* anular, rejeitar; ‹*claim*› indeferir

overrun /əʊvə'rʌn/ *vt* (*pt* **-ran**, *pp* **-run**, *pres p* **-running**) invadir; ‹*a limit*› exceder, ultrapassar

overseas /əʊvə'si:z/ *a* ultramarino; (*abroad*) estrangeiro ● *adv* no ultramar, no estrangeiro

oversee /əʊvə'si:/ *vt* (*pt* **-saw**, *pp* **-seen**) supervisionar. **~r** /'əʊvəsɪə(r)/ *n* capataz *m*

overshadow /əʊvə'ʃædəʊ/ *vt fig* eclipsar; ofuscar

oversight /'əʊvəsaɪt/ *n* lapso *m*

oversleep /əʊvə'sli:p/ *vi* (*pt* **-slept**) acordar tarde, dormir demais

overt /'əʊvɜ:t/ *a* manifesto, claro, patente

overtake /əʊvə'teɪk/ *vt/i* (*pt* **-took**, *pp* **-taken**) ultrapassar

overthrow /əʊvə'θrəʊ/ *vt* (*pt* **-threw**, *pp* **-thrown**) derrubar, depor ● *n* /'əʊvəθrəʊ/ *Pol* derrubada *f*, (*P*) deposição

overtime /'əʊvətaɪm/ *n* horas *fpl* extras

overtones /'əʊvətəʊnz/ *npl fig* tom *m*; implicação *f*

overture /'əʊvətjʊə(r)/ *n Mus* abertura *f*; *fig* proposta *f*; abordagem *f*

overturn /əʊvə'tɜ:n/ *vt/i* virar(-se); ‹*car, plane*› capotar, virar-se

overweight /əʊvə'weɪt/ *a* **be ~** ter excesso de peso

overwhelm /əʊvə'welm/ *vt* oprimir; (*defeat*) esmagar; (*amaze*) assoberbar. **~ing** *a* esmagador; ‹*urge*› irresistível

overwork /əʊvə'wɜ:k/ *vt/i* sobrecarregar(-se) com trabalho ● *n* excesso *m* de trabalho

overwrought /əʊvə'rɔ:t/ *a* muito agitado, superexcitado

ow|e /əʊ/ *vt* dever. **~ing** *a* devido; **~ing to** devido a

owl /aʊl/ *n* coruja *f*

own[1] /əʊn/ *a* próprio; **a house**/*etc* **of one's ~** uma casa/*etc* própria; **get one's ~ back** [!] ir à forra, (*P*) desforrar-se; **hold one's ~** aguentar-se; **on one's ~** sozinho

own[2] /əʊn/ *vt* possuir; **~ up (to)** [!] confessar. **~er** *n* proprietário *m*, dono *m*. **~ership** *n* posse *f*, propriedade *f*

ox /ɒks/ *n* (*pl* **oxen**) boi *m*

> **Oxbridge** Termo usado para se referir simultaneamente às universidades mais antigas e prestigiadas do Reino Unido, Oxford e Cambridge, especialmente quando se quer destacar o meio privilegiado com que estão relacionadas. Ultimamente, foram feitos grandes esforços para atrair alunos de todos os meios sociais.

oxygen /'ɒksɪdʒən/ *n* oxigênio *m*, (*P*) oxigénio *m*

oyster /'ɔɪstə(r)/ *n* ostra *f*

ozone /'əʊzəʊn/ *n* ozônio *m*, (*P*) ozono *m*; **~ layer** camada *f* de ozônio, (*P*) ozono *m*

Pp

pace /peɪs/ *n* passo *m*; *fig* ritmo *m*; **keep ~ with** acompanhar, manter-se a par de ● *vt* percorrer passo a passo ● *vi* ~ **up and down** andar de um lado para o outro

pacemaker /ˈpeɪsmeɪkə(r)/ *n Med* marca-passo *m*, (*P*) pacemaker *m*

Pacific /pəˈsɪfɪk/ *a* pacífico ● *n* ~ **(Ocean)** (Oceano) Pacífico *m*

pacifist /ˈpæsɪfɪst/ *n* pacifista *mf*

pacify /ˈpæsɪfaɪ/ *vt* pacificar, apaziguar

pack /pæk/ *n* pacote *m*; *Mil* mochila *f*; (*of hounds*) matilha *f*; (*of lies*) porção *f*; (*of cards*) baralho *m* ● *vt* empacotar; ‹*suitcase*› fazer; ‹*box, room*› encher; (*press down*) atulhar, encher até não caber mais ● *vi* fazer as malas; ~ **into** (*cram*) apinhar em, comprimir em; **send ~ing** pôr a andar, mandar passear. **~ed** *a* apinhado; **~ed lunch** merenda *f*

package /ˈpækɪdʒ/ *n* pacote *m*, embrulho *m* ● *vt* embalar; ~ **deal** pacote *m* de propostas; ~ **holiday** pacote *m* turístico

packet /ˈpækɪt/ *n* pacote *m*; (*of cigarettes*) maço *m*

pact /pækt/ *n* pacto *m*

pad /pæd/ *n* (*in clothing*) chumaço *m*; (*for writing*) bloco *m* de papel/de notas; (*for ink*) almofada (de carimbo) *f*; **(launching)** ~ rampa *f* de lançamento ● *vt* (*pt* **padded**) enchumaçar, acolchoar; *fig* ‹*essay etc*› encher linguiça, (*P*) pôr palha em [!]. **~ding** *n* chumaço *m*; *fig* linguiça *f*, (*P*) palha *f* [!]

P

paddle[1] /ˈpædl/ *n* remo *m* de canoa

paddl|e[2] /ˈpædl/ *vi* chapinhar, molhar os pés; **~ing pool** piscina *f* de plástico para crianças

paddock /ˈpædək/ *n* cercado *m*; (*at racecourse*) paddock *m*

padlock /ˈpædlɒk/ *n* cadeado *m* ● *vt* fechar com cadeado

paediatrician /piːdɪəˈtrɪʃn/ *n* pediatra *mf*

pagan /ˈpeɪgən/ *a & n* pagão *m*, pagã *f*

page[1] /peɪdʒ/ *n* (*of book etc*) página *f*

page[2] /peɪdʒ/ *vt* mandar chamar

pageant /ˈpædʒənt/ *n* espetáculo *m* (histórico); (*procession*) cortejo *m*. **~ry** *n* pompa *f*

paid /peɪd/ ▶ PAY ● *a* **put ~ to** [!] (*end*) pôr fim a

pail /peɪl/ *n* balde *m*

pain /peɪn/ *n* dor *f*; **~s** esforços *mpl*; **be in ~** sofrer, ter dores; **take ~s to** esforçar-se por ● *vt* magoar. **~killer** *n* analgésico *m*. **~ful** *a* doloroso; (*grievous*) (*laborious*) penoso. **~less** *a* sem dor, indolor

painstaking /ˈpeɪnzteɪkɪŋ/ *a* cuidadoso, esmerado, meticuloso

paint /peɪnt/ *n* tinta *f*; **~s** (*in box*) tintas *fpl* ● *vt/i* pintar. **~er** *n* pintor *m*. **~ing** *n* pintura *f*

paintbrush /ˈpeɪntbrʌʃ/ *n* pincel *m*

pair /peə(r)/ *n* par *m*; **a ~ of scissors** uma tesoura; **a ~ of trousers** um par de calças; **in ~s** aos pares ● *vi* ~ **off** formar pares

Pakistan /pɑːkɪˈstɑːn/ *n* Paquistão *m*. **~i** *a & n* paquistanês *m*

pal /pæl/ *n* [!] colega *mf*; amigo *m*

palace /ˈpælɪs/ *n* palácio *m*

palat|e /ˈpælət/ *n* palato *m*. **~able** *a* saboroso, gostoso; *fig* agradável

palatial /pəˈleɪʃl/ *a* suntuoso, (*P*) sumptuoso

pale /peɪl/ *a* (**-er, -est**) pálido; ‹*colour*› claro ● *vi* empalidecer. **~ness** *n* palidez *f*

Palestin|e /ˈpælɪstaɪn/ *n* Palestina *f*. **~ian** /-ˈstɪnɪən/ *a & n* palestino *m*, (*P*) palestiniano

palette /ˈpælɪt/ *n* paleta *f*

palm /pɑːm/ *n* (*of hand*) palma *f*; (*tree*) palmeira *f* ● *vt* ~ **off** impingir (**on** a); **P~ Sunday** Domingo *m* de Ramos

palpable /ˈpælpəbl/ *a* palpável

palpitat|e /ˈpælpɪteɪt/ *vi* palpitar. **~ion** /-ˈteɪʃn/ *n* palpitação *f*

paltry /ˈpɔːltrɪ/ *a* (**-ier, -iest**) irrisório

pamper /ˈpæmpə(r)/ *vt* mimar, paparicar or apaparicar

pamphlet /ˈpæmflɪt/ *n* panfleto *m*, folheto *m*

pan /pæn/ *n* panela *f*; (*for frying*) frigideira *f* ● *vt* (*pt* **panned**) [!] criticar severamente

panacea /pænəˈsɪə/ *n* panaceia *f*

panache /pæˈnæʃ/ *n* brio *m*, estilo *m*, panache *m*

pancake /ˈpænkeɪk/ *n* crepe *m*, panqueca *f*

panda /ˈpændə/ *n* panda *m*

pandemonium /pændɪˈməʊnɪəm/ *n* pandemônio *m*, (*P*) pandemónio *m*, caos *m*

pander /ˈpændə(r)/ *vi* **~ to** prestar-se a servir, ir ao encontro de, fazer concessões a

pane /peɪn/ *n* vidraça *f*

panel /ˈpænl/ *n* painel *m*; (*jury*) júri *m*; (*speakers*) convidados *mpl*; **(instrument) ~** painel *m* de instrumentos, (*P*) de bordo. **~ling** *n* apainelamento *m*. **~list** *n* convidado *m* de painel

pang /pæŋ/ *n* pontada *f*, dor *f* aguda e súbita; **~s** (*of hunger*) ataques *mpl* de fome; **~s of conscience** remorsos *mpl*

panic /ˈpænɪk/ *n* pânico *m* ● *vt/i* (*pt* **panicked**) desorientar(-se), (fazer) entrar em pânico. **~-stricken** *a* tomado de pânico

panoram|a /pænəˈrɑːmə/ *n* panorama *m*. **~ic** /-ˈræmɪk/ *a* panorâmico

pansy /ˈpænzɪ/ *n* amor-perfeito *m*

pant /pænt/ *vi* ofegar, arquejar

panther /ˈpænθə(r)/ *n* pantera *f*

panties /ˈpæntɪz/ *npl* [!] calcinhas *fpl*, (*P*) cuecas *fpl*

pantomime /ˈpæntəmaɪm/ *n* pantomima *f*

pantry /ˈpæntrɪ/ *n* despensa *f*

pants /pænts/ *npl* [!] (*underwear*) cuecas *fpl*; [!] (*trousers*) calças *fpl*

paper /ˈpeɪpə(r)/ *n* papel *m*; (*newspaper*) jornal *m*; (*exam*) prova *f* escrita; (*essay*) comunicação *f*; **on ~** por escrito ● *vt* forrar com papel. **~s** *npl* (*for identification*) documentos *mpl*. **~ clip** *n* clipe *m*

paperback /ˈpeɪpəbæk/ *a & n* **~ (book)** livro *m* de capa mole

paperweight /ˈpeɪpəweɪt/ *n* pesa-papéis *m invar*, (*P*) pisa-papéis *m invar*

paperwork /ˈpeɪpəwɜːk/ *n* trabalho *m* de secretária; *pej* papelada *f*

paprika /ˈpæprɪkə/ *n* páprica *f*, (*P*) paprica *f*

par /pɑː(r)/ *n* **be below ~** estar abaixo do padrão desejado; **on a ~ with** em igualdade com

parable /ˈpærəbl/ *n* parábola *f*

parachut|e /ˈpærəʃuːt/ *n* pára-quedas *m invar* ● *vi* descer de paraquedas. **~ist** *n* paraquedista *mf*

parade /pəˈreɪd/ *n Mil* parada *f* militar; (*procession*) procissão *f* ● *vi* desfilar ● *vt* alardear

paradise /ˈpærədaɪs/ *n* paraíso *m*

paradox /ˈpærədɒks/ *n* paradoxo *m*. **~ical** /-ˈdɒksɪkl/ *a* paradoxal

paraffin /ˈpærəfɪn/ *n* querosene *m*, (*P*) petróleo *m*

paragon /ˈpærəgən/ *n* modelo *m* de perfeição

paragraph /ˈpærəgrɑːf/ *n* parágrafo *m*

parallel /ˈpærəlel/ *a & n* paralelo *m* ● *vt* (*pt* **parelleled**) comparar(-se) a

paralyse /ˈpærəlaɪz/ *vt* paralisar

paraly|sis /pəˈræləsɪs/ *n* paralisia *f*. **~tic** /-ˈlɪtɪk/ *a & n* paralítico *m*

paramedic /pærəˈmedɪk/ *n* paramédico

parameter /pəˈræmɪtə(r)/ *n* parâmetro *m*

paramount /ˈpærəmaʊnt/ *a* supremo, primordial

parapet /ˈpærəpɪt/ *n* parapeito *m*

paraphernalia /pærəfəˈneɪlɪə/ *n* equipamento *m*, parafernália *f*; tralha *f* [!]

paraphrase /ˈpærəfreɪz/ *n* paráfrase *f* ● *vt* parafrasear

paraplegic /pærəˈpliːdʒɪk/ *n* paraplégico *m*

parasite /ˈpærəsaɪt/ *n* parasita *mf*

parasol /ˈpærəsɒl/ *n* sombrinha *f*; (*on table*) parasol *m*, guarda-sol *m*

parcel /ˈpɑːsl/ *n* embrulho *m*; (*for post*) encomenda *f*

parch /pɑːtʃ/ *vt* ressecar; **be ~ed** estar com muita sede

parchment /ˈpɑːtʃmənt/ *n* pergaminho *m*

pardon /ˈpɑːdn/ *n* perdão *m*; *Jur* perdão *m*, indulto *m*; **I beg your ~** perdão, desculpe; **(I beg your) ~?** como? ● *vt* (*pt* **pardoned**) perdoar

parent /ˈpeərənt/ *n* pai *m*, mãe *f*. **~s** *npl* pais *mpl*. **~al** /pəˈrentl/ *a* dos pais, paterno, materno

parenthesis /pəˈrenθəsɪs/ *n* (*pl* **-theses** /-siːz/) parêntese *m*, parêntesis *m*

parish /ˈpærɪʃ/ *n* paróquia *f*; (*municipal*) freguesia *f*. **~ioner** /pəˈrɪʃənə(r)/ *n* paroquiano *m*

park /pɑːk/ *n* parque *m* ● *vt* estacionar. **~ing** *n* estacionamento *m*; **no ~ing** estacionamento proibido. **~ing meter** *n* parquímetro *m*

parliament /ˈpɑːləmənt/ *n* parlamento *m*, assembleia *f*. **~ary** /-ˈmentrɪ/ *a* parlamentar

Parliament O Parlamento britânico, o órgão legislativo mais importante, é formado pela Câmara dos Lordes e pela Câmara

P

dos Comuns. A primeira tem de mais de 750 membros, a maioria deles nomeados, com um número de cargos hereditários, algo que está sendo reformado no momento. A Câmara dos Comuns tem de 650 membros eleitos. Ver *Dáil Éireann*, *Scottish Parliament*, *Welsh Assembly*.

parochial /pə'rəʊkɪəl/ *a* paroquial; *fig* provinciano; tacanho

parody /'pærədɪ/ *n* paródia *f* ● *vt* parodiar

parole /pə'rəʊl/ *n* **on ~** em liberdade condicional ● *vt* pôr em liberdade condicional

parquet /'pɑːkeɪ/ *n* parquê *m*, parquete *m*

parrot /'pærət/ *n* papagaio *m*

parsley /'pɑːslɪ/ *n* salsa *f*

parsnip /'pɑːsnɪp/ *n* cherovia *f*, pastinaga *f*

parson /'pɑːsn/ *n* pároco *m*, pastor *m*

part /pɑːt/ *n* parte *f*; (*of serial*) episódio *m*; (*of machine*) peça *f*; *Theat* papel *m*; (*side in dispute*) partido *m*; **in ~** em parte; **on the ~ of** da parte de; **~ of speech** categoria *f* gramatical; **take ~ in** tomar parte em; **these ~s** estas partes ● *a* parcial ● *adv* em parte ● *vt/i* separar(-se) (**from** de). **~-time** *a & adv* a tempo parcial, em part-time

partial /'pɑːʃl/ *a* (*incomplete, biased*) parcial; **be ~ to** gostar de. **~ity** /-ɪ'ælətɪ/ *n* parcialidade *f*; (*liking*) predileção *f* (**for** por). **~ly** *adv* parcialmente

P

particip|ate /pɑː'tɪsɪpeɪt/ *vi* participar (**in** em). **~ant** *n* /-ənt/ participante *mf*. **~ation** /-'peɪʃn/ *n* participação *f*

particle /'pɑːtɪkl/ *n* partícula *f*; (*of dust*) grão *m*; *fig* mínimo *m*

particular /pə'tɪkjʊlə(r)/ *a* especial, particular; (*fussy*) exigente; (*careful*) escrupuloso. **~s** *npl* pormenores *mpl*. **in ~** *adv* em especial, particularmente. **~ly** *adv* particularmente

parting /'pɑːtɪŋ/ *n* separação *f*; (*in hair*) risca *f* ● *a* de despedida

partisan /pɑːtɪ'zæn/ *n* partidário *m*; *Mil* guerrilheiro *m*

partition /pɑː'tɪʃn/ *n* (*of room*) tabique *m*, divisória *f*; *Pol* (*division*) partilha *f*, divisão *f* ● *vt* dividir, repartir; **~ off** dividir por meio de tabique

partly /'pɑːtlɪ/ *adv* em parte

partner /'pɑːtnə(r)/ *n* sócio *m*; *Cards, Sport* parceiro *m*; *Dancing* par *m*. **~ship** *n* associação *f*, parceria *f*; *Comm* sociedade *f*

partridge /'pɑːtrɪdʒ/ *n* perdiz *f*

party /'pɑːtɪ/ *n* festa *f*, reunião *f*; (*group*) grupo *m*; *Pol* partido *m*; *Jur* parte *f*; **~ line** (*telephone*) linha *f* coletiva

pass /pɑːs/ *vt/i* (*pt* **passed**) passar; (*overtake*) ultrapassar; ‹*exam*› passar; (*approve*) passar; ‹*law*› aprovar; **~ (by)** passar por; **~ away** falecer; **~ out** or **round** distribuir; **~ out** [!] (*faint*) perder os sentidos, desmaiar; **~ over** (*disregard, overlook*) passar por cima de; **~ up** [!] (*forgo*) deixar perder ● *n* (*permit*) *Sport* passe *m*; *Geog* desfiladeiro *m*, garganta *f*; (*in exam*) aprovação *f*; **make a ~ at** [!] atirar-se para *or* (*P*) a [!]

passable /'pɑːsəbl/ *a* passável; ‹*road*› transitável

passage /'pæsɪdʒ/ *n* passagem *f*; (*voyage*) travessia *f*; (*corridor*) corredor *m*, passagem *f*

passenger /'pæsɪndʒə(r)/ *n* passageiro *m*

passer-by /pɑːsə'baɪ/ *n* (*pl* **passers-by**) transeunte *mf*

passion /'pæʃn/ *n* paixão *f*. **~ate** *a* apaixonado, exaltado

passive /'pæsɪv/ *a* passivo. **~ smoking** *n* fumo *m* passivo

passport /'pɑːspɔːt/ *n* passaporte *m*

password /'pɑːswɜːd/ *n* senha *f*

past /pɑːst/ *a* passado; (*former*) antigo; **these ~ months** estes últimos meses ● *n* passado *m* ● *prep* para além de; (*in time*) mais de; (*in front of*) diante de ● *adv* em frente; **be ~ it** já não ser capaz; **it's five ~ eleven** são onze e cinco

pasta /'pæstə/ *n* prato *m* de massa(s)

paste /peɪst/ *n* cola *f*; *Culin* massa(s) *f(pl)*; (*dough*) massa *f*; (*jewellery*) strass *m*, (*P*) vidro *m* ● *vt* colar

pastel /'pæstl/ *n* pastel *m* ● *a* pastel *invar*

pasteurize /'pæstʃəraɪz/ *vt* pasteurizar

pastime /'pɑːstaɪm/ *n* passatempo *m*

pastry /'peɪstrɪ/ *n* massa *f* (de pastelaria); (*tart*) pastel *m*

pasture /'pɑːstʃə(r)/ *n* pastagem *f*

pasty[1] /'pæstɪ/ *n* empadinha *f*

pasty[2] /'peɪstɪ/ *a* pastoso

pat /pæt/ *vt* (*pt* **patted**) (*hit gently*) dar pancadinhas em; (*caress*) fazer festinhas a ● *n* pancadinha *f*; (*caress*) festinha *f* ● *adv* a propósito; (*readily*) prontamente ● *a* preparado, pronto

patch /pætʃ/ *n* remendo *m*; (*over eye*) tapa-olho *m*; (*spot*) mancha *f*; (*small area*) pedaço *m*; (*of vegetables*) canteiro *m*, (*P*) leira *f*; **bad ~** mau bocado *m*; **not be a ~ on** não chegar aos pés de ● *vt* **~ up** remendar; **~ up a quarrel** fazer as pazes. **~work** *n* obra *f* de retalhos. **~y** *a* desigual

pâté /ˈpæteɪ/ *n* patê *m*

patent /ˈpeɪtnt/ *a & n* patente *f*; **~ leather** verniz *m*, polimento *m* ● *vt* patentear

paternal /pəˈtɜːnl/ *a* paternal; ‹*relative*› paterno

paternity /pəˈtɜːnətɪ/ *n* paternidade *f*

path /pɑːθ/ *n* (*pl* **-s** /pɑːðz/) caminho *m*, trilha *f*; (*in park*) aleia *f*, (*P*) alameda *f*; (*of rocket*) trajetória *f*

pathetic /pəˈθetɪk/ *a* patético; [!] (*contemptible*) desgraçado [!], desprezível

patholog|y /pəˈθɒlədʒɪ/ *n* patologia *f*. **~ist** *n* patologista *mf*

patience /ˈpeɪʃns/ *n* paciência *f*

patio /ˈpætɪəʊ/ *n* (*pl* **-os**) pátio *m*

patriot /ˈpætrɪət/ *n* patriota *mf*. **~ic** /-ˈɒtɪk/ *a* patriótico. **~ism** /-ɪzəm/ *n* patriotismo *m*

patrol /pəˈtrəʊl/ *n* patrulha *f* ● *vt/i* patrulhar. **~ car** *n* carro *m* de patrulha

patron /ˈpeɪtrən/ *n* (*of the arts etc*) patrocinador *m*, mecenas *mf*; protetor *m*; (*of charity*) benfeitor *m*; (*customer*) freguês *m*, cliente *mf*; **~ saint** padroeiro *m*, patrono *m*

patron|age /ˈpætrənɪdʒ/ *n* freguesia *f*, clientela *f*; (*support*) patrocínio *m*. **~ize** *vt* ser cliente de; (*support*) patrocinar; (*condescend*) tratar com ares de superioridade

patter[1] /ˈpætə(r)/ *n* (*of rain*) tamborilar *m*, chuviscar *m*; **~ of steps** som *m* leve de passos miúdos, corridinha *f* leve

patter[2] /ˈpætə(r)/ *n* (*of class, profession*) gíria *f*, jargão *m*; (*chatter*) conversa *f* fiada

pattern /ˈpætn/ *n* padrão *m*; (*for sewing*) molde *m*; (*example*) modelo *m*

paunch /pɔːntʃ/ *n* pança *f*

pause /pɔːz/ *n* pausa *f* ● *vi* pausar, fazer (uma) pausa

pav|e /peɪv/ *vt* pavimentar; **~e the way** preparar o caminho (**for** para). **~ing stone** *n* paralelepípedo *m*, laje *f*

pavement /ˈpeɪvmənt/ *n* passeio *m*

pavilion /pəˈvɪlɪən/ *n* pavilhão *m*

paw /pɔː/ *n* pata *f* ● *vt* dar patadas em; ‹*horse*› escarvar; [!] ‹*person*› pôr as patas em cima de

pawn[1] /pɔːn/ *n Chess* peão *m*; *fig* joguete *m*

pawn[2] /pɔːn/ *vt* empenhar; **~-shop** casa *f* de penhores, prego *m* [!]

pawnbroker /ˈpɔːnbrəʊkə(r)/ *n* penhorista *mf*, dono *m* de casa de penhores, agiota *mf*

pay /peɪ/ *vt/i* (*pt* **paid**) pagar; ‹*interest*› render; ‹*visit, compliment*› fazer; **~ attention** prestar atenção; **~ back** restituir; **~ for** pagar; **~ homage** prestar homenagem; **~ in** depositar ● *n* pagamento *m*; ‹*wages*› vencimento *m*, ordenado *m*, salário *m*; **in the ~ of** em pagamento de. **~slip** *n* contracheque *m*, (*P*) folha *f* de pagamento

payable /ˈpeɪəbl/ *a* pagável

pay as you go *n* pagamento *m* de acordo com o uso, (*P*) pré-pagamento *m*

payment /ˈpeɪmənt/ *n* pagamento *m*; *fig* (*reward*) recompensa *f*

payroll /ˈpeɪrəʊl/ *n* folha *f* de pagamentos; **be on the ~** fazer parte da folha de pagamentos de uma firma

pea /piː/ *n* ervilha *f*

peace /piːs/ *n* paz *f*; **disturb the ~** perturbar a ordem pública

peaceful /ˈpiːsfl/ *a* pacífico; (*calm*) calmo, sereno

peacemaker /ˈpiːsmeɪkə(r)/ *n* mediador *m*, pacificador *m*

peach /piːtʃ/ *n* pêssego *m*

peacock /ˈpiːkɒk/ *n* pavão *m*

peak /piːk/ *n* pico *m*, cume *m*, cimo *m*; (*of cap*) pala *f*; (*maximum*) máximo *m*; **~ hours** horas *fpl* de ponta; *Electr* horas *fpl* de carga máxima; **~ed cap** boné *m* de pala

peal /piːl/ *n* (*of bells*) repique *m*; (*of laughter*) gargalhada *f*, risada *f*

peanut /ˈpiːnʌt/ *n* amendoim *m*; **~s** [x] (*small sum*) uma bagatela *f*

pear /peə(r)/ *n* pera

pearl /pɜːl/ *n* pérola *f*

peasant /ˈpeznt/ *n* camponês *m*, aldeão *m*

peat /piːt/ *n* turfa *f*

pebble /ˈpebl/ *n* seixo *m*, calhau *m*

peck /pek/ *vt/i* bicar; (*attack*) dar bicadas (em) ● *n* bicada *f*; [!] (*kiss*) beijo *m* seco or (*P*) repenicado, beijoca *f*; **~ing order** hierarquia *f*, ordem *f* de importância

P

peckish /'pekɪʃ/ *a* **be ~** [!] ter vontade de comer

peculiar /pɪ'kju:lɪə(r)/ *a* bizarro, singular; (*special*) peculiar (**to** a) característico (**to** de). **~ity** /-'ærətɪ/ *n* singularidade *f*; (*feature*) peculiaridade *f*

pedal /'pedl/ *n* pedal *m* ● *vi* (*pt* **pedalled**) pedalar

pedantic /pɪ'dæntɪk/ *a* pedante

peddle /'pedl/ *vt* vender de porta em porta; ‹*drugs*› fazer tráfico de

pedestal /'pedɪstl/ *n* pedestal *m*

pedestrian /pɪ'destrɪən/ *n* pedestre *mf*, (*P*) peão *m* ● *a* pedestre; *fig* prosaico; **~ crossing** faixa *f* para pedestres, (*P*) passadeira *f*

pedigree /'pedɪgri:/ *n* estirpe *f*, linhagem *f*; (*of animal*) raça *f* ● *a* de raça

pedlar /'pedlə(r)/ *n* vendedor *m* ambulante

peek /pi:k/ *vi* espreitar ● *n* espreitadela *f*

peel /pi:l/ *n* casca *f* ● *vt* descascar ● *vi* ‹*skin*› pelar; ‹*paint*› escamar-se, descascar; ‹*wallpaper*› descolar-se

peep /pi:p/ *vi* espreitar ● *n* espreitadela *f*. **~hole** *n* vigia *f*; (*in door*) olho *m* mágico

peer[1] /pɪə(r)/ *vi* **~ at/into** (*searchingly*) perscrutar; (*with difficulty*) esforçar-se por ver

peer[2] /pɪə(r)/ *n* (*equal, noble*) par *m*

peeved /pi:vd/ *a* ⊠ irritado; chateado ⊠

peevish /'pi:vɪʃ/ *a* irritável

peg /peg/ *n* cavilha *f*; (*for washing*) pregador *m* de roupa, (*P*) mola *f*; (*for coats etc*) cabide *m*; (*for tent*) estaca *f* ● *vt* (*pt* **pegged**) prender com estacas; **off the ~** prêt-à-porter, (*P*) pronto-a-vestir *m* inv

pejorative /pɪ'dʒɒrətɪv/ *a* pejorativo

pelican /'pelɪkən/ *n* pelicano *m*; **~ crossing** passagem *f* com sinais manobrados pelos pedestres, (*P*) peões

pellet /'pelɪt/ *n* bolinha *f*; (*for gun*) grão *m* de chumbo

pelt[1] /pelt/ *n* pele *f*

pelt[2] /pelt/ *vt* bombardear (**with** com) ● *vi* chover a cântaros; (*run fast*) correr em disparada or disparado

pelvis /'pelvɪs/ *n* *Anat* pélvis *m*, bacia *f*

pen[1] /pen/ *n* (*enclosure*) cercado *m* ● *vt* encurralar. **play-~** *n* cercado *m*, (*P*) parque *m*

pen[2] /pen/ *n* caneta *f* ● *vt* (*pt* **penned**) escrever. **~friend** *n* correspondente *mf*

penal /'pi:nl/ *a* penal. **~ize** *vt* impôr uma penalidade a; *Sport* penalizar

penalty /'penltɪ/ *n* pena *f*; (*fine*) multa *f*; *Sport* penalidade *f*; **~ kick** pênalti *m*, (*P*) penálti *f*

penance /'penəns/ *n* penitência *f*

pence /pens/ ▶ PENNY

pencil /'pensl/ *n* lápis *m* ● *vt* (*pt* **pencilled**) escrever or desenhar a lápis. **~ sharpener** *n* apontador *m*, (*P*) apara-lápis *m* invar or afia-lápis *m* inv

pendant /'pendənt/ *n* berloque *m*

pending /'pendɪŋ/ *a* pendente ● *prep* (*during*) durante; (*until*) até

pendulum /'pendjʊləm/ *n* pêndulo *m*

penetrat|e /'penɪtreɪt/ *vt/i* penetrar (em). **~ing** *a* penetrante. **~ion** /-'treɪʃn/ *n* penetração *f*

penguin /'peŋgwɪn/ *n* pinguim *m*

penicillin /penɪ'sɪlɪn/ *n* penicilina *f*

peninsula /pə'nɪnsjʊlə/ *n* península *f*

penis /'pi:nɪs/ *n* pênis *m*, (*P*) pénis *m*

penitentiary /penɪ'tenʃərɪ/ *n* *Amer* penitenciária *f*, cadeia *f*

penknife /'pennaɪf/ *n* (*pl* **-knives**) canivete *m*

penniless /'penɪlɪs/ *a* sem vintém, sem um tostão

penny /'penɪ/ *n* (*pl* **pennies**, *or* **pence**) pêni *m*, (*P*) péni *m*; *fig* centavo *m*; vintém *m*

pension /'penʃn/ *n* pensão *f*; (*in retirement*) aposentadoria *f*, (*P*) reforma *f* ● *vt* **~ off** reformar, aposentar. **~er** *n* **(old-age) ~er** reformado *m*

pensive /'pensɪv/ *a* pensativo

penthouse /'penthaʊs/ *n* cobertura *f*, (*P*) apartamento de luxo (no último andar)

pent-up /'pentʌp/ *a* reprimido

penultimate /pen'ʌltɪmət/ *a* penúltimo

people /'pi:pl/ *npl* pessoas *fpl* ● *n* gente *f*, povo *m* ● *vt* povoar; **the Portuguese ~** os portugueses *mpl*; **~ say** dizem, diz-se

pep /pep/ *n* vigor *m* ● *vt* **~ up** animar; **~ talk** discurso *m* de encorajamento

pepper /'pepə(r)/ *n* pimenta *f*; (*vegetable*) pimentão *m*, (*P*) pimento *m* ● *vt* apimentar. **~y** *a* apimentado, picante

peppermint /'pepəmɪnt/ *n* hortelã-pimenta *f*; (*sweet*) bala *f*, (*P*) pastilha *f* de hortelã-pimenta

per /pɜː(r)/ *prep* por; **~ annum** por ano; **~ cent** por cento; **~ kilo**/*etc* o quilo/*etc*

perceive /pəˈsiːv/ *vt* perceber; (*notice*) aperceber-se de

percentage /pəˈsentɪdʒ/ *n* percentagem *f*

perceptible /pəˈseptəbl/ *a* perceptível, (*P*) percetível

percept|ion /pəˈsepʃn/ *n* percepção *f*, (*P*) perceção *f*. **~ive** /-tɪv/ *a* perceptivo, (*P*) percetivo, penetrante, perspicaz

perch[1] /pɜːtʃ/ *n* poleiro *m* ● *vi* empoleirar-se, pousar

perch[2] /pɜːtʃ/ *n* (*fish*) perca *f*

percolat|e /ˈpɜːkəleɪt/ *vt/i* filtrar(-se), passar. **~or** *n* máquina *f* de café com filtro, cafeteira *f*

percussion /pəˈkʌʃn/ *n* percussão *f*

perennial /pəˈrenɪəl/ *a* perene; (*plant*) perene

perfect[1] /ˈpɜːfɪkt/ *a* perfeito. **~ly** *adv* perfeitamente

perfect[2] /pəˈfekt/ *vt* aperfeiçoar. **~ion** /-ʃn/ *n* perfeição *f*. **~ionist** *n* perfeccionista *mf*, (*P*) perfecionista *mf*

perform /pəˈfɔːm/ *vt* ‹*a task*› *Mus* executar; ‹*a function*› *Theat* desempenhar ● *vi* representar; ‹*function*› funcionar. **~ance** *n* (*of task*) *Mus* execução *f*; (*of function*) *Theat* desempenho *m*; (*of car*) performance *f*, comportamento *m*, rendimento *m*; [!] (*fuss*) drama *m*; cena *f*. **~er** *n* artista *mf*

perfume /ˈpɜːfjuːm/ *n* perfume *m*

perhaps /pəˈhæps/ *adv* talvez

peril /ˈperəl/ *n* perigo *m*. **~ous** *a* perigoso

perimeter /pəˈrɪmɪtə(r)/ *n* perímetro *m*

period /ˈpɪərɪəd/ *n* período *m*, época *f*; (*era*) época *f*; (*lesson*) hora *f* de aula; período *m* letivo; *Med* período *m*; (*full stop*) ponto (final) *m* ● *a* (*of novel*) de costumes; (*of furniture*) de estilo. **~ic** /-ˈɒdɪk/ *a* periódico. **~ical** /-ˈɒdɪkl/ *n* periódico *m*. **~ically** /-ˈɒdɪklɪ/ *adv* periodicamente

peripher|y /pəˈrɪfərɪ/ *n* periferia *f*. **~al** *a* periférico; *fig* marginal; à margem

perish /ˈperɪʃ/ *vi* morrer, perecer; (*rot*) estragar-se, deteriorar-se. **~able** *a* (*of goods*) deteriorável

perjur|e /ˈpɜːdʒə(r)/ *vpr* **~e o.s.** jurar falso, perjurar. **~y** *n* perjúrio *m*

perk[1] /pɜːk/ *vt/i* **~ up** [!] arrebitar(-se). **~y** *a* [!] vivo; animado

perk[2] /pɜːk/ *n* [!] regalia *f*; extra *m*

perm /pɜːm/ *n* permanente *f* ● *vt* **have one's hair ~ed** fazer uma permanente

permanen|t /ˈpɜːmənənt/ *a* permanente. **~ce** *n* permanência *f*. **~tly** *adv* permanentemente, a título permanente

permissible /pəˈmɪsəbl/ *a* permissível, admissível

permission /pəˈmɪʃn/ *n* permissão *f*, licença *f*

permissive /pəˈmɪsɪv/ *a* permissivo; **~ society** sociedade *f* permissiva. **~ness** *n* permissividade *f*

permit[1] /pəˈmɪt/ *vt* (*pt* **permitted**) permitir; consentir (**sb to** a alguém que)

permit[2] /ˈpɜːmɪt/ *n* licença *f*; (*pass*) passe *m*

permutation /pɜːmjuːˈteɪʃn/ *n* permutação *f*, permuta *f*

perpendicular /pɜːpənˈdɪkjʊlə(r)/ *a & n* perpendicular *f*

perpetrat|e /ˈpɜːpɪtreɪt/ *vt* perpetrar. **~or** *n* autor *m*

perpetual /pəˈpetʃʊəl/ *a* perpétuo

perpetuate /pəˈpetʃʊeɪt/ *vt* perpetuar

perplex /pəˈpleks/ *vt* deixar perplexo. **~ed** *a* perplexo

persecut|e /ˈpɜːsɪkjuːt/ *vt* perseguir. **~ion** /-ˈkjuːʃn/ *n* perseguição *f*

persever|e /pɜːsɪˈvɪə(r)/ *vi* perseverar. **~ance** *n* perseverança *f*

Persian /ˈpɜːʃn/ *a & n Lang* persa *m*

persist /pəˈsɪst/ *vi* persistir (**in doing** em fazer). **~ence** *n* persistência *f*. **~ent** *a* persistente; (*obstinate*) teimoso; (*continual*) contínuo, constante. **~ently** *adv* persistentemente

person /ˈpɜːsn/ *n* pessoa *f*; **in ~** em pessoa

personal /ˈpɜːsənl/ *a* pessoal; ‹*secretary*› particular; **~ stereo** estéreo *m* pessoal, walkman *m*. **~ly** *adv* pessoalmente

personality /pɜːsəˈnælətɪ/ *n* personalidade *f*; (*on TV*) vedete *f*, (*P*) vedeta *f*

personify /pəˈsɒnɪfaɪ/ *vt* personificar

personnel /pɜːsəˈnel/ *n* pessoal *m*

perspective /pəˈspektɪv/ *n* perspectiva *f*, (*P*) perspetiva *f*

perspir|e /pəˈspaɪə(r)/ *vi* transpirar. **~ation** /-əˈreɪʃn/ *n* transpiração *f*

persua|de /pəˈsweɪd/ *vt* persuadir (**to** a). **~sion** /-ˈsweɪʒn/ *n* persuasão *f*; (*belief*) crença *f*, convicção *f*. **~sive** /-ˈsweɪsɪv/ *a* persuasivo

P

pert /pɜːt/ *a* (*saucy*) atrevido, descarado; (*lively*) vivo

pertinent /ˈpɜːtɪnənt/ *a* pertinente

perturb /pəˈtɜːb/ *vt* perturbar, transtornar

Peru /pəˈruː/ *n* Peru *m*. **~vian** *a & n* peruano *m*

peruse /pəˈruːz/ *vt* ler com atenção

perva|de /pəˈveɪd/ *vt* espalhar-se por, invadir. **~sive** *a* penetrante

pervers|e /pəˈvɜːs/ *a* que insiste no erro; (*wicked*) perverso; (*wayward*) caprichoso. **~ity** *n* obstinação *f*; (*wickedness*) perversidade *f*; (*waywardness*) capricho *m*, birra *f*

perver|t¹ /pəˈvɜːt/ *vt* perverter. **~sion** *n* perversão *f*

pervert² /ˈpɜːvɜːt/ *n* pervertido *m*, tarado *m*

pessimis|t /ˈpesɪmɪst/ *n* pessimista *mf*. **~m** /-zəm/ *n* pessimismo *m*. **~tic** /-ˈmɪstɪk/ *a* pessimista

pest /pest/ *n* praga *f*, inseto *m* novico; (*animal*) animal *m* daninho; (*person*) peste *f*

pester /ˈpestə(r)/ *vt* incomodar ⓘ

pesticide /ˈpestɪsaɪd/ *n* pesticida *m*

pet /pet/ *n* animal *m* de estimação; (*favourite*) preferido *m*, querido *m* ● *a* ‹*rabbit etc*› de estimação ● *vt* (*pt* **petted**) acariciar; **~ name** nome *m* usado em família

P

petal /ˈpetl/ *n* pétala *f*

peter /ˈpiːtə(r)/ *vi* **~ out** extinguir-se, acabar pouco a pouco, morrer *fig*

petition /pɪˈtɪʃn/ *n* petição *f* ● *vt* requerer

petrify /ˈpetrɪfaɪ/ *vt* petrificar

petrol /ˈpetrəl/ *n* gasolina *f*; **~ pump** bomba *f* de gasolina; **~ station** posto *m* de gasolina; **~ tank** tanque *m* de gasolina

petroleum /pɪˈtrəʊlɪəm/ *n* petróleo *m*

petticoat /ˈpetɪkəʊt/ *n* combinação *f*, anágua *f*

petty /ˈpetɪ/ *a* (**-ier**, **-iest**) pequeno, insignificante; (*mean*) mesquinho; **~ cash** fundo *m* para pequenas despesas, caixa *f* pequena

petulan|t /ˈpetjʊlənt/ *a* petulante, irritável. **~ce** *n* irritabilidade *f*

pew /pjuː/ *n* banco (de igreja) *m*

phantom /ˈfæntəm/ *n* fantasma *m*

pharmaceutical /fɑːməˈsjuːtɪkl/ *a* farmacêutico

pharmac|y /ˈfɑːməsɪ/ *n* farmácia *f*. **~ist** *n* farmacêutico *m*

phase /feɪz/ *n* fase *f* ● *vt* **~ in/out** introduzir/retirar progressivamente

PhD *abbr of* **Doctor of Philosophy** *n* doutorado *m*, (*P*) doutoramento *m*

pheasant /ˈfeznt/ *n* faisão *m*

phenomen|on /fɪˈnɒmɪnən/ *n* (*pl* **-ena**) fenômeno *m*, (*P*) fenómeno *m*. **~al** *a* fenomenal

philanthrop|ist /fɪˈlænθrəpɪst/ *n* filantropo *m*. **~ic** /-ənˈθrɒpɪk/ *a* filantrópico

Philippines /ˈfɪlɪpiːnz/ *npl* **the ~** as Filipinas *fpl*

philistine /ˈfɪlɪstaɪn/ *n* filisteu *m*

philosoph|y /fɪˈlɒsəfɪ/ *n* filosofia *f*. **~er** *n* filósofo *m*. **~ical** /-əˈsɒfɪkl/ *a* filosófico

phlegm /flem/ *n* *Med* catarro *m*, fleuma *f*

phobia /ˈfəʊbɪə/ *n* fobia *f*

phone /fəʊn/ *n* ⓘ telefone *m*; **on the ~** no *or* (*P*) ao telefone; **~ book** lista *f* telefônica, (*P*) telefónica; **~ box** cabine *f* telefônica *or* (*P*) telefónica; **~ call** chamada *f*, telefonema *m* ● *vt/i* ⓘ telefonar (para); **~ back** voltar a telefonar, ligar de volta. **~-in** *n* programa *m* de rádio ou tv com participação dos ouvintes

phonecard /ˈfəʊnkɑːd/ *n* cartão *m* para uso em telefone público

phonetic /fəˈnetɪk/ *a* fonético. **~s** *n* fonética *f*

phoney /ˈfəʊnɪ/ *a* (**-ier**, **-iest**) ⊠ falso; fingido ● *n* ⊠ (*person*) fingido *m*; ⊠ (*thing*) falso *m*, (*P*) falsificação *f*

photo /ˈfəʊtəʊ/ *n* (*pl* **-os**) ⓘ retrato *m*; foto *f*

photocop|y /ˈfəʊtəʊkɒpɪ/ *n* fotocópia *f* ● *vt* fotocopiar. **~ier** *n* fotocopiadora *f*

photogenic /fəʊtəʊˈdʒenɪk/ *a* fotogênico, (*P*) fotogénico

photograph /ˈfəʊtəgrɑːf/ *n* fotografia *f* ● *vt* fotografar. **~er** /fə-ˈtɒgrəfə(r)/ *n* fotógrafo *m*. **~ic** /-ˈgræfɪk/ *a* fotográfico. **~y** /fə-ˈtɒgrəfɪ/ *n* fotografia *f*

phrase /freɪz/ *n* expressão *f*, frase *f*; *Gram* locução *f*, frase *f* elíptica ● *vt* exprimir. **~ book** *n* livro *m* de expressões idiomáticas

physical /ˈfɪzɪkl/ *a* físico

physician /fɪˈzɪʃn/ *n* médico *m*

physicist /ˈfɪzɪsɪst/ *n* físico *m*

physics /ˈfɪzɪks/ *n* física *f*

physiology /fɪzɪˈɒlədʒɪ/ *n* fisiologia *f*

physiotherap|y /fɪzɪəʊ'θerəpɪ/ *n* fisioterapia *f.* **~ist** *n* fisioterapeuta *mf*

physique /fɪ'zi:k/ *n* físico *m*

pian|o /pɪ'ænəʊ/ *n* (*pl* **-os**) piano *m.* **~ist** /'pɪənɪst/ *n* pianista *mf*

pick[1] /pɪk/ *n* (*tool*) picareta *f*

pick[2] /pɪk/ *vt* escolher; ‹*flowers, fruit etc*› colher; ‹*lock*› forçar; ‹*teeth*› palitar; **~ a quarrel with** puxar *or* (*P*) pedir uma briga com; **~ holes in an argument** descobrir os pontos fracos dum argumento; **~ sb's pocket** bater *or* (*P*) roubar a carteira de alguém; **~ off** tirar, arrancar; **~ on** implicar com; **~ out** escolher; (*identify*) identificar, reconhecer ● *n* escolha *f*; (*best*) o/a melhor; **take one's ~** escolher livremente □ **~ up** *vt* apanhar; ‹*speed*› ganhar

pickaxe /'pɪkæks/ *n* picareta *f*

picket /'pɪkɪt/ *n* piquete *m*; (*single striker*) grevista *mf* de piquete ● *vt* (*pt* **picketed**) colocar um piquete em ● *vi* fazer piquete

pickings /'pɪkɪŋz/ *npl* restos *mpl*

pickle /'pɪkl/ *n* vinagre *m*; **~s** picles *mpl*, (*P*) pickles *mpl*; **in a ~** [!] numa encrenca [!] ● *vt* conservar em vinagre

pickpocket /'pɪkpɒkɪt/ *n* batedor *m* de carteiras, (*P*) carteirista *m*

picnic /'pɪknɪk/ *n* piquenique *m* ● *vi* (*pt* **picnicked**) piquenicar, (*P*) fazer um piquenique

picture /'pɪktʃə(r)/ *n* imagem *f*; (*illustration*) estampa *f*, ilustração *f*; (*painting*) quadro *m*, pintura *f*; (*photo*) fotografia *f*, retrato *m*; (*drawing*) desenho *m*; *fig* descrição *f*; quadro *m*; **the ~s** o cinema ● *vt* imaginar; (*describe*) pintar, descrever

picturesque /pɪktʃə'resk/ *a* pitoresco

pie /paɪ/ *n* torta *f*, (*P*) tarte *f*; (*of meat*) empada *f*

piece /pi:s/ *n* pedaço *m*, bocado *m*; (*of machine, in game*) peça *f*; (*of currency*) moeda *f*; **a ~ of advice/furniture/***etc* um conselho/um móvel/*etc*; **take to ~s** desmontar ● *vt* **~ together** juntar, montar

piecemeal /'pi:smi:l/ *a* aos poucos, pouco a pouco

pier /pɪə(r)/ *n* molhe *m*

pierc|e /pɪəs/ *vt* furar, penetrar. **~ing** *a* penetrante; (*of scream, pain*) lancinante

piety /'paɪətɪ/ *n* piedade *f*, devoção *f*

pig /pɪg/ *n* porco *m.* **~-headed** *a* cabeçudo, teimoso

pigeon /'pɪdʒɪn/ *n* pombo *m.* **~hole** *n* escaninho *m*

piggy /'pɪgɪ/ *a* como um porco; **~ bank** cofre *m* de criança. **~back** *adv* nas costas, (*P*) porquinho-mealheiro *m*

pigment /'pɪgmənt/ *n* pigmento *m.* **~ation** /-'teɪʃn/ *n* pigmentação *f*

pigsty /'pɪgstaɪ/ *n* pocilga *f*, chiqueiro *m*

pigtail /'pɪgteɪl/ *n* trança *f*

pilchard /'pɪltʃəd/ *n* peixe *m* pequeno da família do arenque, sardinha *f* europeia

pile /paɪl/ *n* pilha *f*; (*of carpet*) pelo *m* ● *vt/i* amontoar(-se); empilhar(-se) (**into** em); **a ~ of** [!] um monte de [!]; **~ up** acumular(-se). **~-up** *n* choque *m* em cadeia

piles /paɪlz/ *npl* hemorroidas *fpl*

pilfer /'pɪlfə(r)/ *vt* furtar

pilgrim /'pɪlgrɪm/ *n* peregrino *m*, romeiro *m.* **~age** *n* peregrinação *f*, romaria *f*

pill /pɪl/ *n* pílula *f*, comprimido *m*

pillar /'pɪlə(r)/ *n* pilar *m.* **~ box** *n* marco *m* do correio

pillow /'pɪləʊ/ *n* travesseiro *m*

pillowcase /'pɪləʊkeɪs/ *n* fronha *f*

pilot /'paɪlət/ *n* piloto *m* ● *vt* (*pt* **piloted**) pilotar. **~ light** *n* piloto *m*; *Electr* lâmpada *f* testemunho; (*gas*) piloto *m*

pimple /'pɪmpl/ *n* borbulha *f*, espinha *f*

pin /pɪn/ *n* alfinete *m*; *Techn* cavilha *f*; **have ~s and needles** estar com uma cãibra ● *vt* (*pt* **pinned**) pregar *or* prender com alfinete(s); (*hold down*) prender, segurar; **~ sb down** *fig* obrigar alguém a definir-se, apertar (com) alguém *fig*; **~ up** pregar. **~point** *vt* localizar com precisão; **~stripe** *a* de listras finas; **~-up** *n* [!] pin-up *f*

PIN /pɪn/ *abbr* (= **personal identification number**) PIN *m*, (*P*) código *m* PIN

pinafore /'pɪnəfɔ:(r)/ *n* avental *m*; **~ dress** veste *f*

pincers /'pɪnsəz/ *npl* (*tool*) torquês *f*, (*P*) alicate *m*; *Med* pinça *f*; *Zool* pinça(s) *f(pl)*, tenaz(es) *f(pl)*

pinch /pɪntʃ/ *vt* apertar; [x] (*steal*) surripiar [!] ● *n* aperto *m*; (*tweak*) beliscão *m*; (*small amount*) pitada *f*; **at a ~** em caso de necessidade

pine[1] /paɪn/ *n* (*tree*) pinheiro *m*; (*wood*) pinho *m*

pine[2] /paɪn/ *vi* **~ away** definhar, consumir-se; **~ for** suspirar por

pineapple /'paɪnæpl/ *n* abacaxi *m*, (*P*) ananás *m*

ping-pong /'pɪŋpɒŋ/ *n* pingue-pongue *m*

pink /pɪŋk/ *a & n* rosa *m*

pinnacle /'pɪnəkl/ *n* pináculo *m*

pint /paɪnt/ *n* quartilho *m* (= 0,57 l, *Amer* = 0,47 l)

pioneer /paɪə'nɪə(r)/ *n* pioneiro *m* ● *vt* ser o pioneiro em, preparar o caminho para

pious /'paɪəs/ *a* piedoso, devoto

pip /pɪp/ *n* (*seed*) pevide *f*

pipe /paɪp/ *n* cano *m*, tubo *m*; (*of smoker*) cachimbo *m* ● *vt* encanar, canalizar; **~ down** calar a boca

pipeline /'paɪplaɪn/ *n* (*for oil*) oleoduto *m*; (*for gas*) gaseoduto *m*, (*P*) gasoduto *m*; **in the ~** *fig* encaminhado

piping /'paɪpɪŋ/ *n* tubagem *f*; **~ hot** muito quente

pira|te /'paɪərət/ *n* pirata *m*. **~cy** *n* pirataria *f*

Pisces /'paɪsi:z/ *n Astr* Peixe *m*

pistol /'pɪstl/ *n* pistola *f*

piston /'pɪstən/ *n* êmbolo *m*, pistão *m*

pit /pɪt/ *n* (*hole*) cova *f*, fosso *m*; (*mine*) poço *m*; (*quarry*) pedreira *f* ● *vt* (*pt* **pitted**) picar, esburacar; *fig* opor; **~ o.s. against** (*struggle*) medir-se com

pitch[1] /pɪtʃ/ *n* breu *m*. **~-black** *a* escuro como breu

pitch[2] /pɪtʃ/ *vt* (*throw*) lançar; ‹*tent*› armar ● *vi* cair ● *n* (*slope*) declive *m*; (*of sound*) som *m*; (*of voice*) altura *f*; *Sport* campo *m*

pitfall /'pɪtfɔ:l/ *n fig* cilada *f*; perigo *m* inesperado

pith /pɪθ/ *n* (*of orange*) parte *f* branca da casca, mesocarpo *m*; *fig* (*essential part*) cerne *m*; âmago *m*

pithy /'pɪθɪ/ *a* (**-ier**, **-iest**) preciso, conciso

piti|ful /'pɪtɪfl/ *a* lastimoso; (*contemptible*) miserável. **~less** *a* impiedoso

pittance /'pɪtns/ *n* salário *m* miserável, miséria *f*

pity /'pɪtɪ/ *n* dó *m*, pena *f*, piedade *f*; **it's a ~** é uma pena; **take ~ on** ter pena de; **what a ~!** que pena! ● *vt* compadecer-se de

pivot /'pɪvət/ *n* eixo *m* ● *vt* (*pt* **pivoted**) girar em torno de

placard /'plækɑ:d/ *n* (*poster*) cartaz *m*

placate /plə'keɪt/ *vt* apaziguar, aplacar

place /pleɪs/ *n* lugar *m*, sítio *m*; (*house*) casa *f*; (*seat, rank etc*) lugar *m* ● *vt* colocar, pôr; **~ an order** fazer uma encomenda; **at/to my ~** em or na/a minha casa. **~ mat** *n* pano *m* de mesa individual

placid /'plæsɪd/ *a* plácido

plagiar|ize /'pleɪdʒəraɪz/ *vt* plagiar. **~ism** *n* plágio *m*

plague /pleɪg/ *n* peste *f*; (*of insects*) praga *f* ● *vt* atormentar, atazanar

plaice /pleɪs/ *n* (*pl invar*) solha *f*

plain /pleɪn/ *a* (**-er**, **-est**) claro; (*candid*) franco; (*simple*) simples; (*not pretty*) sem beleza; (*not patterned*) liso; **in ~ clothes** à paisana ● *adv* com franqueza ● *n* planície *f*. **~ly** *adv* claramente; (*candidly*) francamente

plaintiff /'pleɪntɪf/ *n* queixoso *m*

plait /plæt/ *vt* entrançar ● *n* trança *f*

plan /plæn/ *n* plano *m*, projeto *m*; (*of a house, city etc*) plano *m*, planta *f* ● *vt* (*pt* **planned**) planear, planejar ● *vi* fazer planos; **~ to do** ter a intenção de fazer

plane[1] /pleɪn/ *n* (*level*) plano *m*; (*aeroplane*) avião *m* ● *a* plano

plane[2] /pleɪn/ *n* (*tool*) plaina *f* ● *vt* aplainar

planet /'plænɪt/ *n* planeta *m*

plank /plæŋk/ *n* prancha *f*

planning /'plænɪŋ/ *n* planeamento *m*, planejamento *m*; **~ permission** permissão *f* para construir

plant /plɑ:nt/ *n* planta *f*; *Techn* aparelhagem *f*; (*factory*) fábrica *f* ● *vt* plantar; **~ a bomb** colocar uma bomba. **~ation** /-'teɪʃn/ *n* plantação *f*

plaque /plɑ:k/ *n* placa *f*; (*on teeth*) tártaro *m*, pedra *f*

plaster /'plɑ:stə(r)/ *n* reboco *m*; (*adhesive*) esparadrapo *m*, band-aid *m*, (*P*) gesso *m*; **in ~** engessado; **~ of Paris** gesso *m* ● *vt* rebocar; (*cover*) cobrir (**with** com, de)

plastic /'plæstɪk/ *a* plástico ● *n* plástica *f*; **~ surgery** cirurgia *f* plástica

plate /pleɪt/ *n* prato *m*; (*in book*) gravura *f* ● *vt* revestir de metal

plateau /'plætəʊ/ *n* (*pl* **-eaux** /-əʊz/) planalto *m*, platô *m*

platform /'plætfɔ:m/ *n* estrado *m*; (*for speaking*) tribuna *f*; *Rail* plataforma *f*, cais *m*; *fig* programa *m* de partido político; **~ ticket** bilhete *m* de gare

platinum /'plætɪnəm/ *n* platina *f*

platitude /ˈplætɪtjuːd/ *n* banalidade *f*, lugar-comum *m*

platonic /pləˈtɒnɪk/ *a* platônico, (*P*) platónico

plausible /ˈplɔːzəbl/ *a* plausível; ‹*person*› convincente

play /pleɪ/ *vt/i* (*for amusement*) brincar; ‹*instrument*› tocar; ‹*cards, game*› jogar; ‹*opponent*› jogar contra; ‹*match*› disputar; **~ down** minimizar; **~ on** (*take advantage of*) aproveitar-se de; **~ safe** jogar pelo seguro; **~ up** [!] dar problemas (a) ● *n* jogo *m*; *Theat* peça *f*; (*movement*) folga *f*, margem *f*. **~group** *n* jardim *m* de infância

playboy /ˈpleɪbɔɪ/ *n* playboy *m*

player /ˈpleɪə(r)/ *n* jogador *m*; *Theat* artista *mf*; *Mus* artista *mf*, executante *mf*, instrumentista *mf*

playful /ˈpleɪfl/ *a* brincalhão *m*

playground /ˈpleɪgraʊnd/ *n* pátio *m* de recreio

playing /ˈpleɪɪŋ/ *n* atuação *f*. **~ card** *n* carta *f* de jogar; **~ field** *n* campo *m* de jogos

playwright /ˈpleɪraɪt/ *n* dramaturgo *m*

plc *abbr of* (= **public limited company**) SARL

plea /pliː/ *n* súplica *f*; (*reason*) pretexto *m*, desculpa *f*; *Jur* alegação *f* da defesa

plead /pliːd/ *vt/i* pleitear; (*as excuse*) alegar; **~ guilty** confessar-se culpado; **~ with** implorar a

pleasant /ˈpleznt/ *a* agradável

pleas|e /pliːz/ *vt/i* agradar (a), dar prazer (a); **they ~e themselves, they do as they ~e** eles fazem como bem entendem ● *adv* por favor, (*P*) se faz favor. **~ed** *a* contente; satisfeito (**with** com). **~ing** *a* agradável

pleasur|e /ˈpleʒə(r)/ *n* prazer *m*. **~able** *a* agradável

pleat /pliːt/ *n* prega *f* ● *vt* preguear

pledge /pledʒ/ *n* penhor *m*, garantia *f*; *fig* promessa *f* ● *vt* prometer; (*pawn*) empenhar

plentiful /ˈplentɪfl/ *a* abundante

plenty /ˈplentɪ/ *n* abundância *f*, fartura *f*; **~ (of)** muito (de); (*enough*) bastante (de)

pliable /ˈplaɪəbl/ *a* flexível

pliers /ˈplaɪəz/ *npl* alicate *m*

plight /plaɪt/ *n* triste *f* situação

plinth /plɪnθ/ *n* plinto *m*

plod /plɒd/ *vi* (*pt* **plodded**) caminhar lentamente; ‹*work*› trabalhar; marrar ☒

plonk /plɒŋk/ *n* ☒ vinho *m* ordinário, (*P*) carrascão *m*

plot /plɒt/ *n* complô *m*, conspiração *f*; (*of novel etc*) trama *f*; (*of land*) lote *m* ● *vt/i* (*pt* **plotted**) conspirar; (*mark out*) traçar

plough /plaʊ/ *n* arado *m* ● *vt/i* arar; **~ back** reinvestir; **~ into** colidir; **~ through** abrir caminho por

ploy /plɔɪ/ *n* [!] estratagema *m*

pluck /plʌk/ *vt* apanhar; ‹*bird*› depenar; ‹*eyebrows*› depilar; *Mus* tanger; **~ up courage** ganhar coragem ● *n* coragem *f*. **~y** *a* corajoso

plug /plʌg/ *n* tampão *m*; *Electr* tomada *f*, (*P*) ficha *f* ● *vt* (*pt* **plugged**) tapar com tampão; [!] (*publicize*) fazer grande propaganda de ● *vi* **~ away** [!] trabalhar com afinco; **~ in** *Electr* ligar

plum /plʌm/ *n* ameixa *f*

plumb /plʌm/ *adv* exatamente ● *vt* sondar

plumb|er /ˈplʌmə(r)/ *n* bombeiro *m*, encanador *m*, (*P*) canalizador *m*. **~ing** *n* encanamento *m*, (*P*) canalização *f*

plummet /ˈplʌmɪt/ *vi* (*pt* **plummeted**) despencar

plump /plʌmp/ *a* (**-er, -est**) rechonchudo, roliço ● *vi* **~ for** optar por

plunder /ˈplʌndə(r)/ *vt* pilhar, saquear ● *n* pilhagem *f*, saque *m*; (*goods*) despojo *m*

plunge /plʌndʒ/ *vt/i* mergulhar, atirar(-se), afundar(-se) ● *n* mergulho *m*; **take the ~** *fig* decidir-se, dar o salto *fig*

plural /ˈplʊərəl/ *a* plural; ‹*noun*› no plural ● *n* plural *m*

plus /plʌs/ *prep* mais ● *a* positivo ● *n* sinal +; *fig* qualidade *f* positiva

plush /plʌʃ/ *n* pelúcia *f*, peluche *m* ● *a* de pelúcia, de peluche; [!] de luxo

ply /plaɪ/ *vt* (*tool*) manejar; (*trade*) exercer; **~ sb with drink** encher alguém de bebidas ● *vi* ‹*ship, bus*› fazer carreira entre dois lugares

plywood /ˈplaɪwʊd/ *n* madeira *f* compensada, (*P*) contraplacado *m*

p.m. /piːˈem/ *adv* da tarde, da noite

pneumatic /njuːˈmætɪk/ *a* pneumático; **~ drill** broca *f* pneumática

pneumonia /njuːˈməʊnɪə/ *n* pneumonia *f*

poach /pəʊtʃ/ *vt/i* (*steal*) caçar/pescar em propriedade alheia or ilegalmente; *Culin* fazer pochê, (*P*) escalfar; **~ed eggs** ovos *mpl* pochês, (*P*) ovos *mpl* escalfados

pocket /ˈpɒkɪt/ *n* bolso *m*, algibeira *f* ● *a* de algibeira ● *vt* meter no bolso. **~book** *n* (*notebook*) livro *m* de apontamentos; *Amer* (*handbag*) carteira *f*; **~ money** *n* (*monthly*) mesada *f*; (*weekly*) semanada *f*, dinheiro *m* para pequenas despesas

pod /pɒd/ *n* vagem *f*

podcast /ˈpɒdkaːst/ *n* podcast *m*

poem /ˈpəʊɪm/ *n* poema *m*

poet /ˈpəʊɪt/ *n* poeta *m*, poetisa *f*. **~ic** /-ˈetɪk/ *a* poético

poetry /ˈpəʊɪtrɪ/ *n* poesia *f*

poignant /ˈpɔɪnjənt/ *a* pungente, doloroso

point /pɔɪnt/ *n* ponto *m*; (*tip*) ponta *f*; (*decimal point*) vírgula *f*; (*meaning*) sentido *m*, razão *m*; *Electr* tomada *f*; **~s** *Rail* agulhas *fpl*; **on the ~ of** prestes a, quase a; **~ of view** ponto *m* de vista; **that is a good ~** (*remark*) é uma boa observação; **to the ~** a propósito; **what is the ~?** de que adianta? ● *vt/i* (*aim*) apontar (**at** para); (*show*) apontar; indicar (**at/to** para); **~ out** apontar, fazer ver. **~-blank** *a & adv* à queima-roupa; *fig* categórico

pointed /ˈpɔɪntɪd/ *a* pontiagudo; (*of remark*) intencional, contundente

pointer /ˈpɔɪntə(r)/ *n* ponteiro *m*; [!] (*hint*) sugestão *f*

pointless /ˈpɔɪntlɪs/ *a* inútil, sem sentido

poise /pɔɪz/ *n* equilíbrio *m*; (*carriage*) porte *m*; *fig* (*self-possession*) presença *f*, segurança *f*. **~d** *a* equilibrado; ‹*person*› seguro de si

poison /ˈpɔɪzn/ *n* veneno *m*, peçonha *f* ● *vt* envenenar. **blood-~ing** *n* envenenamento *m* do sangue. **food-~ing** *n* intoxicação *f* alimentar. **~ous** *a* venenoso

poke /pəʊk/ *vt/i* espetar; (*with elbow*) acotovelar; ‹*fire*› atiçar ● *n* espetadela *f*; (*with elbow*) cotovelada *f*; **~ about** esgaravatar, remexer, procurar; **~ fun at** fazer troça/pouco de; **~ out** ‹*head*› enfiar

poker[1] /ˈpəʊkə(r)/ *n* atiçador *m*

poker[2] /ˈpəʊkə(r)/ *n Cards* pôquer *m*, (*P*) póquer *m*

poky /ˈpəʊkɪ/ *a* (**-ier, -iest**) acanhado, apertado

Poland /ˈpəʊlənd/ *n* Polônia *f*, (*P*) Polónia *f*

polar /ˈpəʊlə(r)/ *a* polar; **~ bear** urso *m* branco

P

pole[1] /pəʊl/ *n* vara *f*; (*for flag*) mastro *m*; (*post*) poste *m*

pole[2] /pəʊl/ *n Geog* polo *m*

Pole /pəʊl/ *n* polaco *m*

police /pəˈliːs/ *n* polícia *f*; **~ state** estado *m* policial; **~ station** distrito *m*, delegacia *f*, (*P*) esquadra *f* de polícia ● *vt* policiar

police|man /pəˈliːsmən/ *n* (*pl* **-men**) policial *m*, (*P*) polícia *m*, guarda *m*, agente *m* de polícia. **~woman** *n* (*pl* **-women**) polícia *f* feminina, (*P*) mulher-polícia *f*

policy[1] /ˈpɒlɪsɪ/ *n* (*plan of action*) política *f*

policy[2] /ˈpɒlɪsɪ/ *n* (*insurance*) apólice *f* de seguro

polio /ˈpəʊlɪəʊ/ *n* polio *f*

polish /ˈpɒlɪʃ/ *vt* polir, dar lustro em; ‹*shoes*› engraxar; ‹*floor*› encerar ● *n* (*for shoes*) graxa *f*; (*for floor*) cera *f*; (*for nails*) esmalte *m*, (*P*) verniz *m*; (*shine*) polimento *m*; *fig* requinte *m*; **~ off** acabar (rapidamente); **~ up** ‹*language*› aperfeiçoar. **~ed** *a* requintado, elegante

Polish /ˈpəʊlɪʃ/ *a & n* polonês *m*, (*P*) polaco *m*

polite /pəˈlaɪt/ *a* polido, educado, delicado. **~ness** *n* delicadeza *f*, cortesia *f*

political /pəˈlɪtɪkl/ *a* político

politician /pɒlɪˈtɪʃn/ *n* político *m*

politics /ˈpɒlətɪks/ *n* política *f*

poll /pəʊl/ *n* votação *f*; (*survey*) sondagem *f*, pesquisa *f*; **go to the ~s** votar, ir às urnas ● *vt* ‹*votes*› obter. **~ing booth** *n* cabine *f* de voto

pollen /ˈpɒlən/ *n* pólen *m*

pollut|e /pəˈluːt/ *vt* poluir. **~ion** /-ʃn/ *n* poluição *f*

polo /ˈpəʊləʊ/ *n* polo *m*; **~ neck** gola *f* rolê

polyester /pɒlɪˈestə/ *n* poliéster *m*

polythene /ˈpɒlɪθiːn/ *n* politeno *m*. **~ bag** *n* saco *m* de plástico

pomegranate /ˈpɒmɪgrænɪt/ *n* romã *f*

pomp /pɒmp/ *n* pompa *f*

pomp|ous /ˈpɒmpəs/ *a* pomposo. **~osity** /-ˈpɒsətɪ/ *n* imponência *f*

pond /pɒnd/ *n* lagoa *f*, lago *m*; (*artificial*) tanque *m*, lago *m*

ponder /ˈpɒndə(r)/ *vt/i* ponderar; meditar (**over** sobre)

pony /ˈpəʊnɪ/ *n* pônei *m*, (*P*) pónei *m*. **~tail** *n* rabo *m* de cavalo

poodle /ˈpuːdl/ *n* caniche *m*

pool[1] /puːl/ *n* (*puddle*) charco *m*, poça *f*; (*for swimming*) piscina *f*

pool[2] /puːl/ *n* (*fund*) fundo *m* comum; *Econ, Comm* pool *m*; (*game*) forma *f* de bilhar; **~s** loteca *f*, (*P*) totobola *m* ● *vt* pôr num fundo comum

poor /pʊə(r)/ *a* (**-er**, **-est**) pobre; (*not good*) medíocre. **~ly** *adv* mal ● *a* doente

pop[1] /pɒp/ *n* estalido *m*, ruído *m* seco ● *vt/i* (*pt* **popped**) dar um estalido, estalar; (*of cork*) saltar; **~ in/out/off** entrar/sair/ir-se embora; **~ up** aparecer de repente, saltar

pop[2] /pɒp/ *n* música *f* pop ● *a* pop *invar*

popcorn /ˈpɒpkɔːn/ *n* pipoca *f*

pope /pəʊp/ *n* papa *m*

poplar /ˈpɒplə(r)/ *n* choupo *m*, álamo *m*

poppy /ˈpɒpɪ/ *n* papoula *f*

popular /ˈpɒpjʊlə(r)/ *a* popular; (*in fashion*) em voga, na moda; **be ~ with** ser popular entre. **~ity** /-ˈlærətɪ/ *n* popularidade *f*. **~ize** *vt* popularizar, vulgarizar

populat|e /ˈpɒpjʊleɪt/ *vt* povoar. **~ion** /-ˈleɪʃn/ *n* população *f*

populous /ˈpɒpjʊləs/ *a* populoso

porcelain /ˈpɔːslɪn/ *n* porcelana *f*

porch /pɔːtʃ/ *n* alpendre *m*; *Amer* varanda *f*

porcupine /ˈpɔːkjʊpaɪn/ *n* porco-espinho *m*

pore[1] /pɔː(r)/ *n* poro *m*

pore[2] /pɔː(r)/ *vi* **~ over** examinar, estudar

pork /pɔːk/ *n* carne *f* de porco

pornograph|y /pɔːˈnɒgrəfɪ/ *n* pornografia *f*. **~ic** /-əˈgræfɪk/ *a* pornográfico

porridge /ˈpɒrɪdʒ/ *n* (papa *f* de) flocos *mpl* de aveia

port[1] /pɔːt/ *n* (*harbour*) porto *m*

port[2] /pɔːt/ *n* (*wine*) (vinho do) Porto *m*

portable /ˈpɔːtəbl/ *a* portátil

porter[1] /ˈpɔːtə(r)/ *n* (*carrier*) carregador *m*

porter[2] /ˈpɔːtə(r)/ *n* (*doorkeeper*) porteiro *m*

portfolio /pɔːtˈfəʊlɪəʊ/ *n* (*pl* **-os**) portfólio *m*; (*case, post*) pasta *f*; (*securities*) carteira *f* de investimentos

porthole /ˈpɔːthəʊl/ *n* vigia *f*

portion /ˈpɔːʃn/ *n* (*share, helping*) porção *f*; (*part*) parte *f*

portrait /ˈpɔːtrɪt/ *n* retrato *m*

portray /pɔːˈtreɪ/ *vt* retratar, pintar; *fig* descrever. **~al** *n* retrato *m*

Portug|al /ˈpɔːtjʊgl/ *n* Portugal *m*. **~uese** /-ˈgiːz/ *a & n invar* português *m*

pose /pəʊz/ *vt/i* (fazer) posar; ‹*question*› fazer, colocar ● *n* pose *f*, postura *f*; **~ as** fazer-se passar por

poser /ˈpəʊzə(r)/ *n* quebra-cabeças *m*

posh /pɒʃ/ *a* ☒ chique *invar*

position /pəˈzɪʃn/ *n* posição *f*; (*job*) lugar *m*, colocação *f*; (*state*) situação *f* ● *vt* colocar

positive /ˈpɒzətɪv/ *a* positivo; (*definite*) categórico, definitivo; ! (*downright*) autêntico; **she's ~ that** ela tem certeza que. **~ly** *adv* positivamente; (*absolutely*) completamente

possess /pəˈzes/ *vt* possuir. **~ion** /-ʃn/ *n* posse *f*; (*thing possessed*) possessão *f*

possessive /pəˈzesɪv/ *a* possessivo

possib|le /ˈpɒsəbl/ *a* possível. **~ility** /-ˈbɪlətɪ/ *n* possibilidade *f*

possibly /ˈpɒsəblɪ/ *adv* possivelmente, talvez; **if I ~ can** se me for possível; **I cannot ~ leave** estou impossibilitado de partir

post[1] /pəʊst/ *n* (*pole*) poste *m* ● *vt* ‹*notice*› afixar, pregar

post[2] /pəʊst/ *n* (*station, job*) posto *m* ● *vt* colocar; (*appoint*) colocar

post[3] /pəʊst/ *n* (*mail*) correio *m*; **P~ Office** agência *f* dos correios, (*P*) estação *f* dos correios; (*corporation*) Departamento *m* dos Correios e Telégrafos, (*P*) Correios, Telégrafos e Telefones *mpl* (CTT) ● *a* postal ● *vt* mandar pelo correio; **keep ~ed** manter informado. **~ code** *n* código *m* postal

post- /pəʊst/ *pref* pós-

postage /ˈpəʊstɪdʒ/ *n* porte *m*

postal /ˈpəʊstl/ *a* postal; **~ order** vale *m* postal

postcard /ˈpəʊstkɑːd/ *n* cartão-postal *m*, (*P*) (bilhete) postal *m*

poster /ˈpəʊstə(r)/ *n* cartaz *m*

posterity /pɒˈsterətɪ/ *n* posteridade *f*

postgraduate /pəʊstˈgrædʒʊet/ *n* pós-graduado *m*

posthumous /ˈpɒstjʊməs/ *a* póstumo. **~ly** *adv* a título póstumo

postman /ˈpəʊstmən/ *n* (*pl* **-men**) carteiro *m*

postmark /ˈpəʊstmɑːk/ *n* carimbo *m* do correio

post-mortem /pəʊstˈmɔːtəm/ *n* autópsia *f*

postpone /pə'spəʊn/ *vt* adiar. **~ment** *n* adiamento *m*

postscript /'pəʊsskrɪpt/ *n* post-scriptum *m*

posture /'pɒstʃə(r)/ *n* postura *f*, posição *f* ● *vi* posar

post-war /'pəʊstwɔ:(r)/ *a* de após-guerra, (*P*) do pós-guerra

pot /pɒt/ *n* pote *m*; (*for cooking*) panela *f*; (*for plants*) vaso *m*; ⊠ (*marijuana*) maconha *f*, (*P*) marijuana *f*; **go to ~** ⊠ ‹*business*› arruinar, degringolar ⊡;⊠ ‹*person*› estar arruinado or liquidado; **take ~ luck** aceitar o que houver; **take a ~-shot** dar um tiro de perto (**at** em); (*at random*) dar um tiro a esmo (**at** em) ● *vt* (*pt* **potted**) **~ (up)** plantar em vaso. **~ belly** *n* pança *f*, barriga *f*

potato /pə'teɪtəʊ/ *n* (*pl* **-oes**) batata *f*

poten|t /'pəʊtnt/ *a* potente, poderoso; ‹*drink*› forte. **~cy** *n* potência *f*

potential /pə'tenʃl/ *a* & *n* potencial *m*. **~ly** *adv* potencialmente

pothol|e /'pɒthəʊl/ *n* caverna *f*, caldeirão *m*; (*in road*) buraco *m*

potion /'pəʊʃn/ *n* poção *f*

potted /'pɒtɪd/ *a* (*of plant*) de vaso; (*preserved*) de conserva

potter[1] /'pɒtə(r)/ *n* oleiro *m*, ceramista *mf*. **~y** *n* olaria *f*, cerâmica *f*

potter[2] /'pɒtə(r)/ *vi* entreter-se com isto ou aquilo

P

potty[1] /'pɒtɪ/ *a* (**-ier**, **-iest**) ⊠ doido, pirado ⊠, (*P*) chanfrado ⊡

potty[2] /'pɒtɪ/ *n* **-ties** ⊡ penico *m* de criança

pouch /paʊtʃ/ *n* bolsa *f*; (*for tobacco*) tabaqueira *f*

poultry /'pəʊltrɪ/ *n* aves *fpl* domésticas, carne *f* de aves domésticas

pounce /paʊns/ *vi* atirar-se (**on** sobre, para cima de)● *n* salto *m*

pound[1] /paʊnd/ *n* (*weight*) libra *f* (= 453 g); (*money*) libra *f*

pound[2] /paʊnd/ *n* (*for dogs*) canil *m* municipal; (*for cars*) parque *m* de viaturas rebocadas

pound[3] /paʊnd/ *vt/i* (*crush*) esmagar, pisar; (*of heart*) bater com força; (*bombard*) bombardear; (*on piano etc*) martelar

pour /pɔ:(r)/ *vt* deitar, derramar ● *vi* correr; ‹*rain*› chover torrencialmente; **~ in/out** (*of people*) afluir/sair em massa; **~ off** or **out** esvaziar, vazar; **~ing rain** chuva *f* torrencial

pout /paʊt/ *vt/i* **~ (one's lips)** (*sulk*) fazer beicinho; (*in annoyance*) ficar de trombas ● *n* beicinho *m*

poverty /'pɒvətɪ/ *n* pobreza *f*, miséria *f*. **~-stricken** *a* pobre

powder /'paʊdə(r)/ *n* pó *m*; (*for face*) pó de arroz *m* ● *vt* polvilhar; ‹*face*› empoar. **~ room** *n* toalete *m*, toucador *m*. **~y** *a* como pó

power /'paʊə(r)/ *n* poder *m*; *Maths*, *Mech* potência *f*; (*energy*) energia *f*; *Electr* corrente *f*; **~ cut** corte *m* de energia, blecaute *m*, (*P*) blackout *m*; **~ station** central *f* elétrica; **~ed by** movido a; ‹*jet etc*› de propulsão. **~ful** *a* poderoso; *Mech* potente. **~less** *a* impotente

practicable /'præktɪkəbl/ *a* viável

practical /'præktɪkl/ *a* prático; **~ joke** brincadeira *f* de mau gosto

practically /'præktɪklɪ/ *adv* praticamente

practice /'præktɪs/ *n* prática *f*; (*of law etc*) exercício *m*; *Sport* treino *m*; (*clients*) clientela *f*; **in ~** (*in fact*) na prática; (*well-trained*) em forma; **out of ~** destreinado, sem prática; **put into ~** pôr em prática

practis|e /'præktɪs/ *vt/i* ‹*skill, sport*› praticar, exercitar-se em; ‹*profession*› exercer; (*put into practice*) pôr em prática. **~ed** *a* experimentado, experiente. **~ing** *a* ‹*Catholic etc*› praticante

practitioner /præk'tɪʃənə(r)/ *n* praticante *mf*; **general ~** médico *m* de clínica geral or de família

pragmatic /præg'mætɪk/ *a* pragmático

praise /preɪz/ *vt* louvar, elogiar ● *n* elogio(s) *m(pl)*, louvor(es) *m(pl)*

praiseworthy /'preɪzwɜ:ðɪ/ *a* louvável, digno de louvor

pram /præm/ *n* carrinho *m* de bebê, (*P*) bebé

prance /prɑ:ns/ *vi* (*of horse*) curvetear, empinar-se; (*of person*) pavonear-se

prank /præŋk/ *n* brincadeira *f* de mau gosto

prawn /prɔ:n/ *n* camarão *m* grande, (*P*) gamba *f*

pray /preɪ/ *vi* rezar, orar

prayer /preə(r)/ *n* oração *f*; **the Lord's P~** o Padre-Nosso. **~ book** *n* missal *m*

pre- /pri:/ *pref* pré-

preach /pri:tʃ/ *vt/i* pregar (**at** a). **~er** *n* pregador *m*

prearrange /priːəˈreɪndʒ/ *vt* combinar or arranjar de antemão

precarious /prɪˈkeərɪəs/ *a* precário; (*of position*) instável, inseguro

precaution /prɪˈkɔːʃn/ *n* precaução *f*. **~ary** *a* de precaução

preced|e /prɪˈsiːd/ *vt* preceder. **~ing** *a* precedente

precedent /ˈpresɪdənt/ *n* precedente *m*

precinct /ˈpriːsɪŋkt/ *n* precinto *m*; *Amer* (*district*) circunscrição *f*; **(pedestrian) ~** área *f* de pedestres, (*P*) zona *f* para peões

precious /ˈpreʃəs/ *a* precioso

precipice /ˈpresɪpɪs/ *n* precipício *m*

precipitat|e /prɪˈsɪpɪteɪt/ *vt* precipitar ● *a* /-ɪtət/ precipitado. **~ion** /-ˈteɪʃn/ *n* precipitação *f*

precis|e /prɪˈsaɪs/ *a* preciso; (*careful*) meticuloso. **~ely** *adv* precisamente. **~ion** /-ˈsɪʒn/ *n* precisão *f*

preclude /prɪˈkluːd/ *vt* evitar, excluir, impedir

precocious /prɪˈkəʊʃəs/ *a* precoce

preconc|eived /priːkənˈsiːvd/ *a* preconcebido. **~eption** /priːkənˈsepʃn/ *n* ideia *f* preconcebida

precursor /priːˈkɜːsə(r)/ *n* precursor *m*

predator /ˈpredətə(r)/ *n* animal *m* de rapina, predador *m*. **~y** *a* predatório

predecessor /ˈpriːdɪsesə(r)/ *n* predecessor *m*, antecessor *m*

predicament /prɪˈdɪkəmənt/ *n* situação *f* difícil

predict /prɪˈdɪkt/ *vt* predizer, prognosticar. **~able** *a* previsível. **~ion** /-ʃn/ *n* predição *f*, (*P*) previção *f*, prognóstico *m*

predictive text messaging *n* previsão *f* de texto, (*P*) escrita *f* inteligente

predominant /prɪˈdɒmɪnənt/ *a* predominante, preponderante. **~ly** *adv* predominantemente, preponderantemente

predominate /prɪˈdɒmɪneɪt/ *vi* predominar

pre-eminent /priːˈemɪnənt/ *a* preeminente, superior

pre-empt /priːˈempt/ *vt* adquirir por preempção. **~ive** *a* antecipado; *Mil* preventivo

preen /priːn/ *vt* alisar; **~ o.s.** enfeitar-se

prefab /ˈpriːfæb/ *n* [!] casa *f* pré-fabricada. **~ricated** /-ˈfæbrɪkeɪtɪd/ *a* pré-fabricado

preface /ˈprefɪs/ *n* prefácio *m*

prefect /ˈpriːfekt/ *n* aluno *m* autorizado a disciplinar outros; (*official*) prefeito *m*

prefer /prɪˈfɜː(r)/ *vt* (*pt* **preferred**) preferir. **~able** /ˈprefrəbl/ *a* preferível

preferen|ce /ˈprefrəns/ *n* preferência *f*. **~tial** /-əˈrenʃl/ *a* preferencial, privilegiado

prefix /ˈpriːfɪks/ *n* (*pl* **-ixes**) prefixo *m*

pregnan|t /ˈpregnənt/ *a* ‹*woman*› grávida; ‹*animal*› prenhe. **~cy** *n* gravidez *f*

prehistoric /priːhɪˈstɒrɪk/ *a* pré-histórico

prejudice /ˈpredʒʊdɪs/ *n* preconceito *m*, ideia *f* preconcebida, prejuízo *m*; (*harm*) prejuízo *m* ● *vt* influenciar. **~d** *a* com preconceitos

preliminar|y /prɪˈlɪmɪnərɪ/ *a* preliminar. **~ies** *npl* preliminares *mpl*, preâmbulos *mpl*

prelude /ˈpreljuːd/ *n* prelúdio *m*

premarital /priːˈmærɪtl/ *a* antes do casamento, pré-marital

premature /ˈprematjʊə(r)/ *a* prematuro

premeditated /priːˈmedɪteɪtɪd/ *a* premeditado

premier /ˈpremɪə(r)/ *a* primeiro ● *n Pol* primeiro-ministro *m*

premises /ˈpremɪsɪz/ *npl* local *m*, edifício *m*; **on the ~** neste estabelecimento, no local

premium /ˈpriːmɪəm/ *n* prêmio *m*, (*P*) prémio *m*; **at a ~** a peso de ouro

premonition /priːməˈnɪʃn/ *n* pressentimento *m*

preoccup|ation /priːɒkjʊˈpeɪʃn/ *n* preocupação *f*. **~ied** /-ˈɒkjʊpaɪd/ *a* preocupado

preparation /prepəˈreɪʃn/ *n* preparação *f*; **~s** preparativos *mpl*

preparatory /prɪˈpærətrɪ/ *a* preparatório; **~ school** escola *f* primária particular

prepare /prɪˈpeə(r)/ *vt/i* preparar(-se) (**for** para); **~d to** pronto a, preparado para

preposition /prepəˈzɪʃn/ *n* preposição *f*

preposterous /prɪˈpɒstərəs/ *a* absurdo, disparatado, ridículo

prerequisite /priːˈrekwɪzɪt/ *n* condição *f* prévia

prerogative /prɪˈrɒgətɪv/ *n* prerrogativa *f*

Presbyterian /prezbɪ'tɪərɪən/ *a & n* presbiteriano *m*

prescri|be /prɪ'skraɪb/ *vt* prescrever; *Med* receitar, prescrever. **~ption** /-ɪpʃn/ *n* prescrição *f*; *Med* receita *f*

presence /'prezns/ *n* presença *f*; **~ of mind** presença *f* de espírito

present[1] /'preznt/ *a & n* presente *mf*; **at ~** no momento, presentemente

present[2] /'preznt/ *n* (*gift*) presente *m*, prenda *f*

present[3] /prɪ'zent/ *vt* apresentar; ‹*film etc*› dar; **~ sb with** oferecer a alguém. **~able** *a* apresentável. **~ation** /prezn'teɪʃn/ *n* apresentação *f*. **~er** *n* apresentador *m*

presently /'prezntlɪ/ *adv* dentro em pouco, daqui a pouco; *Amer* (*now*) neste momento

preservative /prɪ'zɜ:vətɪv/ *n* preservativo *m*, conservante *m*

preserv|e /prɪ'zɜ:v/ *vt* preservar; (*maintain*) *Culin* conservar ● *n* reserva *f*; *fig* área *f*; terreno *m*; (*jam*) compota *f*. **~ation** /prezə'veɪʃn/ *n* conservação *f*

preside /prɪ'zaɪd/ *vi* presidir (**over** a)

presiden|t /'prezɪdənt/ *n* presidente *mf*. **~cy** *n* presidência *f*. **~tial** /-'denʃl/ *a* presidencial

press /pres/ *vt/i* carregar (**on** em); (*squeeze*) espremer; (*urge*) pressionar; (*iron*) passar a ferro; **be ~ed for** estar apertado com falta de; **~ on (with)** continuar (com), prosseguir (com) ● *n* imprensa *f*; *Mech* prensa *f*; (*for wine*) lagar *m*; **~ conference** entrevista *f* coletiva, (*P*) conferência *f* de imprensa

pressing /'presɪŋ/ *a* premente, urgente

pressure /'preʃə(r)/ *n* pressão *f*; **~ group** grupo *m* de pressão ● *vt* fazer pressão sobre. **~ cooker** *n* panela *f* de pressão

pressurize /'preʃəraɪz/ *vt* pressionar, fazer pressão sobre

prestige /pre'sti:ʒ/ *n* prestígio *m*

prestigious /pre'stɪdʒəs/ *a* prestigioso

presumably /prɪ'zju:məblɪ/ *adv* provavelmente, presumivelmente

presum|e /prɪ'zju:m/ *vt* presumir; **~e to** tomar a liberdade de, atrever-se a. **~ption** /-'zʌmpʃn/ *n* presunção *f*

presumptuous /prɪ'zʌmptʃʊəs/ *a* presunçoso

pretence /prɪ'tens/ *n* fingimento *m*; (*claim*) pretensão *f*; (*pretext*) desculpa *f*, pretexto *m*

pretend /prɪ'tend/ *vt/i* fingir (**to do** fazer); **~ to** (*lay claim to*) ter pretensões a, ser pretendente a; (*profess to have*) pretender ter

pretentious /prɪ'tenʃəs/ *a* pretencioso

pretext /'pri:tekst/ *n* pretexto *m*

pretty /'prɪtɪ/ *a* (**-ier**, **-iest**) bonito, lindo ● *adv* bastante

prevail /prɪ'veɪl/ *vi* prevalecer; **~ on sb to** convencer alguém a. **~ing** *a* dominante

prevalen|t /'prevələnt/ *a* geral, dominante. **~ce** *n* frequência *f*

prevent /prɪ'vent/ *vt* impedir (**from doing** de fazer). **~able** *a* que se pode evitar, evitável. **~ion** /-ʃn/ *n* prevenção *f*. **~ive** *a* preventivo

preview /'pri:vju:/ *n* pré-estréia *f*, (*P*) anteestreia *f*

previous /'pri:vɪəs/ *a* precedente, anterior; **~ to** antes de. **~ly** *adv* antes, anteriormente

pre-war /pri:'wɔ:(r)/ *a* do pré-guerra, (*P*) de antes da guerra

prey /preɪ/ *n* presa *f* ● *vi* **~ on** dar caça a; (*worry*) preocupar, atormentar; **bird of ~** ave *f* de rapina, predador *m*

price /praɪs/ *n* preço *m* ● *vt* marcar o preço de. **~less** *a* inestimável; [!] (*amusing*) impagável

prick /prɪk/ *vt* picar, furar ● *n* picada *f*; **~ up one's ears** arrebitar a(s) orelha(s)

prickl|e /'prɪkl/ *n* pico *m*, espinho *m*; (*sensation*) picada *f*. **~y** *a* espinhoso, que pica; ‹*person*› irritável

pride /praɪd/ *n* orgulho *m* ● *vpr* **~ o.s. on** orgulhar-se de

priest /pri:st/ *n* padre *m*, sacerdote *m*. **~hood** *n* sacerdócio *m*; (*clergy*) clero *m*

prim /prɪm/ *a* (**primmer**, **primmest**) formal, cheio de nove-horas [!]; (*prudish*) pudico

primary /'praɪmərɪ/ *a* primário; (*chief, first*) primeiro; **~ school** escola *f* primária

prime[1] /praɪm/ *a* primeiro, principal; (*first-rate*) de primeira qualidade; **P~ Minister** Primeiro-Ministro *m*; **~ number** número *m* primo

prime[2] /praɪm/ *vt* aprontar, aprestar; (*with facts*) preparar; ‹*surface*› preparar, aparelhar

primeval /praɪ'mi:vl/ *a* primitivo

primitive /'prɪmɪtɪv/ *a* primitivo

primrose /'prɪmrəʊz/ *n* primavera *f*, prímula *f*

P

prince /prɪns/ *n* príncipe *m*
princess /prɪn'ses/ *n* princesa *f*
principal /'prɪnsəpl/ *a* principal ● *n* *Schol* diretor *m*. **~ly** *adv* principalmente
principle /'prɪnsəpl/ *n* princípio *m*; **in/on ~** em/por princípio
print /prɪnt/ *vt* imprimir; (*write*) escrever em letra de imprensa; **~ed matter** impressos *mpl* ● *n* marca *f*, impressão *f*; (*letters*) letra *f* de imprensa; (*photo*) prova (fotográfica) *f*; (*engraving*) gravura *f*; **out of ~** esgotado. **~out** *n* cópia *f* impressa
print|er /'prɪntə(r)/ *n* tipógrafo *m*; *Comput* impressora *f*. **~ing** *n* impressão *f*, tipografia *f*
prior /'praɪə(r)/ *a* anterior, precedente; **~ to** antes de
priority /praɪ'ɒrətɪ/ *n* prioridade *f*
prise /praɪz/ *vt* forçar (com alavanca); **~ open** arrombar
prison /'prɪzn/ *n* prisão *f*. **~er** *n* prisioneiro *m*
pristine /'prɪstiːn/ *a* primitivo; ‹*condition*› perfeito, como novo
privacy /'prɪvəsɪ/ *n* privacidade *f*, intimidade *f*; (*solitude*) isolamento *m*
private /'praɪvət/ *a* privado; (*confidential*) confidencial; ‹*lesson, life, house etc*› particular; ‹*ceremony*› íntimo ● *n* soldado *m* raso; **in ~** em particular; (*of ceremony*) na intimidade. **~ly** *adv* particularmente; (*inwardly*) no fundo, interiormente
privilege /'prɪvəlɪdʒ/ *n* privilégio *m*. **~d** *a* privilegiado; **be ~d to** ter o privilégio de
prize /praɪz/ *n* prêmio *m*, (*P*) prémio *m* ● *a* premiado; ‹*fool etc*› perfeito ● *vt* ter em grande apreço, apreciar muito. **~-giving** *n* distribuição *f* de prêmios, (*P*) prémios; **~winner** *n* premiado *m*, vencedor *m*
pro /prəʊ/ *n* **the ~s and cons** os prós e os contras
pro- /prəʊ/ *pref* (*acting for*) pro-; (*favouring*) pró-
probab|le /'prɒbəbl/ *a* provável. **~ility** /-'bɪlətɪ/ *n* probabilidade *f*. **~ly** *adv* provavelmente
probation /prə'beɪʃn/ *n* (*testing*) estágio *m*, tirocínio *m*; *Jur* liberdade *f* condicional
probe /prəʊb/ *n* *Med* sonda *f*; *fig* (*investigation*) inquérito *m* ● *vt/i* **~ (into)** sondar, investigar
problem /'prɒbləm/ *n* problema *m* ● *a* difícil. **~atic** /-'mætɪk/ *a* problemático
procedure /prə'siːdʒə(r)/ *n* procedimento *m*, processo *m*, norma *f*
proceed /prə'siːd/ *vi* prosseguir, ir para diante, avançar; **~ to do** passar a fazer; **~ with sth** continuar or avançar com alguma coisa. **~ing** *n* procedimento *m*
proceedings /prə'siːdɪŋz/ *npl* *Jur* processo *m*; (*report*) ata *f*
proceeds /'prəʊsiːdz/ *npl* produto *m*, lucro *m*, proventos *mpl*
process /'prəʊses/ *n* processo *m*; **in ~** em curso; **in the ~ of doing** sendo feito ● *vt* tratar; *Photo* revelar
procession /prə'seʃn/ *n* procissão *f*, cortejo *m*
procl|aim /prə'kleɪm/ *vt* proclamar. **~amation** /prɒklə'meɪʃn/ *n* proclamação *f*
procure /prə'kjʊə(r)/ *vt* obter
prod /prɒd/ *vt/i* (*pt* **prodded**) (*push*) empurrar; (*poke*) espetar; *fig* (*urge*) incitar ● *n* espetadela *f*; *fig* incitamento *m*
prodigy /'prɒdɪdʒɪ/ *n* prodígio *m*
produc|e[1] /prə'djuːs/ *vt/i* produzir; (*bring out*) tirar, extrair; (*show*) apresentar, mostrar; (*cause*) causar, provocar; *Theat* pôr em cena. **~er** *n* produtor *m*. **~tion** /-'dʌkʃn/ *n* produção *f*; *Theat* encenação *f*
produce[2] /'prɒdjuːs/ *n* produtos (agrícolas) *mpl*
product /'prɒdʌkt/ *n* produto *m*
productiv|e /prə'dʌktɪv/ *a* produtivo. **~ity** /prɒdʌk'tɪvətɪ/ *n* produtividade *f*
profess /prə'fes/ *vt* professar; **~ to do** alegar fazer
profession /prə'feʃn/ *n* profissão *f*. **~al** *a* profissional; (*well done*) de profissional; ‹*person*› que exerce uma profissão liberal ● *n* profissional *mf*
professor /prə'fesə(r)/ *n* professor (universitário) *m*
proficien|t /prə'fɪʃnt/ *a* proficiente, competente. **~cy** *n* proficiência *f*, competência *f*
profile /'prəʊfaɪl/ *n* perfil *m*
profit /'prɒfɪt/ *n* proveito *m*; (*money*) lucro *m* ● *vi* (*pt* **profited**) **~ by** aproveitar-se de; **~ from** tirar proveito de. **~able** *a* proveitoso; (*of business*) lucrativo, rentável
profound /prə'faʊnd/ *a* profundo
profus|e /prə'fjuːs/ *a* profuso. **~ion** /-ʒn/ *n* profusão *f*

P

program /ˈprəʊɡræm/ *n* **(computer)** **~** programa *m* ● *vt* (*pt* **programmed**) programar. **~mer** *n* programador *m*

programme /ˈprəʊɡræm/ *n* programa *m*

progress[1] /ˈprəʊɡres/ *n* progresso *m*; **in ~** em curso, em andamento

progress[2] /prəˈɡres/ *vi* progredir. **~ion** /-ʃn/ *n* progressão *f*

progressive /prəˈɡresɪv/ *a* progressivo; (*reforming*) progressista. **~ly** *adv* progressivamente

prohibit /prəˈhɪbɪt/ *vt* proibir (**sb from doing** alguém de fazer)

project[1] /prəˈdʒekt/ *vt* projetar ● *vi* ressaltar, sobressair. **~ion** /-ʃn/ *n* projeção *f*; (*protruding*) saliência *f*, ressalto *m*

project[2] /ˈprɒdʒekt/ *n* projeto *m*

projectile /prəˈdʒektaɪl/ *n* projétil *m*

projector /prəˈdʒektə(r)/ *n* projetor *m*

prolific /prəˈlɪfɪk/ *a* prolífico

prologue /ˈprəʊlɒɡ/ *n* prólogo *m*

prolong /prəˈlɒŋ/ *vt* prolongar

> *i*
>
> **prom** Nos Estados Unidos, um *prom* é o baile de formatura que se celebra para os estudantes que terminam o *High School*. Em Londres, *the Proms* são uma série de concertos de música clássica aos quais uma grande parte do público assiste de pé. Ocorre no *Royal Albert Hall* no verão, durante oito semanas. Oficialmente, são conhecidos como os *Henry Wood Promenade Concerts*, em memória ao seu fundador.

P

promenade /prɒməˈnɑːd/ *n* passeio *m* ● *vt/i* passear

prominen|t /ˈprɒmɪnənt/ *a* (*projecting; important*) proeminente; (*conspicuous*) bem à vista, conspícuo. **~ce** *n* proeminência *f*. **~tly** *adv* bem à vista

promiscu|ous /prəˈmɪskjʊəs/ *a* promíscuo, de costumes livres. **~ity** /prɒmɪsˈkjuːətɪ/ *n* promiscuidade *f*, liberdade *f* de costumes

promis|e /ˈprɒmɪs/ *n* promessa *f* ● *vt/i* prometer. **~ing** *a* prometedor, promissor

promot|e /prəˈməʊt/ *vt* promover. **~ion** /-ˈməʊʃn/ *n* promoção *f*

prompt /prɒmpt/ *a* pronto, rápido, imediato; (*punctual*) pontual ● *adv* em ponto ● *vt* levar; *Theat* soprar, servir de ponto para. **~er** *n* ponto *m*. **~ly** *adv* prontamente; pontualmente

prone /prəʊn/ *a* deitado (de bruços); **~ to** propenso a

pronoun /ˈprəʊnaʊn/ *n* pronome *m*

pron|ounce /prəˈnaʊns/ *vt* pronunciar; (*declare*) declarar. **~ounced** *a* pronunciado. **~ouncement** *n* declaração *f*. **~unciation** /-ʌnsɪˈeɪʃn/ *n* pronúncia *f*

proof /pruːf/ *n* prova *f*; (*of liquor*) teor *m* alcoólico, graduação *f* ● *a* **~ against** à prova de

prop[1] /prɒp/ *n* suporte *m*; *lit & fig* apoio *m*; esteio *m* ● *vt* (*pt* **propped**) sustentar, suportar, apoiar; **~ against** apoiar contra

prop[2] /prɒp/ *n* ! *Theat* acessório *m*, (*P*) adereço *m*

propaganda /prɒpəˈɡændə/ *n* propaganda *f*

propel /prəˈpel/ *vt* (*pt* **propelled**) propulsionar, impelir

propeller /prəˈpelə(r)/ *n* hélice *f*

proper /ˈprɒpə(r)/ *a* correto; (*seemly*) conveniente; (*real*) propriamente dito; ! (*thorough*) belo; **~ noun** substantivo *m* próprio. **~ly** *adv* corretamente; (*rightly*) com razão, acertadamente; (*accurately*) propriamente

property /ˈprɒpətɪ/ *n* (*house*) imóvel *m*; (*land, quality*) propriedade *f*; (*possessions*) bens *mpl*

prophecy /ˈprɒfəsɪ/ *n* profecia *f*

prophesy /ˈprɒfɪsaɪ/ *vt/i* profetizar; **~ that** predizer que

prophet /ˈprɒfɪt/ *n* profeta *m*. **~ic** /prəˈfetɪk/ *a* profético

proportion /prəˈpɔːʃn/ *n* proporção *f*. **~al**, **~ate** *adjs* proporcional

proposal /prəˈpəʊzl/ *n* proposta *f*; (*of marriage*) pedido *m* de casamento

propos|e /prəˈpəʊz/ *vt* propor ● *vi* pedir em casamento; **~e to do** propor-se fazer. **~ition** /prɒpə-ˈzɪʃn/ *n* proposição *f*; ! (*matter*) caso *m*; questão *f*

proprietor /prəˈpraɪətə(r)/ *n* proprietário *m*

propriety /prəˈpraɪətɪ/ *n* propriedade *f*, correção *f*

prose /prəʊz/ *n* prosa *f*

prosecut|e /ˈprɒsɪkjuːt/ *vt Jur* processar. **~ion** /-ˈkjuːʃn/ *n Jur* acusação *f*

prospect[1] /ˈprɒspekt/ *n* perspectiva *f*

prospect[2] /prəˈspekt/ *vt/i* pesquisar, prospectar, (*P*) prospetar

prospective /prəˈspektɪv/ *a* futuro; (*possible*) provável

prosper /ˈprɒspə(r)/ *vi* prosperar

prosper|ous /ˈprɒspərəs/ *a* próspero. **~ity** /-ˈsperətɪ/ *n* prosperidade *f*

prostitut|e /ˈprɒstɪtjuːt/ *n* prostituta *f*. **~ion** /-ˈtjuːʃn/ *n* prostituição *f*

prostrate /ˈprɒstreɪt/ *a* prostrado

protect /prəˈtekt/ *vt* proteger. **~ion** /-ʃn/ *n* proteção *f*. **~ive** *a* protetor. **~or** *n* protetor *m*

protégé /ˈprɒtɪʒeɪ/ *n* protegido *m*. **~e** *n* protegida *f*

protein /ˈprəʊtiːn/ *n* proteína *f*

protest[1] /ˈprəʊtest/ *n* protesto *m*

protest[2] /prəˈtest/ *vt/i* protestar. **~er** *n* *Pol* manifestante *mf*

Protestant /ˈprɒtɪstənt/ *a & n* protestante *mf*

protocol /ˈprəʊtəkɒl/ *n* protocolo *m*

prototype /ˈprəʊtətaɪp/ *n* protótipo *m*

protract /prəˈtrækt/ *vt* prolongar, arrastar

protrud|e /prəˈtruːd/ *vi* sobressair, sair do alinhamento

proud /praʊd/ *a* (**er, -est**) orgulhoso

prove /pruːv/ *vt* provar, demonstrar ● *vi* **~ (to be) easy/** *etc* verificar-se ser fácil/*etc*; **~ o.s.** dar provas de si. **~n** /-n/ *a* provado

proverb /ˈprɒvɜːb/ *n* provérbio *m*. **~ial** /prəˈvɜːbɪəl/ *a* proverbial

provid|e /prəˈvaɪd/ *vt* prover; munir (**sb with sth** alg de alguma coisa) ● *vi* **~ for** providenciar para; ‹*person*› prover de, cuidar de; (*allow for*) levar em conta; **~ed, ~ing (that)** desde que, contanto que

providence /ˈprɒvɪdəns/ *n* providência *f*

province /ˈprɒvɪns/ *n* província *f*; *fig* competência *f*

provincial /prəˈvɪnʃl/ *a* provincial; (*rustic*) provinciano

provision /prəˈvɪʒn/ *n* provisão *f*; (*stipulation*) disposição *f*; **~s** (*food*) provisões *fpl*

provisional /prəˈvɪʒənl/ *a* provisório. **~ly** *adv* provisoriamente

proviso /prəˈvaɪzəʊ/ *n* (*pl* **-os**) condição *f*

provo|ke /prəˈvəʊk/ *vt* provocar. **~cation** /prɒvəˈkeɪʃn/ *n* provocação *f*. **~cative** /-ˈvɒkətɪv/ *a* provocante

prowess /ˈpraʊɪs/ *n* proeza *f*, façanha *f*

prowl /praʊl/ *vi* rondar ● *n* **be on the ~** andar à espreita

proximity /prɒkˈsɪmətɪ/ *n* proximidade *f*

proxy /ˈprɒksɪ/ *n* **by ~** por procuração

prude /pruːd/ *n* puritano *m*, pudico *m*

pruden|t /ˈpruːdnt/ *a* prudente. **~ce** *n* prudência *f*

prune[1] /pruːn/ *n* ameixa *f* seca

prune[2] /pruːn/ *vt* podar

pry /praɪ/ *vi* bisbilhotar; **~ into** meter o nariz em, intrometer-se em

psalm /sɑːm/ *n* salmo *m*

pseudo- /ˈsjuːdəʊ/ *pref* pseudo-

pseudonym /ˈsjuːdənɪm/ *n* pseudônimo *m*, (*P*) pseudónimo *m*

psychiatr|y /saɪˈkaɪətrɪ/ *n* psiquiatria *f*. **~ic** /-ɪˈætrɪk/ *a* psiquiátrico. **~ist** *n* psiquiatra *mf*

psychic /ˈsaɪkɪk/ *a* psíquico; ‹*person*› com capacidade de telepatia

psychoanalys|e /saɪkəʊˈænəlaɪz/ *vt* psicanalisar. **~t** /-ɪst/ *n* psicanalista *mf*

psychoanalysis /saɪkəʊəˈnæləsɪs/ *n* psicanálise *f*

psycholog|y /saɪˈkɒlədʒɪ/ *n* psicologia *f*. **~ical** /-əˈlɒdʒɪkl/ *a* psicológico. **~ist** *n* psicólogo *m*

psychopath /ˈsaɪkəʊpæθ/ *n* psicopata *mf*

pub /pʌb/ *n* pub *m*

> **pub** Na Grã-Bretanha, é o estabelecimento onde se vende cerveja e outras bebidas (alcoólicas e não alcoólicas) para consumo no local. *Pub* é a forma abreviada de *public house*. Os pubs costumam oferecer comida e uma série de jogos, sobretudo dardos, bilhar, etc. O horário de abertura depende da licença, sendo o horário normal das 11 às 23 horas.

puberty /ˈpjuːbətɪ/ *n* puberdade *f*

public /ˈpʌblɪk/ *a* público; ‹*holiday*› feriado; **in ~** em público; **~ house** pub *m*; **~ relations** relações *fpl* públicas; **~ school** escola *f* particular; *Amer* escola *f* oficial. **~-spirited** *a* de espírito cívico, patriótico. **~ly** *adv* publicamente

publication /pʌblɪ'keɪʃn/ *n* publicação *f*

publicity /pʌ'blɪsətɪ/ *n* publicidade *f*

publicize /'pʌblɪsaɪz/ *vt* fazer publicidade de/a

> **public school** Em Inglaterra e no País de Gales, é um colégio privado para alunos entre os 13 e os 18 anos. A maioria desses colégios são internatos só para rapazes ou só para raparigas. Nos Estados Unidos e na Escócia, o termo refere-se a uma escola pública.

publish /'pʌblɪʃ/ *vt* publicar. **~er** *n* editor *m*. **~ing** *n* publicação *f*; **~ing house** editora *f*

pudding /'pʊdɪŋ/ *n* pudim *m*; (*dessert*) doce *m*

puddle /'pʌdl/ *n* poça *f* de água, charco *m*

puff /pʌf/ *n* baforada *f* ● *vt/i* lançar baforadas; (*breathe hard*) arquejar, ofegar; **~ at** ‹*cigar etc*› dar baforadas em; **~ out** (*swell*) inchar(-se). **~ pastry** *n* massa *f* folhada

puffy /'pʌfɪ/ *a* inchado

pull /pʊl/ *vt/i* puxar; ‹*muscle*› distender; **~ a face** fazer uma careta; **~ one's weight** *fig* fazer a sua quota-parte; **~ sb's leg** brincar com alguém, meter-se com alguém; **~ away** or **out** *Auto* arrancar; **~ down** puxar para baixo; ‹*building*› demolir; **~ in** *Auto* encostar(-se); **~ off** tirar; *fig* sair-se bem em, conseguir alcançar; **~ o.s. together** recompor-se, refazer-se; **~ out** partir; (*extract*) arrancar, tirar; **~ through** sair-se bem; **~ up** puxar para cima; (*uproot*) arrancar; *Auto* parar ● *n* puxão *m*; *fig* (*influence*) influência *f*; empenho *m*; **give a ~** dar um puxão

pullover /'pʊləʊvə(r)/ *n* pulôver *m*

pulp /pʌlp/ *n* polpa *f*; (*for paper*) pasta *f* de papel

pulpit /'pʊlpɪt/ *n* púlpito *m*

pulsat|e /pʌl'seɪt/ *vi* pulsar, bater, palpitar. **~ion** /-'seɪʃn/ *n* pulsação *f*

pulse /pʌls/ *n* pulso *m*; **feel sb's ~** tirar o pulso de alguém

pummel /'pʌml/ *vt* (*pt* **pummelled**) esmurrar

pump[1] /pʌmp/ *n* bomba *f* ● *vt/i* bombear; ‹*person*› arrancar or extrair informações de; **~ up** encher com bomba

pump[2] /pʌmp/ *n* (*shoe*) sapato *m*

pumpkin /'pʌmpkɪn/ *n* abóbora *f*

pun /pʌn/ *n* trocadilho *m*, jogo *m* de palavras

punch[1] /pʌntʃ/ *vt* esmurrar, dar um murro or soco; (*perforate*) furar, perfurar; ‹*a hole*› fazer ● *n* murro *m*, soco *m*; (*device*) furador *m*. **~line** *n* remate *m*; **~-up** *n* [!] pancadaria *f*

punch[2] /pʌntʃ/ *n* (*drink*) ponche *m*

punctual /'pʌŋktʃʊəl/ *a* pontual. **~ity** /-'ælətɪ/ *n* pontualidade *f*

punctuat|e /'pʌŋktʃʊeɪt/ *vt* pontuar. **~ion** /-'eɪʃn/ *n* pontuação *f*

puncture /'pʌŋktʃə(r)/ *n* (*in tyre*) furo *m* ● *vt/i* furar

pungent /'pʌndʒənt/ *a* acre, pungente

punish /'pʌnɪʃ/ *vt* punir, castigar. **~able** *a* punível. **~ment** *n* punição *f*, castigo *m*

punt /pʌnt/ *n* (*boat*) chalana *f*

punter /'pʌntə(r)/ *n* (*gambler*) jogador *m*; [!] (*customer*) freguês *m*, cliente *m*

puny /'pju:nɪ/ *a* (**-ier**, **-iest**) fraco, débil

pup(py) /'pʌpɪ/ *n* cachorro *m*, cachorrinho *m*

pupil /'pju:pl/ *n* aluno *m*; (*of eye*) pupila *f*

puppet /'pʌpɪt/ *n lit* & *fig* fantoche *m*; marionete *f*

purchase /'pɜ:tʃəs/ *vt* comprar (**from sb** de alguém) ● *n* compra *f*. **~r** /-ə(r)/ *n* comprador *m*

pur|e /'pjʊə(r)/ *a* (**-er**, **-est**) puro. **~ely** *adv* puramente. **~ity** *n* pureza *f*

purge /pɜ:dʒ/ *vt* purgar; *Pol* sanear ● *n Med* purgante *m*; *Pol* saneamento *m*

purif|y /'pjʊərɪfaɪ/ *vt* purificar. **~ication** /-ɪ'keɪʃn/ *n* purificação *f*

puritan /'pjʊərɪtən/ *n* puritano *m*. **~ical** /-'tænɪkl/ *a* puritano

purple /'pɜ:pl/ *a* roxo, purpúreo ● *n* roxo *m*, púrpura *f*

purpose /'pɜ:pəs/ *n* propósito *m*; (*determination*) firmeza *f*; **on ~** de propósito; **to no ~** em vão. **~-built** *a* construído especialmente

purposely /'pɜ:pəslɪ/ *adv* de propósito, propositadamente

purr /pɜ:r/ *n* ronrom *m* ● *vi* ronronar

purse /pɜ:s/ *n* carteira *f*; *Amer* bolsa *f* ● *vt* franzir

pursue /pə'sju:/ *vt* perseguir; (*go on with*) prosseguir; (*engage in*)

P

entregar-se a, dedicar-se a. **~r** /-ə(r)/ *n* perseguidor *m*

pursuit /pəˈsjuːt/ *n* perseguição *f*; *fig* atividade *f*

pus /pʌs/ *n* pus *m*

push /pʊʃ/ *vt/i* empurrar; ‹*button*› apertar, premir, carregar; (*thrust*) enfiar; [!] (*recommend*) insistir; **be ~ed for** ‹*time etc*› estar com pouco; **be ~ing thirty**/*etc* [!] estar beirando os *or* (*P*) à beira dos trinta/*etc*; **give the ~ to** [✖] dar o fora em alguém; **~ sb around** fazer alguém de bobo *or* (*P*) de parvo; **~ back** repelir; **~ off** [✖] dar o fora, (*P*) mandar embora; **~ on** continuar; **~ up** (*lift*) levantar; ‹*prices*› forçar o aumento de ● *n* empurrão *m*; (*effort*) esforço *m*; (*drive*) energia *f*. **~chair** *n* carrinho *m* (de criança); **~over** *n* canja *f* [!], coisa *f* fácil; **~-up** *n Amer* flexão *f*. **~er** *n* fornecedor *m* (de droga). **~y** *a* [!] agressivo, furão

put /pʊt/ *vt/i* (*pt* **put**, *pres p* **putting**) colocar, pôr; ‹*question*› fazer, colocar; **~ the damage at a million** estimar os danos em um milhão; **I'd ~ it at a thousand** eu diria mil; **~ sth tactfully** dizer alguma coisa com tato; **~ across** comunicar; **~ away** guardar; **~ back** repor; (*delay*) retardar, atrasar; **~ by** pôr de lado; **~ down** pôr em lugar baixo; (*write*) anotar; (*pay*) pagar; (*suppress*) sufocar, reprimir; **~ forward** ‹*plan*› submeter; **~ in** (*insert*) introduzir; (*fix*) instalar; submeter; **~ in for** fazer um pedido, candidatar-se; **~ off** (*postpone*) adiar; (*disconcert*) desanimar; (*displease*) desagradar; **~ sb off sth** tirar o gosto de alguém por algo; **~ on** ‹*clothes*› pôr, vestir; ‹*radio*› ligar; ‹*light*› acender; ‹*speed, weight*› ganhar; ‹*accent*› adotar; **~ out** pôr para fora; (*stretch*) esticar; (*extinguish*) extinguir, apagar; (*disconcert*) desconcertar; (*inconvenience*) incomodar; **~ up** levantar; ‹*building*› erguer, construir; colocar; aumentar; hospedar; oferecer; **~-up job** embuste *m*; **~ up with** suportar, aturar

putty /ˈpʌtɪ/ *n* massa de vidraceiro *f*, betume *m*

puzzl|e /ˈpʌzl/ *n* puzzle *m*, quebra-cabeça(s) *m* ● *vt* deixar perplexo, intrigar ● *vi* quebrar a cabeça, ser intrigante. **~ing** *a* intrigante

pyjamas /pəˈdʒɑːməz/ *npl* pijama *m*

pylon /ˈpaɪlɒn/ *n* poste *m*

pyramid /ˈpɪrəmɪd/ *n* pirâmide *f*

python /ˈpaɪθn/ *n* píton *m*

Qq

quack[1] /kwæk/ *n* (*of duck*) grasnido *m* ● *vi* grasnar

quack[2] /kwæk/ *n* charlatão *m*

quadrangle /ˈkwɒdræŋgl/ *n* quadrângulo *m*; (*of college*) pátio *m* quadrangular

quadruped /ˈkwɒdrʊped/ *n* quadrúpede *m*

quadruple /ˈkwɒdrʊpl/ *a & n* quádruplo *m* ● /kwɒˈdrʊpl/ *vt/i* quadruplicar. **~ts** /-plɪts/ *npl* quadrigêmeos *mpl*, (*P*) quadrigémeos *mpl*

quaint /kweɪnt/ *a* (**-er**, **-est**) pitoresco; (*whimsical*) estranho, bizarro

quake /kweɪk/ *vi* tremer ● *n* [!] tremor *m* de terra

qualification /kwɒlɪfɪˈkeɪʃn/ *n* qualificação *f*; (*accomplishment*) habilitação *f*; (*diploma*) diploma *m*, título *m*; (*condition*) requisito *m*, condição *f*; *fig* restrição *f*; reserva *f*

qualif|y /ˈkwɒlɪfaɪ/ *vt* qualificar; *fig* (*moderate*) atenuar; moderar; *fig* (*limit*) pôr ressalvas or restrições a ● *vi fig* (*be entitled to*) ter os requisitos (**for** para); *Sport* classificar-se; **he ~ied as a vet** ele formou-se em veterinária. **~ied** *a* formado; (*able*) qualificado, habilitado; (*moderated*) atenuado; (*limited*) limitado

quality /ˈkwɒlətɪ/ *n* qualidade *f*

qualm /kwɑːm/ *n* escrúpulo *m*

quandary /ˈkwɒndərɪ/ *n* dilema *m*

quantity /ˈkwɒntətɪ/ *n* quantidade *f*

quarantine /ˈkwɒrəntiːn/ *n* quarentena *f*

quarrel /ˈkwɒrəl/ *n* zanga *f*, questão *f*, discussão *f* ● *vi* (*pt* **quarrelled**) zangar-se, questionar, discutir. **~some** *a* conflituoso, brigão

quarry[1] /ˈkwɒrɪ/ *n* (*prey*) presa *f*, caça *f*

quarry[2] /ˈkwɒrɪ/ *n* (*excavation*) pedreira *f*

quarter /ˈkwɔːtə(r)/ *n* quarto *m*; (*of year*) trimestre *m*; *Amer* (*coin*) quarto *m* de dólar; 25 cêntimos *mpl*; (*district*) bairro *m*, quarteirão *m*; **~s** (*lodgings*) alojamento *m*, residência *f*; *Mil* quartel *m*; **from all ~s** de todos os lados; **~ of an hour** quarto *m* de hora; **(a) ~ past six** seis e quinze; **(a) ~ to seven** quinze para as sete ● *vt* dividir em quarto;

Mil aquartelar. **~-final** *n Sport* quarta *f or* (*P*) quartos *mpl* de final. **~ly** *a* trimestral ● *adv* trimestralmente

quartet /kwɔː'tet/ *n* quarteto *m*

quartz /kwɔːts/ *n* quartzo *m* ● *a* ‹*watch etc*› de quartzo

quash /kwɒʃ/ *vt* reprimir; *Jur* revogar

quaver /'kweɪvə(r)/ *vi* tremer, tremular ● *n Mus* colcheia *f*

quay /kiː/ *n* cais *m*

queasy /'kwiːzɪ/ *a* delicado; **feel ~** estar enjoado

queen /kwiːn/ *n* rainha *f*; *Cards* dama *f*

queer /kwɪə(r)/ *a* (**-er, -est**) estranho; (*slightly ill*) indisposto; ⊠ (*homosexual*) bicha; maricas ⊠; (*dubious*) suspeito ● *n* ⊠ bicha *m*; maricas *m* ⊠

quell /kwel/ *vt* reprimir, abafar, sufocar

quench /kwentʃ/ *vt* ‹*fire, flame*› apagar; ‹*thirst*› matar, saciar

query /'kwɪərɪ/ *n* questão *f* ● *vt* questionar

quest /kwest/ *n* busca *f*, procura *f*; **in ~ of** em demanda de

question /'kwestʃən/ *n* pergunta *f*, interrogação *f*; (*problem, affair*) questão *f*; **in ~** em questão or em causa; **out of the ~** fora de toda a questão, (*P*) fora de questão; **there's no ~ of** nem pensar em; **without ~** sem dúvida; **~ mark** ponto *m* de interrogação ● *vt* perguntar, interrogar; (*doubt*) pôr em dúvida or em causa. **~able** *a* discutível

questionnaire /kwestʃə'neə(r)/ *n* questionário *m*

queue /kjuː/ *n* fila *f* ● *vi* (*pres p* **queuing**) fazer fila

quibble /'kwɪbl/ *vi* tergiversar, usar de evasivas; (*raise petty objections*) discutir por coisas insignificantes

quick /kwɪk/ *a* (**-er, -est**) rápido; **be ~** despachar-se; **have a ~ temper** exaltar-se facilmente ● *adv* depressa. **~ly** *adv* rapidamente, depressa. **~ness** *n* rapidez *f*

quicken /'kwɪkən/ *vt/i* apressar(-se)

quicksand /'kwɪksænd/ *n* areia *f* movediça

quid /kwɪd/ *n invar* ⊠ libra *f*

quiet /'kwaɪət/ *a* (**-er, -est**) quieto, sossegado, tranquilo ● *n* quietude *f*, sossego *m*, tranquilidade *f*; **keep ~** calar-se; **on the ~** às escondidas, na calada. **~ly** *adv* sossegadamente, silenciosamente. **~ness** *n* sossego *m*, tranquilidade *f*, calma *f*

quieten /'kwaɪətn/ *vt/i* sossegar, acalmar(-se)

quilt /kwɪlt/ *n* coberta *f* acolchoada; **(continental) ~** edredão *m* de penas ● *vt* acolchoar

quintet /kwɪn'tet/ *n* quinteto *m*

quirk /kwɜːk/ *n* mania *f*, singularidade *f*

quit /kwɪt/ *vt* (*pt* **quitted**) deixar ● *vi* ir-se embora; (*resign*) demitir-se, desistir; **~ doing** *Amer* parar or deixar de fazer

quite /kwaɪt/ *adv* completamente, absolutamente; (*rather*) bastante; **~ (so)!** isso mesmo!, exatamente! **~ a few** bastante, alguns/algumas; **~ a lot** bastante

quiver /'kwɪvə(r)/ *vi* tremer, estremecer ● *n* tremor *m*, estremecimento *m*

quiz /kwɪz/ *n* (*pl* **quizzes**) teste *m*; (*game*) concurso *m* ● *vt* (*pt* **quizzed**) interrogar

quizzical /'kwɪzɪkl/ *a* zombeteiro, (*P*) gozão *m* [!]

quota /'kwəʊtə/ *n* cota *f*, quota *f*

quotation /kwəʊ'teɪʃn/ *n* citação *f*; (*estimate*) orçamento *m*; **~ marks** aspas *fpl*

quote /kwəʊt/ *vt* citar; (*estimate*) fazer um orçamento ● *n* [!] (*passage*) citação *f*; [!] (*estimate*) orçamento *m*

Rr

rabbi /'ræbaɪ/ *n* rabino *m*

rabbit /'ræbɪt/ *n* coelho *m*

rabid /'ræbɪd/ *a fig* fanático; ferrenho; ‹*dog*› raivoso

rabies /'reɪbiːz/ *n* raiva *f*

race[1] /reɪs/ *n* corrida *f* ● *vt* ‹*horse*› fazer correr ● *vi* correr, dar or fazer uma corrida; (*rush*) ir em grande or a toda (a) velocidade. **~track** *n* pista *f*

race[2] /reɪs/ *n* (*group*) raça *f* ● *a* racial

racecourse /'reɪskɔːs/ *n* hipódromo *m*

racehorse /'reɪshɔːs/ *n* cavalo *m* de corrida

racial /'reɪʃl/ *a* racial

racing /'reɪsɪŋ/ *n* corridas *fpl*; **~ car** carro *m* de corridas

racis|t /'reɪsɪst/ *a & n* racista *mf*. **~m** /-zəm/ *n* racismo *m*

rack[1] /ræk/ *n* (*for luggage*) porta-bagagem *m*, bagageiro *m*; (*for plates*) escorredor *m* de prato ● *vt* ~ **one's brains** dar tratos à imaginação, (*P*) dar voltas à cabeça

rack[2] /ræk/ *n* **go to ~ and ruin** arruinar-se; (*of buildings etc*) cair em ruínas

racket[1] /'rækɪt/ *n Sport* raquete *f*, (*P*) raqueta *f*

racket[2] /'rækɪt/ *n* (*din*) barulheira *f*; (*swindle*) roubalheira *f*; ⊠ (*business*) negociata *f* ⊡

racy /'reɪsɪ/ *a* (**-ier**, **-iest**) vivo, vigoroso

radar /'reɪdɑː(r)/ *n* radar *m* ● *a* de radar

radian|t /'reɪdɪənt/ *a* radiante. **~ce** *n* brilho *m*

radiator /'reɪdɪeɪtə(r)/ *n* radiador *m*

radical /'rædɪkl/ *a & n* radical *m*

radio /'reɪdɪəʊ/ *n* (*pl* **-os**) rádio *f*; (*set*) (aparelho de) rádio *m*; **~ station** estação *f* de rádio, emissora *f* ● *vt* transmitir pela rádio

radioactiv|e /reɪdɪəʊ'æktɪv/ *a* radioativo. **~ity** /-'tɪvətɪ/ *n* radioatividade *f*

radish /'rædɪʃ/ *n* rabanete *m*

radius /'reɪdɪəs/ *n* (*pl* **-dii** /-dɪaɪ/) raio *m*

raffle /'ræfl/ *n* rifa *f* ● *vt* rifar

raft /rɑːft/ *n* jangada *f*

rafter /'rɑːftə(r)/ *n* trave *f*, viga *f*

rag[1] /ræg/ *n* farrapo *m*; (*for wiping*) trapo *m*; *pej* (*newspaper*) jornaleco *m*. **~s** *npl* farrapos *mpl*, andrajos *mpl*; **in ~s** maltrapilho.

rag[2] /ræg/ *vt* (*pt* **ragged**) zombar de

rage /reɪdʒ/ *n* raiva *f*, fúria *f* ● *vi* estar furioso; (*of storm*) rugir; (*of battle*) estar acesa; **be all the ~** ⊡ fazer furor, estar na moda ⊡

ragged /'rægɪd/ *a* ‹*clothes, person*› esfarrapado, roto; ‹*edge*› esfiapado, esgarçado

raid /reɪd/ *n Mil* ataque *m*; (*by police*) batida *f*; (*by criminals*) assalto *m* ● *vt* fazer um ataque or uma batida or um assalto. **~er** *n* atacante *m*, assaltante *m*

rail /reɪl/ *n* (*of stairs*) corrimão *m*; (*of ship*) amurada *f*; (*on balcony*) parapeito *m*; (*for train*) trilho *m*, (*P*) carril *m*; (*for curtain*) varão *m*; **by ~** por estrada, (*P*) caminho de ferro

railings /'reɪlɪŋz/ *npl* grade *f*

railroad /'reɪlrəʊd/ *n Amer* ▶ RAILWAY

railway /'reɪlweɪ/ *n* estrada *f*, (*P*) caminho *m* de ferro; **~ line** linha *f* do trem *or* (*P*) do comboio; **~ station** estação *f* ferroviária, (*P*) estação *f* de caminho de ferro

rain /reɪn/ *n* chuva *f*; **~ forest** floresta *f* tropical ● *vi* chover. **~storm** *n* tempestade *f* com chuva; **~water** *n* água *f* da chuva

rainbow /'reɪnbəʊ/ *n* arco-íris *m*

raincoat /'reɪnkəʊt/ *n* impermeável *m*

raindrop /'reɪndrɒp/ *n* pingo *m* de chuva

rainfall /'reɪnfɔːl/ *n* precipitação *f*, pluviosidade *f*

rainy /'reɪnɪ/ *a* (**-ier**, **-iest**) chuvoso

raise /reɪz/ *vt* levantar, erguer; (*breed*) criar; ‹*voice*› levantar; ‹*question*› fazer, levantar; ‹*price etc*› aumentar, subir; ‹*funds*› angariar; ‹*loan*› obter ● *n Amer* aumento *m*

raisin /'reɪzn/ *n* passa *f*

rake /reɪk/ *n* ancinho *m* ● *vt* juntar, alisar com ancinho; (*search*) revolver, remexer; **~ in** ‹*money*› ganhar a rodos; **~ up** desenterrar, ressuscitar

rally /'rælɪ/ *vt/i* reunir(-se); (*reassemble*) reagrupar(-se), reorganizar(-se); ‹*health*› restabelecer(-se); ‹*strength*› recuperar as forças ● *n* (*recovery*) recuperação *f*; (*meeting*) comício *m*, assembleia *f*; *Auto* rally *m*, rali *m*

ram /ræm/ *n* (*sheep*) carneiro *m* ● *vt* (*pt* **rammed**) (*beat down*) calcar; (*push*) meter à força; (*crash into*) bater contra

rambl|e /'ræmbl/ *n* caminhada *f*, perambulação *f* ● *vi* perambular, vaguear; **~ on** divagar. **~er** *n* caminhante *mf*; (*plant*) trepadeira *f*. **~ing** *a* ‹*speech*› desconexo

ramp /ræmp/ *n* rampa *f*

rampage /ræm'peɪdʒ/ *vi* causar distúrbios violentos

rampant /'ræmpənt/ *a* **be ~** vicejar, florescer; ‹*diseases etc*› grassar

ramshackle /'ræmʃækl/ *a* ‹*car*› desconjuntado; ‹*house*› caindo aos pedaços

ran /ræn/ ▶ RUN

ranch /rɑːntʃ/ *n* rancho *m*, estância *f*

rancid /'rænsɪd/ *a* rançoso

random /'rændəm/ *a* feito, tirado *etc* ao acaso ● *n* **at ~** ao acaso, a esmo, aleatoriamente

randy /'rændɪ/ *a* (**-ier**, **-iest**) lascivo, sensual

rang /ræŋ/ ▶ RING[2]

range /reɪndʒ/ *n* (*distance*) alcance *m*; (*scope*) âmbito *m*; (*variety*) gama *f*, variedade *f*; (*stove*) fogão *m*; (*of voice*) registro *m*, (*P*) registo *m*; (*of temperature*) variação *f*; **~ of mountains** cordilheira *f*, serra *f* ● *vt* dispor, ordenar ● *vi* estender-se; (*vary*) variar. **~r** *n* guarda-florestal *m*

rank[1] /ræŋk/ *n* fila *f*, fileira *f*; *Mil* posto *m*; (*social position*) classe *f*, categoria *f*; **the ~ and file** a massa *f*, gente *f* comum ● *vt/i* **~ among** contar(-se) entre

rank[2] /ræŋk/ *a* (**-er**, **-est**) ‹*plants*› luxuriante; ‹*smell*› fétido; (*out-and-out*) total

ransack /ˈrænsæk/ *vt* (*search*) espionar, (*P*) espiar, revistar, remexer; (*pillage*) pilhar, saquear

ransom /ˈrænsəm/ *n* resgate *m* ● *vt* resgatar; **hold to ~** prender como refém

rant /rænt/ *vi* usar linguagem bombástica

rap /ræp/ *n* pancadinha *f* seca ● *vt/i* (*pt* **rapped**) bater, dar uma pancada seca em

rape /reɪp/ *vt* violar, estuprar ● *n* violação *f*, estupro *m*

rapid /ˈræpɪd/ *a* rápido. **~ity** /rəˈpɪdətɪ/ *n* rapidez *f*

rapids /ˈræpɪdz/ *npl* rápidos *mpl*

rapist /ˈreɪpɪst/ *n* violador *m*, estuprador *m*

rapport /ræˈpɔː(r)/ *n* bom *m* relacionamento

raptur|e /ˈræptʃə(r)/ *n* êxtase *m*. **~ous** *a* extático; ‹*welcome etc*› entusiástico

rar|e[1] /reə(r)/ *a* (**-er**, **-est**) raro. **~ely** *adv* raramente, raras vezes. **~ity** *n* raridade *f*

rare[2] /reə(r)/ *a* (**-er**, **-est**) *Culin* malpassado

rarefied /ˈreərɪfaɪd/ *a* rarefeito; (*refined*) requintado

rascal /ˈrɑːskl/ *n* (*dishonest*) patife *m*; (*mischievous*) maroto *m*

rash[1] /ræʃ/ *n* erupção *f* cutânea; irritação *f* na pele [!]

rash[2] /ræʃ/ *a* (**-er**, **-est**) imprudente, precipitado. **~ly** *adv* imprudentemente, precipitadamente

rasher /ˈræʃə(r)/ *n* fatia *f* (de presunto ou de bacon)

raspberry /ˈrɑːzbrɪ/ *n* framboesa *f*

rat /ræt/ *n* rato *m*, (*P*) ratazana *f*; **~ race** *fig* luta *f* renhida para vencer na vida, arrivismo *m*

rate /reɪt/ *n* (*ratio*) razão *f*; (*speed*) velocidade *f*; (*price*) tarifa *f*; (*of exchange*) (taxa *f* de) câmbio *m*; (*of interest*) taxa *f*; **~s** (*taxes*) impostos *mpl* municipais, taxas *fpl*; **at this ~** desse jeito, desse modo; **at any ~** de qualquer modo, pelo menos; **at the ~ of** à razão de ● *vt* avaliar; *fig* (*consider*) considerar

rather /ˈrɑːðə(r)/ *adv* (*by preference*) antes; (*fairly*) muito, bastante; (*a little*) um pouco; **I would ~ go** preferia ir

rating /ˈreɪtɪŋ/ *n Comm* rating *m*, (*P*) valor *m*; (*sailor*) praça *f*, marinheiro *m*; *Radio, TV* índice *m* de audiência

ratio /ˈreɪʃɪəʊ/ *n* (*pl* **-os**) proporção *f*

ration /ˈræʃn/ *n* ração *f* ● *vt* racionar

rational /ˈræʃnəl/ *a* racional; ‹*person*› sensato, razoável. **~ize** *vt* racionalizar

rattle /ˈrætl/ *vt/i* matraquear; (*of door, window*) bater; (*of bottles*) chocalhar; [!] agitar; mexer com os nervos de ● *n* (*baby's toy*) guizo *m*, chocalho *m*; (*of football fan*) matraca *f*; (*sound*) matraquear *m*, chocalhar *m*; **~ off** despejar [!]

rattlesnake /ˈrætlsneɪk/ *n* cobra *f* cascavel

raucous /ˈrɔːkəs/ *a* áspero, rouco

ravage /ˈrævɪdʒ/ *vt* devastar, causar estragos a. **~s** *npl* devastação *f*, estragos *mpl*

rave /reɪv/ *vi* delirar; (*in anger*) urrar; **~ about** delirar (de entusiasmo) com

raven /ˈreɪvn/ *n* corvo *m*

ravenous /ˈrævənəs/ *a* esfomeado; (*greedy*) voraz

ravine /rəˈviːn/ *n* ravina *f*, barranco *m*

raving /ˈreɪvɪŋ/ *a* **~ lunatic** doido *m* varrido ● *adv* **~ mad** loucamente

ravish /ˈrævɪʃ/ *vt* (*rape*) violar; (*enrapture*) arrebatar, encantar. **~ing** *a* arrebatador, encantador

raw /rɔː/ *a* (**-er**, **-est**) cru; (*not processed*) bruto; (*wound*) em carne viva; (*weather*) frio e úmido, (*P*) húmido; (*immature*) inexperiente, verde; **~ deal** tratamento *m* injusto; **~ material** matéria-prima *f*

ray /reɪ/ *n* raio *m*

razor /ˈreɪzə(r)/ *n* navalha *f* de barba. **~ blade** *n* lâmina *f* de barbear

re /riː/ *prep* a respeito de, em referência a, relativo a

re- /ri/ *pref* re-

reach /riːtʃ/ *vt* chegar a atingir; (*contact*) contatar; (*pass*) passar; **~ for** estender a mão para agarrar ● *vi* estender-se, chegar ● *n* alcance *m*; **out of ~** fora de alcance; **within ~ of** ao alcance de; (*close to*) próximo de

react /rɪˈækt/ *vi* reagir

reaction /rɪ'ækʃn/ *n* reação *f*. **~ary** *a & n* reacionário *m*

reactor /rɪ'æktə(r)/ *n* reator *m*

read /ri:d/ *vt/i* (*pt* **read** /red/) ler; *fig* (*interpret*) interpretar; (*study*) estudar; (*of instrument*) marcar, indicar ● *n* [!] leitura *f*; **~ about** ler um artigo sobre; **~ out** ler em voz alta. **~able** *a* agradável or fácil de ler; (*legible*) legível. **~er** *n* leitor *m*; (*book*) livro *m* de leitura. **~ing** *n* leitura *f*; (*of instrument*) registro *m*, (*P*) registo *m*

readily /'redɪlɪ/ *adv* de boa vontade, prontamente; (*easily*) facilmente

readjust /ri:ə'dʒʌst/ *vt* reajustar, readaptar ● *vi* readaptar-se, reajustar-se

ready /'redɪ/ *a* (**-ier**, **-iest**) pronto; **~ money** dinheiro *m* vivo, (*P*) pagamento *m* à vista ● *n* **at the ~** pronto para disparar. **~-made** *a* pronto; **~-to-wear** *a* prêt-à-porter, (*P*) pronto-a-vestir

real /rɪəl/ *a* real, verdadeiro; (*genuine*) autêntico; **~ estate** *Amer* bens *mpl* imobiliários ● *adv Amer* [!] realmente

realis|t /'rɪəlɪst/ *n* realista *mf*. **~m** /-zəm/ *n* realismo *m*. **~tic** /-'lɪstɪk/ *a* realista. **~tically** /-'lɪstɪkəlɪ/ *adv* realisticamente

reality /rɪ'ælətɪ/ *n* realidade *f*. **~ TV** *n* reality show *m*, (*P*) reality TV *f*; televisão *f* de reality shows

realiz|e /'rɪəlaɪz/ *vt* dar-se conta de, aperceber-se de, perceber; (*fulfil; turn into cash*) realizar. **~ation** /-'zeɪʃn/ *n* consciência *f*, noção *f*; (*fulfilment*) realização *f*

really /'rɪəlɪ/ *adv* realmente, na verdade

realm /relm/ *n* reino *m*; *fig* domínio *m*; esfera *f*

reap /ri:p/ *vt* (*cut*) ceifar; (*gather*) *fig* colher

reappear /ri:ə'pɪə(r)/ *vi* reaparecer

rear[1] /rɪə(r)/ *n* traseira *f*, retaguarda *f*; **bring up the ~** ir na retaguarda, fechar a marcha ● *a* traseiro, de trás, posterior. **~-view mirror** *n* espelho *m* retrovisor

rear[2] /rɪə(r)/ *vt* levantar, erguer; ‹*children, cattle*› criar; **~ one's head** levantar a cabeça ● *vi* (*of horse etc*) empinar-se

rearrange /ri:ə'reɪndʒ/ *vt* arranjar doutro modo, reorganizar

reason /'ri:zn/ *n* razão *f*; **within ~** razoável ● *vt/i* raciocinar, argumentar; **~ with sb** procurar convencer alguém. **~ing** *n* raciocínio *m*

reasonable /'ri:znəbl/ *a* razoável

reassur|e /ri:ə'ʃʊə(r)/ *vt* tranquilizar, sossegar. **~ance** *n* garantia *f*. **~ing** *a* animador, reconfortante

rebate /'ri:beɪt/ *n* (*refund*) reimbolso *m*; (*discount*) desconto *m*, abatimento *m*

rebel[1] /'rebl/ *n* rebelde *mf*

rebel[2] /rɪ'bel/ *vi* (*pt* **rebelled**) rebelar-se, revoltar-se, sublevar-se. **~lion** *n* rebelião *f*, revolta *f*. **~lious** *a* rebelde

rebound[1] /rɪ'baʊnd/ *vi* repercutir, ressoar; *fig* (*backfire*) recair (**on** sobre)

rebound[2] /'ri:baʊnd/ *n* ricochete *m*

rebuff /rɪ'bʌf/ *vt* receber mal; repelir [!] ● *n* rejeição *f*

rebuild /ri:'bɪld/ *vt* (*pt* **rebuilt**) reconstruir

rebuke /rɪ'bju:k/ *vt* repreender ● *n* reprimenda *f*

recall /rɪ'kɔ:l/ *vt* chamar, mandar regressar; (*remember*) lembrar-se de ● *n* (*summons*) ordem *f* de regresso

recant /rɪ'kænt/ *vi* retratar-se

recap /'ri:kæp/ *vt/i* (*pt* **recapped**) [!] recapitular ● *n* recapitulação *f*

recapitulat|e /ri:kə'pɪtʃʊleɪt/ *vt/i* recapitular

reced|e /rɪ'si:d/ *vi* recuar, retroceder. **his hair is ~ing** ele está ficando *or* (*P*) a ficar com entradas. **~ing** *a* ‹*forehead, chin*› recuado, voltado para dentro

receipt /rɪ'si:t/ *n* recibo *m*; (*receiving*) recepção *f*, (*P*) receção; **~s** *Comm* receitas *fpl*

receive /rɪ'si:v/ *vt* receber. **~r** /-ə(r)/ *n* (*of stolen goods*) receptador *m*, (*P*) recetador *m*; (*of phone*) fone *m*, (*P*) auscultador *m*; *Radio, TV* receptor *m*, (*P*) recetor *m*; **(official) ~r** síndico *m* de massa falida

recent /'ri:snt/ *a* recente. **~ly** *adv* recentemente

receptacle /rɪ'septəkl/ *n* recipiente *m*, receptáculo *m*, (*P*) recetáculo *m*

reception /rɪ'sepʃn/ *n* recepção *f*, (*P*) receção *f*; (*welcome*) acolhimento *m*; (*signal*) recepção *f*, (*P*) receção *f* (de sinal). **~ist** *n* recepcionista *mf*, (*P*) rececionista *mf*

receptive /rɪ'septɪv/ *a* receptivo, (*P*) recetivo

recess /rɪ'ses/ *n* recesso *m*; (*of legislature*) recesso *m*; *Amer Schol* recreio *m*

recession /rɪ'seʃn/ *n* recessão *f*, depressão *f* (económica)

recharge /ri:'tʃɑ:dʒ/ *vt* tornar a carregar, recarregar

recipe /'resəpı/ *n Culin* receita *f*

recipient /rı'sıpıənt/ *n* recipiente *mf*; (*of letter*) destinatário *m*

reciprocate /rı'sıprəkeıt/ *vt/i* reciprocar(-se), retribuir, fazer o mesmo

recital /rı'saıtl/ *n* (*music etc*) recital *m*

recite /rı'saıt/ *vt* recitar; (*list*) enumerar

reckless /'reklıs/ *a* inconsciente, imprudente, estouvado

reckon /'rekən/ *vt/i* calcular; (*judge*) considerar; (*think*) supor, pensar; **~ on** contar com, depender de; **~ with** contar com, levar em conta

reclaim /rı'kleım/ *vt* (*demand*) reclamar; ‹*land*› recuperar

reclin|e /rı'klaın/ *vt/i* reclinar(-se)

recluse /rı'klu:s/ *n* solitário *m*, recluso *m*

recognition /rekəg'nıʃn/ *n* reconhecimento *m*; **beyond ~** irreconhecível; **gain ~** ganhar nome, ser reconhecido

recogniz|e /'rekəgnaız/ *vt* reconhecer. **~able** /'rekəgnaızəbl/ *a* reconhecível

recoil /rı'kɔıl/ *vi* recuar; ‹*gun*› dar coice ● *n* recuo *m*; (*gun*) coice *m*; **~ from doing** recusar-se a fazer

recollect /rekə'lekt/ *vt* recordar-se de. **~ion** /-ʃn/ *n* recordação *f*, memória *f*

recommend /rekə'mend/ *vt* recomendar. **~ation** /-'deıʃn/ *n* recomendação *f*

recompense /'rekəmpens/ *vt* recompensar ● *n* recompensa *f*

reconcil|e /'rekənsaıl/ *vt* ‹*people*› reconciliar; ‹*facts*› conciliar; **~e o.s. to** resignar-se a, conformar-se com. **~iation** /-sılı'eıʃn/ *n* reconciliação *f*

reconnaissance /rı'kɒnısns/ *n* reconhecimento *m*

reconnoitre /rekə'nɔıtə(r)/ *vt/i* (*pres p* **-tring**) *Mil* reconhecer, fazer um reconhecimento (de)

reconsider /ri:kən'sıdə(r)/ *vt* reconsiderar

reconstruct /ri:kən'strʌkt/ *vt* reconstruir. **~ion** /-ʃn/ *n* reconstrução *f*

record[1] /rı'kɔ:d/ *vt* registar; ‹*disc, tape etc*› gravar; **~ that** referir/relatar que. **~ing** *n* (*disc, tape etc*) gravação *f*

record[2] /'rekɔ:d/ *n* (*register*) registro *m*, (*P*) registo *m*; (*mention*) menção *f*, nota *f*; (*file*) arquivo *m*; *Mus* disco *m*; *Sport* record(e) *m*; **have a (criminal) ~** ter cadastro; **off the ~** (*unofficial*) oficioso; (*secret*) confidencial ● *a* record(e) *invar*. **~ player** *n* toca-discos *m invar*, (*P*) gira-discos *m invar*

recorder /rı'kɔ:də(r)/ *n Mus* flauta *f* de ponta; *Techn* instrumento *m* registrador, (*P*) de registo

recount[1] /rı'kaʊnt/ *vt* narrar em pormenor, relatar

recount[2] /'ri:kaʊnt/ *n Pol* nova contagem *f*

recoup /rı'ku:p/ *vt* compensar; (*recover*) recuperar

recover /rı'kʌvə(r)/ *vt* recuperar ● *vi* restabelecer-se. **~y** *n* recuperação *f*; ‹*health*› recuperação *f*, restabelecimento *m*

recreation /rekrı'eıʃn/ *n* recreação *f*, recreio *m*; (*pastime*) passatempo *m*. **~al** *a* recreativo

recruit /rı'kru:t/ *n* recruta *m* ● *vt* recrutar. **~ment** *n* recrutamento *m*

rectang|le /'rektæŋgl/ *n* retângulo *m*. **~ular** /-'tæŋgjʊlə(r)/ *a* retangular

rectify /'rektıfaı/ *vt* retificar

recuperate /rı'kju:pəreıt/ *vt/i* recuperar(-se)

recur /rı'kɜ:(r)/ *vi* (*pt* **recurred**) repetir-se; (*come back*) voltar (**to** a)

recurren|t /rı'kʌrənt/ *a* frequente, (*P*) frequente, repetido, periódico. **~ce** *n* repetição *f*

recycle /ri:'saıkl/ *vt* reciclar

red /red/ *a* (**redder**, **reddest**) encarnado, vermelho; ‹*hair*› ruivo; **~ carpet** *fig* recepção *f or* (*P*) receção *f* solene, tratamento *m* especial; **R~ Cross** Cruz *f* Vermelha; **~ herring** *fig* pista *f* falsa; **~ light** luz *f* vermelha; **~ tape** *fig* papelada *f*, burocracia *f*; **~ wine** vinho *m* tinto ● *n* encarnado *m*, vermelho *m*; **in the ~** em déficit. **~-handed** *a* em flagrante (delito); com a boca na botija [!]; **~-hot** *a* escaldante, incandescente

redden /'redn/ *vt/i* avermelhar(-se); (*blush*) corar, ruborizar-se

redecorate /ri:'dekəreıt/ *vt* decorar/pintar de novo

red|eem /rı'di:m/ *vt* ‹*sins etc*› redimir; ‹*sth pawned*› tirar do prego [!]; ‹*voucher etc*› resgatar. **~emption** /rı'dempʃn/ *n* resgate *m*; (*of honour*) salvação *f*

redirect /ri:daı'rekt/ *vt* ‹*letter*› reendereçar

redness /'rednıs/ *n* vermelhidão *f*, cor *f* vermelha

redo /ri:'du:/ *vt* (*pt* **-did**, *pp* **-done**) refazer

redress /rɪ'dres/ *vt* reparar; (*set right*) remediar, emendar; **~ the balance** restabelecer o equilíbrio ● *n* reparação *f*

reduc|e /rɪ'dju:s/ *vt* reduzir; ‹*temperature etc*› baixar. **~tion** /rɪ-'dʌkʃən/ *n* redução *f*

redundan|t /rɪ'dʌndənt/ *a* redundante, supérfluo; ‹*worker*› desempregado; **be made ~t** ficar desempregado. **~cy** *n* demissão *f* por excesso de pessoal

reed /ri:d/ *n* cara *f*, junco *m*; *Mus* palheta *f*

reef /ri:f/ *n* recife *m*

reek /ri:k/ *n* mau cheiro *m* ● *vi* cheirar mal, tresandar; **he ~s of wine** ele está com cheiro de or tresanda a vinho

reel /ri:l/ *n* carretel *m*; (*spool*) bobina *f* ● *vi* cambalear, vacilar ● *vt* **~ off** recitar [!]

refectory /rɪ'fektərɪ/ *n* refeitório *m*

refer /rɪ'fɜ:(r)/ *vt/i* (*pt* **referred**) **~ to** referir-se a; (*concern*) aplicar-se a, dizer respeito a; (*consult*) consultar; (*direct*) remeter a/para

referee /refə'ri:/ *n* árbitro *m*; (*for job*) pessoa *f* que dá referências ● *vt* (*pt* **refereed**) arbitrar

reference /'refrəns/ *n* referência *f*; (*testimonial*) referências *fpl*; **in** or **with ~ to** com referência a; **~ book** livro *m* de consulta, obra *f* de referência

referendum /refə'rendəm/ *n* (*pl* **-dums**, *or* **-da**) referendo *m*, plebiscito *m*

refill[1] /ri:'fɪl/ *vt* encher de novo; ‹*pen etc*› pôr carga nova em

refill[2] /'ri:fɪl/ *n* ‹*pen etc*› carga *f* nova, (*P*) recarga *f*

refine /rɪ'faɪn/ *vt* refinar. **~d** *a* refinado; ‹*taste, manners etc*› requintado. **~ment** *n* ‹*taste, manners etc*› refinamento *m*, requinte *m*; *Tech* refinação *f*. **~ry** /-ərɪ/ *n* refinaria *f*

reflect /rɪ'flekt/ *vt/i* refletir (**on/upon** em). **~ion** /-ʃn/ *n* reflexão *f*; (*image*) reflexo *m*. **~or** *n* refletor *m*

reflective /rɪ'flektɪv/ *a* refletor; (*thoughtful*) refletido, ponderado

reflex /'ri:fleks/ *a & n* reflexo *m*

reflexive /rɪ'fleksɪv/ *a Gram* reflexivo, (*P*) reflexo

reform /rɪ'fɔ:m/ *vt/i* reformar(-se) ● *n* reforma *f*. **~er** *n* reformador *m*

refrain[1] /rɪ'freɪn/ *n* refrão *m*, estribilho *m*

refrain[2] /rɪ'freɪn/ *vi* abster-se (**from** de)

refresh /rɪ'freʃ/ *vt* refrescar; (*of rest etc*) restaurar; **~ one's memory** avivar or refrescar a memória. **~ing** *a* refrescante; (*of rest etc*) reparador. **~ments** *npl* refeição *f* leve; (*drinks*) refrescos *mpl*

refresher /rɪ'freʃə(r)/ *n* **~ course** curso *m* de reciclagem

refrigerat|e /rɪ'frɪdʒəreɪt/ *vt* refrigerar. **~or** *n* frigorífico *m*, refrigerador *m*, geladeira *f*

refuel /ri:'fju:əl/ *vt/i* (*pt* **refuelled**) reabastecer(-se) (de combustível)

refuge /'refju:dʒ/ *n* refúgio *m*, asilo *m*; **take ~** refugiar-se

refugee /refjʊ'dʒi:/ *n* refugiado *m*

refund[1] /rɪ'fʌnd/ *vt* reembolsar

refund[2] /'ri:fʌnd/ *n* reembolso *m*

refus|e[1] /rɪ'fju:z/ *vt/i* recusar(-se). **~al** *n* recusa *f*; **first ~al** preferência *f*, primeira opção *f*

refuse[2] /'refju:s/ *n* refugo *m*, lixo *m*. **~ collector** *n* lixeiro *m*, (*P*) homem *m* do lixo

refute /rɪ'fju:t/ *vt* refutar

regain /rɪ'geɪn/ *vt* recobrar, recuperar

regal /'ri:gl/ *a* real, régio

regard /rɪ'gɑ:d/ *vt* considerar; (*gaze*) olhar ● *n* consideração *f*, estima *f*; (*gaze*) olhar *m*; **~s** cumprimentos *mpl*; (*less formally*) lembranças *fpl*, saudades *fpl*. **as ~s ~ing** *prep* no que diz respeito a, quanto a. **~less** *adv* apesar de tudo; **~less of** apesar de

regatta /rɪ'gætə/ *n* regata *f*

regenerate /rɪ'dʒenəreɪt/ *vt* regenerar

regime /reɪ'ʒi:m/ *n* regime *m*

regiment /'redʒɪmənt/ *n* regimento *m*. **~al** /-'mentl/ *a* de regimento, regimental

region /'ri:dʒən/ *n* região *f*; **in the ~ of** por volta de. **~al** *a* regional

regist|er /'redʒɪstə(r)/ *n* registro *m*, (*P*) registo *m* ● *vt* (*record*) anotar; (*notice*) fixar, registar, prestar atenção a; ‹*birth, letter*› registrar, (*P*) registar; ‹*vehicle*› matrícular; ‹*emotions etc*› exprimir ● *vi* inscrever-se. **~er office** *n* registro *m*, (*P*) registo *m*. **~ration** /-'streɪʃn/ *n* registro *m*, (*P*) registo *m*; (*for course*) inscrição *f*, matricula *f*; **~ration (number)** número *m* de placa or de matrícula

registrar /redʒɪ'strɑ:(r)/ *n* oficial *m* do registro, (*P*) registo *m* civil; *Univ* secretário *m*

regret /rɪ'gret/ *n* pena *f*, pesar *m*; (*repentance*) remorso *m*; **I have no**

~s não estou arrependido ● *vt* (*pt* **regretted**) lamentar; sentir (**to do** fazer); (*feel repentance*) arrepender-se de, lamentar. **~fully** *adv* com pena, pesarosamente. **~table** *a* lamentável. **~tably** *adv* infelizmente

regular /'regjʊlə(r)/ *a* regular; (*usual*) normal; 🅸 (*thorough*) perfeito; verdadeiro; autêntico ● *n* 🅸 ‹*client*› cliente *mf* habitual. **~ity** /-'lærətɪ/ *n* regularidade *f*. **~ly** *adv* regularmente

regulat|e /'regjʊleɪt/ *vt* regular. **~ion** /-'leɪʃn/ *n* regulação *f*; (*rule*) regulamento *m*, regra *f*

rehabilitat|e /riːə'bɪlɪteɪt/ *vt* reabilitar. **~ion** /-'teɪʃn/ *n* reabilitação *f*

rehears|e /rɪ'hɜːs/ *vt* ensaiar. **~al** *n* ensaio *m*; **dress ~al** ensaio *m* geral

reign /reɪn/ *n* reinado *m* ● *vi* reinar (**over** em)

reimburse /riːɪm'bɜːs/ *vt* reembolsar. **~ment** *n* reembolso *m*

rein /reɪn/ *n* rédea *f*

reincarnation /riːɪnkɑː'neɪʃn/ *n* reencarnação *f*

reindeer /'reɪndɪə(r)/ *n invar* rena *f*

reinforce /riːɪn'fɔːs/ *vt* reforçar; **~d concrete** concreto *m* armado, (*P*) cimento *m* or betão *m* armado. **~ment** *n* reforço *m*; **~ments** reforços *mpl*

reinstate /riːɪn'steɪt/ *vt* reintegrar, reintroduzir

reiterate /riː'ɪtəreɪt/ *vt* reiterar

reject[1] /rɪ'dʒekt/ *vt* rejeitar. **~ion** /-ʃn/ *n* rejeição *f*

reject[2] /'riːdʒekt/ *n* (artigo de) refugo *m*

r

rejoic|e /rɪ'dʒɔɪs/ *vi* regozijar-se (**at/ over** com). **~ing** *n* regozijo *m*

rejuvenate /riː'dʒuːvəneɪt/ *vt* rejuvenescer

relapse /rɪ'læps/ *n* recaída *f* ● *vi* recair

relate /rɪ'leɪt/ *vt* relatar; (*associate*) relacionar ● *vi* **~ to** ter relação com, dizer respeito a; (*get on with*) entender-se com. **~d** *a* aparentado; ‹*ideas etc*› afim, relacionado

relation /rɪ'leɪʃn/ *n* relação *f*; (*person*) parente *mf*. **~ship** *n* parentesco *m*; (*link*) relação *f*; (*affair*) ligação *f*

relative /'relətɪv/ *n* parente *mf* ● *a* relativo. **~ly** *adv* relativamente

relax /rɪ'læks/ *vt/i* relaxar(-se); *fig* descontrair(-se). **~ation** /riːlæk'seɪʃn/ *n* relaxamento *m*; *fig* descontração *f*; (*recreation*) distração *f*. **~ing** *a* relaxante

relay[1] /'riːleɪ/ *n* turma *f*, (*P*) turno *m*; **~ race** corrida *f* de revezamento, (*P*) estafetas

relay[2] /rɪ'leɪ/ *vt* (*message*) retransmitir

release /rɪ'liːs/ *vt* libertar, soltar; *Mech* desengatar, soltar; ‹*bomb, film, record*› lançar; ‹*news*› dar, publicar; ‹*gas, smoke*› soltar, libertar, emitir ● *n* libertação *f*; *Mech* desengate *m*; (*bomb, film, record*) lançamento *m*; (*news*) publicação *f*; (*gas, smoke*) emissão *f*; **new ~** estreia *f*

relegate /'relɪgeɪt/ *vt* relegar

relent /rɪ'lent/ *vi* ceder. **~less** *a* implacável, inexorável, inflexível

relevan|t /'reləvənt/ *a* relevante, pertinente, a propósito; **be ~ to** ter a ver com, dizer respeito a. **~ce** *n* pertinência *f*, relevância *f*

reliab|le /rɪ'laɪəbl/ *a* de confiança, com que se pode contar; ‹*source etc*› fidedigno; ‹*machine etc*› seguro, confiável. **~ility** /-'bɪlətɪ/ *n* confiabilidade *f*

reliance /rɪ'laɪəns/ *n* (*dependence*) segurança *f*; (*trust*) confiança *f*; fé *f* (**on** em)

relic /'relɪk/ *n* relíquia *f*; **~s** vestígios *mpl*, ruínas *fpl*

relief /rɪ'liːf/ *n* alívio *m*; (*assistance*) auxílio *m*, assistência *f*; (*outline, design*) relevo *m*; **~ road** estrada *f* alternativa

relieve /rɪ'liːv/ *vt* aliviar; (*help*) socorrer; (*take over from*) revezar, substituir; *Mil* render

religion /rɪ'lɪdʒən/ *n* religião *f*

religious /rɪ'lɪdʒəs/ *a* religioso

relinquish /rɪ'lɪŋkwɪʃ/ *vt* abandonar, renunciar a

relish /'relɪʃ/ *n* prazer *m*, gosto *m*; *Culin* molho *m* condimentado ● *vt* saborear, apreciar, gostar de

relocate /riːləʊ'keɪt/ *vt/i* transferir(-se), mudar(-se)

reluctan|t /rɪ'lʌktənt/ *a* relutante (**to** em); pouco inclinado (**to** a). **~ce** *n* relutância *f*. **~tly** *adv* a contragosto, relutantemente

rely /rɪ'laɪ/ *vi* **~ on** contar com; (*depend*) depender de

remain /rɪ'meɪn/ *vi* ficar, permanecer. **~s** *npl* restos *mpl*; (*ruins*) ruínas *fpl*. **~ing** *a* restante

remainder /rɪ'meɪndə(r)/ *n* restante *m*, remanescente *m*

remand /rɪ'mɑːnd/ *vt* reconduzir à prisão para detenção provisória ● *n* **on**

~ sob prisão preventiva

remark /rɪ'mɑ:k/ *n* observação *f*, comentário *m* ● *vt* observar, comentar ● *vi* ~ **on** fazer observações or comentários sobre. **~able** *a* notável

remarr|y /ri:'mærɪ/ *vt/i* tornar a casar(-se) (com)

remed|y /'remədɪ/ *n* remédio *m* ● *vt* remediar. **~ial** /rɪ'mi:dɪəl/ *a Med* corretivo

rememb|er /rɪ'membə(r)/ *vt* lembrar-se de, recordar-se de. **~rance** *n* lembrança *f*, recordação *f*

remind /rɪ'maɪnd/ *vt* (fazer) lembrar (**sb of sth** algo a alguém); ~ **sb to do** lembrar a alguém que faça. **~er** *n* o que serve para fazer lembrar; (*note*) lembrete *m*

reminisce /remɪ'nɪs/ *vi* (re) lembrar (coisas passadas). **~nces** *npl* reminiscências *fpl*

reminiscent /remɪ'nɪsnt/ *a* ~ **of** que faz lembrar, evocativo de

remit /rɪ'mɪt/ *vt* (*pt* **remitted**) (*money*) remeter. **~tance** *n* remessa (de dinheiro) *f*

remnant /'remnənt/ *n* resto *m*; (*trace*) vestígio *m*; (*of cloth*) retalho *m*

remorse /rɪ'mɔ:s/ *n* remorsos *m*. **~ful** *a* arrependido, com remorsos. **~less** *a* implacável

remote /rɪ'məʊt/ *a* remoto, distante; ‹*person*› distante; (*slight*) vago, leve; ~ **control** comando *m* à distância, telecomando *m*. **~ly** *adv* de longe; vagamente

remov|e /rɪ'mu:v/ *vt* tirar, remover; (*lead away*) levar; (*dismiss*) demitir; (*get rid of*) eliminar. **~al** *n* remoção *f*; (*dismissal*) demissão *f*; (*from house*) mudança *f*

remunerat|e /rɪ'mju:nəreɪt/ *vt* remunerar. **~ion** /-'reɪʃn/ *n* remuneração *f*

rename /ri:'neɪm/ *vt* rebatizar

render /'rendə(r)/ *vt* retribuir; ‹*services*› prestar; *Mus* interpretar; (*translate*) traduzir

renegade /'renɪgeɪd/ *n* renegado *m*

renew /rɪ'nju:/ *vt* renovar; (*resume*) retomar. **~able** *a* renovável. **~al** *n* renovação *f*; (*resumption*) reatamento *m*

renounce /rɪ'naʊns/ *vt* renunciar a; (*disown*) renegar, repudiar

renovat|e /'renəveɪt/ *vt* renovar. **~ion** /-'veɪʃn/ *n* renovação *f*

renown /rɪ'naʊn/ *n* renome *m*. **~ed** *a* conceituado, célebre, de renome

rent /rent/ *n* aluguel *m*, (*P*) aluguer *m*, renda *f* ● *vt* alugar, arrendar. **~al** *n* (*charge*) aluguel *m*, (*P*) aluguer *m*; renda *f*; (*act of renting*) aluguel *m*, (*P*) aluguer *m*

renunciation /rɪnʌnsɪ'eɪʃn/ *n* renúncia *f*

reopen /ri:'əʊpən/ *vt/i* reabrir(-se)

reorganize /ri:'ɔ:gənaɪz/ *vt/i* reorganizar(-se)

rep /rep/ *n* [!] vendedor *m*; caixeiro-viajante *m*

repair /rɪ'peə(r)/ *vt* reparar, consertar ● *n* reparo *m*, conserto *m*; **in good** ~ em bom estado (de conservação)

repatriat|e /ri:'pætrɪeɪt/ *vt* repatriar. **~ion** /-'eɪʃn/ *n* repatriamento *m*

repay /ri:'peɪ/ *vt* (*pt* **repaid**) pagar, devolver, reembolsar; (*reward*) recompensar. **~ment** *n* pagamento *m*, reembolso *m*

repeal /rɪ'pi:l/ *vt* revogar ● *n* revogação *f*

repeat /rɪ'pi:t/ *vt/i* repetir(-se) ● *n* repetição *f*; (*broadcast*) retransmissão *f*. **~edly** *adv* repetidas vezes, repetidamente

repel /rɪ'pel/ *vt* (*pt* **repelled**) repelir. **~lent** *a* & *n* repelente *m*

repent /rɪ'pent/ *vi* arrepender-se (**of** de). **~ance** *n* arrependimento *m*. **~ant** *a* arrependido

repercussion /ri:pə'kʌʃn/ *n* repercussão *f*

repertoire /'repətwɑ:(r)/ *n* repertório *m*

repertory /'repətrɪ/ *n* repertório *m*

repetit|ion /repɪ'tɪʃn/ *n* repetição *f*. **~ious ~ive** /rɪ-'petətɪv/ *a* repetitivo

repetitive strain injury *n* lesão *f* por esforço repetitivo

replace /rɪ'pleɪs/ *vt* colocar no mesmo lugar, repor; (*take the place of*) substituir. **~ment** *n* reposição *f*; (*substitution*) substituição *f*; (*person*) substituto *m*

replenish /rɪ'plenɪʃ/ *vt* voltar a encher, reabastecer; (*renew*) renovar

replica /'replɪkə/ *n* réplica *f*, cópia *f*, reprodução *f*

reply /rɪ'plaɪ/ *vt/i* responder, replicar ● *n* resposta *f*, réplica *f*

report /rɪ'pɔ:t/ *vt* relatar; (*notify*) informar; (*denounce*) denunciar, apresentar queixa de ● *vi* fazer um relatório; ~ **(on)** ‹*news item*› fazer uma reportagem (sobre); ~ **to** (*go*) apresentar-se a ● *n* (*in newspapers*) reportagem *f*; (*of company, doctor*) relatório *m*; *Schol* boletim *m* escolar; (*sound*) detonação *f*; (*rumour*) rumores *mpl*. **~edly** *adv* segundo consta. **~er** *n* repórter *m*

repossess /ri:pəˈzes/ *vt* reapossar-se de, retomar

represent /reprɪˈzent/ *vt* representar. **~ation** /-ˈteɪʃn/ *n* representação *f*

representative /reprɪˈzentətɪv/ *a* representativo ● *n* representante *mf*

repress /rɪˈpres/ *vt* reprimir. **~ion** /-ʃn/ *n* repressão *f*. **~ive** *a* repressor, repressivo

reprieve /rɪˈpri:v/ *n* suspensão *f* temporária; (*temporary relief*) tréguas *fpl* ● *vt* suspender temporariamente; *fig* dar tréguas a

reprimand /ˈreprɪmɑ:nd/ *vt* repreender ● *n* repreensão *f*, reprimenda *f*

reprint /ˈri:prɪnt/ *n* reimpressão *f*, reedição *f* ● *vt* reimprimir

reproach /rɪˈprəʊtʃ/ *vt* censurar; repreender (**sb for sth** alguém por algo, algo a alguém) ● *n* censura *f*; **above ~** irrepreensível. **~ful** *a* repreensivo, reprovador

reproduc|e /ri:prəˈdju:s/ *vt/i* reproduzir(-se). **~tion** /-ˈdʌkʃn/ *n* reprodução *f*. **~tive** /-ˈdʌktɪv/ *a* reprodutivo, reprodutor

reptile /ˈreptaɪl/ *n* réptil *m*

republic /rɪˈpʌblɪk/ *n* república *f*. **~an** *a & n* republicano *m*

repugnan|t /rɪˈpʌgnənt/ *a* repugnante. **~ce** *n* repugnância *f*

repuls|e /rɪˈpʌls/ *vt* repelir, repulsar. **~ion** /-ʃn/ *n* repulsa *f*. **~ive** *a* repulsivo, repelente, repugnante

reputable /ˈrepjʊtəbl/ *a* respeitado, honrado; ‹*firm, make etc*› de renome, conceituado

reputation /repjʊˈteɪʃn/ *n* reputação *f*

repute /rɪˈpju:t/ *n* reputação *f*. **~d** /-ɪd/ *a* suposto, putativo; **~d to be** tido como, tido na conta de. **~dly** /-ɪdlɪ/ *adv* segundo consta, com fama de

request /rɪˈkwest/ *n* pedido *m* ● *vt* pedir; solicitar (**of, from** a)

require /rɪˈkwaɪə(r)/ *vt* requerer. **~d** *a* requerido; (*needed*) necessário, preciso. **~ment** *n fig* requisito *m*; (*need*) necessidade *f*; (*demand*) exigência *f*

resale /ˈri:seɪl/ *n* revenda *f*

rescue /ˈreskju:/ *vt* salvar; socorrer (**from** de) ● *n* salvamento *m*; (*help*) socorro *m*, ajuda *f*. **~r** /-ə(r)/ *n* salvador *m*

research /rɪˈsɜ:tʃ/ *n* pesquisa *f*, investigação *f* ● *vt/i* pesquisar; fazer investigação (**into** sobre). **~er** *n* investigador *m*

resembl|e /rɪˈzembl/ *vt* assemelhar-se a, parecer-se com. **~ance** *n* semelhança *f*; similaridade *f* (**to** com)

resent /rɪˈzent/ *vt* ressentir(-se de), ficar ressentido com. **~ful** *a* ressentido. **~ment** *n* ressentimento *m*

reservation /rezəˈveɪʃn/ *n* (*booking*) reserva *f*; *Amer* reserva (de índios) *f*

reserve /rɪˈzɜ:v/ *vt* reservar ● *n* reserva *f*; *Sport* suplente *mf*; **in ~** de reserva. **~d** *a* reservado

reservoir /ˈrezəvwɑ:(r)/ *n* (*lake, supply etc*) reservatório *m*; (*container*) depósito *m*

reshuffle /ri:ˈʃʌfl/ *vt Pol* remodelar ● *n Pol* reforma (do Ministério) *f*, remodelação *f* (ministerial)

reside /rɪˈzaɪd/ *vi* residir

residen|t /ˈrezɪdənt/ *a* residente ● *n* morador *m*, habitante *mf*; (*foreigner*) residente *mf*; (*in hotel*) hóspede *mf*. **~ce** *n* residência *f*; (*of students*) residência *f*, lar *m*; **~ce permit** visto *m* de residência

residential /rezɪˈdenʃl/ *a* residencial

residue /ˈrezɪdju:/ *n* resíduo *m*

resign /rɪˈzaɪn/ *vt* (*post*) demitir-se; **~ o.s. to** resignar-se a ● *vi* demitir-se, apresentar a demissão. **~ation** /rezɪgˈneɪʃn/ *n* resignação *f*; (*from job*) demissão *f*. **~ed** *a* resignado

resilien|t /rɪˈzɪlɪənt/ *a* (*springy*) elástico; (*person*) resistente. **~ce** *n* elasticidade *f*; (*of person*) resistência *f*

resin /ˈrezɪn/ *n* resina *f*

resist /rɪˈzɪst/ *vt/i* resistir (a). **~ance** *n* resistência *f*. **~ant** *a* resistente

resolut|e /ˈrezəlu:t/ *a* resoluto. **~ion** /-ˈlu:ʃn/ *n* resolução *f*

resolve /rɪˈzɒlv/ *vt* resolver; **~ to do** resolver fazer ● *n* resolução *f*. **~d** *a* (*resolute*) resoluto; (*decided*) resolvido (**to** a)

resonan|t /ˈrezənənt/ *a* ressonante. **~ce** *n* ressonância *f*

resort /rɪˈzɔ:t/ *vi* **~ to** recorrer a, valer-se de ● *n* recurso *m*; (*place*) estância *f*, local *m* turístico; **as a last ~** em último recurso; **seaside ~** praia *f*, balneário *m*, (*P*) estância *f* balnear

resound /rɪˈzaʊnd/ *vi* reboar; ressoar (**with** com). **~ing** *a* ressoante; *fig* retumbante

resource /rɪ'sɔːs/ *n* recurso *m*; **~s** recursos *mpl*, riquezas *fpl*. **~ful** *a* expedito, engenhoso, desembaraçado. **~fulness** *n* expediente *m*, engenho *m*

respect /rɪ'spekt/ *n* respeito *m* ● *vt* respeitar; **with ~ to** a respeito de, com respeito a, relativamente a. **~ful** *a* respeitoso

respectab|le /rɪ'spektəbl/ *a* respeitável; (*passable*) passável, aceitável

respective /rɪ'spektɪv/ *a* respectivo, (*P*) respetivo. **~ly** *adv* respectivamente, (*P*) respetivamente

respiration /respə'reɪʃn/ *n* respiração *f*

respite /'respaɪt/ *n* pausa *f*, trégua *f*, folga *f*

respond /rɪ'spɒnd/ *vi* responder (**to** a); (*react*) reagir (**to** a)

response /rɪ'spɒns/ *n* resposta *f*; (*reaction*) reação *f*

responsib|le /rɪ'spɒnsəbl/ *a* responsável; ‹*job*› de responsabilidade. **~ility** /-'bɪlətɪ/ *n* responsabilidade *f*

responsive /rɪ'spɒnsɪv/ *a* receptivo, (*P*) recetivo, que reage bem; **~ to** sensível a

rest[1] /rest/ *vt/i* descansar, repousar; (*lean*) apoiar(-se) ● *n* descanso *m*, repouso *m*; (*support*) suporte *m*. **~room** *n Amer* banheiro *m*, (*P*) toaletes *mpl*

rest[2] /rest/ *vi* (*remain*) ficar; **it ~s with him** cabe a ele ● *n* (*remainder*) resto *m* (**of** de); **the ~ (of the)** (*others*) os outros

restaurant /'restrɒnt/ *n* restaurante *m*

restful /'restfl/ *a* sossegado, repousante, tranquilo

restless /'restlɪs/ *a* agitado, desassossegado

restor|e /rɪ'stɔː(r)/ *vt* restaurar; (*give back*) restituir, devolver. **~ation** /restə'reɪʃn/ *n* restauração *f*

restrain /rɪ'streɪn/ *vt* conter, reprimir; **~ o.s.** controlar-se; **~ sb from** impedir alguém de. **~ed** *a* comedido, reservado. **~t** *n* controle *m*; (*moderation*) moderação *f*, comedimento *m*

restrict /rɪ'strɪkt/ *vt* restringir, limitar. **~ion** /-ʃn/ *n* restrição *f*. **~ive** *a* restritivo

result /rɪ'zʌlt/ *n* resultado *m* ● *vi* resultar (**from** de); **~ in** resultar em

resum|e /rɪ'zjuːm/ *vt/i* reatar, retomar; ‹*work, travel*› recomeçar. **~ption** /rɪ'zʌmpʃn/ *n* reatamento *m*, retomada *f*; (*of work*) recomeço *m*

résumé /'rezjuːmeɪ/ *n* resumo *m*, (*P*) CV *m*

resurgence /rɪ'sɜːdʒəns/ *n* reaparecimento *m*, ressurgimento *m*

resurrect /rezə'rekt/ *vt* ressuscitar. **~ion** /-ʃn/ *n* ressureição *f*

resuscitat|e /rɪ'sʌsɪteɪt/ *vt* ressuscitar, reanimar. **~ion** /-'teɪʃn/ *n* reanimação *f*

retail /'riːteɪl/ *n* retalho *m* ● *a & adv* a retalho ● *vt/i* vender(-se) a retalho. **~er** *n* retalhista *mf*

retain /rɪ'teɪn/ *vt* reter; (*keep*) conservar, guardar

retaliat|e /rɪ'tælɪeɪt/ *vi* retaliar, exercer represálias, desforrar-se. **~ion** /-'eɪʃn/ *n* retaliação *f*, represália *f*, desforra *f*

retarded /rɪ'tɑːdɪd/ *a* retardado, atrasado

retch /retʃ/ *vi* fazer esforço para vomitar, estar com ânsias de vômito *or* (*P*) vómito

retention /rɪ'tenʃn/ *n* retenção *f*

reticen|t /'retɪsnt/ *a* reticente. **~ce** *n* reticência *f*

retina /'retɪnə/ *n* retina *f*

retinue /'retɪnjuː/ *n* séquito *m*, comitiva *f*

retire /rɪ'taɪə(r)/ *vi* reformar-se, aposentar-se; (*withdraw*) retirar-se; (*go to bed*) ir deitar-se ● *vt* reformar, aposentar. **~d** *a* reformado, aposentado. **~ment** *n* reforma *f*, aposentadoria *f*, (*P*) aposentação *f*

retiring /rɪ'taɪərɪŋ/ *a* reservado, retraído

retort /rɪ'tɔːt/ *vt/i* retrucar, retorquir ● *n* réplica *f*

retrace /riː'treɪs/ *vt* **~ one's steps** refazer o mesmo caminho; *fig* recordar, recapitular

retract /rɪ'trækt/ *vt/i* retratar(-se), desdizer(-se); ‹*wheels*› recolher; ‹*claws*› encolher, recolher

retreat /rɪ'triːt/ *vi* retirar-se; *Mil* retirar, bater em retirada ● *n* retirada *f*; (*seclusion*) retiro *m*

retrial /riː'traɪəl/ *n* novo *m* julgamento

retribution /retrɪ'bjuːʃn/ *n* castigo (merecido) *m*; (*vengeance*) vingança *f*

retriev|e /rɪ'triːv/ *vt* ir buscar; (*rescue*) salvar; (*recover*) recuperar; (*put right*) reparar. **~er** *n* (*dog*) perdigueiro *m*, (*P*) retriever *m*

retrograde /'retrəgreɪd/ *a* retrógrado ● *vt* retroceder, recuar

retrospect /'retrəspekt/ *n* **in ~** retrospectivamente, (*P*) retrospetivamente. **~ive** /-'spektɪv/ *a* retrospetivo; (*of law, payment*) retroativo

return /rɪ'tɜ:n/ *vi* voltar; regressar; retornar (**to** a) ● *vt* devolver; ‹*compliment, visit*› retribuir; (*put back*) pôr de volta ● *n* volta *f*, regresso *m*, retorno *m*; (*profit*) lucro *m*, rendimento *m*; (*restitution*) devolução *f*; **in ~ for** em troca de; **~ journey** viagem *f* de volta; **~ match** *Sport* desafio *m* de desforra; **~ ticket** bilhete *m* de ida e volta; **many happy ~s (of the day)** muitos parabéns

reunion /ri:'ju:nɪən/ *n* reunião *f*

reunite /ri:ju:'naɪt/ *vt* reunir

rev /rev/ *n* 🄸 *Auto* rotação *f* ● *vt/i* (*pt* **revved**) **~ (up)** 🄸 *Auto* acelerar (o motor)

reveal /rɪ'vi:l/ *vt* revelar; (*display*) expor. **~ing** *a* revelador

revel /'revl/ *vi* (*pt* **revelled**) divertir-se; **~ in** deleitar-se com. **~ry** *n* festas *fpl*, festejos *mpl*

revelation /revə'leɪʃn/ *n* revelação *f*

revenge /rɪ'vendʒ/ *n* vingança *f*; *Sport* desforra *f* ● *vt* vingar

revenue /'revənju:/ *n* receita *f*, rendimento *m*; **Inland R~** Fisco *m*

reverberate /rɪ'vɜ:bəreɪt/ *vi* ecoar, repercutir

revere /rɪ'vɪə(r)/ *vt* reverenciar, venerar

reverend /'revərənd/ *a* reverendo; **R~** Reverendo

reveren|t /'revərənt/ *a* reverente. **~ce** *n* reverência *f*, veneração *f*

revers|e /rɪ'vɜ:s/ *a* contrário, inverso ● *n* contrário *m*; (*back*) reverso *m*; (*gear*) marcha *f* à ré *or* (*P*) atrás ● *vt* virar ao contrário; ‹*order*› inverter; (*turn inside out*) virar do avesso; ‹*decision*› anular ● *vi Auto* fazer marcha à ré *or* (*P*) atrás. **~al** *n* inversão *f*, mudança *f* em sentido contrário; (*of view etc*) mudança *f*

revert /rɪ'vɜ:t/ *vi* **~ to** reverter a

review /rɪ'vju:/ *n* (*inspection; magazine*) revista *f*; (*of a situation*) revisão *f*; (*critique*) crítica *f* ● *vt* revistar, passar *or* (*P*) fazer revista em; ‹*situation*› rever; ‹*book, film etc*› fazer a crítica de. **~er** *n* crítico *m*

revis|e /rɪ'vaɪz/ *vt* rever; (*amend*) corrigir. **~ion** /-ɪʒn/ *n* revisão *f*; (*amendment*) correção *f*

reviv|e /rɪ'vaɪv/ *vt/i* ressuscitar, reavivar; ‹*play*› reapresentar; ‹*person*› reanimar(-se). **~al** *n* reflorescimento *m*, renascimento *m*

revoke /rɪ'vəʊk/ *vt* revogar, anular, invalidar

revolt /rɪ'vəʊlt/ *vt/i* revoltar(-se) ● *n* revolta *f*

revolting /rɪ'vəʊltɪŋ/ *a* (*disgusting*) repugnante

revolution /revə'lu:ʃn/ *n* revolução *f*. **~ary** *a* & *n* revolucionário *m*. **~ize** *vt* revolucionar

revolv|e /rɪ'vɒlv/ *vi* girar; **~ing door** porta *f* giratória

revolver /rɪ'vɒlvə(r)/ *n* revólver *m*

revulsion /rɪ'vʌlʃn/ *n* repugnância *f*, repulsa *f*

reward /rɪ'wɔ:d/ *n* prêmio *m*, (*P*) prémio *m*; (*for criminal, for lost/stolen property*) recompensa *f* ● *vt* recompensar. **~ing** *a* compensador; ‹*task etc*› gratificante

rewind /ri:'waɪnd/ *vt* (*pt* **rewound**) rebobinar

rewrite /ri:'raɪt/ *vt* (*pt* **rewrote**, *pp* **rewritten**) reescrever

rhetoric /'retərɪk/ *n* retórica *f*. **~al** /rɪ'tɒrɪkl/ *a* retórico; ‹*question*› retórico

rheumati|c /ru:'mætɪk/ *a* reumático. **~sm** /'ru:mətɪzm/ *n* reumatismo *m*

rhinoceros /raɪ'nɒsərəs/ *n* (*pl* **-oses**) rinoceronte *m*

rhubarb /'ru:bɑ:b/ *n* ruibarbo *m*

rhyme /raɪm/ *n* rima *f*; (*poem*) versos *mpl* ● *vt/i* (fazer) rimar

rhythm /'rɪðəm/ *n* ritmo *m*. **~ic(al)** /'rɪðmɪk(l)/ *a* rítmico, compassado

rib /rɪb/ *n* costela *f*

ribbon /'rɪbən/ *n* fita *f*; **in ~s** em tiras

rice /raɪs/ *n* arroz *m*

rich /rɪtʃ/ *a* (**-er**, **-est**) rico; ‹*food*› rico em açúcar e gordura. **~es** *npl* riquezas *fpl*. **~ly** *adv* ricamente

rickety /'rɪkətɪ/ *a* (*shaky*) desconjuntado

ricochet /'rɪkəʃeɪ/ *n* ricochete *m* ● *vi* (*pt* **ricocheted** /-ʃeɪd/) fazer ricochete, ricochetear

rid /rɪd/ *vt* (*pt* **rid**, *pres p* **ridding**) desembaraçar (**of** de); **get ~ of** desembaraçar-se de, livrar-se de

riddance /'rɪdns/ *n* **good ~!** que alívio!, vai com Deus!

ridden /'rɪdn/ ▶ RIDE

riddle[1] /'rɪdl/ *n* enigma *m*; (*puzzle*) charada *f*

riddle[2] /'rɪdl/ *vt* **~ with** crivar de

ride /raɪd/ *vi* (*pt* **rode**, *pp* **ridden**) andar (de bicicleta, a cavalo, de carro) ● *vt* ‹*horse*› montar; ‹*bicycle*› andar de; ‹*distance*› percorrer ● *n* passeio *m* or volta *f* (de carro, a cavalo etc); (*distance*) percurso *m*. **~r** /-ə(r)/ *n* cavaleiro *m*, amazona *f*; (*cyclist*) ciclista *mf*; (*in document*) aditamento *m*

ridge /rɪdʒ/ *n* aresta *f*; (*of hill*) cume *m*

ridicule /ˈrɪdɪkju:l/ *n* ridículo *m* ● *vt* ridicularizar

ridiculous /rɪˈdɪkjʊləs/ *a* ridículo

riding /ˈraɪdɪŋ/ *n* equitação *f*

rife /raɪf/ *a* **be ~** estar espalhado; (*of illness*) grassar; **~ with** cheio de

riff-raff /ˈrɪfræf/ *n* gentinha *f*, povinho *m*, ralé *f*

rifle /ˈraɪfl/ *n* espingarda *f* ● *vt* revistar e roubar, saquear

rift /rɪft/ *n* fenda *f*, brecha *f*; *fig* (*dissension*) desacordo *m*; desavença *f*; desentendimento *m*

rig[1] /rɪg/ *vt* (*pt* **rigged**) equipar; **~ out** enfarpelar [!]; **~ up** arranjar ● *n* (*for oil*) plataforma *f* de poço de petróleo

rig[2] /rɪg/ *vt* (*pt* **rigged**) *pej* manipular

right /raɪt/ *a* (*correct, moral*) certo; correto; (*fair*) justo; (*not left*) direito; (*suitable*) certo, próprio ● *n* (*entitlement*) direito *m*; (*not left*) direita *f*; (*not evil*) o bem; **~ of way** *Auto* prioridade *f* ● *vt* ‹*a wrong*› reparar; ‹*sth fallen*› endireitar ● *adv* (*not left*) à direita; (*directly*) direito; (*exactly*) mesmo, bem; (*completely*) completamente; **~ away** logo, imediatamente; **be ~** ‹*person*› ter razão (**to** em); **be in the ~** ter razão; **on the ~** à direita; **put ~** acertar, corrigir. **~ angle** *n* ângulo reto *m*; **~-hand** *a* à or de direita; **~-handed** *a* (*person*) destro; **~-wing** *a Pol* de direita

righteous /ˈraɪtʃəs/ *a* justo, virtuoso

rightful /ˈraɪtfl/ *a* legítimo

rightly /ˈraɪtlɪ/ *adv* devidamente, corretamente; (*with reason*) justificadamente

rigid /ˈrɪdʒɪd/ *a* rígido. **~ity** /rɪˈdʒɪdətɪ/ *n* rigidez *f*

rig|our /ˈrɪgə(r)/ *n* rigor *m*. **~orous** *a* rigoroso

rile /raɪl/ *vt* [!] irritar; exasperar

rim /rɪm/ *n* borda *f*; (*of wheel*) aro *m*

rind /raɪnd/ *n* (*on cheese, fruit*) casca *f*; (*on bacon*) pele *f*

ring[1] /rɪŋ/ *n* (*on finger*) anel *m*; (*for napkin, key etc*) argola *f*; (*circle*) roda *f*, círculo *m*; *Boxing* ringue *m*; (*arena*) arena *f*; (*of people*) grupo *m* ● *vt* rodear, cercar. **~ road** *n* estrada *f* periférica or perimetral *or* (*P*) circular *f*

ring[2] /rɪŋ/ *vt/i* (*pt* **rang**, *pp* **rung**) tocar; (*of words etc*) soar ● *n* toque *m*; [!] (*phone call*) telefonadela *f* [!]; **~ the bell** tocar a campaínha; **~ back** telefonar de volta; **~ off** desligar; **~ up** telefonar (a). **~tone** *n* toque *m*, (*P*) tom de toque *m*

ringleader /ˈrɪŋli:də(r)/ *n* cabeça *m*, cérebro *m*

rink /rɪŋk/ *n* rinque *m* de patinação *or* (*P*) patinagem

rinse /rɪns/ *vt* enxaguar ● *n* enxaguada *f*, (*P*) enxaguadela *f*; (*hair tint*) enxaguada *f*, (*P*) enxaguadela *f*

riot /ˈraɪət/ *n* distúrbio *m*, motim *m*; (*of colours*) festival *m* ● *vi* fazer distúrbios or motins; **run ~** desenfrear-se, descontrolar-se; (*of plants*) crescer em matagal. **~er** *n* desordeiro *m*

riotous /ˈraɪətəs/ *a* desenfreado, turbulento, desordeiro

rip /rɪp/ *vt/i* (*pt* **ripped**) rasgar(-se) ● *n* rasgão *m*; **~ off** [x] (*defraud*) defraudar, enrolar [x]. **~-off** *n* [x] roubalheira *f* [!]

ripe /raɪp/ *a* (**-er**, **-est**) maduro. **~ness** *n* madureza *f*, (*P*) amadurecimento *m*

ripen /ˈraɪpən/ *vt/i* amadurecer

ripple /ˈrɪpl/ *n* ondulação *f* leve; (*sound*) murmúrio *m* ● *vt/i* encrespar(-se), agitar(-se), ondular

rise /raɪz/ *vi* (*pt* **rose**, *pp* **risen**) subir, elevar-se; (*stand up*) erguer-se, levantar-se; ‹*rebel*› sublevar-se; ‹*sun*› nascer; ‹*curtain, prices*› subir ● *n* (*increase*) aumento *m*; (*slope*) subida *f*, ladeira *f*; (*origin*) origem *f*; **give ~ to** originar, causar, dar origem a. **~r** /-ə(r)/ *n* **early ~r** madrugador *m*

rising /ˈraɪzɪŋ/ *n* (*revolt*) insurreição *f* ● *a* ‹*sun*› nascente

risk /rɪsk/ *n* risco *m* ● *vt* arriscar; **at ~** em risco, em perigo; **at one's own ~** por sua conta e risco; **~ doing** (*venture*) arriscar-se a fazer. **~y** *a* arriscado

risqué /ˈri:skeɪ/ *a* picante

rite /raɪt/ *n* rito *m*; **last ~s** últimos sacramentos *mpl*

ritual /ˈrɪtʃʊəl/ *a* & *n* ritual *m*

rival /ˈraɪvl/ *n* & *a* rival *mf*; *fig* concorrente *mf*; competidor *m* ● *vt* (*pt* **rivalled**) rivalizar com. **~ry** *n* rivalidade *f*

river /ˈrɪvə(r)/ *n* rio *m* ● *a* fluvial

rivet /ˈrɪvɪt/ *n* rebite *m* ● *vt* (*pt* **riveted**) rebitar; *fig* prender; cravar. **~ing** *a* fascinante

road /rəʊd/ *n* estrada *f*; (*in town*) rua *f*; (*small*) *fig* caminho *m*; **~ tax** imposto *m* de circulação. **~block** *n* barricada *f*; **~ map** *n* mapa *m* das estradas; **~ sign** *n* sinal *m*, placa *f* de sinalização; **~works** *npl* obras *fpl* (na via)

roadside /'rəʊdsaɪd/ *n* beira *f* da estrada

roadway /'reʊdweɪ/ *n* pista *f* de rolamento, (*P*) faixa *f* de rodagem

roadworthy /'reʊdwɜ:ðɪ/ *a* em condições de ser utilizado na rua/estrada

roam /rəʊm/ *vi* errar, andar sem destino ● *vt* percorrer

roaming /'rəʊmɪŋ/ *n Telecom* roaming *m*

roar /rɔ:(r)/ *n* berro *m*, rugido *m*; (*of thunder*) ribombo *m*, troar *m*; (*of sea, wind*) bramido *m* ● *vt/i* berrar, rugir; (*of lion*) rugir; (*of thunder*) ribombar, troar; (*of sea, wind*) bramir; **~ with laughter** rir às gargalhadas

roaring /'rɔ:rɪŋ/ *a* ‹*trade*› florescente; ‹*success*› enorme; ‹*fire*› com grandes chamas

roast /rəʊst/ *vt/i* assar ● *a* & *n* assado *m*

rob /rɒb/ *vt* (*pt* **robbed**) roubar (**sb of sth** algo de/a alguém); ‹*bank*› assaltar; (*deprive*) privar (**of** de). **~ber** *n* ladrão *m*. **~bery** *n* roubo *m*; (*of bank*) assalto *m*

robe /rəʊb/ *n* veste *f* comprida e solta; (*dressing gown*) robe *m*

robin /'rɒbɪn/ *n* papo-roxo *m*, (*P*) pintarroxo *m*

robot /'rəʊbɒt/ *n* robô *m*, (*P*) robot *m*, autômato *m*, (*P*) autómato *m*

robust /rəʊ'bʌst/ *a* robusto

rock[1] /rɒk/ *n* rocha *f*; (*boulder*) penhasco *m*, rochedo *m*; (*sweet*) pirulito *m*, (*P*) chupa-chupa *m* comprido; **on the ~s** [!] (*of marriage*) em crise; [!] (*of drinks*) com gelo. **~ bottom** *n* ponto *m* mais baixo ● *a* (*of prices*) baixíssimo [!]

rock[2] /rɒk/ *vt/i* balouçar(-se); (*shake*) abanar, sacudir; ‹*child*› embalar ● *n Mus* rock *m*. **~ing chair** *n* cadeira *f* de balanço, (*P*) cadeira *f* de balouço; **~ing horse** *n* cavalo *m* de balanço, (*P*) cavalo *m* de balouço

rocket /'rɒkɪt/ *n* foguete *m*

rocky /'rɒkɪ/ *a* (**-ier, -iest**) ‹*ground*› pedregoso; ‹*hill*› rochoso; [!] (*unsteady*) instável; [!] (*shaky*) tremido [!]

rod /rɒd/ *n* vara *f*, vareta *f*; *Mech* haste *f*; (*for curtains*) bastão *m*, (*P*) varão *m*; (*for fishing*) vara (de pescar) *f*, (*P*) cana *f* de pesca

rode /rəʊd/ ▶ RIDE

rodent /'rəʊdnt/ *n* roedor *m*

rogue /rəʊg/ *n* (*dishonest*) patife *m*, velhaco *m*; (*mischievous*) brincalhão *m*

role /rəʊl/ *n* papel *m*

roll /rəʊl/ *vt/i* (fazer) rolar; (*into ball or cylinder*) enrolar(-se); **be ~ing in money** [!] nadar em dinheiro [!]; **~ over** (*turn over*) virar-se ao contrário ● *n* rolo *m*; (*list*) rol *m*, lista *f*; (*bread*) pãozinho *m*; (*of ship*) balanço *m*; (*of drum*) rufar *m*; (*of thunder*) ribombo *m* □ **~ up** *vi* [!] aparecer ● *vt* ‹*sleeves*› arregaçar; ‹*umbrella*› fechar. **~-call** *n* chamada *f*; **~ing pin** *n* rolo *m* de pastel

roller /'rəʊlə(r)/ *n* cilindro *m*; (*wave*) vagalhão *m*; (*for hair*) rolo *m*. **~ blind** *n* estore *m*; **~ coaster** *n* montanha *f* russa; **~ skate** *n* patim *m* de rodas

Roman /'rəʊmən/ *a* & *n* romano *m*; **~ numerals** algarismos *mpl* romanos. **R~ Catholic** *a* & *n* católico *m*

romance /rəʊ'mæns/ *n* (*love affair*) romance *m*, romantismo *m*

Romania /rʊ'meɪnɪə/ *n* Romênia *f*, (*P*) Roménia *f*. **~n** *a* & *n* romeno *m*

romantic /rəʊ'mæntɪk/ *a* romântico. **~ism** *n* romantismo *m*. **~ize** *vi* fazer romance ● *vt* romantizar

romp /rɒmp/ *vi* brincar animadamente ● *n* brincadeira *f* animada

roof /ru:f/ *n* (*pl* **roofs**) telhado *m*; (*of car*) teto *m*, (*P*) capota *f*; (*of mouth*) palato *m*, céu *m* da boca; **hit the ~** [!] ficar furioso ● *vt* cobrir com telhado. **~ rack** *n* porta-bagagem *m*; **~top** *n* cimo *m* do telhado

rook[1] /rʊk/ *n* (*bird*) gralha *f*

rook[2] /rʊk/ *n Chess* torre *f*

room /rʊ:m/ *n* quarto *m*, divisão *f*; (*bedroom*) quarto *m* de dormir; (*large hall*) sala *f*; (*space*) espaço *m*, lugar *m*; **~s** (*lodgings*) apartamento *m*, cômodo *m*. **~-mate** *n* companheiro *m* de quarto. **~y** *a* espaçoso; ‹*clothes*› amplo, largo

roost /ru:st/ *n* poleiro *m* ● *vi* empoleirar-se. **~er** *n Amer* galo *m*

root[1] /ru:t/ *n* raiz *f*; *fig* origem *f*; **take ~** criar raízes ● *vt/i* enraizar(-se), radicar(-se); **~ out** extirpar, erradicar

root[2] /ru:t/ *vi* **~ about** revolver, remexer; **~ for** *Amer* [x] torcer por

rope /rəʊp/ *n* corda *f*; **know the ~s** estar por dentro (do assunto) ● *vt* atar; **~ in** convencer a participar de/em

rose[1] /rəʊz/ *n* rosa *f*; (*nozzle*) ralo *m* (de regador)

rose[2] /rəʊz/ ▶ RISE

rosé /ˈrəʊzeɪ/ *n* rosé *m*

roster /ˈrɒstə(r)/ *n* lista (de serviço) *f*, escala (de serviço) *f*

rostrum /ˈrɒstrəm/ *n* tribuna *f*; (*for conductor*) estrado *m*; *Sport* pódio *m*

rosy /ˈrəʊzɪ/ *a* (**-ier**, **-iest**) rosado; *fig* risonho

rot /rɒt/ *vt/i* (*pt* **rotted**) apodrecer ● *n* putrefação *f*, podridão *f*; ☒ (*nonsense*) disparate *m*; asneiras *fpl*

rota /ˈrəʊtə/ *n* escala *f* de serviço

rotary /ˈrəʊtərɪ/ *a* rotativo, giratório

rotat|e /rəʊˈteɪt/ *vt/i* (fazer) girar, (fazer) revolver; (*change round*) alternar. **~ion** /-ʃn/ *n* rotação *f*

rote /rəʊt/ *n* **by ~** de cor, maquinalmente

rotten /ˈrɒtn/ *a* podre; (*corrupt*) corrupto; [!] (*bad*) mau; ruim; **~ eggs** ovos *mpl* podres; **feel ~** (*ill*) não se sentir nada bem

rough /rʌf/ *a* (**-er**, **-est**) rude; (*to touch*) áspero, rugoso; (*of ground*) acidentado, irregular; (*violent*) violento; (*of sea*) agitado, encapelado; (*of weather*) tempestuoso; (*not perfect*) tosco, rudimentar; (*of estimate etc*) aproximado; **~ paper** rascunho *m*, borrão *m* ● *n* (*ruffian*) rufia *m*, desordeiro *m* ● *adv* (*live*) ao relento; (*play*) bruto, (*P*) à bruita ● *vt* **~ it** viver de modo primitivo, não ter onde morar [!]; **~ out** fazer um esboço preliminar de. **~ly** *adv* asperamente, rudemente; (*approximately*) aproximadamente. **~ness** *n* rudeza *f*, aspereza *f*; (*violence*) brutalidade *f*

roughage /ˈrʌfɪdʒ/ *n* alimentos *mpl* fibrosos

roulette /ruːˈlet/ *n* roleta *f*

round /raʊnd/ *a* (**-er**, **-est**) redondo; **~ trip** viagem *f* de ida e volta ● *n* (*circle*) círculo *m*; (*slice*) fatia *f*; (*postman's*) entrega *f*; (*patrol*) ronda *f*; (*of drinks*) rodada *f*; (*competition*) partida *f*, rodada *f*, (*P*) ronda *f*; *Boxing* round *m*; (*of talks*) ciclo *m*, série *f*; **~ of applause** salva *f* de palmas ● *prep & adv* em volta (de), em torno (de); **come ~** (*into consciousness*) voltar a si; **go** or **come ~ to** (*a friend etc*) dar um pulo na casa de, passar pela casa de; **~ about** (*nearby*) por aí; *fig* mais ou menos; **~ the clock** noite e dia sem parar ● *vt* arredondar; ‹*cape, corner*› dobrar, virar; **~ off** terminar; **~ up** (*gather*) juntar; ‹*a figure*› arredondar. **~-up** *n* (*of cattle*) rodeio *m*; (*of suspects*) captura *f*

roundabout /ˈraʊndəbaʊt/ *n* carrossel *m*; (*for traffic*) rotatória *f*, (*P*) rotunda *f* ● *a* indireto

rous|e /raʊz/ *vt* acordar, despertar; **be ~ed** (*angry*) exaltar-se, inflamar-se, ser provocado. **~ing** *a* ‹*speech*› inflamado, exaltado; ‹*music*› vibrante; ‹*cheers*› frenético

route /ruːt/ *n* percurso *m*, itinerário *m*; *Naut, Aviat* rota *f*

routine /ruːˈtiːn/ *n* rotina *f*; *Theat* número *m*; **daily ~** rotina *f* diária ● *a* de rotina, rotineiro

row[1] /rəʊ/ *n* fila *f*, fileira *f*; (*in knitting*) carreira *f*; **in a ~** (*consecutive*) seguido em fila *or* (*P*) a fio

row[2] /rəʊ/ *vt/i* remar. **~ing** *n* remo *m*. **~ing boat** *n* barco *m* a remo

row[3] /raʊ/ *n* [!] (*noise*) barulho *m*, bagunça *f*, banzé *m* [!]; [!] (*quarrel*) discussão *f*, briga *f* ● *vi* **~ (with)** [!] brigar (com), discutir (com)

rowdy /ˈraʊdɪ/ *a* (**-ier**, **-iest**) desordeiro

royal /ˈrɔɪəl/ *a* real

royalty /ˈrɔɪəltɪ/ *n* família *f* real; (*payment*) direitos (de autor, de patente, etc) *mpl*

RSI *abbr* = REPETITIVE STRAIN INJURY

rub /rʌb/ *vt/i* (*pt* **rubbed**) esfregar; (*with ointment etc*) esfregar, friccionar ● *n* esfrega *f*; (*with ointment etc*) fricção *f*; **~ it in** repisar/insistir em; **~ off on** comunicar-se a, transmitir-se a; **~ out** (*with rubber*) apagar

rubber /ˈrʌbə(r)/ *n* borracha *f*; **~ band** elástico *m*; **~ stamp** carimbo *m*

rubbish /ˈrʌbɪʃ/ *n* (*refuse*) lixo *m*; (*nonsense*) disparates *mpl*. **~ dump** *n* lixeira *f*

rubble /ˈrʌbl/ *n* entulho *m*

ruby /ˈruːbɪ/ *n* rubi *m*

rucksack /ˈrʌksæk/ *n* mochila *f*

rudder /ˈrʌdə(r)/ *n* leme *m*

ruddy /ˈrʌdɪ/ *a* (**-ier**, **-iest**) avermelhado; (*of cheeks*) corado, vermelho; ☒ (*damned*) maldito [!]

rude /ruːd/ *a* (**-er**, **-est**) mal-educado, malcriado, grosseiro. **~ness** *n* má-educação *f*, má-criação *f*, grosseria *f*

rudiment /ˈruːdɪmənt/ *n* rudimento *m*. **~ary** /-ˈmentrɪ/ *a* rudimentar

ruffian /ˈrʌfɪən/ *n* desordeiro *m*

ruffle /ˈrʌfl/ *vt* ‹*feathers*› eriçar; ‹*hair*› despentear; ‹*clothes*› amarrotar; *fig* perturbar ● *n* (*frill*) franzido *m*, (*P*) folho *m*

rug /rʌg/ *n* tapete *m*; (*covering*) manta *f*

rugged /ˈrʌgɪd/ *a* rude, irregular; ‹*coast, landscape*› acidentado; ‹*character*› forte; ‹*features*› marcado

ruin /ˈruːɪn/ *n* ruína *f* ● *vt* arruinar; *fig* estragar

rule /ruːl/ *n* regra *f*; (*regulation*) regulamento *m*; *Pol* governo *m*; **as a ~** regra geral, por via de regra ● *vt* governar; (*master*) dominar; *Jur* decretar; (*decide*) decidir ● *vi* governar; **~ out** excluir; **~d paper** papel *m* pautado. **~r** /-ə(r)/ *n* (*sovereign*) soberano *m*; (*leader*) governante *m*; (*measure*) régua *f*

ruling /ˈruːlɪŋ/ *a* ‹*class*› dirigente; *Pol* no poder ● *n* decisão *f*

rum /rʌm/ *n* rum *m*

rumble /ˈrʌmbl/ *vi* ribombar, ressoar; (*of stomach*) roncar ● *n* ribombo *m*, estrondo *m*

rummage /ˈrʌmɪdʒ/ *vt* revistar, remexer

rumour /ˈruːmə(r)/ *n* boato *m*, rumor *m* ● *vt* **it is ~ed that** corre o boato de que, consta que

rump /rʌmp/ *n* (*of horse etc*) garupa *f*; (*of fowl*) mitra *f*. **~ steak** *n* bife *m* de alcatra

run /rʌn/ *vi* (*pt* **ran**, *pp* **run**, *pres p* **running**) correr; (*flow*) correr; (*pass*) passar; (*function*) andar, funcionar; (*melt*) derreter, pingar; ‹*bus etc*› circular; ‹*play*› estar em cartaz; ‹*colour*› desbotar; (*in election*) candidatar-se (**for** a); **~ away** fugir; **~ down** descer correndo; **~ out** esgotar-se; ‹*lease*› expirar; **I ran out of sugar** o açúcar acabou; **~ over** (*of vehicle*) atropelar; **~ up** deixar acumular ● *vt* (*manage*) dirigir, gerir; ‹*a risk*› correr; ‹*a race*› participar em; ‹*water*› deixar correr; ‹*a car*› ter, manter; **~ across** encontrar por acaso, dar com; **~ down** (*of vehicle*) atropelar; (*belittle*) dizer mal de, denegrir; **be ~ down** estar exausto; **~ in** ‹*engine*› ligar; **~ into** (*meet*) encontrar por acaso; (*hit*) bater em, ir de encontro a ● *n* corrida *f*; (*excursion*) passeio *m*, ida *f*; (*rush*) corrida *f*, correria *f*; (*in cricket*) ponto *m*; **be on the ~** estar foragido; **have the ~ of** ter à sua disposição; **in the long ~** a longo prazo; **the ~-up to** o período que precede □ **~ off** *vt* ‹*copies*› tirar; ‹*water*› deixar correr ● *vi* fugir. **~-of-the-mill** *a* vulgar

runaway /ˈrʌnəweɪ/ *n* fugitivo *m* ● *a* fugitivo, em fuga; ‹*horse*› desembestado; ‹*vehicle*› desarvorado; ‹*success*› grande

rung[1] /rʌŋ/ *n* (*of ladder*) degrau *m*

rung[2] /rʌŋ/ ▶ RING[2]

runner /ˈrʌnə(r)/ *n* (*person*) corredor *m*; (*carpet*) passadeira *f*; **~ bean** feijão *m* verde. **~-up** *n* segundo classificado *m*

running /ˈrʌnɪŋ/ *n* corrida *f*; (*functioning*) funcionamento *m*; **be in the ~** (*competitor*) ter probabilidades de êxito ● *a* consecutivo, seguido; (*water*) corrente; **four days ~** quatro dias seguidos or a fio; **~ commentary** reportagem *f*, comentário *m*

runny /ˈrʌnɪ/ *a* derretido

runway /ˈrʌnweɪ/ *n* pista *f* de decolagem, (*P*) descolagem

rupture /ˈrʌptʃə(r)/ *n* ruptura *f*, (*P*) rutura *f*; *Med* hérnia *f* ● *vt/i* romper(-se), rebentar

rural /ˈrʊərəl/ *a* rural

ruse /ruːz/ *n* ardil *m*, estratagema *m*, manha *f*

rush[1] /rʌʃ/ *n* (*plant*) junco *m*

rush[2] /rʌʃ/ *vi* (*move*) precipitar-se; (*be in a hurry*) apressar-se ● *vt* fazer, mandar *etc* a toda a pressa; (*person*) pressionar; *Mil* tomar de assalto ● *n* tropel *m*; (*haste*) pressa *f*; **in a ~** a(s) pressa(s); **~ hour** rush *m*, (*P*) hora *f* de ponta

Russia /ˈrʌʃə/ *n* Rússia *f*. **~n** *a* & *n* russo *m*

rust /rʌst/ *n* (*on iron, plants*) ferrugem *f* ● *vt/i* enferrujar(-se). **~proof** *a* inoxidável. **~y** *a* ferrugento, enferrujado; *fig* enferrujado

rustic /ˈrʌstɪk/ *a* rústico

rustle /ˈrʌsl/ *vt/i* restolhar, (fazer) farfalhar; *Amer* (*steal*) roubar; **~ up** [!] ‹*food etc*› arranjar

rut /rʌt/ *n* sulco *m*; *fig* rotina *f*; **in a ~** numa vida rotineira

ruthless /ˈruːθlɪs/ *a* implacável

rye /raɪ/ *n* centeio *m*

Ss

sabbath /ˈsæbəθ/ *n* (*Jewish*) sábado *m*; (*Christian*) domingo *m*

sabbatical /səˈbætɪkl/ *n* *Univ* período *m* de licença, licença *f* sabática

sabot|age /ˈsæbətɑːʒ/ *n* sabotagem *f* ● *vt* sabotar. **~eur** /-ˈtɜː(r)/ *n* sabotador *m*

sachet /ˈsæʃeɪ/ *n* saché *m*, saqueta *f*

sack /sæk/ *n* saco *m*, saca *f* ● *vt* [!] despedir; **get the ~** [!] ser despedido
sacred /ˈseɪkrɪd/ *a* sagrado
sacrifice /ˈsækrɪfaɪs/ *n* sacrifício *m*; *fig* sacrifício *m* ● *vt* sacrificar
sacrileg|e /ˈsækrɪlɪdʒ/ *n* sacrilégio *m*. **~ious** /-ˈlɪdʒəs/ *a* sacrílego
sad /sæd/ *a* (**sadder**, **saddest**) ‹*person*› triste; ‹*story, news*› triste. **~ly** *adv* tristemente; (*unfortunately*) infelizmente. **~ness** *n* tristeza *f*
sadden /ˈsædn/ *vt* entristecer
saddle /ˈsædl/ *n* sela *f* ● *vt* ‹*horse*› selar; **~ sb with** sobrecarregar alguém com
sadis|m /ˈseɪdɪzəm/ *n* sadismo *m*. **~t** /-ɪst/ *n* sádico *m*. **~tic** /səˈdɪstɪk/ *a* sádico
safe /seɪf/ *a* (**-er**, **-est**) (*not dangerous*) seguro; (*out of danger*) fora de perigo; (*reliable*) confiável; **~ from** salvo de risco de; **~ and sound** são e salvo; **~ conduct** salvo-conduto *m*; **~ keeping** custódia *f*, (*P*) proteção *f*; **to be on the ~ side** por via das dúvidas ● *n* cofre *m*, caixa-forte *f*. **~ly** *adv* (*arrive etc*) em segurança; (*keep*) seguro
safeguard /ˈseɪfgɑːd/ *n* salvaguarda *f* ● *vt* salvaguardar
safety /ˈseɪftɪ/ *n* segurança *f*. **~ belt** *n* cinto *m* de segurança; **~ pin** *n* alfinete *m* de fralda, (*P*) alfinete *m* de ama
sag /sæg/ *vi* (*pt* **sagged**) afrouxar
saga /ˈsɑːgə/ *n* saga *f*
sage[1] /seɪdʒ/ *n* (*herb*) salva *f*
sage[2] /seɪdʒ/ *a* sensato, prudente ● *n* sábio *m*
Sagittarius /sædʒɪˈteərɪəs/ *n Astrol* Sagitário *m*
said /sed/ ▶ SAY
sail /seɪl/ *n* vela *f*; (*trip*) viagem *f* em barco à vela ● *vi* navegar; (*leave*) partir; *Sport* velejar ● *vt* navegar. **~ing** *n* navegação *f* à vela. **~ing boat** *n* barco *m* à vela
sailor /ˈseɪlə(r)/ *n* marinheiro *m*
saint /seɪnt/ *n* santo *m*. **~ly** *a* santo, santificado
sake /seɪk/ *n* **for the ~ of** em consideração a; **for my/your/ its own ~** por mim/por você/por isso
salad /ˈsæləd/ *n* salada *f*. **~ dressing** *n* molho *m* para salada
salary /ˈsælərɪ/ *n* salário *m*
sale /seɪl/ *n* venda *f*; (*at reduced prices*) liquidação *f*; **for ~** "vende-se"; **on ~** à venda; **~s assistant**, *Amer* **~s clerk** vendedor *m*; **~s department** departamento *m* de vendas
sales|man /ˈseɪlzmən/ *n* (*pl* **-men**) (*in shop*) vendedor *m*; (*traveller*) caixeiro-viajante *m*. **~woman** *n* (*pl* **-women**) (*in shop*) vendedora *f*; (*traveller*) caixeira-viajante *f*
saliva /səˈlaɪvə/ *n* saliva *f*
salmon /ˈsæmən/ *n* (*pl invar*) salmão *m*
saloon /səˈluːn/ *n* (*on ship*) salão *m*; (*bar*) botequim *m*; **~ (car)** sedã *m*
salt /sɔːlt/ *n* sal *m*; **~ water** água *f* salgada, água *f* do mar ● *a* salgado ● *vt* (*season*) salgar; (*cure*) pôr em salmoura. **~ cellar** *n* saleiro *m*. **~y** *a* salgado
salute /səˈluːt/ *n* saudação *f* ● *vt/i* saudar
salvage /ˈsælvɪdʒ/ *n Naut* salvamento *m*; (*of waste*) reciclagem *f* ● *vt* salvar
salvation /sælˈveɪʃn/ *n* salvação *f*
same /seɪm/ *a* mesmo (**as** que); **at the ~ time** (*at once*) ao mesmo tempo ● *pron* **the ~** o mesmo ● *adv* **the ~** o mesmo; **all the ~** (*nevertheless*) mesmo assim, apesar de tudo
same-sex *a* ‹*couple, marriage*› do mesmo sexo
sample /ˈsɑːmpl/ *n* amostra *f* ● *vt* experimentar, provar
sanatorium /sænəˈtɔːrɪəm/ *n* (*pl* **-iums**) sanatório *m*
sanctify /ˈsæŋktɪfaɪ/ *vt* santificar
sanctimonious /sæŋktɪˈməʊnɪəs/ *a* santarrão, carola
sanction /ˈsæŋkʃn/ *n* (*approval*) aprovação *f*; (*penalty*) pena *f*, sanção *f* ● *vt* sancionar
sanctuary /ˈsæŋktʃʊərɪ/ *n Relig* santuário *m*; (*refuge*) refúgio *m*; (*for animals*) reserva *f*
sand /sænd/ *n* areia *f*; (*beach*) praia *f* ● *vt* (*with sandpaper*) lixar
sandal /ˈsændl/ *n* sandália *f*
sandbank /ˈsændbæŋk/ *n* banco *m* de areia
sandcastle /ˈsændkɑːsl/ *n* castelo *m* de areia
sandpaper /ˈsændpeɪpə(r)/ *n* lixa *f* ● *vt* lixar
sandpit /ˈsændpɪt/ *n* caixa *f* de areia
sandwich /ˈsænwɪdʒ/ *n* sanduíche *m*, (*P*) sandes *f invar* ● *vt* **~ed between** encaixado entre; **~ course** curso *m* profissionalizante envolvendo estudo teórico e estágio em local de trabalho
sandy /ˈsændɪ/ *a* (**-ier**, **iest**) arenoso; ‹*beach*› arenoso; ‹*hair*› ruivo

sane /seɪn/ *a* (**-er**, **-est**) (*not mad*) são *m*; (*sensible*) sensato, ajuizado

sang /sæŋ/ ▶ SING

sanitary /ˈsænɪtrɪ/ *a* sanitário; (*system*) sanitário; **~ towel**, *Amer* **~ napkin** toalha *f* absorvente, (*P*) penso *m* higiénico

sanitation /sænɪˈteɪʃn/ *n* condições *fpl* sanitárias, saneamento *m*

sanity /ˈsænɪtɪ/ *n* sanidade *f*

sank /sæŋk/ ▶ SINK

Santa Claus /ˈsæntəklɔːz/ *n* Papai *m* Noel, Pai *m* Natal

sap /sæp/ *n* seiva *f* ● *vt* (*pt* **sapped**) esgotar, minar

sapphire /ˈsæfaɪə(r)/ *n* safira *f*

sarcas|m /ˈsɑːrkæzəm/ *n* sarcasmo *m*. **~tic** /sɑːrˈkæstɪk/ *a* sarcástico

sardine /sɑːˈdiːn/ *n* sardinha *f*

sash /sæʃ/ *n* (*around waist*) cinto *m*; (*over shoulder*) faixa *f*

sat /sæt/ ▶ SIT

satchel /ˈsætʃl/ *n* sacola *f*

satellite /ˈsætəlaɪt/ *n* satélite *m*; **~ dish** antena *f* de satélite; **~ television** televisão *f* via satélite

satin /ˈsætɪn/ *n* cetim *m*

satir|e /ˈsætaɪə(r)/ *n* sátira *f*. **~ical** /səˈtɪrɪkl/ *a* satírico. **~ist** /ˈsætərɪst/ *n* satirista *mf*. **~ize** *vt* satirizar

satisfact|ion /sætɪsˈfækʃn/ *n* satisfação *f*. **~ory** /-ˈfæktərɪ/ *a* satisfatório

satisfy /ˈsætɪsfaɪ/ *vt* satisfazer; (*convince*) convencer; (*fulfil*) atender. **~ing** *a* satisfatório

saturat|e /ˈsætʃəreɪt/ *vt* saturar; *fig* cansar

Saturday /ˈsætədɪ/ *n* sábado *m*

sauce /sɔːs/ *n* molho *m*; [I] (*cheek*) atrevimento *m*

saucepan /ˈsɔːspən/ *n* panela *f*, (*P*) caçarola *f*

saucer /ˈsɔːsə(r)/ *n* pires *m invar*

saucy /ˈsɔːsɪ/ *a* (**-ier**, **-iest**) picante

Saudi Arabia /saʊdɪəˈreɪbɪə/ *n* Arábia *f* Saudita

sauna /ˈsɔːnə/ *n* sauna *f*

saunter /ˈsɔːntə(r)/ *vi* perambular

sausage /ˈsɒsɪdʒ/ *n* salsicha *f*, linguiça *f*; (*pre-cooked*) salsicha *f*

savage /ˈsævɪdʒ/ *a* (*wild*) selvagem; (*fierce*) cruel; (*brutal*) brutal ● *n* selvagem *mf* ● *vt* atacar ferozmente. **~ry** *n* selvageria *f*, ferocidade *f*

sav|e /seɪv/ *vt* (*rescue*) salvar; (*keep*) guardar; (*collect*) colecionar; ‹*money*› economizar, poupar; ‹*time*› ganhar; (*prevent*) evitar; impedir (**from** de) ● *n Sport* salvamento *m* ● *prep* salvo, exceto. **~er** *n* poupador *m*. **~ing** *n* economia *f*, poupança *f*. **~ings** *npl* economias *fpl*, poupanças *fpl*

saviour /ˈseɪvɪə(r)/ *n* salvador *m*

savour /ˈseɪvə(r)/ *n* sabor *m* ● *vt* saborear. **~y** *a* (*tasty*) saboroso; (*not sweet*) salgado

saw[1] /sɔː/ ▶ SEE[1]

saw[2] /sɔː/ *n* serra *f* ● *vt* (*pt* **sawed**, *pp* **sawn** *or* **sawed**) serrar

sawdust /ˈsɔːdʌst/ *n* serragem *f*

saxophone /ˈsæksəfəʊn/ *n* saxofone *m*

say /seɪ/ *vt/i* (*pt* **said** /sed/) dizer, falar ● *n* **have a ~ (in sth)** ter direito a opinar sobre algo; **have one's ~** exprimir sua (a) opinião; **I ~!** olhe! *or* escute!. **~ing** *n* ditado *m*, provérbio *m*

scab /skæb/ *n* casca *f*, crosta *f*; [I] (*blackleg*) fura-greve *mf invar*

scaffold /ˈskæfəʊld/ *n* cadafalso *m*, andaime *m*. **~ing** /-əldɪŋ/ *n* andaime *m*

scald /skɔːld/ *vt* escaldar, queimar ● *n* escaldadura *f*, queimadura *f*

scale[1] /skeɪl/ *n* (*of fish etc*) escama *f*

scale[2] /skeɪl/ *n* (*ratio, size*) escala *f*; *Mus* escala *f*; (*of salaries, charges*) tabela *f*; **on a small/large/*etc*~** numa pequena/grande/*etc* escala ● *vt* (*climb*) escalar; **~ down** reduzir

scales /skeɪlz/ *npl* (*for weighing*) balança *f*

scallop /ˈskɒləp/ *n Culin* concha *f* de vieira; (*shape*) concha *f* de vieira

scalp /skælp/ *n* couro *m* cabeludo ● *vt* escalpar

scalpel /ˈskælpl/ *n* bisturi *m*

scamper /ˈskæmpə(r)/ *vi* sair correndo, (*P*) a correr *or* à(s) pressa(s)

scampi /ˈskæmpɪ/ *npl* camarões *mpl* fritos

scan /skæn/ *vt* (*pt* **scanned**) (*intently*) perscrutar, esquadrinhar; (*quickly*) passar os olhos em; *Med* examinar; (*radar*) explorar ● *n Med* exame *m*

scandal /ˈskændl/ *n* (*disgrace*) escândalo *m*; (*gossip*) fofoca *f*. **~ous** *a* escandaloso

Scandinavia /skændɪˈneɪvɪə/ *n* Escandinávia *f*. **~n** *a* & *n* escandinavo *m*

scanty /ˈskæntɪ/ *a* (**-ier**, **-iest**) escasso; ‹*clothing*› sumário

scapegoat /'skeɪpgəʊt/ *n* bode *m* expiatório

scar /skɑː(r)/ *n* cicatriz *f* ● *vt* (*pt* **scarred**) marcar; *fig* deixar marcas

scarc|e /skeəs/ *a* (**-er**, **-est**) escasso, raro; **make o.s. ~e** [!] sumir, dar o fora [!], (*P*) desaparecer sem deixar rasto. **~ity** *n* escassez *f*. **~ely** *adv* mal, apenas

scare /skeə(r)/ *vt* assustar, apavorar; **be ~d** estar com medo (**of** de) ● *n* pavor *m*, pânico *m*; **bomb ~** pânico *m* causado por suspeita de bomba num local

scarecrow /'skeəkrəʊ/ *n* espantalho *m*

scarf /skɑːf/ *n* (*pl* **scarves**) (*oblong*) cachecol *m*; (*square*) lenço *m* de cabelo

scarlet /'skɑːlət/ *a* escarlate *m*

scary /'skeərɪ/ *a* (**-ier**, **-iest**) [!] assustador; apavorante

scathing /'skeɪðɪŋ/ *a* mordaz

scatter /'skætə(r)/ *vt* (*strew*) espalhar; (*disperse*) dispersar ● *vi* espalhar-se

scavenge /'skævɪndʒ/ *vi* procurar comida *etc* no lixo. **~r** /-ə(r)/ *n* (*person*) que procura comida *etc* no lixo; (*animal*) que se alimenta de carniça, (*P*) necrófago

scenario /sɪ'nɑːrɪəʊ/ *n* (*pl* **-os**) sinopse *f*, resumo *m* detalhado

scene /siːn/ *n* cena *f*; (*of event*) cenário *m*; (*sight*) vista *f*, panorama *m*; **behind the ~s** nos bastidores; **make a ~** fazer um escândalo

scenery /'siːnərɪ/ *n* cenário *m*, paisagem *f*; *Theat* cenário *m*

scenic /'siːnɪk/ *a* pitoresco, cênico, (*P*) cénico

scent /sent/ *n* (*perfume*) perfume *m*, fragância *f*; (*trail*) rastro *m*, pista *f* ● *vt* (*discern*) sentir. **~ed** *a* perfumado, aromático

sceptic /'skeptɪk/ *n* cético *m*. **~al** *a* cético. **~ism** /-sɪzəm/ *n* ceticismo *m*

schedule /'ʃedjuːl/ *n* programa *m*; (*timetable*) horário *m* ● *vt* marcar, programar; **according to ~** conforme planejado *or* (*P*) planeado; **behind ~** atrasado; **on ~** ‹*train*› na hora, à hora prevista; ‹*work*› em dia

scheme /skiːm/ *n* esquema *m*; (*plan of work*) plano *m*; (*plot*) conspiração *f*, maquinação *f* ● *vi* planejar, (*P*) planear; *pej* intrigar; maquinar; tramar

schizophreni|a /skɪtsəʊ'friːnɪə/ *n* esquizofrenia *f*. **~c** /-'frenɪk/ *a* esquizofrênico, (*P*) esquizofrénico

scholar /'skɒlə(r)/ *n* erudito *m*, estudioso *m*, escolar *m*. **~ly** *a* erudito. **~ship** *n* erudição *f*, saber *m*; (*grant*) bolsa *f* de estudo

school /skuːl/ *n* escola *f*; (*of university*) escola *f*, faculdade *f* ● *a* ‹*age, year, holidays*› escolar ● *vt* ensinar; (*train*) treinar, adestrar. **~ing** *n* instrução *f*; (*attendance*) escolaridade *f*

school|boy /'skuːlbɔɪ/ *n* aluno *m*. **~girl** *n* aluna *f*

school|master /'skuːlmɑːstə(r)/, **~mistress**, **~teacher** *ns* professor *m*, professora *f*

scien|ce /'saɪəns/ *n* ciência *f*; **~ce fiction** ficção *f* científica. **~tific** /-'tɪfɪk/ *a* científico

scientist /'saɪəntɪst/ *n* cientista *mf*

scissors /'sɪzəz/ *npl* **(pair of) ~** tesoura *f*

scoff[1] /skɒf/ *vi* **~ at** zombar de, (*P*) troçar de

scoff[2] /skɒf/ *vt* ☒ (*eat*) devorar; tragar

scold /skəʊld/ *vt* ralhar com

scone /skɒn/ *n Culin* scone *m*, bolinho *m* para o chá

scoop /skuːp/ *n* (*for grain, sugar etc*) pá *f*; (*ladle*) concha *f*; (*news*) furo *m* ● *vt* **~ out** (*hollow out*) escavar, tirar com concha or pá; **~ up** (*lift*) apanhar

scoot /skuːt/ *vi* [!] fugir, mandar-se [!], (*P*) pôr-se a milhas [!]

scooter /'skuːtə(r)/ *n* (*child's*) patinete *f*, (*P*) trotinete *m*; (*motor cycle*) motoreta *f*, lambreta *f*

scope /skəʊp/ *n* âmbito *m*; *fig* (*opportunity*) oportunidade *f*

scorch /skɔːtʃ/ *vt/i* chamuscar(-se), queimar de leve. **~ing** *a* [!] escaldante; abrasador

score /skɔː(r)/ *n Sport* contagem *f*, escore *m*; *Mus* partitura *f* ● *vt* marcar com corte(s), riscar; ‹*a goal*› marcar; *Mus* orquestrar ● *vi* marcar pontos; (*keep score*) fazer a contagem; *Football* marcar um gol *or* (*P*) golo; **a ~ (of)** (*twenty*) uma vintena (de), vinte; **~s** muitos, dezenas; **on that ~** nesse respeito, quanto a isso. **~board** *n* marcador *m*. **~r** /-ə(r)/ *n* (*score-keeper*) marcador *m*; (*of goals*) autor *m*

scorn /skɔːn/ *n* desprezo *m* ● *vt* desprezar. **~ful** *a* desdenhoso, escarninho

Scorpio /'skɔːpɪəʊ/ *n Astr* Escorpião *m*

scorpion /'skɔːpɪən/ *n* escorpião *m*

Scot /skɒt/ *n*, **~tish** *a* escocês *m*

Scotch /skɒtʃ/ *a* escocês ● *n* uísque *m*

Scotland /'skɒtlənd/ *n* Escócia *f*

Scots /skɒts/ *a* escocês

> **Scottish Parliament** O Parlamento Escocês foi estabelecido em Edimburgo em 1999. Tem competência legislativa e executiva em assuntos internos na Escócia e poderes tributários limitados. Há 129 *MSPs* (*Members of the Scottish Parliament*), dos quais 73 são eleitos diretamente e o restante através do sistema de representação proporcional.

scoundrel /ˈskaʊndrəl/ *n* patife *m*, canalha *m*

scour[1] /ˈskaʊə(r)/ *vt* (*clean*) esfregar, arear. **~er** *n* esfregão *m* de palha de aço or de nylon

scour[2] /ˈskaʊə(r)/ *vt* (*search*) percorrer, esquadrinhar

scourge /skɜːdʒ/ *n* açoite *m*; *fig* flagelo *m*

scout /skaʊt/ *n Mil* explorador *m* ● *vi* **~ about (for)** andar à procura de

Scout /skaʊt/ *n* escoteiro *m*, (*P*) escuteiro *m*

scowl /skaʊl/ *n* carranca *f*, ar *m* carrancudo ● *vi* fazer um ar carrancudo

scramble /ˈskræmbl/ *vi* trepar; (*crawl*) avançar de rastros, rastejar, arrastar-se ● *vt* ‹*eggs*› mexer ● *n* luta *f*, confusão *f*

scrap[1] /skræp/ *n* bocadinho *m*; **~ heap** monte *m* de ferro-velho; **~ merchant** sucateiro *m* ● *vt* (*pt* **scrapped**) jogar fora, (*P*) deitar fora; ‹*plan etc*› abandonar, pôr de lado. **~s** *npl* restos *mpl*. **~book** *n* álbum *m* de recortes; **~ iron** *n* ferro *m* velho, sucata *f*; **~ paper** *n* papel *m* de rascunho. **~py** *a* fragmentário

scrap[2] /skræp/ *n* [!] (*fight*) briga *f*; pancadaria *f* [!]; rixa *f*

S

scrape /skreɪp/ *vt* raspar; (*graze*) esfolar, arranhar; **~ through** escapar pela tangente, (*P*) à tangente or por um triz; ‹*exam*› passar pela tangente, (*P*) à tangente; **~ together** conseguir juntar ● *vi* (*graze, rub*) roçar ● *n* (*act of scraping*) raspagem *f*; (*mark*) raspão *m*, esfoladura *f*; *fig* encrenca *f*; maus lençóis *mpl* [!]

scratch /skrætʃ/ *vt/i* arranhar(-se); ‹*a line*› riscar; (*to relieve itching*) coçar(-se) ● *n* arranhão *m*; (*line*) risco *m*; (*wound with claw, nail*) unhada *f*; **start from ~** começar do princípio; **up to ~** à altura, ao nível requerido

scrawl /skrɔːl/ *n* rabisco *m*, garrancho *m*, garatuja *f* ● *vt/i* rabiscar, fazer garranchos, garatujar

scrawny /ˈskrɔːnɪ/ *a* (**-ier**, **-iest**) descarnado, ossudo, magricela

scream /skriːm/ *vt/i* gritar ● *n* grito (agudo) *m*

screech /skriːtʃ/ *vi* guinchar, gritar; (*of brakes*) chiar, guinchar ● *n* guincho *m*, grito *m* agudo

screen /skriːn/ *n* écran *m*, tela *f*; (*folding*) biombo *m*; *fig* (*protection*) manto *m*; *fig* capa *f fig* ● *vt* resguardar, tapar; ‹*film*› passar; ‹*candidates etc*› fazer a triagem de. **~ing** *n Med* exame *m* médico

screw /skruː/ *n* parafuso *m* ● *vt* aparafusar, atarraxar; **~ up** ‹*eyes, face*› franzir; [⊠] (*ruin*) estragar; **~ up one's courage** cobrar arranjar coragem

screwdriver /ˈskruːdraɪvə(r)/ *n* chave *f* de parafusos or de fenda(s)

scribble /ˈskrɪbl/ *vt/i* rabiscar, garatujar ● *n* rabisco *m*, garatuja *f*

script /skrɪpt/ *n* escrita *f*; (*of film*) roteiro *m*, (*P*) guião *m*. **~writer** *n Film* roteirista *m*, (*P*) autor *m* do guião, guionista *mf*

scroll /skrəʊl/ *n* rolo (de papel ou pergaminho) *m*; *Archit* voluta *f* ● *vt/i Comput* passar na tela, (*P*) no ecrã

scrounge /skraʊndʒ/ *vt* [!] (*cadge*) filar [⊠], (*P*) cravar [⊠] ● *vi* (*beg*) parasitar, viver à(s) custa(s) de alguém. **~r** /-ə(r)/ *n* parasita *mf*; filão *m* [⊠], (*P*) crava *mf* [⊠]

scrub[1] /skrʌb/ *n* (*land*) mato *m*

scrub[2] /skrʌb/ *vt/i* (*pt* **scrubbed**) esfregar, lavar com escova e sabão; [!] (*cancel*) cancelar ● *n* esfrega *f*

scruff /skrʌf/ *n* **by the ~ of the neck** pelo cangote, (*P*) pelo cachaço

scruffy /ˈskrʌfɪ/ *a* (**-ier**, **-iest**) desmazelado; desleixado

scrum /skrʌm/ *n* rixa *f*; *Rugby* placagem *f*

scruple /ˈskruːpl/ *n* escrúpulo *m*

scrupulous /ˈskruːpjʊləs/ *a* escrupuloso. **~ly** *adv* escrupulosamente; **~ly clean** impecavelmente limpo

scrutin|y /ˈskruːtɪnɪ/ *n* averiguação *f*, escrutínio *m*. **~ize** *vt* examinar em detalhe

scuffle /ˈskʌfl/ *n* tumulto *m*, briga *f*

sculpt /skʌlpt/ *vt/i* esculpir. **~or** *n* escultor *m*. **~ure** /-tʃə(r)/ *n* escultura *f* ● *vt/i* esculpir

scum /skʌm/ *n* (*on liquid*) espuma *f*; *pej* (*people*) gentinha *f*; escumalha *f*; ralé *f*

scurry /ˈskʌrɪ/ *vi* dar corridinhas; (*hurry*) apressar-se; **~ off** escapulir-se

scuttle[1] /ˈskʌtl/ *n* ‹*bucket, box*› balde *m* para carvão

scuttle[2] /ˈskʌtl/ *vt* (*ship*) afundar abrindo rombos or as torneiras de fundo, afundar voluntariamente

scuttle[3] /ˈskʌtl/ *vi* **~ away** or **off** fugir, escapulir-se

sea /siː/ *n* mar *m*; **at ~** no alto mar, ao largo; **all at ~** desnorteado; **by ~** por mar ● *a* do mar, marinho, marítimo; **~ bird** ave *f* marinha; **~ horse** cavalo-marinho *m*, hipocampo *m*; **~ level** nível *m* do mar; **~ lion** leão-marinho *m*; **~ shell** concha *f*; **~ water** água *f* do mar. **~shore** *n* litoral *m*, costa *f*; (*beach*) praia *f*

seafood /ˈsiːfuːd/ *n* marisco(s) *m(pl)*

seagull /ˈsiːgʌl/ *n* gaivota *f*

seal[1] /siːl/ *n* (*animal*) foca *f*

seal[2] /siːl/ *n* selo *m*, sinete *m* ● *vt* selar; (*with wax*) lacrar; **~ off** ‹*area*› vedar

seam /siːm/ *n* (*in cloth etc*) costura *f*; (*of mineral*) veio *m*, filão *m*. **~less** *a* sem costura

seaman /ˈsiːmən/ *n* (*pl* **-men**) marinheiro *m*, marítimo *m*

seance /ˈseɪɑːns/ *n* sessão *f* espírita

search /sɜːtʃ/ *vt/i* revistar, dar busca (a); ‹*one's heart, conscience etc*› examinar ● *n* revista *f*, busca *f*; (*quest*) procura *f*, busca *f*; (*official*) inquérito *m*; **in ~ of** à procura de; **~ for** procurar. **~ party** *n* equipe *f* or (*P*) equipa de busca; **~ warrant** *n* mandado *m* de busca. **~ing** *a* (*of look*) penetrante; (*of test etc*) minucioso

searchlight /ˈsɜːtʃlaɪt/ *n* holofote *m*

seasick /ˈsiːsɪk/ *a* enjoado. **~ness** *n* enjoo *m*

seaside /ˈsiːsaɪd/ *n* costa *f*, praia *f*, beira-mar *f*

season /ˈsiːzn/ *n* (*of year*) estação *f*; (*proper time*) época *f*; *Cricket, Football etc* temporada *f*; **in ~** na época ● *vt* temperar; ‹*wood*› secar. **~able** *a* próprio da estação. **~al** *a* sazonal. **~ed** *a* (*of people*) experimentado. **~ing** *n* tempero *m*. **~ ticket** *n* (*train etc*) passe *m*; (*theatre etc*) assinatura *f*

seat /siːt/ *n* assento *m*; (*place*) lugar *m*; (*of bicycle*) selim *m*; (*of chair*) assento *m*; (*of trousers*) fundilho *m*; **~ of learning** centro *m* de cultura ● *vt* sentar; (*have seats for*) ter lugares sentados para; **be ~ed, take a ~** sentar-se. **~ belt** *n* cinto *m* de segurança

seaweed /ˈsiːwiːd/ *n* alga *f* marinha

seaworthy /ˈsiːwɜːðɪ/ *a* navegável, em condições de navegabilidade

seclu|de /sɪˈkluːd/ *vt* isolar. **~ded** *a* isolado, retirado. **~sion** /sɪˈkluːʒn/ *n* isolamento *m*

second[1] /ˈsekənd/ *a* segundo; **~ thoughts** dúvidas *fpl*; **on ~ thoughts** pensando melhor ● *n* segundo *m*; (*in duel*) testemunha *f*; **~ (gear)** *Auto* segunda (velocidade) *f*; **the ~ of April** dois de Abril; **~s** (*goods*) artigos *mpl* de segunda (categoria) or de refugo ● *adv* (*in race etc*) em segundo lugar ● *vt* secundar. **~-best** *a* escolhido em segundo lugar; **~-class** *a* de segunda classe; **~-hand** *a* de segunda mão ● *n* (*on clock*) ponteiro *m* dos segundos; **~-rate** *a* medíocre, de segunda ordem or categoria. **~ly** *adv* segundo, em segundo lugar

second[2] /sɪˈkɒnd/ *vt* (*transfer*) destacar (**to** para)

secondary /ˈsekəndrɪ/ *a* secundário; **~ school** escola *f* secundária

secrecy /ˈsiːkrəsɪ/ *n* segredo *m*

secret /ˈsiːkrɪt/ *a* secreto ● *n* segredo *m*; **in ~** em segredo. **~ agent** *n* agente *mf* secreto. **~ly** *adv* em segredo, secretamente

secretar|y /ˈsekrətrɪ/ *n* secretário *m*, secretária *f*; **S~y of State** ministro *m* de Estado, (*P*) Secretário *m* de Estado; *Amer* ministro *m* dos Negócios Estrangeiros. **~ial** /-ˈteərɪəl/ *a* ‹*work, course etc*› de secretária

secret|e /sɪˈkriːt/ *vt* segregar; (*hide*) esconder. **~ion** /-ʃn/ *n* secreção *f*

secretive /ˈsiːkrətɪv/ *a* misterioso, reservado

sect /sekt/ *n* seita *f*. **~arian** /-ˈteərɪən/ *a* sectário

section /ˈsekʃn/ *n* seção *f*; (*of country, community etc*) setor *m*, (*P*) sector *m*; (*district of town*) zona *f*

sector /ˈsektə(r)/ *n* setor *m*

secular /ˈsekjʊlə(r)/ *a* secular, leigo, (*P*) laico; ‹*art, music etc*› profano

secure /sɪˈkjʊə(r)/ *a* seguro, em segurança; ‹*firm*› seguro, sólido; (*in mind*) tranquilo ● *vt* prender bem or com segurança; (*obtain*) conseguir, arranjar; (*ensure*) assegurar; ‹*windows, doors*› fechar bem. **~ly** *adv* solidamente; (*safely*) em segurança

securit|y /sɪˈkjʊərətɪ/ *n* segurança *f*; (*for loan*) fiança *f*, caução *f*. **~ies** *npl* *Finance* títulos *mpl*

sedate /sɪ'deɪt/ *a* sereno, comedido ● *vt* *Med* tratar com sedativos

sedation /sɪ'deɪʃn/ *n Med* sedação *f*; **under ~** sob o efeito de sedativos

sedative /'sedətɪv/ *n Med* sedativo *m*

sediment /'sedɪmənt/ *n* sedimento *m*, depósito *m*

seduce /sɪ'dju:s/ *vt* seduzir

seduct|ion /sɪ'dʌkʃn/ *n* sedução *f*. **~ive** /-tɪv/ *a* sedutor, aliciante

see[1] /si:/ *vt/i* (*pt* **saw**, *pp* **seen**) ver; (*escort*) acompanhar; **~ about** or **to** tratar de, encarregar-se de; **~ through** ‹*task*› levar a cabo; (*not be deceived by*) não se deixar enganar por; **~ (to it) that** assegurar que, tratar de fazer com que; **~ing that** visto que, uma vez que; **~ you later!** [!] até logo! [!] □ **~ off** *vt* (*wave goodbye*) ir despedir-se de; (*chase*) acompanhar

see[2] /si:/ *n* sé *f*, bispado *m*

seed /si:d/ *n* semente *f*; *fig* (*origin*) germe(n) *m*; *Tennis* cabeça *f* de série; (*pip*) caroço *m*; **go to ~** produzir sementes; *fig* desmazelar-se [!]. **~ling** *n* planta *f* brotada a partir da semente

seedy /'si:dɪ/ *a* (**-ier**, **-iest**) (com um ar) gasto, surrado; [!] (*unwell*) abatido; deprimido; em baixo astral [!] *or* (*P*) em baixo

seek /si:k/ *vt* (*pt* **sought**) procurar; ‹*help etc*› pedir

seem /si:m/ *vi* parecer. **~ingly** *adv* aparentemente, ao que parece

seen /si:n/ ▶ SEE[1]

seep /si:p/ *vi* (*ooze*) filtrar-se; (*trickle*) pingar, escorrer, passar

see-saw /'si:sɔ:/ *n* gangorra *f*, (*P*) balanço *m*

S

seethe /si:ð/ *vi* **~ with** ‹*anger*› ferver de; ‹*people*› fervilhar de

segment /'segmənt/ *n* segmento *m*; (*of orange*) gomo *m*

segregat|e /'segrɪgeɪt/ *vt* segregar, separar. **~ion** /-'geɪʃn/ *n* segregação *f*

seize /si:z/ *vt* agarrar, (*P*) deitar a mão a, apanhar; (*take possession by force*) apoderar-se de; (*by law*) apreender; confiscar; (*P*) apresar ● *vi* **~ on** ‹*opportunity*› aproveitar; **~ up** ‹*engine etc*› grimpar, emperrar; **be ~d with** ‹*fear, illness*› ter um ataque de

seizure /'si:ʒə(r)/ *n Med* ataque *m*, crise *f*; (*law*) apreensão *f*, captura *f*

seldom /'seldəm/ *adv* raras vezes, raramente, raro

select /sɪ'lekt/ *vt* escolher, selecionar ● *a* seleto. **~ion** /-ʃn/ *n* seleção *f*; *Comm* sortido *m*

selective /sɪ'lektɪv/ *a* seletivo

self /self/ *n* (*pl* **selves**) **the ~** o eu, o ego

self- /self/ *pref*. **~assurance** *n* segurança *f*; **~assured** *a* seguro de si; **~catering** *a* em que os hóspedes têm condicões de cozinhar; **~centred** *a* egocêntrico; **~confidence** *n* autoconfiança *f*, confiança *f* em si mesmo; **~confident** *a* que tem confiança em si mesmo; **~conscious** *a* inibido, constrangido; **~contained** *a* independente; **~control** *n* autodomínio *m*; **~controlled** *a* senhor de si; **~defence** *n* legítima defesa *f*; **~employed** *a* autónomo, independent; **~esteem** *n* amor *m* próprio; **~evident** *a* evidente; **~indulgent** *a* que não resiste a tentações; (*for ease*) comodista; **~interest** *n* interesse *m* pessoal; **~portrait** *n* auto-retrato *m*; **~possessed** *a* senhor de si; **~respect** *n* amor *m* próprio; **~righteous** *a* que se tem em boa conta; **~sacrifice** *n* abnegação *f*, sacrifício *m*; **~satisfied** *a* cheio de si; convencido [!]; **~seeking** *a* egoísta; **~service** *a* auto-serviço, self-service; **~styled** *a* pretenso; **~sufficient** *a* auto-suficiente

self-harm *n* automutilação *f*

selfish /'selfɪʃ/ *a* egoísta; ‹*motive*› interesseiro. **~ness** *n* egoísmo *m*

selfless /'selflɪs/ *a* desinteressado

sell /sel/ *vt/i* (*pt* **sold**) vender(-se); **~-by date** válido até; **~ off** liquidar; **be sold out** estar esgotado. **~-out** *n* ‹*show*› sucesso *m*; [!] (*betrayal*) traição *f*. **~er** *n* vendedor *m*

Sellotape® /'seləʊteɪp/ *n* fita *f* adesiva, (*P*) fita-cola *f*

semen /'si:mən/ *n* sêmen *m*, (*P*) sémen *m*, esperma *m*

semester /sɪ'mestə(r)/ *n Univ* semestre *m*

semi- /'semɪ/ *pref* semi-, meio

semibreve /'semɪbri:v/ *n Mus* semibreve *f*

semicirc|le /'semɪsɜ:kl/ *n* semicírculo *m*. **~ular** /-sɜ:kjʊlə(r)/ *a* semicircular

semicolon /semɪ'kəʊlən/ *n* ponto e vírgula *m*

semi-detached /semɪdɪ'tætʃt/ *a* **~ house** casa *f* geminada

semi-final /semɪ'faɪnl/ *n* semifinal *f*, (*P*) meia-final *f*

seminar /'semɪnɑ:(r)/ *n* seminário *m*

semiquaver /'semɪkweɪvə(r)/ *n Mus* semicolcheia *f*

semitone /'semɪtəʊn/ *n Mus* semitom *m*

senat|e /'senɪt/ *n* senado *m*. **~or** /-ətə(r)/ *n* senador *m*

send /send/ *vt/i* (*pt* **sent**) enviar, mandar; **~ back** devolver; **~ for** ‹*person*› chamar, mandar vir; ‹*help*› pedir; **~ (away** or **off) for** encomendar, mandar vir; **~ up** [!] parodiar. **~-off** *n* despedida *f*, bota-fora *m*. **~er** *n* expedidor *m*, remetente *m*

senil|e /'si:naɪl/ *a* senil. **~ity** /sɪ'nɪlətɪ/ *n* senilidade *f*

senior /'si:nɪə(r)/ *a* mais velho; mais idoso (**to** do que); (*in rank*) superior; (*in service*) mais antigo; (*after surname*) sênior, (*P*) sénior; **~ citizen** pessoa *f* de idade or da terceira idade, idoso *m* ● *n* pessoa *f* mais velha; *Schol* finalista *mf*. **~ity** /-'ɒrətɪ/ *n* (*in age*) idade *f*; (*in service*) antiguidade *f*

sensation /sen'seɪʃn/ *n* sensação *f*. **~al** *a* sensacional. **~alism** *n* sensacionalismo *m*

sense /sens/ *n* sentido *m*; (*wisdom*) bom-senso *m*; (*sensation*) sensação *f*; (*mental impression*) sentimento *m*; **~s** (*sanity*) razão *f*; **make ~** fazer sentido; **make ~ of** compreender ● *vt* pressentir. **~less** *a* disparatado, sem sentido; *Med* sem sentidos, inconsciente

sensible /'sensəbl/ *a* sensato, razoável; ‹*clothes*› prático

sensitiv|e /'sensətɪv/ *a* sensível (**to** a); (*touchy*) susceptível. **~ity** /-'tɪvətɪ/ *n* sensibilidade *f*

sensory /'sensərɪ/ *a* sensorial

sensual /'senʃʊəl/ *a* sensual. **~ity** /-'ælətɪ/ *n* sensualidade *f*

sensuous /'senʃʊəs/ *a* sensual

sent /sent/ ▶ SEND

sentence /'sentəns/ *n* frase *f*; *Jur* (*decision*) sentença *f*; (*punishment*) pena *f* ● *vt* **~ to** condenar a

sentiment /'sentɪmənt/ *n* sentimento *m*; (*opinion*) modo *m* de ver

sentimental /sentɪ'mentl/ *a* sentimental; **~ value** valor *m* estimativo. **~ity** /-men'tælətɪ/ *n* sentimentalidade *f*, sentimentalismo *m* or sentimental

sentry /'sentrɪ/ *n* sentinela *f*

separable /'sepərəbl/ *a* separável

separate[1] /'seprət/ *a* separado, diferente. **~s** *npl* (*clothes*) conjuntos *mpl*. **~ly** *adv* separadamente, em separado

separat|e[2] /'sepəreɪt/ *vt/i* separar(-se). **~ion** /-'reɪʃn/ *n* separação *f*

September /sep'tembə(r)/ *n* setembro *m*

septic /'septɪk/ *a* séptico, (*P*) sético, infetado

sequel /'si:kwəl/ *n* resultado *m*, sequela *f*; (*of novel, film*) continuação *f*

sequence /'si:kwəns/ *n* sequência *f*

sequin /'si:kwɪn/ *n* lantejoula *f*

serenade /serə'neɪd/ *n* serenata *f* ● *vt* fazer uma serenata para or (*P*) a

seren|e /sɪ'ri:n/ *a* sereno. **~ity** /-'enətɪ/ *n* serenidade *f*

sergeant /'sɑ:dʒənt/ *n* sargento *m*

serial /'sɪərɪəl/ *n* folhetim *m* ● *a* ‹*number*› de série. **~ize** /-laɪz/ *vt* publicar em folhetim

series /'sɪərɪ:z/ *n invar* série *f*

serious /'sɪərɪəs/ *a* sério; (*very bad, critical*) grave, sério. **~ly** *adv* seriamente, gravemente, a sério; **take ~ly** levar a sério. **~ness** *n* seriedade *f*, gravidade *f*

sermon /'sɜ:mən/ *n* sermão *m*

serpent /'sɜ:pənt/ *n* serpente *f*

servant /'sɜ:vənt/ *n* criado *m*, criada *f*, empregado *m*, empregada *f*

serv|e /sɜ:v/ *vt/i* servir; ‹*a sentence*› cumprir; *Jur* (*a writ*) entregar; *Mil* servir, prestar serviço; ‹*apprenticeship*› fazer ● *n Tennis* saque *m*, (*P*) serviço *m*; **~e as/to** servir de/para; **~e its purpose** servir para o que é [!], servir os seus fins; **it ~es you/him** *etc* **right** é bem feito. **~ing** *n* (*portion*) dose *f*, porção *f*

server /'sɜ:və(r)/ *n Comput* servidor *m*

service /'sɜ:vɪs/ *n* serviço *m*; *Relig* culto *m*; *Tennis* saque *m*, (*P*) serviço *m*; (*maintenance*) revisão *f*; **~s** *Mil* forças *fpl* armadas; **of ~ to** útil a/para, de utilidade a/para; **~ area** área *f* de serviço; **~ charge** serviço *m*; **~ station** posto *m* de gasolina, (*P*) posto *m* de abastecimento ● *vt* ‹*car etc*› fazer a revisão de

serviceman /'sɜ:vɪsmən/ *n* (*pl* **-men**) militar *m*

serviette /sɜ:vɪ'et/ *n* guardanapo *m*

session /'seʃn/ *n* sessão *f*; *Univ* ano *m* acadêmico, (*P*) académico; *Amer Univ* semestre *m*; **in ~** (*sitting*) em sessão, reunidos

set /set/ *vt* (*pt* **set**, *pres p* **setting**) pôr, colocar; (*put down*) pousar; ‹*limit etc*› fixar; ‹*watch, clock*› regular, acertar; ‹*example*› dar; ‹*exam, task*› marcar; (*in plaster*) engessar; **~ about** or **to**

começar a, pôr-se a; **~ fire to** atear fogo a, (*P*) deitar fogo a; **~ free** pôr em liberdade; **~ off** ‹*mechanism*› pôr para funcionar, (*P*) pôr a funcionar; **~ out** (*state*) expor; (*arrange*) dispor; **~ sail** partir, içar as velas; **~ square** esquadro *m*; **~ the table** pôr a mesa; **~ theory** teoria *f* de conjuntos; **~ up** (*establish*) fundar, estabelecer ● *vi* ‹*sun*› pôr-se; ‹*jelly*› endurecer, solidificar(-se); **~ in** ‹*rain etc*› pegar, (*P*) vir para ficar; **~ off** or **out** partir, começar a viajar ● *n* (*of people*) círculo *m*, roda *f*; (*of books*) coleção *f*; (*of tools, chairs etc*) jogo *m*; *TV, radio* aparelho *m*; (*hair*) mise *f*; *Theat* cenário *m*; *Tennis* partida *f*, set *m* ● *a* fixo; ‹*habit*› inveterado; ‹*jelly*› duro, sólido; ‹*book*› do programa; ‹*meal*› a preço fixo; **be ~ on doing** estar decidido a fazer; **~ back** ‹*plans etc*› atrasar; ☒ ‹*cost*› custar. **~-back** *n* revés *m*; contratempo *m*; atraso *m* [!]; **~-to** *n* briga *f*; **~-up** *n* (*system*) sistema *m*, organização *f*; (*situation*) situação *f*

settee /se'ti:/ *n* sofá *m*

setting /'setɪŋ/ *n* (*framework*) quadro *m*; (*of jewel*) engaste *m*; *Typ* composição *f*; *Mus* arranjo *m* musical

settle /'setl/ *vt* (*arrange*) resolver; ‹*date*› marcar; ‹*nerves*› acalmar; ‹*doubts*› esclarecer; ‹*new country*› colonizar, povoar; ‹*bill*› pagar ● *vi* assentar; (*in country*) estabelecer-se; (*in house, chair etc*) instalar-se; ‹*weather*› estabilizar(-se); **~ down** acalmar-se; (*become orderly*) assentar; (*sit, rest*) instalar-se; **~ for** aceitar; **~ up (with)** fazer contas (com); *fig* ajustar contas (com). **~r** /-ə(r)/ *n* colono *m*, colonizador *m*

settlement /'setlmənt/ *n* (*agreement*) acordo *m*; (*payment*) pagamento *m*; (*colony*) colônia *f*, (*P*) colónia *f*; (*colonization*) colonização *f*

S

seven /'sevn/ *a & n* sete *m*. **~th** *a & n* sétimo *m*

seventeen /sevn'ti:n/ *a & n* dezessete *m*, (*P*) dezassete *m*. **~th** *a & n* décimo sétimo *m*

sevent|y /'sevntɪ/ *a & n* setenta *m*. **~ieth** *a & n* septuagésimo *m*

sever /'sevə(r)/ *vt* cortar. **~ance** *n* corte *m*

several /'sevrəl/ *a & pron* vários, diversos

sever|e /sɪ'vɪə(r)/ *a* (**-er**, **-est**) severo; ‹*pain*› forte, violento; ‹*illness*› grave; ‹*winter*› rigoroso. **~ely** *adv* severamente; (*seriously*) gravemente. **~ity** /sɪ-'verɪtɪ/ *n* severidade *f*; (*seriousness*) gravidade *f*

sew /səʊ/ *vt/i* (*pt* **sewed**, *pp* **sewn** *or* **sewed**) coser, costurar. **~ing** *n* costura *f*. **~ing machine** *n* máquina *f* de costura

sewage /'sju:ɪdʒ/ *n* efluentes *mpl* dos esgotos, detritos *mpl*

sewer /'sju:ə(r)/ *n* cano *m* de esgoto

sewn /səʊn/ ▶ SEW

sex /seks/ *n* sexo *m*; **have ~** ter relações sexuais ● *a* sexual; **~ maniac** tarado *m* sexual □ **~ up** *vt/i* tornar mais apelativo. **~y** *a* sexy *invar*, que tem sex-appeal

sexist /'seksɪst/ *a & n* sexista *mf*

sexual /'sekʃʊəl/ *a* sexual; **~ harassment** assédio *m* sexual; **~ intercourse** relações *fpl* sexuais. **~ity** /-'ælətɪ/ *n* sexualidade *f*

shabb|y /'ʃæbɪ/ *a* (**-ier**, **-iest**) (*clothes, object*) gasto, surrado; (*person*) maltrapilho, mal vestido; (*mean*) miserável. **~ily** *adv* miseravelmente

shack /ʃæk/ *n* cabana *f*, barraca *f*

shackles /'ʃæklz/ *npl* grilhões *mpl*, algemas *fpl*

shade /ʃeɪd/ *n* sombra *f*; (*of colour*) tom *m*, matiz *m*; (*of opinion*) matiz *m*; (*for lamp*) abat-jour *m*, quebra-luz *m*; *Amer* (*blind*) estore *m*; **a ~ bigger/** *etc* ligeiramente maior/*etc*; **in the ~** à sombra ● *vt* resguardar da luz; (*darken*) sombrear

shadow /'ʃædəʊ/ *n* sombra *f* ● *vt* cobrir de sombra; (*follow*) seguir, vigiar; **S~ Cabinet** gabinete *m* formado pelo partido da oposição. **~y** *a* ensombrado, sombreado; *fig* vago; indistinto

shady /'ʃeɪdɪ/ *a* (**-ier**, **-iest**) sombreiro, (*P*) que dá sombra; (*in shade*) à sombra; *fig* (*dubious*) suspeito; duvidoso

shaft /ʃɑ:ft/ *n* (*of arrow, spear*) haste *f*; (*axle*) eixo *m*, veio *m*; (*of mine, lift*) poço *m*; (*of light*) raio *m*

shaggy /'ʃægɪ/ *a* (**-ier**, **-iest**) ‹*beard*› hirsuto; ‹*hair*› desgrenhado; ‹*animal*› peludo, felpudo

shake /ʃeɪk/ *vt* (*pt* **shook**, *pp* **shaken**) abanar, sacudir; ‹*bottle*› agitar; ‹*belief, house etc*› abalar ● *vi* estremecer, tremer; **~ hands with** apertar a mão de; **~ off** (*get rid of*) sacudir, livrar-se de; **~ one's head** (*to say no*) fazer que não com a cabeça; **~ up** agitar ● *n* (*violent*) abanão *m*, safanão *m*; (*light*) sacudidela *f*. **~-up** *n* (*upheaval*) reviravolta *f*

shaky /'ʃeɪkɪ/ *a* (**-ier**, **-iest**) ‹*hand, voice*› trêmulo, (*P*) trémulo; (*unsteady, unsafe*) pouco firme, inseguro; (*weak*) fraco

shall /ʃæl unstressed ʃəl/ *v aux* **I/we ~ do** (*future*) farei/faremos; **I/you/he ~ do** (*command*) eu hei-de/você há-de/tu hás-de/ele há-de fazer

shallot /ʃəˈlɒt/ *n* cebolinha *f*, (*P*) chalota *f*

shallow /ˈʃæləʊ/ *a* (**-er**, **-est**) pouco fundo, raso; *fig* superficial

sham /ʃæm/ *n* fingimento *m*; ‹*jewel etc*› imitação *f*; ‹*person*› impostor *m*, fingido *m* ● *a* fingido; (*false*) falso ● *vt* (*pt* **shammed**) fingir

shambles /ˈʃæmblz/ *npl* [!] (*mess*) balbúrdia *f*; trapalhada *f*

shame /ʃeɪm/ *n* vergonha *f*; **it's a ~** é uma pena; **what a ~!** que pena! ● *vt* (fazer) envergonhar. **~ful** *a* vergonhoso. **~less** *a* sem vergonha, descarado; (*immodest*) despudorado, desavergonhado

shampoo /ʃæmˈpuː/ *n* xampu *m*, (*P*) champô *m*, shampoo *m* ● *vt* lavar com xampu, (*P*) champô or shampoo

shan't /ʃɑːnt/ (= **shall not**) = SHALL

shanty /ˈʃæntɪ/ *n* barraca *f*; **~ town** favela *f*, (*P*) bairro(s) *m(pl)* da lata

shape /ʃeɪp/ *n* forma *f* ● *vt* moldar ● *vi* **~ (up)** andar bem, fazer progressos; **take ~** concretizar-se, avançar. **~less** *a* informe, sem forma; (*of body*) deselegante, disforme

shapely /ˈʃeɪplɪ/ *a* (**-ier**, **-iest**) ‹*leg, person*› bem feito, elegante

share /ʃeə(r)/ *n* parte *f*, porção *f*; *Comm* ação *f* ● *vt/i* partilhar (**with** com **in** de)

shareholder /ˈʃeəhəʊldə(r)/ *n* acionista *mf*

shark /ʃɑːk/ *n* tubarão *m*

sharp /ʃɑːp/ *a* (**-er**, **-est**) ‹*knife, pencil etc*› afiado; ‹*pin, point etc*› pontiagudo, aguçado; ‹*words, reply*› áspero; (*of bend*) fechado; (*acute*) agudo; (*sudden*) brusco; (*dishonest*) pouco honesto; (*well-defined*) nítido; (*brisk*) rápido, vigoroso; (*clever*) vivo; **six o'clock ~** seis horas em ponto ● *adv* (*stop*) de repente ● *n Mus* sustenido *m*. **~ly** *adv* (*harshly*) rispidamente; (*suddenly*) de repente

sharpen /ˈʃɑːpən/ *vt* aguçar; ‹*pencil*› fazer a ponta de, (*P*) afiar; ‹*knife etc*› afiar, amolar. **~er** *n* afiadeira *f*; (*for pencil*) apontador *m*, (*P*) apara-lápis *m*, (*P*) afia-lápis *m*

shatter /ˈʃætə(r)/ *vt/i* despedaçar(-se), esmigalhar(-se); ‹*hopes*› destruir(-se); ‹*nerves*› abalar(-se). **~ed** *a* (*upset*) passado; (*exhausted*) estourado [!]

shav|e /ʃeɪv/ *vt/i* barbear(-se), fazer a barba (de) ● *n* **have a ~e** barbear-se; **have a close ~e** *fig* escapar por um triz. **~er** *n* aparelho *m* de barbear, (*P*) máquina *f* de barbear. **~ing brush** *n* pincel *m* para a barba; **~ing cream** *n* creme *m* de barbear

shaving /ˈʃeɪvɪŋ/ *n* apara *f*

shawl /ʃɔːl/ *n* xale *m*, (*P*) xaile *m*

she /ʃiː/ *pron* ela ● *n* fêmea *f*

shear /ʃɪə(r)/ *vt* (*pp* **shorn** *or* **sheared**) ‹*sheep etc*› tosquiar

shears /ʃɪəz/ *npl* tesoura *f* para jardim

sheath /ʃiːθ/ *n* (*pl* **s** /ʃiːðz/) bainha *f*; (*condom*) preservativo *m*, camisa de Vênus *f*

shed[1] /ʃed/ *n* (*hut*) casinhola *f*; (*for cows*) estábulo *m*

shed[2] /ʃed/ (*pres p* **shedding**) perder, deixar cair; (*spread*) espalhar; (*blood, tears*) deitar, derramar; **~ light on** lançar luz sobre

sheep /ʃiːp/ *n* (*pl invar*) carneiro *m*, ovelha *f*. **~dog** *n* cão *m* de pastor

sheepish /ˈʃiːpɪʃ/ *a* encabulado

sheepskin /ˈʃiːpskɪn/ *n* pele *f* de carneiro; (*leather*) carneira *f*

sheer /ʃɪə(r)/ *a* mero, simples; (*steep*) íngreme, a pique; ‹*fabric*› diáfano, transparente ● *adv* a pique, verticalmente

sheet /ʃiːt/ *n* lençol *m*; (*of glass, metal*) chapa *f*, placa *f*; (*of paper*) folha *f*

sheikh /ʃeɪk/ *n* xeque *m*, sheik *m*

shelf /ʃelf/ *n* (*pl* **shelves**) prateleira *f*

shell /ʃel/ *n* (*of egg, nut etc*) casca *f*; (*of mollusc*) concha *f*; (*of ship, tortoise*) casco *m*; (*of building*) estrutura *f*, armação *f*; (*of explosive*) cartucho *m* ● *vt* descascar; *Mil* bombardear

S

shellfish /ˈʃelfɪʃ/ *n* (*pl invar*) crustáceo *m*; (*as food*) marisco *m*

shelter /ˈʃeltə(r)/ *n* abrigo *m*, refúgio *m* ● *vt* abrigar; (*protect*) proteger; (*harbour*) dar asilo a ● *vi* abrigar-se, refugiar-se. **~ed** *a* ‹*life etc*› protegido; ‹*spot*› abrigado

shelve /ʃelv/ *vt* pôr em prateleiras; (*fit with shelves*) pôr prateleiras em; *fig* engavetar; pôr de lado

shelving /ˈʃelvɪŋ/ *n* (*shelves*) prateleiras *fpl*

shepherd /ˈʃepəd/ *n* pastor *m*; **~'s pie** empadão *m* de batata e carne moída ● *vt* guiar

sheriff /ˈʃerɪf/ *n* xerife *m*

sherry /'ʃerɪ/ *n* Xerez *m*

shield /ʃi:ld/ *n* (*armour, heraldry*) escudo *m*; (*screen*) anteparo *m* ● *vt* proteger (**from** contra, de)

shift /ʃɪft/ *vt/i* mudar de posição, deslocar(-se); (*exchange, alter*) mudar de ● *n* mudança *f*; (*workers, work*) turno *m*; **make ~** arranjar-se

shifty /'ʃɪftɪ/ *a* (**-ier**, **-iest**) velhaco, duvidoso

shimmer /'ʃɪmə(r)/ *vi* luzir suavemente ● *n* luzir *m*

shin /ʃɪn/ *n* perna *f*. **~ bone** *n* tíbia *f*, canela *f*; **~ pad** *n Football* caneleira *f*

shin|e /ʃaɪn/ *vt/i* (*pt* **shone**) (fazer) brilhar, (fazer) reluzir; ‹*shoes*› engraxar; **the sun is ~ing** faz sol ● *n* lustro *m*; **~e a torch (on)** iluminar com uma lanterna de mão

shingle /'ʃɪŋgl/ *n* (*pebbles*) seixos *mpl*

shingles /'ʃɪŋglz/ *npl Med* zona *f*, herpes-zóster *f*, (*P*) herpes *m*

shiny /'ʃaɪnɪ/ *a* (**-ier**, **-iest**) brilhante; (*of coat, trousers*) lustroso

ship /ʃɪp/ *n* barco *m*, navio *m* ● *vt* (*pt* **shipped**) transportar; (*send*) mandar por via marítima; (*load*) embarcar. **~ment** *n* (*goods*) carregamento *m*; (*shipping*) embarque *m*. **~per** *n* expedidor *m*. **~ping** *n* navegação *f*; (*ships*) navios *mpl*

shipbuilding /'ʃɪpbɪldɪŋ/ *n* construção *f* naval

shipshape /'ʃɪpʃeɪp/ *adv & a* em (perfeita) ordem, impecável

shipwreck /'ʃɪprek/ *n* naufrágio *m*. **~ed** *a* naufragado; **be ~ed** naufragar

shipyard /'ʃɪpjɑ:d/ *n* estaleiro *m*

shirk /ʃ3:k/ *vt* fugir a, furtar-se a, (*P*) baldar-se a ⊠

S **shirt** /ʃ3:t/ *n* camisa *f*; (*of woman*) blusa *f*; **in ~-sleeves** em mangas de camisa

shiver /'ʃɪvə(r)/ *vi* arrepiar-se, tiritar ● *n* arrepio *m*

shoal /ʃəʊl/ *n* (*of fish*) cardume *m*

shock /ʃɒk/ *n* choque *m*, embate *m*; *Electr* choque *m* elétrico; *Med* choque *m* ● *a* de choque; **~ absorber** *Mech* amortecedor *m* ● *vt* chocar. **~ing** *a* chocante; 🄸 (*very bad*) horrível

shodd|y /'ʃɒdɪ/ *a* (**-ier**, **-iest**) mal feito, ordinário, de má qualidade. **~ily** *adv* mal

shoe /ʃu:/ *n* sapato *m*; (*footwear*) calçado *m*; (*horse*) ferradura *f*; (*brake*) sapata *f*, (*P*) calço (de travão) *m*; **on a ~string** 🄸 com/por muito pouco dinheiro, na pindaíba 🄸, por uma tuta e meia 🄸 ● *vt* (*pt* **shod**, *pres p* **shoeing**) ‹*horse*› ferrar. **~ polish** *n* pomada *f*, (*P*) graxa *f* para sapatos; **~ shop** *n* sapataria *f*

shoehorn /'ʃu:hɔ:n/ *n* calçadeira *f*

shoelace /'ʃu:leɪs/ *n* cordão *m* de sapato, (*P*) atacador *m*

shoemaker /'ʃu:meɪkə(r)/ *n* sapateiro *m*

shone /ʃɒn/ ▶ SHINE

shoo /ʃu:/ *vt* enxotar ● *int* xô

shook /ʃuk/ ▶ SHAKE

shoot /ʃu:t/ *vt* (*pt* **shot**) ‹*gun*› disparar; ‹*glance, missile*› lançar; (*kill*) matar a tiro; (*wound*) ferir a tiro; (*execute*) executar, fuzilar; (*hunt*) caçar; (*film*) filmar, rodar; **~ down** abater (a tiro) ● *vi* disparar; atirar (**at** contra, sobre); **~ in/out** (*rush*) entrar/sair correndo, (*P*) correr/surgir abruptamente; **~ up** (*spurt*) jorrar; (*grow quickly*) crescer a olhos vistos, dar um pulo; ‹*prices*› subir em disparada *or* (*P*) disparar ● *n Bot* rebento *m*. **~ing** *n* (*shots*) tiroteio *m*; **~ing star** estrela *f* cadente. **~ing range** *n* carreira *f* de tiro

shop /ʃɒp/ *n* loja *f*; (*workshop*) oficina *f*; **~ assistant** empregado *m*, caixeiro *m*, vendedor *m*; **~ steward** delegado *m* sindical; **~ window** vitrina *f*, (*P*) montra *f*; **talk ~** falar de coisas profissionais ● *vi* (*pt* **shopped**) fazer compras; **~ around** procurar, ver o que há nas lojas. **~ floor** *n* (*workers*) trabalhadores *mpl*; **~-soiled** *Amer* **~worn** *adjs* enxovalhado. **~per** *n* comprador *m*

shopkeeper /'ʃɒpki:pə(r)/ *n* lojista *mf*, comerciante *mf*

shoplift|er /'ʃɒplɪftə(r)/ *n* gatuno *m* de lojas. **~ing** *n* furto *m or* (*P*) ladrão *m* de lojas

shopping /'ʃɒpɪŋ/ *n* (*goods*) compras *fpl*; **go ~** ir às compras; **~ bag** sacola *f or* (*P*) saco *m* de compras; **~ centre** centro *m* comercial

shore /ʃɔ:(r)/ *n* (*of sea*) praia *f*, costa *f*; (*of lake*) margem *f*

short /ʃɔ:t/ *a* (**-er**, **-est**) curto; ‹*person*› baixo; (*brief*) breve, curto; (*curt*) seco, brusco; **be ~ of** (*lack*) ter falta de; **a ~ time** pouco tempo; **he is called Tom for ~** o diminutivo dele é Tom; **in ~** em suma; **~ circuit** *Electr* curto-circuito *m*; **~ cut** atalho *m*; **~ list** pré-seleção *f*; **~ story** conto *m*; **~ wave** *Radio* onda(s) *f(pl)* curta(s) ● *adv* (*abruptly*) bruscamente, de repente; **cut ~** abreviar; (*interrupt*) interromper ● *n Electr* curto-circuito *m*; (*film*) curta-metragem *f*, short *m*;

~s (*trousers*) calção *m*, (*P*) calções *mpl*, short *m*. **~-change** *vt* (*cheat*) enganar; **~-circuit** *vt/i Electr* fazer or dar um curto-circuito (em); **~-lived** *a* de pouca duração; **~-sighted** *a* míope; **~-tempered** *a* irritadiço

shortage /ˈʃɔːtɪdʒ/ *n* falta *f*, escassez *f*

shortbread /ˈʃɔːtbred/ *n* shortbread *m*, biscoito *m* de massa amanteigada

shortcoming /ˈʃɔːtkʌmɪŋ/ *n* falha *f*, imperfeição *f*

shorten /ˈʃɔːtn/ *vt/i* encurtar(-se), abreviar(-se), diminuir

shorthand /ˈʃɔːthænd/ *n* estenografia *f*; **~ typist** estenodactilógrafa *f*, (*P*) estenodatilógrafa *f*, (*P*) estenógrafo *m*

shortly /ˈʃɔːtlɪ/ *adv* (*soon*) em breve, dentro em pouco

shot /ʃɒt/ ▶ SHOOT *n* (*firing, bullet*) tiro *m*; (*person*) atirador *m*; (*pellets*) chumbo *m*; (*photograph*) fotografia *f*; (*injection*) injeção *f*; (*in golf, billiards*) tacada *f*; **go like a ~** ir disparado; **have a ~ (at sth)** experimentar (fazer algo). **~gun** *n* espingarda *f*, caçadeira *f*

should /ʃʊd *unstressed* ʃəd/ *v aux* **you ~ help me** você devia me ajudar, (*P*) devias ajudar-me; **I ~ have stayed** devia ter ficado; **I ~ like to** ; gostaria de or gostava de; **if he ~ come** se ele vier

shoulder /ˈʃəʊldə(r)/ *n* ombro *m* ● *vt* ‹*responsibility*› tomar, assumir; ‹*burden*› carregar, arcar com. **~ blade** *n Anat* omoplata *f*; **~ pad** *n* enchimento *m* de ombro, ombreira *f*, (*P*) chumaço *m*

shout /ʃaʊt/ *n* grito *m*, brado *m*; (*very loud*) berro *m* ● *vt/i* gritar (**at** com); (*very loudly*) berrar (**at** com); **~ down** fazer calar com gritos. **~ing** *n* gritaria *f*, berraria *f*

shove /ʃʌv/ *n* empurrão *m* ● *vt/i* empurrar; [!] (*put*) meter, enfiar; **~ off** [!] (*depart*) começar or pôr-se a andar [!], dar o fora [!], (*P*) cavar [!]

shovel /ˈʃʌvl/ *n* pá *f*; (*machine*) escavadora *f* ● *vt* (*pt* **shovelled**) remover com pá

show /ʃəʊ/ *vt* (*pt* **showed**, *pp* **shown**) mostrar; (*of dial, needle*) marcar; (*put on display*) expor; ‹*film*› dar, passar; **~ in** mandar entrar; **~ out** acompanhar à porta ● *vi* ver-se, aparecer, estar à vista; **~ up** ser claramente visível, ver-se bem; [!] (*arrive*) aparecer ● *n* mostra *f*, demonstração *f*, manifestação *f*; (*ostentation*) alarde *m*, espalhafato *m*; (*exhibition*) mostra *f*, exposição *f*; *Theatre, Cinema* espetáculo *m*, show *m*; **for ~** para fazer vista, (*P*) para dar nas vistas; **on ~** exposto, em exposição □ **~ off** *vt* exibir, ostentar ● *vi* exibir-se, querer fazer figura. **~down** *n* confrontação *f*; **~jumping** *n* concurso *m* hípico; **~-off** *n* exibicionista *mf*; **~piece** *n* peça *f* digna de se expor. **~ing** *n* (*performance*) atuação *f*, performance *f*; *Cinema* exibição *f*

shower /ˈʃaʊə(r)/ *n* (*of rain*) aguaceiro *m*, chuvarada *f*; (*of blows etc*) saraivada *f*; (*in bathroom*) chuveiro *m*; ducha *f*; (*P*) duche *m* ● *vt* **~ with** cumular de, encher de ● *vi* tomar um banho de chuveiro or uma ducha, (*P*) um duche. **~y** *a* chuvoso

shown /ʃəʊn/ ▶ SHOW

showroom /ˈʃəʊrʊm/ *n* espaço *m* de exposição, show-room *m*; (*for cars*) stand *m*

showy /ˈʃəʊɪ/ *a* (**-ier**, **-iest**) vistoso; (*too bright*) berrante; *pej* espalhafatoso

shrank /ʃræŋk/ ▶ SHRINK

shred /ʃred/ *n* tira *f*, retalho *m*, farrapo *m*; *fig* mínimo *m*; sombra *f* ● *vt* (*pt* **shredded**) reduzir a tiras, estraçalhar; *Culin* desfiar. **~der** *n* trituradora *f*; (*for paper*) fragmentadora *f*, (*P*) trituradora *f*

shrewd /ʃruːd/ *a* (**-er**, **-est**) astucioso, fino, perspicaz. **~ness** *n* astúcia *f*, perspicácia *f*

shriek /ʃriːk/ *n* grito *m* agudo, guincho *m* ● *vt/i* gritar, guinchar

shrill /ʃrɪl/ *a* estridente, agudo

shrimp /ʃrɪmp/ *n* camarão *m*

shrine /ʃraɪn/ *n* (*place*) santuário *m*; (*tomb*) túmulo *m*; (*casket*) relicário *m*

shrink /ʃrɪŋk/ *vt/i* (*pt* **shrank**, *pp* **shrunk**) encolher; (*recoil*) encolher-se; **~ from** esquivar-se a, fugir a (+ *inf*) /de (+ *noun*), retrair-se de

shrivel /ˈʃrɪvl/ *vt/i* (*pt* **shrivelled**) encarquilhar(-se)

Shrove /ʃrəʊv/ *n* **~ Tuesday** Terça-feira *f* Gorda or de Carnaval

shrub /ʃrʌb/ *n* arbusto *m*. **~bery** *n* arbustos *mpl*

shrug /ʃrʌg/ *vt* (*pt* **shrugged**) **~ one's shoulders** encolher os ombros; **~ off** não dar importância a ● *n* encolher *m* de ombros

shrunk /ʃrʌŋk/ ▶ SHRINK

shudder /ˈʃʌdə(r)/ *vi* arrepiar-se, estremecer, tremer; **I ~ to think** tremo só de pensar ● *n* arrepio *m*, tremor *m*, estremecimento *m*

shuffle /'ʃʌfl/ *vt* ‹*feet*› arrastar; ‹*cards*› embaralhar, (*P*) baralhar ● *vi* arrastar os pés ● *n* marcha *f* arrastada (*P*)

shun /ʃʌn/ *vt* (*pt* **shunned**) evitar, fugir de

shunt /ʃʌnt/ *vt/i* (*train*) mudar de linha, manobrar

shut /ʃʌt/ *vt* (*pt* **shut**, *pres p* **shutting**) fechar; ~ **in** or **up** trancar ● *vi* fechar-se; ‹*shop, bank etc*› encerrar, fechar; ~ **down** or **up** fechar; ~ **up!** [!] cale-se!, cale a boca! □ ~ **up** *vi* [!] (*stop talking*) calar-se ● *vt* [!] (*silence*) mandar calar

shutter /'ʃʌtə(r)/ *n* taipais *mpl*, (*P*) portada *f* de madeira; (*of laths*) persiana *f*; (*in shop*) taipais *mpl*; *Photo* obturador *m*

shuttle /'ʃʌtl/ *n* (*of spaceship*) ônibus *m* espacial, (*P*) nave *f* espacial; ~ **service** (*plane*) ponte *f* aérea; (*bus*) ônibus *m*, (*P*) autocarro *m*

shuttlecock /'ʃʌtlkɒk/ *n* volante *m*

shy /ʃaɪ/ *a* (**-er**, **-est**) tímido, acanhado, envergonhado ● *vi* ‹*horse*› espantar-se (**at** com); *fig* assustar-se (**at** or **away from** com). **~ness** *n* timidez *f*, acanhamento *m*, vergonha *f*

Sicily /'sɪsɪlɪ/ *n* Sicília *f*

sick /sɪk/ *a* doente; ‹*humour*› negro; **be** ~ (*vomit*) vomitar; **be** ~ **of** estar farto de; **feel** ~ estar enjoado. **~bay** *n* enfermaria *f*; ~ **leave** *n* licença *f* por doença; **~room** *n* quarto *m* de doente

sicken /'sɪkn/ *vt* (*distress*) desesperar; (*disgust*) repugnar ● *vi* **be ~ing for flu** começar a pegar *or* (*P*) chocar uma gripe [!]

sickly /'sɪklɪ/ *a* (**-ier**, **-iest**) ‹*person*› doentio, achacado; ‹*smell*› enjoativo; (*pale*) pálido

S **sickness** /'sɪknɪs/ *n* doença *f*; (*vomiting*) náusea *f*; vômito *m*, (*P*) vómito *m*

side /saɪd/ *n* lado *m*; (*of road, river*) beira *f*; (*of hill*) encosta *f*; *Sport* equipe *f*, (*P*) equipa *f*; **on the** ~ (*extra*) nas horas vagas; (*secretly*) pela calada; ~ **by** ~ lado a lado ● *a* lateral ● *vi* ~ **with** tomar o partido de, alinhar com. **~car** *n* sidecar *m*; **~-effect** *n* efeito *m* secundário; **~show** *n* espetáculo *m* suplementar; **~step** *vt* evitar; **~track** *vt* (fazer) desviar dum propósito

sideboard /'saɪdbɔːd/ *n* aparador *m*

sideburns /'saɪdbɜːnz/ *npl* suíças *fpl*, costeletas *fpl*, (*P*) patilhas *fpl*

sidelight /'saɪdlaɪt/ *n Auto* luz *f* lateral, (*P*) farolim *m*

sideline /'saɪdlaɪn/ *n* atividade *f* secundária; *Sport* linha *f* lateral

sidelong /'saɪdlɒŋ/ *adv & a* de lado

sidewalk /'saɪdwɔːk/ *n Amer* passeio *m*

sideways /'saɪdweɪz/ *adv & a* de lado

siding /'saɪdɪŋ/ *n* desvio *m*, ramal *m*

siege /siːdʒ/ *n* cerco *m*

siesta /sɪ'estə/ *n* sesta *f*

sieve /sɪv/ *n* peneira *f*; (*for liquids*) coador *m* ● *vt* peneirar; ‹*liquids*› passar, coar

sift /sɪft/ *vt* peneirar; (*sprinkle*) polvilhar; ~ **through** examinar minuciosamente, esquadrinhar

sigh /saɪ/ *n* suspiro *m* ● *vt/i* suspirar

sight /saɪt/ *n* vista *f*; (*scene*) cena *f*; (*on gun*) mira *f* ● *vt* avistar, ver, divisar; **at** or **on** ~ à vista; **catch** ~ **of** avistar; **in** ~ à vista, visível; **lose** ~ **of** perder de vista; **out of** ~ longe dos olhos, longe da vista

sightsee|ing /'saɪtsiːɪŋ/ *n* visita *f*, turismo *m*; **go ~ing** visitar lugares turísticos. **~r** /'saɪtsiːə(r)/ *n* turista *mf*

sign /saɪn/ *n* sinal *m*; (*symbol*) signo *m* ● *vt* (*in writing*) assinar ● *vi* (*make a sign*) fazer sinal; ~ **on** or **up** ‹*worker*› assinar contrato. ~ **language** *n* mímica *f*, linguagem *f* gestual

signal /'sɪgnəl/ *n* sinal *m* ● *vi* (*pt* **signalled**) fazer signal ● *vt* comunicar (por sinais); ‹*person*› fazer sinal para

signature /'sɪgnətʃə(r)/ *n* assinatura *f*; ~ **tune** indicativo *m* musical

significan|t /sɪg'nɪfɪkənt/ *a* importante; (*meaningful*) significativo. **~ce** *n* importância *f*; (*meaning*) significado *m*

signify /'sɪgnɪfaɪ/ *vt* significar

signpost /'saɪnpəʊst/ *n* poste *m* de sinalização ● *vt* sinalizar

silence /'saɪləns/ *n* silêncio *m* ● *vt* silenciar, calar

silent /'saɪlənt/ *a* silencioso; (*not speaking*) calado; ‹*film*› mudo. **~ly** *adv* silenciosamente

silhouette /sɪlu'et/ *n* silhueta *f* ● *vt* **be ~d against** estar em silhueta contra

silicon /'sɪlɪkən/ *n* silicone *m*; ~ **chip** circuito *m* integrado

silk /sɪlk/ *n* seda *f*. **~en**, **~y** *adjs* sedoso

sill /sɪl/ *n* (*of window*) parapeito *m*; (*of door*) soleira *f*, limiar *m*

sill|y /'sɪlɪ/ *a* (**-ier**, **-iest**) tolo, idiota. **~iness** *n* tolice *f*, idiotice *f*

silt /sɪlt/ *n* aluvião *m*, sedimento *m*

silver /ˈsɪlvə(r)/ *n* prata *f*; (*silverware*) prataria *f*, pratas *fpl* ● *a* de prata; **~ paper** papel *m* prateado; **~ wedding** bodas *fpl* de prata

silversmith /ˈsɪlvəsmɪθ/ *n* ourives *m*

silverware /ˈsɪlvəweə(r)/ *n* prataria *f*, pratas *fpl*

SIM card /ˈsɪm kɑːd/ *n* SIM *m*, (*P*) cartão SIM

similar /ˈsɪmɪlə(r)/ *a* **~ (to)** semelhante (a), parecido (com). **~ity** /-əˈlærətɪ/ *n* semelhança *f*

simmer /ˈsɪmə(r)/ *vt/i* cozinhar em fogo brando; *fig* (*smoulder*) ferver; fremir; **~ down** acalmar(-se)

simpl|e /ˈsɪmpl/ *a* (**-er**, **-est**) simples. **~e-minded** *a* simples; (*feeble-minded*) pobre de espírito, tolo. **~icity** /-ˈplɪsətɪ/ *n* simplicidade *f*. **~y** *adv* simplesmente; (*absolutely*) absolutamente, simplesmente

simpleton /ˈsɪmpltən/ *n* simplório *m*

simplif|y /ˈsɪmplɪfaɪ/ *vt* simplificar. **~ication** /-ɪˈkeɪʃn/ *n* simplificação *f*

simulat|e /ˈsɪmjʊleɪt/ *vt* simular, imitar. **~ion** /-ˈleɪʃn/ *n* simulação *f*, imitação *f*

simultaneous /sɪmlˈteɪnɪəs/ *a* simultâneo, concomitante. **~ly** *adv* simultaneamente

sin /sɪn/ *n* pecado *m* ● *vi* (*pt* **sinned**) pecar

since /sɪns/ ● *prep*

····➤ desde; **I haven't seen him ~ Monday** não o vejo desde segunda-feira; **I have been waiting ~ yesterday** estou esperando desde ontem; **she had been living in Lisbon ~ 1985** ela estava vivendo em Lisboa desde 1985

● *adv*

····➤ desde então; **he hasn't been seen ~** ninguém o viu desde então

● *conj*

····➤ (*in time expressions*) desde que; **~ she's been working here** desde que ela trabalha aqui

····➤ (*because*) como, visto que; **~ he was ill, he couldn't go** como estava doente, não pôde ir

sincer|e /sɪnˈsɪə(r)/ *a* sincero. **~ely** *adv* sinceramente. **~ity** /-ˈserətɪ/ *n* sinceridade *f*

sinful /ˈsɪnfl/ *a* (*wicked*) pecaminoso; (*shocking*) escandaloso

sing /sɪŋ/ *vt/i* (*pt* **sang**, *pp* **sung**) cantar. **~er** *n* cantor *m*

singe /sɪndʒ/ *vt* (*pres p* **singeing**) chamuscar

single /ˈsɪŋgl/ *a* único, só; (*unmarried*) solteiro; ‹*bed*› de solteiro; ‹*room*› individual; ‹*ticket*› de ida, simples; **in ~ file** em fila indiana; **~ parent** pai *m* solteiro, mãe *f* solteira ● *n* (*ticket*) bilhete *m* de ida or simples; (*record*) disco *m* de 45 r.p.m.; **~s** *Tennis* singulares *mpl* ● *vt* **~ out** escolher. **~-handed** *a* sem ajuda, sozinho; **~-minded** *a* decidido, aferrado à sua ideia, (*P*) determinado, tenaz. **singly** *adv* um a um, um por um

singular /ˈsɪŋgjʊlə(r)/ *n* singular *m* ● *a* (*uncommon*) *Gramm* singular; (*noun*) no singular

sinister /ˈsɪnɪstə(r)/ *a* sinistro

sink /sɪŋk/ *vt* (*pt* **sank**, *pp* **sunk**) ‹*ship*› afundar, ir a pique; (*well*) abrir; (*invest money*) empatar; (*lose money*) enterrar ● *vi* afundar-se; (*of ground*) ceder; (*of voice*) baixar; **~ in** *fig* ficar gravado, entrar [!]; **~ or swim** ou vai ou racha [!] ● *n* pia *f*, (*P*) lava-louça *m*

sinner /ˈsɪnə(r)/ *n* pecador *m*

sip /sɪp/ *n* gole *m* ● *vt* (*pt* **sipped**) bebericar, beber aos golinhos

siphon /ˈsaɪfn/ *n* sifão *m* ● *vt* **~ off** extrair por meio de sifão

sir /sɜː(r)/ *n* senhor *m*; **~** (*title*) Sir *m*; **Dear S~** Exmo Senhor; **excuse me, ~** desculpe, senhor; **no, ~** não, senhor

siren /ˈsaɪərən/ *n* sereia *f*, sirene *f*

sister /ˈsɪstə(r)/ *n* irmã *f*; (*nun*) irmã *f*, freira *f*; (*nurse*) enfermeira-chefe *f*; **~-in-law** cunhada *f*

sit /sɪt/ *vt/i* (*pt* **sat**, *pres p* **sitting**) sentar(-se); (*of committee etc*) reunir-se; **~ for an exam** fazer um exame, prestar uma prova; **be ~ting** estar sentado; **~ around** não fazer nada; **~ down** sentar-se; **~ up** endireitar-se na cadeira; (*not go to bed*) passar a noite acordado. **~ting** *n* reunião *f*, sessão *f*; (*in restaurant*) serviço *m*. **~ting room** *n* sala *f* de estar

site /saɪt/ *n* local *m*; **(building) ~** terreno *m* para construção, lote *m* ● *vt* localizar, situar

situat|e /ˈsɪtʃʊeɪt/ *vt* situar. **be ~ed** estar situado. **~ion** /-ˈeɪʃn/ *n* (*position, condition*) situação *f*; (*job*) emprego *m*, colocação *f*

six /sɪks/ *a & n* seis *m*. **~th** *a & n* sexto *m*

sixteen /sɪkˈstiːn/ *a & n* dezesseis *m*, (*P*) dezasseis *m*. **~th** *a & n* décimo sexto *m*

sixt|y /ˈsɪkstɪ/ *a & n* sessenta *m*. **~ieth** *a & n* sexagésimo *m*

size /saɪz/ *n* tamanho *m*; (*of person, garment etc*) tamanho *m*, medida *f*, (*P*) número *m*; (*of shoes*) número *m*; (*extent*) grandeza *f* ● *vt* **~ up** calcular o tamanho de; ▣ (*judge*) formar um juízo sobre, avaliar. **~able** *a* bastante grande, considerável

sizzle /ˈsɪzl/ *vi* chiar, rechinar

skate[1] /skeɪt/ *n* (*pl invar*) (*fish*) (ar)raia *f*

skat|e[2] /skeɪt/ *n* patim *m* ● *vi* patinar. **~er** *n* patinador *m*. **~ing** *n* patinação *f*, (*P*) patinagem *f*. **~ing rink** *n* rinque *m* de patinação *or* (*P*) patinagem *f*

skateboard /ˈskeɪtbɔːd/ *n* skate *m*

skelet|on /ˈskelɪtən/ *n* esqueleto *m*; (*framework*) armação *f*; **~on crew** *or* **staff** pessoal *m* reduzido; **~on key** chave *f* mestra. **~al** *a* esquelético

sketch /sketʃ/ *n* esboço *m*, croqui(s) *m*; *Theat* sketch *m*, peça *f* curta e humorística; (*outline*) ideia *f or* (*P*) ideia *f* geral, esboço *m* ● *vt* esboçar, delinear ● *vi* fazer esboços. **~-book** *n* caderno *m* de desenho

sketchy /ˈsketʃɪ/ *a* (**-ier**, **-iest**) incompleto, esboçado

skewer /ˈskjʊə(r)/ *n* espeto *m*

ski /skiː/ *n* (*pl* **-s**) esqui *m* ● *vi* (*pt* **ski'd**, *or* **skied**, *pres p* **skiing**) esquiar; (*go skiing*) fazer esqui. **~er** *n* esquiador *m*. **~ing** *n* esqui *m*

skid /skɪd/ *vi* (*pt* **skidded**) derrapar, patinar ● *n* derrapagem *f*

skilful /ˈskɪlfl/ *a* hábil, habilidoso

skill /skɪl/ *n* habilidade *f*, jeito *m*; (*craft*) arte *f*; **~s** aptidões *fpl*. **~ed** *a* hábil, habilidoso; (*worker*) especializado

S

skim /skɪm/ *vt* (*pt* **skimmed**) tirar a espuma de; (*milk*) desnatar, tirar a nata de; (*pass or glide over*) deslizar sobre, roçar ● *vi* **~ through** ler por alto, passar os olhos por; **~med milk** leite *m* desnatado

skimp /skɪmp/ *vt* (*use too little*) poupar em ● *vi* ser poupado

skimpy /ˈskɪmpɪ/ *a* (**-ier**, **-iest**) ‹*clothes*› sumário, mínimo; ‹*meal*› escasso; racionado *fig*

skin /skɪn/ *n* (*of person, animal*) pele *f*; (*of fruit*) casca *f* ● *vt* (*pt* **skinned**) ‹*animal*› esfolar, tirar a pele de; ‹*fruit*› descascar

skinny /ˈskɪnɪ/ *a* (**-ier**, **-iest**) magricela, escanzelado

skint /skɪnt/ *a* ▣ sem dinheiro; na última lona ▣, (*P*) nas lonas ▣

skip[1] /skɪp/ *vi* (*pt* **skipped**) saltar, pular; (*jump about*) saltitar; (*with rope*) pular corda, (*P*) saltar à corda ● *vt* ‹*page*› saltar; ‹*class*› faltar a ● *n* salto *m*. **~ping rope** *n* corda *f* de pular *or* (*P*) de saltar

skip[2] /skɪp/ *n* (*container*) container *m or* (*P*) contentor *m* grande para entulho

skipper /ˈskɪpə(r)/ *n* capitão *m*

skirmish /ˈskɜːmɪʃ/ *n* escaramuça *f*

skirt /skɜːt/ *n* saia *f* ● *vt* contornar, ladear. **~ing board** *n* rodapé *m*

skittle /ˈskɪtl/ *n* pino *m*. **~s** *npl* boliche *m*, (*P*) jogo *m* da laranjinha

skive /skaɪv/ *vi* ▣ eximir-se de um dever; evitar trabalhar, (*P*) furtar-se ao trabalho ▣

skull /skʌl/ *n* caveira *f*, crânio *m*

skunk /skʌŋk/ *n* (*animal*) gambá *m*, (*P*) doninha *f*

sky /skaɪ/ *n* céu *m*. **~-blue** *a & n* azul-celeste *m*

skylight /ˈskaɪlaɪt/ *n* claraboia *f*

skyscraper /ˈskaɪskreɪpə(r)/ *n* arranha-céus *m invar*

slab /slæb/ *n* (*of marble*) placa *f*; (*of paving stone*) laje *f*; (*of metal*) chapa *f*; (*of cake*) fatia *f* grossa

slack /slæk/ *a* (**-er**, **-est**) ‹*rope*› bambo, frouxo; ‹*person*› descuidado, negligente; ‹*business*› parado, fraco; ‹*period, season*› morto ● *n* **the ~** (*in rope*) a parte bamba ● *vt/i* (*be lazy*) estar com preguiça; fazer cera *fig*

slacken /ˈslækən/ *vt/i* ‹*speed, activity etc*› afrouxar, abrandar

slain /sleɪn/ ▶ SLAY

slam /slæm/ *vt* (*pt* **slammed**) bater violentamente com; (*throw*) atirar; ▣ (*criticize*) criticar; malhar ● *vi* ‹*door etc*› bater violentamente ● *n* (*noise*) bater *m*, pancada *f*

slander /ˈslɑːndə(r)/ *n* calúnia *f*, difamação *f* ● *vt* caluniar, difamar. **~ous** *a* calunioso, difamatório

slang /slæŋ/ *n* calão *m*, gíria *f*. **~y** *a* de calão

slant /slɑːnt/ *vt/i* inclinar(-se); ‹*news*› apresentar de forma tendenciosa ● *n* inclinação *f*; (*bias*) tendência *f*; (*point of view*) ângulo *m*; **be ~ing** ser/estar inclinado or em declive

slap /slæp/ *vt* (*pt* **slapped**) (*strike*) bater, dar uma palmada em; (*on face*) esbofetear, dar uma bofetada em; (*put* *forcefully*) atirar com ● *n* palmada *f*, bofetada *f* ● *adv* em cheio. **~-up** *a* ⊠ (*excellent*) excelente

slapdash /'slæpdæʃ/ *a* descuidado; (*impetuous*) precipitado

slapstick /'slæpstɪk/ *n* farsa *f* com palhaçadas

slash /slæʃ/ *vt* (*cut*) retalhar, dar golpes em; (*sever*) cortar; ‹*a garment*› golpear; *fig* (*reduce*) reduzir drasticamente; fazer um corte radical em ● *n* corte *m*, golpe *m*

slat /slæt/ *n* (*in blind*) ripa *f*, (*P*) lâmina *f*

slate /sleɪt/ *n* ardósia *f* ● *vt* ⊡ (*criticize*) criticar severamente

slaughter /'slɔ:tə(r)/ *vt* chacinar, massacrar; ‹*animals*› abater ● *n* chacina *f*, massacre *m*, mortandade *f*; (*animals*) abate *m*

slaughterhouse /'slɔ:təhaʊs/ *n* matadouro *m*

slave /sleɪv/ *n* escravo *m* ● *vi* mourejar, trabalhar como um escravo. **~-driver** *n* *fig* o que obriga os outros a trabalharem como escravos; condutor *m* de escravos. **~ry** /-ərɪ/ *n* escravatura *f*

slay /sleɪ/ *vt* (*pt* **slew**, *pp* **slain**) matar

sleazy /'sli:zɪ/ *a* (**-ier**, **-iest**) ⊡ esquálido; sórdido

sledge /sledʒ/ *n* trenó *m*. **~hammer** *n* martelo *m* de forja, marreta *f*

sleek /sli:k/ *a* (**-er**, **-est**) liso, macio e lustroso

sleep /sli:p/ *n* sono *m* ● *vi* (*pt* **slept**) dormir ● *vt* ter lugar para, alojar; **go to ~** ir dormir, adormecer; **put to ~** (*kill*) mandar matar; **~ around** ser promíscuo. **~er** *n* aquele que dorme; *Rail* (*beam*) dormente *m*; (*berth*) couchette *f*. **~ing bag** *n* saco *m* de dormir, (*P*) saco-cama *m*. **~less** *a* insone; (*night*) em claro, insone. **~walker** *n* sonâmbulo *m*

sleep|y /'sli:pɪ/ *a* (**-ier**, **-iest**) sonolento; **be ~y** ter or estar com sono

sleet /sli:t/ *n* geada *f* miúda ● *vi* cair geada miúda

sleeve /sli:v/ *n* manga *f*; (*of record*) capa *f*; **up one's ~** de reserva, escondido, (*P*) na manga. **~less** *a* sem mangas

sleigh /sleɪ/ *n* trenó *m*

sleight /slaɪt/ *n* **~ of hand** prestidigitação *f*, passe *m* de mágica

slender /'slendə(r)/ *a* esguio, esbelto; *fig* (*scanty*) escasso

slept /slept/ ▶ SLEEP

sleuth /slu:θ/ *n* ⊡ detetive *m*

slew[1] /slu:/ *vi* (*turn*) virar-se

slew[2] /slu:/ ▶ SLAY

slice /slaɪs/ *n* fatia *f* ● *vt* cortar em fatias; *Golf*, *Tennis* cortar

slick /slɪk/ *a* (*slippery*) escorregadio; (*cunning*) astuto, habilidoso; (*unctuous*) melífluo ● *n* **(oil) ~** mancha *f* de óleo, (*P*) derrame *m* de petróleo

slid|e /slaɪd/ *vt/i* (*pt* **slid**) escorregar, deslizar ● *n* escorregadela *f*, escorregão *m*; (*in playground*) escorrega *m*; (*for hair*) prendedor *m*, (*P*) travessa *f*; *Photo* diapositivo *m*, slide *m*. **~ing** *a* ‹*door, panel*› corrediço, de correr; **~ing scale** escala *f* móvel

slight /slaɪt/ *a* (**-er**, **-est**) (*slender, frail*) delgado, franzino; (*inconsiderable*) leve, ligeiro; **not in the ~est** em absoluto ● *vt* desconsiderar, desfeitear ● *n* desconsideração *f*, desfeita *f*. **the ~est** *a* o/a menor. **~ly** *adv* ligeiramente, um pouco

slim /slɪm/ *a* (**slimmer**, **slimmest**) magro, esbelto; ‹*chance*› pequeno, remoto ● *vi* (*pt* **slimmed**) emagrecer

slim|e /slaɪm/ *n* lodo *m*. **~y** *a* lodoso; (*slippery*) escorregadio; *fig* (*servile*) servil; bajulador

sling /slɪŋ/ *n* (*weapon*) funda *f*; (*for arm*) tipoia *f* ● *vt* (*pt* **slung**) atirar, lançar

slip /slɪp/ *vt/i* (*pt* **slipped**) escorregar; (*move quietly*) mover-se de mansinho; **~ away** esgueirar-se; **~ by** passar sem se dar conta, passar despercebido; **~ into** (*go*) entrar de mansinho, enfiar-se em; ‹*clothes*› enfiar; **~ped disc** disco *m* deslocado; **~ sb's mind** passar pela cabeça de alguém; **~ up** ⊡ cometer uma gafe ● *n* escorregadela *f*, escorregão *m*; (*mistake*) engano *m*, lapso *m*; (*petticoat*) combinação *f*; (*of paper*) tira *f* de papel; **give the ~ to** livrar-se de, escapar(-se) de; **~ of the tongue** lapso *m*. **~ road** *n* acesso *m* a autoestrada; **~-up** *n* ⊡ gafe *f*

slipper /'slɪpə(r)/ *n* chinelo *m*

slippery /'slɪpərɪ/ *a* escorregadio; *fig* ‹*person*› que não é de confiança; sem escrúpulos

slipshod /'slɪpʃɒd/ *a* ‹*person*› desleixado, desmazelado; ‹*work*› feito sem cuidado, desleixado

slit /slɪt/ *n* fenda *f*; (*cut*) corte *m*; (*tear*) rasgão *m* ● *vt* (*pt* **slit**, *pres p* **slitting**) fender; (*cut*) fazer um corte em, cortar

slither /'slɪðə(r)/ *vi* escorregar, resvalar

sliver /'slɪvə(r)/ *n* (*of cheese etc*) fatia *f*; (*splinter*) lasca *f*

slog /slɒg/ *vt* (*pt* **slogged**) (*hit*) bater com força ● *vi* (*walk*) caminhar com passos pesados e firmes; (*work*) trabalhar duro ● *n* (*work*) trabalheira *f*; (*walk, effort*) estafa *f*

slogan /ˈsləʊgən/ *n* slogan *m*, lema *m*, palavra *f* de ordem

slop /slɒp/ *vt/i* (*pt* **slopped**) transbordar, entornar. **~s** *npl* (*dirty water*) água(s) *f(pl)* suja(s); (*liquid refuse*) despejos *mpl*

slop|e /sləʊp/ *vt/i* inclinar(-se), formar declive ● *n* (*of mountain*) encosta *f*; (*of street*) rampa *f*, ladeira *f*. **~ing** *a* inclinado, em declive

sloppy /ˈslɒpɪ/ *a* (**-ier**, **-iest**) ‹*ground*› molhado, com poças de água; ‹*food*› aguado; ‹*clothes*› desleixado; ‹*work*› descuidado; feito de qualquer jeito or maneira [!]; ‹*person*› desmazelado; (*maudlin*) piegas

slosh /slɒʃ/ *vt* entornar; [!] (*splash*) esparrinhar, (*P*) salpicar; ⊠ (*hit*) bater em; dar (uma) sova em ● *vi* chapinhar

slot /slɒt/ *n* ranhura *f*; (*in timetable*) horário *m*; *TV* espaço *m*; *Aviat* slot *m* ● *vt/i* (*pt* **slotted**) enfiar(-se), meter(-se), encaixar(-se). **~ machine** *n* (*for stamps, tickets etc*) distribuidor *m* automático; (*for gambling*) caça-níqueis *m*, (*P*) slot machine *f*

slouch /slaʊtʃ/ *vi* (*stand, move*) andar com as costas curvadas; (*sit*) sentar-se em má postura

slovenly /ˈslʌvnlɪ/ *a* desmazelado, desleixado

slow /sləʊ/ *a* (**-er**, **-est**) lento, vagaroso ● *adv* devagar, lentamente ● *vt/i* **~ (up** or **down)** diminuir a velocidade, afrouxar; *Auto* desacelerar; **be ~** ‹*clock etc*› atrasar-se, estar atrasado; **in ~ motion** em câmara lenta. **~ly** *adv* devagar, lentamente, vagarosamente

S

slow|coach /ˈsləʊkəʊtʃ/, **~poke** *Amer ns* lesma *m/f*; pastelão *m fig*

sludge /slʌdʒ/ *n* lama *f*, lodo *m*

slug /slʌg/ *n* lesma *f*

sluggish /ˈslʌgɪʃ/ *a* (*slow*) lento, moroso; (*lazy*) indolente, preguiçoso

sluice /slu:s/ *n* (*gate*) comporta *f*; (*channel*) canal *m* ● *vt* lavar com jorros de água

slum /slʌm/ *n* favela *f*, (*P*) bairro *m* da lata; (*building*) cortiço *m*

slumber /ˈslʌmbə(r)/ *n* sono *m* ● *vi* dormir

slump /slʌmp/ *n* (*in prices*) baixa *f*, descida *f*; (*in demand*) quebra *f* na procura; *Econ* depressão *f* ● *vi* (*fall limply*) cair, afundar-se; (*of price*) baixar bruscamente

slung /slʌŋ/ ▶ SLING

slur /slɜ:(r)/ *vt/i* (*pt* **slurred**) (*speech*) pronunciar indistintamente, mastigar ● *n* (*in speech*) som *m* indistinto; (*discredit*) nódoa *f*, estigma *m*

slush /slʌʃ/ *n* (*snow*) neve *f* meio derretida; **~ fund** *Comm* fundo *m* para subornos, (*P*) saco *m* azul. **~y** *a* ‹*road*› coberto de neve derretida, lamacento

slut /slʌt/ *n* (*dirty woman*) porca *f*, desmazelada *f*; (*immoral woman*) desavergonhada *f*, (*P*) galdéria *f*

sly /slaɪ/ *a* (**slyer**, **slyest**) (*crafty*) manhoso; (*secretive*) sonso, subreptício ● *n* **on the ~** na calada

smack[1] /smæk/ *n* palmada *f*; (*on face*) bofetada *f* ● *vt* dar uma palmada or um tapa em; (*on the face*) esbofetear, dar uma bofetada em ● *adv* [!] em cheio; direto

smack[2] /smæk/ *vi* **~ of sth** cheirar a algo

small /smɔ:l/ *a* (**-er**, **-est**) pequeno; **~ change** trocado *m*, dinheiro *m* miúdo; **~ talk** conversa *f* fiada, bate-papo *m* ● *n* **~ of the back** zona *f* dos rins ● *adv* (*cut etc*) em pedaços pequenos, aos bocadinhos

smallpox /ˈsmɔ:lpɒks/ *n* varíola *f*

smarmy /ˈsmɑ:mɪ/ *a* (**-ier**, **-iest**) [!] bajulador; puxa-saco [!], (*P*) lambe-botas *mf inv*

smart /smɑ:t/ *a* (**-er**, **-est**) elegante; (*clever*) esperto, vivo; (*brisk*) rápido ● *vi* (*sting*) arder, picar

smarten /ˈsmɑ:tn/ *vt/i* **~ (up)** arranjar(-se), dar um ar mais cuidado a; **~ (o.s.) up** embelezar-se, arrumar-se, (*P*) pôr-se elegante/bonito; (*tidy*) arranjar-se

smash /smæʃ/ *vt/i* (*to pieces*) despedaçar(-se); espatifar(-se) [!]; ‹*a record*› quebrar, (*P*) partir; ‹*opponent*› esmagar; (*ruin*) (fazer) falir; (*of vehicle*) espatifar(-se) ● *n* (*noise*) estrondo *m*; (*blow*) pancada *f* forte, golpe *m*; (*collision*) colisão *f*; *Tennis* smash *m*

smashing /ˈsmæʃɪŋ/ *a* [!] formidável; estupendo [!]

smattering /ˈsmætərɪŋ/ *n* leves noções *fpl*, conhecimento *m* superficial

smear /smɪə(r)/ *vt* (*stain; discredit*) manchar; (*coat*) untar, besuntar ● *n* mancha *f*, nódoa *f*; *Med* esfregaço *m*

smell /smel/ *n* cheiro *m*, odor *m*; (*sense*) cheiro *m*; olfato *m* ● *vt/i* (*pt* **smelt**, *or*

smelled) **~ (of)** cheirar (a). **~y** *a* mal-cheiroso

smelt[1] /smelt/ ▶ SMELL

smelt[2] /smelt/ *vt* (*ore*) fundir

smil|e /smaɪl/ *n* sorriso *m* ● *vi* sorrir

smirk /smɜːk/ *n* sorriso *m* falso or afetado

smock /smɒk/ *n* guarda-pó *m*

smog /smɒg/ *n* mistura *f* de nevoeiro e fumaça, smog *m*

smoke /sməʊk/ *n* fumo *m*, fumaça *f* ● *vt* fumar; ‹*bacon etc*› fumar, defumar ● *vi* fumar, fumegar. **~screen** *n lit & fig* cortina *f* de fumaça *or* (*P*) de fumo. **~less** *a* ‹*fuel*› sem fumo. **~r** /-ə(r)/ *n* (*person*) fumante *mf*, (*P*) fumador *m*. **smoky** *a* ‹*air*› enfumaçado, fumacento, fumoso

smooth /smuːð/ *a* (**-er**, **-est**) liso; (*soft*) macio; (*movement*) regular, suave; (*manners*) lisonjeiro, conciliador, suave ● *vt* alisar; **~ out** *fig* aplanar, remover

smother /ˈsmʌðə(r)/ *vt* (*stifle*) abafar, sufocar; (*cover, overwhelm*) cobrir (**with** de); (*suppress*) abafar, reprimir

smoulder /ˈsməʊldə(r)/ *vi lit & fig* arder; abrasar-se

SMS *abbr* (= **Short Message** or **Messaging Service**) mensagem *f* de texto

smudge /smʌdʒ/ *n* mancha *f*, borrão *m* ● *vt/i* sujar(-se), manchar(-se), borrar(-se)

smug /smʌg/ *a* (**smugger**, **smuggest**) presunçoso; convencido [!]

smuggl|e /ˈsmʌgl/ *vt* contrabandear, fazer contrabando de. **~er** *n* contrabandista *mf*. **~ing** *n* contrabando *m*

smut /smʌt/ *n* fuligem *f*. **~ty** *a* cheio de fuligem; [!] (*obscene*) indecente; sujo [!]

snack /snæk/ *n* refeição *f* ligeira. **~ bar** *n* lanchonete *f*, (*P*) snack(-bar) *m*

snag /snæg/ *n* (*obstacle*) obstáculo *m*; (*drawback*) problema *m*, contra *m*, contratempo *m*; (*in cloth*) rasgão *m*; (*in stocking*) fio *m* puxado, (*P*) malha *f*

snail /sneɪl/ *n* caracol *m*; **at a ~'s pace** em passo de tartaruga *or* (*P*) caracol

snake /sneɪk/ *n* serpente *f*, cobra *f*

snap /snæp/ *vt/i* (*pt* **snapped**) (*whip, fingers*) (fazer) estalar; (*break*) estalar(-se), partir(-se) com um estalo, rebentar; (*say*) dizer irritadamente ● *n* estalo *m*; (*photo*) instantâneo *m*, (*P*) instantânea *f*; *Amer* (*fastener*) mola *f* ● *a* súbito, repentino; **~ at** (*bite*) abocanhar, tentar morder; (*speak angrily*) retrucar *or* (*P*) retorquir asperamente; **~ up** (*buy*) comprar rapidamente

snappy /ˈsnæpɪ/ *a* (**-ier**, **-iest**) [!] vivo; animado; **make it ~** [!] vai rápido!, apresse-se! [!]

snapshot /ˈsnæpʃɒt/ *n* instantâneo *m*, (*P*) (fotografia *f*) instantânea *f*

snare /sneə(r)/ *n* laço *m*, cilada *f*, armadilha *f*

snarl /snɑːl/ *vi* rosnar ● *n* rosnadela *f*

snatch /snætʃ/ *vt* (*grab*) agarrar, apanhar; (*steal*) roubar; **~ from sb** arrancar de/a alguém ● *n* (*theft*) roubo *m*; (*bit*) bocado *m*, pedaço *m*

sneak /sniːk/ *vi* (*slink*) esgueirar-se furtivamente; [✱] (*tell tales*) fazer queixa(s); delatar ● *vt* [✱] (*steal*) rapinar [!] ● *n* [✱] dedo-duro *m*; queixinhas *mf* [✱]. **~ing** *a* secreto. **~y** *a* sonso

sneer /snɪə(r)/ *n* sorriso *m* de desdém ● *vi* sorrir desdenhosamente

sneeze /sniːz/ *n* espirro *m* ● *vi* espirrar

snide /snaɪd/ *a* [!] sarcástico

sniff /snɪf/ *vi* fungar ● *vt/i* **~ (at)** (*smell*) cheirar; (*dog*) farejar; **~ at** *fig* (*in contempt*) desprezar ● *n* fungadela *f*

snigger /ˈsnɪgə(r)/ *n* riso *m* abafado ● *vi* rir dissimuladamente

snip /snɪp/ *vt* (*pt* **snipped**) cortar com tesoura ● *n* pedaço *m*, retalho *m*; [✱] (*bargain*) pechincha *f*

snipe /snaɪp/ *vi* dar tiros de emboscada. **~r** /-ə(r)/ *n* franco-atirador *m*

snivel /ˈsnɪvl/ *vi* (*pt* **snivelled**) choramingar, lamuriar-se

snob /snɒb/ *n* esnobe *mf*, (*P*) snob *mf*. **~bery** *n* esnobismo *m*, (*P*) snobismo *m*. **~bish** *a* esnobe, (*P*) snob

snog /snɒg/ *Brit vt/i* (*pres p etc.* **-gg-**) [!] beijar apaixonadamente ● *n* [!] longa troca de carícias e beijos *f*

snooker /ˈsnuːkə(r)/ *n* snooker *m*, sinuca *f*

snoop /snuːp/ *vi* [!] bisbilhotar; meter o nariz em toda a parte; **~ on** espiar, espionar

snooty /ˈsnuːtɪ/ *a* (**-ier**, **-iest**) [!] convencido; arrogante

snooze /snuːz/ *n* [!] soneca *f* [!] ● *vi* [!] tirar *or* (*P*) fazer uma soneca

snore /snɔː(r)/ *n* ronco *m* ● *vi* roncar, (*P*) ressonar

snorkel /ˈsnɔːkl/ *n* tubo *m* de respiração, snorkel *m*

snort /snɔːt/ *n* resfôlego *m*, bufido *m* ● *vi* resfolegar, bufar

snout /snaʊt/ *n* focinho *m*

snow /snəʊ/ *n* neve *f* ● *vi* nevar; **be ~ed under** *fig* (*be overwhelmed*) estar sobrecarregado de *fig*. **~board** *n* snowboard *m*; **~drift** *n* banco *m* de neve; **~plough** *n* limpa-neve *m*. **~y** *a* nevado, coberto de neve

snowball /ˈsnəʊbɔːl/ *n* bola *f* de neve ● *vi* atirar bolas de neve (em); *fig* acumular-se; ir num crescendo; aumentar rapidamente

snowdrop /ˈsnəʊdrɒp/ *n Bot* fura-neve *m*

snowfall /ˈsnəʊfɔːl/ *n* nevada *f*, (*P*) nevão *m*

snowflake /ˈsnəʊfleɪk/ *n* floco *m* de neve

snowman /ˈsnəʊmæn/ *n* (*pl* **-men**) boneco *m* de neve

snub /snʌb/ *vt* (*pt* **snubbed**) desdenhar, tratar com desdém ● *n* desdém *m*

snuffle /ˈsnʌfl/ *vi* fungar

snug /snʌg/ *a* (**snugger**, **snuggest**) (*cosy*) aconchegado; (*close-fitting*) justo

snuggle /ˈsnʌgl/ *vt/i* (*nestle*) aninhar-se, aconchegar-se; (*cuddle*) aconchegar

so /səʊ/ *adv* tão, de tal modo; (*thus*) assim, deste modo ● *conj* por isso, portanto, por consequinte; **~ am I** eu também; **~ does he** ele também; **that is ~** é isso; **I think ~** acho que sim; **five or ~** uns cinco; **~ as to** de modo a; **~ far** até agora, até aqui; **~ long!** 🅸 até já! 🅸; **~ many** tantos; **~ much** tanto; **~ that** para que, de modo que; **~-and-~** fulano *m*. **~-called** *a* pretenso, soi-disant, chamado; **~-so** *a & adv* assim assim, mais ou menos

soak /səʊk/ *vt/i* molhar(-se), ensopar(-se), encharcar(-se); **leave to ~** pôr de molho; **~ through** repassar □ **~ in**, **~ up** *vt* absorver, embeber. **~ing** *a* ensopado, encharcado

soap /səʊp/ *n* sabão. *m*; **(toilet) ~** sabonete *m* ● *vt* ensaboar; **~ opera** *Radio* novela *f* radiofônica, (*P*) radiofónica; *TV* telenovela *f*; **~ flakes** flocos *mpl* de sabão; **~ powder** sabão *m* em pó. **~y** *a* ensaboado

soar /sɔː(r)/ *vi* voar alto; (*go high*) elevar-se; (*hover*) pairar

sob /sɒb/ *n* soluço *m* ● *vi* (*pt* **sobbed**) soluçar

sober /ˈsəʊbə(r)/ *a* (*not drunk, calm, of colour*) sóbrio; (*serious*) sério, grave ● *vt/i* **~ up** (fazer) ficar sóbrio 🅸, (fazer) curar a bebedeira 🅸

soccer /ˈsɒkə(r)/ *n* 🅸 futebol *m*

S

sociable /ˈsəʊʃəbl/ *a* sociável

social /ˈsəʊʃl/ *a* social; (*sociable*) sociável; ‹*gathering, life*› de sociedade; **~ security** previdência *f* social, (*P*) segurança *f* social; (*for old age*) pensão *f*, (*P*) reforma *f*; **~ worker** assistente *mf* social ● *n* reunião *f* social. **~ media** *n* mídia *m* social, (*P*) meios *mpl* de comunicação social; **~ networking site** *n* rede *f* social. **~ly** *adv* socialmente; (*meet*) em sociedade

socialis|t /ˈsəʊʃəlɪst/ *n* socialista *mf*. **~m** /-zəm/ *n* socialismo *m*

socialize /ˈsəʊʃəlaɪz/ *vi* socializar(-se), reunir-se em sociedade; **~ with** frequentar, conviver com

society /səˈsaɪətɪ/ *n* sociedade *f*

sociolog|y /səʊsɪˈɒlədʒɪ/ *n* sociologia *f*. **~ist** *n* sociólogo *m*

sock[1] /sɒk/ *n* meia *f* curta; (*men's*) meia *f* (curta), (*P*) peúga *f*; (*women's*) soquete *f*

sock[2] /sɒk/ *vt* ☒ (*hit*) esmurrar; dar um murro em 🅸

socket /ˈsɒkɪt/ *n* cavidade *f*; (*for lamp*) suporte *m*; *Electr* tomada *f*; (*of tooth*) alvéolo *m*

soda /ˈsəʊdə/ *n* soda *f*; **(baking) ~** *Culin* bicarbonato *m* de soda; **~(-water)** água *f* gasosa, soda *f* limonada, (*P*) água *f* gaseificada

sodden /ˈsɒdn/ *a* ensopado, empapado

sodium /ˈsəʊdɪəm/ *n* sódio *m*

sofa /ˈsəʊfə/ *n* sofá *m*

soft /sɒft/ *a* (**-er**, **-est**) (*not hard, feeble*) mole; (*not rough, not firm*) macio; (*gentle, not loud, not bright*) suave; (*tender-hearted*) sensível; ‹*fruit*› sem caroço; ‹*wood*› de coníferas; ‹*drink*› não-alcoólico; **~ spot** *fig* fraco *m*. **~ness** *n* moleza *f*; (*to touch*) maciez *f*; (*gentleness*) suavidade *f*, brandura *f*

soften /ˈsɒfn/ *vt/i* amaciar, amolecer; (*tone down, lessen*) abrandar

software /ˈsɒftweə(r)/ *n* software *m*

soggy /ˈsɒgɪ/ *a* (**-ier**, **-iest**) ensopado, empapado

soil[1] /sɔɪl/ *n* solo *m*, terra *f*

soil[2] /sɔɪl/ *vt/i* sujar(-se). **~ed** *a* sujo

solace /ˈsɒlɪs/ *n* consolo *m*; (*relief*) alívio *m*

solar /ˈsəʊlə(r)/ *a* solar

sold /səʊld/ ▶ SELL *a* **~ out** esgotado

soldier /ˈsəʊldʒə(r)/ *n* soldado *m* ● *vi* **~ on** 🅸 perseverar com afinco, batalhar 🅸

sole[1] /səʊl/ *n* (*of foot*) planta *f*, sola *f* do pé; (*of shoe*) sola *f*

sole[2] /səʊl/ *n* (*fish*) solha *f*

sole[3] /səʊl/ *a* único. **~ly** *adv* unicamente

solemn /'sɒləm/ *a* solene

solicit /sə'lɪsɪt/ *vt* (*seek*) solicitar ● *vi* (*of prostitute*) aproximar-se de homens na rua, angariar clientes

solicitor /sə'lɪsɪtə(r)/ *n* advogado *m*

solicitous /sə'lɪsɪtəs/ *a* solícito

solid /'sɒlɪd/ *a* sólido; (*not hollow*) maciço, cheio, compacto; ‹*gold etc*› maciço; ‹*meal*› substancial ● *n* sólido *m*; **~s** (*food*) alimentos *mpl* sólidos

solidarity /sɒlɪ'dærətɪ/ *n* solidariedade *f*

solidify /sə'lɪdɪfaɪ/ *vt/i* solidificar(-se)

solitary /'sɒlɪtrɪ/ *a* solitário, só; (*only one*) um único; **~ confinement** prisão *f* celular, solitária *f*

solitude /'sɒlɪtju:d/ *n* solidão *f*

solo /'səʊləʊ/ *n* (*pl* **os**) solo *m* ● *a* solo; **~ flight** voo *m* (a) solo. **~ist** *n* solista *mf*

soluble /'sɒljʊbl/ *a* solúvel

solution /sə'lu:ʃn/ *n* solução *f*

solv|e /sɒlv/ *vt* resolver, solucionar. **~able** *a* resolúvel, solúvel

solvent /'sɒlvənt/ *a* (dis)solvente; *Comm* solvente ● *n* (dis)solvente *m*

sombre /'sɒmbə(r)/ *a* sombrio

some /sʌm/ ● *a*

····➤ (*unspecified number*) uns, umas; **he ate ~ olives** ele comeu umas azeitonas; **have ~ more vegetables** coma mais uns vegetais; (*unspecified amount*) algum(a); **there's still ~ milk in the fridge** ainda há algum leite no congelador; **I need to buy ~ bread** preciso comprar pão; **would you like ~ coffee?** quer café?

····➤ (*certain, not all*) alguns, algumas; **~ people say...** algumas pessoas dizem...; **I like ~ modern writers** gosto de alguns escritores modernos

····➤ (*indefinite*) um(a)... qualquer, uns... quaisquer, umas... quaisquer; **~ man came to the house** um homem entrou na casa; **there must be ~ mistake** deve haver um erro qualquer; **for ~ reason** por algum motivo; **~ day next week** algum dia da semana que vem

····➤ (*considerable amount*) **we've known each other for ~ time** nos conhecemos há algum tempo

● *pron*

····➤ (*part of an amount*) um pouco; **would you like ~?** quer um pouco?; **if you want sugar, I'll give you ~** se quiser açúcar, lhe dou um pouco

····➤ (*a number of*) alguns, algumas; **here are ~ of our suggestions** aqui estão algumas das nossas sugestões; **~ are mine, but ~ aren't** alguns são meus, mas os outros não

● *adv*

····➤ (*approximately*) uns, umas; **~ thirty people attended the funeral** umas trinta pessoas estiveram no funeral

somebody /'sʌmbədɪ/ *pron* alguém ● *n* **be a ~** ser alguém

somehow /'sʌmhaʊ/ *adv* (*in some way*) de algum modo, de alguma maneira; (*for some reason*) por alguma razão

someone /'sʌmwʌn/ *pron & n* = SOMEBODY

somersault /'sʌməsɔ:lt/ *n* cambalhota *f*; (*in the air*) salto *m* mortal ● *vi* dar uma cambalhota/um salto mortal

something /'sʌmθɪŋ/ *pron & n* uma/alguma/qualquer coisa *f*, algo; **~ good/***etc* uma coisa boa/*etc*, qualquer coisa de bom/*etc*; **~ like** um pouco como

sometime /'sʌmtaɪm/ *adv* a certa altura, um dia ● *a* (*former*) antigo; **~ last summer** a certa altura no verão passado; **I'll go ~** hei-de ir um dia

sometimes /'sʌmtaɪmz/ *adv* às vezes, de vez em quando

somewhat /'sʌmwɒt/ *adv* um pouco, um tanto (ou quanto)

somewhere /'sʌmweə(r)/ *adv* (*position*) em algum lugar; (*direction*) para algum lugar

son /sʌn/ *n* filho *m*. **~-in-law** *n* (*pl* **~s-in-law**) genro *m*

sonata /sə'nɑ:tə/ *n Mus* sonata *f*

song /sɒŋ/ *n* canção *f*

soon /su:n/ *adv* (**-er, -est**) em breve, dentro em pouco, daqui a pouco; (*early*) cedo; **as ~ as possible** o mais rápido possível; **I would ~er stay** preferia ficar; **~ after** pouco depois; **~er or later** mais cedo ou mais tarde

soot /sʊt/ *n* fuligem *f*

sooth|e /su:ð/ *vt* acalmar, suavizar; ‹*pain*› aliviar. **~ing** *a* ‹*remedy*› calmante, suavizante; ‹*words*› (re)confortante

sophisticated /sə'fɪstɪkeɪtɪd/ *a* sofisticado, refinado, requintado; ‹*machine etc*› sofisticado

sopping /'sɒpɪŋ/ *a* encharcado, ensopado

soppy /'sɒpɪ/ *a* (**-ier**, **-iest**) [!] (*sentimental*) piegas; [!] (*silly*) bobo, (*P*) tonto

soprano /sə'prɑːnəʊ/ *n* (*pl* **~s**) & *a* soprano *mf*

sorbet /'sɔːbeɪ/ *n* (*water ice*) sorvete *m* feito sem leite

sorcerer /'sɔːsərə(r)/ *n* feiticeiro *m*

sordid /'sɔːdɪd/ *a* sórdido

sore /sɔː(r)/ *a* (**-er**, **-est**) dolorido; (*vexed*) aborrecido (**at, with** com) ● *n* ferida *f*; **have a ~ throat** ter a garganta inflamada, ter dores de garganta

sorely /'sɔːlɪ/ *adv* fortemente, seriamente

sorry /'sɒrɪ/ *a* (**-ier**, **-iest**) (*state, sight etc*) triste; **be ~ to/that** (*regretful*) sentir muito/que, lamentar que; **be ~ about/for** (*repentant*) ter pena de, estar arrependido de; **feel ~ for** ter pena de; **~!** desculpe!, perdão!

sort /sɔːt/ *n* gênero *m*, (*P*) género *m*, espécie *f*, qualidade *f*; **of ~s** [!] uma espécie de [!] *pej*; **out of ~s** indisposto ● *vt* separar por grupos; (*tidy*) arrumar; **~ out** ‹*problem*› resolver; (*arrange, separate*) separar, distribuir

soufflé /'suːfleɪ/ *n Culin* suflê *m*, (*P*) soufflé *m*

sought /sɔːt/ ▶ SEEK

soul /səʊl/ *n* alma *f*; **the life and ~ of** *fig* a alma *f* de *fig*

soulful /'səʊlfl/ *a* emotivo, expressivo, cheio de sentimento

S

sound[1] /saʊnd/ *n* som *m*, barulho *m*, ruído *m*; **~ barrier** barreira *f* de/do som ● *vt/i* soar; (*seem*) dar a impressão de; parecer (**as if** que); **~ a horn** tocar uma buzina, buzinar; **~ like** parecer ser, soar como. **~proof** *a* à prova de som ● *vt* fazer o isolamento sonoro de, isolar; **~track** *n* (*of film*) trilha *f* sonora, (*P*) banda *f* sonora

sound[2] /saʊnd/ *a* (**-er**, **-est**) (*healthy*) saudável, sadio; (*sensible*) sensato, acertado; (*secure*) firme, sólido; **~ asleep** profundamente adormecido. **~ly** *adv* solidamente

sound[3] /saʊnd/ *vt* (*test*) sondar; *Med* (*views*) auscultar

soup /suːp/ *n* sopa *f*

sour /'saʊə(r)/ *a* (**-er**, **-est**) azedo ● *vt/i* azedar, envinagrar

source /sɔːs/ *n* fonte *f*; (*of river*) nascente *f*

south /saʊθ/ *n* sul *m* ● *a* sul, do sul; (*of country, people etc*) meridional; **S~ Africa/America** África/América do Sul *f* ● *adv* a, ao/para (o) sul. **S~ African/American** *a* & *n* sul-africano/sul-americano *m*; **~-east** *n* sudeste *m*; **~-west** *n* sudoeste *m*. **~erly** /'sʌðəlɪ/ *a* do sul, meridional. **~ward(s)** *adv* para (o) sul

southern /'sʌðən/ *a* do sul, meridional, austral

souvenir /suːvə'nɪə(r)/ *n* recordação *f*, lembrança *f*

sovereign /'sɒvrɪn/ *n* & *a* soberano *m*. **~ty** *n* soberania *f*

Soviet /'səʊvɪət/ *a* soviético; **the ~ Union** a União Soviética

sow[1] /səʊ/ *vt* (*pt* **sowed**, *pp* **sowed** *or* **sown**) semear

sow[2] /saʊ/ *n Zool* porca *f*

soy /'sɔɪ/ *n* **~ sauce** molho *m* de soja

soya /'sɔɪə/ *n* soja *f*; **~-bean** semente *f* de soja

spa /spɑː/ *n* termas *fpl*

space /speɪs/ *n* espaço *m*; (*room*) lugar *m*; (*period*) espaço *m*, período *m* ● *a* ‹*research etc*› espacial ● *vt* **~ out** espaçar

space|craft /'speɪskrɑːft/ *n* (*pl invar*) **~ship** *n* nave *f* espacial

spacious /'speɪʃəs/ *a* espaçoso

spade /speɪd/ *n* (*gardener's*) pá *f* de ferro; (*child's*) pá *f*; **~s** *Cards* espadas *fpl*

spaghetti /spə'getɪ/ *n* espaguete *m*, (*P*) esparguete *m*

Spain /speɪn/ *n* Espanha *f*

spam /spæm/ *n* **Spam®** *Culin* marca barata de carne de porco enlatada; *Comput* spam *m* ● *vt* (*pres p etc.* **-mm-**) enviar spam

span[1] /spæn/ *n* (*of arch*) vão *m*; (*of wings*) envergadura *f*; (*of time*) espaço *m*, duração *f*; (*measure*) palmo *m* ● *vt* (*pt* **spanned**) (*extend across*) transpor; (*measure*) medir em palmos; (*in time*) abarcar, abranger, estender-se por

span[2] /spæn/ ▶ SPIN

Spaniard /'spænɪəd/ *n* espanhol *m*

Spanish /'spænɪʃ/ *a* espanhol ● *n Lang* espanhol *m*

spank /spæŋk/ *vt* dar palmadas or chineladas em. **~ing** *n* (*with hand*) palmada *f*; (*with slipper*) chinelada *f*

spanner /'spænə(r)/ *n* (*tool*) chave *f* de porcas; (*adjustable*) chave *f* inglesa

spar /spɑ:(r)/ *vi* (*pt* **sparred**) jogar boxe, esp para treino; *fig* (*argue*) discutir

spare /speə(r)/ *vt* (*not hurt; use with restraint*) poupar; (*afford to give*) dispensar, ceder; **have an hour to ~** dispor de uma hora; **have no time to ~** não ter tempo a perder ● *a* (*in reserve*) de reserva, de sobra; ‹*tyre*› sobressalente; ‹*bed*› extra; ‹*room*› de hóspedes ● *n* (*part*) sobressalente *m*; **~ time** horas *fpl* vagas, tempo *m* livre

sparing /'speərɪŋ/ *a* poupado; **be ~ of** poupar em, ser poupado com. **~ly** *adv* frugalmente

spark /spɑ:k/ *n* centelha *f*, faísca *f* ● *vt* lançar faíscas; **~ off** (*initiate*) desencadear, provocar

sparkle /'spɑ:kl/ *vi* cintilar, brilhar ● *n* brilho *m*, cintilação *f*

sparkling /'spɑ:klɪŋ/ *a* ‹*wine*› espumante

sparrow /'spærəʊ/ *n* pardal *m*

sparse /spɑ:s/ *a* esparso; ‹*hair*› ralo. **~ly** *adv* ‹*furnished etc*› escassamente

spasm /'spæzəm/ *n* (*of muscle*) espasmo *m*; (*of coughing, anger etc*) ataque *m*, acesso *m*

spasmodic /spæz'mɒdɪk/ *a* espasmódico; (*at irregular intervals*) intermitente

spastic /'spæstɪk/ *n* deficiente *mf* motor

spat /spæt/ ▶ SPIT[1]

spate /speɪt/ *n* (*in river*) enxurrada *f*, cheia *f*; **a ~ of** ‹*letters etc*› uma avalanche de

spatter /'spætə(r)/ *vt* salpicar (**with** de, com)

spawn /spɔ:n/ *n* ovas *fpl* ● *vi* desovar ● *vt* gerar em quantidade

speak /spi:k/ *vt/i* (*pt* **spoke**, *pp* **spoken**) falar (**to/with sb about sth** com alguém de/sobre alg coisa); (*say*) dizer; **~ out/ up** falar abertamente; (*louder*) falar mais alto; **~ one's mind** dizer o que se pensa; **so to ~** por assim dizer; **English/ Portuguese spoken** fala-se inglês/ português

speaker /'spi:kə(r)/ *n* (*in public*) orador *m*; (*loudspeaker*) alto-falante *m*; (*of a language*) pessoa *f* de língua nativa, falante *mf* nativo/a de uma língua

spear /spɪə(r)/ *n* lança *f*

spearhead /'spɪəhed/ *n* ponta *f* de lança ● *vt* (*lead*) estar à frente de, encabeçar

special /'speʃl/ *a* especial. **~ity** /-ɪ'ælətɪ/ *n* especialidade *f*. **~ly** *adv* especialmente. **~ty** *n* especialidade *f*

specialist /'speʃəlɪst/ *n* especialista *mf*

specialize /'speʃəlaɪz/ *vi* especializar-se (**in** em). **~d** *a* especializado

species /'spi:ʃɪz/ *n* (*pl invar*) espécie *f*

specific /spə'sɪfɪk/ *a* específico. **~ally** *adv* especificamente, explicitamente

specif|y /'spesɪfaɪ/ *vt* especificar. **~ication** /-ɪ'keɪʃn/ *n* especificação *f*. **~ications** *npl* (*of work etc*) caderno *m* de encargos

specimen /'spesɪmɪn/ *n* espécime(n) *m*, amostra *f*

speck /spek/ *n* (*stain*) mancha *f* pequena; (*dot*) pontinho *m*, pinta *f*; (*particle*) grão *m*

speckled /'spekld/ *a* salpicado, manchado

specs /speks/ *npl* [!] óculos *mpl*

spectacle /'spektəkl/ *n* espetáculo *m*; **(pair of) ~s** (par *m* de) óculos *mpl*

spectacular /spek'tækjʊlə(r)/ *a* espetacular

spectator /spek'teɪtə(r)/ *n* espectador *m*

spectrum /'spektrəm/ *n* (*pl* **-tra**) espectro *m*; (*of ideas etc*) faixa *f*, gama *f*, leque *m*

speculat|e /'spekjʊleɪt/ *vi* especular; fazer especulações or conjecturas; (*P*) conjeturas (**about** sobre); *Comm* especular; fazer especulação (**in** em). **~ion** /-'leɪʃn/ *n* especulação *f*, conjetura *f*; *Comm* especulação *f*. **~or** *n* especulador *m*

speech /spi:tʃ/ *n* (*faculty*) fala *f*; (*diction*) elocução *f*; (*dialect*) falar *m*; (*address*) discurso *m*. **~less** *a* mudo; sem fala, (*P*) sem palavras (**with** com, de)

speed /spi:d/ *n* velocidade *f*, rapidez *f* ● *vt/i* (*pt* **sped**, **move**) (*send*) despedir, mandar; (*drive too fast*) ultrapassar o limite de velocidade; (*drive too fast*) ultrapassar o limite de velocidade; **~ camera** radar *m*; **~ limit** limite *m* de velocidade; **~ up** acelerar(-se). **~ dating** *n*: forma rápida de conhecer vários possíveis namorados, através de conversas breves; **~ dial** *n* discagem *f* rápida, (*P*) marcação *f* rápida. **~ing** *n* excesso *m* de velocidade

speedometer /spi:'dɒmɪtə(r)/ *n* velocímetro *m*

speed|y /ˈspiːdɪ/ *a* (**-ier**, **-iest**) rápido; (*prompt*) pronto. **~ily** *adv* rapidamente; (*promptly*) prontamente

spell[1] /spel/ *n* (*magic*) sortilégio *m*

spell[2] /spel/ *vt/i* (*pt* **spelled**, *or* **spelt**) escrever; *fig* (*mean*) significar; ter como resultado; **~ out** soletrar; *fig* (*explain*) explicar claramente. **~ing** *n* ortografia *f*

spell[3] /spel/ *n* (*short period*) período *m* curto, breve espaço *m* de tempo; (*turn*) turno *m*

spend /spend/ *vt* (*pt* **spent**) ‹*money, energy*› gastar (**on** em); ‹*time, holiday*› passar

spendthrift /ˈspendθrɪft/ *n* perdulário *m*, esbanjador *m*

spent /spent/ ▶ SPEND *a* (*used*) gasto

sperm /spɜːm/ *n* (*pl* **~s** or **~**) (*semen*) esperma *m*, sêmen *m*, (*P*) sémen *m*; (*cell*) espermatozóide *m*

spew /spjuː/ *vt/i* vomitar, lançar

sphere /sfɪə(r)/ *n* esfera *f*

spic|e /spaɪs/ *n* especiaria *f*, condimento *m*; *fig* picante *m* ● *vt* condimentar. **~y** *a* condimentado; *fig* picante

spider /ˈspaɪdə(r)/ *n* aranha *f*

spik|e /spaɪk/ *n* (*of metal etc*) bico *m*, espigão *m*, ponta *f*. **~y** *a* guarnecido de bicos or pontas, pontiagudo

spill /spɪl/ *vt/i* (*pt* **spilled**, *or* **spilt**) derramar(-se), entornar(-se), espalhar(-se); **~ over** transbordar, extravasar

spin /spɪn/ *vt/i* (*pt* **spun**, *pres p* **spinning**) ‹*wool, cotton*› fiar; ‹*web*› tecer; ‹*turn*› (fazer) girar, (fazer) rodopiar; **~ out** ‹*money, story*› fazer durar; ‹*time*› (fazer) parar ● *n* volta *f*; *Aviat* parafuso *m*; **go for a ~** dar uma volta or um giro *or* (*P*) um passeio. **~ drier** *n* centrifugadora *f* para a roupa, secadora *f*, (*P*) máquina *f* de secar (a roupa); **~-off** *n* bônus *m*, (*P*) bónus *m* inesperado; (*by-product*) derivado *m*

spinach /ˈspɪnɪdʒ/ *n* (*plant*) espinafre *m*; (*as food*) espinafres *mpl*

spindl|e /ˈspɪndl/ *n* roca *f*, fuso *m*; *Mech* eixo *m*. **~y** *a* alto e magro; (*of plant*) espigado

spine /spaɪn/ *n* espinha *f*, coluna *f* vertebral; (*prickle*) espinho *m*, pico *m*; (*of book*) lombada *f*

spineless /ˈspaɪnlɪs/ *a fig* (*cowardly*) covarde; sem fibra *fig*

spinster /ˈspɪnstə(r)/ *n* solteira *f*; *pej* solteirona *f*

spiral /ˈspaɪərəl/ *a* (em) espiral; (*staircase*) em caracol ● *n* espiral *f* ● *vi* (*pt* **spiralled**) subir em espiral

spire /ˈspaɪə(r)/ *n* agulha *f*, flecha *f*

spirit /ˈspɪrɪt/ *n* espírito *m*; (*boldness*) coragem *f*, brio *m*; **~s** (*morale*) moral *m*; (*drink*) bebidas *fpl* alcoólicas; **in high ~s** alegre ● *vt* **~ away** dar sumiço em, arrebatar

spirited /ˈspɪrɪtɪd/ *a* fogoso; ‹*attack, defence*› vigoroso, enérgico

spiritual /ˈspɪrɪtʃʊəl/ *a* espiritual

spiritualism /ˈspɪrɪtʃʊəlɪzəm/ *n* espiritismo *m*

spit[1] /spɪt/ *vt/i* (*pt* **spat**, *or* **spit**, *pres p* **spitting**) cuspir; (*of rain*) chuviscar; (*of cat*) bufar ● *n* cuspe *m*, (*P*) cuspo *m*; **the ~ting image of** o retrato vivo de, a cara chapada de [!]

spit[2] /spɪt/ *n* (*for meat*) espeto *m*; (*of land*) restinga *f*, (*P*) língua *f* de terra

spite /spaɪt/ *n* má vontade *f*, despeito *m*, rancor *m* ● *vt* aborrecer, mortificar. **in ~ of** a despeito de, apesar de. **~ful** *a* rancoroso, maldoso

splash /splæʃ/ *vt* salpicar, respingar ● *vi* esparrinhar, salpicar, esparramar-se; **~ (about)** chapinhar ● *n* (*act, mark*) salpico *m*; (*sound*) chape *m*; (*of colour*) mancha *f*; **make a ~** (*striking display*) fazer um vistão, causar furor

splendid /ˈsplendɪd/ *a* esplêndido, magnífico; (*excellent*) estupendo [!]; ótimo

splendour /ˈsplendə(r)/ *n* esplendor *m*

splint /splɪnt/ *n Med* tala *f*

splinter /ˈsplɪntə(r)/ *n* lasca *f*, estilhaço *m*; (*under the skin*) farpa *f*, lasca *f* ● *vi* estilhaçar-se, lascar-se; **~ group** grupo *m* dissidente

split /splɪt/ *vt/i* (*pt* **split**, *pres p* **splitting**) rachar, fender(-se); (*divide, share*) dividir; (*tear*) romper(-se) ● *n* racha *f*, fenda *f*; (*share*) quinhão *m*, parte *f*; *Pol* cisão *f*; **~ on** [x] (*inform on*) denunciar; **~ one's sides** rebentar de riso, (*P*) desmanchar-se a rir; **~ up** (*of couple*) separar-se; **a ~ second** uma fração de segundo; **~ting headache** dor *f* de cabeça forte

splurge /splɜːdʒ/ *n* [!] espalhafato *m*; estardalhaço *m* ● *vi* [!] (*spend*) gastar os tubos, (*P*) gastar à doida [!]

splutter /ˈsplʌtə(r)/ *vi* falar cuspindo; ‹*engine*› cuspir; ‹*fat*› crepitar

spoil /spɔɪl/ *vt* (*pt* **spoilt** *or* **spoiled**) estragar; (*pamper*) mimar ● *n* **~(s)** (*plunder*) despojo(s) *m(pl)*, espólios *mpl*. **~sport** *n* desmancha-prazeres *mf invar.*

~t *a* (*pampered*) mimado, estragado com mimos

spoke[1] /spəʊk/ *n* raio *m*

spoke[2] **spoken** /spəʊk, 'spəʊkən/ ▶ SPEAK

spokes|man /'spəʊksmən/ *n* (*pl* **-men**); **~woman** *n* (*pl* **-women**) porta-voz *mf*

sponge /spʌndʒ/ *n* esponja *f* ● *vt* (*clean*) lavar com esponja; (*wipe*) limpar com esponja ● *vi* **~ on** [!] (*cadge*) viver à(s) custa(s) de. **~ bag** *n* bolsa *f* de toalete; **~ cake** *n* pão de ló *m*. **~r** /-ə(r)/ *n* [!] parasita *mf* ⊠

sponsor /'spɒnsə(r)/ *n* patrocinador *m*; (*for membership*) (sócio) proponente *m* ● *vt* patrocinar; (*for membership*) propor. **~ship** *n* patrocínio *m*

spontaneous /spɒn'teɪnɪəs/ *a* espontâneo

spoof /spu:f/ *n* [!] paródia *f*

spooky /'spu:kɪ/ *a* (**-ier**, **-iest**) [!] fantasmagórico; que dá arrepios

spool /spu:l/ *n* (*of sewing machine*) bobina *f*; (*for thread, line*) carretel *m*, (*P*) carrinho *m*

spoon /spu:n/ *n* colher *f*. **~-feed** *vt* (*pt* **-fed**) alimentar de colher; *fig* (*help*) dar na bandeja para *fig*, (*P*) dar de bandeja a *fig*. **~ful** *n* colherada *f*

sporadic /spə'rædɪk/ *a* esporádico, acidental

sport /spɔ:t/ *n* esporte *m*, (*P*) desporto *m*; **(good) ~** ⊠ (*person*) gente *f* fina, (*P*) bom tipo *m*, (*P*) tipo *m* fixe [!]; **~s car/ coat** carro *m* /casaco *m* esporte *or* (*P*) de desporto ● *vt* (*display*) exibir, ostentar. **~y** *a* [!] esportivo; (*P*) desportivo

sporting /'spɔ:tɪŋ/ *a* esportivo, (*P*) desportivo; **a ~ chance** uma certa possibilidade de sucesso, uma boa chance

sports|man *n* (*pl* **-men**); **~woman** (*pl* **women**) desportista *mf*. **~manship** *n* (*spirit*) espírito *m* esportivo, (*P*) desportivo; (*activity*) esportismo *m*, (*P*) desportismo *m*

spot /spɒt/ *n* (*mark, stain*) mancha *f*; (*in pattern*) pinta *f*, bola *f*; (*drop*) gota *f*; (*place*) lugar *m*, ponto *m*; (*pimple*) borbulha *f*, espinha *f*; *TV* spot *m* televisivo; **a ~ of** [!] um pouco de; **be in a ~** [!] estar numa encrenca [!], (*P*) estar metido numa alhada [!]; **on the ~** no local; (*there and then*) ali mesmo, logo ali ● *vt* (*pt* **spotted**) manchar; [!] (*detect*) descobrir; detectar [!]; **~ check** inspeção *f* de surpresa; (*of cars*) fiscalização *f* de surpresa. **~ on** *a* [!] certo, exacto. **~ted** *a* manchado; (*with dots*) de pintas, de bolas; (*animal*) malhado. **~ty** *a* (*with pimples*) com borbulhas

spotless /'spɒtlɪs/ *a* impecável, imaculado

spotlight /'spɒtlaɪt/ *n* foco *m*; *Cine, Theat* refletor *m*, holofote *m*

spouse /spaʊz/ *n* cônjuge *mf*, esposo *m*

spout /spaʊt/ *n* (*of vessel*) bico *m*; (*of liquid*) esguicho *m*, jorro *m*; (*pipe*) cano *m* ● *vi* jorrar, esguichar; **up the ~** ⊠ (*ruined*) liquidado ⊠ (*P*) acabado

sprain /spreɪn/ *n* entorse *f*, mau jeito *m* ● *vt* torcer, dar um mau jeito a

sprang /spræŋ/ ▶ SPRING

sprawl /sprɔ:l/ *vi* (*sit*) estirar-se, esparramar-se; (*fall*) estatelar-se; ‹*town*› estender-se, espraiar-se

spray[1] /spreɪ/ *n* (*of flowers*) raminho *m*, ramalhete *m*

spray[2] /spreɪ/ *n* (*water*) borrifo *m*, salpico *m*; (*from sea*) borrifo *m* de espuma; (*device*) bomba *f*, aerossol *m*; (*for perfume*) vaporizador *m*, atomizador *m* ● *vt* aspergir, borrifar, pulverizar; (*with insecticide*) pulverizar

spread /spred/ *vt/i* (*pt* **spread**) (*extend, stretch*) estender(-se); ‹*news, fear, illness etc*› alastrar(-se), espalhar(-se), propagar(-se); ‹*butter etc*› passar, (*P*) barrar; ‹*wings*› abrir ● *n* (*expanse*) expansão *f*, extensão *f*; (*spreading*) propagação *f*; (*paste*) pasta *f* para passar no pão, (*P*) para barrar no pão; [!] (*meal*) banquete *m*. **~sheet** *n Comput* folha *f* de cálculo

spree /spri:/ *n* **go on a ~** [!] cair na farra, (*P*) ir para a farra

sprightly /'spraɪtlɪ/ *a* (**-ier**, **-iest**) vivo, animado

spring /sprɪŋ/ *vi* (*pt* **sprang**, *pp* **sprung**) (*arise*) nascer; (*jump*) saltar, pular; **~ up** surgir ● *vt* (*produce suddenly*) sair-se com; (*a surprise*) fazer (**on sb** a alguém); **~ from** vir de, originar-se de, provir de ● *n* salto *m*, pulo *m*; (*device*) mola *f*; (*season*) primavera *f*; (*of water*) fonte *f*, nascente *f*; **~ onion** cebolinha *f*. **~-clean** *vt* fazer limpeza geral

springboard /'sprɪŋbɔ:d/ *n* trampolim *m*

springtime /'sprɪŋtaɪm/ *n* primavera *f*

springy /'sprɪŋɪ/ *a* (**-ier**, **-iest**) elástico

sprinkle /'sprɪŋkl/ *vt* (*with liquid*) borrifar, salpicar; (*with salt, flour*) polvilhar (**with** de); **~ sand**/*etc* espalhar areia/*etc*. **~r** /-ə(r)/ *n* (*in garden*) regador *m*; (*for fires*) sprinkler *m*

sprinkling /ˈsprɪŋklɪŋ/ *n* (*amount*) pequena quantidade *f*; (*number*) pequeno número *m*

sprint /sprɪnt/ *n Sport* corrida *f* de pequena distância, sprint *m* ● *vi* correr em sprint or a toda a velocidade; *Sport* correr

sprout /spraʊt/ *vt/i* brotar, germinar; (*put forth*) deitar ● *n* (*on plant etc*) broto *m*; **(Brussels) ~s** couves *f* de Bruxelas

sprung /sprʌŋ/ ▶ SPRING *a* ‹*mattress etc*› de molas

spry /spraɪ/ *a* (**spryer**, **spryest**) vivo, ativo; (*nimble*) ágil

spud /spʌd/ *n* ⊠ batata *f*

spun /spʌn/ ▶ SPIN

spur /spɜː(r)/ *n* (*of rider*) espora *f*; *fig* (*stimulus*) aguilhão *m*; *fig* espora *f fig* ● *vt* (*pt* **spurred**) esporear, picar com esporas; *fig* (*incite*) aguilhoar; esporear; **on the ~ of the moment** impulsivamente, no calor do momento

spurn /spɜːn/ *vt* desdenhar, desprezar, rejeitar

spurt /spɜːt/ *vi* jorrar, esguichar; *fig* (*accelerate*) acelerar subitamente; dar um arranco súbito ● *n* jorro *m*, esguicho *m*; (*of energy, speed*) arranco *m*, arrancada *f*, surto *m*

spy /spaɪ/ *n* espião *m* ● *vt* (*make out*) avistar, descortinar ● *vi* **~ (on)** espiar, espionar; **~ out** descobrir. **~ing** *n* espionagem *f*

squabble /ˈskwɒbl/ *vi* discutir, brigar ● *n* briga *f*, disputa *f*

squad /skwɒd/ *n Mil* pelotão *m*; (*team*) equipe *f*, (*P*) equipa *f*; **firing ~** pelotão *m* de fuzilamento; **flying ~** brigada *f* móvel

squadron /ˈskwɒdrən/ *n Mil* esquadrão *m*; *Aviat* esquadrilha *f*; *Naut* esquadra *f*

squal|id /ˈskwɒlɪd/ *a* esquálido, sórdido. **~or** *n* sordidez *f*

squall /skwɔːl/ *n* borrasca *f*

squander /ˈskwɒndə(r)/ *vt* desperdiçar

square /skweə(r)/ *n* quadrado *m*; (*in town*) largo *m*, praça *f*; (*T-square*) régua-tê *f*; (*set square*) esquadro *m*; **go back to ~ one** recomeçar tudo do princípio, voltar à estaca zero ● *a* (*of shape*) quadrado; ‹*metre, mile etc*› quadrado; (*honest*) direito, honesto; (*of meal*) abundante, substancial; **(all) ~** (*quits*) quite(s); **~ brackets** parênteses *mpl* retos ● *vt Math* elevar ao quadrado; (*settle*) acertar; **~ up to** enfrentar ● *vi* (*agree*) concordar. **~ly** *adv* diretamente; (*fairly*) honestamente

squash /skwɒʃ/ *vt* (*crush*) esmagar; (*squeeze*) espremer; (*crowd*) comprimir, apertar ● *n* (*game*) squash *m*; *Amer* (*marrow*) abóbora *f*; **lemon ~** limonada *f*; **orange ~** laranjada *f*. **~y** *a* mole

squat /skwɒt/ *vi* (*pt* **squatted**) acocorar-se, agachar-se; (*be a squatter*) ser ocupante ilegal ● *a* (*dumpy*) atarracado. **~ter** *n* ocupante *mf* ilegal de casa vazia, posseiro *m*

squawk /skwɔːk/ *n* grasnido *m*, crocito *m* ● *vi* grasnar, crocitar

squeak /skwiːk/ *n* guincho *m*, chio *m*; (*of door, shoes etc*) rangido *m* ● *vi* guinchar, chiar; (*of door, shoes etc*) ranger. **~y** *a* ‹*shoe etc*› que range; ‹*voice*› esganiçado

squeal /skwiːl/ *vi* dar gritos agudos, guinchar ● *n* grito *m* agudo, guincho *m*; **~ (on)** ⊠ (*inform on*) delatar, (*P*) denunciar

squeamish /ˈskwiːmɪʃ/ *a* (*nauseated*) que enjoa à toa, impressionável, delicado

squeeze /skwiːz/ *vt* ‹*lemon, sponge etc*› espremer; ‹*hand, arm*› apertar; (*extract*) arrancar; extorquir (**from** de) ● *vi* (*force one's way*) passar à força, meter-se por ● *n* aperto *m*, apertão *m*; (*hug*) abraço *m*; *Comm* restrições *fpl* de crédito

squid /skwɪd/ *n* lula *f*

squiggle /ˈskwɪgl/ *n* rabisco *m*, floreado *m*

squint /skwɪnt/ *vi* ser estrábico or vesgo; (*with half-shut eyes*) franzir os olhos, (*P*) semicerrar os olhos ● *n Med* estrabismo *m*

squirm /skwɜːm/ *vi* (re)torcer-se, contorcer-se

squirrel /ˈskwɪrəl/ *n* esquilo *m*

squirt /skwɜːt/ *vt/i* esguichar ● *n* esguicho *m*

stab /stæb/ *vt* (*pt* **stabbed**) apunhalar; (*knife*) esfaquear ● *n* punhalada *f*; (*with knife*) facada *f*; (*of pain*) pontada *f*; [!] (*attempt*) tentativa *f*

stabilize /ˈsteɪbəlaɪz/ *vt* estabilizar

stab|le[1] /ˈsteɪbl/ *a* (**-er**, **-est**) estável. **~ility** /stəˈbɪlətɪ/ *n* estabilidade *f*

stable[2] /ˈsteɪbl/ *n* cavalariça *f*, estrebaria *f*

stack /stæk/ *n* pilha *f*, montão *m*; (*of hay etc*) meda *f* ● *vt* ~ **(up)** empilhar, amontoar

stadium /'steɪdɪəm/ *n* estádio *m*

staff /stɑːf/ *n* pessoal *m*; (*in school*) professores *mpl*; *Mil* estado-maior *m*; (*stick*) bordão *m*, cajado *m*; (*pl* **staves**) *Mus* pauta *f* ● *vt* prover de pessoal

stag /stæg/ *n* veado (macho) *m*, cervo *m*. ~ **party** *n* [!] reunião *f* masculina; (*before wedding*) despedida *f* de solteiro

stage /steɪdʒ/ *n Theat* palco *m*; (*phase*) fase *f*, ponto *m*; (*platform in hall*) estrado *m*; **go on the** ~ seguir a carreira teatral, ir para teatro [!]; ~ **door** entrada *f* dos artistas ● *vt* encenar, pôr em cena; *fig* (*organize*) organizar. **~-fright** *n* nervosismo *m*, medo *m* do palco

stagger /'stægə(r)/ *vi* vacilar, cambalear ● *vt* (*shock*) atordoar, chocar; ‹*holidays etc*› escalonar. **~ing** *a* atordoador, chocante

stagnant /'stægnənt/ *a* estagnado, parado

stagnat|e /stæg'neɪt/ *vi* estagnar

stain /steɪn/ *vt* manchar, pôr nódoa em; (*colour*) tingir, dar cor a ● *n* mancha *f*, nódoa *f*; (*colouring*) corante *m*; **~ed glass window** vitral *m*; **~less steel** aço *m* inoxidável

stair /steə(r)/ *n* degrau *m*; **~s** escada(s) *f(pl)*

stair|case /'steəkeɪs/, **~way** /-weɪ/ *ns* escada(s) *f(pl)*, escadaria *f*

stake /steɪk/ *n* (*post*) estaca *f*, poste *m*; (*wager*) parada *f*, aposta *f*; **at** ~ em jogo; **have a ~ in** ter interesse em ● *vt* ‹*area*› demarcar, delimitar; (*wager*) jogar, apostar; ~ **a claim to** reivindicar

stale /steɪl/ *a* (**-er**, **-est**) estragado, velho; ‹*bread*› duro, mofado; ‹*smell*› rançoso; ‹*air*› viciado; ‹*news*› velho

stalemate /'steɪlmeɪt/ *n* (*chess*) empate *m*; *fig* (*deadlock*) impasse *m*; beco sem saída *m*

stalk[1] /stɔːk/ *n* (*of plant*) caule *m*

stalk[2] /stɔːk/ *vi* andar com um ar empertigado ● *vt* ‹*prey*› perseguir furtivamente, tocaiar

stall /stɔːl/ *n* (*in stable*) baia *f*; (*in market*) tenda *f*, barraca *f*; **~s** *Theat* poltronas *fpl* de orquestra; *Cinema* plateia *f* ● *vt/i Auto* enguiçar, (*P*) ir abaixo; ~ **(for time)** ganhar tempo, empatar

stalwart /'stɔːlwət/ *a* forte, rijo; (*supporter*) fiel

stamina /'stæmɪnə/ *n* resistência *f*

stammer /'stæmə(r)/ *vt/i* gaguejar ● *n* gagueira *f*, (*P*) gaguez *f*

stamp /stæmp/ *vt/i* ~ **(one's foot)** bater com o pé (no chão), pisar com força ● *vt* estampar; ‹*letter*› estampilhar, selar; (*with rubber stamp*) carimbar; ~ **out** ‹*fire, rebellion etc*› esmagar; ‹*disease*› erradicar ● *n* estampa *f*; (*for postage*) selo *m*; *fig* (*mark*) cunho *m*; **rubber** ~ carimbo *m*. ~ **collecting** *n* filatelia *f*

stampede /stæm'piːd/ *n* (*scattering*) debandada *f*; (*of horses, cattle etc*) debandada *f*; *fig* (*rush*) corrida *f* ● *vt/i* (fazer) debandar; ‹*horses, cattle etc*› tresmalhar

stance /stæns/ *n* posição *f*, postura *f*

stand /stænd/ *vi* (*pt* **stood**) estar em pé; (*keep upright position*) ficar em pé; (*rise*) levantar-se; (*be situated*) encontrar-se, ficar, situar-se; *Pol* candidatar-se (**for** por); ~ **back** recuar; ~ **by** or **around** estar parado sem fazer nada; ~ **by** (*be ready*) estar a postos; ‹*promise, person*› manter-se fiel a; ~ **down** desistir, retirar-se; ~ **out** (*be conspicuous*) sobressair; ~ **still** estar/ficar imóvel; ~ **still!** não se mexa!, fique, quieto!; ~ **to reason** ser lógico; ~ **up** levantar-se, pôr-se em or de pé ● *vt* pôr (de pé), colocar; (*tolerate*) suportar, aguentar; ~ **a chance** ter uma possibilidade; ~ **for** representar, simbolizar; [!] (*tolerate*) aturar; ~ **in for** substituir; ~ **up for** defender, apoiar; ~ **up to** enfrentar ● *n* posição *f*; (*support*) apoio *m*; *Mil* resistência *f*; (*at fair*) stand *m*, pavilhão *m*; (*in street*) quiosque *m*; (*for spectators*) arquibancada *f*, (*P*) bancada *f*; *Amer* (*witness box*) banco *m* das testemunhas. **~by** *a* (*for emergency*) de reserva; ‹*ticket*› de stand-by, (*P*) de reserva ● *n* (*at airport*) stand-by *m*; **on ~by** *Mil* de prontidão; *Med* de plantão; **~-in** *n* substituto *m*, suplente *mf*; **~-offish** *a* [!] (*aloof*) reservado, distante

standard /'stændəd/ *n* norma *f*, padrão *m*; (*level*) nível *m*; (*flag*) estandarte *m*, bandeira *f*; **~s** (*morals*) princípios *mpl*; ~ **of living** padrão *m* de vida, (*P*) nível *m* de vida ● *a* regulamentar; (*average*) standard, normal; ~ **lamp** candeeiro *m* de pé

standardize /'stændədaɪz/ *vt* padronizar

standing /'stændɪŋ/ *a* em pé, de pé *invar*; ‹*army, committee etc*› permanente ● *n* posição *f*; (*reputation*) prestígio *m*; (*duration*) duração *f*; ~ **order** (*at bank*) ordem *f* permanente, (*P*) autorização *f* de pagamento por transferência bancária

standpoint /'stændpɔɪnt/ *n* ponto *m* de vista

standstill /'stændstɪl/ *n* paralisação *f*; **at a ~** parado, paralisado; **bring/ come to a ~** (fazer) parar, paralisar(-se), imobilizar(-se)

stank /stæŋk/ ▶ STINK

staple[1] /'steɪpl/ *n* (*for paper*) grampo *m*, (*P*) agrafo *m* ● *vt* ‹*paper*› grampear, (*P*) agrafar. **~r** /-ə(r)/ *n* grampeador *m*, (*P*) agrafador *m*

staple[2] /'steɪpl/ *a* principal, básico ● *n* *Comm* artigo *m* básico

star /stɑ:(r)/ *n* estrela *f*; (*cinema*) estrela *f*, vedete *f*, (*P*) vedeta *f*; (*celebrity*) celebridade *f* ● *vt* (*pt* **starred**) (*of film*) ter no papel principal, (*P*) ter como ator principal ● *vi* **~ in** ser a vedete *or* (*P*) vedeta, ter o papel principal em. **~dom** *n* celebridade *f*, estrelato *m*

starch /stɑ:tʃ/ *n* amido *m*, fécula *f*; (*for clothes*) goma *f* ● *vt* pôr em goma, engomar. **~y** *a* (*of food*) farináceo, feculento; *fig* (*of person*) rígido; formal

stare /steə(r)/ *vi* **~ at** olhar fixamente ● *n* olhar *m* fixo

stark /stɑ:k/ *a* (**-er**, **-est**) (*desolate*) árido, desolado; (*severe*) austero, severo; (*utter*) completo, rematado; ‹*fact etc*› brutal ● *adv* completamente; **~ naked** nu em pelo, (*P*) em pelota [!]

starling /'stɑ:lɪŋ/ *n* estorninho *m*

starry /'stɑ:rɪ/ *a* estrelado. **~-eyed** *a* [!] sonhador; idealista

start /stɑ:t/ *vt/i* começar; ‹*machine*› ligar, pôr em andamento; ‹*fashion etc*› lançar; (*leave*) partir; (*cause*) causar, provocar; (*jump*) sobressaltar-se, estremecer; (*of car*) arrancar, partir ● *n* começo *m*, início *m*; (*of race*) largada *f*, partida *f*; (*lead*) avanço *m*; (*jump*) sobressalto *m*, estremecimento *m*; **by fits and ~s** aos arrancos, intermitentemente; **for a ~** para começar; **give sb a ~** sobressaltar alguém, pregar um susto a alguém; **~ to do** começar a or pôr-se a fazer. **~er** *n Auto* arranque *m*; (*competitor*) corredor *m*; *Culin* entrada *f*. **~ing point** *n* ponto *m* de partida

startl|e /'stɑ:tl/ *vt* (*make jump*) sobressaltar, pregar um susto a; (*shock*) alarmar, chocar. **~ing** *a* alarmante; (*surprising*) surpreendente

starv|e /stɑ:v/ *vi* (*suffer*) passar fome; (*die*) morrer de fome; **be ~ing** [!] (*very hungry*) ter muita fome, (*P*) estar esfomeado, morrer de fome [!] ● *vt* fazer passar fome a; (*deprive*) privar. **~ation** /-'veɪʃn/ *n* fome *f*

stash /stæʃ/ *vt* [x] guardar; esconder; enfurnar [!]

state /steɪt/ *n* estado *m*, condição *f*; (*pomp*) pompa *f*, gala *f*; *Pol* Estado *m*; **in a ~** muito abalado ● *a* de Estado, do Estado; ‹*school*› público; ‹*visit etc*› oficial ● *vt* afirmar (**that** que); ‹*views*› exprimir; (*fix*) marcar, fixar

stately /'steɪtlɪ/ *a* (**-ier**, **-iest**) majestoso; **~ home** solar *m*, palácio *m*

statement /'steɪtmənt/ *n* declaração *f*; (*of account*) extrato *m* de conta

> *i*
> **state school** Na Grã-Bretanha, é um colégio federal de educação gratuita, financiado direta ou indiretamente pelo governo. Inclui educação primária e secundária, colégios especializados, *comprehensive schools*, etc.

statesman /'steɪtsmən/ *n* (*pl* **-men**) homem *m* de estado, estadista *m*

static /'stætɪk/ *a* estático ● *n Radio, TV* estática *f*, interferência *f*

station /'steɪʃn/ *n* (*position*) posto *m*; (*rail, bus, radio*) estação *f*; (*rank*) condição *f*, posição *f* social ● *vt* colocar; **~ed at** or **in** *Mil* estacionado em. **~ wagon** *n* perua *f*, (*P*) carrinha *f*

stationary /'steɪʃnrɪ/ *a* estacionário, parado, imóvel; ‹*vehicle*› estacionado, parado

stationer /'steɪʃənə(r)/ *n* dono *m* de papelaria; **~'s shop** papelaria *f*. **~y** *n* artigos *mpl* de papelaria; (*writing paper*) papel *m* de carta

statistic /stə'tɪstɪk/ *n* dado *m* estatístico. **~s** *n* (*as a science*) estatística *f*. **~al** *a* estatístico

statue /'stætʃu:/ *n* estátua *f*

stature /'stætʃə(r)/ *n* estatura *f*

status /'steɪtəs/ *n* (*pl* **-uses**) situação *f*, posição *f*, categoria *f*; (*prestige*) prestígio *m*, importância *f*, status *m*; **~ quo** status quo *m*; **~ symbol** símbolo *m* de status

statut|e /'stætju:t/ *n* estatuto *m*, lei *f*. **~ory** /-ʊtrɪ/ *a* estatutário, regulamentar; ‹*holiday*› legal

staunch /stɔ:ntʃ/ *a* (**-er**, **-est**) ‹*friend*› fiel, leal

S

stave /steɪv/ *n Mus* pauta *f* ● *vt* **~ off** (*keep off*) conjurar, evitar; (*delay*) adiar

stay /steɪ/ *vi* estar, ficar, permanecer; (*dwell temporarily*) ficar, alojar-se, hospedar-se; (*spend time*) demorar-se; **~ behind** ficar para trás; **~ in** ficar em casa; **~ put** [!] não se mexer; **~ up (late)** deitar-se tarde, ficar acordado até tarde ● *vt* ‹*hunger*› enganar ● *n* estada *f*, visita *f*, permanência *f*. **~ing power** *n* resistência *f*

steadfast /'stedfɑːst/ *a* firme, constante

stead|y /'stedɪ/ *a* (**-ier**, **-iest**) (*stable*) estável, firme, seguro; (*regular*) regular, constante; ‹*hand, voice*› firme ● *vt* firmar, fixar, estabilizar; (*calm*) acalmar; **go ~y with** [!] namorar, ter uma relação estável com. **~ily** *adv* firmemente; (*regularly*) regularmente, de modo constante

steak /steɪk/ *n* bife *m*

steal /stiːl/ *vt/i* (*pt* **stole**, *pp* **stolen**) roubar (**from sb** de alguém); **~ away/in/***etc* sair/entrar/*etc* furtivamente, esgueirar-se; **~ the show** pôr os outros na sombra, roubar a atenção de todos

stealth /stelθ/ *n* **by ~** furtivamente, na calada, às escondidas. **~y** *a* furtivo

steam /stiːm/ *n* vapor *m* de água; (*on window*) condensação *f*; **~ iron** ferro *m* a vapor ● *vt* (*cook*) cozinhar a vapor ● *vi* soltar vapor, fumegar; (*move*) avançar; **~ up** ‹*window*› embaciar. **~ engine** *n* máquina *f* a vapor; (*locomotive*) locomotiva *f* a vapor. **~y** *a* (*heat*) úmido, (*P*) húmido

steamer /'stiːmə(r)/ *n* (*ship*) (barco a) vapor *m*; *Culin* utensílio *m* para cozinhar a vapor

steel /stiːl/ *n* aço *m*; **~ industry** siderurgia *f* ● *a* de aço ● *vpr* **~ o.s.** endurecer-se, fortalecer-se

steep[1] /stiːp/ *vt* (*soak*) mergulhar, pôr de molho; (*permeate*) passar, impregnar; **~ed in** *fig* ‹*vice, misery etc*› mergulhado em; *fig* ‹*knowledge, wisdom etc*› impregnado de, repassado de

steep[2] /stiːp/ *a* (**-er**, **-est**) íngreme, escarpado; [!] exagerado; exorbitante; **rise ~ly** ‹*slope*› subir a pique; ‹*price*› disparar

steeple /'stiːpl/ *n* campanário *m*, torre *f*

steeplechase /'stiːpltʃeɪs/ *n* (*race*) corrida *f* de obstáculos

steer /stɪə(r)/ *vt/i* guiar, conduzir, dirigir; ‹*ship*› governar, (*P*) comandar; *fig* guiar; orientar; **~ clear of** evitar passar perto de. **~ing** *n Auto* direção *f*. **~ing wheel** *n Auto* volante *m*

stem[1] /stem/ *n* caule *m*, haste *f*; (*of glass*) pé *m*; (*of pipe*) boquilha *f*; (*of word*) radical *m* ● *vi* (*pt* **stemmed**) **~ from** provir de, vir de

stem[2] /stem/ *vt* (*pt* **stemmed**) (*check*) conter; (*stop*) estancar

stem cell *n* célula-tronco *f*, célula *f* estaminal

stench /stentʃ/ *n* mau cheiro *m*, fedor *m*

stencil /'stensl/ *n* estênsil *m*, (*P*) stencil *m* ● *vt* (*pt* **stencilled**) ‹*document*› policopiar

step /step/ *vi* (*pt* **stepped**) ir andar; **~ down** (*resign*) demitir-se; **~ in** (*intervene*) intervir ● *vt* **~ up** aumentar ● *n* passo *m*, passada *f*; (*of stair, train*) degrau *m*; (*action*) medida *f*, passo *m*; **~s** (*ladder*) escada *f*; **in ~** no mesmo passo, a passo certo; *fig* em conformidade (**with** com). **~ladder** *n* escada *f* portátil; **~ping stone** *n fig* (*means to an end*) ponte *f*; trampolim *m*

step|brother /'stepbrʌðə(r)/ *n* meio-irmão *m*. **~daughter** *n* nora *f*, (*P*) enteada *f*. **~father** *n* padrasto *m*. **~mother** *n* madrasta *f*. **~sister** *n* meia-irmã *f*. **~son** *n* genro *m*, (*P*) enteado *m*

stereo /'sterɪəʊ/ *n* (*pl* **-os**) estéreo *m*; (*record player etc*) equipamento or sistema *m* estéreo *m* ● *a* estéreo *invar*. **~phonic** /-ə'fɒnɪk/ *a* estereofônico, (*P*) estereofónico

stereotype /'sterɪətaɪp/ *n* estereótipo *m*

steril|e /'steraɪl/ *a* estéril

steriliz|e /'sterəlaɪz/ *vt* esterilizar. **~ation** /-'zeɪʃn/ *n* esterilização *f*

sterling /'stɜːlɪŋ/ *n* libra *f* esterlina ● *a* esterlino; (*silver*) de lei; *fig* excelente; de (primeira) qualidade

stern[1] /stɜːn/ *a* (**-er**, **-est**) severo

stern[2] /stɜːn/ *n* (*of ship*) popa *f*, ré *f*

stethoscope /'steθəskəʊp/ *n* estetoscópio *m*

stew /stjuː/ *vt/i* estufar, guisar; (*fruit*) cozer ● *n* ensopado *m*; **~ed fruit** compota *f*

steward /'stjʊəd/ *n* (*of club etc*) ecônomo *m*, (*P*) ecónomo *m*; administrador *m*; (*on ship etc*) camareiro *m* (de bordo), (*P*) comissário *m* (de bordo). **~ess** /-'des/ *n* aeromoça *f*; (*P*) assistente *f* de bordo

stick[1] /stɪk/ *n* pau *m*; (*for walking*) bengala *f*; (*of celery*) talo *m*

stick[2] /stɪk/ *vt* (*pt* **stuck**) ‹*glue*› colar; (*thrust*) cravar, espetar; ⊡ (*put*) enfiar, meter; ⊠ (*endure*) aguentar, aturar, suportar; **be stuck with sb/sth** ⊡ não conseguir descartar-se or livrar-se de alguém/algo ⊡; **~ to** ‹*promise*› ser fiel a ● *vi* (*pt* **stuck**) (*adhere*) colar, aderir; (*remain*) ficar enfiado or metido; (*be jammed*) emperrar, ficar engatado; **~ in one's mind** ficar na memória; **~ up for** ⊡ tomar o partido de, defender □ **~ out** *vt* ‹*head*› esticar, pôr de fora; ‹*tongue etc*› mostrar ● *vi* (*protrude*) sobressair. **~-up** *n* ⊠ assalto à mão armada *m*; **~ing plaster** *n* esparadrapo *m*, (*P*) adesivo *m*

sticker /'stɪkə(r)/ *n* adesivo *m*, etiqueta *f* (adesiva)

sticky /'stɪkɪ/ *a* (**-ier**, **-iest**) pegajoso; ‹*label, tape*› adesivo; ‹*weather*› abafado, mormacento

stiff /stɪf/ *a* (**-er**, **-est**) teso, hirto, rígido; ‹*limb, joint*› (*hard*) duro; (*unbending*) inflexível; ‹*price*› elevado; puxado ⊡; ‹*penalty*› severo; ‹*drink*› forte; ‹*manner*› reservado, formal; **be bored/scared ~** ⊡ estar muito aborrecido/com muito medo, ⊡ estar morto de aborecimento/medo; **~ neck** torcicolo *m*. **~ness** *n* rigidez *f*

stiffen /'stɪfn/ *vt/i* (*harden*) endurecer; ‹*limb, joint*› emperrar

stifl|e /'staɪfl/ *vt/i* abafar, sufocar. **~ing** *a* sufocante

stigma /'stɪgmə/ *n* estigma *m*. **~tize** *vt* estigmatizar

stiletto /stɪ'letəʊ/ *n* (*pl* **-os**) estilete *m*. **~ heel** *n* salto *m* alto fino

still[1] /stɪl/ *a* imóvel, quieto; (*quiet*) sossegado; **~ life** natureza *f* morta ● *n* silêncio *m*, sossego *m* ● *adv* ainda; (*nevertheless*) apesar disso, apesar de tudo; **keep ~!** fique quieto!, não se mexa!

still[2] /stɪl/ *n* (*apparatus*) alambique *m*

stillborn /'stɪlbɔːn/ *a* natimorto, (*P*) nado-morto

stilted /'stɪltɪd/ *a* afetado, (*P*) afetado

stilts /stɪlts/ *npl* pernas *fpl* de pau, (*P*) andas *fpl*

stimul|ate /'stɪmjʊleɪt/ *vt* estimular. **~ant** *n* estimulante *m*. **~ating** *a* estimulante. **~ation** /-'leɪʃn/ *n* estimulação *f*

stimulus /'stɪmjʊləs/ *n* (*pl* **-li** /-laɪ/) (*spur*) estímulo *m*

sting /stɪŋ/ *n* picada *f*; (*organ*) ferrão *m* ● *vt* (*pt* **stung**) picar ● *vi* picar, arder

stingy /'stɪndʒɪ/ *a* (**-ier**, **-iest**) pão-duro *m*; sovina (**with** com)

stink /stɪŋk/ *n* fedor *m*, catinga *f*, mau cheiro *m* ● *vi* (*pt* **stank** *or* **stunk**, *pp* **stunk**) **~ (of)** cheirar (a), tresandar (a) ● *vt* **~ out** ‹*room etc*› empestar. **~ing** *a* malcheiroso; **~ing rich** ⊠ podre de rico ⊡

stint /stɪnt/ *vi* **~ on** poupar em, apertar em ● *n* (*work*) tarefa *f*, parte *f*, quinhão *m*

stipulat|e /'stɪpjʊleɪt/ *vt* estipular. **~ion** /-'leɪʃn/ *n* condição *f*, estipulação *f*

stir /stɜːr/ *vt/i* (*pt* **stirred**) (*move*) mexer(-se), mover(-se); (*excite*) excitar; ‹*a liquid*› mexer; **~ up** ‹*trouble etc*› provocar, fomentar ● *n* agitação *f*, rebuliço *m*

stirrup /'stɪrəp/ *n* estribo *m*

stitch /stɪtʃ/ *n* (*in sewing*) *Med* ponto *m*; (*in knitting*) malha *f*, ponto *m*; (*pain*) pontada *f*; **in ~es** ⊡ às gargalhadas ⊡ ● *vt* coser

stock /stɒk/ *n Comm* estoque *m*, (*P*) stock *m*, provisão *f*; *Finance* valores *mpl*, fundos *mpl*; (*family*) família *f*, estirpe *f*; *Culin* caldo *m*; (*flower*) goivo *m*; **in ~** em estoque; **out of ~** esgotado; **take ~** *fig* fazer um balanço; **~ market** Bolsa (de Valores) *f*; (de Valores) ● *a* (*goods*) corrente, comum; (*hackneyed*) estereotipado ● *vt* ‹*shop etc*› abastecer, fornecer; (*sell*) vender ● *vi* **~ up with** abastecer-se de. **~ cube** *n* cubo *m* de caldo; **~taking** *n Comm* inventário *m*

stockbroker /'stɒkbrəʊkə(r)/ *n* corretor *m* da Bolsa

stocking /'stɒkɪŋ/ *n* meia *f*

stockist /'stɒkɪst/ *n* armazenista *m*

stockpile /'stɒkpaɪl/ *n* reservas *fpl* ● *vt* acumular reservas de, estocar

stocky /'stɒkɪ/ *a* (**-ier**, **-iest**) atarracado

stoic /'stəʊɪk/ *n* estoico *m*

stoke /stəʊk/ *vt* ‹*boiler, fire*› alimentar, carregar

stole[1] /stəʊl/ *n* (*garment*) estola *m*

stole[2], **stolen** /stəʊl, stəʊlən/ ▶ STEAL

stomach /'stʌmək/ *n* estômago *m*; (*abdomen*) barriga *f*, ventre *m* ● *vt* (*put up with*) aturar. **~ ache** *n* dor *f* de estômago; (*abdomen*) dores *fpl* de barriga

ston|e /stəʊn/ *n* pedra *f*; (*pebble*) seixo *m*; (*in fruit*) caroço *m*; (*weight*) 6,348 kg; *Med* cálculo *m*, pedra *f* ● *vt* apedrejar; ‹*fruit*› tirar o caroço de; **within a ~e's throw (of)** muito perto (de). **~e-cold**

a gelado. **~e-deaf** totalmente surdo. **~ed** *a* [!] (*drunk*) bebão *m* [!], (*P*) bêbado *m* [!]; [!] (*drugged*) drogado, (*P*) pedrado [!]. **~y** *a* pedregoso.

stood /stʊd/ ▶ STAND

stool /stuːl/ *n* banco *m*, tamborete *m*

stoop /stuːp/ *vi* (*bend*) curvar-se, baixar-se; (*condescend*) condescender, dignar-se; **~ to sth** rebaixar-se a (fazer) algo ● *n* **walk with a ~** andar curvado

stop /stɒp/ *vt/i* (*pt* **stopped**) parar; (*prevent*) impedir (**from** de); ‹*hole, leak etc*› tapar, vedar; ‹*pain, noise etc*› parar; [!] (*stay*) ficar; **~ it!** acabe logo com isso!, (*P*) para com isso! ● *n* (*of bus*) parada *f*; (*P*) paragem *f*; (*full stop*) ponto *m* final; **put a ~ to** pôr fim a. **~watch** *n* cronômetro *m*, (*P*) cronómetro

stopgap /ˈstɒpgæp/ *n* substituto *m* provisório; tapa-buracos *mpl* [!] ● *a* temporário

stoppage /ˈstopɪdʒ/ *n* parada *f*, (*P*) paragem *f*; (*of work*) paralização *f* de trabalho; (*of pay*) suspensão *f*

stopper /ˈstɒpə(r)/ *n* rolha *f*, tampa *f*

storage /ˈstɔːrɪdʒ/ *n* (*of goods, food etc*) armazenagem *f*, armazenamento *m*; **in cold ~** no frigorífico

store /stɔː(r)/ *n* reserva *f*, provisão *f*; (*warehouse*) armazém *m*, entreposto *m*; (*shop*) grande armazém *m*; *Amer* loja *f*; (*in computer*) memória *f*; **be in ~** estar guardado; **have in ~ for** reservar para; **set ~ by** dar valor a ● *vt* (*for future*) pôr de reserva, juntar, fazer provisão de; (*in warehouse*) armazenar. **~room** *n* depósito *m*, almortarifado *m*, (*P*) armazém *m*

storey /ˈstɔːrɪ/ *n* (*pl* **-eys**) andar *m*

stork /stɔːk/ *n* cegonha *f*

storm /stɔːm/ *n* tempestade *f*; **a ~ in a teacup** uma tempestade num copo de água ● *vt* tomar de assalto ● *vi* enfurecer-se. **~y** *a* tempestuoso

story /ˈstɔːrɪ/ *n* estória *f*, (*P*) história *f*; (*in press*) artigo *m*, matéria *f*; *Amer* (*storey*) andar *m*; [!] (*lie*) cascata *f*, (*P*) peta *f*

stout /staʊt/ *a* (**-er**, **-est**) (*fat*) gordo, corpulento; (*strong, thick*) resistente, sólido, grosso; (*brave*) resoluto ● *n* cerveja *f* preta forte

stove /stəʊv/ *n* (*for cooking*) fogão (de cozinha) *m*

stow /stəʊ/ *vt* **~ (away)** (*put away*) guardar, arrumar; (*hide*) esconder ● *vi* **~ away** viajar clandestinamente

stowaway /ˈstəʊəweɪ/ *n* passageiro *m* clandestino

straggle /ˈstrægl/ *vi* (*lag behind*) desgarrar-se, ficar para trás; (*spread*) estender-se desordenadamente. **~r** /-ə(r)/ *n* retardatário *m*

straight /streɪt/ *a* (**-er**, **-est**) direito; (*tidy*) em ordem; (*frank*) franco; direto; (*of hair*) liso; (*of drink*) puro; **keep a ~ face** não se desmanchar, manter um ar sério ● *adv* (*in straight line*) reto; (*directly*) direito; direto; diretamente; **~ ahead** or **on** (sempre) em frente; **~ away** logo, imediatamente; **go ~** viver honestamente ● *n* linha *f* reta

straighten /ˈstreɪtn/ *vt* endireitar; (*tidy*) arrumar, pôr em ordem

straightforward /streɪtˈfɔːwəd/ *a* franco, sincero; (*easy*) simples

strain[1] /streɪn/ *n* (*breed*) raça *f*; (*streak*) tendência *f*, veia *f*

strain[2] /streɪn/ *vt* (*rope*) esticar, puxar; (*tire*) cansar; (*filter*) filtrar, passar; ‹*vegetables, tea etc*› coar; *Med* distender, torcer; *fig* forçar; pôr à prova ● *vi* esforçar-se ● *n* tensão *f*; *fig* (*effort*) esforço *m*; *Med* distensão *f*; **~s** (*music*) melodias *fpl*; **~ one's ears** apurar o ouvido. **~ed** *a* forçado; ‹*relations*› tenso. **~er** *n* coador *m*, (*P*) passador *m*

strait /streɪt/ *n* estreito *m*; **~s** estreito *m*; *fig* apuros *mpl*, dificuldades *fpl*. **~-laced** *a* severo, puritano

strand /strænd/ *n* (*thread*) fio *m*; (*lock of hair*) mecha *f*, madeixa *f*

stranded /ˈstrændɪd/ *a* (*person*) em dificuldades, deixado para trás, abandonado

strange /streɪndʒ/ *a* (**-er**, **-est**) estranho. **~ly** *adv* estranhamente

stranger /ˈstreɪndʒə(r)/ *n* estranho *m*, desconhecido *m*

strangle /ˈstrængl/ *vt* estrangular, sufocar

strap /stræp/ *n* (*of leather etc*) correia *f*; (*of dress*) alça *f*; (*of watch*) pulseira *f* com correia ● *vt* (*pt* **strapped**) prender com correia

strapping /ˈstræpɪŋ/ *a* robusto, grande

strata ▶ STRATUM

strategic /strəˈtiːdʒɪk/ *a* estratégico; (*of weapons*) estratégico de longo alcance

strategy /ˈstrætədʒɪ/ *n* estratégia *f*

stratum /ˈstrɑːtəm/ *n* (*pl* **strata**) estrato *m*, camada *f*

straw /strɔː/ *n* palha *f*; (*for drinking*) canudo *m*, (*P*) palhinha *f*; **the last ~** a última gota *f*

strawberry /ˈstrɔːbrɪ/ *n* (*fruit*) morango *m*; (*plant*) morangueiro *m*

stray /streɪ/ *vi* (*deviate from path etc*) extraviar-se; desencaminhar-se; afastar-se (**from** de); (*lose one's way*) perder-se; (*wander*) vagar, (*P*) vaguear, errar ● *a* perdido, extraviado; (*isolated*) isolado, raro, esporádico ● *n* animal *m* perdido or vadio

streak /striːk/ *n* risca *f*, lista *f*; (*strain*) veia *f*; (*period*) período *m*; **~ of lightning** relâmpago *m* ● *vt* listrar, riscar ● *vi* ir como um raio

stream /striːm/ *n* riacho *m*, córrego *m*, regato *m*; (*current*) corrente *f*; *fig* (*flow*) jorro *m*; torrente *f*; *Schol* nível *m*, grupo *m* ● *vi* correr; (*of banner, hair*) flutuar; (*sweat*) escorrer, pingar

streamer /ˈstriːmə(r)/ *n* (*of paper*) serpentina *f*; (*flag*) flâmula *f*, bandeirola *f*

streamline /ˈstriːmlaɪn/ *vt* dar forma aerodinâmica a; *fig* racionalizar. **~d** *a* ‹*shape*› aerodinâmico

street /striːt/ *n* rua *f*; **the man in the ~** *fig* o homem da rua, (*P*) o cidadão *m* comum; **~ lamp** poste *m* de iluminação

streetcar /ˈstriːtkɑː(r)/ *n Amer* bonde *m*, (*P*) (carro *m*) elétrico *m*

strength /streŋθ/ *n* força *f*; (*of wall*) solidez *f*; (*of fabric etc*) resistência *f*; **on the ~ of** à base de, em virtude de

strengthen /ˈstreŋθn/ *vt* fortificar, fortalecer, reforçar

strenuous /ˈstrenjʊəs/ *a* enérgico; (*arduous*) árduo; estrênuo, (*P*) estrénuo; (*tiring*) fatigante, esgotante

stress /stres/ *n* acento *m*; (*pressure*) pressão *f*, tensão *f*; *Med* stress *m*, (*P*) (e) stress(e) *m* ● *vt* acentuar, sublinhar; (*sound*) acentuar. **~ful** *a* estressante, (*P*) (e)stressant(e)

stretch /stretʃ/ *vt* (*pull taut*) esticar; ‹*arm, leg, neck*› estender, esticar; ‹*clothes*› alargar; ‹*truth*› forçar, torcer ● *vi* estender-se; (*after sleep etc*) espreguiçar-se; (*of clothes*) alargar-se; **~ one's legs** esticar as pernas ● *n* extensão *f*, trecho *m*; (*period*) período *m*; (*of road*) troço *m*; **at a ~** sem parar ● *a* (*of fabric*) com elasticidade

stretcher /ˈstretʃə(r)/ *n* maca *f*, padiola *f*

strew /struː/ *vt* (*pt* **strewed**, *pp* **strewed**, *or* **strewn**) (*scatter*) espalhar; (*cover*) juncar, cobrir

strict /strɪkt/ *a* (**-er**, **-est**) estrito, rigoroso. **~ly** *adv* estritamente; **~ly speaking** a rigor, (*P*) em rigor

stride /straɪd/ *vi* (*pt* **strode**, *pp* **stridden**) caminhar a passos largos ● *n* passada *f*; **make great ~s** *fig* fazer grandes progressos; **take sth in one's ~** fazer algo sem problemas

strident /ˈstraɪdnt/ *a* estridente

strife /straɪf/ *n* conflito *m*, dissensão *f*, luta *f*

strike /straɪk/ *vt* (*pt* **struck**) bater (em); ‹*blow*› dar; ‹*match*› riscar, acender; ‹*gold etc*› descobrir; (*of clock*) soar, dar, bater (horas); (*of lightning*) atingir ● *vi* fazer greve; (*attack*) atacar; **~ a bargain** fechar negócio; **~ off** or **out** riscar; **~ up** *Mus* começar a tocar; ‹*friendship*› travar ● *n* (*of workers*) greve *f*; *Mil* ataque *m*; (*find*) descoberta *f*; **on ~** em greve

striker /ˈstraɪkə(r)/ *n* grevista *mf*

striking /ˈstraɪkɪŋ/ *a* notável, impressionante; (*attractive*) atraente

string /strɪŋ/ *n* corda *f*, fio *m*; (*of violin, racket etc*) corda *f*; (*of pearls*) fio *m*; (*of onions, garlic*) réstia *f*; (*of lies etc*) série *f*; (*row*) fila *f*; **pull ~s** usar pistolão, (*P*) puxar os cordelinhos ● *vt* (*pt* **strung**) (*thread*) enfiar; **~ out** espaçar-se. **~ed** *a* ‹*instrument*› de cordas. **~y** *a* filamentoso, fibroso; ‹*meat*› com nervos

stringent /ˈstrɪndʒənt/ *a* rigoroso, estrito

strip[1] /strɪp/ *vt/i* (*pt* **stripped**) (*undress*) despir(-se); ‹*machine*› desmontar; (*deprive*) despojar, privar. **~per** *n* artista *mf* de strip-tease; (*solvent*) removedor *m*, (*P*) decapante *m*

strip[2] /strɪp/ *n* tira *f*; (*of land*) faixa *f*; **comic ~** história *f* em quadrinhos, (*P*) banda *f* desenhada; **~ light** tubo *m* de luz fluorescente

stripe /straɪp/ *n* risca *f*, lista *f*, barra *f*. **~d** *a* listrado, com listras

strive /straɪv/ *vi* (*pt* **strove**, *pp* **striven**) esforçar-se (**to** por)

strode /strəʊd/ ▶ STRIDE

stroke[1] /strəʊk/ *n* golpe *m*; (*of pen*) penada *f*, (*P*) traço *m*; (*in swimming*) braçada *f*; (*in rowing*) remada *f*; *Med* ataque *m*, congestão *f*; **~ of genius** rasgo *m* de genialidade or de génio; **~ of luck** golpe *m* de sorte

stroke[2] /strəʊk/ *vt* (*with hand*) acariciar, fazer festas em

stroll /strəʊl/ *vi* passear, dar uma volta; **~ in/***etc* entrar/*etc* tranquilamente ● *n* volta *f*, (*P*) passeio *m*

strong /strɒŋ/ *a* (**-er**, **-est**) forte; ‹*shoes, fabric etc*› resistente; **be a hundred/***etc***~** ser em número de cem/*etc*; **~ language** linguagem *f* grosseira, palavrões *mpl*. **~room** *n* casa-forte *f*. **~ly** *adv* (*greatly*) fortemente, grandemente; (*with energy*) com força; (*deeply*) profundamente

stronghold /ˈstrɒŋhəʊld/ *n* fortaleza *f*; *fig* baluarte *m*; bastião *m*

strove /strəʊv/ ▶ STRIVE

struck /strʌk/ ▶ STRIKE ● *a* **~ on** ☒ apaixonado por, (*P*) apanhado por ☒

structur|e /ˈstrʌktʃə(r)/ *n* estrutura *f*; (*of building etc*) edifício *m*, construção *f*. **~al** *a* estrutural, de estrutura, de construção

struggle /ˈstrʌgl/ *vi* (*to get free*) debater-se; (*contend*) lutar; (*strive*) esforçar-se (**to, for** por); **~ to one's feet** levantar-se a custo ● *n* luta *f*; (*effort*) esforço *m*; **have a ~ to** ter dificuldade em

strum /strʌm/ *vt* (*pt* **strummed**) ‹*banjo etc*› dedilhar

strung /strʌŋ/ ▶ STRING

strut /strʌt/ *n* (*support*) suporte *m*, escora *f* ● *vi* (*pt* **strutted**) (*walk*) pavonear-se

stub /stʌb/ *n* (*of pencil, cigarette*) ponta *f*; (*of tree*) cepo *m*, toco *m*; (*counterfoil*) talão *m*, canhoto *m* ● *vt* (*pt* **stubbed**) **~ one's toe** dar uma topada; **~ out** esmagar

stubble /ˈstʌbl/ *n* (*on chin*) barba *f* por fazer; (*of crop*) restolho *m*

stubborn /ˈstʌbən/ *a* teimoso, obstinado. **~ness** *n* teimosia *f*, obstinação *f*

stubby /ˈstʌbɪ/ *a* (**-ier**, **-iest**) ‹*finger*› curto e grosso; ‹*person*› atarracado

stuck /stʌk/ ▶ STICK² *a* emperrado. **~-up** *a* [!] (*snobbish*) convencido; esnobe, (*P*) snob

stud¹ /stʌd/ *n* tacha *f*; (*for collar*) botão *m* de colarinho ● *vt* (*pt* **studded**) enfeitar com tachas; **~ded with** salpicado de

stud² /stʌd/ *n* (*horses*) haras *m*, (*P*) coudelaria. **~ (farm)** *n* coudelaria *f*; **~ (horse)** *n* garanhão *m*

student /ˈstjuːdnt/ *n Univ* estudante *mf*, aluno *m*; *Schol* aluno *m* ● *a* ‹*life, residence*› universitário

studio /ˈstjuːdɪəʊ/ *n* (*pl* **-os**) estúdio *m*; **~ flat** estúdio *m*

studious /ˈstjuːdɪəs/ *a* ‹*person*› estudioso; (*deliberate*) estudado

study /ˈstʌdɪ/ *n* estudo *m*; (*office*) escritório *m* ● *vt/i* estudar

stuff /stʌf/ *n* substância *f*, matéria *f*; ☒ (*things*) coisa(s) *f* ● *vt* encher; ‹*animal*› empalhar; (*cram*) apinhar, encher ao máximo; *Culin* rechear; (*block up*) entupir; (*put*) enfiar, meter. **~ing** *n* enchimento *m*; *Culin* recheio *m*

stuffy /ˈstʌfɪ/ *a* (**-ier**, **-iest**) abafado, mal arejado; (*dull*) enfadonho

stumbl|e /ˈstʌmbl/ *vi* tropeçar; **~e across** or **on** dar com, encontrar por acaso, topar com. **~ing block** *n* obstáculo *m*

stump /stʌmp/ *n* (*of tree*) cepo *m*, toco *m*; (*of limb*) coto *m*; (*of pencil, cigar*) ponta *f*

stumped /stʌmpt/ *a* [!] (*baffled*) atrapalhado; perplexo

stun /stʌn/ *vt* (*pt* **stunned**) aturdir, estontear

stung /stʌŋ/ ▶ STING

stunk /stʌŋk/ ▶ STINK

stunning /ˈstʌnɪŋ/ *a* atordoador; [!] (*delightful*) fantástico; sensacional

stunt¹ /stʌnt/ *vt* ‹*growth*› atrofiar. **~ed** *a* atrofiado

stunt² /stʌnt/ *n* (*feat*) façanha *f*, proeza *f*; (*trick*) truque *m*; *Aviat* acrobacia *f* aérea. **~ man** *n* dublê *m*, (*P*) duplo *m*

stupefy /ˈstjuːpɪfaɪ/ *vt* estupefazer, (*P*) estupeficar, espantar

stupendous /stjuːˈpendəs/ *a* estupendo, assombroso, prodigioso

stupid /ˈstjuːpɪd/ *a* estúpido, obtuso. **~ity** /-ˈpɪdətɪ/ *n* estupidez *f*. **~ly** *adv* estupidamente

stupor /ˈstjuːpə(r)/ *n* estupor *m*, torpor *m*

sturdy /ˈstɜːdɪ/ *a* (**-ier**, **-iest**) robusto, vigoroso, forte

stutter /ˈstʌtə(r)/ *vi* gaguejar ● *n* gagueira *f*, (*P*) gaguez *f*

sty /staɪ/ *n* (*pigsty*) pocilga *f*, chiqueiro *m*

styl|e /staɪl/ *n* estilo *m*; (*fashion*) moda *f*; (*kind*) gênero *m*, (*P*) género *m*; tipo *m*; (*pattern*) feitio *m*, modelo *m*; **in ~e** (*live*) em grande estilo; (*do things*) com classe ● *vt* (*design*) desenhar, criar; **~e sb's hair** fazer um penteado em *or* (*P*) a alguém. **~ist** *n* (*of hair*) cabeleireiro *m*

stylish /ˈstaɪlɪʃ/ *a* elegante, na moda

suave /swɑːv/ *a* polido, de fala mansa, (*P*) melífluo

subconscious /sʌb'kɒnʃəs/ *a & n* subconsciente *m*

subcontract /sʌbkən'trækt/ *vt* dar de subempreitada, (*P*) subcontratar

subdivide /sʌbdɪ'vaɪd/ *vt* subdividir

subdue /səb'dju:/ *vt* ‹*enemy, feeling*› dominar, subjugar; ‹*sound, voice*› abrandar. **~d** *a* (*weak*) submisso; (*quiet*) recolhido; ‹*light*› velado

subject[1] /'sʌbdʒɪkt/ *a* (*state etc*) dominado; **~ to** sujeito a ● *n* sujeito *m*; *Schol, Univ* disciplina *f*, matéria *f*; (*citizen*) súdito *m*, (*P*) súbdito *m*. **~ matter** *n* conteúdo *m*, tema *m*, assunto *m*

subject[2] /səb'dʒekt/ *vt* submeter

subjective /sʌb'dʒektɪv/ *a* subjetivo

subjunctive /səb'dʒʌŋktɪv/ *a & n* subjuntivo *m*, (*P*) conjuntivo *m*

sublime /sə'blaɪm/ *a* sublime

submarine /sʌbmə'ri:n/ *n* submarino *m*

submerge /səb'mɜ:dʒ/ *vt* submergir, mergulhar ● *vi* submergir, mergulhar

submissive /səb'mɪsɪv/ *a* submisso

submi|t /səb'mɪt/ *vt/i* (*pt* **submitted**) submeter(-se) (**to** a); *Jur* (*argue*) alegar. **~ssion** /-'mɪʃn/ *n* submissão *f*

subnormal /sʌb'nɔ:ml/ *a* subnormal; ‹*temperature*› abaixo do normal

subordinate[1] /sə'bɔ:dɪnət/ *a* subordinado, subalterno; *Gram* subordinado ● *n* subordinado *m*, subalterno *m*

subordinate[2] /sə'bɔ:dɪneɪt/ *vt* subordinar (**to** a)

subscribe /səb'skraɪb/ *vt/i* subscrever; contribuir (**to** para); **~ to** ‹*theory, opinion*› subscrever, aceitar; ‹*newspaper*› assinar. **~r** /-ə(r)/ *n* subscritor *m*, assinante *m*

subscription /səb'skrɪpʃn/ *n* subscrição *f*; (*to newspaper*) assinatura *f*

subsequent /'sʌbsɪkwənt/ *a* subsequente, posterior. **~ly** *adv* subsequentemente, a seguir, posteriormente

subservient /səb'sɜ:vɪənt/ *a* servil, subserviente

subside /səb'saɪd/ *vi* ‹*flood, noise etc*› baixar; ‹*land*› ceder, afundar; ‹*wind, storm, excitement*› abrandar, acalmar. **~nce** /-əns/ *n* (*of land*) afundamento *m*

subsidiary /səb'sɪdɪərɪ/ *a* subsidiário ● *n Comm* filial *f*, sucursal *f*

subsid|y /'sʌbsədɪ/ *n* subsídio *m*, subvenção *f*. **~ize** /-ɪdaɪz/ *vt* subsidiar, subvencionar

subsist /səb'sɪst/ *vi* subsistir; **~ on** viver de. **~ence** *n* subsistência *f*; **~ence allowance** ajudas *fpl* de custo

substance /'sʌbstəns/ *n* substância *f*

substandard /sʌb'stændəd/ *a* de qualidade inferior

substantial /səb'stænʃl/ *a* substancial. **~ly** *adv* substancialmente

substitut|e /'sʌbstɪtju:t/ *n* (*person*) substituto *m*; suplente *mf* (**for** de); (*thing*) substituto *m* (**for** de) ● *vt* substituir (**for** por). **~ion** /-'tju:ʃn/ *n* substituição *f*

subtitle /'sʌbtaɪtl/ *n* subtítulo *m*, (*P*) legenda *f*

subtle /'sʌtl/ *a* (**-er**, **-est**) sutil, (*P*) subtil. **~ty** *n* sutileza *f*, (*P*) subtileza *f*

subtotal /'sʌbtəʊtl/ *n* soma *f* parcial

subtract /səb'trækt/ *vt* subtrair, diminuir. **~ion** /-kʃn/ *n* subtração *f*, diminuição *f*

suburb /'sʌbɜ:b/ *n* subúrbio *m*, arredores *mpl*. **~an** /sə'bɜ:bən/ *a* dos subúrbios, suburbano. **~ia** /sə'bɜ:bɪə/ *n pej* os arredores, os subúrbios

subver|t /səb'vɜ:t/ *vt* subverter. **~sion** /-ʃn/ *n* subversão *f*. **~sive** /-sɪv/ *a* subversivo

subway /'sʌbweɪ/ *n* passagem *f* subterrânea; *Amer* (*underground*) metropolitano *m*, (*P*) metro *m*

succeed /sək'si:d/ *vi* ser bem-sucedido, ter êxito; **~ in doing sth** conseguir fazer algo ● *vt* (*follow*) suceder a. **~ing** *a* seguinte, sucessivo

success /sək'ses/ *n* sucesso *m*, êxito *m*

succession /sək'seʃn/ *n* sucessão *f*; (*series*) série *f*; **in ~** seguidos, consecutivos

successive /sək'sesɪv/ *a* sucessivo, consecutivo

successor /sək'sesə(r)/ *n* sucessor *m*

succinct /sək'sɪŋkt/ *a* sucinto

succulent /'sʌkjʊlənt/ *a* suculento

succumb /sə'kʌm/ *vi* sucumbir

such /sʌtʃ/ ● *a*

····➤ (*of that kind*) tal, semelhante, assim; **~ a book** um tal livro; **~ a person** uma tal pessoa; **~ people** essas pessoas; **there is no ~ thing** uma coisa assim não existe

····➤ (*so much*) tanto; **I've got ~ a headache!** tenho uma dor de cabeça tão grande!; **it was ~ fun!** foi tão divertido!

● *adv*

····➤ tão; **~ a big house** uma casa tão grande; **he has ~ lovely blue eyes** ele tem uns olhos azuis tão bonitos; **~ a long time** tanto tempo

····➤ (*in phrases*) **as ~: the new job is not a promotion as ~** o novo emprego não é bem uma promoção; **there is no garden as ~** não existe um jardim no real sentido da palavra; **in ~ a way that** de tal maneira que; **~ as** tal como; **wild flowers ~ as primroses are becoming rare** as flores selvagens, tais como as prímulas, estão ficando raras; **~ as?** por exemplo?; **~ is: ~ is life** assim é a vida

such-and-such *a* **on ~-and-~ day in July** em tais e tais dias de julho

suck /sʌk/ *vt* chupar; ‹*breast*› mamar; **~ in** or **up** (*absorb*) absorver, aspirar; (*engulf*) tragar; **~ up to** puxar o saco a [!]; **~ one's thumb** chuchar no dedo. **~er** *n* [✖] (*greenhorn*) trouxa *mf* [!]; *Bot* broto *m*

suction /ˈsʌkʃn/ *n* sucção *f*

sudden /ˈsʌdn/ *a* súbito, repentino; **all of a ~** de repente, de súbito. **~ly** *adv* subitamente, repentinamente

sue /su:/ *vt* (*pres p* **suing**) processar

suede /sweɪd/ *n* camurça *f*

suet /ˈsu:ɪt/ *n* sebo *m*

suffer /ˈsʌfə(r)/ *vt/i* sofrer; (*tolerate*) tolerar, suportar. **~er** *n* sofredor *m*, o que sofre; (*patient*) doente *mf*, vítima *f*. **~ing** *n* sofrimento *m*

suffice /səˈfaɪs/ *vi* bastar, chegar, ser suficiente

sufficien|t /səˈfɪʃnt/ *a* suficiente, bastante

suffocat|e /ˈsʌfəkeɪt/ *vt/i* sufocar. **~ion** /-ˈkeɪʃn/ *n* sufocação *f*, asfixia *f*

sugar /ˈʃʊgə(r)/ *n* açúcar *m*; **brown ~** açúcar *m* preto, (*P*) açúcar *m* amarelo ● *vt* adoçar, pôr açúcar em. **~ lump** *n* torrão *m* de açúcar, (*P*) quadradinho *m* de açúcar. **~y** *a* açucarado; *fig* (*too sweet*) delico-doce, (*P*) adocicado

suggest /səˈdʒest/ *vt* sugerir. **~ion** /-tʃn/ *n* sugestão *f*. **~ive** *a* sugestivo; (*improper*) brejeiro, picante; **be ~ive of** sugerir, fazer lembrar

suicid|e /ˈsu:ɪsaɪd/ *n* suicídio *m*; **commit ~e** suicidar-se. **~ attack** *n* ataque *m* suicida; **~ bomber** *n* terrorista *mf* suicida, (*P*) bombista *mf* suicida. **~al** /-ˈsaɪdl/ *a* suicida

suit /su:t/ *n* terno *m*, (*P*) fato *m*; (*woman's*) costume *m*, (*P*) fato *m* de saia e casaco; *Cards* naipe *m*; **follow ~** *fig* seguir o exemplo ● *vt* convir a; (*of garment, style*) ficar bem em *or* (*P*) a; (*adapt*) adaptar. **~able** *a* conveniente; apropriado (**for** para). **~ably** *adv* convenientemente. **~ed** *a* **be ~ed to** ser feito para, servir para; **be well ~ed** (*matched*) combinar-se bem; (*of people*) ser o ideal

suitcase /ˈsu:tkeɪs/ *n* mala *f* (de viagem)

suite /swi:t/ *n* (*of rooms; mus*) suíte *f*, (*P*) suite *f*; (*of furniture*) mobília *f*

suitor /ˈsu:tə(r)/ *n* pretendente *m*

sulk /sʌlk/ *vi* amuar, ficar emburrado. **~y** *a* amuado; emburrado [!]

sullen /ˈsʌlən/ *a* carrancudo

sulphur /ˈsʌlfə(r)/ *n* enxofre *m*

sultana /sʌlˈtɑ:nə/ *n* (*fruit*) passa *f* branca, (*P*) sultana *f*

sultry /ˈsʌltrɪ/ *a* (**-ier**, **-iest**) abafado, opressivo; *fig* sensual

sum /sʌm/ *n* soma *f*; (*amount of money*) soma *f*, quantia *f*, importância *f*; (*in arithmetic*) conta *f* ● *vt* (*pt* **summed**) somar; **~ up** recapitular, resumir; (*assess*) avaliar, medir

summar|y /ˈsʌmərɪ/ *n* sumário *m*, resumo *m* ● *a* sumário. **~ize** *vt* resumir

summer /ˈsʌmə(r)/ *n* verão *m*, estio *m* ● *a* de verão, veranil. **~ time** *n* verão *m*, época *f* de verão. **~y** *a* estival, próprio de verão, veranil

> *i* **summer camp** Nos Estados Unidos, é o acampamento de verão, considerado um aspecto importante na vida de muitas crianças. Praticam-se atividades ao ar livre em ambiente natural, como natação, montanhismo, sobrevivência ao ar livre. Nesses acampamentos, milhares de estudantes trabalham como supervisores.

summit /ˈsʌmɪt/ *n* cume *m*, cimo *m*; **~ conference** *Pol* conferência *f* de cúpula, (*P*) (reunião *f* de) cimeira

summon /ˈsʌmən/ *vt* mandar chamar; (*to meeting*) convocar; **~ up** ‹*strength, courage etc*› chamar a si, fazer apelo a

summons /ˈsʌmənz/ *n Jur* citação *f*, intimação *f* ● *vt* citar, intimar

S

sumptuous /'sʌmptʃʊəs/ *a* suntuoso, (*P*) sumptuoso, luxuoso

sun /sʌn/ *n* sol *m* ● *vt* (*pt* **sunned**) **~ o.s.** aquecer-se ao sol. **~glasses** *npl* óculos *mpl* de sol. **~roof** *n* teto *m* solar; **~tan** *n* bronzeado *m*. **~tanned** *a* bronzeado. **~tan oil** *n* óleo *m* de bronzear

sunbathe /'sʌnbeɪð/ *vi* tomar um banho de sol

sunburn /'sʌnbɜːn/ *n* queimadura *f* solar. **~t** *a* queimado pelo sol

Sunday /'sʌndɪ/ *n* domingo *m*; **~ school** catecismo *m*, (*P*) catequese *f*

sundr|y /'sʌndrɪ/ *a* vários, diversos; **all and ~y** todo o mundo, todo e cada um. **~ies** *npl* artigos *mpl* diversos

sunflower /'sʌnflaʊə(r)/ *n* girassol *m*

sung /sʌŋ/ ▶ SING

sunk /sʌŋk/ ▶ SINK

sunken /'sʌŋkən/ *a* ‹*ship etc*› afundado; ‹*eyes*› fundo

sunlight /'sʌnlaɪt/ *n* luz *f* do sol, sol *m*

sunny /'sʌnɪ/ *a* (**-ier**, **-iest**) ‹*room, day etc*› ensolarado

sunrise /'sʌnraɪz/ *n* nascer *m* do sol

sunset /'sʌnset/ *n* pôr *m* do sol

sunshade /'sʌnʃeɪd/ *n* (*awning*) toldo *m*; (*parasol*) para-sol *m*, (*P*) guarda-sol *m*

sunshine /'sʌnʃaɪn/ *n* sol *m*, luz *f* do sol

sunstroke /'sʌnstrəʊk/ *n Med* insolação *f*

super /'suːpə(r)/ *a* [!] (*excellent*) formidável

superb /suː'pɜːb/ *a* soberbo, esplêndido

superficial /suːpə'fɪʃl/ *a* superficial

superfluous /su'pɜːflʊəs/ *a* supérfluo

superhuman /suːpə'hjuːmən/ *a* sobre-humano

superimpose /suːpərɪm'pəʊz/ *vt* sobrepor (**on** a)

superintendent /suːpərɪn'tendənt/ *n* superintendente *m*; (*of police*) comissário *m*, chefe *m* de polícia

superior /suː'pɪərɪə(r)/ *a & n* superior *m*. **~ity** /-'ɒrətɪ/ *n* superioridade *f*

superlative /suː'pɜːlətɪv/ *a* supremo, superlativo ● *n Gram* superlativo *m*

supermarket /'suːpəmɑːkɪt/ *n* supermercado *m*

supernatural /suːpə'nætʃrəl/ *a* sobrenatural

superpower /'suːpəpaʊə(r)/ *n* superpotência *f*

S

supersede /suːpə'siːd/ *vt* suplantar, substituir

superstiti|on /suːpə'stɪʃn/ *n* superstição *f*. **~ous** *a* /-'stɪʃəs/ supersticioso

superstore /'suːpəstɔː(r)/ *n* hipermercado *m*

supervis|e /'suːpəvaɪz/ *vt* supervisar, fiscalizar, supervisionar. **~ion** /-'vɪʒn/ *n* supervisão *f*. **~or** *n* supervisor *m*; (*shop*) chefe *mf* de seção *or* (*P*) secção; (*firm*) chefe *mf* de serviço

supper /'sʌpə(r)/ *n* jantar *m*; (*late at night*) ceia *f*

supple /'sʌpl/ *a* flexível, maleável

supplement[1] /'sʌplɪmənt/ *n* suplemento *m*. **~ary** /-'mentrɪ/ *a* suplementar

supplement[2] /'sʌplɪment/ *vt* suplementar

supplier /sə'plaɪə(r)/ *n* fornecedor *m*

suppl|y /sə'plaɪ/ *vt* suprir, prover; *Comm* fornecer, abastecer ● *n* provisão *f*; (*of goods, gas etc*) fornecimento *m*, abastecimento *m* ● *a* ‹*teacher*› substituto; **~ies** (*food*) víveres *mpl*; *Mil* suprimentos *mpl*; **~y and demand** oferta e procura

support /sə'pɔːt/ *vt* (*hold up, endure*) suportar, aguentar; (*provide for*) sustentar, suster; (*back*) apoiar, patrocinar; *Sport* torcer por ● *n* apoio *m*; *Techn* suporte *m*. **~er** *n* partidário *m*; *Sport* torcedor *m*, (*P*) adepto *m*

suppos|e /sə'pəʊz/ *vt/i* supor; **~e that** supondo que, na hipótese de que; **he's ~ed to do** ele deve fazer; (*believed to*) consta que ele faz. **~ed** *a* suposto. **~edly** /-ɪdlɪ/ *adv* segundo dizem; (*probably*) supostamente, em princípio. **~ing** *conj* se. **~ition** /sʌpə-'zɪʃn/ *n* suposição *f*

suppress /sə'pres/ *vt* (*put an end to*) suprimir; (*restrain*) conter, reprimir; (*stifle*) abafar, sufocar; *Psych* recalcar. **~ion** /-ʃn/ *n* supressão *f*; (*restraint*) repressão *f*; *Psych* recalque *m*, (*P*) recalcamento *m*

suprem|e /suː'priːm/ *a* supremo. **~acy** /-eməsɪ/ *n* supremacia *f*

surcharge /'sɜːtʃɑːdʒ/ *n* sobretaxa *f*; (*on stamp*) sobrecarga *f*

sure /ʃʊə(r)/ *a* (**-er**, **-est**) seguro, certo ● *adv* [!] (*certainly*) deveras; não há dúvida que; de certeza; **be ~ about** or **of** ter a certeza de; **be ~ to** (*not fail*) não deixar de; **he is ~ to find out**

ele vai descobrir com certeza; **make ~** assegurar. **~ly** *adv* com certeza, certamente

surf /sɜːf/ *n* (*waves*) ressaca *f*, rebentação *f*. **~er** *n* surfista *mf*. **~ing** *n* surfe *m*, (*P*) surf *m*, jacaré-na-praia *m*

surface /ˈsɜːfɪs/ *n* superfície *f* ● *a* superficial ● *vt/i* revestir; (*rise, become known*) emergir; **~ mail** via *f* marítima

surfboard /ˈsɜːfbɔːd/ *n* prancha *f* de surfe, (*P*) surf

surge /sɜːdʒ/ *vi* ‹*waves*› ondular, encapelar-se; (*move forward*) avançar ● *n* (*wave*) onda *f*, vaga *f*; (*motion*) arremetida *f*

surgeon /ˈsɜːdʒən/ *n* cirurgião *m*

surg|ery /ˈsɜːdʒərɪ/ *n* cirurgia *f*; (*office*) consultório *m*; (*session*) consulta *f*; (*consulting hours*) horas *fpl* de consulta. **~ical** *a* cirúrgico

surly /ˈsɜːlɪ/ *a* (**-ier**, **-iest**) carrancudo, trombudo

surmise /səˈmaɪz/ *vt* imaginar, supor, calcular ● *n* conjetura *f*; hipótese *f*

surmount /səˈmaʊnt/ *vt* sobrepujar, vencer, (*P*) superar

surname /ˈsɜːneɪm/ *n* sobrenome *m*, (*P*) apelido *m*

surpass /səˈpɑːs/ *vt* superar, ultrapassar, exceder

surplus /ˈsɜːpləs/ *n* excedente *m*, excesso *m*; *Finance* saldo *m* positivo ● *a* excedente, em excesso

surpris|e /səˈpraɪz/ *n* surpresa *f* ● *vt* surpreender. **~ed** *a* surpreendido; admirado (**at** com). **~ing** *a* surpreendente. **~ingly** *adv* surpreendentemente

surrender /səˈrendə(r)/ *vi* render-se ● *vt* (*hand over*) *Mil* entregar ● *n Mil* rendição *f*; (*of rights*) renúncia *f*

surrogate /ˈsʌrəgeɪt/ *n* delegado *m*; **~ mother** mãe *f* de aluguel, (*P*) aluguer

surround /səˈraʊnd/ *vt* rodear, cercar; *Mil etc* cercar. **~ing** *a* circundante, vizinho. **~ings** *npl* arredores *mpl*, (*P*) redondezas *fpl*; (*setting*) meio *m*, ambiente *m*

surveillance /sɜːˈveɪləns/ *n* vigilância *f*

survey[1] /səˈveɪ/ *vt* ‹*landscape etc*› observar; (*review*) passar em revista; (*inquire about*) pesquisar; ‹*land*› fazer o levantamento de; ‹*building*› vistoriar; inspecionar. **~or** *n* (*of buildings*) fiscal *m*; (*of land*) agrimensor *m*

survey[2] /ˈsɜːveɪ/ *n* (*inspection*) vistoria *f*; inspeção *f*; (*general view*) panorâmica *f*; (*inquiry*) pesquisa *f*

survival /səˈvaɪvl/ *n* sobrevivência *f*; (*relic*) relíquia *f*, vestígio *m*

surviv|e /səˈvaɪv/ *vt/i* sobreviver (a). **~or** *n* sobrevivente *mf*

susceptib|le /səˈseptəbl/ *a* (*prone*) susceptível (**to** a); (*sensitive, impressionable*) susceptível, sensível

suspect[1] /səˈspekt/ *vt* suspeitar; (*doubt, distrust*) desconfiar de, suspeitar de

suspect[2] /ˈsʌspekt/ *a* & *n* suspeito *m*

suspen|d /səˈspend/ *vt* (*hang, stop*) suspender; (*from duty etc*) suspender; **~ded sentence** suspensão *f* de pena. **~sion** *n* suspensão *f*; **~sion bridge** ponte *f* suspensa or pênsil

suspender /səˈspendə(r)/ *n* (presilha *f* de) liga *f*; **~s** *Amer* (*braces*) suspensórios *mpl*. **~ belt** *n* cinta-liga *f*, (*P*) cinta *f* de ligas, (*P*) cinto *m* de ligas

suspense /səˈspens/ *n* ansiedade *f*, incerteza *f*; (*in book etc*) suspense *m*, tensão *f*

suspicion /səˈspɪʃn/ *n* suspeita *f*; (*distrust*) desconfiança *f*; (*trace*) vestígio *m*, (*P*) traço *m*

suspicious /səsˈpɪʃəs/ *a* desconfiado; (*causing suspicion*) suspeito; **be ~ of** desconfiar de

sustain /səˈsteɪn/ *vt* (*support*) suster, sustentar; (*suffer*) sofrer; (*keep up*) sustentar; *Jur* (*uphold*) sancionar; ‹*interest, effort*› manter; **~ed effort** esforço *m* contínuo

sustenance /ˈsʌstɪnəns/ *n* (*food*) alimento *m*, sustento *m*

SUV *abbr* (= **sport utility vehicle**) carro *m* esporte, (*P*) veículo *m* utilitário desportivo

swagger /ˈswægə(r)/ *vi* pavonear-se, andar com arrogância

swallow[1] /ˈswɒləʊ/ *vt/i* engolir; **~ up** (*absorb, engulf*) devorar, tragar

swallow[2] /ˈswɒləʊ/ *n* (*bird*) andorinha *f*

swam /swæm/ ▶ **SWIM**

swamp /swɒmp/ *n* pântano *m*, brejo *m* ● *vt* (*flood, overwhelm*) inundar, submergir

swan /swɒn/ *n* cisne *m*

swank /swæŋk/ *vi* [!] (*show off*) gabar-se; mostrar-se [!]

swap /swɒp/ *vt/i* (*pt* **swapped**) [!] trocar (**for** por) ● *n* [!] troca *f*

swarm /swɔːm/ *n* (*of insects, people*) enxame *m* ● *vi* formigar; **~ into** or **round** invadir

swarthy /ˈswɔːðɪ/ *a* (**-ier**, **-iest**) moreno, trigueiro

swat /swɒt/ *vt* (*pt* **swatted**) ‹*fly etc*› esmagar, esborrachar

sway /sweɪ/ *vt/i* oscilar, balançar(-se); (*influence*) mover, influenciar ● *n* oscilação *f*, balanceio *m*; (*rule*) domínio *m*, poder *m*

swear /sweə(r)/ *vt/i* (*pt* **swore**, *pp* **sworn**) jurar; (*curse*) praguejar; rogar pragas (**at/a** contra); **~ by** jurar por; [!] (*recommend*) ter grande fé em. **~ word** *n* palavrão *m*

sweat /swet/ *n* suor *m* ● *vi* suar. **~y** *a* suado

sweater /ˈswetə(r)/ *n* suéter *m*, (*P*) camisola *f*

sweatshirt /ˈswetʃɜːt/ *n* suéter *m* or (*P*) camisola *f* de malha or algodão

Swed|e /swiːd/ *n* sueco *m*. **~en** *n* Suécia *f*. **~ish** *a & n* sueco *m*

sweep /swiːp/ *vt/i* (*pt* **swept**) varrer; (*go majestically*) avançar majestosamente; (*carry away*) arrastar; ‹*chimney*› limpar ● *n* (*with broom*) varredela *f*; (*curve*) curva *f*; (*movement*) gesto *m* largo; **(chimney-)~** limpa-chaminés *m*. **~ing** *a* ‹*gesture*› largo; ‹*action*› de grande alcance; **~ing statement** generalização *f* fácil

sweet /swiːt/ *a* (**-er**, **-est**) doce; [!] (*charming*) doce; gracinha, (*P*) encanto; [!] (*pleasant*) agradável ● *n* doce *m*; **~ corn** milho *m*; **~ pea** ervilha-de-cheiro *f*; **~ shop** confeitaria *f*; **have a ~ tooth** gostar de doce, (*P*) ser guloso. **~ness** *n* doçura *f*

sweeten /ˈswiːtn/ *vt* adoçar; *fig* (*mitigate*) suavizar. **~er** *n* (*for tea, coffee*) adoçante (artificial) *m*; [!] (*bribe*) agrado *m*, (*P*) suborno *m*

sweetheart /ˈswiːthɑːt/ *n* namorado *m*, namorada *f*; (*term of endearment*) querido *m*, querida *f*, amor *m*

swell /swel/ *vt/i* (*pt* **swelled**, *pp* **swollen**, *or* **swelled**) (*expand*) inchar; (*increase*) aumentar ● *n* (*of sea*) ondulação *f* ● *a* [!] (*excellent*) excelente; [!] (*smart*) chique. **~ing** *n Med* inchação *f*, inchaço *m*

swelter /ˈsweltə(r)/ *vi* fazer um calor abrasador; (*person*) abafar (com calor)

swept /swept/ ▶ SWEEP

swerve /swɜːv/ *vi* desviar-se, dar uma guinada

swift /swɪft/ *a* (**-er,**, **-est**) rápido, veloz

swig /swɪg/ *vt* (*pt* **swigged**) [!] (*drink*) emborcar [!]; beber em longos tragos ● *n* [!] trago *m*; gole *m*

swim /swɪm/ *vi* (*pt* **swam**, *pp* **swum**, *pres p* **swimming**) nadar; ‹*room, head*› rodar ● *vt* atravessar a nado; (*distance*) nadar ● *n* banho *m*. **~mer** *n* nadador *m*. **~ming** *n* natação *f*. **~ming bath**, **~ming pool** *ns* piscina *f*; **~ming cap** *n* touca *f* de banho *or* (*P*) de natação; **~ming costume**, **~-suit** *ns* maiô *m*, (*P*) fato *m* de banho; **~ming trunks** *npl* calção *m or* (*P*) calções *mpl* de banho

swindle /ˈswɪndl/ *vt* trapacear, fraudar, (*P*) vigarizar ● *n* vigarice *f*. **~r** /-ə(r)/ *n* vigarista *mf*

swine /swaɪn/ *npl* (*pigs*) porcos *mpl* ● *n* (*pl invar*) [!] (*person*) animal *m*; canalha *m* [!]. **~ flu** *n* gripe *f* suína

swing /swɪŋ/ *vt/i* (*pt* **swung**) balançar(-se); (*turn round*) girar ● *n* (*seat*) balanço *m*; (*of opinion*) reviravolta *f*; *Mus* swing *m*; (*rhythm*) ritmo *m*; **in full ~** no máximo, em plena atividade; **~ round** (*of person*) virar-se

swipe /swaɪp/ *vt* [!] (*hit*) bater em; dar uma pancada em; [!] (*steal*) afanar [!]; roubar ● *n* [!] (*hit*) pancada *f*; **~ card** cartão *m* magnético

swirl /swɜːl/ *vi* rodopiar, redemoinhar ● *n* turbilhão *m*, redemoinho *m*

swish /swɪʃ/ *vt/i* sibilar, zunir, (fazer) cortar o ar; (*with brushing sound*) roçar ● *a* [!] chique, fino

Swiss /swɪs/ *a & n* suíço *m*

switch /swɪtʃ/ *n* interruptor *m*; (*change*) mudança *f* ● *vt* (*transfer*) transferir; (*exchange*) trocar ● *vi* desviar-se; **~ off** desligar

switchboard /ˈswɪtʃbɔːd/ *n* (*telephone*) PBX *m*, mesa *f* telefônica *or* (*P*) telefónica

Switzerland /ˈswɪtsələnd/ *n* Suíça *f*

swivel /ˈswɪvl/ *vt/i* (*pt* **swivelled**) (fazer) girar; **~ chair** cadeira *f* giratória

swollen /ˈswəʊlən/ ▶ SWELL *a* inchado

swoop /swuːp/ *vi* ‹*bird*› lançar-se; cair (**down on** sobre); ‹*police*› dar uma batida policial, (*P*) fazer uma rusga

sword /sɔːd/ *n* espada *f*

swore /swɔː(r)/ ▶ SWEAR

sworn /swɔːn/ ▶ SWEAR *a* ‹*enemy*› jurado, declarado; ‹*ally*› fiel

swot /swɒt/ *vt/i* (*pt* **swotted**) [!] (*study*) estudar muito, (*P*) marrar [x] ● *n* [!]

estudante *m* muito aplicado, (*P*) marrão *m* ⊠

swum /swʌm/ ▶ **SWIM**

swung /swʌŋ/ ▶ **SWING**

syllable /ˈsɪləbl/ *n* sílaba *f*

syllabus /ˈsɪləbəs/ *n* (*pl* **-uses**) programa *m*

symbol /ˈsɪmbl/ *n* símbolo *m*. **~ic(al)** /-ˈbɒlɪk(l)/ *a* simbólico. **~ism** *n* simbolismo *m*

symbolize /ˈsɪmbəlaɪz/ *vt* simbolizar

symmetr|y /ˈsɪmətrɪ/ *n* simetria *f*. **~ical** /sɪˈmetrɪkl/ *a* simétrico

sympathize /ˈsɪmpəθaɪz/ *vi* **~ with** ter pena de, condoer-se de; *fig* compartilhar os sentimentos de. **~r** *n* simpatizante *mf*

sympath|y /ˈsɪmpəθɪ/ *n* (*pity*) pena *f*, compaixão *f*; (*solidarity*) solidariedade *f*; (*condolences*) pêsames *mpl*, condolências *fpl*; **be in ~y with** estar de acordo com. **~etic** /-ˈθetɪk/ *a* compreensivo, simpático; (*likeable*) simpático; (*showing pity*) compassivo

symphon|y /ˈsɪmfənɪ/ *n* sinfonia *f* ● *a* sinfônico, (*P*) sinfónico

symptom /ˈsɪmptəm/ *n* sintoma *m*

synagogue /ˈsɪnəgɒg/ *n* sinagoga *f*

synchronize /ˈsɪŋkrənaɪz/ *vt* sincronizar

syndrome /ˈsɪndrəʊm/ *n Med* síndrome *f*, (*P*) síndroma *f*

synonym /ˈsɪnənɪm/ *n* sinônimo *m*, (*P*) sinónimo *m*. **~ous** /sɪˈnɒnɪməs/ *a* sinônimo; (*P*) sinónimo (**with** de)

synopsis /sɪˈnɒpsɪs/ *n* (*pl* **-opses** /-siːz/) sinopse *f*, resumo *m*

synthesis /ˈsɪnθəsɪs/ *n* (*pl* **-theses** /-siːz/) síntese *f*

synthetic /sɪnˈθetɪk/ *a* sintético

Syria /ˈsɪrɪə/ *n* Síria *f*

syringe /sɪˈrɪndʒ/ *n* seringa *f* ● *vt* seringar, injetar

syrup /ˈsɪrəp/ *n* (*liquid*) xarope *m*; (*treacle*) calda *f* de açúcar. **~y** *a fig* melado; enjoativo

system /ˈsɪstəm/ *n* sistema *m*; (*body*) organismo *m*; (*order*) método *m*. **~atic** /sɪstəˈmætɪk/ *a* sistemático

Tt

tab /tæb/ *n* (*flap*) lingueta *f*; (*for fastening, hanging*) aba *f*; (*label*) etiqueta *f*; (*loop*) argola *f*; *Amer* [!] (*bill*) conta *f*; **keep ~s on** [!] vigiar

table /ˈteɪbl/ *n* mesa *f*; (*list*) tabela *f*, lista *f*; **at ~** à mesa; **lay** or **set the ~** pôr a mesa; **turn the ~s** inverter as posições; **~ tennis** pingue-pongue *m*; **~ of contents** índice *m* (das matérias) ● *vt* (*submit*) apresentar; (*postpone*) adiar. **~cloth** *n* toalha de mesa *f*

tablespoon /ˈteɪblspuːn/ *n* colher *f* grande de sopa

tablet /ˈtæblɪt/ *n* (*of stone*) lápide *f*, placa *f*; (*drug*) comprimido *m*

tabloid /ˈtæblɔɪd/ *n* tablóide *m*; **~ journalism** *pej* jornalismo *m* sensacionalista, imprensa *f* marrom

taboo /təˈbuː/ *n* & *a* tabu *m*

taciturn /ˈtæsɪtɜːn/ *a* taciturno

tack /tæk/ *n* (*nail*) tacha *f*; (*stitch*) ponto *m* de alinhavo; *Naut* amura *f*; *fig* (*course of action*) rumo *m* ● *vt* (*nail*) pregar com tachas; (*stitch*) alinhavar ● *vi Naut* bordejar; **~ on** (*add*) acrescentar, juntar

tackle /ˈtækl/ *n* equipamento *m*, apetrechos *mpl*; *Sport* placagem *f* ● *vt* ‹*problem etc*› atacar; *Sport* placar; ‹*a thief etc*› agarrar-se a

tacky /ˈtækɪ/ *a* (**-ier**, **-iest**) peganhento, pegajoso

tact /tækt/ *n* tato *m*. **~ful** *a* cheio de tato, diplomático. **~fully** *adv* com tato. **~less** *a* sem tato

tactic /ˈtæktɪk/ *n* (*expedient*) tática *f*. **~s** *n(pl)* (*procedure*) tática *f*. **~al** *a* tático

tadpole /ˈtædpəʊl/ *n* girino *m*

tag /tæg/ *n* (*label*) etiqueta *f*; (*on shoelace*) agulheta *f*; (*phrase*) chavão *m*, clichê *m* ● *vi* (*pt* **tagged**) etiquetar; (*add*) juntar ● *vi* **~ along** [!] andar atrás, seguir

tail /teɪl/ *n* cauda *f*, rabo *m*; (*of shirt*) fralda *f*; **~s!** (*tossing coin*) coroa! ● *vt* (*follow*) seguir, vigiar ● *vi* **~ away** or **off** diminuir, baixar. **~back** *n* (*traffic*) fila *f*, (*P*) bicha *f*; **~ light** *n Auto* farolete *m* traseiro, (*P*) farolim *m* traseiro

tailor /ˈteɪlə(r)/ *n* alfaiate *m* ● *vt* ‹*garment*› fazer; *fig* (*adapt*) adaptar. **~-made** *a* feito sob medida, (*P*) por

s t

medida; **~-made for** *fig* feito para, talhado para

take /teɪk/ *vt/i* (*pt* **took**, *pp* **taken**) (*get hold of*) agarrar em, pegar em; (*capture*) tomar; ‹*a seat, a drink, train, bus etc*› tomar; (*carry*) levar (**to** a, para); (*contain, escort*) levar; (*tolerate*) suportar, aguentar; ‹*choice, exam*› fazer; ‹*photo*› tirar; (*require*) exigir; **be ~n by** or **with** ficar encantado com; **be ~n ill** adoecer; **it ~s time to** leva tempo para; **~ after** parecer-se a; **~ away** levar; **~ away from sb/sth** tirar de alguém/de algo; **~ back** aceitar de volta; (*return*) devolver; (*accompany*) acompanhar; (*statement*) retirar, retratar; **~ down** ‹*object*› tirar para baixo; ‹*notes*› tirar, tomar; **~ in** ‹*garment*› meter para dentro; (*include*) incluir; (*cheat*) enganar, levar [!]; (*grasp*) compreender; (*receive*) receber; **~ it that** supor que; **~ on** ‹*task*› encarregar-se de; ‹*staff*› admitir, contratar; **~ out** tirar; (*on an outing*) levar para sair; **~ part** participar or tomar parte (**in** em); **~ place** ocorrer, suceder; **~ sides** tomar partido; **~ sides with** tomar o partido de; **~ to** gostar de, simpatizar com; ‹*activity*› tomar gosto por, entregar-se a; **~ up** ‹*object*› apanhar, pegar em; ‹*hobby*› dedicar-se a; (*occupy*) ocupar, tomar □ **~ off** *vt* (*remove*) tirar; (*mimic*) imitar, macaquear ● *vi Aviat* decolar, levantar voo, (*P*) descolar. **~ over** *vt* tomar conta de, assumir a direção de ● *vi* tomar o poder; **~ over from** (*relieve*) render, substituir; (*succeed*) suceder a. **~-away** *n* (*meal*) comida *f* para levar, take-away *m*; (*shop*) loja *f* que só vende comida para ser consumida em outro lugar; **~-off** *n* imitação *f*; *Aviat* decolagem *f*, (*P*) descolagem *f*; **~over** *n Pol* tomada *f* de poder; *Comm* take-over *m*

t

takings /'teɪkɪŋz/ *npl* receita *f*

talcum /'tælkəm/ *n* talco *m*; **~ powder** pó *m* (de) talco

tale /teɪl/ *n* conto *m*, história *f*

talent /'tælənt/ *n* talento *m*. **~ed** *a* talentoso, bem dotado

talk /tɔ:k/ *vt/i* falar; (*chat*) conversar; **~ into doing** convencer a fazer; **~ nonsense** dizer disparates; **~ over** discutir; **~ shop** falar de assuntos profissionais; **~ to o.s.** falar sozinho, falar com os seus botões ● *n* conversa *f*; (*mode of speech*) fala *f*; (*lecture*) palestra *f*; **small ~** conversa *f* banal; **there's ~ of** fala-se de

talkative /'tɔ:kətɪv/ *a* falador, conversador, tagarela

tall /tɔ:l/ *a* (**-er**, **-est**) alto; **~ story** [!] história *f* do arco-da-velha

tally /'tælɪ/ *vi* corresponder (**with** a); conferir (**with** com)

tame /teɪm/ *a* (**-er**, **-est**) manso; (*domesticated*) domesticado; (*dull*) insípido ● *vt* amansar, domesticar

tamper /'tæmpə(r)/ *vi* **~ with** mexer indevidamente em; (*text*) alterar

tampon /'tæmpən/ *n Med* tampão *m*; (*sanitary towel*) toalha *f* higiênica, (*P*) tampão *m*

tan /tæn/ *vt/i* (*pt* **tanned**) queimar, bronzear; ‹*hide*› curtir ● *n* bronzeado *m* ● *a* castanho amarelado

tandem /'tændəm/ *n* (*bicycle*) tandem *m*; **in ~** em tandem, um atrás do outro

tang /tæŋ/ *n* (*taste*) sabor *m* or gosto *m* característico *m*; (*smell*) cheiro *m* característico

tangerine /tændʒə'ri:n/ *n* tangerina *f*

tangible /'tændʒəbl/ *a* tangível

tangle /'tæŋgl/ *vt* emaranhar, enredar; **become ~d** emaranhar-se, enredar-se ● *n* emaranhado *m*

tank /tæŋk/ *n* tanque *m*, reservatório *m*; (*for petrol*) tanque *m*, (*P*) depósito *m*; (*for fish*) aquário *m*; *Mil* tanque *m*

tanker /'tæŋkə(r)/ *n* carro-tanque *m*, camião-cisterna *m*; (*ship*) petroleiro *m*

tantaliz|e /'tæntəlaɪz/ *vt* atormentar, tantalizar. **~ing** *a* tentador

tantamount /'tæntəmaʊnt/ *a* **be ~ to** equivaler a

tantrum /'tæntrəm/ *n* chilique *m*, ataque *m* de mau gênio, (*P*) génio, birra *f*

tap[1] /tæp/ *n* (*for water etc*) torneira *f*; **on ~** [!] (*available*) disponível ● *vt* (*pt* **tapped**) ‹*resources*› explorar; ‹*telephone*› grampear [!], pôr escutas em or colocar sob escuta

tap[2] /tæp/ *vt/i* (*pt* **tapped**) bater levemente. **~ dance** *n* sapateado *m*

tape /teɪp/ *n* (*for dressmaking*) fita *f*; (*sticky*) fita *f* adesiva, (*P*) fita-cola *f*; **(magnetic) ~** fita (magnética) *f* ● *vt* (*tie*) atar, prender; (*stick*) colar; (*record*) gravar. **~ measure** *n* fita *f* métrica; **~ recorder** *n* gravador *m*

taper /'teɪpə(r)/ *n* vela *f* comprida e fina ● *vt/i* **~ (off)** estreitar(-se), afilar(-se). **~ed ~ing** *adjs* ‹*fingers etc*› afilado; ‹*trousers*› afunilado

tapestry /'tæpɪstrɪ/ *n* tapeçaria *f*

tar /tɑ:(r)/ *n* alcatrão *m* ● *vt* (*pt* **tarred**) alcatroar

target /ˈtɑ:gɪt/ *n* alvo *m* ● *vt* ter como alvo

tariff /ˈtærɪf/ *n* tarifa *f*; (*on import*) direitos *mpl* aduaneiros

Tarmac® /ˈtɑ:mæk/ *n* macadame (alcatroado) *m*, (*P*) asfalto *m*; (*runway*) pista *f*

tarnish /ˈtɑ:nɪʃ/ *vt/i* (fazer) perder o brilho; (*stain*) manchar

tarpaulin /tɑ:ˈpɔ:lɪn/ *n* lona *f* impermeável (alcatroada *or* (*P*) asfaltada or encerada)

tart[1] /tɑ:t/ *a* (**-er**, **-est**) ácido; *fig* (*cutting*) mordaz; azedo

tart[2] /tɑ:t/ *n Culin* torta *f* de fruta, (*P*) tarte *f*; ⊠ (*prostitute*) prostituta *f*; mulher *f* da vida ⊠ ● *vt* **~ up** ! embonecar(-se)

tartan /ˈtɑ:tn/ *n* tecido *m* escocês ● *a* escocês

task /tɑ:sk/ *n* tarefa *f*, trabalho *m*; **take to ~** repreender, censurar. **~ force** *n Mil* força-tarefa *f*, (*P*) unidade *f* especial

tassel /ˈtæsl/ *n* borla *f*

taste /teɪst/ *n* gosto *m*; *fig* (*sample*) amostra *f*; **have a ~ of** (*experience*) provar ● *vt* (*eat, enjoy*) saborear; (*try*) provar; (*perceive taste of*) sentir o gosto de ● *vi* **~ of** or **like** ter o sabor de, saber a. **~ful** *a* de bom gosto. **~less** *a* insípido, insosso; *fig* (*not in good taste*) sem gosto; *fig* (*in bad taste*) de mau gosto

tasty /ˈteɪstɪ/ *a* (**-ier**, **-iest**) saboroso, gostoso

tat /tæt/ ▶ TIT[2]

tatter|s /ˈtætəz/ *npl* farrapos *mpl*. **~ed** /-əd/ *a* esfarrapado

tattoo /təˈtu:/ *vt* tatuar ● *n* tatuagem *f*

tatty /ˈtætɪ/ *a* (**-ier**, **-iest**) ! enxovalhado; em mau estado

taught /tɔ:t/ ▶ TEACH

taunt /tɔ:nt/ *vt* escarnecer de, zombar de ● *n* escárnio *m*

Taurus /ˈtɔ:rəs/ *n Astr* Touro *m*

taut /tɔ:t/ *a* esticado, retesado; *fig* (*of nerves*) tenso

tawdry /ˈtɔ:drɪ/ *a* (**-ier**, **-iest**) espalhafatoso e ordinário

tax /tæks/ *n* taxa *f*, imposto *m*; (*on income*) imposto *m* de renda, (*P*) sobre o rendimento; **~ relief** isenção *f* de imposto; **~ return** declaração *f* do imposto de renda, (*P*) sobre o rendimento; **~ year** ano *m* fiscal ● *vt* taxar, lançar impostos sobre, tributar; *fig* (*put to test*) pôr à prova. **~-free** *a* isento de imposto. **~able** *a* tributável, passível de imposto. **~ation** /-ˈseɪʃn/ *n* impostos *mpl*, tributação *f*. **~ing** *a* penoso, difícil

taxi /ˈtæksɪ/ *n* (*pl* **-is**) táxi *m*; **~ rank, ~ stand** ponto *m* de táxis, (*P*) praça *f* de táxis ● *vi* (*pt* **taxied**, *pres p* **taxiing**) *Aviat* rolar na pista, taxiar. **~cab** *n* táxi *m*; **~-driver** *n* motorista *mf* de táxi

taxpayer /ˈtækspeɪə(r)/ *n* contribuinte *mf*

tea /ti:/ *n* chá *m*; **high ~** refeição *f* leve à noite. **~bag** *n* saquinho *m* de chá; **~ break** *n* intervalo *m* para o chá; **~ leaf** *n* folha *f* de chá; **~ shop** *n* salão *m* or casa *f* de chá; **~time** *n* hora *f* do chá; **~ towel** *n* pano *m* de prato

teach /ti:tʃ/ *vt* (*pt* **taught**) ensinar, dar aulas de, lecionar (**sb sth** alg coisa a alguém) ● *vi* ensinar, ser professor. **~er** *n* professor *m*. **~ing** *n* ensino *m*; (*doctrines*) ensinamento(s) *m(pl)* ● *a* pedagógico, de ensino; ‹*staff*› docente

teacup /ˈti:kʌp/ *n* xícara *f* de chá, (*P*) chávena *f*

teak /ti:k/ *n* teca *f*

team /ti:m/ *n* equipe *f*, (*P*) equipa *f*; (*of oxen*) junta *f*; (*of horses*) parelha *f* ● *vi* **~ up** juntar-se, associar-se (**with** a). **~work** *n* trabalho *m* de equipe, (*P*) equipa

teapot /ˈti:pɒt/ *n* bule *m*

tear[1] /teə(r)/ *vt/i* (*pt* **tore**, *pp* **torn**) rasgar(-se); (*snatch*) arrancar, puxar; (*rush*) lançar-se, ir numa correria; *fig* dividir ● *n* rasgão *m*; **~ o.s. away** arrancar-se (**from** de)

tear[2] /tɪə(r)/ *n* lágrima *f*. **~ gas** *n* gases *mpl* lacrimogênios, (*P*) gás *m* lacrimogénio

tearful /ˈtɪəfl/ *a* lacrimoso, choroso. **~ly** *adv* choroso, com (as) lágrimas nos olhos

tease /ti:z/ *vt* implicar; (*make fun of*) caçoar de, (*P*) fazer troça de

teaspoon /ˈti:spu:n/ *n* colher *f* de chá

teat /ti:t/ *n* (*of bottle*) bico *m*; (*of animal*) teta *f*

technical /ˈteknɪkl/ *a* técnico. **~ity** /-ˈkælətɪ/ *n* questão *f* de ordem técnica. **~ly** *adv* tecnicamente

technician /tekˈnɪʃn/ *n* técnico *m*

technique /tekˈni:k/ *n* técnica *f*

technolog|y /tekˈnɒlədʒɪ/ *n* tecnologia *f*. **~ical** /-əˈlɒdʒɪkl/ *a* tecnológico

teddy /'tedɪ/ *a* **~ (bear)** ursinho *m* de pelúcia, (*P*) peluche
tedious /'ti:dɪəs/ *a* maçante
tedium /'ti:dɪəm/ *n* tédio *m*
tee /ti:/ *n Golf* tee *m*
teem[1] /ti:m/ *vi* **~ (with)** (*swarm*) pulular (de), fervilhar (de), abundar (em)
teem[2] /ti:m/ *vi* **~ (with rain)** chover torrencialmente
teenage /'ti:neɪdʒ/ *a* juvenil, de/para adolescente. **~r** /-ə(r)/ *n* jovem *mf*, adolescente *mf*
teens /ti:nz/ *npl* **in one's ~** na adolescência, entre os 13 e os 19 anos
teeter /'ti:tə(r)/ *vi* cambalear
teeth /ti:θ/ ▶ TOOTH
teeth|e /ti:ð/ *vi* começar a ter dentes; **~ing troubles** *fig* problemas *mpl* iniciais
teetotaller /ti:'təʊtlə(r)/ *n* abstêmio *m*, (*P*) abstémio *m*
telecommunications /telɪkəmju:nɪ'keɪʃnz/ *npl* telecomunicações *fpl*
telegram /'telɪgræm/ *n* telegrama *m*
telepath|y /tɪ'lepəθɪ/ *n* telepatia *f*
telephone /'telɪfəʊn/ *n* telefone *m* ● *vt* ‹*person*› telefonar a; ‹*message*› telefonar ● *vi* telefonar; **~ book** lista *f* telefônica, (*P*) telefónica; **~ box, ~ booth** cabine *f* telefônica, (*P*) telefónica; **~ call** chamada *f*; **~ directory** lista *f* telefônica, (*P*) telefónica, guia *m* telefônico; **~ number** número *m* de telefone
telephoto /telɪ'fəʊtəʊ/ *n* **~ lens** teleobjetiva *f*
telescop|e /'telɪskəʊp/ *n* telescópio *m* ● *vt/i* encaixar(-se). **~ic** /-'skɒpɪk/ *a* telescópico
televise /'telɪvaɪz/ *vt* televisionar, transmitir pela televisão
t
television /'telɪvɪʒn/ *n* televisão *f*; **~ set** aparelho *m* de televisão, televisor *m*
teleworking /'telɪwɜ:kɪŋ/ *n* teletrabalho *m*
tell /tel/ *vt* (*pt* **told**) dizer (**sb sth** alg coisa a alguém); ‹*story*› contar; (*distinguish*) distinguir, diferençar, diferenciar; **I told you so** bem lhe disse; **~ off** 🅸 (*scold*) ralhar com, dar uma bronca em; **~ tales** mexericar, fofocar ● *vi* (*know*) ver-se, saber; **~ of** falar de; **~ on** (*have effect on*) afetar; 🅸 (*inform on*) fazer queixa de 🅸. **~tale** *n* mexeriqueiro *m*, fofoqueiro *m* ● *a* (*revealing*) revelador
telly /'telɪ/ *n* 🅸 TV *f* 🅸
temp /temp/ *n* 🅸 empregado *m* temporário
temper /'tempə(r)/ *n* humor *m*, disposição *f*; (*anger*) mau humor *m* ● *vt* temperar; **keep/lose one's ~** manter a calma/perder a calma or a cabeça, zangar-se
temperament /'temprəmənt/ *n* temperamento *m*. **~al** /-'mentl/ *a* caprichoso
temperate /'tempərət/ *a* moderado, comedido; ‹*climate*› temperado
temperature /'temprətʃə(r)/ *n* temperatura *f*; **have a ~** estar com or ter febre
tempestuous /tem'pestʃʊəs/ *a* tempestuoso
template /'templ(e)ɪt/ *n* molde *m*
temple[1] /'templ/ *n* templo *m*
temple[2] /'templ/ *n Anat* têmpora *f*, fonte *f*
tempo /'tempəʊ/ *n* (*pl* **-os**) *Mus* tempo *m*; (*pace*) ritmo *m*
temporar|y /'temprərɪ/ *a* temporário, provisório
tempt /tempt/ *vt* tentar; **~ sb to do** tentar alguém a fazer, dar a alguém vontade de fazer. **~ation** /-'teɪʃn/ *n* tentação *f*. **~ing** *a* tentador
ten /ten/ *a & n* dez *m*
tenac|ious /tɪ'neɪʃəs/ *a* tenaz. **~ity** /-æsətɪ/ *n* tenacidade *f*
tenant /'tenənt/ *n* inquilino *m*, locatário *m*
tend[1] /tend/ *vt* tomar conta de, cuidar de
tend[2] /tend/ *vi* **~ to** (*be apt to*) tender a, ter tendência para
tendency /'tendənsɪ/ *n* tendência *f*
tender[1] /'tendə(r)/ *a* (*soft, delicate*) terno; (*sore, painful*) sensível, dolorido; (*loving*) terno, meigo. **~-hearted** *a* compassivo. **~ly** *adv* (*lovingly*) ternamente, meigamente; (*delicately*) delicadamente. **~ness** *n* (*love*) ternura *f*, meiguice *f*
tender[2] /'tendə(r)/ *vt* ‹*money*› oferecer; ‹*apologies, resignation*› apresentar ● *vi* **~ (for)** apresentar orçamento (para) ● *n Comm* orçamento *m*; **legal ~** (*money*) moeda *f* corrente
tendon /'tendən/ *n* tendão *m*
tenement /'tenəmənt/ *n* prédio *m* de apartamentos de renda moderada; *Amer* (*slum*) prédio *m* pobre

tennis /ˈtenɪs/ *n* tênis *m*, (*P*) ténis *m*; **~ court** quadra *f* de tênis, (*P*) court *m* de ténis

tenor /ˈtenə(r)/ *n* (*meaning*) teor *m*; *Mus* tenor *m*

tense[1] /tens/ *n Gram* tempo *m*

tense[2] /tens/ *a* (**-er**, **-est**) tenso ● *vt* ‹*muscles*› retesar

tension /ˈtenʃn/ *n* tensão *f*

tent /tent/ *n* tenda *f*, barraca *f*

tentative /ˈtentətɪv/ *a* provisório; (*hesitant*) hesitante

tenterhooks /ˈtentəhʊks/ *npl* **on ~** em suspense

tenth /tenθ/ *a & n* décimo *m*

tenuous /ˈtenjʊəs/ *a* tênue, (*P*) ténue

tepid /ˈtepɪd/ *a* tépido, morno

term /tɜːm/ *n* (*word*) termo *m*; (*limit*) prazo *m*, termo *m*; *Schol etc* período *m*, trimestre *m*; *Amer* semestre *m*; (*of imprisonment*) (duração de) pena *f*; **~ of office** *Pol* mandato *m*; **come to ~s with** chegar a um acordo com; (*become resigned to*) resignar-se a; **~s** (*conditions*) condições *fpl*; **on good/bad ~s** de boas/más relações; **not on speaking ~s** de relações cortadas ● *vt* designar, denominar, chamar

terminal /ˈtɜːmɪnl/ *a* terminal, final; ‹*illness*› fatal, mortal, terminal ● *n* (*oil, computer*) terminal *m*; *Rail* estação *f* terminal; *Electr* borne *m*; **(air) ~** terminal *m* (de avião)

terminat|e /ˈtɜːmɪneɪt/ *vt* terminar, pôr termo a ● *vi* terminar. **~ion** /-ˈneɪʃn/ *n* término *m*, (*P*) terminação *f*, termo *m*

terminology /tɜːmɪˈnɒlədʒɪ/ *n* terminologia *f*

terminus /ˈtɜːmɪnəs/ *n* (*pl* **-ni** /-naɪ/) (*rail, coach*) estação *f* terminal

terrace /ˈterəs/ *n* terraço *m*; (*in cultivation*) socalco *m*; (*houses*) casas *fpl* em fileira contínua, lance *m* de casas; **the ~s** *Sport* arquibancada *f*, (*P*) bancada *f* (principal); **~d house** casa *f* ladeada por outras casas

terrain /teˈreɪn/ *n* terreno *m*

terribl|e /ˈterəbl/ *a* terrível. **~y** *adv* terrivelmente; [!] (*very*) extremamente; espantosamente

terrific /təˈrɪfɪk/ *a* terrífico, tremendo; [!] (*excellent; great*) tremendo, fantástico. **~ally** *adv* [!] (*very*) tremendamente [!]; [!] (*very well*) lindamente; maravilhosamente

terrif|y /ˈterɪfaɪ/ *vt* aterrar, aterrorizar; **be ~ied of** ter pavor de

territorial /terɪˈtɔːrɪəl/ *a* territorial

territory /ˈterɪtərɪ/ *n* território *m*

terror /ˈterə(r)/ *n* terror *m*, pavor *m*

terrorism /ˈterərɪzəm/ *n* terrorismo *m*

terroris|t /ˈterərɪst/ *n* terrorista *mf*. **~m** /-zəm/ *n* terrorismo *m*

terrorize /ˈterəraɪz/ *vt* aterrorizar, aterrar

terse /tɜːs/ *a* conciso, lapidar; (*curt*) lacônico, (*P*) lacónico

test /test/ *n* teste *m*, exame *m*, prova *f*; *Schol* prova *f*, teste *m*; (*of goods*) controle *m*; (*of machine etc*) ensaio *m*; (*of strength*) prova *f*; **put to the ~** pôr à prova; **~ match** jogo *m* internacional ● *vt* examinar; (*check*) controlar; (*try*) ensaiar; ‹*pupil*› interrogar, (*P*) examinar. **~ tube** *n* proveta *f*; **~-tube baby** bebê *m* de proveta, (*P*) bebé-proveta *mf*

testament /ˈtestəmənt/ *n* testamento *m*; **Old/New T~** Antigo/Novo Testamento *m*

testicle /ˈtestɪkl/ *n* testículo *m*

testify /ˈtestɪfaɪ/ *vt/i* testificar, testemunhar, depôr

testimonial /testɪˈməʊnɪəl/ *n* carta *f* de recomendação

testimony /ˈtestɪmənɪ/ *n* testemunho *m*

tetanus /ˈtetənəs/ *n* tétano *m*

tether /ˈteðə(r)/ *vt* prender com corda ● *n* **be at the end of one's ~** estar nas últimas

text /tekst/ *n* texto *m*; **~ message** mensagem *f* escrita *or* (*P*) sms *m* ● *vt* enviar uma mensagem de texto a

textbook /ˈtekstbʊk/ *n* compêndio *m*, manual *m*, livro *m* de texto

textile /ˈtekstaɪl/ *n & a* têxtil *m*

texture /ˈtekstʃə(r)/ *n* (*of fabric*) textura *f*; (*of paper*) grão *m*

Thai /taɪ/ *a & n* tailandês *m*. **~land** *n* Tailândia *f*

Thames /temz/ *n* Tâmisa *m*

than /ðæn unstressed ðən/ *conj* que, do que; (*with numbers*) de; **more/less ~ ten** mais/menos de dez

thank /θæŋk/ *vt* agradecer; **~ you!** obrigado! **~s!** [!] obrigado. **~s** *npl* agradecimentos *mpl*; **~s to** graças a; **T~sgiving (Day)** *Amer* Dia *m* de Ação de Graças

t

thankful /ˈθæŋkfl/ *a* grato; agradecido; reconhecido (**for** por). **~ly** *adv* com gratidão; (*happily*) felizmente

thankless /ˈθæŋklɪs/ *a* ingrato

that /ðæt *unstressed* ðət/ ● *a*

····➤ (*nearer*) esse/essa; **I want ~ drink** quero essa bebida; **give me ~ one** me dê esse; (*further away*) aquele/aquela; **~ drink over there** aquela bebida lá

● *pron*

····➤ esse/essa; (*indefinite*) isso; **what's ~ on your shirt?** o que é isso na sua camiseta?; (*further away*) aquele/aquela; (*indefinite*) aquilo; **who's ~?** quem é?; **~'s Peter over there** aquele ali é o Peter; **those are my parents** aqueles são os meus pais; **what's ~ over there on the hill?** o que é aquilo lá na montanha?

● *rel pron*

····➤ que; **where's the letter ~ came yesterday?** onde está a carta que veio ontem?; **the man ~ stole the car** o homem que roubou o carro

! With a preposition, use *o qual*, *a qual* when referring to objects: **the chair that I was sitting on** *a cadeira na qual eu estava sentada*

! With a preposition, use *quem* when referring to people: **the people that I've talked about** *as pessoas de quem falei*; **the girls that I was talking to** *as meninas com quem eu estava falando* (*referring to time*) em que; **the year ~ he died** o ano em que ele morreu; **the day ~ we went to the beach** o dia em que fomos para a praia

● *adv*

····➤ tão, tanto assim; **he's not ~ stupid** ele não é assim tão estúpido; **it isn't ~ cold** não está assim tanto frio

● *conj*

····➤ que; **I don't think ~ he'll come** não me parece que ele venha; **we know ~ you're right** sabemos que você tem razão

····➤ (*in phrases*) **~ is (to say)** isto é; **~'s right** é isso mesmo; **like ~** assim; **don't be like ~!** não seja assim!

thatch /θætʃ/ *n* colmo *m*. **~ed** *a* de colmo; **~ed cottage** casa *f* com telhado de colmo

thaw /θɔː/ *vt/i* derreter(-se), degelar; ‹*food*› descongelar ● *n* degelo *m*, derretimento *m*

the *before vowel* /ðɪ *before consonant* ðə *stressed* ðiː/ ● *definite article*

····➤ o, a; *pl* os, as; **~ dog** o cão; **~ tree** a árvore; **go to ~ dentist** ir ao dentista; **in ~ garden** no jardim

! When the articles *o* and *a* follow the prepositions *a*, *de*, and *em*, they often contract to form *ao*, *à*, *do*, *da* and *no*, *na*. (*+ adjective to form noun*) **~ blind** os cegos; **~ unemployed** os desempregados; **~ impossible** o impossível; (*+ nationality*) **~ French** os franceses; **~ Portuguese** os portugueses; (*per*) **paid by ~ hour** pago por hora; **sold by ~ dozen** vendido por dúzia

● *adv*

····➤ **~ more...~ more...** quanto mais...tanto mais...

theatre /ˈθɪətə(r)/ *n* teatro *m*

theatrical /θɪˈætrɪkl/ *a* teatral

theft /θeft/ *n* roubo *m*

their /ðeə(r)/ *a* deles, delas, seu

theirs /ðeəz/ *poss pron* o(s) seu(s), a(s) sua(s), o(s) deles, a(s) delas; **it is ~** é (o) deles/delas *or* o seu

them /ðem *unstressed* ðəm/ *pron* os, as; (*after prep*) eles, elas; **(to) ~** lhes

theme /θiːm/ *n* tema *m*; **~ park** parque *m* temático

themselves /ðəmˈselvz/ *pron* eles mesmos/próprios, elas mesmas/próprias; (*reflexive*) se; (*after prep*) si (mesmos, próprios); **by ~** sozinhos; **with ~** consigo

then /ðen/ *adv* (*at that time*) então, nessa altura; (*next*) depois, em seguida; (*in that case*) então, nesse caso; (*therefore*) então, portanto, por conseguinte

theolog|y /θɪˈɒlədʒɪ/ *n* teologia *f*. **~ian** /θɪəˈləʊdʒən/ *n* teólogo *m*

theor|y /ˈθɪərɪ/ *n* teoria *f*. **~etical** /-ˈretɪkl/ *a* teórico

therapeutic /θerəˈpjuːtɪk/ *a* terapêutico

therap|y /ˈθerəpɪ/ *n* terapia *f*. **~ist** *n* terapeuta *mf*

there /ðeə(r)/ *adv* aí, ali, lá; (*over there*) lá, acolá ● *int* (*triumphant*) pronto, aí está; (*consoling*) então, vamos lá; **he goes ~** ele vai aí *or* lá; **~ he goes** aí vai ele; **~ is, ~ are** há; **~ you are** (*giving*) toma; **~ and then** logo ali. **~abouts** *adv* por aí. **~by** *adv* desse modo

t

therefore /'ðeəfɔ:(r)/ *adv* por isso, portanto, por conseguinte

thermal /'θɜ:ml/ *a* térmico

thermometer /θə'mɒmɪtə(r)/ *n* termômetro *m*, (*P*) termómetro *m*

Thermos® /'θɜ:məs/ *n* garrafa *f* térmica, (*P*) termo *m*

thermostat /'θɜ:məstæt/ *n* termostato *m*

thesaurus /θɪ'sɔ:rəs/ *n* (*pl* **-ri** /-raɪ/) dicionário *m* de sinônimos, (*P*) sinónimos

these /ði:z/ ▶ THIS

thesis /'θi:sɪs/ *n* (*pl* **theses** /-si:z/) tese *f*

they /ðeɪ/ *pron* eles, elas; **~ say (that)...** diz-se or dizem que

thick /θɪk/ *a* (**-er, -est**) espesso, grosso; [!] (*stupid*) estúpido ● *adv* = THICKLY ● *n* **in the ~ of** no meio de. **~-skinned** *a* insensível. **~ly** *adv* espessamente; (*spread*) em camada espessa. **~ness** *n* espessura *f*, grossura *f*

thicken /'θɪkən/ *vt/i* engrossar, espessar(-se); **the plot ~s** o enredo complica-se

thief /θi:f/ *n* (*pl* **thieves** /θi:vz/) ladrão *m*, gatuno *m*

thigh /θaɪ/ *n* coxa *f*

thimble /'θɪmbl/ *n* dedal *m*

thin /θɪn/ *a* (**thinner, thinnest**) (*slender*) estreito, fino, delgado; (*lean, not plump*) magro; (*sparse*) ralo, escasso; (*flimsy*) leve, fino; ‹*soup*› aguado; ‹*hair*› ralo ● *adv* = THINLY ● *vt/i* (*pt* **thinned**) (*of liquid*) diluir(-se); (*of fog etc*) dissipar(-se); (*of hair*) rarear; **~ out** (*in quantity*) diminuir, reduzir; ‹*seedlings etc*› desbastar. **~ly** *adv* (*sparsely*) esparsamente. **~ness** *n* (*of board, wire etc*) finura *f*; (*of person*) magreza *f*

thing /θɪŋ/ *n* coisa *f*; **~s** (*belongings*) pertences *mpl*; **the best ~ is to** o melhor é; **for one ~** em primeiro lugar; **just the ~** exatamente o que era preciso; **poor ~** coitado

think /θɪŋk/ *vt/i* (*pt* **thought**) pensar (**about, of** em); (*carefully*) refletir (**about, of** em, sobre); **I ~ so** eu acho que sim; **~ better of it** (*change one's mind*) pensar melhor; **~ nothing of** achar natural; **~ of** (*hold opinion of*) pensar de, achar de; **~ over** pensar bem em; **~ up** inventar. **~ tank** *n* comissão *f* de peritos

third /θɜ:d/ *a* terceiro; **T~ World** Terceiro Mundo *m*; **~-party insurance** seguro *m* contra terceiros ● *n* terceiro *m*; (*fraction*) terço *m*. **~-rate** *a* inferior, medíocre. **~ly** *adv* em terceiro lugar

thirst /θɜ:st/ *n* sede *f*. **~y** *a* sequioso, sedento; **be ~y** estar com or ter sede

thirteen /θɜ:'ti:n/ *a & n* treze *m*. **~th** *a & n* décimo terceiro *m*

thirt|y /'θɜ:tɪ/ *a & n* trinta *m*. **~ieth** *a & n* trigésimo *m*

this /ðɪs/ (*pl* **these**) ● *a*

····➤ este, esta; **I don't like ~ car** não gosto deste carro; **~ morning** esta manhã; **~ Wednesday** esta quarta-feira; **~ one** este, esta; **these ones** estes, estas; **I'll have ~ one, please** quero este, por favor

● *pron*

····➤ este, esta; (*indefinite*) isto; **what's ~?** o que é isto?; **what are these?** o que são (estes/estas)?; **~ is the kitchen** esta é a cozinha; **after ~** depois disto

● *adv*

····➤ **~ far** tão longe; **I didn't think we would get ~ far** nunca pensei que chegássemos tão longe; **~ high** desta altura; **it's about ~ high** é mais ou menos desta altura

····➤ (*in phrases*) **like ~** assim, desta forma; **do it like ~** faça assim; **~ and that** isto e aquilo; **'what did you talk about?'– 'oh, ~ and that'** 'de que falaram?'– 'oh, disto e daquilo'

thistle /'θɪsl/ *n* cardo *m*

thorn /θɔ:n/ *n* espinho *m*, pico *m*. **~y** *a* espinhoso; *fig* bicudo; espinhoso

thorough /'θʌrə/ *a* consciencioso; (*deep*) completo, profundo; ‹*cleaning, washing*› a fundo. **~ly** *adv* ‹*clean, study etc*› completo, a fundo; (*very*) perfeitamente, muito bem

thoroughbred /'θʌrəbred/ *n* ‹*horse etc*› puro-sangue *m invar*

those /ðəʊz/ ▶ THAT

though /ðəʊ/ *conj* se bem que, embora, conquanto ● *adv* [!] contudo; no entanto

thought /θɔ:t/ ▶ THINK ● *n* pensamento *m*; ideia *f*; **on second ~s** pensando bem

thoughtful /'θɔ:tfl/ *a* pensativo; (*considerate*) atencioso, solícito. **~ly** *adv* pensativamente; (*considerately*) com consideração, atenciosamente

thoughtless /'θɔ:tlɪs/ *a* irrefletido; (*inconsiderate*) pouco atencioso. **~ly**

t

adv sem pensar; (*inconsiderately*) sem consideração

thousand /'θaʊznd/ *a & n* mil *m*; **~s of** milhares de. **~th** *a & n* milésimo *m*

thrash /θræʃ/ *vt* surrar, espancar; (*defeat*) dar uma surra or sova em; **~ about** debater-se; **~ out** debater a fundo, discutir bem

thread /θred/ *n* fio *m*; (*for sewing*) linha *f* de coser; (*of screw*) rosca *f* ● *vt* enfiar; **~ one's way** abrir caminho, furar

threadbare /'θredbeə(r)/ *a* puído, surrado

threat /θret/ *n* ameaça *f*

threaten /'θretn/ *vt/i* ameaçar

three /θri:/ *a & n* três *m*

thresh /θreʃ/ *vt* ‹*corn etc*› malhar, debulhar

threshold /'θreʃəʊld/ *n* limiar *m*, soleira *f*; *fig* limiar *m*

threw /θru:/ ▶ THROW

thrift /θrɪft/ *n* economia *f*, poupança *f*. **~y** *a* econômico, (*P*) económico, poupado

thrill /θrɪl/ *n* arrepio *m* de emoção, frêmito *m*, (*P*) frémito *m* ● *vt* excitar(-se), emocionar(-se), (fazer) vibrar; **be ~ed** estar/ficar encantado. **~ing** *a* excitante, emocionante

thriller /'θrɪlə(r)/ *n* livro or filme de suspense *m*

thriv|e /θraɪv/ *vi* (*pt* **thrived** *or* **throve**, *pp* **thrived** *or* **thriven**) prosperar, florescer; (*grow strong*) dar-se bem (**on** com). **~ing** *a* próspero

throat /θrəʊt/ *n* garganta *f*; **have a sore ~** ter dores de garganta

throb /θrɒb/ *vi* (*pt* **throbbed**) ‹*wound, head*› latejar; ‹*heart*› palpitar, bater; ‹*engine*› *also fig* vibrar, trepidar ● *n* (*of pain*) latejo *m*, espasmo *m*; (*of heart*) palpitação *f*, batida *f*; (*of engine*) vibração *f*, trepidação *f*

throes /θrəʊz/ *npl* **in the ~ of** *fig* às voltas com, no meio de

throne /θrəʊn/ *n* trono *m*

throttle /'θrɒtl/ *n Auto* válvula-borboleta *f*, estrangulador *m*, acelerador *m* de mão ● *vt* estrangular

through /θru:/ *prep* através de, por; (*during*) durante; (*by means or way of, out of*) por; (*by reason of*) por, por causa de ● *adv* através; (*entirely*) completamente, até o fim; **be ~** ter acabado (**with** com); *Telephone* estar ligado; **come** or **go ~** (*cross, pierce*) atravessar; **get ~** ‹*exam*› passar; **be wet ~** estar ensopado or encharcado ● *a* ‹*train, traffic etc*› direto

throughout /θru:'aʊt/ *prep* durante, por todo; **~ the country** por todo o país (afora); **~ the day** durante todo a dia, pelo dia afora ● *adv* completamente; (*place*) por toda a parte; (*time*) durante todo o tempo

throw /θrəʊ/ *vt* (*pt* **threw**, *pp* **thrown**) atirar, jogar, lançar; [!] (*baffle*) desconcertar; **~ a party** [!] dar uma festa; **~ away** jogar fora, (*P*) deitar fora; **~ off** (*get rid of*) livrar-se de; **~ out** ‹*person*› expulsar; (*reject*) rejeitar; **~ over** (*desert*) abandonar, deixar; **~ up** ‹*one's arms*› levantar; (*resign from*) abandonar; [!] (*vomit*) vomitar ● *n* lançamento *m*; (*of dice*) lançe *m*

thrush /θrʌʃ/ *n* (*bird*) tordo *m*

thrust /θrʌst/ *vt* (*pt* **thrust**) arremeter, empurrar, impelir ● *n* empurrão *m*, arremetida *f*; **~ into** (*put*) enfiar em, mergulhar em; **~ upon** (*force on*) impôr a

thud /θʌd/ *n* som *m* surdo, baque *m*

thug /θʌg/ *n* bandido *m*, facínora *m*, malfeitor *m*

thumb /θʌm/ *n* polegar *m*; **under sb's ~** completamente dominado por alguém ● *vt* ‹*book*› manusear; **~ a lift** pedir carona, (*P*) boleia

thumbtack /'θʌmtæk/ *n Amer* percevejo *m*

thump /θʌmp/ *vt/i* bater (em), dar pancadas (em); (*with fists*) dar murros (em); ‹*piano*› martelar (em); (*of heart*) bater com força ● *n* pancada *f*; (*thud*) baque *m*

thunder /'θʌndə(r)/ *n* trovão *m*, trovoada *f*; (*loud noise*) estrondo *m* ● *vi* ‹*weather, person*› trovejar; **~ past** passar como um raio. **~y** *a* ‹*weather*› tempestuoso

thunderbolt /'θʌndəbəʊlt/ *n* raio *m* e ribombo *m* de trovão; *fig* raio *m* fulminante *fig*

thunderstorm /'θʌndəstɔ:m/ *n* tempestade *f* com trovoadas, temporal *m*

Thursday /'θɜ:zdɪ/ *n* quinta-feira *f*

thus /ðʌs/ *adv* assim, desta maneira; **~ far** até aqui

thwart /θwɔ:t/ *vt* frustrar, contrariar

thyme /taɪm/ *n* tomilho *m*

tick[1] /tɪk/ *n* (*sound*) tique-taque *m*; (*mark*) sinal *m*; [!] (*moment*) instantinho *m* ● *vi* fazer tique-taque ● *vt* **~ (off)**

marcar com sinal; **~ off** [!] (*scold*) dar uma bronca em [!] (*P*) ralhar com; **~ over** ‹*engine, factory*› funcionar em marcha lenta, (*P*) em 'ralenti'

tick[2] /tɪk/ *n* (*insect*) carrapato *m*

ticket /'tɪkɪt/ *n* bilhete *m*; (*label*) etiqueta *f*; (*for traffic offence*) aviso *m* de multa. **~ collector** *n* (*railway*) guarda *m*; **~ office** *n* bilheteira *f*

tickle /'tɪkl/ *vt* fazer cócegas; *fig* (*amuse*) divertir ● *n* cócegas *fpl*, comichão *m*

ticklish /'tɪklɪʃ/ *a* coceguento, sensível a cócegas; *fig* delicado; melindroso

tidal /'taɪdl/ *a* de marés, que tem marés; **~ wave** onda *f* gigantesca; *fig* onda *f* de sentimento popular, vaga *f* de fundo

tide /taɪd/ *n* maré *f*; (*of events*) marcha *f*, curso *m*; **high ~** maré *f* cheia, preia-mar *f*; **low ~** maré *f* baixa, baixa-mar *f* ● *vt* **~ over** (*help temporarily*) aguentar

tid|y /'taɪdɪ/ *a* (**-ier**, **-iest**) ‹*room*› arrumado; ‹*appearance, work*› asseado, cuidado; (*methodical*) bem ordenado; [!] ‹*amount*› belo [!] ● *vt* arrumar, arranjar. **~iness** *n* arrumação *f*, ordem *f*

tie /taɪ/ *vt* (*pres p* **tying**) atar, amarrar, prender; (*link*) ligar, vincular; ‹*a knot*› dar, fazer ● *vi Sport* empatar ● *n* fio *m*, cordel *m*; (*necktie*) gravata *f*; (*link*) laço *m*, vínculo *m*; *Sport* empate *m*; **~ in with** estar ligado com, relacionar-se com; **~ up** amarrar, atar; ‹*animal*› prender; ‹*money*› imobilizar; (*occupy*) ocupar

tier /tɪə(r)/ *n* cada fila *f*, camada *f*, prateleira *f etc* colocada em cima de outra; (*in stadium*) bancada *f*; (*of cake*) andar *m*; (*of society*) camada *f*

tiger /'taɪgə(r)/ *n* tigre *m*

tight /taɪt/ *a* (**-er**, **-est**) ‹*clothes*› apertado, justo; ‹*rope*› esticado, tenso; ‹*control*› rigoroso; ‹*knot, schedule, lid*› apertado; [!] (*drunk*) embriagado [!]; **be in a ~ corner** *fig* estar em apuros or num aperto, (*P*) estar entalado [!] ● *adv* = TIGHTLY. **~ly** *adv* bem; (*squeeze*) com força

tighten /'taɪtn/ *vt/i* ‹*rope*› esticar; ‹*bolt, control*› apertar; **~ up on** apertar o cinto

tightrope /'taɪtrəʊp/ *n* corda (de acrobacias) *f*; **~ walker** funâmbulo *m*

tights /taɪts/ *npl* collants *mpl*, meias-colant *fpl*

tile /taɪl/ *n* (*on wall, floor*) ladrilho *m*, azulejo *m*; (*on roof*) telha *f* ● *vt* ladrilhar, pôr azulejos em; (*roof*) telhar, cobrir com telhas

till[1] /tɪl/ *vt* ‹*land*› cultivar

till[2] /tɪl/ *prep & conj* = UNTIL

till[3] /tɪl/ *n* caixa (registadora) *f*

tilt /tɪlt/ *vt/i* inclinar(-se), pender ● *n* (*slope*) inclinação *f*; **(at) full ~** a toda a velocidade

timber /'tɪmbə(r)/ *n* madeira (de construção) *f*; (*trees*) árvores *fpl*

time /taɪm/ *n* tempo *m*; (*moment*) momento *m*; (*epoch*) época *f*, tempo *m*; (*by clock*) horas *fpl*; (*occasion*) vez *f*; (*rhythm*) compasso *m*; **~s** (*multiplying*) vezes; **at ~s** às vezes; **for the ~ being** por agora, por enquanto; **from ~ to ~** de vez em quando; **have a good ~** divertir-se; **have no ~ for** não ter paciência para; **in no ~** num instante; **in ~** a tempo; (*eventually*) com o tempo; **in two days' ~** daqui a dois dias; **on ~** na hora, (*P*) a horas; **take your ~** não se apresse; **what's the ~?** que horas são?; **~ bomb** bomba-relógio *f*; **~ off** tempo *m* livre; **~ zone** fuso *m* horário ● *vt* escolher a hora para; (*measure*) marcar o tempo de; *Sport* cronometrar; (*regulate*) acertar. **~ limit** *n* prazo *m*

timeless /'taɪmlɪs/ *a* intemporal; (*unending*) eterno

timely /'taɪmlɪ/ *a* oportuno

timer /'taɪmə(r)/ *n Techn* relógio *m*; (*with sand*) ampulheta *f*

timetable /'taɪmteɪbl/ *n* horário *m*

timid /'tɪmɪd/ *a* tímido; (*fearful*) assustadiço, medroso

timing /'taɪmɪŋ/ *n* (*measuring*) cronometragem *f*; (*of artist*) ritmo *m*; (*moment*) cálculo *m* do tempo, timing *m*; **good/bad ~** (*moment*) momento *m* bem/mal escolhido

tin /tɪn/ *n* estanho *m*; (*container*) lata *f*; **~ foil** papel *m* de alumínio; **~ plate** lata *f*, folha(-de-Flandes) *f* ● *vt* (*pt* **tinned**) estanhar; ‹*food*› enlatar; **~ned foods** conservas *fpl*. **~ opener** *n* abridor *m* de latas, (*P*) abre-latas *m*. **~ny** *a* ‹*sound*› metálico

tinge /tɪndʒ/ *vt* **~ (with)** tingir (de); *fig* dar um toque (de) ● *n* tom *m*, matiz *m*; *fig* toque *m*

tingle /'tɪŋgl/ *vi* (*sting*) arder; (*prickle*) picar ● *n* ardor *m*; (*prickle*) picadela *f*

tinker /'tɪŋkə(r)/ *n* latoeiro *m* ambulante ● *vi* **~ (with)** mexer (em), tentar consertar

tinkle /'tɪŋkl/ *n* tinido *m*, tilintar *m* ● *vt/i* tilintar

tinsel /ˈtɪnsl/ *n* fio *m* prateado/dourado, enfeites *mpl* metálicos de Natal; *fig* falso brilho *m*; ouropel *m*

tint /tɪnt/ *n* tom *m*, matiz *m*; (*for hair*) tintura *f*, tinta *f* ● *vt* tingir, colorir

tiny /ˈtaɪnɪ/ *a* (**-ier**, **-iest**) minúsculo, pequenino

tip[1] /tɪp/ *n* ponta *f*; **(have sth) on the ~ of one's tongue** ter algo na ponta da língua

tip[2] /tɪp/ *vt/i* (*pt* **tipped**) (*tilt*) inclinar(-se); (*overturn*) virar(-se); (*pour*) colocar, (*P*) deitar; (*empty*) despejar(-se); **~ off** avisar, prevenir ● *n* (*money*) gorjeta *f*; (*advice*) sugestão *f*; dica *f* [!]; (*for rubbish*) lixeira *f*. **~-off** *n* (*warning*) aviso *m*; (*information*) informação *f*

tipsy /ˈtɪpsɪ/ *a* ligeiramente embriagado, alegre, tocado [!]

tiptoe /ˈtɪptəʊ/ *n* **on ~** na ponta dos pés

tir|e[1] /ˈtaɪə(r)/ *vt/i* cansar(-se) (**of** de). **~eless** *a* incansável, infatigável. **~ing** *a* fatigante, cansativo

tire[2] /ˈtaɪə(r)/ *n Amer* pneu *m*

tired /taɪəd/ *a* cansado, fatigado; **~ of** (*sick of*) farto de; **~ out** morto de cansaço

tiresome /ˈtaɪəsəm/ *a* maçador; aborrecido; chato [✖]

tissue /ˈtɪʃuː/ *n* tecido *m*; (*handkerchief*) lenço *m* de papel. **~ paper** *n* papel *m* de seda

tit[1] /tɪt/ *n* (*bird*) chapim *m*, canário-da-terra *m*

tit[2] /tɪt/ *n* **give ~ for tat** pagar na mesma moeda

titbit /ˈtɪtbɪt/ *n* petisco *m*

title /ˈtaɪtl/ *n* título *m*

to /tuː *unstressed* tə/ ● *prep*

····➤ (*direction*) a; **go ~ the beach** ir para a praia; **go ~ the dentist** ir ao dentista; **go ~ a party** ir a uma festa; **go ~ Portugal** (*for a short time*) ir a Portugal; (*for good*) ir para Portugal; **go ~ bed** ir para a cama; **go ~ school/university** ir para a escola/faculdade

! The preposition *a* often contracts with the definite articles *o* and *a* to form *ao* and *à*.

····➤ (*up to*) até; **go ~ the end of the street** ir até ao fim da rua; **~ this day** até hoje; **from Monday ~ Friday** de segunda a sexta

····➤ (*expressing indirect object*) **give sth ~ sb** dar algo para alguém; **give the book ~ her** dá o livro para ela; **give it ~ me** me dá isso

····➤ (*attitude*) para (com); **she was nice ~ him** ela foi simpática para com ele

····➤ (*in telling time*) para; **it's ten ~ six** são dez para as seis

····➤ (*expressing duration*) **it lasts three ~ four hours** dura entre três a quatro horas

● *infinitive particle*

····➤ (*forming infinitive*) **~ eat** comer

! In an infinitive **to** is not translated: **to sing** *cantar*; **to go** *ir* (*purpose*) para; **I set out ~ buy food** saí para ir buscar comida

····➤ (*after be + adjectives*) de; **be easy/difficult ~ read** ser fácil/difícil de ler; **it's easy ~ forget** é fácil esquecer

····➤ (*in phrases*) **go ~ and fro** andar de um lado para o outro.

~-do *n* [!](*fuss*) agitação *f*; **he made a great ~-do about being left off the guest list** causou muita agitação por ter sido excluído da lista de convidados; **-~-be** *adj* **her husband-~-be** o seu futuro marido →For verbal expressions using the infinitive **to** such as **to tell sb to do sth** and **to help sb to do sth** see entries **tell** and **help**

toad /təʊd/ *n* sapo *m*

toady /ˈtəʊdɪ/ *n* lambe-botas [!] *mf*, puxa-saco [!] *m* ● *vi* puxar saco [!] bajular, ser um(a) lambe-botas

toast /təʊst/ *n* fatia *f* de pão torrado, torrada *f*; (*drink*) brinde *m*, saúde *f* ● *vt* (*bread*) torrar; (*drink to*) brindar, beber à saúde de. **~er** *n* torradeira *f*

tobacco /təˈbækəʊ/ *n* tabaco *m*

toboggan /təˈbɒgən/ *n* tobogã *m*

today /təˈdeɪ/ *n & adv* hoje *m*

toddler /ˈtɒdlə(r)/ *n* criança *f* que está aprendendo a andar *or* (*P*) a aprender a andar

toe /təʊ/ *n* dedo *m* do pé; (*of shoe, stocking*) biqueira *f*; **on one's ~s** alerta, vigilante ● *vt* **~ the line** andar na linha. **~nail** *n* unha *f* do dedo do pé

i **TOEFL – Test of English as a Foreign Language** Exame que se faz para se candidatar a qualquer

t

universidade americana e que certifica o domínio do inglês dos estudantes que falam outros idiomas como língua materna.

toffee /'tɒfɪ/ *n* puxa-puxa *m*, (*P*) caramelo *m*. **~ apple** *n* maçã *f* caramelizada

together /tə'geðə(r)/ *adv* junto, juntamente, juntos; (*at the same time*) ao mesmo tempo; **~ with** juntamente com. **~ness** *n* camaradagem *f*, companheirismo *m*

toil /tɔɪl/ *vi* labutar ● *n* labuta *f*, labor *m*

toilet /'tɔɪlɪt/ *n* banheiro *m*, (*P*) casa *f* de banho; (*grooming*) toalete *f*; **~ water** água-de-colônia *f*, (*P*) água-de-colónia. **~ paper** *n* papel *m* higiênico *or* (*P*) higiénico; **~ roll** *n* rolo *m* de papel higiênico, (*P*) higiénico

toiletries /'tɔɪlɪtrɪz/ *npl* artigos *mpl* de toalete

token /'təʊkən/ *n* sinal *m*, prova *f*; (*voucher*) cheque *m*; (*coin*) ficha *f* ● *a* simbólico

told /təʊld/ ▶ TELL ● *a* **all ~** (*all in all*) ao todo

tolerabl|e /'tɒlərəbl/ *a* tolerável; (*not bad*) sofrível, razoável

toleran|t /'tɒlərənt/ *a* tolerante (**of** para com). **~ce** *n* tolerância *f*

tolerate /'tɒləreɪt/ *vt* tolerar

toll[1] /təʊl/ *n* pedágio *m*, (*P*) portagem *f*; **death ~** número *m* de mortos; **take its ~** (*of age*) fazer sentir o seu peso

toll[2] /təʊl/ *vt/i* (*of bell*) dobrar

tomato /tə'mɑ:təʊ/ *n* (*pl* **-oes**) tomate *m*

tomb /tu:m/ *n* túmulo *m*, sepultura *f*

tomboy /'tɒmbɔɪ/ *n* menina *f* levada (e masculinizada), (*P*) maria-rapaz *f*

tombstone /'tu:mstəʊn/ *n* lápide *f*, pedra *f* tumular

tomorrow /tə'mɒrəʊ/ *n & adv* amanhã *m*; **~ morning/night** amanhã de manhã/à noite

ton /tʌn/ *n* tonelada *f* (= 1016 kg); **(metric) ~** tonelada *f* (= 1000 kg); **~s of** [!] montes de [!], (*P*) carradas de [!]

tone /təʊn/ *n* tom *m*; (*of radio, telephone etc*) sinal *m*; (*colour*) tom *m*, tonalidade *f*; *Med* tonicidade *f* ● *vt* **~ down** atenuar ● *vi* **~ in** combinar-se, harmonizar-se (**with** com); **~ up** ‹*muscles*› tonificar. **~-deaf** *a* sem ouvido musical

tongs /tɒŋz/ *n* tenaz *f*; (*for sugar*) pinça *f*; (*for hair*) pinça *f*

tongue /tʌŋ/ *n* língua *f*. **~-in-cheek** *a & adv* sem ser a sério, com ironia, a brincar. **~-tied** *a* calado. **~-twister** *n* trava-língua *m*

tonic /'tɒnɪk/ *n Med* tônico *m*, (*P*) tónico *m*; *Mus* tônica *f*, (*P*) tónica *f* ● *a* tônico, (*P*) tónico

tonight /tə'naɪt/ *adv & n* hoje à noite, logo à noite, esta noite *f*

tonne /tʌn/ *n* (*metric*) tonelada *f*

tonsil /'tɒnsl/ *n* amígdala *f*

tonsillitis /tɒnsɪ'laɪtɪs/ *n* amigdalite *f*

too /tu:/ *adv* demasiado, demais; (*also*) também, igualmente; [!] (*very*) muito

took /tʊk/ ▶ TAKE

tool /tu:l/ *n* (*carpenter's, plumber's etc*) ferramenta *f*; (*gardener's*) utensílio *m*; *fig* (*person*) joguete *m*. **~bag** *n* saco *m* de ferramenta(s)

toot /tu:t/ *n* toque *m* de buzina ● *vt/i* **~ (the horn)** buzinar

tooth /tu:θ/ *n* (*pl* **teeth**) dente *m*. **~less** *a* desdentado

toothache /'tu:θeɪk/ *n* dor *f* de dentes

toothbrush /'tu:θbrʌʃ/ *n* escova *f* de dentes

toothpaste /'tu:θpeɪst/ *n* pasta *f* de dentes, dentifrício *m*, (*P*) dentífrico

toothpick /'tu:θpɪk/ *n* palito *m*

top[1] /tɒp/ *n* (*highest point; upper part*) alto *m*, cimo *m*, topo *m*; (*of hill; also fig*) cume *m*; (*upper surface*) cimo *m*, topo *m*; (*surface of table*) tampo *m*; (*lid*) tampa *f*; (*of bottle*) rolha *f*; (*of list*) cabeça *f*; **from ~ to bottom** de alto a baixo; **on ~ of** em cima de; *fig* além de; **on ~ of that** ainda por cima ● *a* ‹*shelf etc*› de cima, superior; (*in rank*) primeiro; (*best*) melhor; (*distinguished*) eminente; (*maximum*) máximo; **~ gear** *Auto* a velocidade mais alta; **~ hat** chapéu *m* alto; **~ secret** ultrassecreto ● *vt* (*pt* **topped**) (*exceed*) ultrapassar, ir acima de; **~ up** encher; (*mobiles*) recarregar; **~ped with** coberto de. **~-heavy** *a* mais pesado na parte de cima

top[2] /tɒp/ *n* (*toy*) pião *m*; **sleep like a ~** dormir como uma pedra

topic /'tɒpɪk/ *n* tópico *m*, assunto *m*

topical /'tɒpɪkl/ *a* da atualidade, corrente

topless /'tɒplɪs/ *a* com o peito nu, topless

topple /'tɒpl/ *vt/i* (fazer) desabar, (fazer) tombar, (fazer) cair

top-up card *n* cartão *m* pré-pago

t

top-up fees *npl*: contribuição complementar às mensalidades da universidade, para fins de matrícula; (*P*) contribuição suplementar acrescida às propinas da universidade

torch /tɔːtʃ/ *n* (*electric*) lanterna *f* elétrica; (*flaming*) archote *m*, facho *m*

tore /tɔː(r)/ ▶ TEAR[1]

torment[1] /ˈtɔːmənt/ *n* tormento *m*

torment[2] /tɔːˈment/ *vt* atormentar, torturar; (*annoy*) aborrecer, chatear

torn /tɔːn/ ▶ TEAR[1]

tornado /tɔːˈneɪdəʊ/ *n* (*pl* **-oes**) tornado *m*

torpedo /tɔːˈpiːdəʊ/ *n* (*pl* **-oes**) torpedo *m* ● *vt* torpedear

torrent /ˈtɒrənt/ *n* torrente *f*. **~ial** /təˈrenʃl/ *a* torrencial

torso /ˈtɔːsəʊ/ *n* (*pl* **-os**) torso *m*

tortoise /ˈtɔːtəs/ *n* tartaruga *f*

tortoiseshell /ˈtɔːtəsʃel/ *n* (*for ornaments etc*) tartaruga *f*

tortuous /ˈtɔːtʃʊəs/ *a* (*of path etc*) que dá muitas voltas, sinuoso; *fig* tortuoso; retorcido

torture /ˈtɔːtʃə(r)/ *n* tortura *f*, suplício *m* ● *vt* torturar

Tory /ˈtɔːrɪ/ *a & n* [!] conservador *m*

toss /tɒs/ *vt* atirar, jogar, (*P*) deitar; (*shake*) agitar, sacudir ● *vi* agitar-se, debater-se; **~ a coin, ~ up** tirar cara ou coroa

tot[1] /tɒt/ *n* criancinha *f*; [!] (*glass*) copinho *m*

tot[2] /tɒt/ *vt/i* (*pt* **totted**) **~ up** [!] somar

total /ˈtəʊtl/ *a & n* total *m* ● *vt* (*pt* **totalled**) (*find total of*) totalizar; (*amount to*) elevar-se a, montar a. **~ity** /-ˈtælətɪ/ *n* totalidade *f*. **~ly** *adv* totalmente

totalitarian /təʊtælɪˈteərɪən/ *a* totalitário

totter /ˈtɒtə(r)/ *vi* cambalear, andar aos tombos; (*of tower etc*) oscilar

touch /tʌtʃ/ *vt/i* tocar; (*of ends, gardens etc*) tocar-se; (*tamper with*) mexer em; (*affect*) comover; **~ down** *Aviat* aterrissar, (*P*) aterrar; **~ off** disparar; (*cause*) dar início a, desencadear; **~ on** (*mention*) tocar em; **~ up** retocar ● *n* (*sense*) tato *m*; (*contact*) toque *m*; (*of colour*) toque *m*, retoque *m*; **a ~ of** (*small amount*) um pouco de; **get in ~ with** entrar em contato, (*P*) contacto com; **lose ~** perder contato, (*P*) contacto. **~-and-go** *a* (*risky*) arriscado; (*uncertain*) duvidoso, incerto; **~line** *n* linha *f* lateral

touching /ˈtʌtʃɪŋ/ *a* comovente, comovedor

touchy /ˈtʌtʃɪ/ *a* melindroso, suscetível, que se ofende facilmente

tough /tʌf/ *a* (**-er**, **-est**) (*hard, difficult; relentless*) duro; (*strong*) forte, resistente ● *n* **~ (guy)** valentão *m*, durão *m* [!]; **~ luck!** [!] pouca sorte!, que azar!

toughen /ˈtʌfn/ *vt/i* (*person*) endurecer; (*strengthen*) reforçar

tour /tʊə(r)/ *n* viagem *f*; (*visit*) visita *f*; (*by team etc*) tournée *f*; **on ~** em tournée ● *vt* visitar

tourism /ˈtʊərɪzəm/ *n* turismo *m*

tourist /ˈtʊərɪst/ *n* turista *mf* ● *a* turístico; **~ office** agência *f* de turismo

tournament /ˈtʊərnəmənt/ *n* torneio *m*

tousle /ˈtaʊzl/ *vt* despentear, esguedelhar

tout /taʊt/ *vi* angariar clientes (**for** para) ● *vt* (*try to sell*) tentar revender ● *n* (*hotel etc*) angariador *m*; (*ticket*) cambista *m*, (*P*) revendedor *m*

tow /təʊ/ *vt* rebocar; **~ away** ‹*vehicle*› rebocar ● *n* reboque *m*; **on ~** a reboque. **~path** *n* caminho *m* de sirga; **~ rope** *n* cabo *m* de reboque

toward(s) /təˈwɔːd(z)/ *prep* para, em direção a, na direção de; (*of attitude*) para com; (*time*) por volta de

towel /ˈtaʊəl/ *n* toalha *f*; (*tea towel*) pano *m* de prato ● *vt* (*pt* **towelled**) esfregar com a toalha. **~ rail** *n* toalheiro *m*. **~ling** *n* atoalhado *m*, (*P*) pano *m* turco

tower /ˈtaʊə(r)/ *n* torre *f*; **~ block** prédio *m* alto ● *vi* **~ above** dominar. **~ing** *a* muito alto; *fig* (*of rage etc*) violento

town /taʊn/ *n* cidade *f*; **go to ~** [!] perder a cabeça [!]; **~ council** município *m*; **~ hall** câmara *f* municipal; **~ planning** urbanização *f*

toxic /ˈtɒksɪk/ *a* tóxico

toy /tɔɪ/ *n* brinquedo *m* ● *vi* **~ with** ‹*object*› brincar com; ‹*idea*› considerar, cogitar

trace /treɪs/ *n* traço *m*, rastro *m*, sinal *m*; (*small quantity*) traço *m*, vestígio *m* ● *vt* seguir or encontrar a pista de; (*draw*) traçar; (*with tracing paper*) decalcar

track /træk/ *n* (*of person etc*) rastro *m*, pista *f*; (*racetrack, of tape*) pista *f*; (*record*) faixa *f*; (*path*) trilho *m*, carreiro *m*; *Rail* via *f* ● *vt* seguir a pista or a trajetória de; **keep ~ of** manter-se em contato com; (*keep oneself informed*) seguir; **~ down**

(*find*) encontrar, descobrir; (*hunt*) seguir a pista de; **~ suit** conjunto *m* de jogging, (*P*) fato *m* de treino

tractor /ˈtræktə(r)/ *n* trator *m*

trade /treɪd/ *n* comércio *m*; (*job*) ofício *m*, profissão *f*; (*swap*) troca *f*; **~ mark** marca *f* de fábrica; **~ union** sindicato *m* ● *vt/i* comerciar (em), negociar (em); **~ on** (*exploit*) tirar partido de, abusar de ● *vt* (*swap*) trocar; **~ in** ‹*used article*› trocar. **~r** /-ə(r)/ *n* negociante *mf*, comerciante *mf*

tradesman /ˈtreɪdzmən/ *n* (*pl* **-men**) comerciante *m*

trading /ˈtreɪdɪŋ/ *n* comércio *m*; **~ estate** zona *f* industrial

tradition /trəˈdɪʃn/ *n* tradição *f*. **~al** *a* tradicional

traffic /ˈtræfɪk/ *n* (*trade*) tráfego *m*, tráfico *m*; (*on road*) trânsito *m*, tráfego *m*; *Aviat* tráfego *m*; **~ circle** *Amer* giratória *f*, (*P*) rotunda *f*; **~ island** ilha *f* de pedestres, (*P*) refúgio *m* para peões; **~ jam** engarrafamento *m*; **~ warden** guarda *mf* or (*P*) polícia *mf* de trânsito ● *vi* (*pt* **trafficked**) traficar (**in** em). **~ lights** *npl* sinal *m* luminoso, (*P*) semáforo *m*. **~ker** *n* traficante *mf*

tragedy /ˈtrædʒədɪ/ *n* tragédia *f*.

tragic /ˈtrædʒɪk/ *a* trágico

trail /treɪl/ *vt/i* arrastar(-se), rastejar; (*of plant, on ground*) rastejar; (*of plant, over wall*) trepar; (*track*) seguir ● *n* (*of powder, smoke etc*) esteira *f*; rastro *m*, (*P*) rasto *m*; (*track*) pista *f*; (*beaten path*) trilho *m*

trailer /ˈtreɪlə(r)/ *n* reboque *m*; *Amer* (*caravan*) reboque *m*; caravana *f*; trailer *m*; (*film*) trailer *m*, apresentação *f* de filme

train /treɪn/ *n Rail* trem *m*, (*P*) comboio *m*; (*procession*) fila *f*; (*of dress*) cauda *f*; (*retinue*) comitiva *f* ● *vt* (*instruct, develop*) educar, formar, treinar; ‹*plant*› guiar; ‹*sportsman, animal*› treinar; ‹*aim*› assestar, apontar ● *vi* estudar, treinar-se. **~ed** *a* (*skilled*) qualificado; ‹*doctor etc*› diplomado. **~er** *n Sport* treinador *m*; (*shoe*) tênis *m*, (*P*) ténis *m*. **~ing** *n* treino *m*

trainee /treɪˈniː/ *n* estagiário *m*

trait /treɪ(t)/ *n* traço *m*, característica *f*

traitor /ˈtreɪtə(r)/ *n* traidor *m*

tram /træm/ *n* bonde *m*, (*P*) (carro) elétrico *m*

tramp /træmp/ *vi* marchar (com passo pesado) ● *vt* percorrer, palmilhar ● *n* som *m* de passos pesados; (*vagrant*) vagabundo *m*, andarilho *m*; (*hike*) longa caminhada *f*

trample /ˈtræmpl/ *vt/i* **~ (on)** pisar com força; *fig* menosprezar

trampoline /ˈtræmpəliːn/ *n* (lona *f* usada como) trampolim *m*

trance /trɑːns/ *n* (*hypnotic*) transe *m*; (*ecstasy*) êxtase *m*, arrebatamento *m*; *Med* estupor *m*

tranquil /ˈtræŋkwɪl/ *a* tranquilo, sossegado. **~lity** /-ˈkwɪlətɪ/ *n* tranquilidade *f*, sossego *m*

tranquillizer /ˈtræŋkwɪlaɪzə(r)/ *n* (*drug*) tranquilizante *m*, calmante *m*

transact /trænˈzækt/ *vt* ‹*business*› fazer; efetuar. **~ion** /-kʃn/ *n* transação *f*

transcend /trænˈsend/ *vt* transcender

transcri|be /trænˈskraɪb/ *vt* transcrever. **~pt**, **~ption** /-ɪpʃn/ *ns* transcrição *f*

transfer[1] /trænsˈfɜː(r)/ *vt* (*pt* **transferred**) transferir; ‹*power, property*› transmitir; **~ the charges** (*telephone*) ligar a cobrar ● *vi* mudar(-se), ser transferido; (*change planes etc*) fazer transferência

transfer[2] /ˈtrænsfɜː(r)/ *n* transferência *f*; (*of power, property*) transmissão *f*; (*image*) decalcomania *f*

transform /trænsˈfɔːm/ *vt* transformar. **~ation** /-əˈmeɪʃn/ *n* transformação *f*. **~er** *n Electr* transformador *m*

transfusion /trænsˈfjuːʒn/ *n* (*of blood*) transfusão *f*

transient /ˈtrænzɪənt/ *a* transitório, transiente, efêmero, (*P*) efémero, passageiro

transistor /trænˈzɪstə(r)/ *n* (*device, radio*) transístor *m*

transit /ˈtrænsɪt/ *n* trânsito *m*; **in ~** em trânsito

transition /trænˈzɪʃn/ *n* transição *f*. **~al** *a* transitório

transitive /ˈtrænsətɪv/ *a* transitivo

transitory /ˈtrænsɪtərɪ/ *a* transitório

translat|e /trænzˈleɪt/ *vt* traduzir. **~ion** /-ʃn/ *n* tradução *f*. **~or** *n* tradutor *m*

transmi|t /trænzˈmɪt/ *vt* (*pt* **transmitted**) transmitir. **~ssion** *n* transmissão *f*. **~tter** *n* transmissor *m*

transparen|t /trænsˈpærənt/ *a* transparente. **~cy** *n* transparência *f*; *Photo* diapositivo *m*

transpire /trænˈspaɪə(r)/ *vi* ‹*secret etc*› transpirar, vir a saber-se; (*happen*) suceder, acontecer

transplant[1] /træns'plɑːnt/ *vt* transplantar

transplant[2] /'trænsplɑːnt/ *n Med* transplantação *f*, (*P*) transplante *m*

transport[1] /træn'spɔːt/ *vt* (*carry, delight*) transportar. **~ation** /-'teɪʃn/ *n* transporte *m*

transport[2] /'trænspɔːt/ *n* (*of goods, delight etc*) transporte *m*

transpose /træn'spəʊz/ *vt* transpor

transvestite /trænz'vestaɪt/ *n* travesti *mf*

trap /træp/ *n* armadilha *f*, ratoeira *f*, cilada *f* ● *vt* (*pt* **trapped**) apanhar na armadilha; (*cut off*) prender, bloquear

trapdoor /træp'dɔː(r)/ *n* alçapão *m*

trapeze /trə'piːz/ *n* trapézio *m*

trash /træʃ/ *n* (*worthless stuff*) porcaria *f*; (*refuse*) lixo *m*; (*nonsense*) disparates *mpl*. **~ can** *n Amer* lata *f* do lixo, (*P*) caixote *m* do lixo. **~y** *a* que não vale nada, porcaria

trauma /'trɔːmə/ *n* trauma *m*, traumatismo *m*. **~tic** /-'mætɪk/ *a* traumático

travel /'trævl/ *vi* (*pt* **travelled**) viajar; (*of vehicle, bullet, sound*) ir ● *vt* percorrer ● *n* viagem *f*; **~ agent** agente *mf* de viagem. **~ler** *n* viajante *mf*; **~ler's cheque** cheque *m* de viagem

travesty /'trævəstɪ/ *n* paródia *f*, caricatura *f*

trawler /'trɔːlə(r)/ *n* traineira *f*, (*P*) arrastão *m*

tray /treɪ/ *n* tabuleiro *m*, bandeja *f*

treacherous /'tretʃərəs/ *a* traiçoeiro

treachery /'tretʃərɪ/ *n* traição *f*, perfídia *f*, deslealdade *f*

treacle /'triːkl/ *n* melaço *m*

tread /tred/ *vt/i* (*pt* **trod**, *pp* **trodden**) (*step*) pisar; (*walk*) andar, caminhar; (*walk along*) seguir; **~ sth into** ‹*carpet*› esmigalhar or pisar algo sobre/em ● *n* passo *m*, maneira *f* de andar; (*of tyre*) trilho *m*

treason /'triːzn/ *n* traição *f*

treasure /'treʒə(r)/ *n* tesouro *m* ● *vt* ter o maior apreço por; (*store*) guardar bem guardado. **~r** *n* tesoureiro *m*

treasury /'treʒərɪ/ *n* (*building*) tesouraria *f*; (*department*) Ministério *m* das Finanças or da Fazenda; *fig* tesouro *m*

treat /triːt/ *vt/i* tratar; **~ sb to sth** convidar alguém para algo ● *n* (*pleasure*) prazer *m*, regalo *m*; (*present*) mimo *m*, gentileza *f*

treatment /'triːtmənt/ *n* tratamento *m*

treaty /'triːtɪ/ *n* (*pact*) tratado *m*

trebl|e /'trebl/ *a* triplo ● *vt/i* triplicar ● *n Mus* (*voice*) soprano *m*

tree /triː/ *n* árvore *f*

trek /trek/ *n* viagem *f* penosa; (*walk*) caminhada *f* ● *vi* (*pt* **trekked**) viajar penosamente; (*walk*) caminhar

trellis /'trelɪs/ *n* grade *f* para trepadeiras, treliça *f*

tremble /'trembl/ *vi* tremer

tremendous /trɪ'mendəs/ *a* (*fearful, huge*) tremendo; [!] (*excellent*) fantástico; formidável

tremor /'tremə(r)/ *n* tremor *m*, estremecimento *m*; **(earth) ~** abalo (sísmico) *m*, tremor *m* de terra

trench /trentʃ/ *n* fossa *f*, vala *f*; *Mil* trincheira *f*

trend /trend/ *n* tendência *f*; (*fashion*) moda *f*. **~y** *a* [!] na (última) moda, (*P*) na berra [!]

trepidation /trepɪ'deɪʃn/ *n* (*fear*) receio *m*, apreensão *f*

trespass /'trespəs/ *vi* entrar ilegalmente (**on** em); **no ~ing** entrada *f* proibida. **~er** *n* intruso *m*

trial /'traɪəl/ *n Jur* julgamento *m*, processo *m*; (*test*) ensaio *m*, experiência *f*, prova *f*; (*ordeal*) provação *f*; **on ~** em julgamento; **~ and error** tentativas *fpl*, (*P*) tentativa *f* e erro

triang|le /'traɪæŋgl/ *n* triângulo *m*. **~ular** /-'æŋgjʊlə(r)/ *a* triangular

trib|e /traɪb/ *n* tribo *f*. **~al** *a* tribal

tribunal /traɪ'bjuːnl/ *n* tribunal *m*

tributary /'trɪbjʊtərɪ/ *n* afluente *m*, tributário *m*

tribute /'trɪbjuːt/ *n* tributo *m*; **pay ~ to** prestar homenagem a, render tributo a

trick /trɪk/ *n* truque *m*; (*prank*) partida *f*; (*habit*) jeito *m* ● *vt* enganar; **do the ~** [!] (*work*) dar resultado

trickle /'trɪkl/ *vi* pingar, gotejar, escorrer ● *n* fio *m* de água *etc*; *fig* (*small number*) punhado *m*

tricky /'trɪkɪ/ *a* (*crafty*) manhoso; ‹*problem*› delicado, complicado

tricycle /'traɪsɪkl/ *n* triciclo *m*

trifle /'traɪfl/ *n* ninharia *f*, bagatela *f*; (*sweet*) sobremesa *f* feita de pão-de-ló, frutas e creme ● *vi* **~ with** brincar com; **a ~** um pouquinho

trifling /'traɪflɪŋ/ *a* insignificante

trigger /'trɪgə(r)/ *n* (*of gun*) gatilho *m* ● *vt* **~ (off)** (*initiate*) desencadear, despoletar

trim /trɪm/ *a* (**trimmer**, **trimmest**) bem arranjado, bem cuidado; ‹*figure*› elegante, esbelto ● *vt* (*pt* **trimmed**) (*cut*) aparar; ‹*sails*› orientar, marear; (*ornament*) enfeitar; guarnecer (**with** com) ● *n* (*cut*) aparadela *f*, corte *m* leve; (*decoration*) enfeite *m*; (*on car*) acabamento(s) *m(pl)*, estofado *m*; **in ~** em ordem; (*fit*) em boa forma. **~ming(s)** *n* (*dress*) enfeite *m*; *Culin* guarnição *f*, acompanhamento *m*

trinket /ˈtrɪŋkɪt/ *n* bugiganga *f*; (*jewel*) bijuteria *f*, berloque *m*

trio /ˈtriːəʊ/ *n* (*pl* **-os**) trio *m*

trip /trɪp/ *vi* (*pt* **tripped**) (*stumble*) tropeçar, dar um passo em falso; (*go or dance lightly*) andar/dançar com passos leves ● *vt* **~ (up)** fazer tropeçar, passar uma rasteira a ● *n* (*journey*) viagem *f*; (*outing*) passeio *m*, excursão *f*; (*stumble*) tropeção *m*, passo *m* em falso

tripe /traɪp/ *n* (*food*) dobrada *f*, tripas *fpl*; [I] (*nonsense*) disparates *mpl*

triple /ˈtrɪpl/ *a* triplo, tríplice ● *vt/i* triplicar. **~ts** /-plɪts/ *npl* trigêmeos *mpl*, (*P*) trigémeos *mpl*

triplicate /ˈtrɪplɪkət/ *n* **in ~** em triplicado

tripod /ˈtraɪpɒd/ *n* tripé *m*

trite /traɪt/ *a* banal, corriqueiro

triumph /ˈtraɪəmf/ *n* triunfo *m* ● *vi* triunfar (**over** sobre); (*exult*) exultar, rejubilar(-se). **~ant** /-ˈʌmfənt/ *a* triunfante

trivial /ˈtrɪvɪəl/ *a* insignificante

trod, **trodden** /trɒd, ˈtrɒdn/ ▶ TREAD

trolley /ˈtrɒlɪ/ *n* carrinho *m*; **(tea-)~** carrinho *m* de chá

trombone /trɒmˈbəʊn/ *n Mus* trombone *m*

troop /truːp/ *n* bando *m*, grupo *m*; **~s** *Mil* tropas *fpl*; **~ing the colour** a saudação da bandeira ● *vi* **~ in/out** entrar/sair em bando or grupo

trophy /ˈtrəʊfɪ/ *n* troféu *m*

tropic /ˈtrɒpɪk/ *n* trópico *m*; **~s** trópicos *mpl*. **~al** *a* tropical

trot /trɒt/ *n* trote *m*; **on the ~** [I] a seguir, a fio ● *vi* (*pt* **trotted**) trotar; (*of person*) correr em passos curtos, ir num or a trote [I]; **~ out** [I] (*produce*) exibir; [I] (*state*) desfiar

trouble /ˈtrʌbl/ *n* (*difficulty*) dificuldade(s) *f(pl)*, problema(s) *m(pl)*; (*distress*) desgosto(s) *m(pl)*, aborrecimento(s) *m(pl)*; (*pains, effort*) cuidado *m*, trabalho *m*, maçada *f*; (*inconvenience*) transtorno *m*; incômodo *m*, (*P*) incómodo *m*; *Med* doença *f*; **~(s)** (*unrest*) agitação *f*, conflito(s) *m(pl)*; **be in ~** estar em apuros, estar em dificuldades; **get into ~** meter-se em encrenca/apuros; **it is not worth the ~** não vale a pena ● *vt/i* (*bother*) incomodar(-se), (*P*) maçar(-se); (*worry*) preocupar(-se); (*agitate*) perturbar. **~maker** *n* desordeiro *m*, provocador *m*; **~shooter** *n* mediador *m*, negociador *m*. **~d** *a* agitado, perturbado; (*of sleep*) agitado; (*of water*) turvo

troublesome /ˈtrʌblsəm/ *a* problemático, importuno, (*P*) maçador

trough /trɒf/ *n* (*drinking*) bebedouro *m*; (*feeding*) comedouro *m*; **~ (of low pressure)** depressão *f*, linha *f* de baixa pressão

trounce /traʊns/ *vt* (*defeat*) esmagar; (*thrash*) espancar

troupe /truːp/ *n Theat* companhia *f*, troupe *f*

trousers /ˈtraʊzəz/ *npl* calça *f*, (*P*) calças *fpl*; **short ~** calções *mpl*

trousseau /ˈtruːsəʊ/ *n* (*pl* **-s** /-əʊz/) (*of bride*) enxoval *m* de noiva

trout /traʊt/ *n* (*pl invar*) truta *f*

trowel /ˈtraʊəl/ *n* (*garden*) colher *f* de jardineiro; (*for mortar*) trolha *f*

truan|t /ˈtruːənt/ *n* absenteísta *mf*, (*P*) absentista *mf*; *Schol* gazeteiro *m*; **play ~t** fazer gazeta. **~cy** *n* absenteísmo *m*, (*P*) absentismo *m*

truce /truːs/ *n* trégua(s) *f(pl)*, armistício *m*

truck /trʌk/ *n* (*lorry*) caminhão *m*, (*P*) camião *m*; (*barrow*) carro *m* de bagageiro; (*wagon*) vagão *m* aberto. **~ driver** *n* motorista *mf* de caminhão, (*P*) camionista *mf*

trudge /trʌdʒ/ *vi* caminhar com dificuldade, caminhar a custo, arrastar-se

true /truː/ *a* (**-er**, **-est**) verdadeiro; (*accurate*) exato; (*faithful*) fiel; **come ~** (*happen*) realizar-se, concretizar-se; **it is ~** é verdade

truffle /ˈtrʌfl/ *n* trufa *f*

truly /ˈtruːlɪ/ *adv* verdadeiramente; (*faithfully*) fielmente; (*truthfully*) sinceramente

trump /trʌmp/ *n* trunfo *m*; **~ card** carta *f* de trunfo; [I] (*valuable resource*) trunfo *m* ● *vt* jogar trunfo, trunfar; **~ up** forjar, inventar

trumpet /ˈtrʌmpɪt/ *n* trombeta *f*

truncheon /ˈtrʌntʃən/ *n* cassetete *m*

trunk /trʌŋk/ *n* (*of tree, body*) tronco *m*; (*of elephant*) tromba *f*; (*box*) mala *f* grande; *Amer Auto* mala *f*; **~s** (*for swimming*) calção *m or* calções *mpl* de banho. **~ call** *n* chamada *f* interurbana; **~ road** *n* estrada *f* nacional

trust /trʌst/ *n* confiança *f*; (*association*) truste *m*, (*P*) trust *m*; consórcio *m*; (*foundation*) fundação *f*; (*responsibility*) responsabilidade *f*; *Jur* fideicomisso *m*; **in ~** em fideicomisso; **on ~** (*without proof*) sem verificação prévia; (*on credit*) a crédito, (*P*) à confiança ● *vt* (*rely on*) ter confiança em, confiar em; (*hope*) esperar; **~ sb with sth** confiar alguma coisa a alguém ● *vi* **~ in** or **to** confiar em. **~ed** *a* ‹*friend etc*› de confiança, seguro. **~ful**, **~ing** *adjs* confiante. **~y** *a* fiel

trustee /trʌs'ti:/ *n* administrador *m*; *Jur* fideicomissário *m*

trustworthy /'trʌstwɜ:ðɪ/ *a* (digno) de confiança

truth /tru:θ/ *n* (*pl* **-s** /tru:ðz/) verdade *f*. **~ful** *a* ‹*account etc*› verídico; ‹*person*› verdadeiro, que fala verdade

try /traɪ/ *vt/i* (*pt* **tried**) tentar, experimentar; (*be a strain on*) cansar, pôr à prova; *Jur* julgar; **~ for** ‹*post, scholarship*› candidatar-se a; ‹*record*› tentar alcançar; **~ on** ‹*clothes*› provar; **~ out** experimentar; **~ to do** tentar fazer ● *n* (*attempt*) tentativa *f*, experiência *f*; ‹*Rugby*› ensaio *m*. **~ing** *a* difícil

T-shirt /'ti:ʃɜ:t/ *n* T-shirt *f*, camiseta *f* de algodão de mangas curtas

tub /tʌb/ *n* selha *f*; [!] (*bath*) tina *f*; banheira *f*

tuba /'tju:bə/ *n Mus* tuba *f*

tubby /'tʌbɪ/ *a* (**-ier**, **-iest**) baixote e gorducho

tub|e /tju:b/ *n* tubo *m*; [!] (*railway*) metrô *m*, (*P*) metro *m*; **inner ~e** câmara *f* de ar. **~ing** *n* tubos *mpl*, tubagem *f*

tuberculosis /tju:bɜ:kjʊ'ləʊsɪs/ *n* tuberculose *f*

tubular /'tju:bjʊlə(r)/ *a* tubular

tuck /tʌk/ *n* (*fold*) prega *f* cosida; (*for shortening or ornament*) refego *m* ● *vt/i* fazer pregas; (*put*) guardar, meter, enfiar; (*hide*) esconder; **~ in** or **into** [!] (*eat*) atacar; **~ in** ‹*shirt*› meter as fraldas para dentro; ‹*blanket*› prender em; ‹*person*› cobrir bem, aconchegar. **~ shop** *n Schol* loja *f* de balas, (*P*) pastelaria *f* (junto à escola)

Tuesday /'tju:zdɪ/ *n* terça-feira *f*

tuft /tʌft/ *n* tufo *m*

tug /tʌg/ *vt/i* (*pt* **tugged**) puxar com força; ‹*vessel*› rebocar ● *n* (*boat*) rebocador *m*; (*pull*) puxão *m*; **~ of war** disputa *f* cabo-de-guerra

tuition /tju:'ɪʃn/ *n* ensino *m*

tulip /'tju:lɪp/ *n* tulipa *f*

tumble /'tʌmbl/ *vi* tombar, baquear, dar um trambolhão ● *n* tombo *m*, trambolhão *m*. **~ drier** *n* máquina *f* de secar (roupa)

tumbledown /'tʌmbldaʊn/ *a* em ruínas

tumbler /'tʌmblə(r)/ *n* copo *m*

tummy /'tʌmɪ/ *n* [!] (*stomach*) estômago *m*; [!] (*abdomen*) barriga *f*. **~ ache** *n* [!] dor *f* de barriga/de estômago

tumour /'tju:mə(r)/ *n* tumor *m*

tumult /'tju:mʌlt/ *n* tumulto *m*. **~uous** /-'mʌltʃʊəs/ *a* tumultuado, barulhento, agitado

tuna /'tju:nə/ *n* (*pl invar*) atum *m*

tune /tju:n/ *n* melodia *f* ● *vt* ‹*engine*› regular, (*P*) afinar; ‹*piano etc*› afinar ● *vi* **~ in (to)** *Radio, TV* ligar (em), (*P*) sintonizar; **~ up** afinar; **be in ~/out of ~** ‹*instrument*› estar afinado/desafinado; ‹*singer*› cantar afinado/desafinado. **~ful** *a* melodioso, harmonioso. **~r** *n* afinador *m*; *Radio* sintonizador *m*

tunnel /'tʌnl/ *n* túnel *m* ● *vi* (*pt* **tunnelled**) abrir um túnel (**into** em)

turban /'tɜ:bən/ *n* turbante *m*

turbine /'tɜ:baɪn/ *n* turbina *f*

turbulen|t /'tɜ:bjʊlənt/ *a* turbulento. **~ce** *n* turbulência *f*

turf /tɜ:f/ *n* (*pl* **turfs** *or* **turves**) gramado *m*, (*P*) relva *f*, relvado *m*; **the ~** (*racing*) turfe *m*, hipismo *m*; **~ accountant** corretor *m* de apostas ● *vt* **~ out** [!] jogar fora, (*P*) deitar fora

Turk /tɜ:k/ *n* turco *m*. **~ey** *n* Turquia *f*. **~ish** *a* turco *m* ● *n Lang* turco *m*

turkey /'tɜ:kɪ/ *n* peru *m*

turmoil /'tɜ:mɔɪl/ *n* agitação *f*, confusão *f*, desordem *f*; **in ~** em ebulição

turn /tɜ:n/ *vt/i* virar(-se), voltar(-se), girar; (*change*) transformar(-se) (**into** em); (*become*) ficar, tornar-se; ‹*corner*› virar, dobrar; ‹*page*› virar, voltar; **~ against** virar-se or voltar-se contra; **~ down** recusar; (*fold*) dobrar para baixo; (*reduce*) baixar; **~ in** (*hand in*) entregar; [!] (*go to bed*) deitar-se; **~ off** ‹*light etc*› apagar; ‹*tap*› fechar; ‹*road*› virar (para rua transversal); **~ on** ‹*light etc*› acender, ligar; ‹*tap*› abrir; **~ round**

virar-se, voltar-se ● *n* volta *f*; (*in road*) curva *f*; (*of mind, events*) mudança *f*; (*occasion, opportunity*) vez *f*; [!] ataque *m*; crise *f*; [!] (*shock*) susto *m*; **do a good ~** prestar (um) serviço; **in ~** por sua vez, sucessivamente; **speak out of ~** dizer o que não se deve, cometer uma indiscrição; **take ~s** revezar-se; **~ of the century** virada *f or* (*P*) viragem *f* do século □ **~ away** *vi* virar-se or voltar-se para o outro lado ● *vt* (*avert*) desviar; (*reject*) recusar; (*send back*) mandar embora. **~ back** *vi* (*return*) devolver; ‹*vehicle*› dar meia volta, voltar para trás ● *vt* (*fold*) dobrar para trás. **~ out** *vt* ‹*light*› apagar; (*empty*) esvaziar, despejar; ‹*pocket*› virar do avesso; (*produce*) produzir ● *vi* (*transpire*) vir a saber-se, descobrir-se; [!] (*come*) aparecer. **~ up** *vi* aparecer, chegar; (*be found*) aparecer ● *vt* (*find*) desenterrar; (*increase*) aumentar; ‹*collar*› levantar. **~out** *n* assistência *f*; **~-up** *n* (*of trousers*) dobra *f*

turning /'tɜːnɪŋ/ *n* rua *f* transversal; (*corner*) esquina *f*. **~ point** *n* momento *m* decisivo

turnip /'tɜːnɪp/ *n* nabo *m*

turnover /'tɜːnəʊvə(r)/ *n* (*pie, tart*) pastel *m*, empada *f*; (*money*) faturamento *m*, (*P*) faturação *f*; (*of staff*) rotatividade *f*

turnpike /'tɜːnpaɪk/ *n Amer* auto-estrada *f* com pedágio, (*P*) portagem

turnstile /'tɜːnstaɪl/ *n* (*gate*) torniquete *m*, borboleta *f*

turntable /'tɜːnteɪbl/ *n* (*for record*) prato *m* do toca-disco, (*P*) gira-discos; (*record player*) toca-disco *m*, (*P*) gira-discos *m*

turquoise /'tɜːkwɔɪz/ *a* turquesa *invar*

turret /'tʌrɪt/ *n* torreão *m*, torrinha *f*

turtle /'tɜːtl/ *n* tartaruga-do-mar *f*. **~neck** *a* de gola alta

tusk /tʌsk/ *n* (*tooth*) presa *f*; (*elephant's*) defesa *f*, dente *m*

tutor /'tjuːtə(r)/ *n* professor *m* particular; *Univ* professor *m* universitário

tutorial /tjuː'tɔːrɪəl/ *n Univ* seminário *m*

TV /tiː'viː/ *n* tevê *f*, (*P*) TV

tweet /twiːt/ *n* pio *m*, pipilo *m* ● *vi* pipilar

tweezers /'twiːzəz/ *npl* pinça *f*

twel|ve /twelv/ *a & n* doze *m*; **~ (o'clock)** doze horas. **~fth** *a & n* décimo segundo *m*; **T~fth Night** véspera *f* de Reis

twent|y /'twentɪ/ *a & n* vinte *m*. **~ieth** *a & n* vigésimo *m*

twice /twaɪs/ *adv* duas vezes

twiddle /'twɪdl/ *vt/i* **~ (with)** (*fiddle with*) torcer, brincar (com); **~ one's thumbs** girar os polegares, não ter nada para fazer

twig /twɪg/ *n* galho *m*, graveto *m*

twilight /'twaɪlaɪt/ *n* crepúsculo *m* ● *a* crepuscular

twin /twɪn/ *n & a* gêmeo *m*, (*P*) gémeo *m* ● *vt* (*pt* **twinned**) (*pair*) emparelhar, emparceirar; **~ beds** par *m* de camas de solteiro

twine /twaɪn/ *n* guita *f*, cordel *m* ● *vt/i* (*weave together*) entrançar; (*wind*) enroscar(-se)

twinge /twɪndʒ/ *n* dor *f* aguda e súbita, pontada *f*; *fig* pontada *f*, (*P*) ferroada *f*

twinkle /'twɪŋkl/ *vi* cintilar, brilhar ● *n* cintilação *f*, brilho *m*

twirl /twɜːl/ *vt/i* (fazer) girar; ‹*moustache*› torcer

twist /twɪst/ *vt* torcer; (*weave together*) entrançar; (*roll*) enrolar; (*distort*) torcer, deturpar; **~ sb's arm** *fig* forçar alguém ● *vi* ‹*rope etc*› torcer-se, enrolar-se; ‹*road*› dar voltas or curvas, serpentear ● *n* (*act of twisting*) torcedura *f*, (*P*) torcedela *f*; (*of rope*) nó *m*; (*of events*) reviravolta *f*

twit /twɪt/ *n* [!] idiota *mf*

twitch /twɪtʃ/ *vt/i* contrair(-se) ● *n* (*tic*) tique *m*; (*jerk*) puxão *m*

two /tuː/ *a & n* dois *m*; **in** or **of ~ minds** indeciso; **put ~ and ~ together** tirar conclusões. **~-faced** *a* de duas caras, hipócrita; **~-piece** *n* (*garment*) duas-peças *m invar*, (*P*) fato *m* de duas peças; **~-seater** *n* (*car*) carro *m* de dois lugares; **~-way** *a* (*of road*) mão dupla

twosome /'tuːsəm/ *n* par *m*

tycoon /taɪ'kuːn/ *n* magnata *m*

tying /'taɪɪŋ/ ▶ TIE

type /taɪp/ *n* (*example, print*) tipo *m*; (*kind*) tipo *m*; gênero *m*, (*P*) género *m*; [!] (*person*) cara *m*, (*P*) tipo *m* [!] ● *vt/i* (*write*) bater à máquina; datilografar, (*P*) dactilografar

typescript /'taɪpskrɪpt/ *n* texto *m* datilografado, (*P*) dactilografado

typewrit|er /'taɪpraɪtə(r)/ *n* máquina *f* de escrever. **~ten** /-ɪtn/ *a* batido à máquina, datilografado, (*P*) dactilografado

t

typhoid /'taɪfɔɪd/ *n* **~ (fever)** febre *f* tifóide
typhoon /taɪ'fu:n/ *n* tufão *m*
typical /'tɪpɪkl/ *a* típico. **~ly** *adv* tipicamente
typify /'tɪpɪfaɪ/ *vt* ser o (protó)tipo de, tipificar, symbolizar
typing /'taɪpɪŋ/ *n* datilografia *f*, (*P*) dactilografia *f*
typist /'taɪpɪst/ *n* datilógrafo *m*, (*P*) dactilógrafo m
tyrann|y /'tɪrənɪ/ *n* tirania *f*. **~ical** /tɪ'rænɪkl/ *a* tirânico
tyrant /'taɪərənt/ *n* tirano *m*
tyre /'taɪə(r)/ *n* pneu *m*

Uu

ubiquitous /ju:'bɪkwɪtəs/ *a* ubíquo, omnipresente
UFO /'ju:fəʊ/ *n* OVNI *m*
ugl|y /'ʌglɪ/ *a* (**-ier**, **-iest**) feio. **~iness** *n* feiura *f*, (*P*) fealdade *f*
UK *abbr* ▶ **United Kingdom**
ulcer /'ʌlsə(r)/ *n* úlcera *f*
ulterior /ʌl'tɪərɪə(r)/ *a* ulterior; **~ motive** razão *f* inconfessada, segundas intenções *fpl*
ultimate /'ʌltɪmət/ *a* último, derradeiro; (*definitive*) definitivo; (*maximum*) supremo; (*basic*) fundamental. **~ly** *adv* finalmente
ultimatum /ʌltɪ'meɪtəm/ *n* (*pl* **-ums**) ultimato *m*
ultra- /'ʌltrə/ *pref* ultra-, super-
ultraviolet /ʌltrə'vaɪələt/ *a* ultravioleta
umbilical /ʌm'bɪlɪkl/ *a* **~ cord** cordão *m* umbilical
umbrella /ʌm'brelə/ *n* guarda-chuva *m*
umpire /'ʌmpaɪə(r)/ *n Sport* árbitro *m* ● *vt* arbitrar
umpteen /'ʌmpti:n/ *a* ⊠ sem conta; montes de [!]; **for the ~th time** ⊠ pela centésima or enésima vez
UN *abbr* (= **United Nations**) ONU *f*
un- /ʌn/ *pref* não, pouco
unable /ʌn'eɪbl/ *a* **be ~ to do** ser incapaz de/não poder fazer
unabridged /ʌnə'brɪdʒd/ *a* ‹*text*› integral
unacceptable /ʌnək'septəbl/ *a* inaceitável, inadmissível
unaccompanied /ʌnə'kʌmpənɪd/ *a* só, desacompanhado
unaccountable /ʌnə'kaʊntəbl/ *a* (*strange*) inexplicável; (*not responsible*) que não tem que dar contas a alguém or que não pode ser responsabilizado
unaccustomed /ʌnə'kʌstəmd/ *a* desacostumado; **~ to** não acostumado or não habituado a
unadulterated /ʌnə'dʌltəreɪtɪd/ *a* (*pure, sheer*) puro
unaided /ʌn'eɪdɪd/ *a* sem ajuda, sozinho, por si só
unanim|ous /ju:'nænɪməs/ *a* unânime. **~ously** *adv* unanimemente, por unanimidade
unarmed /ʌn'ɑ:md/ *a* desarmado, indefeso
unashamed /ʌnə'ʃeɪmd/ *a* desavergonhado, sem vergonha. **~ly** /-ɪdlɪ/ *adv* sem vergonha
unassuming /ʌnə'sju:mɪŋ/ *a* modesto, despretencioso
unattached /ʌnə'tætʃt/ *a* ‹*person*› livre
unattainable /ʌnə'teɪnəbl/ *a* inacessível
unattended /ʌnə'tendɪd/ *a* ‹*person*› desacompanhado; ‹*car, luggage*› abandonado
unattractive /ʌnə'træktɪv/ *a* sem atrativos; ‹*offer*› de pouco interesse, pouco apetecível
unauthorized /ʌn'ɔ:θəraɪzd/ *a* não-autorizado, sem autorização
unavoidabl|e /ʌnə'vɔɪdəbl/ *a* inevitável. **~y** *adv* inevitavelmente
unaware /ʌnə'weə(r)/ *a* **be ~ of** desconhecer, ignorar, não ter consciência de. **~s** /-eəz/ *adv* (*unexpectedly*) inesperadamente; **catch sb ~s** apanhar alguém desprevenido or de surpresa
unbalanced /ʌn'bælənst/ *a* ‹*mind, person*› desequilibrado or instável
unbearable /ʌn'beərəbl/ *a* insuportável
unbeat|able /ʌn'bi:təbl/ *a* imbatível. **~en** *a* não vencido, invicto; (*unsurpassed*) insuperado
unbelievable /ʌnbɪ'lɪ:vəbl/ *a* inacreditável, incrível
unbiased /ʌn'baɪəst/ *a* imparcial

unblock /ʌn'blɒk/ *vt* desbloquear, desobstruir; ‹*pipe*› desentupir

unbreakable /ʌn'breɪkəbl/ *a* inquebrável

unbroken /ʌn'brəʊkən/ *a* (*intact*) intato, inteiro; (*continuous*) ininterrupto

unburden /ʌn'bɜːdn/ *vpr* **~ o.s.** (*open one's heart*) desabafar (**to** com)

unbutton /ʌn'bʌtn/ *vt* desabotoar

uncalled-for /ʌn'kɔːldfɔː(r)/ *a* injustificável, gratuito

uncanny /ʌn'kænɪ/ *a* (**-ier**, **-iest**) estranho, misterioso

unceasing /ʌn'siːsɪŋ/ *a* incessante

uncertain /ʌn'sɜːtn/ *a* incerto; **be ~ whether** não saber ao certo se, estar indeciso quanto a. **~ty** *n* incerteza *f*

unchang|ed /ʌn'tʃeɪndʒd/ *a* inalterado, sem modificação. **~ing** *a* inalterável, imutável

uncivilized /ʌn'sɪvɪlaɪzd/ *a* não civilizado, bárbaro

uncle /'ʌŋkl/ *n* tio *m*

uncomfortable /ʌn'kʌmfətəbl/ *a* ‹*thing*› desconfortável; incômodo, (*P*) incómodo; (*unpleasant*) desagradável; **feel** or **be ~** (*uneasy*) sentir-se or estar pouco à vontade

uncommon /ʌn'kɒmən/ *a* pouco vulgar, invulgar, fora do comum. **~ly** *adv* invulgarmente, excepcionalmente

uncompromising /ʌn'kɒmprəmaɪzɪŋ/ *a* intransigente

unconcerned /ʌnkən'sɜːnd/ *a* (*indifferent*) indiferente (**by** a)

unconditional /ʌnkən'dɪʃənl/ *a* incondicional

unconscious /ʌn'kɒnʃəs/ *a* inconsciente (**of** de). **~ly** *adv* inconscientemente

unconventional /ʌnkən'venʃənl/ *a* não convencional, fora do comum

uncooperative /ʌnkəʊ'ɒpərətɪv/ *a* ‹*person*› pouco cooperativo; do contra [!]

uncork /ʌn'kɔːk/ *vt* desarrolhar, tirar a rolha de

uncouth /ʌn'kuːθ/ *a* rude, grosseiro

uncover /ʌn'kʌvə(r)/ *vt* descobrir, revelar

undecided /ʌndɪ'saɪdɪd/ *a* (*irresolute*) indeciso; (*not settled*) por decidir, pendente

undeniable /ʌndɪ'naɪəbl/ *a* inegável, incontestável

under /'ʌndə(r)/ *prep* debaixo de, sob; (*less than*) com menos de; (*according to*) conforme, segundo; **~ age** menor de idade; **~ way** em preparo, (*P*) em preparação ● *adv* por baixo, debaixo

under- /'ʌndə(r)/ *pref* sub-

undercarriage /'ʌndəkærɪdʒ/ *n* *Aviat* trem *m* de aterrissagem or (*P*) de aterragem

underclothes /'ʌndəkləʊðz/ *npl* ▶ **UNDERWEAR**

undercoat /'ʌndəkəʊt/ *n* (*of paint*) primeira mão *f*, (*P*) primeira demão *f*

undercover /ʌndə'kʌvə(r)/ *a* ‹*agent, operation*› secreto

undercurrent /'ʌndəkʌrənt/ *n* corrente *f* subterrânea; *fig* filão *m*; *fig* tendência *f* oculta

undercut /ʌndə'kʌt/ *vt* (*pt* **undercut**, *pres p* **undercutting**) *Comm* vender a preços mais baixos do que a concorrência

underdeveloped /ʌndədɪ'veləpt/ *a* atrofiado; ‹*country*› em vias de desenvolvimento

underdog /ʌndə'dɒg/ *n* desprotegido *m*; o mais fraco

underdone /'ʌndədʌn/ *a* (*of meat*) mal passado

underestimate /ʌndə'restɪmeɪt/ *vt* subestimar, não dar o devido valor a

underfed /ʌndə'fed/ *a* subalimentado, subnutrido

underfoot /ʌndə'fʊt/ *adv* debaixo dos pés; (*on the ground*) no chão

undergo /ʌndə'gəʊ/ *vt* (*pt* **-went**, *pp* **-gone**) (*be subjected to*) sofrer; (*treatment*) ser submetido a

undergraduate /ʌndə'grædʒʊət/ *n* estudante *mf* universitário

underground[1] /ʌndə'graʊnd/ *adv* debaixo da terra; *fig* (*secretly*) clandestinamente

underground[2] /'ʌndəgraʊnd/ *a* subterrâneo; *fig* (*secret*) clandestino ● *n Rail* metro(politano) *m*, (*P*) metro *m*

undergrowth /'ʌndəgrəʊθ/ *n* mato *m*

underhand /'ʌndəhænd/ *a* (*deceitful*) sonso, dissimulado

under|lie /ʌndə'laɪ/ *vt* (*pt* **-lay**, *pp* **-lain**, *pres p* **-lying**) estar por baixo de. **~lying** *a* subjacente

underline /ʌndə'laɪn/ *vt* sublinhar, ressaltar

undermine /ʌndə'maɪn/ *vt* minar, solapar

U

underneath /ʌndə'ni:θ/ *prep* sob, debaixo de, por baixo de ● *adv* abaixo, em baixo, por baixo

underpaid /ʌndə'peɪd/ *a* mal pago

underpants /'ʌndəpænts/ *npl* (*man's*) cuecas *fpl*

underpass /'ʌndəpɑ:s/ *n* (*for cars, people*) passagem *f* inferior

underprivileged /ʌndə'prɪvɪlɪdʒd/ *a* desfavorecido

underrate /ʌndə'reɪt/ *vt* subestimar, depreciar

underside /'ʌndəsaɪd/ *n* lado *m* inferior, base *f*

underskirt /'ʌndəskɜ:t/ *n* anágua *f*

understand /ʌndə'stænd/ *vt/i* (*pt* **-stood**) compreender, entender. **~able** *a* compreensível. **~ing** *a* compreensivo ● *n* compreensão *f*; ‹*agreement*› acordo *m*, entendimento *m*

understatement /'ʌndəsteɪtmənt/ *n* versão *f* atenuada da verdade, litotes *f*, eufemismo *m*

understudy /'ʌndəstʌdɪ/ *n* substituto *m*

undertak|e /ʌndə'teɪk/ *vt* (*pt* **-took**, *pp* **-taken**) empreender; ‹*responsibility*› assumir; **~e to** encarregar-se de. **~ing** *n* (*task*) empreendimento *m*; (*promise*) compromisso *m*

undertaker /'ʌndəteɪkə(r)/ *n* agente *m* funerário; papa-defuntos *m* [!], (*P*) coveiro *m*

undertone /'ʌndətəʊn/ *n* **in an ~** a meia voz or em surdina

undervalue /ʌndə'vælju:/ *vt* avaliar por baixo, subestimar

underwater /ʌndə'wɔ:tə(r)/ *a* submarino ● *adv* debaixo de água

underwear /'ʌndəweə(r)/ *n* roupa *f* interior or de baixo

underweight /'ʌndəweɪt/ *a* **be ~** estar com o peso abaixo do normal, ter peso a menos

U

underwent /ʌndə'went/ ▶ UNDERGO

underworld /'ʌndəwɜ:ld/ *n* (*of crime*) submundo *m*, (*P*) bas-fonds *mpl*

underwriter /'ʌndəraɪtə(r)/ *n* segurador *m*, subscritor *m*; (*marine*) underwriter *m*, segurador *m*

undeserved /ʌndɪ'zɜ:vd/ *a* imerecido, injusto

undesirable /ʌndɪ'zaɪərəbl/ *a* indesejável, inconveniente

undies /'ʌndɪz/ *npl* [!] roupa *f* de baixo or interior

undignified /ʌn'dɪgnɪfaɪd/ *a* pouco digno, sem dignidade

undisputed /ʌndɪ'spju:tɪd/ *a* incontestado

undo /ʌn'du:/ *vt* (*pt* **-did**, *pp* **-done** /dʌn/) desfazer; ‹*knot*› desfazer, desatar; ‹*coat, button*› abrir; **leave ~ne** não fazer, deixar por fazer. **~ing** *n* desgraça *f*, ruína *f*

undoubted /ʌn'daʊtɪd/ *a* indubitável. **~ly** *adv* indubitavelmente

undress /ʌn'dres/ *vt/i* despir(-se); **get ~ed** despir-se

undu|e /ʌn'dju:/ *a* excessivo, indevido. **~ly** *adv* excessivamente, indevidamente

undying /ʌn'daɪɪŋ/ *a* eterno, perene

unearth /ʌn'ɜ:θ/ *vt* desenterrar; *fig* descobrir

unearthly /ʌn'ɜ:θlɪ/ *a* sobrenatural, misterioso; **~ hour** [!] hora *f* absurda or inconveniente

uneasy /ʌn'i:zɪ/ *a* (*ill at ease*) pouco à vontade; (*worried*) preocupado

uneconomic /ʌni:kə'nɒmɪk/ *a* antieconômico

uneducated /ʌn'edʒʊkeɪtɪd/ *a* ‹*person*› inculto, sem instrução

unemploy|ed /ʌnɪm'plɔɪd/ *a* desempregado. **~ment** *n* desemprego *m*; **~ment benefit** auxílio-desemprego *m*, (*P*) subsídio *m* de desemprego

unending /ʌn'endɪŋ/ *a* interminável, sem fim

unequal /ʌn'i:kwəl/ *a* desigual. **~led** *a* sem igual, inigualável

unequivocal /ʌnɪ'kwɪvəkl/ *a* inequívoco, claro

uneven /ʌn'i:vn/ *a* desigual, irregular

unexpected /ʌnɪk'spektɪd/ *a* inesperado. **~ly** *a* inesperadamente

unfair /ʌn'feə(r)/ *a* injusto (**to** com). **~ness** *n* injustiça *f*

unfaithful /ʌn'feɪθfl/ *a* infiel

unfamiliar /ʌnfə'mɪlɪə(r)/ *a* estranho, desconhecido; **be ~ with** desconhecer, não conhecer, não estar familiarizado com

unfashionable /ʌn'fæʃənəbl/ *a* fora de moda

unfasten /ʌn'fɑ:sn/ *vt* ‹*knot*› desatar, soltar; ‹*button*› abrir

unfavourable /ʌn'feɪvərəbl/ *a* desfavorável

unfeeling /ʌn'fi:lɪŋ/ *a* insensível

unfit /ʌn'fɪt/ *a* sem preparo físico, (*P*) preparação física, fora de forma;

(*unsuitable*) impróprio (**for** para)

unfold /ʌn'fəʊld/ *vt* desdobrar; (*expose*) expor, revelar ● *vi* desenrolar-se

unforeseen /ʌnfɔː'siːn/ *a* imprevisto, inesperado

unforgettable /ʌnfə'getəbl/ *a* inesquecível

unforgivable /ʌnfə'gɪvəbl/ *a* imperdoável, indesculpável

unfortunate /ʌn'fɔːtʃənət/ *a* (*unlucky*) infeliz; (*regrettable*) lamentável; **it was very ~ that** foi uma pena/ lamentável que. **~ly** *adv* infelizmente

unfounded /ʌn'faʊndɪd/ *a* ‹*rumour etc*› infundado, sem fundamento

unfriendly /ʌn'frendlɪ/ *a* pouco amável, antipático, frio

unfurnished /ʌn'fɜːnɪʃt/ *a* sem mobília

ungainly /ʌn'geɪnlɪ/ *a* desajeitado, deselegante

ungrateful /ʌn'greɪtfl/ *a* ingrato

unhapp|y /ʌn'hæpɪ/ *a* (**-ier**, **-iest**) infeliz, triste; (*not pleased*) descontente; pouco contente (**with** com). **~iness** *n* infelicidade *f*, tristeza *f*

unharmed /ʌn'hɑːmd/ *a* incólume, são e salvo, ileso

unhealthy /ʌn'helθɪ/ *a* (**-ier**, **-iest**) ‹*climate etc*› doentio, insalubre; ‹*person*› adoentado, com pouca saúde

unholy /ʌn'həʊlɪ/ *a* (**-ier**, **-iest**) ‹*person, act etc*› ímpio; [!] (*great*) incrível; espantoso

unhurt /ʌn'hɜːt/ *a* ileso, incólume

unicorn /'juːnɪkɔːn/ *n* unicórnio *m*

uniform /'juːnɪfɔːm/ *n* uniforme *m* ● *a* uniforme, sempre igual. **~ity** /-'fɔːmətɪ/ *n* uniformidade *f*. **~ly** *adv* uniformemente

unif|y /'juːnɪfaɪ/ *vt* unificar. **~ication** /-ɪ'keɪʃn/ *n* unificação *f*

unilateral /juːnɪ'lætrəl/ *a* unilateral

unimaginable /ʌnɪ'mædʒɪnəbl/ *a* inimaginável

unimportant /ʌnɪm'pɔːtnt/ *a* sem importância, insignificante

uninhabited /ʌnɪn'hæbɪtɪd/ *a* desabitado

unintentional /ʌnɪn'tenʃənl/ *a* involuntário, não propositado

uninterest|ed /ʌn'ɪntrəstɪd/ *a* desinteressado (**in** em), indiferente (**in** a). **~ing** *a* desinteressante, sem interesse

union /'juːnɪən/ *n* união *f*; (*trade union*) sindicato *m*; **U~ Jack** bandeira *f* britânica. **~ist** *n* sindicalista *mf*; *Pol* unionista *mf*

unique /juː'niːk/ *a* único, sem igual

unisex /'juːnɪseks/ *a* unissexo

unison /'juːnɪsn/ *n* **in ~** em uníssono

unit /'juːnɪt/ *n* unidade *f*; (*of furniture*) peça *f*; unidade *f*, (*P*) módulo *m*

unite /juː'naɪt/ *vt/i* unir(-se). **U~d Kingdom** *n* Reino *m* Unido; **U~d Nations (Organization)** *n* Organização *f* das Nações Unidas; **U~d States (of America)** Estados *mpl* Unidos (da América)

unity /'juːnətɪ/ *n* unidade *f*; *fig* (*harmony*) união *f*

universal /juːnɪ'vɜːsl/ *a* universal

universe /'juːnɪvɜːs/ *n* universo *m*

university /juːnɪ'vɜːsətɪ/ *n* universidade *f* ● *a* universitário; ‹*student, teacher*› universitário, da universidade

unjust /ʌn'dʒʌst/ *a* injusto

unkempt /ʌn'kempt/ *a* desmazelado, desleixado; (*of hair*) despenteado, desgrenhado

unkind /ʌn'kaɪnd/ *a* desagradável, duro

unknowingly /ʌn'nəʊɪŋlɪ/ *adv* sem saber, inconscientemente

unknown /ʌn'nəʊn/ *a* desconhecido ● *n* **the ~** o desconhecido

unleaded /ʌn'ledɪd/ *a* sem chumbo

unless /ʌn'les/ *conj* a não ser que, a menos que, salvo se, se não

unlike /ʌn'laɪk/ *a* diferente ● *prep* ao contrário de

unlikely /ʌn'laɪklɪ/ *a* improvável

unlimited /ʌn'lɪmɪtɪd/ *a* ilimitado

unload /ʌn'ləʊd/ *vt* descarregar

unlock /ʌn'lɒk/ *vt* abrir (com chave), (*P*) destrancar

unluck|y /ʌn'lʌkɪ/ *a* (**-ier**, **-iest**) infeliz, sem sorte; ‹*number*› que dá azar; **be ~y** ter pouca sorte, ter azar. **~ily** *adv* infelizmente

unmarried /ʌn'mærɪd/ *a* solteiro, celibatário

unmask /ʌn'mɑːsk/ *vt* desmascarar

unmistakable /ʌnmɪs'teɪkəbl/ *a* ‹*voice etc*› inconfundível; (*clear*) claro, inequívoco

unnatural /ʌn'nætʃrəl/ *a* que não é natural; (*wicked*) desnaturado

unnecessary /ʌn'nesəserɪ/ *a* desnecessário; (*superfluous*) supérfluo, dispensável

u

unnerve /ʌn'nɜːv/ *vt* desencorajar, desmoralizar, intimidar

unnoticed /ʌn'nəʊtɪst/ *a* **go ~** passar despercebido

unobtrusive /ʌnəb'truːsɪv/ *a* discreto

unofficial /ʌnə'fɪʃl/ *a* oficioso, que não é oficial; ‹*strike*› ilegal, não autorizado

unorthodox /ʌn'ɔːθədɒks/ *a* pouco ortodoxo, não ortodoxo

unpack /ʌn'pæk/ *vt* ‹*suitcase etc*› desfazer; ‹*contents*› desembalar, desempacotar ● *vi* desfazer a mala

unpaid /ʌn'peɪd/ *a* não remunerado; ‹*bill*› a pagar, por pagar

unpalatable /ʌn'pælətəbl/ *a* ‹*food, fact etc*› desagradável, intragável

unparalleled /ʌn'pærəleld/ *a* sem paralelo or comparação, incomparável

unpleasant /ʌn'pleznt/ *a* desagradável (**to** com); ‹*person*› antipático

unplug /ʌn'plʌg/ *vt* (*pt* **-plugged**) *Electr* desligar a tomada, (*P*) tirar or desligar a ficha da tomada

unpopular /ʌn'pɒpjʊlə(r)/ *a* impopular

unprecedented /ʌn'presɪdentɪd/ *a* sem precedentes, inaudito, nunca visto

unpredictable /ʌnprə'dɪktəbl/ *a* imprevisível

unprepared /ʌnprɪ'peəd/ *a* sem preparação, improvisado; ‹*person*› desprevenido

unpretentious /ʌnprɪ'tenʃəs/ *a* despretencioso, sem pretensões

unprincipled /ʌn'prɪnsəpld/ *a* sem princípios, sem escrúpulos

unprofessional /ʌnprə'feʃənl/ *a* ‹*work*› de amador; ‹*conduct*› sem consciência profissional, pouco profissional

unprofitable /ʌn'prɒfɪtəbl/ *a* não lucrativo

u

unqualified /ʌn'kwɒlɪfaɪd/ *a* sem habilitações; ‹*success etc*› total, absoluto; **be ~ to** não estar habilitado or ter qualificações para

unquestionable /ʌn'kwestʃənəbl/ *a* incontestável, indiscutível, inquestionável

unravel /ʌn'rævl/ *vt* (*pt* **unravelled**) desenredar, desemaranhar; ‹*knitting*› desmanchar

unreal /ʌn'rɪəl/ *a* irreal

unreasonable /ʌn'riːznəbl/ *a* pouco razoável, disparatado; (*excessive*) excessivo

unrecognizable /ʌn'rekəgnaɪzəbl/ *a* irreconhecível

unrelated /ʌnrɪ'leɪtɪd/ *a* ‹*facts*› desconexo; sem relação (**to** com); ‹*people*› não aparentado (**to** com)

unreliable /ʌnrɪ'laɪəbl/ *a* que não é de confiança

unrest /ʌn'rest/ *n* agitação *f*, distúrbios *mpl*

unrivalled /ʌn'raɪvld/ *a* sem igual, incomparável

unroll /ʌn'rəʊl/ *vt* desenrolar

unruly /ʌn'ruːlɪ/ *a* indisciplinado, turbulento

unsafe /ʌn'seɪf/ *a* (*dangerous*) que não é seguro, perigoso; ‹*person*› em perigo

unsatisfactory /ʌnsætɪs'fæktərɪ/ *a* insatisfatório, pouco satisfatório

unsavoury /ʌn'seɪvərɪ/ *a* desagradável, repugnante

unscathed /ʌn'skeɪðd/ *a* ileso, incólume

unscrew /ʌn'skruː/ *vt* desenroscar, desaparafusar

unscrupulous /ʌn'skruːpjʊləs/ *a* sem escrúpulos, pouco escrupuloso, sem consciência

unseemly /ʌn'siːmlɪ/ *a* inconveniente, indecoroso, impróprio

unsettle /ʌn'setl/ *vt* perturbar, agitar. **~d** *a* perturbado; ‹*weather*› instável, variável; ‹*bill*› não saldado, por pagar

unshakeable /ʌn'ʃeɪkəbl/ *a* ‹*person, belief etc*› inabalável

unshaven /ʌn'ʃeɪvn/ *a* com a barba por fazer, por barbear

unsightly /ʌn'saɪtlɪ/ *a* feio

unskilled /ʌn'skɪld/ *a* inexperiente; ‹*work, worker*› não especializado; ‹*labour*› mão-de-obra *f* não especializada

unsociable /ʌn'səʊʃəbl/ *a* insociável, misantropo

unsophisticated /ʌnsə'fɪstɪkeɪtɪd/ *a* simples, natural

unsound /ʌn'saʊnd/ *a* pouco sólido; **of ~ mind** *Jur* que não está em plena posse das suas faculdades mentais

unspeakable /ʌn'spiːkəbl/ *a* indescritível; (*bad*) inqualificável

unstable /ʌn'steɪbl/ *a* instável

unsteady /ʌn'stedɪ/ *a* ‹*step*› vacilante, incerto; ‹*ladder*› instável; ‹*hand*› pouco firme

unstuck /ʌn'stʌk/ *a* (*not stuck*) descolado; **come ~** 🅸 (*fail*) falhar

unsubscribe /ˌʌnsəb'skraɪb/ *vi* descadastrar-se, (*P*) anular uma inscrição/subscrição

unsuccessful /ʌnsək'sesfl/ *a* ‹*candidate*› malsucedido; ‹*attempt*› malogrado, fracassado; **be ~** não ter êxito

unsuit|able /ʌn's(j)u:təbl/ *a* impróprio; pouco apropriado; inadequado (**for** para)

unsure /ʌn'ʃʊə(r)/ *a* incerto

unsuspecting /ʌnsə'spektɪŋ/ *a* sem desconfiar de nada, insuspeitado

untangle /ʌn'tæŋgl/ *vt* desemaranhar, desenredar, desembaraçar

unthinkable /ʌn'θɪŋkəbl/ *a* impensável, inconcebível

untid|y /ʌn'taɪdɪ/ *a* (**-ier, -iest**) ‹*room, desk etc*› desarrumado; ‹*appearance*› desleixado, desmazelado; ‹*hair*› despenteado. **~iness** *n* desordem *f*; (*of appearance*) desmazelo *m*

untie /ʌn'taɪ/ *vt* ‹*knot, parcel*› desatar, desfazer; ‹*person*› desamarrar

until /ən'tɪl/ *prep* até. **not ~** não antes de ● *conj* até que

untimely /ʌn'taɪmlɪ/ *a* inoportuno, intempestivo; ‹*death*› prematuro

untold /ʌn'təʊld/ *a* incalculável

untoward /ʌntə'wɔ:d/ *a* inconveniente, desagradável

untrue /ʌn'tru:/ *a* falso

unused[1] /ʌn'ju:zd/ *a* (*new*) novo, por usar; (*not in use*) não utilizado

unused[2] /ʌn'ju:st/ *a* **~ to** não habituado a, não acostumado a

unusual /ʌn'ju:ʒʊəl/ *a* insólito, fora do comum

unveil /ʌn'veɪl/ *vt* descobrir, revelar; ‹*statue, portrait etc*› desvelar

unwanted /ʌn'wɒntɪd/ *a* (*useless*) que já não serve; ‹*child*› indesejado

unwelcome /ʌn'welkəm/ *a* desagradável; ‹*guest*› indesejável

unwell /ʌn'wel/ *a* indisposto

unwieldy /ʌn'wi:ldɪ/ *a* difícil de manejar, pouco jeitoso

unwilling /ʌn'wɪlɪŋ/ *a* relutante (**to** em), pouco disposto (**to** a)

unwind /ʌn'waɪnd/ *vt/i* (*pt* **unwound** /ʌn'waʊnd/) desenrolar(-se); 🅸 (*relax*) descontrair(-se)

unwise /ʌn'waɪz/ *a* imprudente, insensato

unwittingly /ʌn'wɪtɪŋlɪ/ *adv* sem querer

unworthy /ʌn'wɜ:ðɪ/ *a* indigno

unwrap /ʌn'ræp/ *vt* (*pt* **unwrapped**) desembrulhar, abrir, desfazer

unwritten /ʌn'rɪtn/ *a* ‹*agreement*› verbal, tácito

up /ʌp/ *adv* (*to higher place*) cima, para cima, para o alto; (*in higher place*) em cima, no alto; (*out of bed*) acordado, de pé, (*P*) a pé; (*up and dressed*) pronto; (*finished*) acabado; ‹*sun*› alto; **be ~ against** defrontar, enfrentar; **be ~ in** 🅸 saber; **be ~ to** (*do*) estar fazendo, (*P*) estar a fazer; (*plot*) estar tramando, (*P*) estar a tramar; ‹*task*› estar à altura de; **come** or **go ~** subir; **feel ~ to doing** (*able*) sentir-se capaz de fazer; **it is ~ to you** depende só de você, (*P*) de ti; **walk ~ and down** andar dum lado para o outro or para a frente e para trás ● *prep* no cimo de, em cima de, no alto de; **~ the street/river/** *etc* pela rua/pelo rio/*etc* acima ● *vt* (*pt* **upped**) (*increase*) aumentar ● *npl* **have ~s and downs** *fig* ter (os seus) altos e baixos. **~-and-coming** *a* prometedor; **~market** *a* requintado, fino

upbringing /'ʌpbrɪŋɪŋ/ *n* educação *f*

update /ʌp'deɪt/ *vt* atualizar

upheaval /ʌp'hi:vl/ *n* pandemônio *m*, (*P*) pandemónio *m*, revolução *f fig*; (*social, political*) convulsão *f*

uphill /'ʌphɪl/ *a* ladeira acima, ascendente; *fig* (*difficult*) árduo ● *adv* /ʌp'hɪl/ **go ~** subir

uphold /ʌp'həʊld/ *vt* (*pt* **upheld**) sustentar, manter, apoiar, defender

upholster /ʌp'həʊlstə(r)/ *vt* estofar. **~y** *n* estofados *mpl*, (*P*) estofo(s) *m(pl)*

upkeep /'ʌpki:p/ *n* manutenção *f*

upon /ə'pɒn/ *prep* sobre

upper /'ʌpə(r)/ *a* superior ● *n* (*of shoe*) gáspea *f*; **have the ~ hand** estar por cima or em vantagem, estar em posição de superioridade; **~ class** classe *f* alta

upright /'ʌpraɪt/ *a* vertical; (*honourable*) honesto, honrado, (*P*) reto

uprising /'ʌpraɪzɪŋ/ *n* insurreição *f*, sublevação *f*, levantamento *m*

uproar /'ʌprɔ:(r)/ *n* tumulto *m*, alvoroço *m*

uproot /ʌp'ru:t/ *vt* desenraizar; *fig* erradicar; desarraigar

upset[1] /ʌp'set/ *vt* (*pt* **upset**, *pres p* **upsetting**) (*overturn*) entornar, virar; ‹*plan*› contrariar, transtornar; ‹*stomach*› desarranjar, (*P*) indispor; ‹*person*› contrariar, transtornar, incomodar ● *a* aborrecido

upset² /'ʌpset/ *n* transtorno *m*; (*of stomach*) indisposição *f*; (*distress*) choque *m*

upshot /'ʌpʃɒt/ *n* resultado *m*

upside-down /ʌpsaɪd'daʊn/ *adv lit & fig* ao contrário; de pernas para o ar, (*P*) de pantanas [!]

upstairs /ʌp'steəz/ *adv* (*at*/*to*) em/para cima, no/para o andar de cima ● /'ʌpsteəz/ *a* ‹*flat etc*› de cima, do andar de cima

upstart /'ʌpstɑːt/ *n* arrivista *mf*

upstream /ʌp'striːm/ *adv* rio acima, contra a corrente

uptake /'ʌpteɪk/ *n* **be quick on the ~** pegar, (*P*) apanhar rapidamente as coisas; *fig* ser de compreensão rápida, ser vivo

up-to-date /'ʌptədeɪt/ *a* moderno, atualizado

upturn /'ʌptɜːn/ *n* melhoria *f*

upward /'ʌpwəd/ *a* ascendente, voltado para cima. **~s** *adv* para cima

uranium /jʊ'reɪnɪəm/ *n* urânio *m*

urban /'ɜːbən/ *a* urbano

urge /ɜːdʒ/ *vt* aconselhar vivamente (**to** a); **~ on** (*impel*) incitar (a) ● *n* (*strong desire*) grande vontade *f*

urgen|t /'ɜːdʒənt/ *a* urgente; **be ~t** urgir, ser insistente. **~cy** *n* urgência *f*

urinal /jʊə'raɪnl/ *n* urinol *m*

urin|e /'jʊərɪn/ *n* urina *f*. **~ate** *vi* urinar

urn /ɜːn/ *n* urna *f*; (*for tea, coffee*) espécie *f* de samovar

us /ʌs unstressed əs/ *pron* nos; (*after preps*) nós; **with ~** connosco; **he knows ~** ele nos conhece, (*P*) ele conhece-nos

US *abbr* (= **United States**) ▶ UNITE

USA *abbr* (= **United States of America**) ▶ UNITE

usable /'juːzəbl/ *a* utilizável

usage /'juːzɪdʒ/ *n* uso *m*

USB *abbr* (= **universal serial bus**) USB. **~ key** *n* pen drive *m*, (*P*) pen *m*; **~ port** porta *f* USB

USB port /juːesbiːpɔːt/ *n* porto *m* USB, (*P*) entrada *f* USB

use¹ /juːz/ *vt* usar, utilizar, servir-se de; (*exploit*) servir-se de; (*consume*) gastar, usar, consumir; **~ up** esgotar, consumir. **~r** /-ə(r)/ *n* usuário *m*, (*P*) utente *mf*. **~r-friendly** *a* fácil de usar

use² /juːs/ *n* uso *m*, emprego *m*; **in ~** em uso; **it is no ~ shouting**/*etc* não serve de nada or não adianta gritar/*etc*; **make ~ of** servir-se de; **of ~** útil

used¹ /juːzd/ *a* (*second-hand*) usado

used² /juːst/ *pt* **he ~ to sing** ele costumava or ele tinha por costume or hábito cantar ● *a* **~ to singing** acostumado a or habituado a cantar

use|ful /'juːsfl/ *a* útil. **~less** *a* inútil; ‹*person*› incompetente

username /'juːzəneɪm/ *n* nome *m* de usuário, (*P*) nome *m* de utilizador

usher /'ʌʃə(r)/ *n* lanterninha *m*, (*P*) arrumador *m* ● *vt* **~ in** mandar or fazer entrar. **~ette** *n* vaga-lume *f*, (*P*) arrumadora *f*

USSR *abbr* URSS

usual /'juːʒʊəl/ *a* usual, habitual, normal; **as ~** como de costume, como habitualmente; **at the ~ time** na hora de costume, (*P*) à(s) hora(s) de costume. **~ly** *adv* habitualmente, normalmente

utensil /juː'tensl/ *n* utensílio *m*

uterus /'juːtərəs/ *n* útero *m*

utilitarian /juːtɪlɪ'teərɪən/ *a* utilitário

utility /juː'tɪlətɪ/ *n* utilidade *f*; **(public) ~** serviço *m* público; **~ room** área *f* de serviço (para as máquinas de lavar a roupa e a louça)

utilize /'juːtɪlaɪz/ *vt* utilizar

utmost /'ʌtməʊst/ *a* (*furthest, most intense*) extremo; **the ~ care**/*etc* (*greatest*) o maior cuidado/*etc* ● *n* **do one's ~** fazer todo o possível or tudo, fazer tudo ao alcance de alguém

utter¹ /'ʌtə(r)/ *a* completo, absoluto. **~ly** *adv* completamente

utter² /'ʌtə(r)/ *vt* proferir; ‹*sigh, shout*› dar

U-turn /'juːtɜːn/ *n* retorno *m*, (*P*) inversão *f* de marcha *fig*, reviravolta *f*

Vv

vacan|t /'veɪkənt/ *a* ‹*post, room, look*› vago; ‹*mind*› vazio; ‹*seat, space, time*› desocupado, livre. **~cy** *n* (*post*) vaga *f*; (*room in hotel*) vago *m*

vacate /və'keɪt/ *vt* vagar, deixar vago

vacation /və'keɪʃn/ *n* férias *fpl*

vaccinat|e /'væksɪneɪt/ *vt* vacinar. **~ion** /-'neɪʃn/ *n* vacinação *f*

u v

vaccine /ˈvæksiːn/ *n* vacina *f*

vacuum /ˈvækjʊəm/ *n* (*pl* **-cuums**, *or* **-cua**) vácuo *m*, vazio *m*. **~ cleaner** *n* aspirador *m* (de pó)

vagina /vəˈdʒaɪnə/ *n* vagina *f*

vagrant /ˈveɪgrənt/ *n* vadio *m*, vagabundo *m*

vague /veɪg/ *a* (**-er**, **-est**) vago; (*outline*) impreciso; **be ~ about** ser vago acerca de, não precisar. **~ly** *adv* vagamente

vain /veɪn/ *a* (**-er**, **-est**) (*conceited*) vaidoso; (*useless*) vão, inútil; (*fruitless*) infrutífero; **in ~** em vão. **~ly** *adv* em vão

valentine /ˈvæləntaɪn/ *n* (*card*) cartão *m* do dia de São Valentim or dia dos Namorados

valiant /ˈvælɪənt/ *a* corajoso, valente

valid /ˈvælɪd/ *a* válido. **~ity** /və-ˈlɪdətɪ/ *n* validade *f*

validate /ˈvælɪdeɪt/ *vt* validar, confirmar, ratificar

valley /ˈvælɪ/ *n* vale *m*

valuable /ˈvæljʊəbl/ *a* (*object*) valioso, de valor; ‹*help, time etc*› precioso. **~s** *npl* objetos *mpl* de valor

valuation /væljʊˈeɪʃn/ *n* avaliação *f*

value /ˈvæljuː/ *n* valor *m* ● *vt* avaliar; (*cherish*) dar valor a; **~ added tax** imposto *m* de valor adicional, (*P*) acrescentado

valve /vælv/ *n Anat, Techn* (*of car tyre*) válvula *f*; (*of bicycle tyre*) pipo *m*; (*of radio*) lâmpada *f*, válvula *f*

vampire /ˈvæmpaɪə(r)/ *n* vampiro *m*

van /væn/ *n* (*large*) caminhão *m*; (*small*) camionete *f*, comercial *m*, (*P*) carrinha *f* (comercial); (*milkman's, baker's etc*) camionete *f*; *Rail* bagageiro *m*, (*P*) furgão *m*

vandal /ˈvændl/ *n* vândalo *m*. **~ism** /-əlɪzəm/ *n* vandalismo *m*

vandalize /ˈvændəlaɪz/ *vt* destruir, estragar, vandalizar

vanilla /vəˈnɪlə/ *n* baunilha *f*

vanish /ˈvænɪʃ/ *vi* desaparecer, sumir-se, desvanecer-se

vanity /ˈvænətɪ/ *n* vaidade *f*. **~ case** *n* bolsa *f* de maquilagem, (*P*) de maquilhagem

vantage point /ˈvɑːntɪdʒpɔɪnt/ *n* (bom) ponto *m* de observação

vapour /ˈveɪpə(r)/ *n* vapor *m*; (*mist*) bruma *f*

vari|able /ˈveərɪəbl/ *a* variável. **~ation** /-ˈeɪʃn/ *n* variação *f*. **~ed** /-ɪd/ *a* variado

variance /ˈveərɪəns/ *n* **at ~** em desacordo (**with** com)

variant /ˈveərɪənt/ *a* diverso, diferente ● *n* variante *f*

varicose /ˈværɪkəʊs/ *a* **~ veins** varizes *fpl*

variety /vəˈraɪətɪ/ *n* variedade *f*; (*entertainment*) variedades *fpl*

various /ˈveərɪəs/ *a* vários, diversos, variados

varnish /ˈvɑːnɪʃ/ *n* verniz *m* ● *vt* envernizar; ‹*nails*› pintar

vary /ˈveərɪ/ *vt/i* variar

vase /vɑːz/ *n* vaso *m*, jarra *f*

vast /vɑːst/ *a* vasto, imenso. **~ly** *adv* imensamente, infinitamente

vat /væt/ *n* tonel *m*, dorna *f*, cuba *f*

VAT /viːeɪˈtiː, væt/ *abbr* ICM *m*, (*P*) IVA *m*

vault[1] /vɔːlt/ *n* (*roof*) abóbada *f*; (*in bank*) casa-forte *f*; (*tomb*) cripta *f*; (*cellar*) adega *f*

vault[2] /vɔːlt/ *vt/i* saltar ● *n* salto *m*

VDU *abbr* ▶ VISUAL DISPLAY UNIT

veal /viːl/ *n* (*meat*) vitela *f*

veer /vɪə(r)/ *vi* virar, mudar de direção

vegan /ˈviːgən/ *a* & *n* vegetariano *m* estrito, (*P*) vegano

vegetable /ˈvedʒɪtəbl/ *n* hortaliça *f*, legume *m* ● *a* vegetal

vegetarian /vedʒɪˈteərɪən/ *a* & *n* vegetariano *m*

vegetation /vedʒɪˈteɪʃn/ *n* vegetação *f*

vehement /ˈviːəmənt/ *a* veemente. **~ly** *adv* veementemente

vehicle /ˈviːɪkl/ *n* veículo *m*

veil /veɪl/ *n* véu *m* ● *vt* velar, cobrir com véu; *fig* esconder; disfarçar

vein /veɪn/ *n* (*in body; mood*) veia *f*; (*in rock*) veio *m*, filão *m*; (*of leaf*) nervura *f*

velocity /vɪˈlɒsətɪ/ *n* velocidade *f*

velvet /ˈvelvɪt/ *n* veludo *m*

vendetta /venˈdetə/ *n* vendeta *f*

vending machine /ˈvendɪŋməʃiːn/ *n* vendedora *f* automática, (*P*) máquina *f* de distribuição, automática

vendor /ˈvendə(r)/ *n* vendedor *m*; **street ~** vendedor *m* ambulante

veneer /vəˈnɪə(r)/ *n* folheado *m*; *fig* fachada *f*; máscara *f*

venerable /ˈvenərəbl/ *a* venerável

Venezuela /venɪzˈweɪlə/ *n* Venezuela *f*. **~n** *a* & *n* venezuelano *m*

vengeance /ˈvendʒəns/ *n* vingança; **with a ~** furiosamente, em excesso, com mais força do que se pretende

venison /ˈvenɪzn/ *n* carne *f* de veado

venom /ˈvenəm/ *n* veneno *m*. **~ous** /ˈvenəməs/ *a* venenoso

vent[1] /vent/ *n* (*in coat*) abertura *f*

vent[2] /vent/ *n* (*hole*) orifício *m*, abertura *f*; (*for air*) respiradouro *m* ● *vt* (*anger*) descarregar (**on** para *or* em cima de); **give ~ to** *fig* desabafar, dar vazão a

ventilat|e /ˈventɪleɪt/ *vt* ventilar. **~ion** /-ˈleɪʃn/ *n* ventilação *f*. **~or** *n* ventilador *m*

ventriloquist /venˈtrɪləkwɪst/ *n* ventríloquo *m*

venture /ˈventʃə(r)/ *n* empreendimento *m* arriscado, aventura *f* ● *vt/i* arriscar(-se)

venue /ˈvenjuː/ *n* porto *m* de encontro

veranda /vəˈrændə/ *n* varanda *f*

verb /vɜːb/ *n* verbo *m*

verbal /ˈvɜːbl/ *a* verbal; (*literal*) literal

verbose /vɜːˈbəʊs/ *a* palavroso, prolixo

verdict /ˈvɜːdɪkt/ *n* veredito *m*; (*opinion*) opinião *f*

verge /vɜːdʒ/ *n* beira *f*, borda *f*; **on the ~ of doing** prestes a fazer ● *vi* **~ on** estar à beira de

verify /ˈverɪfaɪ/ *vt* verificar

vermin /ˈvɜːmɪn/ *n* animais *mpl* nocivos, verme *m*; (*lice, fleas etc*) parasitas *mpl*

vermouth /ˈvɜːməθ/ *n* vermute *m*

vernacular /vəˈnækjʊlə(r)/ *n* vernáculo *m*; (*dialect*) dialeto *m*

versatil|e /ˈvɜːsətaɪl/ *a* versátil; ‹*tool*› que serve para vários fins, multiuso. **~ity** /-ˈtɪlətɪ/ *n* versatilidade *f*

verse /vɜːs/ *n* (*poetry*) verso *m*, poesia *f*; (*stanza*) estrofe *f*; (*of Bible*) versículo *m*

version /ˈvɜːʃn/ *n* versão *f*

versus /ˈvɜːsəs/ *prep* contra

vertical /ˈvɜːtɪkl/ *a* vertical. **~ly** *adv* verticalmente

V

vertigo /ˈvɜːtɪgəʊ/ *n* vertigem *f*

verve /vɜːv/ *n* verve *f*, vivacidade *f*

very /ˈverɪ/ *adv* muito; **the ~ first/best/***etc* (*emph*) o primeiro/melhor/*etc* de todos; **~ much** muito; **~ well** muito bem ● *a* (*actual*) mesmo, próprio; (*exact*) preciso; exato; **at the ~ end** mesmo *or* precisamente no fim; **the ~ day/***etc* o próprio *or* o mesmo dia/*etc*

vessel /ˈvesl/ *n* vaso *m*, recipiente *m*

vest[1] /vest/ *n* corpete *m*, (*P*) camisola *f* interior; *Amer* (*waistcoat*) colete *m*

vest[2] /vest/ *vt* conferir (**in** a); **~ed interests** interesses *mpl*

vestige /ˈvestɪdʒ/ *n* vestígio *m*

vestry /ˈvestrɪ/ *n* sacristia *f*

vet /vet/ *n* [!] veterinário *m* ● *vt* (*pt* **vetted**) ‹*candidate etc*› examinar atentamente, estudar

veteran /ˈvetərən/ *n* veterano *m*; **(war) ~** veterano *m* de guerra

veterinary /ˈvetərɪnərɪ/ *a* veterinário. **~ surgeon** *n* veterinário *m*

veto /ˈviːtəʊ/ *n* (*pl* **-oes**) veto *m*; (*right*) direito *m* de veto ● *vt* vetar, opor o veto a

vex /veks/ *vt* aborrecer, irritar, contrariar; **~ed question** questão *f* muito debatida, assunto *m* controverso

via /ˈvaɪə/ *prep* por, via

viab|le /ˈvaɪəbl/ *a* viável. **~ility** /-ˈbɪlətɪ/ *n* viabilidade *f*

viaduct /ˈvaɪədʌkt/ *n* viaduto *m*

vibrant /ˈvaɪbrənt/ *a* vibrante

vibrat|e /vaɪˈbreɪt/ *vt/i* (fazer) vibrar. **~ion** /-ʃn/ *n* vibração *f*

vicar /ˈvɪkə(r)/ *n* (*Anglican*) pastor *m*; (*Catholic*) vigário *m*, pároco *m*. **~age** *n* presbitério *m*, (*P*) vicariato *m*

vice[1] /vaɪs/ *n* (*depravity*) vício *m*

vice[2] /vaɪs/ *n Techn* torno *m*

vice- /vaɪs/ *pref* vice-. **~chairman** *n* vice-presidente *m*; **~chancellor** *n* vice-chanceler *m*; *Univ* reitor *m*; **~president** *n* vice-presidente *mf*

vice versa /ˈvaɪsɪˈvɜːsə/ *adv* vice-versa

vicinity /vɪˈsɪnətɪ/ *n* vizinhança *f*, cercania(s) *fpl*, arredores *mpl*; **in the ~ of** nos arredores de

vicious /ˈvɪʃəs/ *a* (*spiteful*) mau, maldoso; (*violent*) brutal, feroz; **~ circle** círculo *m* vicioso. **~ly** *adv* maldosamente; (*violently*) brutalmente, ferozmente

victim /ˈvɪktɪm/ *n* vítima *f*

victimiz|e /ˈvɪktɪmaɪz/ *vt* perseguir. **~ation** /-ˈzeɪʃn/ *n* perseguição *f*

victor /ˈvɪktə(r)/ *n* vencedor *m*

victor|y /ˈvɪktərɪ/ *n* vitória *f*. **~ious** /-ˈtɔːrɪəs/ *a* vitorioso

video /ˈvɪdɪəʊ/ *a* vídeo ● *n* (*pl* **-os**) [!] vídeo ● *vt* (*record*) gravar em vídeo; **~ cassette** videocassete *m*, (*P*) cassete *f* de vídeo; **~ recorder** (gravador *m* de) vídeo *m*, (*P*) câmara *f* de vídeo

vie /vaɪ/ *vi* (*pres p* **vying**) rivalizar; competir (**with** com)

view /vjuː/ *n* vista *f* ● *vt* ver; (*examine*) examinar; (*consider*) considerar, ver; ‹*a house*› visitar, ver; **in my ~** a meu ver, na minha opinião; **in ~ of** em vista de; **on ~** em exposição, à mostra; (*open to the public*) aberto ao público; **with a ~ to** com a intenção de, com o fim de. **~er** *n TV* telespectador *m*; (*for slides*) visor *m*

viewfinder /'vjuːfaɪndə(r)/ *n* visor *m*

viewpoint /'vjuːpɔɪnt/ *n* ponto *m* de vista

vigil /'vɪdʒɪl/ *n* vigília *f*; (*over corpse*) velório *m*; *Relig* vigília *f*

vigilan|t /'vɪdʒɪlənt/ *a* vigilante. **~ce** *n* vigilância *f*. **~te** /vɪdʒɪ'læntɪ/ *n* vigilante *m*

vig|our /'vɪgə(r)/ *n* vigor *m*. **~orous** /'vɪgərəs/ *a* vigoroso

vile /vaɪl/ *a* (*base*) infame, vil; 🄸 (*bad*) horroroso; péssimo

vilify /'vɪlɪfaɪ/ *vt* difamar

villa /'vɪlə/ *n* vivenda *f*, vila *f*; (*country residence*) casa *f* de campo

village /'vɪlɪdʒ/ *n* aldeia *f*, povoado *m*. **~r** *n* aldeão *m*, aldeã *f*

villain /'vɪlən/ *n* patife *m*, mau-caráter *m*

vindicat|e /'vɪndɪkeɪt/ *vt* vindicar, justificar. **~ion** /-'keɪʃn/ *n* justificação *f*

vindictive /vɪn'dɪktɪv/ *a* vingativo

vine /vaɪn/ *n* (*plant*) vinha *f*

vinegar /'vɪnɪgə(r)/ *n* vinagre *m*

vineyard /'vɪnjəd/ *n* vinha *f*, vinhedo *m*

vintage /'vɪntɪdʒ/ *n* (*year*) ano *m* de colheita de qualidade excepcional, ano *m* vintage ● *a* ‹*wine*› de colheita excepcional e de um determinado ano; ‹*car*› de museu 🄸; fabricado entre 1917 e 1930

viola /vɪ'əʊlə/ *n Mus* viola *f*, violeta *f*

violat|e /'vaɪəleɪt/ *vt* violar. **~ion** /-'leɪʃn/ *n* violação *f*

violen|t /'vaɪələnt/ *a* violento. **~ce** *n* violência *f*. **~tly** *adv* violentamente, com violência

violet /'vaɪələt/ *n Bot* violeta *f*; (*colour*) violeta *m* ● *a* violeta

violin /vaɪə'lɪn/ *n* violino *m*. **~ist** *n* violinista *mf*

VIP /viːaɪ'piː/ *abbr* (= **very important person**) VIP *m*, personalidade *f* importante

viper /'vaɪpə(r)/ *n* víbora *f*

virgin /'vɜːdʒɪn/ *a & n* virgem *f*. **~ity** /və'dʒɪnətɪ/ *n* virgindade *f*

Virgo /'vɜːgəʊ/ *n Astr* Virgem *f*

viril|e /'vɪraɪl/ *a* viril, varonil. **~ity** /vɪ'rɪlətɪ/ *n* virilidade *f*

virtual /'vɜːtʃʊəl/ *a* verdadeiro, que é na prática (embora não em teoria); **a ~ failure**/*etc* praticamente um fracasso/*etc*. **~ly** *adv* praticamente

virtue /'vɜːtʃuː/ *n* (*goodness, chastity*) virtude *f*; (*merit*) mérito *m*; **by** or **in ~ of** por or em virtude de

virtuos|o /vɜːtʃʊ'əʊsəʊ/ *n* (*pl* **-si** /-siː/) virtuoso *m*

virtuous /'vɜːtʃʊəs/ *a* virtuoso

virus /'vaɪərəs/ *n* (*pl* **-es**) vírus *m*; 🄸 (*disease*) virose *f*

visa /'viːzə/ *n* visto *m*

vise /vaɪs/ *n Amer* (*vice*) torno *m*

visib|le /'vɪzəbl/ *a* visível. **~ility** /-'bɪlətɪ/ *n* visibilidade *f*. **~ly** *adv* visivelmente

vision /'vɪʒn/ *n* (*dream, insight*) visão *f*; (*seeing, sight*) vista *f*, visão *f*

visionary /'vɪʒənərɪ/ *a* visionário; ‹*plan, scheme etc*› fantasista, quimérico ● *n* visionário *m*

visit /'vɪzɪt/ *vt* (*pt* **visited**) ‹*person*› visitar, fazer uma visita a; ‹*place*› visitar ● *vi* estar de visita ● *n* (*tour, call*) visita *f*; (*stay*) estada *f*, visita *f*. **~or** *n* visitante *mf*; (*guest*) visita *f*

visor /'vaɪzə(r)/ *n* viseira *f*; (*in vehicle*) visor *m*

vista /'vɪstə/ *n* vista *f*, panorama *m*

visual /'vɪʒʊəl/ *a* visual. **~ display unit** *n* terminal *m* de vídeo. **~ly** *adv* visualmente

visualize /'vɪʒʊəlaɪz/ *vt* visualizar; (*foresee*) imaginar, prever

vital /'vaɪtl/ *a* vital. **~ statistics** *npl* estatísticas *fpl* demográficas; 🄸 (*of woman*) medidas *fpl*

vitality /vaɪ'tælətɪ/ *n* vitalidade *f*

vitamin /'vɪtəmɪn/ *n* vitamina *f*

vivac|ious /vɪ'veɪʃəs/ *a* cheio de vida, vivo, animado. **~ity** /-'væsətɪ/ *n* vivacidade *f*, animação *f*

vivid /'vɪvɪd/ *a* vívido; ‹*imagination*› vivo. **~ly** *adv* vividamente

vixen /'vɪksn/ *n* raposa *f* fêmea

vocabulary /və'kæbjʊlərɪ/ *n* vocabulário *m*

vocal /'vəʊkl/ *a* vocal; *fig* ‹*person*› eloquente; **~ cords** cordas *fpl* vocais. **~ist** *n* vocalista *mf*

vocation /və'keɪʃn/ *n* vocação *f*; (*trade*) profissão *f*. **~al** *a* vocacional, profissional

vociferous /və'sɪfərəs/ *a* vociferante

vodka /'vɒdkə/ *n* vodka *m*

vogue /vəʊg/ *n* voga *f*, moda *f*, popularidade *f*; **in ~** em voga, na moda
voice /vɔɪs/ *n* voz *f* ● *vt* (*express*) exprimir. **~mail** *n* (*system*) correio *m* de voz, (*P*) caixa *f* de correio de voz; (*message*) mensagem *f* de voz
void /vɔɪd/ *a* vazio; *Jur* nulo, sem validade ● *n* vácuo *m*, vazio *m*; **make ~** anular, invalidar; **~ of** sem, destituído de
volatile /ˈvɒlətaɪl/ *a* ‹*substance*› volátil; *fig* (*changeable*) instável, volúvel
volcan|o /vɒlˈkeɪnəʊ/ *n* (*pl* **-oes**) vulcão *m*. **~ic** /-ænɪk/ *a* vulcânico
volition /vəˈlɪʃn/ *n* **of one's own ~** de sua própria vontade
volley /ˈvɒlɪ/ *n* (*of blows etc*) saraivada *f*; (*of gunfire*) salva *f*; *Tennis* voleio *m*. **~ball** *n* voleibol *m*, vôlei *m*, (*P*) vólei *m*
volt /vəʊlt/ *n* volt *m*. **~age** *n* voltagem *f*
voluble /ˈvɒljʊbl/ *a* falante, loquaz
volume /ˈvɒljuːm/ *n* (*book, sound*) volume *m*; (*capacity*) capacidade *f*
voluntar|y /ˈvɒləntərɪ/ *a* voluntário; (*unpaid*) não remunerado. **~ily** /-trəlɪ/ *adv* voluntariamente
volunteer /vɒlənˈtɪə(r)/ *n* voluntário *m* ● *vi* oferecer-se or voluntariar-se (**to do** para fazer); *Fld* alistar-se como voluntário ● *vt* oferecer espontaneamente
voluptuous /vəˈlʌptʃʊəs/ *a* voluptuoso, sensual
vomit /ˈvɒmɪt/ *vt/i* (*pt* **vomited**) vomitar ● *n* vômito *m*, (*P*) vómito *m*
voodoo /ˈvuːduː/ *n* vodu *m*, (*P*) vudu *m*
voraci|ous /vəˈreɪʃəs/ *a* voraz. **~ty** /vəˈræsətɪ/ *n* voracidade *f*
vot|e /vəʊt/ *n* voto *m*; (*right*) direito *m* de voto ● *vt/i* votar. **~er** *n* eleitor *m*
vouch /vaʊtʃ/ *vi* **~ for** responder por, garantir
voucher /ˈvaʊtʃə(r)/ *n* (*for meal, transport*) vale *m*; (*receipt*) comprovante *m*
vow /vaʊ/ *n* voto *m* ● *vt* ‹*loyalty etc*› jurar (**to** a); **~ to do** jurar fazer
vowel /ˈvaʊəl/ *n* vogal *f*
voyage /ˈvɔɪɪdʒ/ *n* viagem (por mar) *f*. **~r** /-ə(r)/ *n* viajante *m*
vulgar /ˈvʌlgə(r)/ *a* ordinário, grosseiro; (*in common use*) vulgar. **~ity** /-ˈgærətɪ/ *n* (*behaviour*) grosseria *f*, vulgaridade *f*
vulnerab|le /ˈvʌlnərəbl/ *a* vulnerável. **~ility** /-ˈbɪlətɪ/ *n* vulnerabilidade *f*
vulture /ˈvʌltʃə(r)/ *n* urubu *m*, (*P*) abutre *m*
vying /ˈvaɪɪŋ/ ▶ VIE

Ww

wad /wɒd/ *n* bucha *f*, tampão *m*; (*bundle*) maço *m*, rolo *m*
wadding /ˈwɒdɪŋ/ *n* enchimento *m*
waddle /ˈwɒdl/ *vi* bambolear-se, rebolar-se, gingar
wade /weɪd/ *vi* **~ through** *fig* avançar a custo por; ‹*mud, water*› patinhar em
wafer /ˈweɪfə(r)/ *n* (*biscuit*) bolacha *f* de baunilha; *Relig* hóstia *f*
waffle[1] /ˈwɒfl/ *n* [!] (*talk*) lenga-lenga *f*; papo *m*; conversa *f*; [!] (*writing*) lenga-lenga *f* ● *vi* [!] escrever muito sem dizer nada de importante
waffle[2] /ˈwɒfl/ *n Culin* waffle *m*
waft /wɒft/ *vi* flutuar ● *vt* espalhar, levar suavemente
wag /wæg/ *vt/i* (*pt* **wagged**) abanar, agitar, sacudir
wage[1] /weɪdʒ/ *vt* ‹*campaign, war*› fazer
wage[2] /weɪdʒ/ *n* **~(s)** (*weekly, daily*) salário *m*, ordenado *m*. **~ earner** *n* trabalhador *m* assalariado; **~ freeze** *n* congelamento *m* de salários
wager /ˈweɪdʒə(r)/ *n* (*bet*) aposta *f* ● *vt* apostar (**that** que)
waggle /ˈwægl/ *vt/i* abanar, agitar, sacudir
wagon /ˈwægən/ *n* (*horse-drawn*) carroça *f*; *Rail* vagão *m* de mercadorias
waif /weɪf/ *n* criança *f* abandonada
wail /weɪl/ *vi* lamentar-se, gemer lamentosamente ● *n* lamentação *f*, gemido *m* lamentoso
waist /weɪst/ *n* cintura *f*. **~line** *n* cintura *f*
waistcoat /ˈweɪskəʊt/ *n* colete *m*
wait /weɪt/ *vt/i* esperar; **~ for** esperar; **~ on** servir; **keep sb ~ing** fazer alguém esperar ● *n* espera *f*; **lie in ~ (for)** estar escondido à espera (de), armar uma emboscada (para). **~ing list** *n* lista *f* de espera; **~ing room** *n* sala *f* de espera
wait|er /ˈweɪtə(r)/ *n* garçon *m*, (*P*) empregado *m* (de mesa). **~ress** *n* garçonete *f*, (*P*) empregada *f* (de mesa)
waive /weɪv/ *vt* renunciar a, desistir de
wake[1] /weɪk/ *vt/i* (*pt* **woke**, *pp* **woken**) **~ (up)** acordar, despertar ● *n* (*before burial*) velório *m*
wake[2] /weɪk/ *n* (*ship*) esteira (de espuma) *f*; **in the ~ of** (*following*) atrás

de, na sequência de

Wales /weɪlz/ *n* País *m* de Gales

walk /wɔːk/ *vi* andar, caminhar; (*not ride*) ir a pé; (*stroll*) passear; **~ out** (*go away*) sair; (*go on strike*) fazer greve; **~ out on** abandonar ● *vt* ‹*streets*› andar por, percorrer; ‹*distance*› andar, fazer a pé, percorrer; ‹*dog*› (levar para/a) passear ● *n* (*stroll*) passeio *m*, volta *f*; (*excursion*) caminhada *f*; (*gait*) passo *m*, maneira *f* de andar; (*pace*) passo *m*; (*path*) caminho *m*; **it's a 5-minute ~** são 5 minutos a pé; **~ of life** meio *m*, condição *f* social. **~over** *n* vitória *f* fácil

walker /ˈwɔːkə(r)/ *n* caminhante *mf*

walkie-talkie /wɔːkɪˈtɔːkɪ/ *n* walkie-talkie *m*

walking /ˈwɔːkɪŋ/ *n* andar (a pé) *m*, marcha (a pé) *f* ● *a* [!] ‹*dictionary*› vivo. **~ stick** *n* bengala *f*

wall /wɔːl/ *n* parede *f*; (*around land*) muro *m*; (*of castle, town; also fig*) muralha *f*; (*of stomach etc*) parede(s) *f(pl)*; **go to the ~** sucumbir, falir; ‹*firm*› ir à falência ● *vt* ‹*city*› fortificar; ‹*property*› murar; **up the ~** [!] fora de si

wallet /ˈwɒlɪt/ *n* carteira *f*

wallflower /ˈwɔːlflaʊə(r)/ *n Bot* goivo *m*; **be a ~** *fig* tomar chá de cadeira, (*P*) esperar sentado

wallop /ˈwɒləp/ *vt* (*pt* **walloped**) [✱] espancar [!] ● *n* [✱] pancada *f* forte

wallow /ˈwɒləʊ/ *vi* (*in mud*) chafurdar; *fig* regozijar-se

wallpaper /ˈwɔːlpeɪpə(r)/ *n* papel *m* de parede ● *vt* forrar com papel de parede

> *i* **Wall Street** Rua, em Manhattan, Nova Iorque, onde se encontram a Bolsa de Valores e as sedes de muitas instituições financeiras. Quando se fala de *Wall Street*, muitas vezes se está falando dessas instituições.

walnut /ˈwɔːlnʌt/ *n* (*nut*) noz *f*; (*tree*) nogueira *f*

waltz /wɔːls/ *n* valsa *f* ● *vi* valsar

wand /wɒnd/ *n* (*magic*) varinha *f* mágica or de condão

wander /ˈwɒndə(r)/ *vi* andar ao acaso, vagar, errar; ‹*river*› serpentear; ‹*mind, speech*› divagar; (*stray*) extraviar-se. **~er** *n* vagabundo *m*, andarilho *m*. **~ing** *a* errante

wane /weɪn/ *vi* diminuir; (*decline*) declinar ● *n* **on the ~** em declínio; ‹*moon*› no quarto minguante

wangle /ˈwæŋgl/ *vt* [!] conseguir algo através de pistolão [!] (*P*) conseguir algo através de persuasão ou manipulação

want /wɒnt/ *vt* querer (**to do** fazer); (*need*) precisar (de); (*ask for*) exigir, requerer; **I ~ you to go** eu quero que você vá/que tu vás ● *vi* **~ for** ter falta de ● *n* (*need*) necessidade *f*, precisão *f*; (*desire*) desejo *m*; (*lack*) falta *f*, carência *f*; **for ~ of** por falta de. **~ed** *a* ‹*criminal*› procurado pela polícia; (*in ad*) precisa(m)-se

WAP /wæp/ *a* WAP

war /wɔː(r)/ *n* guerra *f*; **at ~** em guerra; **on the ~-path** em pé de guerra

warble /ˈwɔːbl/ *vt/i* gorjear

ward /wɔːd/ *n* (*in hospital*) enfermaria *f*; *Jur* (*minor*) pupilo *m*; *Pol* círculo *m* eleitoral ● *vt* **~ off** ‹*a blow*› aparar; ‹*anger*› desviar; ‹*danger*› prevenir, evitar

warden /ˈwɔːdn/ *n* (*of institution*) diretor *m*; (*of park*) guarda *m*

warder /ˈwɔːdə(r)/ *n* guarda (de prisão) *m*, carcereiro *m*

wardrobe /ˈwɔːdrəʊb/ *n* (*place*) armário *m*; guarda-roupa *m*, (*P*) guarda-fato *m*, (*P*) roupeiro *m*; (*clothes*) guarda-roupa *m*

warehouse /ˈweəhaʊs/ *n* (*pl* **-s** /-haʊzɪz/) armazém *m*, depósito *m* de mercadorias

wares /weəz/ *npl* (*goods*) mercadorias *fpl*, artigos *mpl*

warfare /ˈwɔːfeə(r)/ *n* guerra *f*

warlike /ˈwɔːlaɪk/ *a* marcial, guerreiro; (*bellicose*) belicoso

warm /wɔːm/ *a* (**-er**, **-est**) quente; (*hearty*) caloroso, cordial; **be** or **feel ~** estar com or ter or sentir calor ● *vt/i* **~ (up)** aquecer(-se). **~-hearted** *a* afetuoso, com calor humano. **~ly** *adv* (*heartily*) calorosamente; **wrap up ~ly** agasalhar-se bem. **~th** *n* calor *m*

warn /wɔːn/ *vt* avisar, prevenir; **~ sb off sth** (*advise against*) pôr alguém de prevenção or de pé atrás com algo; (*forbid*) proibir algo a alguém. **~ing** *n* aviso *m*; **~ing light** lâmpada *f* de advertência; **without ~ing** sem aviso, sem prevenir

warp /wɔːp/ *vt/i* ‹*wood etc*› empenar; *fig* (*pervert*) torcer; deformar; desvirtuar. **~ed** *a fig* deturpado; pervertido

warrant /ˈwɒrənt/ *n* autorização *f*; (*for arrest*) mandato (de captura) *m*; *Comm* título *m* de crédito, warrant *m* ● *vt* justificar; (*guarantee*) garantir

warranty /'wɒrəntɪ/ *n* garantia *f*

warrior /'wɒrɪə(r)/ *n* guerreiro *m*

warship /'wɔːʃɪp/ *n* navio *m* de guerra

wart /wɔːt/ *n* verruga *f*

wartime /'wɔːtaɪm/ *n* **in ~** em tempo de guerra

wary /'weərɪ/ *a* (**-ier**, **-iest**) cauteloso, prudente

was /wɒz unstressed wəz/ ▶ BE

wash /wɒʃ/ *vt/i* lavar(-se); (*flow over*) molhar, inundar; **~ one's hands of** lavar as mãos de; **~ out** ‹*cup etc*› lavar; ‹*stain*› tirar lavando; **~ up** lavar a louça; *Amer* (*wash oneself*) lavar-se ● *n* lavagem *f*; (*dirty clothes*) roupa *f* para lavar; (*of ship*) esteira *f*; (*of paint*) fina camada *f* de tinta; **have a ~** lavar-se. **~basin** *n* pia *f*, (*P*) lavatório *m*; **~cloth** *n Amer* (*facecloth*) toalha *f* de rosto; **~-out** *n* ☒ fiasco *m*; **~room** *n Amer* banheiro *m*, (*P*) casa *f* de banho. **~able** *a* lavável. **~ing** *n* (*dirty*) roupa *f* suja; (*clean*) roupa *f* lavada. **~ing machine** *n* máquina *f* de lavar roupa; **~ing powder** *n* detergente *m* em pó; **~ing-up** *n* lavagem *f* da louça

washed-out /wɒʃt'aʊt/ *a* (*faded*) desbotado; (*exhausted*) exausto

washer /'wɒʃə(r)/ *n* (*machine*) máquina *f* de lavar roupa, louça *f*; (*ring*) anilha *f*

wasp /wɒsp/ *n* vespa *f*

waste /weɪst/ *vt* desperdiçar, esbanjar; ‹*time*› perder ● *vi* **~ away** consumir-se ● *a* (*useless*) inútil; ‹*material*› de refugo; **~ paper** papéis *mpl* velhos or usados; **~-paper basket** cesto *m* de papéis ● *n* desperdício *m*, perda *f*; (*of time*) perda *f*; (*rubbish*) lixo *m*; **lay ~** assolar, devastar; **~ (land)** (*desolate*) região *f* desolada, ermo *m*; (*unused*) (terreno) baldio *m*; **~-disposal unit** triturador *m* de lixo

wasteful /'weɪstfl/ *a* dispendioso; ‹*person*› esbanjador, gastador, perdulário

watch /wɒtʃ/ *vt/i* ver bem, olhar com atenção, observar; ‹*game, TV*› ver; (*guard, spy on*) vigiar; (*be careful about*) tomar or ter cuidado com; **~ out** (*look out*) estar à espreita (**for** de); (*take care*) acautelar-se ● *n* vigia *f*, vigilância *f*; *Naut* quarto *m*; (*for telling time*) relógio *m*. **~dog** *n* cão *m* de guarda; **~tower** *n* torre *f* de observação. **~ful** *a* atento, vigilante

watchmaker /'wɒtʃmeɪkə(r)/ *n* relojoeiro *m*

watchman /'wɒtʃmən/ *n* (*pl* **-men**) (*of building*) guarda *m*; **(night-)~** guarda-noturno *m*

water /'wɔːtə(r)/ *n* água *f*; **~ polo** polo *m* aquático ● *vt* regar; **~ down** juntar água a, diluir; ‹*milk, wine*› aguar, batizar [!]; *fig* (*tone down*) suavizar ● *vi* (*of eyes*) lacrimejar, chorar. **~ closet** *n* WC *m*, banheiro *m*, (*P*) lavabos *mpl*; **~colour** *n* aquarela *f*; **~melon** *n* melancia *f*; **~ pistol** *n* pistola *f* de água; **~ polo** *n* polo *m* aquático; **~skiing** *n* esqui *m* aquático

watercress /'wɔːtəkres/ *n* agrião *m*

waterfall /'wɔːtəfɔːl/ *n* queda *f* de água, cascata *f*

watering can /'wɔːtərɪŋkæn/ *n* regador *m*

waterlogged /'wɔːtəlɒgd/ *a* saturado de água; ‹*land*› empapado, alagado; ‹*vessel*› inundado, alagado

waterproof /'wɔːtəpruːf/ *a* impermeável; ‹*watch*› à prova de água

watershed /'wɔːtəʃed/ *n fig* momento *m* decisivo; (*in affairs*) ponto *m* crítico

watertight /'wɔːtətaɪt/ *a* à prova de água, hermético; *fig* ‹*argument etc*› inequívoco; irrefutável

waterway /'wɔːtəweɪ/ *n* via *f* navegável

watery /'wɔːtərɪ/ *a* ‹*colour*› pálido; ‹*eyes*› lacrimoso; ‹*soup*› aguado; ‹*tea*› fraco

watt /wɒt/ *n* watt *m*

wav|e /weɪv/ *n* onda *f*; (*in hair*) *Radio* onda *f*; (*sign*) aceno *m* ● *vt* acenar com; ‹*sword*› brandir; ‹*hair*› ondular; **~e goodbye** dizer adeus ● *vi* acenar (com a mão); ‹*hair etc*› ondular; ‹*flag*› tremular. **~elength** *n* comprimento *m* de onda. **~y** *a* ondulado

waver /'weɪvə(r)/ *vi* vacilar; (*hesitate*) hesitar

wax[1] /wæks/ *n* cera *f* ● *vt* encerar; ‹*car*› polir

wax[2] /wæks/ *vi* (*of moon*) aumentar, crescer

waxwork /'wækswɜːk/ *n* (*dummy*) figura *f* de cera. **~s** *npl* (*exhibition*) museu *m* de figuras de cera

way /weɪ/ *n* (*road, path*) caminho *m*, estrada *f*, rua *f* (**to** para); (*distance*) percurso *m*; (*direction*) (*P*) direção *f*; (*manner*) modo *m*, maneira *f*; (*means*) meios *mpl*; (*respect*) respeito *m*; **~s** (*habits*) costumes *mpl*; **be in the ~** atrapalhar; **be on one's** or **the ~** estar a caminho; **by the ~** a propósito; **by ~ of** por, via, através; **get one's own ~** conseguir o que quer; **give ~** (*yield*) ceder; (*collapse*) desabar; *Auto* dar a preferência *or* (*P*) a prioridade; **in a ~** de certo modo; **make one's ~** ir; **that ~** dessa maneira; **this ~** desta maneira; **~ in** entrada *f*; **~ out** saída *f* ● *adv* [!] consideravelmente; de longe. **~-out** *a* [!] excêntrico

waylay /weɪ'leɪ/ *vt* (*pt* **-laid**) (*assail*) armar uma cilada para; (*stop*) interceptar, (*P*) intercetar

wayward /'weɪwəd/ *a* (*wilful*) teimoso; (*perverse*) caprichoso, difícil

WC /dʌb(ə)lju:'si:/ *n* WC *m*, banheiro *m*, (*P*) casa *f* de banho

we /wi:/ *pron* nós

weak /wi:k/ *a* (**-er**, **-est**) fraco; (*delicate*) frágil. **~en** *vt/i* enfraquecer; (*give way*) fraquejar. **~ness** *n* fraqueza *f*; (*fault*) ponto *m* fraco; **a ~ness for** (*liking*) um fraco por

weakling /'wi:klɪŋ/ *n* fraco *m*

wealth /welθ/ *n* riqueza *f*; (*riches, resources*) riquezas *fpl*; (*quantity*) abundância *f*

wealthy /'welθɪ/ *a* (**-ier**, **-iest**) rico

wean /wi:n/ *vt* ‹*baby*› desmamar; (*from habit etc*) desabituar

weapon /'wepən/ *n* arma *f*

wear /weə(r)/ *vt* (*pt* **wore**, *pp* **worn**) (*have on*) usar, trazer; (*put on*) pôr; (*expression*) ter; (*damage*) gastar; **~ black/red/***etc* vestir-se de preto/vermelho/*etc*; **~ down** gastar; ‹*person*› extenuar; **~ off** passar; **~ on** ‹*time*› passar lentamente; **~ out** gastar; ‹*tire*› esgotar ● *vi* (*last*) durar; (*become old, damaged etc*) gastar-se ● *n* (*use*) uso *m*; (*deterioration*) gasto *m*, uso *m*; (*endurance*) resistência *f*; (*clothing*) roupa *f*; **~ and tear** desgaste *m*

wear|y /'wɪərɪ/ *a* (**-ier**, **-iest**) fatigado, cansado; (*tiring*) fatigante, cansativo ● *vi* **~y of** cansar-se de

weasel /'wi:zl/ *n* doninha *f*

weather /'weðə(r)/ *n* tempo *m*; **under the ~** [!] (*ill*) indisposto, achacado ● *a* meteorológico ● *vt* (*survive*) aguentar, resistir a. **~-beaten** *a* curtido pelo tempo; **~ forecast** *n* boletim *m* meteorológico

weav|e[1] /wi:v/ *vt* (*pt* **wove**, *pp* **woven**) ‹*cloth etc*› tecer; ‹*plot*› urdir, criar ● *n* (*style*) tipo *m* de tecido. **~er** /-ə(r)/ *n* tecelão *m*, tecelã *f*

weave[2] /wi:v/ *vi* (*move*) serpear; (*through traffic, obstacles*) ziguezaguear

web /web/ *n* (*of spider*) teia *f*; (*fabric*) tecido *m*; *Comput* web *m*, rede *f*; (*on foot*) membrana *f* interdigital. **~bed** *a* ‹*foot*› palmado. **~-footed** *a* palmípede; **~log** blog *m*, (*P*) blogue *m*; **to keep/write a ~log** ter um blog *or* (*P*) blogue; **~ page** *n* página *f* web; **~site** *n* site *m*, síto *m*

wed /wed/ *vt/i* (*pt* **wedded**) casar(-se)

wedding /'wedɪŋ/ *n* casamento *m*. **~ cake** *n* bolo *m* de noiva; **~ ring** *n* aliança (de casamento) *f*

wedge /wedʒ/ *n* calço *m*, cunha *f*; (*cake*) fatia *f*; (*of lemon*) quarto *m*; (*under wheel etc*) calço *m*, cunha *f* ● *vt* calçar; (*push*) meter or enfiar à força; (*pack in*) entalar

Wednesday /'wenzdɪ/ *n* quarta-feira *f*

weed /wi:d/ *n* erva *f* daninha ● *vt/i* arrancar as ervas, capinar; **~ out** suprimir, arrancar. **~killer** *n* herbicida *m*. **~y** *a fig* ‹*person*› fraco

week /wi:k/ *n* semana *f*; **a ~ today/tomorrow** de hoje/de amanhã a oito dias. **~ly** *a* semanal ● *a & n* (*periodical*) (jornal) semanário *m* ● *adv* semanalmente, todas as semanas

weekday /'wi:kdeɪ/ *n* dia *m* de semana

weekend /'wi:kend/ *n* fim *m* de semana

weep /wi:p/ *vt/i* (*pt* **wept**) chorar (**for sb** por alguém); **~ing willow** (salgueiro-)chorão *m*

weigh /weɪ/ *vt/i* pesar; **~ anchor** levantar âncora or ferro, zarpar; **~ down** (*weight*) sobrecarregar; (*bend*) envergar; *fig* acabrunhar; **~ up** [!] (*examine*) pesar

weight /weɪt/ *n* peso *m*; **lose ~** emagrecer; **put on ~** engordar. **~lifter** *n* halterofilista *m*; **~lifting** *n* halterofilia *f*. **~y** *a* pesado; ‹*subject etc*› de peso; (*influential*) influente

weir /wɪə(r)/ *n* represa *f*, açude *m*

weird /wɪəd/ *a* (**-er**, **-est**) misterioso; (*strange*) estranho, bizarro

welcom|e /'welkəm/ *a* agradável; (*timely*) oportuno; **~e to do** livre para fazer ● *int* bem-vindo! ● *n* acolhimento *m* ● *vt* acolher, receber; (*as greeting*) dar as boas vindas a; **be ~e** ser bem-vindo; **you're ~e!** (*after thank you*) não tem de quê!, de nada!. **~ing** *a* acolhedor

weld /weld/ *vt* soldar ● *n* solda *f*. **~er** *n* soldador *m*

welfare /'welfeə(r)/ *n* bem-estar *m*; (*aid*) assistência *f*, previdência *f* social; **W~ State** Estado-Providência *m*

well[1] /wel/ *n* (*for water, oil*) poço *m*; (*of stairs*) vão *m*; (*of lift*) poço *m*

well[2] /wel/ *adv* (**better**, **best**) bem; **we may as ~ go** é melhor irmos andando; **as ~ as** tão bem como; (*in addition*) assim como; **be ~** (*healthy*) ir or passar bem; **do ~** (*succeed*) sair-se bem, ser bem-sucedido; **very ~** muito bem; **~ done!** bravo!, muito bem! ● *a* bem *invar* ● *int* bem!. **~-behaved** *a* bem-comportado, educado; **~-being** *n* bem-estar *m*; **~-done** *a* (*of meat*) bem passado; **~-dressed** *a* bem-vestido; **~-heeled** *a* 🅸 (*wealthy*) rico; **~-informed** *a* versado, bem informado; **~-known** *a* (bem-)conhecido; **~-meaning** *a* bem-intencionado; **~-off** *a* rico, próspero; **~-read** *a* instruído; **~-spoken** *a* bem-falante; **~-timed** *a* oportuno; **~-to-do** *a* rico; **~-wisher** *n* admirador *m*, simpatizante *mf*

wellington /ˈwelɪŋtən/ *n* (*boot*) bota *f* alta de borracha

Welsh /welʃ/ *a* galês ● *n Lang* galês *m*

> *i*
> **Welsh Assembly** A Assembleia Nacional de Gales começou a funcionar em Cardiff, em 1999. Embora a Assembleia não tenha poderes para criar impostos, ela passou a ter poderes legislativos depois de um referendo em 2011. É formada por 60 membros ou *AMs* (*Assembly Members*); 40 são eleitos diretamente e os restantes, das listas regionais, através do sistema de representação proporcional.

went /went/ ▶ GO

wept /wept/ ▶ WEEP

were /wɜː(r) unstressed wə(r)/ ▶ BE

west /west/ *n* oeste *m*; **the W~** *Pol* o Oeste, o Ocidente ● *a* ocidental, do oeste; **the W~ Indies** as Antilhas ● *adv* a oeste, para oeste. **~erly** *a* ocidental, oeste. **~ward(s)** *adv* para oeste

western /ˈwestən/ *a* ocidental, do oeste; *Pol* ocidental ● *n* (*film*) filme *m* de cowboys, bangue-bangue *m*

westernize /ˈwestənaɪz/ *vt* ocidentalizar

wet /wet/ *a* (**wetter**, **wettest**) molhado; (*of weather*) chuvoso, de chuva; 🅸 ‹*person*› fraco; **get ~** molhar-se; **~ blanket** 🅸 desmancha-prazeres *mf invar* 🅸; **~ paint** pintado de fresco; **~ suit** roupa *f* de mergulho ● *vt* (**wetted**) molhar

whack /wæk/ *vt* 🅸 bater em ● *n* 🅸 pancada *f*. **~ed** *a* 🅸 morto de cansaço; rebentado 🅸

whale /weɪl/ *n* baleia *f*

wharf /wɔːf/ *n* (*pl* **wharfs**) cais *m*

> **what** /wɒt/ ● *pron*
>
> ····▶ (*in questions*) o que; **~ is it?** o que é?; **~ do you want?** o que você quer?; **~ is your name?** como você se chama?; **~ is your favourite?** qual é o seu favorito?; **~ happened?** o que aconteceu?; **~?** (*say that again*) o quê?/como?
>
> ····▶ (*introducing clause*) o que; **I don't know ~ he wants** não sei o que ele quer; **tell me ~ happened** conte-me o que aconteceu; **I don't agree with ~ you're saying** não concordo com o que diz; **do ~ I tell you** faça o que lhe digo
>
> ····▶ (*with prepositions*) que; **~ are you thinking about?** em que você está pensando?; **~'s it for?** para o que é isso?
>
> ····▶ (*in phrases*) **~ about me/him?** e eu/ele?; **~ about a cup of coffee?** que tal uma xícara de café?; **~ if the train is late?** e se o trem se atrasar?; **~ for?** para quê?; **so ~?** e depois?
>
> ● *a*
>
> ····▶ (*in questions*) qual; **~ train did you catch?** qual foi o trem que você pegou?; **~ time is it?** que horas são?; **~ colour is it?** que cor é essa?; **~ shoes should I wear?** que sapatos eu uso?; **~ time does it start?** a que horas começa?
>
> ····▶ (*in exclamations*) que; **~ an idea!** que ideia!; **~ luck!** que sorte!; **~ a huge house!** que casa enorme!

whatever /wɒtˈevə(r)/ *a* **~ book/***etc* qualquer livro/*etc* que seja ● *pron* (*no matter what*) qualquer que seja; (*anything that*) o que quer que, tudo o que; **~ happens** aconteça *o* que acontecer; **do ~ you like** faça o que quiser; **nothing ~** absolutamente nada

whatsoever /wɒtsəʊˈevə(r)/ *a & pron* = WHATEVER

wheat /wiːt/ *n* trigo *m*

wheel /wiːl/ *n* roda *f*; **at the ~** (*of vehicle*) ao volante; (*helm*) ao leme ● *vt* empurrar ● *vi* rodar, rolar

wheelbarrow /ˈwiːlbærəʊ/ *n* carrinho *m* de mão

wheelchair /ˈwiːltʃeə(r)/ *n* cadeira *f* de rodas

when /wen/ *adv, conj & pron* quando; **the day/moment ~** o dia/momento em que

whenever /wenˈevə(r)/ *conj & adv* (*at whatever time*) quando quer que, quando; (*every time that*) (de) cada vez que, sempre que

where /weə(r)/ *adv, conj & pron* onde, aonde; (*in which place*) em que, onde; (*whereas*) enquanto que, ao passo que; **~ is he going?** aonde é que ele vai?. **~abouts** *adv* onde ● *n* paradeiro *m*. **~by** *adv* pelo que. **~upon** *adv* após o que, depois do que

whereas /weərˈæz/ *conj* enquanto que, ao passo que

wherever /weərˈevə(r)/ *conj & adv* onde quer que; **~ can it be?** onde pode estar?

whether /ˈweðə(r)/ *conj* se; **not know ~** não saber se; **~ I go or not** caso eu vá ou não

which /wɪtʃ/ ● *a*

····➤ (*in questions*) que, qual; **~ book do you need?** de que/qual livro precisa?; **~ bag is yours?** qual das malas é a sua?; **~ way is the bank/hospital/supermarket?** como se vai para o banco/hospital/supermercado?

● *pron*

····➤ (*in questions*) qual; **~ is yours?** qual é o seu/a sua?; **there are three peaches, ~ do you want?** há três pêssegos, qual você quer?; **~ is the biggest?** qual é a maior?

····➤ (*relative*) que, o qual/a qual; (*pl*) os quais/as quais; **the book ~ is on the table** o livro que está em cima da mesa; **she made a serious mistake, ~ was unusual for her** ela fez um erro grave, o que era incomum para ela; **her work about ~ I know nothing** o trabalho dela, do qual nada sei; **the play ~ I took part in** a peça da qual eu participei

! Note that if *o qual* or *a qual* are preceded by the prepositions *em* or *de*, they often contract with them to form *no qual*, *na qual*, *do qual*, *da qual*.

whichever /wɪtʃˈevə(r)/ *a* **~ book**/*etc* qualquer livro/*etc* que seja; **take ~ book you wish** leve o livro que quiser ● *pron* qualquer, quaisquer

whiff /wɪf/ *n* (*of fresh air*) sopro *m*, lufada *f*; (*smell*) baforada *f*

while /waɪl/ *n* (espaço de) tempo *m*, momento *m*; **once in a ~** de vez em quando ● *conj* (*when*) enquanto; (*while*) embora; (*whereas*) enquanto que ● *vt* **~ away** ‹*time*› passar

whim /wɪm/ *n* capricho *m*

whimper /ˈwɪmpə(r)/ *vi* gemer; ‹*baby*› choramingar ● *n* gemido *m*; (*baby*) choro *m*

whimsical /ˈwɪmzɪkl/ *a* ‹*person*› caprichoso; (*odd*) bizarro

whine /waɪn/ *vi* lamuriar-se, queixar-se; ‹*dog*› ganir ● *n* lamúria *f*, queixume *m*; (*dog*) ganido *m*

whip /wɪp/ *n* chicote *m* ● *vt* (*pt* **whipped**) chicotear; *Culin* bater; **~ up** excitar; (*cause*) provocar; [I] ‹*meal*› preparar rapidamente; **~ped cream** creme *m* chantilly ● *vi* (*move*) ir a toda a pressa. **~-round** *n* [I] coleta *f*; vaquinha *f*

whirl /wɜːl/ *vt/i* (fazer) rodopiar, girar ● *n* rodopio *m*

whirlpool /ˈwɜːlpuːl/ *n* redemoinho *m*

whirlwind /ˈwɜːlwɪnd/ *n* redemoinho *m* de vento, turbilhão *m*

whirr /wɜː(r)/ *vi* zunir, zumbir

whisk /wɪsk/ *vt/i* (*snatch*) levar/tirar bruscamente; *Culin* bater; ‹*flies*› sacudir ● *n Culin* batedeira *f*; **~ away** (*brush away*) sacudir

whisker /ˈwɪskə(r)/ *n* fio *m* de barba. **~s** *npl* (*of animal*) bigode *m*; (*beard*) barba *f*; (*sideboards*) suíças *fpl*

whisky /ˈwɪskɪ/ *n* uísque *m*

whisper /ˈwɪspə(r)/ *vt/i* sussurrar, murmurar; (*of stream, leaves*) sussurrar ● *n* sussurro *m*, murmúrio *m*; **in a ~** baixinho, em voz baixa

whistle /ˈwɪsl/ *n* assobio *m*; (*instrument*) apito *m* ● *vt/i* assobiar; (*with instrument*) apitar

white /waɪt/ *a* (**-er**, **-est**) branco, alvo; (*pale*) pálido; **go ~** (*turn pale*) empalidecer; (*of hair*) branquear, embranquecer; **~ coffee** café *m* com leite; **~-collar worker** empregado *m* de escritório; **~ elephant** *fig* trambolho *m*, elefante *m* branco; **~ lie** mentirinha *f* ● *n* (*colour; of eyes; person*) branco *m*; (*of egg*) clara (de ovo) *f*. **~ness** *n* brancura *f*

whiten /ˈwaɪtn/ *vt/i* branquear

Whitsun /ˈwɪtsn/ *n* Pentecostes *m*

whizz /wɪz/ *vi* (*pt* **whizzed**) (*through air*) zunir, sibilar; (*rush*) passar a toda a velocidade. **~-kid** *n* [I] prodígio *m*

who /huː/ *interr pron* quem ● *rel pron* que, o(a) qual, os(as) quais

whoever /huːˈevə(r)/ *pron* (*no matter who*) quem quer que, seja quem for; (*the one who*) aquele que

whole /həʊl/ *a* inteiro, todo; (*not broken*) intacto; **the ~ house**/*etc* toda a casa/*etc* ● *n* totalidade *f*; (*unit*) todo *m*; **as a ~** no conjunto, como um todo; **on the ~** de um modo geral. **~hearted** *a* de todo o coração; ‹*person*› dedicado; **~heartedly** *adv* sem reservas, sinceramente

wholefood /ˈhəʊlfuːd/ *n* comida *f* integral

wholemeal /ˈhəʊlmiːl/ *a* **~ bread** pão *m* integral

wholesale /ˈhəʊlseɪl/ *n* venda *f* por grosso or por atacado ● *a* ‹*firm*› por grosso, por atacado; *fig* sistemático; em massa ● *adv* (*in large quantities*) por atacado; *fig* em massa; em grande escala. **~r** /-ə(r)/ *n* grossista *mf*, atacadista *mf*

wholesome /ˈhəʊlsəm/ *a* sadio, saudável

wholewheat /ˈhəʊlwiːt/ *a* = WHOLEMEAL

wholly /ˈhəʊlɪ/ *adv* inteiramente, completamente

whom /huːm/ *interr pron* quem ● *rel pron* (*that*) que; (*after prep*) quem, que, o qual

whore /hɔː(r)/ *n* prostituta *f*

whose /huːz/ *rel pron & a* cujo, de quem ● *interr pron* de quem; **~ hat is this?**, **~ is this hat?** de quem é este chapéu?; **~ son are you?** de quem é que o senhor é filho?

why /waɪ/ *adv* porque, por que motivo, por que razão, porquê; **she doesn't know ~ he's here** ela não sabe porque or por que motivo ele está aqui; **she doesn't know ~** ela não sabe porquê; **do you know ~?** você sabe porquê? ● *int* (*protest*) ora, ora essa; (*discovery*) oh; **~ yes**/*etc* ah, sim

wick /wɪk/ *n* torcida *f*, mecha *f*, pavio *m*

wicked /ˈwɪkɪd/ *a* mau, malvado; (*mischievous, spiteful*) maldoso

wicker /ˈwɪkə(r)/ *n* verga *f*, vime *m*

wicket /ˈwɪkɪt/ *n Cricket* arco *m*

wide /waɪd/ *a* (**-er**, **-est**) largo; (*extensive*) vasto, grande, extenso; **two metres ~** com dois metros de largura ● *adv* longe; (*fully*) completamente; **open ~** ‹*door, window*› abrir(-se) de par em par, escancarar(-se); ‹*mouth*› abrir bem; **~ awake** (bem) desperto, (bem) acordado; **far and ~** por toda a parte. **~ly** *adv* largamente; (*travel, spread*) muito; (*generally*) geralmente; (*extremely*) extremamente

widen /ˈwaɪdn/ *vt/i* alargar(-se)

widespread /ˈwaɪdspred/ *a* muito espalhado, difundido, generalizado

widow /ˈwɪdəʊ/ *n* viúva *f*. **~ed** *a* ‹*man*› viúvo; ‹*woman*› viúva; **be ~ed** enviuvar, ficar viúvo or viúva. **~er** *n* viúvo *m*

width /wɪdθ/ *n* largura *f*

wield /wiːld/ *vt* ‹*axe etc*› manejar; *fig* ‹*power*› exercer

wife /waɪf/ *n* (*pl* **wives**) mulher *f*, esposa *f*

wi-fi, **Wi-Fi**®, **wifi** /ˈwaɪfaɪ/ *n* wi-fi *m*

wig /wɪg/ *n* cabeleira (postiça) *f*; (*judge's etc*) peruca *f*

wiggle /ˈwɪgl/ *vt/i* remexer(-se), retorcer(-se), mexer(-se) dum lado para outro

wild /waɪld/ *a* (**-er**, **-est**) selvagem; (*of plant*) silvestre; (*mad*) louco; (*enraged*) furioso, violento; **~-goose chase** falsa pista *f*, tentativa *f* inútil, (*P*) caça *f* aos gambozinos ● *adv* a esmo; (*without control*) à solta. **~s** *npl* regiões *fpl* selvagens. **~ly** *adv* violentamente; (*madly*) loucamente

wilderness /ˈwɪldənɪs/ *n* deserto *m*

wildlife /ˈwaɪldlaɪf/ *n* animais *mpl* selvagens

wilful /ˈwɪlfl/ *a* ‹*person*› voluntarioso; (*act*) intencional, propositado

will[1] /wɪl/ *v aux* **you ~ sing**/**he ~ do**/*etc* tu cantarás or tu vais cantar/ele fará or ele vai fazer/*etc*; (*1st person: future: expressing will or intention*) **I ~ sing**/**we ~ do**/*etc* eu cantarei or eu vou cantar/nós faremos or nós vamos fazer/*etc*; **~ you have a cup of coffee?** quer tomar um cafezinho?; **~ you shut the door?** quer fazer o favor de fechar a porta?

will[2] /wɪl/ *n* vontade *f*; (*document*) testamento *m*; **at ~** à vontade, quando or como se quiser ● *vt* (*wish*) querer; (*bequeath*) deixar em testamento. **~power** *n* força *f* de vontade

willing /ˈwɪlɪŋ/ *a* pronto, de boa vontade; **~ to** disposto a. **~ly** *adv* (*with pleasure*) de boa vontade, de bom grado; (*not forced*) voluntariamente. **~ness** *n* boa vontade *f*; disposição *f* (**to do** em para fazer)

willow /ˈwɪləʊ/ *n* salgueiro *m*

willy-nilly /wɪlɪ'nɪlɪ/ *adv* de bom ou de mau grado, quer queira ou não

wilt /wɪlt/ *vi* murchar, definhar

wily /'waɪlɪ/ *a* (**-ier**, **-iest**) manhoso, matreiro

win /wɪn/ *vt/i* (*pt* **won**, *pres p* **winning**) ganhar ● *n* vitória *f* □ **~ over** *vt* convencer, conquistar

winc|e /wɪns/ *vi* estremecer, contrair-se

winch /wɪntʃ/ *n* guincho *m* ● *vt* içar com guincho

wind[1] /wɪnd/ *n* vento *m*; (*breath*) fôlego *m*; (*flatulence*) gases *mpl*; **get ~ of** *fig* ouvir rumor de; **put the ~ up** assustar; **in the ~** no ar; **~ farm** central *f* eólica; **~ instrument** *Mus* instrumento *m* de sopro. **~swept** *a* varrido pelo vento

wind[2] /waɪnd/ *vt/i* (*pt* **wound**) enrolar(-se); (*wrap*) envolver, pôr em volta; (*of path, river*) serpentear; **~ (up)** ‹*clock etc*› dar corda em/a; **~ up** (*end*) terminar, acabar; *fig* ‹*speech etc*› concluir; ‹*firm*› liquidar; **he'll ~ up in jail** ele vai acabar na cadeia

windfall /'wɪndfɔːl/ *n* fruta *f* caída; *fig* (*money*) sorte *f* grande

windmill /'wɪndmɪl/ *n* moinho *m* de vento

window /'wɪndəʊ/ *n* janela *f*; (*of shop*) vitrine *f*, (*P*) montra *f*; (*counter*) guichê *m*, (*P*) guichet *m*; **go ~-shopping** ir ver vitrines/montras. **~ box** *n* jardineira *f*, (*P*) floreira *f*; **~ cleaner** *n* limpador *m* de janelas; **~pane** *n* vidro *m*, vidraça *f*; **~ sill** *n* peitoril *m*

windpipe /'wɪndpaɪp/ *n* traqueia *f*

windscreen /'wɪndskriːn/ *n* para-brisa *m*, (*P*) para-brisas *m invar*. **~ wiper** /-waɪpə(r)/ *n* limpador *m* de para-brisa, (*P*) limpa *m* para-brisas

windshield /'wɪndʃiːld/ *n Amer* = WINDSCREEN

windsurf|er /'wɪndsɜːfə(r)/ *n* surfista *mf*, (*P*) praticante *mf* de windsurf. **~ing** *n* surfe *m*, (*P*) windsurf *m*

windy /'wɪndɪ/ *a* (**-ier**, **-iest**) ventoso; **it is very ~** está ventando muito, (*P*) está muito ventoso

wine /waɪn/ *n* vinho *m*; **~ bar** bar *m* para degustação de vinhos; **~ waiter** garçon *m*, (*P*) empregado *m* de vinhos. **~ cellar** *n* adega *f*, cave *f*; **~ list** *n* lista *f* de vinhos; **~ tasting** *n* prova *f* or degustação *f* de vinhos

wine glass /'waɪnglɑːs/ *n* copo *m* de vinho; (*with stem*) cálice *m*

wing /wɪŋ/ *n* asa *f*; *Mil* flanco *m*; *Archit* ala *f*; *Auto* para-lamas *m invar*, (*P*) guarda-lamas *m invar*; **~s** *Theat* bastidores *mpl*; **under sb's ~** debaixo das asas de alguém

wink /wɪŋk/ *vi* piscar o olho; ‹*light, star*› cintilar, piscar ● *n* piscadela *f*; **not sleep a ~** não pregar olho

winner /'wɪnə(r)/ *n* vencedor *m*

winning /'wɪnɪŋ/ *a* vencedor, vitorioso; (*number*) premiado; (*smile*) encantador, atraente. **~s** *npl* ganhos *mpl*

wint|er /'wɪntə(r)/ *n* inverno *m* ● *vi* hibernar. **~ry** *a* de inverno, invernoso; ‹*smile*› glacial

wipe /waɪp/ *vt* limpar; (*dry*) enxugar, limpar ● *n* limpadela *f*; **~ off** limpar; **~ out** (*destroy*) aniquilar, limpar [!]; (*cancel*) cancelar; **~ up** enxugar

wir|e /'waɪə(r)/ *n* arame *m*; [!] (*telegram*) telegrama *m*; **(electric) ~e** fio elétrico *m* ● *vt* ‹*a house*› montar a instalação elétrica em; [!] (*telegraph*) telegrafar. **~ing** *n Electr* instalação *f* elétrica

wireless /'waɪələs/ *n* rádio *f*; (*set*) rádio *m*

wisdom /'wɪzdəm/ *n* sagacidade *f*, sabedoria *f*; (*common sense*) bom senso *m*, sensatez *f*; **~ tooth** dente *m* (do) siso

wise /waɪz/ *a* (**-er**, **-est**) ‹*person*› sábio, avisado, sensato; ‹*look*› entendedor; **~ guy** [!] sabichão *m*, [!] sabe-tudo *m* [!]; **none the ~r** sem entender nada

wisecrack /'waɪzkræk/ *n* [!] (boa) piada *f*

wish /wɪʃ/ *n* (*desire, aspiration*) desejo *m*, vontade *f*; (*request*) pedido *m*; (*greeting*) desejo *m*, voto *m*; **I have no ~ to go** não tenho nenhum desejo or nenhuma vontade de ir; **with best ~es** (*formal*) (*in letter*) com os melhores cumprimentos, com saudações cordiais; (*on greeting card*) com desejos or votos (**for** de) ● *vt* (*desire, bid*) desejar; (*want*) apetecer; ter vontade de; desejar (**to do** fazer); **~ sb well** desejar felicidades a alguém; **I don't ~ to go** não me apetece ir, não tenho vontade de ir, não desejo ir; **I ~ he'd leave** eu gostaria que ele partisse, quem dera que ele partisse ● *vi* **~ for** desejar

wishful /'wɪʃfl/ *a* **~ thinking** sonhar acordado, impossível de concretizar

wishy-washy /'wɪʃɪwɒʃɪ/ *a* sem expressão, fraco, inexpressivo

wistful /'wɪstfl/ *a* melancólico, saudoso

wit /wɪt/ *n* inteligência *f*; (*humour*) presença *f* de espírito, humor *m*; (*person*) senso *m or* (*P*) sentido *m* de humor; **be at one's ~'s** or **~s' end** não saber o que fazer; **keep one's ~s about one** estar alerta; **live by one's ~s** ganhar a vida de maneira suspeita; **scared out of one's ~s** apavorado

witch /wɪtʃ/ *n* feiticeira *f*, bruxa *f*. **~craft** *n* feitiçaria *f*, bruxaria *f*, magia *f*

with /wɪð/ *prep* com; (*having*) de; (*because of*) de; (*at the house of*) em casa de; **the man ~ the beard** o homem de barbas; **fill/***etc***~** encher/*etc* de; **laughing/shaking/***etc* **~** a rir/a tremer/*etc* de; **I'm not ~ you** [!] não estou compreendendo-o, (*P*) não te estou a compreender

withdraw /wɪð'drɔː/ *vt/i* (*pt* **withdrew**, *pp* **withdrawn**) retirar(-se); ‹*money*› tirar. **~al** *n* retirada *f*; *Med* estado *m* de privação. **~n** *a* ‹*person*› retraído, fechado

wither /'wɪðə(r)/ *vt/i* murchar, secar. **~ed** *a* ‹*person*› mirrado. **~ing** *a fig* (*scornful*) desdenhoso

withhold /wɪð'həʊld/ *vt* (*pt* **withheld**) negar, recusar; (*retain*) reter; (*conceal, not tell*) esconder (**from** de)

within /wɪ'ðɪn/ *prep & adv* dentro (de), por dentro (de); (*in distances*) a menos de; **~ a month** (*before*) dentro de um mês; **~ sight** à vista

without /wɪ'ðaʊt/ *prep* sem; **~ fail** sem falta; **go ~ saying** não ser preciso dizer

withstand /wɪð'stænd/ *vt* (*pt* **withstood**) resistir a, opor-se a

witness /'wɪtnɪs/ *n* testemunha *f*; (*evidence*) testemunho *m* ● *vt* testemunhar, presenciar; ‹*document*› assinar como testemunha; **bear ~ to** testemunhar, dar testemunho de. **~ box** *n* banco *m* das testemunhas

witticism /'wɪtɪsɪzəm/ *n* dito *m* espirituoso

witty /'wɪtɪ/ *a* (**-ier,**, **-iest**) espirituoso

wives /waɪvz/ ▶ WIFE

wizard /'wɪzəd/ *n* feiticeiro *m*; *fig* (*genius*) gênio *m*, (*P*) génio *m*

wizened /'wɪznd/ *a* encarquilhado

W

wobbl|e /'wɒbl/ *vi* (*of jelly, voice, hand*) tremer; (*stagger*) cambalear, vacilar; (*of table, chair*) balançar. **~y** *a* (*trembling*) trêmulo, (*P*) trémulo; (*staggering*) cambaleante, vacilante; ‹*table, chair*› pouco firme

woe /wəʊ/ *n* dor *f*, infortúnio *m*

woke, **woken** /wəʊk, 'wəʊkən/ ▶ WAKE[1]

wolf /wʊlf/ *n* (*pl* **wolves** /wʊlvz/) lobo *m*; **cry ~** dar alarme falso, (*P*) falso alarme ● *vt* ‹*food*› devorar. **~ whistle** *n* assobio *m* de admiração

woman /'wʊmən/ *n* (*pl* **women**) mulher *f*. **~ly** *a* feminino

womb /wuːm/ *n* seio *m*, ventre *m*; *Med* útero *m*; *fig* seio *m*

women /'wɪmɪn/ ▶ WOMAN; **~'s movement** movimento *m* feminista

won /wʌn/ ▶ WIN

wonder /'wʌndə(r)/ *n* admiração *f*; (*thing*) maravilha *f* ● *vt* perguntar-se a si mesmo (**if** se) ● *vi* admirar-se (**at** de, com) , ficar admirado (**at** de, com); espantar-se (**at** de, com); (*reflect*) pensar (**about** em); **it is no ~** não admira (**that** que)

wonderful /'wʌndəfl/ *a* maravilhoso. **~ly** *adv* maravilhosamente; **it works ~ly** funciona às mil maravilhas

won't /wəʊnt/ (= **will not**) = WILL[1]

wood /wʊd/ *n* madeira *f*, pau *m*; (*for burning*) lenha *f*. **~(s)** *n* (*area*) bosque *m*, mata *f*, floresta *f*. **~ed** *a* arborizado. **~en** *a* de or em madeira, de pau; *fig* (*stiff*) rígido; *fig* (*inexpressive*) inexpressivo; de pau

woodcut /'wʊdkʌt/ *n* gravura *f* em madeira

woodland /'wʊdlənd/ *n* região *f* arborizada, bosque *m*, mata *f*

woodpecker /'wʊdpekə(r)/ *n* (*bird*) pica-pau *m*

woodwind /'wʊdwɪnd/ *n Mus* instrumentos *mpl* de sopro de madeira

woodwork /'wʊdwɜːk/ *n* (*of building*) madeiramento *m*; (*carpentry*) carpintaria *f*

woodworm /'wʊdwɜːm/ *n* caruncho *m*

wool /wʊl/ *n* lã *f*. **~len** *a* de lã. **~lens** *npl* roupas *fpl* de lã. **~ly** *a* de lã; (*vague*) confuso ● *n* [!] (*garment*) roupa *f* de lã

word /wɜːd/ *n* palavra *f*; (*news*) notícia(s) *f(pl)*; (*promise*) palavra *f* ● *vt* exprimir, formular; **by ~ of mouth** de viva voz, por via oral; **have a ~ with** dizer duas palavras a; **in other ~s** em outras palavras, (*P*) por outras palavras. **~ processor** *n* processador *m* de texto(s). **~ing** *n* termos *mpl*, redação *f*. **~y** *a* prolixo

wore /wɔː(r)/ ▶ WEAR

work /wɜːk/ *n* trabalho *m*; (*product, book etc*) obra *f*; (*building etc*) obras *fpl*; **at ~** no trabalho; **out of ~** desempregado ● *vt/i* (*of person*) trabalhar; *Techn* (fazer) funcionar, (fazer) andar; (*of drug etc*) agir, fazer efeito; ‹*farm, mine*› explorar; ‹*land*› lavrar; **~ sb** (*make work*) fazer alguém trabalhar; **~ in** introduzir, inserir; **~ loose** soltar-se; **~ off** (*get rid of*) descarregar; **~ed up** ‹*person*› enervado, transtornado, agitado. **~ out** *vt* (*solve*) resolver; (*calculate*) calcular; (*devise*) planejar, (*P*) planear ● *vi* (*succeed*) resultar; *Sport* treinar-se; **~ up** *vt* criar ● *vi* (*to climax*) ir num crescendo. **~s** *npl Techn* mecanismo *m*; (*factory*) fábrica *f*

workable /'wɜːkəbl/ *a* viável, praticável

workaholic /wɜːkə'hɒlɪk/ *n* **be a ~** [!] trabalhar como um possesso, [!] ser viciado em trabalho

worker /'wɜːkə(r)/ *n* trabalhador *m*, trabalhadora *f*; (*factory*) operário *m*

working /'wɜːkɪŋ/ *a* ‹*day, clothes, hypothesis, lunch etc*› de trabalho; **the ~ class(es)** a classe operária, a(s) class(es) trabalhadora(s), o proletariado; **~ mother** mãe *f* que trabalha; **~ party** comissão *f* consultiva, de estudo *etc*; **in ~ order** em condições de funcionamento. **~-class** *a* operário, trabalhador. **~s** *npl* mecanismo *m*

workman /'wɜːkmən/ *n* (*pl* **-men**) trabalhador *m*; (*factory*) operário *m*. **~ship** *n* trabalho *m*, execução *f*, mão-de-obra *f*; (*skill*) arte *f*, habilidade *f*

workshop /'wɜːkʃɒp/ *n* oficina *f*, (*P*) workshop *m*

world /wɜːld/ *n* mundo *m*; **a ~ of** muito(s), grande quantidade de, um mundo de ● *a* mundial. **~wide** *a* mundial, universal

worldly /'wɜːldlɪ/ *a* terreno; (*devoted to the affairs of life*) mundano; **~ goods** bens *mpl* materiais. **~-wise** *a* com experiência do mundo

worm /wɜːm/ *n* verme *m*; (*earthworm*) minhoca *f* ● *vt* **~ one's way into** insinuar-se, introduzir-se, enfiar-se

worn /wɔːn/ *a* usado. **~-out** *a* ‹*thing*› completamente gasto; ‹*person*› esgotado

worr|y /'wʌrɪ/ *vt/i* preocupar(-se); **don't ~y** fique descansado, não se preocupe ● *n* preocupação *f*. **~ied** *a* preocupado. **~ying** *a* preocupante, inquietante

worse /wɜːs/ *a & adv* pior ● *n* pior *m*; **get ~** piorar; **from bad to ~** de mal a pior; **~ luck** pouca sorte, pena

worsen /'wɜːsn/ *vt/i* piorar

worship /'wɜːʃɪp/ *n* (*reverence*) reverência *f*, veneração *f*; (*religious*) culto *m*; **Your/His W~** Vossa/Sua Excelência *f* ● *vt* (*pt* **worshipped**) adorar, venerar ● *vi* fazer as suas devoções, praticar o culto

worst /wɜːst/ *a & n* **(the) ~** (o/a) pior *mf*; **if the ~ comes to the ~** se o pior acontecer, na pior das hipóteses; **do one's ~** fazer todo o mal que se quiser; **get the ~ of it** ficar a perder; **the ~ (thing) that** o pior que ● *adv* pior

worth /wɜːθ/ *a* **be ~** valer; (*deserving*) merecer ● *n* valor *m*, mérito *m*; **ten pounds ~ of** dez libras de; **it's ~ it, it's ~ while** vale a pena; **it's not ~ my while** não vale a pena; **it's ~ waiting/***etc* vale a pena esperar/*etc*; **for all one's ~** [!] dando tudo por tudo. **~less** *a* sem valor

worthwhile /'wɜːθwaɪl/ *a* que vale a pena; ‹*cause*› louvável, meritório

worthy /'wɜːðɪ/ *a* **(-ier, -iest)** (*deserving*) digno; merecedor (**of** de); (*laudable*) meritório, louvável ● *n* (*person*) pessoa *f* ilustre

would /wʊd unstressed wəd/ *v aux* **he ~ do/you ~ sing/***etc* (conditional tense) ele faria/você cantaria/*etc*; **he ~ have done** ele teria feito; **she ~ come every day** (*used to*) ela vinha or costumava vir aqui todos os dias; **~ you please come here?** chegue aqui por favor; **~ you like some tea?** você quer um chá?; **he ~n't go** (*refused to*) ele não queria ir; **~-be author/doctor/***etc* aspirante a autor/médico/*etc*

wound[1] /wuːnd/ *n* ferida *f* ● *vt* ferir; **the ~ed** os feridos *mpl*

wound[2] /waʊnd/ ▶ WIND[2]

wove, **woven** /wəʊv, 'wəʊvn/ ▶ WEAVE[2]

wrangle /'ræŋgl/ *vi* disputar, discutir, brigar ● *n* disputa *f*, discussão *f*, briga *f*

wrap /ræp/ *vt* (*pt* **wrapped**) **~ (up)** embrulhar (**in** em); (*in cotton wool, mystery etc*) envolver (**in** em); **~ped up in** (*engrossed*) absorto em, mergulhado em ● *vi* **~ up** (*dress warmly*) abrigar-se bem, agasalhar-se bem ● *n* xaile *m*. **~per** *n* (*of sweet*) papel *m*; (*of book*) capa *f* de papel. **~ping** *n* embalagem *f*

wrath /rɒθ/ *n* ira *f*

wreath /riːθ/ *n* (*pl* **-s** /-ðz/) (*of flowers, leaves*) coroa *f*, grinalda *f*

wreck /rek/ *n* (*sinking*) naufrágio *m*; (*ship*) navio *m* naufragado; restos *mpl* de navio; (*remains*) destroços *mpl*; (*vehicle*) veículo *m* destroçado; **be a nervous**

~ estar com os nervos arrasados ● *vt* destruir; ‹*ship*› fazer naufragar, afundar; *fig* ‹*hope*› acabar. **~age** *n* (*pieces*) destroços *mpl*

wren /ren/ *n* (*bird*) carriça *f*

wrench /rentʃ/ *vt* (*pull*) puxar; (*twist*) torcer; (*snatch*) arrancar (**from** a) ● *n* (*pull*) puxão *m*; (*of ankle, wrist*) torcedura *f*; (*tool*) chave *f* inglesa; *fig* dor *f* de separação

wrestl|e /ˈresl/ *vi* lutar; debater-se (**with** com *or* contra). **~er** *n* lutador *m*. **~ing** *n* luta *f*

wretch /retʃ/ *n* desgraçado *m*, miserável *mf*; (*rascal*) miserável *mf*

wretched /ˈretʃɪd/ *a* (*pitiful, poor*) miserável; (*bad*) horrível, desgraçado

wriggle /ˈrɪɡl/ *vt/i* remexer(-se), contorcer-se

wring /rɪŋ/ *vt* (*pt* **wrung**) (*twist; clothes*) torcer; **~ out of** (*obtain from*) arrancar a; **~ing wet** encharcado; (*of person*) encharcado até aos ossos

wrinkle /ˈrɪŋkl/ *n* (*on skin*) ruga *f*; (*crease*) prega *f* ● *vt/i* enrugar(-se)

wrist /rɪst/ *n* pulso *m*. **~watch** *n* relógio *m* de pulso

write /raɪt/ *vt/i* (*pt* **wrote**, *pp* **written**) escrever; **~ back** responder; **~ down** escrever, tomar nota de; **~ off** ‹*debt*› dar por liquidado; ‹*vehicle*› destinar à sucata; **~ out** (*in full*) escrever por extenso; **~ up** (*from notes*) redigir. **~-off** *n* perda *f* total; **~-up** *n* relato *m*; (*review*) crítica *f*

writer /ˈraɪtə(r)/ *n* escritor *m*, autor *m*

writhe /raɪð/ *vi* contorcer(-se)

writing /ˈraɪtɪŋ/ *n* escrita *f*; **~(s)** (*works*) escritos *mpl*, obras *fpl*; **in ~** por escrito. **~ paper** *n* papel *m* de carta

written /ˈrɪtn/ ▶ WRITE

wrong /rɒŋ/ *a* (*incorrect, mistaken*) mal, errado; (*unfair*) injusto; (*wicked*) mau; (*amiss*) que não está bem; *Mus* ‹*note*› falso; ‹*clock*› que não está certo; **what's ~?** qual é o problema?; **what's ~ with it?** (*amiss*) o que é que não está bem?; (*morally*) que mal há nisso?, que mal tem? ● *adv* mal; **go ~** (*err*) desencaminhar-se, correr mal; (*fail*) ir mal; ‹*vehicle*› quebrar ● *n* mal *m*; (*injustice*) injustiça *f*; **he's in the ~** (*his fault*) ele não tem razão ● *vt* (*be unfair to*) ser injusto com; (*do a wrong to*) fazer mal a. **~ly** *adv* mal; (*blame etc*) sem razão, injustamente

wrongful /ˈrɒŋfl/ *a* injusto, ilegal

wrote /rəʊt/ ▶ WRITE

wrung /rʌŋ/ ▶ WRING

wry /raɪ/ *a* (**wryer, wryest**) torto; ‹*smile*› forçado; **~ face** careta *f*

Xx

Xmas /ˈkrɪsməs/ *n* ▶ CHRISTMAS

X-ray /ˈeksreɪ/ *n* raio X *m*; (*photograph*) radiografia *f* ● *vt* radiografar; **have an ~** tirar uma radiografia

xylophone /ˈzaɪləfəʊn/ *n* xilofone *m*

Yy

yacht /jɒt/ *n* iate *m*. **~ing** *n* iatismo *m*, andar *m* de iate; (*racing*) regata *f* de iate

yank /jæŋk/ *vt* [!] puxar bruscamente ● *n* [!] puxão *m*

Yank /jæŋk/ *n* [!] ianque *mf*

yap /jæp/ *vi* (*pt* **yapped**) latir

yard[1] /jɑːd/ *n* (*measure*) jarda *f* (=0,9144 m)

yard[2] /jɑːd/ *n* (*of house*) pátio *m*; *Amer* (*garden*) jardim *m*; (*for storage*) depósito *m*

yardstick /ˈjɑːdstɪk/ *n* jarda *f*; *fig* bitola *f*; craveira *f*

yarn /jɑːn/ *n* (*thread*) fio *m*; [!] (*tale*) longa *f* história

yawn /jɔːn/ *vi* bocejar; (*be wide open*) abrir-se, escancarar-se ● *n* bocejo *m*

year /jɪə(r)/ *n* ano *m*; **school/tax ~** ano *m* escolar/fiscal; **be ten ~s old/etc** ter dez/*etc* anos de idade. **~book** *n* anuário *m*. **~ly** *a* anual ● *adv* anualmente

yearn /jɜːn/ *vi* **~ for, to** desejar, ansiar por, suspirar por. **~ing** *n* desejo *m*; anseio *m* (**for** de)

yeast /jiːst/ *n* levedura *f*

yell /jel/ *vt/i* gritar, berrar ● *n* grito *m*, berro *m*

yellow /ˈjeləʊ/ *a* amarelo; [!] (*cowardly*) covarde; poltrão ● *n* amarelo *m*

yelp /jelp/ *n* (*of dog etc*) ganido *m* ● *vi* ganir

yes /jes/ *n* & *adv* sim *m*. **~-man** *n* [!] lambe-botas *m invar*; puxa-saco *m*

yesterday /ˈjestədɪ/ *n & adv* ontem *m*; **~ morning/afternoon/evening** ontem de manhã/à tarde/à noite; **the day before ~** anteontem; **~ week** há oito dias, há uma semana

yet /jet/ *adv* ainda; (*already*) já; **as ~** até agora, por enquanto; **his best book ~** o seu melhor livro até agora ● *conj* contudo, no entanto

Yiddish /ˈjɪdɪʃ/ *n* ídiche *m*, (*P*) iídiche *m*

yield /jiːld/ *vt* (*produce*) produzir, dar; ‹*profit*› render; (*surrender*) entregar ● *vi* (*give way*) ceder or dar prioridade ● *n* produção *f*; *Comm* rendimento *m*

yoga /ˈjəʊgə/ *n* ioga *f*

yoghurt /ˈjɒgət/ *n* iogurte *m*

yoke /jəʊk/ *n* jugo *m*, canga *f*; (*of garment*) pala *f* ● *vt* jungir; (*unite*) unir, ligar

yolk /jəʊk/ *n* gema (de ovo) *f*

yonder /ˈjɒndə(r)/ *adv* acolá, além

you /juː/ *pron* (*familiar*) tu, você; *pl* vocês; (*polite*) vós, o(s) senhor(es), a(s) senhora(s); (*object*) (*familiar*) te, lhe; *pl* vocês; (*polite*) o(s), a(s), lhes, vós, o(s) senhor(es), a(s) senhora(s); (*after prep*) ti, si, você; *pl* vocês; (*polite*) vós, o senhor, a senhora; *pl* os senhores, as senhoras; (*indefinite*) se; (*after prep*) si, você; **with ~** (*familiar*) contigo, consigo, com você; *pl* com vocês; (*polite*) com o senhor/a senhora; *pl* convosco, com os senhores/as senhoras; **I know ~** (*familiar*) eu te conheço, (*P*) eu conheço-te, eu o/a conheço, (*P*) eu conheço-o/a; *pl* eu os/as conheço, (*P*) eu conheço-os/as; (*polite*) eu vos conheço, (*P*) eu conheço-vos, conheço o senhor/a senhora; *pl* conheço os senhores/as senhoras; **~ can see the sea** você pode ver o mar, (*P*) tu podes ver o mar

young /jʌŋ/ *a* (**-er**, **-est**) jovem, novo, moço ● *n* ‹*people*› jovens *mpl*, a juventude *f*, a mocidade *f*; (*of animals*) crias *fpl*, filhotes *mpl*

youngster /ˈjʌŋstə(r)/ *n* jovem *mf*, moço *m*, rapaz *m*

your /jɔː(r)/ *a* (*familiar*) teu, tua, seu, sua; *pl* teus, tuas, seus, suas; (*polite*) vosso, vossa, do senhor, da senhora; *pl* vossos, vossas, dos senhores, das senhoras

yours /jɔːz/ *poss pron* (*familiar*) o teu, a tua, o seu, a sua; *pl* os teus, as tuas, os seus, as suas; (*polite*) o vosso, a vossa, o/a do senhor, o/a da senhora; *pl* os vossos, as vossas, os/as do(s) senhor(es), os/as da(s) senhora(s); **a book of ~** um livro seu; **~ sincerely/faithfully** atenciosamente, com os cumprimentos de

yourself /jɔːˈself/ (*pl* **-selves**) *pron* (*familiar*) tu mesmo/a, você mesmo/a; *pl* vocês mesmos/as; (*polite*) vós mesmo/a, o senhor mesmo, a senhora mesma; *pl* vós mesmos/as, os senhores mesmos, as senhoras mesmas; (*reflexive*) (*familiar*) te; a ti mesmo/a; se; a si mesmo/a; *pl* a vocês mesmos/as; (*polite*) ao senhor mesmo, à senhora mesma; *pl* aos senhores mesmos, às senhoras mesmas; (*after prep: familiar*) ti mesmo/a, si mesmo/a, você mesmo/a; *pl* vocês mesmos/as; (*after prep: polite*) vós mesmo/a, o senhor mesmo, a senhora mesma; *pl* vós mesmos/as, os senhores mesmos, as senhoras mesmas; **with ~** (*familiar*) contigo mesmo/a, consigo mesmo/a, com você; *pl* com vocês; (*polite*) convosco, com o senhor, com a senhora; *pl* com os senhores, com as senhoras; **by ~** sozinho

youth /juːθ/ *n* (*pl* **-s** /-ðz/) mocidade *f*, juventude *f*; (*young man*) jovem *m*, moço *m*; **~ club** centro *m* de jovens; **~ hostel** albergue *m* da juventude. **~ful** *a* juvenil, jovem

yo-yo® /ˈjəʊjəʊ/ *n* (*pl* **-os**) ioiô *m*

Yugoslav /ˈjuːgəslɑːv/ *a & n* iugoslavo *m*, (*P*) jugoslavo *m*. **~ia** /-ˈslɑːvɪə/ *n* Iugoslávia *f*, (*P*) Jugoslávia *f*

Zz

zany /ˈzeɪnɪ/ *a* **-ier, -iest** tolo, bobo, pateta

zeal /ziːl/ *n* zelo *m*

zealous /ˈzeləs/ *a* zeloso

zebra /ˈzebrə, ˈziːbrə/ *n* zebra *f*; **~ crossing** faixa *f* para pedestres, (*P*) passagem *f* para peões, passadeira *f*

zenith /ˈzenɪθ/ *n* zênite *m*, (*P*) zénite *m*, auge *m*

zero /ˈzɪərəʊ/ *n* (*pl* **-os**) zero *m*; **~ hour** a hora H; **below ~** abaixo de zero

zest /zest/ *n* (*gusto*) entusiasmo *m*; *fig* (*spice*) sabor *m* especial; (*lemon or orange peel*) casca *f* de limão/laranja ralada

zigzag /ˈzɪgzæg/ *n* ziguezague *m* ● *a & adv* em ziguezague ● *vi* (*pt* **zigzagged**) ziguezaguear

zinc /zɪŋk/ *n* zinco *m*

zip /zɪp/ *n* (*vigour*) energia *f*, alma *f*; **~ (fastener)** fecho *m* ecler ● *vt* (*pt* **zipped**) fechar o fecho ecler de ● *vi* ir a toda a velocidade. **Z~ code** *n Amer* CEP de endereçamento postal *m*, (*P*) código *m* postal

zipper /ˈzɪpə(r)/ *n* (= **zip(-fastener)**) ▶ **ZIP**

zodiac /ˈzəʊdɪæk/ *n* zodíaco *m*

zombie /ˈzɒmbɪ/ *n* zumbi *m*; [!] zumbi *m*, (*P*) autómato *m*, zombie *m*

zone /zəʊn/ *n* zona *f*

zoo /zuː/ *n* jardim *m* zoológico

zoolog|y /zəʊˈɒlədʒɪ/ *n* zoologia *f*. **~ical** /-əˈlɒdʒɪkl/ *a* zoológico. **~ist** *n* zoólogo *m*

zoom /zuːm/ *vi* (*rush*) sair roando; **~ off** or **past** passar zunindo; **~ lens** zum *m*, zoom *m*

zucchini /zuːˈkiːnɪ/ *n* (*pl invar*) *Amer* courgette *f*

Portuguese verbs

Portuguese verbs can be divided into three categories: regular verbs, those with spelling peculiarities determined by their sound and irregular verbs.

Regular verbs:

in **-ar** (e.g. **comprar**)

Present: compr|o, **~as, ~a, ~amos, ~ais, ~am**
Future: comprar|ei, **~ás, ~á, ~emos, ~eis, ~ão**
Imperfect: compr|ava, **~avas, ~ava, ~ávamos, ~áveis, ~avam**
Preterite: compr|ei, **~aste, ~ou, ~amos (P: ~ámos), ~astes, ~aram**
Pluperfect: compr|ara, **~aras, ~ara, ~áramos, ~áreis, ~aram**
Present subjunctive: compr|e, **~es, ~e, ~emos, ~eis, ~em**
Imperfect subjunctive: compr|asse, **~asses, ~asse, ~ássemos, ~ásseis, ~assem**
Future subjunctive: compr|ar, **~ares, ~ar, ~armos, ~ardes, ~arem**
Conditional: comprar|ia, **~ias, ~ia, ~íamos, ~íeis, ~iam**
Personal infinitive: comprar, **~es, ~, ~mos, ~des, ~em**
Present participle: comprando
Past participle: comprado
Imperative: compra, comprai

in **~er** (e.g. **bater**)

Present: bat|o, **~es, ~e, ~emos, ~eis, ~em**
Future: bater|ei, **~ás, ~á, ~emos, ~eis, ~ão**
Imperfect: bat|ia, **~ias, ~ia, ~íamos, ~íeis, ~iam**
Preterite: bat|i, **~este, ~eu, ~emos, ~estes, ~eram**
Pluperfect: bat|era, **~eras, ~era, ~êramos, ~êreis, ~eram**
Present subjunctive: bat|a, **~as, ~a, ~amos, ~ais, ~am**
Imperfect subjunctive: bat|esse, **~esses, ~esse, ~êssemos, ~êsseis, ~essem**
Future subjunctive: bat|er, **~eres, ~er, ~ermos, ~erdes, ~erem**
Conditional: bater|ia, **~ias, ~ia, ~íamos, ~íeis, ~iam**
Personal infinitive: bater, **~es, ~, ~mos, ~des, ~em**
Present participle: batendo
Past participle: batido
Imperative: bate, batei

in **~ir** (e.g. **admitir**)

Present: admit|o, **~es, ~e, ~imos, ~is, ~em**
Future: admitir|ei, **~ás, ~á, ~emos, ~eis, ~ão**
Imperfect: admit|ia, **~ias, ~ia, ~íamos, ~íeis, ~iam**
Preterite: admit|i, **~iste, ~iu, ~imos, ~istes, ~iram**
Pluperfect: admit|ira, **~iras, ~ira, ~íramos, ~íreis, ~iram**
Present subjunctive: admit|a, **~as, ~a, ~amos, ~ais, ~am**
Imperfect subjunctive: admit|isse, **~isses, ~isse, ~íssemos, ~ísseis, ~issem**
Future subjunctive: admit|ir, **~ires, ~ir, ~irmos, ~irdes, ~irem**
Conditional: admitir|ia, **~ias, ~ia, ~íamos, ~íeis, ~iam**
Personal infinitive: admitir, **~es, ~, ~mos, ~des, ~em**
Present participle: admitindo
Past participle: admitido
Imperative: admite, admiti

Regular verbs with spelling changes:

-ar verbs:

in **-car** (e.g. **ficar**)

Preterite: fiquei, ficaste, ficou, ficamos (P: ficámos), ficais, ficam
Present subjunctive: fique, fiques, fique, fiquemos, fiqueis, fiquem

in **-çar** (e.g. **abraçar**)

Preterite: abracei, abraçaste, abraçou, abraçamos (P: abraçámos), abraçastes, abraçaram
Present subjunctive: abrace, abraces, abrace, abracemos, abraceis, abracem

in **-ear** (e.g. **passear**)

Present: passeio, passeias, passeia, passeamos, passeais, passeiam
Present subjunctive: passeie, passeies, passeie, passeemos, passeeis, passeiem
Imperative: passeia, passeai

in **-gar** (e.g. **apagar**)

Preterite: apaguei, apagaste, apagou, apagamos (P: apagámos), apagastes, apagaram
Present subjunctive: apague, apagues, apague, apaguemos, apagueis, apaguem

in **-oar** (e.g. **voar**)

Present: voo, voas, voa, voamos, voais, voam

averiguar

Preterite: averiguei, averiguaste, averiguou, averiguamos (P: averiguámos), averiguastes, averiguaram
Present subjunctive: averigue, averigues, averigue, averiguemos, averigueis, averiguem

enxaguar

Present: enxaguo, enxaguas, enxagua, enxaguamos, enxaguais, enxaguam
Preterite: enxaguei, enxaguaste, enxaguou, enxaguamos (P: enxaguámos), enxaguastes, enxaguaram
Present subjunctive: enxágue, enxagues, enxague, enxaguemos, enxagueis, enxaguem
Similarly: aguar, desaguar

saudar

Present: saúdo, saúdas, saúda, saudamos, saudais, saúdam
Present subjunctive: saúde, saúdes, saúde, saudemos, saudeis, saúdem
Imperative: saúda, saudai

-er verbs:

in **-cer** (e.g. **tecer**)

Present: teço, teces, tece, tecemos, teceis, tecem
Present subjunctive: teça, teças, teça, teçamos, teçais, teçam

in **-ger** (e.g. **proteger**)

Present: protejo, proteges, protege, protegemos, protegeis, protegem
Present subjunctive: proteja, protejas, proteja, protejamos, protejais, protejam

in **-guer** (e.g. **erguer**)

Present: ergo, ergues, ergue, erguemos, ergueis, erguem
Present subjunctive: erga, ergas, erga, ergamos, ergais, ergam

in **-oer** (e.g. **roer**)

Present: roo, róis, rói, roemos, roeis, roem
Imperfect: roía, roías, roía, roíamos, roíeis, roíam
Preterite: roí, roeste, roeu, roemos, roestes, roeram
Past participle: roído
Imperative: rói, roei

-ir verbs:

in **-ir** with **-e-** in stem (e.g. **vestir**)

Present: visto, vestes, veste, vestimos, vestis, vestem
Present subjunctive: vista, vistas, vista, vistamos, vistais, vistam
Similarly: mentir, preferir, refletir, repetir, seguir, sentir, servir

in **-ir** with **-o-** in stem (e.g. **dormir**)

Present: durmo, dormes, dorme, dormimos, dormis, dormem
Present subjunctive: durma, durmas, durma, durmamos, durmais, durmam
Similarly: cobrir, descobrir, tossir

in **-ir** with **-u-** in stem (e.g. **subir**)

Present: subo, sobes, sobe, subimos, subis, sobem
Similarly: consumir, cuspir, fugir, sacudir, sumir

in **-air** (e.g. **sair**)

Present: saio, sais, sai, saímos, saís, saem
Imperfect: saía, saías, saía, saíamos, saíeis, saíam
Preterite: saí, saíste, saiu, saímos, saístes, saíram
Pluperfect: saíra, saíras, saíra, saíramos, saíreis, saíram
Present subjunctive: saia, saias, saia, saiamos, saiais, saiam
Imperfect subjunctive: saísse, saísses, saísse, saíssemos, saísseis, saíssem
Future subjunctive: sair, saíres, sair, sairmos, sairdes, saírem
Personal infinitive: sair, saíres, sair, sairmos, sairdes, saírem
Present participle: saindo
Past participle: saído
Imperative: sai, saí

in **-gir** (e.g. **dirigir**)

Present: dirijo, diriges, dirige, dirigimos, dirigis, dirigem
Present subjunctive: dirija, dirijas, dirija, dirijamos, dirijais, dirijam

in **-guir** (e.g. **distinguir**)

Present: distingo, distingues, distingue, distinguimos, distinguis, distinguem
Present subjunctive: distinga, distingas, distinga, distingamos, distingais, distingam

in **-uir** (e.g. **atribuir**)

Present: atribuo, atribuis, atribui, atribuímos, atribuís, atribuem
Imperfect: atribuía, atribuías, atribuía, atribuíamos, atribuíeis, atribuíam
Preterite: atribuí, atribuíste, atribuiu, atribuímos, atribuístes, atribuíram
Pluperfect: atribuíra, atribuíras, atribuíra, atribuíramos, atribuíreis, atribuíram
Present subjunctive: atribua, atribuas, atribua, atribuamos, atribuais, atribuam
Imperfect subjunctive: atribuísse, atribuísses, atribuísse, atribuíssemos, atribuísseis, atribuíssem
Future subjunctive: atribuir, atribuíres, atribuir, atribuirmos, atribuirdes, atribuírem
Personal infinitive: atribuir, atribuíres, atribuir, atribuirmos, atribuirdes, atribuírem
Present participle: atribuindo
Past participle: atribuído
Imperative: atribui, atribuí

proibir

Present: proíbo, proíbes, proíbe, proibimos, proibis, proíbem
Present subjunctive: proíba, proíbas, proíba, proibamos, proibais, proíbam
Imperative: proíbe, proibi
Similarly: coibir

reunir

Present: reúno, reúnes, reúne, reunimos, reunis, reúnem

Present subjunctive: reúna, reúnas, reúna, reunamos, reunais, reúnam
Imperative: reúne, reuni

in **-struir** (e.g. **construir**) – like **atribuir** except:

Present: construo, constróis/construis, constrói/construi, construímos, construís, constroem/construem
Imperative: constrói/construi, construí

in **-duzir** (e.g. **produzir**)

Present: produzo, produzes, produz, produzimos, produzis, produzem
Imperative: produz(e), produzi
Similarly: luzir, reluzir

Irregular verbs

caber

Present: caibo, cabes, cabe, cabemos, cabeis, cabem
Preterite: coube, coubeste, coube, coubemos, coubestes, couberam
Pluperfect: coubera, couberas, coubera, coubéramos, coubéreis, couberam
Present subjunctive: caiba, caibas, caiba, caibamos, caibais, caibam
Imperfect subjunctive: coubesse, coubesses, coubesse, coubéssemos, coubésseis, coubessem
Future subjunctive: couber, couberes, couber, coubermos, couberdes, couberem

dar

Present: dou, dás, dá, damos, dais, dão
Preterite: dei, deste, deu, demos, destes, deram
Pluperfect: dera, deras, dera, déramos, déreis, deram
Present subjunctive: dê, dês, dê, demos, deis, deem
Imperfect subjunctive: desse, desses, desse, déssemos, désseis, dessem
Future subjunctive: der, deres, der, dermos, derdes, derem
Imperative: dá, dai

dizer

Present: digo, dizes, diz, dizemos, dizeis, dizem
Future: direi, dirás, dirá, diremos, direis, dirão
Preterite: disse, disseste, disse, dissemos, dissestes, disseram
Pluperfect: dissera, disseras, dissera, disséramos, disséreis, disseram
Present subjunctive: diga, digas, diga, digamos, digais, digam
Imperfect subjunctive: dissesse, dissesses, dissesse, disséssemos, dissésseis, dissessem
Future subjunctive: disser, disseres, disser, dissermos, disserdes, disserem
Conditional: diria, dirias, diria, diríamos, diríeis, diriam
Present participle: dizendo
Past participle: dito
Imperative: diz, dizei

estar

Present: estou, estás, está, estamos, estais, estão
Preterite: estive, estiveste, esteve, estivemos, estivestes, estiveram
Pluperfect: estivera, estiveras, estivera, estivéramos, estivéreis, estiveram
Present subjunctive: esteja, estejas, esteja, estejamos, estejais, estejam
Imperfect subjunctive: estivesse, estivesses, estivesse, estivéssemos, estivésseis, estivessem
Future subjunctive: estiver, estiveres, estiver, estivermos, estiverdes, estiverem
Imperative: está, estai

fazer

Present: faço, fazes, faz, fazemos, fazeis, fazem
Future: farei, farás, fará, faremos, fareis, farão
Preterite: fiz, fizeste, fez, fizemos, fizestes, fizeram

Pluperfect: fizera, fizeras, fizera, fizéramos, fizéreis, fizeram
Present subjunctive: faça, faças, faça, façamos, façais, façam
Imperfect subjunctive: fizesse, fizesses, fizesse, fizéssemos, fizésseis, fizessem
Future subjunctive: fizer, fizeres, fizer, fizermos, fizerdes, fizerem
Conditional: faria, farias, faria, faríamos, faríeis, fariam
Present participle: fazendo
Past participle: feito
Imperative: faz(e), fazei

frigir

Present: frijo, freges, frege, frigimos, frigis, fregem
Present subjunctive: frija, frijas, frija, frijamos, frijais, frijam
Imperative: frege, frigi

haver

Present: hei, hás, há, hemos/havemos, haveis/heis, hão
Preterite: houve, houveste, houve, houvemos, houvestes, houveram
Pluperfect: houvera, houveras, houvera, houvéramos, houvéreis, houveram
Present subjunctive: haja, hajas, haja, hajamos, hajais, hajam
Imperfect subjunctive: houvesse, houvesses, houvesse, houvéssemos, houvésseis, houvessem
Future subjunctive: houver, houveres, houver, houvermos, houverdes, houverem
Imperative: há, havei

ir

Present: vou, vais, vai, vamos, ides, vão
Imperfect: ia, ias, ia, íamos, íeis, iam
Preterite: fui, foste, foi, fomos, fostes, foram
Pluperfect: fora, foras, fora, fôramos, fôreis, foram
Present subjunctive: vá, vás, vá, vamos, vades, vão
Imperfect subjunctive: fosse, fosses, fosse, fôssemos, fôsseis, fossem
Future subjunctive: for, fores, for, formos, fordes, forem
Present participle: indo
Past participle: ido
Imperative: vai, ide

ler

Present: leio, lês, lê, lemos, ledes, leem
Imperfect: lia, lias, lia, líamos, líeis, liam
Preterite: li, leste, leu, lemos, lestes, leram
Pluperfect: lera, leras, lera, lêramos, lêreis, leram
Present subjunctive: leia, leias, leia, leiamos, leiais, leiam
Imperfect subjunctive: lesse, lesses, lesse, lêssemos, lêsseis, lessem
Future subjunctive: ler, leres, ler, lermos, lerdes, lerem
Present participle: lendo
Past participle: lido
Imperative: lê, lede
Similarly: crer

odiar

Present: odeio, odeias, odeia, odiamos, odiais, odeiam
Present subjunctive: odeie, odeies, odeie, odiemos, odieis, odeiem
Imperative: odeia, odiai
Similarly: incendiar

ouvir

Present: ouço (P also: oiço), ouves, ouve, ouvimos, ouvis, ouvem
Present subjunctive: ouça, ouças, ouça, ouçamos, ouçais, ouçam (P also: oiça, oiças, oiça, oiçamos, oiçais, oiçam)

pedir

Present: peço, pedes, pede, pedimos, pedis, pedem
Present subjunctive: peça, peças, peça, peçamos, peçais, peçam
Similarly: despedir, impedir, medir

perder

Present: perco, perdes, perde, perdemos, perdeis, perdem
Present subjunctive: perca, percas, perca, percamos, percais, percam

poder

Present: posso, podes, pode, podemos, podeis, podem
Preterite: pude, pudeste, pôde, pudemos, pudestes, puderam
Pluperfect: pudera, puderas, pudera, pudéramos, pudéreis, puderam
Present subjunctive: possa, possas, possa, possamos, possais, possam
Imperfect subjunctive: pudesse, pudesses, pudesse, pudéssemos, pudésseis, pudessem
Future subjunctive: puder, puderes, puder, pudermos, puderdes, puderem

polir

Present: pulo, pules, pule, polimos, polis, pulem
Present subjunctive: pula, pulas, pula, pulamos, pulais, pulam
Imperative: pule, poli

pôr

Present: ponho, pões, põe, pomos, pondes, põem
Future: porei, porás, porá, poremos, poreis, porão
Imperfect: punha, punhas, punha, púnhamos, púnheis, punham
Preterite: pus, puseste, pôs, pusemos, pusestes, puseram
Pluperfect: pusera, puseras, pusera, puséramos, puséreis, puseram
Present subjunctive: ponha, ponhas, ponha, ponhamos, ponhais, ponham
Imperfect subjunctive: pusesse, pusesses, pusesse, puséssemos, pusésseis, pusessem
Future subjunctive: puser, puseres, puser, pusermos, puserdes, puserem
Conditional: poria, porias, poria, poríamos, poríeis, poriam
Present participle: pondo
Past participle: posto
Imperative: põe, ponde
Similarly: compor, depor, dispor, opor, supor etc

prover

Present: provejo, provês, provê, provemos, provedes, proveem
Present subjunctive: proveja, provejas, proveja, provejamos, provejais, provejam
Imperative: provê, provede

querer

Present: quero, queres, quer, queremos, quereis, querem
Preterite: quis, quiseste, quis, quisemos, quisestes, quiseram
Pluperfect: quisera, quiseras, quisera, quiséramos, quiséreis, quiseram
Present subjunctive: queira, queiras, queira, queiramos, queirais, queiram
Imperfect subjunctive: quisesse, quisesses, quisesse, quiséssemos, quisésseis, quisessem
Future subjunctive: quiser, quiseres, quiser, quisermos, quiserdes, quiserem
Imperative: quer, querei

requerer

Present: requeiro, requeres, requer, requeremos, requereis, requerem
Present subjunctive: requeira, requeiras, requeira, requeiramos, requeirais, requeiram
Imperative: requer, requerei

rir

Present: rio, ris, ri, rimos, rides, riem
Present subjunctive: ria, rias, ria, riamos, riais, riam
Imperative: ri, ride
Similarly: sorrir

saber

Present: sei, sabes, sabe, sabemos, sabeis, sabem

Preterite: soube, soubeste, soube, soubemos, soubestes, souberam
Pluperfect: soubera, souberas, soubera, soubéramos, soubéreis, souberam
Present subjunctive: saiba, saibas, saiba, saibamos, saibais, saibam
Imperfect subjunctive: soubesse, soubesses, soubesse, soubéssemos, soubésseis, soubessem
Future subjunctive: souber, souberes, souber, soubermos, souberdes, souberem
Imperative: sabe, sabei

ser

Present: sou, és, é, somos, sois, são
Imperfect: era, eras, era, éramos, éreis, eram
Preterite: fui, foste, foi, fomos, fostes, foram
Pluperfect: fora, foras, fora, fôramos, fôreis, foram
Present subjunctive: seja, sejas, seja, sejamos, sejais, sejam
Imperfect subjunctive: fosse, fosses, fosse, fôssemos, fôsseis, fossem
Future subjunctive: for, fores, for, formos, fordes, forem
Present participle: sendo
Past participle: sido
Imperative: sê, sede

ter

Present: tenho, tens, tem, temos, tendes, têm
Imperfect: tinha, tinhas, tinha, tínhamos, tínheis, tinham
Preterite: tive, tiveste, teve, tivemos, tivestes, tiveram
Pluperfect: tivera, tiveras, tivera, tivéramos, tivéreis, tiveram
Present subjunctive: tenha, tenhas, tenha, tenhamos, tenhais, tenham
Imperfect subjunctive: tivesse, tivesses, tivesse, tivéssemos, tivésseis, tivessem
Future subjunctive: tiver, tiveres, tiver, tivermos, tiverdes, tiverem
Present participle: tendo
Past participle: tido
Imperative: tem, tende

trazer

Present: trago, trazes, traz, trazemos, trazeis, trazem
Future: trarei, trarás, trará, traremos, trareis, trarão
Preterite: trouxe, trouxeste, trouxe, trouxemos, trouxestes, trouxeram
Pluperfect: trouxera, trouxeras, trouxera, trouxéramos, trouxéreis, trouxeram
Present subjunctive: traga, tragas, traga, tragamos, tragais, tragam
Imperfect subjunctive: trouxesse, trouxesses, trouxesse, trouxéssemos, trouxésseis, trouxessem
Future subjunctive: trouxer, trouxeres, trouxer, trouxermos, trouxerdes, trouxerem
Conditional: traria, trarias, traria, traríamos, traríeis, trariam
Imperative: traze, trazei

valer

Present: valho, vales, vale, valemos, valeis, valem
Present subjunctive: valha, valhas, valha, valhamos, valhais, valham

ver

Present: vejo, vês, vê, vemos, vedes, veem
Imperfect: via, vias, via, víamos, víeis, viam
Preterite: vi, viste, viu, vimos, vistes, viram
Pluperfect: vira, viras, vira, víramos, víreis, viram
Present subjunctive: veja, vejas, veja, vejamos, vejais, vejam
Imperfect subjunctive: visse, visses, visse, víssemos, vísseis, vissem
Future subjunctive: vir, vires, vir, virmos, virdes, virem
Present participle: vendo
Past participle: visto
Imperative: vê, vede

vir

Present: venho, vens, vem, vimos, vindes, vêm

Imperfect: vinha, vinhas, vinha, vínhamos, vínheis, vinham

Preterite: vim, vieste, veio, viemos, viestes, vieram

Pluperfect: viera, vieras, viera, viéramos, viéreis, vieram

Present subjunctive: venha, venhas, venha, venhamos, venhais, venham

Imperfect subjunctive: viesse, viesses, viesse, viéssemos, viésseis, viessem

Future subjunctive: vier, vieres, vier, viermos, vierdes, vierem

Present participle: vindo

Past participle: vindo

Imperative: vem, vinde

Verbos irregulares ingleses

Infinitivo	*Pretérito*	*Particípio passado*
be	was	been
bear	bore	borne
beat	beat	beaten
become	became	become
begin	began	begun
bend	bent	bent
bet	bet, betted	bet, betted
bid	bade, bid	bidden, bid
bind	bound	bound
bite	bit	bitten
bleed	bled	bled
blow	blew	blown
break	broke	broken
breed	bred	bred
bring	brought	brought
build	built	built
burn	burnt, burned	burnt, burned
burst	burst	burst
buy	bought	bought
catch	caught	caught
choose	chose	chosen
cling	clung	clung
come	came	come
cost	cost, costed (*vt*)	cost, costed
cut	cut	cut
deal	dealt	dealt
dig	dug	dug
do	did	done
draw	drew	drawn
dream	dreamt, dreamed	dreamt, dreamed
drink	drank	drunk
drive	drove	driven
eat	ate	eaten
fall	fell	fallen
feed	fed	fed
feel	felt	felt
fight	fought	fought

Infinitivo	*Pretérito*	*Particípio passado*
find	found	found
flee	fled	fled
fly	flew	flown
freeze	froze	frozen
get	got	got, gotten *US*
give	gave	given
go	went	gone
grow	grew	grown
hang	hung, hanged	hung, hanged
have	had	had
hear	heard	heard
hide	hid	hidden
hit	hit	hit
hold	held	held
hurt	hurt	hurt
keep	kept	kept
kneel	knelt	knelt
know	knew	known
lay	laid	laid
lead	led	led
lean	leaned, leant	leaned, leant
learn	learnt, learned	learnt, learned
leave	left	left
lend	lent	lent
let	let	let
lie	lay	lain
lose	lost	lost
make	made	made
mean	meant	meant
meet	met	met
pay	paid	paid
put	put	put
read	read	read
ride	rode	ridden
ring	rang	rung
rise	rose	risen
run	ran	run

Infinitivo	*Pretérito*	*Particípio passado*
say	said	said
see	saw	seen
seek	sought	sought
sell	sold	sold
send	sent	sent
set	set	set
sew	sewed	sewn, sewed
shake	shook	shaken
shine	shone	shone
shoe	shod	shod
shoot	shot	shot
show	showed	shown
shut	shut	shut
sing	sang	sung
sink	sank	sunk
sit	sat	sat
sleep	slept	slept
sling	slung	slung
smell	smelt, smelled	smelt, smelled
speak	spoke	spoken
spell	spelled, spelt	spelled, spelt
spend	spent	spent
spit	spat	spat
spoil	spoilt, spoiled	spoilt, spoiled
spread	spread	spread
spring	sprang	sprung
stand	stood	stood
steal	stole	stolen
stick	stuck	stuck
sting	stung	stung
stride	strode	stridden
strike	struck	struck
swear	swore	sworn
sweep	swept	swept
swell	swelled	swollen, swelled
swim	swam	swum
swing	swung	swung
take	took	taken
teach	taught	taught
tear	tore	torn
tell	told	told
think	thought	thought
throw	threw	thrown
thrust	thrust	thrust
tread	trod	trodden
understand	understood	understood
wake	woke	woken
wear	wore	worn
win	won	won
write	wrote	written